# Indian hieroglyphs

## Invention of writing

S. Kalyanaraman

Sarasvati Research Center

Library of Congress Control Number LCCN: 2011963130



Printed in the USA

First paperback printing, January 2012



ISBN: 098289712X

ISBN-13: 978-0982897126

CONTENTS

# S. Kalyanaraman


ABSTRACT

*Indian hieroglyphs – Invention of writing*

This book is a hermeneutic interpretation of Indian hieroglyphs in the context of invention and evolution of writing systems c. 3500 BCE, general semantics of Indian linguistic area (*sprachbund*, language union) and cryptography. Semantics (plain text) and cipher (glyphics) are presented, for e.g.

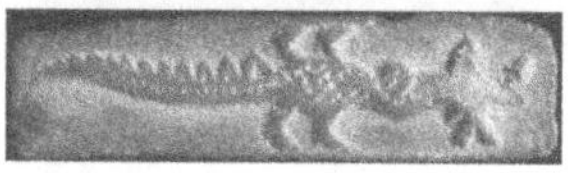

1. m0314 seal impression: Line 1: Turner workshop; forge, stone ore, ingot; excellent cast metal; Line 2: Metal workshop, ingot furnace, casting, riveting smithy, forge; furnace (stone ore) account scribe; Line 3: Smithy, lump of silver (forging metal); mint, gold furnace; smithy/forge; turner wheelwright.

2. *mẽṛhet, meḍ* 'iron' [*meḍho* 'ram']; *karba, ib* 'hard iron' [*karibha* 'elephant']; *kol* 'iron smith' [*kola* 'tiger']; *koḍ* 'artisan's workshop' [*koḍ* 'horns']; *mũh* 'ingot' [mũhe 'face']; *padm* 'temper of iron' [*phaṭa* cobra's hood]; *dhatu* 'mineral' [*dhaṭu* 'scarf (on neck)']; *koḍ* 'artisan's workshop' [*koḍiyum* 'rings on neck'] Inscription text glyphics: turner's workshop, casting (metal) furnace (stone ore) account scribe.

3. *kōdā* 'to turn in a lathe' [*khōṇḍa* 'heifer']; *karmāraśāla* 'smithy, forge' [*kammarsāla* 'pannier']; *loa* 'copper' [*lo* 'overflow']; *kaṇḍa kanka* 'stone (ore) metal furnace account scribe'.[*kaṇḍa kanka* 'rim of jar']; *koṭha jangaḍiyo* 'treasury military guard' [*koṭhla* 'bag'; *sangaḍa* 'lathe, portable furnace'].

4. *adur ḍhangar khũṭ ayaskāṇḍa* 'native metalsmith guild; stone (ore) metal'; *khũṭ* 'community' [*adar ḍangra khũṭ* 'zebu, *bos indicus; aya* 'fish'; *gaṇḍa* 'four'].

5. *ayakāra* 'blacksmith' -- Pāṇini's *aṣṭādhāyī* : kārukarma, 'artisan's work' (*Arthaśāstra*: 2.14.17); *kāru* 'artisan' [*aya* 'fish'; *karā* 'crocodile'].

6. *kol kammara* 'iron smith' [*kola* 'tiger'; *krammaru* 'head turned back']; *eraka* 'copper' [*heraka* 'spy']; *kōdār* 'turner' [*khōṇḍa* 'leafless tree'.] Inscription text glyphics: Lathe-turner workshop; brass-worker, furnace (stone ore) account (scribe); metal artisan's workshop.

This book finally solves a cryptography problem of Indus Script inscriptions. Using evidence from almost all the 6000 + inscriptions, this book makes a contribution to an understanding of the middle phase in evolution of writing systems, a phase which bridged pictographic writing with syllabic writing to represent sounds of a language called meluhha (mleccha) in Indian language union – *lingua franca* of Harosheth hagoyim (*kharoṣṭī goya*), smithy of nations. A revolution in thought occurred with the invention, by artisan-traders, of Indian hieroglyphs as an unambiguous, precise writing system, to document the material revolution of the bronze-age c. 3500 BCE.

# Indian Hieroglyphs

Some examples of hieroglyphs are presented from Plates v to vii called 'field symbols' in the concordance of Mahadevan concordance. Guidance provided by Shri D.M. Gautam, Financial Adviser, Indian Railways in selecting these examples, is gratefully acknowledged. Decoding of many of these hieroglyphs will be presented in this book.

**PLATE IV**

62 63 64 65 66

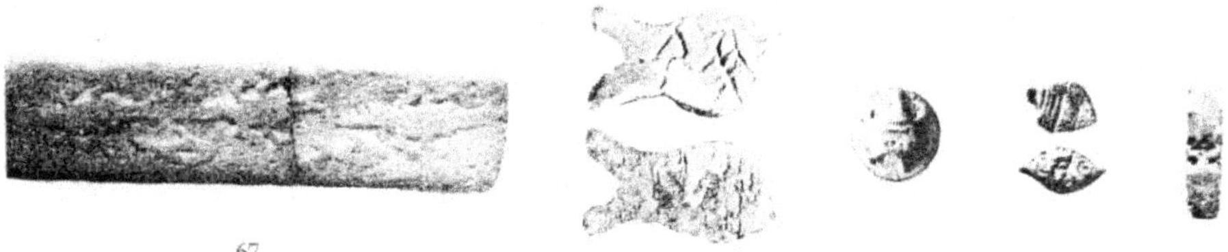

67 68 69 70 71

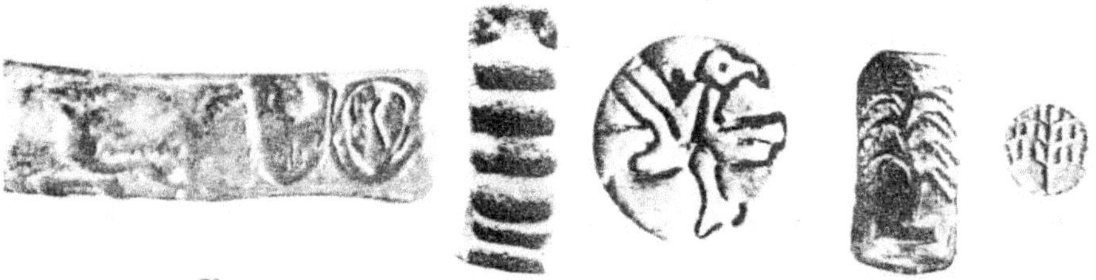

72 73 74 75 76

77 78 79 80 81

82 83 84 85 86 87 88

PLATE V

89

90

91

92

93

94

95

96

97

98

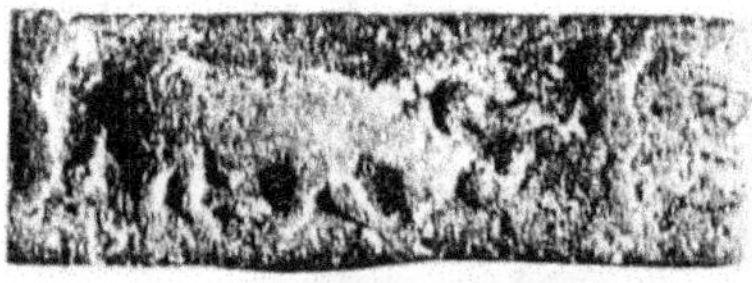
99

100

101

102

103

104

105

PLATE VI

106

107

108

109

110

111

112

113

114

115

116

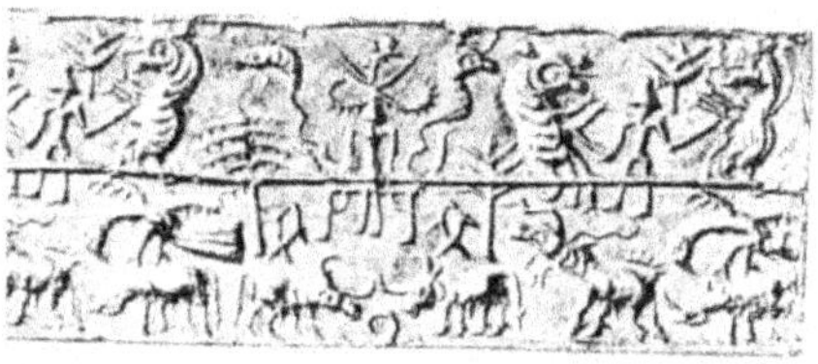
117

118

119

121

122

123

124

PLATE VII

125

126

127

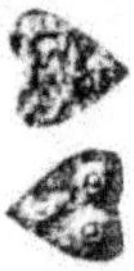
128

29

130

131

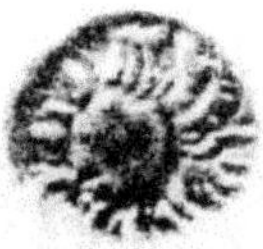
132

133

134

135

136

137

138

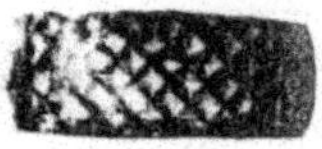
139

140

141

142

143

144

145

Painting of Sarasvati (divinity of vidyā, 'learning' and vāk, 'language') is by Raja Ravi Varma (1848-1906). Figures of Indus script inscriptions are referenced from the public domain and/or Archaeological Survey of India, Department of Archaeology and Museums, Govt. of Pakistan, British and other museums of the world.

(Cover image is smelter/furnace fire which heralded the bronze-age c. 3500 BCE. Fire-workers, who worked on earth's minerals, invented the world's earliest writing system called Indus Script).

Sources for the analyses of language and images of Indian hieroglyphs adapted after sources are duly referenced and gratefully acknowledged.

Language dictionaries of the Indian linguistic area and etymological dictionaries for Indo-Aryan, Dravidian and Munda groups are essential resources for understanding the semantics of the *sprachbund* (language union). For this purpose, a comprehensive *Indian Lexicon* (S. Kalyanarman, 1998) is available.

Kalyanaraman

January 10, 2012

1 INDUS VALLEY MYSTERY— *HAROSHETH HAGOYIM*, 'SMITHY OF NATIONS'

Archaeology and language: Archaeological context of Indus script cipher.

One key to unlock the Indus valley mystery is to enter through the archaeological context of Uruk which, together with Elam and Susa was in the Meluhha interaction sphere.

Uruk (Warka) has produced artifacts which parallel Indus script glyphs, for example, hieroglyphs on Warka vase and Susa ritual basin. These are intimations of an early writing system by mleccha (meluhha) speakers who were settlers in Sumer. Many languages of the Indian linguistic area (language union or *sprachbund*) provide multiple keys – over 1500 lexemes – which are plain texts to decode, rebus, the ciphertext hieroglyphs of the writing system.

Another archaeological context is the well-documented find of Harvard Archaeological Research Project (HARP) excavations at Harappa (1986 to 2007) -- a potsherd inscribed with Indus script, dated stratigraphically to c. 3500 BCE.

Narmer Palette with Egyptian hieroglyphs N'r M'r (Cuttle-fish, chisel) was dated c. 3300 BCE. [(Great Hierakonpolis Palette) Cairo J.E. 14716, C.G. 32169 Hierakonpolis (Horus Temple 'Main Deposit')].

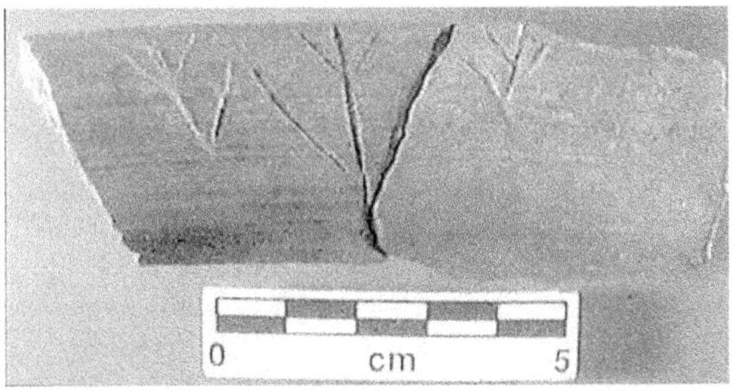


h1522 (Harappa potsherd with the earliest writing system dated to c. 3500 BCE).

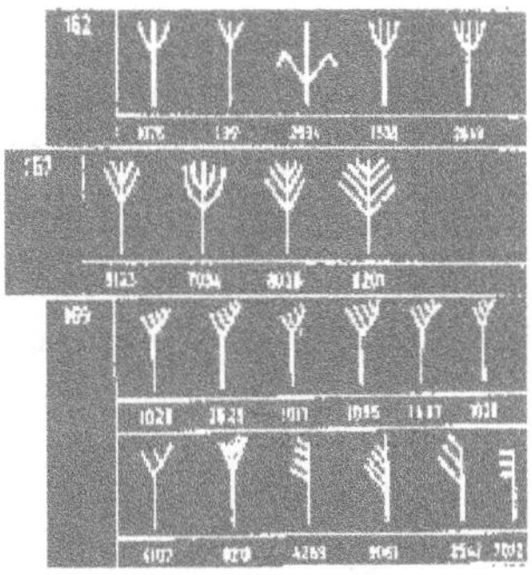

A unique characteristic of languages of the Indian language union (*sprachbund* or Indian linguistic area), is reduplication of words. In English, such a reduplication occurs in phrases like humpty-dumpty, hocus-pocus. This hieroglyph on a potsherd is seen to represent such reduplications, conveying an emphasis on the intended meaning. The glyph is read rebus: Glyph: *ṭagara-kolmo* '*tabernae montana* (wild tulip flower)'-'rice-plant'). Rebus: *tagara-kolami* 'tin furnace/smithy'. Tin as an alloying mineral to create bronze is represented by allographs connoting two words for tin: *ṭagara* and *ranku* (three or five-petlled sprout; liquid measure; antelope). An allograph also connoted smithy: a procession of animals. Glyph: *pasara* 'animals'. Rebus: *pasra* 'smithy'. The two words for tin, *ṭagara* and *ranku* may connote cassiterite (tin ore -- tin oxide mineral, $SnO_2$ -- translucent thin crystals.with multiple crystal faces) or smelted, ingoted pure tin (tin mineral - Sn) as in the two pure tin ingots – with Indian hieroglyphs -- found in a shipwreck in Haifa. The two words *kolmo* and *pasra* for a smithy, may similarly denote distinguishing between a smithy for tin mineral and a smithy for all minerals. Hence, the use of variant glyphs to connote a smithy/forge. (Variants of Sign 162, 167, 169). Association of a smithy with a temple by a mleccha (meluhha) word, *kole.l* which means 'smithy, temple'. Is indicative of the reason why some glyphs of the writing system, to represent the creative metallurgists' repertoire, get associated with sacredness or divinity in the traditions of Indian language union.

BBC titled the report of May 4, 1999 'Earliest writing'. Citing this find, the report quoted one of the excavators, Richard Meadow: "...these primitive inscriptions found on pottery may pre-date all other known writing."

http://news.bbc.co.uk/2/hi/science/nature/334517.stm

***Harosheth hagoyim*, 'smithy of nations' of the bronze-age**

Indian hieroglyphs of Indus script constitute some of the earliest writing systems in the history of civilizations.

This work demonstrates that the invention of writing was related to *Harosheth ha-goy-im*, חרשת הגוים 'smithy of nations' (Hebrew). In the Bible, Harosheth-hagoyim is the home of general Sisera, who was killed by Jael during the war of Naphtali and Zebulun against Jabin, king of Hazor in Canaan (Judges 4:2). The lead players of this war are the general Barak and the judge Deborah. Harosheth is derived from the root חרש

The Biblical phrase is relatable to two lexemes of Indian linguistic area: *kharoṣṭī* (name a writing system) and *gōya* ('clan' Pkt.)

The semantics of *harosheth,*'engraving' justify the identification of *kharoṣṭī* (a writing system) as a cognate. An added justification is the prefix '*khar-*' in *kharoṣṭī*. In Kashmiri, *khar* means 'blacksmith'.

The suffix '*-oṣṭ*' is related to semantics 'lip': ŏ́ṣṭha m. ' lip ' RV. Paš. lauṛ. *ūṭh* f. ← Ind. (?), gul. *ūṣṭ* ' lip ', dar. weg. *uṣṭ* ' bank of a river ' (IIFL iii 3, 22); Kal. rumb. *ūṣṭ, uṣṭ* ' lip '; Sh. *ŏṭụ* m. ' upper lip ', *ŏṭi̯* f. ' lower lip ' (→ Ḍ *ōṭe* pl.); K. *wuṭh*, dat. *°ṭhas* m. ' lip '; L. *hoṭh* m., P. *hoṭh, hõṭh* m., WPah. bhal. *oṭh* m., jaun. *hõṭh*, Ku. *ũṭh*, gng. *ōṭh*, N. *oṭh*, A. *ő̃ṭh*, MB. Or.*oṭha*, Mth. Bhoj. *oṭh*, Aw. lakh. *ő̃ṭh*, *hő̃ṭh*, H. *oṭh, õṭh, hoṭh, hõṭh* m., G. *oṭh, hoṭh* m., M. *oṭh, õṭh, hoṭ* m., Si. *oṭa*. ŏ́ṣṭha -- : WPah.poet. *oṭhḷu* m. ' lip ', *hoṭru*, kṭg. *hóṭṭh*, kc. *ōṭh*, Garh. *hoṭh, hõṭ*. (CDIAL 2563).This semantic is consistent with one meaning (from Dictionary of Old Testament Proper Names) of *harosheth* as 'manufactory'.

Other lexemes relate *kharoṣṭī* to semant. 'sounds' : Gy. wel.*khār* -- ' to call aloud ', germ. *kar* -- , gr. rum. boh. *akhar* -- ' to call, cry out, groan ' Turner BSOAS xxii 493 (CDIAL 4067). garhā f. ' blame ' MBh. Pa. Pk. *garahā* -- f. ' blame ' L. *gall*, pl. *°lā* f. ' word, thing '; P. *gall* f. ' word '; OH. *gāl(h)anā* ' to talk '; -- poss. X gāli -- : S. *g̱ālhi* f., *°hu* m. 'talk '; L. *gālh* f. ' word ', pl. *gālhī* ' abuse ', (Ju.) *g̱ālh* f. (CDIAL 4068).

Thus, *kharoṣṭī* as a lexeme is relatable to meanings of cognate phonemes: 'metalsmith's lip or, word-lip (spoken word)' – a vikalpa (representation or cryptography) to denote sounds of language in written characters (in the case of *kharoṣṭī*, syllables of *lingua franca* or the language repertoire of artisans).

Thus, etymology of *kharoṣṭī* as a writing system is a representation of sounds of blacksmiths' language repertoire of Indian linguistic area (language union or *sprachbund*). This etymological excursus is consistent with the interpretation of *harosheth*, as 'smithy'.

In the case of Indian hieroglyphs of Indus script, the writing system represented words themselves while *kharoṣṭī* used symbols or characters to denote syllables of sounds of a language. Some claim that choice of symbols for *kharoṣṭī* syllables were patterned after Aramaic. It is not clear if any Indian hieroglyphs of Indus script are orthographically comparable to cursive, syllabic characters of *kharoṣṭī*.

In the word, *hagoyim*, 'ha' is a definite article, 'the'. It relates to the noun which it precedes. *Goyim* is plural for *goy* 'nation, people, usually non-Hebrew people.' Romans 11:25 uses the phrase *Melo-Ha-Goyim* which is Hebrew for 'completeness of the nations (Gentiles)'.

See the following lexemes of Indian linguistic area semant. 'to plough'; 'to engrave':

karṣá m. ' dragging ' Pāṇ., ' agriculture ' Āp. [Cf. *ka´rṣl* -- ' ploughing ' TS., *karṣí* -- Kapiṣṭh.: √kr̥ṣ] Pk. *karisa* -- m. ' dragging ', *kassa* -- m. ' mud '; Paš. *kaṣ* ' pulling '; Or. *kāsa* ' time or turn of ploughing a field '. <-> Poss. Wg. *koṣ* ' snake ', Ash.*kəreš* ' snake ', Wg. *koṣ* (< ' dragging or trailing on the ground ')(CDIAL 2905).

<uzra> {V} ``to ^engrave (cut incised designs)". !literally. @V0282. #25401. <okhar> {V2} ``to ^drag a field after planting". @1212. #21091. <okhaR> {V2} ``to ^seed one row at a time". @1211. #21101. <kari>(F), <kAri>(F), <kaRi>(B), <khaRi> {N} ``^pen, ^pencil". Pl. <-le>. (Munda etyma) útkirati ' digs out or up ' VS., ' piles up, engraves ' Kālid [√kr̥̄1] 1. Pk. *ukkiraï*, °*kīraï* ' digs, engraves on stone '; S. *ukiraṇu* ' to engrave ' 2. Pk. *ukkaraï* ' digs up '; L. awāṇ. *ukruṇ* ' to inscribe '; P. *ukkarṇā* ' to dig, engrave '; Garh. *ukarṇū* ' to collect '; M. *ukarṇẽ* ' to scrape up, rake out (a fire), scratch, mark ' (or < 1) 3. Pa. Pk. *ukkiṇṇa* -- ' dug up '.4. Ku. *ukerṇo* ' to dig out earth '. (CDIAL 1723). Ta. kuṟl (-pp-, -tt-) to form pits, hollows, cavities, sink, excavate, inscribe, engrave *Te.* kṟōce, kṟocce be engraved *Kuwi* (F.) graiyū (*pl.* grānga) hole; (S.) glāyu a well; (Su. P.) gṟāyu hole, pit. *Br.* xurrum grainpit. (DEDR 1818). Ta. kīṟu to scratch, scrape; *Ka.* gīṟu to scratch, scrape; *Te.* gīṟu to scratch, scrape; geṟa line; *Kuwi* (S.) lōki garri grīnai to underline; (Ṭ.) giri line; (Isr.) gīra line on the palm of the hand. / Cf. Or. girā a line. ? Cf. Skt. kiraka- a scribe. (DEDR 1623).

One interpretation for the etymon *goy* is that the primitive root is *ga-ah* 'rise up, exalted in triumph, to be lifted up'. The word '*-goy*' in *hagoyim* means 'a nation' (Hebrew). In Indian Prākṛt, *gōy*, 'clan' is a semantic cognate of the Hebrew etymon, *goy*.

Other cognate etyma of Indian linguistic area: గోత్ర [ gōtra ] *gōtra*. [Skt.] n. The earth. నేల. గోత్రము *gōtramu*. n. A mountain. కొండ. A family, tribe or lineage. వంశము. అన్యగోత్రుడు an alien, one of another family or clan. గోత్రభిత్తు *gōtra-bhittu*. n. Lit. the 'destroyer of mountains', i.e., Indra. a caste, tribe, caste according to families. (-त्रः) a mountain; 'गोत्रं नाम्नि कुले$प्यद्रौ' इति यादवः; Śi.9.8. Hence गोत्रोद्दलनः means Indra; cf. इन्द्रे तु गोत्रोद्दलनः कुलघ्ने गिरिदारणे Nm. (-त्रा) 1 a multitude of cows. -2 the earth. gōtrá n. ' cowpen, enclosure ' RV., ' family, clan ' ChUp., *gōtrā* -- f. ' herd of cows ' Pāṇ.

2. gōtraka -- n. ' family ' Yājñ. [gṓ -- 1. Pa. *gotta* -- n. ' clan ', Pk. *gotta* -- , *gutta* -- , amg. *gōya* -- n.; Gau. *gū* ' house ' (in Kaf. and Dard. several other words for ' cowpen ' > ' house ': *gōśrayaṇa -- , gōṣṭhá -- , *gōstha -- (?), ghōṣa -- ); Pr. *gū´ṭu* ' cow '; S. *goṭru* m. ' parentage ', L. *got* f. ' clan ', P. *gotar, got* f.; Ku. N. *got* ' family '; A. *got* -- *nāti* ' relatives '; B. *got* ' clan '; Or. *gota* ' family, relative '; Bhoj. H. *got* m. ' family, clan ', G. *got* n.; M. *got* ' clan, relatives '; -- Si. *gota* ' clan, family ' ← Pa. 2. B. H. *gotā* m. ' relative '. (CDIAL 4279).

gava (in cmpd.) ' cow or bull '. 2. *gavu -- . [Cf. -- *gavī* -- in cmpd. e.g. *strīgavī* -- f. ' milch -- cow ' Pāṇ. com. <-> gṓ -- ] 1. Pa. *gava* -- in cmpd. e.g. *gavāssa* -- ' cows and horses '; Pk. *gava* -- m. ' cattle ', *gavā* -- f. ' cow '; WPah. bhal. *go* m. ' horned reddish wild animal like a cow '; -- Tir. *gọ̄* ' bull '; Paš. kuṛ. ar. *gō*, dar. *gā* f.; Bshk. *gṓ* ' bull ', Tor. *gō*, Phal. *gū*, pl. *gūwa*; Sh. *gō*, pl. *gavĕ´* f. rather than direct < *gaúḥ*, *gā´m*, &c. -- Si. *gava* ' bullock ' or < gāva -- .2. Pa. acc. *gavuṁ* ~ °*vaṁ*, Pk. *gaü* -- , °*ua* -- m., °*uā* -- f., S. *gaū̃* f., L. *gaū̃* f., P. *gaū* f., N. *gau*, *gauwā* f.; Or. *gaü* ' cattle '; Aw. lakh. *gaū* f., H. *gau* m.f., *gaū* f., G. *gaü* f., M. *gau* f. Brj. *gaw* m. ' Bos gavaeus '. (CDIAL 4093). gavala 'wild buffalo' (Skt. Pkt.); *gauri gāi (N.)*(CDIAL 4096).

[quote] HAW Theological Wordbook of the Old Testament relates this root semantically to four distinct etyma (*harash* I, II, III, & IV).

The verb חרש (*harash* I) means to engrave or plough. HAW Theological Wordbook of the Old Testament reads, "The basic idea is cutting into some material, e.g. engraving metal or plowing soil." Derivatives of this verb are:

חרש (*harash*), meaning engraver;

חרשת (*haroshet*) a noun meaning a carving. This word is equal to the first part of the name Harosheth-hagoyim;

חריש (*harish*), meaning plowing or plowing time;

מחרשה (*maharesha*) meaning ploughshare;

חרישי (*harishi*), a word which is only used in Jona 4:8 to indicate a certain characteristic of the sun - vehement (King James) or scorching (NIV).

The verb חרש (*harash* II) most commonly denotes refraining from speech or response, either because one is deaf or mute, or because one doesn't want to respond. None of the sources indicates a relation with the previous root, and perhaps there is none, but on the other hand, perhaps deafness was regarded in Biblical as either being marked or else cut or cut off.

The noun חרש (*horesh*) from root חרש (*hrsh* III) occurs only in Isaiah 17:9 and has to do with a wood or forest. The noun חרש (*heresh*) from root חרש(*hrsh* IV) occurs only in Isaiah 3:3 and probably means magical art or expert enchanter, or something along those lines.

The second part of the name, *hagoyim*, comes from the definite article (*ha*plus the common word גוי (*goy*) meaning nation, people, gentile. This word comes from the assumed root גוה (*gwh*), which is not translated but which seems to denote things that are surpassed or left behind. Other derivatives are: גו (*gaw* a and *gew*), meaning back, as in "cast behind the back," i.e. put out of mind (1 Kings 14:9, Nehemiah 9:26, Isaiah 38:17); גויה (*gewiya*), meaning body, either dead or alive (Genesis 47:18, Judges 14:8, Daniel 10:6).

The meaning of the name Harosheth-hagoyim can be found as any combination of the above. NOBS Study Bible Name List reads Carving Of The Nations, but equally valid would be Silence Of The Gentiles or Engraving Of What's Abandoned. Jones' Dictionary of Old Testament Proper Names reads Manufactory for Harosheth and "of the Gentiles" for Hagoyim. [unquote]

Source: http://www.abarim-publications.com/Meaning/Harosheth.html#.TwVThTVd6a8

Richard Salomon (On The Origin Of The Early Indian Scripts: A Review Article by Richard Salomon, *Journal of the American Oriental Society* 115.2 (1995), 271-279) has presented a lucid account on the evolution of *kharoṣṭī* and *brāhmī* scripts while reviewing the following works:

1. Der Beginn der Schrift und frühe Schriftlichkeit in Indien. By Oscar von Hinüber. *Akademie der Wissenschaften und der Literatur, Abhandlungen der Geistes- und Sozialwissenschaftlichen Klasse, Jahrgang 1989, Nr.11*. Mainz: Akademie Der Wissenschaften Und Der Literatur} / Stuttgart: Franz Steiner Verlag Wiesbaden}, 1990. 75 pp; and

2. *Schrift im alten Indien: Ein Forschungsbericht mit Anmerkungen.* By Harry Falk. ScriptOralia 56. Tübingen: Gunter Narr Verlag, 1993. 355 pp. DM 136.

Origin of the scripts *kharoṣṭī* and *brāhmī* are generally assigned to the early Mauryan era (late 4th-mid 3rd centuries BCE), and said to be derived from prototypes in Semitic or Semitic-derived scripts. von Hinuber has left the door open by allowing for the possibility of a 'very early form' of *kharoṣṭī*. Harry Falk notes that *kharoṣṭī* must have been created at one stroke at some later date not before 325 BCE (p. 104). "The argument for this date is based on the theory that the new script could only have originated when the professional monopoly of the Aramaic scribe-bureaucrats of the Achaemenian empire (cf. pp. 78-81) had broken down in the wake of the Greek conquest." Salomon notes that *kharoṣṭī* characters have different phonetic values from the Aramaic letters that they most closely resemble in shape *(e.g.* Aramaic *pe/kharoṣṭī a).*

I posit a hypothesis that a very early form of *kharoṣṭī* had existed, and contacts for Meluhhan traders existed with Aramaic users (perhaps related to Achaemenid arrival in northwest India c. 500 BCE). Considering that many mints of the region used both Indian hieroglyphs and *kharoṣṭī* scripts on early punch-marked coins, the possibility of existence of a syllabic script together with Indian hieroglyphs on birchbark manuscripts by metallurgists cannot be ruled out. There is evidence of birtchbark manuscripts of Gandhara with Bauddham texts dated to the first century. It should be underscored that in Uruk (Warka) and Susa, cuneiform coexisted with hieroglyphic writing sytems of the type evidenced by the Uruk (Warka) vase and inscribed ritual basin of middle Elamite period (c. 15$^{th}$ century BCE), Susa. The basin showed a ligature of goat-fish. Many ligatures of this type and even more complex ligatures such as a composite animal, are used extensively on Indus script inscriptions.

Choice of glyphs such as goat or fish and ligaturing as an orthographic medium links Susa/Uruk and Meluhha (Indus script) as a cultural interaction sphere. There are other parallels such as the architectural model of mudhif (reed hut), imageries of Sit shamshi bronze (c.125h century BCE, Susa) and are discussed in this book.

*kharoṣṭī* is an ancient *Arapacana* syllabary order used by the Gandhara culture ancient South Asia to write the Gāndhārī and Sanskrit languages: *a ra pa ca na la da ba ḍa ṣa va ta ya ṣṭa ka sa ma ga stha ja śva dha śa kha kṣa sta jñā rtha* (or *ha) bha cha sma hva tsa gha ṭha ṇa pha ska ysa śca ṭa ḍha*. It was also in use in Kushan, Sogdiana and along the Silk Road where there is some evidence it may have survived until the 7th century in the remote way stations of Khotan and Niya. The study of the *Kharoṣṭī* script was recently invigorated by the discovery of the Gandharan Buddhist Texts, a set of birch-bark manuscripts written in *Kharoṣṭī*, discovered near the Afghan city of Hadda just west of the Khyber Pass in modern Pakistan. The manuscripts were donated to the British Library in 1994. The entire set of manuscripts Kharoṣṭī script and the Gāndhārī language are dated to the 1st century CE, making them the oldest Buddhist manuscripts yet discovered. (cf. Early Buddhist Manuscript Project http://ebmp.org/)

*kharoṣṭī* included a set of numerals that are reminiscent of Roman numerals. The symbols were I for the unit, X for four (perhaps representative of four lines or directions), ↄ for ten (doubled for twenty), and ʌ for the hundreds multiplier. The system is based on an additive and a multiplicative principle, but does not have the subtractive feature used in the Roman number system.

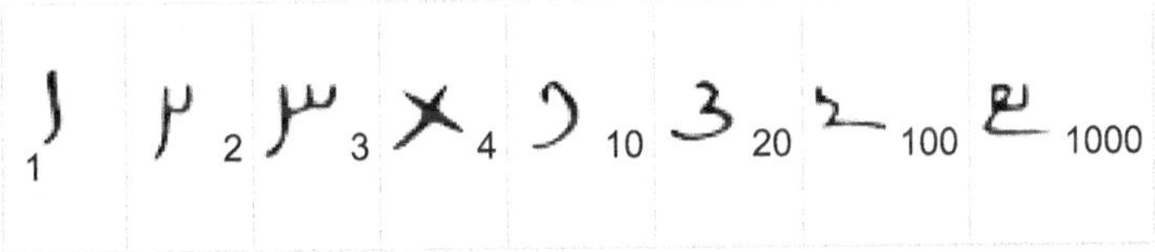


The corpora of Indus script show over 600 glyphs. Such a large number of glyphs cannot all be abstractions unrelated to an underlying language, if the glyphs were intended to convey 'meaning'. Language words are powerful tools for communication of 'meaning' in any messaging system.

This book establishes that inventors of Indian hieroglyphs were literate and used hieroglyphs to represent their sounds of speech.

Archaeology context has shown that the users of Indian hieroglyphs were innovators in the technology of using minerals, stones and creating alloys of the bronze-age: alloying copper with tin, arsenic and zinc, heralding a true industrial revolution managed by corporate formations called *śreṇi*, 'economic guilds'.

The total number of inscribed objects with Indian hieroglyphs has now reached a critical mass of over 6,000 – an adequate database for solving a mathematical problem in cryptography of matching *ciphertext* with *plaintext*.

Svastika Indus script seals. Urn with svastikas. North Elmham, Norfolk. 5th-6th century. British Museum.

This book is a sequel to *Indus Script Cipher – Hieroglyphs of Indian Linguistic Area* (S. Kalyanaraman, 2010) and presents a hermeneutics interpretation. As an exercise in cryptanalysis, the *cyphertext* is unraveled with specific, matching evidences of *plaintext* of Indian linguistic area, in an archaeo-metallurgical context.

References

Corpora of Indus script texts have been compiled by many scholars. A comprehensive illustrated corpus is still in process (2012) with only three volumes published so far, edited by Asko Parpola (and others) with UNESCO involvement, as a contribution to heritage studies (hereinafter referred to as Parpola concordance). It is hoped that the corpora will be available online open access to promote further researches in languages of ancient times, many of which survive even today in Indian linguistic area (language union, *sprachbund*). Part 1 of Volume 3 containing additional inscriptions from Mohenjo-daro and Harappa has been published in 2010.

Iravatham Mahadevan compiled a corpus of texts in 1977 together with a concordance list. Out of a total of 2906 inscribed objects (according to Mahadevan concordance), the one-horned, young bull occurs on 1159 objects; on 900 of these objects, the young bull (heifer) is shown in front of a standard device. If the inscribed objects 'without texts' but with only pictographs are also taken into reckoning, the number of inscribed objects discovered according to Parpola concordance, Volumes 1 and 2 are 3692 (Collections in India: 1537; Collections in Pakistan: 2138; West Asia: 17). Volume 3, Part 1 of Parpola concordance reckons an additional number of 472 inscribed objects from Mohenjo-daro and of 1570 inscribed objects from Harappa. Thus, the total number of inscribed objects according to Parpola concordance totals 5,734. There are also a few hundred cognate epigraphs listed in Schoyen and other museum collections which may be included in forthcoming Volume 3, Part 2.

The following objects discovered outside of Sarasvati-Sindhu river basins are also evaluated in this book:

95 seal and fragments of seals at Saar

220 sealings or fragments of sealings at Saar

16 Gadd's list of "seals of ancient Indian style found at Ur"

10 Persian Gulf seals and one Persian Gulf sealing reported by Brunswig, Parpola and Potts

2 Yale tablets

Over 10 Mesopotamian cylinder seals from Met Museum and British Museum

1 Mcmohan cylinder seal

1 Legrain's seal impression

2 seals reported by Frankfort

2 inscribed tin ingots of a Haifa shipwreck

1 Akkadian cylinder seal showing a Meluhhan

9851 Telloh

Texts related to West Asian inscriptions (either not illustrated or not linked):

[Pierre de talc. Louvre, AO 9036. P. Amiet, Bas-relliefs imaginaries de l'Orient ancien, Paris, 1973, p. 94, no. 274...ils proviendrait de Tello, l'ancienne Girsu, une des cites de l'Etat sumerien de Lagash. Musee National De Arts Asiatiques Guimet, 1988-1989, *Les cites oubliees de l'Indus Archeologie du Pakistan*.]

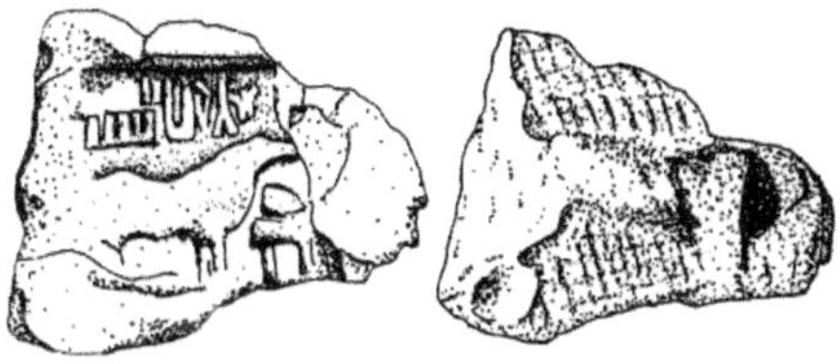

Impression of a seal from Umma. One-horned heifer. Scheil 1925. Indicative of the receipt of goods from the Sarasvati-Sindhu and of the possible presence of Indus traders in Mesopotamia. Tell Asmar seals, together with ceramics, knobbed ware, etched beads and kidney shaped inlay of bone provide supporting evidence for this possibility.

M0592 double-axe shown on a copper plate, which depicts a double-axe identical to the one unearthed in Sumer, Mesopotamia, ca. 3000 BCE.

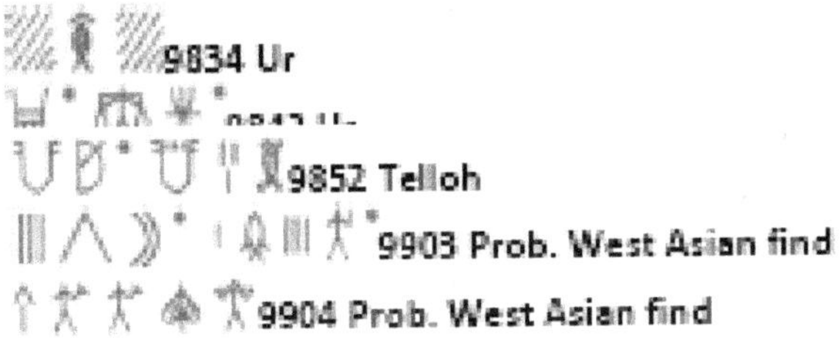

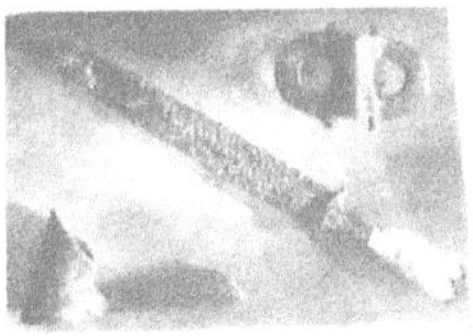

Chanhu-daro 23 seal: double-axe shown in front of antelope

Dagger and axes found in an Ur grave. Sumerian double-bladed axe, Ur (V. Gordon Childe, 1929, *The most ancient East: the oriental prelude to European history*, London, Kegan Paul, Trench, Trubner and Co. Ltd., Fig. 72b).

A double-axe comparable in shape to the double-axe found in Ur occurs as a glyph on a Mohenjo-daro copper tablet (m0592) with Indus script inscription .

m0592At

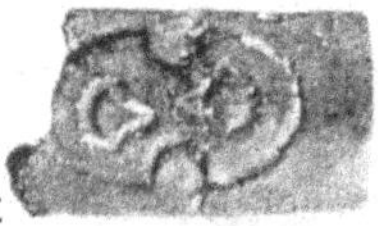

m0592Bt

3413 Pict-133: Double-axe (?) without shaft. [The sign is also comparable to the glyph which appears on the text of a Chanhu-daro seal: Text 6402, Chanhu-daro Seal 23].

Chanhu-daro is called the 'Sheffield' of ancient India by the excavator, Ernest Mackay. This work will relate this observation to *Harosheth Hagoyim* [cognate: *kharoṣṭī goy* (Meluhha/mleccha)] 'smithy of nations'.

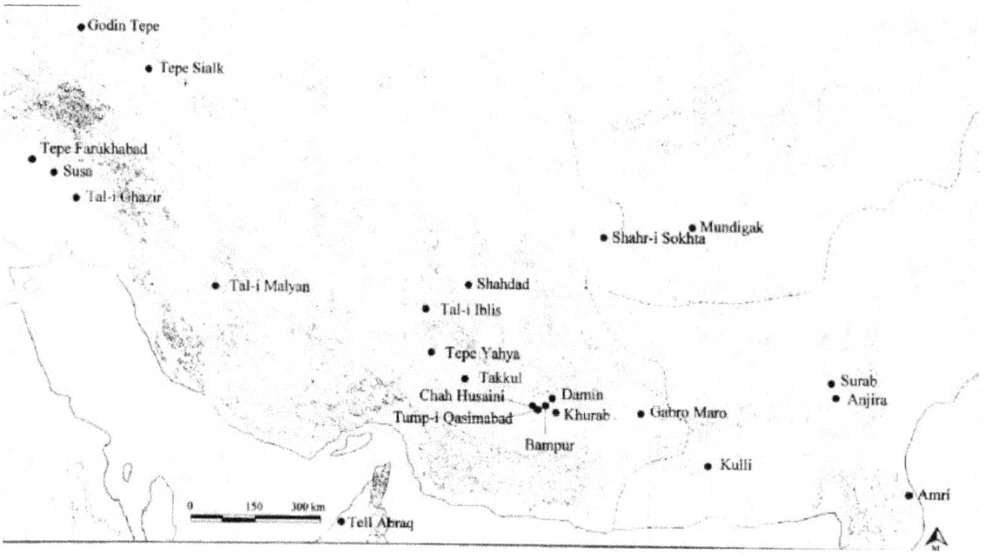


Map showing interaction areas from Susa to Meluhha (Amri), 3rd millennium BCE

Bahrain seal: four antelope heads emanating from a star. Dotted circles on the obverse. meḍha 'polar star' (Marathi). meḍ 'iron' (Ho.Mu.) Allograph: meḍh 'ram'.

The glyphics are repeated on a circular seal of Mohenjo-daro. It shows a warrior. Mohenjo-daro seal m0417 six heads from a core.

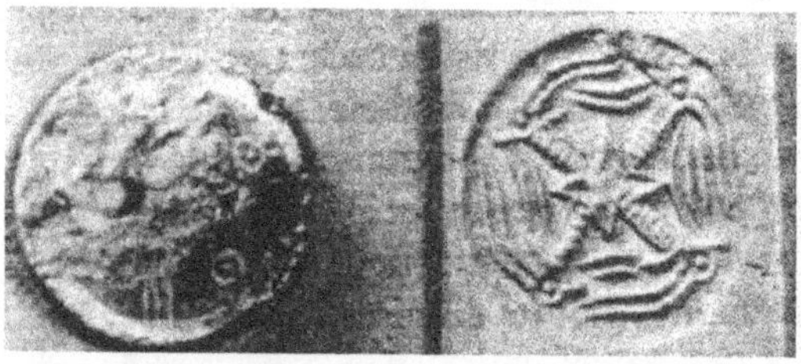

The core is a glyphic 'chain' or 'ladder'. Glyph 'linked chain': kaḍī a chain; a hook; a link (G.); kaḍum a bracelet, a ring (G.) Rebus: kaḍiyo [Hem. Des. kaḍaio = Skt. sthapati a mason] a bricklayer; a mason; kaḍiyaṇa, kaḍiyeṇa a woman of the bricklayer caste; a wife of a bricklayer (G.) Glyph: 'ladder': H. *sainī, senī* f. ' ladder ' Rebus: Pa. *sēṇi* -- f. ' guild, division of army '; Pk. *sēṇi* -- f. ' row, collection '; śrēṇi (metr. often *śrayaṇi* -- ) f. ' line, row, troop ' RV. The lexeme in Tamil means: Limit, boundary; □ □ □ □.□ □ □ □ □ □□□ □ □ □ □ □ □ □ □ □ □(□ □ □ □.35, 1). Country, territory.

The glyphics are:

Semantics: 'group of animals/quadrupeds': paśu 'animal' (RV), *pasaramu, pasalamu* = an animal, a beast, a brute, quadruped (Te.) Rebus: *pasra* 'smithy' (Santali)

> paśú m., *páśu* -- n. ' domestic or sacrificial animal ' RV. m. ' goat ' lex. Pa. *pasu* -- , *°uka* -- m. ' cattle '; Aś.shah. man. *paśu* -- , gir. kāl. dh. jau. *pasu* -- ' beast ', NiDoc. *paśu*; Pk. *pasu*<-> m. ' animal, horned quadruped, goat, sheep ', Ap. *pasuva* -- m.; Kt. *paćə* -- *moč* ' shepherd '; S. *paha* f. ' goat '; A. *pâha* ' animal of the deer class, any quadruped '; H. *pas* f. ' buffalo -- heifer ', *pasū* m. ' animal (such as goat or sheep) '. paśú -- : S.kcch. *paū* f. ' she -- goat '; WPah.poet. *pəśu* m. ' cattle, head of cattle, animal ' (Him.I 117 ← H.). (CDIAL 7984).

Glyph: 'six': bhaṭa 'six'. Rebus: bhaṭa 'furnace'.

Glyph (the only inscription on the Mohenjo-daro seal m417): 'warrior': bhaṭa. Rebus: bhaṭa 'furnace'. Thus, this glyph is a semantic determinant of the message: 'furnace'. It appears that the six heads of 'animal' glyphs are related to 'furnace' work.

There are other seals/tablets which depict 5 or 6 animals surrounding a crocodile glyph. [The examples are nine inscribed objects: m02015 A,B, m2016, m1393, m1394, m1395, m0295, m0439, m440, m0441 A,B]. On some tablets, such a glyphic composition is also accompanied (on obverse side, for example, cf. m2015A and m0295) with a glyphic of two joined tiger heads to a single body. In one inscription (m0295), the text inscriptions are also read. The animals shown are: composite animal of three tigers, crocodile, heifer, tiger-looking-back, elephant, rhinoceros, zebu (bos indicus), a pair of bulls, monkey(?).

It is a reasonable inference that these glyphics are related to the community, or guild of artisans. This gets confirmed and unraveled as decipherment provides for rebus readings of all the clearly identifiable glyphic elements.

m2015Am2015Bm2016Am1393tm1394tm 1395Atm1395Bt

m0439tm440ACm0441Atm0441Bt m0295 Pict-61: Composite motif of three tigers joined together. 1386

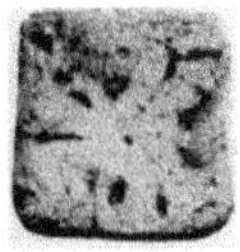

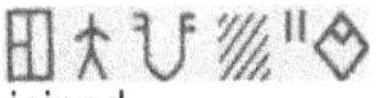

The identifiable joined animals on m0417 may relate to the lexeme *sangaḍa* 'joined animals' (Marathi). Rebus: *sangāta* 'association, guild'.

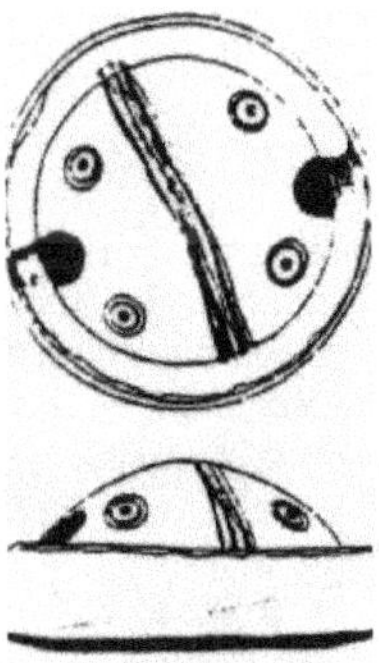

1. Glyph: 'one-horned heifer': *kondh* 'heifer'. *kūdār* 'turner, brass-worker'.
2. Glyph: 'bull': *ḍhangra* 'bull'. *Rebus: ḍhangar* 'blacksmith'. Pair of bulls: *dula* 'pair'. Rebus: *dul* 'casting (metal)'.
3. Glyph: 'ram': *meḍh* 'ram'. Rebus: *meḍ* 'iron'
4. Glyph: 'antelope': *mṛeka* 'goat'. Rebus: *milakkhu* 'copper'. Vikalpa 1: *meluhha* '*mleccha*' 'copper worker'. Vikalpa 2: *meṛh* 'helper of merchant'.
5. Glyph: 'zebu': *khūṭ* 'zebu'. Rebus: *khūṭ* 'guild, community' (Semantic determinant of the 'jointed animals' glyphic composition). *kūṭa* joining, connexion, assembly, crowd, fellowship (DEDR 1882) Pa. *gotta* 'clan'; Pk. *gotta, gōya* id. (CDIAL 4279) Semantics of Pkt. lexeme *gōya* is concordant with Hebrew *'goy'* in *ha-goy-im* (lit. the-nation-s)
6. The sixth animal can only be guessed. Perhaps, a monkey, a tiger, or a rhinoceros

Glyph: 'monkey': kuṭhāru = a monkey (Skt.lex.) Ta. kōṭaram monkey. Ir. kōḍa (small) monkey; kūḍag monkey. Ko. korṇ small monkey. To. kwṛṇ monkey. Ka. kōḍaga monkey, ape. Koḍ. koḍë monkey. Tu. koḍañji, koḍañja, koḍaṅ baboon (DEDR 2196) Konḍa (BB) kōnza red-faced monkey. Kui kōnja black-faced monkey. Kuwi (F.) kōnja monkey (small); (S.) konja ape; konzu monkey; (P.) kōnja black-faced monkey. (DEDR 2194) Rebus: kuṭhāru 'armourer or weapons maker'(metal-worker), also an inscriber or writer.

Glyph: 'tiger?': *kol* 'tiger'. Rebus: *kol* 'worker in iron'. Vikalpa (alternative): perhaps, rhinoceros. Glyph: *baḍhi* 'castrated boar'. Rebus: *baḍhoe* 'worker in wood and iron'.

Thus, the entire glyphic composition of six animals on the Mohenjo-daro seal m417 is semantically a representation of a *śrēṇi*, 'guild', a *khūṭ*, 'community' of smiths and masons.

Pa. *gotta* -- n. ' clan ', Pk. *gotta* -- , *gutta* -- , amg. *gōya* -- n.; Gau. *gū* ' house ' (in Kaf. and Dard. several other words for ' cowpen ' > ' house ': gōṣṭhá -- , Pr. *gū́ṭu* ' cow '; S. *goṭru* m. ' parentage ', L. *got* f. ' clan ', P. *gotar, got* f.; Ku. N. *got* ' family '; A. *got -- nāti* ' relatives '; B. *got* ' clan '; Or. *gota* ' family, relative '; Bhoj. H. *got* m. ' family, clan ', G. *got* n.; M. *got* ' clan, relatives '; -- Si. *gota* ' clan, family ' ← Pa. (CDIAL 4279).

This guild, community of smiths and masons evolves into Harosheth Hagoyim, 'a smithy of nations'.

It appears that the Meluhhans were in contact with many interaction areas, Dilmun and Susa (elam) in particular. There is evidence for Meluhhan settlements outside of Meluhha. It is a reasonable inference that the Meluhhans with bronze-age expertise of creating arsenical and bronze alloys and working with other metals constituted the 'smithy of nations', Harosheth Hagoyim.

Dilmun seal from Barbar; six heads of antelope radiating from a circle; similar to animal protomes in Failaka, Anatolia and Indus. Obverse of the seal shows four dotted circles. [Poul Kjaerum, The Dilmun Seals as evidence of long distance relations in the early second millennium BC, pp. 269-277.] A tree is shown on this Dilmun seal.

Glyph: 'tree': *kuṭi* 'tree'. Rebus: *kuṭhi* 'smelter furnace' (Santali).

Izzat Allah Nigahban, 1991, *Excavations at Haft Tepe, Iran*, The University Museum, UPenn, p. 97. furnace' Fig.96a.

There is a possibility that this seal impression from Haft Tepe had some connections with Indian hieroglyphs. This requires further investigation. "From Haft Tepe (Middle Elamite period, ca. 13th century) in Ḵūzestān an unusual pyrotechnological installation was associated with a craft workroom containing such materials as mosaics of colored stones framed in bronze, a dismembered elephant skeleton used in manufacture of bone tools, and several hundred bronze arrowpoints and small tools. "Situated in a courtyard directly in front of this workroom is a most unusual kiln. This kiln is very large, about 8 m long and 2 and one half m wide, and contains two long compartments with chimneys at each end, separated by a fuel chamber in the middle. Although the roof of the kiln had collapsed, it is evident from the slight inturning of the walls which remain in situ that it was barrel vaulted like the roofs of the tombs. Each of the two long heating chambers is divided into eight sections by partition walls. The southern heating chamber contained metallic slag, and was apparently used for making bronze objects. The northern heating chamber contained pieces of broken pottery and other material, and thus was apparently used for baking clay objects including tablets . . ." (loc.cit. Bronze in pre-Islamic Iran, *Encyclopaedia Iranica*, http://www.iranicaonline.org/articles/bronze-i Negahban, 1977; and forthcoming).

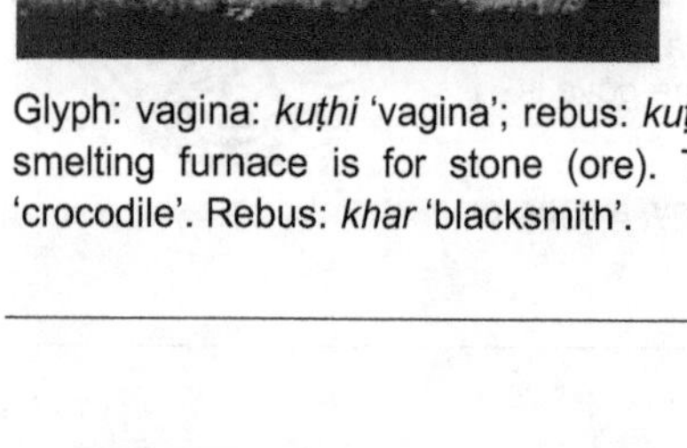

Allograph for *kāmaṭhum*, 'bow'.

The glyphic elements shown on the tablet are: copulation, vagina, crocodile. h180 tablet. Gyphic: 'copulation': *kamḍa, khamḍa* 'copulation' (Santali) Rebus: *kammaṭi* a coiner (Ka.); *kampaṭṭam* coinage, coin, mint (Ta.) *kammaṭa* = mint, gold furnace (Te.) Vikalpa: kaṇḍa 'stone (ore)'.

Glyph: vagina: *kuṭhi* 'vagina'; rebus: *kuṭhi* 'smelting furnace'. The descriptive glyphics indicates that the smelting furnace is for stone (ore). This is distinquished from sand ore. Glyph: 'crocodile': *karā* 'crocodile'. Rebus: *khar* 'blacksmith'.

Thus, the message of the glyphic composition is: *kammaṭa kaṇḍa kuṭhi khar* mint (coiner) stone (ore) smelting furnace, blacksmith.

A comparable glyphic composition is a naked woman seated with her legs spread out flanked by two scorpions. Cylinder-seal impression from Ur showing a squatting female. L. Legrain, 1936, Ur excavations, Vol. 3, Archaic Seal Impressions. This glyphic composition depicts a smelting furnace for stone ore as distinguished from a smelting furnace for sand ore. *meṛed-bica* = iron stone ore, in contrast to *bali-bica*, iron sand ore (Mu.lex.)

byucu बिचु; । वृश्चिकः m. (sg. dat. bicis बिचिस्), a scorpion. bici-zötsü bici-zötsü । परोपतापनस्वभावः adj. c.g. scorpion - natured, malignant, malicious, spiteful, maleficent. -ṭŏph -ट्वफ् । वृश्चिकदंशः f. (sg. dat. -ṭŏpi -ट्वपि), the sting of a scorpion; met. a secret malignant act. (Kashmiri) vṛ́ścika m. (vṛścana -- m. lex.) ' scorpion ' RV., ' cater- pillar covered with bristles ' lex. [Variety of form for ' scorpion ' in MIA. and NIA. due to taboo? <-> √vraśc?] Pa. vicchika -- m. ' scorpion ', Pk. vicchia -- , viṁchia -- m., Sh.koh. bičh m. (< *vṛści -- ?), Ku. bichī, A. bisā (also ' hairy caterpillar ': -- ī replaced by m. ending -- ā), B. Or. bichā, Mth. bīch, Bhoj. Aw.lakh. bīchī, H. poet. bīchī f., bīchā m., G. vīchī, vīchī m.; -- *vicchuma -- : Paš.lauṛ. ućúm, dar. učum, S. vichū̃ m., (with greater deformation) L.mult. vaṭhūhā, khet. vaṭṭhūha; -- Pk. vicchua -- , viṁchua -- m., L. vichū m., awāṇ. vicchū, P. bicchū m., Or. G. vīchu m.; -- Pk. viccu -- , ua -- , viṁcua -- m., K. byucu m. (← Ind.), P.bhaṭ. biccū, WPah.bhal. biććū m., cur. biccū, bhiḍ. biććoṭū n. ' young scorpion ', M. vīćū, vīćū m. (vīćḍā m. ' large scorpion '), vīćvī, ćvīṇ, ćīṇ f., Ko. viccu, viṁcu,iṁcu. -- N. bacchiū ' large hornet '? (Scarcely < *vapsi -- ~ *vaspi -- ).vṛścikapattrikā -- .Addenda: vṛ́ścika -- : Garh. bicchū, chī ' scorpion ', A. also bichā (phonet. -- s -- ) AFD 218. (CDIAL 12081) Rebus: bica, bica-diri (Sad. bicā; Or. bicī) stone ore; meṛeḍ bica, stones containing iron; tambabica, copper-ore stones; samṛobica, stones containing gold (Mundari.lex.)

A pair of scorpions: *dula* 'pair'. Rebus: *dul* 'casting (metal)'. Thus the entire composition reads rebus: *dul bica kuṭhi* 'casting, ore smelter.

The entire composition of glyphic elements on h180:

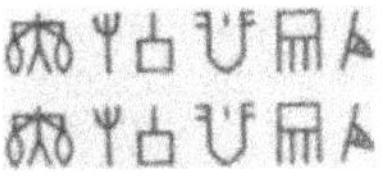

4304

Other glyphic elements of the tablet:

Two tigers rearing on their hindlegs standing face to face.

Glyph: tiger: kola 'tiger'. Rebus: kol 'working in iron'

Glyph: dula 'pair'. Rebus: dul 'casting (metal).

A person carrying a sickle-shaped weapon and a wheel on his bands faces a woman with disheveled hair and upraised arm. *kuṭhāru* 'armourer' (Skt.) salae sapae = untangled, combed out, hair hanging loose (Santali.lex.) Rebus: *sal* workshop (Santali) The glyptic composition is decoded as *kuṭhāru sal* 'armourer workshop.' *eṛaka* 'upraised arm' (Ta.). Rrebus: *eraka* = copper (Ka.) Thus, the entire composition of these glyphic elements relate to an armourer's copper workshop.

Glyphics on text inscription 4304:

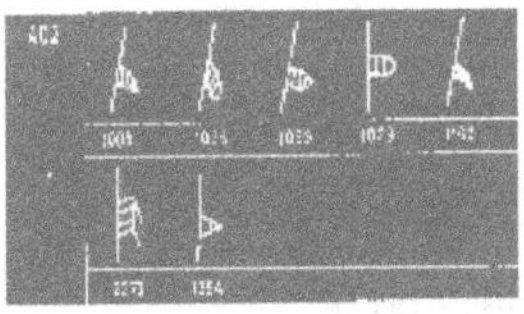

*koḍi* 'flag' (Ta.)(DEDR 2049). *koḍ* 'workshop' (Kuwi)

Sign 187 is comparable to the sign used to depict a *koṣhāgāra* 'warehouse' on Sohgaura copper plate. Rebus: *kuṭhāru* 'armourer' (Skt.) Ta. *koṭṭakai* shed with sloping roofs, cow-stall; marriage pandal; koṭṭam cattle-shed; koṭṭil cow-stall, shed, hut; (STD) koṭambe feeding place for cattle. Ma. koṭṭil cowhouse, shed, workshop, house. Ka. koṭṭage, koṭige, koṭṭige stall or outhouse (esp. for cattle), barn, room. Koḍ. koṭṭï shed. Tu.koṭṭa hut or dwelling of Koragars; koṭya shed, stall. Te. koṭṭămu stable for cattle or horses; koṭṭāyi thatched shed. Kol. (Kin.) koṛka, (SR.) korkā cowshed; (Pat., p. 59) konṭoḍi henhouse. Nk. khoṭa cowshed. Nk. (Ch.) koṛka id. Go. (Y.) koṭa, (Ko.) koṭam (pl. koṭak) id. (Voc. 880); (SR.) koṭkashed; (W. G. Mu. Ma.) koṛka, (Ph.) korka, kurka cowshed (Voc. 886); (Mu.) koṭorla, koṭorli shed for goats (Voc. 884). Malt. koṭa hamlet. / Influenced by Skt. goṣṭha- Ta. koṭi banner, flag, streamer; kōṭu summit of a hill, peak, mountain; kōṭai mountain; kōṭar peak, summit of a tower; kuvaṭu mountain, hill, peak;kuṭumi summit of a mountain, top of a building, crown of the head, bird's crest, tuft of hair (esp. of men), crown, projecting corners on which a door swings.Ma. koṭi top, extremity, flag, banner, sprout; kōṭu end; kuvaṭu hill, mountain-top; kuṭuma, kuṭumma narrow point, bird's crest, pivot of door used as hinge, lock of hair worn as caste distinction; koṭṭu head of a bone. Ko. koṛy flag on temple; koṭ top tuft of hair (of Kota boy, brahman), crest of bird; kuṭ clitoris.To. kwïṭ tip, nipple, child's back lock of hair. Ka. kuḍi pointed end, point, extreme tip of a creeper, sprout, end, top, flag, banner; guḍi point, flag, banner;kuḍilu sprout, shoot; kōḍu a point, the peak or top of a hill; koṭṭu a point, nipple, crest, gold ornament worn by women in their plaited hair; koṭṭa state of being extreme; koṭṭa-kone the extreme point; (Hav.) koḍi sprout; Koḍ. koḍi top (of mountain, tree, rock, table), rim of pit or tank, flag. Tu. koḍi point, end, extremity, sprout, flag; koḍipuni to bud, germinate; (B-K.) koḍipu, koḍipel; a sprout; koḍirè the top-leaf; koṭṭu cock's comb, peacock's tuft. Te.koḍi tip, top, end or point of a flame; koṭṭa-kona the very end or extremity. Kol. (Kin.) koṛi point. Pa. kūṭor cock's comb. Go. (Tr.) koḍḍī tender tip or shoot of a plant or tree; koḍḍi (S.) end, tip, (Mu.) tip of bow; (A.) koḍi point (Voc. 891). Malt. qoṛgo comb of a cock; ? qóru the end, the top (as of a tree). Cf. 2081 Ta. koṇṭai and 2200 Ta Ta. koṇṭai and 2200 Ta. kōṭu.(DEDR 2058)

Sign 343 sal 'splinter'; rebus: sal 'workshop' (Santali) kaṇḍa kanka 'rim of jar' (Santali); rebus: 'furnace scribe' Thus the first three glyphs (signs) from left read: koḍ kuṭhāru sal kaṇḍa kanka 'armourer workshop furnace account scribe'. The Santali gloss kan-ka is instructive.It may be a dimunitive form of *kan-khar 'copper smith' comparable to the cognate gloss: kaṉṉār 'coppersmiths, blacksmiths' (Tamil) If so, kaṇḍa kan-khār connotes: 'copper-smith furnace.'

The set of next three glyphs (signs) read rebus: ranku 'liquid measure'; rebus: ranku 'tin' (Santali) kolmo 'paddy plant' (Santali); rebus: kolami 'forge, smithy' (Telugu) kuṭi 'water-carrier' (Te.); rebus: kuṭhi 'smelter,furnace'. *ranku kolami kuṭhi* 'tin forge smithy furnace'.

Thus, the entire composition of the two-sided tablet h180 with Indus script inscription is read rebus:

workshop furnace account (scribe); tin forge smithy stone ore furnace blacksmith; armourer copper workshop. Casting (metal) working in iron.

*Harosheth ha-goy-im*, Indian hieroglyphs (*mlecchita vikalpa*) and *kharoṣṭī gōya*

A bas-relief in a fragment of a vessel has been reported from Salut, Oman on December 22, 2011. The site has also yielded a seal with Indus script. It has a hieroglyph: A pair of hoods of snakes.

Hood of a snake, *phaṭa*, is shown on some Indus script inscriptions.

Rebus reading: 'cast, sharp (tempered) alloy (metal, iron?)'

"Tempering is a heat treatment technique for metals, alloys and glass...The temperatures used in tempering are often too low to be gauged by the color of the workpiece. In this case, the blacksmith will heat the work piece for a known amount of time. Doing this ensures a certain degree of consistency in the tempering process from work piece to work piece. The cumulative effects of time and temperature can also be gauged by monitoring the color of the oxide film formed while tempering a well-polished blade."

Glyph: 'pair': dula 'pair'. Rebus: dul 'cast (metal)

Glyph: 'snake's hood': *paṭam* , *n.* < *phaṭa.* 1. Cobra's hood (CDIAL 9040). Rebus: 'sharpness of iron': padm (obl.padt-) temper of iron (Ko.)(DEDR 3907). *patam* 'sharpness, as of the edge of a knife' (Ta.)

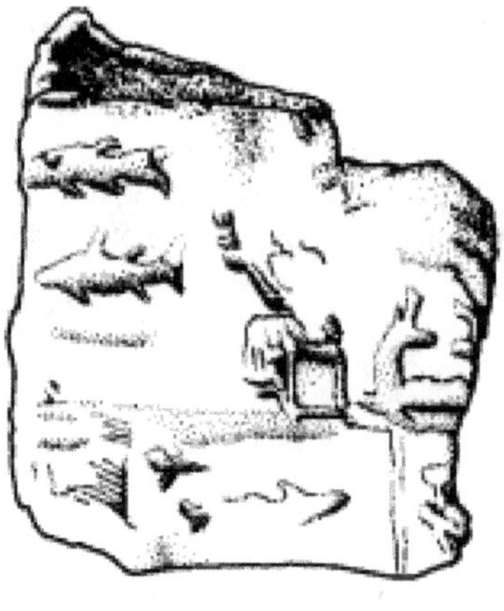

*Ill. 46*

415 Seal Impression *H.T.S. 128*
Plate 48; Ill. 46

This seal impression is incomplete, but the remaining part contains a figure, possibly a deity, at the center, with head smeared and unclear, wearing a long garment with vertical folded skirt, seated on a simple bench with one arm bent at the elbow and the hand touching his waist while the other is extended, holding some object. In front of this seated figure, are two large fish above each other, with some distance between, with clearly detailed eyes, fins, and tails. Behind the seated deity, at ground level as shown by a horizontal band, is a recumbent animal, possibly a mountain goat, with straight horns sprouting from the head which is turned backward. Behind this recumbent goat part of a tree with rounded flowers or fruit appears at the border edge of the broken side. Two more fish appear below the ground lines, similar in shape and details to those in front of the seated deity. Other incomplete parts of objects appear on panels divided by straight vertical lines under the seated figure.

Fish are rather unusual in seal designs, but they do sometimes appear. An early representation of fish appears on two seals in the Ashmolean Museum, classified by Buchanan to the Proto-historic art of the Jemdet Nasr period (Buchanan 1966: V. I, Pl. 4 Nos. 49, 50, pp. 13-14), while he assigns another seal with a fish design to Early Egyptian cylinder seals with a suggested attribution of the Proto-historic period for which, he adds, there is evidence of a connection of some sort with the Proto-historic of southern Mesopotamia and southwestern Iran (Buchanan 1966: Pl. 64 No. 1053, pp. 210-11). More seals with fish designs, in the British Museum, are classified by Wiseman as Jemdat Nasr-Early Dynastic I Period (Wiseman 1962: Pl. 1 a, d, pp. 15-16) and other seals with fish designs are also classified to Jemdat Nasr Period by Frankfort (Frankfort 1939: Pl. VII c, Pl. VIII a).

Some seals with fish designs are described by Legrain as Elamite (Legrain 1921: Pl. III Nos. 50, 51, 53, pp. 19, 45, Pl. XXIII No. 334, p. 59), while more seals with fish designs from Susa are attributed by Pezard to the native and indigenous art of Elam (Pezard 1911: Pl. I Nos. 142, 143, pp. 125-26, 334, 59). One group of seals with fish designs from Susa is attributed by Amiet to the Proto-Elamite period (Amiet 1972: V. II, Pl. 20 Nos. 766-68, 777, Pl. 92 Nos. 769-94, Pl. 126 Nos. 1315, 1318; V.I, pp. 117-19, 166), and another group to the middle of the second millennium B.C. (Amiet 1972: Pl. 178 Nos. 2050, 2052, pp. 263-64) and to the Medeo-Elamite period (Amiet 1972: Pl. 178 No. 2054, p. 267), while one example is described as a seal of the early first millennium B.C. (Amiet 1972: Pl. 186 No. 2160). Two seals in the Ashmolean are described by Buchanan as Mitannean style (Buchanan 1966: Pl. 58 Nos. 951, 952) as are many seal impressions with fish designs from Nuzi which are classified by Porada with Group XXVI of Elaborate Mitannean Style, dated to the second half of the fifteenth century B.C. (Porada 1947b: Pl. XLIV Nos. 896, 903, 905, pp. 11, 82-90). A cylinder seal with a fish design, in the Morgan collection, is described by Ward as perhaps an Assyrian cylinder seal of the Syro-Hittite region, with a suggested date of around 1000-500 B.C. (Ward 1909: Pl. XXI No. 144, p. 72).

These comparable examples with fish designs belong to different periods, and it seems that the design of a fish was not limited to a single time, but appears in various periods from the Proto-historic to the Late Elamite Period.

Decoding Salut seal with Indian hieroglyphs (Indus script)

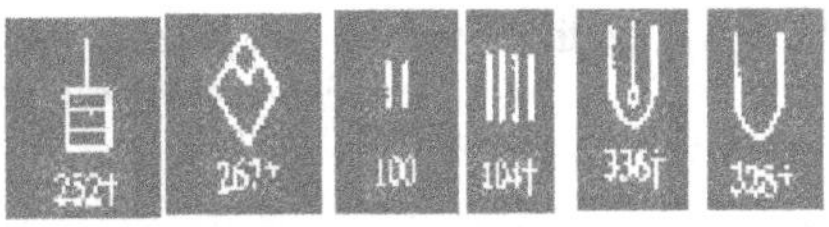

Field symbol: Ox with a trough (?) in front.

[Note: the glyphic readings may need some edits – as and when a high resolution photograph becomes available – and, the glyphic elements have been read rebus, tentatively, consonant with Indus script hieroglyphs.]

This was a stone seal with a perforated boss and was perhaps tied to a trade load from Meluhha.

An Indus Seal from the excavation of the Salut Early Bronze Age tower

December, 22, 2011

The remarkable findings reported from Salut, Oman are consistent with the central thesis of *Indus Script Cipher*. The writing in Indus Script is of artisan ancestors of Harosheth, (cognate *kharoṣṭī*) tradition. It was *harosheth hagoyim*, a smithy of nations, indeed. Harosheth is spelt in pronunciation: *khar-o'-sheth. Harosheth* and cognate *kharoṣṭī* may mean 'workmanship' or 'art of writing', apart from connoting specifically blacksmiths' writing system as artisans who invented early writing systems necessitated by the economic imperative of bronze-age trade.

http://bharatkalyan97.blogspot.com/2011/12/indus-seal-from-excavation-of-salut.html

What differentiates writing from art seen, for e.g., in rock art petroglyphs? Petroglyphs are pictures of reality (simple pictographs), for e.g., a hunting scene. Writing systems use 'glyphics' to denote sounds of speech. It took over two millennia of civilizational history to graduate from pictographs to writing. Intimations of syllabic writing evidenced by Egyptian hieroglyphs, cuneiform, proto-Elamite (?), Aramaic, *kharoṣṭī* and *brāhmī* were phases in the invention of writing before a true phonetic-alphabetic system of writing was adopted to represent speech.

There was an evolutionary phase between pictographic writing and syllabic writing. That stage was represented by Indian hieroglyphs which constituted a major breakthrough in the process of inventing writing. Indian hieroglyphs were direct representations of spoken words using a technique which is also used in Egyptian hieroglyphs: rebus glyphic representation of homophones (or, similar sounding words) which did NOT connote the phonemes related to the words associated with pictographs but connoted their homophones to create messages about bronze-age repertoire.

I call this double-imaging of impressions in the mind, *sphoṭa* (flash of thought) in imaging or writing – a representation through symbols of at least two or more *associated substratum sounds* of speech. A 'written record' is created of impressions in the minds of the sender and recipient of communicated messsages. How did this *sphoṭa* come about? I suggest that this was necessitated by an economic imperative: arrival of the bronze-age and resultant need to create bills of lading of trade loads. For over two millennia before the dawn of the bronze-age, pictographs served the needs of inter-personal communication. The dawn of bronze-age created a game-changer; artisans were able to organize themselves to trade bronze-age artifacts which were surplus to their own needs of personal consumption and were available for *trade* exchanges with neighboring settlements. The industrial revolution heralded by bronze-age was supported by the concomitant revolution in messaging systems using writing to represent sounds of *lingua franca*, spoken language to message about bronze-age repertoire of artisans.

"Spoken words are the symbols of mental experience and written words are the symbols of spoken words. Just as all men have not the same writing, so all men have not the same speech sounds, but the mental experiences, which these directly symbolize, are the same for all, as also are those things of which our experiences are the images. " [Aristotle, *On interpretation*, tr. by E.M. Edghill]

http://ebooks.adelaide.edu.au/a/aristotle/interpretation/

Invention of writing as *sphoṭa*, using Indian hieroglyphs for Meluhha language

The mental experience that Aristotle recognizes is *sphoṭa*, a flash of understanding. When a person from the Indian linguistic area (*sprachbund*) looked at a glyph which looked like a ram, the word-sound which flashed in his or her mind was *meḍha*.

This flash of word-sound also invokes – simultaneously -- a similar sounding word *meḍ* which has a meaning for him or her. This meaning is, 'iron' or semantically, some hard stone. In a cultural interaction setting of Meluhha speakers/traders, when two or more persons have contracted – in a *sprachbund* -- to associate meanings with sounds of words, the image of a 'ram' will automatically flash in both the sender of the written message and the receiver of the written message, the words *meḍha* and *meḍ* will flash the moment a glyphic of 'ram' is written down or seen in the document. Both have contracted to understand this to be *meḍ* as the word which designates 'iron' -- a hard stone that has economic value and value in use when the metal is used to make tools or weapons. This flash, this *sphoṭa*, results in the invention of a writing system, c. 3500 BCE, and occurs together with or necessitated by the invention of the economic use of 'metal' – native metal (meteoric iron?) or alloyed arsenical copper or bronze or brass or bell-metal (that is, mixed minerals: copper + tin/arsenic/zinc) -- in the bronze-age. In a flash of genius, writing stands invented to represent sounds of words and expands the use of tallies (and bullae) to keep account of material such as 'iron' of economic value and adds a 'verbal' tag to it using the method of rebus reading of glyphics.

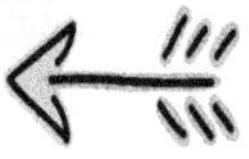

Citing a parallel from Egyptian hieroglyphic writing

The Narmer Palette (Great Hierakonpolis Palette)

Cairo J.E. 14716, C.G. 32169 Hierakonpolis

(Horus Temple 'Main Deposit')

The inventor of Egyptian hieroglyph represented *Narmer* (a name) by using two glyphics: cuttle-fish (*N'r*) + awl (chisel)(*M'r*). The writing system evolved further with some syllabic representations.

At the top of both sides of the Palette are the central serekhs bearing the rebus symbols n'r (catfish) and m'r (chisel) inside, being the phonetic representation of Narmer's name. The Narmer Palette is a 63-centimetre tall (2.07 ft), shield-shaped, ceremonial palette, carved from a single piece of flat, soft dark gray-green siltstone.

The Narmer Palette, also known as the Great ierakonpolis Palette or the Palette of Narmer, is a significant Egyptian archeological find, dating from about the 31st century BC, containing some of the earliest hieroglyphic inscriptions ever found. It is thought by some to depict the unification of Upper and Lower Egypt under the king Narmer. On one side, the king is depicted with the bulbed White crown of Upper (southern) Egypt, and the other side depicts the king wearing the level Red Crown of Lower (northern) Egypt. Along with the Scorpion Macehead and the Narmer Maceheads, also found together in the "Main Deposit" at Hierakonopolis, the Narmer Palette provides one of the earliest known depictions of an Egyptian king. The Palette shows many of the classic conventions of Egyptian art which must already have been formalized by the time of the Palette's creation."

The Egyptologist Bob Brier has referred to the Narmer Palette as "the first historical document in the world". (Brier, Bob. *Daily Life of the Ancient Egyptians*, A. Hoyt Hobbs 1999, p.202).

Cylinder seal of Uruk displaying a confronted tiger motif sometimes described as a *"serpopard"* - 3000 BCE - Louvre Jasper cylinder seal: tiger-headed eagle, tiger-headed snake hood, tiger's paws on the two animal's bodies, Mesopotamia, Uruk.

The motif is similar to the entwined snake hoods shown on Narmer Palette c. 31st century BCE. Reverse and obverse sides of Narmer Palette. Ht. 63 cm. Graygreen siltstone. Egyptian Museum in Cairo.

Obverse side

The obverse side of the Narmer Palette shows some images which link with images used in Uruk. The bottom registers shows a bull and two entwined snake-hoods. At the top of both sides of the Palette are the central serekhs bearing the rebus symbols *n'r* (catfish) and *mr* (chisel) inside, being the phonetic representation of Narmer's name. (Wengrow, David, *The Archaeology of Ancient Egypt* Cambridge University Press). The serekh on each side are flanked by a pair of bovine heads with highly curved horns, thought to represent the cow goddess Bat.

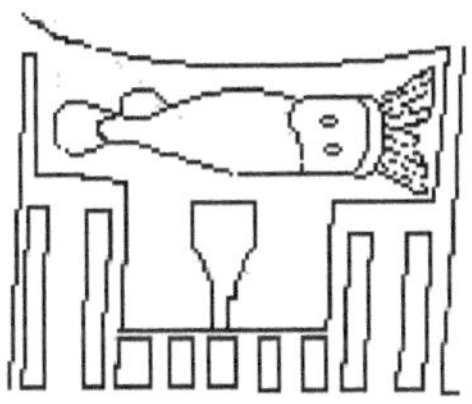

Below the bovine heads is what appears to be a procession, with Narmer depicted at almost the full height of the register (a traditional artistic representation emphasizing his importance) shown wearing the Red Crown of Lower Egypt, whose symbol was the papyrus.

He holds a mace and a flail, two traditional symbols of kingship. To his right are the hieroglyphic symbols for his name.

Behind him is his sandal bearer, whose name may be represented by the rosette appearing adjacent to his head, and a second rectangular symbol that has no clear interpretation but which has been suggested may represent a town or citadel. (Janson, Horst Woldemar; Anthony F. Janson *History of Art: A Survey of the Major Visual Arts from the Dawn of History to the Present Day* Prentice Hall 1986). Immediately in front of the pharaoh is a long-haired man, accompanied by a pair of hieroglyphs that have been interpreted as his name: *Tshet* (this assumes that these symbols had the same phonetic value used in later hieroglyphic writing). Before this man are four standard bearers, holding aloft an animal skin, a dog, and two falcons. At the far right of this scene are ten decapitated corpses, with heads at their feet, possibly symbolizing the victims of Narmer's conquest. Above them are the symbols for a ship, a falcon, and a harpoon, which has been interpreted as representing the names of the towns that were conquered.

Below the procession, two men are holding ropes tied to the outstretched, intertwining necks of two serpopards confronting each other, mythical felines with bodies of leopards (or more likely lionesses, given that there are no spots indicated) and snakelike necks. The circle formed by their exaggeratedly curving necks is the central part of the Palette, which is the area where the cosmetics would be ground. These animals have been considered an additional symbol for the unification of Egypt, but it is a unique image in Egyptian art and there is nothing to suggest that either animal represents an identifiable part of Egypt, although each had lioness war goddesses as protectors and the intertwined necks may represent the unification of the state. Similar images of such mythical animals are known from other contemporaneous cultures, and there are other examples of late-predynastic objects (including other palettes and knife handles) which borrow similar elements from Mesopotamian iconography. (Wilkinson, Toby A.H. *Early Dynastic Egypt*. p.6, Routledge, London. 1999.)

At the bottom of the Palette, a bovine image is seen knocking down the walls of a city while trampling on a fallen foe. Because of the lowered head in the image, this is interpreted as a presentation of the king vanquishing his foes, "Bull of his Mother" being a common epithet given to Egyptian kings as the son of the patron cow goddess. (Breasted, , James Henry. *Ancient Records of Egypt*, Chicago 1906, part Two, §§ 143, 659, 853; part Three §§ 117, 144, 147, 285 etc). This posture of a bovine has the meaning of "force" in later hieroglyphics.

A comparable glyphic composition occurs on a Chanhu-daro seal.

Bison (gaur) trampling a prostrate person (?) underneath. Impression of a seal from Chanhujodaro (Mackay 1943: pl. 51: 13). The prostrate 'person' is seen to have a very long neck, possibly with neck-rings, reminiscent of the rings depicted on the neck of the one-horned bull normally depicted in front of a standard device.

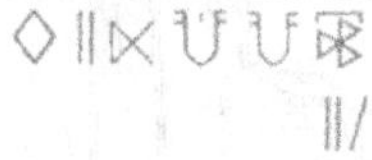

6113 Pict-98

Reverse side

Repeating the format from the other side, two human-faced bovine heads, thought to represent the patron cow goddess Bat, flank the serekhs. Some authors suggest that the images represent the vigor of the king as a pair of bulls.

A large picture in the center of the Palette depicts Narmer wearing the White Crown of Upper Egypt, whose symbol was the flowering lotus, and wielding a mace. To his left is a man bearing the king's sandals, again flanked by a rosette symbol. To the right of the king is a kneeling prisoner, who is about to be struck by the king. A pair of symbols appear next to his head, perhaps indicating his name or indicating the region where he was from.

Above the prisoner is a falcon, representing Horus, perched above a set of papyrus flowers, the symbol of Lower Egypt. In his talons, he holds a rope-like object which appears to be attached to the nose of a man's head that also emerges from the papyrus flowers, perhaps indicating that he is drawing life from the head. The papyrus has often been interpreted as referring to the marshes of the Nile Delta region in Lower Egypt, or that the battle happened in a marshy area, or even that each papyrus flower represents the number 1,000, indicating that 6,000 enemies were subdued in the battle.

Below the king's feet is a third section, depicting two naked, bearded men. They are either running or are meant to be seen as sprawling dead upon the ground. Appearing to the left of the head of each man is a hieroglyphic sign, the first a walled town, the second a type of knot, likely indicating the name of a defeated town.

Source: http://en.wikipedia.org/wiki/Narmer_Palette

It appears that the entwined snakes has a Sumerian connection.

This is a scene from a ceremonial make-up palette c. 3300 BCE. Two jackals face standing up face each other. Two snakes flanking a circle have tiger-heads in place of the snake-hoods, licking a ram. Some suggest that this may be an import from Sumer to the Nile Valley. Source: The depiction of rams in the context of faces of tigers is determinative that the sharpness, tempered metal sought to be achieved by the process of alloying is related to copper. Hence, the tiger glyphs could connot bronze or arsenic alloys of copper. A pair tiger glyphs then indicate cast bronze or arsenic alloys – cast perhaps into bun ingots or cast into weapon or tool shapes hardened enough to be made with sharpened edges.
http://www.nemo.nu/ibisportal/0egyptintro/2aegypt/index.htm

The two tigers standing on their hindlegs and facing each other on the Sumerian palette are comparable to *kola*, the jackals or tigers shown on the Harappa tablet h1971.

h1971B Harappa. Three tablets with identical glyphic compositions on both sides: h1970, h1971 and h1972. Seated figure or deity with reed house or shrine at one side. Left: H95-2524; Right: H95-2487.

The glyph of entwined snake-hoods together with an eagle appear on a Uruk cylinder seal.

H 14.5 cm. dia. 8.5 cm. black steatite. Late 3rd-early 2n millennium BCE. Leopard fighting a snake.
Source: http://www.louvre.fr/en/oeuvre-notices/vase-depicting-leopard-fighting-snake

The Sumerian deity, Ningizzida, is accompanied by two gryphons; it is the oldest known image of two snakes coiling around an axial rod, dating from before 2000 BCE.

(Kohl, 1978; idem, 1979)

Rebus readings: Glyph: *kola* 'tiger'. Rebus: *kol* working

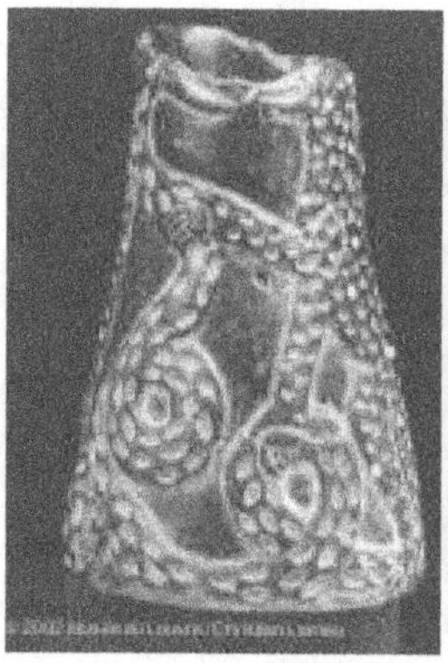
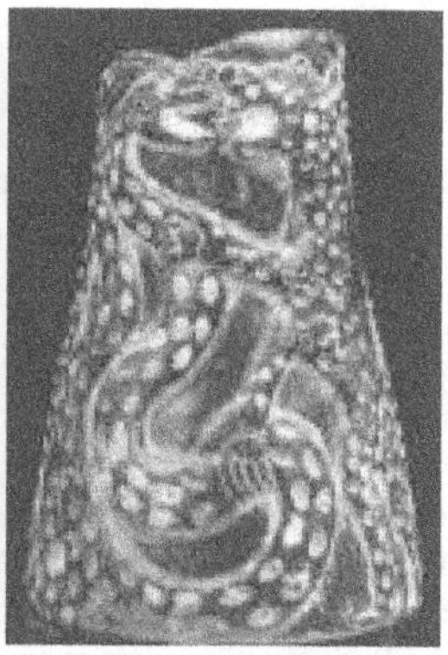
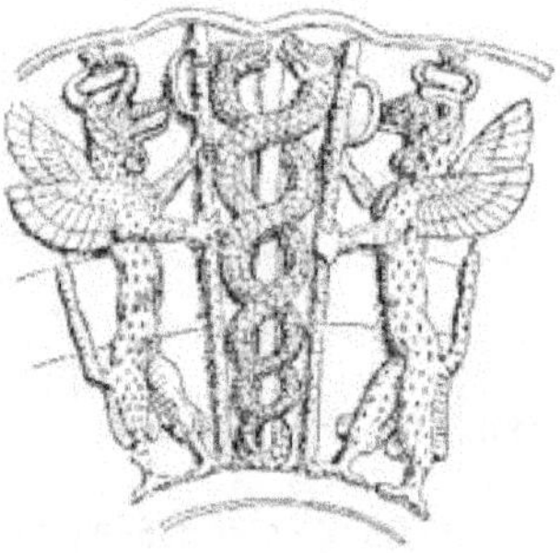

'pañcaloha, alloy of five metals, in iron'. Glyph: when the head of the tiger is elongaged to appear like a snake's hood: Glyph: 'snake's hood': *paṭam.* Rebus: *padm* 'temper, sharpness (of metal)'. If the ram glyph denotes *melakku* 'copper'. or meḍ 'metal', the tiger glyph denotes an alloy of minerals: kol. When elongated like a snake's hood, the tiger represents a sharpened, tempered alloy – *padm kol* -- which can produce sharp tools, sharp as the edge of a knife and weapons. Pair of snake-hoods is relatable to the glyph: dola 'pair'. Rebus: dul 'cast (metal). Thus a pair of tigers with elongated necks made to look like snake-hoods cnnote 'cast alloy tempered metal.' Such a snake-hood is shown on Indus script inscriptions by the tail of a composite animal to look like a snake's hood. Ligaturing tiger (jackal) with a snake's hood is a way of celebrating the creation by the artisan of an alloy which could produce sharp-edged tools and weapons.

This vase in the shape of a truncated cone is decorated with a motif often found on steatite recipients from the 3rd millennium BC: a leopard fighting a snake. The fight certainly refers to an episode in trans-Elamite mythology. Chlorite vases were luxury objects produced for export.

Comparable to the elongated necks tigers entwined as serpents on Narmer Palette and on Uruk cylinder seal, there is a fantastic composition on some copper plates of Mohenjo-daro. One example of m0578 copper tablet is shown.

m0578At

m0578Bt Orthography seems to have been effectively used to depict the hood of snake etymon: paṭam (Rebus: padm 'sharpness, temper like the edge of a knife'. Maybe, the intention is to depict 'cast tempered metal' by a worker in iron, *badhi* (since part of the rump of the composite animal looks like a rhinoceros).

On a composite animal m1175, the tail is depicted to mimic a snake's hood.

m1175

Worship of entwined snakes carved on stone, roadsite temple, Hampi

PLATE XLVIII

Two views of chlorite handle with opposed "combatant" snakes, Tepe Yahya IVB2. Courtesy of The Peabody Museum, Harvard University.

Narmer palette is rebus method of writing . The name of the king ca. 31st century BCE was depicted by two glyphs (on top of the palette between two ox-heads): n'r 'cat-fish' + mr 'awl or chisel'. Similar method of rebus representation of hieroglyphs was adopted on Indus script glyphs — to detail technical specifications of products made by artisans (and NOT names).

About the same time or perhaps a few centuries earlier than 3300 BCE when Narmer Palette was composed using rebus method of hieroglyphs. Indus script was evolving using a similar rebus method of hieroglyphs. Just as orthography and glyph patterns on Narmer Palette show interconnections with Uruk, Indian hieroglyphs also show interconnections with Uruk. If Narmer Palette is a candidate for the earliest writing system using hieroglyphs, Indus script inscriptions also are also to be reckoned for identifying the earliest writing system using hieroglyphs as glyphic representation of sounds of speech. Both evolutionary phases in the evolution of writing systems used for words or morphemes together with cuneiform and later Aramaic or kharoṣṭī systems of writing used for syllables should be deemed major contributions on the road to a breakthrough in bronze age trade communications.

A note on Bat, the goddess depicted on Narmer Palette

It is unclear if the rebus reading of the name Bat is relatable to *baṭha, baṭhi* 'furnace' in Mleccha (Meluhha).

Godess Bat is shown as a pair on Narmer Palette flanking both sides of the rebus inscription N'r M'r.

She has a human face with horns and 'cow' ears, depicting a petal, leaf *daḷa*, a lexeme which may also explain the rosette with six petals, shown as a phonetic determinative of the sandal bearer accompanying Narmer and shown on obverse and reverse sides of the Narmer Palette. (Rebus readings: *daḷa* 'leaf, petal'. Rebus: 'arsenic', 'army, guild'.) This sandal bearer could be a Meluhhan who prepared the hieroglyphic inscription. (Rebus readings of Bat, goddess: Glyph: *baṭa* 'six'. Rebus: *bhaṭa* 'furnace').

Note the six flower-buds shown below the eagle's talon. Six is an Indian hieroglyph shown on the hair-do of a woman with one-eye holding back two rearing tigers on a few tablet duplicates of Harappa with Indus inscriptions. (Rebus reading of eagle glyph: pajhaṛ 'kite'. Rebus: pasra 'smithy, forge'.) Thus, the glyphic composition depicts a smithy/forge with a (metal smelting) furnace for copper. Glyph: ``^flower'':Sa. *baha* `flower, blossom, to flower'.Mu. *tarai-ba*(A) `a kind of marsh-flower'. ~ *baa*(H) ~ *baha*(N) `flower, blossom, to flower'.Ho *ba* `flower, blossom, to flower'.Bh. *baha* `flower, blossom, to flower'. KW *baha*|Cf. So. *ba'a* `to blossom'.@(V021,M111) Allograph: *Ta.* eruvai a kind of kite whose head is white and whose body is brown; eagle. *Ma.* eruva eagle, kite.(DEDR 818). Rebus: eruvai 'copper' (Tamil). B. khāg, khāgṛā ' reed for pens ', Or. khagaṛā ' the reed Saccharum spontaneum '. Allograph: Pk. khaggi -- ' rhinoceros '.(CDIAL 3786). Rebus: kãgar portable brazier (Kashmiri) Glyph: *mũh* 'face'. *mũhe* 'ingot'. The entire glyphic composition is a depiction of a 'smithy/forge with copper ingot furnace'.

Significanceof 'six' as a glyphic notation may be seen from Mohenjo-daro seals: m0112 and m0241.

Sign 147 which is the first glyphic on the inscription is relatable to 'ingots' from Glyph: *baṭa* 'six'.Rebus: *bhaṭa* 'furnace'.

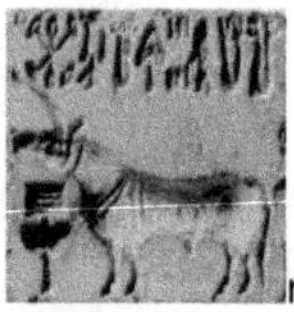
m0112  2099

m0241  1536

The glyph sequence Sign 403 (Glyph: bangles) and Sign 87 (Glyph: two) are read rebus: Glyph: sangaḍa 'bangles' (Pali). Rebus: sangāta 'association, guild' (Skt.) Glyph: ib 'two'. Rebus: *ib* 'iron'. The pair thus reads: *ib* sangaḍa 'iron (worker) guild'.

h0723 Harappa tablet obverse.

h0669 Harappa seal. Flipped to show as the sequence of glyphs would appear on a seal impression.

The pair of glyphs is seen on Mohenjo-daro faience tablet m0453 in the context of kamaḍha 'penance'. Rebus: *kampaṭṭa* 'mint, coiner'. Vikalpa *kaṇḍ* 'stone ore metal'. The pair of glyphs of 'snake hoods': Glyph: dula 'pair'. Rebus: dul 'cast (metal)'. Glyph: *paṭam* 'snake's hood'. Rebus: *padm* 'tempered, sharp (metal), like the edge of knife'. The message of the inscription: iron guild mint producing sharp, tempered (hard) metal.

m453BC 1629 Pict-82 Person seated on a pedestal flanked on either side by a kneeling adorant and a hooded serpent rearing up.

The procession showing four standard bearers (including two standards showing a bird perched on top) is similar to the procession shown on a Mohenjo-daro tablet carrying three standards showing glyphs: 'scarf', 'one-horned heifer' and 'standard device'. The bird perhed on top of the first two standards carried may be read rebus: Glyph: *baṭa* 'quail'. Rebus: *bhaṭa* 'furnace'. The third and fourth standards could also denote 'one-horned heifer' and 'scarf'. (Rebus readings: kondho 'one-horned heifer'. Rebus: *kũdār* 'turner, brass-worker'. Glyph: *dhaṭu* 'scarf'. Rebus: *dhatu* 'mineral'.)

[quote]

By the time of the Middle Kingdom Bat's identity and attributes were subsumed within the goddess Hathor. (Wilkinson, Richard H. *The Complete Gods and Goddesses of Ancient Egypt*, p.172 Thames & Hudson. 2003. )

The worship of Bat dates to earliest times and may have its origins in Late Paleolithic cattle herding. Bat was the chief goddess of Seshesh, otherwise known as Hu or Diospolis Parva, the 7th nome of Upper Egypt.

The epithet Bat may be linked to the word *ba* with the feminine suffix 't'. Ba means something like personality or emanation and is often translated as 'soul' . The word can also be read as 'power' or 'god'. Bat became strongly associated with the sistrum and the center of her cult, was known as the 'Mansion of the sistrum'. (Hart, George. *The Routledge Dictionary of Egyptian Gods and Goddesses*, p. 47 2nd Edition Routledge. 2005.)

The sistrum is a musical instrument whose shape is very similar to that of the ankh.

This instrument is depicted with her head and neck as the handle and base, with rattles placed between her horns. The imagery is repeated on each side, having two faces. The sistrum was one of the most frequently used sacred instruments in temples.

The Egyptian Pyramid Texts say:

*I am Praise; I am Majesty; I am Bat with Her Two Faces; I am the One Who Is Saved, and I have saved myself from all things evil.* (R. O. Faulkner, The Ancient Egyptian Pyramid Texts, Oxford 1969, p. 181, Utterance 506)

Both Hathor on the left and Bat on the right flank Menkaure (2532–2503 BCE) in this fourth Dynasty triad statue, the goddesses are providing the authority for him to be king; note the feather of Ma'at held by the emblem on Bat's crown –Stone statue. *Cairo Museum* Another interpretation reads: Triad statue of pharaoh Menkaura, accompanied by the goddess Hathor (on his right) and the personification of the nome of Diospolis Parva (on his left). The hieroglyphs at the bottom of the statue have not been read.

On another statue, vikalpa (alternative) hieroglyphs of 'jackal nome', 'reed' and 'currycomb' are depicted to denote Bat. Glyph: jackal: *kola* 'jackal'. Rebus: *kol* 'woman', *kol* 'working in iron, alloy of five metals.' Nome is a geographic division which divided ancient Egypt. Linked to Sistrum nome, Diospolis parva (Greek) relates to Hut (Het)(Egyptian name) and Hu (name today) http://www.toutankharton.com/Nomes The 'reed' glyph which is shown on mudhifs and on Uruk trough, links the region to Sumer.

M.V.T., triad of the Jackall-nome, no. 11, upper part. Plate 43

(Triad No. 12, inscription, left half) (Triad No. 12, inscription, right half)

Source: Plate 46.
http://www.gizapyramids.org/pdf%20library/reisner_gn_books/mycerinus/plates_43to57.pdf

Although it was rare for Bat to be clearly depicted in painting or sculpture, two exceptions are displayed below, one in bovine form and the other in human form. In rare instances she was pictured as a celestial bovine creature surrounded by stars. More commonly, Bat was depicted on amulets, with a human face, but with bovine features, such as the ears of a cow and the inward-curving horns of the type of cattle first herded by the Egyptians.

She is found, on a significant Egyptian archaeological find. This stone object dates from about the 31st century BC and contains some of the earliest hieroglyphic inscriptions. It is thought by some to depict the unification of Upper and Lower Egypt during the first dynasty under the pharaoh Narmer. Bat appears at the top of each side of the object.

The imagery of Bat as a divine cow was remarkably similar to that of Hathor the parallel goddess from Lower Egypt. The significant difference in their depiction is that Bat's horns curve*inward* and Hathor's curve *outward* slightly. It is possible that this could be based in the different breeds of cattle herded at different times.

In two dimensional images, both goddesses often are depicted straight on, facing the onlooker and not in profile in accordance with the usual Egyptian convention.

Hathor's cult centre was in the 6th Nome of Upper Egypt, adjacent to the 7th where Bat was the cow goddess, which may indicate that they were once the same goddess.

In the image to the right a king of the fourth dynasty is flanked by both goddesses, Hathor and Bat. They are remarkably similar in this large sculpture, however, their crowns identify them clearly. The emblem on Bat repeats the sistrum imagery and her zoomorphic face is present upon it (wearing another sistrum). The image on her crown carries the feather of Ma'at.

[unquote]

Source: http://en.wikipedia.org/wiki/Bat_(goddess)

The glyph of a woman's face on the hieroglyph is comparable to the glyph shown on a metal linchpin of a war chariot dated to c. 1500 BCE, discovered by University of Haifa, from El-ahwat, near Katzir in Israel.

This is the hieroglyph composition shown above Bat's head. Bat is shown together with Hathore and Mendaure on the stone statue. Between the horns, is a reed symbol shown with a mudhif of Sumer on

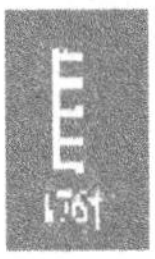

Uruk trough. The ears on the human face are orthographically comparable to two petals or two leaves. A comb is shown athwart a pole, together with scarves hanging down the pole.

Reading hieroglyphs rebus: Glyph: Composition of Bat goddess. Rebus: *bhaṭa, bhaṭi* 'furnace'. Glyph: *koḍ* 'horns'. Rebus: *koḍ* 'artisan's workshop'. Glyph: *kola* 'woman'. Rebus: *kol* 'pañcaloha, alloy of five metals, working in iron.' Glyph: *mũh* 'face'. *mũhe* 'ingot'. Glyph: *dhaṭu* 'scarf'. Rebus: *dhatu* 'mineral'. Glyph: *karṇaka* 'ear'. Rebus: *karṇaka* 'account scribe'. Glyph: *daḷa* 'leaf, petal'. Rebus: 'arsenic (alloying mineral for arsenical copper, brass)', 'army, guild'. *khareḍo* = a currycomb (G.) Rebus: *kharādī* ' turner' (G.) [Comparable to an Indian hieroglyph, Indus Script Sign 176.] Glyph: 'reed': *Ta. eruvai* European bamboo reed. Rebus: *eruvai* 'copper' (Tamil). A pair (of leaves): *dula* 'pair'. Rebus: *dul* 'cast (metal)'.

The entire mleccha (meluhhan) composition: *koḍ bhaṭa dul mũhe eruva dhatu kharādī karṇaka daḷa* (Glyphs: horns, face,two leaves, reed, currycomb, scarf, ear). Rebus: 'artisan's workshop,furnace,cast arsenical-copper ingot, copper mineral smith (metal-turner), account-scribe-guild'.

The 'reed' glyph and the 'humanface' glyph are the key hieroglyphic links to Uruk trough and Indian hieroglyphs of Indus script.

The Meluhhan settlers of Uruk who created the hieroglyphs of Uruk trough, of Indus script and of the Nar Mer Palette are of the same scribe guild whose language was Indus language, mleccha (meluhha) and who had learnt the literate art of writing to represent (vikalpa) human speech sounds.

The Meluhhan, the *kaṇḍakanka,* the account scribes have produced evidence for *mlecchita vikalpa* (cryptographic representation of *deśabhāṣā jñānam* 'knowledge of dialects of language' of the Indian *sprachbund* (language union or linguistic area). Both *mlecchita vikalpa* and *deśabhāṣā jñānam* are listed by Vātsyāyana (c. $8^{th}$ cent. BCE) together with *akṣaramuṣṭika kathanam* (narration using fingers and wrist – mudra) as three language related arts to be learnt by youth.

This account scribes' evidence is presented in this book as a contribution to a phase of evolution of writing systems to represent sounds of human speech.

Meadow: "The earliest (Indus) inscriptions date back to 3500 BC."

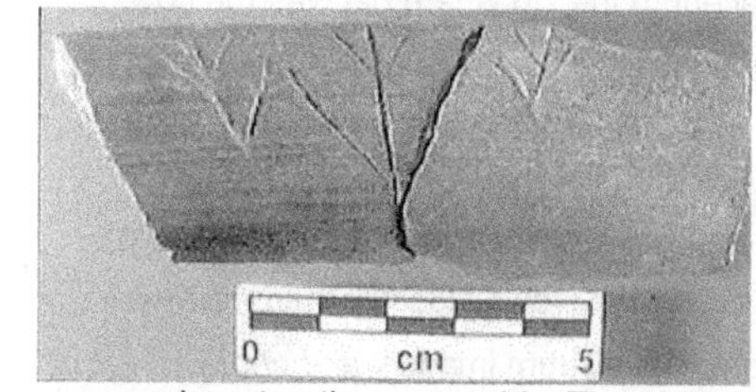


h1522A sherd. Slide 124. Inscribed Ravi sherd. The origins of Indus writing can now be traced to the Ravi Phase (c. 3300-2800 BCE) at Harappa. Some inscriptions were made on the bottom of the pottery before firing. Other inscriptions such as this one were made after firing. This inscription (c. 3300 BCE) appears to be three plant symbols arranged to appear almost anthropomorphic. The trident looking projections on these symbols seem to set the foundation for later symbols such as those seen in 131 (shown below).

Slide 131. Inscribed sherd, Kot Dijian Phase. This sign was carved onto the pottery vessel after it was fired and may indicate the type of goods being stored in the vessel or the owner of the vessel itself...This symbol becomes very common in the later Indus script.

I suggest that the word associated with this glyph is *tagaraka, tabernae montana.* Rebus: *tagara* 'tin' (Ka.); tamara id. (Skt.) Allograph: *ṭagara* 'ram'. Since *tagaraka* is used as an aromatic unguent for the hair, fragrance, the glyph gets depicted on an ivory comb of Tell Abraq. The semant. 'tin' may explain why a ram (or goat) is ligatured to a 'fish' glyph. Tin alloyed with copper mineral yields bronze: *aya* 'fish'. Rebus: *aya* 'metal'.+ *ṭagara* 'ram'. Rebus: *tagara* 'tin' yields bronze. Hence, the celebration and documenting the ligatured goat-fish on the Susa vat.

Susa, limestone vat, Middle Elamite period (c. 1500 BC – 1100 BCE). Louvre Musuem.

Indian hieroglyphs were not syllabic writing. Indian hieroglyphs were word-writing (sometimes called logographic or morphemic writing) to denote the bronze-age repertoire experienced by artisan guilds. Thus, process of writing moved from the stage of tally-bullae system of accounting to a written accout of a furnace scribe, an associate of the bronze-age trader, to support economic transactions using bills of lading for bronze-age trade loads. A corollary to the account presented in this book of this stage of evolution of writing, is the identification of over 1000 glosses of the *lingua franca* of the artisans, scribes, and traders who used Indian hieroglyphs.

The inventor of Indian hieroglyphs represented a smith, *ayakāra* by presenting two glyphics: fish (*aya*) + crocodile (*karā*). The writing system evolved further with combinations of glyphics as ligatures, to connote word-phrases. For syllabic representations, new methods – syllabic scripts -- were invented, called: *kharoṣṭī* and *brāhmī* which were used together with Indian hieroglyphics, on, for example, punch-marked coins.

Indian hieroglyph composition comparable to Egyptian hieroglyph reading 'Narmer'

Glyph: *ayo* 'fish' (Mu.) Rebus: *aya* = iron (G.); *ayah, ayas* = metal (Skt.)

Glyph: *kāru* a wild crocodile or alligator (Te.) Rebus: *khār* a blacksmith, an iron worker (cf. bandūka-khār) (Kashmiri)

Combined rebus reading: *ayakāra* 'iron-smith' (Pali)

One side of a prism tablet;

m0410, m0482 Seal

m0482A One side of a two-sided tablet m1429C

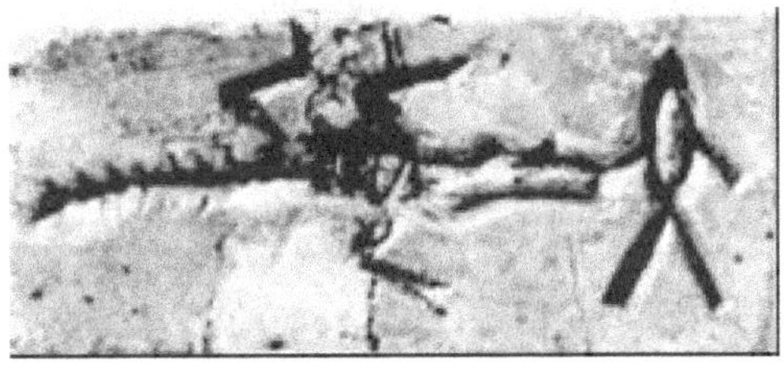

m2033B One side of a prism tablet.

The *lingua franca* was Meluhha (mleccha). An *Indian Lexicon* read with this book and *Indus Script Cipher* provide the methodological framework and resource base for language studies of Indian linguistic area (*sprachbund* or language union) and to promote further researches into the evolution of syllabic scripts: Aramaic, *kharoṣṭī* and *brāhmī*.

This work avers that invention of writing using Indian hieroglyphs was necessitated by the economic imperative of the bronze age, c. 3500 BCE. Indus script was composed of hieroglyphs written and read rebus. The Indian hieroglyphs were orthographic representations of lexemes (phonetic-semantic) of an underlying language of artisans. The language was meluhha (cognate mleccha) of Indian linguistic area (*sprachbund*).

Indus script stands unraveled in an archaeological context of 19 circular platforms found in Harappa some with Indus script tablets — close to a furnace/kiln used for smelting.

Advancing from tallies which were used extensively in Elam-Susa to tablets (used widely in Harappa and Mohenjo-daro) inscribed with hieroglyphs read rebus phonetically, counting was taken to the next stage of evolution of writing to record an account of categories and descriptions of traded products.

Invention of writing: an economic imperative of bronze age

In the pre-bronze era, tallies served the needs of tracking property items inventoried as lists of personal possessions such as farm animals or textiles or food items.

Bronze age brought in its wake many organizational changes. A lapidary who was working with clay or shell or stone beads had graduated from chalcolithic phase to be a miner or a smith capable of creating alloys, working with a variety of furnaces, a variety of mineral sand or stone ores such as copper, gold, silver, lead, tin, zinc, and experimenting with creating alloys using techniques for mixing copper and tin, copper and zinc, using furnaces to create metal ingots, or create sculptures or tools, or weapons using moulds, learnt the use of anvils to forge metals into plates or vessels. Thus, lapidaries graduated to become professionals with special competence as coppersmiths, blacksmiths, turners, carvers, turners. Tallies of unique shapes or even complex tallies with markings were inadequate to cope with the sudden multiplication of professions and products handled by the artisans. A new invention was needed to categorise, sort and consolidate the account for trade loads.

The metallurgical techniques of mixing minerals in furnaces, to create alloys like bronze or brass were also paralleled by the techniques of ligaturing glyphic elements to create unique sets of Indian hieroglyphs. Good examples of such mixing in orthographic representation are 'composite animal' glyphs; 'ram' glyphic ligatured to 'human-face' glyphic element; 'one-horned heifer' glyph with characteristic 'pannier' glyphic element, and 'rings-on-neck' glyphic element; a 'short-horned bull or elephant or rhinoceros or tiger or buffalo' glyphic elements shown in front of a 'trough' glyphic; 'water-carrier' glyphic in 'parenthesis' glyphic enclosure with 'star' glyphic elements; 'seated-person' glyphic in 'penance' posture with 'star' glyphic elements; 'rim' glyphic element emphasized on a 'narrow-necked jar' glyphic element.

Complex tokens evolved as Indus tablets (many miniatures with incisions as in Harappa) with Indus script inscriptions, based on an underlying spoken speech, to designate categories of products from artisan's workshops.

That the tablets were tokens with writing becomes evident by the numbers of duplicates discovered in excavations. The inscriptions on tablets were category identifiers for trade goods.

Tallies shaped in various types could serve the needs of 15 or 16 categories of property items or inventory lists: for e.g., shapes identified by Denise Schmandt-Besserat of cones, spheres, disks, cylinders, tetrahedrons, ovoids, quadrangles, triangles, biconoids, paraboloids, bent coils, ovals, rhomboids, vessels, tools, animals. In some cases such as shapes of tools or shapes of animals – as pictographs – identified the particular tools, particular vessels and particular animals as property items or inventory lists of tools or animals (sheep, goat, ewe, cow etc.) or vessels (plates, pans, pots, etc.)

To categorise numbers of categories larger than 15 or 16, not enough numbers of clearly identifiable tally shapes could be invented. Hundreds of industrial goods which were coming out of workshops of organized guilds of artisans – lapidaries, shell-workers, miners, metal workers, ivory-carvers and alloy-makers, ingot-producers and makers of metallic tools and weapons needed hundreds of identifier tokens. Even distinct markings on tokens were inadequate to cope with the large number of categories of goods. The markings could only be meaningless graphics.

This imperative of coping with a large inventory list of goods and varieties of processes of bronze age, necessitated the invention of writing by making the graphic markings *meaningful*. This is the crux of semantic representation as the hall-mark of Indian hieroglyphic writing.

Pictographs had graduated to be logographs as hieroglyphs – an abstraction connoting the sounds (phonemes) used to represent the animals, semantically in the language used by the artisans and traders. The leap in writing systems occurred when the sounds instantenously evoked by the logographs became associated with rebus (similar sounding) semantics, not connoting the animal –

crocodile, tiger or rhinoceros etc. – itself but a similar sound in the spoken language, *lingua franca*, which connoted a bronze-age trade item or related professional competence.

A crocodile, tiger or rhinoceros, respectively, with meaningful semantics – *khara, kola or badhi* – were not themselves the trade items but were read rebus connoting rebus semantics: 'smith, metal-worker, worker in wood and iron'. So it is that what were mentioned in Cuneiform texts as trade in 'fish-eyes' were not fish-eyes themselves as trade items but a rebus reading of what the 'dotted circles' as glyphic elements connoted semantically, in meaningful representations of bronze-age artifacts or bronze-age technology processes. An 'eye' was kaṇḍ; read rebus: kaṇḍ 'stone (ore) of iron (metal)' as in *ayaskāṇḍa* a phrase attested (c. 6th century BCE) by Pāṇini, meaning 'excellent or stony (hard) iron (metal)'.

This was how semantics were introduced into the systems of identifiers or potters' marks using the underlying phonetics of the spoken language, *lingua franca*, which identified the goods with remarkable precision and uniqueness.

This is how hieroglyphic writing of Indus script came about, to match with the invention of bronze-age metalwork and a consequent revolution in industrial organization through corporate forms of guilds and long-distance trade (using seal impressions to authenticate/describe trade consignments).

Just as bronze or brass were alloys created by mixing copper and tin or copper and zinc, hieroglyphs were also mixed or ligatured to connote multiple trade goods or professional competences.

m0702 Mohenjo-daro seal. Glyphic on h859 Harappa two-sided tablet (31 duplicates found). Such an arched reed roof might have adorned each of the 19 circular platforms of Harappa. Who knows?

Etyma in Indian linguistic area denote this multiplicity of trade goods: *mā̃ḍ* m. 'array of instruments &c.' (Marathi); Si. *maḍa -- ya* 'adornment, ornament' (Sinhala). (CDIAL 9736) *muṭṭu* 'instrument, tool' (Telugu) (DEDR 4937). This array could be denoted orthographically and read rebus, by an arch comparable to the Toda *munda* hut or Sumerian *mudhif* – a *caitya* roof or barrel-vaulted, arched or curved roof – a unique architectural marvel in Indian linguistic area.

Hence, the invention of composite animal glyphs as combination hieroglyphs – combining the rebus semantics connoted by the glyphs of elephant (trunk), tiger (forelegs), bull (hindlegs), serpent (tail), horns (zebu or *bos indicus*), human face (*mukha – rebus mū̃h 'ingot'*).

Representation of syntax, morphological modifications to sememes and grammar in language was the next stage in evolution of writing which resulted in syllabic abstract graphics of cuneiform, *kharoṣṭī* or *brāhmī*.

Many of the bronze-age manufactured or industrial goods were surplus to the needs of the producing community and had to be traded, together with a record of types of goods and types of processes such as native metal or minerals, smelting of minerals, alloying of metals using two or more minerals, casting ingots, forging and turning metal into shapes such as plates or vessels, using anvils, *cire perdue* technique for creating bronze statues – in addition to the production of artifacts such as bangles and ornaments made of śankha or shell (*turbinella pyrum*), semi-precious stones, gold or silver beads. Thus writing was invented to maintain production-cum-trade accounts, to cope with the economic imperative of bronze age technological advances to take the artisans of guilds into the stage of an industrial production-cum-trading community.

Tablets and seals inscribed with hieroglyphs, together with the process of creating seal impressions took inventory lists to the next stage of trading property items using bills of lading of trade loads of industrial goods. Such bills of lading describing trade loads were created using tablets and seals with the invention of writing based on phonetics and semantics of language – the hallmark of Indian hieroglyphs.

m0491 Tablet. Line drawing (right)

Dawn of the bronze age is best exemplified by a Mohenjo-daro tablet which shows a procession of three hieroglyphs carried on the shoulders of three persons. The

hieroglyphs are: 1. Scarf carried on a pole; 2. A heifer carried on a stand; 3. Portable standard device (lathe-gimlet).

Three professions are described by the three hieroglyphs: *dhatu kōdā sãgāḍī* 'Associates (guild): mineral worker; metals turner-joiner (forge); worker on a lathe'.

The rebus readings are:

1. WPah.kṭg. dhàṭṭu m. ' woman's headgear, kerchief ', kc. dhaṭu m. (also dhaṭhu m. ' scarf ', J. dhāṭ(h)u m. Him.I 105). dhaṭu m. (also dhaṭhu) m. 'scarf' (WPah.) (CDIAL 6707) Rebus: dhatu = mineral (Santali) dhātu 'mineral (Pali) dhātu 'mineral' (Vedic); a mineral, metal (Santali); dhāta id. (G.) H. dhāṛnā 'to send out, pour out, cast (metal)' (CDIAL 6771).
2. koḍiyum 'heifer' (G.) [ kōḍiya ] kōḍe, kōḍiya. [Tel.] n. A bullcalf. . k* దూడA young bull. Plumpness, prime. తరుణము. జోడుకోడయులు a pair of bullocks. kōḍe adj. Young. kōḍe-kāḍu. n. A young man.పడుచువాడు. [ kārukōḍe ] kāru-kōḍe. [Tel.] n. A bull in its prime. खोंड [ khōṇḍa ] m A young bull, a bullcalf. (Marathi) గోద [ gōda ] gōda. [Tel.] n. An ox. A beast. kine, cattle.(Telugu) koḍiyum (G.) Rebus: koḍ artisan's workshop (Kuwi); B. kōdā 'to turn in a lathe'; Or. kũnda 'lathe', kũdibā, kũd 'to turn' (→ Drav. Kur. kũd 'lathe') (CDIAL 3295)
3. Drawing. Reconstruction of the glyphic elements in 'standard device' shown in front of a heifer on many Indus inscriptions.

san:gaḍa, 'lathe, portable furnace'; śagaḍī (G.) = lathe san:gāḍo a lathe; sãghāḍiyo a

worker on a lathe (G.lex.) sãgaḍ part of a turner's apparatus (M.); sãgāḍī lathe (Tu.)(CDIAL 12859). sāṅgaḍa That member of a turner's apparatus by which the piece to be turned is confined and steadied. सांगडीस धरणें To take into linkedness or close connection with, lit. fig. (Marathi) सांगाडी [ sāṅgāḍī ] f The machine within which a turner confines and steadies the piece he has to turn. (Marathi) सगडी [ sagaḍī ] f (Commonly शेगडी) A pan of live coals or embers. (Marathi) san:ghāḍo, saghaḍī (G.) = firepan; saghaḍī, śaghaḍi = a pot for holding fire (G.)[culā sagaḍī portable hearth (G.)] Rebus 1: Guild. सांगडणी [ sāṅgaḍaṇī ] *f* (Verbal of सांगडणें) Linking or joining together (Marathi). संगति [ saṅgati ] *f* (S) pop. संगत *f* Union, junction, connection, association. संगति [ saṅgati ] *c* (S) pop. संगती *c* or संगत *c* A companion, associate, comrade, fellow. संगतीसोबती [ saṅgatīsōbatī ] *m* (संगती & सोबती) A comprehensive or general term for Companions or associates. संग [ saṅga ] *m* (S) Union, junction, connection, association, companionship, society. संगें [ saṅgēṃ ] *prep* (संग S) With, together with, in company or connection with. संघात [ saṅghāta ] *m* S Assembly or assemblage; multitude or heap; a collection together (of things animate or inanimate). संघट्टणें [ saṅghaṭṭaṇēṃ ] *v i* (Poetry. संघट्टन) To come into contact or meeting; to meet or encounter. (Marathi) G. *sãghāṛɔ* m. ' lathe '; M. *sãgaḍ* f. part of a turner's apparatus ' (CDIAL 12859) Rebus 2: stone-cutting. sanghāḍo (G.)

cutting stone, gilding (G.); san:gatarāśū = stone cutter; san:gatarāśi = stone-cutting; san:gsāru karan.u = to stone (S.) san:ghāḍiyo, a worker on a lathe (G.) Rebus 3: saṁghaṭayati ' strikes (a musical instrument) ' R., ' joins together ' Kathās. [√ghaṭ]Pa. *saṅghaṭita* -- ' pegged together '; Pk. *saṁghaḍia*<-> ' joined ', caus. *saṁghaḍāvēi*; M. *sā̃gaḍṇē* ' to link together '. (CDIAL 12855). Rebus 3: battle. jangaḍiyo 'military guard who accompanies treasure into the treasury' (G.)

Glyph: 'dotted circles': *kaṇḍ* 'eye'. Rebus: *kaṇḍ* 'stone (ore) metal'.

Allograph 1: M. *sā̃gaḍ* f. ' a body formed of two or more fruits or animals or men &c. linked together (CDIAL 12859). Oriya. *saṅghāṛibā* ' to mix up many materials, stir boiling curry, tie two cattle together and leave to graze ' (CDIAL 12860). A body formed of two or more animals is a 'composite animal' glyphic ligature.

Allograph 2: *sā̃gāḍā* m. ' frame of a building ' (M.)(CDIAL 12859)

Allographs to denote rebus: dhatu = mineral (Santali)

Glyph: 'waist-band':Ta. taṭṭi drawers. Ka. daṭṭi waist-band, sash, zone. Tu. daṭṭi waist-band. Te. daṭṭi waist-band or girdle of cloth, sash. Kui ḍaṭa a long cloth. / ? Cf. Skt. dhaṭī- piece of cloth worn over the privities; (Vaijayantī) dhaṭinī- string round the loins; Mar. dhaḍī dhotee (DEDR 3038). *dhaṭa2, dhaṭī -- f. ' old cloth, loincloth ' lex. [Drav., Kan. daṭṭi ' waistband ' etc., DED 2465] Ku. dhaṛo ' piece of cloth ', N. dharo, B. dhaṛā; Or. dhaṛā ' rag, loincloth ', dhaṛi ' rag '; Mth. dhariā ' child's narrow loincloth '.*dhaṭa -- 2. 2. †*dhaṭṭa -- (CDIAL 6707).

Glyph: 'headless body': *dhaḍa ' trunk of body '. Pk. dhaḍa -- n. ' trunk of body ', S. dhaṛu m., P. dhaṛ f.; Ku. dhaṛ m. ' trunk of body or tree, middle part of anything '; B. dhaṛ 'trunk of body', Or. dhaṛa ' trunk of body or tree '; Mth. dhar ' headless body '; OAw. dhara m. ' body, heart '; H. dhaṛ m. ' trunk of body ' (→ Mth. N. dhaṛ), OMarw. dhaṛa m., G. dhaṛ n.; M. dhaḍ n. ' headless body '. (CDIAL 6712).The procession is a celebration of the graduation of a stone-cutter as a metal-turner in a smithy/forge.A *san:gatarāśū* 'stone-cutter' or engraver/lapidary of neolithic/chalolithic age had graduated into a metal turner's workshop (*koḍ*), working with metallic minerals (dhatu) of the bronze age.

h0006. Harappa seal. The glyphs of heifer, together with a standard device are the most frequently used hieroglyphs on Indus script inscriptions.

The entire message on the seal – of field symbol + glyphics on text inscription is a description of the professional metallurgical repertoire or artisans of a mint (coiners) guild.

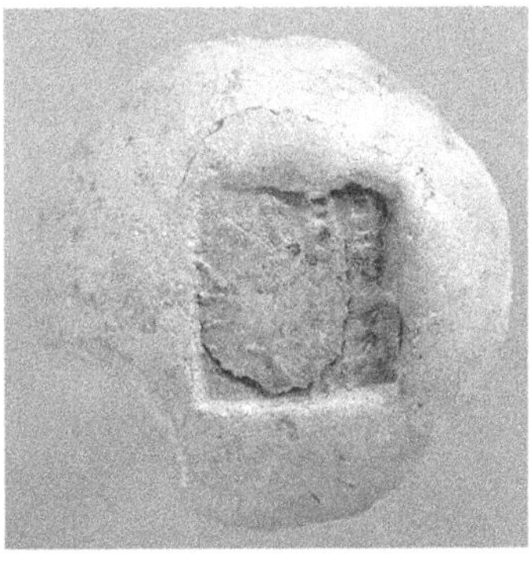

1. Glyphics of one-horned heifer (pannier, rings on face/neck, one-horn) + lathe/furnace: *kūdharsangaḍa kammārasāla* 'workshop, association (or guild) of brass-work turners, (ore)stone-workers, stone-engravers'

2. Reading rebus the text inscription glyphs on h0006 seal: Mint (Coiner) Guild (with) iron workshop, smithy, forge, furnace (of) turner.

Glyph: *Sēni* 'ladder'. Rebus: *sēṇi* 'guild'.

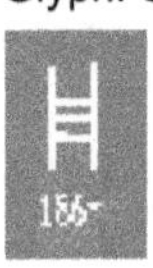

Glyph: *koḍ* 'one'. Rebus: *koḍ* 'workshop'.

Glyph: 'two' ib 'two'. Rebus: ib 'iron'.

Glyph: pot + three ingots. baṭi 'pot. Rebus: *baṭhi* 'furnace'. *kolmo* 'three'. Rebus: *kolami* 'smithy, forge'. Thus the ligatured glyphic reads; *kolami baṭhi* 'smithy, forge, furnace'

Glyph: khoṇḍ square (Santali) 'rhombus or angle'. *koṇḍ* 'angle'. Rebus: B. kõdā 'to turn in a lathe'. *kũdar* 'brass-worker, turner'.

Glyph: *kāmaṭhum* = a bow; *kāmaḍ, kāmaḍum* = a chip of bamboo (G.) *kāmaṭhiyo* a bowman; an archer (Skt.lex.) Rebus: *kammaṭi* a coiner (Ka.); *kampaṭṭam* coinage, coin, mint (Ta.) *kammaṭa* = mint, gold furnace (Te.)

Sign 186 on Slide 137. Harappa.com This Early Harappan seal impression or sealing of a square seal has several script signs and two ladder like motifs (Kot Diji Phase, c. 2800 BCE). The wet clay was probably placed on a bundle of goods to seal it and then was broken off when the bundle was opened. Since this sealing was found in a hearth area, it is probable that the raw clay was hardened accidentally when it was swept into the fire along with other trash, possibly even the rope or reeds used to bundle the goods.

A possible array of three ladder glyphs on the Harappa seal impression (Slide 137)? If so, kolmo 'three'. Rebus: kolami 'forge, smithy'. Hence, the entire text inscription phrase on this seal impression may connote: guild of forge,smithy.

Glyph: 'ladder' (cf. first sign on text of inscription on h0006 seal): H. *sainī, senī* f. ' ladder '; Si. *hiṇi, hiṇa, iṇi* ' ladder, stairs ' (GS 84 < *śrēṇi* -- ). (CDIAL 12685). niśrayaṇī´ f. ' ladder, staircase ' ŚBr., *nihśrayaṇī* -- , °*yiṇī* -- , *ni(ḥ)śrēṇī* -- f. MBh. [√śri] Pa. *nissēni* -- f. ' ladder ', Pk. *ṇissēṇī* -- , *ṇīsēṇi* -- , *ṇīsaṇī* -- , °*ṇiā* -- f., Or. *nisiṇi*, °*suṇi*, (Sambhalpur) *nisānī* (< **niśrāyaṇa* -- ?), OAw. *nisenī*, OH. *nasīnī* f., H. *nisenī* f., M. *niśīṇ*, *nisaṇ* f., Ko. *nisaṇi*, Si. *nisiṇiya.* -- G. *nisarṇī* (P. B. Paṇḍit IL xvi 123) rather < niḥsaraṇa -- . (CDIAL 7458). S. *sīṇa* f. ' the threads of the loom between which the warp runs '; Or. *seṇi* ' row of rafters in a thatched roof, the wooden plates on which the rafters are put crosswise '; Bi. *senī* 'the broad flat metal plates in a tobacconist's shop'.(CDIAL 12718).
Rebus: Pa. *sēṇi* -- f. ' guild, division of army '; Pk. *sēṇi* -- f. ' row, collection '; śrēṇi (metr. often *śrayaṇi* -- ) f. ' line, row, troop ' RV. [Same as **śrayaṇī* -- (for ' line ~ ladder ' cf. *śrēṣṭrī -- 2)? -- √śri] (CDIAL 12718). ஏணி[1] ēṇi , *n.* < எண்-. cf. *śrēṇi.* 1. Number; எண். ஏணிபோகிய கீழ்நிலைப்படலமும் (ஞானா. 54, 1). 2. Tier; அடுக்கு. அண்டத்தேணியின் பரப்பும் (கந்தபு. சூரன்வதை. 485). 3. [K. M. Tu. *ēṇi.*] cf. *niśśrēṇī.* Ladder; ஏறுதற்கருவி. மண்டலத்தூ டேற்றிவைத் தேணிவாங்கி (திவ். பெரியாழ். 4, 9, 3). 4. Limit, boundary; எல்லை. நளியிரு முந்நீரேணி யாக (புறநா. 35, 1). 5. Country, territory; நாடு. (திவா.)

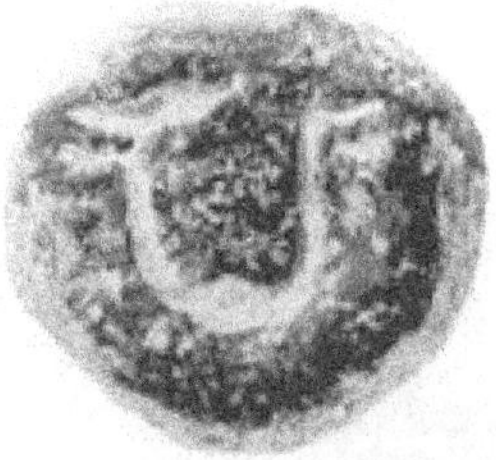

Daimabad seal. 'Rim of jar' hieroglyph is shown on a circular seal.

Another hieroglyph used with comparable high frequency of occurrence is that of a 'rim-of-jar'. This is decoded rebus: kaṇḍ kanka, kaṇḍ karṇaka 'rim of jar' (Santali. Sanskrit). Rebus: furnace account (scribe). This hieroglyph announces the arrival of a new professional, an expert carver who can keep accounts of the industrial goods produced in guild workshops and sorted out or displayed on circular working platforms. This hieroglyph is often the terminal signature tune of many inscriptions conveying the message that goods tallied using tablets have been consolidated together to create seal impressions as bills of lading for multi-commodity trade loads. The invention of writing has created a new professional: (accountant) scribe.

Bronze Head in High Relief. Cast in high relief, depicting a youthful face rising from a plaque. From the Gandhara culture, circa 3rd century AD. Northern Pakistan Dimensions - Height: 5.8 cm. Width: 5.0 cm. A 3,200-year-old round bronze tablet with a carved face of a woman, found at El-ahwat excavation site near Katzir in central Israel, is part of a linchpin that held the wheel of a battle chariot in place.

Why was the face of a woman carved on the bronze tablet? I suggest that the pictograph was a hieroglyph connoting glyphic:

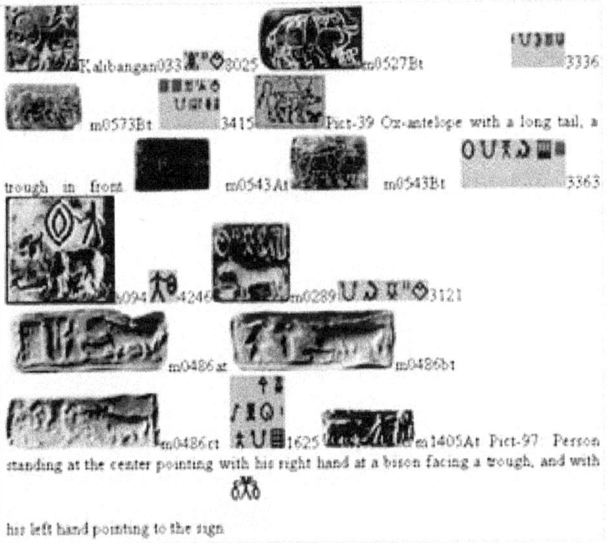


*kola* 'woman' (Nahali). Rebus: *kol* 'working in metal' (Tamil). kola 'blacksmith' (Ka.); Koḍ. kollë blacksmith (DEDR 2133). kolhe 'iron smelter' (Santali) kol, kolhe 'the koles, an aboriginal tribe of iron smelters akin to that of the Santals' (Santali) kulhu 'a hindu caste, mostly oil men'; kulhu 'an oil press' (Santali) WPah.kṭg. kóllhu m. ' sugar -- cane or oil press '. (CDIAL 3536).

Another breakthrough in advancing writing systems, beyond phonetic hieroglyphs to categorise trade items and prepare bills of lading, was the invention of abstract graphics in syllabic writing system such as cuneiform, aramaic, *kharoṣṭī, brāhmī*. Syllabic writing was used to write names of trade partners or names of places of origin or destination of traded goods, or words of common parlance (beyond the list of glosses which could be directly logographically connoted by hieroglyphs). Together with syllabic systems of writing, hieroglyphs were used to write designations of professions or descriptions of materials used, production processes (such as smelting, casting, forging, turning) or to name the products manufactured. A good example of such combined deployment of syllabic writing and hieroglyphic writing is in the set of devices used on punch-marked coins, from c. 6th cent. BCE.

The interactions which led to the diffusion of the idea of writing is evidenced by the fact that *kharoṣṭī* and *harosheth* in *harosheth-hagoyim* 'smithy of nations' are cognate etyma. Haroshesh-hagoyim is the site which produced the bronze linchpin used for battle chariots. The linchpin had used a hieroglyph: profile of the face of a woman.

Thanks to the work of Randall Law, Kenoyer, Meadow, HARP recent Harappa excavations and Susa pot reported by Maurizio Tosi (with a 'fish' glyph painted on the pot which yielded metal artifacts from

Meluhha?)—all who have raised thoughtful questions and provided the archaeological finds which complete the picture of the ancient work of ancient bronze age artisans of Indus-Sarasvati civilization.

Circular working platform as a workshop (anvil, smithy, forge).

A lexeme of Indian linguistic area which described a circular working platform of the type found at Harappa: Ku. Pathrauṭī f. ' pavement of slates and stones '(CDIAL 8858) Ta. paṭṭaṭai, paṭṭaṟai anvil, smithy, forge. Ka. Paṭṭaḍe, paṭṭaḍi anvil, workshop. Te. Paṭṭika, paṭṭeḍa anvil; paṭṭaḍa workshop.(DEDR 3865). Pathürü f. ' level piece of ground, plateau, small village '; S. patharu m. ' rug, mat '; Or. Athuripathuri ' bag and baggage '; M. pāthar f. ' flat stone '; OMarw. Pātharī ' precious stone '.(CDIAL 8857) Allograph Indus script glyph: pātra 'trough' in front of wild/domesticated/composite animals. Pattar 'trough' (DEDR 4079) 4080 Ta. Cavity, hollow, deep hole; pattar (DEDR 4080) Rebus: பத்தர்² pattar , n. < T. battuḍu. A caste title of goldsmiths. It was a smiths' guild at work on circular platforms of Harappa using tablets as category 'tallies' for the final shipment of package with a seal impression.

Trough as a hieroglyph
See examples of 'trough' glyph are shown in front of wild, domesticated and composite animals — an evidence for the use of 'trough' glyph as a hieroglyph, together with the 'animal' glyph. Maybe, the 19 circular working platforms of Harappa were used for assembling 19 'types' of products — the 'trough' glyph denoting the working platform and the 'animal' glyph denoting the product type (e.g. copper, gold, metal alloy, output of furnaces (of various types), minerals).

**ಪಟ್ಟಡಿ paṭṭu 2-aḍi 4. = ಪಟ್ಟಡೆ, q. v. (My.; Ši. 399). 2, = ಪಟ್ಟಡಿಮನೆ (My.). — ಪಟ್ಟಡಮನೆ. A workshop (ಅದೇಶಶ, ಕಲ್ಸಾಲೆ Bl. 108; My.).**

**ಪಟ್ಟಲೆ paṭṭalĕ. A district, a community. (R.).** Kittel Kannada dictionary (p. 926). A possible allograph used in Indus script glyphs: X a place where four roads meet — *paṭṭa* (Kannada)

 6131This is the only text on a large Chanhu-daro seal and occurs together with 'one-horned heifer' glyph.

Orthographically comparable glyphs including ligatured glyphs (or glyphs with modified glyphic elements) on texts:

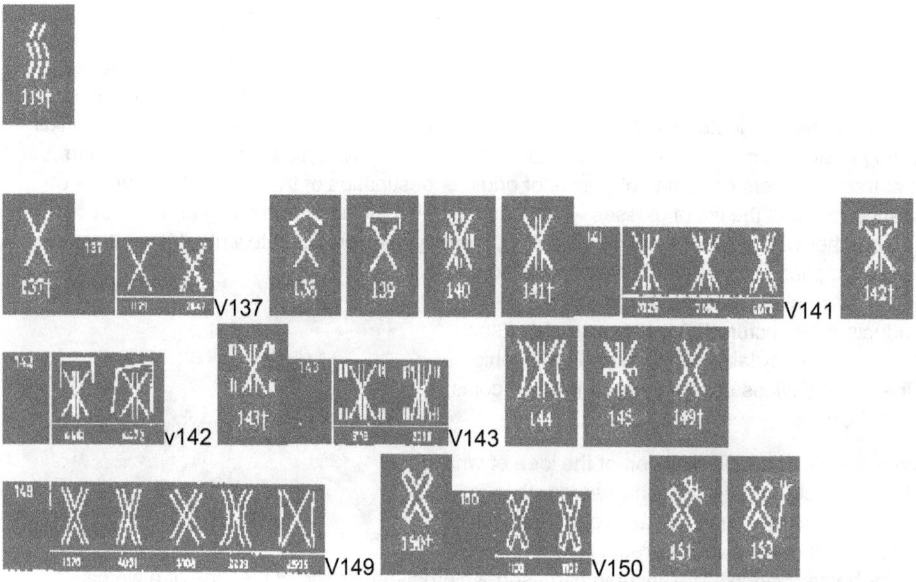

Glyphic elements on Sign 140, 143 (Sign 119 depicts four sets of two short strokes or a total of eight short strokes as shown on h351 miniature tablet) may connote depiction of a fraction $1/8^{th}$. This is conjectured from the orthography of Sign 120 which shows eight short slanted strokes.

The glyph is read as *vaṭṭa, bāṭa* 'road'. Rebus: *bhaṭa* 'furnace, smelter'. vártman n. ' track of a wheel, path ' RV. [J. Bloch StudII 19 **vartmā* nom. sg. m. after *ádhvā* m. (cf. pánthā -- ) became f. in MIA. -- √vr̥t1] Vaṭuma (nt.) [cp. Vedic vartman, fr. vr̥t] a road, path D ii.8; S iv.52 (chinna˚); J iii.412; Vism 123 (sa˚ & a˚). (Pali) Pa. *vaṭuma* -- n. ' path, road ', Pk. *vaṭṭa* -- n.m., *vaṭṭā* <-> f., *vaṭṭamaya* -- , *vaḍū̆maga* -- n., K. *wath*, dat. *°ti* f., pog. *wat*, S. *vāṭa* f., P. *vāṭ,bāṭ* f., ḍog. *batta* f., kgr. *bat* f., bhaṭ. *batt*, WPah.bhad. bhal. paṅ. cam. *batt* f., pāḍ. cur. *bat*; Ku. *bāṭ* ' path, pass ', *bāṭo* m. ' path ', N. *bāṭo* (obl. *bāṭa* postp. ' from '), A. B. *bāṭ*; Or. *bāṭa* ' path, place '; Mth. *bāṭ* ' path ', Bhoj. *bāt*, OAw. OMarw. *bāṭa* f., H. *bāṭ* f., G. M. Ko. *vāṭ* f.; Si.*vaṭuma* ' road ' (← Pa.?), *devaṭa* ' lane ' (*de* -- < dēśá -- ?); -- Sh. *bāṭu̯* m. ' wheel '; G. *vāṭɔ* m. ' tire ' (semant. cf. *vartaní* -- f. ' felly of wheel, path ' RV., Pa. *vattanī* -- f. ' track, path ', Pk. *vaṭṭaṇī* -- f. ' road '). -- Deriv.: N. *baṭuwā* ' traveller '; B. *beṭo* ' of the road ' < **bāṭuā* ODBL 491; Or. *bāṭuā* ' traveller ', G. *vāṭvɔ* m. -- X mārga -- q.v. -- Si. *vat* ' road ' (LM 404, EGS 155) extracted from *māvat* < *mahāpanthā -- . (CDIAL 11366) బాట [ bāṭa ] *bāṭa*. [Tel.] n. A road, way. రాజమార్గము. బాటసారి *bāṭasāri*. n. A wayfarer, a traveller, దారినడచువాడు.

பாட்டை[1] pāṭṭai , *n*. perh. *vāṭa*. 1. [T. *bāṭa*, K. *bāṭe*.] cf. U. *bāt*. Road, way; பாதை. இராஜபாட்டை.

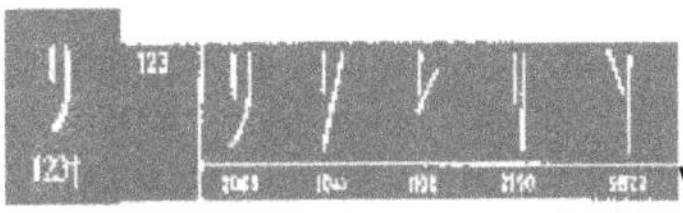
V123

Glyph: text sign 123: taṭṭai 'mechanism made of split bamboo for scaring away parrots from grain fields (Ta.); taṭṭe 'a thick bamboo or an areca-palm stem, split in two' (Ka.) (DEDR 3042) toṭxin, toṭ.xn goldsmith (To.); taṭṭāṉ 'gold- or silver-smith' (Ta.); taṭṭaravāḍu 'gold- or silver-smith' (Te.); *ṭhaṭṭakāra 'brass-worker' (Skt.)(CDIAL 5493). Ta. taṭṭumuṭṭu furniture, goods and chattels, utensils, luggage. Ma. taṭṭumuṭṭu kitchen utensils, household stuff. Tu. taṭṭimuṭṭu id.(DEDR 3041).

Thus, the glyphs frequently occurring in a pair are read rebus: *bhaṭa* 'furnace, smelter' + ṭhaṭṭakāra 'brass-worker' or, smelter of brass-worker.

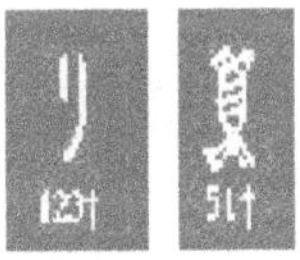

Some pairs of texts containing Sign 123:

A pair V051 is read rebus: cundakāra 'ivory turner' (cognate kundār) + ṭhaṭṭakāra 'brass-worker' or, smelter-turner of brass-work.

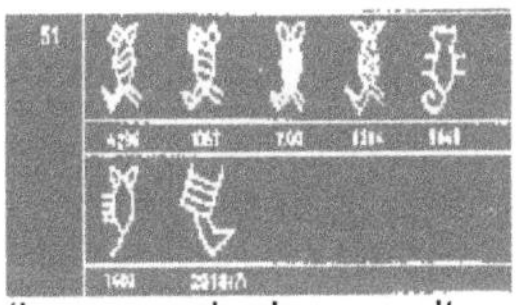

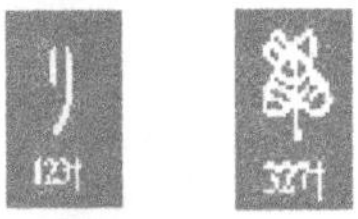

A pair is read rebus: lohakāra 'metal worker' + ṭhaṭṭakāra 'brass-worker' or, smelter of brass-work.

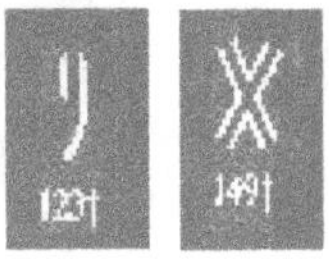

Other examples where the X text glyph appears:

Person kneeling under a tree facing a tiger. [*Chanhu-daro Excavations*, Pl. LI, 18]

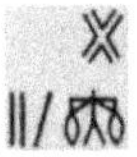
6118

Chanhu-daro Seal obverse and reverse. The 'water-carrier' and X signs of this so-called Jhukar culture seal are comparable to other inscriptions. Fig. 3 and 3a of Plate L. After Mackay, 1943.

6120

Miniature tablet. Harappa (Vats 581=IM 77:4581=CISI-I:H-351)

Line 1

Glyph: gaṇḍa 'four'. kaṇḍa 'furnace, altar'. Glyph: baṭa 'pot'. Rebus: bhaṭa 'smelter'. Thus, the text line is read as: *gaṇḍa bhaṭa* smelter furnace.

Line 2

Glyph: A pair of linear strokes (two long linear strokes) Decoded as casting workshop dula 'pair'; rebus: dul 'cast (metal)(Santali) goṭ = one (Santali); goṭi = silver (G.) koḍa 'one' (Santali); koḍ 'workshop' (G.) That is, one-eighth share to workshop (guild)[i.e. *ā̃s*, 'share' to *koṭ* ] or, *koṭṭhāsa* -- m. ' share, portion ' (Pali)

kaṇḍa kanka 'rim of jar'. Rebus: kaṇḍa karṇaka 'furnace account (scribe).

kharedo = a currycomb (G.) Rebus: kharādī ' turner' (G.)

*baṭa* 'road'. *paṭṭa* 'road' (Kannada) Rebus 1: *paṭṭaḍe* 'a workshop; smithy/forge' (Kannada); *paṭṭaṭai* id. (Tamil) పట్టడ [paṭṭaḍa] *paṭṭaḍu* n. A smithy (Telugu). Rebus 2:

*bhaṭa* 'furnace, smelter'. In this orthographically descriptive glyphic variant, the ligaturing glyphic element on top of X may be read rebus as: *aḍi* (semant. 'prop, support; anvil') as in S. *aḍī* f. ' rail across bottom of a lathe ', *āḏo* ' transverse '; B. *āṛ* ' aslant ', *āṛā* ' beam '; Or. *āṛa* ' width ', *āṛā* ' cross -- beam ', Mth. *āṛ*, *āṛi* ' boundary between fields '; H. *āṛ* f ' horizontal line painted across forehead ', *āṛā* ' transverse '; OMarw. *āḍo* ' transverse '; G. *āḍū* ' slanting ', *āḍ* f. ' curved piece of mica worn as ornament by women on forehead '; M. *āḍẽ* n. ' ridgepole, cross -- bar, keel ', *aḍvā* ' transverse '; Ko. *āḍa* ' crosswise ' (CDIAL 189). L. P. *aḍḍī* f. ' heel '; H. *aḍḍā* m. ' heel of shoe '; -- Si. *aḍiya* ' foot, footstep ' (CDIAL 191). H. *āṛ* f. ' interruption, covering ', *āṛnā* ' to cause to stop ' (perh. rather der. *aṛnā*< *aḍ -- ); G. *āḍi* f. ' obstacle ', *aḍvū* ' to stop ', *āḍṇī* f. ' a stand ' (CDIAL 188). *Go.* (G.) aḍi beneath (Mu.) aḍit below; aḍita lower; aṛke below; (Ma.) aḍita, aḍna lower; (M.) aḍ(ḍ)i below, low; (L.) aḍī down (Ko.) aṛgi underneath; *Koḍ.* aḍi place below, down. *Tu.* aḍi bottom, base; kār aḍi footsole, footstep (DEDR 72) aḍḍa id., horizontal, intervening; across, athwart; rafter; *Br.*aḍ sheltered; shelter, protection (DEDR 83) *Ta.* aṭai prop. slight support; aṭai-kal anvil. *Ma.* aṭa-kkallu anvil of goldsmiths. *Ko.* aṛ gal small anvil. *Ka.* aḍe, aḍa, aḍi the piece of wood on which the five artisans put the article which they happen to operate upon, a support; aḍegal, aḍagallu, aḍigallu anvil. *Tu.* aṭṭè a support, stand. *Te.*ḍā-kali, ḍā-kallu, dā-kali, dā-gali, dāyi anvil. (DEDR 86).

h351A

h351B
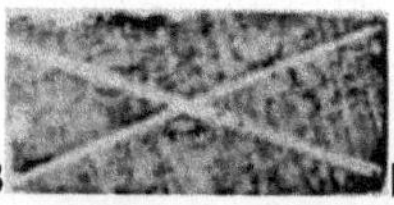
h351C

4581

Text on h351 tablet.

h351A inscription has many duplicates as seen from the following examples of texts from Mahadevan concordance:

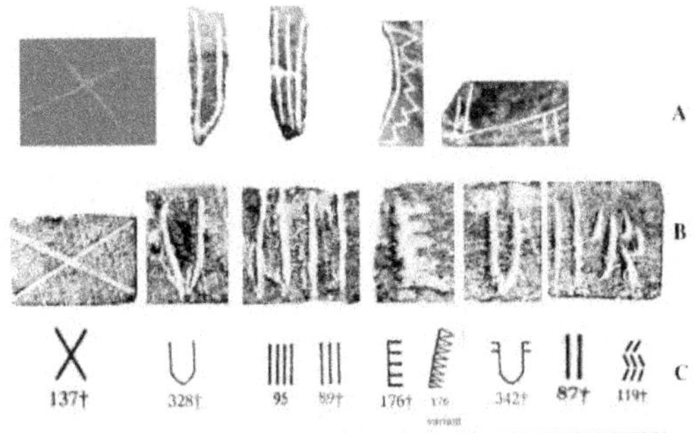


Figure 3: Photographic Comparison of Sulur Dish and Harappa Tablet.
A: Symbols from Sulur Dish. B: Signs from Harappa Tablet. C: Normalized Signary.
†These have variants (Mahadevan 1977). 176: Variant from Parpola 1994: 107c.

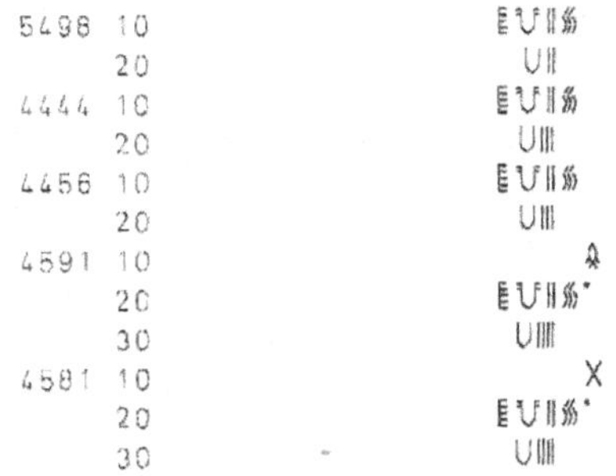

5498 10
20
4444 10
20
4456 10
20
4591 10
20
30
4581 10
20
30


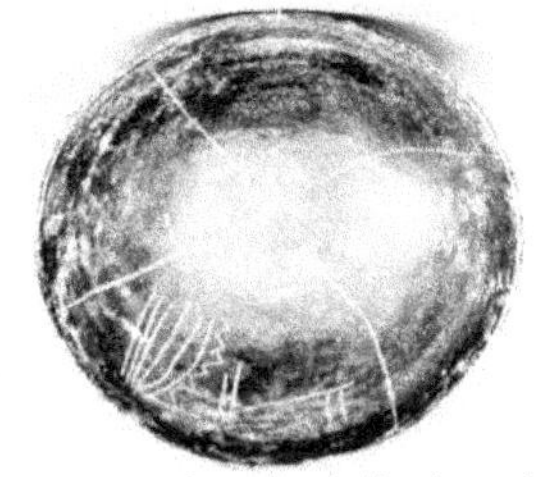

Inscribed terracotta dish from Sulur, a megalithic site near Coimbatore. c. 100 BCE (British Museum No. 1935.4-19.15)

(After Mahadevan, I., A megalithic pottery inscription and a Harappan tablet: a case of extraordinary resemblance)

Furnace (output) tally: *kuṭhi kanka*; glyph: water-carrier glyph + rim-of-jar glyph

Ligatured glyph on Harappa seal h1682A: water-carrier glyph ligatured with a 'rim of jar' glyph.

That a glyphic element in this ligature is a 'water-carrier' is demonstrated by a variant shown on a seal impression (Gadd seal PBA 18)

kuṭi 'water-carrier (woman)' (Telugu); rebus: kuṭhi 'furnace, smelter' (Santali) The pair of polar

stars flanking the water-carrier are also related to smithy/trade. मेढ [*mēḍha*] polar star (Marathi); Rebus: *mēḍh* 'helper of merchant' (Prakrit). meḍ 'iron' (Ho.) dula 'pair' (Kashmiri); dul 'cast (metal)' (Santali). Thus the 'water-carrier' glyph + pair of stars on the glyphic composition of the Gadd seal impression (PBA 18) read rebus: *dul mēḍ kuṭhi* 'cast metal (iron) from furnace'. With the ligature of the 'rim of jar' glyph, the message about the furnace account (from the smithy) is accounted for and documented by the furnace account scribe. Once this documentation is accomplished by creating a seal as in h1682A as bill of lading information, the tablets which provided the product inputs, from smiths of the guild, can be thrown away.

Tally, account, hence the most frequently used glyph: *kanaka* 'rim-of-jar' (Santali) *karṇaka* id. (Sanskrit)kárṇaka m. ' projection on the side of a vessel, handle ' ŚBr. [kárṇa -- ] Pa. kaṇṇaka -- ' having ears or corners '; Wg. Kaṇə ' ear — ring ' NTS xvii 266; S. kano m. ' rim, border '; P. kannā m. ' obtuse angle of a kite ' (→ H. kannā m. ' edge, rim, handle '); N. kānu ' end of a rope for supporting a burden '; B. kāṇā ' brim of a cup ', G. kānɔ m.; M. kānā m. ' touch — hole of a gun '.(CDIAL 2831).

Rebus: கணக்கு kaṇakku , n. cf. gaṇaka. [M. kaṇakku.] 1. Number, account, reckoning, calculation, computation; எண். (திவா.) 2. The four simple rules of arithmetic, viz., கூட்டல், கழித்தல், பெருக்கல், வகுத்தல். 3. Account book, ledger; வரவுசெலவுக்கணக்குக் குறிப்பு. காவலர் கணக் காய் வகையின் வருந்தி (குறுந். 261). 4. Science of arithmetic; கணிதசாஸ்திரம். (Tamil)gaṇáyati ' counts ' MBh. [Prob. Like guṇáyati1 < gr̥ṇ- (MIA. Gaṇ -- , giṇ -- , guṇ -- ) in gr̥ṇā́ti, ' addresses, praises ' RV., cf. gārayatē ' teaches ' Dhātup., *girati3, *gr̥ta<-> (J. C. Wright). --

√g&rcirclemacr;3. See Add. S.v. gr̥ṇā´ti] Pa. gaṇēti ' counts, takes notice of '; Aś. Ganīyati ' is counted '; Pk. Gaṇēi, °ṇaï ' counts '; Ash. Gäṇ -- ' to count, read ', Wg. Gaṇ -- NTS xvii 255; Dm. gaṇ -- ' to say '; Paš. Gaṇ -- ' to count ', Bshk. Gän -- , K. ḍoḍ. gaṇṇo, S. gaṇaṇu, L. gaṇaṇ, (Ju.) g°, Wpah. Jaun. Gaṇnȭ, Ku. Gaṇṇo, N. gannu, A. gaṇiba, B. gaṇā, Or. Gaṇibā, Mth. Ganab, Bhoj. Ganal, Aw. Lakh. Ganab, G. gaṇvũ, M. gaṇṇẽ, Si. Gaṇinavā. — Gy. As. Gen -- , eur. Gin -- , Bashg. Gīr -- , L. giṇaṇ, P. giṇṇā, Bi. Ginab, H. ginnā. (CDIAL 3993)

Each platform was for a smiths' guild at work using tablets as category 'tallies' for the final shipment of package with a seal impression...(a bill of lading). The trade transaction is thus processed and recorded for the shipment of a package. Hence, the use of tablets together with seals (and their seal impressions) in trade stands explained in an archaeological context. Thanks again, to Kenoyer and Meadow for the thoughtful questions they had raised for further researches using Indus script corpora.

The tablets were the tallies defining the product in process in guild workshops. The seal was a consolidation of the tally for preparing the seal impression as a bill of lading from a guild.

Many Indus script inscriptions recovered from excavations lack precise stratigraphic information. Some are surface finds, some even lack provenance information. The lacunae have been remedied significantly by the recent HARP excavations in Harappa in which scores of tablets have been recovered in the context of circular working platforms, providing a basis for reasonable inferences being drawn by archaeologists. However, the cumulative, large assemblage of inscriptions now totaling over 6,000 provide a reasonably adequate database resource to identify types and subtypes of inscriptions. The large number of inscriptions make it possible to infer functions served by inscription types (e.g., tablets, seals, seal impressions).

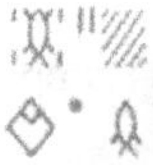

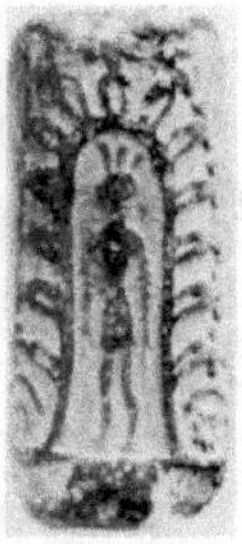

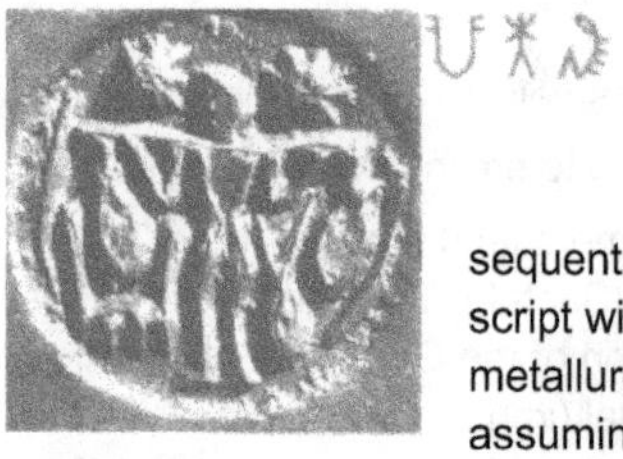

An approach demonstrated by RPN Rao et al, using a simple Markov chain model to capture sequential dependencies between hieroglyphs of Indus script will also be helpful in anticipating sequences of glyphs in an archaeo-metallurgical context or identification of allographs in an inscription, without assuming any *a priori* syntactical dependencies as in language representations in a meaningful sentence of meluhha (mlecchа) of Indian linguistic area. [cf. A Markov model of the Indus script by Rajesh P. N. Rao,Nisha Yadav, Mayank N. Vahia, Hrishikesh Joglekar, R. Adhikari and Iravatham Mahadevan (2009) Proceedings of the National Academy of Sciences of the United States of America, pnas.0906237106].

One technique which has been used in this book is to use glyphic elements within a glyhic composition. For instance, in the following example of groups of inscriptions, the enquiry begins from the glyphic element, 'a pair of stars'. Associated sets of glyphics are identified. Groups of inscriptions containing glyphic elements revealed through such associated sets of glyphics helps categorise the rebus readings of inscriptions. Many are identified as allographs (alternative glyphics) but connoting comparable phonemes. Some allographs which occur on the same inscription may perhaps be inferred to be phonetic determinatives. For example, 'polar star' glyphic is read: *meḍha*. An allograph is the 'ram' glyph is read rebus as: *meḍha*. Another allograph is the glyphic: *mēḍi* 'glamorous fig tree or racemosa'. Yet another allograph is a 'pot-shape with projecting base': *mẽhi bāṭi* ' vessel with a projecting base '(Maithili) [See m1186A which shows glyphic of a vessel with a projecting base and decorated with leaves of fig tree or racemosa]; *meḍ(h)* post (Marathi) *meṭṭa* 'projecting' (Te.)

A transition from tokens can be seen in inscribed tablets of a very small size (many almost the size of a thumbnail) mostly from Harappa. It is also possible to infer how these tablets were used to create an account of transactions and record them on s. Seal impressions (in some cases, using more than one seal with inscription) create the description of trade loads as compilations of bills of lading.

Gadd seal (PBA 18), h179B, m0305. These three inscriptions depict 'a pair of stars' glyphic.

Associated allograph glyphics (e.g. glyphics of 'a kneeling adorant', 'an offering vessel', 'a ram') with comparable inscriptions showing a person within an architectural embellishment.

h178B

h177B

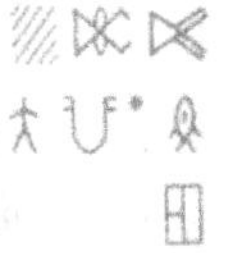

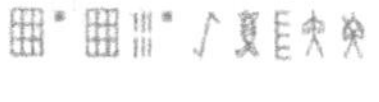

m1186A

m0488ct(One side of a prism tablet)

Many glyphic elements on these inscriptions (pictographs + text signs) can be read rebus as connoting the following semantics:

Category 1: meḍ 'iron' (Ho.) मेधा = धन, wealth Naigh._ii , 10. (Monier-Williams, p. 832)

*Te.* meṇḍu abundance, plenty, much, a good or great deal; abundant, plentiful, ample, much, great. *Go.* (Tr.) mēnḍ (*obl.* mēṭ-, *pl.* mēhk) full (used suffixally, e.g. ḍoppō-mēnḍ a leafplate full); (W. Ph.) mēṟ full, whole, entire, complete; (Mu.) menḍ (*pl.* mehk) id., e.g. gappa menḍ (*pl.*gappa mehk) basketful; (Mu.) meṭaŋ having the total of; (Ma.) nāṟ menḍu the whole village; nāṟ meṭor all the people of the village (*Voc.* 2950). (DEDR 5060). मेंढसर [ mēṇḍhasara ] *m* A bracelet of gold thread (Marathi)

Category 2: मेटींव [ mēṭīṃva ] *p* of मेटणें A verb not in use. Roughly hewn or chiseled--a stone. (Marathi)

Category 3: मेढ 'merchant's helper' (Pkt.); *m.* an elephant-keeper Gal._(cf. मेठ). *Ta.* mēṭṭi haughtiness, excellence, chief, head, land granted free of tax to the headman of a village; mēṭṭimai haughtiness; leadership, excellence. *Ka.* mēṭi loftiness, greatness, excellence, a big man, a chief, a head, head servant. *Te.* mēṭari, mēṭi chief, head, leader, lord; (prob. mēṭi < *mēl-ti [cf. 5086]; Ka. Ta. < Te.; Burrow 1969, p. 277) (DEDR 5091).மேட்டி mēṭṭi, *n.* Assistant house-servant; waiting-boy. மேட்டி +. Headman of the Toṭṭiya caste; தொட்டியர் தலைவன். (E. T. vii, 185.) మేటి [ mēṭi ] *mēṭi.* n. Lit: a helper. A servant, a cook, a menial who cleans plates, dishes, lamps and shoes, &c. (Eng. 'mate') మేటి [ mēṭi ] or మేటరి *mēṭi* [Tel.] n. A chief, leader, head man, lord, శ్రేష్ఠుడు, అధిపుడు. adj. Chief, excellent, noble. శ్రేష్ఠమైన. మేటిదొర a noble man, lord. Bilh. ii. 50. మెరయుచు నుండెడి మేటీరంబులు మేటీరంబులు, అనగా మేటి, గొప్పలైన, ఈరంబులు, పొదలు large bushes. "తేటైనపన్నీట తీర్థంబులాడి, మేటికస్తూరిమేనెల్లబూసి." Misc. iii. 22. మేటిగా = మెండుగా. మేటిల్లు *mētillu.* v. n. To excel. అతిశయించు. Medinī (f.) [Vedic medin an associate or companion fr. mid in meaning to be friendly] मेथ् 1 U. (मेथति-ते) 1 To associate with; मिथु मिथुः *ind.* Together, mutually (मिथः); ब्रह्मादयस्तनुभृतो मिथुरर्द्यमानाः Bhāg.11.6.14. मिद् To love, feel affection (Apte. Lexicon) Mettāyati [Denom. fr. mettā] to feel friendly, to show love, to be benevolent A iv.151; DhsA 194; VbhA 75. With loc. to show friendship or be affectionate towards J i.365; iii.96; Dāvs iii.34. Metta (adj. nt.) [cp. Vedic maitra "belonging to Mitra"; Epic Sk. maitra "friendly," fr. mitra] friendly, benevolent, kind as adj. at D iii.191 (mettena kāya -- kammena etc.), 245 (˚ŋ vacī -- kammaŋ); as nt. for mettā in cpds. of mettā (cp. mettaŋsa) and by itself at D i.227 (mettaŋ+cittaŋ), perhaps also at Sn 507. (Pali)

Other semantics of possible rebus readings:

Rebus 1: manḍī मंडी f. an exchange, a place where merchants meet to transact business (Gr.M.). *மண்டி³ maṇṭi, n. < U. maṇḍī. 1. Large grain market; தானியம் மிகுதியாக விற்குமிடம். மண்டித் தெரு. 2. Shop, stall, warehouse; large shop where things are sold wholesale or in large quantities; பெருவியாபாரம் செய்யும் பண்டசாலை. (W.)* మండువా [ maṇḍuvā ] *manḍuvā*. [Tel.] n. A courtyard. A booth. A stable for horses, గుర్రాలపాక, గుర్రపుసాల. స్వా. i. మండి [ maṇḍi ] or మండీ *manḍi*. [Tel.] [H.] n. A wholesale shop, భారీ సరుకులు అమ్మేచోటు.

Rebus 2: *மண்டூரம் maṇṭūram, n. < maṇḍūra. Iron dross, oxide of iron, refuse of melted iron; இருப்புக் கிட்டம். (W.)* మండూరము [ maṇḍūramu ] *manḍūramu*. [Skt.] n. The rust of iron, or refuse of melted iron, used as a medicine. ఇనుపచిట్టము, ఇనుప చిట్టముతో చేసిన సిందూరము. mā̃ḍ माँड् I मिश्रीकरणम् f. mixing (Gr.Gr. 126), esp. mixing up or kneading (by rubbing with the palms of the hands) of flour or other food with water, buttermilk, etc. (Gr.Gr. 1); cf. mā̃ḍay and namda-mō̃ḍ. -- diñü -- दिञ्&below; I मिश्रीकरणम् f.inf. to mix food, as ab. mā̃ḍi onu-

Rebus 3: 'are written': maṇḍáyati ' adorns, decorates ' ariv., *máṇḍatē*, *°ti* Dhātup. [√maṇḍ] Pa. *maṇḍēti* ' adorns ', Pk. *maṁḍēi*, *°ḍaï*; Ash. *mū˘ṇḍ* -- , *moṇ* -- intr. ' to put on clothes, dress ', *muṇḍaā´* -- tr. ' to dress '; K. *manḍun* ' to adorn ', H. *maṇḍnā*; OMarw. *māṁḍaï* ' writes '; OG. *māṁḍīṁ* 3 pl. pres. pass. ' are written ', G. *mā̃ḍvũ* ' to arrange, dispose, begin ', M.*mā̃ḍṇē*, Ko. *mā̃ṇḍtā*.(CDIAL 9747). மண்டர் maṇṭar , *n.* Heroes, champions, soldiers; படைவீரர். (திவா.) மண்டலமாக்கள் maṇṭala-mākkaḷ , *n.* < id. +. 1. Kings, rulers; அரசர். மண்டலமாக் கள் பிறிதோருருவங் கொண்டும் (சிலப். 8, 89, உரை மேற்.) மண்டலர் maṇṭalar , *n.* < *maṇḍala*. A class of Arhats; அருகபதம் பெற்றவரில் ஒருசாரார். (சி. சி. பர. ஆசீவகன்மறுதலை, 2.) *மண்டலீகன் maṇṭalīkan̲, n. < maṇḍalīka. 1. King; அரசன். பலமன்னியர் மண்டலீகர் (உத்தர ரா. திருவோலக். 11). 2. Viceroy; petty ruler; ruler of a limited region; நாட்டின் பகுதியை யாளும் அதிகாரி.*

Glyph 'kneeling (adorant)': మండి [ maṇḍi ] or మండీ *manḍi*. [Tel.] n. Kneeling down with one leg, an attitude in archery, ఒక కాలితో నేలమీద మోకరించుట, ఆలీఢపాదము. मेट [ mēṭa ] *n* (मिटणें) The knee-joint or the bend of the knee. मेटें खुंटीस बसणें To kneel down. 4677 *Ta.* maṇṭi kneeling, kneeling on one knee as an archer. *Ma.* maṇṭuka to be seated on the heels. *Ka.* maṇḍi what is bent, the knee. *Tu.* maṇḍi knee. *Te.* maṇḍī kneeling on one knee. *Pa.* maḍtel knee; maḍi kuḍtel kneeling position. *Go.* (L.) meṇḍā, (G. Mu. Ma.) minḍa knee (*Voc.* 2827). *Konḍa* (BB) meḍa, meṇḍa id. *Pe.* menḍa id. *Manḍ.* menḍe id. *Kui* menḍa id. *Kuwi* (F.) menda, (S. Su. P.) menḍa, (Isr.) meṇḍa id. Cf. 4645 Ta. maṭaṅku (maṇi-forms). / ? Cf. Skt. maṇḍūkī- part of an elephant's hind leg; Mar. meṭ knee-joint. (DEDR 4677)

Glyph 'oblation, offering': mḗdha m. ' sacrificial oblation ' RV. Pa. *mēdha* -- m. ' sacrifice '; Si. *mehe*, *mē* sb. ' eating ' ES 69.(CDIAL 10327).

Glyph 'star': मेढ [ mēḍha ] The polar star (Marathi). मेढेमत [ mēḍhēmata ] *n* (मेढ Polar star, मत Dogma or sect.) A persuasion or an order or a set of tenets and notions amongst the Shúdra-people. Founded upon certain astrological calculations proceeding upon the North star. Hence मेढेजोशी or डौरीजोशी. mēṭan̲ , *n.* < மேடம்¹. The planet Mars, as the lord of the sign Aries; [மேஷ ராசிக்கு உடையவன்] செவ்வாய் (நாமதீப. 98.)

Glyph 'crookedness of horns': Meṇḍa [dial., cp. Prk. mĕṇṭha & miṇṭha: Pischel, *Prk. Gr.* § 293. The Dhtm (156) gives a root meṇḍ (meḍ) in meaning of "koṭilla," i. e. crookedness. (Pali) M. *mēḍhā* m. ' crook or curved end (of a horn, stick, &c.) '.

Glyph: ‘ram with curling horns’: H. *mẽṛā*, *mẽḍā* m. ‘ ram with curling horns ’, °*ḍī* f. ‘ she -- goat do. ’ (CDIAL 10120) Bi. *mẽṛhwā* ‘ a bullock with curved horns like a ram's ’; M. *mẽḍhrū̃* n. ‘ sheep ’.(CDIAL 10311).Glyph ‘ram’: मेंढा [ mēṇḍhā ] *m* (मेष S through H) A male sheep, a ram or tup. मेंढरूं [ mēṇḍharūṃ ] *n* (मेंढा) A sheep Pr. मेलें में0 आगीला भिईल काय? (Marathi) mēṇḍha m. ‘ ram ’, °*aka* -- , *mēṇḍa* -- 4, *miṇḍha* -- 2, °*aka* -- , *mēṭha* -- 2, *mēṇḍhra* -- , *mēḍhra* -- 2, °*aka* -- m. lex. 2. *mēṇṭha- (*mēṭha* -- m. lex.). 3. *mējjha -- . [*r* -- forms (which are not attested in NIA.) are due to further sanskritization of a loan -- word prob. of Austro -- as. origin (EWA ii 682 with lit.) and perh. related to the group s.v. bhēḍra -- ] 1. Pa. *meṇḍa* -- m. ‘ ram ’, °*aka* -- ‘ made of a ram's horn (e.g. a bow) ’; Pk. *meḍḍha* -- , *meṁḍha* -- (°*ḍhī* -- f.), °*ṁḍa* -- , *miṁḍha* -- (°*dhiā* -- f.), °*aga* -- m. ‘ ram ’, Dm. Gaw. *miṇ* Kal.rumb. *amŕn/aŕə* ‘ sheep ’ (*a* -- ?); Bshk. *minā´l* ‘ ram ’; Tor. *miṇḍ* ‘ ram ’, *miṇḍā´l* ‘ markhor ’; Chil.*mindh**l/ ‘ ram ’ AO xviii 244 (*dh*!), Sv. *yēṛo -- miṇ*; Phal. *miṇḍ*, *miṇ* ‘ ram ’, *miṇḍṓl* m. ‘ yearling lamb, gimmer ’; P. *mẽḍhā* m., °*ḍhī* f., ludh.*mīḍḍhā*, *mī˜ḍhā* m.; N. *meṛho*, *meṛo* ‘ ram for sacrifice ’; A. *mersāg* ‘ ram ’ ( -- *sāg* < *chāgya -- ?), B. *meṛā* m., °*ṛi* f., Or. *meṇḍhā*, °*ḍā* m., °*ḍhi*f., H. *meṛh*, *meṛhā*, *mẽḍhā* m., G. *mẽḍhɔ*, M. *mẽḍhā* m., Si. *mäḍayā*.2. Pk. *meṁṭhī* -- f. ‘ sheep ’; H. *meṭhā* m. ‘ ram ’. 3. H. *mejhukā* m. ‘ ram ’. mēṇḍha -- 2: A. also *mer* (phonet. *mer*) ‘ ram ’ AFD 235. (CDIAL 10310) मेठ a ram L. (Monier-Williams, p. 832) Meṇḍa [dial., cp. Prk. mĕṇṭha & miṇṭha: Pischel, *Prk. Gr.* § 293. The Ved. (Sk.) word for ram is meṣa] 1. a ram D i.9; J iv.250, 353 (˚visāṇa -- dhanu, a bow consisting of a ram's horn). -- ˚pathaNpl. "ram's road" Nd1 155=415. -- ˚yuddha ram fight D i.6. –Meṇḍaka (adj.) [fr. meṇḍa] 1. made of ram(s) horn, said of a (very strong) bow J ii.88 (˚dhanu); v.128 (˚singadhanu). -- 2. belonging to a ram, inmeṇḍaka -- pañha "question about the ram" Miln 90 alluding to the story of a ram in the Ummagga -- jātaka (J vi.353 -- 55), which is told in form of a question, so difficult & puzzling that nobody "from hell to heaven" (J vi.354) can answer it except the Bodhisatta. Cp. Trenckner's remark Miln 422. (Pali) मेंढा [ mēṇḍhā ] *m* (मेष S through H) A male sheep, a ram or tup. मेंढरूं चेंढरूं [ mēṇḍharū ñcēṇḍharūṃ ] *n* (मेंढरूं by redup.) A sheep and suchlike. (Marathi) मेंढका or क्या [ mēṇḍhakā or kyā ] *a* (मेंढा) A shepherd (Marathi) మెంఠము [ meṇṭhamu ] *menṭhamu*. [Mahrati.] n. A ram. పొట్టేలు. "రణములోనైన తనువికారంబులెల్ల, దేవతలకు శమించెవద్దేవుకరుణ, దాల్చెదకుండువీతన్యధా బలమున, గంఠ నాళాగ్ర మున నుండమెంఠశిరము." Kasi Khand. vii. 139.మేండము [ mēṇḍamu ] *mēnḍamu*. [Skt.] n. A ram, పొట్టేలు.மேண்டம் mēṇṭam , *n.* < *mēṇḍha*. Ram; ஆடு. (பரி. அக.) மேடகம் mēṭakam< *mēḍaka*. மேடம் mēṭam , *n.* < *mēṣa*. 1. Sheep, ram; ஆடு. (பிங்.) 2. Aries of the zodiac; ராசிமண்டலத்தின் முதற்பகுதி. (பிங்.) 3. The first solar month. See சித்திரை[1], 2. மேடமாமதி (கம்பரா. திருவவதா. 110).

Glyph ‘fig, ficus racemosa’: మేడి [ mēḍi ] *mēḍi*. [Tel.] అత్తి, ఉదుంబరము. మేడిపండు the fruit of this tree.

5090 *Ka.* mēḍi glomerous fig tree, *Ficus racemosa*; opposite-leaved fig tree, *F. oppositifolia*. *Te.* mēḍi *F. glomerata*. *Kol.* (Kin.) mēṛi id. [*F. glomerata* Roxb. = *F. racemosa* Wall.](DEDR 5090).

Sign 130. Glyph ‘curved end of stick’: मेंढा [ mēṇḍhā ] *m* A crook or curved end (of a stick, horn &c.) and *attrib*. such a stick, horn, bullock.

Possible allographs (which can be found on other inscriptions):

Glyph 'eyelashes’: *Kol.* (SR.) kaṇlā mindī, (Kin.) kandl mindig (*pl.*) eyelash. *Go.* (A. Ch. Ma.) mindi, (Tr. W. Ph.) mindī id.; (M.) konḍā-mindī eyebrow; (Ko.) konḍa-minḍi eyelid, eyelash (*Voc.* 2831). / Cf. Halbi mendī eyelashes. (DEDR 4864).

Glyph ‘pot’: *Konḍa* manḍi earthen pan, a covering dish. *Pe.* manḍi cooking pot. *Kui* manḍi brass bowl. *Kuwi* (S.) mandi basin; (Isr.) manḍi plate, bowl. (DEDR 4678). Pk. *maṁḍaya* -- ‘ adorning ’; Ash. *mōṇḍa*, *mōnda*, *mūnda* NTS ii 266, *mōṇə* NTS vii 99 ‘ clothes ’; G. *mā̃ḍ* m. ‘ arrangement, disposition, vessels or pots for decoration ’, *māṇ* f. ‘ beautiful array of household vessels ’; M. *mā̃ḍ* m. ‘ array of instruments &c. ’; Si. *maḍa -- ya* ‘ adornment, ornament ’. (CDIAL 9736)

Glyph 'spot': *Kui* meda scar, spot or blotch on skin. *Malt.* medgo discoloured by bruise; medgre to discolour, blacken.(DEDR 5063).

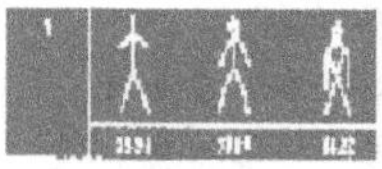

Ia. 18

Sign variants 001. Glyph 'body, foot': meḍ 'body', 'dance' (Santali) Vikalpa: B. dhaṛ 'trunk of body'. Hence, rebus reading could be either meḍ 'iron' or, dhatu 'mineral' (Santali> மெட்டு¹-தல் meṭṭu-, v. tr. cf. நெட்டு-. [K. meṭṭu.] To spurn or push with the foot;

காலால் தாக்குதல். நிகளத்தை மெட்டி மெட்டிப் பொடிபடுத்தி (பழனிப்பிள்ளைத். 12). (Tamil) meṭṭu 'to put or place down the foot or feet; to step, to pace, to walk (Ka.); meṭṭisu 'to cause to step or walk, to cause to tread on' (Ka.) meḍ 'dance' (Santali) మెట్ట [ meṭṭa ] or మెట్ట *meṭṭa.* மெட்டு¹-தல் meṭṭu-, v. tr. cf. நெட்டு-. [K. meṭṭu.] To spurn or push with the foot; காலால் தாக்குதல். நிகளத்தை மெட்டி மெட்டிப் பொடிபடுத்தி (பழனிப்பிள்ளைத். 12). (Tamil) meṭṭu 'to put or place down the foot or feet; to step, to pace, to walk (Ka.); meṭṭisu 'to cause to step or walk, to cause to tread on' (Ka.) meḍ 'dance' (Santali); Rebus: meḍ, mẽṛhẽt 'iron'(Mu.Ho.) *Ko.* meṭ- (mec-) to trample on, tread on; meṭ sole of foot, footstep, footprint. *To.* möṭ- (möṭy-) to trample on; möṭ step, tread, wooden-soled sandal. *Ka.* meṭṭu to put or place down the foot or feet, step, pace, walk, tread or trample on, put the foot on or in, put on (as a slipper or shoe); *n.* stepping, step of the foot, stop on a stringed instrument; sandal, shoe, step of a stair;meṭṭisu to cause to step; meṭṭige, meṭla step, stair. *Koḍ.* moṭṭï footprint, foot measure, doorsteps. *Tu.* muṭṭu shoe, sandal; footstep; steps, stairs.*Te.* meṭṭu step, stair, treading, slipper, stop on a lute; maṭṭu, (K. also) meṭṭu to tread, trample, crush under foot, tread or place the foot upon; *n.* treading; maṭṭincu to cause to be trodden or trampled. *Ga.* (S.3) meṭṭu step (< Te.). *Konḍa* maṭ- (-t-) to crush under foot, tread on, walk, thresh (grain, as by oxen); *caus.* maṭis-. *Kuwi* (S.) mettunga steps. *Malt.* maḍye to trample, tread. (DEDR 5057).

'Dance step' hieroglyph

m0493Bm1428C Mohenjo-daro.

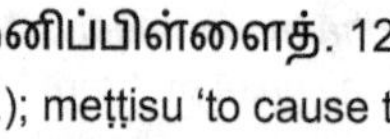

Three dancers in step on one side of a prism tablet. *kolmo* 'three' (Mu.) Rebus: *kolami* 'smithy, forge' (Telugu) *meṭ* 'dance step' (Telugu); Rebus: *meḍ* 'iron' (Ho.Mu.) The message conveyed rebus by this hieroglyph set: iro smithy/forge.

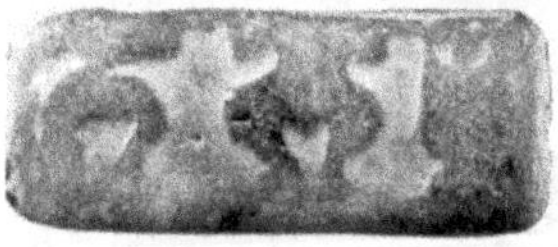
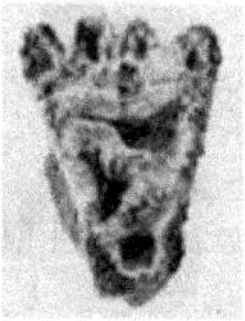

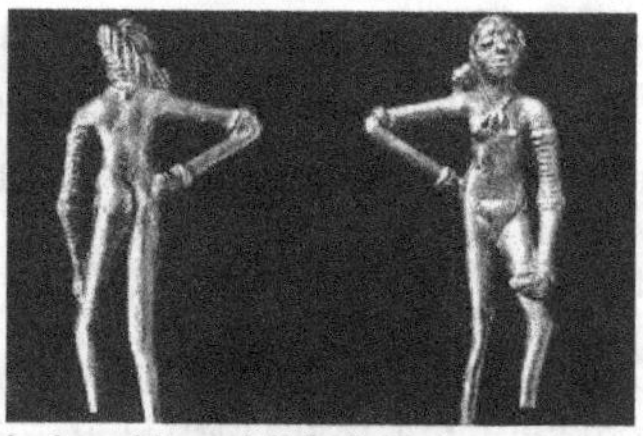

Bronze statue, Mohenjo-daro. 'Dance step' glyph on Bhirran potsherd.

Tepe Yahya. Seal impressions of two sides of a seal. Six-legged lizard and opposing footprints shown on opposing sides of a double-sided steatite stamp seal perforated along the lateral axis. Lamberg-Karlovsky 1971: fig. 2C Shahr-i-Soktha Stamp seal shaped like a foot. Shahdad seal (Grave 78)

Reproduction of drawing on a pottery vessel found in Shahr-i Sokhta, Iran. Late half of 3rd Millennium B.C. In five pictures a goat steps toward a tree, climbs it up, eats leaves and comes down. This picture is one of earliest examples of artist's attempt to show motion in means of animation. Source: Trace of a photo of the reproduction presented together with the vase in National Museum of Iran. Covering an area of 151 hectares, Shahr-i Sokhta was one of the world's largest cities at the dawn of the urban era. In the western part of the site is a vast graveyard, measuring 25 hk.s. It contains between 25,000 to 40,000 ancient graves. (Sandro Salvatori And Massimo Vidale, Shahr-I Sokhta 1975-1978: Central Quarters Excavations: Preliminary Report, Istituto italiano per l'Africa e l'Oriente, 1997.) Two glyphs: ram and tree. *meḍ 'ram'. Rebus: meḍ* 'iron' (Ho.Mu.) *kuṭi* 'tree'. Rebus: *kuṭhi* 'smelter furnace'.

Glyph: *meṭṭu* 'foot'. Rebus: *meḍ* 'iron' (Ho.Mu.) dula 'pair' (Kashmiri); dul 'cast (metal)(Santali). Six legs of a lizard is an enumeration of six 'portable furnaces' ; rebus: kakra. 'lizard'; kan:gra 'portable furnace'. bhaṭa 'six' (G.) rebus: baṭa = kiln (Santali); baṭa = a kind of iron (G.) bhaṭṭhī f. 'kiln, distillery', awāṇ. bhaṭh; P. bhaṭṭh m., °ṭhī f. 'furnace', bhaṭṭhā m. 'kiln'; S. bhaṭṭhī keṇī 'distil (spirits)'. Read rebus as : *dul (pair) meḍ* 'cast iron'; *kan:gra bhaṭa* 'portable furnace'.

Glyph 'neck': మెడ [ meḍa ] or మెడకాయ *meḍa*. [Tel.] n. The neck, కంఠము, గళము.

Glyph 'mountain': మెట్ట [ meṭṭa ] or మిట్ట *meṭṭa*. [Tel.] n. Rising ground, high lying land, uplands. A hill, a rock. ఉన్నతభూమి, మెరక, పర్వతము, దిబ్బ. மேடு mēṭu , *n.* [T. *meṭṭa*, M. K. *mēḍu*.] 1. Height; உயரம். (பிங்.) 2. Eminence, little ridge, rising ground; சிறுதிடர். hill, hillock, (பிங்.) *Ka.* mede heap. *Te.* (*VPK*, intro. p. 128) meda id. (DEDR 5065) *Ta.* meṭṭu place where custom is paid, custom-house. *Tu.* (K. Ramakrishnaiya, *Dravidian Cognates*, p. 181) moṭṭu place where custom is paid. *Te.* meṭṭu id., place where toll is levied, toll-gate.(DEDR 5059). *Ta.* meṭṭu mound, heap of earth; mēṭu height, eminence, hillock; muṭṭu rising ground, high ground, heap. *Ma.* mēṭu rising ground, hillock; māṭu hillock, raised ground; miṭṭāl rising ground, an alluvial bank; (Tiyya) maṭṭa hill. *Ka.* mēḍu height, rising ground, hillock; miṭṭu rising or high ground, hill; miṭṭe state of being high, rising ground, hill, mass, a large number; (Hav.) muṭṭe heap (as of straw). *Tu.* miṭṭè prominent, protruding; muṭṭe heap. *Te.* meṭṭa raised or high ground, hill; (K.) meṭṭu mound; miṭṭa high ground, hillock, mound; high, elevated, raised, projecting; (*VPK*) mēṭu, mēṭa, mēṭi stack of hay; (Inscr.) meṇṭa-cēnu dry field (cf. meṭṭu-nēla, meṭṭu-vari). *Kol.* (SR.) meṭṭā hill; (Kin.) meṭṭ, (Hislop) met mountain. *Nk.* meṭṭ hill, mountain. *Ga.* (S.3, *LSB* 20.3) meṭṭa high land. *Go.* (Tr. W. Ph.) maṭṭā, (Mu.) maṭṭa mountain; (M. L.) meṭā id., hill; (A. D. Ko.) meṭṭa, (Y. Ma. M.) meṭa hill; (SR.) meṭṭā hillock (*Voc.* 2949). *Konḍa* meṭa id. *Kuwi* (S.) metta hill; (Isr.) meṭa sand hill. Cf. 5474 Ta.viṭam. DED(S, N) (DEDR 5058).

Rebus: M. *mãḍ* m. ' array of instruments &c. '; Si. *maḍa -- ya* ' adornment, ornament '. (CDIAL 9736)

Glyphic element 'vessel with projecting base' on m1186A and h179B. Semantics denoted by the orthography of the ornamented glyph: arbour, temporary pavilon, canopy.

Glyph 'vessel with projecting base': మండకంచము *manḍa-kantsamu*. n. A platter that has a rim like a soup plate. అంచుకట్టిన కంచము. అనుకంచము a platter that has no rim. *Konḍa* manḍi earthen pan, a covering dish. *Pe.* manḍi cooking pot. *Kui* manḍi brass bowl. *Kuwi* (S.) mandi basin; (Isr.) manḍi plate, bowl. (DEDR 4678). miṭṭa projecting (Te.)(DEDR 5058). *manḍa* ' some sort of framework (?) '. [In *nau -- manḍḗ* n. du. ' the two sets of poles rising from the thwarts or the two bamboo covers of a boat (?) ' ŚBr. (as illustrated in BPL p. 42); and in BHSk. and Pa. *bōdhi -- manḍa* -- n. perh. ' thatched cover ' rather than ' raised platform ' (BHS ii 402). If so, it may belong to manḍapá -- and maṭha -- ] Ku. *mãṛā* m. pl. ' shed, resthouse ' (if not < **mãṛhā* < **manḍhaka* -- s.v. manḍapá -- ).(CDIAL 9737). మండితము [manḍitamu] [Skt.] adj. Dressed, decorated, decked. అలంకరింపబడ్డ. మండితుడు *manḍituḍu*. n. One who is dressed, arrayed, or decorated. అలంకరింప బడినవాడు. మండనము [ manḍanamu ] *manḍanamu*.

[Skt.] n. Adorning, dressing, decorating, decoration. An ornament, jewel, భూషణము,

అలంకరణము.మండనుడు *manḍanuḍu*. n. One who is dressed or ornamented. "ఏకాంతభక్తి మహితమండనుడు"

he who is adorned with faith. BD. v. 1. maṇḍapa m.n. ' open temporary shed, pavilion ' Hariv., °*pikā* -- f. ' small pavilion, customs house ' Kād. 2. maṇṭapa -- m.n. lex. 3. *maṇḍhaka -- . [Variation of *ṇḍ* with *ṇṭ* supports supposition of non -- Aryan origin in Wackernagel AiGr ii 2, 212: see EWA ii 557. -- Prob. of same origin as maṭha -- 1 and maṇḍa -- 6 with which NIA. words largely collide in meaning and form] 1. Pa. *maṇḍapa* -- m. ' temporary shed for festive occasions '; Pk. *maṁḍava* -- m. ' temporary erection, booth covered with creepers ', °*viā* -- f. ' small do. '; Phal. *manḍau* m. ' wooden gallery outside a house '; K. *manḍav* m. ' a kind of house found in forest villages '; S. *manahū* m. ' shed, thatched roof '; Ku. *mā̃ṛyā, manyā* ' resthouse '; N. *kāṭhmā̃ṛau* ' the city of Kathmandu ' (*kāṭh* -- < kāṣṭhá -- ); Or. *maṇḍuā̃* ' raised and shaded pavilion ', *paṭā* -- *maṇḍoi* ' pavilion laid over with planks below roof ', *muṇḍoi*, °*ḍei* ' raised unroofed platform '; Bi. *mā̃ṛo* ' roof of betel plantation ', *mā̃ṛuā, maṛ°, malwā* ' lean -- to thatch against a wall ', *maṛaī* ' watcher's shed on ground without platform '; Mth. *māṛab* ' roof of betel plantation ', *maṛwā* ' open erection in courtyard for festive occasions '; OAw. *māṁḍava* m. ' wedding canopy '; H. *mā̃ṛwā* m., °*wī* f., *manḍwā* m.,°*wī* f. ' arbour, temporary erection, pavilion ', OMarw. *maṁḍavo, māḍhivo* m.; G. *mā̃ḍav* m. ' thatched open shed ', *mā̃ḍvɔ* m. ' booth ', *mā̃ḍvī*f. ' slightly raised platform before door of a house, customs house ', *mā̃ḍaviyɔ* m. ' member of bride's party '; M. *mā̃ḍav* m. ' pavilion for festivals ',*mā̃ḍvī* f. ' small canopy over an idol '; Si. *maḍu* -- *va* ' hut ', *maḍa* ' open hall ' SigGr ii 452. 2. Ko. *māṁṭav* ' open pavilion '. 3. H. *mā̃ḍhā, māṛhā, māḍhā* m. ' temporary shed, arbour ' (cf. OMarw. *māḍhivo* in 1); -- Ku. *mā̃ṛā* m.pl. ' shed, resthouse ' (or < maṇḍa -- 6?] *chāyāmaṇḍapa -- . maṇḍapa -- : S.kcch. *mānḍhvo* m. ' booth, canopy '. (CDIAL 9740). G. *māḍāṇ* n. ' wooden frame on a well for irrigation bucket '? (CDIAL 9745). மண்டகம் maṇṭakam , *n.* See மண்டபம்¹. மண்டகம் எடுத்த நிலத்தொடும் (S. I. i, 150, 61). மண்டபச்செலவு maṇṭapa-c-celavu , *n.* < மண்டபம்¹ +. Expense incurred for receiving a deity in a *maṇṭapamW.)* மண்டபம்¹ +. Tent or pavilion resembling a hall; கூடாரம். கணடங்குத்திய மண்டபவெழினியுள் (பெருங். உஞ்சைக். 37, 103). *மண்டபம்¹ maṇṭapam , n.* < *maṇḍapa. 1. Pavilion in a temple or other place used during festivals for the reception of idols when they are carried in procession, generally a square or rectangular hall with a flat roof* supported by pillars; திருநாளில் சுவாமி தங்கு வதற்காகக் கட்டப்பட்ட கற்கட்டடம். 2. Temporary saloon or open shed decorated for festive occasions; அலங்காரப்பந்தல். (W.) 3. Public hall or rest house; சாவடி. మండపము [ maṇḍapamu ] *manḍapamu*.

[Skt.] n. A porch, a portico, స్తంభములమీద కట్టిన కట్టడము. A bower, pavilion, చావడి, సభాభేదము, నాలుగు

కాళ్లమండపము a four pillared portico. ముఖమండపము a porch of a temple. మండపి or గర్భమండపి *manḍapi*.

n. A shrine, a sanctuary. గర్భగృహము. A small portico. చిన్నమండపము. "గర్భమండపి గడిగిన కలశజలము." A. vi. 7.

Glyph: 'heap or ears of millet': మండె [ maṇḍe ] or మండియ *manḍe*. [Tel.] A stock or heap of the

unthrashed ears of the great millet, or of cut tobacco. జొన్న కుచ్చెలను దించికంకికోసి ప్రోగువేసి ఆరవేసిన

పొగాకుకుప్ప. Glyph: scorpion: మండ్రగబ్బ [ maṇḍragabba ] *manḍra-gabba*. [Tel.] n. A large black

scorpion. పుట్టతేలు, నల్లని పెద్దతేలు.

Glyph 'stack of hay': mēṭu, mēṭa, mēṭi stack of hay (Te.)(DEDR 5058).

Glyph 'serpent': मेद Meda N. of a serpent-demon MBh. (Monier-Williams, p. 832)

मेंढरी [ mēṇḍharī ] *f* A piece in architecture. मेंधला [mēndhalā] *m* In architecture. A common term for the two upper arms of a double चौकठ (door-frame) connecting the two. Called also मेंढरी & घोडा. It answers to छिली the name of the two lower arms or connections. (Marathi)

Glyph 'forked stake': Medhi (f.) [Vedic methī pillar, post (to bind cattle to); BSk. medhi Divy 244; Prk. meḍhi Pischel *Gr.* § 221. See for etym. Walde, *Lat. Wtb.* s. v. meta] pillar, part of a stūpa [not in the Canon?].(Pali) mọ̃nḍu स्थाणुः m. the trunk or stump of a tree, including the solid part of the root (cf. mŏnḍü 1) (El. *múnd*) (cf. khŏḍa-mo, p. 392*a,* l. 5, and nasta-mo, s.v. nast); a log, a heavy block of wood (Gr.Gr. 37, Śiv. 1856); a pillar (Kashmiri) मेढा [ mēḍhā ] *m* A stake, esp. as forked. 2 A dense arrangement of stakes, a palisade, a paling. 3 fig. A supporter or backer. 4 A twist or tangle arising in thread or cord, a curl or snarl. मेढी [ mēḍhī ] *f* (Dim. of मेढ) A small bifurcated stake: also a small stake, with or without furcation, used as a post to support a cross piece. मेढाविणें [ mēḍhāviṇēṃ ] *v c* C (मेढा) To enclose a place with मेढे pales or stakes. मेड [ mēḍa ] *f* (Usually मेढ q. v.) मेडका *m* A stake, esp. as bifurcated. मेढेकोट [ mēḍhēkōṭa ] *m* (मेढा & कोट) A dense paling; a palisade or stoccade; any defence of stakes. मेढ्या [ mēḍhyā ] *a* (मेढ Stake or post.) A term for a person considered as the pillar, prop, or support (of a household, army, or other body), the *staff* or *stay*. मेढ [ mēḍha ] *f* A forked stake. Used as a post. Hence a short post generally whether forked or not. Pr. हातीं लागली चेड आणि धर मांडवाची मेढ. मेड [ mēḍa ] *f* (Usually मेढ q. v.) मेडका *m* A stake, esp. as bifurcated. मेढकी [ mēḍhakī ] *f* मेढकें *n* (Dim. of मेढ) A small stake or post, esp. as bifurcated. (Marathi) मित् *f.* Ved. A column, post. mēthí m. ' pillar in threshing floor to which oxen are fastened, prop for supporting carriage shafts ' AV., °*thī* -- f. KātyŚr.com.,*mēdhī* -- f. Divyāv. 2. mēṭhī -- f. PañcavBr.com., *mēḍhī* -- , *mēṭī* -- f. BhP.1. Pa. *mēdhi* -- f. ' post to tie cattle to, pillar, part of a stūpa '; Pk. *mēhi* -- m. ' post on threshing floor ', N. *meh(e)*, *miho*, *miyo*, B. *mei*, Or. *maï* -- *dāṇḍi*, Bi. *mēh*, *mēhā* ' the post ', (SMunger) *mehā* ' the bullock next the post ', Mth. *meh*, *mehā* ' the post ', (SBhagalpur) *mīhā̃* ' the bullock next the post ', (SETirhut) *mēhi bāṭi* ' vessel with a projecting base '.2. Pk. *mēḍhi* -- m. ' post on threshing floor ', *mēḍhaka*<-> ' small stick '; K. *mīr*, *mīrü* f. ' larger hole in ground which serves as a mark in pitching walnuts ' (for semantic relation of ' post -- hole ' see kūpa -- 2); L. *meṛh* f. ' rope tying oxen to each other and to post on threshing floor '; P. *mehṛ*f., *mehaṛ* m. ' oxen on threshing floor, crowd '; OA *meṛha*, *mehra* ' a circular construction, mound '; Or. *meṛhī*, *meri* ' post on threshing floor '; Bi.*mēṛ* ' raised bank between irrigated beds ', (Camparam) *mēṛhā* ' bullock next the post ', Mth. (SETirhut) *mēṛhā* ' id. '; M. *meḍ(h)*, *meḍhī* f.,*meḍhā* m. ' post, forked stake '. (CDIAL 10317) Middha (nt.) [orig. pp. perhaps to Vedic mid (?) to be fat=medh, as DhsA 378 gives "medhatī ti middhaŋ." -- More likely however connected with Sk. methi (pillar=Lat. meta), cp. Prk. medhi. The meaning is more to the point too, viz. "stiff." (Pali) Glyph: 'root or stump (of tree)': mọ̃nḍu 1 म्वं&above;ड्&below; । स्थाणुः m. the trunk or stump of a tree, including the solid part of the root (cf. mŏnḍü 1) (El. *múnd*) (cf. khŏḍa-mo, p. 392*a,* l. 5, and nasta-mo, s.v. nast); a log, a heavy block of wood (Gr.Gr. 37, Śiv. 1856); a pillar; -- ° any clumsy lump (Rām. 631), cf.gala-mọ̃nḍu, p. 282*a,* l. 5, or used in the names of various cakes (cf. alapōshĕ-mọ̃nḍu, p. 22*b,* l. 27; lāyĕ-mọ̃nḍu, p. 543*a,* l. 48), or in such compounds as kana-mọ̃nḍu, p. 448*a,* l. 11, the root of the ear; murkha-mŏnḍu, a fool-block, an utter fool. mŏnḍi-ala mŏnḍi-ala म्वं&above;डि&below;-अल । मूलोद्धारः m. tottering of the trunk, rooting up; hence, utter destruction; cf. ala 4. -pākh -पाख् । चिरकालपाकः m. (sg. dat. -pākas -पाकस), log-cooking, i.e. cooking on a fire on which a whole chopped log is consumed; met. cooking for a very long time. -zyunu -ज़िनु&below; । स्थाण्विन्धनम् m. log firewood, a log chopped up for firewood. (Kashmiri)

Glyph 'composite (animals)' or ligatured glyphs: మేడము [ mēḍamu ] *mēḍamu.* [Telugu] n. Joining,union, కూడిక.

Glyph 'oppositon': *mētha ' opposing, quarrelling with '. [√mith] Pa. *mēdhaka* -- , °*aga* -- m. ' quarrel, abuse '; L. *mīˆhā̃* m. ' accusation, reproach '. (CDIAL 10314) *mēḍamu.* A fight, battle, యుద్ధము. మేడము

పొడుచు *mēdamu-poḍuṭsu*. v. n. To fight a battle.యుద్ధముచేయు, కోడిమేడము a cock fight. మేండ్రించు [ mēṇḍriñcu ] *mēnḍrinṭsu*. [Tel.] v. a. To divide, cut, sever; భేదించు. (Telugu)

Glyph 'curl of hair': *mēṇḍhī ' lock of hair, curl '. [Cf. **mēṇḍha* -- 1 s.v. *miḍḍa -- ] S. *mīˇḍhī* f., *°ḍho* m. ' braid in a woman's hair ', L. *mẽḍhī* f.; G. *mīḍlɔ*, *miḍ°* m. 'braid of hair on a girl's forehead'(CDIAL 10312)

Glyph 'tangled cord': M. *meḍhā* m. ' curl, snarl, twist or tangle in cord or thread ' (CDIAL 10312)

Glyph 'spear': మేడెము [ mēḍemu ] or మేడియము *mēḍemu*. [Tel.] n. A spear or dagger. ఈటె, బాకు. The rim of a bell-shaped earring, set with ems.రాళ్లుచెక్కిన□మికీ అంచుయొక్క పనితరము. "క ఓడితినన్నన్ వారక మేడెముపొడుతురె." BD. vi. 116.

Background

Many savants have tried to unravel the Indus valley mystery. Many mysteries remain unresolved: for e.g., the ziggurat under stupa mound in Mohenjo-daro, function of tablets distinct from seals and other inscriptions. With an evaluation of the evidences reported from Harappa Archaeological Research Project (HARP) excavations (1986-2007), it is inferred that the function of the Indus script was to enable the helper of the merchants in the guild workshop to tally and record bills of lading for products to be packaged, sealed and couriered to trade partners (for e.g. those in Meluhha settlements of Mesopotmia or associates along the settlements of the Persian Gulf or Elam.)

Earlier notes 1) from Mackay, 2) on the use of script on metal objects, 3) rebus readings of 'animal' glyphs on Indus script inscriptions, 4) analyses of copper tablets are also embedded for ready reference.

Bronze age and the evolution of writing

In the context of the bronze age, the comments of James D. Muhly are apposite to further evaluate the role played by Indus artisans (and the possible diffusion of Indus script glyphs) in the interaction areas of Eurasia, in general and of Elam (BMAC), Persian gulf region, and Mesopotamia, in particular: "The Early Bronze Age of the 3rd millennium BCE saw the first development of a truly international age of metallurgy… The question is, of course, why all this took place in the 3rd millennium BCE… It seems to me that any attempt to explain why things suddenly took off about 3000 BCE has to explain the most important development, the birth of the art of writing… As for the concept of a Bronze Age one of the most significant events in the 3rd millennium was the development of true tin-bronze alongside an arsenical alloy of copper…" (J.D. Muhly, 1973, *Copper and Tin*, Conn.: Archon., Hamden; Transactions of Connecticut Academy of Arts and Sciences, vol. 43, p. 221f. )

Arsenical bronze occurs in the archaeological record across the globe, the earliest artefacts so far known have been found on the Iranian plateau in the 5th millennium BCE. [Thornton, C.P.; Lamberg-Karlovsky, C.C.; Liezers, M.; Young, S.M.M. (2002). "On pins and needles: tracing the evolution of copper-based alloying at Tepe Yahya, Iran, via ICP-MS analysis of Common-place items.".*Journal of Archaeological Science* 29 (29): 1451–1460.] Early occurrences of realgar – a reddish-yellow arsenic sulfide mineral -- as a red painting pigment are known for works of art from China, India, Central Asia, and Egypt.

Earliest inscriptions on copper tablets were found at Mohenjo-daro. Indus Writing on Metal was found at Harappa also.

Copper tablet (H2000-4498/9889-01) with raised script was found in Trench 43. Harappa. (Source: Slide 351 harappa.com) Eight such duplicates of tablets have been found (HARP, 2005); these were recovered from circular platforms. This example of a uniquely scripted tablet with raised Indus script glyphs shows that copper tablets were also used in Harappa, while hundreds of copper tablets with incised script inscriptions were found in Mohenjo-daro. See also: http://bharatkalyan97.blogspot.com/2011/11/decoding-longest-inscription-of-indus.html The copper tablet with raised script contains a 'backbone' glyph; decoding: kaśēru 'the backbone' (Bengali. Skt.); kaśēruka id. (Skt.) Rebus: kasērā' metal worker ' (Lahnda)(CDIAL 2988, 2989) An alternate (vikalpa) reading is: *kaṇḍa* 'backbone'. Rebus: *kaṇḍa* 'stone (ore) metal'. Glyph: 'ingot shape': *mũh* 'ingot'.mũhã̄ = the quantity of iron produced at one time in a native smelting furnace of the Kolhes; iron produced by the Kolhes and formed like a four-cornered piece a little pointed at each end (Santali). *dula* 'pair'. Rebus: *dul* 'cast (metal)'. Thus, the three glyphs are read together sequentially as: *dul mũh kaṇḍa* 'cast ingot stone (ore) metal'.

Recovered from circular platforms? Clearly, the circular platforms functioned as sorting, marketing platforms if, in the center of the circle, a storage pot containing metal artefacts, beads, ivory products etc. were kept for display, marketing, trade. [The center of the circle may also have held a drill-lathe.] Prastará m. ' anything strewn, grass to sit on ' RV., ' flat surface ' Mn., ' (v.l. prastāra -- ) plain ' Hariv., ' rock, stone ' Hit. [√stṛ]K. pathur, °thuru (dat. °tharas, °tharis) m. 'area, bare floor ', pathürü f. ' level piece of ground, plateau, small village '; S. patharu m. ' rug, mat '; Or. Athuripathuri ' bag and baggage '(CDIAL 8857).Pa. pattharati tr. ' spreads out, scatters ', Pk. Pattharaï patthuraï; L. (Ju.) patharaṇ ' to spread, turn over '; Mth. Pathrab intr. ' to lie scattered '; G. pātharvũ tr. ' to spread '; Si. Paturanavā ' to spread abroad, proclaim ' (whence caus. Paturuvanavā and intr. Pätirenavā ' to be extended '); Md. Faturān ' to spread out '; -- Pk. Pattharia<-> ' spread out '; Si. Pätali ' flat, level, plain ' (rather than < pattralá -- ). — See *prastārayati, *prastṛta -- .Addenda: *prastarati: S.kcch. pātharṇū ' to spread '; caus. Ko. Pātlāytā ' spreads out (bed, etc.) ' S. M. Katre, Md. Faturuvanī tr. ' spreads ', feturenī intr. (absol. Feturi).(CDIAL 8860). Circular platforms as guild trade platforms for artisans of forge/smithy and lapidaries

Pattharati [pa+tharati] to spread, spread out, extend J i.62; iv.212; vi.279; DhA i.26; iii.61 (so read at J vi.549 in cpd ˚pāda with spreading feet, v. l. patthaṭa˚). — pp. patthaṭa (q. v.). — Caus. Patthāreti with

pp. patthārita probably also to be read at Th 1, 842 for padhārita. (Pali)

Pattharika [fr. Patthara] a merchant Vin ii.135 (kaŋsa˚). (Pali)

[An allograph pattara 'trough' is a glyph used in front of many types of animals including wild animals and composite animal glyphs. Pātra 'trough'; pattar 'merchant'. The lexeme also connotes a 'guild'.]

Glyph: पात्र pātra, (l.) s. Vessel, cup, plate; receptacle. [lw. Sk. Id.] (Nepali) pātramu A utensil, ఉపకరణము.

Hardware. Metal vessels. (Telugu) பத்தல் pattal, n. பத்தர்¹ pattar 1. A wooden bucket; மரத்தாலான நீரிறைக்குங் கருவி. தீம்பிழி யெந்திரம் பத்தல் வருந்த (பதிற்றுப். 19, 23).

Rebus: பத்தர்² pattar , n. < T. battuḍu. A caste title of goldsmiths; தட்டார் பட்டப்பெயருள் ஒன்று. பட்டடை¹ paṭṭaṭai , n. prob. படு¹- + அடை¹-. 1. [T. paṭṭika, K. paṭṭaḍe.] Anvil; அடைகல். (பிங்.)

சீரிடங்காணி னெறிதற்குப் பட்ட டை (குறள், 821). 2. [K. paṭṭaḍi.] Smithy, forge; கொல்லன் களரி பத்தல் pattal , n. 1. A wooden bucket; மரத்தாலான நீரிறைக்குங் கருவி. தீம்பிழி யெந்திரம் பத்தல் வருந்த (பதிற்றுப். 19, 23). பத்தர்¹ pattar , n. 1. See பத்தல், 1, 4, 5. 2. Wooden trough for feeding animals; தொட்டி. பன்றிக் கூழ்ப்பத்தரில் (நாலடி, 257). Paṭṭar-ai community; guild as of workmen (Ta.); pattar merchants; perh. Vartaka (Skt.) Patthara [cp. Late Sk. Prastara. The ord. meaning of Sk. Pr. Is "stramentum"] 1. Stone, rock S i.32. — 2. Stoneware Miln 2. (Pali) Pa. Pk. Patthara — m. ' stone ', S. patharu m., L. (Ju.) pathar m., khet. Patthar, P. patthar m. (→

forms of Bi. Mth. Bhoj. H. G. below with atth or ath), Wpah.jaun. pātthar; Ku. Pāthar m. ' slates, stones ', gng. Pāth*Ir ' flat stone '; A. B. pāthar ' stone ', Or. Pathara; Bi. Pāthar, patthar, patthal ' hailstone '; Mth. Pāthar, pathal ' stone ', Bhoj. Pathal, Aw.lakh. pāthar, H. pāthar, patthar, pathar, patthal m., G. patthar, pathrɔ m.; M. pāthar f. ' flat stone '; Ko. Phāttaru ' stone '; Si. Patura ' chip, fragment '; -- S. pathirī f. ' stone in the bladder '; P. pathrī f. ' small stone '; Ku. Patharī ' stone cup '; B. pāthri ' stone in the bladder, tartar on teeth '; Or. Pathurī ' stoneware '; H. patthrī f. ' grit ', G. pathrī f. *prastarapaṭṭa -- , *prastaramṛttikā -- , *prastarāsa -- .Addenda: prastará -- : Wpah.kṭg. pátthər m. ' stone, rock '; pəthreuṇõ ' to stone '; J. pāthar m. ' stone '; Omarw. Pātharī ' precious stone '. (CDIAL 8857) paṭṭarai 'workshop' (Ta.) pattharika [fr. Patthara] a merchant Vin ii.135 (kaŋsa˚).(Pali) cf. Pattharati [pa+tharati] to spread, spread out, extend J i.62; iv.212; vi.279; DhA i.26; iii.61 (so read at J vi.549 in cpd ˚pāda with spreading feet, v. l. patthaṭa˚). — pp. patthaṭa (q. v.). பத்தர்&sup5; pattar, n. perh. Vartaka. Merchants; வியாபாரிகள். (W.) battuḍu. n.

8 cast copper tablets recovered from circular platforms, Harappa (2005);

The caste title of all the five castes of artificers as vaḍla b*, carpenter. The circular platforms could have served as prastara for the articles taken for display from out of the storage pots. "During excavations of the circular platform area on Mound F numerous Cemetery H-type sherds and some complete vessels were recovered in association with pointed base goblets and large storage vessels that are usually associated with Harappa Period 3C." South fo the platforms was a furnace. "A large kiln was also found just below the surface of the mound to the south of the circular platforms." http://www.harappa.com/indus4/e6.html The circular platforms are used in conjunction with the products taken out of the kiln (furnace) and large storage vessels which could have been plced in the center of any of the street platforms, constituting the main market street of early times of Harappa settlement. Circular platforms (with a dia. Of 1.5 m) found within rooms (of a coppersmith) as in Padri might have served as working platforms for the brass-workers, lapidaries, artisans of the civilization or as a display counter if the room was used as a shop for sales.

Glyph (Middle glyph of the three-glyph inscription): Sign 48: S.*kaṇḍo* m. ' back ', L. *kaṇḍ* f., *kaṇḍā* m. 'backbone' (CDIAL 2670). Rebus: *kaṇḍa* 'stone (ore)(Gadba)'. . Ga. (Oll.) kanḍ, (S.) kanḍu (pl. kanḍkil) stone (DEDR 1298). Vikalpa: kaśēru 'the backbone' (Bengali. Skt.); kaśēruka id. (Skt.) Rebus: kasērā' metal worker ' (Lahnda)(CDIAL 2988, 2989) L. awāṇ. Kasērā ' metal worker ', P. kaserā m. ' worker in pewter ' (both ← E with — s -- ); N. kasero ' maker of brass pots '; Bi. H. kaserā m. ' worker in pewter '. (CDIAL 2988) கசம்¹ kacam , n. cf. ayas. (அக. நி.) 1. Iron; இரும்பு. 2. Mineral fossil; தாதுப்பொருள் (Tamil) N. kasār ' maker of brass pots '; A. kãhār ' worker in bell — metal '; B. kā̃sāri ' pewterer, brazier, coppersmith ', Or. Kāsārī; H. kasārī m. ' maker of brass pots '; G.kāsārɔ, kas m. ' coppersmith '; M. kā̃sār, kās m. ' worker in white metal ', kāsārḍā m. ' contemptuous term for the same '. (CDIAL 2989)

Two identical glyphs which flank the 'backbone' glyph on these tablets is an oval (variant 'rhombus') sign — like a metal ingot — and is ligatured with an infixed sloping stroke: ḍhāḷiyum = adj. sloping, inclining (G.) The ligatured glyph is read rebus as: ḍhālako = a large metal ingot (G.) ḍhālakī = a metal heated and poured into a mould; a solid piece of metal; an ingot (G.)

h2249A. This tablet shows that a pair of ovals with infixed stroke flank the 'backbone' glyph.

Glyph of 'pairing': dula 'pair' (Kashmiri); dul 'cast (metal)' (Santali).

A pair of ḍhālako shown on the seal impression on a pot (Mohenjo-daro. Text 2937) may connote *dul ḍhālako* 'cast metal ingot'.

Thus the inscription of the copper tablet with inscription in raised script (bas relief) is decoded as: maker of brass pots, (bronze) ingots: dul ḍhālako kasērā lit. cast ingot, brass worker.

The Trench 43 is the same trench which exposed many circular platforms.

Slide 336 harappa.com Overview of Trench 43 in 2000 looking north, showing the HARP-exposed circular platform in the foreground and the "granary" area in the background. Note the wall voids to the west, south, and east of the circular platform (see also image 356).

Slide 356.Detail view of the HARP-excavated platform in Trench 43 with Wheeler's platform to the east (toward the top of the image). Note the mud-brick wall foundations that surround each platform to the east, south, and west (the north walls remain unexposed). Traces of baked brick thresholds can be seen on the right (south).

Slide 158. Harappa.com Circular platform. In 1998, the circular platform first exposed by Sir Mortimer Wheeler in 1946 was re-exposed and the area around the platform was expanded to reveal the presence of the room in which it was enclosed. The brick walls had been removed by brick robbers and only the mud brick foundations were preserved along with a few tell-tale baked bricks. This particular platform is dated to the beginning of the Harappa Phase Period 3C (c. 2200 BC).

Slide 159 (Harappa.com). New circular platform. To the west of Wheeler's circular platform a new platform was discovered. This platform was excavated using modern stratigraphic procedures and detailed documentation. Charcoal, sediment, animal bone, charred plant and other botanical samples were collected from each stratum to complement the other artifacts such as pottery, seals and domestic debris. These samples should allow a more precise reconstruction of the function of these enigmatic structures. Slide 353. Circular platforms in the southwestern part of Mound F excavated by M.S. Vats in the 1920s and 1930s, as conserved by the Department of Archaeology and Museums, Government of Pakistan.

Slide 355 (Harappa.com). The circular platform excavated by Wheeler in 1946 (left) and the one excavated by HARP in 1998 (right). Both of these platforms were found inside small square rooms that originally had baked brick walls, subsequently removed by brick robbers (Trench 43).

An overview of the area on Mound F as seen from the city wall on Mound AB. The circular working platforms are in the background and a row of identical houses that were clearly made all at one time, possibly a housing project of some wealthy merchant or perhaps sponsored by the city council.

Connected with the circular working platforms is the kiln discovered close-by.

Large updraft kiln of the Harappan period (ca. 2400 BCE) found during excavations on Mound E Harappa, 1989 (After Fig. 8.8, Kenoyer, 2000) After Figure 9. Harappa 1999, Mound F, Trench 43: Period 5 kiln, plan and section views. http://www.harappa.com/indus4/e6.html

Hypothesis 1: It is reasonable to infer that the kiln of the type used a

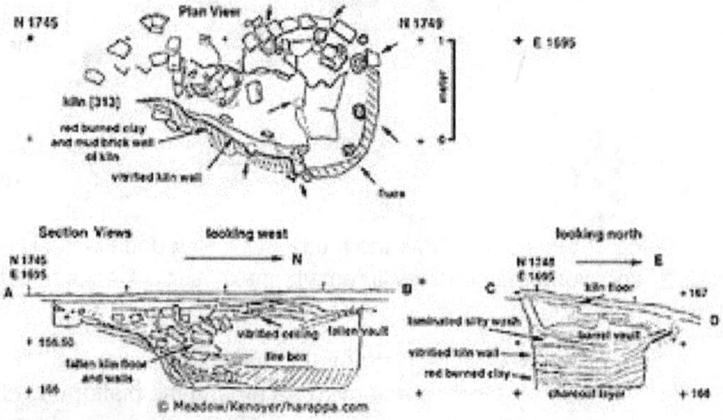


smelting furnace is also relatable both to the circular working platforms and the copper tablets with Indus script glyphs. The shape of the kiln shown in this Figure 9 diagram is comparable to another kiln which was unearthed. "During excavations of the circular

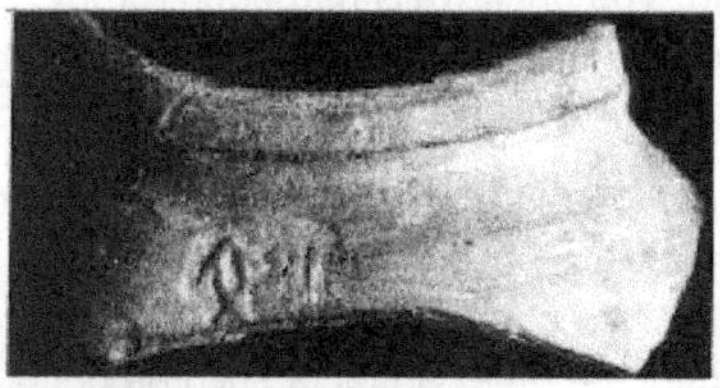

platform area on Mound F numerous Cemetery H-type sherds and some complete vessels were recovered in association with pointed base goblets and large storage vessels that are usually associated with Harappa Period 3C. A large kiln was also found just below the surface of the mound to the south of the circular platforms. The upper portion of the kiln had been eroded, but the floor of the firing chamber was found preserved along with the fire-box. Upon excavation it became clear that this was a new form of kiln with a barrel vault and internal flues (Figure 8). This unique installation shows a clear discontinuity with the form of Harappan pottery kilns, which were constructed with a central column to support the floor (Dales and Kenoyer 1991). Radiocarbon samples taken from Harappa Phase hearths in the domestic areas and from the bottom of the Late Harappan kiln will help to determine if these installations were in use at the same time or if the kiln was built in an abandoned area after the Harappa Phase occupation. It is possible that people using Late Harappan style pottery were living together with people using Harappan style pottery during the Period 4 transition between Periods 3C and 5." http://www.harappa.com/indus4/e6.html

Hypothesis 2: It is reasonable to infer a close link between the functions served by the circular platform and the copper tablet with raised Indus script glyphs. "During his excavations, Vats identified 17 circular brick platforms (Vats 1940:19ff) and in 1946 Wheeler excavated an 18th example (Wheeler 1947). Earlier interpretations about the circular platforms suggested that they were used for husking grain and that they may have had a central wooden mortar. In the 1998 excavations one additional circular platform was located and detailed documentation and sampling was conducted to determine its function and chronology." Contra view: "The new excavations did not reveal any evidence for grain processing and there was no evidence for a wooden mortar in the center. Some straw impressions were found on the floor to the south of the circular platform, but microscopic examination by Dr. Steve Weber confirmed that these impressions were of straw and not of chaff or grain processing byproducts."

Susa pot (reported by Maurizio Tosi) — containing metal artifacts possibly sent from Meluhha traders or received by merchants with links to Meluhha trading community?)

Hypothesis 3: Considering that the circular platforms were located in close proximity to one another, it is reasonable to infer that the workers who worked on these platforms belonged to a guild or metalworker community.Indus language (Indian linguistic area: mleccha/meluhha): bharatiyo = a caster of metals; a brazier; bharatar, bharatal, bharataḷ = moulded; an article made in a mould; bharata = casting metals in moulds; bharavum = to fill in; to put in; to pour into (G.lex.) bhart = a mixed metal of copper and lead; bhartīyā = a barzier, worker in metal; bhaṭ, bhrāṣṭra = oven, furnace (Skt.)

Hypothesis 4: It is reasonable to infer that the center of the circular platform could have held a storage pot of the type unearthed in Susa with metal objects (and with a 'fish' Indus script glyph written below the rim of the pot) — evidenced by Maurizio Tosi as a link with Meluhha (aka Indus valley).
h1085 h1083

Hypothesis 5: It is reasonable to infer that the pots with inscriptions (either embossed using a seal or inscribed as on the Susa pot) were used as containers for despatch to traders, while other storage pots (without inscriptions) might have been kept in the center of the circular platforms.

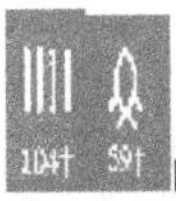

Reading glyphs on Side B: *aḍar ḍangra khũṭ* (zebu, *bos indicus*). *aya* (fish) *gaṇḍa* (four) Rebus (the composite message of three glyphs): *aduru ḍhangar khũṭ ayaskāṇḍa* 'nativemetal smith guild stone ore metal'.

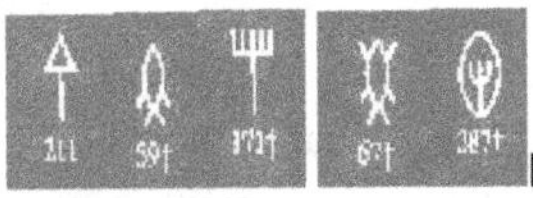

Reading glyphs on Side A: Part 1: *kuṭila* 'bent'; Rebus: *kuṭila* 'bronze (8 parts copper, 2 parts tin); reduplication of ( ) may indicate a specified number of 'ingots' [dula 'likeness' (Kashmiri). Rebus: *dul* 'cast (metal)'(Santali)]'; *kolom* (rice plant). Rebus: *kolami* 'smithy, forge'. *añcu* (*amśu*) *aya* 'fish + fins'. Rebus: 'iron (stony) metal'. Part 2: *aḍar* (harrow) *aya* (fish) *kāṇḍa* (arrow) Rebus: *aduru ḍhangar ayaskāṇḍa* 'nativemetal smith stone ore metal'. The composite message of five glyphs: tin-alloyed bronze cast smithy, forge; iron (stony) metal; nativemetalsmith stone ore metal.

h1953B and A. Two sides of a seal: One side showed a zebu with 'fish' and 'four strokes' glyphs. The other had a five-glyph inscription including the 'fish' and 'arrow' glyphs which are allographs of the 'fish' and 'four strokes' glyphs on the obverse of the seal. It has been suggested that the zebu connoted a guild (community): aya 'fish'; aya 'metal' (G.); kāṇḍa 'arrow'; 'four'; rebus: kāṇḍa 'furnace stone ore metal': hence, the two glyphs connote: *ayaskāṇḍa* (of) Zebu: *aḍar ḍhangar khūṭ* 'native-metal-blacksmith community (guild)(making) excellent metal'. Kūṭa a house, dwelling (Skt.lex.) khūṭ = a community, sect, society, division, clique, schism, stock; khūṭren peṛa kanako = they belong to the same stock (Santali)khūṭ Nag. Khūṭ, kūṭ Has. (Or. Khūṭ) either of the two branches of the village family.Rebus: kūdār 'turner' (B.)

m1118 Seal. Shows the glyphs: zebu, fish, four strokes (circumscript), all read rebus in mleccha/meluhha.

A zebu bull tied to a post; a bird above. Large painted storage jar discovered in burned rooms at Nausharo, ca. 2600 to 2500 BCE. Cf. Fig. 2.18, J.M. Kenoyer, 1998, Cat. No. 8. This storage pot is shown with a zebu (khūṭ) painted on it; perhaps used to store artifacts of the guild (*khūṭ*) nativemetal furnace (*bhaṭa*): glyph: *baṭa* 'quail'.

Hypothesis 6: *khūṭ*,'zebu' rebus: 'guild'. [khūṭ Brahmani bull (Kathiawar G.); khūṭro entire bull used for agriculture, not for breeding (G.)(CDIAL 3899). Khūṭro = entire bull; khūṭ= brahmaṇi bull (G.) khuṇṭiyo = an uncastrated bull (Kathiawad. G.lex.) khūṭaḍum a bullock (used in Jhālwāḍ)(G.) kuṇṭai = bull (Ta.lex.) cf. khū̃dhi hump on the back; khuīdhū hump-backed (G.)(CDIAL 3902).] Rebus: kūṭa a house, dwelling (Skt.lex.) khūṭ = a community, sect, society, division, clique, schism, stock; khūṭren peṛa kanako = they belong to the same stock (Santali) khūṭ Nag. khūṭ, kūṭ Has. (Or. Khūṭ) either of the two branches of the village family.

Text 2937.

Seal impression on pot. Glyphs: Pair of dotted ovals; rim-of-jar. The glyphs are part of the three glyphs

used on copper tablet with raised script.

The same sequence of three signs (Glyphs of a pair of dotted ovals + rim-of-jar)occurs on one side of a prism tablet: m1429A (The other two sides show a boat and a crocodile holding fish glyph on its jaw).

m1429B. Glyphs: crocodile + fish

(Te.) Pali: ayakāra 'iron-smith'. ] Both ayaskāma and ayaskāra are attested in Panini ayakāra 'blacksmith' (Pali) kāruvu = mechanic, artisan, Viśvakarma, the celestial artisan (Pan. Viii.3.46; ii.4.10). Wpah. Bhal. Kamīṇ m.f. labourer (man or woman) ; MB. Kāmiṇā labourer (CDIAL 2902) N. kāmi blacksmith (CDIAL 2900). Khār 1 खार् । लोहकारः m. (sg. Abl. Khāra 1 खार; the pl. dat. Of this word is khāran 1 खारन्, which is to be distinguished from khāran 2, q.v., s.v.), a blacksmith, an iron worker (cf. bandūka-khār, p. 111b, l. 46; K.Pr. 46; H. xi, 17); a farrier (El.). This word is often a part of a name, and in such case comes at the end (W. 118) as in Wahab khār, Wahab the smith (H. ii, 12; vi, 17). Khāra-basta खार-बस्ֺत । चर्मप्रसेविका f. the skin bellows of a blacksmith. —būṭhū —ब&above;ठ्&below; । लोहकारभित्तिः f. the wall of a blacksmith's furnace or hearth. —bāy —बाय् ।

लोहकारपत्नी f. a blacksmith's wife (Gr.Gr. 34). —dŏkuru; । लोहकारायोघनः m. a blacksmith's hammer, a sledge-hammer.-gȧji —ग&above;जि&below; or —güjü; । लोहकारचुल्लिः f. a blacksmith's furnace or hearth. —hāl —हाल् । लोहकारकन्दुः f. (sg. Dat. —höjü —हा&above;जू&below;), a blacksmith's smelting furnace; cf. hāl 5. —kūrü; । लोहकारकन्या f. a blacksmith's daughter. —koṭu; । लोहकारपुत्रः m. the son of a blacksmith, esp. a skilful son, who can work at the same profession. —küṭü; । लोहकारकन्या f. a blacksmith's daughter, esp. one who has the virtues and qualities properly belonging to her father's profession or caste. —mĕ˘ʦü लोहकारमृत्तिका f. (for 2, see [khāra 3] ), 'blacksmith's earth,' i.e. iron-ore. —nĕcyuwu —न्यचिवु&below; । लोहकारात्मजः m. a blacksmith's son. —nay —नय् । लोहकारनालिका f. (for khāranay 2, see [khārun] ), the trough into which the blacksmith allows melted iron to flow after smelting. -ʦañĕ लोहकारशान्ताङ्गाराः f.pl. charcoal used by blacksmiths in their furnaces. —wān लोहकारापणः m. a blacksmith's shop, a forge, smithy (K.Pr. 3). —waṭh —वठ् । आघाताधारशिला m. (sg. Dat. —waṭas —वटि), the large stone used by a blacksmith as an anvil. (Kashmiri) kāruvu = mechanic, artisan, Viśvakarma, the celestial artisan (Te.); కారువు [ kāruvu ] kāruvu. [Skt.] n. An artist, artificer. An agent; gāre = affix of noun denoting one who does it, e.g. samagāre = cobbler (Tu.); garuva (Ka.); gar_uva = an important man (Te.) cf. –ka_ra suffix. 'worker' (Skt.) kā́ri— m. 'artisan, worker' Pāṇ. 2. F. 'action, work' Bhaṭṭ. [√KR̥ 1] 1. P.kārī m. 'worker'. 2. Kt. kå̄r 'work', Wg.kō̜, Pr. Kā̃; S. kāri f. 'work, occupation, use'; L. kār f. 'work'; P. kārī f. 'remedy'; Or. Kāri 'work'. (CDIAL 3064) karuvu n. Melting: what is melted (Te.)कारु [ kāru ] m (S) An artificer or artisan. 2 A common term for the twelve बलुतेदार q. v. Also कारुनारु m pl q. v. in नारुकारु. (Marathi) कारिगर, कारिगार, कारागीर, कारेगार, कारागार [ kārigara, kārigāra, kārāgīra, kārēgāra, kārāgāra ] m ( P) A good workman, a clever artificer or artisan. 2 Affixed as an honorary designation to the names of Barbers, and sometimes of सुतार, गवंडी, & चितारी. 3 Used laxly as adj and in the sense of Effectual, availing, effective of the end. बलुतें [ balutēṃ ] n A share of the corn and garden-produce assigned for the subsistence of the twelve public servants of a village, for whom see below. 2 In some districts. A share of the dues of the hereditary officers of a village, such as पाटील, कुळकरणी &c. बलुतेदार or बलुता [ balutēdāra or balutā ] or त्या m (बलुतें &c.) A public servant of a village entitled to बलुतें. There are twelve distinct from the regular Governmentofficers पाटील, कुळकरणी &c.; viz. सुतार, लोहार, महार, मांग (These four constitute पहिली or थोरली कास or वळ the first division. Of three of them each is entitled to चार पाचुंदे, twenty bundles of Holcus or the thrashed corn, and the महार to आठ पाचुंदे); कुंभार, चाम्हार, परीट, न्हावी constitute दुसरी orमधली कास or वळ, and are entitled, each, to तीन पाचुंदे; भट, मुलाणा, गुरव, कोळी form तिसरी or धाकटी कास or वळ, and have, each, दोन पाचुंदे. Likewise there are twelve अलुते or supernumerary public claimants, viz. तेली, तांबोळी, साळी, माळी, जंगम, कळवांत, डवऱ्या, ठाकर, घडशी, तराळ, सोनार, चौगुला. Of these the allowance of corn is not settled. The learner must be prepared to meet with other enumerations of the बलुतेदार (e. g. पाटील, कुळ- करणी, चौधरी, पोतदार, देशपांड्या, न्हावी, परीट, गुरव, सुतार, कुंभार, वेसकर, जोशी; also सुतार, लोहार, चाम्हार, कुंभार as constituting the first-class and claiming the largest division of बलुतें; next न्हावी, परीट, कोळी, गुरव as constituting the middle class and claiming a subdivision of बलुतें; lastly, भट, मुलाणा, सोनार, मांग; and, in the Konkaṇ, yet another list); and with other accounts of the assignments of corn; for this and many similar matters, originally determined diversely, have undergone the usual influence of time, place, and ignorance. Of the बलुतेदार in the Indápúr pergunnah the list and description stands thus:--First class, सुतार, लोहार, चाम्हार, महार; Second, परीट, कुंभार, न्हावी, मांग; Third, सोनार, मुलाणा, गुरव, जोशी, कोळी, रामोशी; in all fourteen, but in no one village are the whole fourteen to be found or traced. In the Panḍharpúr districts the order is:--पहिली or थोरली वळ (1st class); महार, सुतार, लोहार, चाम्हार, दुसरी or मधली वळ(2nd class); परीट, कुंभार, न्हावी, मांग, तिसरी or धाकटी वळ (3rd class); कुळकरणी, जोशी, गुरव, पोतदार; twelve बलुते and of अलुते there are eighteen. According to Grant Duff, the बलतेदार are सुतार, लोहार, चाम्हार, मांग, कुंभार, न्हावी, परीट, गुरव, जोशी, भाट, मुलाणा; and the अलुते are सोनार, जंगम, शिंपी, कोळी, तराळ or वेसकर, माळी, डवऱ्यागोसावी, घडशी, रामोशी, तेली, तांबोळी, गोंधळी. In many villages of Northern Dakhaṇ the महार receives the बलुतें of the first, second, and third classes; and, consequently, besides the महार, there are but nine बलुतेदार. The following are the only अलुतेदार or नारू now to be found;--सोनार, मांग, शिंपी, भट गोंधळी, कोर- गू, कोतवाल, तराळ, but of the अलुतेदार & बलुते- दार there is much confused intermixture, the अलुतेदार of one district being the बलुतेदार of another, and vice  lls . (The word कास used above, in पहिली कास, मध्यम कास, तिसरी कास requires explanation. It means Udder; and, as the बलुतेदार are, in the phraseology of endearment or fondling, termed वासरें (calves), their allotments or divisions are figured by successive bodies of calves drawing at the कास or under of the गांव under the figure of a गाय or cow.) (Marathi)kruciji 'smith' (Old Church Slavic)

kāru a wild crocodile or alligator (Te.) కారు mosale 'wild crocodile or alligator. S. ghaṛyālu m. ' long —snouted porpoise '; N. ghaṛiyāl ' crocodile' (Telugu)'; A. B. ghāṛiyāl ' alligator ', Or. Ghaṛiāḷa, H. ghaṛyāl, ghariār m. (CDIAL 4422) கரவு² karavu, n. < கரா. Cf. grāha. Alligator; முதலை. கரவார்தடம் (திவ். திருவாய். 8, 9, 9). கரா karā, n. prob. Grāha. 1. A species of alligator; முதலை. கராவதன் காலினைக்கதுவ (திவ். பெரியதி. 2, 3, 9). 2. Male alligator; ஆண்முதலை. (பிங்.) கராம் karām n. prob. Grāha. 1. A species of alligator ; முதலைவகை. முதலையு மிடங்கருங் கராமும் (குறிஞ்சிப். 257). 2. Male alligator; ஆண் முதலை. (திவா.) Ta. Ayil iron. Ma. Ayir, ayiram any ore. Ka. aduru native metal. Tu. ajirda karba very hard iron (DEDR 192).

m1429C. Glyph: Boat.

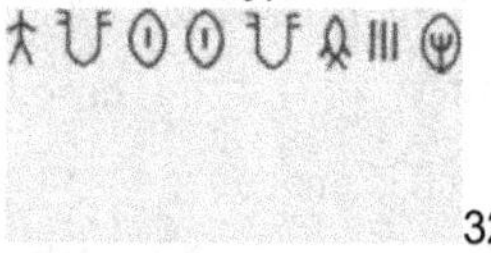

3246 Text of inscription.

bagalo = an Arabian merchant vessel (G.) bagala = an Arab boat of a particular description (Ka.); bagalā (M.); bagarige, bagarage = a kind of vessel (Ka.)(Ka.lex.); rebus: ban:gala = kumpaṭi = an:gāra śakaṭī = a chafing dish a portable stove a goldsmith's portable furnace (Te.lex.) cf. ban:garu ban:garamu = gold (Te.) baṭa= quail (Santali) A pair of quails. dula 'pair'. Rebus: dul 'cast (metal)'. Together, the quails connote: 'cast (metal) furnace. Glyph: 'a pair of squares': khoṇḍ square (Santali) Rebus: B. kõdā 'to turn in a lathe'. dula 'pair'. Rebus: dul 'cast (metal)'.Together, the squares connote: cast (metal) turner. Glyph: 'tree'. *kuṭi* 'tree'. Rebus: *kuṭhi* 'smelter furnace'. Thus, the entire message of the boat composition glyphics read: cast (metal) smelter furnace, turner; goldsmith's furnace.

Glyphs of inscription text: This is a two-part text.

Part 1

Glyph: kolom 'graft, plant'. Rebus: kolami 'smithy, forge'. ( ) 'curved, bent'; rebus: *dul kuṭila* 'cast bronze'. *kuṭila* 'bent'; Rebus: *kuṭila* 'bronze (8 parts copper, 2 parts tin); reduplication may indicate a specified number of 'ingots' [dula 'likeness' (Kashmiri). Rebus: dul 'cast (etal)(Santali)]'. Thus, the ligatured glyph is read rebus: *dul kuṭila*

Glyph: kolom 'three. Rebus: kolami 'smithy, forge'.

Glyph: aya 'fish'. Rebus: aya 'metal'.

Glyph: rim of jar. *kaṇḍa kanka* Rebus: stone (ore) furnace account (scribe).

Part 2

Glyph: *dula* 'pair'. Rebus: *dul* 'cast (metal). *ḍhāḷako* 'ingot'. Together, as a pair: Rebus: cast (metal) ingot.

Glyph: (infixed) splinter: sal 'splinter'. Rebus: sal 'workshop'.

Glyph: rim of jar. *kaṇḍa kanka* Rebus: stone (ore) furnace account (scribe).

Glyph: 'body'. *meḍ* 'body'. *Rebus: meḍ* 'iron'.

Thus the two parts of the text glyphs are read rebus – one deals with bronze, the other with cast (metal) ingots: 1. Bronze metal smithy, forge; stone (ore) furnace account. 2. Cast (metal) iron ingot workshop, stone (ore) furnace account.

The entire composition on three sides of the prism with hieroglyphs denotes: blacksmith; cast (metal) smelter furnace, turner,goldsmith's furnace; bronze metal smithy, forge and cast (metal) iron ingot workshop, stone (ore) furnace account. The artisan is a worker dealing with gold, iron and bronze and smelting in furnaces, casting and ingots. The inscription is a stone (ore) furnace account of all these metallurgical process sequences.

Archaeological context unravels the purposes served by inscribed tablets vis-à-vis inscribed seals and seal impressions

Hypothesis 7: Seal impression on pot (Mohenjo-daro. Text 2937) The pot was used as a container to trade the products described by the inscription. In their contribution to theorpus of Indus Inscriptions, Volume 3, Part 1, Kenoyer and Meadow observe: "Square seals with script alone are found first in Period 3B...We are also obtaining important chronological information with respect to inscribed tablets, which are particularly common at Harappa, more so than seals. Through careful stratigraphic cutting-back of Vats' section in Trench I of Mound F and comparison with his report of that trench (Vats 1940), we have determined that he was not correct in reporting that small steatite tablets with incised script are from the earliest levels of the site. Instead it is evident that such tablets appeare toward the middle of Period 3B and continued to be used well into Period 3C (Meadow & kenoyer 1997; 2000). Furthermore, these inscribed steatite tablets, which Vats (1940) called 'tiny steatite seals', are not seals at all but are incised with script that was to be read directly from the tablet. And along with the steatite tablets are found terracotta and glazed faience tablets with molded bas-relief script, motifs, and narrative scenes, which also start appearing in mid-Period 3B and continue into Period 3C (Meadow & Kenoyer 1997; 2000)...

Group of incised baked steatite tablets. A group of 16 three-sided incised baked steatite tablets, all with the same inscriptions, were *uncovered* in mid- to late Period 3B debris outside of the curtain wall. (See 146). These tablets may originally been enclosed in a perishable container such as a small bag of cloth or leather.

Life and death of Harappan seals and tablets. An additional six copies of these tablets, again all with the same inscriptions, were found elsewhere in the debris outside of perimeter wall [250] including two near the group of 16 and two in debris between the perimeter and curtain walls. Here all 22 tablets are displayed together with a unicorn intaglio seal from the Period 3B street inside the perimeter wall, which has two of the same signs as those found on the tablets. (See also 145, 146, 147, 148, 149, 150). Quoting from R.H. Meadow and J.M. Kenoyer's article in South Asian Archaeology 1997 (Rome, 2001): "It is tempting to think that the evident loss of utility and subsequent discard of the tablets is related to the "death" of the seal. Seals are almost always found in trash or street deposits (and never yet in a grave) indicating that they were either lost or intentionally discarded, the latter seeming the more likely in most instances. The end of the utility of a seal must relate to some life event of its owner, whether change of status, or death, or the passing of an amount of time during which the seal was considered current. A related consideration is that apparently neither seals nor tablets could be used by just anyone or for any length of time because otherwise they would not have fallen out of circulation. Thus the use of seals — and of tablets — was possible only if they were known to be current. Once they were no longer current, they were discarded. This would help explain why a group of 16 (or 18) tablets with the same inscriptions, kept together perhaps in a cloth or leather pouch, could have been deposited with other trash outside of the perimeter wall of Mound E."

Period 3B debris related to: c. 2450 BCE — c. 2200 BCE.

A tribute has to be paid in particular to Kenoyer, Meadow and participants in the HARP multi-disciplinary team work and many including Marshall and Mackay who have tried to explain the function served by Indus script inscriptions. The focus is on tablets [made of either steatite (terracotta) or copper] with Indus script. Many duplicates, that is, tablets with the same inscription have been unearthed and Kenoyer & Meadow discuss the stratigraphic context in which 22 such samples were found in Harappa during the 1986-2007 excavations. Earlier excavations were under the late George F. Dale Jr. in Mohenjo-daro and other sites, following the pioneering archaeological investigations of Banerjee, Dikshit, Marshall, Mackay and earlier exploratory surveys of Ahmad Hasan Dani, Brij Basi Lal, Nani Gopal Majumdar, and Sir Marc Aurel Stein.

Examples of 22 duplicates steatite triangular tablets h-2218 to h-2239
h2219A First side of three-sided tablet

h2219B Second side of three-sided tablet

h2219C Third side of three-sided tablet

The two glyphs which appear on the h2219A example also appear on a seal. "In a street deposit of similar age just inside the wall, a seal was found with two of the same characters as seen on one side of the tablets."

While the 22 tablets were meant to help in 'tallying' the products produced by the artisans, the `seal was meant to be used in preparing a bill of lading for the products to be couriered through containers.

h1682A. The seal which contained the two glyphs used on the 'tally' three-sided tablets. The seal showed a one-horned heifer + standard device and two segments of inscriptions: one segment showing the two glyphs shown on one side of the 'tally' tablet; the other segment showing glyphs of a pair of 'rectangle with divisions' + 'three long linear strokes'.

Decoding a pair of glyphs, a pair of 'rectangle with divisions': khaṇḍ 'field, division' (Skt.); Rebus: kaṇḍ 'furnace' (Skt.) Thus, reduplicated glyph connotes dul kaṇḍ 'casting furnace'. Vikalpa: khonḍu 'divided into parts' (Kashmiri)khonḍu I खण्डितः, विकलावयवः adj. (f. khünḍü 1, sg. Dat. khanjĕ 1 खंज्य), broken, divided into parts; hence, deprived of a part or limb or member, maimed, mutilated; unevenly formed, irregularly angled. (Kashmiri) A pair of such glyphs divided into parts, may thus be decoded as: dul kaṇḍ khonḍu khonḍ 'casting furnace workshop'. Vikalpa 1: jaṇḍ khaṇḍ = ivory (Jaṭkī) khaṇḍi_ = ivory in rough (Jaṭkī); gaṭī = piece of elephant's tusk (S.) Vikalpa 2: Pa.kandi (pl. —l) necklace, beads. Ga. (P.) kandi (pl. —l) bead, (pl.) necklace; (S.2) kandiṭ bead (DEDR 1215). kandil, kandīl = a globe of glass, a lantern (Ka.lex.) The pair of glyphs 'rectangle with divisions' may thus also connote 'cast beads'. If so, the seal text inscription connotes two sets of products assembled for a freight consignment through a courier: furnace metal products + furnace bead products.

Both sets of products are from the sangatarāsu stone-engraver, metal-turner's workshop.

Decoding the glyph, 'three long linear strokes': 'three'; rebus: 'smithy' (Santali)

Glyph of standard device in front of the one-horned heifer: sā̃gāḍī lathe (Tu.)(CDIAL 12859). sāṅgaḍa That member of a turner's apparatus by which the piece to be turned is confined and steadied. सांगडीस धरणें To take into linkedness or close connection with, lit. fig. (Marathi) सांगाडी [ sāṅgāḍī ] f The machine within which a turner confines and steadies the piece he has to turn. (Marathi)सगडी [ sagaḍī ] f (Commonly शेगडी) A pan of live coals or embers. (Marathi) san:ghāḍo, saghaḍī (G.) = firepan; saghaḍī, śaghaḍi = a pot for holding fire (G.)[*culā sagaḍī* portable hearth (G.)]

Thus, the entire set of glyphs on the h1682A seal [denoting the heifer + standard device] can be decoded: koḍiyum 'heifer'; [ kōḍiya ] kōḍe, kōḍiya. [Tel.] n. A bullcalf. . k* దూడA young bull. Plumpness, prime. తరుణము. కోడెకోడయులు a pair of bullocks. Kōḍe adj. Young. Kōḍe-kāḍu. n. A young man.పడుచువాడు. [ kārukōḍe ] kāru-kōḍe. [Tel.] n. A bull in its prime. खोंड [ khōṇḍa ] m A young bull, a bullcalf. (Marathi) గోద [ gōda ] gōda. [Tel.] n. An ox. A beast. Kine, cattle.(Telugu) koḍiyum (G.) rebus: koḍ 'workshop' (G.) B. kõdā 'to turn in a lathe'; Or. kū̃nda 'lathe', kū̃dibā, kū̃d 'to turn' (→ Drav. Kur. kū̃d 'lathe') (CDIAL 3295)

The two glyphs (heifer + lathe) together thus refer to a turner's workshop with a portable hearth. The two sets of the text of the inscription refer to the products assembled together (perhaps on the circular working platforms) by this workshop of the guild. The sets of products denoted by the two sets of glyphic sequences can be lls des rebus:

kuṭi 'water carrier' (Te.) Rebus: kuṭhi 'smelter furnace' (Santali) kuṛī f. 'fireplace' (H.); krvṛī f. 'granary (Wpah.); kuṛī, kuṛo house, building'(Ku.)(CDIAL 3232) kuṭi 'hut made of boughs' (Skt.) guḍi temple (Telugu)

kaṇḍa kanka 'rim of jar' (Santali); rebus: furnace scribe. *Kaṇḍa kanka* may be a dimunitive form of *kan-khār 'copper smith' comparable to the cognate gloss: kaṉṉār 'coppersmiths, blacksmiths' (Tamil) If so, kaṇḍa kan-khār connotes: 'copper-smith furnace.'kaṇḍa 'fire-altar (Santali); kan 'copper' (Ta.)

kanka 'Rim of jar' (Santali); karṇaka rim of jar'(Skt.) Rebus: karṇaka 'scribe' (Te.); gaṇaka id. (Skt.) (Santali)

Thus, the 'rim-of-jar' glyph connotes: furnace account (scribe). Together with the glyph showing 'water-carrier', the ligatured glyphs of 'water-carrier' + 'rim-of-jar' can thus be read as: kuṭhi kaṇḍa kanka 'smelting furnace account (scribe)'.

Thus, the inscription on seal h1682A can be explained in the context of the tablets used as tally tokens to account for consolidated trade load of the assembled products (delivered by the guild artisans) using the impression of the seal as a bill of lading.

The use of tablets in conjunction with the seal has been elaborated. Once the accounting is completed using the seal and the seal impression on the package to be couriered, the tablets used as tallying instruments by the guild helper of merchant have served their purpose and can be disposed of in the debris. The new seal with consolidated description of categories can itself serve as the bill of lading. Using the perforated boss on the back of some seals, the seal itself can be tied to the package.

Use of seals to create sealings: context trade with interaction areas such as Mesopotamia

Archaeological finds of tablets (sometimes called bas-relief tablets or incised miniature tablets) and seals are in association with kilns and working platforms. Metallurgical context is shown by the use of copper to create tablets with Indus script glyphs. Archaeological finds of seal impressions used as tags on chunks of burnt clay for sealing packages (since textile or reed impressions have been found on the obverse of such tags) show the trade context in which these examples of Indus writing have been used. About 32% of all Indus inscriptions found at Lothal are on such tags (seal impressions).

h119 Seal. The of four long strokes, seal impression on Lewan-Dheri 1 Decoding glyph of gaṇḍa 'four'

glyph of four sets compares with the Lothal 174 and (shown below) 'four long strokes'. (Santali); rebus:

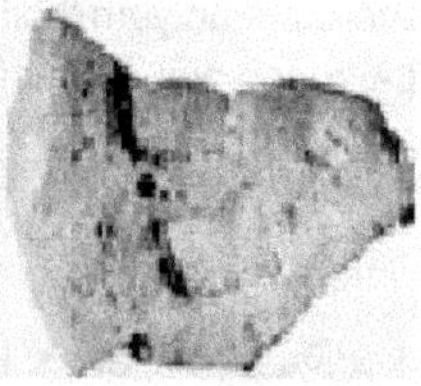

'furnace, kaṇḍ fire-altar'. pon 'four' (Santali) rebus: pon 'gold' (Ta.) Thus, the four sets of four long strokes may denote: (output) from gold furnaces.

Lewan-dheri 1 Seal impression.

m0037 Seal impression.

m0650 Seal. This seal contains in its inscription, the same three glyphs shown on m0037 Seal

impression. Thus, the example of the seal is an assemblage of two sets of descriptions of two sets of goods which may be put into the same trade package to be couriered with a bill of lading. Thus combinations of inscriptions achieved the purpose of completing part of the message required for a bill of lading.

m0425 Seal impression with three 'tags' from three seals is an example of such assemblage of messages to complete the detailed description of goods in a trade package.

Thus, it is clear that the combinations of seal impressions are likely to be more complete assemblage of messages for preparing bills of lading. This assemblage uses the descriptions of goods is achieved through multiple tablets used as tallies for compiling the bill of lading.

Banawali 23 Seal impression. This uses an assemblage of glyphs: a person standing with raised arm, a ram, a one-horned heifer, two glyphs: fish and arrow. Eache of these glyphs can be read rebus to complete the reading of the message conveyed by the inscription, as a bill of lading on a consignment, a trade package. Decoding: meḍ 'body'(Mu.); rebus: 'iron' (Ho.) eṛaka 'upraised arm' (Ta.); rebus: eraka = copper (Ka.) Glyph: kaṇḍa 'arrow' (Skt.) rebus: kaṇḍa 'fire-altar, furnace'. Glyph: aya 'fish'; rebus: aya 'metal' (G.) ayaskāṇḍa 'excellent quantity of iron' (Pāṇ.) koḍiyum 'heifer'(G.) koḍe 'heifer' (Telugu) खोंड [ khōṇḍa ] m A young bull, a bullcalf. Rebus: कोंडण [ kōṇḍaṇa ] f A fold or pen. (Marathi) koḍ 'workshop' (G.)Glyph: miṇḍāl markhor (Tor.wali) meḍho a ram, a sheep (G.)(CDIAL 10120) kunda 'turner' kundār turner (A.); kũdār, kũdāri (B.); kundāru (Or.); kundau to turn on a lathe, to carve, to chase; kundau dhiri = a hewn stone; kundau murhut = a graven image (Santali) kunda a turner's lathe (Skt.)(CDIAL 3295) Rebus: meḍ iron (Ho.) meṛed-bica = iron stone ore, in contrast to bali-bica, iron sand ore (Mu.lex.)

Thus, the Banawali seal impression connotes an assemblage of categories of copper (smelted metal); iron (native metal); iron (smelted metal); (turner's) workshop. The load prepared in package decribes these categories of products.

Rakhigarhi 65 Seal impression. This shows a duplicate set of impressions from perhaps the same seal. As to why two seal impressions were affixed can only be conjectured. Maybe, there were two consignments in the package from the same guild workshop. Is the third glyph comparable to the man on the Banawali seal impression with an upraised arm?

Over 80 single seal impressions have been found [Lothal (66), Mohenjo-daro (5), Kalibangan (4), Harappa (1), Banawali (1), Rohira (2), Lewan-dheri (1). 36 multiple impressions have been identified [Lothal (27), Kalibangan (6), Mohenjo-daro (2) and Rakhigarhi (1)]. Such seal impressions containing two long Indus inscription (m0304 and m0314) has been decoded rebus at http://bharatkalyan97.blogspot.com/2011/11/decoding-longest-inscription-of-indus.html. The bills of lading are restricted only with descriptions of trade goods and do not indicate names of trading partners or destinations of the packages.

It is clear that multiple seal impressions complete the process of compiling the details needed for a bill of lading and contain complete descriptions of the trade consignments loads since the compilation is an assemblage of inscriptions of individual seals.

The Indus writing was mainly used to provide a detailed description of the goods in packages and seal impressions served as parts of bills of lading.

An example of 'sealing' is presented by Mackay. Mackay, EJH, 1938, Further Excavations at Mohenjo-daro, Vol. II, New Delhi, Government of India, Pl. XC, no. 17. Note: "No. 17 in Pl. XC is certainly a true sealing (i.e. a clay seal impression) and it owes its preservation to having been slightly burnt; it was once fastened to some such object as a smooth wooden rod." (Mackay,ibid.,1938, Vol. I, p. 349). One can only conjecture as to the reason why a pair of seal impressions were created on clay around a wooden rod: perhaps, the rod served as the bill of lading for a particular category of goods/artifacts. The three glyphs can be read rebus. The set of three glyphs is read rebus as: *bhaṭa ḍab ranku* 'furnace ingot tin'. Glyph 1: A glyphic ligature is the 'ladle or spoon' glyph (ligatured to the 'pot' glyph). *ḍabu* 'an iron spoon' (Santali) Rebus: *ḍab, ḍhimba, ḍhompo* 'lump (ingot?)', clot, make a lump or clot, coagulate, fuse, melt together (Santali) baṭhu m. 'large pot in which grain is parched (S.) Rebus: *baṭa* = a kind of iron (G.) bhaṭa 'furnace' (G.) *bhaṭa* = kiln (Santali). Thus the ligatured glyph of 'pot + spoon' reads rebus: *ḍab* '(furnace) ingot'. Glyph 2: Glyph of rectangle with divisions: *baṭai* = to divide, share (Santali) [Note the glyphs of nine rectangles divided.] Rebus: *bhaṭa* = an oven, kiln, furnace (Santali) *baṭhi* furnace for smelting ore (the same as kuṭhi) (Santali) *bhaṭa* = an oven, kiln, furnace; make an oven, a furnace; iṭa bhaṭa = a brick kiln; kun:kal bhaṭa a potter's kiln; cun bhaṭa = a lime kiln; cun tehen dobon bhaṭaea = we shall prepare the lime kiln today (Santali); *bhaṭṭhā* (H.) *bhart* = a mixed metal of copper and lead; *bhart-īyā* = a barzier, worker in metal; *bhaṭ, bhrāṣṭra* = oven, furnace (Skt.) *mẽṛhẽt baṭi* = iron (Ore) furnaces. [Synonyms are: mẽt = the eye, rebus for: the dotted circle (Santali.lex) baṭha [H. *baṭṭhī* (Sad.)] any kiln, except a potter's kiln, which is called coa; there are four kinds of kiln: cunabat.ha, a lime-kin, iṭabaṭha, a brick-kiln, ērēbaṭha, a lac kiln, kuilabaṭha, a charcoal kiln; trs. Or intrs., to make a kiln; cuna rapamente ciminaupe baṭhakeda? How many limekilns did you make? Baṭha-sen:gel = the fire of a kiln; baṭi [H. Sad. Baṭṭhi, a furnace for distilling) used alone or in the cmpds. Arkibut.i and bat.iora, all meaning a grog-shop; occurs also in ilibaṭi, a (licensed) rice-beer shop (Mundari.lex.) bhaṭi = liquor from mohwa flowers (Santali) Glyph 3: ranku 'liquid measure'; rebus: ranku 'tin' (Santali)

One more question. Why were there three sides of the disposed of tally tablets?

The purpose of side 1 as part of the seal used for sealing the package has been explained. Side 1 (glyphs: 'water-carrier ligatured with rim-of-jar' glyph + 'three linear strokes' glyph) connoted that the tally was meant for products taken out from the smelter/furnace. Side 1 glyphs were used to tally furnace output, i.e. output of *kuṭhi*, 'smelter'.

Side 2 glyphs: rhombus with corner + three linear strokes. kōṇṭa corner (Nk.); Tu. kōṇṭu angle, corner (Tu.); Rebus: *kõdā* 'to turn in a lathe' (B.) kolmo 'three' (Mu.) Rebus: kolami 'forge' (Te.) Side 2 glyphs were used to tally forged products from the turner's lathe, i.e., output of *kõdā*, 'lathe'.

Side 3 glyphs: rimless pot + four linear strokes. *baṭa* = rimless pot (Kannada). Rebus: baṭa = furnace (Santali) bhrāṣṭra = furnace (Skt.) pon 'four' (Santali) rebus: pon 'gold' (Ta.) Vikalpa: gaṇḍa set of four (Santali) kaṇḍa 'fire-altar'. Side 3 glyphs were used to tally gold furnace (products), i.e. output of *baṭa*, 'furnace'.

Kudos to Kenoyer and Meadow whose insights provided the leads for further researches on the functions of the script, for e.g., by raising the question of the use and disposal of tablet multiples with the same inscription. Credit goes to Kenoyer and Meadow who have raised incisive questions for further researches to unravel the purpose served by the tablets which occur in multiple copies carrying the same impression, clearly indicating that the inscriptions are unlikely to refer to names (of artisans or residents of the citadel or the lower town). Based on the rebus readings of the glyphs, the inscriptions refer to the categories of artifacts produced from three distinct processes—1) furnace output, 2) turners' or forge output, 3) gold furnace output -- by the workers in stone, workers in semi-precious stones (for bead work), workers in minerals, metal, alloys, furnace/ smelter workers, and helpers of merchants who script the entire process of manufacture and preparation of bills of lading. Hence, the importance of the 'rim-of-jar' sign denoting the scribe, the furnace account (scribe).

The miniature incised tablets of Harappa might have served the same functions that the copper tablets of Mohenjo-daro served: as tallying instruments for the outputs from furnaces/smelters.

The use of the circular working platforms was to store the products in storage pots kept in the center of the circle and the articles spread out around the circumference of the circular platform as wares for display, marketing and sale or, for preparing bills of lading using the seals. It is also possible that the center of the platform was used to install a drill-lathe of the type shown in front of the one-horned heifer on over 1000 inscribed objects of the corpora.

The advance accounting practices for categorizing the stages of metallurgical processed involved in producing final trade load of the guild workshops gets completed with the stamping of the seal impression on the package, thus securing the package tied with cords of fibre and authenticated by the seal impression. The merchant associates in the Meluhha settlements in distant lands would understand the language and writing and unpack the material for further recording the trade transactions using cuneiform script documenting the trade contracts and after invoking the divinities — e.g. Mitra-Varuṇa, as witnesses (one as contract divinity and the other as law divinity)(as in Bogazkoi inscriptions). It is suggested that both cuneiform script and Indian hieroglyphs were used to finalise the trade transactions since the Indian hieroglyphs provided only descriptive bills of lading of products traded; specifying names of contracting parties and quantities involved were done using cuneiform.

Examples of 31 duplicates, double-sided terracotta tablets

Executive summary: rebus decoding of the text hieroglyphs: Associates (guild) workshop, excellent iron (stone ore metal)

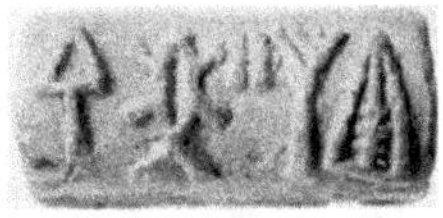

Text 5207 etc. (From 2-sided tablets h859-870, samples of the 31 duplicates mentioned herein.)... Glyph: 'arch': *māḍvī* f. ' small canopy over an idol '(Marathi). *mēṭa* raised place, tower, upper story, palace (Ma.) *maṇḍua* 'booth, shed' Rebus: *mā̃ḍ* m. 'array of instruments &c.' (Marathi); Si. *maḍa -- ya* 'adornment, ornament' (Sinhala). (CDIAL 9736) Vikalpa: Glyph: 'lathe': *sā̃gāḍā* 'lathe'. Glyph: *sā̃gāḍā* m. ' frame of a building ' (M.)(CDIAL 12859) Rebus: *sangata* 'associates (guild)'.

Glyph: 'sprout': pajhaṛ = to sprout from a root (Santali); Rebus: *pasra* 'smithy, forge' (Santali) Vikalpa: *kodo* 'millet' (Mu.); rebus: *koḍ* 'artisan's workshop' (Kuwi).

`Glyph: 'splinter' sal 'splinter'. Rebus: sal 'artisan's workshop'. *ayaskāṇḍa* 'iron stone (metal)'. The text message thus connotes: an array of instruments from smithy/forge workshop, iron stone (metal). The animal glyph on the obverse: kond 'heifer'. Rebus: kond '(metal) turner workshop'.

Copies of incised tablets and duplicates of molded tablets have been found in large numbers in two noteworthy instances at Harappa: (1) script copies incised into 22 rectangular steatite tablets, triangular in section, from secondary deposits of Period 3B on the outside of the perimeter wall in Trench 11 on East side of Mound E (Meadow & Kenoyer 2000, fig. 4; this volume: H-2218 through H-2239) and (2) 31 duplicates bearing iconography and script, made of regular molded terracotta, biconvex in section, from the northern portion of Trench II in Area G (Vats 1940: 195; CISI 1: H-252 through H-265 and H-276 & H-277; CISI 2: H-859 through H-870; this volume: H-1155). Other copies and duplicates have been found scattered across the site where, like the multiples above, they are always found in trash, fill, or street deposits. Why tablets were made, how they were used, and why they were discarded remain intriguing unanswered questions. Their intrinsic interest lies not only in the script that they often bear, but even more so in the iconography, which provides an important glimpse, however fragmentary, into details of Harappan ideology, particularly for the time frame from ca.2400 to ca. 2000 BC (Harappa Period 3B through much of Period 3C). For a more detailed discussion see Meadow & Kenoyer 2000." (J. Mark Kenoyer & Richard H. Meadow, 2010, Inscribed objects from Harappa excavations 1986-2007 in: Asko Parpola, B.M. Pande and Petteri Koskikallio (eds.), *Corpus of Indus seals and inscriptions, Volume 3: New material, untraced objects and collections outside India and Pakistan, Part 1: Mohenjo-daro and Harappa*, Helsinki, Suomalainen Tiedeakatemia, pp. xlix-l) http://www.harappa.com/indus/Kenoyer-Meadow-2010-HARP.pdf

In the reference Kenoyer & Meadow 2000, it is noted: "The tablets (or tokens) are common at Harappa, and multiple copies were often produced. In 1997, HARP excavators found 22 three-sided steatite tablets, all with the same inscriptions, from the middle Harappan Phase (about 2300 BCE). Sixteen were discovered in a single group, as if they had been in a perishable container that was thrown over the city wall with other trash. In a street deposit of similar age just inside the wall, a seal was found with two of the same characters as seen on one side of the tablets. Why were these intact seals or tablets discarded? They were individually made by craftsmen from models or molds at the demand of an individual or group. They were used for a time, then discarded. Unlike coins, they apparently had value only in relation to the individual or group permitted to employ them. They have never been found in graves — either the grave of a seal-owning individual has not been excavated, or the seals were not integral to n individual's identity. Perhaps a change in an individual's status made a specific seal or

tablet invalid. Or perhaps the use of a seal or tablet was validated only when competent authority used it, otherwise, it was worthless." (Richard H. Meadow and Jonathan Mark Kenoyer, 2000, The Indus valley mystery, one of the world's first great civilizations is still a puzzle, in: *Scientific American Discovering Archaeology*, March/April 2000, p. 41)
Source:
http://www.anthropology.wisc.edu/pdfs/Kenoyer%20Articles/The%20Indus%20Valley%20Mystery.pdf

h252A Inscription on one side of the 2-sided tablet (in bas relief). The other side shows a one-horned heifer (as in h254B).

h254B. Two-sided tablet. The other side shows an inscription as in h252A.

This is one set of the 31 duplicates. Tablets in bas relief. The first sign looks like an arch around a pillar with ring-stones. Obverse: One-horned bull.

The inscription on these 31 duplicates can be read rebus in three parts:

1. Composite glyph of arch-around-a-pillar with ring-stones: storehouse
2. Unsmelted native metal
3. Furnace (with)a quantity of iron, excellent iron (metal) from stone ore

h739B & A (Standard device; obverse: tree)

A variant glyph comparable to the 'pillar with ring-stones' which is part of the composite glyph with an arch over the glyph is provided by one side of a Harappa tablet: h739B Obverse: H739A: glyph:*kuṭi* 'tree'; rebus: *kuṭhi* 'smelter furnace' (Santali) Vikalpa: *ḍāḷ*= a branch of a tree (G.) Rebus: *ḍhāḷako* = a large ingot (G.) ḍhāḷakī = a metal heated and poured into a mould; a solid piece of metal; an ingot (G.)

If this comparison of glyphs is valid, the 'pillar with ring-stones' may, in fact, represent a churning motion of a lathe-drill: Allograph: A sack slung on the front shoulder of the young bull is khōṇḍā , khōṇḍī , kothḷɔ Rebus: B. kōdā 'to turn in a lathe'; Or. kū̃nda 'lathe', kū̃dibā, kū̃d 'to turn' (→ Drav. Kur. Kū̃d 'lathe') (CDIAL 3295) Rebus: koṭṭil 'workshop' (Ma.)(DEDR 2058). Koṭe 'forged metal' (Santali) koḍ 'artisan's workshop' (Kuwi) Vikalpa: saṅgaḍa, portable brazier and lathe; rebus: sanga 'guild (of turners)'.

Thus, the arched drill glyph may connote a turner's workshop. This is a vikalpa reading, if the 'arch' is not to be read as roof of a 'storehouse'. The arch over the drill-lathe glyph may connote semantics of a guild: *pattar.* (Tamil); battuḍu 'guild of goldsmiths' (Telugu). This may be consistent with the semant. patthar 'stones' (Hindi) pattar 'trough'; rebus: . patthara — m. ' stone; pattar 'merchants, guild (smiths)' (The word may, thus, denote a lapidary).(CDIAL 8857).

Glyph and rebus decoding: patthara [cp. Late Sk. prastara. The ord. meaning of Sk. Pr. Is "stramentum"] 1. Stone, rock S i.32. — 2. Stoneware Miln 2. (Pali) Pa. Pk. Patthara — m. ' stone ', S. patharu m., L. (Ju.) pathar m., khet. Patthar, P. patthar m. (→ forms of Bi. Mth. Bhoj. H. G. below with atth or ath), Wpah.jaun. pātthar; Ku. Pāthar m. ' slates, stones ', gng. Pāth*lr ' flat stone '; A. B. pāthar ' stone ', Or. Pathara; Bi. Pāthar, patthar, patthal ' hailstone '; Mth. Pāthar, pathal ' stone ', Bhoj. Pathal, Aw.lakh. pāthar, H. pāthar, patthar, pathar, patthal m., G. patthar, pathrɔ m.; M. pāthar f. ' flat stone '; Ko. Phāttaru ' stone '; Si. Patura ' chip, fragment '; -- S. pathirī f. ' stone in the bladder '; P. pathrī f. ' small stone '; Ku. Patharī ' stone cup '; B. pāthri ' stone in the bladder, tartar on teeth '; Or. Pathurī ' stoneware '; H. patthrī f. ' grit ', G. pathrī f. prastará -- : Wpah.kṭg. páthər m. ' stone, rock '; pəthreuṇõ ' to stone '; J. pāthar m. ' stone '; Omarw. Pātharī ' precious stone '. (CDIAL 8857)

Glyph: 'spread feet': Pattharati [pa+tharati] to spread, spread out, extend J i.62; iv.212; vi.279; DhA i.26; iii.61 (so read at J vi.549 in cpd °pāda with spreading feet, v. l. patthaṭa°). — pp. patthaṭa (q. v.). Rebus: paṭṭarai 'workshop' (Ta.) pattharika [fr. Patthara] a merchant Vin ii.135 (kaŋsa°).(Pali) பத்தர்&sup5; pattar, n. perh. Vartaka. Merchants; வியாபாரிகள். (W.) battuḍu. n. The caste title of all the five castes of artificers as vaḍla b*, carpenter.

Together with meḍ 'body', rebus: meḍ 'iron', the rebus reading of the 'body with spread feet' may read rebus: *meḍ pattar* 'iron (workers) guild'.

The seal inscription shows the pattern of tally accomplished by bringing into the storehouse 1. Unsmelted native metal; and 2. (output from) furnace of worker in wood and iron. The assumption made is that the the two categories brought into the storehouse would have been tallied by the furnace account scribe or merchant, using tablets with inscriptions denoting: 1. Unsmelted metal; and 2. (output from) stone iron (metal) ore furnace.

Glyph (arch-around a pillar with ring-stones may denote a storehouse): koḍ = a cow-pen; a cattlepen; a byre (G.) कोठी cattle-shed (Marathi) कोंडी [ kōṇḍī ] A pen or fold for cattle. गोठी [ gōṭhī ] f C (Dim. Of गोठा) A pen or fold for calves. (Marathi)koḍ = a cow-pen; a cattlepen; a byre (G.) कोठी cattle-shed (Marathi) कोंडी [ kōṇḍī ] A pen or fold for cattle. गोठी [ gōṭhī ] f C (Dim. Of गोठा) A pen or fold for calves. (Marathi) Rebus: koḍ = place where artisan's work (Kur.) कोठी [ kōṭhī] f (कोष्ट S) A granary, garner, storehouse, warehouse, treasury, factory, bank. (Marathi) [An attempt has been made to provide rebus readings of some 'architectural' glyphs and the use of 'dot or circle' as a hieroglyph atop a bull on Urseal 18; the note is appended in Annex 2.]

Glyph: kolmo 'seedling, paddy plant'; rebus: kolami 'forge, smithy' (Te.) Vikalpa: pajhaṛ = to sprout from a root (Santali); Rebus: pasra 'smithy, forge' (Santali)[It is possible that two variants of the glyph: one with three pronged representation of seedling; and the other with five-pronged representation of seedling might have been intended to specify a fine distinction between the two lexemes: *kolmo, pajhaṛ* perhaps denoting two types of forge – *kolami, pasra*; it is possible that *kolami* was a smithy related to stone ore metal (*kol* 'working in iron); *pasra* was a smithy related to variety of metals and alloys (rebus glyph: *pasaramu* 'domestic animals [representing working in wood (*baḍhi* - boar), iron (*kol* - tiger), copper (*meḍ* - ram), tin (*ranku* - antelope).'] Other glyphs used to denote alloying minerals: 1. tin, 2. zinc, 3. arsenic respectively : 1. *tagaraka* (*tabernae montana* or *ranku* 'liquid measure'), 2. *sattiya* (svastika glyph), 3. *daḷ* (branch of tree, twig).

Glyph: aṭar 'a splinter' (Ma.) aṭaruka 'to burst, crack, sli off,fly open; aṭarcca ' splitting, a crack'; aṭarttuka 'to split, tear off, open (an oyster) (Ma.); aḍaruni 'to crack' (Tu.) (DEDR 66) Rebus: *aduru* 'native, unsmelted metal' (Kannada) aduru = *gaṇiyinda tegadu karagade iruva aduru* = ore taken from the mine and not subjected to melting in a furnace (Ka. Siddhānti Subrahmaṇya śastri's *New interpretation of the Amarakośa,* Bangalore, Vicaradarpana Press, 1872, p. 330) Vikalpa: sal 'splinter'; rebus: sal 'workshop' (Santali)

Thus the two glyphs of the text of the tablet inscription showing arch-around a pillar with ring-stones + paddy plant + splinter glyph may connote, rebus: *kolami koḍ aduru*, 'forge unsmelted metal workshop'.

Glyph: Fish + scales aya ās [amśu or, añcu 'iron' (Tocharian)] 'metllic stalks of stone ore' (See http://bharatkalyan97.blogspot.com/2011/11/decoding-longest-inscription-of-indus.html) Vikalpa 1: badhoṛ 'a species of fish with many bones' (Santali) Rebus: badhoria 'expert in working in wood'(Santali) Vikalpa 2: 'fish + scales'. Aya + Ku. *ā̃s, ā̃so* m. ' share '. Hence, the ligatured glyphic may connote a share of metal for workshop (guild). Vikalpa: *ā̃s*, cognate with *añc* 'iron' (Tocharian) may be a determinative of 'iron' as the 'metal'. Hence, the ligatured glyph may connote 'iron or stony metal'.

Slanting is perhaps an orthographic notation of a fraction. An Asokan pillar inscription at Lumbini reads: *lummini-gāme ubalike kaṭe aṭṭha-bhāgiye ca.* "The village of Lumbini was made free of taxes and to pay (only) an eighth share (of the produce)". (Inscriptions of Asoka, ed. E. Hultzsch, Rummindei Pillar Inscription.) Hultzsch cites Fleet (JRAS 1908: 479) that aṭṭha-bhāga (from Skt.

aṣṭa-bhāga) is an 'eighth share' which the king is permitted by Manu (VII: 130) to levy on grains" Pa. *koṭṭhāsa* -- m. ' share, portion ', adj. ' divided into ' (*ā* felt as contraction of *a* -- *a* and preserved before *ṁs*; consequent *āṁs* > *ās*: cf. re -- establishment of prefix *ā* before MIA. double consonant, e.g. Pk. *āṇavēdi* < **āṇṇ°* replacing *aṇṇ* -- < Sk. *ājñ* -- ); Si. *koṭasa*, *kohoṭa* ' share, part, piece '.(CDIAL 3549).

áṁśa m. ' share, part ' RV. [√aś1] Pa. Pk. *aṁsa* -- m., Pk. *°siyā* -- f.; Wg. (Lumsden) "*onshái*" ' lot, chance ' (Morgenstierne NTS xvii 227 with ?); Ku. *ā̃s*, *ā̃so* m. ' share ', *ā̃si* f. ' measure of land '; B. *do* -- *ā̃ś* ' consisting of two parts or two grains ', *do* -- *ā̃ślā* ' cross -- bred '; Or. *ā̃siā* ' having angles ' (if not rather < áśri -- ); Bi. *ā̃sī* ' the smallest sheaf ' (or poss. < *adhamāṁśa -- ); Si. *asa* ' part, half '.(CDIAL 2)

*aṁśú* m. ' filament esp. of soma -- plant ' RV., ' thread, minute particle, ray'. Pa. *aṁsu* -- m. ' thread '; Pk. *aṁsu* -- m. ' sunbeam '; A. *ā̃h* ' fibre of a plant ', OB. *ā̃su*; B. *ā̃s* ' fibre of tree or stringy fruit, nap of cloth '; Or. *ā̃su*' fibrous layer at root of coconut branches, edge or prickles of leaves ', *ā̃s* f. ' fibre, pith '; -- with -- *i* -- in place of -- *u* -- : B. *ā̃iś* ' fibre '; M. *ā̃sī̃* n. ' fine particles of flattened rice in winnowing fan '; A. *āhiyā* ' fibrous '.(CDIAL 4)

Glyph: kaṇḍa 'arrow' (Skt.) Rebus: kaṇḍa 'fire-altar, furnace'. Vikalpa: kaṇḍ 'stone (ore)'.

The two glyphs together denote furnace of a worker in wood and iron: *aya ās (amśu) 'metallic stalks of stone ore' aya ās kanḍa* 'furnace (with) a quantity of iron, excellent iron (or metal) from stone ore' Vikalpa: badhor kanḍa 'furnace (of) worker in wood and iron'. *Ayaskanḍa* is a lexeme attested in: Pāṇini.gan. The phrase might have indicated 'stony metal'.

'Each platform is 11 feet in diameter and consists of a single course of four continuous concentric rings of brick-on-edge masonry with a hollow at the center equal to the length of three bricks. The mortar used in them is mud but the pointing is of gypsum. (Pl. XIII, c) (Picture 26.4) Their purpose is not clear. While digging the hollow of P8 there was found a small quantity of burnt wheat and husked barley and about two pounds of animal bones. Some bits of bones were also found in two or three others. As, however, the bones etc., lay about a foot below the central hollow, that is to say distinctly below the brickwork of these platforms, and similar fragments of bones were also found sticking at the same level among the edges of the platforms, it appears certain that they were merely a part of the debris and by no means the contents of the hollow.' (Vats, MS, 1940, *Excavation at Harappa*, Delhi, ASI, p. 182).

Picture 26.4

The hypotheses, in the context of trade from the working platforms, are 1) that the tablets were used in the consolidation process to prepare a composite bill of lading describing the artifacts and 2) that a guild of workshops used the tablets for such consolidation of the trade loads.

Note: HARP excavators surmised the possible production of indigo. An alternative explanation is possible and deserves further investigation in the context of metalwork on the circular working platforms.

HARP excavations of one of the circular brick floors in mound F at Harappa revealed a deep depression containing greenish layers of clay. The greenish layers may have been caused by the presence of zinc particles which have a bluish green color. Zinc dust is flammable when exposed to heat and burns with a bluish-green flame. In an identification of the corrosion minerals identified on the Great Buddha, Kamakura, Japan it is noted that "some of the compounds found on the Buddha were mixed copper-zinc salts...and schulenbergite, a mixed copper-zinc basic sulfate, that is rhombohedral with a pearly, light green-blue color." (David A. Scott, Getty Conservation Institute, 2002, Copper and Bronze in Art: corrosion, colorants, conservation, Getty Publications, p. 162)

"Ancient Indian literature has even recorded a breakthrough in zinc extraction in those days. Such process included high temperature distillation that was developed and then applied in future zinc extraction and purification from their metal ore sources. Zinc ores were broken with the use of iron hammers or pestles. Then, such broken ores were again crushed by larger pestles. Then, the ore would have to be thoroughly roasted in order to reduce the levels of sulphur. After which, a high proportion of calcined dolomite was mixed with the crushed and roasted ores. An interesting ingredient in this process is the addition of common salt. This is for the reason that salt would help in the distillation process, thereby, producing soda vapor that assists in amassing calcium and magnesium oxides. This allows zinc vapor to freely flow and increasing zinc yield. This zinc yield was poured on clay containers for heating."

Example of Rosasite. Minor ore of zinc and copper and as a mineral specimen. Colour: Blue to green.Rosasite forms in the oxidation zones of zinc-copper deposits. It typically is found as crusts and botryoidal masses or nodules. Crystals are fibrous and found in tufted aggregates. The color is an attractive bluish green. Rosasite crystals are harder than aurichalcite; 4 versus 1 — 2 respectively. Rosasite is associated with red limonite and other such colorful minerals as aurichalcite, smithsonite and hemimorphite. Nodules of rosasite certainly add color to what are termed "landscape" specimens. http://www.mineralgallery.co.za/rosasite.htm

It will be necessary to test, by chemical analysis, the greenish layers of clay found in the circular platform for the presence of such alloying mineral clays. Is it possible that the working platforms were also used by the smiths to work on their anvils to forge metal artifacts, using portable furnaces – the way crucible steel was produced during the iron age?

Ernest Mackay, Chapter XXI. Seals and seal impressions, copper tablets, with tabulation (pp.370-405).

As of 1927, 558 objects with inscriptions had been found. Discussing 80 copper tablets found, Mackay notes (p. 398): "The rectangular pieces are of various sizes, ranging from 1.2 by 0.5 in. to 1.5 by 1.0 in. The square pieces, which are rare, average 0.92 by 0.92 in. in size. These tablets vary greatly in thickness, from 0.07 in. to 0.12 in. One especially substantial tablet (HR 4799) measures 0.85 in. square by 0.23 in. thick...On most of the tablets there is the figure of an animal on one side, and on the other three or more signs forming an inscription. The figures and signs were in every case carefully cut with a burin...Below is a list of the animals on the legible tablets with the numbers found, up to the present, of each: elephant (6), antelope (5), hare (5), rhinoceros (4), buffalo(?) (4), short- horned bull (4), human figure (3), goat (2), brahmani bull (2), tiger (2), two-headed animal (2), composite animal (1), monkey (?)(1)...The above list shows that most of the animals that appear on the seals are also represented on the copper tablets...composite animal...It has the hind-quarters of a rhinoceros and the fore-quarters of a leopard or tiger. It has the unicorn's horn, and a manger stands before it. (Pl.

CXVIII,2). A very curious animal on two sides of the tablets appears to have the body of an antelope with a head at either end. The fact that more than one example has been found of this animal proves that it is not a vagary of the engraver (Pl. CXVII,3). The tablet bearing the figure of a man dressed in what seems to be a costume of leaves is exceptionally interesting (Pl. CXVII, 16). He is apparently a hunter armed with a bow and arrow...The antelope appears on five of the tablets, represented in a typical attitude with his head turned to look behind him (Pl. CXVII, 1 and 2; Pl. CXVIII,1). This attitude is very common in Elamitic art, especially on the pottery and seals. The position is also well known on both the archaic seals and pottery of Mesopotamia. For the present, the elephant appears to take first place amongst the animals on these copper tablets. An excellent example is seen in Pl. CXVII,11, of which the original was found at a depth of 1 foot below the surface in House XXVI, VS Area...The exceptionally powerful-looking animal with long curling horns (Pl. CXVII, 8 and 12, and Pl. CXVIII, 4 and 6), and with a manger placed in front of it, does not appear on any of the seals. The long tail of the animal with a tuft at the end is carried well in the air, as if the creature were about to charge...The rope pattern on the obverse of Tablet No. 5 in Pl. CXVIII is unique at Mohenjo-daro...The fact that all of the tablets bearing the representation of a hare have the same inscription on the obverse (Pl. CXVII, 5 and 6), and that the animals with long curling horns and long tail also bear the same inscription – different, however, from the inscription on the tablet refers in some way to the animal on the tablet. Of three tablets, each with an elephant engraved upon it, all bear the same inscription (Pl. CXII, 11), and lastly those with the figures of antelopes looking backwards over their shoulders all have the same characters on the reverse (Pl. CXVII, 1 and 2; Pl. CXVIII,1). Some, if not all the animals on the copper tablets were possibly dedicated to certain gods. As on some of the seals, we find a manger placed before certain of them, as, for instance, the unicorn, the rhinoceros, antelope, and Brahmani bull. This suggests that these animals were kept in captivity, and, if so, it is likely to have been for religious purposes; a rhinoceros is obviously quite useless for any domestic purpose. A manger is placed before the composite animal on the tablet illustrated in Pl. CXVIII,2, despite the fact that such an animal could never have existed." (pp. 400-401).

The 'manger' is a 'trough' hieroglyph.

http://www.scribd.com/doc/32303649/Indus-Writing-on-Metal
Indus Writing on Metal

Copper tablets from Mohenjo-daro: an analysis – 46 tablet groups (After Parpola, 1994, fig. 7.14). The 46 tablet groups are shown with distinctive pictorial motifs and glyphs sequenced together to constitute the Indus script inscriptions on copper tablets.

See:

1. Parpola, A. 1992 Copper Tablets from Mohenjo-daro and the study of the Indus Script. In:*Proceedings of the Second International Conference on Mohenjo-daro*, edited by I. M. Nadiem, pp. Karachi, Department of Archaeology.

2. Pande, B. M. 1979 Inscribed Copper Tablets from Mohenjo daro: A Preliminary Analysis. In : *Ancient Cities of the Indus*, edited by G. L. Possehl, pp. 268-288. New Delhi, Vikas Publishing House PVT LTD.

3. Pande, B. M. 1991 Inscribed Copper Tablets from Mohenjo-daro: Some Observations.*Puratattva* (21): 25-28.

Brij Mohan Pande had first analysed (1979 and 1991) the importance and significance of copper tablets with unique sets of inscriptions. This contribution is just scintillating and was later (1992) followed up by Asko Parpola identifying 36 groups. The find by HARP recently, of a copper tablet — and 8 duplicates — (bas relief with raised script) in Harappa was a stunner, together with 31 and 22 sets of duplicate tablets with identical inscriptions.

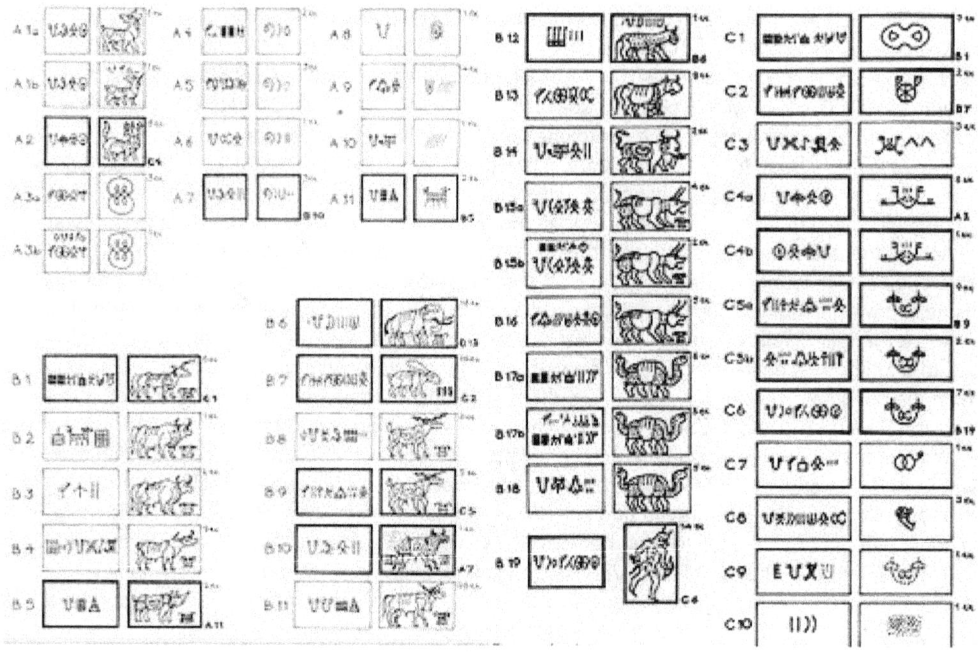

http://www.scribd.com/doc/32588163/Animal-Glyphs-of-Indus-Script
Animal Glyphs of Indus Script

See catalogue of seals and seal impressions in: Harriet Crawford, 2001, Early Dilmun Seals from Saar, Archaeology International, Upper House, Stoke Saint Milborough, Ludlow. Many glyphs shown in the catalogues are concordant with Indus script glyphs, pointing to trade interactions across the Persian Gulf from Meluhha.

Early Dilmun Seals from Saar (Harriet Crawford, 2001)

'Architectural' glyphs of Indus script: mudhif (reedhouse,Mesopotamia) and a 'dot, circle' glyph of Indus script depicted atop a bull on Urseal 18 (Gadd)

m0702 Text 2206 showing Sign 39, a glyph which compares with the Sumerian mudhif structure.

Modern mudhif structure (Iraq)

with figures seated on

The Toda mund, from, Richard Barron, 1837, “View in India, chiefly among the Nilgiri Hills’. Oil on canvas. The architecture of Iraqi mudhif and Toda mund — of Indian linguistic area — is comparable.

284 x 190 mm. Close up view of a Toda hut, the stone wall in front of the building.

Photograph taken circa 1875-1880, numbered 37 elsewhere. Royal Commonwealth Society Library. Cambridge University Library. University of Cambridge.

A Toda temple in Muthunadu Mund near Ooty, India.

http://en.wikipedia.org/wiki/Toda_people Tribe of Nilgiris, India. Note the decoration of very small door.

The hut of a Toda the front wall, and the

Text 1330 (appears showing Sign 39. (*Bos indicus*) This the cattle byre of Southern Mesopotamia

with Zebu glyph) Pictorial motif: Zebu sign is comparable to dated to c. 3000 BCE.

goṭ = the place where cattle are collected at mid-day (Santali); goṭh (Brj.)(CDIAL 4336). Goṣṭha (Skt.); cattle-shed (Or.) koḍ = a cow-pen; a cattlepen; a byre (G.) कोठी cattle-shed (Marathi) कोंडी [ kōṇḍī ] A pen or fold for cattle. गोठी [ gōṭhī ] f C (Dim. Of गोठा) A pen or fold for calves. (Marathi)

Sumerian mudhif (reed house) http://www.laputanlogic.com/articles/2004/01/24-0001.html

Cattle Byres c.3200-3000 B.C. Late Uruk-Jemdet Nasr period. Magnesite. Cylinder seal. In the lower field of this seal appear three reed cattle byres. Each byre is surmounted by three reed pillars topped by rings, a motif that has been suggested as symbolizing a male god, perhaps Dumuzi. Within the huts calves or vessels appear alternately; from the sides come calves that drink out of a vessel between them. Above each pair of animals another small calf appears. A herd of enormous cattle moves in the upper field. Cattle and cattle byres in Southern Mesopotamia, c. 3500 BCE.

Drawing of an impression from a Uruk period cylinder seal. (After Moorey, PRS, 1999, Ancient materials and industries: the archaeological evidence,

Eisenbrauns.)

Koṭṭhaka1 (nt.) "a kind of koṭṭha," the stronghold over a gateway, used as a store — room for various things, a chamber, treasury, granary Vin ii.153, 210; for the purpose of keeping water in it Vin ii.121=142; 220; treasury J i.230; ii.168; -- store — room J ii.246; koṭṭhake pāturahosi appeared at the gateway, i. e. arrived at the mansion Vin i.291.; -- udaka — k a bath — room, bath cabinet Vin i.205 (cp. Bdhgh's expln at Vin. Texts ii.57); so also nahāna — k° and piṭṭhi — k°, bath — room behind a hermitage J iii.71; DhA ii.19; a gateway, Vin ii.77; usually in cpd. Dvāra — k° "door cavity," i. e. room over the gate: gharaŋ satta — dvāra — koṭṭhakapaṭimaṇḍitaŋ "a mansion adorned with seven gateways" J i.227=230, 290; VvA 322. Dvāra — koṭṭhakesu āsanāni paṭṭhapenti "they spread mats in the gateways" VvA 6; esp. with bahi: bahi — dvārakoṭṭhakā nikkhāmetvā "leading him out in front of the gateway" A iv.206; °e thiṭa or nisinna standing or sitting in front of the gateway S i.77; M i.161, 382; A iii.30. — bala — k. a line of infantry J i.179. — koṭṭhaka — kamma or the occupation connected with a storehouse (or bathroom?) is mentioned as an example of a low occupation at Vin iv.6; Kern, Toev. S. v. "someone who sweeps away dirt." (Pali)

urseal15 Gadd, PBA 18 (1932), p. 13, Pl. III, no. 15; Legrain, MJ (1929), p. 306, pl. XLI, no. 119; found at Ur in the cemetery area, in a ruined grave. There is a round spot upon the bull's back. गोदा [ gōdā ] m A circular brand or mark made by actual cautery (Marathi) गोटा [ gōṭā ] m A roundish stone or pebble. 2 A marble (of stone, lac, wood &c.) 2 A marble. 3 A large lifting stone. Used in trials of strength among the Athletæ. 4 A stone in temples described at length underउचला 5 fig. A term for a round, fleshy, well-filled body. 6 A lump of silver: as obtained by melting down lace or fringe. गोटुळा or गोटोळा [ gōṭuḷā or gōṭōḷā ] a (गोटा) Spherical or spheroidal, pebble-form. (Marathi)

Rebus: krvṛi f. 'granary (Wpah.); kuṛī, kuṛo house, building'(Ku.)(CDIAL 3232) कोठी [ kōṭhī ] f (कोष्ट S) A granary, garner, storehouse, warehouse, treasury, factory, bank. (Marathi)

कोठी The grain and provisions (as of an army); the commissariat supplies. Ex. लशकराची कोठी चालली-उतरली- आली-लुटली. कोठ्या [ kōṭhyā ] कोठा [ kōṭhā ] m (कोष्ट S) A large granary, store-room, warehouse, water-reservoir &c. 2 The stomach. 3 The chamber of a gun, of water-pipes &c. 4 A bird's nest. 5 A cattle-shed. 6 The chamber or cell of a huṇḍí in which is set down in figures the amount. कोठारें [ kōṭhārēṃ ] n A storehouse gen (Marathi)

Sumerian mudhif facade, with uncut reed fonds and sheep entering, carved into a gypsum trough from Uruk, c. 3200 BCE (British Museum WA 120000). Photo source.

See also: *Expedition* 40:2 (1998), p. 33, fig. 5b Life on edge of the marshes.

Two views of carved gypsum trough from Uruk. Two lambs exit a reed structure identifical to the present-day mudhif on this ceremonial trough from the site of Uruk in northern Iraq. Neither the leaves or plumes have been removed from the reds which are tied together to form the arch. As a result, the crossed-over, feathered reeds create a decorative pattern along the length of the roof, a style more often seen in modern animal shelters built by the Mi'dan. Dating to ca. 3000 BCE, the trough documents the length of time, such arched reed buildings have been in use

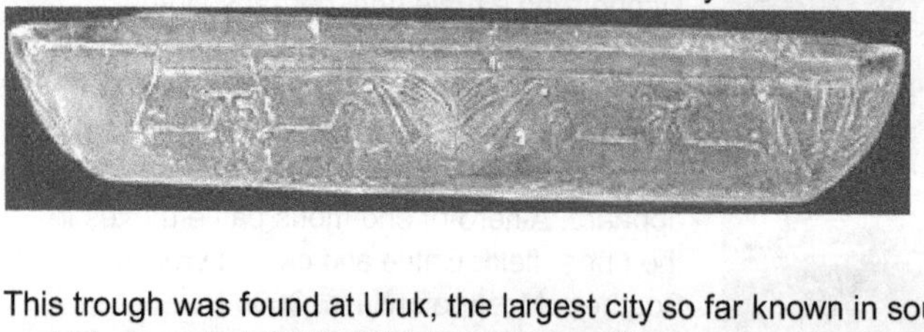

A cult object in the Temple of Inanna?

This trough was found at Uruk, the largest city so far known in southern Mesopotamia in the late prehistoric period (3300-3000 BC). The carving on the side shows a procession of sheep (a goat and a ram) approaching a reed hut (of a type still found in southern Iraq) and two lambs emerging. The decoration is only visible if the trough is raised above the level at which it could be conveniently used, suggesting that it was probably a cult object, rather than of practical use. It may have been a cult object in the Temple of Inana (Ishtar), the Sumerian goddess of love and fertility; a bundle of reeds (Inanna's symbol) can be seen projecting from the hut and at the edges of the scene. Later documents make it

clear that Inanna was the supreme goddess of Uruk. Many finely-modelled representations of animals and humans made of clay and stone have been found in what were once enormous buildings in the center of Uruk, which were probably temples. Cylinder seals of the period also depict sheep, cattle, processions of people and possibly rituals. Part of the right-hand scene is cast from the original fragment now in the Vorderasiatisches Museum, Berlin

J. Black and A. Green, Gods, demons and symbols of -1 (London, The British Museum Press, 1992)

P.P. Delougaz, 'Animals emerging from a hut', Journal of Near Eastern Stud-1, 27 (1968), pp. 186-7

H.W.F. Saggs, Babylonians (London, The British Museum Press, 1995)

D. Collon, Ancient Near Eastern art (London, The British Museum Press, 1995)

H. Frankfort, The art and architecture of th (London, Pelican, 1970)
http://www.britishmuseum.org/explore/highlights/highlight_objects/me/t/the_uruk_trough.aspx

Life on the edge of the marshes (Edward Ochsenschlaer, 1998)

ARC08002FU1

http://www.youtube.com/watch?v=AB8zsBH1rP8&feature=player_embedded Pergamonmuseum der Staatlichen Museen zu Berlin (Pergamon Museum, Museum Island Berlin)

Ur contained one of the largest ziggurats and had two ports that welcomed ships from as far as India. The Ur's ziggurat is a pyramid-like brick tower built in 2100 B.C. as a tribute to Sin, the moon god. It originally rose 65 feet from a base measuring 135 by 200 feet and had three platforms, each a different color, and a silver shrine at the top. About a third of it remains. Reaching a height of about 50 feet, it looks sort of like a castle wall filled in with dirt and ascended by a staircase. Some regard best preserved structure similar to the Tower of Babel.

Uruk (Warka) vase describes using hieroglyphs, the process of making copper and alloy ingots

I suggest that the scribes of this vase were Meluhha speakers. The hieroglyphs on the narratives on the vase depict the storage and transport of copper and bronze ingots.

Warka Vase

<u>bibliography and image source</u>: Strommenger, Eva:*Fünf Jahrtausende Mesopotamien*. München: Hirmer Verlag, fig. 19. 106 cm. high and 36 cm. dia. on top. The narrative on the vase showing a pair of glyphs: scarf + reed staff which glyphic is repeated on a Uruk (Warka) stone vessel with additional hieroglyphs. The bottom registers show an array of goats/animals and *taberna montana.* These glyphs are read rebus:

*melh, mṛeka* 'goat'; rebus: *milakkhu* 'copper' (Pali). *pasara*

'domestic animals'. *pasra* 'smithy, forge'.

*Tabernae Montana*, a flowering plant of the family Apocynaceae.

Glyphs on the bottom register of Uruk vase.

*tagaraka 'tabernae montana'.* Rebus: *tagara* 'tin'. Mineral tin alloyed with mineral copper yields bronze metal. One variant glyphic is an Indus script glyph (Sign 162) found on a potsherd dated to c. 3500 BCE. This writing on Harappa potsherd is the most ancient script document on the globe. Mleccha (meluhha) of Harappa had settled in Uruk (Warka) and made the Inanna temple with such artifacts attesting an early writing system of the 'smithy of nations' – harosheth ha-goy-im or

*kharoṣṭī gōya* [cognate *got* 'clan' (Pkt.); semant.'lip of blacksmith clan'].

Ur was unearthed in the 1920s and 30s by a team led by the British archaeologist Leonard Woolley, who found a great temple complex, royal tombs, and the remains of houses on city streets. In the tombs were treasures—including scores of stunning objects made with gold, silver and precious stones—that rivaled treasures found at famous burial sites in ancient Egypt. Most of the objects were taken to the British Museum. Bombing raids during the first Persian Gulf War left four craters in the temple precinct and 400 holes on the ziggurat.

The stone relief of reed + scarf glyphic is also shown on the narrative of Uruk vase (cf. drawing).

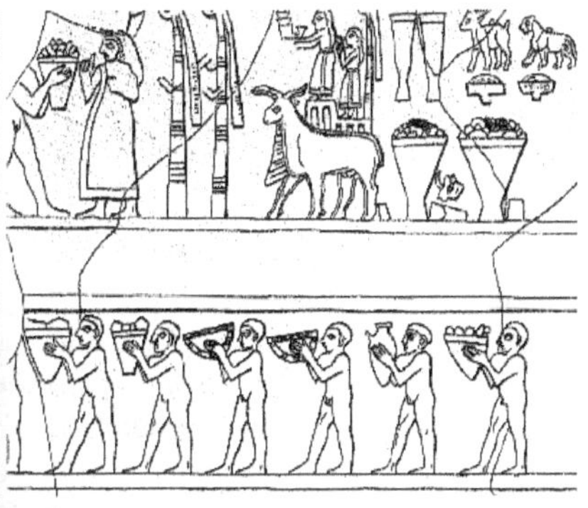

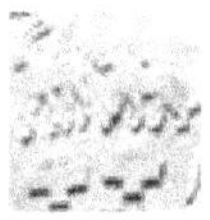

On the top register right corner, two animal glyphs are shown;: goat and tiger. *mṛeka* 'goat'. Rebus: *milakkhu* 'copper. *kola* 'tiger'. Rebus: *kol* 'pañcaloha, alloy of five metals', 'working in iron'. The pots are shown to contain stone ore ingots. below these animals two fire-altars with metal ingots (sometimes called 'bun ingots') are shown: *kaṇḍ* 'fire-altar'. These glyphs recur on Indus script inscriptions.

Another line drawing of top register of the Uruk vase. The head of a bull is shown between two pots containing copper ingots. This is a semantic determinant of the contents of the pots. The bull, glyphic: *adar ḍangra*. Rebus: aduru *ḍhangar* 'native metalsmith'. That is, the pots contain aduru 'unsmelted native metal'.

(Kohl, 1978; idem, 1979)

The limestone cup from Uruk is similarly likely to show that the bearded person holding a bull (as a semantic determinant) is a blacksmith.

Limestone cup from Uruk: Ht 12.7 cm. 3,100-3,000 BCE, Uruk in Southern Iraq (Photo from pg. 53 of D. Collon's 1995 *Ancient Near Eastern Art*). The figure on the front wears only a belt and has his curled hair parted in the center. He embraces a bull on either side of his torso, his arm around their neck. On the back of each bull stands a large bird.

Spreadout drawing of the Uruk vase in four registers. The third register shows a procession of animals: ram, goat, heifer are clearly identifiable.

Based on the occurrence of other animals on sculptural fragments, and the stone vase, it may also be assumed that one of the animals is also a bull.

Uruk vase detail. Ram in front of a pot containing metal ingots. Stone vase from Mesopotamia
Late Uruk period, about 3400-3200 BCE. Ht. 1.2 cm. It shows a bull, goat and ram.

A cow and a stable of reeds with sculpted columns in the background. Fragment of another vase of alabaster (era of Djemet-Nasr) from Uruk, Mesopotamia. Limestone 16 X 22.5 cm. AO 8842, Louvre, Departement des Antiquites Orientales, Paris, France. Six circles decorated on the reed post are semantic determinants of Glyph: *bhaṭa* 'six'. Rebus: *bhaṭa* 'furnace'.

A bearded figure wearing a netted skirt and hat is understood to be the ruler of Uruk, whose role as priest, provider, and protector seems to be emphasized. On the over one meter tall Warka vase, he is depicted in relief presenting an offering to Inanna. Below him runs a row of naked servants or priests carrying offerings. Below them is a row of dometi animals and a row of plants growing from a river.

Uruk (modern Warka)

Introduction
The site of Uruk, modern Warka, is located in southern Iraq about 35 kilometers east of the modern course of the Euphrates river. Settlement at the site began in the Ubaid period (5th millennium BC). In the Uruk period (4000-3000 BC) the site was the largest in Mesopotamia at 100 hectares. Uruk continued to grow in the Early Dynastic period (2900-2350 BC), reaching a size of about 400 hectares. After the end of the Early Dynastic period, the city declined in size and significance until the Ur III period (2100-2000 BC), when the ruling dynasty pursued new building projects in the Eanna precinct. It is to this period that the massive ziggurat still visible today dates. Uruk declined again after the Ur III period, and was resettled in the Neo-Assyrian (883-612 BC) and Neo-Babylonian periods (612-539 BC). Occupation continued at Uruk in the Achaemenid, Seleucid, and Parthian periods. Settlement at Uruk finally came to an end during the Sassanian period (224-633 AD).

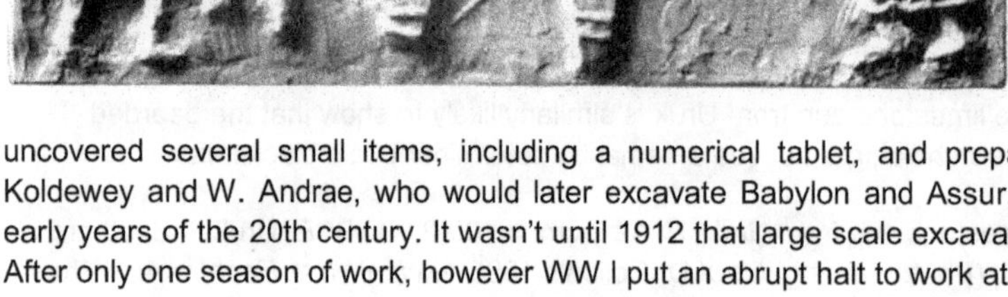

History of Excavation
W. K. Loftus was the first archaeologist to visit Uruk in 1850 and 1854. During his excavations, he uncovered several small items, including a numerical tablet, and prepared a map of the site. R. Koldewey and W. Andrae, who would later excavate Babylon and Assur, each visited the site in the early years of the 20th century. It wasn't until 1912 that large scale excavations began under J. Jordan. After only one season of work, however WW I put an abrupt halt to work at Uruk. Jordan returned to the site in 1928, with A. Falkenstein serving as epigrapher. Jordon's excavation set a precedent by concentrating primarily in the Eanna district of the site, the main religious complex in the center of Uruk. When Jordan became Director of Antiquities in Baghdad in 1931, German excavations continued under A. Nöldeke, E. Heinrich, and H. J. Lenzen until WW II forced a halt in 1939. Lenzen continued to direct

excavations for the German Archaeological Institute after the war from 1953 to 1967. He was succeed by H. J. Schmidt until 1977, and R. M. Boehmer after 1980. The 39 campaigns of German excavations came to a halt in 1989 and in 2001, a team direected by M. van Ess returned to Uruk to begin mapping the site using subsurface magnetometry.

The Eanna Precinct in the Late Uruk Period

The Late Uruk period (3600-3200 BC) saw an explosion of Mesopotamian cultural development. Construction activities expanded, writing developed, pottery technology advanced, and great works of monumental art were produced. At Uruk, levels VIII to IV correspond to the Late Uruk period, though the greatest achievements are apparent in levels V and IV. The most prominent area of Uruk during the Uruk period was the sacred Eanna ("House of Heaven") precinct dedicated to the goddess Inanna. Excavations there uncovered several monumental cult, administrative, and other public buildings, each rebuilt and reused over several occupation phases.

*Uruk V*

Uruk temples continued the architectural tradition of the preceding Ubaid period. Tripartite temple plans (i.e., a long central hall with rows of smaller rooms on either side) and niched and buttressed facades were characteristic of the earliest levels of the Uruk period. In Level V, the Limestone Temple, so called because the wall foundations (and possibly the entire building) were constructed of large slabs of limestone quarried from a site 80km from Uruk on the west side of the Euphrates, exhibited both of these classical Mesopotamian features.

Outside of the Eanna precinct, the earliest phases of the White Temple dedicated to the god Anu also probably date to the end of Level V. The niched and buttressed walls of the White Temple were covered with white gypsum plaster. The whole building was set upon a platform 13 meters high, a clear precursor to the ziggurat (a temple set on top of several stacked platforms) that would become so ubiquitous in later periods of Mesopotamian history.

*Uruk IVb*

In this level, the sacred precinct was entered from the south through the Mosaic Court. This building and its columns were made of small mud bricks, which were then faced with a layer of mud plaster. Red, white, or black baked clay cones were then pushed into the mud plaster walls, creating colorful geometric patterns along the pillars and walls.

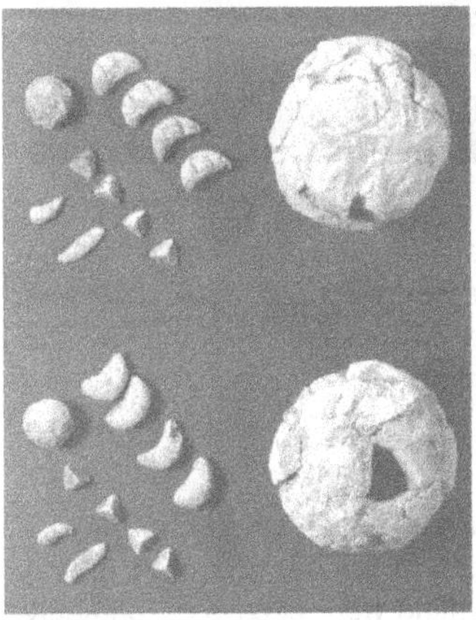

To the southwest of the Mosaic Court, the Square Building had a large square courtyard with a long rectangular hall on each side. Both the interior courtyard and exterior facade of the building had the niching characteristic of Uruk temples, but the plan of the building was unique, and its function is not certain.

Northwest of the Mosaic Court, several buildings with tripartite plans may have been temples. Three other buildings may have been the residences of the officials in charge of the temples in the Eanna precinct.

The Stone Cone Mosaic Temple was constructed to the west, apart from the complex of temples and ceremonial buildings attached to the Mosaic Court. A buttressed wall surrounded the tripartite temple building, and the temple itself was decorated with colored stone cones which formed geometric patterns on the walls in the same fashion as the Mosaic Court.

*Uruk IVa*

In level IVa, the new buildings were constructed over the level IVb Eanna complex. The large Temple D (80x50 meters) stood on the filled-in courtyard of the building below it. Slightly smaller, Temple C lay to the northwest of Temple D, and exhibited a clear tripartite plan. Northwest of this building, the Pillared Hall was decorated with another stone cone mosaic. Just west of the Pillared Hall, the Great Court may have been a sunken area surrounded by benches.

Above the Stone Cone Mosaic Temple of Level IVb, and odd building named theRiemchengebäude was constructed. It was given its name by the excavators because of the 'riemchen' bricks characteristic of Late Uruk architecture. These are small compact bricks with a square section. The building consisted of a long corridor surrounding a central chamber with a separate room to the southeast. The function of the building is unclear, but it may have been the site of a religious ritual.

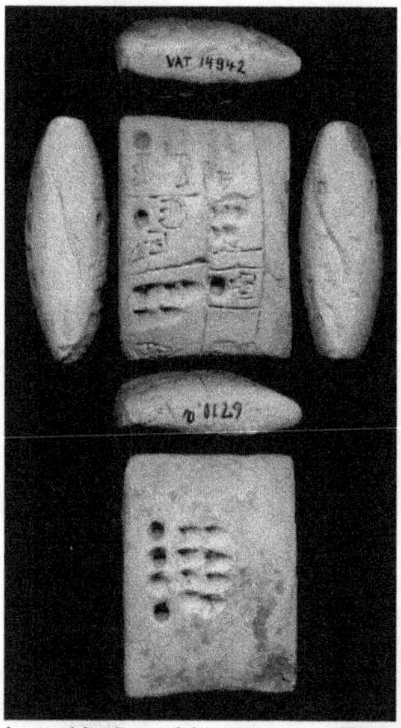


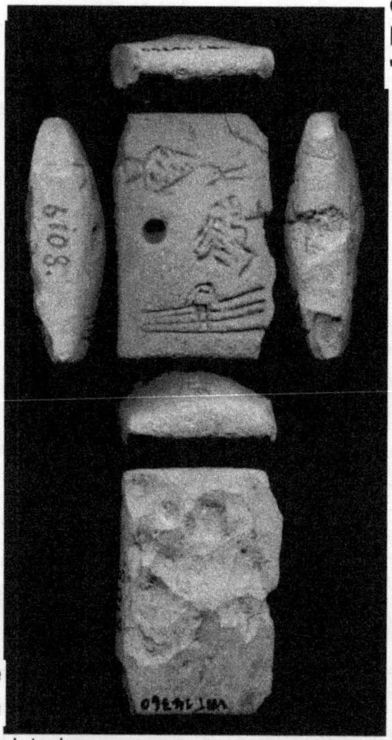

The City Wall
In the Early Dynastic I period in the first half of the third millennium BC, the citizens of Uruk probably first contructed the 9km long mud brick wall that enclosed the city. Although it has not been thoroughly excavated, this early date for the construction of the wall is inferred based on evidence from a cylinder seal impression. Throughout the history of occupation of the city, the wall underwent many repairs, the last of which dates to the 18h century BC.

The Development of Writing in the Uruk Period
Among the other technological advances that the Uruk period witnessed was the advent of pictographic representations on clay tablets and the development in stages of written language. From the Eanna complex of Uruk itself, nearly 5000 tablets from this earliest phase of writing were excavated primarily from rubbish dumps. Other more complete tablets from the same period have been found at sites in both in the northern and southern extents of southern Mesopotamia (see also proto-cuneiform).

These archaic tablets were used to fill in pits left by the levelling the Uruk IV buildings in order to build foundations for level III buildings. The tablets themselves, therefore, must date to a period prior to level

III. The earliest phases of writing then dates to Uruk level IV, and more specifically, it probably dates to the latest subphase of that level, IVa. A second phase of writing is dated to Uruk level III, also called the Jemdet Nasr period because a large number of texts from this date were found at the site of Jemdet Nasr, just south of modern day Baghdad.

Although the first written tablets that appear in theUruk IV period are quite underdeveloped in relation to the fully formed cuneiform systems of later periods, they did not appear spontaneously. Precursors to the Uruk tablets took the form of clay "tokens" sealed in "bullae" and clay tablets impressed with numerical notations. Tokens were simply lumps of clay fashioned into standardized shapes. Each shape represented a numerical unit (i.e., 1 or 10, etc.), and some may have represented a type of object (i.e., sheep or cloth). Often tokens were encased in bullae, hollow clay balls that were officially sealed by means of an incised cylinder seal which, when rolled over the surface of the bullae would leave a unique impression.

The second precursor to Uruk IV writing were simple clay tablets, sometimes with cylinder seal impressions, with rounded impressions representing numbers. These are very difficult to date and to interpret, as the shape of the impressions and the units of counting do not always correspond to what is know about counting systems in later periods.

In the Uruk IV phase, written documents come in three varieties:

(1) Clay "tags" with incised drawings that probably corresponded to the person receiving or selling the item(s) to which the tag was attached.

(2) Small tablets that combine impressed rounded numerical signs with incised pictographs representing objects or personal names.

(3) Larger tablets divided into sections, each containing impressions of numerical signs and incised pictographs representing objects or personal names. Sometimes, the numerical signs are added together and the total is incised on the back of the tablet.

In the Jemdet Nasr period, the majority of the texts fall into the third category, lists of numbers and associated commodities. A new category of texts also develops during the Jemdet Nasr period, though they may be a continuation of a type which has not been discovered in Uruk IV contexts. This lexical category continues into the following periods.

It is important to note that the purpose of all of these early forms of writing, including theUruk IV and Jemdet Nasr period texts, along with their precursors, was to record economic transactions. Writing itself developed out of a need to remember exchanges of large numbers of goods among the inhabitants of those cities whose population had increased throughout the Uruk period so that face-to-face contact was no longer the norm. It was a tool of economic administration, not a means to record literature, history, or sacred ideas.

It took several centuries for the written language to develop so that it could represent the complexities of grammar and syntax. The earliest signs used in the Uruktexts, which were either pictographic representations of objects, symbols representing deities, abstract images, or numerical signs, eventually developed into the more abstract cuneiform signs characterized by horizontal and vertical wedges. In theUruk IV and Jemdet Nasr phases, signs represented concepts or nouns, and perhaps simple verbs, but there is no grammatical relationship between those ideas represented on the texts. Sometimes signs were combined to form ideas related to both signs (such as the sign for disbursement which combines the sign for head with the sign for ration), and other times signs were combined to form words that sounded like those signs. In this way, signs which originally had a pictographically assigned meaning became associated with abstract concepts that sounded similar. For example, the Sumerian word for "life" is pronounced "til," and the word for "arrow" is pronounced "ti." In writing, the same sign, TI, is used for both ideas presumably because it is easier to draw an arrow than it is to draw the more abstract notion of life.

Later, the TI sign might be combined with other signs, whose sounds would act as the syllables that make up a longer word. Although it is generally agreed that the language represented on the archaic texts is Sumerian, it is only once the syllabic function of the signs was applied that language could truly be represented in a permanent medium.

The form of the signs also changed over time. Originally, pictographs were incised in clay using a sharp stylus. By the Jemdet Nasr phase, the sharp stylus was replaced by an angled stylus with a triangular tip. The result of pushing a stylus of this shape into wet clay is a wedge with a triangular shaped "head" and a long straight "tail." The shape of these wedges provide the name we use for the writing system of Mesopotamia, "cuneiform," Latin for wedge-shaped. As the use of the triangular stylus continued, the signs themselves became more and more abstracted into combinations of horizontal and vertical wedges that no longer bore much resemblance to their original forms. The range of sign forms used also decreased as the number of similar-looking signs reduced. <br>

The Spread of Uruk Culture

The name Uruk is also applied to the archaeological period corresponding to the fourth millennium BC (Uruk levels VIII-IVa). Not only did the written documents appear in this period, but the Uruk period also saw the rise of the first cities, monumental art and complex political structures. Prior to the Uruk period, maps of settlement in southern Mesopotamia show several sites of a small size, mostly under 10 hectares (0.1 km$^2$). These sites are evenly distributed over the landscape, and some may have been economic or religious centers. At the start of the Uruk period, the number and size of sites increased dramatically. Uruk itself swelled to 70 hectares (0.7 km$^2$). The reasons for such an extraordinary change are unclear. There may have been a sudden influx of new population groups or favorable changes in climate, but the trend continued into the Late Uruk period. By the end of the Uruk period, the site of Urukoccupied about 100 hectares (1 km$^2$), and more than half of the settled area of southern Mesopotamia was located in its vicinity.

*Cylinder seal and impression showing ruler on a boat with icons symbolizing the goddess Inanna (ADFU 1, Plate 17).*

The rapid increase in the size of the settled area ofUruk meant that new developments in the social structure of society were inevitable. The archaic texts, cylinder seals and monumental art all provide information about these changes. In the cylinder seals and seal impressions on tablets of levels IV and III, a bearded figure wearing a netted skirt and hat appears in religious, agricultural, or military scenes. This figure is generally understood to represent the ruler of Uruk, whose role as priest, provider, and protector is emphasized. The same figure also appears on the Lion Hunt Stela, a basalt stone monument which shows him attacking lions with a spear and with a bow and arrow. On the WarkaVase, an alabaster vessel over a meter tall, he is depicted in relief presenting an offering to Inanna. Below him runs a row of naked servants or priests carry offerings, and below them is a row of domestic animals and a row of plants growing from a river. The remarkable vessel clearly shows the shared view of a social hierarchy, at the bottom of which were the plants an animals that sustained society, and at the top of which were the ruler and the god, who managed and distributed those staples. The Urukperiod marks the first instance

when these roles were expressed in figurative art, and this type of royal propaganda is a theme that continues in the millennia of Near Eastern history that follow.

The types of artifacts found in Uruk levels V-IVa have been found at sites from the same period throughout the entire Near East. The most easily recognizable identifier of this period is the bevelled-rim bowl, a crude, handmade, mass-produced ceramic type with a distinctive rim. This type of pottery has been found in fourth millennium sites in southwest Iran, Syria, Turkey, and Egypt. Other aspects of Uruk culture, such as the tripartite temple plan and niched and buttressed facades of the Eanna precinct buildings are found in northern and southern Mesopotamian contexts. Cylinder seals of a type that was developed in Uruk also spread throughout the Near East. The convergence of these artifact classes at sites outside of Uruk has prompted theories of the expansion of Urukpolitical control over Mesopotamia by the establishment of merchant colonies north and east of Uruk itself. Now archaeologists recognize the unique cultural development of northern Mesopotamia that can be seen at sites alongside or in place of Uruk culture, which suggests that the methods by which Uruk influence expanded are much more complicated than originally thought. There is no doubt, however, that the Uruk period, which saw innovations including writing, the cylinder seal, the plow, and wheeled vehicles constituted a crucial phase in the history of the Near East.

References

*Ausgrabungen der Deutschen Forschungsgemeinschaft in Uruk-Warka.* Berlin: Mann. 17 volumes. 1946-2001

*Ausgrabungen in Uruk-Warka, Endberichte.* Mainz: Philipp von Zabern GmbH. 25 volumes. 1987-2003.

Boehmer, R. M. Uruk-Warka In *Oxford Encyclopedia of Archaeology in the Near East,* vol. 5, 294-298. New York: Oxford University, 1997.

Crawford, H. *Sumer and the Sumerians.* Cambridge: Cambridge, 1991.

Englund, R. K. Texts From the Late Uruk Period In *Mesopotamien 1: Späturuk-Zeit und Frühdynastische Zeit. OBO* 160, 15-233. Freiburg and Göttingen: Universitätsverlag and Vandenhoeck & Ruprecht, 1998.

Nissen, H., P. Damerow, and R. K. Englund. *Archaic Bookkeeping: Writing and Techniques of Economic Administration in the Ancient Near East.* P. Larsen, trans. Chicago: University of Chicago, 1993

Postgate, J. N. *Early Mesopotamia: Society and Economy at the Dawn of History.* London: Routledge, 1992.

Roaf, M. *The Cultural Atlas of Mesopotamia and the Ancient Near East.* Oxford and New York: Facts on File, 1990.

Source: http://cdli.ucla.edu/wiki/doku.php/uruk_mod._warka

Shell plaque From Ur, Southern Iraq (c. 2,600-2,400 B.C.) Entwined in the branches of a flowering tree, two goats appear to be nibbling on its leaves. This decorative plaque, which was carved from shell and highlighted with bitumen, was also excavated from the Royal Tombs of UR.

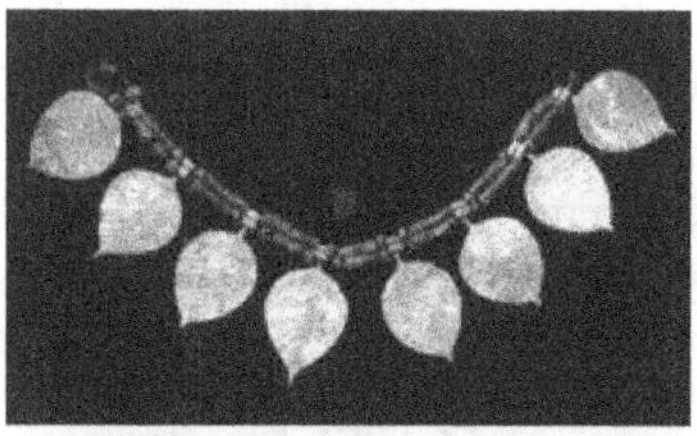

Headdress and necklace of gold, lapis lazuli and cornelian from the Royal Cemetery of Ur, Southern Iraq. (c. 2,600 B.C.)

Silver lyre from Ur, Southern Iraq (c. 2,600-2,400 B.C.). Entirely covered in sheet silver attached by small silver nails. The plaques down the front of the sounding box are made of shell. The silver cow's head decorating the front has inlaid eyes of shell and lapis lazuli. Eleven silver tubes acted as the tuning pegs. Most Sumerian lyres had eleven strings, and it is assumed that each string produced a different sound.

Gold cup from Ur, Southern Iraq. (c. 2,600-2,400 B.C.)

Gold dagger with lapis handle and sheath, from the Royal Cemetery at Ur (c. 2,400 B.C.)

The Standard of Ur from Ur, Southern Iraq, (c. 2,600-2,400 B.C.)The object has two main panels called "War and Peace." The "War" section shows one of the earliest representations of a Sumerian army: soldiers on chariots trampling enemies; infantry with cloaks carry spears; enemy soldiers are killed with axes, and prisoners are paraded and presented to the king who holds a spear. The "Peace" panel depicts various scenes of life: animals, fish and other goods are brought in procession to a banquet; seated figures, wearing woolen fleeces or fringed skirts, drink to the accompaniment of a musician playing a lyre.

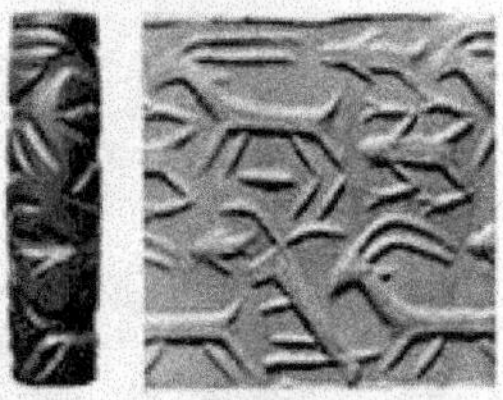

Cylinder seals were invented around 3,500 B.C. in Southern Mesopotamia (now Iraq) and were used as an administrative tool to seal documents and other items - such as legal documents or records - by rolling the seals with their carving on them across a malleable surface and creating a raised impression. Running from one-half inch in size to a couple of inches, the cylindrical seal "embodies the essence of Mesopotamia." Cylinder seals give us an unbroken chain of information from the 4th millennium down to the 1st millennium, and this information

covers aesthetics, art, imagery, mythology, history, and administration. Cylinder seals led to the invention of cuneiform writing on clay.

Cuneiform clay tablet with a message signed, "Your loving wife who has had a child." (2,900 – 2,700 B.C.). "The origin of writing", began with the cuneiform clay tablets of Mesopotamia about 3,200 B.C. Written in various languages, the tablets contained letters, dictionaries, hymns, political tracts, sales slips, astronomy, and student notebooks of schoolboys learning to read and write in Sumeria. Humorous stories have been found such as a debate between a plow and a hoe arguing the moral of valuing humility over pride.

Source: http://www.hmc.org.qa/hmc/heartviews/H-V-v4%20N1/10.htm

I suggest that the pair of reed glyphs with scarfs on the Uruk stone vessel carved in alabaster stone denote: *dhatu eruva* 'mineral copper'. It is a narrative relief sculpture, dated to c. 3,200–3,000 BCE. A thousand Sumerian economic texts were found in Uruk (Warka) which are 'the most ancient script documents of the world' (Werner Ekschmitt). The other two glyphic pairs: goat + eight-petaled flower: *milakkhu ara ḍhāḷako* 'copper, large metal ingot' (G.) Eight petals (*daḷa*) denote 8 parts of copper alloyed with one part arsenic, *daḷa* to create the brass alloy. *are* 'eight' (Mu.). Rebus: *ara* 'copper'. dula 'pair'. Rebus: dul 'cast (metal)'. The document reads: *dhatu eruva milakkhu dul ara ḍhāḷako* 'mineral copper smelter copper, cast copper (metal) ingot'.

Glyph: 'reed': *Ta.* eruvai European bamboo reed. Rebus: eruvai 'copper' (Tamil). Glyph: dhaṭu 'scarf' (WPah.). Rebus: dhatu 'mineral' (Santali).

Glyph: ``^flower":Sa. *baha* `flower, blossom, to flower'.Mu. *tarai-ba*(A) `a kind of marsh-flower'. ~ *baa*(H) ~ *baha*(N) `flower, blossom, to flower'.Ho *ba* `flower, blossom, to flower'.Bh. *baha* `flower, blossom, to flower'. KW *baha*|Cf. So. *ba'a* `to blossom'.@(V021,M111)

Rebus:``^make":Sa. *bai* `to make'.Mu. *bai* `to make'.KW *bai* @(M100)

Glyph: *melh, mṛeka* 'goat'; rebus: *meḍh* 'merchant's clerk' (Pkt.) *milakkhu* 'copper' (Pali)

dhaṭu 'scarf'; rebus: dhatu 'mineral' (Santali) dhātu 'mineral (Pali) dhātu 'mineral' (Vedic); a mineral, metal (Santali); dhāta id. (G.) H. dhāṛnā 'to send out, pour out, cast (metal)' (CDIAL 6771).

The 'petals' glyphic element may relate to an alloying mineral, arsenic.

Representing arsenic in Indian hieroglyphs. Possible allographs:

Glyph: 'petal': దళము [daḷamu] *daḷamu*. [Skt.] n. A leaf. ఆకు. A petal. A part, భాగము. dala n. ' leaf, petal ' MBh. Pa. Pk. *dala* -- n. ' leaf, petal ', G. M. *daḷ* n.(CDIAL 6214). <DaLO>(MP) {N} ``^branch, ^twig". *Kh.<DaoRa>(D) `dry leaves when fallen', ~<daura>, ~<dauRa> `twig', Sa.<DAr>, Mu.<Dar>, ~<Dara> `big branch of a tree', ~<DauRa> `a twig or small branch with fresh leaves on it', So.<kOn-da:ra:-n> `branch', H.<DalA>, B.<DalO>, O.<DaLO>, Pk.<DAlA>. %7811. #7741.(Munda etyma)

Glyph: ḍāla1 m. ' branch ' Śīl. 2. *ṭhāla -- . 3. *ḍāḍha -- . [Poss. same as *dāla -- 1 and dāra -- 1: √dal, √d&rcirclemacr;. But variation of form supports PMWS 64 ← Mu.] 1. Pk. *ḍāla* -- n. ' branch '; S. *ḏāru* m. ' large branch ', *ḏārī* f. ' branch '; P. *ḍāl* m. ' branch ', *°lā* m. ' large do. ', *°lī* f. ' twig '; WPah. bhal. *ḍā* m. ' branch '; Ku. *ḍālo* m. ' tree '; N. *ḍālo* ' branch ', A. B. *ḍāl*, Or. *ḍāḷa*; Mth. *ḍār* ' branch ', *°ri* ' twig '; Aw. lakh. *ḍār* ' branch ', H. *ḍāl*, *°lā* m., G.*ḍāḷi*, *°ḷī* f., *°ḷũ* n. 2. A. *ṭhāl* ' branch ', *°li* ' twig '; H. *ṭhāl*, *°lā* m. ' leafy branch (esp. one lopped off) '. 3. Bhoj. *ḍāṛhī* ' branch '; M. *ḍāhaḷ* m. ' loppings of trees ', *ḍāhḷā* m. ' leafy branch ', *°ḷī* f. ' twig ', *ḍhāḷā* m. ' sprig ', *°ḷī* f. ' branch '. (CDIAL 5546).

Glyph: dálati intr. ' cracks, splits ' Suśr., *dalayati* tr. Dhātup. dala2 n. ' piece split off, fragment ' Suśr., ' a half ' VarBṛS. [~ dara -- 2. -- Cf. dala -- 1. -- √dal1]Pk. *dala* -- n. ' piece '; K. *düjü* f. ' small piece of cloth, small plot of ground (e.g. seed -- bed) '; S. *ḏaru* m. ' a breadth of cloth '; WPah.jaun. *dalī* bundle of lighted sticks of pine '; B. *dal* ' fragment, thickness (of a board, &c.) '; M. *daḷ* n. ' half ' (CDIAL 6213,

6216). దళించు *dalinṭsu*. v. t. To cut, split, divide. ఖండించు, భేదించు. దళనము *daḷanamu*. n. Breaking, cutting, severing. ఖండించుట, భేదించుట. Rebus: *ḍhāḷako* 'a large metal ingot' (G.)

Glyph: H. *hāriyal* ' green ', m. ' green pigeon '. P. *haryal* ' green ', m. ' green pigeon '; B. *hariyāl* ' green pigeon ', Or. *hariāḷ caṛhei*, H. *har(i)yāl* m.; M. *har(i)yaḷ* m. ' bee -- eater ' (CDIAL 13986).

*Glyph: Or. har(i)yāḷ* m. ' small green snake '(CDIAL 13987).

Glyph: மத்தளம் mattaḷam , *n.* < *mardala*. A kind of drum; பறைவகை. மத்தளங் கொட்ட (திவ். நாய்ச். 6, 6). தாளம் tāḷam , *n.* < *tāla*. A small cymbal for keeping time in music; (Mus.) Time-measure; பாடுகையிற் காலத்தை அறுதியிடும் அளவு. இத்தாளங்களின் வழிவரும் . . . ஏழு தூக்குக்களும் (சிலப். 3, 16, உரை) (Tamil)

Rebus 1: தாளம் tāḷam Yellow orpiment (Tamil) తాళకము [ tāḷakamu ] *tāḷakamu*. [Skt.] n. Yellow orpiment. Yellow sulphuret of arsenic. హరిదళము, తొగరిమన్ను. Pa. *haritāla* -- m. ' yellow orpiment ', Pk*. *hariāla* -- , *haliāra* -- m.n.,(CDIAL 13987). hartāl हर्ताल् । हरितालकम् f. (sg. dat. hartāli हर्तालि), orpiment, sulphuret of arsenic, yellow arsenic, ratsbane. హరిదళము [ haridaḷamu ] or అరిదళము *hari-daḷamu*. [from Skt. హరితాళమ్.] n. Yellow orpiment, *Arsenicum flavum.* వేషగాండ్రు మూతికి పూసుకొనేటిది. స్వర్ణతాళము gold coloured orpiment, *auri-pigmentum.*

Rebus 2: dala n. ' party, band '. [T. Burrow BSOAS xii 381 ← Drav.]Pk. *dala* -- n. ' army '; Sh. (Lor.) *d*ʻl*o* ' party, group '; K. *dal*, *ḍal* m. ' company, party '; L. *dal*, *ḍal* m. ' army, flight of locusts '; P. *dal* m. ' army, swarm '; N. *dal* ' army, band, flock '; A. B. *dal* ' company '; Or. *daḷa* ' party, herd '; OAw. *dara* ' army '; H. *dal* m. ' troop, company ' (→ Bhoj. *dal*); G. M. *daḷ* n. ' army '. -- Kho. (Lor.) *ḍ*ʻl*l*, *ḍāl*, *dāl* ' party, section, herd of horses ' (with *ā*) is obscure. (CDIAL 6215).

Rebus 3: A. *dalā* ' clod ', *dali* ' lump, piece of stone used as a missile '; B. *dalā*, *°li*, *dalni* ' lump, clod '; Or.*daḷi* ' clod ', *daḷanī* ' clod, brickbat '; H. *dalī* f. ' clod ' (CDIAL 5536).

End of the Uruk trough. Length: 96.520 cm Width: 35.560 cm Height: 15.240 cm. .

Importance of 'eight' count: Glyph 'eight': Ta. eṭṭu eight; eṇ-patu eighty; eṇ-ṇūṟu 800; eṇṇ-eṭṭu eight eights (= 64); eṇmar, eṇvar eight persons; evv-eṭṭu eight each. Ma. eṭṭu eight; eṇ-patu eighty; eṇ-ṇūṟu 800; eṇmar eight persons. Ko. eṭ eight; em bat eighty. To. öṭ eight; pu·ṭ eighteen. Ka. eṇṭu eight; eṇbar eight persons; eṇ-pattu, em-battu eighty. Koḍ. ëṭṭï eight; ëṭṭane eighth; ëm-badï eighty; ëṭ-ṇu·rï 800. Tu. eṇma, eṇůma eight; eṇpa eighty. Te. enimidi eight; enamaṇḍru eight persons; enu-badi, enabhai, (inscr., p. 354) eṇumbodi, eṇbodi, enubodi eighty; enaman(n)ūṟu 800. Kol. (SR.) enumadī, enumidī, (Kin.) enumdi eight; (SR.) enmāter, enmāṭar eight persons. Go. (Tr.) aṛmur, aṛmul, (W. ChD.) armur, (Hislop) yermud eight (Voc. 354); (L.) enmīdī, (Pat.) tenmidi id.; (Tr.) aṛmuhk eight each. (DEDR 784)

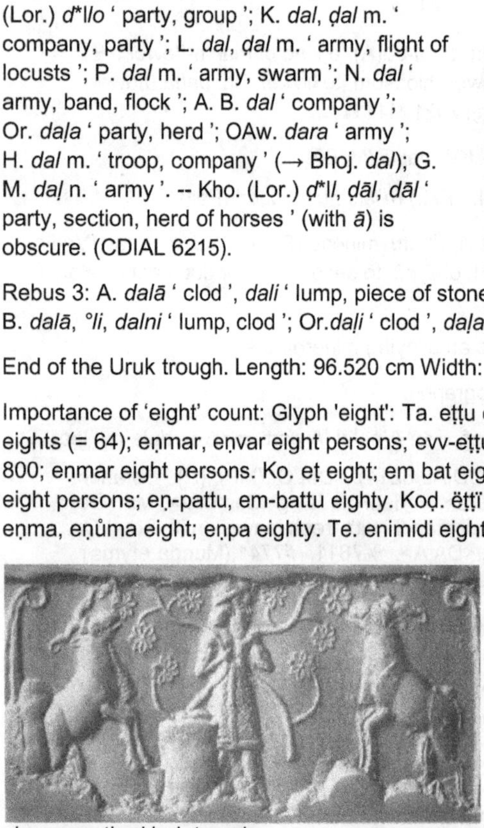

Silver ornaments found at Lothal. The flower motif is comparable to the head-dress of a terracotta figure of Mohenjo-daro and the eight-petal flower shown on the Uruk trough

Rebus 'mathematician':Ta. eṇ thought, intention, deliberation, esteem, calculation, mathematics, number; eṇṇu (eṇṇi-) to think, consider, determine, esteem, conjecture, count, reckon, compute, set a price upon; eṇṇam thought, idea, respect, deliberation, anxiety, mathematics; eṇṇar, eṇṇalar mathematicians; eṇṇal intention, counting, deliberation; eṇṇikkai numbering, esteem, reverence; ēṇi number; ēṭal meaning, intention, thought. Ma. eṇ number, thought; eṇṇam number, counting; eṇṇuka to count, number, esteem, relate; eṇṇikka to get counted, account for; n. counting. To. öṇ- (öṇy-) to count; öṇm (obl. öṇt-) counting, numbers. Ka. eṇike, eṇṇike counting, number, thinking, observation; eṇisu, eṇasu, eṇusu, eṇṇisu to add together, enumerate, count, estimate, appreciate, consider, think, plan, compare; eṇṇu to count, think. Koḍ. ëṇṇ- (ëṇṇi-) to say, tell. Tu. eṇṇuni to count, think, presume, expect; eṇṇige, eṇike, eṇe, eṇke calculation, estimation. Te. ennu to count, reckon, think, believe, esteem, care for, criticize; ennika counting, number, esteem, regard, opinion, hope; encu to count, reckon, enumerate, think, consider, believe, judge, esteem. Pa. eja number; eja cāj- to count (cāj- to do). Pe. eja ki- id. Manḍ. eji ki- id. Kuwi (S.) eji kīnai id. (DEDR 793).

A set of eight-petalled flowers are shown on a cylinder seal: c.3200-3000 B.C. Late Uruk-Jemdet Nasr period. Marble. Cylinder seal. Mesopotamia. A bearded male figure wears a round cap and a skirt with netlike pattern. This man appears on many artifacts excavated at Inanna's city, Uruk, and may represent the en, or priest-king, of the city, who assumes the role of divine consort of Inanna in the sacred marriage ceremony. Clasped to his chest are two curving branches ending in rosette-flowers. These rosette symbols of Inanna are nibbled by maned sheep, literally portraying the nourishment of the flocks ensured by the union of the goddess and her consort. The emblems of Inanna that flank the scene suggest that it is taking place within the sacred precinct of her temple.

Glyph: 'creeper': vēlli f. ' creeping plant ' lex. [Cf. vallī -- ] Pk. *vellī* -- , *°lā* -- f. ' creeper ', P. *vel*, *bel* f., Ku. *bel*, N. *beli*; B. *bel* ' jasmine '; Mth. *belī* ' a kind of flower '; OAw. *beli* ' creeper ', H. *bel*, *belī* f., G. *vel*, *velī* f., *velɔ* m., M. *vel* f. Garh. *bel* ' creeper (CDIAL 12123). Rebus: Ta. *veḷḷi whiteness, silver, silver coin, star, planet Venus, Friday; Ma.* veḷḷi silver, Venus, Friday, white speck on the eye; Ka. beḷḷi silver, planet Venus; *Koḍ*boḷḷi star, silver; Te. venḍi silver; Kui. wenḍi silver; Pkt. (*DNM*) villa- bright, clear; vilha- white (DEDR 5496). Vikalpa: *Ta.* koṭi creeper, umbilical cord. *Ma.* koṭi creeper, what is long and thin, umbilical cord, etc. *Ko.* koṛy creeper; koc binding (for firewood, etc.) made from plant. *To.* kwïṛy creeper. *Koḍ.* koḍi ele betel leaf. *Pe.* goḍi creeper. *Manḍ.* kuṛi id. Rebus: *koḍ* 'artisan's workshop' (Kuwi) Vikalpa: Glyph: H. *ḍaṭhā* m. ' stalk '.(CDIAL 5527). Rebus: dhatu 'mineral' (Santali). . Glyph: *mēḍā* 'ram (with crooked horns)'. Rebus: *meṛeḍ* 'iron' (Mundari)

The trough shows a pair of reed flags (with scarfs), a pair of goats and a pair of eight-petalled flowers.

Glyph: Ta. Tu. koṭi flag; *Ka.* kuḍi top, flag, banner; guḍi point, flag, banner (DEDR 2049). Rebus 1: kuṭikai hut made of leaves, temple; Ko. guṛy temple; To. kuṛy Hindu temple; Ka.Te.Pa.Ga. guḍi house, temple; Go. guḍi, (Mu.) guḍḍi, (S. Ko.) guṛi temple (DEDR 1655). Rebus 2: *koḍ* 'artisan's workshop' (Kuwi.G.)

The glyphic elements on the Uruk trough and comparable glyphs on other cylinder seals of the interaction area are thus: dhatu 'mineral' (scarf) + milakku 'copper' (goat) + meḍ 'iron' (ram) + ayas 'metal' (fish) + bel 'silver' (creeper) + tala 'arsemoc' (petal).

Thus glyphic elements read rebus: *koḍ bai meṛeḍ* 'workshop, make (metal)'

Ewe and Ram Flanking Plant with a Gatepost. Cylinder seal and impression Mesopotamia, Late Uruk period (ca.3500–3100 B.C.) Serpentine 16 x 13 mm Seal no. 5 http://www.themorgan.org/collections/collections.asp?id=612

Three Stags with a Plant Cylinder seal and impression Mesopotamia, Late Uruk period/Jamdat Nasr period (ca. 3500–2900 B.C.) Serpentine 25 x 22 mm

Seal no. 20

http://www.themorgan.org/collections/collections.asp?id=614

Glyph: 'reed': *Ta.* eruvai European bamboo reed; a species of Cyperus; straight sedge tuber. *Ma.* eruva a kind of grass. (DEDR 819). Rebus: *Ta.* eruvai blood, (?) copper. *Ka.* ere a dark-red or dark-brown colour, a dark or dusky colour; (Badaga) erande sp. fruit, red in colour. *Te.*rēcu, rēcu-kukka a sort of ounce or lynx said to climb trees and to destroy tigers; (B.) a hound or wild dog. *Kol.* resn a·te wild dog (i.e. *res na·te; see 3650). *Pa.* iric netta id. *Ga.* (S.3) rēs nete hunting dog, hound. *Go.* (Ma.) erm ney, (D.) erom nay, (Mu.) arm/aṛm nay wild dog (*Voc.* 353); (M.) rac nāī, (Ko.) rasi ney id. (*Voc.* 3010). For 'wild dog', cf. 1931 Ta. ce- red, esp. the items for 'red dog, wild dog'. (DEDR 817). Allograph: *Ta.* eruvai a kind of kite whose head is white and whose body is brown; eagle. *Ma.* eruva eagle, kite.(DEDR 818).

Assuming that a Meluhha merchant is associated with the Uruk (Warka) trough glyphic composition, the composition of glyphs on the Uruk trough read rebus in meluhha (mleccha): glyphs: a pair of flags, scarves (on reed), flower, eight-petals, pair of goats *koḍ dul dhatu ĕṇṇ meḍh ere bai*, 'artisan's workshop (for) cast minerals, copper, trader's clerk – making, (ac)counting or enumerating mathematician (*ĕṇṇ bai*, lit. counting making)'.

This is an example of Indian meluhha hieroglyph composition.

Terracotta head of ewe. Probably from Uruk, southern Iraq Late Prehistoric period, about 3300-3000 BC Length: 13.650 cm Height: 9.520 cm

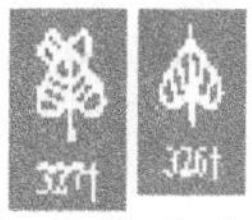

Probably from the decoration of a temple. Sheep played an important role in the ancient Sumerian economy. Documents show that lls d textiles were sometimes produced in large factories, employing hundreds of women, and probably exported throughout the region. Images on cylinder seals from this period appear to show lines of weavers, with their hair in pig tails.

Although it is not clear exactly where this baked clay head came from, other very similar examples made of stone and terracotta have been excavated from the city of Uruk. Indeed, it seems that images of sheep were especially common there at this time. The extraordinary lls des of this piece is characteristic of fine objects of this period. Scenes of sheep on stone sculpture (for example, the 'Uruk Trough' in The British Museum) and cylinder seals at this time show a close relationship with the symbol of the goddess Inana (Ishtar), a fertility deity.

J.E. Reade, *Mesopotamia* (London, The British Museum Press, 1991)

M. Roaf, *Cultural atlas of Mesopotamia* (New York, 1990)

J. Rawson, *Animals in art* (London, The British Museum Press, 1977)

Etymology concordant with *gashshu*,'gypsum, whitewash' (Sumerian)[See doc. A Discussion of the Use of im-babbar 2 by the Craft Workers of Ancient Mesopotamia]*kasiṅgala ' rubbish '. [Cf. kásāmbu — n. ' (prob.) rubbish ', Pa. kasambu — n. ' rubbish ': see *kasaṭa -- .] P. kahigal f. ' plaster of mud and chaff ';

N. kasiṅar ' dirt, rubbish '.(CDIAL 2982).Konḍa (BB) kaR- to smear, daub, whitewash. Pe. Kāz- (kāst-) to plaster, rub on (medicine); kāspa- to rub on, smear on. Kui kāja (kāji-) to daub, plaster over holes; n. daubing, plastering; kahpa (kaht-) to smear, plaster. Kuwi (F.) kūdū kaiyali to plaster with mud (kūdū for Su. Isr. Kūḍu wall, IIJ 6.238); (Isr.) kah- to daub, smear. Kur. Xasnā id. (DEDR 1503).

Sargonid seal. Uruk.

Fascinating is the relief decoration carved on these plaques, often in two or three registers. They

include several ritual scenes, scenes of offering to the temple, libation and festival activities. Very informative about temple household and the social practices that went on in the temples. Therefore these plaques were the really first major attempts towards visual narrative in the Early Mesopotamian art. For some of these wall plaques we know that they were commemorating not a generic but a specific event, celebrating a particular achievement on the behalf of the king and his people. Later examples from EDIII are inscribed too that makes this certain. These plaques therefore, which most of the time depict celebration, of especially a societal kind, derives its meaning from its very making. The same of human figure is also evident in these reliefs.

Note: The 'door' shown on the right-side of the plaque compares with an Indus script glyph (discussed elsewhere in this book).

Glyph 'leaf, petal': A 'leaf' glyph has to be distinguished from a 'petals' glyph because the leaf orthography is clearly representative of the *ficus* genus which attains sacredness in later historical periods in the Indian linguistic area.

Glyptic elements of m296 seal impression: 1. Two heads of one-horned heifers; 2. ligatured to a pair of rings and a standard device; 3. ligatured to a precise count of nine leaves. Read rebus: koḍiyum 'heifer, rings on neck'; rebus: koḍ 'workshop' (Kuwi.G.); dula 'pair' (Kashmiri); rebus: dul 'cast metal' (Mu.) lo, no 'nine' (B.); loa 'ficus religiosa' (Santali); rebus: loh 'metal' (Skt.); loa 'copper' (Santali) sangaḍa 'jointed animals' (Marathi); sangaḍa 'lathe' (G.) Part of the pictorial motif is thus decoded rebus: loh dul koḍ 'metal cast(ing) smithy turner (lathe) workshop '. Part of the inscription is read rebus: *ayaskāṇḍa kole.l* 'smithy, excellent quantity of iron'.

The stem in the orthographic composition relates to *sangaḍa* 'lathe/furnace' (yielding crucible stone ore nodules), the standard device which is depicted frequently in front of 'one-horned heifer'. Rebus: *sangāta* 'association, guild' or, *sangatarāsu* 'stone-cutter' (Telugu). The 'globules' glyphic joining the two ringed necks of a pair of one-horned heifers may connote: goṭi. It may connote a forge.

Glyph: 'piece': guḍá—1. — In sense 'fruit, kernel' cert. ← Drav., cf. Tam. koṭṭai 'nut, kernel'; A. goṭ 'a fruit, whole piece', °ṭā 'globular, solid', guṭi 'small ball, seed, kernel'; B. goṭā 'seed, bean, whole'; Or. goṭā 'whole, undivided', goṭi 'small ball, cocoon', goṭāli 'small round piece of chalk'; Bi. goṭā 'seed'; Mth. goṭa 'numerative particle' (CDIAL 4271) Rebus: koṭe 'forging (metal)(Mu.) Rebus: goṭī f. 'lump of silver' (G.) goṭi = silver (G.) koḍ 'workshop' (G.). Glyph: 'two links in a chain': kaḍī a chain; a hook; a link (G.); kaḍum a bracelet, a ring (G.) Rebus: kaḍiyo [Hem. Des. kaḍaio = Skt. sthapati a mason] a bricklayer; a mason; kaḍiyaṇa, kaḍiyeṇa a woman of the bricklayer caste; a wife of a bricklayer (G.) The stone-cutter is also a mason.

kamaḍha = *ficus religiosa* (Skt.); kamar.kom 'ficus' (Santali) rebus: kamaṭa = portable furnace for melting precious metals (Te.); kampaṭṭam = mint (Ta.) Vikalpa: Fig leaf 'loa'; rebus: loh '(copper) metal'. loha-kāra 'metalsmith' (Skt.).

Text on m296 seal.

Glyphs: ayas 'fish'. Rebus: aya 'metal'. Glyph: kaṇḍa 'arrow' Rebus: 'stone (ore)metal'; kaṇḍa 'fire-altar'. ayaskāṇḍa is explained in Panini as 'excellent quantity of iron'. It can also be explained as 'metal of stone (ore) iron.'

The last sign on epigraph 5477 and 1554 (m296 seal) is read as: kole.l = smithy, temple in Kota village (Ko.)

Thus, the three text sign sequence can be explained rebus as smithy for metal of stone (ore) iron.

taṭṭai 'mechanism made of split bamboo for scaring away parrots from grain fields (Ta.); taṭṭe 'a thick bamboo or an areca-palm stem, split in two' (Ka.) (DEDR 3042) toṭxin, toṭ.xn goldsmith (To.); taṭṭāṉ 'gold- or silver-smith' (Ta.); taṭṭaravāḍu 'gold- or silver-smith' (Te.); *ṭhaṭṭakāra 'brass-worker' (Skt.)(CDIAL 5493). Thus, the glyph is decoded: taṭṭara 'worker in gold, brass'.

This is a complex, ligatured glyph with a number of glyphic elements. May denote a cast metal (copper) worker guild working with 4 types of pure metal and alloyed ingots (copper + arsenic/tin/zinc).

Glyphic element: erako nave; era = knave of wheel. Glyphic element: āra 'spokes'. Rebus: āra 'brass' as in ārakūṭa (Skt.) Rebus: Tu. eraka molten, cast (as metal); eraguni to melt (DEDR 866) erka = ekke (Tbh. of arka) aka (Tbh. of arka) copper (metal); crystal (Ka.lex.) cf. eruvai = copper (Ta.lex.) eraka, er-aka = any metal infusion (Ka.Tu.); erako molten cast (Tu.lex.) Glyphic element: kund opening in the nave or hub of a wheel to admit the axle (Santali) Rebus: kundam, kund a sacrificial fire-pit (Skt.) kunda 'turner' kundār turner (A.); kūdār, kūdāri (B.); kundāru (Or.); kundau to turn on a lathe, to carve, to chase; kundau dhiri = a hewn stone; kundau murhut = a graven image (Santali) kunda a turner's lathe (Skt.)(CDIAL 3295)

Glyphic element: 'corner': *khuṇṭa2 ' corner '. 2. *kuṇṭa -- 2. [Cf. *khōñca -- ] 1. Phal. khun ' corner '; H. khū̃ṭ m. ' corner, direction ' (→ P. khū̃ṭ f. ' corner, side '); G. khū̃ṭrī f. ' angle '. <-> X kōṇa -- : G. khuṇ f., khū̆ṇɔ m. ' corner '.2. S. kuṇḍa f. ' corner '; P. kū̃ṭ f. ' corner, side ' (← H.). (CDIAL 3898). Rebus: khū̃ṭ 'community, guild' (Mu.)

The 'U' glyphic could be baṭi 'broad-mouthed, rimless metal vessel'; rebus: baṭi 'smelting furnace'. The 'U' glyphic is a semantic determinant to emphasise that this is a temple with a smithy furnace. The structural form within which this sign is enclosed may represent a temple: kole.l 'temple, smithy' (Ko.); kolme smithy' (Ka.)

Cylinder seal: hunting scene Period: Akkadian Date: ca. 2250–2150 B.C.E. Geography:Mesopotamia Culture: Akkadian Medium: Chert Dimensions: H. 1 1/8 in. (2.8 cm) Classification: Stone-Cylinder Seal, Inscribed Credit Line: Bequest of W. Gedney Beatty, 1941 Accession Number: 41.160.192 This artwork is currently on display in Gallery 403. The pair of bull men on Akkadian cylinder seal are *ḍhangar* 'bulls'. Rebus: *ḍã̄gar* '(casting) smiths'.

m1427At One side of a two-sided Mohenjo-daro tablet. Glyph: 'heifer with two horns'.

Glyph: 'a pair of divided rectangles.

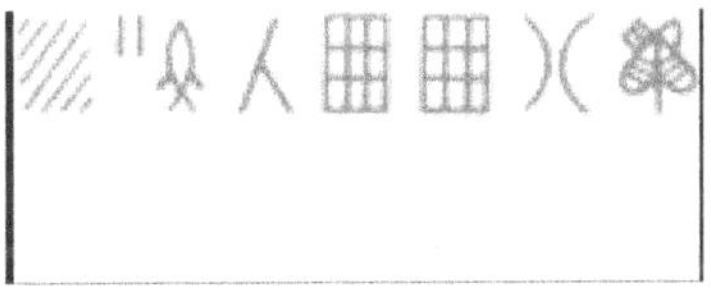

Association of glyphic element 'ficus' with glyphic element 'mountain'.*loa* 'ficus'; rebus: 'copper' gets associated with *ḍã̄ga* 'mountain', denoting *ḍã̄gar* a coppersmith. Together with a pair of goats flanking the 'mountain' glyph, the message is of a meluhhan. *mṟeka* 'goat'. milakku, mleccha 'copper'; meluhha.

Glyphic element: 'pair of divided rectangles': A comparable glyphic of two divided squares is seen on a Yale tablet. A blacksmith, turner, casting (metal) workshop.

Bull's head (bucranium) between two seated figures drinking from two vessels through straws. Decoding the bull: ḍhangar 'bull'; ḍhangar 'blacksmith' (H.) We find that on the top register, above the bull's head, the Yale tablet shows two squares with divisions flanking a circle while in the Failaka tablet shows two birds with wings flanking a tree (or corn stalk). Glyph: Skt. kuṭī- intoxicating liquor. *Ta.* kuṭi (-pp-, -tt-) to drink, inhale; *n.* drinking, beverage (DEDR 1654). Rebus: *kuṭhi* 'smelting furnace'. Glyph: ḍangra 'bull'. Rebus: ḍhangar 'blacksmith'.

Glyph: 'circle': कोंड [kōṇḍa ] *m* C A circular hedge or field-fence. 2 A circle described around a person under adjuration. 3 The circle at marbles. 4 A circular hamlet; a division of aमौजा or village, composed generally of the huts of one caste. 5 Grounds under one occupancy or tenancy. (Marathi) koṭṭa 'seed' (Ma.); •*gōṭṭa— 'something round'. [Cf. guḍá—1. — In sense 'fruit, kernel' cert. ← Drav., cf. Tam. koṭṭai 'nut, kernel'; A. goṭ 'a fruit, whole piece', °ṭā 'globular, solid', guṭi 'small ball, seed, kernel'; B. goṭā 'seed, bean, whole'; Or. goṭā 'whole, undivided', goṭi 'small ball, cocoon', goṭāli 'small round piece of chalk'; Bi. goṭā 'seed'; Mth. goṭa 'numerative particle' (CDIAL 4271) Rebus: koṭe 'forging (metal)(Mu.)

Rebus: B. kōdā 'to turn in a lathe'; Or. kũnda 'lathe', kũdibā, kũd 'to turn' (→ Drav. Kur. kũd 'lathe') (CDIAL 3295)

khaṇḍ 'field, division' (Skt.); Rebus: kaṇḍ 'furnace' (Skt.) Thus, reduplicated glyph connotes dul kaṇḍ 'casting furnace'. khonḍu 'divided into parts' (Kashmiri) A pair of such glyphs divided into parts, may thus be decoded as: dul kaṇḍ khonḍ 'casting furnace workshop'.

Kalibangan053 Sign 232

Reduplicated (mirror-imaged) mountain ridge can be decoded:

ḍagara]A slope or ascent (as of a river's bank, of a small hill). 2 unc An eminence, a mount, a little hill [ḍāṅga] m n ( H Peak or summit of a hill.) (Marathi). ṭākuro = hill top (N.); ṭāngī = hill, stony country (Or.); ṭān:gara = rocky hilly land (Or.); ḍān:gā = hill, dry upland (B.); ḍā̃g = mountain-ridge (H.)(CDIAL 5476). Rebus: ḍhaṅgar 'blacksmith' (H.) Mirror-reflected glyph: dul ḍāṅgar 'pair of hill-ranges'; rebus: dul ḍāṅgar 'caster, metalsmith'. Grapheme: kōḍu a point, the peak or top of a hill (DEDR 2049) Rebus: koḍ 'workshop' (Kuwi) koṭe 'forge' (Santali) Kui (K.) koḍi hoe. (DEDR 2064) Pa. koṭṭēti 'hews, breaks, crushes', Pk. koṭṭēi (CDIAL 3241)

Thus, the hill glyph is read rebus: dul ḍāṅgar koḍ 'blacksmith cast, forge workshop.'

Sign 17 and variants. This is a ligature of a body (with a shoulder stick) and *ficus religiosa* leaf.

m1653 ivory plaque. Text 1905

bhaṭa 'warrior'; bhaṭa 'six' (G.) rebus: baṭa = kiln (Santali); baṭa = a kind of iron (G.) bhaṭṭhī f. 'kiln, distillery', awāṇ. bhaṭh; P. bhaṭṭh m., °ṭhī f. 'furnace', bhaṭṭhā m. 'kiln'; S. bhaṭṭhī keṇī 'distil (spirits) dhātu 'mineral' (Pali)

loa 'ficus religiosa' (Santali) rebus: loh 'metal' (Skt.) Sign 17 is decode rebus: loh bhaṭa 'metal furnace'

daṭhi, daṭi the petioles and mid-ribs of a compound leaf after the leaflets have been plucked off, stalks of certain plants, as Indian corn, after the grain has been taken off (Santali) Rebus: dhatu 'mineral' (Santali)

Vikalpa: kamaṛkom = fig leaf (Santali.lex.) kamarmaṛā (Has.), kamaṛkom (Nag.); etiole or stalk of a leaf (Mundari.lex.)

kampaṭṭam coinage, coin (Ta.)(DEDR 1236) kampaṭṭa- muḷai die, coining stamp (Ta.) kammaṭṭam, kammiṭṭam coinage, mint (Ma.); kammatia coiner (Ka.)(DEDR 1236) kammaṭa = coinage, mint (Ka.M.) kampaṭṭa-k-kūṭam mint; kampaṭṭa-k-kāran- coin-maker.

m1748

The superscript ligatures can be read as suffixes: - kāra 'artisan'. kāruvu = mechanic, artisan, Vis'vakarma, the celestial artisan (Te.); kāruvu. [Skt.] n. An artist, artificer. An agent . One is a loha-kāra (metalsmith). the other is a cunda-kāra (ivory turner). Vikalpa: *kūdār* 'turner'.

Glyph: 'summit of hill': Ta. kōṭu summit of a hill, peak, mountain; kōṭar peak, summit of a tower; To. kōḍu a point, the peak or top of a hill; Tu. koḍi point, end, extremity, sprout, flag; Go. koḍi point (DEDR 2049). Rebus: 'guild': Ka. kūṭa joining, connexion, assembly; Tu. kūḍuni to join (tr.), unite, copulate, embrace, adopt; meet (intr.), assemble; Tu. kūṭa assembly, meeting, mixture; Te. kūṭami meeting, union, copulation; kūṭakamu addition, mixture (DEDR 1882).

Archaic book-keeping. Hans Jorg Nissen, Peter Damerow, Robert K. Englund, 1993, *Archaic bookkeeping: early writing and techniques of economic administration in the ancient Near East*, Univ. of Chicago Press. *Archaic Book-keeping* brings together the most current scholarship on the earliest true writing system in human history. Invented by the Babylonians at the end of the fourth millennium B.C., this script, called proto-cuneiform, survives in the form of clay tablets that have until now posed formidable barriers to interpretation. Many tablets, excavated in fragments from ancient dump sites, lack a clear context. In addition, the purpose of the earliest tablets was not to record language but to monitor the administration of local economies by means of a numerical system. Using the latest philological research and new methods of computer analysis, the authors have for the first time deciphered much of the numerical information. In reconstructing both the social context and the function of the notation, they consider how the development of our earliest written records affected patterns of thought, the concept of number, and the administration of household economies. Complete with computer-generated graphics keyed to the discussion and reproductions of all documents referred to in the text, Archaic Bookkeeping will interest specialists in Near Eastern civilizations, ancient history, the history of science and mathematics, and cognitive psychology.

Excerpted below is an article by Andrew Lawler on the problems related to decipherment of Indus script:

The Indus Script—Write or Wrong? — Andrew Lawler

Cited in a Univ. of Bern Bachelor thesis:
http://www.indoeurohome.com/LucyZuberbuehlerindusscriptmss2009.pdf

Science 17 December 2004:
Vol. 306 no. 5704 pp. 2026-2029
DOI: 10.1126/science.306.5704.2026

The Indus Script—Write or Wrong?

1. Andrew Lawler

For 130 years scholars have struggled to decipher the Indus script. Now, in a proposal with broad academic and political implications, a brash outsider claims that such efforts are doomed to failure because the Indus symbols are not writing

Academic prizes typically are designed to confer prestige. But the latest proposed award, a $10,000 check for finding a lengthy inscription from the ancient Indus civilization, is intended to goad rather than honor. The controversial scholar who announced the prize cheekily predicts that he will never have to pay up. Going against a century of scholarship, he and a growing number of linguists and archaeologists assert that the Indus people—unlike their Egyptian and Mesopotamian contemporaries 4000 years ago—could not write.

That claim is part of a bitter clash among academics, as well as between Western scientists and Indian nationalists, over the nature of the Indus society, a clash that has led to shouting matches and death threats. But the provocative proposal, summed up in a paper published online, is winning adherents within the small community of Indus scholars who say it is time to rethink an enigmatic society that spanned a vast area in today's Pakistan, India, and Afghanistan—the largest civilization of its day.

The Indus civilization has intrigued and puzzled researchers for more than 130 years, with their sophisticated sewers, huge numbers of wells, and a notable lack of monumental architecture or other signs of an elite class (see sidebar on p. 2027). Most intriguing of all is the mysterious system of symbols, left on small tablets, pots, and stamp seals. But without translations into a known script—the "Rosetta stones" that led to the decipherment of Egyptian hieroglyphics and Sumerian cuneiform in the 19th century—hundreds of attempts to understand the symbols have so far failed. And what language the system might have expressed—such as a Dravidian language similar to tongues of today's southern India, or a Vedic language of northern India—is also a hot topic. This is no dry discussion: Powerful Indian nationalists of the Hindutva movement see the Indus civilization as the direct ancestor to Hindu tradition and Vedic culture.

Searching for script.

Richard Meadow excavates at Harappa.

CREDITS: COURTESY OF THE HARAPPA ARCHAEOLOGICAL RESEARCH PROJECT/PHOTOS BY R. H. MEADOW

Now academic outsider Steve Farmer (see sidebar on p. 2028) and two established Indus scholars argue that the signs are not writing at all but rather a collection of religious-political symbols that held together a diverse and multilingual society. The brevity of most inscriptions, the relative frequencies of symbols, and the lack of archaeological evidence of a manuscript tradition add up to a sign system that does not encode language, argue historian Farmer and his co-authors, Harvard University linguist Michael Witzel and computational theorist Richard Sproat of the University of Illinois, Urbana-Champaign. Instead, they say the signs may have more in common with European medieval heraldry, the Christian cross, or a bevy of magical symbols used by prehistoric peoples.

This idea has profound implications for how the Indus civilization lived and died. Instead of the monolithic, peaceful, and centralized empire envisioned by some scholars, the authors say that the new view points to a giant multilingual society in which a system of religious-political signs provided cohesion.

Their thesis has bitterly divided the field of Indus studies, made up of a small and close-knit bunch dominated by Americans. Some respected archaeologists and linguists flatly reject it. "I categorically disagree that the script does not reflect a language," says archaeologist J. Mark Kenoyer of the University of Wisconsin, Madison, who co-directs a dig at the key site of Harappa in Pakistan. "What the heck were they doing if not encoding language?" Asko Parpola, a linguist at Finland's University of Helsinki who has worked for decades to decipher the signs, says. "There is no chance it is not a script; this is a fully formed system. It was a phonetic script." Linguist Gregory Possehl of the University of Pennsylvania in Philadelphia says that it is not possible to "prove" the script cannot be deciphered. All three argue that Farmer's thesis is a pessimistic and defeatist approach to a challenging problem. Meanwhile, the very idea that the Indus civilization was not literate is deeply offensive to many Indian nationalists.

Yet since a 2002 meeting at Harvard University at which Farmer laid out a detailed theory—and was greeted with shouts of derision—he has attracted important converts, including his co-authors. A growing cadre of scholars back the authors' approach as a fresh way to look at a vexing problem and an opportunity to shed new light on many of the mysteries that haunt Indus research. Harvard anthropologist Richard Meadow, who with Kenoyer directs the Harappa project, calls the paper "an extremely valuable contribution" that could cut the Gordian knot bedeviling the field. Sanskrit and South Asian linguist Witzel says he was shocked when he first heard Farmer's contention in 2001. "I thought I could read a few of the signs," Witzel recalls. "So I was very skeptical." Now he is throwing his scholarly weight behind the new thesis, as a co-author of the paper and also editor of the *Electronic Journal of Vedic Studies*, an online journal aimed at rapid publication, which published the paper. Adds archaeologist Steven Weber of Washington State University in Vancouver: "Sometimes it takes someone from the outside to ask the really basic questions." Weber, who is now collaborating with Farmer, adds that "the burden of proof now has to be on the people who say it is writing."

SEEKING THE WRITE STUFF

Since the 1870s, archaeologists have uncovered more than 4000 Indus inscriptions on a variety of media. Rudimentary signs appear around 3200 B.C.E.—the same era in which hieroglyphics and cuneiform began to appear in Egypt and Iraq. By 2800 B.C.E., the signs become more durable, continuing in use in later periods; the greatest diversity starts to appear around 2400 B.C.E. Some signs are highly abstract, whereas others seem to have obvious pictographic qualities, such as one that looks like a fish and another that resembles a jar. Both are used frequently; the jar sign accounts for one in 10 symbols, says Possehl. As in Mesopotamia, the signs typically appear on small tablets made of clay as well as on stamp seals. The seals often are accompanied by images of animals and plants, both real and mythical.

The signs start to diminish around 1900 B.C.E. and vanish entirely by 1700 B.C.E., when the Indus culture disappears. Oddly, the inscriptions are almost all found in trash dumps rather than in graves or in primary contexts such as the floor of a home. "They were thrown away like expired credit cards," says Meadow.

No one had ever seriously questioned whether the signs are a form of writing. But scholars hotly debate whether the system is phonetic like English or Greek or logosyllabic—using a combination of symbols that encode both sound and concepts—like cuneiform or hieroglyphics. Even the number of signs is controversial. Archaeologist and linguist S. R. Rao of India's University of Goa has proposed a sign list of only 20, but Harvard graduate student Bryan Wells is compiling a revised list now numbering 700; most estimates hover in the 400 range.

Farmer and colleagues reanalyzed the signs, drawing on published data from many sites and unpublished data from the Harappa project provided by Meadow. They found that the average Indus inscription, out of a total of 4000 to 5000 in a 1977 compilation, has 4.6 signs. The longest known inscription contains 17 signs, and fewer than 1% are as long as 10 symbols. The authors argued that such short "texts" are unprecedented for actual writing. Although many scholars assert that longer inscriptions may have been made on perishable materials, the authors note that there is no archaeological evidence of the imperishable paraphernalia that typically accompanies literate culture, such as inkpots, rock inscriptions, or papermaking devices.

Farmer and colleagues also take apart a long-held assumption that the frequent repetition of a small number of Indus signs is evidence of a script encoding language. About 12% of an average English text, for example, consists of the letter "E," often used repeatedly in a single sentence to express a certain sound. In contrast, the paper notes that very few Indus symbols are repeated within individual inscriptions, implying that the signs do not encode sounds.

Further, the authors note that many Indus symbols are incredibly rare. Half of the symbols appear only once, based on Wells's catalog; three-quarters of the signs appear five times or fewer. According to the 1977 compilation put together by Iravatham Mahadevan, an Indian linguist now retired in Chennai, India, more than one-fourth of all signs appear only once, and more than half show up five times or fewer. Rarely used signs likely would not encode sound, says Farmer. It is as if many symbols "were invented on the fly, only to be abandoned after being used once or a handful of times," he, Witzel, and Sproat write.

Short and sweet.

Most Indus inscriptions are short.

CREDIT: COURTESY OF THE HARAPPA ARCHAEOLOGICAL RESEARCH PROJECT/PHOTOS BY R. H. MEADOW

Farmer believes that the symbols have nonlinguistic meaning. He speculates that the signs may have been considered magical—as the Christian cross can be—and indicated individuals or clans, cities or professions, or gods. He and his colleagues compare the Indus script to inscriptions found in prehistoric southeastern Europe around 4000 B.C.E., where the Vinca culture produced an array of symbols often displayed in a linear form, including a handful used frequently.

But these conclusions are not accepted by key archaeologists and linguists who have spent their careers digging at Harappa or trying to decipher the symbols. "Regularities in the frequency and distribution of signs are possible only in a linguistic script," says Mahadevan. Wells is more blunt. "He is utterly wrong," he says of Farmer. "There is something you recognize as an epigrapher immediately, such as long linear patterns."

As to the brevity of inscriptions, Wells says averages can be misleading. The longer Indus inscriptions, he says, can't be explained as magical symbols. Vinca symbols, for example, rarely are grouped in numbers greater than five. "And you don't get repetitive ordering" as with Indus signs, he adds. "The Indus script is a highly patterned, highly ordered system with a syntax—it just looks too much like writing." Wells also says that a mere 30 signs are used only once, rather than the 1000 Farmer postulates, because many of the "singletons" transform into compound signs used repeatedly.

Parpola agrees that the pattern of symbols argues for an organized script. "There are a limited number of standardized signs, some repeated hundreds of times—with the same shape, recurring combinations, and regular lines," he says. But Wells and Parpola, like most linguists in the field, agree on little beyond their opposition to Farmer. Wells rejects Parpola's method of deciphering the signs, and Parpola dismisses Wells's contention that there are significant differences between the signs of upper and lower Indus.

Wells and some other scholars believe that the attraction of Farmer's idea has less to do with science than with the long history of decipherment failures. "Some have turned to this idea that it is not writing out of frustration," he says.

Sign or script?

Farmer says Indus seals (left), like Vinca signs (right) are not writing.

CREDIT: COURTESY OF THE HARAPPA ARCHAEOLOGICAL RESEARCH PROJECT/PHOTOS BY R. H. MEADOW

But many others are convinced that Farmer, Witzel, and Sproat have found a way to move away from sterile discussions of decipherment, and they find few flaws in their arguments. "They have settled the issue for me," says George Thompson, a Sanskrit scholar at Montserrat College of Art in Beverly, Massachusetts. "We have the work of a comparative historian, a computational linguist, and a Vedicist," he adds. "Together they have changed the landscape regarding the whole question." In a forthcoming book on South Asian linguistic archaeology, Frank Southworth of the University of Pennsylvania calls the paper an "unexpected solution" to the old troubles with decipherment.

Meanwhile, Farmer is injecting a bit of fun into the melee. "Find us just one inscription with 50 symbols on it, in repeating symbols in the kinds of quasi-random patterns associated with true scripts, and we'll consider our model falsified," he wrote on a listserve devoted to the Indus. And he is putting his money—or, rather, that of a donor he won't reveal—where his mouth is, promising the winner $10,000. The orthodox dismiss the prize as grandstanding, whereas Farmer boasts that "no one is ever going to collect that money."

RETRENCHING

Each side clearly has far to go to convince its opponents. "I'm not sure the case is strong enough on either side," says linguist Hans Hock of the University of Illinois, Urbana-Champaign. "Let each side of the controversy make their case."

Yet there already is a retreat from earlier claims that the Indus symbols represent a full-blown writing system and that they encoded speech. Many scholars such as Possehl now acknowledge that the signs likely are dominated by names of places, people, clans, plants, and gods rather than by the narratives found in ancient Sumer or Egypt. They say the script may be more similar to the first stages of writing in those lands. Harvard archaeologist Carl Lamberg-Karlovsky says the meanings of the Indus signs likely are "impenetrable and imponderable" and adds that whether or not the signs are considered writing, they clearly are a form of communication—and that is what really counts. Recent research in Central and South America has highlighted how complex societies prospered without traditional writing, such as the knotted strings or khipu of the vast Incan empire (*Science*, 2 July, p. 30).

Literacy promoter.

J. Mark Kenoyer, on the dig at Harappa, thinks Indus signs are script.

CREDIT: COURTESY OF THE HARAPPA ARCHAEOLOGICAL RESEARCH PROJECT/PHOTOS BY R. H. MEADOW

Farmer adds that a society does not need to be literate to be complex. "A big, urban civilization can be held together without writing," he says. He and his co-authors suggest that the Indus likely had many tongues and was a rich mix of ethnicities like India today. Wells has found marked differences between signs in the upper and lower Indus River regions, backing up the theory of a more diverse society. But some, such as D. P. Agrawal, an independent archaeologist based in Almora, India, doubt that a civilization spread over more than 1 million square kilometers, and with uniform weights, measures, and developed trade, could manage its affairs without a script.

This debate over Indus literacy has political as well as academic consequences. "This will be seen as an attack on the greatness of Indian civilization—which would be unfortunate," says Shereen Ratnagar, a retired archaeologist who taught at Delhi's Nehru University. Tension is already high between some Western and Indian scholars and Indian nationalists. "Indologists are at war with the Hindutva polemicists," says statistical linguist Lars Martin Fosse of the University of Oslo, and the issue of the script "is extremely sensitive." Farmer says he regularly receives e-mail viruses and death threats from Indian nationalists who oppose his views.

For decades, Indus researchers have tended to stick with their established positions, as on the script, a tendency that has kept the field from moving forward, says one archaeologist who compares the small cadre of Indus scholars to a "dysfunctional family" with a proclivity for secrecy, ideological positions, and intolerance. Meadow is among those who argue that it is time to set aside old ideas, no matter how much time and effort has been invested in them, in order to push the field forward. "We're here to do science, and it is always valuable to have new models," he says. Adds Ratnagar: "We must get back to an open mind." Given the strong emotions swirling around the Indus symbols, discovering the key to that open mind may prove the hardest code to break.

http://www.sciencemag.org/content/306/5704/2026.full

Bryan Wells' thesis has been published in 2011. Bryan Wells, 2011, *Epigraphic Approaches to Indus Writing*, Oxbow Books, David Brown Book Co., ISBN 9781842179949 "Epigraphic Approaches to Indus Writing is a comprehensive look at one of the last undeciphered Old World scripts. It has defied decipherment for 90 years because of the terse nature of the texts and the lack of a comprehensive corpus and detailed sign list. This book presents the analysis of a comprehensive, computer-based corpus using the most detailed sign list yet compiled for the Indus script. Custom computer programs allowed the verification of the sign list and the compilation of statistics regarding sign distribution and use. Questions such as: How do you create an epigraphic database? How do you define a sign? What is the Indus number system like? Where did the Indus Script come from? and What is the Indus Language(s)? are all addressed." The book has a forward by C. C. Lamberg-Karlovsky.

Wells has studied the Indus Script since 1992. It was a controversial topic for his Ph.D. thesis (Harvard U.), because he had to defend his conviction that it is, indeed, script. The subject continues to be controversial. He distinguishes 676 graphemes in the Indus script and argues that the Indus language can't possibly be Dravidian but most likely is Munda. Bryan Wells is almost right, but he has to take a new look at the Indian *sprachbund*, as has been done in this book using the over 8000 semantic clusters in my *Indian Lexicon* to show that the hieroglyphs encoded speech. So did, for e.g., the hieroglyphs on Narmer Palette – to name N'r M'r -- and the Uruk (Warka) vase – goat-fish ligatured animal to name the metallurgical processes of the evolving bronze age artisans. I suggest that the Indus Language was a *sprachbund*, a language union.

There is evidence that Meluhha people settled in Mesopotamia (Vermaak 2008).

As Asko Parpola notes ('Hind leg' + 'fish': towards further understanding of the Indus script, 2008, Hunmin jeongeum Society's 'Scripta 2008' Conference, 9-10 October 2008, Seoul. SCRIPTA, Volume 1 (September 2009: 37-76). http://www.harappa.com/script/script-indus-parpola.pdf): "Proto-Elamite texts have been found as far east as Tepe Yahya in Kerman (cf. Damerow & Englund 1989) and Shahr-i Sokht in Seistan (cf. Englund 2004: 103; Lamberg-Karlovsky 1978; Potts 1999: 81-83. Shahr-i Sokhta was in contact with the Early Harappan sites of Pakistani Baluchistan in 3000-2600 BCE (cf. Biscione 1984). In 1994, at Miri Qalat, a site later occupied y the Indus Civilization (cf. Besenval 1997: 207-210). A some iconogrpahic motifs of the Indus seals moreover seem to go back to Proto-Elamite models (cf. Parpola 1984), it appears possible that the Early Harappans obtained the idea of writing from the Proto-Elamites during the first quarter of the third millennium. In any case the Early Harappans did not copy Proto-Elamite script signs, but devised their own, adopting local symbols, some of which we know from the 'potter's marks' and motifs of painted pottery." The notion that Early Harappans obtained the idea of writing from Proto-Elamites during the first quarter of the third millennium is belied by the evidence of HARP which produced a potsherd with inscription dated to c. 3300 BCE. There is evidence for contact and interactions between Meluhha and Proto-Elamite people. There is not enough enough to surmise who learnt the art of writing from whom. Just as Abydos evidence shows that a single sign could represent a word, the evidence of Indus script inscriptions also shows that a single glyph can connote the sounds of speech related to single words.

On Archaic Egyptian script, dated to c. 3200 BCE, Baines notes: "The earliest recognizable writing from a secure archaeological context is on tags originally attached to grave goods in the royal tomb U-j at Abydos and on pottery from the same tomb...Its system, although very limited, appears well formed and its repertoire includes the royal throne and palace facade' which accompany the names of later Predynastic kings. At least four pre-1st Dynasty kings can be identified...Although the readings of their names are uncertain, the script was quite developed; words were encoded both in logographic form -- with a single sign writing a complete word -- and phonetically... By the early 1st Dynasty, almost all the uniconsonantl signs are attested, as well as the use of classifiers or determinatives, so that the writing system was in essence fully formed even though a very limited range of material was written. Many inscribed artifacts are preserved from the first two Dynasties, the most numerous categories being cylinder seals and sealings, cursive annotations on pottery, and tags originally attached to tomb equipment, especially of the 1st Dynasty kings. Continuous language was stil not recorded." (Baines 1999: 882-883). [The tomb U-j of a Predynastic king (probably 'Scorpion') at Umm el-Qa'ab near Abydos was excavated in 1988 and its c. 150 bone tags, as well as the pottery inscriptions and sealings were published ten years later (Dreyer 1998).]

Baines, John (1999), Writing, invention and early development, pp. 882-885 in: Kathryn A. Bard (ed.), *Encyclopedia of the archaeology of ancient Egypt*. London and New York: Routledge.

-- (2004), The earliest Egyptian writing: development, context, purpose, pp. 150-189 in: Houston, Stephen D. (ed.) 2004, *The first writing: Script invention as history and process.* Cambridge: Cambridge University Press.

Besenval, R. (1997), The chronology of ancient occupation in Makran: Results of the 1994 season at Miri Qalat, Pakistani Makran, pp. 199-216 in: Raymond Allchin and Bridget Allchin (eds.), *South Asian Archaeology,* 1995, I. Cambridge: The Ancient India and Iran Trust.

Biscione, Raffaele (1984), Baluchistan presence in the ceramic assemblage of Period I at Shahr-i Sokhta, pp. 69-84 in: Bridget and Raymond Allchin (eds.), *South Asian Archaeology 1981.* Cambridge: Cambridge University Press.

Damerow, Peter and Robert K. Englund (1989), *The Proto-Elamite texts from Tepe Yahya* (The American School of Prehistoric Research Bulletin 39). Cambridge, MA: Peabody Museum of Archaeology and Ethnology.

Daniels, Peter T. (1996), Methods of decipherment, pp. 141-159 in: Peter T. Daniels and William Bright (eds.), *The world's writing systems.* New York: Oxford University Press.

Dreyer, Günter (1998), *Umm el-Qaab I: Das prädynastische Königsgrab U-j und seine frühen Schriftzeugnisse* (Archäologische Veröffentlichungen 86). Mainz: Verlag Philipp von Zabern.

Englund, Robert K. (1996), The Proto-Elamite script, pp. 160-164 in: Peter T. Daniels and William Bright (eds.), *The world's writing systems*, New York: Oxford University Press.

-- (1998), Texts from the Late Uruk Period, pp. 13-233 in: Josef Bauer, Robert K. Englund & Manfred Krebernik, *Mesopotamien: Spaturuk-Zeit und Fruhdynastische Zeit* (Orbis Biblicus et Orientalis 160/1). Freiburg (Schweiz): Univrsitatsverlag & Gottingen:Vandenhoeck & Ruprecht.

-- (2004), The state of decipherment of Proto-Elamite, pp. 100-149 in: Houston (ed.) 2004.

Honoré, Emmanuelle (2007), Earliest cylinder-seal glyptic in Egypt: From Greater Mesopotamia to Naqada, pp. 31-45 in: Hany Hanna (ed.), *The international conference on heritage of Naqada and Qus region, January 22-28, 2007, Naqada, Egypt*, Vol. I. Alexandria: ICOM.

Koskenniemi, Kimmo (1981), Syntactic methods in the study of the Indus script, *Studia Orientalia* 50: 125-136.

Koskenniemi, Kimmo & Asko Parpola (1979), Corpus of texts in the Indus script (Department of Asian and African Studies, University of Helsinki, Research reports 1). Helsinki.

______ (1980), Documentation and duplicates of the texts in the Indus script (Department of Asian and African Studies, University of Helsinki, Research reports 2). Helsinki.

______ (1982), A concordance to the texts in the Indus script (Department of Asian and African Studies, University of Helsinki, Research reports 3). Helsinki.

Koskenniemi, Seppo, Asko Parpola & Simo Parpola (1970), A method to classify characters of unknown ancient scripts, *Linguistics* 61: 65-91.

______ (1973), *Materials for the study of the Indus script, I: A concordance to the Indus inscriptions* (Annales Academiae Scientiarum Fennicae, B 185). Helsinki: Suomalainen Tiedeakatemia.

Parpola, Asko (1975a), Tasks, methods and results in the study of the Indus script, *Journal of the Royal Asiatic Society of Great Britain and Ireland* 1975(2): 178-209.

______ (1975b), Isolation and tentative interpretation of a toponym in the Harappan inscriptions, pp. 121-143 in: Jean Leclant (ed.), *Le déchiffrement des écritures et des langues: Colloque du XXIXe Congrès International des Orientalistes.* Paris: L'Asiathèque.

______ (1990), Astral proper names in India: An analysis of the oldest sources, with argumentation of an ultimately Harappan origin, *The Adyar Library Bulletin* 53: 1-53.

______ (1994), *Deciphering the Indus Script.* Cambridge: Cambridge University Press.

______ (1997a), *Deciphering the Indus script: Methods and select interpretations*, Keynote address delivered at the 25th Annual South Asia Conference, University of Wisconsin, Madison, Wisconsin, 18-20 October 1996 (Occasional Papers Series, 2). Madison: Center for South Asia, University of Wisconsin-Madison.

______ (1997b), Dravidian and the Indus script: On the interpretation of some pivotal signs, *Studia Orientalia* 82: 167-191.

______ (2005), Study of the Indus script, *Proceedings of the International Conference of Eastern Studies* 50: 28-66. Tokyo: The Tôhô Gakkai.

______ (2008a), Is the Indus script indeed not a writing system?, pp. 111-131 in: *Airāvati: Felicitation volume in honour of Iravatham Mahadevan*. Chennai: Varalaaru.com. http://www.harappa.com/script/indus-writing.pdf

______ (2008b), Copper tablets from Mohenjo-daro and the study of the Indus script, pp. 132-139 in: Eric Olijdam & Richard H. Spoor (eds.), *Intercultural relations between South and Southwest Asia: Studies in commemoration of E. C. L. During Caspers (1934-1996)* (BAR International Series 1826). Oxford: Archaeopress.

______ (2009) (in press), The Indus script as a key to the Harappan language and religion: Methods and results of a limited decipherment, *Horizons: Seoul Journal of Humanities* 1.

---------- (2009). 'Hind leg' + 'fish': towards further understanding of the Indus script, 2008, Hunmin jeongeum Society's 'Scripta 2008' Conference, 9-10 October 2008, Seoul. *SCRIPTA*, Volume 1 (September 2009: 37-76)

Parpola, Asko, Seppo Koskenniemi, Simo Parpola & Pentti Aalto (1969a), Decipherment of the Proto-Dravidian inscriptions of the Indus Civilization: A first announcement (The Scandinavian Institute of Asian Studies, Special Publications, 1). Copenhagen.

______ (1969b), Progress in the decipherment of the Proto-Dravidian Indus script (The Scandinavian Institute of Asian Studies, Special Publications, 2). Copenhagen.

______ (1970), Further progress in the Indus script decipherment (The Scandinavian Institute of Asian Studies, Special Publications 3). Copenhagen.

Parpola, Päivikki (1988), On the synthesis of context-free grammars, pp. 133-141 in: Matti Mäkelä, Seppo Linnainmaa and Esko Ukkonen (eds.), *STeP-88 (Finnish artificial intelligence symposium, University of Helsinki, August 15-18, 1988)* I. Helsinki.

Pope, Maurice (1999), *The story of decipherment: From Egyptian Hieroglyphic to Maya script*, Revised ed. London: Thames and Hudson Ltd.

Potts, D. T. (1999), *The archaeology of Elam: Formation and transformation of an ancient Iranian state*. Cambridge: Cambridge University Press.

Ray, John D. (1986), The emergence of writing in Egypt, *World Archaeology* 17(3): 307-316.

Ritner, Robert K. (1996), Egyptian writing, pp. 73-87 in: Peter T. Daniels and William Bright (eds.), *The world's writing systems*. New York: Oxford University Press.

Robinson, Andrew (2002), *Lost Languages: The enigma of the world's undeciphered scripts.* New York: McGraw Hill.

Vermaak, P.S. (2008), Guabba, the Meluh□h□an village in Mesopotamia, *Journal for Semitics* 17(2): 454-71.

The inscription showing a 'five-petal glyph' on potsherd h1522A finds many parallels. Impression from a cylinder seal. urseal6 Cylinder seal; BM 122947; U. 16220 (cut down into Ur III mausolea from Larsa level; U. 16220), enstatite; Legrain, 1951, No. 632; Collon, 1987, Fig. 611.Humped bull stands before a plant, feeding from a round manger or a bundle of fodder (or, probably, a cactus); behind the bull is a scorpion and two snakes; above the whole a human figure, placed horizontally, with fantastically long arms and legs, and rays about his head.

adar ḍangra 'zebu or humped bull'; rebus: aduru 'native metal' (Ka.); ḍhangar 'blacksmith' (H.)

The glyph is *taberna Montana*, 'mountain tulip'.

Glyph, taberna montana

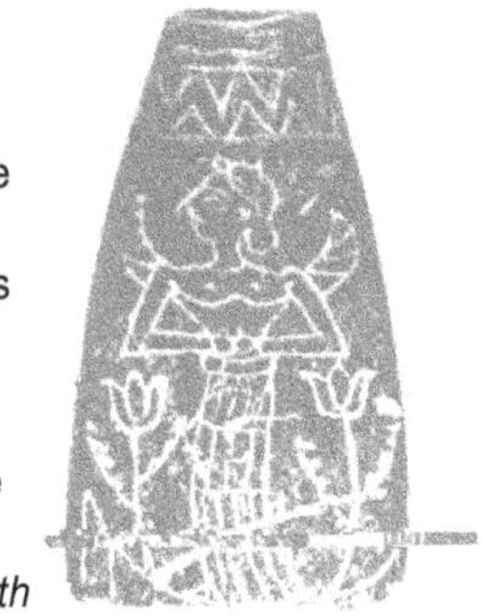

A soft-stone flask, 6 cm. tall, from Bactria (northern Afghanistan) showing a winged female deity (?) flanked by two flowers similar to those shown on the comb from Tell Abraq.(After Pottier, M.H., 1984, *Materiel funeraire e la Bactriane meridionale de l'Age du Bronze*, Paris, Editions Recherche sur les Civilisations: plate 20.150)

Ivory comb with Mountain Tulip motif and dotted circles. TA 1649 Tell Abraq.(D.T. Potts, South and Central Asian elements at Tell Abraq (Emirate of Umm al-Qaiwain, United Arab Emirates), c. 2200 BC—AD 400, in Asko Parpola and Petteri Koskikallio, *South Asian Archaeology 1993*: , pp. 615-666).

Tell Abraq axe with epigraph ('tulip' glyph + a person raising his arm above his shoulder and wielding a tool + dotted circles on body) [After Fig. 7 Holly Pittman, 1984, *Art of the Bronze Age: Southeastern Iran, Western Central Asia, and the Indus Valley*, New York, The Metropolitan Museum of Art, pp. 29-30].

Glyph: eṛaka 'upraised arm' (Ta.); rebus: eraka = copper (Ka.) kandi 'beads' (Pa.)(DEDR 1215). Rebus: khaṇḍaran, khaṇḍrun 'pit furnace' (Santali) meḍ 'body' (M.); Rebus: meḍh 'helper of merchant' (Pkt.)

tagar = a flowering shrub; a plant in bloom (G.lex.) tagara = the shrub tabernaemontana coronaria, and a fragrant powder or perfume obtained from it, incense (Vin 1.203); tagara-mallika_ two kinds of gandha_ (P.lex.) ṭagara (tagara) a spec. plant; fragrant wood (Pkt.Skt.) tagara = a kind of flowering tree (Te.lex.) This is a flower, tagaraka, used as a hair-fragrance (Skt.) and hence is also depicted on a bonecomb. Signs, 162, 163, 169 sign variants. Rebus: takaram 'tin' (Ta.) Thus the set of glyphics carved on the Tell Abraq axe can be read rebus: *tagara eraka khaṇḍaran* '(out of) tin copper furnace', a description of the ingredients of the bronze alloy used to produce the axe.

Glyphic element 'thorny, thorn': ran:ga ron:ga, ran:ga con:ga = thorny, spikey, armed with thorns; edel dare ran:ga con:ga dareka = this cotton tree grows with spikes on it (Santali)

Rebus: tagromi 'tin, metal alloy' (Kuwi) ran:ga, ran: pewter is an alloy of tin lead and antimony (añjana) (Santali). takaram tin, white lead, metal sheet, coated with tin (Ta.); tin, tinned iron plate (Ma.); tagarm tin (Ko.); tagara, tamara, tavara id. (Ka.) tamaru, tamara, tavara id. (Ta.): tagaramu, tamaramu, tavaramu id. (Te.); ṭagromi tin metal, alloy (Kuwi); tamara id. (Skt.)(DEDR 3001). trapu tin (AV.); tipu (Pali); tau, taua lead (Pkt.); tū_ tin (P.); ṭau zinc, pewter (Or.); tarūaum lead (OG.); tarvu~ (G.); tumba lead (Si.)(CDIAL 5992).

Glyph: ṭakkarā f. ' blow on the head ' Rājat. [Cf. *ṭakk -- 2] Pk. ṭakkara -- m. ' collision ', K. ṭakara m.; S. ṭakaru m. ' knocking the head against anything, butting ', ṭakiraṇu ' to knock against, encounter, be compared with '; L. ṭakkaraṇ ' to meet, agree '; P. ṭakkar f. ' pushing, knocking ', ṭakkarṇā ' to collide, meet '; Ku. ṭakkar ' shock, jerk, loss '; N. ṭakar ' obstacle, collision '; B. ṭakkar ' blow ', Or. ṭakkara, ṭākara, H. G. M. ṭakkar f. (CDIAL 6701) தகரார் takarār , n. < Arab. takrar. Colloq. 1. Altercation, objection. ṭakkarā -- : S.kcch. ṭakrāṇū ' to collide ', G. ṭakrāvũ AKŚ 37. *dhakk ' push, strike '. [dhakkayati ' annihilates ' Dhātup.]K. daka m. ' a push, blow ', S. dhaku m., L. P. dhakkā m.; Ku. dhakkā ' collision ', dhǎ̄kā ' forcibly pushing '; N. dhakkā ' collision, push '; B. dhǎ̄kkā ' push ', Or. dhakā; H. dhak m. ' shock, sudden terror ', dhakkā m. ' push '; OMarw. dhakā -- dhakī f. ' rush '; G. dhakkɔ m. ' push ', M. dhakā, ḍhakā m.; -- P. dhakkṇā ' to push, oust '; -- S. dhakiṛaṇu ' to half -- clean rice by beating it in a mortar '; -- Ku. dhakelṇo ' to push ', N. dhakelnu, H. dhakelnā, ḍha°, G. dhakelvũ. *dhakk -- : S.kcch. dhakko ḍeṇo ' to push '; WPah.kṭg. dhàkkɔ m. ' push, dash ', J. dhākā m.(CDIAL 5424). L. *ḍakkaṇ*, (Ju.) *ḍa°* ' to stop, obstruct '; P. *ḍakkṇā* ' to block up, hinder ', *ḍakk* m. ' hindrance ', *ḍakkā* m. ' plug '. (CDIAL 5518). Ka. (Jenu Kuruba, LSB 4.12) dūku, (HavS.) dūku, (Bark.) dūki, (Coorg) dūku to push (or with 3722 Ta. nūkku). Kur. tukknā to give a push to, shove. Malt. tuke to push, remove. (DEDR 3286) Ka. tagalu, tagilu, tagulu to come in contact with, touch; taguḷisu to chase, drive away; Te. tagulucu to cause to touch; taguluḍu, taguludala touching, contact, catching, addictedness; taguluvaḍu to be caught, seized, or entangled. Konḍa tagli (-t-) to touch, hit. (DEDR 3004) Ta. takai (-v-, -nt-) to stop, resist, check, deter, obstruct or forbid by oath, seize, take hold of, overpower, subdue, shut in, enclose, include, bind, fasten, yoke; (-pp-, -tt-) to check, resist, stop, deter, bind, fasten; n. binding, fastening, garland, obstruction, check, hindrance, armour, coat of mail; takaippu surrounding wall, fortress, palatial building, section of house, apartment, battle array of an army. Ka. taga, tagave, tagahu, tage delay, obstacle, hindrance, impediment; tage to stop, arrest, obstruct, impede, stun; tagar to be stopped or impeded, impede, etc. (DEDR 3006).

Allograph: Ta. takar sheep, ram, goat, male of certain other animals (yāḷi, elephant, shark). பொருநகர் தாக்கற்குப் பேருந் தகைத்து (குறள், 486).Ma. takaran huge, powerful as a man, bear, etc. Ka. tagar, ṭagaru, ṭagara, ṭegaru ram. Tu. tagaru, ṭagarů id. Te. tagaramu, tagaru id. / Cf. Mar. tagar id. (DEDR 3000).

Allograph: ṭagara1 ' squinting ' lex. [Cf. ṭēraka -- ] H. ṭagrā ' cross -- eyed ' (CDIAL 5425).

Rebus: worker in stone: टकारी or टंकारी [ ṭakārī or ṭaṅkārī ] m (टंक) A caste or an individual of it. They are workers in stone, makers of handmills &c. टंकशाला [ ṭaṅkaśālā ] f (S) pop. टंकसाळ or टकसाळ f A mint. ṭaṅka1 m.n. ' weight of 4 māṣas ' ŚārṅgS., ' a stamped coin ' Hit., °aka -- m. ' a silver coin ' lex. 2. ṭaṅga -- 1 m.n. ' weight of 4 māṣas ' lex. 3. *ṭakka -- 1. [Bloch IA 59 ← Tatar tanka (Khot. tanka = kārṣāpaṇa S. Konow Saka Studies 184)]1. Pk. ṭaṁka -- m. ' a stamped coin H. ṭā̃k m. ' a partic. weight '; G. ṭā̃k f. ' a partic. weight equivalent to 1/72 ser '; M. ṭā̃k m. ' a partic. weight '.2. H. ṭaṅgā m. ' a coin worth 2 paisā '. P. ṭakā m. ' a copper coin '; Ku. ṭākā ' two paisā '; N. ṭako ' money '; A. ṭakā ' rupee ', B. ṭākā; Mth. ṭakā, ṭakkā, ṭakwā ' money ', Bhoj. ṭākā; H. ṭakā m. ' two paisā coin ', G. ṭakɔ m., M. ṭakā (CDIAL 5426). ṭaṅka2 m.n. ' spade, hoe, chisel ' R. 2. ṭaṅga -- 2 m.n. ' sword, spade ' lex. 1. Pa. ṭaṅka -- m. ' stone mason's chisel '; Pk. ṭaṁka -- m. ' stone -- chisel, sword '; Woṭ. ṭhõ ' axe '; Bshk. ṭhoṅ ' battleaxe ', ṭheṅ ' small axe ' (< *ṭaṅkī); Tor. (Biddulph) "tunger" m. ' axe ' (ṭ? AO viii 310), Phal. ṭhõ˘ṅgi f.; K. ṭõṅguru m. ' a kind of hoe '; N. (Tarai) ṭā̃gi ' adze '; H. ṭā̃kī f. ' chisel '; G. ṭā̃k f. ' pen nib '; M. ṭā̃k m. ' pen nib ', ṭā̃kī f. ' chisel '.2. A. ṭāṅgi ' stone chisel '; B. ṭāṅg, °gi ' spade, axe '; Or. ṭāṅgi ' battle -- axe '; Bi. ṭā̃gā, °gī ' adze '; Bhoj. ṭāṅī ' axe '; H. ṭā̃gī f. ' hatchet '.(CDIAL 5427).*ṭaṅkati2 ' chisels '. [ṭaṅka -- 2] Pa. ṭaṅkita -- mañca -- ' a stone (i.e. chiselled) platform '; G. ṭā̃kvũ ' to chisel ', M. ṭā̃kṇẽ. (CDIAL 5433).ṭaṅkaśālā -- , ṭaṅkakaś° f. ' mint ' lex. [ṭaṅka -- 1, śā'lā -- ] N. ṭaksāl, °ār, B. ṭāksāl, ṭā̃k°, ṭek°, Bhoj. ṭaksār, H. ṭaksāl, °ār f., G. ṭā̃ksāḷ f., M. ṭā̃ksāl, ṭāk°, ṭāk°, ṭak°. -- Deriv. G. ṭaksāḷī m. ' mint -- master ', M. ṭāksāḷyā m. ṭaṅkaśālā -- : Brj. ṭaksāḷī, °sārī m. ' mint -- master '.(CDIAL 5434).

Rebus 2: soldering: ṭáṅkati1, ṭaṅkáyati ' ties ' Dhātup. 2. *ṭañcati.1. S. ṭākaṇu ' to stitch ', ṭā̃ko m. ' a stitch '; Ku. ṭā̃ko ' sewing, joining, patch '; N. ṭā̃knu ' to join, tack, button up ', ṭā̃ko ' stitch, seam '; A. ṭākiba ' to tie loosely '; B. ṭā̃kā ' to stitch ', Or. ṭāṅkibā, ṭāk ' hand -- stitching '; Bhoj. ṭā̃kal ' to sew '; H.

ṭā̃knā ' to stitch, join, rivet, solder ', ṭā̃kā m. ' stitch, join '; G. ṭā̃kvũ ' to stitch ', ṭā̃kɔ m., M. ṭā̃kā, ṭākā m.2. G. ṭā̃cvũ ' to stitch ', ṭā̃cṇī f. ' small pin '; M. ṭā̃ċṇẽ, ṭāċ° ' to sew lightly ', ṭā̃ċṇī, ṭāċ° f. ' pin '.

Wild tulip motif

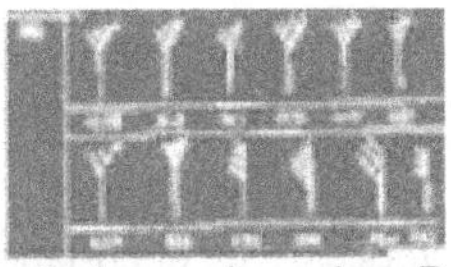

Wild tulip is a motif that occurs on southeast Iranian cylinder seals and on Persian Gulf seals. 1st row: Bactrian artifacts; 2nd row: a comb from the Gulf area and late trans-Elamite seals [After Marie-Helene Pottier, 1984, Materiel funeraire de la Bactriane meridionale de l'age du bronze, Recherche sur les Civilizations, Memoire 36, Paris, fig. 21; Sarianidi, V.I., 1986, Le complexe culturel de Togolok 21 en Margiane, Arts Asiatiques 41: fig. 6,21; Potts, 1994, fig. 53,8; Amiet, 1986, fig. 132]. Bone comb with Mountain Tulip motif and dotted circles. TA 1649 Tell Abraq, United Arab Emirates. Ivory comb with Mountain Tulip motif and dotted circles. TA 1649 Tell Abraq. [D.T. Potts, South and Central Asian elements at Tell Abraq (Emirate of Umm al-Qaiwain, United Arab Emirates), c. 2200 BC—AD 400, in Asko Parpola and Petteri Koskikallio, South Asian Archaeology 1993: , pp. 615-666] The ivory comb found at Tell Abraq measures 11 X 8.2 X .4 cm. Both sides of the comb bear identical, incised decoration in the form of two long-stemmed flowers with crenate or dentate leaves, flanking three dotted circles arranged in a triangular pattern. Bone and ivory combs with dotted-circle decoration are well-known in the Harappan area (e.g. at Chanhu-daro and Mohenjo-daro), but none of the Harappan combs bear the distinctive floral motif of the Tell Abraq comb. These flowers are identified as tulips, perhaps Mountain tulip or Boeotian tulip (both of which grow in Afghanistan) which have an undulate leaf. There is a possibility that the comb is an import from Bactria, perhaps transmitted through Meluhha to the Oman Peninsula site of Tell Abraq.

Indus script sign variants show such a five-petalled tulip, a glyph on the Early Harappan Ravi phase potsherd – h1522A (with five petals as in *taberna montana*, tagaraka). The variants are stylized as Sign 162 (with three prongs) and Sign 165 (with five petals). Sign 167 shows five petals (and variants show many more branches or petals (and somet times less number of petals):

Variants of Sign 169 (One possibility is that the scribe chose to represent two distinct rebus readings: Sign 162 with three petals to be read as kolmo 'paddy plant'; and Sign 169 with five petals to be read as tagaraka '*taberna montana* wild tulip'.

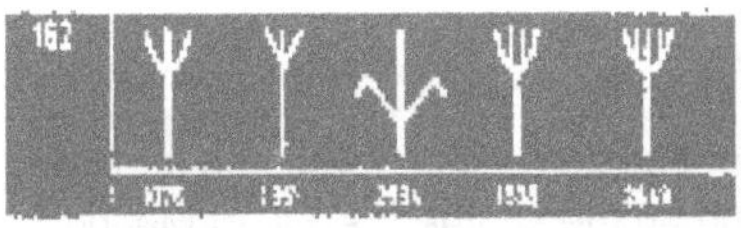

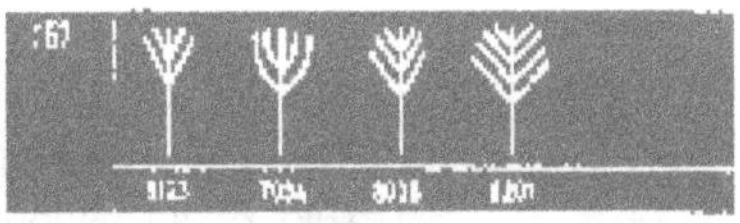

Seal impression from Harappa (Kenoyer, 1998); a woman is carrying a three-petalled flower.

If a three-petalled glyph is a variant of the 'tulip – five-petalled' glyph, the following occurrences including the seal of Altyn-tepe have to be viewed as a representation of 'tin' mineral – and not tht of a *kolmo* 'paddy-plant', but *tagaraka*, 'taberna montana'. The sign also is ligatured to form other signs:

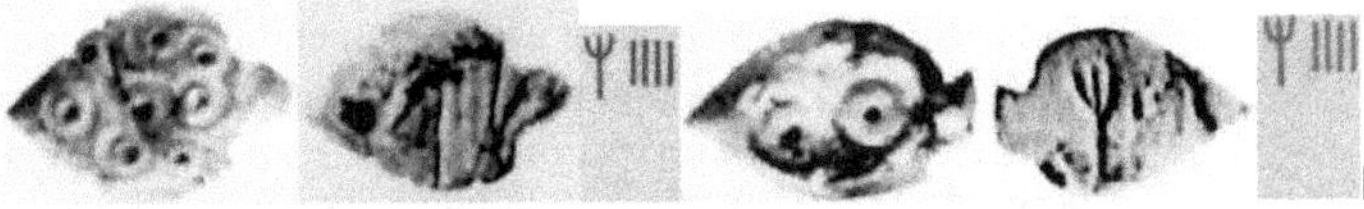

h337, h338 Texts 4417, 4426 (les on leaf-shaped tablets)

Decoding inscription on Indus seal of Mitathal

Abstract

The seal belongs to an artisan. Used as a calling card and for sealing on packages, the seal describes the workshop of the artisan.

Provenance of the seal

Excerpts from: Prabhakar VN, Tejas Garge, Randall Law, 2010, Mitathal: New observations based on surface reconnaissance and geologic provenance studies, Man and Environment XXXV (1): 54-61 http://tinyurl.com/3nay3dg

Mirror: http://www.docstoc.com/docs/88327056/Indus-steatite-seal-in-Mitathal Indus seal found in Mitathal.

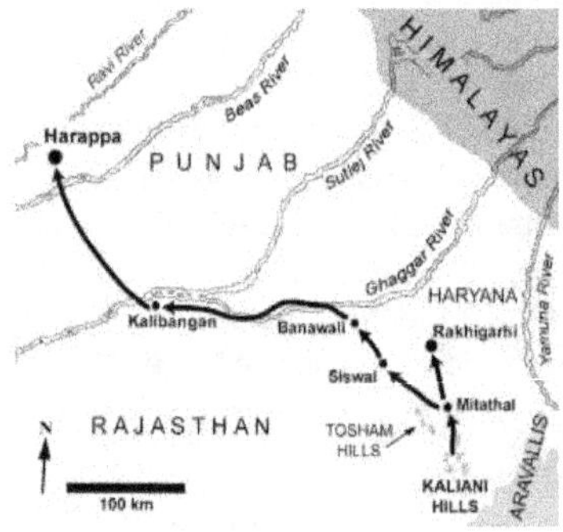


[quote] Abstract

The Indus Civilization settlement of Mitathal, District Bhiwani, Haryana is rapidly being leveled due to agricultural activities. A short surface reconnaissance was conducted during which, among other things, a steatite seal was recovered. A small fragment of that seal was analyzed using instrumental neutron activation analysis (INAA) and determined to have been made from raw steatite that most probably originated in the Alwar District of northern Rajasthan. This, along with evidence that rock outcrops near the Haryana/Rajasthan border were being exploited for manufacture of grinding stones, indicates that residents of the site had important trade relationships extending towards the south...

Mitathal is situated on the alluvial plain near a channel between the Chautang and the Yamuna rivers and is in close proximity (25 to 30 km) to the hilly outcrops of Kaliana and Tosham, which are rich in quartzite and metavolcanic rocks respectively. The site is approximately 120 km west-northwest of New Delhi, 10 km northeast of Bhiwani – the headquarters of the district of the same name, and 1.5 km northwest of Mitathal village...

When walking across Mitathal one is struck by the large number of blue-green faience bangle fragments visible on the site's surface...Ash pits and kilns of considerable size were observed on the northwestern and eastern peripheries of the site. One among these was a feature that is suspected to be a series of faience kilns...Other common surface finds were non-diagnostic bits of copper and identifiable copper-alloy objects such as bangle fragments (Fig. 4)...

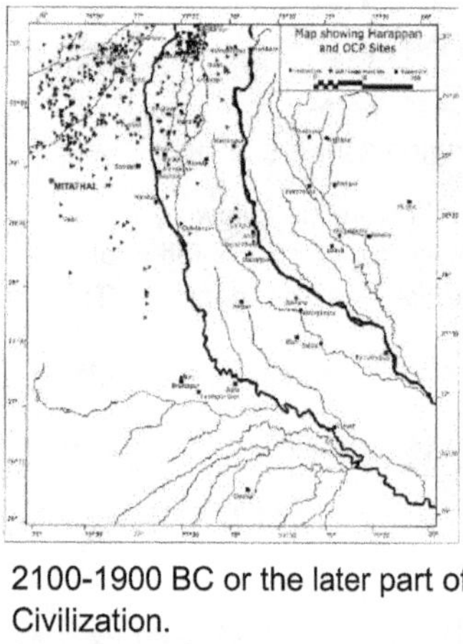

The most significant find by our team was of a broken steatite seal (Fig. 6). It was found on the southern slope of Mound 2 not far from the canal. Suraj Bhan's excavation report makes note of a seal (Bhan 1975: 82, Fig. 16) collected from the surface of Rakhi Shahpur (Rakhigarhi), but no seal or sealing had previously been reported from Mitathal itself. The seal recovered by our team is rectangular in shape, trapezoidal in section and inscribed on one side. The surviving portion measures 15.50 x 14.51 mm. The section of the top and bottom suggests that it was, when complete, convex backed with a perforated hole through the width. Seals of this type were used at the site of Harappa only during Period 3C (Meadow and Kenoyer 2001: 27) and so we can confidently date this surface find to ca. 2100-1900 BC or the later part of what is commonly called the Mature Harappan Phase of the Indus Civilization.

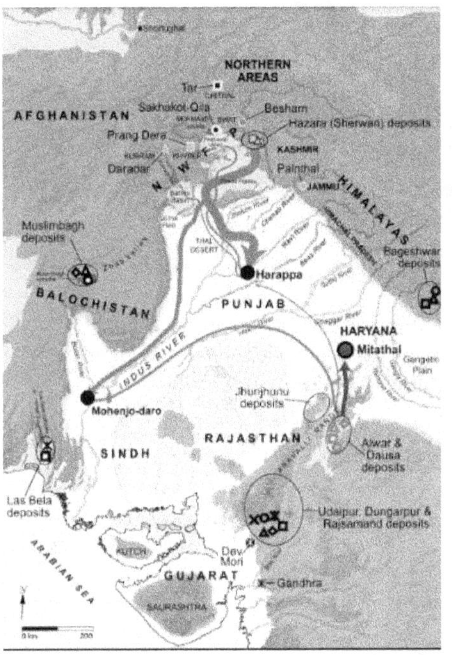


The first sign on the face of the seal resembles a vertical eye enclosing a vertical flaring stroke attached with three short oblique strokes. This sign corresponds to the sign no. 354 in Parpola's "Sign List of Indus Script" (Parpola 1994: 77). The second sign, which corresponds to sign no. 134 in the "Sign List" (Parpola 1994:73), is composed of seven vertical strokes/bars – having four strokes in the first row and three in the second. Scanning electron microscopy (SEM) of the first sign (Fig. 7) was performed at the Department of Materials and Metallurgical Engineering, IIT, Kanpur and suggested that the seal's deeply incised characters were created with a sharp-edged metal tool...

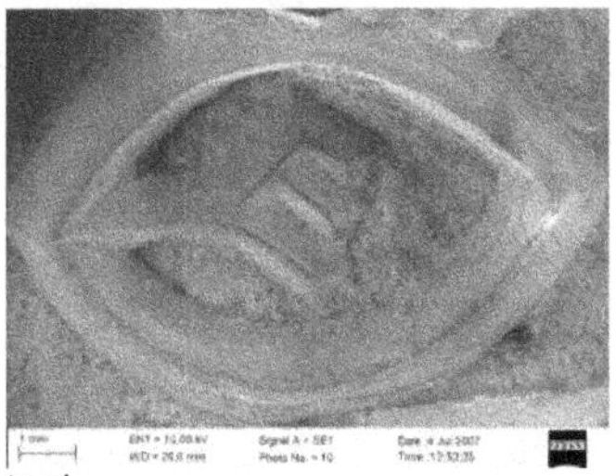

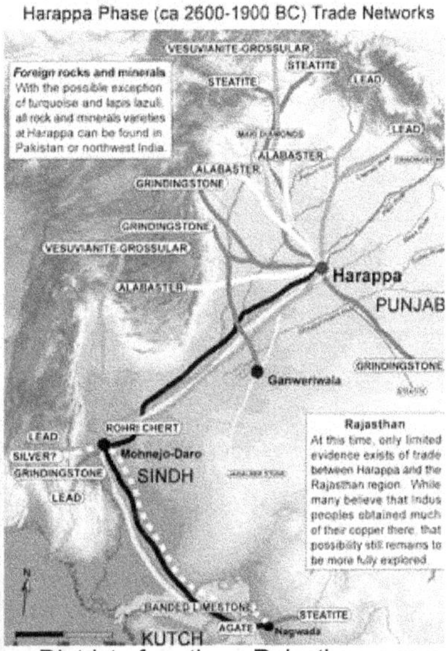


The elemental data produced during the analysis of the Mitathal seal are listed in Table 1 in parts per million (ppm). Using canonical distriminant analysis (a multivariate statistical technique that is well-suited to differentiating various raw material sources and assigning a possible provenance to artefacts), the elemental composition of the Mitathal seal was compared to INAA-derived geologic data from 37 steatite sources within and adjacent to the area across which peoples of the Indus Civilization dwelled (Law 2008: Chapter 7). The locations of those 37 sources are noted on Fig. 11. The results of the analysis – displayed as a bivariate plot (Fig. 12) – indicate that the steatite the seal is composed of most closely resembles that from a deposit (Nangalhari-Bairaswas) in the Alwar District of northern Rajasthan, some 150 km south of Mitathal...It was not surprising to find that the Mitathal seal is composed of steatite from the Alwar District, as that would have been one of the nearest raw material source areas for people dwelling in Haryana. However, a small percentage of the samples analyzed from Harappa and Mohenjo-Daro also appears to have come from Alwar and other northern Rajasthan sources. What we might be seeing at Mitathal then is a node near the beginning of a steatite trade route through which raw material was transported westward towards those distant cities. Hopefully, large-scale analysis of steatite artefacts from major sites like Rakhigarhi can one day be carried out in order to more effectively evaluate the extent to which raw steatite from northern Rajasthan and other source areas was utilized in the "Eastern Domain."

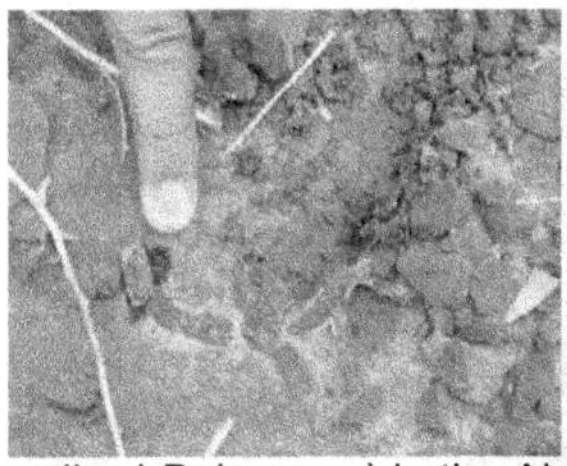

...The acquisition of raw material for grinding stones from the Kaliana Hills and steatite from the Alwar region of northern Rajasthan likely put residents of Mitathal in contact with, if only indirectly, peoples of the Ganeshwar-Jodhpur cultural phase. Further evidence for this southern connection may come when the provenance of some of the many copper artefacts recovered from the site is determined. [unquote]

Fig. 1: Location of Mitathal in the 'Eastern Domain' of the Indus Civilization

Fig.4: Copper bangle fragment

Fig. 7: SEM imge of the seal from Mitathal

Fig. 6: Drawing of the seal from Mitathal

Fig. 11: Steatite sources and select acquisition networks ca. 2200-1900 BCE

Fig. 10: Possible Harappan period distribution route of Kiliana quartzite

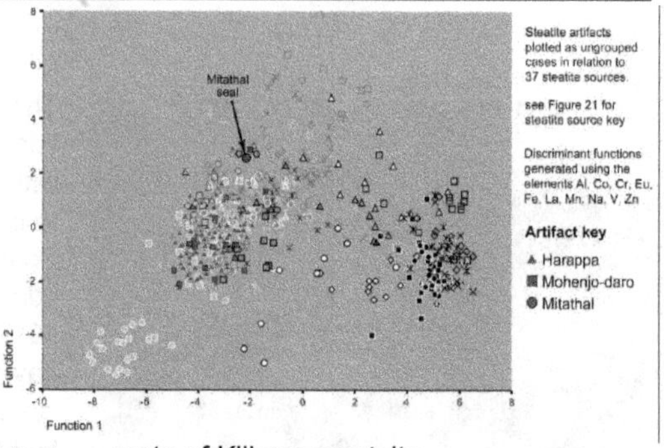


Fig. 12: Bivariate plot comparing Harappan steatite artifacts to samples from 37 geologic sources

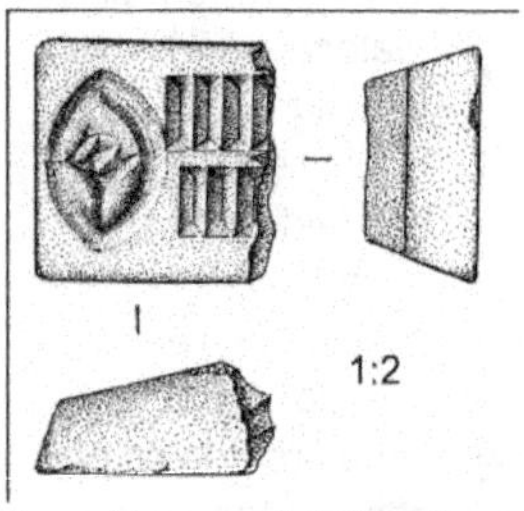


Table 1: INAA data for the Mitathal seal

| Element | ppm |
|---|---|
| Al | 2272 |
| Co | 2.264 |
| Cr | 2.87 |
| Eu | 4.018 |
| Fe | 1939 |
| La | 0.9789 |
| Mn | 16.23 |
| Na | 1457 |
| Sc | 0.0614 |
| V | 9.567 |
| Zn | 16.13 |

Exquisite posters prepared to depict Indus rock and mineral trade networks by Randall Law may be seen at "Indus Rock and Mineral Trade Networks: The View from Harappa" https://mywebspace.wisc.edu/rwlaw/posters/pmain.htm Poster series presented at the 18th International Conference of the European Association of South Asian Archaeologists London, England, July 4–8, 2005. The poster analyzing steatite sources is at: https://mywebspace.wisc.edu/rwlaw/posters/Poster_4s.jpg

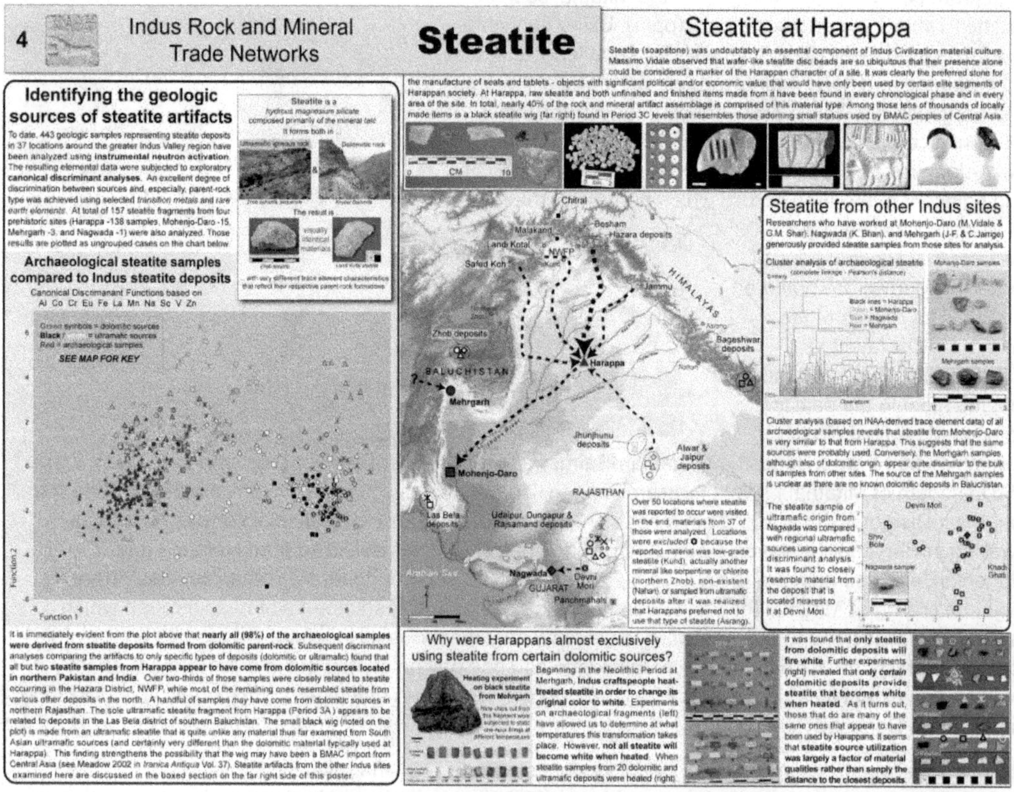

Evaluating the trade networks of Harappa between ca 2600 to 1900 BCE, Randall Law notes: "A total of 2586 grindingstones (whole and fragmentary) from Harappa were compared with the geologic source

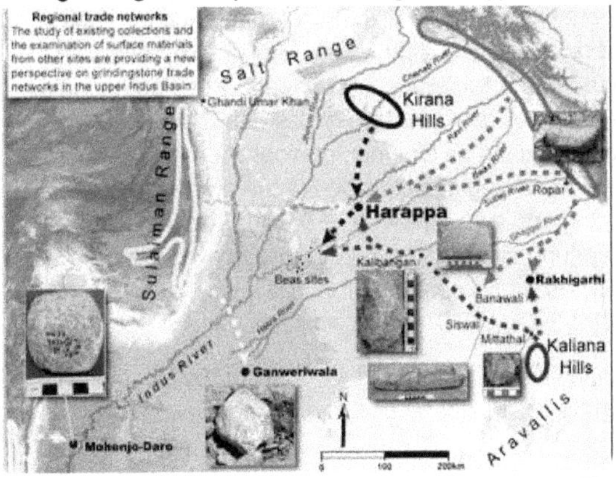


samples and assigned a regional provenance...(The map presented shows the sources as Kirana Hills on the westbank of Chenab river and Kaliana Hills near Mitathal)...For approximately 1000 years following Harappa's initial settlement the majority (85%) of grindingstones were brought to the site from the nearest possible sources in the Kirana Hills – 120 km away. A trend toward the acquisition of higher-quality stone from more distant sources (225 to 400 km) slowly began in the proto-urban phase (Period 2) and culminated in the middle of the urban phase (Period 3B) when only 2% of grinding stones used at the site came from the Kirana Hills...The use of Delhi quartzite from the distant Kaliana Hills increased steadily throughout the sequence... Foreign rocks and minerals. With the possible exception of turquoise and lapis lazuli, all rock and minerals varieties at Harappa can be found in Pakistan or northwest India...Harappa's expanding trade networks. The early 4th millennium BCE founders of Harappa were participants in already established long-distance interaction networks through which certin materials like lapis lazuli and marine shell were brought to the Punjab region from sources more than 800 km away. However, the majority of rocks and minerals from site's first two occupational phases reflect an emphasis on the utilization of much closer, albeit still distant, sources. Most large griding stones were acquired in the Kirana Hills, which at 120 km were the closest rock outcrops of any kind. The black chert used by Early Harappans was from the Salt Range - 250 km away. Steatite came from regions 350 to 450 km away - the closest ocurrences in which material that would fire white could be found. All of these sources, as well as those for the lead and alabaster used during periods 1 and 2, were located in regions north of Harappa...By Period 3A, most of the chert at Harappa *probably* came from the Rohri Hills, 500 km to the southwest. The use of Kirana Hills sources for grindstone steadily diminished and by Period 3B most querns and mullers came from areas farther away to the west (Sulaiman Range - 225 km) and east (Kaliana Hills - 400 km)."

See also: Randall William Law, 2008, Inter-regional interaction and urbanism in the ancient Indus valley: a geologic provenience study of Harappa's rock and mineral assemblage, University of Wisconsin-Madison http://tinyurl.com/3s22o4m

Decoding the inscription on Mitathal seal

Two clearly visible glyphs on the broken seal constitute the (partial) inscription. Some comparable glyphs may be seen on other Indus inscriptions.

H1522 (Paropola, Asko, BM Pande and Petteri Koskikallio, 2010, *Corpus of Indus Seals and Inscriptions 3.1 supplement to Mohenjoo-daro and Harappa,* Helsinki, Suomalainen Tiedeakatemia). This inscription is dated ca. 3300 BCE. The glyph of a 'rice plant' (or 'maize cob') recurs on many Indus inscriptions in many vaiant forms and in ligatured glyphs.

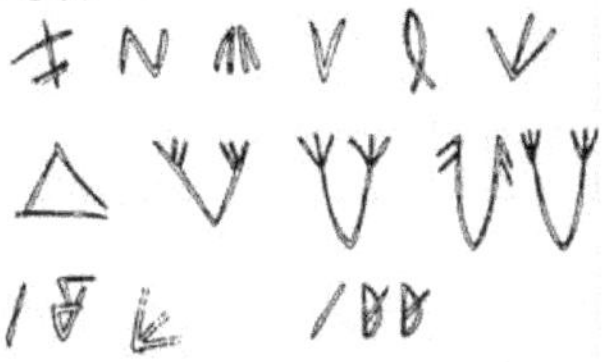

"Mitathal (28-50; 76-10), Dt. Bhiwani, about 10 km to the nw of Bhiwani railway station, with a twin mound...The site was for the first time put on the archaeological map by the discovery of gold Gupta coins in 1915-16. Two copper harpoons, the typical Copper Hoard tools, were accidentally discovered at the site in 1965, one of them now housed in the Arch. Museum at Gurukul, Jhajjar. Subsequently a hoard of 13 copper rings, since lost, was discovered. The true archaeological potential of the site and its Harappa affiliations were first recognized in 1967 when a few potsherd and beads of semiprecious stones, paste and faience were shown to the writer, who conducted excavations here in 1968 on behalf of the Panjab Univ...An unfinished bead and an unworked nodule of agate from the site point to the local manufacture of the beads... The large number of faience bangles with a rich variety of shapes and designs represent the popular ornament...Among toys mention may be made of the terracotta cart wheels, wheeled animals,

discs with nail marks and clay balls. A quartzite hammer-stone, saddle querns and pestles, discoid balls, perhaps used as weights, cubical chert and cuboid sandstone weights, chert blades and ring stone comprise the stone artefacts. A bone or ivory stylus or pin, a ring and a square wire of copper and terracotta triangular cakes, discs with tapering sides and sling balls have also been recovered..." (Ghosh, A. 1989, *An encyclopaedia of Indian archaeology*, Delhi, Munshiram Manoharlal, pp. 289-290).

A database is presented of select lexemes from Indian linguistic area and samples of inscriptions with a bearing on the glyphs of Indus script on Mitathal seal. Using this database, the Mitathal inscription is decoded, read rebus.

Glyph1 This is a ligatured glyph comprising: four numeral strokes and three numeral strokes. Each glyph denotes a lexeme and is read rebus.

*gaṇḍa* 'four' (Santali); rebus: *kaṇḍ* fire-altar, furnace' (Santali)

*kolmo* 'three' (Mu.); *kolami* 'smithy, forge' (Te.)

Thus, the glyph reads: *kolmo gaṇḍa* 'smithy with fire-altar'.

Glyph 2 This is a ligatured glyph comprising: 'plant' infixed within a 'hole'.

*dulo* 'hole' (N.); rebus: *dul* 'to cast metal in a mould' (Santali)

*kodo* 'millet' (Mu.); rebus: *koḍ* 'artisan's workshop' (Kuwi).

Thus, the glyph reads: *dul koḍ* 'casting (metal) workshop.'

The entire inscription thus connotes the repertoire of the artisan: casting metal workshop with smithy (forge) and fire-altar (furnace).

Database of select lexemes from Indian linguistic area and samples of inscriptions with a bearing on the glyphs of Indus script on Mitathal seal (cf. Indus Script Cipher – Hieroglyphs of Indian linguistic area by S. Kalyanaraman)

dula 'pair, likeness'; rebus: dul 'cast (metal)'. Thus, dul kuṭila 'cast bronze'. dula दुल । युग्मम् m. a pair, a

couple, esp. of two similar things (Rām. 966) (Kashmiri); dol 'likeness, picture, form' (Santali) Rebus: dul 'to cast metal in a mould' (Santali) Pkt. *dula* second (CDIAL 6402) Ku. *dulo* m., *°li* f., *dulno* m. 'hole, cavity, animal's den'; N. *dulo* 'hole, animal's hole (e.g. of a mouse)', *nāka ko dulo* 'nostril', *dulko* 'little hole'; — M. *ḍuḷū̃* n. 'little hole', *ḍolā* m.; — poss. Ash. *dūra* 'hole' (*kāsāra-dū́ra*'nostril', *dum—durē̃k* 'smoke—hole'); Wg. *dúri*, *dorī́g* 'smoke—hole': but these poss. < DÚR—. — Con- nexion, if any, with P.*duḍ*(*h*) f. 'wolf's den', *ḍuḍḍ* f. 'mouse—hole' (CDIAL 6452)

கோடு kōṭu : ***•நடுநிலை நீங்குகை. கோடிறீக் கூற் றம்*** (***நாலடி***, 5). 3. [K. kōḍu.] Tusk; ***யானை பன்றிகளின் தந்தம். மத்த யானையின் கோடும்*** (***தேவா.*** 39, 1).

<gaGgai>(P),,<gOGgei>(M) {N} ``Indian ^millet, a cultivated food grain". Cf. <jiJjari> `various sp. of grain'. *Kh.<gaGgai>(B), ~<gaGgoi>(B) `maize'; Mu.<gaGgae>, ~<gaGai>, Ho<gaGgai>, Sad.<gA~gAi>, H.<kA~gAni>. %10641. #10561.

kā̃g 'boar's tusk'; khāg, khā̃g m. ' rhinoceros horn, boar's tusk (H.) khaḍgá1 m. ' rhinoceros ' MaitrS. 2. khāḍga- ' coming from a rhinoceros ' ŚāṅkhŚr., khaḍga -- m. ' rhinoceros horn ' lex. 3. *khāḍgin -- . [Of non -- Aryan origin: cf. gaṇḍá -- 4 EWA i 318] 1. Pa. Pk. khagga -- m. ' rhinoceros ', Si. kagayā; <-> OAw. khagahā. 2. Ku. N. khāg, khāgo ' rhinoceros horn '; B. khāg ' rhinoceros horn, boar's tusk ', H. khāg, khā̃g m. ' rhinoceros horn, boar's tusk, cock's spur '. -- Altern. < khaḍgá -- 2: P.khaggā m. ' leaf of Aloe perfoliata ', B. khāg, khāgṛā ' reed for pens ', Or. khagaṛā ' the reed Saccharum spontaneum '.3. Pk. Khaggi -- ' rhinoceros '.(CDIAL 3786).

kā̃gar portable brazier (Kashmiri) kangar 1 कंगर् m. a large portable brazier (El.). kā̃gürü काँग्; or kā̃gürü काँग; or kā̃gar काँग्ꣳर्ꣳ । हसब्तिका f. (sg. dat. kā̃grĕ काँग्र्य or kā̃garĕ काँगर्य, abl. kā̃gri काँग्रि), the portable brazier, or kāngrī, much used in Kashmīr (K.Pr. kángár, 129, 131, 178; káṅgrí, 5, 128, 129). For particulars see El. s.v. kángri; L. 7, 25, kangar; and K.Pr. 129. The word is a fem. dim. of kang, q.v. (Gr.Gr. 37). kā̃gri-khŏphürü काँग्रि-ख्वफ्ꣳ; । भग्ना काष्ठाङ्गारिका f. a worn-out brazier. -khôru -खोरु; । काष्ठाङ्गारिका<-> र्धभागः m. the outer half (made of woven twigs) of a brazier, remaining after the inner earthenware bowl has been broken or removed; see khôru. -kŏnḍolu -क्वंड&above;लु&below; । हसन्तिकापात्रम् m. the circular earthenware bowl of a brazier, which contains the burning fuel. -kõñü -काञ्; । हसन्तिकालता f. the covering of woven twigs outside the earthenware bowl of a brazier (Kashmiri)

kaṇḍ = altar, furnace (Santali) kaṇḍ = altar, furnace (Santali) *लोहकारकन्दुः* f. a blacksmith's smelting furnace (Grierson Kashmiri lex.) payĕn-kõda *पयन्-कोंद / परिपाककन्दुः* f. a kiln (a potter's, a lime-kiln, and brick-kiln, or the like); a furnace (for smelting) ]. kāndavika = a baker; kandu = an iron plate or pan for baking cakes etc. (Ka.lex.)

Glyp: 'one long linear stroke': koṛa = in arithmetic one; 4 koṛa or koḍa = 1 gaṇḍa = 4 (Santali) Rebus: koḍ, 'artisan's workshop' (Kuwi.)

Four + three strokes are read (since the strokes are shown on two lines one below the other) : gaṇḍa 'four' (Santali); rebus: 'furnace, kaṇḍ fire-altar'; kolmo 'three' (Mu.); rebus: kolami 'smithy' (Te.)

gaṇḍa 'four' (Santali);

kaṇḍa 'fire-altar' cf. ayaskāṇḍa a quantity of iron, excellent iron (Pāṇ.gaṇ)

kolom 'cob'; kolami 'forge, smithy' kolmo 'rice plant' (Mu.)

kolmo 'three'; kolami 'forge, smithy' (Te.)

kol 'furnace, forge' (Kuwi) kol 'alloy of five metals, pancaloha' (Ta.)

kōnṭa corner (Nk.); Tu. kōṇṭu angle, corner (Tu.); Rebus: kõdā 'to turn in a lathe' (B.)

kundār turner (A.); kūdār, kūdāri (B.); kundāru (Or.); kundau to turn on a lathe, to carve, to chase; kundau dhiri = a hewn stone; kundau murhut = a graven image (Santali) kunda a turner's lathe (Skt.)(CDIAL 3295) Grapheme (Sign 261): *khuṇṭa2 ' corner '. 2. *kuṇṭa -- 2. [Cf. *khōñca -- ] 1. Phal. khun ' corner '; H. khū̃ṭ m. ' corner, direction ' (→ P. khū̃ṭ f. ' corner, side '); G. khū̃ṭrī f. ' angle '. <-> X kōṇa -- : G. khuṇ f., khū˘ṇɔ m. ' corner '.2. S. kuṇḍa f. ' corner '; P. kū̃ṭ f. ' corner, side ' (← H.). (CDIAL 3898)

*kōtr ' dig '. 2. *khōtr -- . [See list s.v. *khōdd -- and √*khuṭ1]
1. G. *kotarvũ* ' to dig, carve ', *kotar* n. ' cave, den '; -- N. *kotranu* ' to scratch ' < **kōtraḍ* --
2. S. *khoṭranu* ' to dig, carve '; L. poṭh. *khotarṇā* ' to poke about '
(X khánati in *khanotarṇā* ' to poke, dig up with any small instrument '), awāṇ. *khōtruṇ* ' to scratch, dig ', G. *khotarvũ* ' to dig, scratch ', *khotarṇā̃* n. pl. ' old errors raked up '; -- N. *khotar* ' burnt sediment of milk ' < **khotraḍ* -- .
Addenda: *kōtr -- . 2. *khōtr -- : S.kcch. *khotarṇū* ' to scratch (for itching) ', P. *khoṭnā* ' to dig, scratch, poke '. (CDIAL 3512) *Ta.* koṭṭu (koṭṭi-) to sting (as a scorpion, wasp); *n.* stinging; hoe with short handle, weeding-hoe, spade; koṭukku sting of a wasp, hornet, scorpion, claws of a crab, lobster; tēṭ-koṭṭāṉ a green insect whose touch produces the same sensation as a scorpion-sting; tēṭ-kuṭicci a black bee (for tēṭ-, see 3470 Ta. tēḷ). *Ma.*koṭṭuka to sting (of scorpion); koṭukka scorpion's sting. *Ko.* koṭk- (koṭky-) (snake) strikes, bites; ? kako·ṭ hoe with sharp, broad blade (for ka-, see 1265). *Ka.*kuṭuku to sting (as a scorpion); kuḍuku to peck; kukku to peck, strike something with a stone, etc., in a pecking manner, dig up the ground slightly with a hoe; (Hav.) koḍappu to peck. *Tu.* koḍapuni, (B-K.) kuḍapu to bite (as a serpent), peck, strike with the beak; kukkuli pecking; kukkuliyuni to peck; koṭṭu, koṭrèspade; (B-K.) kuḍpoḷu a hornet. *Nk.* koṛk- to peck. *Pa.* koḍk- id.; koṭṭ- id., dig; koṭal hoe. *Ga.* (Oll.) koṭ- to dig, (fowl) to peck; koṭal hoe, spade; (S.) koṭ- to bite (as a snake). *Go.* koṭṭānā (SR. Tr.) to peck, pierce leaves and sew them for platters, (Ph.) to pierce, thrust; (A.) koṭṭ- to hoe; (M.) koṭāna to sew; (Tr.)goṭṭānā to poke or thrust with a stick or finger; kōṭstānā to have one's ears pierced (*Voc.* 888); (Sr. Tr. W. Ph.) kohkānā to prick, puncture, tattoo; (Mu. Ko.)kohk-, (Ma.) koʔk- to peck (*Voc.* 959). *Pe.* koṭ- (-t-) to dig, hoe, (snake) to bite; koḍgi hoe. *Manḍ.* kuṭ- (-t-) (snake) to bite, (hen) to peck. *Kui* (K.) koḍi hoe.*Kuwi* (Su. Mah. Isr.) koṛgi, (F.) kūrgi, (S.) korgi hoe, mattock. *Malt.* koḍkare woodpecker. Cf. 1672 Ka. kuṭṭu, 2080 Ka. konḍi, and 2126 Pa. gorka. / Cf. Turner, *CDIAL*, no. 3241(2) (forms with meanings 'prick, hoe'). (DEDR 2064).

<kodo>(P) {N} ``a certain ^millet''. *Kh.<kuda>(D), ~<koday>(D) `millet', Sa., Mu., Ho<kodey>, H. Nep.<kodo>; Sk.<kodrAUA>. %17771. #17641. kōdrava m. ' Paspalum scrobiculatum (a grain eaten by the poor) ' MBh., °*aka* -- m. BHSk. [Cf. *kōradūṣa*<-> m. ' id. ' Suśr., °*aka* -- m. KātyŚr., Pa. *kudrūsa* -- , °*aka* -- m., Pk. *kōdūsaga* -- , *kōdū*° m. E. H. Johnston JRAS 1931, 577] Pk. *koddava* -- , *kud*° m., K. *kuduru* m., S. *koḍrirī* f., P. *kodrā* m. (*kodā̃*, °*dõ* m. ← H.), WPah. *koḍlo* m.; Ku. *kodo* ' a small edible grain '; N. *kodo* ' Eleusine indica '; B. *kodo* ' P. scrobiculatum ', Or. *kodua*; Bi. *kodo* ' P. frumentaceum ', °*daī* ' a smaller variety '; Mth. *kodo* ' P. scorbiculatum ', H. *kodo*, °*dõ*, °*daw* m.,°*daī* f. (*kodrā* m. ← P.), G. *kodrā* m. pl. ' the grain ', °*drī* f. ' the grain separated from the chaff ' (→ M. *kodrū* m.). kōnālaka -- see kuṇāla -- .Addenda: kōdrava -- : WPah.kc. *kodo* m. ' certain coarse grain ', kṭg. *kodrɔ* m. ← P. †*kōdravapiṣṭa -- . (CDIAL 3515). *kōdravapiṣṭa -- ' flour of Paspalum scrobiculatum '. [kōdrava -- , piṣṭá -- ] WPah.kc. *kodtho, kədiṭṭho*, kṭg. *kədríṭṭhɔ* m. ' flour of this grain ', J. *kdiṭhā* m. (CDIAL 3515a)

<kODu>(:),,<kaDu>(MP) {N} ``^bracelet, ^wristlet, ^bangle''. Cf. <gaDua>. *So.<kaddu:-n>, Kh.<karam>(D), ~<kaRam>(AB) `wrist [D], bracelet [ABD]', H.<kARa> `bangle', O.<kORa>, Guj.<kADU~>, cf. Kh.<kaDu'-> `to embrace'. %17781. #17651.

``^grinding_^stone'':

Sa. *guRgu* `grinding stone'.

Mu. *guRu* `grinding stone'. !sic; recte *guRgu*??

KW *guRgu*

@(M064)

``^stone'':

So. *arEG*(R)/ *rEG* `stone'.

Go. *a:reG* `stone'.

Kh. *sOrEG* `rock, stone'.

~ *ku~R~u~-sOr* `grinding cylinder'.

~ *pa'D-sOr* `grind-stone'.

~ *thOm-sOr* `to stone, to smash with a stone'.

Mu. *sErEG* `a large, flat stone'.

@(V183)

<kikin>(Z) {INDECL} ``^small, ^tiny''. #16820.

<kikin areG>(Z) [kikIn areG],[ki'kIn areG] {N} ``^pebble, ^small ^stone''. |<areG> `stone'. #16830.

<areG>(ZA) {N} ``^stone, ^rock''. Cf. <reG> `id.'. #2910.

<areG=lo?o>(Z) {N} ``^white ^stone''. |<lo?o> `?to dig up'. #2940. <raGni areG>(A) {N} ``^rock''. |<raGni> `?'. #28102.

<riD=saG=reG>(Z) {N} ``^grind^stone for ^turmeric''. |<rid=saG> `grindstone for spices'. #28465.

<guDlu>(P) {NI} ``a cultivated food ^grain of the ^millet kind''. *@. #11081.

<guRudi>(P) {N} ``a cultivated food ^grain of the ^millet kind''. *Kh.<guDlu>(P), Sa.<gundli>, Mu.<guDlu>, ~<guRulu>, Ho<guDlu>, O.<guRlu>, H.<go~Deli>. %12281. #12191.

<guRumO>(K) {N} ``parched ^paddy''. %12291. #12201.

<juaRi>(P),,<juaNi>(MP) {N} ``^maize; Indian ^corn''. *Sa.<joNDra>, Mu.<jonDra>, Sad.<jonlA>, B.<jOnarO>, H.<joarA>, ~<jAvara>; H.<jUarA> `millet'. %15311. #15201.

<arig>(Z),,<ari>(A),,<ari>(Z) [arig'] {N} ``^millet''. *Dr.<ariki>. #2960.

<ari=saG>(Z) {N} ``^millet ^gruel''. |<saG> `gruel?'. #2970. <ari=saG>(Z) {N} ``^millet ^gruel''. #2972.

<siDay>(Z) [siRay] {N} ``^millet(:)''. #30780.

<jebmol siDay>(Z) [siRay] {N} ``^rice (or ^millet?) for ^seed''. |<jebmol> `paddy seed, rice for sowing'. #30791.

<Deray siDay>(Z) [siRay] {N} ``^<ragi> ^millet (%Eleusine sp.)''. |<Deray> `hill millet'. #30800.

<Dej=ara?> `millet plant'. #34000.

|<Der> `hill millet, a grain'. #35380.

<ja~ta>(Z) [dza~ta] {N} ``^mill^stone, ^grindstone''. #14000.

``^grind'':

So. *riD* `to grind (in a mill)'.

Kh. *ri'D* `to grind'.

Sa. *ri'd* `to grind (in a stone), to crush'.

Mu. *ri'd* `to grind (in a stone), to crush'.

Ho *rid* `to grind (in a stone), to crush'.

Bh. *rid* `to grind (in a stone), to crush'.

KW *rid*

Ku. *rid* `to grind (in a stone), to crush'.

@(V076,M054)

riṛ 'ridge formed by the backbone' (Santali) rīḍhaka -- m. ' backbone ' lex. WPah.bhal. rī`ṛ f. ' backbone, high mountain '; Aw.lakh. rīṛh ' backbone ', H. rīṛh f. (CDIAL 10749a). [ roṇḍi ] roṇḍi. [Tel.] n. The haunch, the side between the ribs and loins. (Telugu) Rebus: rīti 'yellow or pale brass , bell-metal' (Skt.) rīti2 f. ' yellow brass, bell metal ' Kathās., rītika -- n. ' calx of brass ', kā -- f. ' brass ' lex. 2. rīrī -- , rirī -- f. ' yellow brass ' lex. [Ac. to AO xviii 248 Dard. forms < *raktikā -- 2] 1. Dm. rit' copper ', Gaw. rīt (→ Sv. rīda NoPhal 49); Bshk. rīd ' brass ', Tor. žit f. 2. Pk. rīrī -- f. ' brass '; Sh. rīl m. ' brass, bronze, copper '.(CDIAL 10752). இரீதி irīti, n. < rīti. Brass; பித்தளை. (W.) **இரதி*, irati , n. cf. rīti. Brass; *பித்தளை. (பிங்.)*

<ganDa>(P) {NUM} ``^four''. Syn. <cari>(LS4), <hunja-mi>(D). *Sa., Mu.<ganDa> `id.', H.<gA~Da> `a group of four cowries'. %10591. #10511.

<ganDa-mi>(KM) {NUM} ``^four''. |<-mi> `one'. %10600. #10520.

Text 4251 h097 Pict-95: Seven robed figures (with stylized twigs on their head and pig-tails) standing in a row. The first sign from right on line 1 of Inscribed text 4251 could be Sign 174 and connotes 'cast bronze'; it is a glyptic formed of a pair of brackets (): kuṭila 'bent'; rebus: kuṭila, katthīl = bronze (8 parts copper and 2 parts tin) [cf. āra-kūṭa, 'brass' (Skt.) (CDIAL 3230) kuṭi— in cmpd. 'curve' (Skt.)(CDIAL 3231). Vikalpa: dula 'hole'. Rebus: dul 'casting (metal)' (Santali)

Allograph

kuṭi— in cmpd. 'curve', kuṭika— 'bent' MBh. (CDIAL 3231); rebus: kuṭhi 'smelter' (Santali) [Shape of oval is consistent with the tradition of Koles to form equilateral lumps pointed at each end of ingots: mũh metal ingot (Santali) mũhã = the quantity of iron produced at one time in a native smelting furnace of the Kolhes; iron produced by the Kolhes and formed like a four-cornered piece a little pointed at each end; mūhā me~ṛhe~t = iron smelted by the Kolhes and formed into an equilateral lump a little pointed at each end; kolhe tehen me~ṛhe~tko mūhā akata = the Kolhes have to-day produced pig iron (Santali.lex.) The paired glyphs may be read as: dul 'likeness'; rebus: dul 'cast (metal)' (Santali)] kuṭika— 'bent' MBh. [√kuṭ 1] Ext. in H. kuṛuk f. 'coil of string or rope'; M. kuḍčā m. 'palm contracted and hollowed', kuḍapṇẽ 'to curl over, crisp, contract'. CDIAL 3231 kuṭilá— 'bent, crooked' KātyŚr., aka— Pañcat., n. 'a partic. plant' lex. [√kuṭ 1] Pa. kuṭila— 'bent', n. 'bend'; Pk. kuḍila— 'crooked', illa— 'humpbacked', illaya— 'bent' DEDR 2054 Ta. koṭu curved, bent, crooked; koṭumai crookedness, obliquity; koṭukki hooked bar for fastening doors, clasp of an ornament. A pair of curved lines: dol 'likeness, picture, form' [e.g., two tigers, two bulls, sign-pair.] Kashmiri. dula दुल । युग्मम् m. a pair, a couple, esp. of two similar things (Rām. 966). Rebus: dul meṛeḍ cast iron (Mundari. Santali) dul 'to cast metal in a mould' (Santali) pasra meṛed, pasāra meṛed = syn. of koṭe meṛed = forged iron, in contrast to dul meṛed, cast iron (Mundari.lex.)

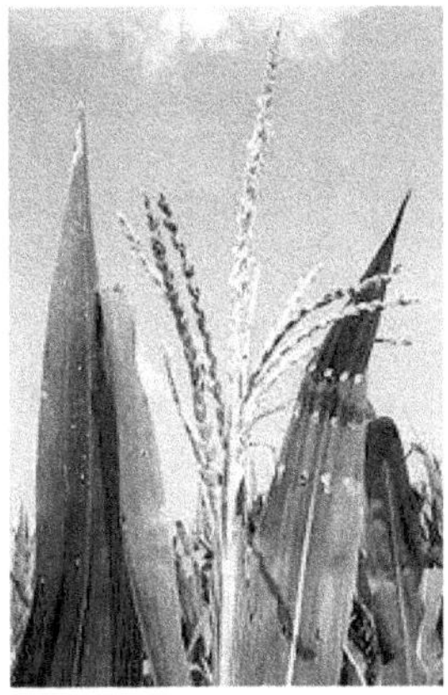

The second glyph from the right on Mitathal seal is comparable to the glyph on another Indus seal (see glyph, second from right).

Seal m898 (The second sign from the right is a ligature: rice plant is ligatured to three long numerical strokes). One conjecture is that the 'rice-plant' glyph is a phonetic determinant of the 'three numerical strokes' glyph. If this conjecture is valid, both the glyphs may be connoted by the same lexeme: kolmo, 'rice plant, three'.

Zebu Seal. Harppa (Kenoyer). The occurrence of these two distinct glyphs indicates that the glyphs may connot two distinct lexemes. The 'plant' glyph may denote a maize cob.

Maize cobs. Millet cob.

Rice plant.

Altyn-tepe seals with hieroglyphs of Indian linguistic area, attesting trade contacts with Meluhha (Masson, 1988, pl. XXIX:9 pl. XVII:14)

"The discovery in Altyn-Depe of a proto-Indian seal with two signs deserves special mention. V.M. Masson pointed out, that what the seal depicted was a pictogram and not just a representation of animals. In his opinion this means that some of the ancient residents of Altyn-Depe were able to read this text."(G. Bongard- Levin, 1989, Archaeological Finds in Central Asia throw light on Ancient India, Jagdish Vibhakar and Usha Gard (Eds.), *Glimpses of Ancient India through Soviet Eyes*, Delhi, Sundeep Prakashan).

Altyn-depe (close to the Caspian sea, in Turkmenistan). Silver seal. Pictograph of ligatured animal with three heads.

Bison: ḍangar 'bull'; rebus: ḍāṅgar 'blacksmith' (H.)

One-horned heifer: koḍiyum 'heifer kundār turner (A.); koḍ 'artisan's workshop' (Kuwi)

Antelope: meḷh 'goat' (Br.) Rebus: meṛha, meḍhi 'merchant's clerk; (G.)

sangaḍa 'jointed naimal' (M.) san:gāḍo a lathe (M.); cutting stone, gilding (G.)

Thus the ligatured animal glyph is read rebus: *san:gāḍo ḍāṅgar kundār meḍh* 'stone-cutter, blacksmith, turner, merchant's clerk.'

One of the two Altyn-tepe seals shows a 'three-petal' glyph together with a 'harrow' glyph. Another seal shows a 'svastika' glyph. If the three-petal glyph connotes: tagaraka rebus: tagara, 'tin', the other two glyphs can also be read rebus in the mineral context: adar 'harrow'; aduru 'native metal'; satthiya 'svastika glyph'; rebus: satthiya 'pewter'.

Thus, the two Altyn-tepe seals are decoded: Seal 1: Glyph: svastika; rebus: jasta 'zinc' (Kashmiri) Seal 2: aḍar 'harrow'; rebus: aduru 'native metal'; tagaraka 'taberna montana'; rebus: tagara 'tin'. Thus, the two-sign sequence on the seal reads: 'native metal, tin'.

Apparently, together with the three-headed composite animal glyph on a separate seal, the two seals belonged to a guild – sangha -- of traders dealing with tin, metalwork, stone-work products from Meluhha.

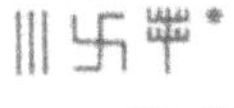

The text of inscription on an Altyn-tepe seals compare with an inscription on a miniature tablet, Text 4500 (Harappa. Incised miniature tablet; not illustrated). Line 2 of inscription: A pair of 'harrows' glyph: dula 'pair'; rebus dul 'cast (metal)'; aḍar 'harrow'; rebus: aduru 'native metal'. Thus, the duplicated 'harrow' glyph read rebus: cast native metal. Glyph: svastika; rebus: jasta 'zinc' (Kashmiri). Glyph 'three liner strokes': kolmo 'three'; rebus: kolami 'smithy'. Line 1 of inscription: Ligatured glyph: cunda 'musk-rat'; rebus: cundakāra 'ivory turner'; kolmo 'three'; rebus: kolami 'smithy'. Thus the Text 4500 on an incised miniature tablet read rebus: ivory turner smithy'; cast native metal, tin, smithy.

'Dotted circle' glyph

Rebus: kandi (pl.–l) beads, necklace (Pa.); kanti (pl.–l) bead, (pl.) necklace; kandiṭ 'bead' (Ga.)(DEDR 1215). Rebus Vikalpa 1: khaṇḍ 'ivory' (H.) Rebus Vikalpa 2: khaṇḍaran, khaṇḍrun 'pit furnace' (Santali)

Finds at Altyn-depe: ivory sticks and gaming pieces (?) obtained from Meluhha; similar objects with dotted circles found in Mohenjo-daro and Harappa.

Bhagawanpura is a site located on the right bank of the River Sarasvati_ in Dist. Kuruṣetra. Remains of semi-circular huts leaving behind only post-holes and rammed floors have been found. From Period IB levels bones of true domesticatd horse, equus caballus have been found. Intersecting dotted circle designs are found on pottery of Painted Grey Ware which overlap the Late Harappan ware.

Mohenjo-daro. Dotted circle decoration on a steatite bowl (DK 3178), DK-B, house 3, room VIII (Jansen and Urban, 1985, RTWH, Aachen).

Vessel fragments with dot-in-circle design from Susa. Louvre Museum. At the Royal Cemetery of Ur, Woolley 1934: 558-59 found a small container with a narrow neck and sides decorated with three dot-incircle designs.

Terracotta female adorned with 'dotted circles'; Period Namazga II; Yalangach Tepe, Geoksyur (Weiner, 1984, Fig. 183) kola 'woman'; rebus: kolami 'smithy, forge'.khaṇḍi = a saṛi, a full dress for a woman, a piece of cloth twelve cubits long by two in width; khaṇḍa = a piece of cloth suitable for the dress of a woman's sar.i; khaṇḍi bande, bande = to dress, of women binding round waist (Santali) khand 'ivory' kandhi 'a lump, a piece' (Santali)Rebus: kandi 'beads' (Pa.)(DEDR 1215). khaṇḍ 'ivory' (H.) kandi (pl. –l) beads, necklace (Pa.); kanti (pl. –l) bead, (pl.) necklace; kandiṭ 'bead' (Ga.)(DEDR 1215).Rebus: khaṇḍaran, khaṇḍrun 'pit furnace' (Santali)

Hence, the depiction of 'dotted circles' (like perforated beads) surrounding a fire-altar and also on ivory objects. काढतें [kāḍhatēṃ] n Among gamesters. An ivory counter &c. placed to represent a sum of money. (Marathi) The dotted circles also adorn the standard device which is a drill-lathe, sangaḍa खंड [ khaṇḍa ] A piece, bit, fragment, portion.(Marathi)

Dotted circle glyph: context, vedi glyph, ivory artifacts

Four 'round spot' glyphs around the 'dotted circle' in the center of the composition: gōṭī 'round pebble; rebus: kōṭhī ] f (कोष्ट S) A granary, garner, storehouse, warehouse, treasury, factory, bank.

गोटी [ gōṭī ] f (Dim. Of गोटा) A roundish stone or pebble. गोदा [ gōdā ] m A circular brand or mark made by actual cautery (Marathi)गोटा [ gōṭā ] m A roundish stone or pebble. 2 A marble (of stone, lac, wood &c.) 2 A marble. 3 A large lifting stone. Used in trials of strength among the Athletæ. 4 A stone in temples described at length underउचला 5 fig. A term for a round, fleshy, well-filled body. 6 A lump of silver: as obtained by melting down lace or fringe. गोटुळा or गोटोळा [ gōṭuḷā or gōṭōḷā ] a (गोटा) Spherical or spheroidal, pebble-form. (Marathi)
Rebus: krvṛi f. 'granary (Wpah.); kuṛī, kuṛo house, building'(Ku.)(CDIAL 3232) कोठी [ kōṭhī ] f (कोष्ट S) A granary, garner, storehouse, warehouse, treasury, factory, bank. (Marathi)

कोठी The grain and provisions (as of an army); the commissariatsupplies. Ex. लशकराची कोठी चालली-उतरली- आली-लुटली. कोठ्या [ kōṭhyā ] कोठा [ kōṭhā ] m (कोष्ट S) A large granary, store-room, warehouse, water-reservoir &c. 2 The stomach. 3 The chamber of a gun, of water-pipes &c. 4 A bird's nest. 5 A cattle-shed. 6 The chamber or cell of a hunḍí in which is set down in figures the amount. कोठारें [ kōṭhārēṃ ] n A storehouse gen (Marathi)

vēdha m. ' hitting the mark ' MBh., ' penetration, hole ' VarBṛS. [√vyadh] Pa. vēdha -- m. ' prick, wound '; Pk. vēha -- m. ' boring, hole ', P. veh, beh m., H. beh m., G. veh m. karṇavēdha -- .(CDIAL 12108) வேதிதம் vētitam , n. < vēdhita. (யாழ். அக.) 1. Perforating, drilling; துளைக்கை. 2. Tube; துளையுடைப்பொருள். வேதை[3] vētai , n. < vēdha. 1. Drilling, boring; துளைக்கை. (Tamil)
Vedhin (adj.) [fr. vidh=vyadh] piercing, shooting, hitting (Pali) Rebus: vḗdi f. ' raised piece of ground serving as an altar and usu. strewed with kuśa grass ' RV., ' stand, bench ' MBh., ' platform for wedding ceremony ' Kāv., vēdika<-> m. ' bench ' R., °kā -- f. MBh. [Cf. vēdá -- m. ' bunch of kuśa grass used as

broom ' AV.] Pa. vēdi -- , °dī -- , °dikā -- f. ' cornice, ledge, rail '; Pk. vēi -- , vēiā -- f. ' platform '; A. bei ' quadrangular frame of greenery forming platform on which ceremonial bathing of bride and bridegroom is performed '.(CDIAL 12107). Vedi & Vedī (f.) [Vedic vedi sacrificial bench] ledge, cornice, rail Mhvs 32, 5; 35, 2; 36, 52 (pāsāṇa°); 36, 103; Vv 8416 (=vedikā VvA 346). -- See on term Dial. ii.210; Mhvs. tsrln220, 296. Vedikā (f.) (& vediyā) [fr. vedi] cornice, ledge, railing D ii.179; Vin ii.120; J iv.229, 266; Vv 786 (vediyā= vedikā VvA 304); 8416 (=vedikā VvA 340); VvA 275. Velli [dial.?] is a word peculiar to the Jātaka. At one passage it is expld by the Commentary as "vedi" (i. e. rail, cornice), where it is applied to the slender waist of a woman (cp. vilāka & vilaggita): J vi.456. At most of the other passages it is expld as "a heap of gold": thus at J v.506 (verse: velli -- vilāka -- majjhā; C.: ettha vellī ti rāsi vilākamajjhā ti vilagga -- majjhā uttattaghana -- suvaṇṇa -- rāsi -- ppabhā c' eva tanu -- dīgha -- majjhā ca"), and vi.269 (verse: kañcana -- velli -- viggaha; C.: "suvaṇṇa -- rāsi -- sassirīka -- sarīrā"). At v.398 in the same passage as vi.269 expld in C. as "kañcana -- rūpakasadisa -- sarīrā"). The idea of "golden" is connected with it throughout. (Pali) vēdi [Skt.] n. A terrace, a piece of raised ground, a platform. An altar. (Telugu)

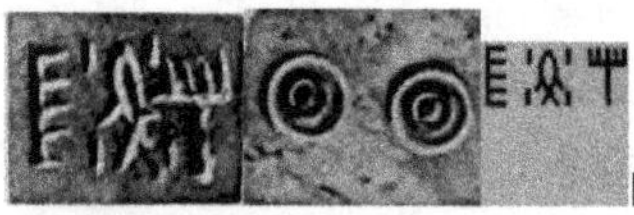
Ropar 1,Text 9021

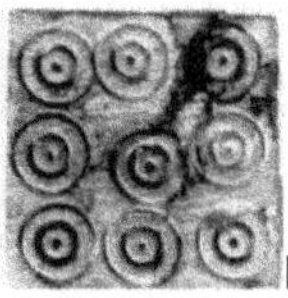
h128

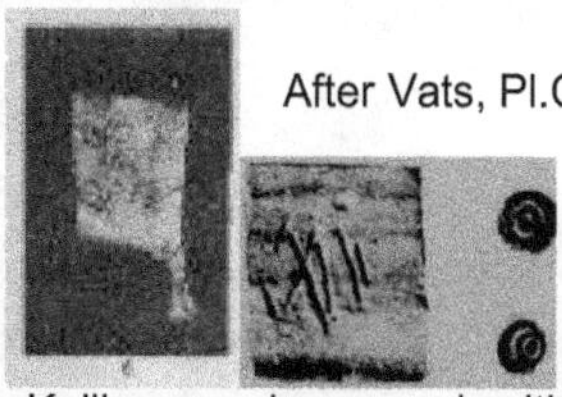
After Vats, Pl.CXIX,.No.6 An ivory comb fragment with one preserved tooth and ornamented with double incised circles (3.8 in. long).

Kalibangan, Ivory comb with three dotted circles; Kalibangan, Period II; Thapar 1979, Pl.XXVII, in: Ancient Cities of the Indus.

Ivory rod, ivory plaque with dotted circles. Mohenjo-daro. [Musee National De Arts Asiatiques Guimet, 1988-1989, Les cites oubliees de l'Indus Archeologie du Pakistan.]

h1017ivorystick

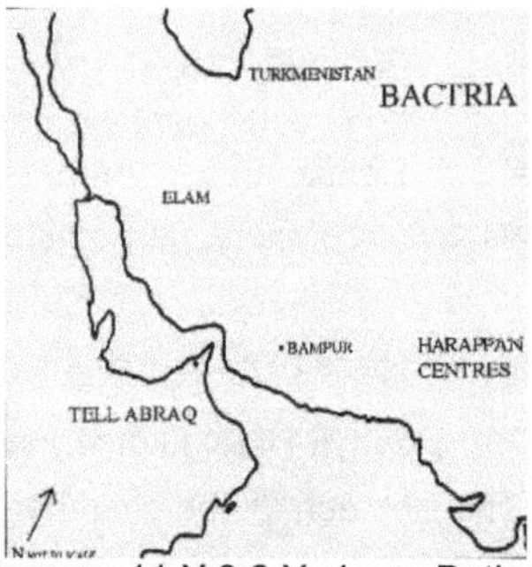


The ivory comb found at Tell Abraq measures 11 X 8.2 X .4 cm. Both sides of the comb bear identical, incised decoration in the form of two long-stemmed flowers with crenate or dentate leaves, flanking three dotted circles arranged in a triangular pattern. Bone and ivory combs with dotted-circle decoration are well-known in the Harappan area (e.g. at Chanhu-daro and Mohenjo-daro), but none of the Harappan combs bear the distinctive floral motif of the Tell Abraq comb. These flowers are identified as tulips, perhaps Mountain tulip or Boeotian tulip (both of which grow in Afghanistan) which have an undulate leaf. There is a possibility that the comb is an import from Bactria, perhaps transmitted through Meluhha to the Oman Peninsula site of Tell Abraq.

Glyph of shawl, a gaudy dress for an idol; rebus: potti 'priest'

The glyphs decorating the shawl are trefoils, that is, three hollow circles. Read rebus, the shawl is potti. potti, pottika n. Same as. Doll's clothes, a gaudy dress for an idol or for a little girl. (Telugu) S. potī f. ' shawl ' Pk. potta -- , °taga -- , °tia -- n. ' cotton cloth ', pottī -- , °tiā -- , °tullayā -- , puttī -- f. ' piece of cloth, man's dhotī, woman's sāṛī ', pottia -- ' wearing clothes ' (CDIAL 8400) pōtramu ' a cloth' (Telugu) போத்து² pōttu , n. < பொத்து. 1. Hole, hollow (Tamil) buḍhi mala 'a bead with wide hole' (Santali) peaṭa 'three' (Santali)

posta 'red thread employed to make borders of cloth' (Santali) pōta2 m. ' cloth ', pōtikā -- f. lex. 2. *pōtta -- 2 (sanskrit- ized as pōtra -- 2 n. ' cloth ' lex.). 3. *pōttha -- 2 ~ pavásta<-> n. ' covering (?) ' RV., ' rough hempen cloth ' AV. T. Chowdhury JBORS xvii 83. 4. pōntī -- f. ' cloth ' Divyāv. 5. *pōcca -- 2 < *pōtya -- ? (Cf. pōtyā = pōtānāṁ samūhaḥ Pāṇ.gaṇa. -- pṓta -- 1?). [Relationship with prōta -- n. ' woven cloth ' lex., plōta -- ' bandage, cloth ' Suśr. or with pavásta -- is obscure: EWA ii 347 with lit. Forms meaning ' cloth to smear with, smearing ' poss. conn. with or infl. by pusta -- 2 n. ' working in clay ' (prob. ← Drav., Tam. pūcu &c. DED 3569, EWA ii 319)] 1. Pk. pōa -- n. ' cloth '; Paš.ar. pōwok ' cloth ', pōg ' net, web ' (but lauṛ. dar. pāwāk ' cotton cloth ', Gaw. pāk IIFL iii 3, 150). 2. Pk. potta -- , °taga -- , °tia -- n. ' cotton cloth ', pottī -- , °tiā -- , °tullayā -- , puttī -- f. ' piece of cloth, man's dhotī, woman's sāṛī ', pottia -- ' wearing clothes '; S. potī f. ' shawl ', potyo m. ' loincloth '; L. pot, pl. °tā f. ' width of cloth '; P. potṛā m. ' child's clout ', potṇā ' to smear a wall with a rag '; N. poto ' rag to lay on lime -- wash ', potnu ' to smear '; Or. potā ' gunny bag '; OAw. potaï ' smears, plasters '; H. potā m. ' whitewashing brush ', potī f. ' red cotton ', potiyā m. ' loincloth ', potṛā m. ' baby clothes '; G. potn. ' fine cloth, texture ', potũ n. ' rag ', potī f., °tiyũ n. ' loincloth ', potṛī f. ' small do. '; M. pot m. ' roll of coarse cloth ', n. ' weftage or texture of cloth ', potrẽ n. ' rag for smearing cowdung '.3. Pa. potthaka -- n. ' cheap rough hemp cloth ', potthakamma -- n. ' plastering '; Pk. pottha -- , °aya -- n.m. ' cloth '; S. potho m. ' lump of rag for smearing, smearing, cloth soaked in opium '. 4. Pa. ponti -- ' rags '. 5. Wg. pōč ' cotton cloth, muslin ', Kt. puč; Pr. puč ' duster, cloth ', pū́čuk ' clothes '; S. poco m. ' rag for plastering, plastering '; P. poccā m. ' cloth or brush for smearing ',pocṇā ' to smear with earth '; Or. pucā̆ra, pucurā ' wisp of rag or jute for whitewashing with, smearing with

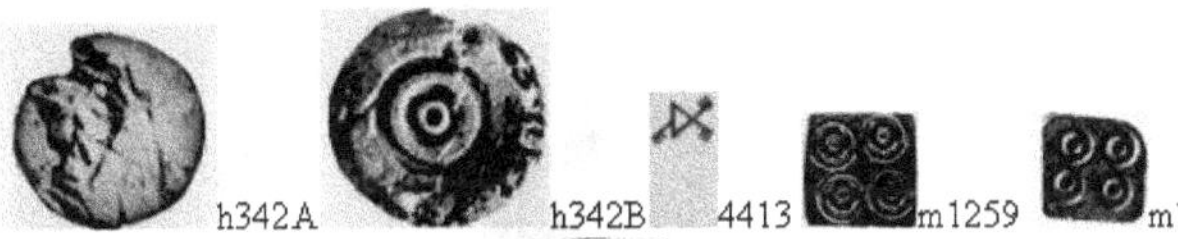

h342A h342B 4413 m1259 m1260

m0352A m0352C m0352D m0352E

m0352F m1654A ivory cube m1654B ivory cube

m1654D ivory cube m1254 m1255 Nausharo10 Slide 187 A faience button seal with geometric motif (H2000-4491/9999-34) was found on the surface of Mound AB at Harappa by one of the workmen.

[Harappa 2000 find].

m1256 m1257 m1258

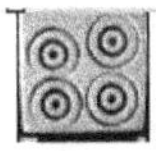

Slide 203 (Kenoyer, 2002). Steatite button seal Fired steatite button seal with four concentric circle designs from the Trench 54 area (H2000-4432/2174-3)

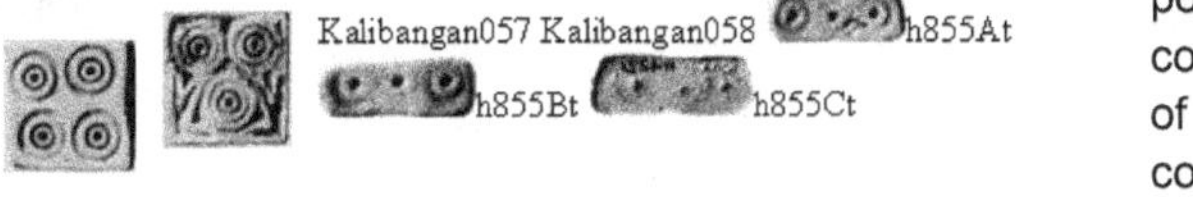

Kalibangan057 Kalibangan058 h855At h855Bt h855Ct

m1259 m1260 h974Ait h974Bit h974Cit 4592 h978Ait h978Bit h978Cit

5412 h888Abit 4466 h889Abit 5477

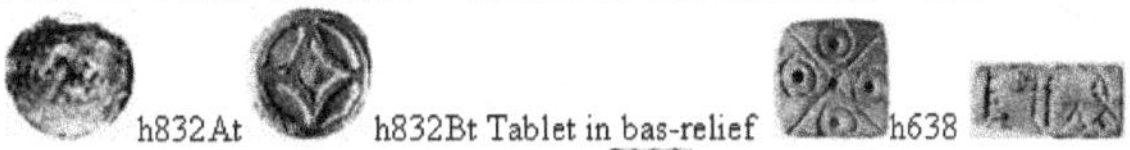

h832At h832Bt Tablet in bas-relief h638

h352A h352B h352C 4575 Pict-120: One or more dotted circles. [54 out of 67 objects on which this glyph occurs, are miniature tablets] The text on top line occurs mainly on miniature tablets of Harappa over 46 times.

such a rag '. (CDIAL 8400) போத்தி pōtti போற்றி pōr̲r̲i , < id. n. 1. Praise, applause, commendation; புகழ்மொழி. (W.) 2. Brahman temple-priest of Malabar; கோயிற் பூசைசெய்யும் மலையாளநாட்டுப் பிராமணன். (W.) 3. See போத்தி, 1.--int. Exclamation of praise; துதிச்சொல்வகை. பொய்த்தீர் காட்சிப் புரையோய் போற்றி (சிலப். 13, 92) (Tamil) potR `" Purifier "'N. of one of the 16 officiating priests at a sacrifice (the assistant of the Brahman (RV. Br. ŚrS. Hariv.)

trika, a group of three (Skt.) The occurrence of a three-fold depiction on a trefoil may thus be a phonetic determinant, a suffix to potṛ as in potṛka

Rebus reading of the hieroglyph: potti 'temple-priest' (Ma.) போத்தி pōtti போற்றி pōr̲r̲i , < id. n. 1. Praise, applause, commendation; புகழ்மொழி. (W.) 2. Brahman temple-priest of Malabar; கோயிற் பூசைசெய்யும் மலையாளநாட்டுப் பிராமணன். (W.) 3. See போத்தி, 1.--int. Exclamation of praise; துதிச்சொல்வகை. பொய்த்தீர் காட்சிப் புரையோய் போற்றி (சிலப். 13, 92) (Tamil) potR `" Purifier "'N. of one of the 16 officiating priests at a sacrifice (the assistant of the Brahman (RV. Br. ŚrS. Hariv.)

Rebus: Bi. *pot* ' jeweller's polishing stone ' (CDIAL 8403). [The 'dotted circle' may denote a polished bead; hence, Pk. *pottī* -- f. 'glass ' (CDIAL 8403).]

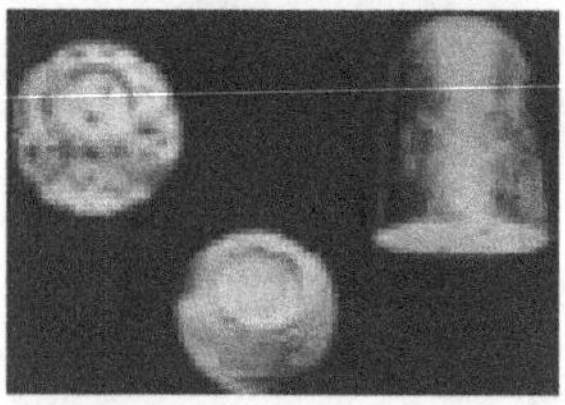

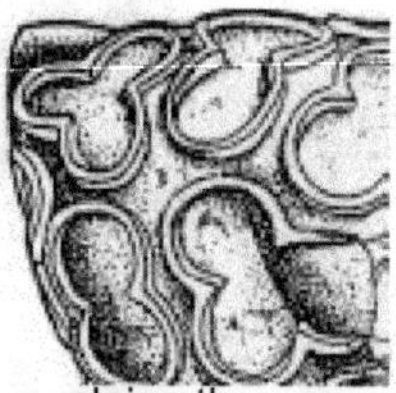

Sacredness connoted by the temple-priest explains the occurrence of the trefoil glyph on the base for holding a śivalinga. Two bases decorated with trefoil and a lingam. Smoothed, polished pedestal of dark red stone. National Museum of Pakistan, Karachi. After Mackay 1938: 1,411; II, pl. 107:35; cf. Parpola, 1994, p. 218.

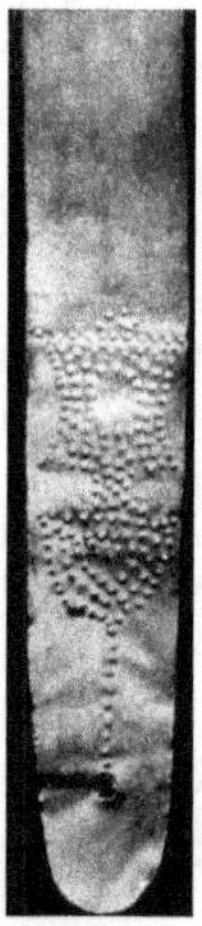

pheṭā̃r a heifer (Santali) Heifer with trefoil inlays, Uruk (W.16017) c. 3000 BCE; shell mass with inlays of lapis lazuli, 5.3 cm long. Vorderasiatisches Museum, Berlin; cf. Parpola, 1994, p. 213.

Trefoil decorated bull; traces of red pigment remain inside the trefoils. Steatite statue fragment. Mohenjo-daro (Sd 767). After Ardeleanu-Jansen, 1989: 196, fig. 1; cf. Parpola, 1994, p. 213. pōtu 'male of animals' (Telugu) A phonetic determinative of the trefoil motif.

Trefoils painted on steatite beads. Harappa (After Vats. Pl. CXXXIII, Fig. 2)

Glyph: pottar, பொத்தல் pottal, n. < id. [Ka.poṭṭare, Ma. pottu, Tu.potre.]

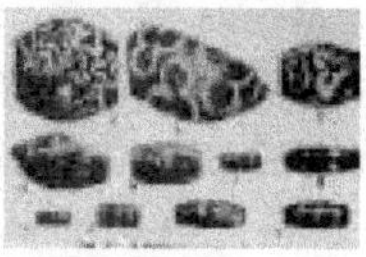

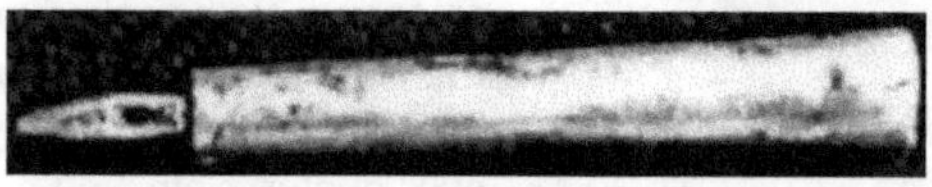

Fillet on the fore-head of the priest statuette, 2700 BCE. Stone. Mohenjo-daro. Karachi Museum. The priest wears a fillet similar to the two fillets of gold which bears the standard device embossed on them. The fillets of gold were discovered at Mohenjo-daro. Similar gold ornaments with embossed standard devices were also reported from an Akkadian burial site in West Asia. [Source: Page 22, Fig. 12 in: Deo Prakash Sharma, 2000, *Harappan seals, sealings and copper tablets*, Delhi, National Museum].

The central ornament worn on the forehead of the famous "priest-king" sculpture from Mohenjo-daro appears to represent an eye bead, possibly made of gold with steatite inlay in the center.

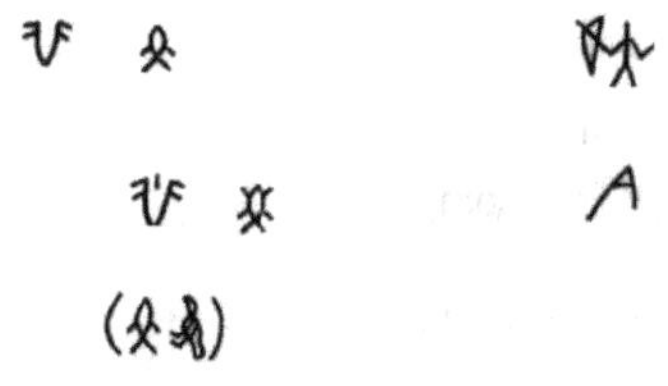

Golden pendant with inscription from jewelry hoard at Mohenjo-daro. Drawing of inscription that encircles the gold ornament. Needle-like pendant with cylindrical body. Two other examples, one with a different series of incised signs were found together. The pendant is made from a hollow cylinder with soldered ends and perforated point. Museum No. MM 1374.50.271; Marshall 1931: 521, pl. CLI, B3. [After Fig. 4.17a, b in: JM Kenoyer, 1998, p. 196].

Gold fillet depicting the standard device, Mohenjo-daro, 2600 BCE. [Source: Page 32 in: Deo Prakash Sharma, 2000, *Harappan seals, sealings and copper tablets*, Delhi, National Museum]. At *a* Marshall, *MIC*, Pl. CLI are specimens of fillets consisting of thin bands of beaten gold with holes for cords at their ends.

Harappa. Standard device shown on faience tablets (left: H90-1687, right, H93-2051) and carved in ivory (center, H93-2092). [After Fig. 5.12 in JM Kenoyer, 1998]. The miniature replica object has been recovered in 1993 from excavations at Harappa. This may be an ivory replica of a device made of basketry and wood. This replica shows a hemispherical lower basin with dotted circles and a cylindrical top portion with cross-hatching. The shaft extending from the base seems to be broken on this replica.

'Dotted circle' is a sacred glyph. It is a hieroglyph.

Epigraphs 5477, 1554; 4604, 5477

Thus, Indus writing is perhaps an indigenous evolution at about the same time (or, perhaps two centuries earlier than the time, c. 3500 BCE) the first human document was created usine hieroglyphs read rebus for Narmer palette of ca. 33rd cent. BCE.

Comparble to m0304 showing a seated person in penance, is a seal showing a scarfed person in penance:

He also has scarf as a pigtail, is horned with two stars shown within the horn-curves.

Glyph of 'a pair of stars' also on the 'water-carrier' glyph of Gadd seal (PBA18).

Other glyphic elements are: twig, horns.

kamaḍha 'penance' (Pkt.) Rebus: kammaṭi a coiner (Ka.) kampaṭṭam 'mint' (Ta.) Kur. Kaṇḍō a stool. Malt. Kanḍo stool, seat. (DEDR 1179) Rebus: kaṇḍ = a furnace, altar (Santali.lex.)

dhaṭu m. (also dhaṭhu) m. 'scarf' (WPah.) (CDIAL 6707) Allograph: ḍato = claws of crab (Santali); dhātu = mineral (Skt.), dhatu id. (Santali)

kūdī, kūṭī bunch of twigs (Skt.lex.) kūdī (also written as kūṭī in manuscripts) occurs in the Atharvaveda (AV 5.19.12) and Kauśika Sūtra (Bloomsfield's ed.n, xliv. Cf. Bloomsfield, American Journal of Philology, 11, 355; 12,416; Roth, Festgruss an Bohtlingk, 98) denotes it as a twig. This is identified as that of Badarī, the jujube tied to the body of the dead to efface their traces. (See Vedic Index, I, p. 177). Rebus: kuṭhi 'smelting furnace' (Santali) koṭe 'forged (metal) (Santali) Vikalpa: మండ [ maṇḍa ] *manḍa*. [Tel.] n. A twig with leaves on it. చెట్టుకొమ్మ. A small branch, ఉపశాఖ. the back of the hand. మీఁజెయ్యి. A frying brush,వేపుడుకుచ్చు.

mēḍha The polar star. (Marathi) Rebus: meḍ 'iron' (Ho.) dula 'pair' (Kashmiri); Rebus: dul 'cast (metal)'(Santali) ḍabe, ḍabea 'large horns, with a sweeping upward curve, applied to buffaloes' (Santali) Rebus: ḍab, ḍhimba, ḍhompo 'lump (ingot?)', clot, make a lump or clot, coagulate, fuse, melt together (Santali)

The glyphic composition of the seal read rebus: *dul meḍ ḍab dhatu kammaṭi* 'cast metal ingot, metallic minerals coiner.'

The text of the inscription shows two types of 'fish' glyphs: one fish + fish with scales circumscribed by four short-strokes: aya 'fish' (Mu.); rebus: aya 'metal' (Skt.)
gaṇḍa set of four (Santali) kaṇḍa 'fire-altar' cf. ayaskāṇḍa a quantity of iron, excellent iron (Pāṇ.gaṇ)
The reading is consistent with the entire glyphic composition related to the mineral, mint forge.

Another comparable glyphic composition is provided by seal m1181.

m1181. Seal. Mohenjo-daro. Three-faced, horned person (with a three-leaved Ils branch on the crown), wearing bangles and armlets and seated on a hoofed platform.

m1181 Text of inscription.

Each glyphic element on this composition and text of inscription is decoded rebus:

Glyph: 'hoof': Ku. *khuṭo* ' leg, foot ', °*ṭī* ' goat's leg '; N. *khuṭo* ' leg, foot '(CDIAL 3894). S. *khuṛī* f. ' heel '; WPah. paṅ. *khūṛ* ' foot '. khura m. ' hoof ' KātyŚr̥. 2. *khuḍa -- 1 (*khuḍaka --* , *khula°* ' ankle -- bone ' Suśr.). [← Drav. T. Burrow BSOAS xii 376: it belongs to the word -- group ' heel <-> ankle -- knee -- wrist ', see *kuṭṭha -- ](CDIAL 3906). *Ta.* kuracu, kuraccai horse's hoof. *Ka.* gorasu, gorase, gorise, gorusu hoof. *Te.* gorija, gorise, (B. also) gorije, korije id. / Cf. Skt.khura- id. (DEDR 1770). Allograph: (Kathiawar) *khūṭ* m. ' Brahmani bull ' (G.) Rebus: *khūṭ* 'community, guild' (Santali)

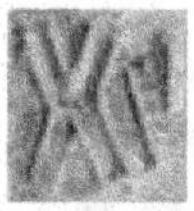

Two glyphs 'cross-road' glyph + 'splice' glyph — which start from right the inscription of Text on Seal m1181.The pair of glyphs on the inscription is decoded: dhatu adaru bāṭa 'furnace (for) mineral, native metal'. Dāṭu 'cross'(Telugu); bāṭa 'road' (Telugu). Aḍar = splinter (Santali); rebus: aduru = native metal (Ka.) aduru = gan.iyinda tegadu karagade iruva aduru = ore taken from the mine and not subjected to melting in a furnace (Kannada. Siddha_nti Subrahman.ya' S'astri's new interpretation of the Amarakos'a, Bangalore, Vicaradarpana Press, 1872, p. 330) Thus, the two glyphs 'cross-road + splice' read rebus: aduru dhatu bāṭa 'native metal (mineral/element) furnace'.

Other glyphic elements: aḍar kuṭhi 'native metal furnace'; soḍu 'fireplace'; sekra 'bell-metal and brass worker'; Glyph of 'fish + infixed stroke': aya sal 'iron (metal) workshop'.

Glyph of 'two curved lines': kuṭila 'bent'; Rebus: kuṭila 'bronze (8 parts copper, 2 parts tin)(Skt.) dula 'pair' (Kashmiri); dul 'cast (metal)' (Santali). Glyph of 'rim of jar': kaṇḍa kanka; rebus: furnace account (scribe). Together with the 'rim-of-jar' glyph, the pair of glyphs read rebus: cast bronze furnace account (scribe).

In a comparable glyphic composition showing a person seated in penance, two serpents are shown flanking the person.

m453BC Seated in penance, the person is flanked on either side by a kneeling adorant, offering a pot and a hooded serpent rearing up. Glyph: *kaṇḍo* 'stool'. Rebus; *kaṇḍ* 'furnace'. Vikalpa: kaṇḍ 'stone (ore) metal'. Rebus: *kamaḍha* 'penance'. Rebus 1: *kaṇḍ 'stone ore'.* Rebus 2*:* *kampaṭṭa* 'mint'. Glyph: 'serpent hood': *paṭa.* Rebus: *pata* 'sharpness (of knife), tempered (metal). padm 'tempered iron' (Ko.) Glyph: rimless pot: *baṭa.* Rebus: *bhaṭa* 'smelter, furnace'. It appears that the message of the glyphics is about a mint or metal workshop which produces sharpened, tempered iron (stone ore) using a furnace.

m0492A,B,C Pict-99: Person throwing a spear at a bison and placing one foot on the head of the bison; a hooded serpent at left.Two bisons standing face-to-face. Person spearing bison. A hooded serpent.

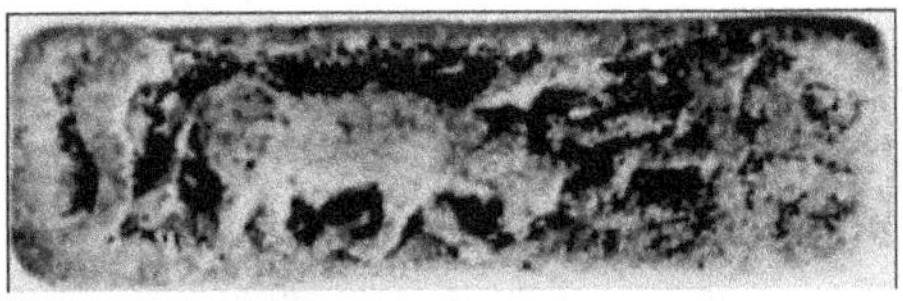 

படம் paṭam , *n.* < *phaṭa.* 1. Cobra's hood; பாம்பின் விரிந்த தலையிடம். பைந்நாப் பட வரவே ரல்குலுமை (திருவாச. 34, 1). phaṭa n. ' expanded hood of snake ' MBh. 2. *phēṭṭa -- 2. [Cf. *phuṭa* -- m., °*ṭā* -- f., *sphuṭa* -- m. lex., °*ṭā* -- f. Pañcat. (Pk.*phuḍā* -- f.), *sphaṭa* -- m., °*ṭā* -- f., *sphōṭā* -- f. lex. and phaṇa -- 1. Conn. words in Drav. T. Burrow BSOAS xii 386] 1. Pk. *phaḍa* -- m.n. ' snake's hood ', °*ḍā* -- f., M. *phaḍā* m., °*ḍī* f.
2. A. *pheṭ*, *phēṭ*.(CDIAL 9040).

Rebus: patam = sharpness (as of the edge of a knife)(Ta.); padm (obl. Padt-) temper of iron (Ko.); pada = keenness of edge or sharpness (Ka.); hada = sharpeness (as of a knife), forming (as metals) to proper degree of hardness (Tu.); padnā sharpness (Go.); padanu, padunu = sharpness, temper (Te.); padnu = sharpening (of knife by heating and hammering)(Konḍa); pato = sharp (as a blade); patter = to sharpen (Malt.)(DEDR 3907). paṭiman पटिमन् *m.* Sharpness, pungency (Skt. Apte.lexicon). పదను *padunu* Goodness of metal; ఉక్కును కాచడములో పదును తప్పినది he failed in giving the right temper to the steel. "పదునైన బలువాడి మెరుగువాలు." HK. iv. 193. పదను పెట్టేరాయి a bone or whetstone; పదునుపెట్టు to set or sharpen. (Telugu)

 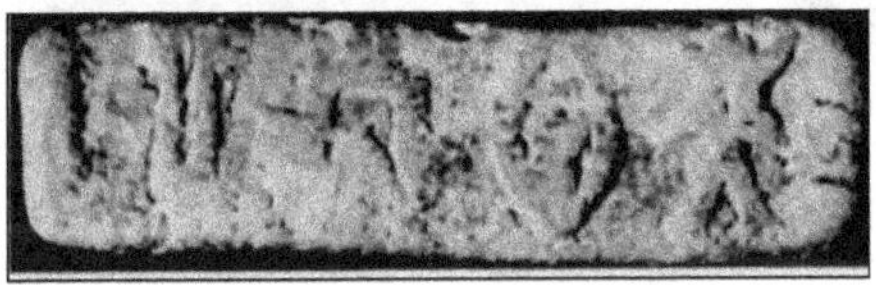

paddu = item, entry in an account (Te.); poddu – thing, item (Pa.)(DEDR 3919).

Vikalpa: Glyph: moṇḍ the tail of a serpent (Santali) Rebus: Md. moḍenī ' massages, mixes '. Kal.rumb. moṇḍ -- ' to thresh ', urt. maṇḍ -- ' to soften ' (CDIAL 9890) mā̃ḍ माँड् । मिश्रीकरणम् f. mixing (Gr.Gr. 126), esp. mixing up or kneading (by rubbing with the palms of the hands) of flour or other food with water, buttermilk, etc. (Gr.Gr. 1); cf. mā̃ḍay and namda-mō̃ḍ. -- diñü -- दिञू&below; । मिश्रीकरणम् f.inf. to mix food, as ab. mā̃ḍi onu- Thus, the ligature of the serpent as a tail of the composite animal glyph is decoded as: polished or mixed (alloyed?) metal (artifact). The glyphic composition can be read rebus: maṇḍ meḍ 'polished iron'; kamaḍa 'penance'. Rebus: kammaṭi 'coiner, mint'. kaṇḍo 'stool'. Rebus; kaṇḍ 'furnace'. Vikalpa: kaṇḍ 'stone (ore) metal'.

AN253198001 British Museum. This seal with zebu (*bos indicus* hieroglyph) of Mohenjo-daro also contains a pair of glyphs comparable to the two glyphs: ‘two curved lines’ + ‘rim of jar’. Preceded by (a) two long linear strokes: ib ‘two’; rebus: ib ‘iron’ (Santali); dula ‘pair’; rebus: dul ‘cast (metal)(Santali) (b) ‘flag’ glyph koḍi ‘flag’ (Ta.)(DEDR 2049). Koḍ ‘workshop’ (Kuwi); and (c) ‘corner of oval’ glyph: kana, kanac = corner (Santali); kañcu = bronze (Te.) kan- copper work (Ta.) Vikalpa: *khuṇṭa ‘ corner ’. 2. *kuṇṭa — 2. [Cf. *khōñca -- ] 1. Phal. Khun ‘ corner ’; H. khũṭ m. ‘ corner, direction ’ (→ P. khūṭ f. ‘ corner, side ’); G. khũṭṛī f. ‘ angle ’. <-> X kōṇa -- : G. khuṇ f., khū˘ṇɔ m. ‘ corner ’.2. S. kuṇḍa f. ‘ corner ’; P. kũṭ f. ‘ corner, side ’ (← H.). (CDIAL 3898) Rebus: kūdār, kūdāri (B.); kundāru (Or.); kundau to turn on a lathe, to carve, to chase; kundau dhiri = a hewn stone; kundau murhut = a graven image (Santali) kunda a turner’s lathe (Skt.)(CDIAL 3295)

Glyph: zebu (*bos indicus*) + rings on shoulder: adar ḍangar ‘zebu’; rebus: aduru ḍangar ‘native metal smith’. Vikalpa: khūṭro = entire bull; khūṭ= brāhmaṇi bull (G.) khuṇṭiyo = an uncastrated bull (Kathiawad. G.lex.) khũṭaḍum a bullock (used in Jhālwāḍ)(G.) kuṇṭai = bull (Ta.lex.) cf. khũdhi hump on the back; khuĩdhū hump-backed (G.)(CDIAL 3902).; rebus: community, guild. koḍiyum ‘rings on neck’; rebus: koḍ ‘workshop’ (Kuwi.G.)

*the person is seated on a hoofed platform (representing a bull): decoding of glyphics read rebus: ḍangar 'bull'; ḍhangar 'blacksmith' (H.); koṇḍo 'stool'; rebus: koḍ 'workshop'. The glyphics show that the seal relates to a blacksmith's workshop.

*the seated person's hair-dress includes a horned twig. Aḍaru twig; aḍiri small and thin branch of a tree; aḍari small branches (Ka.); aḍaru twig (Tu.)(DEDR 67). Aḍar = splinter (Santali); rebus: aduru = native metal (Ka.) Vikalpa: kūtī = bunch of twigs (Skt.) Rebus: kuṭhi = furnace (Santali)

*tiger's mane on face: The face is depicted with bristles of hair, representing a tiger's mane. Cūḍā, cūlā, cūliyā tiger's mane (Pkt.)(CDIAL 4883) Rebus: cuḷḷai = potter's kiln, furnace (Ta.); cūḷai furnace, kiln, funeral pile (Ta.); cuḷḷa potter's furnace; cūḷa brick kiln (Ma.); cullī fireplace (Skt.); cullī, ullī id. (Pkt.)(CDIAL 4879; DEDR 2709). Sulgao, salgao to light a fire; sen:gel, sokol fire (Santali.lex.) hollu, holu = fireplace (Kuwi); soḍu fireplace, stones set up as a fireplace (Mand.); ule furnace (Tu.)(DEDR 2857).

*bangles on arms *cūḍā* 'bracelets' (H.); rebus: *soḍu* 'fireplace'. Vikalpa: sekeseke, sekseke covered, as the arms with ornaments; sekra those who work in brass and bell metal; sekra sakom a kind of armlet of bell metal (Santali)

*fish + splinter glyph ayo, hako 'fish'; a~s = scales of fish (Santali); rebus: aya = iron (G.); ayah, ayas = metal (Skt.)sal stake, spike, splinter, thorn, difficulty (H.); sal 'workshop' (Santali) Vikalpa: Glyph: ḍhāḷiyum = adj. sloping, inclining; rebus: ḍhāḷako = a large metal ingot (G.) H. dhāṛnā 'to send out, pour out, cast (metal)' (CDIAL 6771). Thus, the ligatured 'fish + sloping (stroke)' is read rebus: metal ingot.

•dāṭu = cross (Te.); dhatu = mineral (Santali) dhātu 'mineral (Pali) dhātu 'mineral' (Vedic); a mineral, metal (Santali); dhāta id. (G.)H. dhāṛnā 'to send out, pour out, cast (metal)' (CDIAL 6771). Aṭar a splinter; aṭaruka to burst, crack, slit off, fly open; aṭarcca splitting, a crack; aṭarttuka to split, tear off, open (an oyster)(Ma.); aḍaruni to crack (Tu.)(DEDR 66). Dāravum = to tear, to break (G.) dar = a fissure, a rent, a trench; darkao = to crack,to break; bhit darkaoena = the wall is cracked (Santali) Rebus: aduru 'native (unsmelted) metl' (Kannada).

Seated person in penance: *kamaḍha* 'penance' (Pkt.); rebus: *kampaṭṭa* 'mint' (Ma.) Glyphics of shoggy, brisltles of hair on the face of the person: Shoggy hair; tiger's mane. Sodo bodo, sodro bodro adj. adv. Rough, hairy, shoggy, hirsute, uneven; sodo [Persian. Sodā, dealing] trade; traffic; merchandise; marketing; a bargain; the purchase or sale of goods; buying and selling; mercantile dealings (G.lex.) sodagor = a merchant, trader; sodāgor (P.B.) (Santali.lex.)

Glyph: clump between the two horns: kuṇḍa n. ' clump ' e.g. darbha—kuṇḍa—Pāṇ.(CDIAL 3236). Kundār turner (A.)(CDIAL 3295). Kuṇḍa n. ' clump ' e.g. darbha—kuṇḍa—Pāṇ. [← Drav. (Tam. Koṇṭai ' tuft of hair ', Kan. Goṇḍe ' cluster ', &c.) T. Burrow BSOAS xii 374] Pk. Kuṁḍa—n. ' heap of crushed sugarcane stalks ' (CDIAL 3266) Ta. Koṇtai tuft, dressing of hair in large coil on the head, crest of a bird, head (as of a nail), knob (as of a cane), round top. Ma. Koṇṭa tuft `of hair. Ko.goṇḍ knob on end of walking-stick, head of pin; koṇḍ knot of hair at back of head. To. Kwïḍy Badaga woman's knot of hair at back of head (< Badaga koṇḍe). Ka. Koṇḍe, goṇḍe tuft, tassel, cluster. Koḍ. Koṇḍe tassels of sash, knob-like foot of cane-stem. Tu. Goṇḍè topknot, tassel, cluster. Te. Koṇḍe, (K. also) koṇḍi knot of hair on the crown of the head. Cf. 2049 Ta. Koṭi. / Cf. Skt. Kuṇḍa- clump (e.g. darbha-kuṇḍa-), Pkt. (DNM) goṇḍī- = mañjarī-; Turner, CDIAL, no. 3266; cf. also Mar. gōḍā cluster, tuft. (DEDR 2081) kuṇḍī = crooked buffalo horns (L.) rebus: kuṇḍī = chief of village. Kuṇḍi-a = village headman; leader of a village (Pkt.lex.) I.e. śreṇi jet.t.ha chief of metal-worker guild. Koḍ 'horns'; rebus: koḍ 'artisan's workshop' (G.) Thus the entire glyphic composition of hieroglyphs on m1185 seal is a message conveyed from a sodagor 'merchant, trader'. The bill of lading lists a variety of repertoire of the artisan guild's trade load from a mint — the native metal and brass workshop of blacksmith (guild) with furnace: aḍar kuṭhi 'native metal furnace'; soḍu 'fireplace'; sekra 'bell-metal and brass worker'; *aya sal* 'iron (metal) workshop'.

Indus script hieroglyphs: composite animal, smithy

Composite animal on Indus script is a composite hieroglyph composed of many glyphic elements. All glyphic elements are read rebus to complete the technical details of the bill of lading of artifacts created by artisans.

m1177 Mohenjo-daro seal. 2450

Glyphic elements on the field symbol (composite animal complex glyphic)

*mẽṛhet, meḍ* 'iron' [*meḍho* 'ram']; *karba, ib* 'hard iron' [*karibha* 'elephant']; *kol* 'iron smith' [*kola* 'tiger']; *koḍ* 'artisan's workshop' [*koḍ* 'horns']; *mũh* 'ingot' [mũhe 'face']; *padm* 'temper of iron' [*phaṭa* cobra's hood]; *dhatu* 'mineral' [*dhaṭu* 'scarf (on neck)']; *koḍ* 'artisan's workshop' [*koḍiyum* 'rings on neck']

Inscription text glyphics: turner's workshop, casting (metal) furnace (stone ore) account scribe.

Glyph: *kōnṭa* 'corner' (Nk.); Tu. *kōṇṭu* 'angle, corner' (Tu.). Rebus: *kõdā* 'to turn in a lathe' (B.)

Glyph: 'splinter' sal 'splinter'. Rebus: sal 'artisan's workshop'.

Glyph: dula 'pair'. Rebus: dul 'casting (metal)' (Santali) Glyph: kolmo 'rice plant'. Rebus: kolami 'smithy'.

Glyph: *kaṇḍa kanka* 'rim of jar'. Rebus: furnace (stone ore) account (scribe).

m1180 Mohenjo-daro seal. Human-faced markhor.

m0301 Mohenjo-daro seal.

m0302 Mohenjo-daro seal.

m0303 Mohenjo-daro seal.

m0299. Mohenjo-daro seal.

m0300. Mohenjo-daro seal.

m1179. Mohenjo-daro seal. Markhor or ram with human face in composite hieroglyph.

h594. Harappa seal. Composite animal (with elephant trunk and rings (scarves) on shoulder visible).koṭiyum = a wooden circle put round the neck of an animal; koṭ = neck (G.) Vikalpa: kaḍum 'neck-band, ring'; rebus: khāḍ 'trench, firepit' (G.) Vikalpa: khaḍḍā f. Hole, mine, cave (CDIAL 3790). Kanduka, kandaka ditch, trench (Tu.); kandakamu id. (Te.); kanda trench made as a fireplace during weddings (Konda); kanda small trench for fireplace (Kui); kandri a pit (Malt)(DEDR 1214) khaḍḍa— 'hole, pit'. [Cf. *gaḍḍa— and list s.v. kartá—1] Pk. Khaḍḍā— f. 'hole, mine, cave', ḍaga— m. 'one who digs a hole', ḍōlaya— m. 'hole'; Bshk. (Biddulph) "kād" (= khaḍ?) 'valley'; K. khŏḍ m. 'pit', khŏ̃ḍü f. 'small pit', khoḍu m. 'vulva'; S. khaḏa f. 'pit'; L. khaḍḍ f. 'pit, cavern, ravine'; P. khaḍḍ f. 'pit, ravine', ḍī f. 'hole for a weaver's feet' (→ Ku. Khaḍḍ, N. khaḍ; H. khaḍ, khaḍḍā m. 'pit, low ground, notch'; Or. Khāḍi 'edge of a deep pit'; M. khaḍḍā m. 'rough hole, pit'); Wpah. Khaś. Khaḍḍā 'stream'; N. khāṛo 'pit, bog', khāṛi

'creek', khāṛal 'hole (in ground or stone)'. — Altern. < *khāḍa—: Gy. Gr. Xar f. 'hole'; Ku. Khāṛ 'pit'; B. khāṛī 'creek, inlet', khāṛal 'pit, ditch'; H. khāṛī f. 'creek, inlet', khaṛ—har, al m. 'hole'; Marw. Khāṛo m. 'hole'; M. khāḍ f. 'hole, creek', ḍā m. 'hole', ḍī f. 'creek, inlet'. 3863 khắtra— n. 'hole' Hpariś., 'pond, spade' Uṇ. [√khan] Pk. Khatta— n. 'hole, manure', aya— m. 'one who digs in a field'; S. khāṭru m. 'mine made by burglars', ṭro m. 'fissure, pit, gutter made by rain'; P. khāt m. 'pit, manure', khāttā m. 'grain pit', ludh. Khattā m. (→ H. khattā m., khatiyā f.); N. khāt 'heap (of stones, wood or corn)'; B. khāt, khāṭrū 'pit, pond'; Or. Khāta 'pit', tā 'artificial pond'; Bi. Khātā 'hole, gutter, grain pit, notch (on beam and yoke of plough)', khattā 'grain pit, boundary ditch'; Mth. Khātā, khattā 'hole, ditch'; H. khāt m. 'ditch, well', f. 'manure', khātā m. 'grain pit'; G. khātar n. 'housebreaking, house sweeping, manure', khātriyũ n. 'tool used in housebreaking' (→ M. khātar f. 'hole in a wall', khātrā m. 'hole, manure', khātryā m. 'housebreaker'); M. khắt n.m. 'manure' ( lls d. khatāviṇẽ 'to manure', khāterẽ n. 'muck pit'). — Unexpl. ṭ in L. khāṭvā̃ m. 'excavated pond', khāṭī f. 'digging to clear or excavate a canal' (~ S. khātī f. 'id.', but khāṭyāro m. 'one employed to measure canal work') and khaṭṭaṇ 'to dig'. (CDIAL 3790) •gaḍa— 1 m. 'ditch' lex. [Cf. *gaḍḍa—1 and list s.v. kartá—1] Pk. Gaḍa— n. 'hole'; Paš. Gaṛu 'dike'; Kho. (Lor.) gōḷ 'hole, small dry ravine'; A. garā 'high bank'; B. gaṛ 'ditch, hole in a husking machine'; Or. Gaṛa 'ditch, moat'; M. gaḷ f. 'hole in the game of marbles'. 3981 *gaḍḍa— 1 'hole, pit'. [G. < *garda—? — Cf. *gaḍḍ—1 and list s.v. kartá—1] Pk. Gaḍḍa— m. 'hole'; Wpah. Bhal. Cur. Gaḍḍ f., paṅ. gaḍḍṛī, pāḍ. Gaḍōṛ 'river, stream'; N. gaṛ—tir 'bank of a river'; A. gārā 'deep hole'; B. gāṛ, ṛā 'hollow, pit'; Or. Gāṛa 'hole, cave', gāṛiā 'pond'; Mth. Gāṛi 'piercing'; H. gāṛā m. 'hole'; G. garāḍ, ḍɔ m. 'pit, ditch' (< *graḍḍa— < *garda—?); Si. Gaḍaya 'ditch'. — Cf. S. giḏi f. 'hole in the ground for fire during Muharram'. — X khānĭ—: K. gān m. 'underground room'; S. (LM 323) gāṇ f. 'mine, hole for keeping water'; L. gāṇ m. 'small embanked field within a field to keep water in'; G. gāṇ f. 'mine, cellar';

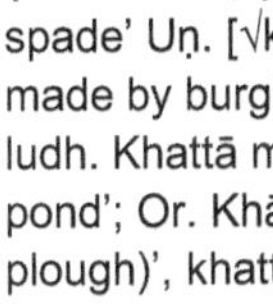

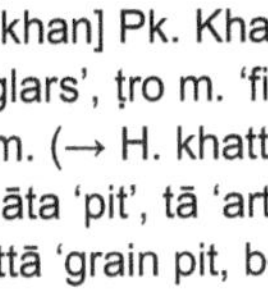

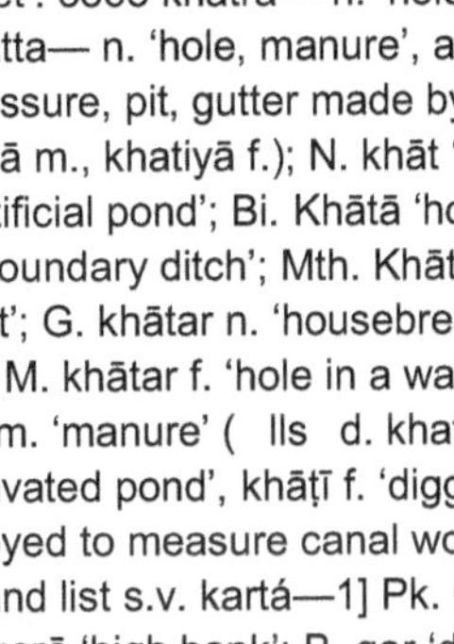

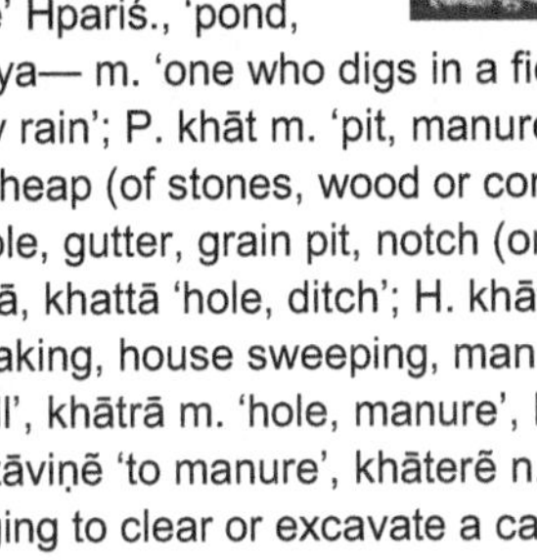

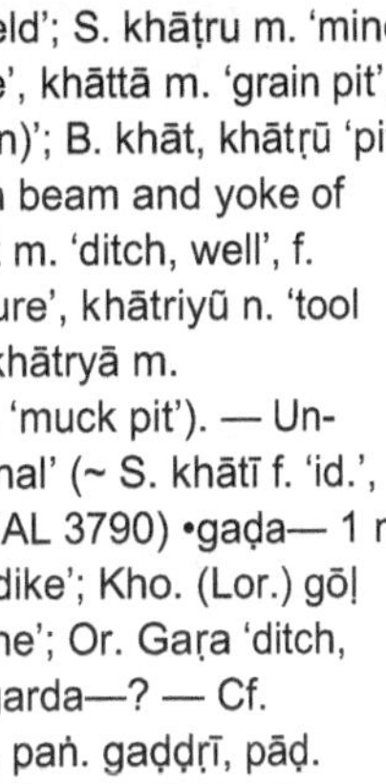

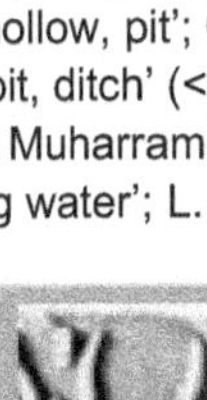

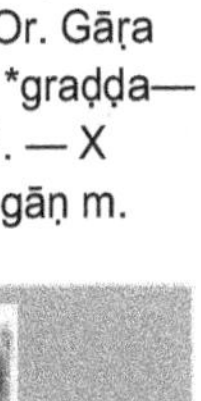

M. gāṇ f. 'cavity containing water on a raised piece of land' Wpah.kṭg. gāṛ 'hole (e.g. after a knot in wood)'. (CDIAL 3947) 3860 *khāḍa— 'a hollow'. [Cf. *khaḍḍa— and list s.v. kartá—1] S. khāṛī f. 'gulf, creek'; P. khāṛ 'level country at the foot of a mountain', ṛī f. 'deep watercourse, creek'; Bi. Khārī 'creek, inlet'; G. khāṛi , ṛī f., ṛɔ m. 'hole'. — Altern. < *khaḍḍa—: Gy. Gr. Xar f. 'hole'; Ku. Khāṛ 'pit'; B. khāṛī 'creek, inlet', khāṛal 'pit, ditch'; H. khāṛī 'creek, inlet', khaṛ—har, al m. 'hole'; Marw. Khāṛo m. 'hole'; M. khāḍ f. 'hole, creek', ḍā m. 'hole', ḍī f. 'creek, inlet'. The neck-bands hung above the shoulder of the composite animal may thus read rebus: trench or fire-pit (i.e. furnace) for the minerals/metals described by the glyphic elements connoting animals: elephant, ram (or zebu, bos indicus).

m1175 Composite glyph inscription (water-'furnace'; road, bata; M1186A Composite Text of inscription (3

animal with a two-carrier, rebus: kuti rebus: bata 'furnace'). animal hieroglyph. lines).

There are many 'human face' ligatured examples of the depiction of to animals:

Ligatured faces: some close-up images.

The animal is a quadruped: pasaramu, pasalamu = an animal, a beast, a brute, quadruped (Te.)Rebus: pasra 'smithy' (Santali) Allograph: panǰā̆r 'ladder, stairs'(Bshk.)(CDIAL 7760) Thus the composite animal connotes a smithy. Details of the smithy are described orthographically by the glyphic elements of the composition.

Rebus reading of the 'face' glyph: mũhe 'face' (Santali) mũh opening or hole (in a stove for stoking (Bi.); ingot (Santali) mũh metal ingot (Santali) mũhã̄ = the quantity of iron produced at one time in a native smelting furnace of the Kolhes; iron produced by the Kolhes and formed like a four-cornered piece a little pointed at each end; mūhā mẽṛhẽt = iron smelted by the Kolhes and formed into an equilateral lump a little pointed at each of four ends; kolhe tehen mẽṛhẽt ko mūhā akata = the Kolhes have to-day produced pig iron (Santali.lex.) kaula mengro 'blacksmith' (Gypsy) mleccha-mukha (Skt.) = milakkhu 'copper' (Pali) The Sanskrit loss mleccha-mukha should literally mean: copper-ingot absorbing the Santali gloss, mũh, as a suffix.

A remarkable phrase in Sanskrit indicates the link between mleccha and use of camels as trade caravans. This is explained in the lexicon of Apte for the lexeme: auṣṭrika 'belonging to a camel'. The lexicon entry cited *Mahābhārata*: औष्ट्रिक a. Coming from a camel (as milk); Mb.8. 44.28; -कः An oil-miller; मानुषाणां मलं म्लेच्छा म्लेच्छाना- मौष्ट्रिका मलम् । औष्ट्रिकाणां मलं षण्ढाः षण्ढानां राजयाजकाः ॥ Mb.8.45.25. From the perspective of a person devoted to śāstra and rigid disciplined life, Baudhāyana thus defines the word म्लेच्छः mlēcchḥ : -- गोमांसखादको यस्तु विरुद्धं बहु भाषते । सर्वाचारविहीनश्च म्लेच्छ इत्यभिधीयते ॥ 'A person who eatrs meat, deviates from traditional practices.'

The 'face' glyph is thus read rebus: *mleccha mũh* 'copper ingot'.

It is significant that Vatsyayana refers to in his lists of 64 arts and calls it mlecchita-vikalpa, lit. 'an alternative representation — in cryptography or cipher — of mleccha words.'

The glyphic of the hieroglyph: tail (serpent), face (human), horns (*bos indicus*, zebu or ram), trunk (elephant), front paw (tiger),

moṇḍ the tail of a serpent (Santali) Rebus: Md. Moḍenī ' massages, mixes '. Kal.rumb. moṇḍ -- ' to thresh ', urt. Maṇḍ -- ' to soften ' (CDIAL 9890) Thus, the ligature of the serpent as a tail of the composite animal glyph is decoded as: polished metal (artifact). Vikalpa: xolā = tail (Kur.); qoli id. (Malt.)(DEDr 2135). Rebus: kol 'pañcalōha' (Ta.)கொல் kol, n. 1. Iron; இரும்பு. மின் வெள்ளி பொன் கொல்லெனச் சொல்லும் (தக்கயாகப். 550). 2. Metal; உலோகம். (நாமதீப. 318.) கொல்லன் kollaṉ, n. < T. golla. Custodian of treasure; கஜானாக்காரன். (P. T. L.) கொல்லிச்சி kollicci, n. Fem. Of கொல்லன். Woman of the blacksmith caste; கொல்லச் சாதிப் பெண். (யாழ். அக.) The gloss kollicci is notable. It clearly evidences that kol was a blacksmith. Kola 'blacksmith' (Ka.); Koḍ. Kollë blacksmith (DEDR 2133). Ta. Kol working in iron, blacksmith; kollaṉ blacksmith. Ma. Kollan blacksmith, artificer. Ko. Kole·l smithy, temple in Kota village. To. Kwala·l Kota smithy. Ka. Kolime, kolume, kulame, kulime, kulume, kulme fire-pit, furnace; (Bell.; U.P.U.) konimi blacksmith;

(Gowda) Ils id. Koḍ. Kollë blacksmith. Te. Kolimi furnace. Go. (SR.) kollusānā to mend implements; (Ph.) kolstānā, kulsānā to forge; (Tr.) kōlstānā to repair (of ploughshares); (SR.) kolmi smithy (Voc. 948). Kuwi (F.) kolhali to forge (DEDR 2133) கொல்² kol Working in iron; கொற்றொழில். Blacksmith; கொல்லன். (Tamil) mūhe 'face' (Santali); Rebus: mūh '(copper) ingot' (Santali);mleccha-mukha (Skt.) = milakkhu 'copper' (Pali) கோடு kōṭu : •நடுநிலை நீங்குகை. கோடிறீக் கூற் றம் (நாலடி, 5). 3. [K. kōḍu.] Tusk; யானை பன்றிகளின் தந்தம். மத்த யானையின் கோடும் (தேவா. 39, 1). 4. Horn; விலங்கின் கொம்பு. கோட்டிடை யாடினை கூத்து (திவ். இயற். திருவிருத். 21). Ko. Kṛ (obl. Kṭ-) horns (one horn is kob), half of hair on each side of parting, side in game, log, section of bamboo used as fuel, line marked out. To. Kwṛ (obl. Kwṭ-) horn, branch, path across stream in thicket. Ka. Kōḍu horn, tusk, branch of a tree; kōṟ horn. Tu. Kōḍů, kōḍu horn. Te. Kōḍu rivulet, branch of a river. Pa. kōḍ (pl. kōḍul) horn (DEDR 2200)Rebus: koḍ = the place where artisans work (G.) kul 'tiger' (Santali); kōlu id. (Te.) kōlupuli = Bengal tiger (Te.)Pk. Kolhuya -- , kulha — m. ' jackal ' < *kōḍhu -- ; H.kolhā, °lā m. ' jackal ', adj. ' crafty '; G. kohlũ, °lũ n. ' jackal ', M. kolhā, °lā m. krōṣṭṛ̊ ' crying ' BhP., m. ' jackal ' RV. = krṓṣṭu — m. Pāṇ. [√kruś] Pa. koṭṭhu -- , °uka — and kotthu -- , °uka — m. ' jackal ', Pk. Koṭṭhu — m.; Si. Koṭa ' jackal ', koṭiya ' leopard ' GS 42 (CDIAL 3615). कोल्हा [ kōlhā ] कोल्हें [ kōlhēṃ ] A jackal (Marathi) Rebus: kol 'furnace, forge' (Kuwi) kol 'alloy of five metals, pañcaloha' (Ta.) Allograph: kōla = woman (Nahali) [The ligature of a woman to a tiger is a phonetic determinant; the scribe clearly conveys that the gloss represented is kōla] karba 'iron' (Ka.)(DEDR 1278) as in ajirda karba 'iron' (Ka.) kari, karu 'black' (Ma.)(DEDR 1278) karbura 'gold' (Ka.) karbon 'black gold, iron' (Ka.) kabbiṇa 'iron' (Ka.) karum pon 'iron' (Ta.); kabin 'iron' (Ko.)(DEDR 1278) Ib 'iron' (Santali) [cf. Toda gloss below: ib 'needle'.] Ta. Irumpu iron, instrument, weapon. A. irumpu,irimpu iron. Ko. Ibid. To. Ib needle. Koḍ. Irïmbï iron. Te. Inumu id. Kol. (Kin.) inum (pl. inmul) iron, sword. Kui (Friend-Pereira) rumba vaḍi ironstone (for vaḍi, see 5285). (DEDR 486)

m0317silver

m1199 silver

Silver seal Mackay 1938, vol. 2, Pl. XC,1: XCVI, 520 ; h018: copper seal, Mohenjodaro Indian museum.

Allograph: karibha — m. ' Ficus religiosa (?) [Semantics of ficus religiosa may be relatable to homonyms used to denote both the sacred tree and rebus gloss: *loa*, ficus (Santali); *loh* 'metal' (Skt.)]

miṇḍāl markhor (Tor.wali) meḍho a ram, a sheep (G.)(CDIAL 10120)bhēḍra -- , bhēṇḍa — m. ' ram ' lex. [← Austro — as. J. Przyluski BSL xxx 200: perh. Austro — as. *mēḍra ~ bhēḍra collides with Aryan mḗḍhra — 1 in mēṇḍhra — m. ' penis ' BhP., ' ram ' lex. — See also bhēḍa — 1, mēṣá -- , ēḍa -- . — The similarity between bhēḍa — 1, bhēḍra -- , bhēṇḍa -- ' ram ' and *bhēḍa — 2 ' defective ' is paralleled by that between mḗḍhra — 1, mēṇḍha — 1 ' ram ' and *mēṇḍa — 1, *mēṇḍha — 2 (s.v. *miḍḍa -- ) ' defective '](CDIAL 9606) mēṣá m. ' ram ', °ṣī́ -- f. ' ewe ' RV. 2. Mēha — 2, miha- m. lex. [mēha — 2 infl. By mḗhati ' emits semen ' as poss. Mēḍhra — 2 ' ram ' (~ mēṇḍha — 2) by mḗḍhra — 1 ' penis '?]1. Pk. Mēsa — m. ' sheep ', Ash. Mišalá; Kt. Məṣe/l ' ram '; Pr. Məṣé ' ram, oorial '; Kal. Meṣ, meṣalák ' ram ', H. mes m.; -- X bhēḍra — q.v.2. K. myã̄ -- pūtu m. ' the young of sheep or goats '; Wpah.bhal. me\i f. ' wild goat '; H. meh m. ' ram '.mēṣāsya -- ' sheep — faced ' Suśr. [mēṣá -- , āsyà -- ](CDIAL 10334) Rebus: meḍ (Ho.); mẽṛhet 'iron' (Mu.Ho.)mẽṛh t iron; ispat m. = steel; dul m. = cast iron (Mu.) Allograph: meḍ 'body ' (Mu.)

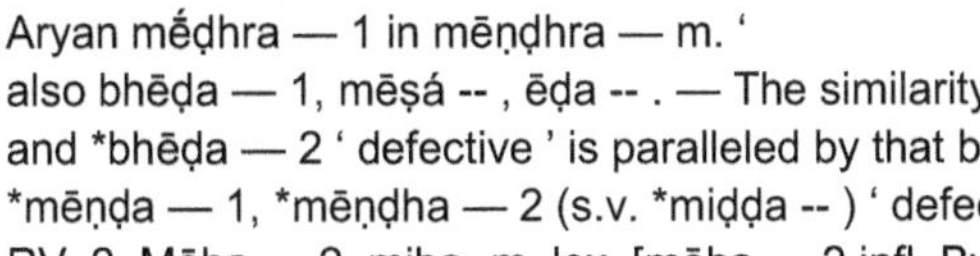

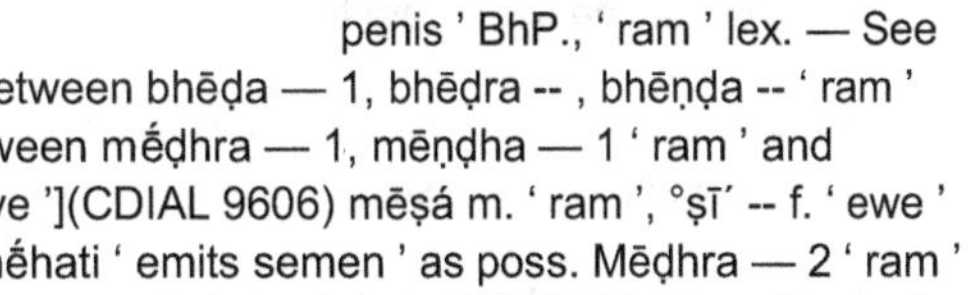

That the smithy guild dealt with silver is evidenced by the discovery of 3 silver seals.

Four-sided tablet with narrative hieroglyphs + text of inscription (m1431 Mohenjo-daro tablet)

m1431 Text of inscription (with some glyphs visible on line 3 — top line).
Each glyphic element on this remarkable tablet contains messages related to the furnace scribe (account) of artisan guild turner-carver workshop.

m1431A. A person seated on a tree-branch. A tiger looking backwards and up. Text of inscription.

Pk. ḍhaṁkhara — m.n. ' branch without leaves or fruit ' (CDIAL 5524) Rebus: ḍhangar 'blacksmith' (H.)

ḍāḷ= a branch of a tree (G.) Rebus: ḍhāḷako = a large ingot (G.) ḍhāḷakī = a metal heated and poured into a mould; a solid piece of metal; an ingot (G.)

eraka, hero = a messenger; a spy (G.lex.) heraka = spy (Skt.); er to look at or for (Pkt.); er uk- to play 'peeping tom' (Ko.) Rebus: eraka 'copper' (Ka.) Thus the person seated like a spy on a leafless tree-branch is decoded: *eraka ḍhangar*, 'coppersmith'. Together with kol 'tiger' glyph; the reading is: ḍhāḷako eraka ḍhangar kolami'copper ingot (copper)smith'.

m1431B. Row of animals in file (a one-horned bull, an elephant and a rhinoceros from right); a gharial with a fish held in its jaw above the animals; a bird (?) at right. Koḍe 'heifer' (Telugu) खोंड [ khōṇḍa ] m A young bull, a bullcalf. Rebus: kōdā 'to turn in a lathe' (B.) कोंडण [kōṇḍaṇa] f A fold or pen. (Marathi) ayakāra 'ironsmith' (Pali)[fish = aya (G.); crocodile = kāru (Te.)]baṭṭai quail (N.Santali) Rebus: bhaṭa = an oven, kiln, furnace (Santali) baṭhi furnace for smelting ore (the same as kuṭhi) (Santali) bhaṭa = an oven, kiln, furnace; make an oven, a furnace; iṭa bhaṭa = a brick kiln; kun:kal bhaṭa a potter's kiln; cun bhaṭa = a lime kiln; cun tehen dobon bhaṭaea = we shall prepare the lime kiln today (Santali); bhaṭṭhā (H.) bhart = a mixed metal of copper and lead; bhartīyā = a barzier, worker in metal; bhaṭ, bhrāṣṭra = oven, furnace (Skt.) mẽṛhẽt baṭi = iron (Ore) furnaces. [Synonyms are: mẽt = the eye, rebus for: the dotted circle (Santali.lex) baṭha [H. baṭṭhī (Sad.)] any kiln, except a potter's kiln, which is called coa; there are four kinds of kiln: cunabat.ha, a lime-kin, it.abat.ha, a brick-kiln, ērēbaṭha, a lac kiln, kuilabaṭha, a charcoal kiln; trs. Or intrs., to make a kiln; cuna rapamente ciminaupe baṭhakeda? How many limekilns did you make? Baṭha-sen:gel = the fire of a kiln; baṭi [H. Sad. baṭṭhi, a furnace for distilling) used alone or in the cmpds. arkibuṭi and baṭiora, all meaning a grog-shop; occurs also in ilibaṭi, a (licensed) rice-beer shop (Mundari.lex.) bhaṭi = liquor from mohwa flowers (Santali)

Long linear stroke is a category grouping or 'descriptive' glyph — a determinative of an artisan's workshop — as may be seen from the following examples of inscriptions.

Decoded read rebus: *koḍ kampaṭṭam dul kolamikaṇḍa kanka*, 'artisan's workshop; copper mint ; cast metal smithy; furnace account scribe'.

The multi-sided prism tablet (m1431) was, therefore, used to collect the products from the guild (smithy) workers' (perhaps, from each of the 19+ working platforms) to create a composite, descriptive bill of lading for a trade load.

Glyph: one long linear stroke. koḍa, koṛa = in arithmetic one; 4 koṛa or koḍa = 1 gaṇḍa = `4 (Santali) Rebus: koḍ, 'artisan's workshop' (Kuwi.)

kamaḍha = ficus religiosa (Skt.) Rebus: kamaṭa = portable furnace for melting precious metals (Te.); kampaṭṭam = mint (Ta.) loa 'ficus religiosa' (Santali) rebus: loh 'metal' (Skt.) Rebus: lo 'copper'. Thus, 'cast copper'.

dula 'pair' (Kashmiri); rebus: dul 'cast (metal)' (Santali) kolmo 'seedling, paddy plant'; rebus: kolami 'forge, smithy' (Te.)

kaṇḍa kanka 'rim of jar' (Santali); rebus: furnace scribe (account). *Kaṇḍa kanka* may be a dimunitive form of *kan-khār 'copper smith' comparable to the cognate gloss: kaṉṉār 'coppersmiths, blacksmiths' (Tamil) If so, kaṇḍa kan-khār connotes: 'copper-smith furnace.'kaṇḍa 'fire-altar (Santali); kan 'copper' (Ta.)

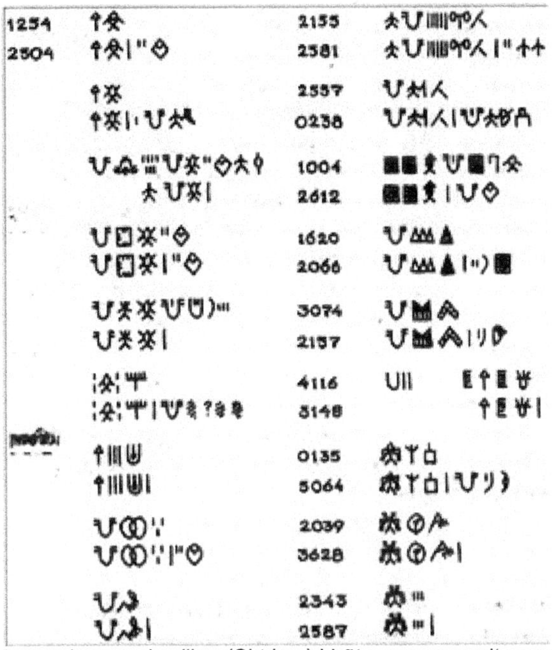


In the m1431 Text, the long linear stroke connotes rebus:

Glyph of 'linear stroke': goṭ = one (Santali); koḍa 'one'(Santali) Rebus: goṭi = silver (G.) koḍ 'workshop' (G.)

baḍhia = a castrated boar, a hog (Santali) baḍhi 'a caste who work both in iron and wood' (Santali)
m1431C. Zebu, *bos indicus* + other (illegible) glyphs. Decoded rebus reading: Guild.

*khũṭ*,'zebu' rebus: 'guild'. [khũṭ Brahmani bull (Kathiawar G.); khũṭro entire bull used for agriculture, not for breeding (G.)(CDIAL 3899). Khũṭro = entire bull; khũṭ= brahmaṇi bull (G.) khuṇṭiyo = an uncastrated bull (Kathiawad. G.lex.) khũ_ṭaḍum a bullock (used in Jhālwāḍ)(G.) kuṇṭai = bull (Ta.lex.) cf. khũ_dhi hump on the back; khuĩ_dhũ hump-backed (G.)(CDIAL 3902).] Rebus: kūṭa a house, dwelling (Skt.lex.) khũṭ = a community, sect, society, division, clique, schism, stock; khũṭren peṛa kanako = they belong to the same stock (Santali)
khūṭ Nag. Khũṭ, kūṭ Has. (Or. Khūṭ) either of the two branches of the village family.

m1431E. From R.—a person holding a vessel; a woman with a platter (?); a kneeling person with a staff in his hands facing the woman; a goat with its forelegs on a platform under a tree. [Or, two antelopes flanking a tree on a platform, with one antelope looking backwards?]

Line drawing of Indus script seal impression on one side of a prism tablet M1431E. Mohenjo-daro. Symmetrically flanking goats with feet on central tree and mountain (ASI).

The turner on a lathe is depicted on this glyphic narrative. kōdā 'to turn in a lathe' (Bengali)

Glyph: 'broken tree branch': khōṇḍa A tree of which the head and branches are broken off, a stock or stump: also the lower portion of the trunk—that below the branches. (Marathi) Rebus 1: koḍ 'workshop' (G.)

Allograph glyph: खोंड [ khōṇḍa ] m A young bull, a bullcalf. (Marathi) గోద [ gōda ] gōda. [Tel.] n. An ox. A beast. kine, cattle.(Telugu) koḍiyum 'heifer' (G.) [ kōḍiya ] kōḍe, kōḍiya. [Tel.] n. A bullcalf. . k* దూడA young bull. Plumpness, prime. తరుణము. జోడుకోడయులు a pair of bullocks. kōḍe adj. Young. kōḍe-kāḍu. n. A young man.పడుచువాడు. [ kārukōḍe ] kāru-kōḍe. [Tel.] n. A bull in its prime. koḍiyum (G.) Rebus 2:

B. kõdā 'to turn in a lathe'; Or. kŭnda 'lathe', kūdibā, kūd 'to turn' (→ Drav. Kur. kūd 'lathe') (CDIAL 3295).

M1431E shows a turner at work, assisted by a person bending on all fours. kunda 'turner' kundār turner (A.); kūdār, kūdāri (B.); kundāru (Or.); kundau to turn on a lathe, to carve, to chase; kundau dhiri = a hewn stone; kundau murhut = a graven image (Santali) kunda a turner's lathe (Skt.)(CDIAL 3295) Glyph: Br. Kōṇḍō on all fours, bent double. (DEDR 2054a) The seated person is shown wearing knot of hair at back. Sūnd gaṭ (Go.) cundī the hairtail as worn by men (Kur.)(DEDR 2670). Rebus: cundakāra a turner J vi.339 (Pali) cundakāra cognate kundār.

m1430C, body of bison, three heads: bison, antelope, bull; a pair of goat(s), tree

bison, bos gaurus 'sal'; rebus: sal 'workshop' (Santali)

mẽḍha 'antelope'; rebus: meḍ 'iron' (Ho.) ḍangar 'bull' ḍangar 'blacksmith'.

Ur. Shell plaque. Shell plaque From Ur, Southern Iraq (c. 2,600-2,400 B.C.) Entwined in the branches of a flowering tree, two goats appear to be nibbling on its leaves. This decorative plaque, which was carved from shell and highlighted with bitumen, was also excavated from the Royal Tombs of Ur. The glyphics on this plaque are comparable to the glyphics on Tablet 1431E showing two goat glyphs flanking a tree glyph.

Orthography of the two goats on the prism tablet is comparable to the glyph on a shell plaque from Ur. Mlekh, mṛeka 'goat' (Br.Telugu); rebus: milakkhu 'copper'. डगर [ ḍagara ]A slope or ascent (as of a river's bank, of a small hill). A pair is dula; rebus: dul 'cast (metal)'(Santali) Rebus: ḍāṅgar 'blacksmith' (H.) Thus, the glyptic composition is read rebus: *dul mlekh ḍāṅgar* 'cast copper-smith'.

A lexeme which may explain the 'mountain' or 'haystack' glyphs; Rebus: Rebus: mẽṛhẽt, meḍ 'iron' (Mu.Ho.): kunda 'hayrick'; rebus: kundār turner (A.)

After Amiet, P., 1961, *La glyptique mesopotamienne archaique*, Paris: 497; Mundigak IV.3; 3.

Sumerian cylinder seal showing flanking goats with hooves on tree and/or mountain. Uruk period. (After Joyce Burstein in: Katherine Anne Harper, Robert L. Brown, 2002, The roots of tantra, SUNY Press, p.100) Hence, two goats + mountain glyph reads rebus: meḍ kundār 'iron turner'. Leaf on mountain: kamaṛkom 'petiole of leaf'; rebus: kampaṭṭam 'mint'. loa = a species of fig tree, ficus glomerata, the fruit of ficus glomerata (Santali) Rebus: lo 'iron' (Assamese, Bengali); loa 'iron' (Gypsy).

The glyphic composition is read rebus: meḍ loa kundār 'iron turner mint'.

kundavum = manger, a hayrick (G.) Rebus: kundār turner (A.); kūdār, kūdāri (B.); kundāru (Or.); kundau to turn on a lathe, to carve, to chase; kundau dhiri = a hewn stone; kundau murhut = a graven image (Santali) kunda a turner's lathe (Skt.)(CDIAL 3295) This rebus reading may explain the hayrick glyph shown on the sodagor 'merchant, trader' seal surrounded by four animals.Two antelopes are put next to the hayrick on the platform of the seal on which the horned person is seated.

mlekh 'goat' (Br.); rebus: milakku 'copper' (Pali); mleccha 'copper' (Skt.) Thus, the composition of glyphs on the platform: pair of antelopes + pair of hayricks read rebus: milakku kundār 'copper turner'. Thus the seal is a framework of glyphic compositions to describe the repertoire of a brazier-mint, 'one who works in brass or makes brass articles' and 'a mint'.

Glyph: Vikalpa lexemes: Ta. meṭṭu mound, heap of earth; mēṭu height, eminence, hillock; muṭṭu rising ground, high ground, heap. Ma. mēṭu rising ground, hillock; māṭu hillock, raised ground; miṭṭāl rising ground, an alluvial bank; (Tiyya) maṭṭa hill. Ka. mēḍu height, rising ground, hillock; miṭṭu rising or high ground, hill; miṭṭe state of being high, rising ground, hill, mass, a large number; (Hav.) muṭṭe heap (as of straw). Tu. miṭṭè prominent, protruding; muṭṭe heap. Te. meṭṭa raised or high ground, hill; (K.) meṭṭu mound; miṭṭa high ground, hillock, mound; high, elevated, raised, projecting; (VPK) mēṭu, mēṭa, mēṭi stack of hay; (Inscr.) meṇṭa-cēnu dry field (cf. meṭṭu-nēla, meṭṭu-vari). Kol. (SR.) meṭṭā hill; (Kin.) meṭṭ, (Hislop) met mountain. Nk. meṭṭ hill, mountain. Ga. (S.3, LSB 20.3) meṭṭa high land. Go. (Tr. W. Ph.) maṭṭā, (Mu.) maṭṭa mountain; (M. L.) meṭā id., hill; (A. D. Ko.) meṭṭa, (Y. Ma. M.) meṭa hill; (SR.) meṭṭā hillock (Voc. 2949). Konḍa meṭa id. Kuwi (S.) metta hill; (Isr.) meṭa sand hill. (DEDR 5058)

Glyph: Vikalpa reading: kamaṛkom = fig leaf (Santali.lex.) kamarmaṛā (Has.), kamaṛkom (Nag.); the petiole or stalk of a leaf (Mundari.lex.)Rebus: kampaṭṭam coinage, coin (Ta.)(DEDR 1236) kampaṭṭa-muḷai die, coining stamp (Ta.) Vikalpa: lo 'iron' (Assamese, Bengali); loa 'iron' (Gypsy)

Glyph: Vikalpa reading: M. ḍagar f. ' little hill, slope '.S. ṭakuru m. ' mountain ' N. ṭākuro, ri ' hill top '. P. ṭekrā m., rī f. ' rock, hill '; H. ṭekar, krā m. ' heap, hillock '; G. ṭekrɔ m., rī f. ' mountain, hillock '.6. K. ṭẽg m. ' hillock, mound '.7. G. ṭũk ' peak '.8. M. ṭũg n. ' mound, lump '. — Ext. — r -- : Or. ṭuṅguri ' hillock '; M. ṭũgar n. ' bump, mound ' (see *uṭṭungara -- ); -- -- l -- : M. ṭũgaḷ, gũḷ n.9. K. ḍáki f. ' hill, rising ground '. — Ext. — r -- : K. ḍakürü f. ' hill on a road '.10. Ext. — r -- : Pk. ḍaggara — m. ' upper terrace of a house '; 11. Ku. ḍā̃g, ḍā̃k ' stony land '; B. ḍāṅ ' heap ', ḍāṅgā ' hill, dry upland '; H. ḍā̃g f. ' mountain — ridge '; M. ḍā̃g m.n., ḍā̃gaṇ, gāṇ, ḍāgāṇ n. ' hill — tract '. — Ext. — r -- : N. ḍaṅgur ' heap '.12. M. ḍũg m. ' hill, pile ', gā m. ' eminence ', gī f. ' heap '. — Ext. — r -- : Pk. ḍuṁgara — m. ' mountain '; Ku. ḍũgar, ḍũgrī; N. ḍuṅgar ' heap '; Or. ḍuṅguri ' hillock ', H. ḍũgar m., G. ḍũgar m., ḍũgrī f. 13. S.ḍū̃garu m. ' hill ', H. M. ḍõgar m. 14. Pa. tuṅga -- ' high '; Pk. Tuṁga -- ' high ', tuṁgīya — m. ' mountain '; K. tŏng, tǫ̃ngu m. ' peak ', P. tuṅg f.; A. tuṅg ' importance '; Si. Tuṅgu ' lofty, mountain '. — Cf. uttuṅga -- ' lofty ' MBh. 15. K. thǫ̃ngu m. ' peak '. 16. H. dā̃g f. ' hill, precipice ', dā̃gī ' belonging to hill country '. Addenda: *ṭakka — 3. 12. *ḍuṅga -- : S.kcch. ḍūṅghar m. ' hillock '. (CDIAL 5423). Unc An eminence, a mount, a little hill (Marathi). ṭākuro = hill top (N.); ṭāngī = hill, stony country (Or.); ṭān:gara = rocky hilly land (Or.); ḍān:gā = hill, dry upland (B.); ḍā~g = mountain-ridge (H.)(CDIAL 5476). Marathi. डांग [ ḍāṅga ] m n ( H Peak or summit of a hill.)

Cylinder seal. Chlorite. AO 22303 H. 3.9 cm. Dia. 2.6 cm. "At the end of the Uruk period (c.3500-3100 BC) appeared the cylindrical seals which were to be used, among other things, to seal the first written documents. The print left by the rolling of these miniature bas-reliefs on the soft clay of the tablet reveals a rich iconography that varies with the different epochs. Thus the dynasty of Akkad (2340-2200

BC) the stone-cutters showed a certain predilection for mythological scenes. On the Sharkalisharri cylinder, fifth king of the Akkad dynasty, two naked heroes, acolytes of Eas, water two buffaloes which carry the inscription, central element of the composition: "the divine Sharkalisharri, king of Akkad, Ibni-sharrum, the scribe, (is) his servant." – Louvre

Fine engraving, elegant drawing, and a balanced composition make this seal one of the masterpieces of glyptic art. The decoration, which is characteristic of the Agade period, shows two buffaloes that have just slaked their thirst in the stream of water spurting from two vases held by two naked kneeling heroes.

A masterpiece of glyptic art

This seal, which belonged to Ibni-Sharrum, the scribe of King Sharkali-Sharri, who succeeded his father Naram-Sin, is one of the most striking examples of the perfection attained by carvers in the Agade period. The two naked, curly-headed heroes are arranged symmetrically, half-kneeling. They are both holding vases from which water is gushing as a symbol of fertility and abundance; it is also the attribute of the god of the river, Enki-Ea, of whom these spirits of running water are indeed the acolytes. Two arni, or water buffaloes, have just drunk from them. Below the scene, a river winds between the mountains represented conventionally by a pattern of two lines of scales. The central cartouche bearing an inscription is held between the buffaloes' horns.

A scene testifying to relations with distant lands

Buffaloes are emblematic animals in glyptic art in the Agade period. They first appear in the reign of Sargon, indicating sustained relations between the Akkadian Empire and the distant country of Meluhha, that is, the present Indus Valley, where these animals come from. These exotic creatures were probably kept in zoos and do not seem to have been acclimatized in Iraq at the end of the 3rd millennium BC. Indeed, it was not until the Sassanid Empire that they reappeared. The engraver has carefully accentuated the animals' powerful muscles and spectacular horns, which are shown as if seen from above, as they appear on the seals of the Indus.

The production of a royal workshop

The calm balance of the composition, based on horizontal and vertical lines, gives this in low relief a classical monumental character, typical of the style of the late Akkadian period. Seals of this quality were the preserve of the entourage of the royal family or high dignitaries and were probably made in a workshop whose production was reserved for this elite.

Bibliography

Amiet Pierre, Bas-reliefs imaginaires de l'ancien Orient : d'après les cachets et les sceaux-cylindres, exp. Paris, Hôtel de la Monnaie, juin-octobre 1973, avec une préface de Jean Nougayrol, Paris, Hôtel de la Monnaie, 1973.

Amiet Pierre, L'Art d'Agadé au musée du Louvre, Paris, Éditions de la Réunion des musées nationaux, 1976.

Art of the First Cities, New York, 2003, n 135.

Boehmer Rainer Michael, Die Entwicklung der Glyptik während der Akkad-Zeit, Berlin, W. De Gruyter und C , 1965, n 724, fig. 232.

Boehmer Rainer Michael, Das Auftreten des Wasserbüffels in Mesopotamien in historischer Zeit und sein sumerische Bezeichnung, ZA 64 (1974), pp. 1-19.

Clercq Louis (de), Collection de Clercq. Catalogue méthodique et raisonné. Antiquités assyriennes, cylindres orientaux, cachets, briques, bronzes, bas-reliefs, etc., t. I, Cylindres orientaux, avec la collaboration de Joachim Menant, Paris, E. Leroux, 1888, n 46.

Collon Dominique, First Impressions : cylinder seals in the Ancient Near-East, Londres, British museum publications, 1987, n 529.

Frankfort Henri, Cylinder Seals, Londres, 1939, pl XVIIc.
Zettler Richard L., "The Sargonic Royal Seal. A Consideration of Sealing in Mesopotamia", in Seals and Sealing in the Ancient Near East,
Bibliotheca Mesopotamica 6, Malibu, 1977, pp. 33-39.

Cylinder seal impression of Ibni-sharrum, a scribe of Shar-kalisharri ca. 2183–2159 BCE The inscription reads “O divine Shar-kali-sharri, Ibni-sharrum the scribe is your servant.”

The overflowing pot is a motif which occurs on a Mesopotamian cylinder seal. Akkadian, reign of Shar-kali-sharri. Mesopotamia. Cuneiform inscription in Old Akkadian. Serpentine; Diam. 2.6 cm (1 in.); H. 3.9 cm Musée du Louvre, Département des Antiquités Orientales, Paris AO 22303.

http://www.metmuseum.org/special/First_Cities/images/135BR3.R.jpg

A glyphic composition of overflowing pot occur on a Mohenjo-daro pectoral, m1656:

m1656 pectoral: Frequency of occurrence of glyph composition: kaṇḍa = a pot of certain shape and size (Santali) Rebus: kaṇḍ = altar, furnace (Santali) kanka ‘rim’. Rebus 1: kanka ‘account (scribe). Rebus 2: khanaka ‘miner’ Glyph of overflowing pot: <dul> {V2} ``to ^pour out water in offering to the gods; to ^water a garden". @5312. #8221.(Munda etyma). Rebus: dul ’casting (metal)(Santali) Thus the glyphic elements related to overflowing pot, on m1656 and on Ibni Sharrum cylinder seal, read rebus: dul kaṇḍ kanka ‘casting furnace account (scribe). M1465 glyphic elements occur together with the one-horned heifer + standard device glyphs (*koḍ + sangaḍa* ‘guild workshop’. Ibni Sharrum cylinder seal occurs with a pair of buffalo glyphs. *dula sal kaḍa* ‘a pair of buffaloes’. Rebus: *dul sal kaḍa* ‘casting workshop of *kaḍa-i-o,* °turner, mason’.

Vikalpa 1: <lo->(B) {V} ``(pot, etc.) to ^overflow". See <lo-> `to be left over'. @B24310. #20851. Re<lo->(B) {V} ``(pot, etc.) to ^overflow". See <lo-> `to be left over'. (Munda etyma)Rebus: <lua>(B),,<loa>(B) {N} ``^iron". Pl. <-le>. @B23760. #21231.

<lowa>(F) {N} ``^iron". *Loan. @N501. #21131.

Vikalpa 2: వారుచు or వార్చు *vāruṭsu.* (causal of వారు) v. a. To touch water with the lips and cast it away. ఆచమించు. To cause to flow, వారజేయు. గంజివార్చు to pour off the water from boiled rice by inclining the vessel, వారు నట్టుచేయు. To expect, ప్రతీ క్షించు, ఉద్దేశించు. సంధ్యవార్చు to offer up prayers: (because while uttering the prayer called సంధ్య they let water run through their hungers.) "హేమకుంభ జలములనొగివార్చి జలకంబుదీర్చి." DRU. 774. "సంధ్యవార్చువేళ." G. vi. 17. వారుపు or వార్పు *vārupu.* n. The act of straining water or letting it flow, ఆచమనము. Water poured off from boiling rice, గంజి.

eṛe = to cast, as metal; to overflow (Ka.) eṛaka = any metal infusion (Ka.Tu.) Vikalpa: Ta. vār (-v-, -nt-) to flow, trickle, overflow (DEDR 535) வார்ப்பு vārppu n. < வார்[2]-. 1. Pouring; ஒழுக்குகை. 2. Casting; உருக்கி வார்க்கை. வார்ப்பி னமைத்த யாப்பமை யரும்பொறி (பெருங். இலாவாண. 18, 24).

வார்ப்பாலை vārppālai, *n.* < வார்ப்பு +. Foundry; இரும்பு முதலியன உருக்கி வார்க்கு மிடம். *Pond.* வார்ப்பு vārppu , *n.* < வார்-. Encasing, as precious stones in an ornament; இரத்தினத்தில் ஏற்றின மேற்பூச்சு. (திவ். பெரியாழ். 3, 3, 3, வ்யா. பக். 567.) வார்ப்புலை vārppulai , *n.* < வார்ப்பு +. See வார்ப்பாலை. *Pond. Ta.* vār (-v-, -nt-) to flow, trickle, overflow; (-pp-, -tt-) to pour, cast (as metal in a mould); vārppu pouring, casting, that which is cast; vāri channel for draining off rain-water from roof, waterway, sluice. *Ma.* vāruka to run, flow down, be strained off (water); vārkka to pour, cast; vārcca issue, flux; vārppu fusion, casting metals, issue. *Ko.* va·ry ditch around fields, acting as moat outside embankment and fence; ? varb- (varby-) (tears) stand in eyes ready to fall. *To.* po·ry ditch. *Ka.* bār to set free a liquid, pour out, purge. *Tu.* (B-K.) barcelů channel to empty surplus water, as from a field. *Te.* vāru to flow down as water from boiled rice, be drained off; vār(u)cu to pour or drain off, as water from boiled rice. *Nk. (Ch.)* vār jav water of boiled rice (cf. *DBIA* 166). *Pa.* vār jāva water in which rice has been boiled; vārp- (vārt-) to strain. *Ga.* (P.)vārp- (vārt-) to strain (water from boiled rice); (S.) vārk- (vārt-) to strain water from food, etc.; (S.3) vār- to be filtered (like boiled rice); vārp- (vārup-) to filter (like boiled rice, etc.). *Go.* (Ma.) vār- to pour (*Voc.* 3225); (A. S.) vāṭ- id. (*Voc.* 3219); (Mu.) var irrigation channel *(Voc. 3177). Koṇḍa* (BB 1972) vāra canal for irrigation. *Pe.* vār- (-t-) to pour. *Kui* vāru (*pl.* vārka) water-channel, stream, torrent. *Kui* (Isr.) vāru flood. (DEDR 5356). phyār 1 फ्यार् । क्षालनजलम् m. strained water, the dirty water squeezed out of something that has been washed, or the water strained off after cooking (cf. atha-pho, p. 61*a,* l. 35) (Gr.Gr. 124). -- gatshun -- गछ&dotbelow;ुन् । अज्ञात्वा अकार्यनिष्पत्तिसमापातः m.inf. refuse water to come into existence; met. something to turn out wrong, a wrong result (causing disappointment) unexpectedly or owing to some mistake to come from any action. -- kaḍun -- कड्डन् । ईषत्पाकयोजनया जलनिःसारणम् m.inf. to pour or strain off the water (in which food has been cooked). -- karun -- करुन् । अकार्यविधानम् m.inf. to make refuse water; hence, to perform some improper work causing disappointment by its results. -- nīrith gatshun -- नीरिथ् गछ&dotbelow;ुन् । अवाच्यगुह्योक्तिसंभवः m.inf. straining water to issue forth; met. some one's secret or opinions to be let out (with deplorable results) in the presence of his enemy (esp. when done ignorantly). -- nīrith tsalun -- नीरिथ् च&dotbelow;लुन् । अवाच्यवदनसंभवः m.inf. unseasonable or objectionable words suddenly and unexpectedly to be uttered or divulged. -- trāwun -- त्रावुन् । जलनिःसारणम् m.inf. to strain off, or wring out, water (after cooking or washing).(Kashmiri). Gy.

pog. *bharnu* ' to fill, draw water ' kash. *bharunŭ* ' to fill ', ḍoḍ. *bharṇō*; S. *bharaṇu* ' to fill ', L. *bharaṇ*; Ku. *bharṇo* ' to support, feed, fill '; N.*bharnu* ' to fill '; A. *bhariba* ' to put in '; B. *bharā* ' to load '; Or. *bharibā* ' to fill '; Bi. *bharab* ' to irrigate '; Mth. *bharab* ' to fill ', Bhoj. *bharal*; OAw.*bharaï* ' bears, endures, fills, covers '; H. *bharnā* ' to fill, be full '; OMarw. *bharaï* ' fills ', G. *bharvũ*; M. *bharṇẽ* ' to carry, fill '; Ko. *bhartā* ' fills '; -- caus.: N. *bharāunu* ' to cram into '; A. *bharāiba* ' to fill '; G. *bharāvvũ* ' to fasten '; M. *bharaviṇẽ* ' to feed '. bhárati: S.kcch. *bharṇū* ' to fill, load, embroider '; WPah.kṭg. (kc.) *bhɔ`rnō* ' to fill, heap, pay, pour (liquids into a bucket etc.) ', J. *bharṇu*, jaun.*bhaurnõ* (WPah.kṭg. (kc.) *bhɔ`ri* ' much, very ' < bahura -- ); Garh. *bharnu* ' to fill up '.(CDIAL 9397).

Importance of a count of 'six'

Elamite lady spinner. Musee du Louvre. Paris. An elegantly coiffed, exquisitely-dressed and well fanned Elamite woman sits on a feline footed stool winding thread on a spindle. The stool on which the lovely Elamite lady sits has the legs of a feline; the fish is also placed on a similar stool in front her.This five-inch fragment is dated 8th century BCE. It was molded and carved from a mix of bitumen, ground calcite, and quartz. The Elamites used bitumen, a naturally occurring mineral pitch, or asphalt, for vessels, sculpture, glue, caulking, and waterproofing. http://www.oznet.net/iran/elamspin.htm

The glyphics represent *kol khũṭ khati,'* working in iron, a guild of wheelwrights *'.*

kola 'tiger' (Telugu); rebus: kol 'working in iron (Tamil). The legs of the two stools shows glyphic of tiger's foot. Glyph: 'foot, hoof': Glyph: 'hoof': Ku. *khuṭo* ' leg, foot ', °*ṭī* ' goat's leg '; N. *khuṭo* ' leg, foot '(CDIAL 3894). S. *khuṛī* f. ' heel '; WPah. paṅ. *khūṛ* ' foot '. khura m. ' hoof ' KātyŚr̥. 2. *khuḍa -- 1 (*khuḍaka* -- , *khula*° ' ankle -- bone ' Suśr.). [← Drav. T. Burrow BSOAS xii 376: it belongs to the word -- group ' heel <-> ankle -- knee -- wrist ', see *kuṭṭha -- ](CDIAL 3906). *Ta.* kuracu, kuraccai horse's hoof. *Ka.* gorasu, gorase, gorise, gorusu hoof. *Te.* gorija, gorise, (B. also) gorije, korije id. / Cf. Skt.khura- id. (DEDR 1770). Allograph: (Kathiawar) *khũṭ* m. ' Brahmani bull ' (G.) Rebus: *khũṭ* 'community, guild' (Santali)

Glyph: kātī 'spinner' (G.) Rebus: khati 'wheelwright' (H.) kāṭi = fireplace in the form of a long ditch (Ta.Skt.Vedic) kāṭya = being in a hole (VS. XVI.37); kāṭ a hole, depth (RV. i. 106.6) khāḍ a ditch, a trench; khāḍ o khaiyo several pits and ditches (G.) khaṇḍrun: 'pit (furnace)' (Santali)

ayo 'fish' (Mu.); rebus: aya 'metal' (G.)

Glyphic: 'count of six': bhaṭa 'six' (G.); rebus: bhaṭa 'furnace' (Santali) kola 'woman' (Nahali); Rebus: kolami 'smithy' (Te.) Vikalpa: goti 'woman'; rebus; goṭ 'cow-pen'; rebus: koḍ 'place where artisans work' (Kuwi) Kur. kaṇḍō a stool. Malt. kaṇdo stool, seat. (DEDR 1179) Rebus: kaṇḍ 'fire-altar, furnace' (Santali) kola 'tiger, jackal' (Kon.); rebus: kolami 'smithy' (Te.) Grapheme as a phonetic determinant of the depiction of woman, kola; rebus: kolami 'smithy' (Te.)

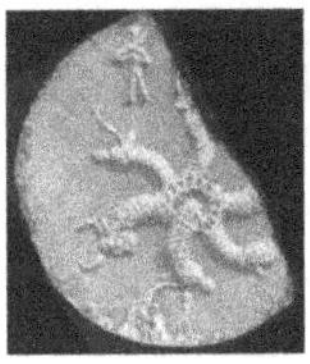

m417 six heads from a core bhaṭa 'six' (G.) rebus: baṭa = kiln (Santali); baṭa = a kind of iron (G.) bhaṭṭhī f. 'kiln, distillery', awāṇ. bhaṭh; P. bhaṭṭh m., °ṭhī f. 'furnace', bhaṭṭhā m. 'kiln'; S. bhaṭṭhī keṇī 'distil (spirits) Glyph: 'animals': asaramu, pasalamu = an animal, a beast, a brute, quadruped (Te.) Rebus: pasra = a smithy, place where a black-smith works, to work as a blacksmith; kamar pasra = a smithy; pasrao lagao akata se ban:?

Has the blacksmith begun to work? pasraedae = the blacksmith is at his work (Santali.lex.) pasra 'smithy' (Santali) pasra meṛed, pasāra meṛed = syn. of koṭe meṛed = forged iron, in contrast to dul meṛed, cast iron (Mundari.)

bhaṭa 'six' (G.) Rebus: bhaṭa 'furnace' (G.)

kola 'woman' (Nahali); Rebus: kolami 'smithy' (Te.)

meḍhi, miḍhī, meṇḍhī = a plait in a woman's hair; a plaited or twisted strand of hair (P.) मेढा [ mēḍhā ] meṇḍa A twist or tangle arising in thread or cord, a curl or snarl. (Marathi) (CDIAL 10312). [dial., cp. Prk. mĕṇṭha & miṇṭha: Pischel, Prk. Gr. § 293. The Dhtm (156) gives a root meṇḍ (meḍ) in meaning of "koṭilla," i. e. crookedness. (Pali) Vikalpa: ḍhompo = knot on a string (Santali) ḍhompo = ingot (Santali) Vikalpa: cūḍa 'diadem, hairdress' (Skt.) Rebus: cūḷa 'furnace' (H.) Rebus: meḍ 'iron' (Ho.) Thus, the glyptic elements of woman, plaited hair and six plaits can be decoded as: meḍ bhaṭa kolami 'iron smelter smithy'.

After "Kunst." Barthel Hrouda. Editor. *Der Alte Orient, Geschichte und Kultur des alten Vorderasien*. Munchen. C. Bertelsmann. Verlag GmbH. 1991, p. 360. A count of six locks of hair on the bearded person in the middle, flanked by – holding apart -- two one-horned heifers.

Scarf as an Indus script hieroglyph, a glyphic element

Terracotta tablet, Mohenjo-daro. Scarf (also shown on pigtail glyphs). Scarf i carried in a procession depicted on a terracotta tablet (together with a banner showing a one-horned heifer and a portable standard device). [After Marshall 1931, Pl. CXVIII,9]

Scarf is ligatured as a pigtail to a standing, horned person wishin a pot decorated with ficus leaves as a torana. Part of the glyphs included in Seal m1186.

Scarf shown ligatured as a pigtail to a horned, standing person. Tablet m0488c (One side of a prism tablet).

Scarf as a pigtail.

A glyphic element ligatured to a horned, kneeling person in front of a horned, standing person (also with scarf as a hieroglyph) within a torana. One side of a tablet.

er-agu = a bow, an obeisance; er-aguha = bowing, coming down (Ka.lex.) er-agisu = to bow, to be bent; tomake obeisance to; to crouch; to come down; to alight (Ka.lex.) cf. arghas = respectful reception of a guest (by the offering of rice, du_rva grass, flowers or often only of water)(S'Br.14)(Skt.lex.) erugu = to bow, to salute or make obeisance (Te.) Rebus: eraka 'copper' (Ka.) erka = ll (Tbh. Of arka) aka (Tbh. Of arka) copper (metal); crystal (Ka.lex.) eraka, er-aka = any metal infusion (Ka.Tu.) eruvai 'copper' (Ta.); ere dark red (Ka.)(DEDR 446). Er-r-a = red; (arka-) agasāle, agasāli, agasālavāḍu = a goldsmith (Te.lex.)

Thus, the horned, scarfed, kneeling person is read rebus: *eraka dhatu* 'copper mineral'.

Decoding 'scarf' glyph: dhaṭu m. (also dhaṭhu) m. 'scarf' (Wpah.) (CDIAL 6707)Rebus: dhatu 'minerals' (Santali)

"Indus inscriptions resemble the Egyptian hieroglyphs…" (John Marshall, 1931, Mohenjo-daro and the Indus civilization, London, Arthur Probsthain, p.424). Yes, indeed, Indus writing was hieroglyphic and was invented ca. 3500 BCE as the artisans gained the expertise in participating in the bronze age innovations and technologies.

The bronze age necessitated writing system as an essential complementary innovation to categorise, compile, and creat bills of lading as authenticated records of trade transactions — by account scribes — of artifacts produced by guilds (workshops) of artisans, miners, lapidaries, turner-carvers.

Thus, the functions served by circular working platforms, the functions served (as preparatory resources for bills of lading) by: 1) use of tablets as category tallies, 2) compilation of seals, 3) creation of seal impressions are explained in the archaeological context of trade evidenced across interaction areas (e.g. Persian Gulf, Sumer: Susa and Uruk).

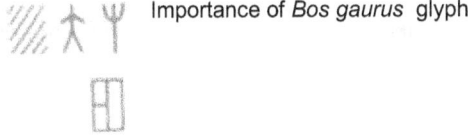

Importance of *Bos gaurus* glyph

Text 2279 Person throwing a spear at a buffalo and placing one foot on the head of the buffalo. 2279 seal impression, Mohenjo-daro (DK 8165); after Mackay 1938: pl.88, no.279 kolsa = to kick the foot forward, the foot to come into contact with anything when walking or running; kolsa pasirkedan = I kicked it over (Santali.lex.) kola = killing, e.g. āḍukola = woman-slaying (Te.) Thus, homa kola = bison slaying. Rebus: hom = gold (Ka.) kol =metal (Ta.) kol sal 'iron workshop'.

This glyhph on line 1 of the inscription on DK 8164 seal impression, could be a phonetic determinant: kwal.el 'smithy, temple in Kota village' (Ko.); kwala.l Kota smithy (To.)(DEDR 2133). Vikalpa: mēṛsa = v.a. toss, kick with the foot, hit with the tail (Santali.lex.) Rebus: mẽṛh t iron; ispat m. = steel; dul m. = cast iron (Mu.); meḍ (Ho.) The glyptic scene is decoded rebus: meḍ kol sal 'iron, metal workshop'

sal 'the Indian gaur, gaveus gaurus'; sal sakwa 'a horn made from a horn of the gaur' (Santali) *சைரிபம்* cairipam, n. < sairibha. buffalo; *எருமை. (பிங்.)* (Skt.Tamil)

Vikalpa: kaḍru 'buffalo' (G.); kaḍa buffalo (Santali) kaṭrā bull calf; kaṭhrā young buffalo bull; kaṭiyā buffalo heifer (H.); kaṭṛa buffalo calf (WPah.); kaṭai buffalo calf (Gaw.); kaṭṛā young buffalo (P.)(CDIAL 245). kaṭādamu = a he-buffalo (Te.lex.)17 kōṛi buffalo (Konḍa); kaḍru (Pe.Mand.); kōru pl. kōrka (Kui); kōḍru, kōdru, gōḍru, kōḍrū (Kuwi)(DEDR 2256). kaḍa, kaḍru, kaṛa 'a buffalo bull' kaḍi 'a female buffalo calf' (Santali) Or. kaṛā ' castrated male buffalo ', kaṛāi ' young buffalo cow that has not calved ', kaṛhi ' lamb that has not borne '; Bi. kāṛā m., ṛī f. ' buffalo calf ', H. kāṛā m. (CDIAL 2658)

goraka. [Tel.] n. A wild buffalo. An iron arrow ఇనుపబాణము. goraka-kaṭṭe. n. A javelin, or slender spear.(Telugu)

The following glosses, kārā in Urdu, Telugu, Tamil and kaṛā, kaṛa in Kurku and Santali of the linguistic area indicate an ancient form, kārā to denote 'buffalo'. Rebus: khār 1 खार् I लोहकारः m. (sg. abl. khāra 1 खार; the pl. dat. of this word is khāran 1 खारन्, which is to be distinguished from khāran 2, q.v., s.v.), a blacksmith, an iron worker (cf.bandūka-khār, p. 111b, l. 46; K.*Pr. 46; H. xi, 17); a farrier (El.). This word is often a part of a name, and in such case comes at the end (W. 118) as in Wahab khār,

Wahab the smith (H. ii, 12; vi, 17). khāra-basta खार-बस्‌त । चर्मप्रसेविका f. the skin bellows of a blacksmith. -büṭhü; । लोहकारभित्तिः f. the wall of a blacksmith's furnace or hearth. -bāy -बाय् । लोहकारपत्नी f. a blacksmith's wife (Gr.Gr. 34). -dŏkuru -द्वकुरु। लोहकारायोघनः m. a blacksmith's hammer, a sledge-hammer. -gȧji or -güjü । लोहकारचुल्लिः f. a blacksmith's furnace or hearth. -hāl -हाल् । लोहकारकन्दुः f. a blacksmith's smelting furnace; cf. hāl 5. -kūrü -कूरू&below; । लोहकारकन्या f. a blacksmith's daughter. -koṭu । लोहकारपुत्रः m. the son of a blacksmith, esp. a skilful son, who can work at the same profession. -küṭü । लोहकारकन्या f. a blacksmith's daughter, esp. one who has the virtues and qualities properly belonging to her father's profession or caste. -mĕ˘tsü । लोहकारमृत्तिका f. (for 2, see [khāra 3] ), 'blacksmith's earth,' i.e. iron-ore. -nĕcyuwu -न्यचिवु। लोहकारात्मजः m. a blacksmith's son. -nay -नय् । लोहकारनालिका f. (for khāranay 2, see [khārun] ), the trough into which the blacksmith allows melted iron to flow after smelting. -tsañĕ । लोहकारशान्ताङ्गाराः f.pl. charcoal used by blacksmiths in their furnaces. -wān वान् । (Kashmiri)

காரா kār-ā n. < கரு-மை + ஆ&sup8;. [T. kārāvu, U. kārā.] Buffalo; எருமை. செங்கண் வன்கட் காரா (தஞ்சைவா. 380).(Tamil) kār-āvu. [Tel.] n. A wild cow. forest cattle. kaarenumu n. wild buffalo (female) (Telugu) गौर gaur, adj. (f. -ī), White, pale; of fair complexion, fair;—yellow;—red, pale red;—s.m. A kind of buffalo, the Bos gaurus (Urdu) kaṛa, kaḍa 'a buffalo bull' (Santali) Kur. kaṛā young male buffalo; kaṛī young female buffalo; kaṛrū, kaḍrū buffalo calf (male or female). Ko. kaṛc ng buffalo calf between two and three years; kaṛc kurl cow calf between two and three years; ? To. kaṛ pen for calves from 6 months to 1-2 years.Ko. (Ph.) kāṛā young buffalo ( Voc.648). Konḍa (BB) gṛālu calf. Kui (K.) grāḍu, (W.) ḍrāḍu (pl. ḍrāṭka) id.; (W.) gāṛo a bullock or buffalo not trained to the plough; kṛai young female buffalo or goat. Br. xarās bull, bullock; xaṛ ram.(DEDR 1123). Gaw. kaṭái 'buffalo calf', Bshk. kaṭṓr, Sh. (Lor.) k *l tu (ṭ?); K. kaṭh, dat. ṭas m. 'ram, sheep in general, (con- temptuous) son'; L. kaṭṭā m., ṭī f. 'buffalo calf'; P. kaṭṭā m., ṭī f. 'yearling buffalo', kaṭṭū m. 'young buffalo bull', kaṭṛā m., ṛī f. 'young buffalo'; WPah. khaś. rudh. marm. kaṭru 'buffalo calf', bhal. kaṭṭā m., ṭī f. 'buffalo calf', kaṭru n. 'bear cub'; Ku. kāṭo 'young buffalo bull', kaṭyāro 'young buffalo'; H. kaṭiyā f. 'buffalo heifer', kaṭrā m. 'buffalo calf', kaṭhṛā m. 'young buffalo bull' (CDIAL 2645).

Vikalpa: ran:gā 'buffalo'; Rebus: ran:ga 'pewter or alloy of tin (ran:ku), lead (nāga) and antimony (an~jana)'(Santali)

Vikalpa: kaḍru 'buffalo' (G.); kaḍa buffalo (Santali) kaṭrā bull calf; kaṭhrā young buffalo bull; kaṭiyā buffalo heifer (H.); kaṭra buffalo calf (WPah.); kaṭai buffalo calf (Gaw.); kaṭrā young buffalo (P.)(CDIAL 245). kaṭādamu = a he-buffalo (Te.lex.)17 kōṛi buffalo (Konḍa); kaḍru (Pe.Mand.); kōru pl. kōrka (Kui); kōḍru, kōdru, gōḍru, kōḍrū (Kuwi)(DEDR 2256). kaḍa, kaḍru, kaṛa 'a buffalo bull' kaḍi 'a female buffalo calf' (Santali) Or. kaṛā ' castrated male buffalo ', kaṛāi ' young buffalo cow that has not calved ', kaṛhi ' lamb that has not borne '; Bi. kāṛā m., ṛī f. ' buffalo calf ', H. kāṛā m. (CDIAL 2658)

goraka. [Tel.] n. A wild buffalo. An iron arrow ఇనుపబాణము. goraka-kaṭṭe. n. A javelin, or slender spear.(Telugu)

Vikalpa: ran:gā 'buffalo'; Rebus: ran:ga 'pewter or alloy of tin (ran:ku), lead (nāga) and antimony (añjana)'(Santali)

Stamp seal with a water-buffalo, Mohenjo-daro. “As is usual on Indus Valley seals that

show a water buffalo,this animal is standing with upraised head and both hornsclearly visible. (Mackay, 1938b, p. 391). A feeding trough isplaced in front of it, and a double row of undecipherable scriptfills the entire space above. The horns are incised to show thenatural growth lines. During the Akkadian period, cylinderseals in Mesopotamia depict water buffaloes in a similar posethat may have been copied from Indus seals (see cat. No.135)(For a Mesopotamian seal with water buffalo, see Parpola1994, p. 252 and Collon 1987, no.529 – Fig. 11).”(JMK –Jonathan Mark Kenoyer, Professor of Anthropology, Universityof Wisconsin, Madison) (p.405)

 m1928 a,b  h0087  m0266

. 1306  m0267 Water-buffalo  2257

 m0268 Water-buffalo  2445  m0269  2663

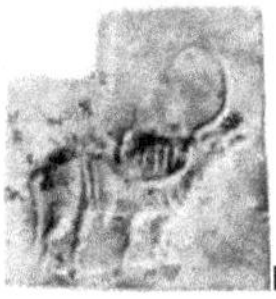 m0270  h171A 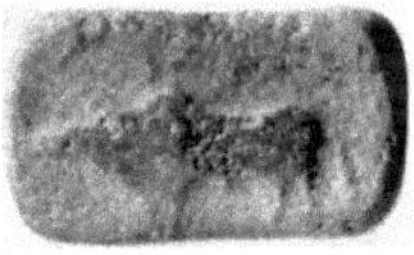 h171B

Buffalo. Pict-100 Person  throwing a spear at a buffalo and placing one foot on the head of the buffalo.

m1430Bt  m1430C

  m1430At Pict-101: Person throwing a spear at a buffalo and placing one foot on its head; three persons standing near a tree at the center.

Impression of an Indus-style cylinder seal of unknown Near Eastern origin in the Musee du Louvre, Paris. One of the two anthropomorphic figures carved on this seal wears the horns of water buffalo while sitting on a throne with hoofed legs, surrounded by snakes, fishes and water buffaloes. Copyrighted photo by M. Chuzeville for the Departement des antiquites orientales, Musee du Louvre.

A pair of buffaloes flank a round spot in the bottom register of the cylinder seal impression.

Glyph: ‘round spot’: गोटी [ gōṭī ] f (Dim. Of गोटा) A roundish stone or pebble. Rebus: कोठी [ kōṭhī ] f (कोष्ट S) A granary, garner, storehouse, warehouse, treasury, factory, bank. (Marathi)

Decoding rebus other hieroglyphs of the cylinder seal

kaṭa-sal 'buffalo'. Rebus: kaḍiyo [Hem. Des. kaḍaio = Skt. sthapati a mason] a bricklayer; a mason; kaḍiyaṇa, kaḍiyeṇa a woman of the bricklayer caste; a wife of a bricklayer (G.)

Viklpa: kaḍacal 'turner's workshop'. meḍh 'ram'. Rebus: meḍ 'iron'. Badhoe 'boar'. Rebus: baḍhi 'worker in wood and iron'. aya 'fish'. Rebus: aya 'metal'. pajhaṛ 'kite'. Rebus: pasra 'smithy'. kuṭi 'tree'. Rebus: kuṭhi 'smelter'. tagaraka 'taberna montana' (five-petalled flower). Rebus: tagara 'tin'. dula kola 'pair of tigers'. Rebus: dul kol 'casting work in iron'. kola 'woman'. Rebus: kolami 'smithy/forge'. ṭhaṭera 'buffalo horns'. ṭhaṭera 'brass worker'. kaṇḍo 'stool'. Rebus: kaṇḍ 'furnace, altar'.

This is a veritable inventory of bronze-age repertoire of the Indus artisans' workshop.

Ligature, a technique used by scribes/artisans of the civilization

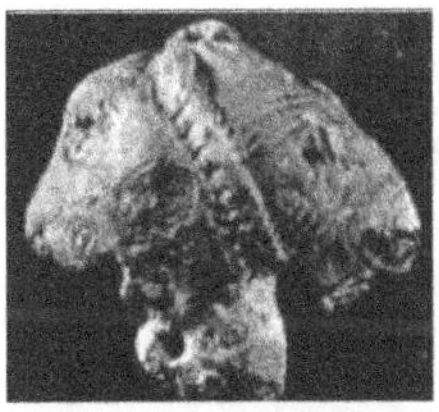

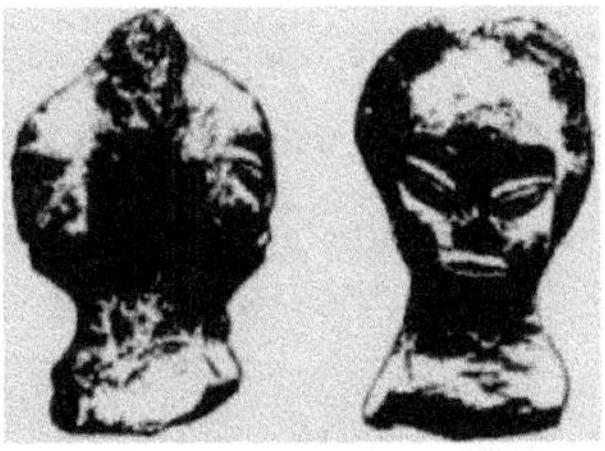

Ligatured sculpture: three-faced: tiger, bovine, elephant, Nausharo NS 92.02.70.04 6.76 cm (h); three-headed: elephant, buffalo, bottom jaw of a feline. NS 91.02.32.01.LXXXII. Dept. of Archaeology, Karachi. EBK 7712. The glyphs of elephant, buffalo and tiger occur on Mohenjo-daro Seal m0304. The glyphic compositions (pictographs + text glyphs) have been explained to be a detailed account of the metal work engaged in by the Indus artisans.

Elephant: ibha (glyph). Rebus: ibbo (merchant of ib 'iron')

Tiger: kola (glyph). Rebus: kol (working in iron, kolami 'smithy/forge')

Buffalo: kaṭā, kaṭamā 'bison' (Ta.)(DEDR 1114) (glyph). Rebus: kaḍiyo [Hem. Des. kaḍa-i-o = (Skt. Sthapati, a mason) a bricklayer, mason (G.)]

A ligatured glyph wad used to connote the professional competence of an artisan who performed the roles of merchant, smith and mason.

h1971B Harappa. Three tablets with identical glyphic compositions on both sides: h1970, h1971 and h1972. Seated figure or deity with reed house or shrine at one side. Left: H95-2524; Right: H95-2487.

Harappa. Planoconvex molded tablet found on Mound ET. A. Reverse. a female deity battling two tigers and standing above an elephant and below a six-spoked wheel; b. Obverse. A person spearing with a barbed spear a buffalo in front of a seated horned deity wearing bangles and with a plumed headdress. The person presses his foot down the buffalo's head. An alligator with a narrow snout is on the top register. "We have found two other broken tablets at Harappa that appear to have been made from the same mold that was used to create the scene of a deity battling two tigers and standing above an elephant. One was found in a room located on the southern slope of Mount ET in 1996 and another example comes from excavations on Mound F in the 1930s. However, the flat obverse of both of these broken tablets does not show the spearing of a buffalo, rather it depicts the more well-known scene showing a tiger looking back over its shoulder at a person sitting on the branch of a tree. Several other flat or twisted rectangular terracotta tablets found at Harappa combine these two narrative scenes of a figure strangling two tigers on one side of a tablet, and the tiger looking back over its shoulder at a figure in a tree on the other side." [JM Kenoyer, 1998, p. 115].

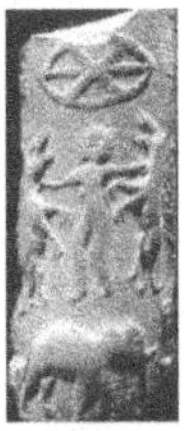

h1973B h1974B Two tablets. One side shows a person seated on a tree branch, a tiger looking up, a crocodile on the top register and other animals in procession in the bottom register. (comparable to h1970, h1971 and h1972) Obverse side shows an elephant, a person strangling two tigers and a six-spoked wheel.

The glyphic which is common to both set 1 (h1970B, h1971B and h1972B) and set 2: (h1973B and h1974B) is: crocodile on the top register. karā 'crocodile' (Telugu). Rebus: khara 'blacksmith' (Kashmiri)

The following glyphics of m1431 prism tablet show the association between the tiger + person on tree glyphic set and crocile + 3 animal glyphic set.

m0489A One side of a prism tablet shows: crocodile + fish glyphic above:

elephant, rhinoceros, tiger, tiger looking back and up.

m1431A m1431B Crocodile+ three animal glyphs: rhinoceros, elephant, tiger

It is possible that the broken portions of set 2 (h1973B and h1974B) showed three animals in procession: tiger looking back and up + rhinoceros + tiger.

Reverse side glyphs:

eraka 'nave of wheel'. Rebus: era 'copper'.

Animal glyph: elephant 'ibha'. Rebus ibbo, 'merchant'.

Composition of glyphics: Woman with six locks of hair + one eye + thwarting + two pouncing tigers + nave with six spokes. Rebus: *kola* 'woman' + kaṇga 'eye' (Pego.), *bhaṭa* 'six'+ *dul* 'casting (metal)' + *kūdā kol* (tiger jumping) + *era āra* (nave of wheel, six spokes), *ibha* (elephant). Rebus: *era* 'copper'; *kūdār dul kol* 'turner, casting, working in iron'; *kan* 'brazier, bell-metal worker';

The glyphic composition read rebus: copper, iron merchant with *taṭu kanḍ kol bhaṭa* 'iron stone (ore) mineral 'furnace'.

Glypg: 'woman': kola 'woman' (Nahali). Rebus kol 'working in iron' (Tamil)

Glyph: 'impeding, hindering': taṭu (Ta.) Rebus: dhatu 'mineral' (Santali) Ta. taṭu (-pp-, -tt) to hinder, stop, obstruct, forbid, prohibit, resist, dam, block up, partition off, curb, check, restrain, control, ward off, avert; n. hindering, checking, resisting; taṭuppu hindering, obstructing, resisting, restraint; Kur. ṭaṇḍnā to prevent, hinder, impede. Br. taḍ power to resist. (DEDR 3031)

Allograph: 'notch': Marathi: खांडा [ khāṇḍā ] *m* A jag, notch, or indentation (as upon the edge of a tool or weapon).

Glyph: 'full stretch of one's arms': kāḍ 2 काड् । पौरुषम् m. a man's length, the stature of a man (as a measure of length) (Rām. 632, zangan kaḍun kāḍ, to stretch oneself the whole length of one's body. So K. 119). Rebus: kāḍ 'stone'. Ga. (Oll.) kanḍ, (S.) kanḍu (pl. kanḍkil) stone (DEDR 1298). maypoṇḍi kanḍ whetstone; (Ga.)(DEDR 4628). (खडा) Pebbles or small stones: also stones broken up (as for a road), metal. खडा [ khaḍā ] *m* A small stone, a pebble. 2 A nodule (of lime &c.): a lump or bit (as of gum, assafœtida, catechu, sugar-candy): the gem or stone of a ring or trinket: a lump of hardened fæces or scybala: a nodule or lump gen. CDIAL 3018 kāṭha m. ' rock ' lex. [Cf. *kānta* -- 2 m. ' stone ' lex.] Bshk. *kōr* ' large stone ' AO xviii 239. கண்டு[3] kaṇṭu , *n.* < *gaṇḍa*. 1. Clod, lump; கட்டி. (தைலவ. தைல. 99.) 2. Wen; கழலைக்கட்டி. 3. Bead or something like a pendant in an ornament for the neck; ஓர் ஆபரணவுரு. புல்லிகைக்கண்ட நாண் ஒன்றிற் கட்டின கண்டு ஒன்றும் (S.I.I. ii, 429). (CDIAL 3023) kāṇḍa cluster, heap ' (in *tṛṇa -- kāṇḍa* -- Pāṇ. Kāś.). [Poss. connexion with gaṇḍa -- 2 makes prob. non -- Aryan origin (not with P. Tedesco Language 22, 190 < *kṛntáti*). Pa. *kaṇḍa* -- m.n. joint of stalk, lump. काठः A rock, stone. kāṭha m. ' rock ' lex. [Cf. *kānta* -- 2 m. ' stone ' lex.]Bshk. *kōr* ' large stone ' AO xviii 239.(CDIAL 3018). অয়স্কঠিন [ aẏaskaṭhina ] as hard as iron; extremely hard (Bengali)

Glyph: 'one-eyed': काण *a.* [कण् निमीलने कर्तरि घञ् Tv.] 1 One-eyed; अक्ष्णा काणः Sk; काणेन चक्षुषा किं वा H. Pr.12; Ms.3.155. -2 Perforated, broken (as a cowrie) <kaNa>(Z) {ADJ} ``^one-^eyed, ^blind''. Ju<kaNa>(DP),,<kana>(K) {ADJ} ``^blind, blind in one eye''. (Munda) Go. (Ma.) kanḍ reppa eyebrow (Voc. 3047(a))(DEDR 5169). *Ka.* kāṇ (kanḍ-) to see; *Ko.* kaṇ-/ka·ṇ- (kaḍ-) to see; *Koḍ.* ka·ṇ- (ka·mb-, kanḍ-) to see; *Ta.* kāṇ (kāṇp-, kaṇṭ-) to see; *Kol.*kanḍt, kanḍakt seen, visible. (DEDR 1443).
*Ta.* kaṇ eye, aperture, orifice, star of a peacock's tail. (DEDR 1159a) Rebus 'brazier, bell-metal worker': கன்னான் kaṉṉāṉ , *n.* < கன்[1]. [M. *kannān.*] Brazier, bell-metal worker, one of the divisions of the

Kammāḷa caste; செம்புகொட்டி. (திவா.) *Ta.* kaṉ copper work, copper, workmanship; kaṉṉāṉ brazier. *Ma.* kannān id. (DEDR 1402). கன்[1] kaṉ , *n.* perh. கன்மம். 1. Workmanship; வேலைப்பாடு. கன்னார் மதில்சூழ் குடந்தை (திவ். திருவாய். 5, 8, 3). 2. Copper work; கன்னார் தொழில். (W.) 3. Copper; செம்பு. (ஈடு, 5, 8, 3.) 4. See கன்னத்தட்டு. (நன். 217, விருத்.) கன்[2] kaṉ , *n.* < கல். 1. Stone; கல். (சூடா.) 2. Firmness; உறுதிப்பாடு. (ஈடு, 5, 8, 3.)

kā̃ḍ 2 काँड् m. a section, part in general; a cluster, bundle, multitude (Śiv. 32). kā̃ḍ 1 काँड् । काण्डः m. the stalk or stem of a reed, grass, or the like, straw. In the compound with dan 5 (p. 221*a,* l. 13) the word is spelt kāḍ.

kõda कोँद । कुलालादिकन्दुः f. a kiln; a potter's kiln (Rām. 1446; H. xi, 11); a brick-kiln (Śiv. 133); a lime-kiln. -bal -बल् । कुलालादिकन्दुस्थानम् m. the place where a kiln is erected, a brick or potter's kiln (Gr.Gr. 165). -- khasūñū -- खस&above;ञ्&below; । कुलालादिकन्दुयथावद्भावः f.inf. a kiln to arise; met. to become like such a kiln (which contains no imperfectly baked articles, but only well-made perfectly baked ones), hence, a collection of good ('pucka') articles or qualities to exist.

**ಕಣಿ kaṇi. 5. A stone** ([illegible] Śm. 96; *cf.* [illegible] 4). [illegible] (Bp. 1, 39). [illegible] (36, 2). [illegible] (My.; see Tbb. [illegible]).

**ಕಣಿ kaṇi. 6. A place** ([illegible] Śm. 96; T. [illegible]).

ಕಣಿ kaṇi. 1. An atom, a minute particle; a trifle. [illegible] (Rśv. 6, after 11).

ಕಣಿ kaṇi. 2. = [illegible], [illegible]. Tbb. of [illegible] (Śmd. 364). That is dug: a ditch, a basin (see [illegible]); a mine ([illegible], [illegible], [illegible] HlA., Mr. 100; [illegible], [illegible] Nr. 91; [illegible] 104; C.). [illegible] ([illegible] Nr.). [illegible] (Dp. 54). See *e. g.* Bp. 22, 62; J. 6, 25; B. 5, 98.

ಕಂಡೆ [ kaṇḍe ] *kaṇḍe.* [Tel.] n. A head or ear of millet or maize. జొన్నకంకి.

*kaṇṭa ' backbone, podex, penis '. 2. *kaṇḍa -- . 3. *karaṇḍa -- 4. (Cf. *kāṭa -- 2, *ḍākka -- 2: poss. same as káṇṭa -- 1] 1. Pa. *piṭṭhi -- kaṇṭaka* -- m. ' bone of the spine '; Gy. eur. *kanro* m. ' penis ' (or < káṇṭaka -- ); Tir. *mar -- kaṇḍḗ* ' back (of the body) '; S.*kaṇḍo* m. ' back ', L. *kaṇḍ* f., *kaṇḍā* m. 'backbone', awāṇ. *kaṇḍ*, °*ḍī* ' back '; P. *kaṇḍ* f. ' back, pubes '; WPah. bhal. *kaṇṭ* f. ' syphilis '; N. *kaṇḍo* ' buttock, rump, anus ',*kaṇḍeulo* ' small of the back '; B. *kā̃ṭ* ' clitoris '; Or. *kaṇṭi* ' handle of a plough '; H. *kā̃ṭā* m. ' spine ', G. *kā̃ṭɔ* m., M. *kā̃ṭā* m.; Si. *äṭa -- kaṭuva* ' bone ', *piṭa -- k°* ' backbone '. 2. Pk. *kaṁḍa* -- m. ' backbone '. 3. Pk. *karaṁḍa* -- m.n. ' bone shaped like a bamboo ', *karaṁḍuya* -- n. ' backbone '. (CDIAL 2670).

<kana.kana>(A) {ADJ} ``^perforated''. #15890. <kaNa>>: *De.<kana>(GM) `a hole; perforated'. ??hole, to make a hole? #10761. <kaNa-gu-nu> {ADJ} ``^perforated''. |<gu> `?perfect/past', <nu> `adjective'. *De.<kana>(GM) `a hole; perforated'. (Munda) Pk. *kāṇa* -- ' full of holes ', G. *kāṇũ* ' full of holes ', n. ' hole ' (CDIAL 3019) Marathi: खड्डा [ khaḍḍā ] *m* A rough hole or pit. M. *khāḍ* f. ' hole, creek ', °*ḍā* m. 'hole' (CDIAL, no. 3874).

Pk. khāṇī -- f. ' mine '; Gy. as. xani, eur. sp. xaní f., boh. xaníg f., gr. xaníng f. ' well '; K. khān f. ' mine '; S. khāṇi f. ' mine, quarry, water in a pit '; L. khāṇ f. ' mine ' (CDIAL 3873)

Rebus: 'to engrave, write; lapidary': <kana-lekhe>(P) {??} ``??''. |. Cf. <kana->. %16123. #16013. <lekhe->(P),,<leke->(KM) {VTC} ``to ^write''. Cf. <kana-lekhe>. *Kh.<likhae>, H.<lIkhAna>, O.<lekhlba>, B.<lekha>; Kh.<likha>(P), Mu.<lika>. %20701. #20541. Kashmiri: khanun खनुन् । खननम् conj. 1 (1 p.p. khonu for 1, see s.v.; f. khüñü to dig (K.Pr. 155, 247; L. 459; Śiv. 59, 746, 994,

143, 1197, 1214, 1373, 1754; Rām. 343, 958, 1147, 1724; H. xii, 6); to engrave (Śiv. 414, 671, 176; Rām. 1583). khonu-motu खनुमतु; I खात: perf. part. (f. khüñümütsü) dug (e.g. a field, or a well); engraved. mŏhara-khonu म्वहर-खनु; or (Gr.M.) mŏhar-kan I मुद्राखननकारु: m. a seal-engraver, a lapidary (El. *mohar-kand*). -wöjü I *अङ्गुलिमुद्रा f. a signet-ring.

DEDR 1170 *Ta.* kaṇṭam iron style for writing on palmyra leaves. *Te.* gaṇṭamu id.

DEDR 1179 *Kur.* kaṇḍō a stool. *Malt.* kanḍo stool, seat. ಗಡಮಂಚೆ *gaḍa-manche*. n. A wooden frame like a bench to keep things on. గంపలు మొదలగువాటిని ఉంచు మంచె.

3986 *gaḍha ' fort '. [Poss. with ODBL 500 < **gr̥dha*- (> gr̥há -- ), Av. *gərəda* -- ]
Pk. *gaḍha* -- m., °*ḍhā* -- f. ' fort '; K. *gaḍ* m. (= vill. **gaṛ*?) ' small masonry fort built in the hills by a local chieftain '; S. *gaṛhu*m. ' fort ', P. *gaṛh* m., Ku. *gaṛ*, A. *gar*, B. *gaṛ*, Or. *gaṛ(h)a*, Mth. Bhoj. *gaṛh*, OAw. *gaḍha* m., H. *gaṛhī* f. (→ N. *gaṛi*), OMarw. OG. *gaḍha* m., G. *gaḍh*, *ghaṛ* m. (whence *gaḍhī* m. ' inhabitant of a hill fort '), M. *gaḍhī*, *gaḍḍī* f. *gaḍhapati -- ; saṁgaḍha -- .Addenda: *gaḍha -- : S.kcch. *gaḍḍh* m. ' fort '.

Allograph: 'rhinoceros': gaṇḍá4 m. ' rhinoceros ' lex., °*aka* -- m. lex. 2. *ga- yaṇḍa -- . [Prob. of same non -- Aryan origin as khaḍgá --1: cf. *gaṇōtsāha* -- m. lex. as a Sanskritized form ← Mu. PMWS 138]1.

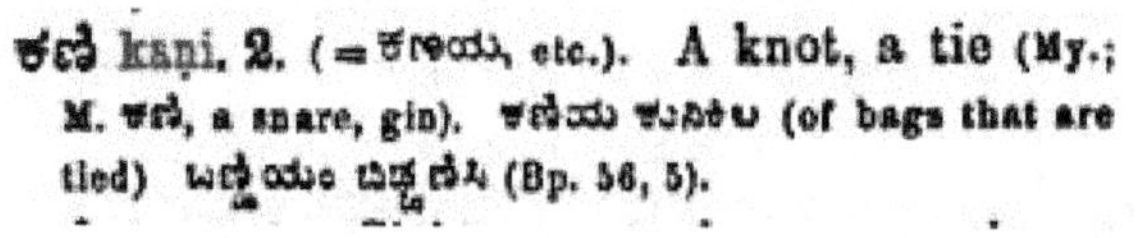
ಕಣಿ kaṇi. 2. (= ಕಣ್ಣು, etc.). A knot, a tie (My.; M. ಕಣಿ, a snare, gin). ಕಣಿಯು ಕಟ್ಟಿದ (of bags that are tied) ಬಿಕ್ಕೆಯು ಬಿಕ್ಕಡೆ (Bp. 56, 5).

Pa. *gaṇḍaka* -- m., Pk. *gaṁḍaya* -- m., A. *gãr*, Or. *gaṇḍā*. 2. K. *gõḍ* m., S. *geṇḍo* m. (lw. with *g* -- ), P. *gaĩḍā* m., °*ḍī* f., N. *gaĩṛo*, H. *gaĩṛā* m., G. *gẽḍɔ* m., °*ḍī* f., M. *gẽḍā* m.Addenda: gaṇḍa -- 4. 2. *gayaṇḍa -- : WPah.kṭg. *geṇḍɔ mirg* m. ' rhinoceros ', Md. *genḍā* ← H. (CDIAL 4000).

1. Pk. *kaṁkaya* -- m. ' comb ', *kaṁkaya* -- , °*kaï* -- m. ' name of a tree '; Gy. eur. *kangli* f.; Wg. *kuṇi* -- *prũ* ' man's comb ' (for *kuṇi* -- cf. *kuṇälík* beside *kuṅälík* s.v. kr̥muka -- ; -- *prũ* see prapavaṇa -- ); Bshk. *kēṅg* ' comb ', Gaw. *khēṅgī´*, Sv. *khẽ́ṅgiā*, Phal. *khyẽ́ṅgia*, *kēṅgī* f., *kāṅga* ' combing ' in *ṣiṣ k° dūm* ' I comb my hair '; Tor. *kyäṅg* ' comb ' (Dard. forms, esp. Gaw., Sv., Phal. but not Sh., prob. ← L. P. type < *kaṅgahiā -- , see 3 below); Sh. kōṅyi̯ f. (→ Ḍ. k*lṅi f.), gil. (Lor.) kōĩ f. ' man's comb ', kōũ m. ' woman's comb ', pales. kōgōm. ' comb '; K. kanguwu m. ' man's comb ', kangañ f. ' woman's '; WPah. bhad. kā´kei ' a comb -- like fern ', bhal. kãkei f. ' comb, plant with comb -- like leaves '; N. kāṅiyo, kāĩyo ' comb ', A. kā̃kai, . kā̃kui; Or. kaṅkāi, kaṅkuā ' comb ', kakuā ' ladder -- like bier for carrying corpse to the burning -- ghat '; Bi. kakwā ' comb ', kakahā, °hī, Mth. kakwā, Aw. lakh. kakawā, Bhoj. kakahī f.; H. kakaiyā ' shaped like a comb (of a brick) '; G. (non -- Aryan tribes of Dharampur) kākhāī f. ' comb '; M. kaṅkvā m. ' comb ', kā̃kaī f. ' a partic. shell fish and its shell '; -- S. kaṅgu m. ' a partic. kind of small fish ' < *kaṅkuta -- ? -- Ext. with -- l -- in Ku. kā̃gilo, kāĩlo ' comb '.2. G. (Soraṭh) kā̃gaṛ m. ' a weaver's instrument '?3. L. kaṅghī f. ' comb, a fish of the perch family ', awāṇ. kaghī ' comb '; P. kaṅghā m. ' large comb ', °ghī f. ' small comb for men, large one for women ' (→ H.kaṅghā m. ' man's comb ', °gahī, °ghī f. ' woman's ', kaṅghuā m. ' rake or harrow '; Bi. kāgahī ' comb ', Or. kaṅgei, M. kaṅgvā); -- G. kā̃gsī f. ' comb ', with metath. kā̃sko m., °kī f.; WPah. khaś. kāgśī, śeu. kāśkī ' a comblike fern ' or < *kaṅkataśikha -- .*kaṅkatakara -- , *kaṅkataśikha -- .Addenda: káṅkata -- : WPah.kṭg. kaṅgi f. ' comb '; J. kāṅgṛu m. ' small comb .kaṅkatakara CDIAL 2599 *kaṅkatakara ' comb -- maker '. [káṅkata -- , kará -- 1]H. *kāgherā* m. ' caste of comb -- makers ', °*rī* f. ' a woman of this caste '.

1161 *Ta.* kaṇ place, site. *Ka.* kaṇi a place.

Kashmiri: khān 2 खान् m. a table (not used by Hindūs)

(El., K.Pr. 13, YZ. 29).

Copper tablets. Mohenjo-daro. Harappa seal h095

The seal shows a professional: *kharā kaḍaio*, 'a blacksmith and mason'.. Yes, the same ancestors of the *kharā* legacy whose legatees of the Indian language union (*sprachbund*) create the *kharoṣṭī* syllabic writing system.

The chain link shown in front the 'hare' glyph on h095: kaḍī a chain; a hook; a link (G.); kaḍum a bracelet, a ring (G.) Rebus: kaḍiyo [Hem. Des. kaḍaio = Skt. sthapati a mason] a bricklayer; a mason; kaḍiyaṇa, kaḍiyeṇa a woman of the bricklayer caste; a wife of a bricklayer (G.)

It is significant that both the glyphs: 'hare' and 'thicket in front of the hare' are related to the cognate word, *khār*. Glyph: 'hare': N. *kharāyo* ' hare ', Or. *kharā*, *°riā*, *kherihā*, Mth. *kharehā*, H. *kharahā* m. (CDIAL 3823). Glyph: 'thicket': khāra 2 खार (= ) or khār 4 खार् (L.V. 96, K.Pr. 47, Śiv. 827) I द्वेष: m. (for 1, see khār 1), a thorn, prickle, spine (K.Pr. 47; Śiv. 827, 153)(Kashmiri) Rebus: khār 'blacksmith' (Kashmiri). Thus, 'hare' glyph is an allograph for 'crocodile' which reads rebus: *kara*. khār 1 खार् I लोहकार: m. (sg. abl. khāra 1 खार; the pl. dat. of this word is khāran 1 खारन्, which is to be distinguished from khāran 2, q.v., s.v.), a blacksmith, an iron worker (cf. bandūka-khār, p. 111*b*, l. 46; K.Pr. 46; H. xi, 17); a farrier (El.). This word is often a part of a name, and in such case comes at the end (W. 118) as in Wahab khār, Wahab the smith (H. ii, 12; vi, 17). khāra-basta

Vikalpa: Glyph: balle a thicket, bush (Tu.); vallai extensive thicket (Ta.); balle thick bush, thick jungle (Ka.); vallara, vallura arbour, bower, thicket (Skt.); vallara id. (Pkt.)(DEDR 5289). Rebus: bali 'iron sand sore'(Mu.) boṭor 'hare' (Santali); Rebus: badhoṛ 'expert in working in wood'(Santali)

Vikalpa: Glyph: 'bush, thorn': Pk. *kaṁṭiya* -- ' thorny '; S. *kaṇḍī* f. ' thorn bush '; N. *kā̃ṛe* ' thorny '; A. *kā̃ṭi* ' point of an oxgoad ', *kā̃iṭīyā* ' thorny '; H. *kā̃ṭī* f. ' thorn bush '; G.*kā̃ṭī* f. ' a kind of fish '; M. *kā̃ṭī*, *kāṭī* f. ' thorn bush '. -- Ext. with -- *la* -- : S. *kaṇḍiru* ' thorny, bony '; -- with -- *lla* -- : Gy. pal. *ķăndī'la* ' prickly pear '; H. *kā̃ṭīlā*, *kaṭ°* ' thorny '.(CDIAL 2679). kāṇṭaka -- ĀpŚr.1. Paš. *kā̃ṛ* ' porcupine ' (cf. *kaṇṭakaśrēṇi* -- , *kaṇṭakāgāra* -- ). 2. S. *kā̃ḍo* ' thorny ', Si. *kaṭu*. -- Deriv.: S. *kā̃ḍero* m. ' camel -- thorn ', *°rī* f. ' a kind of thistle '(CDIAL 3022). Rebus: *Tu.* kandůka, kandaka ditch, trench. *Te.* kandakamu id. *Konḍa* kanda trench made as a fireplace during weddings. *Pe.* Kanda fire trench. *Kui* kanda small trench for fireplace. *Malt.* kandri a pit.(DEDR 1214).

Indus script "fish-eyes" traded with Ur

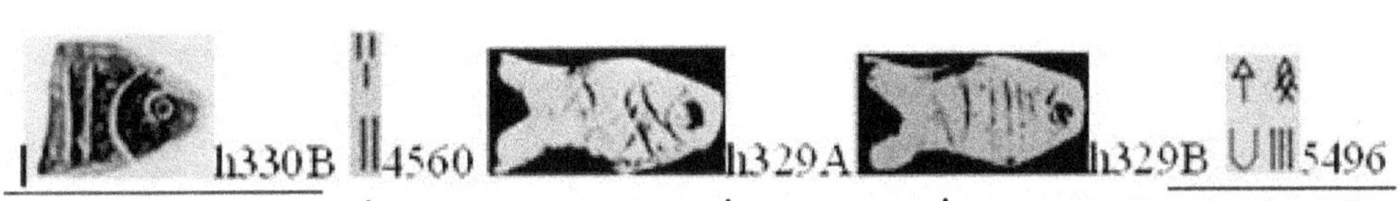


kaṇi 'stone' (Kannada) கன்¹ kaṉ Copper (Tamil) கன்² kaṉ , n. < கல். stone (Tamil) खडा (Marathi) is 'metal, nodule, stone, lump'. *kaṇi* 'stone' (Kannada) with Tadbhava *khaḍu*. *khaḍu, kaṇ* 'stone/nodule (metal)'. . Ga. (Oll.) kanḍ, (S.) kanḍu (pl. kanḍkil) stone (DEDR 1298). These could be the substratum glosses for *kāṇḍa* in ayas *kāṇḍa* 'excellent iron' (Pan.) h329A has a fish-shaped tablet with two signs: fish + arrow (which has been decoded as *ayaskāṇḍa* on a *bos indicus* seal). The 'fish-eye' is a reinforcement of the gloss *kāṇḍ*'stone/nodule (metal)'. The dotted circle (eye) is decoded rebus as *kaṇ* 'aperture' (Tamil); kāṇũ hole (Gujarati) (i.e. glyph showing dotted-circle); kāṇa 'one eye' and these glyphs may have been interpreted as the 'fish-eyes' or 'eye stones' (Akkadian IGI-HA, IGI-KU6) mentioned in Mesopotamian texts. The commodities denoted may be nodules of mined stones/nodules of chalcopyrite. See Annex. 'Eye stones' elucidating, based on textual and archaeological contexts, that ‘fish-eyes’ do NOT refer to pearls. Donkin surmises that they refer to agate stones. This monograph argues that the glyphs of ‘dotted circles’ denoting ‘fish-eyes’ or ‘antelope-eyes’, refer to ‘stone/nodules of mineral (perhaps, chalcopyrite)’, decoded rebus as *kāṇḍ* as in *ayaskāṇḍa* ‘excellent iron’.

m0308 One-eyed glyph: *kāṇa* ‘one-eyed’; rebus: *kāṇḍa* ‘metal (stone ore)’; *bhaṭa* ‘six (hair-knots)’; rebus: *bhaṭa* ‘furnace’. Slide 90 harappa.com (one-eye glyph)

Pict-123 Standard device which is normally in front of a one-horned bull. The device is flanked by columns of dotted circles.

Glyphs and rebus readings: kolami ‘smithy, forge’ + *kanka, karṇaka ‘account’* + *bhaṭa* ‘furnace’ + *kūdā* ‘turner’ + kol ‘working in iron’ + era ‘copper’ + āra ‘brass’ as in ārakūṭa (Skt.)

The glyphs of ‘woman’, ‘face’, ‘six’, ‘one-eye’: kola ‘woman’. Rebus: *kol* ‘smithy’. *bhaṭa* ‘six’. Rebus: *bhaṭa* ‘furnace’. *mũh* ‘face’. Rebus: *mũhe* ‘ingot’. *kāṇ* ‘one-eye, blind’. Rebus: *kāṇḍ* ‘stone ore’ as in *ayaskāṇḍa* ‘excellent quantity of iron’. The glyphic composition thus read rebus: ‘furnace stone ore ingot smithy/forge’.

Glyph on text of inscription: *panǰắr* ‘ladder, stairs’(Bshk.)(CDIAL 7760). Rebus: *pasra* ‘smithy’. *ayaskāṇḍa* is denoted on the text by ‘fish’ + ‘arrow’ glyphs: *aya* + *kāṇḍa.* The penultimate glyph (before the ‘ladder’ glyph) may be an orthographic variant of ‘standard device’: *sangaḍa* ‘lathe, portable furnace’. Rebus: sangāta ‘association, guild’. Thus the text reads: excellent iron workshop, smithy guild – an intimation of the Harosheth hagoyim, ‘smithy of nations’.

Glyph: ‘pair of tigers’: kola ‘tiger’. dula ‘pair’. Rebus: dula kol ‘casting work in iron’. Rebus: kol , *n.* < கொல்-. Working in iron; கொற்றொழில். 4. Blacksmith; கொல்லன். *கொல்லன் kollan , n.* < *கொல்[2]. [M. kollan.] Blacksmith; கருமான். மென்றோன் மிதியுலைக் கொல்லன் (பெரும்பாண். 207).* கொற்றுறை korrurai , *n.* < கொல்[2] + துறை. Blacksmith's workshop, smithy; கொல்லன் பட் டடை. கொற்றுறைக் குற்றில (புறநா. 95). கொற்று[1] korru , *n.* prob. கொல்-. 1. Masonry, brickwork; கொற்றுவேலை. கொற்றுள விவரில் (திரு வாலவா. 30, 23). 2. Mason, bricklayer; கொத் தன். *Colloq.* 3. The measure of work turned out by a mason; ஒரு கொத்தன் செய்யும் வேலை யளவு. இந்தச் சுவர் கட்ட எத்தனை கொற்றுச் செல்லும்?

Thus side 1 glyphs refer to: merchant (of) furnace (outputs) account (from) smithy/forge of turner, working in copper and brass.

Obverse side glyphs are of two sets:

Set 1: crocodile + person with foot on head of animal + spearing + bison + horned (with twig) seated person in penance

ayakāra ‘ironsmith’ (fish, *aya* + crocodile, *karā*) + kolami ‘smithy/forge’ (kolsa ‘kicking’) + sal ‘workshop’ (sal ‘bison’) + kol ‘working in iron’ (kol ‘killing’) + kammaṭi ‘coiner’; kammaṭa ‘mint’ (kamaḍha ‘penance’) + kuṭhi ‘smelter’ (kūdī ‘twig’) + koḍ ‘artisan’s workshop’ (koḍ ‘horns’)

Set 2: crocodile + person seated on branch of tree + tiger looking back and up + rhinoceros + tiger in procession.

ayakāra ‘ironsmith’ (fish, *aya* + crocodile, *karā*) + era ‘copper’ (eraka ‘spy’) + ḍhālako, ‘large metal ingot’ (ḍāḷ, ‘branch of a tree’) + three animals in procession: badhoe ‘worker in wood and iron’ [badhi ‘castrated boar’] + kol ‘smith working in iron with smithy/forge’ [kol + kammara ‘tiger looking up’] + kolami ‘smithy/forge’ [kola ‘tiger’]

Details of the tiger + spy + leafless tree glyphics are clearly seen on a Mohenjo-daro seal m0309.

m0309  2522

Glyphics read rebus: *kol kammara* 'iron smith' [*kola* 'tiger' (Telugu); *krammaru* 'head turned back' (Telugu)]; *eraka* 'copper' [*heraka* 'spy']; *kõdār* 'turner' (Bengali) [*khōṇḍa* 'leafless tree' (Marathi).]

Glyphs on text inscription

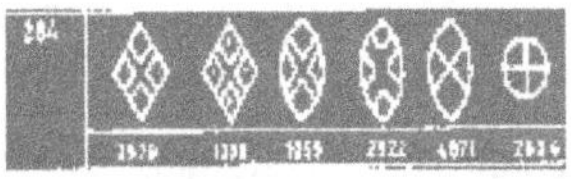

V284 Glyph: *kōnṭa* 'corner' (Nk.); Tu. *kōṇṭu* 'angle, corner' (Tu.). Rebus: *kõdā* 'to turn in a lathe' (B.) Four corners marked may denote a worker guild working with 4 types of pure metal and alloyed ingots (copper + arsenic/tin/zinc).

Glyph: 'splinter' sal 'splinter'. Rebus: sal 'artisan's workshop'.

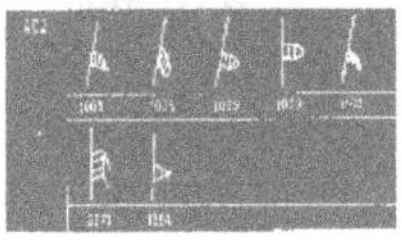

Glyph: taṭṭai 'mechanism made of split bamboo for scaring away parrots from grain fields (Ta.); taṭṭe 'a thick bamboo or an areca-palm stem, split in two' (Ka.) (DEDR 3042)Rebus: toṭxin, toṭ.xn goldsmith (To.); taṭṭāṉ 'gold- or silver-smith' (Ta.); taṭṭaravāḍu 'gold- or silver-smith' (Te.); *ṭhaṭṭakāra 'brass-worker' (Skt.)(CDIAL 5493). Thus, the glyph is decoded: taṭṭara 'worker in gold, brass'.

Glyph: *kaṇḍa kanka* 'rim of jar'. Rebus: furnace (stone ore) account (scribe).

V402

Glyph: *koḍi* 'flag' (Ta.)(DEDR 2049). Rebus: *koḍ* 'workshop' (Kuwi)

Glyph: *ayo, hako* 'fish'; a~s = scales of fish (Santali). Rebus: aya = iron (G.); ayah, ayas = metal (Skt.)

Glyph: one long linear stroke. koḍa, koṛa = in arithmetic one; 4 koṛa or koḍa = 1 gaṇḍa = 4 (Santali) Rebus: koḍ, 'artisan's workshop' (Kuwi.)

The text inscription reads rebus: Lathe-turner workshop; brass-worker, furnace (stone ore) account (scribe); metal artisan's workshop.

*kõdā* 'lathe-turner'; *sal* 'artisan's workshop'. taṭṭara 'worker in gold, brass'; *kaṇḍa kanka* furnace (stone ore) account (scribe); *koḍ* 'workshop'; *aya* 'metal'; *koḍ* 'artisan's workshop'

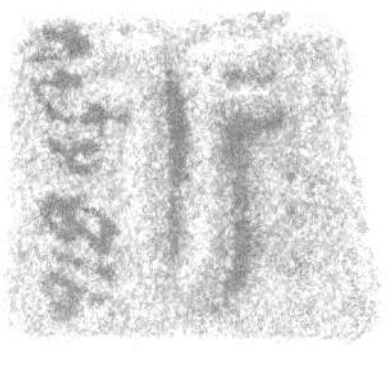

Thus set 2 is distinctively a different set of trade loads compared to set 1.

Set
in

2 has copper ingots of ironsmith, worker in wood and iron, smith working iron with smithy/forge.

Set

1 has the trade loads of ironsmith with smithy/forge workshop, smith

working as coiner in mint, with a smelter and artisan's workshop.

Thus, two specialist guilds of workers' bronze age products are being collected together to further compile the bills of lading for the two trade loads.

saman: = to offer an offering, to place in front of; front, to front or face (Santali) Rebus: samr.obica, stones containing gold(Mundari). nāga = snake (Skt.) Rebus: nāga = lead (Skt.)

கடை-தல் kaṭai- , *4 v.* [K. *kaḍa.*] *tr.* 1. To churn with a churning rod; மத்தாற்கடைதல். பாம்பு கயிறாக் கடல் கடைந்த மாயவன் (சிலப். 17, 2). 2. To turn in a lathe; to form, as moulds on a wheel; மரமுதலியன கடைதல். கடைந்த மணிச்செப் பென வீங்கு (கூர்மபு. தக்கன்வே. 52). கடைச்சல் kaṭaiccal, *n.* < கடை-. 1. Turning on a lathe or on a brazier's wheel; மரமுதலிய வற்றைக் கடைகை. 2. Turning work; கடைசல் வேலை. 3. That which is turned on a lathe; கடையப்பட்ட பொருள். கடைச்சற்பட்டை kaṭaiccaṟ-paṭṭai , *n.* < id. +. Turner's lathe; கடைச்சலுளியின் சுற் றுக்கட்டை. (C.E.M.) கடைசல் kaṭaical

*கடவன் kaṭavaṉ Master, lord; எசமானன். ஒருவன் ஒருகிருகத்துக்குக் கடவனா யிருக்கும் (ஈடு, 1, 1, 5).*

, *n.* < கடை-. 1. Polishing, enamelling; மெருகிடுகை. 2. Turned work in wood. See கடைச்சல். *Colloq.*

கடைசற்பட்டறை kaṭaicaṟ-paṭṭarai , *n.* < id. +. Turner's shop; கடைசல்வேலைசெய்யுஞ் சாலை. *Loc.*

கடையல் kaṭaiyal , *n.* < கடை. [K. *kaḍeca- lu*, M. *kaḍaccal.*] 1. Turning in a lathe; கடை கை. 2. Turner's work; கடையும்வேலை.

கடையாணி kaṭai-y-āṇi *n.* < id. +. [K. *kaḍāṇi.*] 1. Linchpin; அச்சாணி. (C.G.) 2. Pin used to keep a tenon in a mortise; பூட் டாணி. (W.)

கடைஞன் kaṭaiñaṉ Man of the labouring caste in an agricultural tract; மருதநிலமகன். (திவா.)

கடையர் kaṭaiyar Name of a sub-division of Paḷḷas, who are lime-burners and divers for pearls; பள்ளரில் சுண்ணாம்புசுடுதலும் முத்துக்குளித் தலும் ஆகிய தொழில்களைச் செய்யும் வகுப்பார். (W.)

*Ta.* kaṭai (-v-, -nt-) to churn, turn in lathe, mash to pulp (as vegetables with the bowl of a ladle); kaṭaical polishing, enamelling, turned work in wood; kaṭaiccal turning on a lathe, that which is turned on a lathe; kaṭaiccal uḷi turner's chisel; kaṭaiyal turning in a lathe, agitating, churning. *Ma.* kaṭayuka to churn, turn on lathe, polish; kaṭa churning; kaṭaccal turning; kaṭaccil turning and polishing (wood, etc.), churning. *Ko.* kaṛv- (kaṛd-) to churn; kaṛc uḷy lathe. *To.* kaṛ- (kaṛQ-) to churn. *Ka.* kaḍe, kaḍi to churn, stir, rub together (as two pieces of wood to excite fire), turn in a lathe;kaḍe, kaḍa, kaḍaha, kaḍeta churning; kaḍayisu to cause to churn. *Koḍ.* kaḍe- (kaḍev-, kaḍand-) to grind with mortar and pestle; (Shanmugam) kaḍev grinding; kaḍace kallï mortar and pestle. *Tu.* kaḍeyuni, kaḍevuni to stir up, turn; kaḍeñcuni to knead; kaḍanda grinding; kaḍavu, kaḍcilů, karcilů a turning lathe; (B-K.) kaḍañjige kneading. *Go.* (Mu.) karrih-, (Ph.) karahtānā, (S.) karah- to churn (*Voc.* 559); (LuS.)

kèrtuna id. *Koṇḍa* (BB) karas- (-t-) to stir with ladle. *Kui* kaṟsa (kaṟsi-) to knead; *n.* act of kneading. *Malt.* gaṭye to churn (DEDR 1141).

*ghaṭṭapāla ' ferryman '. [ghaṭṭa -- 1, pālá -- ] B. *ghāṭoāl*, *°ṭāl* 'man in charge of a ghāṭ '; Or. *ghāṭuāḷa* ' ferryman, toll -- collector ', *°ārā* ' ferryman '; H. *ghaṭwāl*, *°ār* m. ' wharfinger '.(CDIAL 4416)

Kaṭakaṭāyati=taṭataṭāyati to crush, grind, creak, snap PugA. i.34; VvA 121 (as v.l.); Vism 264.

*Ta.* karaṇṭi spoon or ladle. *Ma.* karaṇṭi spoon. *Te.* garīṭe, gaṇṭe, geṇṭe spoon, ladle. *Kol.* (SR.) gāṭe spoon; (Kamaleswaran). *Kuwi* (S.) garti (brass) spoon. (DEDR 1267) Pk. *caṭṭu* -- , *°ua* -- , *°ula* -- , *caṭua* -- m. ' wooden spoon '; P. *caṭṭū*, *caṭṭhū* m. ' wooden mortar '; M. *ċāṭū* m. ' wooden spoon '.(CDIAL 457) 2309 *Ta.* caṭṭukam, caṭṭuvam ladle, metal spatula with a long handle for turning and removing a cooked cake. *Ma.* caṭṭukam ladle, metal spoon; ?caṭṭuvam shoulder-bone (or with 2303 Kol. saṭṭa). *Ko.* caṭy go·l iron ladle with flat, round blade, for taking rice from pot. *Ka.* saṭuka, saṭṭu, saṭṭuga, soṭaka ladle, spoon. *Koḍ.* caṭṭuva wooden spoon used for stirring. *Tu.* saṭṭi a kind of wooden ladle; saṭṭuga, taṭṭuga a flat kind of trough for serving boiled rice. *Te.* caṭṭuvamu a sort of spoon with a shallow bowl having holes in it. *Ga.* (P.) saṭve ladle. *Koṇḍa* saṭva ladle made of wood for serving soup or curry. *Pe.* haṭva ladle; oar. *Kuwi* (Su.) haṭva ladle. / Cf. Skt. caṭuka- a wooden vessel for taking up fluid; Pkt. (*DNM*; Norman) caṭṭu- wooden spoon. Kaṭacchu [cp. on etym. Morris in *J.P.T.S.* 1887, 163] a ladle, a spoon; expld by uḷunka DhA iv.75, 123; by dabbi PvA 135. Used for butter VvA 68, otherwise for cooked food in general, esp. rice gruel. -- Vin ii.216; J i.454; iii.277. -- gāha "holding on to one's spoon," i. e. disinclination to give food, niggardliness, stinginess DhsA 376, cp. Dhs trsl. 300 n2. -- gāhika "spoon in hand," serving with ladles (in the distribution of food at the Mahādāna) PvA 135. -- parissāvana a perforated ladle Vin ii.118. -- bhikkhā "ladle -- begging," i. e. the food given with a ladle to a bhikkhu when he calls at a house on his begging tour Th 1, 934; Miln 9; DhA iv.123; as representing a small gift to one individual, opposed to the Mahādanā Pv ii.957; as an individual meal contrasted with public feeding (salāka -- bhatta) DhA i.379. -- matta (bhatta) "only a spoonful of rice" Miln 8; DhA iv.75.

4417 ghaṭṭáyati1 ' rubs, touches, shakes ' Suśr., *gháṭṭatē* Dhātup., *ghaṭṭita* -- MBh. 2. *ghōṭṭ -- . [Derivation of *ghaṭṭ* -- from ghr̥ṣṭa -- is phonet. difficult in view of *ghaṭṭēti* in Pa. canonical texts and co - - existence of **ghōṭṭ* -- (Sanskritized as *ghuṣṭa* -- ' rubbed ') in NIA. They are prob. words of non -- Aryan, perhaps Mu., origin (PMWS 56) which have collided with MIA. *ghaṭṭha* -- . -- √ghaṭṭ1]
1. Pa. *ghaṭṭēti* ' dashes against, touches '; Pk. *ghaṭṭaï* ' touches, rubs against '; B. *ghā̃ṭā* ' to stir with the fingers '; Or. *ghāṭibā* ' to brand with a hot iron '; M. *ghāṭṇē* ' to bruise, mash, beat '; Si. *gaṭanavā*, pret. *gäṭuvā* ' to dash together '.
2. S. *ghoṭaṇu* ' to bruise, grind ', *ghoṭo* m. ' rub with a pestle '; L. awāṇ. *ghōṭuṇ* ' to rub ', *ghuṭṭuṇ* ' to be pressed '; P. *ghoṭṇā* ' to grind, rub, smoothe ', *ghoṭṭā* m. ' a paper -- polishing instrument '; Ku. *ghoṭṇo* ' to powder '; N. *ghoṭnu* ' to rub, polish, wear away '; A. *ghõṭiba* ' to mix by stirring '; B. *ghõṭā*, *ghũṭā* ' to rub, stir, dig up '; Or. *ghoṭibā* ' to pound, stir up '; H. *ghoṭnā*, *ghõṭ°* ' to rub ', *ghoṭā*, *ghõṭā* m. ' wooden pestle '; M. *ghõṭṇē* ' to grind, rub, polish '.

Mth. *kūṛ* ' pot ', *kūṛā* ' churn '(CDIAL 3264). A. *ghõṭiba* also ' to churn '(CDIAL 4417) 4417 ghaṭṭáyati1 ' rubs, touches, shakes ' Suśr., *gháṭṭatē* Dhātup., *ghaṭṭita* -- MBh. 2. *ghōṭṭ -- . [Derivation of *ghaṭṭ* -- from ghr̥ṣṭa -- is phonet. difficult in view of *ghaṭṭēti* in Pa. canonical texts and co -- existence of **ghōṭṭ* -- (Sanskritized as *ghuṣṭa* -- ' rubbed ') in NIA. They are prob. words of non -- Aryan, perhaps Mu., origin (PMWS 56) which have collided with MIA. *ghaṭṭha* -- . -- √ghaṭṭ1]
1. Pa. *ghaṭṭēti* ' dashes against, touches '; Pk. *ghaṭṭaï* ' touches, rubs against '; B. *ghā̃ṭā* ' to stir with the fingers '; Or. *ghāṭibā* ' to brand with a hot iron '; M. *ghāṭṇē* ' to bruise, mash, beat '; Si. *gaṭanavā*, pret. *gäṭuvā* ' to dash together '.
2. S. *ghoṭaṇu* ' to bruise, grind ', *ghoṭo* m. ' rub with a pestle '; L. awāṇ. *ghōṭuṇ* ' to rub ', *ghuṭṭuṇ* ' to be pressed '; P. *ghoṭṇā* ' to grind, rub, smoothe ', *ghoṭṭā* m. ' a paper -- polishing instrument '; Ku. *ghoṭṇo* ' to powder '; N. *ghoṭnu* ' to rub, polish, wear away '; A. *ghõṭiba* ' to mix by stirring '; B. *ghõṭā*, *ghũṭā* ' to rub, stir, dig up '; Or. *ghoṭibā* ' to pound, stir up '; H. *ghoṭnā*, *ghõṭ°* ' to rub ', *ghoṭā*, *ghõṭā* m. ' wooden pestle '; M. *ghõṭṇē* ' to grind, rub, polish '.

గర్గరి [ gargari ] *gargari*. [Skt.] n. A churning pot. పెరుగుతరిచేకుండ. 4043 gargara2 m. ' churn ' MBh., *°rī* -- f. ' churn, waterpot ' Hariv. [Onom. and prob. same as gárgara -- 1, cf. similar onom. formation in Eng. *guggle*, *guglet* NED s.vv. -- Ac. to PMWS 55 with *karkarī* -- f. ' waterjar ' Bhartr̥. ← Mu.] Pk. *gaggarī* -- f. ' small waterpot '; Ku. *gāgro* ' waterpot ', gng. *gāgar;* N. *gāgro* ' earthen jar ', *°ri* ' copper jar '; A. *gāgarī* ' waterpot ', B.*gāgrī*; Or. *gagarā* ' large metal water vessel ', *gǎgari* ' earthen pot '; Bi. *gagrā*, *°rī* ' copper or brass water vessel ', Mth. *gāgari*; Bhoj. *gagarī* ' earthen pot '; Aw. lakh. *gagarā* ' jar ', *°rī* ' small jar '; H. *gǎgar* f., *gagrā* m., *gāgrī* f. ' waterpot ', G. *gāgar*, *°ger* f. -- K. *gāgürü* f. ' waterpot ', L. *gāgir* f., P. *gāggar*, *gāgar*, *°rī* f. are ← E. gargara -- 2: WPah.kṭg. *gaggər* f. (obl. -- *i*) ' brass water vessel ', J. *gāgar* f.; Garh. *gāgar* ' pitcher '.

3295 kunda1 m. ' a turner's lathe ' lex. [Cf. *cunda -- 1] N. *kũdnu* ' to shape smoothly, smoothe, carve, hew ', *kũduwā* ' smoothly shaped '; A. *kund* ' lathe ', *kundiba* ' to turn and smooth in a lathe ',*kundowā* ' smoothed and rounded '; B. *kũd* ' lathe ', *kũdā*, *kõdā* ' to turn in a lathe '; Or. *kū̆nda* ' lathe ', *kũdibā*, *kũd°* ' to turn ' (→ Drav. Kur.*kũd* ' lathe '); Bi. *kund* ' brassfounder's lathe '; H. *kunnā* ' to shape on a lathe ', *kuniyā* m. ' turner ', *kunwā* m.

3495 kōṭáyatē ' breaks ' Dhātup. [Cf. *prakuṭya* ' having cut into small pieces ' MBh., Pa. *ākōṭēti* ' breaks, beats down, stamps '. -- √kuṭ2] K. *kūrun* ' to gouge out, extract (an eye, kernel of walnut, etc.) '; N. *kornu* ' to tear, scratch, comb '; A. *koriba* ' to hoe '; B. *koṛā* ' to dig, borethrough, pierce '; Bi. *koṛab* ' to dig, cut through (e.g. a field embankment to let out flood water) '; H. *koṛnā*, *kornā* ' to dig up, scrape out, carve '

1142 *Ta.* kaṭai shop, bazaar, market. *Ma.* kaṭa market (DEDR 1142).

கடவுநர் kaṭavunar , *n.* < கடவு-. Those who conduct, lead or manage; செலுத்துவோர். கடும்பரி கடவுநர் (சிலப். 5, 54).

*கடவன் kaṭavaṉ , n. < கட-மை. 1. One who is under obligation; கடமைப்பட்டவன். கட வன் பாரி கைவண்மையே (புறநா. 106). 2. Master, lord; எசமானன். ஒருவன் ஒருகிருகத்துக்குக் கடவனா யிருக்கும் (ஈடு, 1, 1, 5).*

*Ta.* kaṭavu, kaṭā, kaṭāy male of sheep or goat, he-buffalo; kiṭā buffalo, bull, ram; kiṭāy male of sheep; kaṭāri, kiṭāri heifer, young cow that has not calved; (PPTI) kaṭamai female of the goat. *Ma.* kaṭā, kiṭā, kiṭāvu male of cattle, young and vigorous; child, young person; kaṭacci heifer, young cow, calf; kiṭāri a cow-calf, heifer; female buffalo. *Ko.* kaṛc na·g buffalo calf between two and three years; kaṛc kurl cow calf between two and three years; ? ke·v calf of buffalo or cow, under one year (? < *kṛe·v); ? ke·n im, ke·no·ṛ im buffalo with its calf; ke·n a·v, ke·no·ṛ a·v cow with its calf. ? *To.* kaṛ pen for calves from 6 months to 1-2 years. *Ka.* kaḍasu young cow or buffalo that has not yet calved. *Koḍ.* kaḍïci id. *Tu.*gaḍasů id. *Te.* krēpu calf (? or with 1594 Ta. ciṟu). *Go.* (Ph.) kāṛā young buffalo (*Voc.* 648). *Konḍa* (BB) gṛālu calf. *Kui* (K.) grāḍu, (W.)ḍrāḍu (*pl.* ḍrāṭka) id.; (W.) gāṛo a bullock or buffalo not trained to the plough; kṛai young female buffalo or goat. *Kuwi* (Su.) ḍālu, (F. S.) dālu calf. *Kur.* kaṛā young male buffalo; kaṛī young female buffalo; kaṛrū, kaḍrū buffalo calf (male or female). *Br.* xarās bull, bullock; xaṛ ram. Cf. 1114 Ta. kaṭamā. / Cf. Turner, *CDIAL*, no. 2645 *kaṭṭa- (also Skt. [*lex.*] kaṭāha- a young female buffalo whose horns are just appearing), and no. 2658 (DEDR 1123)

*Ta.* kaṭamā, kaṭamāṉ bison; kaṭamai, kaṭampai elk. *Ma.* kaṭamān elk, fallow deer. *Ka.* kaḍave, kaḍava, kaḍaba, kaḍabe, kaḍavu, kaḍaha elk; Indian stag, *Rusa aristotelis*; kaḍiti, gaṇaje a kind of deer or elk; (Gowda) kaḍE stag. *Koḍ.* kaḍamë sambur. *Tu.* kaḍama stag, elk. *Te.* kaḍāti, kaṇāti musk deer; kaḍāju, kaḍiti, kaṇāju, kaṇiti nilgao, a species of antelope; (B.) kaṇuju sambur deer. *Kol.* kaḍas id. *Nk.*kaṛas id. *Kur.* kā̃ṛsā, (Tiga, Bleses) kāṛsā male of the bādō-deer. (DEDR 1114)

*Ta.* kaṭuvaṉ male monkey, tom-cat; kaṭuvaṉ-paṉṟi boar. *Ma.* kaṭuvan male of cats, pigs, etc.; kāṭan wild hog, tom-cat, male tiger. *Ko.*kaṛvn tom-cat. *Ka.* gaḍava a stout male monkey; (Hav.) kaṇṭā male cat. *Go.* (A. Y.) gaḍḍi black-faced monkey; (Haig) gaḍḍe id. (male) (*Voc.*1028). *Malt.* gaḍa-berge, gaḍo a wildcat. (DEDR 1140 )

కడుపు [ kaḍupu ] *kadupu*. [Tel.] n. A herd of cattle or flock of sheep. సమూహము, మంద. ఎనుపకడుపు a herd of buffaloes. పందికడుపు a herd of swine. లేటికడుపు a herd of antelopes. గూబకడుపు a flock of owls. చిలకకడుపు a flock of parrots. తేటికడుపు a swarm of bees.

*கடாய் kaṭāy, n. < கடா² See கடா. (தொல். பொ. 602, உரை.)* கடா kaṭā , *n.* < கடா-. 1. Interrogation, question; வினா. கடாவிடை (ஞானா. 63, 10). 2. cf. G. *gaḍār*. Male of sheep or goat; ஆட்டின் ஆண். (திவா.) 3. Sheep; ஆட்டின்பொது. (திவா.) 4. cf. M. *kiḍāvu*. He-buffalo; எருமைக்கடா. *Colloq.* கடவு³ kaṭavu , *n.* < கடா. 1. Male buffalo; எருமைக்கடா. முதுகடவு கடவி (அழகர்கல. 33). 2. Male goat or sheep; ஆட்டுக்கடா. *கடாய்க்கன்று kaṭāy-k-kaṉṟu , n. < கடாய்¹ +. Bull-calf; காளைக்கன்று. (யாப். வி. 3.)*

*கடாவடி kaṭā-v-aṭi , n. < கடா² + அடி-. Treading out grain a second time by buffaloes or bulls; களத்தில் கடாக்களைவிட்டுப் பிணையடிக் கை. (W.) கடாவிடு-தல் kaṭā-viṭu- , v. intr. < id. +. To thresh out grain with buffaloes or bulls after beating the sheaves upon the threshing floor; பிணையடித்தல். (பதிற்றுப். 62, 15, உரை.)*

*gaḍḍa4 ' sheep '. 2. gaḍḍara -- , °*ḍala* -- m. Apte. [Cf. *gaḍḍārikā* -- f. ' ewe in front of a flock ' lex., *gaḍḍālikā*<-> f. ' sheep ' → Psht. *gaḍūrai* ' lamb ' NTS ii 256] 1. Ash. *gaḍewä* m. ' sheep ', °*wī* f.; Wg. *gáḍawā, goḍṓ* ' ram ', *guḍsok* ' lamb '; Paš. *giḍī́* f. ' sheep '; L. *gaḍ* m. ' wild sheep '. 2. Pk. *gaḍḍarī* -- f. ' goat, ewe ', °*riyā* -- f. ' ewe '; Woṭ. *gaḍūre* ' lamb '; B. *gāṛal*, °*ṛar* ' the long -- legged sheep '; Or. *gāraṛa, gaṛera*, °*ṛarā* ' ram ', *gāraṛi* ' ewe ', *garaṛa* ' sheep '; H. *gāḍar* f. ' ewe '; G. *gāḍar*, °*ḍrū* n. ' sheep '. -- Deriv. B. *gāṛle* ' shepherd ', H. *gaḍariyā* m. (CDIAL 3983) Allograph: 'hill goat': P. *khāḍū* m. ' hill goat '; WPah.J. *khāḍū* m. ' ram ', kṭg. (kc.) *kháḍḍu* m., poet. *khaṛu* m. (Him.I 31 all prob. conn. K. *kaṭh*, stem *kaṭ* -- , < *kaṭṭa -- 2). (CDIAL 3790a).

கடா³ kaṭā , *n.* < *kaṭāha*. [U. *karāh*.] Shallow iron boiler for boiling sugar; *கடாகம் kaṭākam, n. < kaṭāha. 1. Sphere, globe; அண்டகோளகை. (பிங்.)* 2. *Brass boiler; கொப்பரை. (சூடா.)*

Kaṭhati [Sk. kvathati; cp. Goth. hvapo scum, hvapjan to seethe. The Dhātumañjūsā (no. 132, ed. Andersen & Smith) comments on kaṭh with "sosāna -- pākesu." See also kuthati] 1. to boil, to stew Bdhgh on Vin i.205, see *Vin. Texts* ii.57 n1, where pp. is given as kuthita. Similarly Th 2, 504 (cp. *Sisters* 174 n4, but cp. *Mil. trs.* ii.271 "distressed"; E. Müller, *J.R.A.S.* 1910, 539). -- 2. to be scorched, pp. kaṭhita (=hot) Miln 323, 325, 357, 397. – (Pali)

*கடாரம் kaṭāram , n. cf. kaṭāha. [M. kiḍāram.] 1. Brass or copper boiler, cauldron; கொப்பரை. (பிங்.) கடாய்² kaṭāy, n. < kaṭāha. [K. kaḍāyi.] Frying pan; a large round boiler of copper, bell-metal or iron; பொரிக்குஞ் சட்டி. Loc.* gaḍḍuka m. ' waterpot, vessel for boiled rice ' lex., *gaḍḍūka* -- m. lex. 2. gaḍu -- 2, *gaḍuka* -- m. W. [Grouped by PMWS 55 with gargara -- 2 and ghaṭa -- as ← Mu.] 1. Sh. (Lor.) *gaḍubī́* ' iron vessel '; K. *güḍüwa* m. ' small metal pot ', S. *gaḍū̃* m., L. *gaḍvī* f., P. *gaḍvā* m.; WPah. bhal. *guḍḍū* m. ' inkpot ',*guḍri* f. ' earthen pot for boiling rice '; B. *gāṛu* ' pitcher '; Si. *kaḷa* -- *geḍiya* ' waterpot '; -- G. *ghāḍvɔ* m. ' earthen pot for ghee ' X ghaṭa -- . 2. P. *gaṛvā* m. ' brass jug '; B. *gaṛu* ' waterpot with spout ', Or. *gaṛu*, °*uā*; OAw. *gaḍuvana* obl. pl. ' waterpot ', H. *gaṛuā* m. ' narrow -- mouthed waterpot ' (→ Ku. N. *gaṛuwā* ' earthen pot '); G. *gaṛvɔ* m. ' metal waterpot '; M. *gaḍū*, °*ḍuvā* m. ' drinking cup '. -- Paš. shut. *garū́* ' belly ', gul. *gaṛém* ' my belly ' (semant. cf. Kt. *kṭol* ' belly ' ← Eng. *kettle*, and Eng. *pot = belly*). -- N. *gariyo* ' wooden oil vessel ', *karuwā* ' spouted brass pot ' X karaka -- .(CDIAL 3984).

*கடாசு-தல் kaṭācu- , 5 v. tr. < கடாவு-. Loc. 1. To drive, as a wedge, a nail; ஆணி* ஆப்பு முதலியன அடித்தல். 2. To throw, fling; எறிதல்.

*கடாவு¹-தல் kaṭāvu- , 5 v. tr. < கடவு-. 1. To discharge, as missiles; to propel; பிரயோகித் தல். கடாயின கொண்டொல்கும் வல்லி (திவ். இயற். திருவிருத். 6). 2. To ride, as an animal; to drive, as a car; செலுத்துதல். தேர்கடாவி (தேவா. 839, 3). 3. To drive in, as a nail, a peg, a wedge; to nail on; to join by nail, as boards; ஆணிமுதலி யன அறைதல். கவியாப்பைக் கடாவுவனே (தனிப்பா. i, 171, 24). 4. To buffet, cuff; குட்டுதல். வேதன் பொற்சிரமீது கடாவி (திருப்பு. 164). 5. To interrogate, question; வினாவுதல். (திவா.) 6. To urge, impel, influence; தூண்டுதல். இயற்கையன் பினானும் . . . செய்கையன்பினானும் கடாவப்பட்டு (திருக்கோ. 11, உரை). கடாவு² kaṭāvu , n. < கடாவு-. Emitting, throwing out; செலுத்துகை. காலை ஞாயிற்றுக் கதிர் கடாவுறுப்ப (சிறுபாண். 10).*

கடாஞ்செய்-தல் kaṭāñ-cey- , *v. intr. < kaṭa கடாட்சம் kaṭāṭcam , n. < kaṭākṣa. 1. The outside corner of the eye; கடைக்கண். 2. Side glance; கடைக்கண்பார்வை. 3. Grace; அருள். திருமகள் கடாட்சமுண்டானால் (குமரே. சத. 67). கடாட்சவீட்சணம் kaṭāṭca-vīṭcaṇam , n. < id. +. Side glance; கடைக்கண்பார்வை.*

*கடாட்சி-த்தல் kaṭāṭci- , 11 v. tr. < id. To condescend to cast a side glance, to look upon with gracious favour; அருணோக்கஞ்செய் தல். அன்பர்மகிழ்வுறக் கடாட்சிக்கும் (சிவரக. தேவி மேருவரை. 13).*

கடவுள் kaṭavuḷ , *n.* < கட-. [K. *kaḍavaḷ.*] 1. God, who transcends speech and mind; இறைவன். (பிங்.) 2. Celestial Being; வானவன். கடவுள ரதனை நோக்கி (கந்தபு. தாரக. 59). 3. Sage; முனிவன். தொன்முது கடவுட்பின்னர் மேய (மதுரைக். 41). 4. Guru, spiritual preceptor; குரு. (பிங்.) 5. Goodness, auspiciousness; நன்மை. கடிமண மியற்றினார் கடவு ணாளினால் (சீவக. 1490). 6. Divine nature; தெய்வத்தன்மை. கடவுட் கடிஞையொடு (மணி. 15, 57).

கடவை kaṭavai , *n.* < கட-. 1. Leap, jump, passing over; கடக்கை. (J.) 2. Way; வழி. 3. Door-way having a raised sill to be stepped over; வாயில். (W.) 4. Ladder; ஏணி. (திவா.) 5. Break or opening in a fence with some obstruction at the bottom; வேலித்திறப்பில் தாண்டிச் செல்லக்கூடிய தடைமரம். (J.) 6.Turnstile; கவரிறுக்குமரம். (பிங்.) 7. Military camp; பாசறை. (பிங்.) 8. [K. *kaḍamē.*] Fault, defect, crime; குற்றம். (பிங்.) 9. cf. கடவு². Whirling-nut. See தணக்கு. (மலை.).

1145 *Ta.* kaṭṭil cot, bedstead, couch, sofa; throne. *Ma.* kaṭṭil bedstead, cot. *Ko.* kaṭl cot. *Koḍ.* kaṭṭï id. *Te.* kaṭli litter, dooly. *Go.* (Tr. Mu.)kaṭṭul (*obl.* kaṭṭud-, *pl.* kaṭṭuhk) bed, cot; (numerous dialects) kaṭṭul, kaṭul id. (*Voc.* 477). *Konḍa* (Sova dial.) kaṭel(i) cot. *Pe.* kaṭel id.*Manḍ.* kaṭel id. *Kui* (K.) gaṭeli id. *Kuwi* (Su.) kaṭeli, (P.) gaṭeli, (S.) kateli, (F.) kuteli (i.e. kaṭeli; *pl.* kutelka, i.e. kaṭelka) id. / Cf. Turner,*CDIAL*, no. 3781, kháṭvā- cot; no. 3785, khaṭṭi- bier (*lex.*); also kaṭāha- cot (*lex.*). From IA: Pa. kaṭeya cot (< Halbi); *Kui* kaṭe id.; *Kur.*khaṭī bedstead, bed; *Malt.* kaṭe, káṭi id. DED(S) 960.

*Ma.* kaṭṭila, kaṭṭala, kaṭṭiḷa door frame. ? *Ko.* kaṭo·ḷ wall of temple compound. *Koḍ.* kaṭṭoḷe door frame.(DEDR 1146).

Kaṭa = kata [pp. of karoti] in meaning of "original," good (cp. sat); as nt. "the lucky die" in phrase kaṭaggaha (see below). Also in combn with su˚ & duk˚ for sukata & dukkata (e. g. Vin ii.289; DhA iii.486; iv.150), and in meaning of "bad, evil" in kaṭana. Cp. also kali.
-- ggaha "he who throws the lucky die," one who is lucky, fortunate, in phrase "ubhayattha k." lucky in both worlds, i. e. here & beyond Th 1, 462; Jiv.322 (=jayaggaha victorious C.); cp. Morris in *J.P.T.S.* 1887, 159. Also in "ubhayam ettha k." S iv.351 sq. -- Opposed to kali the unlucky die, in

phrase kaliŋ gaṇhāti to have bad luck J vi.206 (kaliggaha=parājayasaŋkhāta, i. e. one who is defeated, as opp. to kaṭaggaha=jayasankhāta), 228, 282.

kaṭa कट com. gen. one who cuts off or destroys, a destroyer, used in compounds such as kaṭa-sankaṭa (Śiv. 161) or sankaṭa-kaṭa (Śiv. 892, 934, 178, 151), a destroyer of perils, an attributive name of Śiva or (Śiv. 151) Pārvatī. (Kashmiri)

See: http://www.scribd.com/doc/2305168/Buffalo-Hieroglyph

Decoding fish and ligatured-fish glyphs of Indus script

Background

Stastistical analyses on 'fish' and related glyphs on Indus writing system are presented in two recent issues of *Bulletin of the Indus Research Center*: No. 1 (Sept. 2009), The Indus script: text and context, a stastical-positional analysis of significant text segments by Sundar Ganesan et al.; No. 2 (August 2011), The Indus fish swam in the great bath: a new solution to an old riddle by Iravatham Mahadevan. Both monographs assume that signs have to be distinguished from pictorial motifs (or field symbols) for determining the semantics of the messages conveyed by the script. Positional analysis of 'fish' glyphs has also been presented in: *The Indus Script: A Positional-statistical Approach* By Michael Korvink, 2007, Gilund Press.

Hypothesis

Any decipherment of Indus script has to consistently explain the writing irrespective of the objects on which the writing is presented. Both signs and pictorial motifs are integral parts of the messages of Indus script. Both types of glyphs are read rebus to decode the hieroglyphs of Indus script based on the underlying Indus language. The hieroglyphs are compiled by artisans (e.g. lapidaries, smiths) of the civilization.

Susa of Mesopotamian civilization received (ca. 3rd millennium BCE) a pot containing metal artefacts shown in the figure. The pictures are thanks to Prof. Maurizio Tosi who made a presentation on the interaction areas of the civilization in an international conference in Delhi (2010). http://www.docstoc.com/docs/63999062/sarasvatiinteractionareas

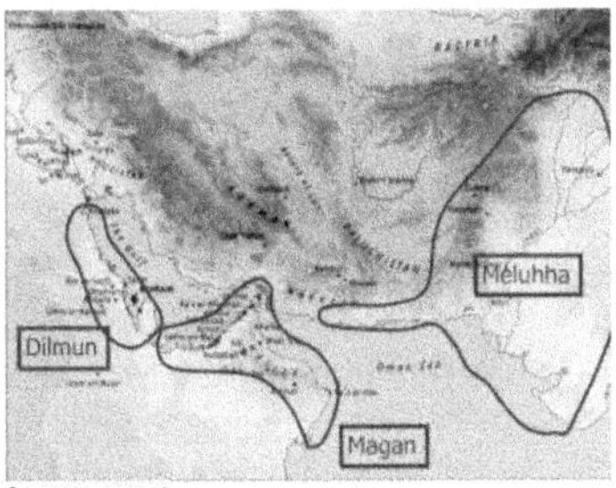


The pot and its contents had perhaps originated from Meluhha since the pot had a 'fish' glyph inscribed. I suggest that this Indus script glyph conveyed the message from Indus artisans to merchant associates of Susa, that the pot had 'metal' contents. The glyph is read rebus in *mleccha* (cognate, *meluhha*), the underlying Indus language. *ayo* 'fish'; rebus: *ayo* 'metal'. With this decoding framework of Indus script cipher, the ligatured-fish glyphs can also be read in the context of metal artifacts archaeologically attested of the bronze-age civilization.

Argument

Picture of Susa pot (cf. Maurizio Tosi) is, in my view, a 'rosetta stone' of Indus script. Other 'rosetta stones' such as the tin ingots with Indus script glyphs are discussed in the book, *Indus script cipher* (2010) by S. Kalyanaraman

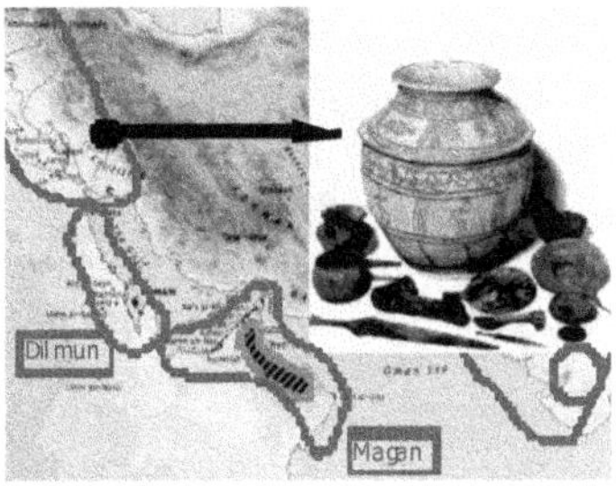


Mahadevan has to explain his reading of the 'meaning' of the fish and related glyphs in the context of the inscribed fish glyph on the Susa pot.

Fish is a frequently-used glyph on Indus script and the glyph together with ligatured glyphs has a consistent positional sequence and contextual occurrence in the inscriptions.

The glyph is frequently paired with 'circumscribed four short strokes' or with 'arrow' glyph.

Table from: The Indus Script: A Positional-statistical Approach By Michael Korvink, 2007, Gilund Press. Mahadevan notes (Para 6.5 opcit.) that 'a unique feature of the FISH signs is their tendency to form clusters, often as pairs, and rarely as triplets also. This pattern has fascinated and baffled scholars from the days of Hunter posing problems in interpretation.' One way to resolve the problem is to interpret the glyptic elements creating ligatured fish signs and read the glyptic elements rebus to define the semantics of the message of an inscription.

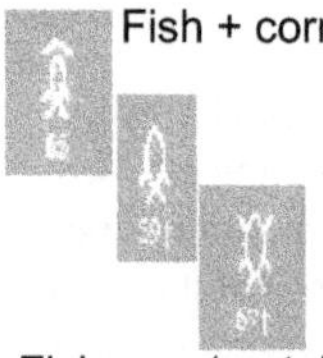

Fish + corner, *aya koṇḍa*, 'metal turned or forged'

Fish, *aya* 'metal'

Fish + scales, *aya ãs (amśu)* 'metallic stalks of stone ore'. Vikalpa: *badhoṛ* 'a species of fish with many bones' (Santali) Rebus: *baḍhoe* 'a carpenter, worker in wood'; *badhoria* 'expert in working in wood'(Santali)

Fish + splinter, *aya aduru* 'smelted native metal'

Fish + sloping stroke, *aya ḍhāḷ* 'metal ingot'

Fish + arrow or allograph, Fish + circumscribed four short strokes

*ayakāṇḍa* 'large quantity of stone (ore) metal' or *aya kaṇḍa,* 'metal fire-altar'. *ayo, hako* 'fish'; *ãs* = scales of fish (Santali); rebus: *aya* 'metal, iron' (G.); *ayah, ayas* = metal (Skt.) Santali lexeme, *hako* 'fish' is concordant with a proto-Indic form which can be identified as *ayo* in many glosses, Munda, Sora glosses in particular, of the Indian linguistic area.

*beḍa hako (ayo)* 'fish' (Santali); *beḍa* 'either of the sides of a hearth' (G.) Munda: So. *ayo* `fish'. Go. ayu `fish'. Go <ayu> (Z), <ayu?u> (Z),, <ayu?> (A) {N} ``^fish''. Kh. kaDOG `fish'. Sa. Hako `fish'. Mu. hai (H) ~ haku(N) ~ haikO(M) `fish'. Ho haku `fish'. Bj. hai `fish'. Bh.haku `fish'. KW haiku ~ hakO |Analyzed hai-kO, ha-kO (RDM). Ku. Kaku`fish'.@(V064,M106) Mu. ha-i, haku `fish' (HJP). @(V341) ayu>(Z), <ayu?u> (Z) <ayu?>(A) {N} ``^fish''. #1370. <yO>\\<AyO>(L) {N} ``^fish''. #3612. <kukkulEyO>,,<kukkuli-yO>(LMD) {N} ``prawn''. !Serango dialect. #32612. <sArjAjyO>,,<sArjAj>(D) {N} ``prawn''. #32622. <magur-yO>(ZL) {N} ``a kind of ^fish''. *Or.<>. #32632. <ur+GOl-Da-yO>(LL) {N} ``a kind of ^fish''. #32642.<bal.bal-yO>(DL) {N} ``smoked fish''. #15163. Vikalpa: Munda: <aDara>(L) {N} ``^scales of a fish, sharp bark of a tree''.#10171. So<aDara>(L) {N} ``^scales of a fish, sharp bark of a tree''.

Indian mackerel Ta. *ayirai, acarai, acalai* loach, sandy colour, *Cobitis thermalis*; *ayilai* a kind of fish. Ma. *ayala* a fish, mackerel, scomber; *aila, ayila* a fish; *ayira* a kind of small fish, loach (DEDR 191) aduru native metal (Ka.); ayil iron (Ta.) ayir, ayiram any ore (Ma.); ajirda karba very hard iron (Tu.)(DEDR 192). Ta. ayil javelin, lance, surgical knife, lancet.Ma. ayil javelin, lance; ayiri surgical knife, lancet. (DEDR 193). aduru = gan.iyinda tegadu karagade iruva aduru = ore taken from the mine and not subjected to melting in a furnace (Ka. Siddhānti Subrahmaṇya' Śastri's new interpretation of the AmarakoŚa, Bangalore, Vicaradarpana Press, 1872, p.330); adar = fine sand (Ta.); ayir – iron dust, any ore (Ma.) Kur. adar the waste of pounded rice, broken grains, etc. Malt. adru broken grain (DEDR 134). Ma. aśu thin, slender;ayir, ayiram iron dust.Ta. ayir subtlety, fineness, fine sand, candied sugar; ? atar fine sand, dust. அய.ர$^3$ ayir, n. 1. Subtlety, fineness; நணசம. (த_வ_.) 2. [M. ayir.] Fine sand; நணமணல. (மலசலப. 92.) ayiram, n. Candied sugar; ayil, n. cf. ayas. 1. Iron; 2. Surgical knife, lancet; Javelin, lance; ayilavaṉ, Skanda, as bearing a javelin (DEDR 341).Tu. gadarů a lump (DEDR 1196)

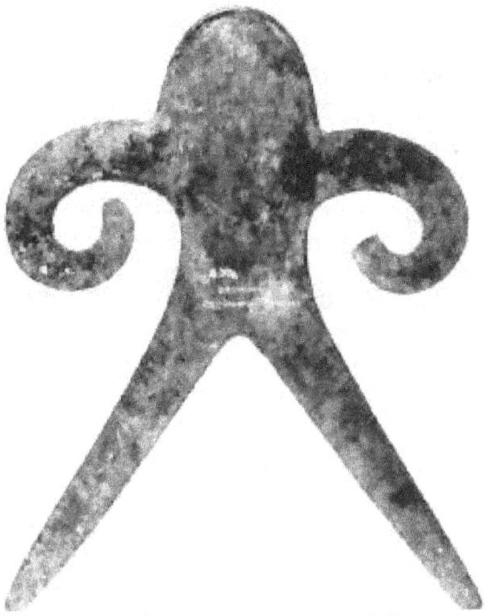

kadara— m. 'iron goad for guiding an elephant' lex. (CDIAL 2711). अयोगू: A blacksmith; Vāj.3.5. अयस् a. [इ-गतौ-असुन्] Going, moving; nimble. n. (-यः) 1 Iron (एति चलति अयस्कान्तसंनिकर्षं इति तथात्वम्; नायसोल्लिख्यते रत्नम् Śukra

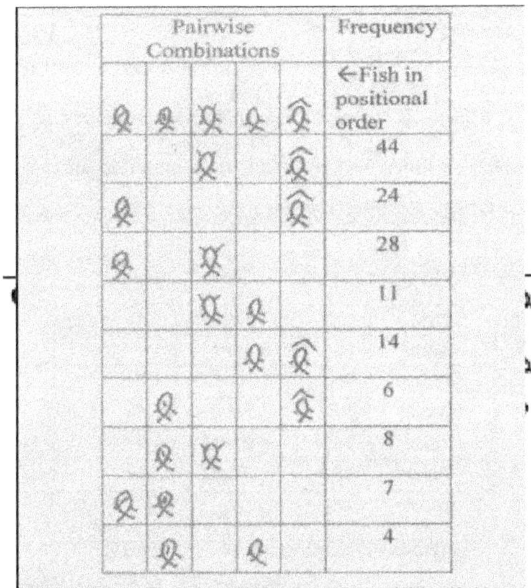

Pairwise Combinations
Frequency
←Fish in positional order
44
24
28
11
14
6
8
7
4

Figure 20: Positional Order of the "Fish" Signs

4.169. अभितप्तमयो$पि मार्दवं भजते कैव कथा शरीरिषु R.8.43. -2 Steel. -3 Gold. -4 A metal in general. ayaskāṇḍa 1 an iron-arrow. -2 excellent iron. -3 a large quantity of iron. -क_नत_(अयसक_नत_) 1 'beloved of iron', a magnet, load-stone; 2 a precious stone; ˚मजण_ a loadstone; ayaskāra 1 an iron-smith,

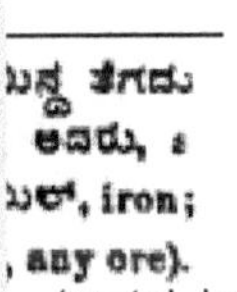


blacksmith (Skt.Apte) ayas-kāntamu. [Skt.] n. The load-stone, a magnet. ayaskāruḍu. n. A black smith, one who works in iron. ayassu. n. ayō-mayamu. [Skt.] adj. made of iron (Te.) áyas— n. 'metal, iron' RV. Pa. ayō nom. sg. n. and m., aya— n. 'iron', Pk. aya— n., Si. ya. AYAŚCŪRṆA—, AYASKĀṆḌA—, *AYASKŪṬA—. Addenda: áyas—: Md. da 'iron', dafat 'piece of iron'. ayaskāṇḍa— m.n. 'a quantity of iron, excellent iron' Pāṇ. gaṇ. viii.3.48 [ÁYAS—, KAA´ṆḌA—]Si.yakaḍa 'iron'.*ayaskūṭa— 'iron hammer'. [ÁYAS—, KUU´ṬA—1] Pa. ayōkūṭa—, ayak m.; Si. yakuḷa'sledge —hammer', yavuḷa (< ayōkūṭa) (CDIAL 590, 591, 592). cf. Lat. aes , aer-is for as-is ; Goth. ais , Thema aisa; Old Germ. e7r , iron ;Goth. eisarn ; Mod. Germ. Eisen.

Context for use of 'fish' glyph. This photograph of a fish and the 'fish' glyph on Susa pot are comparable to the 'fish' glyph on an Indus seal.

Kalibangan 37, 34

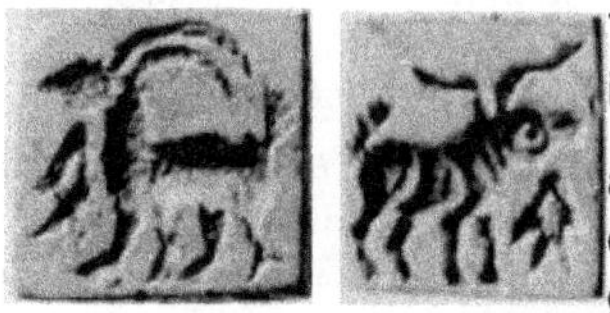

Two Kalibangan seals show an antelope and fish glyphs as the inscription. mēḍha 'antelope'; rebus: meḍ 'iron' (Ho.)

ayo 'fish'; rebs: ayo 'metal' (G.) [These are examples which clearly demonstrate that Indus script is a glyptic writing system and hence, all glyphs and glyptic elements have to be decoded.]

A copper anthropomorph had a 'fish' glyph incised. Anthropomorph with 'fish' sign incised on the chest and with curved arms like the horns of a markhor. Sheorajpur (Kanpur Dist., UP, India). State Museum, Lucknow (O.37) Typical find of Gangetic Copper Hoards. 47.7 X 39 X 2.1 cm. C. 4 kg. Early 2nd millennium BCE.

miṇḍāl markhor (Tor.wali) meḍho a ram, a sheep (G.)(CDIAL 10120) meḍ iron (Ho.) meṛed-bica = iron stone ore, in contrast to bali-bica, iron sand ore (Mu.lex.)

aya 'fish'. Rebus: aya 'metal' (G.) The glyphic composition reads*:* *aya meḍ* 'iron metal'.

Fish on an Indus seal. National Museum 135.

Fish glyph occurs on a cylinder seal together with the glyphs of 'bull', 'heifer' and also of 'bird'. Tell Suleimeh Cylinder seal. A fish over a short-horned bull and a bird over a one-horned bull; (Akkadian to early Old Long 1.6 cm. Dia. Tell 87798; (al-Gailani

cylinder seal impression, Babylonian). Gypsum. 2.6 cm. Suleimeh (level IV), Iraq; IM Werr,1983, p. 49 No. 7).

[Drawing by Larnia Al-GailaniWerr. Cf. Dominique Collon 1987, First impressions: cylinder seals in the ancient Near East, London: 143, no. 609] baṭa = quail (Santali) Rebus: baṭa = furnace (Santali) bhrāṣṭra = furnace (Skt.) baṭa = a kind of iron (G.) bhaṭa 'furnace' (G.) baṭa = kiln (Santali).

mẽḍha 'antelope'; rebus: meḍ 'iron' (Ho.)

ḍangar 'bull'; rebus: ḍangar 'blacksmith' (H.)

koḍe 'heifer' (Telugu) खोंड [ khōṇḍa ] *m* A young bull, a bullcalf. Rebus: koḍ = place where artisans work (G.) कोंडण [ kōṇḍaṇa ] *f* A fold or pen. (Marathi)

"...we have Toch. A. *ancu 'iron', the basis of the derived adjective ancwaashi 'made of iron', to which corresponds Toch. B encuwo, with the parallel derived adjective encuwanne 'made of iron'...The two forms go back to CToch. oencuwoen- non.sg. *oencuwo, the final part of which is a regular product of IE *-on...This noun is deprived of any convincing IE etymology...The term Ved. ams'u-, Av . asu- goes back to a noun borrowed from some donor language of Central Asia, as confirmed by CToch. *oencuwoen-...the BMAC language would not belong to the Indo-European family; it does not seem to be related to Dravidian either...New identifications and reconstructions will certainly help to define more precisely the contours of the BMAC vocabulary in Indo-Iranian, as well as in Tocharian."( Georges-Jean Pinault, 2006,

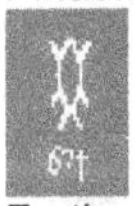

Further links between the Indo-Iranian substratum and the BMAC language in: Bertil Tikkanen & Heinrich Hettrich, eds., 2006, T*hemes and tasks in old and middle Indo-Aryan linguistics*, Delhi, Motilal Banarsidass, p.192) As the term Ved. *amśu* relatable to Tocharian *ancu* 'iron', the early meaning of *amśu* may be close to the protrusions of a mineral stone ore block explained in lexical meanings as 'stalk, ray of light'. It is possible that the Santali lexeme *ā̃s,* 'scales of fish' may be read rebus as *amśu,* 'metallic stalks of stone ore'. http://bharatkalyan97.blogspot.com/2011/09/central-asian-seals-seal-impressions.html

Vikalpa: badhoṛ 'a species of fish with many bones' (Santali) Rebus: *baḍhoe* 'a carpenter, worker in wood'; *badhoria* 'expert in working in wood'(Santali)

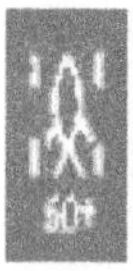
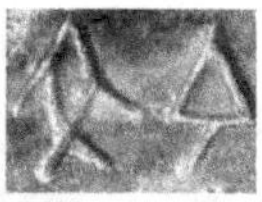

Four short strokes circumscribed or prefixed with arrow sign Ayo 'fish' (Mu.) + kaṇḍa 'arrow' (Skt.) H. kā̃ḍerā m. ' a caste of bow -- and arrow -- makers (CDIAL 3024). S.kānu m. reed ', nī f. ' topmost joint of the reed Sara, reed pen, stalk, straw, porcupine's quill '; L. kānā̃ m. ' stalk of the reed Sara ', nī~ f. ' pen, small spear '; P. kānnā m. ' the reed Saccharum munja, reed in a weaver's warp Or. kāṇḍa, kā̃ṛ ' stalk, arrow '; Bi. kā̃ṛā ' stem of muñja grass (used for thatching) '; Mth. kā̃ṛ ' stack of stalks of large millet '; Bhoj. kaṇḍā ' reeds '; H. kaṇḍā m. ' reed, bush ' (← EP.?); G.kā̃ḍ m. ' joint, bough, arrow (CDIAL 3023). kāṇḍīra ' armed with arrows ' Pāṇ., m. ' archer ' lex. [kāṇḍa-- ]H. kanīrā m. ' a caste (usu. of arrow -- makers) (CDIAL 3026) L. kanērā m. ' mat -- maker ' H. kā̃ḍerā m. ' a caste of bow -- and arrow -- makers '. (CDIAL 3024). Ta. katuppu herd of cattle. Ka. kadupu herd, flock; kadale, kadaḷi a mass, multitude. Te. kadupu id. / ? Cf. Skt. kadamba(ka)- multitude, troop. (DEDR 1198) kolom kaṭhi 'a reed pen' (Santali)

Rebus: *ayaskāṇḍa* 'a quantity of iron, excellent iron' (Pāṇ.gaṇ) aya = iron (G.); ayah, ayas = metal (Skt.) kaṇḍa 'fish, arrow' rebus: metal, fire-altar. *gaṇḍa* 'four' (Santali) *kaṇḍa* 'fire-altar (Santali)

kandhi 'a lump, a piece' (Santali) काढतें [ kāḍhatēṃ ] n Among gamesters. An ivory counter &c. placed to represent a sum of money. (Marathi) The dotted circles also adorn the standard device which is a drill-lathe, sangaḍa खंड [ khaṇḍa ] A piece, bit, fragment, portion.(Marathi) Rebus: *kandi* 'beads' (Pa.)(DEDR 1215). kandi (pl. –l) beads, necklace (Pa.); kanti (pl. –l) bead, (pl.) necklace; kandiṭ 'bead' (Ga.)(DEDR 1215). khaṇḍ 'ivory' (H.) Rebus: khaṇḍaran, khaṇḍrun 'pit furnace' (Santali)

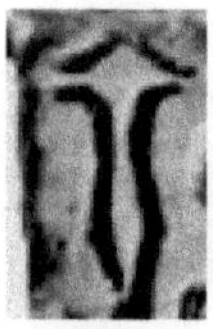

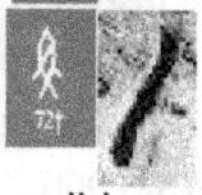

Fish-eye: kan 'copper' (Ta.) Vikalpa: *kaṇḍa* 'stone ore metal'.

*aḍaren kaṇḍa kanka* 'native metal furnace account scribe'.

aḍaren, ḍaren lid, cover (Santali) Rebus: aduru 'native metal' (Ka.) aduru = gan.iyinda tegadu karagade iruva aduru = ore taken from the mine and not subjected to melting in a furnace (Ka. Siddha_nti Subrahman.ya' S'astri's new interpretation of the Amarakos'a, Bangalore, Vicaradarpana Press, 1872, p. 330)

ḍhāḷ = a slope; the inclination of a plane;m ḍhāḷiyum = adj. sloping, inclining (G.) Rebus: ḍhāḷako = a large metal ingot (G.)

Vikalpa: डगर [ ḍagara ]A slope or ascent (as of a river's bank, of a small hill). M. ḍagar f. ' little hill, slope '.S. ṭakuru m. ' mountain ' N. ṭākuro, ri ' hill top '. P. ṭekrā m., rī f. ' rock, hill '; H. ṭekar, krā m. ' heap, hillock '; G. ṭekrɔ m., rī f. ' mountain, hillock '.6. K. ṭę̄g m. ' hillock, mound '.7. G. ṭūk ' peak '.8. M. ṭūg n. ' mound, lump '. -- Ext. -- r -- : Or. ṭuṅguri ' hillock '; M. ṭũgar n. ' bump, mound ' (see *uṭṭungara -- ); -- -- l -- : M. ṭũgaḷ, gūḷ n.9. K. ḍąki f. ' hill, rising ground '. -- Ext. -- r -- : K. ḍakürü f. ' hill on a road '.10. Ext. -- r -- : Pk. ḍaggara -- m. ' upper terrace of a house '; 11. Ku. ḍā̃g, ḍā̃k ' stony land '; B. ḍāṅ ' heap ', ḍāṅgā ' hill, dry upland '; H. ḍā̃g f. ' mountain -- ridge '; M. ḍā̃g m.n., ḍā̃gaṇ, gāṇ, ḍāgāṇ n. ' hill -- tract '. -- Ext. -- r -- : N. ḍaṅgur ' heap '.12. M. ḍūg m. ' hill, pile ', gā m. ' eminence ', gī f. ' heap '. -- Ext. -- r -- : Pk. ḍuṁgara -- m. ' mountain '; Ku. ḍũgar, ḍũgrī; N. ḍuṅgar ' heap '; Or. ḍuṅguri ' hillock ', H. ḍũgar m., G. ḍũgar m., ḍũgrī f. 13. S.ḍ̱ũgaru m. ' hill ', H. M. ḍõgar m. 14. Pa. tuṅga -- ' high '; Pk. tuṁga -- ' high ', tuṁgī̆ya -- m. ' mountain '; K. tōng, tọ̄ngu m. ' peak ', P. tuṅg f.; A. tuṅg ' importance '; Si. tuṅgu ' lofty, mountain '. -- Cf. uttuṅga -- ' lofty ' MBh. 15. K. thọ̄ngu m. ' peak '. 16. H. dā̃g f. ' hill, precipice ', dā̃gī ' belonging to hill country '. Addenda: *ṭakka -- 3. 12. *ḍuṅga -- : S.kcch. ḍūṅghar m. ' hillock '. (CDIAL 5423). unc An eminence, a mount, a little hill (Marathi). ṭākuro = hill top (N.); ṭāṅgī = hill, stony country (Or.); ṭān:gara = rocky hilly land (Or.); ḍān:gā = hill, dry upland (B.); ḍā~g = mountain-ridge (H.)(CDIAL 5476). Marathi. डांग [ ḍāṅga ] m n ( H Peak or summit of a hill.) Rebus: ḍhaṅgar 'blacksmith' (H.)

Vikalpa: dāṭu 'cross' (Te.); dhātu = mineral (Skt.)

*Read as aya koṇḍa*, 'metal turned, i.e. forged.

*koṇḍa* bend (Ko.); Tu. kōḍi corner; kōṇṭu angle, corner, crook. Nk. kōnṭa corner (DEDR 2054b) G. khū̃ṭrī f. 'angle' Rebus: *kōdā* 'to turn in a lathe'(B.) कोंद kōnda 'engraver, lapidary setting or infixing gems' (Marathi) koḍ 'artisan's workshop' (Kuwi) koḍ = place where artisans work (G.) ācāri koṭṭya 'smithy' (Tu.) कोंडण [kōṇḍaṇa] f A fold or pen. (Marathi) B. kōdā 'to turn in a lathe'; Or.kū̃nda 'lathe', kū̃dibā, kū̃d 'to turn' (→ Drav. Kur. kū̃d ' lathe') (CDIAL 3295) A. kundār, B. kū̃dār, ri, Or. kundāru; H. kū̃derā m. 'one who works a lathe, one who scrapes', rī f., kū̃dernā 'to scrape, plane, round on a lathe'; kundakara— m. 'turner' (Skt.)(CDIAL 3297). कोंदण [ kōndaṇa ] n (कोंदणें) Setting or infixing of gems.(Marathi) খোদকার [ khōdakāra ] n an engraver; a carver. **খোদকারি** n. engraving; carving; interference in other's work. খোদাই [ khōdāi ] n engraving; carving. **খোদাই করা** v. to engrave; to carve. **খোদানো** v. & n. en graving; carving. খোদিত [ khōdita ] a engraved. (Bengali) खोदकाम [ khōdakāma ] n Sculpture; carved work or work for the carver. खोदगिरी [ khōdagirī ] f Sculpture, carving, engraving: also sculptured or carved work. खोदणावळ [ khōdaṇāvaḷa ] f (खोदणें) The price or cost of sculpture or carving. खोदणी [ khōdaṇī ] f (Verbal of खोदणें) Digging, engraving &c. 2 fig. An exacting of money by importunity. v लाव, मांड. 3 An instrument to scoop out and cut flowers and figures from paper. 4 A goldsmith's die. खोदणें [ khōdaṇēṃ ] v c & i ( H) To dig. 2 To engrave. खोद खोदून विचारणें or -पुसणें To question minutely and searchingly, to probe. खोदाई [ khōdāī ] f (H.) Price or cost of digging or of sculpture or carving. खोदींव [ khōdīṃva ] p of खोदणें Dug. 2 Engraved, carved, sculptured. (Marathi)

*aṭar* 'a splinter' (Ma. *aṭar* 'a splinter'; *aṭaruka* 'to burst, crack, sli off,fly open; *aṭarcca* ' splitting, a crack'; *aṭarttuka* 'to split, tear off, open (an oyster) (Ma.); *aḍaruni* 'to crack' (Tu.) (DEDR 66) *aṭaruka* 'to burst, crack, sli off,fly open; *aṭarcca* 'splitting, a crack'; *aṭarttuka* 'to split, tear off, open (an oyster) (Ma.); *aḍaruni* 'to crack' (Tu.) (DEDR 66) Rebus: *aṭar aya* variant reading of *aduru ayas*, 'unsmelted metal'.

Vikalpa: goṭ = one (Santali); goṭi = silver (G.) koḍa 'one'(Santali); koḍ 'workshop' (G.)

*sal* stake, spike, splinter, thorn, difficulty (H.); Rebus: *sal* 'workshop' (Santali) **ஆலை*[3] ālai, n. < šālā. 1. Apartment, hall; *சாலை. ஆலைசேர் வேள்வி* (*தேவா.* 844. 7). 2. Elephant stable or stall; *யானைக்கூடம். களிறு சேர்ந் தல்கிய வழுங்க லாலை* (*புறநா.* 220, 3).*ஆலைக்குழி* ālai-k-kuḻi, n. < *ஆலை*[1] +. Receptacle for the juice underneath a sugar-cane press; *கரும்பாலையிற் சாறேற்கும் அடிக்கலம்.***ஆலைத்தொட்டி* ālai-t-toṭṭi, n. < id. +. Cauldron for boiling sugar-cane juice; *கருப்பஞ் சாறு காய்ச்சும் சால்.ஆலைபாய்-தல்* ālai-pāy-, v. intr. < id. +. 1. To work a sugar-cane mill; *ஆலையாட்டுதல். ஆலைபாயோதை* (*சேதுபு. நாட்டு.* 93). 2. To move, toss, as a ship; *அலைவுறுதல்*. (R.) 3. To be undecided, vacillating; *மனஞ் சுழலுதல். நெஞ்ச மாலைபாய்ந் துள்ள மழிகின்றேன்* (*அருட்பா,*) Vikalpa: sal 'splinter'; rebus: workshop (sal) '

Glyptic elements read rebus include the following:

The zebu (brāhmaṇi bull) is: aḍar ḍangra (Santali); ḍhangar 'bull'; rebus: dhan:gar 'blacksmith' (Mth.) ḍangar 'blacksmith' (H.)

koḍiyum koḍiyum 'heifer' (G.) [kōḍiya] kōḍe, kōḍiya. [Tel.] n. A bullcalf. . k* దూడA young bull. Plumpness, prime. తరుణము. జోడుకోడయలు a pair of bullocks. kōḍe adj. Young. kōḍe-kāḍu. n. A young man.పడుచువాడు. [ kārukōḍe ] kāru-kōḍe. [Tel.] n. A bull in its prime. खोंड [ khōṇḍa ] m A young bull, a bullcalf. (Marathi) గోద [ gōda ] gōda. [Tel.] n. An ox. A beast. kine, cattle.(Telugu) koḍiyum (G.) koḍiyum 'heifer' (G.) koḍiyum; खोंड [ khōṇḍa ] m A young bull, a bullcalf. (Marathi) [kōḍe ] kōḍe. [Tel.] n. A bullcalf. *-దూడ. A young bull. kāru-kōḍe. [Tel.] n. A bull in its prime. [ kōḍiya ] G. godhɔ m. ' bull ', dhũ n. ' young bull ', OG. godhalu m. ' entire bull ', G. godhliyũ n. ' young bull ' (CDIAL 4315). Te. kōḍiya, kōḍe young bull; adj. male (e.g. kōḍe dūḍa bull calf), young, youthful; kōḍek;ḍu a young man. Kol. (Haig) kōḍē bull. Nk. khoṛe male calf. Konḍa kōḍi cow; kōṛe young bullock. Pe.kōḍi cow. Manḍ. kūḍi id. Kui kōḍi id., ox. Kuwi (F.) kōdi cow; (S.) kajja kōḍi bull ; (Su. P.) kōḍi cow (DEDR 2199) cf. koṛa 'a boy, a young man' (Santali)

- A young bull is kōḍe, khōṇḍa
- One horn is koḍ, kōṇḍa Pa. kōḍ (pl. kōḍul) horn; Ka. kōḍu horn, tusk, branch of a tree; kōṟ horn Tu. kōḍů, kōḍu horn Ko. kṛ (obl. kṭ-)( (DEDR 2200) Paš. kōṇḍā́'bald', Kal. rumb. kōṇḍa 'hornless'.(CDIAL 3508). Kal. rumb.khōṇḍ a' half' (CDIAL 3792).
- Rings on neck are: koṭiyum (G.) koṭiyum = a wooden circle put round the neck of an animal; koṭ = neck (G.) Vikalpa: kaḍum 'neck-band, ring'; rebus: khāḍ 'trench, firepit' (G.) Vikalpa: khaḍḍā f. hole, mine, cave (CDIAL 3790) kanduka, kandaka ditch, trench (Tu.); kandakamu id. (Te.); kanda trench made as a fireplace during weddings (Konda); kanda small trench for fireplace (Kui); kandri a pit (Malt)(DEDR 1214) khaḍḍa— 'hole, pit'. [Cf. *gaḍḍa— and list s.v. kartá—1] Pk. khaḍḍā— f. 'hole, mine, cave', ḍaga— m. 'one who digs a hole', ḍōlaya— m. 'hole'; Bshk. (Biddulph) "kād" (= khaḍ?) 'valley'; K. khōḍ m. 'pit', khŏḍü f. 'small pit', khoḍu m. 'vulva'; S. khaḏa f. 'pit'; L. khaḍḍ f. 'pit, cavern, ravine'; P. khaḍḍ f. 'pit, ravine', ḍī f. 'hole for a weaver's feet' (→ Ku. khaḍḍ, N. khaḍ; H. khaḍ, khaḍḍā m. 'pit, low ground, notch'; Or. khāḍi 'edge of a deep pit'; M. khaḍḍā m. 'rough hole, pit'); WPah. khaś. khaḍḍā 'stream'; N. khāṛo 'pit, bog', khāṛi 'creek', khāṛal 'hole (in ground or stone)'. — Altern. < *khāḍa—: Gy. gr. xar f. 'hole'; Ku. khāṛ 'pit'; B. khāṛī 'creek, inlet', khāṛal 'pit, ditch'; H. khāṛī f. 'creek, inlet', khaṛ—har, al m. 'hole'; Marw. khāṛo m. 'hole'; M. khāḍ f. 'hole, creek', ḍā m. 'hole', ḍī f. 'creek, inlet'. 3863 khā́tra— n. 'hole' HPariś., 'pond, spade' Uṇ. [√khan] Pk. khatta— n. 'hole, manure', aya— m. 'one who digs in a field'; S. khāṭru m. 'mine made by burglars', ṭro m. 'fissure, pit, gutter made by rain'; P. khāt m. 'pit, manure', khāttā m. 'grain pit', ludh. khattā m. (→ H. khattā m., khatiyā f.); N. khāt 'heap (of stones, wood or corn)'; B. khāt, khāṭrū 'pit, pond'; Or. khāta 'pit', tā 'artificial pond'; Bi. khātā 'hole, gutter, grain pit, notch (on beam and yoke of plough)', khattā 'grain pit, boundary ditch'; Mth. khātā, khattā 'hole, ditch'; H. khāt m. 'ditch, well', f. 'manure', khātā m. 'grain pit'; G. khātar n. 'housebreaking, house sweeping, manure', khātriyũ n. 'tool used in housebreaking' (→ M. khātar f. 'hole in a wall', khātrā m. 'hole, manure', khātryā m. 'housebreaker'); M. khā̆t n.m. 'manure' (deriv. khatāviṇẽ 'to manure', khāterẽ n. 'muck pit'). — Unexpl. ṭ in L. khāṭvā̃ m. 'excavated pond', khāṭī f. 'digging to clear or excavate a canal' (~ S. khātī f. 'id.', but khāṭyāro m. 'one employed to measure canal work') and khaṭṭaṇ 'to dig'. (CDIAL 3790) •gaḍa— 1 m. 'ditch' lex. [Cf. *gaḍḍa—1 and list s.v. kartá—1] Pk. gaḍa— n. 'hole'; Paš. gaṛu 'dike'; Kho. (Lor.) gōḷ 'hole, small dry ravine'; A. garā 'high bank'; B. gaṛ 'ditch, hole in a husking machine'; Or. gaṛa 'ditch, moat'; M. gaḷ f. 'hole in the game of marbles'. 3981 *gaḍḍa— 1 'hole, pit'. [G. < *garda—? — Cf. *gaḍḍ—1 and list s.v. kartá—1] Pk. gaḍḍa— m. 'hole'; WPah. bhal. cur. gaḍḍ f., paṅ. gaḍḍṛī, pāḍ. gaḍōṛ 'river, stream'; N. gaṛ—tir 'bank of a river'; A. gārā 'deep hole'; B. gāṛ, ṛā 'hollow, pit'; Or. gāṛa 'hole, cave', gāṛiā 'pond'; Mth. gāṛi 'piercing'; H. gāṛā m. 'hole'; G. garāḍ, ḍɔ m. 'pit, ditch' (< *graḍḍa— < *garda—?); Si. gaḍaya 'ditch'. — Cf. S. giḏi f. 'hole in the ground for fire during Muharram'. — X khānī̆—: K. gān m. 'underground room'; S. (LM 323) gāṇ f. 'mine, hole for keeping water'; L. gāṇ m. 'small embanked field within a field to keep water in'; G. gāṇ f. 'mine, cellar'; M. gāṇ f. 'cavity containing water on a raised piece of land' WPah.kṭg. gāṛ 'hole (e.g. after a knot in wood)'. (CDIAL 3947) 3860 *khāḍa— 'a hollow'. [Cf. *khaḍḍa— and list s.v. kartá—1] S.

khāṛī f. 'gulf, creek'; P. khāṛ 'level country at the foot of a mountain', ṛī f. 'deep watercourse, creek'; Bi. khārī 'creek, inlet'; G. khāṛi , ṛī f., ṛɔ m. 'hole'. — Altern. < *khaḍḍa—: Gy. gr. xar f. 'hole'; Ku. khāṛ 'pit'; B. khāṛī 'creek, inlet', khāṛal 'pit, ditch'; H. khāṛī 'creek, inlet', khaṛ—har, al m. 'hole'; Marw. khāṛo m. 'hole'; M. khāḍ f. 'hole, creek', ḍā m. 'hole', ḍī f. 'creek, inlet'.

- A sack slung on the front shoulder of the young bull is khōṇḍā, khōṇḍī , kothḷɔ

खोंडा [ khōṇḍā ] m A कांबळा of which one end is formed into a cowl or hood. खोंडी [ khōṇḍī ] f An outspread shovelform sack (as formed temporarily out of a कांबळा, to hold or fend off grain, chaff &c. (Marathi) khŏdrang, khudrang ख्वद्ःरंग adj. c.g. self-coloured; as subst. m. N. of a kind of blanket having the natural colour of the wool (L. 37). khudürü और्णशाटकविशेषः f. a kind of coarse woollen blanket. (Kashmiri) Pa. kotthalī -- f. ' sack (?) '; Pk. kotthala -- m. ' bag, grainstore ' (kōha -- m. ' bag ' < *kōtha?); K. kŏthul, lu m. ' large bag or parcel ', kothüjü f. ' small do. '; S. kothirī f. ' bag '; Ku. kuthlo ' large bag, sack '; B. kūthlī ' satchel, wallet '; Or. kuthaḷi, thuḷi, kothaḷi, thiḷi ' wallet, pouch '; H. kothlā m. ' bag, sack, stomach (see *kōttha -- ) ', lī f. ' purse '; G.kothḷɔ m. ' large bag ', ḷī f. ' purse, scrotum '; M. kothḷā m. ' large sack, chamber of stomach (= peṭā ċā k) ', ḷẽ n. ' sack ', ḷī f. ' small sack '; -- X gōṇī´ -- : S. gothirī f. ' bag ', L. gutthlā m.(CDIAL 3511) Ta. kaṇṭāḷam travelling sack placed on a bullock, pack-saddle. Ka. kaṇṭale, kaṇṭāḷa, kaṇṭāḷe, kaṇṭle double bag carried across a beast. Te. kaṇṭalamu, kaṇṭlamubullock-load consisting of two bags filled with goods. / Cf. Mar. kaṇṭhāḷī a bag having opening in the middle (DEDR 1174) gōṇī´ f. ' sack ' Pāṇ., gōṇikā -- f. ' blanket ' BHS ii 215. [← Drav. EWA i 345 with lit.]Pa. gōṇa -- saṁthata -- ' covered with a woollen rug ', gōṇaka -- m. ' woollen rug with a long fleece '; NiDoc. goni ' sack '; Gy. pal. gŏni ' bag, purse ', eur. gono m. ' sack '; Ash.gō˜ ' carpet ', Wg. gṙŏī, gṙẽ, Dm. gūni; Paš. gōnī ' saddlebag '; K. guna f. ' pair of large saddlebags usu. of goat's hair for carrying grain '; S. guṇī f. ' coarse sackcloth '; L. ```gūṇī˜f. ' sack '; P. gūṇ f. ' hair cloth, hempen sacking ', gūṇī f. ' sack '; B. gun ' sacking '; Or. goṇī ' sackcloth, sack, corn measure, ragged garment '; Bi. gon ' grain sack '; H. gon f. ' sack '; G. gū˜ṇi f. ' sacking, sack '; M. goṇ f. ' sack ', ṇī f. ' sackcloth ', ṇā m. ' large grain sack '.Addenda: gōṇī´ -- : WPah.kṭg. gv̄ṇ f. (obl. -- i) ' sack for corn '; <-> Md. (RTMV1) gōni ' sack ' ← Ind. (CDIAL 4275) gōṇamu. [Tel. of Tam. కోమణము.] n. A waist cloth or modesty piece. [ gōṇi ] gōṇi. [Skt.] n. A sack, sackcloth. a sackful. [Tel.] gōtamu. [Tel.] n. A sack, a bag. (Telugu)

Rebus: B. *kõdā* 'to turn in a lathe'; Or. kū̃nda 'lathe', kūdibā, kū̃d 'to turn' (→ Drav. Kur. kū̃d 'lathe') (CDIAL 3295)

Rebus: koṭṭil 'workshop' (Ma.)(DEDR 2058). koṭe 'forged metal' (Santali) koḍ 'artisan's workshop' (Kuwi) koḍ = place where artisans work (G.) कोंडण [ kōṇḍaṇa ] f A fold or pen. (Marathi) koṭṭil cowhouse, shed, workshop, house; Malt. koṭa hamlet. / Influenced by Skt. goṣṭha-. (DEDR 2059). kūṭam = workshop (Tamil); கோட்டம் kōṭṭam,n. <kōṣṭha. 1. Room, enclosure; அறை. சுடுமணோங்கிய நெடு நிலைக் கோட்டமும் (மணி. 6, 59). 2. Temple; கோயில். கோழிச் சேவற் கொடியோன் கோட்டமும் (சிலப். 14, 10). koṭe meṛed = forged iron (Mu.) meḍ 'iron' (Ho.) dul meṛed, cast iron (Mu.) koṭe 'forged metal' (Santali) கொட்டுக்கன்னார் koṭṭu-k-kaṉṉār , n. < கொட்டு² +. Braziers who work by beating plates into shape and not by casting; செம் படிக்குங் கன்னார். (W.)

dāmṛa, damrā ' young bull (A.)(CDIAL 6184). Glyph: *ḍaṅgara1 ' cattle '. 2. *daṅgara -- . [Same as ḍaṅgara -- 2 s.v. *ḍagga -- 2 as a pejorative term for cattle] 1. K. ḍangur m. ' bullock ', L. ḍaṅgur, (Ju.) ḍā̃gar m. ' horned cattle '; P. ḍaṅgar m. ' cattle ', Or. ḍaṅgara; Bi. ḍā̃gar ' old worn -- out beast, dead cattle ', dhūr ḍā̃gar ' cattle in general '; Bhoj. ḍāṅgar ' cattle '; H. ḍā̃gar, ḍā̃grā m. ' horned cattle '.2. H. dā̃gar m. = prec. (CDIAL 5526) Rebus: ḍaṅgar 'blacksmith'. ḍāṅgar 'blacksmith' (H.); ḍhā~gar., dhā~gar blacksmith; digger of wells (H.) Nepali. डाङ्रे ḍāṅre , or ḍā̃gre, adj. Large; lazy; working with- out thoroughness or seriousness; -- s. A partic. kind of bird, the mainā; -- a contemptuous term for a blacksmith डाङ्रो ḍāṅro , or ḍā̃gro, s. A term of contempt used for a blacksmith (kāmi). [v.s.v. ḍāṅre.] ḍān:ro = a term of contempt for a blacksmith (N.)(CDIAL 5524). ṭhākur = blacksmith (Mth.) (CDIAL 5488). ठाकूर [ ṭhākūra ] m (ठक्कुर S through H) A tribe or an individual of t. They inhabit woods and wilds (esp. of N. Konkaṇ). 2 A chief among certain castes of Rájpúts, Bhíls &c., a title or compellation of respect. 3 The Supreme God: also an idol or a god. 4 A family priest among certain tribes of Shúdras. ठाकूरजी [ ṭhākūrajī ] m (ठक्कुर S) A name for the Deity. Among Byrágís. ठाकूरद्वार [ ṭhākūradvāra] n sometimes ठाकूरदारा m (ठाकूर The Deity, द्वार A door.) Among Byrágís. A temple or idol-house: also the adytum or penetralia.ठकूरदारा मांडून बसणें To make an outlay or great display (of sanctity or piety). ṭhakkaru, ṭhakkaruḍu = a deity; an idol; an honorific title same as ṭhākūru = a father; a religious preceptor (Te.lex.) ṭhākur blacksmith (Mth.)(CDIAL 5488).

damya ' tameable ', m. ' young bullock to be tamed ' Mn. [~ *dāmiya -- . -- √dam] Pa. damma -- ' to be tamed (esp. of a young bullock) '; Pk. damma -- ' to be tamed '; S. ḍamu ' tamed '; -- ext. -- ḍa -- : A. damrā ' young bull ', dāmuri ' calf '; B. dāmṛā ' castrated bullock '; Or. dāmaṛī ' heifer ', dāmaṛiā ' bullcalf, young castrated bullock ', dāmuṛ, ṛi ' young bullock '. Addenda: damya -- : WPah.kṭg. dām m. 'young ungelt ox'.(CDIAL 6184).

kolmo 'three' (Mu.); rebus: kolami 'smithy' (Te.) hence, *ayo kolmo* 'iron, smithy'.

*bhaṭa* 'six' (G.); rebus: *bhaṭa* 'furnace' (Santali) henca ayo *bhaṭa* 'iron, furnace'.

Four + three strokes are read (since the strokes are shown on two lines one below the other) : gaṇḍa 'four' (Santali); rebus: 'furnace, kaṇḍ fire-altar'; kolmo 'three' (Mu.) dula 'pair' (Kashmiri); rebus: dul 'cast metal' (Mu.) hence, *ayo dul kāṇḍa* 'iron, cast stone ore'.

2 INDUS SEAL AND SEAL IMPRESSION

*"Indus inscriptions resemble the Egyptian hieroglyphs...":* John Marshall (1931)

The context is the bronze age. Examples of metal artifacts are provided (including a report of Mackay about Chanhu-daro calling it the 'sheffield' of the ancient east denoting that Chanhu-daro yielded many types of products – tools and weapons -- of metal workers.

An Indus seal is an assemblage or clubbing together of tally (token) information from tablets (which contain Indus script inscriptions).

A seal impression creates description of goods for a bill of lading (Duplicate seal impressions can also serve the purpose of tokens as demonstrated in the examples of Kanmer).

Multiple seal impressions on the same trade load provide a complete message of a consolidated, composite bill of lading and indicate the descriptions of the consolidated trade consignment.

Most of the seals and seal impressions which conain the 'rim of jar' glyph are furnace scribe accounts. Most of the seals and seal impressions which contain the 'heifer +/or standard device' define the source of the consignment: turner workshop guild.

This is an example of an Indus seal and its seal impression.

Dimensions
Height: 2.4 centimetres (Of the seal)
Width: 2.5 centimetres
Depth: 1.4 centimetres
Height: 2.8 centimetres (Of the impression)
Width: 2.7 centimetres
Depth: 0.6 centimetres

A precise account on the functions of an Indus seal is provided by British Museum, excerpted below:

[quote] Indus seal AN145081001

Harappa and Mohenjo-Daro, modern Pakistan, about 2600 to 1900 BCE. Some of the earliest evidence of the use of symbols and script in India, from the Indus Valley cities of Mohenjo-Daro and Harappa.

An organized system of government and culture developed at around the same time in the river valleys of the Nile in Egypt, Euphrates in Mesopotamia and Indus in India and Pakistan. The best-known sites from this period in the Indus Valley are Mohenjo-Daro and Harappa, though in recent years hundreds of other sites with similar cultural patterns have been discovered in India, including Dholavira in Kutch. This is currently thought to have extended from the north-western parts of the subcontinent to Gujarat, Haryana and Indian Punjab.

Unlike the other early in the world, these sites were not isolated city-states, but apparently part of an integrated and interconnected urban culture. There is also evidence of trade with central Asia, Sumer and Mesopotamia. Among the material remains are a wide variety of terracotta figurines, gold adornments, beads of gold and precious and semi-precious stone, ivory, terracotta and glass, a few bronze figures and vessels and thousands of small square and rectangular seals and their impressions. These seals are useful in reconstructing the economy, art and religion of India from 2500 to 1700 BC. They were probably used in trade, as they and their impressions have been found in lands further afield.

The patterns on the soft steatite stone were carved in intaglio, and then the finished seal baked to whiten and harden its surface. The designs often carry complex motifs of humans, animals and a uniform and developed pictographic script. Approximately 400 different signs have been catalogued, though despite scholarly efforts for nearly 80 years, it has yet to be deciphered. On most of these examples we can see the script above the animals. The finely drawn animals are often composite creatures, or at times partly human with animal features. Until the script is decoded, these seals suggest to us belief in the supernatural, the widespread nature of the Harappan civilization and the far-reaching trading relations they held with other ancient cultures in the world.

Further reading

J.M. Kenoyer, *Ancient Cities of the Indus Valley Civilization* (Oxford, 1999)

N. Lahiri, *Finding Forgotten Cities: How the Indus Civilization was Discovered* (London, 2005)

J. McIntosh, *A Peaceful Realm: The Rise And Fall of the Indus Civilization* (New York, 2001)

J. McIntosh, *The Ancient Indus Valley: New Perspectives* (Santa Barbara, 2007).

G. Possehl, *The Indus Civilization: a Contemporary Perspective* (Walnut Creek, 2002)

R. Wright, *The Ancient Indus: Urbanism Economy and Society* (Cambridge, 2010)

[unquote]

http://www.britishmuseum.org/explore/highlights/highlight_objects/asia/s/indus_seal.aspx

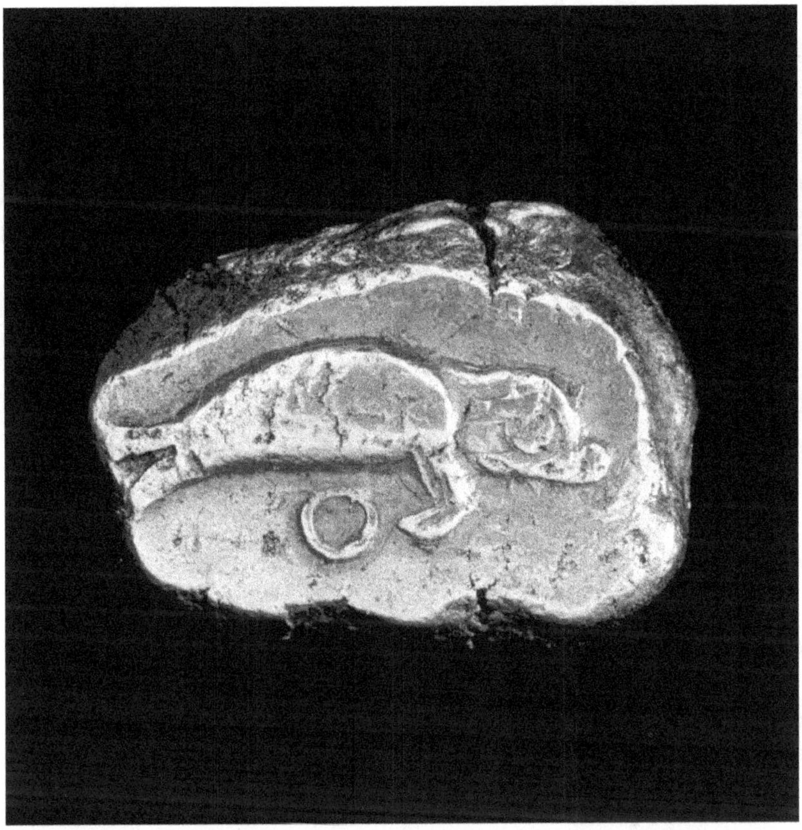

Greek, around 600-550 BC. Phocaea, Ionia (modern Turkey)

[quote] An early electrum coin with a 'talking' design

The earliest coins come from Lydia in Asia Minor (modern Turkey). From there, electrum coinage (made from the alloy of gold and silver) soon spread to the Greek cities on the west coast of Asia Minor. From its beginnings there in the late seventh century BC, the use and production of coins reached the Greek Islands and the Greek mainland during the course of the sixth century. It is often difficult to tell where a particular coin was produced, because none of these early coins was inscribed with a place name.

However, educated guesses can be made. This electrum coin has the design of a seal on its obverse (front). The Greek word for seal is *phoce* and this coin is therefore usually attributed to the Greek city of Phocaea, in Ionia. This is an early instance of the phenomenon of the *type parlant*, or 'talking type', where the design on the coin somehow illustrates the name of the city that produced it.

G.K. Jenkins, *Ancient Greek coins* (London, Seaby, 1990)

C.M. Kraay, *Archaic and Classical Greek co* (London, Methuen, 1976)

I.A. Carradice, *Greek coins* (London, The British Museum Press, 1996)

I.A. Carradice and M.J. Price, *Coinage in the Greek world*(London, Seaby, 1988) [unquote]

http://www.britishmuseum.org/explore/highlights/highlight_objects/cm/e/electrum_stater_with_a_seal.as
px

Indus seal. British Museum.Trough in front of a rhinoceros. Trough is a hieroglyph. So is the rhinoceros. So is the text shown above the animal, an assemblage of hieroglyphs.

The principal function of a seal with Indus script inscription is to create a seal impression for trade loads. When multiple seal impressions are affixed on a trade consignment, each seal impression is intended to be a part of the bill of lading, describing the contents of the trade consignment. Whenever a 'trough' hieroglyph is shown on any inscription, it connotes a guild. Glyph: pattar 'trough'; Rebus: pattar 'guild (of smiths)'. Every glyph in th corpora of Indus inscriptions – be it a pictorial motif or field symbol, be it a sign or text glyph – is read rebus as a hieroglyph. Such glyphs range from a list of animals [heifer, short-horned bull, zebu (bos indicus), rhinoceros, elephant, tiger, antelope etc.] to a list of pictographs [rim-of-jar, fish, lathe-gimlet, crocodile, leafless branch of tree, rimless pot, nave-of-wheel, mountain, svastika, liquid measure etc.] The underlying language for rebus renderings is meluhha/mleccha of Indian linguistic area.

A bronze age interaction area of Meluhha was Susa.

There is a possibility that there was a Meluhha settlement of traders in Susa who could read the messages conveyed by Indus script inscriptions.

Some glyphics of the bronze model have parallels in Indian hieroglyphs. Glyph: 'stump of tree': M. khũṭ m. 'stump of tree'; P. khuṇḍ, °ḍā m. 'peg, stump'; G. *khũṭ* f. 'landmark', *khũṭɔ* m., °*ṭī* f. ' peg ', °*ṭũ* n. 'stump' (CDIAL 3893). Allograph: (Kathiawar) khũṭ m. 'Brahmani bull'(G.) Rebus: khũṭ 'community, guild' (Munda) The ceremony involved lo 'pouring (water) oblation' (Munda) for the setting sun. Rebus: loa 'copper' (Santali) The glyphic representations connote a guild of coppersmiths in front of a ziggurat, temple and is a veneration of ancestors. The authors of the bronze model seem to have interacted with the groups of artisans of Mohenjo-daro who had a ziggurat in front of the 'great bath'.

Sit Shamshi. Model of a place of worship, known as the Sit Shamshi, or "Sunrise (ceremony)" Middle-Elamite period, toward the 12th century BC Acropolis mound, Susa, Iran; Bronze; H. 60 cm; W. 40 cm Excavations led by Jacques de Morgan, 1904-5; Sb 2743; Near Eastern Antiquities, Musée du Louvre/C. Larrieu. Two nude figures squat on the bronze slab, one knee bent to the ground. One of the figures holds out open hands to his companion who prepares to pour the contents of a lipped vase onto them.The scene takes place in a stylized urban landscape, with reduced-scale architectural features: a tiered tower or ziggurat flanked with pillars, a temple on a high terrace. There is also a large jar resembling the ceramic pithoi decorated with rope motifs that were used to store water and liquid foodstuffs. An arched stele stands by some rectangular basins. Rows of 8 dots in relief flank the ziggurat; jagged sticks represent trees.An inscription tells us the name of the piece's royal dedicator and its meaning in part: "I Shilhak-Inshushinak, son of Shutruk-Nahhunte, beloved servant of Inshushinak, king of Anshan and Susa [...], I made a bronze sunrise."

Three jagged sticks on the Sit Shamshi bronze, in front of the water tank (Great Bath replica?)

If the sticks are orthographic representations of 'forked sticks' and if the underlying language is Meluhha (mleccha), the borrowed or substratum lexemes which may provide a rebus reading are:

kolmo 'three'; rebus; kolami 'smithy' (Telugu)
Glyph: मेंढा [ mēṇḍhā ] A crook or curved end (of a stick, horn &c.) and attrib. such a stick, horn, bullock. मेढा [ mēḍhā ] m A stake, esp. as forked. meḍ(h), meḍhī f., meḍhā m. ' post, forked stake '.(Marathi)(CDIAL 10317) Rebus: mẽṛhẽt, meḍ 'iron' (Mu.Ho.) Vikalpa: khuṇṭ 'stump'. Rebus: khũṭ 'community, guild' (Mu.)
Thus, three jagged sticks on the Sit Shamshi bronze may be decoded as *khũṭ kolami* 'smithy guild' or, *meḍ kolami* 'iron (metal) smithy'. 'Iron' in such lexical entries may refer to 'metal'.

Sit Shamshi bronze illustrates the complex technique of casting separate elements joined together with rivets, the excavations at Susa have produced one of the largest bronze statues of Antiquity: dating from the 14th century BC, the effigy of "Napirasu, wife of Untash-Napirisha," the head of which is missing, is 1.29 m high and weighs 1,750 kg. It was made using the solid-core casting method.

These metallurgical techniques find an expression on Indus script inscriptions as seen on a long inscription on a seal impression found in Mohenjo-daro (m-314)-- all glyphs of the inscription relate to the repertoire of artisans engaged in metal work.

Text 1429 This  long inscription –with 11 glyphs, included in Mahadevan concordance -- is not illustrated with the inscribed object.

Another example is Mohenjo-daro seal m0038a:

m0038a

1087

See related links:

http://bharatkalyan97.blogspot.com/2011/11/mohenjo-daro-stupa-great-bath-modeled.html
http://bharatkalyan97.blogspot.com/2011/11/decoding-indus-scipt-susa-cylinder-seal.html
Origins of iron-working in India, Rakesh Tiwari

Damaged circular clay furnace, comprising iron slag and tuyeres and other waste materials stuck with its body, exposed at Lohsanwa mount, Period II, Malhar, Dist. Chandauli, India.

This report is significant because recent excavations have produced clear evidence of iron-working at Malhar, Dist. Chandali -- Lat. 24deg.-59'-16"N; Long. 83deg.-15'-46" where a damaged circular clay furnace, comprising iron slag and tuyeres and other waste materials stuck with its body in a stratigraphically dated location. (See Figure 6, page 542). "As discussed elsewhere (Tewari et al. 2000) the sites at Malhar, the Baba Wali Pahari, and the Valley are archaeologically linked to the area of Geruwarwa Pahar which appears to have been a major source of iron ore. The Geruwarwa Pahar situated to the southeast of the Baba Wali Pahari, is full of hematite. Villagers reported (as a tradition passed down from several generations), that the agarias (a particular tribe known for their iron smelting skills) from Robertsganj side, used to come in this area to procure iron by smelting the hematite...The presence of tuyeres, slags, finished iron artefacts, above-mentioned clay structures with burnt internal surface and arms, revealed at Malhar, suggest a large scale activity related to manufacture of iron tools." (p. 542). Malhar is located on river Karamnasa which joins River Ganga at Varanasi. Two radiocarbon dates recorded at this site range around 1800 cal. BCE (Table 2, p. 540) -- precise dates are: 1882 and 2012 BCE.

Rakesh Tewari provides the following summary of the evidence from Malhar and other Central Ganga Plain and Eastern Vindhya sites: [Quote]Discussion These results indicate that iron using and iron working was prevalent in the Central Ganga Plain and the Eastern Vindhyas from the early second millennium BC. The dates obtained so far group into three: three dates between c. 1200-900 cal BC, three between c. 1400-1200 cal BC, and five between c. 1800-1500 cal BC. The types and shapes of the associated pottery are comparable to those to be generally considered as the characteristics of the Chalcolithic Period and placed in early to late second millennium BC. Taking all this evidence together it may be concluded that knowledge of iron smelting and manufacturing of iron artefacts was well known in the Eastern Vindhyas and iron had been in use in the Central Ganga Plain, at least from the early second millennium BC. The quantity and types of iron artefacts, and the level of technical advancement indicate that the introduction of iron working took place even earlier. The beginning of the use of iron has been traditionally associated with the eastward migration of the later Vedic people, who are also considered as an agency which revolutionised material culture particularly in eastern Uttar Pradesh and Bihar (Sharma 1983: 117-131). The new finds and their dates suggest that a fresh review is needed. Further, the evidence corroborates the early use of iron in other areas of the country, and attests that India was indeed an independent center for the development of the working of iron. [unquote](pp. 543-544).

Thus, both the Gufkral evidence evaluated by Possehl and Gullapalli and the evidence from Malhar and other Central Ganga Plain and Eastern Vindhya sites discussed by Rakesh Tewari point to an indigenous evolution of iron-working in India dated to early 2nd millennium BCE.

The evidence leads to a reasonable hypothesis that the metal-workers of the chalcolithic periods of Sarasvati Civilization moved into the Ganga and Eastern Vindhya iron-age sites to continue the tradition of metal-working, exemplified by the asur-s of Mundarica tradition. No wonder, the Sarasvati hieroglyphs have a significant number of homonyms from the Mundarica tradition to represent metal-working artefacts such as furnaces and minerals used to produce metal products.

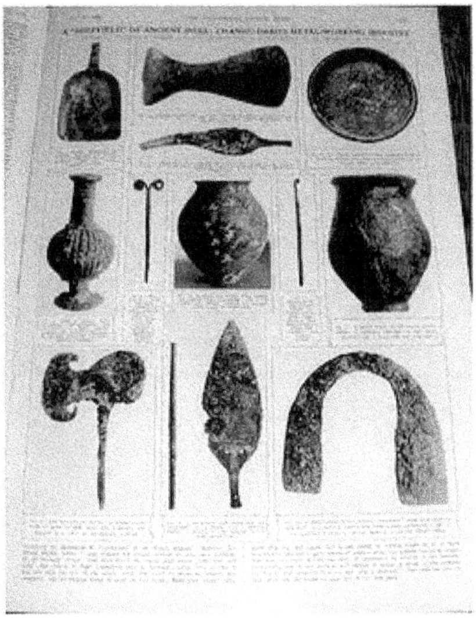

The cultural continuity and the indigenous origins of metal-working are areas for further research as excavations proceed on over 2000 Sarasvati River basin sites.

Examples of metallurgical skills of Indus artisans: bronze statue of a woman holding a small bowl, Mohenjo-daro; copper alloy made using cire perdue method (DK 12728; Mackay 1938: 274, Pl. LXXIII, 9-11)

Foot with anklet; copper alloy.

Mohenjo-daro (After Fig. 5.11 in Agrawal. D.P. 2000. *Ancient Metal Technology & Archaeology of South Asia*. Delhi: Aryan Books International.)

Possehl, Gregory L. and Gullampalli, Praveena, 1999, The early iron age in South Asia. In Vincent Piggott, ed., The Archaeometallurgy of the Asian Old World. University Museum Monograph 89, MASCA research papers in science and archaeology Vol. 16, Philadephia: The Univrsity Museum, UPenn, pp. 153-175

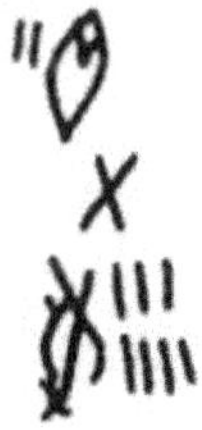

Gold pendant with Indus script inscription. The pendant is needle-like with cylindrical body. It is made from a hollow cylinder with soldered ends and perforated oint. Museum No. MM 1374.50.271; Marshall 1931: 521, pl. CLI, B3 (After Fig. 4.17 a,b in: JM Kenoyer, 1998, p. 196)

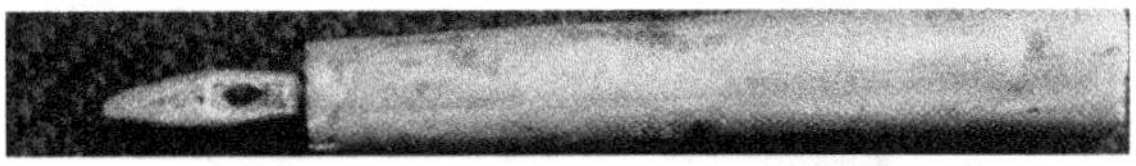

Illustrated London News 1936 - November 21st. A 'Sheffield of Ancient India: Chanhu-Daro's metal working industry 10 X photos of copper knives, spears, razors, axes and dishes.

http://www.iln.org.uk/iln_years/year/1936a.htm

Copper model of a passsenger box on a cart. Chanhu-daro, 'a Sheffield of ancient India'.

Inscribed metal tools, copper tablets: Mohenjo-daro, Harappa.

Axe with inscription and other tools, Chanhu-daro, Kalibangan

Text 6306 on Chanhu-daro broken axe, 40A and 40B.

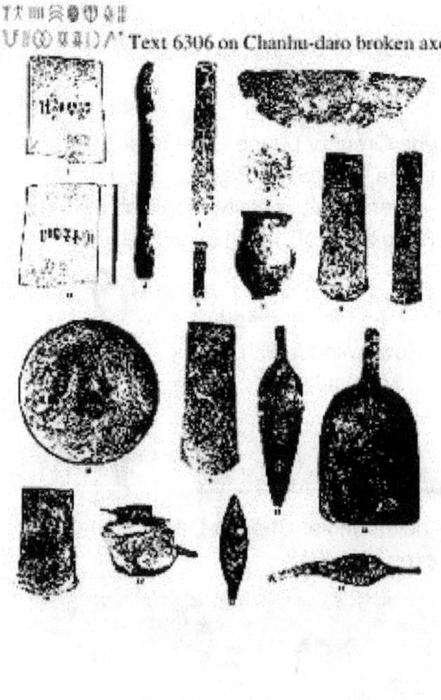

h380 4902 Bronze dagger

h381 4901 Bronze dagger

2924 Inscribed bronze implement (MIC Plate CXXVI-3)
2926 Inscribed bronze implement (MIC Plate CXXVII-1)
2928 Inscribed bronze implement (MIC Plate CXXXIII-1)

**Inscribed Copper tablets**

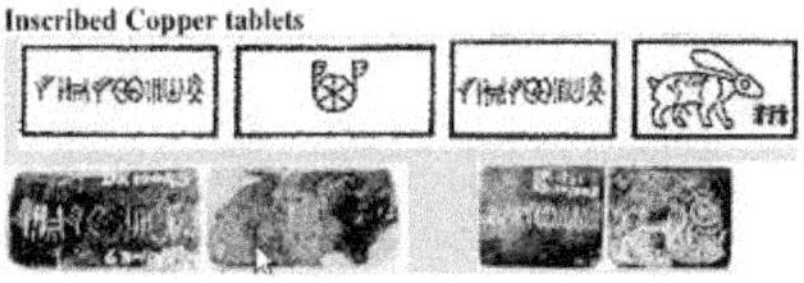

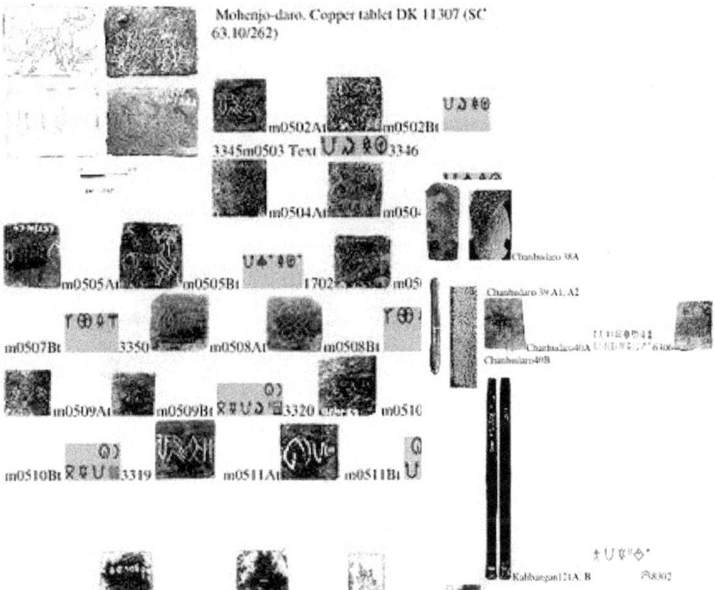

Copper model. Chariot box, Chanhu-daro. Copper tablets m0438; m1449; m1452; m1486; m1493; m1498; m1501; m0582 (123 copper tablets)

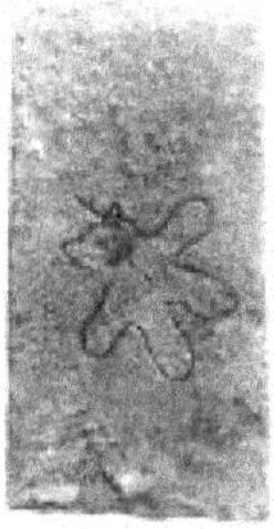
m0475

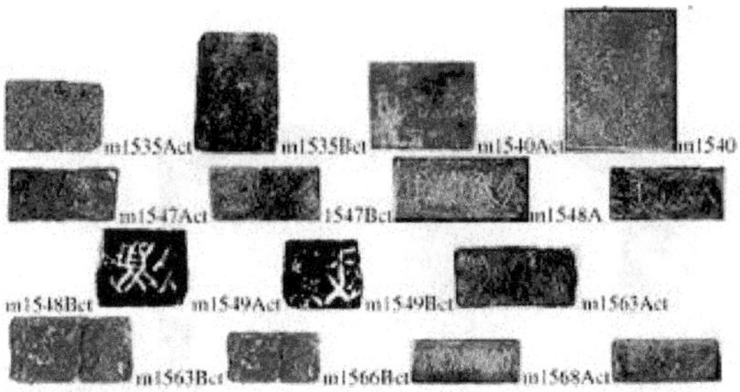


Incised copper tablet

2903 Incised copper tablet

2911 Incised copper tablets. Markhor.

2915

Copper plate, Mohenjo-daro with Indus script glyph.

m0317silver

m1199 silver

Silver seal Mackay 1938, vol. 2, Pl. XC,1: XCVI, 520 ; h018: copper seal, Mohenjodaro Indian museum.

Silver seals with Indus script inscriptions, Mohenjo-daro

Inscribed lead celt, Harappa.(Slide 209 Harappa.com HARP)

Two pure tin ingots with Indus script inscription. Shipwreck in Haifa.
More examples in embedded document (attached at the end).
Chanhu-daro was called Sheffield of ancient India. It was part of Harosheth Hagoyyim, 'smithy of nations'.

Indus script cipher: Hieroglyphs of Indian linguistic area (2010) Kalyanaraman

Indus writing on utensils and metal tools

Decoded smith guild tokens

Bhirrana artefacts (See the dancing step glyph shown on a potsherd, decoded as 'iron').

Copper celts, Bhirrana.

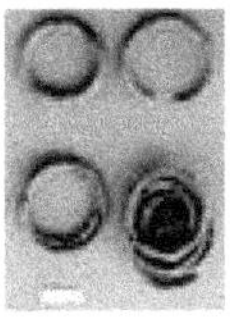  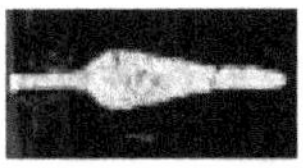  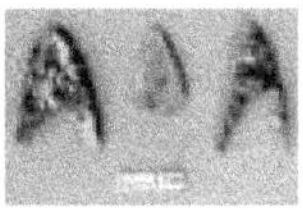 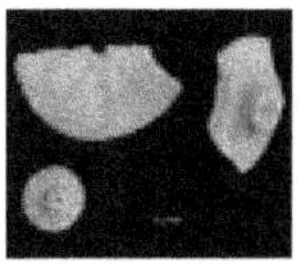

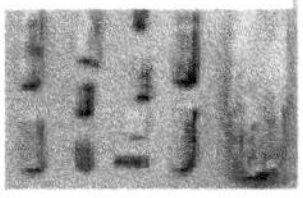 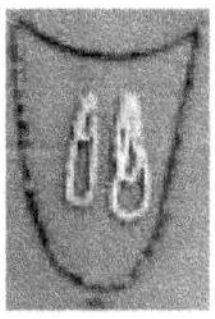 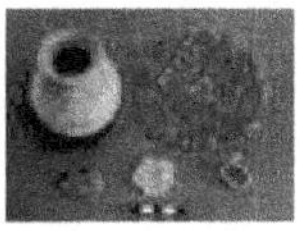

Daimabad bronzes. Buffalo on four-legged platform attached to four solid wheels 31X25 cm.; elephanton four-legged platform with axles 25 cm.; rhinoceros on axles of four solid wheels 25X19 cm. (MK Dhavalikar, 'Daimabad bronzes' in: Harappan civilization, ed. by GL Possehl, New Delhi, 1982, pp. 361-6; SA Sali, Daimabad 1976-1979, New Delhi, 1986).

Researching Indus writing

Daimabad bronze chariot. c. 1500 BCE. 22X52X17.5 cm.

Buffalo. Daimabad bronze. Prince of Wales Museum, Mumbai.

"A good many important facts can be determined, however, to clear the ground for more satisfactory research. In the first place this script is in no way even remotely connected with either the Sumerian or Proto-Elamitic signs. I have compared some of the signs with the signs of these scripts. For the references to the Sumerian pictographs, or the earliest forms of the Sumerian signs, I have referred the reader to the numbers of REC. (Thureau-Dangin, "Recherches sur l'Origine de l'Ecriture Cuneiforme") and for the Proto-Elamitic signs to Professor Scheil's "Textes de Comptabilite Proto-Elamites", in vol. xvii of Memoires de la Mission Archeologique de Perse, pp. 31-66. This series is commonly cited as Del. Per. (Delegation en Perse). The Indus inscriptions resemble the Egyptian hieroglyphs far more than they do the Sumerian linear and cuneiform system." [John Marshall, 1996 (Repr.), *Mohenjo-Daro and the Indus Civilization: Being an official account of Archaeological Excavations at Mohenjo-Daro carried out by the Government of India between the years 1922 and 1927*, Asian Educational Services, pp. 423-424] http://books.google.com/books?id=SZWE7O-5vusC&dq=elam+indus&source=gbs_navlinks_s

Duplicate tablets and Indus inscriptions

There are two tablets with identical seal impressions which contain a long Indus inscription composed of 23 glyphs. Reported in Marshall 1931 (Vol. II, p.402); repeated in Vol. III, Pl. CXVI.23.

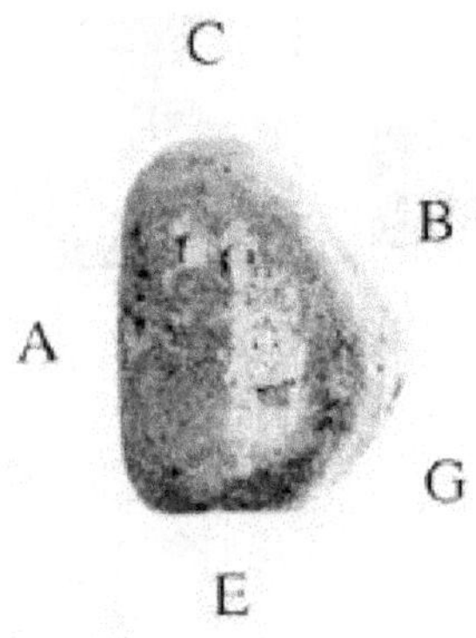


M-494 F

m0494A,BGt Prism Tablet in bas-relief. (BGt is a side view of two sides – B and G -- the prism tablet).

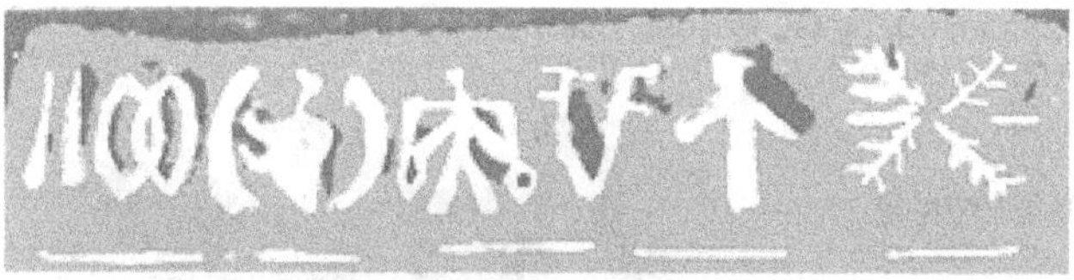

A reading of m0495G shown and discussed in http://indusscriptmore.blogspot.com/2011/09/indus-signs-of-17-and-18-strokes.html with particular reference to the first sign read as 'X'. If the glyph is a composite glyphic of four forked sticks, a vikalpa (alternative) reading is: मेंढा [ mēṇḍhā ] A crook or curved end (of a stick, horn &c.) and attrib. such a stick, horn, bullock. मेढा [ mēḍhā ] m A stake, esp. as forked. meḍ(h), meḍhī f., meḍhā m. ' post, forked stake '.(Marathi)(CDIAL 10317) Rebus: mẽṛhẽt, meḍ 'iron' (Mu.Ho.) gaṇḍa 'four'; rebus: kaṇḍa 'furnace, altar'. Thus, the composite glyphis is read rebus: iron (metal) furnace, *meḍ kaṇḍa*.

m0495A,B,Gt Prism Tablet in bas-relief

Inscription on tablet m0495 serves as a reinforcement of the reading of inscription on tablet m0494 (see the side shot of sides B and G reproduced above). The organizer of the photographic corpus, Asko Parpola, should be complimented for a painstaking effort to produce a high resolution reading of 3 lines of the text on the prism tablets (which almost look like five- sided object as may be seen from the photograph M-494F).
Sharper resolution images of the two tablets (3.6 cm. long) with three sides of a prism are as follows:

m-0495A
m-0495B
m-0495G

The reading of the text of the inscription on the two prism tablets provided in Mahadevan concordance is as follows:

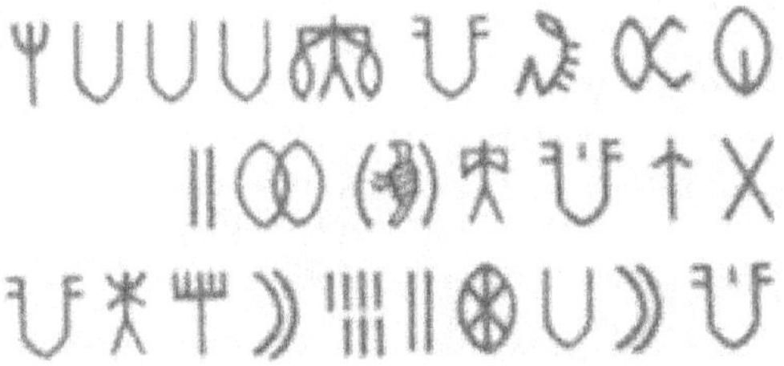

Text 1623/Text 2847

Decoding the identical inscription on Prism tablets m0494 and m0495

Line 1 Turner, mint, brass-work, furnace scribe, smelter, gridiron smithy, smithy/forge
Line 2 Mineral (ore), furnace/altar, furnace scribe workshop; metal (a kind of iron), casting furnace; cast metal ingot; casting workshop
Line 3 Furnace scribe workshop; cast bronze; kiln; gridiron; casting workshop; smithy (with) furnace; cast bronze; native metal; metal turner; furnace scribe.

Thus, line 1 is a description of the repertoire of a smithy/forge including mint and brass-work; line 2 is a smelting, casting workshop for ingots; line 3 is furnace scribe workshop for caste bronze, with kiln, furnace and native metal turning.

Line 1

1.1 Corner (of a room) glyph.

S. kuṇḍa f. 'corner'; P. kū̃ṭ f. 'corner, side' (← H.). (CDIAL 3898) Rebus 1: kundār turner (A.) kūdār, kūdāri (B.); kundāru (Or.); kundau to turn on a lathe, to carve, to chase; kundau dhiri = a hewn stone; kundau murhut = a graven image (Santali) kunda a turner's lathe (Skt.)(CDIAL 3295). Rebus 2: *khū̃ṭ* 'community, guild' (Mundari)

1.2 Crab glyph

Sign 57. Crab or claws of crab. kamaṭha crab (Skt.) Rebus: kammaṭa = portable furnace (Te.) kampaṭṭam coiner, mint (Ta.) Vikalpa: ḍato 'claws or pincers (chelae) of crabs'; ḍaṭom, ḍiṭom to seize with the claws or pincers, as crabs, scorpions; ḍaṭkop = to pinch, nip (only of crabs) (Santali) Rebus: dhātu 'mineral' (Vedic); dhatu 'a mineral, metal' (Santali) Vikalpa: erā 'claws'; Rebus: era 'copper'.

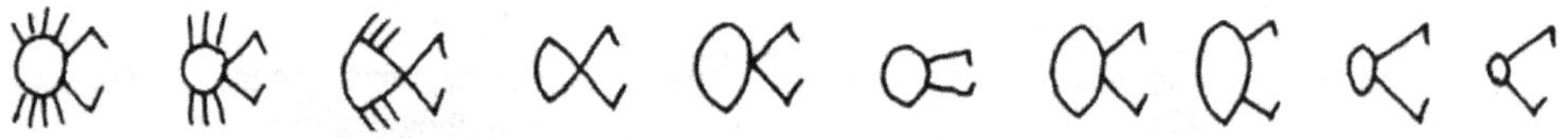

Allographs of the 'crab' glyph on Indus script (After Parpola 1994: 232, cf. 71-72.

The following are likely to be allographs of glyph described as three-branched fig tree Sign

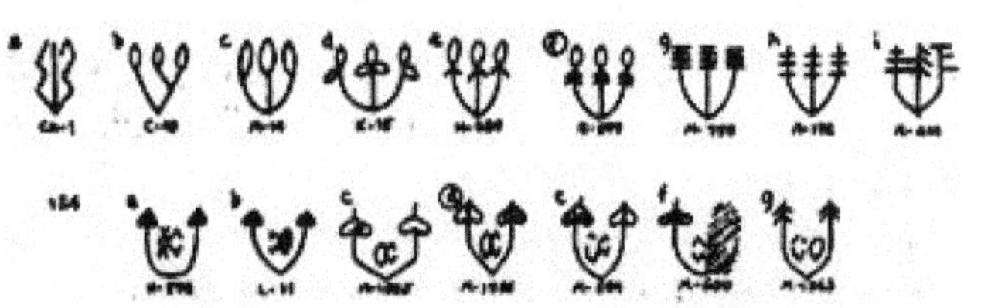

Argument: Allographs of a leaf sign, ligature with crab sign [After Parpola, 1994, fig. 13.15] The archer shown on one copper tablet seems to be equivalent to a glyph on another copper plate -- that of ligatured U (rimless wide-mouthed pot) with leaves and crab's claws. The archer has been decoded: *kamāṭhiyo* = archer; *kāmaṭhum* = a bow; *kāmaḍ, kāmaḍum* = a chip of bamboo (G.) *kāmaṭhiyo* a bowman; an archer (Skt.lex.) Rebus: *kammaṭi* a coiner (Ka.); *kampaṭṭam* coinage, coin, mint (Ta.) *kammaṭa* = mint, gold furnace (Te.)

Copper tablets from Mohenjo-daro which Parpola calls a 'pictorial translation' of the Indus glyph 'crab inside fig tree'. (After Parpola 1994: 234, fig. 13.13). The significance of this 'translation' becomes clear from the rebus readings of spoken words (of speech of Meluhha, mleccha artisans) connoting the allographs: *kamāṭhiyo* = archer. *kamaṛkom* 'fig'. *kamaḍha* 'crab'. The message is: *kammaṭa* = mint, gold furnace (Te.)

Vikalpa (alternative): *kaṇḍa* 'stone ore (metal)', as in *ayas kāṇḍa* 'excellent iron' (Pāṇini).

Harappa tablet (H0178) A ram-headed anthropoorph stands inside a fig tree. Glyph: meḍha 'ram'. Rebus1: meḍ 'iron'. Rebus 2: meḍha 'helper of (iron) merchant'.

The inscribed objects referenced in the list of allographs of Sign 371 are seen in a bronze-age metallurgical context. Some allographs occur on copper plate inscriptions.

Chanhudaro40A

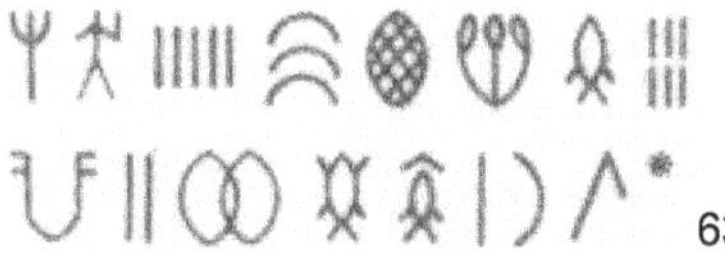

6306

Chanhudaro40B

copper ID 1701

Guild nodule (ore)/stone, workshop, native metal, bell-metal-brass, guild blacksmith-artisan, mine-worker-scribe, cast metal smithy, iron, iron-smithy,nodule (ore)/stone, nodule-ore-stone-smithy, smithy-workshop, copper-iron-smithy

अकडा *m* A hook or crook, a curved end gen. (M.) Rebus: अखाडा [ akhāḍā ] *m* ( H) A community, or the common place of residence or of assembly, of persons engaged in study or some particular pursuit; a college, a disputation-hall, a gymnasium, circus, arena. Hence, A club or clubroom; a stand of idlers, loungers, newsmongers, gossips, scamps. 2 An order of men. Ex. गोसाव्यांचे अठरा अखाडे आहेत.(M.)

khaḍā 'circumscribe' (M.); Rebs: khaḍā 'nodule (ore), stone' (M.)

*koḍa* 'in arithmetic, one' (Santali); rebus: *koḍ* 'artisan's workshop' (Kuwi)

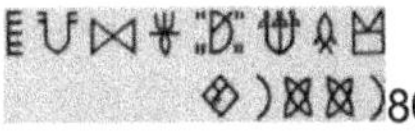

Kalibangan015 8056

 h289A  h289B  5467

 h577 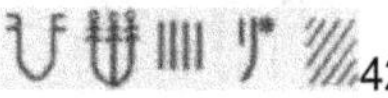 4243

 m0758a  2184

m0172  1071

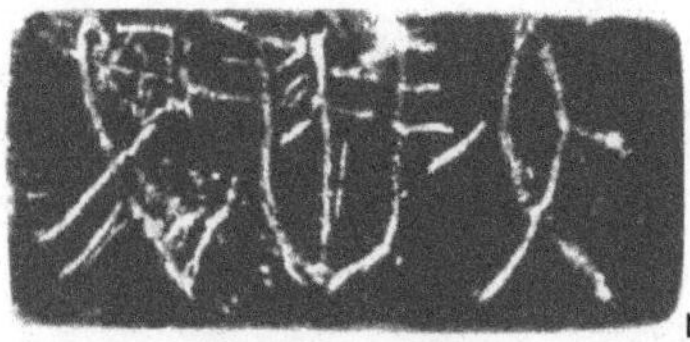 m0414A 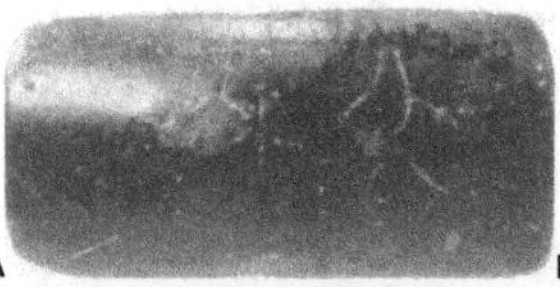 m0414B Seal with incision on obverse  2004

Modern seal impression of m0414  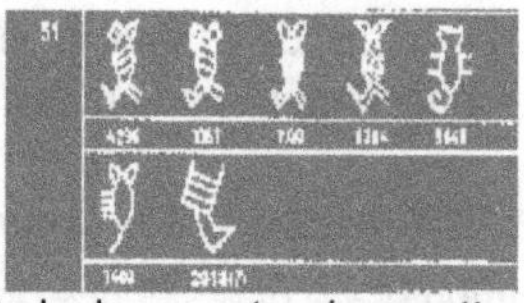

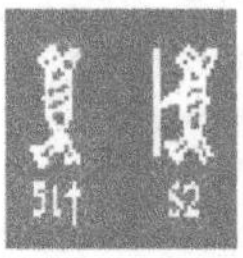

The first glyph from right connotes *kũdār* 'turner'. The second glyph connotes *kampaṭṭa* 'mint, coiner'. The third glyph: *aya* 'fish'. Rebus: *aya* 'metal'.

 h598A  h598D 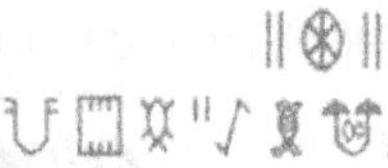 5073 [The ligature infixed on the last sign of the second line may be Sign 54 ]

 Lothal011  7026

 m0604At  m0604Bt  3315

 m0600At  m0600Bt  3375

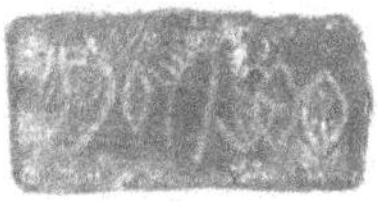 m1563Act 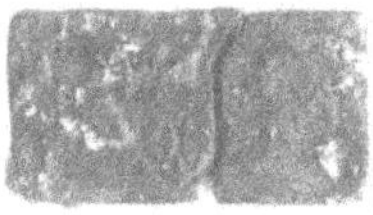 m1563Bct

1.3 Backbone, rib cage

Sign 48. kaśēru 'the backbone' (Bengali. Skt.); kaśēruka id. (Skt.) Rebus: kasērā 'metal worker' (Lahnda)(CDIAL 2988, 2989) Spine, rib-cage: A comparable glyptic representation is on a seal published by Omananda Saraswati. In Pl. 275: Omananda Saraswati 1975. Ancient Seals of Haryana (in Hindi). Rohtak." (I. Mahadevan, 'Murukan' in the Indus Script, The Journal of the Institute of Asian Studies, March 1999). B.B. Lal, 1960. From Megalithic to the Harappa: Tracing back the graffiti on pottery. Ancient India, No.16, pp. 4-24.

1.4 Rim of jar glyph

kaṇḍa kanka (Santali); Rebus: kaṇḍa kanka 'furnace scribe'. kaṇḍa 'fire-altar, furnace' (Santali); kan 'copper' (Ta.) karṇaka 'scribe, accountant' (Skt.) Vikalpa: kaṇḍ kanaka 'gold furnace'. kánaka n. ' gold ' (Skt.) கன் kan̠ ,n. perh. கன்மம். 1. workmanship; வேலைப்பாடு. கன்னார் மதில்சூழ் குடந்தை (திவ். திருவாய். 5, 8, 3). 2. copper work; கன்னார் தொழில். (W.) 3. copper; செம்பு. (ஈடு, 5, 8, 3.) MBh. Pa. kanaka -- n., Pk. kaṇaya -- n., MB. kanayā ODBL 659, Si. kanā EGS 36.(CDIAL 2717) కనకము [ kanakamu ] kanakamu. [Skt.] n. Gold. (Telugu) கனகம் kan̠akam, n. < kanaka. 1. Gold; பொன். காரார்வண்ணன் கனகமனையானும் (தேவா. 502, 9 (Tamil) kanaka (nt.) [cp. Sk. kanaka; Gr. knh_kos yellow; Ags. hunig=E. honey. See also kañcana] gold, usually as uttatta˚ molten gold; said of the colour of the skin Bu i.59; Pv iii.32; J v.416; PvA 10 suvaṇṇa).-- agga gold -- crested J v.156; -- chavin of golden complexion J vi.13; -- taca (adj.) id. J v.393; -- pabhā golden splendour Bu xxiii.23; -- vimāna a fairy palace of gold VvA 6; PvA 47, 53; -- sikharī a golden peak, in ˚rājā king of the golden peaks (i. e. Himālayas): Dāvs iv.30. (Pali) Vikalpa: kan̠ 'copper work' (Ta.) The sequence of two glyphs discussed in 1.3 and 1.4 above occur with high frequency on copper tablets. The pair of glyphs is read rebus as: metal work, furnace scribe -- *kasērā kaṇḍa kanka*.

This is a professional calling card of the artisan engaged in metal work.

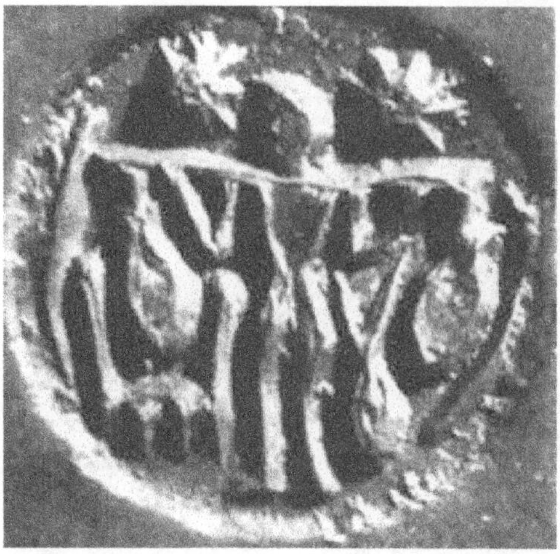

1.5 Water-carrier glyph

kuṭi 'water-carrier' (Telugu); Rebus: kuṭhi 'smelter furnace' (Santali) kuṛī f. 'fireplace' (H.); krvṛl f. 'granary (WPah.); kuṛī, kuṛo house, building'(Ku.)(CDIAL 3232) kuṭi 'hut made of boughs' (Skt.) guḍi temple (Telugu) A comparable glyptic representation is provided in a Gadd seal found in an interaction area of the Persian Gulf. Gadd notes that the 'water-carrier' seal is is an unmistakable example of an 'hieroglyphic' seal. Seal impression, Ur (Upenn; U.16747); [After Edith Porada, 1971, Remarks on seals found in the Gulf States. Artibus Asiae 33 (4): 331-7: pl.9, fig.5]; water carrier with a skin (or pot?) hung on each end of the yoke across his shoulders and another one below the crook of his left arm; the vessel on the right end of his yoke is over a receptacle for the water; a star on either side of the head (denoting supernatural?). The whole object is enclosed by 'parenthesis' marks. The parenthesis is perhaps a way of splitting of the ellipse (Hunter, G.R., JRAS, 1932, 476).

1.6 Three (rimless) pots

kolmo 'three' (Mu.); rebus: kolami 'smithy' (Te.)

S. baṭhu m. 'large pot in which grain is parched, Rebus; bhaṭṭhā m. 'kiln' (P.) baṭa = a kind of iron (G.) Vikalpa: meṛgo = rimless vessels (Santali) bhaṭa 'furnace' (G.) baṭa = kiln (Santali); baṭa = a kind of iron (G.) bhaṭṭha -- m.n. ' gridiron (Pkt.) baṭhu large cooking fire' baṭhī f. 'distilling furnace'; L. bhaṭṭh m. 'grain—parcher's oven', bhaṭṭhī f. 'kiln, distillery', awāṇ. bhaṭh; P. bhaṭṭh m., ṭhī f. 'furnace', bhaṭṭhā m. 'kiln'; S. bhaṭṭhī keṇī 'distil (spirits)'. (CDIAL 9656) Rebus: meḍ iron (Ho.)

kolmo 'rice plant' (Mu.) Rebus: kolami 'furnace,smithy' (Te.) Vikalpa: pajhaṛ = to sprout from a root (Santali); Rebus: pasra 'smithy, forge' (Santali)

Line 2

2.1 Cross
dāṭu = cross (Te.); Rebus: dhatu = mineral (ore)(Santali) dhātu 'mineral (Pali) dhātu 'mineral' (Vedic); a mineral, metal (Santali); dhāta id. (G.)

2.2 Arrow
kaṇḍa 'arrow'; Rebus: kaṇḍ = a furnace, altar (Santali)

2.3 Rim of jar + infixed short stroke

Rim of jar is decoded as: kaṇḍa kanka 'furnace scribe'. (See line 1.4) sal stake, spike, splinter, thorn, difficulty (H.); sal 'workshop' (Santali) Vikalpa: aṭar 'a splinter' (Ma.) aṭaruka 'to burst, crack, sli off,fly open; aṭarcca ' splitting, a crack'; aṭarttuka 'to split, tear off, open (an oyster) (Ma.); a ḍ aruni 'to crack' (Tu.) (DEDR 66) Rebus: aduru 'native, unsmelted metal' Rebus: adaru = native metal (Ka.) aduru = gan.iyinda tegadu karagade iruva aduru = ore taken from the mine and not subjected to melting in a furnace (Ka. Siddhānti Subrahman.ya' S'astri's new interpretation of the Amarakos'a, Bangalore, Vicaradarpana Press, 1872, p. 330)

Thus, the ligatured glyph is read rebus as: scribe (of) native,unsmelted metal furnace.

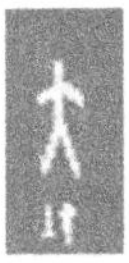

2.4 Body
mēd 'body' (Kur.)(DEDR 5099); meḍ 'iron' (Ho.)

2.5 Bird (circumscribed in bracket) Decoding: Furnace for riveting metal (a kind of iron)
baṭa= quail (Santali) Rebus: baṭa = a kind of iron (G.) bhaṭa 'furnace' (G.) baṭa = kiln (Santali) Vikalpa: pota 'pigeon'; pot 'beads' (H.G.M.)(CDIAL 8403). Vikalpa: baṭṭai quail (N.) vartaka = a duck (Skt.)(CDIAL 11361). batak = a duck (G.) vartikā = quail (RV.); wuwrc partridge (Ash.); barti = quail, partridge (Kho.); vaṭṭaka_ quail (Pali); vaṭṭaya (Pkt.) (CDIAL 11361).
Rebus: vartaka 'merchant' (Skt.)

( ) A pair of enclosures: *jāḍa -- ' joining, pair '. [← Drav. LM 333]; 2. S. jāṛo m. ' twin ', L. P. jāṛā m.; M. jāḍī f. ' a double yoke '. (CDIAL 5091) Rebus: *jaḍati ' joins, sets '. 1. Pk. jaḍia -- ' set (of jewels), joined '; K. jarun ' to set jewels ' (← Ind.); S. jaṛaṇu ' to join, rivet, set ', jaṛa f. ' rivet, boundary between two fields '; P.jaṛāuṇā ' to have fastened or set '; A. zarāiba ' to collect '; B. jaṛāna ' to set jewels, wrap round, entangle ', jaṛ ' heaped together '; Or. jaṛibā ' to unite '; OAw.jaraï ' sets jewels, bedecks '; H. jaṛnā ' to join, stick in, set ' (→ N. jaṛnu ' to set, be set '); OMarw. jaṛāū ' inlaid '; G. jaṛvū ' to join, meet with, set jewels '; M.jaḍṇẽ ' to join, connect, inlay, be firmly established ', jaṭṇẽ ' to combine, confederate '. (CDIAL 5091)

Vikalpa: dula दुल । युग्मम् m. a pair, a couple, esp. of two similar things (Rām. 966) (Kashmiri); dol 'likeness, picture, form' (Santali) Rebus: dul 'to cast metal in a mould' (Santali) dul meṛeḍ cast iron (Mundari. Santali)
'cast bronze'; it is a glyptic formed of a pair of brackets (): kuṭila 'bent'; rebus: kuṭila, katthīl = bronze (8 parts copper and 2 parts tin)

2.6 Two over-lapping (or pair of) ovals: Oval is the shape of an ingot (of metal). Paired ovals (ingots) are decoded as 'cast' 'metal ingots'.

mūh metal ingot (shaped like an oval) (Santali) mūhā̃ = the quantity of iron produced at one time in a native smelting furnace of the Kolhes; iron produced by the Kolhes and formed like a four-cornered piece a little pointed at each end; mūhā me~r.he~t = iron smelted by the Kolhes and formed into an equilateral lump a little pointed at each end; kolhe tehen me~r.he~tko mūhā akata = the Kolhes have to-day produced pig iron (Santali.lex.) kaula mengro 'blacksmith' (Gypsy) paired: dul 'likeness'; dul 'cast (metal)']

2.7 A pair of linear strokes (two long linear strokes) Decoded as casting workshop
dula 'pair'; rebus: dul 'cast (metal)(Santali) goṭ = one (Santali); goṭi = silver (G.) koḍa 'one' (Santali); koḍ 'workshop' (G.)

Line 3

3.1 Rim of jar + infixed short stroke as in Line 2.3 above. Decoded as: furnace scribe workshop.

3.2 Two bent (curved) lines. Decoded as 'cast bronze'.

kuṭila 'bent'; rebus: kuṭila, katthīl = bronze (8 parts copper and 2 parts tin)
dula 'pair'; rebus: dul 'cast (metal)(Santali)

3.3 Rimless pot. Decoded as: gridiron. See 1.6 above (for three rimless pots).
S. baṭhu m. 'large pot in which grain is parched, Rebus; bhaṭṭhā m. 'kiln' (P.) baṭa = a kind of iron (G.) Vikalpa: meṛgo = rimless vessels (Santali) bhaṭa 'furnace' (G.) baṭa = kiln (Santali); baṭa = a kind of iron (G.) bhaṭṭha -- m.n. ' gridiron (Pkt.) baṭhu large cooking fire' baṭhī f. 'distilling furnace'; L. bhaṭṭh m. 'grain—parcher's oven', bhaṭṭhī f. 'kiln, distillery', awāṇ. bhaṭh; P. bhaṭṭh m., ṭhī f. 'furnace', bhaṭṭhā m. 'kiln'; S. bhaṭṭhī keṇī 'distil (spirits)'. (CDIAL 9656)Rebus: meḍ iron (Ho.)

3.4 Nave of spoked wheel. Decoded as (molten cast copper) turner, kundār 'turner'.

era = knave of wheel; rebus: era = copper; erako = molten cast (G.) eraka, (copper) 'metal infusion'; āra 'spokes'; rebus: āra 'brass' as in ārakūṭa (Skt.) kund opening in the nave or hub of a wheel to admit the axle (Santali) Rebus: kundam, kund a sacrificial fire-pit (Skt.) kunda 'turner' kundār turner (A.); kūdār, kūdāri (B.); kundāru (Or.); kundau to turn on a lathe, to carve, to chase; kundau dhiri = a hewn stone; kundau murhut = a graven image (Santali) kunda a turner's lathe (Skt.)(CDIAL 3295) Vikalpa: era, er-a = eraka = ?nave; erako_lu = the iron axle of a carriage (Ka.M.); cf. irasu (Ka.lex.) [Note Sign 391 and its ligatures Signs 392 and 393 may connote a spoked-wheel, nave of the wheel through which the axle passes; cf. ara_, spoke] ஆரம்² āram , n. < āra. 1. Spoke of a wheel. See ஆரக்கால். ஆரஞ்சூழ்ந்த வயில்வாய் நேமியொடு (சிறுபாண். 253) (Tamil) 3.5 As in 2.7 above. A pair of linear strokes (two long linear strokes) Decoded as 'casting workshop'. dula 'pair'; rebus: dul 'cast (metal)(Santali) goṭ = one (Santali); goṭi = silver (G.) koḍa 'one' (Santali); koḍ 'workshop' (G.) 3.6 Four + Three short strokes. Decoded as smithy (with) furnace. Four + three strokes are read (since the strokes are shown on two lines one below the other) : gaṇḍa 'four' (Santali); Rebus: kaṇḍa 'furnace' (Santali); kolmo 'three' (Mu.); rebus: kolami 'smithy' (Te.) Vikalpa: ?ea 'seven' (Santali); rebus: ?eh-ku 'steel' (Te.) Vikalpa: pon 'four' (Santali) rebus: pon 'gold' (Ta.) 3.7 As in 3.2 above. Two bent (curved) lines. Decoded as 'cast bronze'. kuṭila 'bent'; rebus: kuṭila, katthīl = bronze (8 parts copper and 2 parts tin) dula 'pair'; rebus: dul 'cast (metal)(Santali) 3.8 Harrow aḍar 'harrow'; rebus: aduru 'native metal' 3.9 Horned body (Body as in 2.4 above.) Decoded as 'metal (iron) turner'. mēd 'body' (Kur.)(DEDR 5099); meḍ 'iron' (Ho.) kōḍ, kōṇḍa 'horn'. Pa. kōḍ (pl. kōḍul) horn; Ka. kōḍu horn, tusk, branch of a tree; kōr̤ horn Tu. kōḍů, kōḍu horn Ko. kṛ (obl. kṭ-)( (DEDR 2200) Paš. kōṇḍā́'bald', Kal. rumb. kōṇḍa 'hornless'.(CDIAL 3508). Kal. rumb.khōṇḍ a' half' (CDIAL 3792). Rebus: कोंडण [kōṇḍaṇa] f A fold or pen. (Marathi) kōdā 'to turn in a lathe' (Bengali) कोंद kōnda 'engraver, lapidary setting or infixing gems' (Marathi) कोंदण [ kōndaṇa ] n (कोंदणें) Setting or infixing of gems.(Marathi) খোদকার [ khōdakāra ] n an engraver; a carver. খোদকারি n. engraving; carving; interference in other's work. খোদাই [ khōdāi ] n engraving; carving. খোদাই করা v. to engrave; to carve. খোদানো v. & n. en graving; carving. খোদিত [ khōdita ] a engraved. (Bengali) खोदकाम [ khōdakāma ] n Sculpture; carved work or work for the carver. खोदगिरी [ khōdagirī ] f Sculpture, carving, engraving: also sculptured or carved work. खोदणावळ [ khōdaṇāvaḷa ] f (खोदणें) The price or cost of sculpture or carving. खोदणी [ khōdaṇī ] f (Verbal of खोदणें) Digging, engraving &c. 2 fig. An exacting of money by importunity. v लाव, मांड. 3 An instrument to scoop out and cut flowers and figures from paper. 4 A goldsmith's die. खोदणें [ khōdaṇēṃ ] v c & i ( H) To dig. 2 To engrave. खोद खोदून विचारणें or -पुसणें To question minutely and searchingly, to probe. खोदाई [ khōdāī ] f ( H) Price or cost of digging or of sculpture or carving. खोदींव [ khōdīṃva ] p of खोदणें Dug. 2 Engraved, carved, sculptured. (Marathi) 3.10 Rim of jar. As in 1.4 above. Decoded as: kaṇḍa kanka 'furnace scribe'.

The following examples are of 8 copper tablets recovered in Harappa by HARP project. A third glyph on these tablets is an oval sign -- like a metal ingot -- and is ligatured with an infixed sloping stroke:

ḍhāḷiyum = adj. sloping, inclining (G.) The ligatured glyph is read rebus as: ḍhālako = a large metal ingot (G.) ḍhālakī = a metal heated and poured into a mould; a solid piece of metal; an ingot (G.) The inscription on these tablets is in bas-relief:

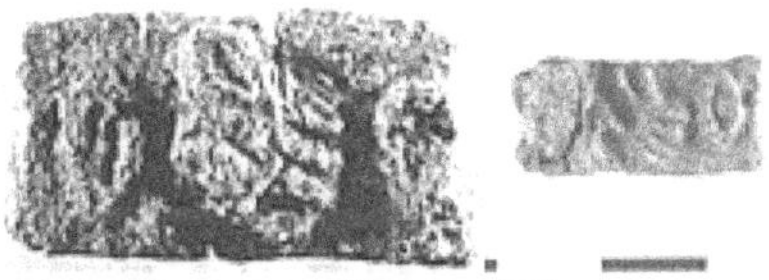

8 cast copper tablets recovered from circular platforms, Harappa (2005);

Copper tablet (H2000-4498/9889-01) with raised script found in Trench 43. Slide 351 harappa.com

Copper tablets with Indus script in bas-relief, Harappa. The three glyphs on the ingots are read in sequence: *ḍhālako kasērā kaṇḍa kanka* 'metal ingot, metal work, furnace scribe'.

Mohenjo-daro Seal impression m0494 and m0495. (Identical impression of three lines on three sides on the prism-shaped tablets). The inscription on m-0494/m-0495 which contains 23 glyphs (adding all the glyphs on three sides of a prism) is decoded -- treating the three lines of inscriptions on the prisms as one composite inscription with a composite message.

> There can only be a conjecture as to why the prism tablets were mass produced with identical three lines of impression: it is likely that the tablets were used by artisans of a guild performing identical metal work for transporting packages with identical contents and hence, identical messages conveyed through the inscription.

An "Early Harappan" polychrome pot with fish design from Nal, South Baluchistan. After Gordon 1960: pl. VI a.

Mohenjo-daro 0314 Seal impression.

Text. Reading of glyphs on m0314 Seal impression.

The indus script inscription on m0314 is a detailed account of the metal work engaged in by the Indus artisans. It is a professional calling card of the metalsmiths' guild of Mohenjo-daro used to affix a sealing on packages of metal artefacts traded by Meluhha (mleccha) speakers.

A notable featue of the sequencing of glyphs is the use of three variants of 'fish' glyphs on line 1 of the inscription. Each variant 'fish' glyph has been distinctively decoded as working with ore, metalwork (forging, turning) and casting.

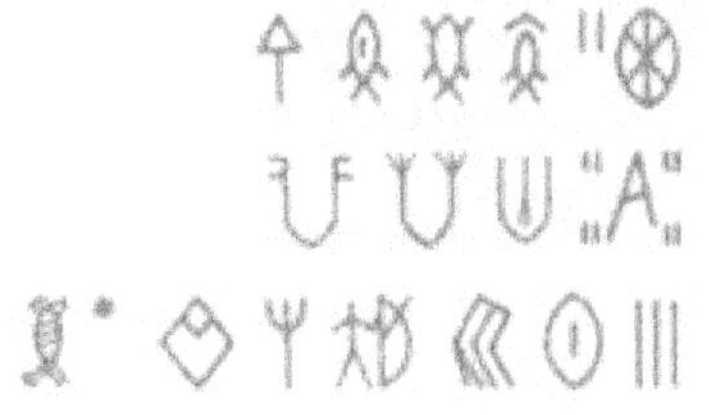

Rebus decoding of glyphs on the seal impression:
Three lines of the inscription with glyphs can be read rebus from right to left -- listing the metallurgical competence of the artisans' guild:

Line 1: Turner workshop; forge, stone ore, ingot; excellent cast metal
Line 2: Metal workshop, ingot furnace, casting, riveting smithy,forge; furnace (stone ore) account scribe
Line 3: Smithy, lump of silver (forging metal); mint, gold furnace; smithy/forge; turner wheelwright.

Details:

Line 1

1.1. Turner workshop

kund opening in the nave or hub of a wheel to admit the axle (Santali) Rebus: kundam, kund a sacrificial fire-pit (Skt.) kunda 'turner' kundār turner (A.)

sal 'splinter'; rebus: sal 'workshop' (Santali)

1.2. Forge, stone ore, ingot

Fish + corner, aya koṇḍa, 'metal turned, i.e. forged'
Fish + scales aya ãs (amśu) 'metllic stalks of stone ore
Fish + sloping stroke, aya dhāḷ 'metal ingot' (Vikalpa: ḍhāḷ = a slope; the inclination of a plane (G.)
Rebus: : ḍhāḷako = a large metal ingot (G.)

1.3. Excellent cast metal

ḍol 'the shaft of an arrow, an arrow' (Santali) Vikalpa: dul 'casting' (Santali)

Vikalpa: kaṇḍa 'arrow' (Skt.) ayaskāṇḍa 'a quantity of iron, excellent iron'

Line 2

2.1 Iron workshop

मेंढा [ mēṇḍhā ] A crook or curved end (of a stick, horn &c.) and attrib. such a stick, horn, bullock. मेढा [ mēḍhā ] m A stake, esp. as forked. Vikalpa: kottaṉ a mason (Ta.) kotti pick-axe, stone-digger, carver (Ma.) Rebus: mẽṛhẽt, meḍ 'iron' (Mu.Ho.)

2.2 Ingot furnace

S. baṭhu m. 'large pot in which grain is parched, Rebus; bhaṭṭhā m. 'kiln' (P.) baṭa = a kind of iron (G.) Vikalpa: meṛgo = rimless vessels (Santali) bhaṭa 'furnace' (G.) baṭa = kiln (Santali); baṭa = a kind of iron (G.) bhaṭṭha -- m.n. ' gridiron (Pkt.) baṭhu large cooking fire' baṭhī f. 'distilling furnace'; L. bhaṭṭh m. 'grain—parcher's oven', bhaṭṭhī f. 'kiln, distillery', awāṇ. bhaṭh; P. bhaṭṭh m., ṭhī f. 'furnace', bhaṭṭhā m. 'kiln'; S. bhaṭṭhī keṇī 'distil (spirits)'. (CDIAL 9656)Rebus: meḍ iron (Ho.)

ḍabu 'an iron spoon' (Santali) Rebus: ḍab, ḍhimba, ḍhompo 'lump (ingot?)', clot, make a lump or clot, coagulate, fuse, melt together (Santali)

2.3 Casting, iron (riveting smithy), forge

kolmo 'rice plant' (Mu.) Rebus: kolami 'furnace,smithy' (Te.) Vikalpa: M. meḍ(h), meḍhī f., meḍhā m. ' post, forked stake '(CDIAL 10317). Rebus: meḍ, mẽṛhẽt 'iron'(Mu.Ho.)

mēthí m. ' pillar in threshing floor to which oxen are fastened, prop for supporting carriage shafts ' AV., °thī -- f. KātyŚr.com., mēdhī -- f. Divyāv. 2. mēṭhī -- f. PañcavBr.com., mēḍhī -- , mēṭī -- f. BhP. 1. Pa. mēdhi -- f. ' post to tie cattle to, pillar, part of a stūpa '; Pk. mēhi -- m. ' post on threshing floor ', N. meh(e), miho, miyo, B. mei, Or. maï -- dāṇḍi, Bi. mēh, mēhā ' the post ', (SMunger) mehā ' the bullock next the post ', Mth. meh, mehā ' the post ', (SBhagalpur) mīhā̃ ' the bullock next the post ', (SETirhut) mēhi bāṭi ' vessel with a projecting base '. 2. Pk. mēḍhi -- m. ' post on threshing floor ', mēḍhaka<-> '

small stick '; K. mīr, mīrü f. ' larger hole in ground which serves as a mark in pitching walnuts ' (for semantic relation of ' post -- hole ' see kūpa -- 2); L. meṛh f. ' rope tying oxen to each other and to post on threshing floor '; P. mehṛ f., mehaṛ m. ' oxen on threshing floor, crowd '; OA meṛha, mehra ' a circular construction, mound '; Or. meṛhī, meri ' post on threshing floor '; Bi. mẽṛ ' raised bank between irrigated beds ', (Camparam) mẽṛhā ' bullock next the post ', Mth. (SETirhut) mẽṛhā ' id. '; M. meḍ(h), meḍhī f., meḍhā m. ' post, forked stake '. (CDIAL 10317)

Vikalpa: pajhaṛ = to sprout from a root (Santali); Rebus: pasra 'smithy, forge' (Santali)

Vikalpa: *jāḍyadhānya ' winter rice '. [jā´ḍya -- , dhānyà -- ]
Bhoj. jaṛahan ' winter rice '; H. jaṛhan m. ' rice reaped at the end of the Rains '.(CDIAL 5181)

*jāḍa -- ' joining, pair '. [← Drav. LM 333]; 2. S. jāṛo m. ' twin ', L. P. jāṛā m.; M. ǰāḍī f. ' a double yoke '. (CDIAL 5091) Rebus: *jaḍati ' joins, sets '. 1. Pk. jaḍia -- ' set (of jewels), joined '; K. jarun ' to set jewels ' (← Ind.); S. jaṛaṇu ' to join, rivet, set ', jaṛa f. ' rivet, boundary between two fields '; P.jaṛāuṇā ' to have fastened or set '; A. zarāiba ' to collect '; B. jaṛāna ' to set jewels, wrap round, entangle ', jaṛ ' heaped together '; Or. jaṛibā ' to unite '; OAw.jaraï ' sets jewels, bedecks '; H. jaṛnā ' to join, stick in, set ' (→ N. jaṛnu ' to set, be set '); OMarw. jaṛāū ' inlaid '; G. jaṛvũ ' to join, meet with, set jewels '; M.ǰaḍṇẽ ' to join, connect, inlay, be firmly established ', ǰaṭṇẽ ' to combine, confederate '. (CDIAL 5091)

Vikalpa: dula दुल । युग्मम् m. a pair, a couple, esp. of two similar things (Rām. 966) (Kashmiri); dol 'likeness, picture, form' (Santali) Rebus: dul 'to cast metal in a mould' (Santali) dul meṛeḍ cast iron (Mundari. Santali)

2.4 Furnace scribe

kaṇḍ kanka 'rim of jar'; Rebus: karṇaka 'scribe'; kaṇḍ 'furnace, fire-altar'. Thus the ligatured sign is decoded: kaṇḍ karṇaka 'furnace scribe

Line 3

3.1 Smithy

kolmo 'three' (Mu.); rebus: kolami 'smithy' (Te.)

3.2 Lump of silver (forging metal)

guḍá—1. — In sense 'fruit, kernel' cert. ← Drav., cf. Tam. koṭṭai 'nut, kernel'; A. goṭ 'a fruit, whole piece', °ṭā 'globular, solid', guṭi 'small ball, seed, kernel'; B. goṭā 'seed, bean, whole'; Or. goṭā 'whole, undivided', goṭi 'small ball, cocoon', goṭāli 'small round piece of chalk'; Bi. goṭā 'seed'; Mth. goṭa 'numerative particle' (CDIAL 4271) Rebus: koṭe 'forging (metal)(Mu.) Rebus: goṭī f. 'lump of silver' (G.)

Fish signs (and variants) seem to be differentiated from, perhaps a loop of threads formed on a loom or loose fringes of a garment. This may be seen from the seal M-9 which contains the sign:

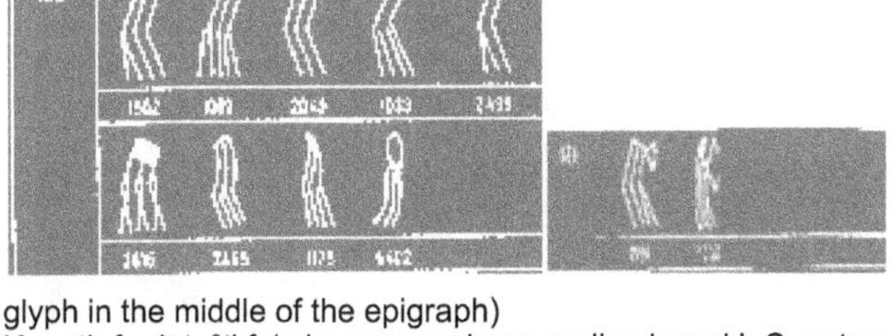

Sign 180 Signs 180, 181 have variants. Warp-pegs kor.i = pegs in the ground in two rooms on which the thread is passed back and forth in preparing the warp (S.)

Edging, trimming (cf. orthography of glyph in the middle of the epigraph)
K. goṭh f., dat. °ṭi f. ' chequer or chess or dice board '; S. goṭu m. ' large ball of tobacco ready for hookah ', °ṭī f. ' small do. '; P. goṭ f. ' spool on which gold or silver wire is wound, piece on a chequer board '; N.

goṭo ' piece ', goṭi ' chess piece '; A. goṭ ' a fruit, whole piece ', °ṭā ' globular, solid ', guṭi ' small ball, seed, kernel '; B. goṭā ' seed, bean, whole '; Or. goṭā ' whole, undivided ', goṭi ' small ball, cocoon ', goṭāli ' small round piece of chalk '; Bi. goṭā ' seed '; Mth. goṭa ' numerative particle '; H. goṭ f. ' piece (at chess &c.) '; G. goṭ m. ' cloud of smoke ', °ṭɔ m. ' kernel of coconut, nosegay ', goṭī f. ' lump of silver, clot of blood ', °ṭilɔm. ' hard ball of cloth '; M. goṭā m. ' roundish stone ', °ṭī f. ' a marble ', goṭuḷā ' spherical '; Si. guṭiya ' lump, ball '; -- prob. also P. goṭṭā ' gold or silver lace ', H.goṭā m. ' edging of such ' (→ K. goṭa m. ' edging of gold braid ', S. goṭo m. ' gold or silver lace '); M. goṭ ' hem of a garment, metal wristlet '. Ko. gōṭu ' silver or gold braid '.(CDIAL 4271)

Rebus: goṭī f. 'lump of silver' (G.)

3.3 Mint, gold furnace

kamāṭhiyo = archer; kāmaṭhum = a bow; kāmaḍ, kāmaḍum = a chip of bamboo (G.) kāmaṭhiyo a bowman; an archer (Skt.lex.) Rebus: kammaṭi a coiner (Ka.); kampaṭṭam coinage, coin, mint (Ta.) kammaṭa = mint, gold furnace (Te.)

3.4 Smithy, forge

kolmo 'rice plant' (Mu.) Rebus: kolami 'furnace,smithy' (Te.) Vikalpa: pajhaṛ = to sprout from a root (Santali); Rebus: pasra 'smithy, forge' (Santali)

3.5 Turner

S. kuṇḍa f. 'corner'; P. kũṭ f. 'corner, side' (← H.). (CDIAL 3898) Rebus: kundār turner (A.) kũdār, kũdāri (B.); kundāru (Or.); kundau to turn on a lathe, to carve, to chase; kundau dhiri = a hewn stone; kundau murhut = a graven image (Santali) kunda a turner's lathe (Skt.)(CDIAL 3295).

The following texts are examples which demonstrate that long texts of inscriptions can be created by combining texts from multiple seals even though the average number of glyphs is about 5 or 6 per inscribed object. It all depends on the multiplicity of the contents of the package described by the seal impressions as bills of lading. This belies the claim of some people that it is impossible to find long texts in inscriptions, say, with 50+ hieroglyphs.

Decoding L211 fifteen glyphs and k089 twenty glyphs as product assemblages in sealings as descriptions of packaged goods incorporated in bills of lading — from multiple guild workshops, hence, multiple lines of the inscription read from multiple seal impressions.

Lothal seal impression created by inscriptions from three seals. L211. "More than a hundred clay tags with ancient seal impressions come from a burnt-down grain warehouse at the Harappan port town of Lothal. Many of these tags also bear impressions of woven cloth, reed matting or other packing material. This shows that the tags were once attached to bales of goods, and that the seals were used, as in ancient West Asia, for controlling economic transactions. Indus seals coming from West Asian sites testify to trade relations entertained by the Indus civilisation with Mesopotamia."

"As many as 65 terracotta sealings recovered from the warehouse bore impressions of Indus seals on th obverse and of packing material such as bamboo matting, reed, woven cloth and cord on the reverse. Substantial part of the warehouse was destroyed in P,III and was never rebuilt. All this elaborate infrastructure for external trade amply reflected in other finds from Lothal. A circular steatite seal of the class known as Persian Gulf seal (Bibby, 1958, pp. 243-4; Wheeler, 1958, p. 246; Rao 1963, p. 37), found aqundantly at Failaka and Rasal Qaila (Bahrain) on the Persian Gillf, is a surface find at Lothal, evidently the Persain Gulf sites were inter mediary in the Indus trade with Mesopotamia. Conversely some of the Indus-like seals found it Mesopotamia may have been imports from Lothal. A bun-shaped copper ingot, weighing 1.438 kg follows the shape, size and weight of Susa ingots, with which tht Lothal specimen shares the lack of arsenic in its composition. In addition to the Indus stone cubes of standard weights. Lothal had another series of weights conforming to the Heavy Assyrian standard for international trade." (Parpola: http://www.harappa.com/script/parpola5.html)

The orthography (M-shape) is similar to the orthography of mangalasūtra (marriage badge) used in some Indian traditions and worn by Indian brides.

(Assuming that the gyph orthographically connotes the architecture of a warehouse with a roof: कोठी [ kōṭhī ] f (कोष्ट S) A granary, garner, storehouse, warehouse, treasury, factory, bank. (Marathi) कोठी The grain and provisions (as of an army); the commissariatsupplies. Ex. लशकराची कोठी चालली-उतरली- आली-लुटली. कोठ्या [ kōṭhyā ] कोठा [ kōṭhā ] m (कोष्ट S) A large granary, store-room, warehouse, water-reservoir &c. 2 The stomach. 3 The chamber of a gun, of water-pipes &c. 4 A bird's nest. 5 A cattle-shed. 6 The chamber or cell of a hunḍí in which is set down in figures the amount. कोठारें [ kōṭhārēṃ ] n A storehouse gen (Marathi) krvṛl f. 'granary (Wpah.); kuṛī, kuṛo house, building'(Ku.)(CDIAL 3232) kuṭi 'hut made of boughs' (Skt.) guḍi temple (Telugu)[Notes on hunḍí: हुंडी [ huṇḍī ] f ( H) A bill of exchange. हुंडी लावणें To present a hunḍí.हुंडी [ huṇḍī ] f ( H) A bill of exchange. हुंडी लावणें To present a hunḍí. हुंडाभाडा [ huṇḍābhāḍā ] m ( H) sometimes हुंडेंभाडें n Contract or agreement (for the transportation of goods &c.) in which the payment of all tolls and duties, and of all charges for hire &c. is included; a lump-contract. (Marathi)

dula 'pair' (Kashmiri); rebus: dul 'cast (metal)'(Santali) kolom = cutting, graft; to graft, engraft, prune; kolma hoṛo = a variety of the paddy plant (Desi)(Santali.) kolmo 'rice plant' (Mu.) Rebus: kolami 'furnace,smithy' (Te.) Thus the ligatured glyph decodes: cast (metal) smithy
L211 Fifteen glyphs

Line 1: Turner's workshop, metal ingot, metal (iron) workshop, furnace scribe (account)
Line 2: (…)workshop, cast metal, copper (metal), furnace scribe (account)
Line 3: (…), furnace scribe account — native metal, metal ingot, warehouse, casting smithy/forge, furnace scribe account

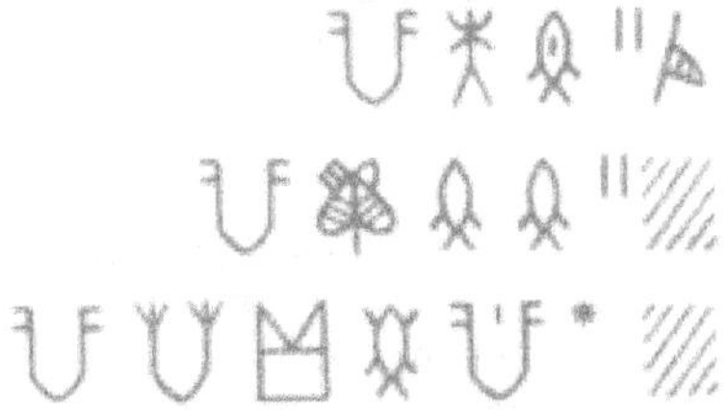

Detailed decoding rebus readings:

Line 1
koḍi 'flag' (Ta.)(DEDR 2049). Rebus: koḍ, 'artisan's workshop' (Kuwi.)
kunda 'turner' kundār turner (A.)
sal 'splinter'; rebus: sal 'workshop' (Santali)
Fish + sloping stroke, aya dhāḷ 'metal ingot' (Vikalpa: ḍhāḷ = a slope; the inclination of a plane (G.) Rebus: : ḍhāḷako = a large metal ingot (G.)
meḍ 'body' (Mu.); rebus: meḍ 'iron' (Ho.)ḍabe, ḍabea 'large horns, with a sweeping upward curve, applied to buffaloes' (Santali) Rebus: ḍab, ḍhimba, ḍhompo 'lump (ingot?)', clot, make a lump or clot, coagulate, fuse, melt together (Santali) Thus, horned body glyph decodes rebus: *ḍab meḍ* 'iron (metal) ingot'.
kaṇḍa kanka 'furnace scribe (account)' kaṇḍ kanka 'rim of jar'; Rebus: karṇaka 'scribe'; kaṇḍ 'furnace, fire-altar'. Thus the ligatured sign is decoded: kaṇḍ karṇaka 'furnace scribe.

Line 2
aya 'fish' (Mu.); rebus: aya 'metal' (G.)
dula 'pair' (Kashmiri); rebus: dul 'cast (metal)'
loa 'ficus religiosa' (Santali) rebus: loh 'metal' (Skt.) Rebus: lo 'copper'. Thus, lls de 'cast copper'
kaṇḍa kanka 'furnace scribe (account)'kaṇḍ kanka 'rim of jar'; Rebus: karṇaka 'scribe'; kaṇḍ 'furnace, fire-altar'. Thus the ligatured sign is decoded: kaṇḍ karṇaka 'furnace scribe

Line 3
kaṇḍa kanka 'furnace scribe (account)' kaṇḍ kanka 'rim of jar'; Rebus: karṇaka 'scribe'; kaṇḍ 'furnace, fire-altar'. Thus the ligatured sign is decoded: kaṇḍ karṇaka 'furnace scribe
aṭar 'a splinter'; aṭaruka 'to burst, crack, sli off,fly open; aṭarcca ' splitting, a crack'; aṭar ttuka 'to split, tear off, open (an oyster) (Ma.); aḍaruni 'to crack' (Tu.) (DEDR 66)
Rebus: aduru 'native, unsmelted metal' (Kannada)

Fish + scales aya ãs (amśu) 'metllic stalks of stone ore

k089 Twenty glyphs

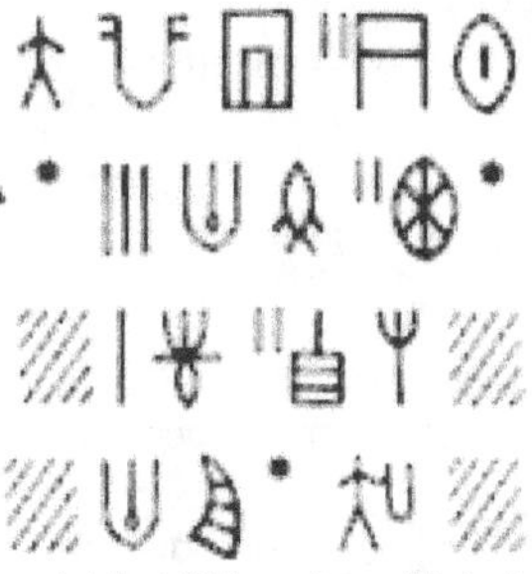

Kalibangan089. Multiple seal impression. 17 glyphs are recognized in the four or five impressions created by multiple (perhaps four or five) seals. Lothal has yielded 27 such multiple impressions, perhaps, on one package.

Line 1: (metal) ingot, guild workshop, stonework, furnace scribe (account), iron (metal)
Line 2: Turner's workshop, metal, ingot furnace, smithy/forge, (metal) furnace
Line 3: Smithy/forge, tin workshop, ingot forge, workshop
Line 4: metal furnace, workshop, smith/forge

Detailed decoding rebus readings:

Line 1
mũh 'metal ingot' (Santali) mũhã = the quantity of iron produced at one time in a native smelting furnace of the Kolhes; iron produced by the Kolhes and formed like a four-cornered piece a little pointed at each end; mūhā mẽṛhẽt = iron smelted by the Kolhes and formed into an equilateral lump a little pointed at each end; kolhe tehen me~ṛhe~t mūhā akata = the Kolhes have to-day produced pig iron (Santali.lex.)

Woṭ. Šen ' roof ', Bshk. Šan, Phal. Šān(AO xviii 251, followed by Buddruss Woṭ 126, < śar(a)ṇa -- ); Wpah. (Joshi) śannī f. ' small room in a house to keep sheep in '. Addenda: śaraṇá — 2. 2. *śarṇa — Wpah. Ktg.śɔ́nni f. ' bottom storey of a house in which young of cattle are kept '. Śaraṇá ' protecting ', n. ' shelter, home ' RV. 2. *śarṇa -- . [√śar] 1. Pa. Pk. Saraṇa — n. ' protection, shelter, house '; Ḍ. Šərɔ́n

m. ' roof ' (← Sh.?), Dm. šaran; P. saraṇ m. ' protection, asylum ', H. saran f.; G. sarṇū n. ' help '; Si.saraṇa ' defence, village, town '; -- < *śarāṇa — or poss. *śāraṇa -- : Kho. Šarān ' courtyard of a house ', Sh. Šarāṇū m. ' fence '. (CDIAL 12326)Rebus: seṇi (f.) [Class. Sk. Śreṇi in meaning "guild"; Vedic= row] 1. A guild Vin iv.226; J i.267, 314; iv.43; Dāvs ii.124; their number was eighteen J vi.22, 427; VbhA 466. ° -- pamukha the head of a guild J ii.12 (text seni -- ). — 2. A division of an army J vi.583; ratha -- ° J vi.81, 49; seṇimokkha the chief of an army J vi.371 (cp. Senā and seniya). (Pali) bharaḍo = cross-beam in the roof of a house (G.lex.) bhāraṭiyum, bhārvaṭiyo, bhāroṭiyo = a beam (G.lex.) bāri = bamboo splits fastened lengthwise to the rafters of a roof from both sides (Tu.lex.) bārapaṭṭe = chief beam lying on pillars (Te.lex.) bharaṇum a piece in architecture; placed at the top of a pillar to support a beam (G.) Rebus: bharatiyo = a caster of metals; a brazier; bharatar, bharatal, bharataḷ = moulded; an article made in a mould; bharata = casting metals in moulds; bharavum = to fill in; to put in; to pour into (G.lex.) bhart = a mixed metal of copper and lead; bhartīyā = a barzier, worker in metal; bhaṭ, bhrāṣṭra = oven, furnace (Skt.) Thus, the glyph 'roof + cross-beam' may read: bharaḍo šen; rebus: *bharatiyo seṇi* 'guild of casters of metal'.

sal 'splinter'; Rebus: sal 'workshop' (Santali) Thus the entire glyphic: 'roof+cross-beam+splinter' may read: *bharatiyo seṇi sal* 'workshop (of) guild of casters of metal'.

L. ḍhok f. ' hut in the fields '; Ku. ḍhwākā m. pl. ' gates of a city or market '; N. ḍhokā (pl. of *ḍhoko) ' door '; -- Omarw. ḍhokaro m. ' basket '; -- N. ḍhokse ' place covered with a mat to store rice in, large basket '. (CDIAL 6880) धोंगडा [ dhōṅgaḍā ] m धोंगडें n Coarse mean clothes: also a coarse mean garment or cloth. Pr. गांडीं घोंगडा पोटाला तुकडा. Rebus: *ḍhōkka2 ' rock '. 2. *ḍhōṅka -- . [Perh. Belongs to same group as *ḍōṅga — 2 s.v. *ṭakka — 3] 1. Kho. (Lor.) ḍok ' high ground, hillock, heap '; H. ḍhok m. ' large piece of broken stone '. 2. Ku. ḍhūgo ' stone ', N. ḍhuṅgo.(CDIAL 5603)

kaṇḍa kanka 'furnace scribe (account)'
meḍ 'body' (Mu.); rebus: meḍ 'iron' (Ho.)

Line 2
Turner workshop: kund opening in the nave or hub of a wheel to admit the axle (Santali) Rebus: kundam, kund a sacrificial fire-pit (Skt.) kunda 'turner' kundār turner (A.)
sal 'splinter'; rebus: sal 'workshop' (Santali)
aya 'fish' (Mu.); rebus: aya 'metal' (G.)
S. baṭhu m. 'large pot in which grain is parched, Rebus; bhaṭṭhā m. 'kiln' (P.) baṭa = a kind of iron (G.)
Vikalpa: meṛgo = rimless vessels (Santali) bhaṭa 'furnace' (G.) baṭa = kiln (Santali); baṭa = a kind of iron (G.) bhaṭṭha — m.n. ' gridiron (Pkt.) baṭhu large cooking fire' baṭhī f. 'distilling furnace'; L. bhaṭṭh m. 'grain—parcher's oven', bhaṭṭhī f. 'kiln, distillery', awāṇ. Bhaṭh; P. bhaṭṭh m., ṭhī f. 'furnace', bhaṭṭhā m. 'kiln'; S. bhaṭṭhī keṇī 'distil (spirits)'. (CDIAL 9656)Rebus: meḍ iron (Ho.)
ḍabu 'an iron spoon' (Santali) Rebus: ḍab, ḍhimba, ḍhompo 'lump (ingot?)', clot, make a lump or clot, coagulate, fuse, melt together (Santali)
kolmo 'three' (Mu.); rebus: kolami 'smithy' (Te.)
kaṇḍa 'arrow'; Rebus: kaṇḍ = a furnace, altar (Santali)

Line 3
kolom = cutting, graft; to graft, engraft, prune; kolma hoṛo = a variety of the paddy plant (Desi)(Santali.)
kolmo 'rice plant' (Mu.) Rebus: kolami 'furnace,smithy' (Te.)
ranku 'liquid measure'; rebus: ranku 'tin' (Santali)
sal 'splinter'; rebus: sal 'workshop' (Santali)
Ligature of 'ingot' glyph + 'paddy plant' glyph: kolom +mũh 'smithy metal ingot'.
Glyph: one long linear stroke. Koḍa, koṛa = in arithmetic one; 4 koṛa or koḍa = 1 gaṇḍa = 4 (Santali)
Rebus: koḍ, 'artisan's workshop' (Kuwi.)

Line 4

meḍ 'body' (Mu.); rebus: meḍ 'iron' (Ho.) ligatured with 'pot' glyph. S. baṭhu m. 'large pot in which grain is parched, Rebus; bhaṭṭhā m. 'kiln' (P.) baṭa = a kind of iron (G.)
கோடு kōṭu : •நடுநிலை நீங்குகை. கோடிறீக் கூற் றம் (நாலடி, 5). 3. [K. kōḍu.] Tusk; யானை பன்றிகளின் தந்தம். மத்த யானையின் கோடும் (தேவா. 39, 1). 4. Horn; விலங்கின் கொம்பு. கோட்டிடை யாடினை கூத்து (திவ். இயற். திருவிருத். 21). Ta. Kōṭu (in cpds. Kōṭṭu-) horn, tusk, branch of tree, cluster, bunch, coil of hair, line, diagram, bank of stream or pool; kuvaṭu branch of a tree; kōṭṭāṉ, kōṭṭuvāṉ rock horned-owl (cf. 1657 Ta. Kuṭiñai). Ko. Kṛ (obl. Kṭ-) horns (one horn is kob), half of hair on each side of parting, side in game, log, section of bamboo used as fuel, line marked out. To. Kwṛ (obl. Kwṭ-) horn, branch, path across stream in thicket. Ka. Kōḍu horn, tusk, branch of a tree; kōṛ horn. Tu. Kōḍů, kōḍu horn. Te. Kōḍu rivulet, branch of a river. Pa. kōḍ (pl. kōḍul) horn (DEDR 2200)

Rebus: koḍ, 'artisan's workshop' (Kuwi.)

S. baṭhu m. 'large pot in which grain is parched, Rebus; bhaṭṭhā m. 'kiln' (P.) baṭa = a kind of iron (G.) Vikalpa: meṛgo = rimless vessels (Santali) bhaṭa 'furnace' (G.) baṭa = kiln (Santali); baṭa = a kind of iron (G.) bhaṭṭha — m.n. ' gridiron (Pkt.) baṭhu large cooking fire' baṭhī f. 'distilling furnace'; L. bhaṭṭh m. 'grain—parcher's oven', bhaṭṭhī f. 'kiln, distillery', awāṇ. Bhaṭh; P. bhaṭṭh m., ṭhī f. 'furnace', bhaṭṭhā m. 'kiln'; S. bhaṭṭhī keṇī 'distil (spirits)'. (CDIAL 9656)Rebus: meḍ iron (Ho.)

ḍabu 'an iron spoon' (Santali) Rebus: ḍab, ḍhimba, ḍhompo 'lump (ingot?)', clot, make a lump or clot, coagulate, fuse, melt together (Santali)
Dholavira signboard.

Each glyph is 35 cm to 37 cm tall and 25 cm to 27 cm wide. The 10 signs constitute a work of great craftsmanship. Each sign is made of several pieces, which have been inlaid on a wooden board.

The signboard must have been placed above the north gate of the citadel that existed at the Harappan city of Dholavira. All the signs are made of thoroughly baked gypsum and their white brilliance must have made the board visible from afar.

A clear indication that the hieroglyphs were recognizable across a vast interaction area. According to Indus Script Cipher, this represents perhaps the first advertisement hoarding atop the gateway of a citadel visible to navigators on ships and boats traversing the Persian Gulf.

http://www.gujarattourism.com/showpage.aspx?contentid=55&webpartid=58

Three types of metallurgical services are announced.
Segment 1: Mint, merchant: mineral, metal infusion, turner-carver

Claws of crab 'kamaṭha'; rebus: kampaṭṭam 'mint'; Vikalpa: ḍato = claws of crab (Santali); dhātu = mineral (Skt.)
Nave of wheel: eraka; rebus: eraka, (copper) 'metal infusion';kund opening in the nave or hub of a wheel to admit the axle (Santali) kundam, kund a sacrificial fire-pit (Skt.) : kundār turner (A.); kūdār, kūdāri (B.); kundāru (Or.); kundau to turn on a lathe, to carve, to chase; kundau dhiri = a hewn stone; kundau murhut = a graven image (Santali)
barea = two (Ka.); baṛea = blacksmith (Santali)[A pair of glyphs showing nave of wheel, i.e. metal-caster-smith] Vikalpa: dul 'cast metal'; dol 'likeness'

Segment 2: Silver, native metal, turner-carver

One 'met'; rebus: meḍ 'iron'; vikalpa: goṭ = one (Santali); goṭi = silver (G.)
aḍaren, ḍaren lid, cover (Santali) Rebus: aduru 'native metal' (Ka.)
kana, kanac = corner (Santali); kañcu = bronze (Te.) kan- copper work (Ta.)
kund opening in the nave or hub of a wheel to admit the axle (Santali) kundam, kund a sacrificial fire-pit (Skt.) : kundār turner (A.); kūdār, kūdāri (B.); kundāru (Or.); kundau to turn on a lathe, to carve, to chase; kundau dhiri = a hewn stone; kundau murhut = a graven image (Santali)

Segment 3: Copper mint, workshop, turner-carver

Fig leaf 'loa'; rebus: loh '(copper) metal' kamaḍha = ficus religiosa (Skt.); kamaṭa = portable furnace for melting precious metals (Te.); kampaṭṭam = mint (Ta.)
Peg 'khuṇṭa'; rebus: kūṭa 'workshop'
khūṭi = pin (M.) kuṭi= furnace (Santali)
kund opening in the nave or hub of a wheel to admit the axle (Santali) kundam, kund a sacrificial fire-pit (Skt.) : kundār turner (A.); kūdār, kūdāri (B.); kundāru (Or.); kundau to turn on a lathe, to carve, to chase; kundau dhiri = a hewn stone; kundau murhut = a graven image (Santali)
The three animals: buffalo, rhinoceros, elephant occur together with a leaping tiger on a seal. cf. Decoding of animal glyphs and other glyphs on the seal as related to lapidaries/metalsmith/metalwork artisan guild/mint Indus script cipher: Hieroglyphs of Indian linguistic area (2010)

Reconstructed as a seal impression using seal m0304 creating a pair of antelopes and a pair of hayricks below the platform (stool) base (After J. Huntington). Mohenjo-daro seal m0304

Rebus readings of hieroglyphs on m0304 (both pictorial motifs + sign glyphs, in two lines)

Note: There are over 27 clearly identifiable, glyphic elements on the seal m0304 (both animal glyphs plus text sign glyphs). Each glyphic element (hieroglyph) is decoded, read rebus.

A person is shown seated in 'penance'.

kamaḍha 'penance' (Pkt.) Rebus: kammaṭi a coiner (Ka.); kampaṭṭam coinage, coin, mint (Ta.)

kammaṭa = mint, gold furnace (Te.) Thus, the over-arching message of the inscription composed of many hieroglyphs (of glyphic elements) thus is a description of the offerings of a 'mint or coiner (workshop with a golf furnace)'.

Rebus readings of the horned head-dress:

tāttāru 'buffalo horns' (Munda); Rebus: ṭhaṭhero 'brassworker'(Ku.) cūḍā, cūlā, cūliyā tiger's mane (Pkt.)(CDIAL 4883) Vikalpa: kuṇḍī = crooked buffalo horns (L.) Rebus: kuṇḍī = chief of village. Kuṇḍi-a = village headman; leader of a village (Pkt.lex.) I.e. śreṇi jeṭṭha chief of metal-worker guild. kūṭī = bunch of twigs (Skt.) Rebus: kuṭhi = furnace (Santali) Vikalpa: clump between the two horns: kuṇḍa n. ' clump ' e.g. darbha—kuṇḍa—Pāṇ.(CDIAL 3236). Kundār turner (A.)(CDIAL 3295). : kundār turner (A.); kūdār, kūdāri (B.); kundāru (Or.); kundau to turn on a lathe, to carve, to chase; kundau dhiri = a hewn stone; kundau murhut = a graven image (Santali) kunda a turner's lathe (Skt.)(CDIAL 3295) Vikalpa: kūdī, kūṭī 'bunch of twigs' (Skt.) Rebus: kuṭhi 'smelter furnace' (Santali)

Rebus reading of glyphic elements of the 'bristled (tiger's mane) face':

There are two glyphic elements denoted on the face.

mũh 'face'; rebus: metal ingot (Santali) mũhā̃ = the quantity of iron produced at one time in a native smelting furnace of the Kolhes; iron produced by the Kolhes and formed like a four-cornered piece a little pointed at each end; mūhā mẽṛhẽt = iron smelted by the Kolhes and formed into an equilateral lump a little pointed at each end; kolhe tehen me~ṛhe~t mūhā akata = the Kolhes have to-day produced pig iron (Santali.lex.)

Shoggy hair; tiger's mane. *Sodo bodo, sodro bodro* adj. adv. Rough, hairy, shoggy, hirsute, uneven;*sodo* [Persian. *Sodā*, dealing] trade; traffic; merchandise; marketing; a bargain; the purchase or sale of goods; buying and selling; mercantile dealings (G.lex.) sodagor = a merchant, trader;*sodāgor* (P.B.) (Santali.lex.) The face is depicted with bristles of hair, representing a tiger's mane.*cūḍā, cūlā, cūliyā* tiger's mane (Pkt.)(CDIAL 4883).Rebus: cūḷai 'furnace, kiln, funeral pile' (Te.)(CDIAL 4879; DEDR 2709). Thus the composite glyphic composition: 'bristled (tiger's mane) face' is read rebus as: sodagor mũh cūḷa 'furnace (of) ingot merchant'.

Reading the glyphic elements on the chest of the person and arms:

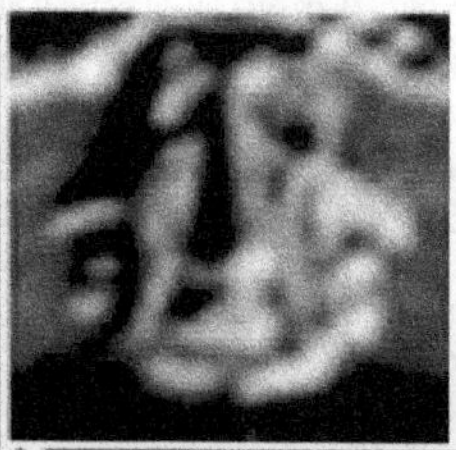

kamarasāla = waist-zone, waist-band, belt (Te.) karmāraśāla = workshop of blacksmith (Skt.) kamar 'blacksmith' (Santali)

sekeseke, sekseke covered, as the arms with ornaments;

Rebus: sekra those who work in brass and bell metal; sekra sakom a kind of armlet of bell metal (Santali) Vikalpa: bāhula n. armour for the arms (Skt.) Rebus: బంగల bangala. [Tel.] n. An oven. కుంపటి. (Telugu) Vikalpa: cūri 'bangles' (H.) Rebus: cūḷai 'furnace, kiln, funeral pile' (Te.)(CDIAL

4879; DEDR 2709).

Thus, together, the glyphic elements on the chest of the person and arms are read rebus: sekra karmāraśāla 'brass/bell-metal workshop of smith (with) furnace'.

Glyphic compositions on the base on which the person is seated; hence, the rebus readings of glyphics: stool, pair of hayricks, pair of antelopes.

Kur. Kaṇḍō a stool. Malt. Kanḍo stool, seat. (DEDR 1179) Rebus: kaṇḍ = a furnace, altar (Santali.lex.) mēṭu, mēṭa, mēṭi stack of hay (Te.)(DEDR 5058). Rebus: meḍ 'iron' (Ho.) Vikalpa: kuntam 'haystack' (Te.)(DEDR 1236) Rebus: kuṇḍamu 'a pit for receiving and preserving consecrated fire' (Te.)

A pair of hayricks, a pair of antelopes: mēṭu, mēṭa, mēṭi stack of hay (Te.)(DEDR 5058). Rebus: meḍ 'iron' (Ho.) Vikalpa: kundavum = manger, a hayrick (G.) Rebus: kundār turner (A.); kūdār, kūdāri (B.); kundāru (Or.); kundau to turn on a lathe, to carve, to chase; kundau dhiri = a hewn stone; kundau murhut = a graven image (Santali) kunda a turner's lathe (Skt.)(CDIAL 3295) Thus, a pair of haystacks can be read as phonetic determinatives of a pair of antelopes.

Decoding a pair: dula दुल । युग्मम् m. a pair, a couple, esp. of two similar things (Rām. 966) (Kashmiri); dol 'likeness, picture, form' (Santali) Rebus: dul 'to cast metal in a mould' (Santali) dul meṛeḍ cast iron (Mundari. Santali)

Antelope: miṇḍāl 'markhor' (Tōrwālī) meḍho a ram, a sheep (G.)(CDIAL 10120); rebus: mēṛhēt, meḍ 'iron' (Mu.Ho.)

Glyph: krammara 'look back' (Te.); Rebus: kamar 'smith' (Santali) Vikalpa 1: mlekh 'antelope'(Br.); milakkhu 'copper' (Pali) Vikalpa 2: kala stag, buck (Ma.) Rebus: kallan mason (Ma.); kalla glass beads (Ma.); kalu stone (Konḍa); xal id., boulder (Br.)(DEDR 1298). Rebus: kallan 'stone-bead-maker'.

Thus, together, the glyphs on the base of the platform are decoded rebus:*meḍ kamar dul meṛeḍ (vikalpa: kūdār)*,'iron (metal) smith, casting (metal) (Vikalpa: ku *kūdār* 'turner').

Animal glyphs around the seated person, glyphics: buffalo (*sal*), boar (rhinoceros, *baḍhoe*), elephant (*ib*), tiger (jumping, *kūdā kol*).

The four animal glyphs surrounding the seated person thus connote, rebus: workshop (*sal*), worker in both iron and wood (*baḍhi*), merchant (*ibbho*), turner-smith (*kūdā kol*),

sal '*bos gaurus*'; rebus: sal 'workshop' (Santali) Vikalpa 1: ran:gā 'buffalo'; ran:ga 'pewter or alloy of tin (ran:ku), lead (nāga) and antimony (añjana)'(Santali) Vikalpa 2: kaṭamā 'bison' (Ta.)(DEDR 1114) Rebus: kaḍiyo [Hem. Des. Kaḍa-i-o = (Skt. Sthapati, a mason) a bricklayer, mason (G.)]

baḍhia = a castrated boar, a hog (Santali) Rebus: baḍhi 'a caste who work both in iron and wood' (Santali) baḍhoe 'a carpenter, worker in wood'; badhoria 'expert in working in wood'(Santali)

ibha 'elephant' (Skt.) Rebus: ibbho 'merchant' (cf.Hemacandra, *Desinamamala*, vaṇika). ib 'iron' (Santali) karibha 'elephant' (Skt.); rebus: karb 'iron' (Ka.)

kolo, koleā 'jackal' (Kon.Santali); kola kukur 'white tiger' (A.); कोल्हा [ kōlhā ] कोल्हें [ kōlhēṃ ] (Marathi) Rebus: kol pañcaloha 'five metals'(Ta.); kol 'furnace, forge' (Kuwi) Ta. kol working in iron, blacksmith; kollaṉ blacksmith. Ma. kollan blacksmith, artificer. Ko. kole·l smithy, temple in Kota village; kolhali to forge (DEDR 2133) kūrda m. ' jump ', gūrda -- m. ' jump ' Kāṭh. [√kūrd] S. kuḏu m. ' leap ', N. kud, Or. kuda, °dā, kudā -- kudi ' jumping about

'.kū´rdati ' leaps, jumps ' MBh. [gū´rdati, khū´rdatē Dhātup.: prob. ← Drav. (Tam. kuti, Kan. gudi ' to spring ') T. Burrow BSOAS xii 375]S. kuḏaṇu ' to leap '; L. kuḏaṇ ' to leap, frisk, play '; P. kuddṇā ' to leap ', Ku. kudṇo, N. kudnu, B. kūdā, kōdā; Or. kudibā ' to jump, dance '; Mth. kūdab ' to jump ', Aw. lakh. kūdab, H. kūdnā, OMarw. kūdaï, G. (CDIAL 3411, 3412) Rebus: kunda 'turner' kundār turner (A.) Vikalpa: puṭi 'to jump'; puṭa 'calcining of metals'. Pouncing tiger glyph is read rebus: kūdā kol 'turner smith'. Allograph: ஏறு ēṟu Pouncing upon, as an eagle; பருந்தின் கவர்ச்சி. பரிந்தி னேறுகுறித் தொரீஇ (புறநா. 43, 5). Rebus: eruvai 'copper' (Ta.); ere dark red (Ka.)(DEDR 446).

Thus, together, the set of animals surround the seated person are decoded rebus: ran:ga baḍhi karb kol dhātu puṭi '(worker in) pewter, iron & wood, iron(metal) forge/furnace for calcining metals.

Decoding the text of the inscription

Text 2420 on m0304

Line 2 (bottom): 'body' glyph. Mēd 'body' (Kur.)(DEDR 5099); meḍ 'iron' (Ho.)

Line 1 (top):

'Body' glyph plus ligature of 'splinter' shown between the legs: mēd 'body' (Kur.)(DEDR 5099); meḍ 'iron' (Ho.) sal 'splinter'; Rebus: sal 'workshop' (Santali) Thus, the ligatured glyph is read rebus as:*meḍ sal* 'iron (metal) workshop'.

Sign 216 (Mahadevan). ḍato 'claws or pincers (chelae) of crabs'; ḍaṭom, ḍiṭom to seize with the claws or pincers, as crabs, scorpions; ḍaṭkop = to pinch, nip (only of crabs) (Santali) Rebus: dhatu 'mineral' (Santali) Vikalpa: erā 'claws'; Rebus: era 'copper'. Allograph: kamaṛkom = fig leaf (Santali.lex.) kamarmaṛā (Has.), kamaṛkom (Nag.); the petiole or stalk of a leaf (Mundari.lex.) kamat.ha = fig leaf, religiosa (Skt.)

Sign 229. Sannī, sannhī = pincers, smith's vice (P.) śannī f. ' small room in a house to keep sheep in ' (Wpah.) Bshk. Šan, Phal.šān 'roof' (Bshk.)(CDIAL 12326). Seṇi (f.) [Class. Sk. Śreṇi in meaning "guild"; Vedic= row] 1. A guild Vin iv.226; J i.267, 314; iv.43; Dāvs ii.124; their number was eighteen J vi.22, 427; VbhA 466. ° -- pamukha the head of a guild J ii.12 (text seni -- ). — 2. A division of an army J vi.583; ratha -- ° J vi.81, 49; seṇimokkha the chief of an army J vi.371 (cp. Senā and seniya). (Pali)

Sign 342. Kaṇḍa kanka 'rim of jar' (Santali): karṇaka rim of jar'(Skt.) Rebus: karṇaka 'scribe, accountant' (Te.); gaṇaka id. (Skt.) (Santali) copper fire-altar scribe (account)(Skt.) Rebus: kaṇḍ 'fire-altar' (Santali) Thus, the 'rim of jar' ligatured glyph is read rebus: fire-altar (furnace) scribe (account)

Sign 344. Ligatured glyph: 'rim of jar' ligature + splinter (infixed); 'rim of jar' ligature is read rebus: kaṇḍa karṇaka 'furnace scribe (account)'.

sal stake, spike, splinter, thorn, difficulty (H.); Rebus: sal 'workshop' (Santali) *ஆலை³ ālai, n. < šālā. 1. Apartment, hall; சாலை. ஆலைசேர் வேள்வி (தேவா. 844. 7). 2. Elephant stable or stall; யானைக்கூடம். களிறு சேர்ந் தல்கிய வழுங்க லாலை (புறநா. 220, 3).ஆலைக்குழி ālai-k-kuḻi, n. < ஆலை¹ +. Receptacle for the juice underneath a sugar-cane press; கரும்பாலையிற் சாறேற்கும் அடிக்கலம்.*ஆலைத்தொட்டி ālai-t-toṭṭi, n. < id. +. Cauldron for boiling sugar-cane juice; கருப்பஞ் சாறு காய்ச்சும் சால்.ஆலைபாய்-தல் ālai-pāy-, v. intr. < id. +. 1. To work a sugar-cane mill; ஆலையாட்டுதல். ஆலைபாயோதை (சேதுபு. நாட்டு. 93). 2. To move, toss, as a ship; அலைவுறுதல். (R.) 3. To be undecided, vacillating; மனஞ் சுழலுதல். நெஞ்ச மாலைபாய்ந் துள்ள மழிகின்றேன் (அருட்பா,) Vikalpa: sal 'splinter'; rebus: workshop (sal)' ālai 'workshop' (Ta.) *ஆலை³ ālai, n. < šālā. 1. Apartment, hall; சாலை. ஆலைசேர் வேள்வி (தேவா. 844. 7). 2. Elephant stable or stall; யானைக்கூடம். களிறு சேர்ந் தல்கிய வழுங்க லாலை (புறநா. 220, 3).ஆலைக்குழி ālai-k-kuḻi, n. < ஆலை¹ +. Receptacle for the juice underneath a sugar-cane press; கரும்பாலையிற் சாறேற்கும் அடிக்கலம்.*ஆலைத்தொட்டி ālai-t-toṭṭi, n. < id. +. Cauldron for boiling sugar-cane juice; கருப்பஞ் சாறு காய்ச்சும் சால்.ஆலைபாய்-தல் ālai-pāy-, v. intr. < id. +. 1. To work a sugar-cane mill; ஆலையாட்டுதல். ஆலைபாயோதை (சேதுபு. நாட்டு. 93) Thus, together with the 'splinter' glyph, the entire ligature 'rim of jar + splinter/splice' is read rebus as: furnace scribe (account workshop). Sign 59. Ayo, hako 'fish'; a~s = scales of fish (Santali); rebus: aya = iron (G.); ayah, ayas = metal (Skt.) Sign 342. Kaṇḍa karṇaka 'rim of jar'; rebus: 'furnace scribe (account)'. Thus the inscription reads rebus: iron, iron (metal) workshop, copper (mineral) guild, fire-altar (furnace) scribe (account workshop), metal furnace scribe (account) As the decoding of m0304 seal demonstrates, the Indus hieroglyphs are the professional repertoire of an artisan (miners'/metalworkers') guild detailing the stone/mineral/metal resources/furnaces/smelters of workshops (smithy/forge/turners' shops).

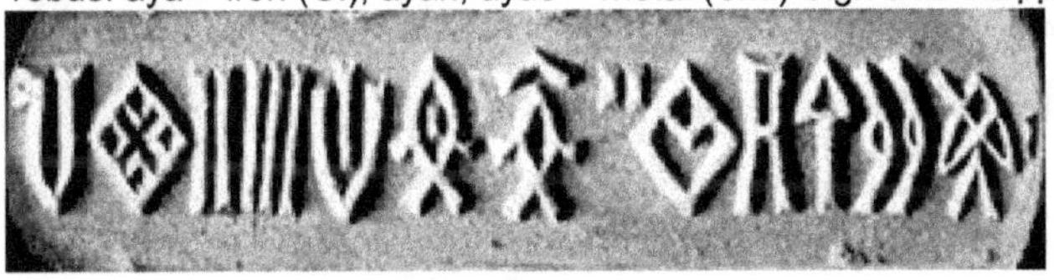

Slide 14. Sealing.
One of the longer inscriptions made from a seal found during Mackay's excavations between 1927-1931 in Mohenjo-daro (D.K. 9134).

The message translation – as a description of the trade load for the bill of lading: Furnace cast excellent iron smithy guild workshop; turning native metal iron smelter furnace/smithy blacksmith. Guild furnace scribe account. [The rhomboid glyph with four corners orthographically identified by denote four smiths' whose account is consolidated by this seal impression called a 'sealing'. Three or four such seal impressions would have completed the descriptions of trade loads meant as consignments to trade partners in interaction areas.]

> Glyph reading: bhaṭa (soldier), dul (pair, eye pupil), kaṇḍa (arrow), kole.l (temple), khũṭ (corner), sal (splinter), ayas kōṇṭu (angle + fish), ayas aḍaruni (crack + fish), mēḍhā baṭa (forked stake + rimless pot), kolmo barea (three + two), khũṭ (corner), kaṇḍ kanka (rim of jar)

Rebus decoding of glyphs: bhaṭa (furnace), dul (casting), kaṇḍa (excellent iron), kole.l (smithy), khũṭ (guild), sal (workshop), ayas kōdā (iron turned in a lathe), ayas aḍar (native metal iron), meḍh baṭa (iron furnace or smelter), kolami baṛea (furnace/'smithy blacksmith)', khũṭ (guild), kaṇḍ kanka (furnace account scribe).

Meluhha/mleccha semantics of some glyphs are explained further:

'Soldier' glyph: Pa. bhaṭa -- m. ' hireling, servant, soldier '; Pk. bhaḍa -- m. ' soldier ', bhaḍaa -- m. ' member of a non -- Aryan tribe '; bhr̥ta m. ' hireling, mercenary ' Yājñ.com., bhr̥taka -- m. ' hired servant ' Mn.: > MIA. bhaṭa -- m. ' hired soldier, servant ' MBh. [√bhr̥]; B. bhaṛ ' soldier, servant, nom. prop. ', bhaṛil ' servant, hero '; G. bhaṛ m. ' warrior, hero, opulent person ', adj. ' strong, opulent ', ubhaṛ m. ' landless worker ' (G. cmpd. with u -- , ' without ', i.e. ' one without servants '?); Si. beḷē ' soldier ' < *baḷaya, st. baḷa -- Addenda: bhr̥ta -- : S.kcch. bhaṛ ' brave '; Garh. (Śrīnagrī dial.) bhɔṛ, (Salānī dial.) bheṛ ' warrior ' (CDIAL 9588).Si. baḷām ' warfare ' (CDIAL 9589).Ku. bhaṛau ' song about the prowess of ancient heroes '. (CDIAL 9590). படை[2] paṭai , n. < படு[2]-. [K. paḍe.] 1. Army; சேனை. (பிங்.) படையியங் கரவம் (தொல். பொ. 58). 2. Forces for the defence of a kingdom, of six kinds, viz., mūla-p-paṭai, kūli-p-paṭai, nāṭṭu-p-paṭai, kāṭṭu-p-paṭai, tuṇai-p-paṭai, pakai-p-paṭai;Colloq. 4. Relations and attendants; பரிவாரம். அவன் படைகளுக்கு யார் போட்டுமுடியும்? 5. Weapons, arms of any kind; ஆயுதம். தொழுதகை யுள்ளும் படையொடுங்கும் (குறள், 828). 6. Instrument, implement, tool; கருவி. A sledge-like weapon, used in war; முசுண்டி. (பிங்.) Ta. paṭai army, crowd, weapons, battle. Ma. paṭa battle, army. To. paṛ crowd; fight (in songs). Ka. paḍe multitude, host, force, army; paḍeyila soldier; paḍevaḷa, paḍevaḷḷa a general. Tu. paḍè multitude, mob, army. Te. paḍava fight, battle; paḍavalamu van of an army; paḍavālu commander of an army. (DEDR 3860).

Rebus: bhaṭa 'furnace'. OA. bhāthi ' bellows ' AFD 206. N. bhā̃ṭi ' bellows ', H. bhāṭhī f.

Allograph: 'quiver, skinbag (bellows)' glyph: Pa. bhastā -- f. ' bellows ' (cf. vāta -- puṇṇa -- bhasta -- camma -- n. ' goat's skin full ofwind '), biḷāra -- bhastā -- f. ' catskin bag ', bhasta -- n. ' leather sack (for flour) '; K. khāra -- basta f. ' blacksmith's skin bellows '; -- S. bathī f. ' quiver ' (< *bhathī); A. Or. bhāti ' bellows ', Bi. bhāthī, (S of Ganges) bh̃āthī; OAw. bhāthā̆ ' quiver '; H. bhāthā m. ' quiver ', bhāthī f. ' bellows '; G. bhāthɔ, bhātɔ, bhāthṛɔ m. ' quiver ' (whence bhāthī m. ' warrior '); M. bhātā m. ' leathern bag, bellows, quiver ', bhātaḍ n. ' bellows, quiver '; bhástrā f. ' leathern bag ' ŚBr., ' bellows ' Kāv., bhastrikā -- f. ' little bag ' Daś.(CDIAL 9424).

Allograph: 'ploughshare' glyph: படை² paṭai Ploughshare; கலப்பை. (பிங்.) படை யுழ வெழுந்த பொன்னும் (கம்பரா. நாட்டு. 7).

Or. doḷā, ḍoḷā 'pupil of eye'(CDIAL 6582); Allograph: ḍol 'the shaft of an arrow, an arrow' (Santali) dula 'pair' (Kashmiri) Rebus: dul 'casting' (Santali)

kaṇḍa 'arrow' (Skt.) Rebus: 'excellent (iron)' as in: ayaskāṇḍa 'a quantity of iron, excellent iron' (Pāṇ.gaṇ.)

Seam impressions as imports of trade goods into Harappa

These are three seal impressions. Eash impression is created by two seals. The excavators surmise that these are imports are into Harappa since the clay used is different from clay found near Harappa.

Slide 138. Three clay sealings from the Harappa Phase levels (2600-1900 BC) that may have come from large bundles of goods shipped to the site from a distant region. The clay does not appear to be the same type of clay as found near Harappa and each sealing has the impression of two different seals.

A pair of glyphs on the bottom seal are 'bow' glyphs. kāmaṭhum = a bow (G.) Rebus: kammaṭi a coiner (Ka.); kampaṭṭam coinage, coin, mint (Ta.) kammaṭa = mint, gold furnace (Te.) dula 'pair' (Kashmiri) Rebus: dul 'casting (metal)(Santali). Read rebus, the pair of glyphs may connote the imports are imports of cast (metal) from a coiner workshop (or mint).

Decoding inscription on a Mohenjo-daro tablet (m1405) and 'rim-of-jar' Indus script glyph

Glyph 'rim-of-jar' is the most frequently occurring text glyph on Indus script inscriptions. It is decoded: kaṇḍ kan-ka, 'rim-of-jar'; rebus: 'furnace account (scribe)' (Santali).

Glyphs on m1405 tablet inscription: (ox, trough, body-shoulder, rim-of-jar, water-carrier)

Decoding: Blacksmith, stone-merchant, copper (metal) smelter-scribe (arrow-maker) - ḍangur, pattar, meḍ eraka, kaṇḍ kan-ka kuṭhi

Indus inscription on a Mohenjo-daro tablet (m1405) including 'rim-of-jar' glyph as component of a ligatured glyph (Sign 15 Mahadevan)

This tablet is a clear and unambiguous example of the fundamental orthographic style of Indus Script inscriptions that: both signs and pictorial motifs are integral components of the message conveyed by the inscriptions. Attempts at 'deciphering' only what is called a 'sign' in Parpola or Mahadevan corpuses will result in an incomplete decoding of the complete message of the inscribed object.

This inscribed object is decoded as a professional calling card: a blacksmith-precious-stone-merchant with the professional role of copper-miner-smelter-furnace-scribe.

m1405At Pict-97: Person standing at the center points with his right hand at a bison facing a trough, and with his left hand points to the ligatured glyph.

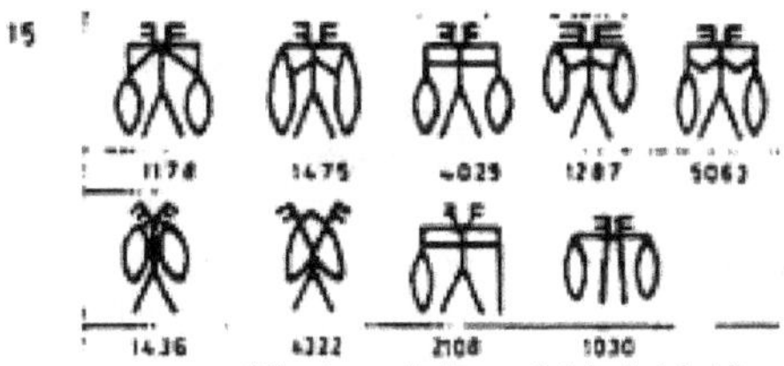

The inscription on the tablet juxtaposes – through the hand gestures of a person - a 'trough' gestured with the right hand; a ligatured glyph composed of 'rim-of-jar' glyph and 'water-carrier' glyph (Sign 15) gestured with the left hand.

The inscription of this tablet is trough, shoulder (person), glyph ligatured to water-carrier

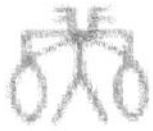

composed of four glyphs: bison, ligatured glyph -- Sign 15 (rim-of-jar glyph).

Variants for Sign 15

(Mahadevan)

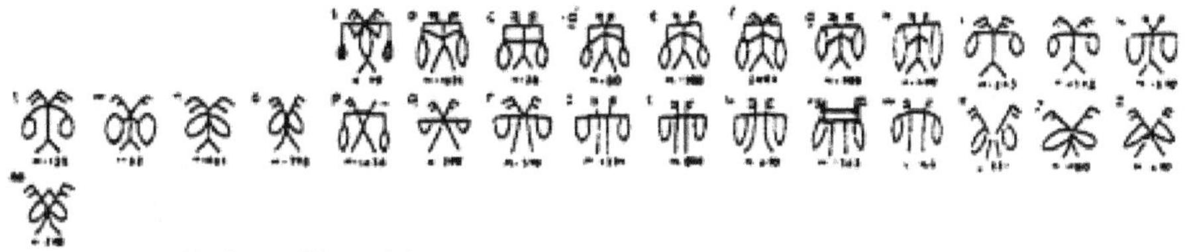

Variants (Parpola)

Each of these four glyphs can be read rebus in mleccha (meluhhan).

ḍangur m. 'bullock', rebus: ḍāṅro 'blacksmith' (N.)

*ḍagga -- 3 ' cattle '. 2. †*ḍhagga -- 2. [Cf. *ḍaṅgara -- 1, *daṅgara -- ] 1. WPah.kṭg. *ḍɔggɔ* m. 'a head of cattle', *ḍɔgge* m.pl. 'cattle', sat. (LSI ix 4, 667) *ḍōgai* ' cattle '.2. S.kcch. *ḍhago* m. ' ox ', L(Shahpur) *ḍhaggā* m. 'small weak ox', *ḍhaggī* f. ' cow ', Garh. *ḍhā̃gu* ' old bull '(CDIAL 5524a) *ḍaṅgara1 'cattle'. 2. *daṅgara -- . [Same as *ḍaṅ- gara* -- 2 s.v. *ḍagga -- 2 as a pejorative term for cattle]1. K. *ḍangur* m. 'bullock', L. *ḍaṅgur*, (Ju.) *ḍā̃gar* m. 'horned cattle'; P. *ḍaṅgar* m. 'cattle', Or. *ḍaṅgara*; Bi. *ḍā̃gar* 'old worn -- out beast, dead cattle', *dhūr ḍā̃gar* 'cattle in general'; Bhoj. *ḍāṅgar* 'cattle'; H. *ḍā̃gar*, *ḍā̃grā* m. ' horned cattle '. 2. H. *dā̃gar* m. = prec.(CDIAL 5526) Rebus: N. *ḍāṅro* ' term of contempt for a blacksmith' (CDIAL 5524) Vikalpa: sal 'bos gaurus'; rebus sal 'workshop' (Santali) <sayEl>(L) {N} ``^bison, wild ^buffalo''. #59041.

pattar 'trough' (Ta.), rebus paṭṭar-ai community; guild as of workmen (Ta.); pattar merchants (Ta.); perh. vartaka (Skt.) pātharī 'precious stone' (OMarw.) (CDIAL 8857)

meḍ 'body' (Mu.); rebus: meḍ 'iron' (Ho.); eṛaka 'upraised arm' (Ta.); rebus: eraka = copper (Ka.)

Ligature 1 in composite glyph: kan-ka 'rim of jar' (Santali), rebus karṇaka 'scribe, accountant' (Pa.); vikalpa: 1. kāraṇika -- m. 'arrow-maker' (Pa.) 2. khanaka 'miner, digger, excavator' (Skt.). Ligature 2 in composite glyph: kuṭi 'water-carrier' (Telugu), rebus: kuṭhi 'smelter furnace' (Santali)

The composite message is thus: blacksmith, merchant, copper smelter scribe.

Vikalpa: pattar 'trough'; rebus pattar, vartaka 'merchant'. பத்தல் pattal, n. பத்தர்[1] pattar 1. A wooden bucket; மரத்தாலான நீரிறைக்குங் கருவி. தீம்பிழி யெந்திரம் பத்தல் வருந்த (பதிற்றுப். 19, 23). பத்தர்[2] pattar , n. < T. battuḍu. A caste title of goldsmiths; தட்டார் பட்டப்பெயருள் ஒன்று. பட்டடை[1] paṭṭaṭai , n. prob. படு[1]- + அடை[1]-. 1. [T. paṭṭika, K. paṭṭaḍe.] Anvil; அடைகல். (பிங்.) சீரிடங்காணி னெறிதற்குப் பட்ட டை (குறள், 821). 2. [K. paṭṭaḍi.] Smithy, forge; கொல்லன் களரி பத்தல் pattal , n. 1. A wooden bucket; மரத்தாலான நீரிறைக்குங் கருவி. தீம்பிழி யெந்திரம் பத்தல் வருந்த (பதிற்றுப். 19, 23). பத்தர்[1] pattar , n. 1. See பத்தல், 1, 4, 5. 2. Wooden trough for feeding animals; தொட்டி. பன்றிக் கூழ்ப்பத்தரில் (நாலடி, 257).
paṭṭar-ai community; guild as of workmen (Ta.); pattar merchants; perh. vartaka (Skt.)

Patthara [cp. late Sk. prastara. The ord. meaning of Sk. pr. is "stramentum"] 1. stone, rock S i.32. -- 2. stoneware Miln 2. (Pali) Pa. Pk. patthara -- m. ' stone ', S. patharu m., L. (Ju.) pathar m., khet. patthar, P. patthar m. (→ forms of Bi. Mth. Bhoj. H. G. below with atth or ath), WPah.jaun. pātthar; Ku. pāthar m. ' slates, stones ', gng. pāth*lr ' flat stone '; A. B. pāthar ' stone ', Or. pathara; Bi. pāthar, patthar, patthal ' hailstone '; Mth. pāthar, pathal ' stone ', Bhoj. pathal, Aw.lakh. pāthar, H. pāthar, patthar, pathar, patthal m., G. patthar, pathrɔ m.; M. pāthar f. ' flat stone '; Ko. phāttaru ' stone '; Si. patura ' chip, fragment '; -- S. pathirī f. ' stone in the bladder '; P. pathrī f. ' small stone '; Ku. patharī ' stone cup '; B. pāthri ' stone in the bladder, tartar on teeth '; Or. pathurī ' stoneware '; H. patthrī f. ' grit ', G. pathrī f. *prastarapaṭṭa -- , *prastaramr̥ttikā -- , *prastarāsa -- .Addenda: prastará -- : WPah.kṭg. pátthər m. ' stone, rock '; pəthreuṇõ ' to stone '; J. pāthar m. ' stone '; OMarw. pātharī ' precious stone '. (CDIAL 8857)

paṭṭarai 'workshop' (Ta.) pattharika [fr. patthara] a merchant Vin ii.135 (kaŋsa˚).(Pali) cf. Pattharati [pa+tharati] to spread, spread out, extend J i.62; iv.212; vi.279; DhA i.26; iii.61 (so read at J vi.549 in cpd ˚pāda with spreading feet, v. l. patthaṭa˚). -- pp. patthaṭa (q. v.). பத்தர் pattar, n. perh. vartaka. Merchants; வியாபாரிகள். (W.) battuḍu. n. The caste title of all the five castes of artificers as vaḍla b*, carpenter.

'rim-of-jar' glyph

The orthography of 'jar' glyph (Sign 342) clearly emphasizes the 'rim' of a jar.

The orthographic focus is on the rim; karṇaka, kanaka; rebus: writer.

The rim of a jar is kaṇḍ kan-ka (Santali). kaṇḍ denotes

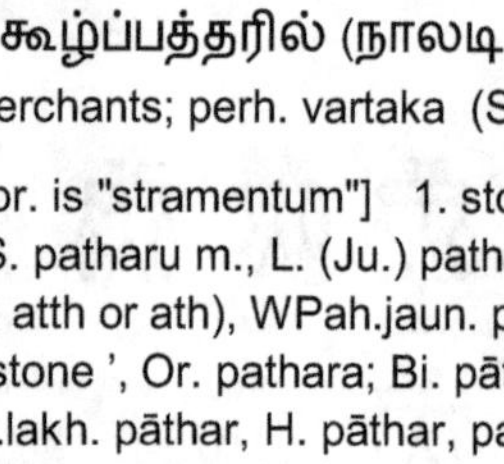

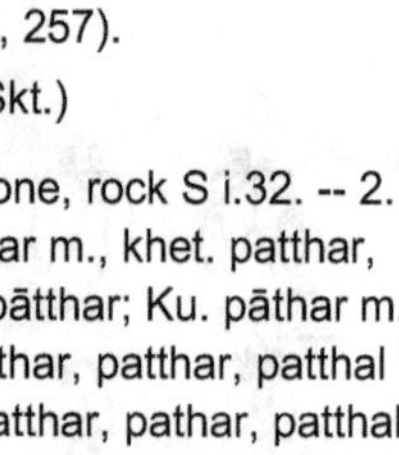

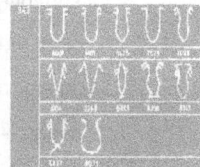

a brass pot; Rebus: kaṇḍ karṇaka 'furnace scribe' (Skt.)

Daimabad seal (ca. 1400 BCE) The orthography on this unique seal is vivid: the focus of the engraver is on the 'rim-of-jar'.

Sign 342 (and variants) is a 'rim-of-jar' glyph and has a frequency of 1395 occurrences in the corpus of inscriptions.

The glyph depicts a rimmed narrow-necked jar and has to be distinguished from Sign 328 which is a 'rimless, wide-mouthed' pot. Sign 328 has a frequency of 350 occurrences in the corpus of inscriptions.

m0478A On this tablet, 'lid' glyph is ligatued to a 'rim-of-jar' glyph.

ḍaren, aḍaren cover, lid (Santali); rebus: aduru 'native metal' (Ka.) Other glyphs of the tablet have been decoded: kola 'tiger, jackal' (Kon.); rebus: kol working in iron, blacksmith, 'alloy of five metals, panchaloha' (Tamil) kol 'furnace, forge' (Kuwi) kolami 'smithy' (Te.) erg a = act of clearing jungle (Kui) [Note image showing two men carrying uprooted trees]. This glyptic composition depicting the act of clearing jungle may be a phonetic determinant for the person seated on the tree branch and the glyph of a woman pushing them apart: eraka, hero = a messenger; a spy (G.lex.) heraka = spy (Skt.); er to look at or for (Pkt.); er uk- to play 'peeping tom' (Ko.) Rebus: eraka 'copper' (Ka.)

kol 'working in iron, blacksmith (Ta.); kollan- blacksmith (Ta.); kollan blacksmith, artificer (Ma.)(DEDR 2133) kolme = furnace (Ka.) kole.l 'temple, smithy' (Ko.); kolme smithy' (Ka.) kol = pañcaloha (five metals); kol metal (Ta.lex.) pan~caloha = a metallic alloy containing five metals: copper, brass, tin, lead and iron (Skt.); an alternative list of five metals: gold, silver, copper, tin (lead), and iron (dhātu;Nānārtharatnākara 82; Mangarāja's Nighaṇṭu. 498)(Ka.) kol, kolhe, 'the koles, an aboriginal tribe if iron smelters speaking a language akin to that of Santals' (Santali)

kuṭi 'water-carrier' (Telugu); Rebus: kuṭhi 'smelter furnace' (Santali)

k020 Glyphs: threaded beads + water-carrier. goṭā 'seed' (Bi.); goṭa 'numerative particle' (Mth.Hindi)(CDIAL 4271) Rebus: koṭe 'forging (metal)(Mu.)

Ligatured Hieroglyphs of Indus writing with rim-of-jar glyph as a component

Gadd notes that the 'water-carrier' seal is is an unmistakable example of an 'hieroglyphic' seal. Seal impression, Ur (Upenn; U.16747); [After Edith Porada, 1971, Remarks on seals found in the Gulf States. *Artibus Asiae* 33 (4): 331-7: pl.9, fig.5]; water carrier with a skin (or pot?) hung on each end of the yoke across his shoulders and another one below the crook of his left arm; the vessel on the right end of his yoke is over a receptacle for the water; a star on either side of the head (denoting supernatural?). The whole object is enclosed by 'parenthesis' marks. The parenthesis is perhaps a way of splitting of the ellipse (Hunter, G.R., JRAS, 1932, 476).

A trough is shown in front of some domesticated animals and also wild animals like rhinoceros, tiger, elephant. The trough glyph is clearly a hieroglyph, in fact, a category classifier. Trough as a glyph occurs on about one hundred inscriptions, though not identified as a distinct pictorial motif in the corpus of inscriptions. Why is a trough shown in front of a rhinoceros which was not a domesticated animal? A reasonable deduction is that 'trough' is a hieroglyph intended to classify the animal 'rhinoceros' in a category.

ḍhangar 'trough'; ḍhangar 'bull'; rebus: ḍhangar 'blacksmith'

The 'standard device' glyph denoted a stone artisan: sangataras. A 'trough' glyph in front of an animal denoted a stone-merchant-goldsmith: pattar.

The glyptic elements on m1405 are: 1. bison, 2. trough, 3. person lifting up his hand, 4. water-carrier. These are hieroglyphs decoded rebus.

1. bison sal 'bos gaurus'; rebus sal 'workshop' (Santali) śāla 'workshop' (Skt.) ālai 'workshop' (Ta.)

2. bison, trough ḍhangar 'trough'; ḍhangar 'bull'; rebus: ḍhangar 'blacksmith' Vikalpa: pātra 'trough'; patthar 'merchant' sal 'bos gaurus'; rebus: sal 'workshop'. Vikalpa (alternative): ḍangra 'bull'; rebus: d.hangar 'blacksmith'.

3. Water-carrier glyph kuṭi 'water-carrier' (Telugu); Rebus: kuṭhi 'smelter furnace' (Santali) kuṛī f. 'fireplace' (H.); krvṛI f. 'granary (WPah.); kuṛī, kuṛo house, building'(Ku.)(CDIAL 3232) kuṭi 'hut made of boughs' (Skt.) guḍi temple (Telugu) [The bull is shown in front of the trough for drinking; hence the semantics of 'drinking'.]

The most frequently occurring glyph is thus explained as a 'furnace scribe' and is consistent with the readings of glyphs which occur together with this glyph. Kan-ka may denote an artisan working with copper, kan̲ (Ta.) kan̲n̲ār 'coppersmiths, blacksmiths' (Ta.) Thus, the phrase kanḍ karṇaka may be decoded rebus as a brassworker, scribe. karṇaka 'scribe, accountant'.

A splinter glyph – two short strokes -- is ligatured within the rim of jar glyph. sal stake, spike, splinter, thorn, difficulty (H.); Rebus: sal 'workshop' (Santali)

kanka 'Rim of jar' (Santali); karṇaka rim of jar'(Skt.) Rebus: karṇaka 'scribe' (Te.); gaṇaka id. (Skt.) (Santali)

Text of inscription on m0892. This is one example of the orthographic emphasis on the 'rim' or 'handle' of the short-necked jar on two glyphs: one shows the rim and the other shows the rim and ligatures two short-strokes. The two short-strokes are a splinter; rebus: sal 'workshop' (Santali); śāla id. (Skt.). ālai id. (Tamil) The two signs thus read, rebus: furnace scribe, workshop furnace scribe.

m1179 The glyphs on this seal are: markhor, scarf, wavy (curved) lines, rim-of-jar.

miṇḍāl 'markhor' (Tōrwālī) meḍho a ram, a sheep (G.)(CDIAL 10120); rebus: mẽṛhet, meḍ 'iron' (Mu.Ho.) ['scarf' glyph is ligatured on the neck of markhor. Scarf [read rebus as dhaṭu m. (also dhaṭhu) m. 'scarf' (WPah.) (CDIAL 6707) Rebus: dhatu 'minerals' (Santali); dhātu 'mineral' (Pali)]. See Decoding standard device, heifer and scarf glyphs of Indus Script]

Wavy(curved) lines glyph is relatable to: kuṭi— in cmpd. 'curve' (Skt.)(CDIAL 3231).

kuṭika— 'bent' MBh. [√kuṭ 1] Ext. in H. kuṛuk f. 'coil of string or rope'; M. kuḍċā m. 'palm contracted and hollowed', kuḍapṇẽ 'to curl over, crisp, contract'. CDIAL 3231 kuṭilá— 'bent, crooked' KātyŚr., aka— Pañcat., n. 'a partic. plant' lex. [√kuṭ 1] Pa. kuṭila— 'bent', n. 'bend'; Pk. kuḍila— 'crooked', illa— 'humpbacked', illaya— 'bent' DEDR 2054 Ta. koṭu curved, bent, crooked; koṭumai crookedness, obliquity; koṭukki hooked bar for fastening doors, clasp of an ornament. A pair of curved lines: dol 'likeness, picture, form' [e.g., two tigers, two bulls, sign-pair.] Kashmiri. dula दुल । युग्मम् m. a pair, a couple, esp. of two similar things (Rām. 966). Rebus: dul meṛeḍ cast iron (Mundari. Santali) dul 'to cast metal in a mould' (Santali) pasra meṛed, pasāra meṛed = syn. of koṭe meṛed = forged iron, in contrast to dul meṛed, cast iron (Mundari.lex.) Rebus: kuṭhi 'smelter' (Santali)

Continuum of Indus script sign sequence on punch-marked coins

gotao to thread, to string; saire sutamko gotaca they thread needles (Santali) Rebus: goṭ, goṭh The place where cattle are collected at mid-day; got.ao, got.hao to collect cattle together for their mid-day rest (Santali) Rebus: kottaṉ a mason (Ta.) kotti pick-axe, stone-digger, carver (Ma.) (DEDR 2091) koḍ Artisans' workplace (G.) gotga.rn treasurer of the village (Ko.)(DEDR 2093) This sequence of chain of beads + rim-of-jar glyph survives on punch-marked coins.

kottukkāran- head of a company of labourers (Ta.); gottugār-a headman (Ka.)(DEDR 2093). goṭ Another name for the Sohrae festival; goṭ gai on the first day of the got. Puja or Sohrae in the evening all the cattle of the village are driven over an egg and the animal which treads on it is called the goṭ gai (Santali).

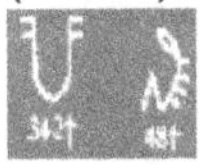


The pair of signs: 342 + 48 can be decoded: Yellow brass/bell metal fire-altar scribe

riṛ 'ridge formed by the backbone' (Santali); rebus: rīti 'brass' (Skt.)

Sign 48: (Grapheme) riṛ 'ridge formed by the backbone' (Santali) rīḍhaka -- m. ' backbone ' lex.WPah.bhal. rī`ṛ f. ' backbone, high mountain '; Aw.lakh. rīrh ' backbone ', H. rīṛh f. (CDIAL 10749a). riṛ 'ridge formed by the backbone' (Santali) rīḍhaka -- m. ' backbone ' lex.WPah.bhal. rī`ṛ f. ' backbone, high mountain '; Aw.lakh. rīrh ' backbone ', H. rīṛh f. (CDIAL 10749a).Rebus (homonym): rlti 'yellow or pale brass , bell-metal' (Skt.) rīti2 f. ' yellow brass, bell metal ' Kathās., rītika -- n. ' calx of brass ', kā -- f. ' brass ' lex. 2. rīrī -- , rirī -- f. ' yellow brass ' lex. [Ac. to AO xviii 248 Dard. forms < *raktikā -- 2] 1. Dm. rit ' copper ', Gaw. rīt (→ Sv. rīda NoPhal 49); Bshk. rīd ' brass ', Tor. žit f. 2. Pk. rīrī -- f. ' brass '; Sh. rīl m. ' brass, bronze, copper '.(CDIAL 10752). இரீதி irīti, n. < rīti. Brass; பித்தளை. (W.) *இரதி, irati , n. cf. rīti. Brass; பித்தளை. (பிங்.) Vikalpa: Pk.kaṁḍa -- m. ' backbone; L.kaṇḍ f., kaṇḍā m. ' backbone ', awāṇ. kaṇḍ, ḍī ' back '; H. kā̃ṭā m. ' spine ', *karaṇḍa -- backbone (Skt.) Pa. piṭṭhi -- kaṇṭaka -- m. ' bone of the spine ';S. kaṇḍo m. ' back ', P. kaṇḍ f. ' back, pubes '; WPah. bhal. kaṇṭ f. ' syphilis '; N. kaṇḍo ' buttock, rump, anus ', kaṇḍeulo ' small of the back '; B. kā̃ṭ ' clitoris '; Or. kaṇṭi ' handle of a plough '; G. kā̃ṭɔ m., M. kā̃ṭā m.; Si. äṭa -- kaṭuva ' bone ',piṭa -- k ' backbone '.Pk. karaṁḍa -- m.n. ' bone shaped like a bamboo ', karaṁḍuya -- n. ' backbone '. (CDIAL 2670) Rebus: Rebus: kampaṭṭam 'coiner, mint' (Ta.)

Glyph Sign 47: Vikalpa: riṛ 'ridge formed by the backbone' (Santali) rīḍhaka -- m. ' backbone ' lex. WPah.bhal. rī`ṛ f. ' backbone, high mountain '; Aw.lakh. rīrh ' backbone ', H. rīṛh f. (CDIAL 10749a). [ roṇḍi ] ronḍi. [Tel.] n. The haunch, the side between the ribs and loins. (Telugu) Rebus: rlti 'yellow or pale brass , bell-metal' (Skt.) rīti2 f. ' yellow brass, bell metal ' Kathās., rītika -- n. ' calx of brass ', kā -- f. ' brass ' lex. 2. rīrī -- , rirī -- f. ' yellow brass ' lex. [Ac. to AO xviii 248 Dard. forms < *raktikā -- 2] 1. Dm. rit' copper ', Gaw. rīt (→ Sv. rīda NoPhal 49); Bshk. rīd ' brass ', Tor. žit f. 2. Pk. rīrī -- f. ' brass '; Sh. rīl m. ' brass, bronze, copper '.(CDIAL 10752). இரீதி irīti, n. < rīti. Brass; பித்தளை. (W.) *இரதி irati , n. cf. rīti. Brass; பித்தளை. (பிங்.)

Vikalpa: bharaḍo 'spine'; Rebus: bharan 'to spread or bring out from a kiln' (P.) baran, bharat (5 copper, 4 zinc and 1 tin)(P.B.) baraḍo = spine; backbone; the back; baraḍo thābaḍavo = lit. to strike on the backbone or back; hence, to encourage; baraḍo bhāre thato = lit. to have a painful backbone, i.e. to do something which will call for a severe beating (G.lex.) baraḍ, baraḍu = barren, childless; baranṭu = leanness (Tu.lex.) maṇuk.o a single vertebra of the back (G.)

The following pair terminates 184 inscriptions:

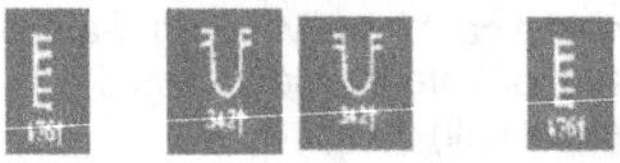

(10) (Variant sign pair, sign sequence reversed).

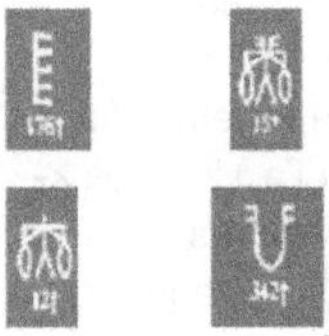

The following pairs of signs terminates 8 and 26 sequences, respectively:

Sign 12: kuṭi 'water-carrier' (Te.); Rebus: kuṭhi 'smelter' (Santali) khareḍo = a currycomb (G.) Rebus: kharādī ' turner' (G.) Vikalpa: kāmsako, kāmsiyo = a large sized comb (G.); Rebus: kãsāri 'pewterer' (Bengali) The ligature of 'rim of jar' glyph is denoted by the ligatured Sign 15; this ligaturing glyptic element has been decoded as 'furnace scribe'. Thus, the pair of Sign 176 together with either Sign 342 or Sign 15 can be read, respectively as: kuṭhi kan-ka kharādī 'smelter-furnace-scribe, turner' or kan-ka kharādī 'scribe, turner'.

Pict-49 Uncertain animal with dotted circles on its body. m1908

This seal has sign 347, 342 sequence, which is a terminal pair with 110 occurrences. An additional glyph shown in front of the animal is: a sloped stroke.

Glyptic element (or sign) on Seal m1908. ḍhāḷ = a slope; the inclination of a plane (G.) Rebus: : ḍhāḷako = a large metal ingot (G.) The three signs can be read: ḍhāḷako dul kolmo baṭa kaṇḍ kanka 'ingot casting smithy (iron) furnace scribe'.

The seal has other glyptic elements: 1. Tusk of a rhinoceros 2. Young spotted animal (?deer or antelope) 3. Dotted circles for the animal's eye and inscribed all over the body.

Antelope: miṇḍāl 'markhor' (Tōrwālī) meḍho a ram, a sheep (G.)(CDIAL 10120); rebus: mẽṛhẽt, meḍ 'iron' (Mu.Ho.)

The indication is that the pasra 'forge' also deals with meḍ 'iron'.

The ligatured animal can be read as a set of hieroglyphs:

piserā 'small deer' ; rebus: pasra 'smithy'; kā̃g 'boar's tusk'; rebus: kā̃gar 'portable brazier'; kandi 'hole, opening' (Ka.); kan 'eye' (Ka.); rebus: kandi (pl. -l) necklace, beads (Pa.) Thus, the entire ligatured animal is decoded rebus: meḍ pasra kā̃gar kandil 'iron smithy, forge, portable furnace, beads'. Pa.kandi (pl. -l) necklace, beads. Ga. (P.) kandi (pl. -l) bead, (pl.) necklace; (S.2) kandiṭ bead (DEDR 1215). kandil, kandīl = a globe of glass, a lantern (Ka.lex.)

A gloss in Telugu explains such a group, lexeme clusters which can, semantically, be interpreted as an 'animal specie'. pasaramu, pasalamu = an animal, a beast, a brute, quadruped (Te.lex.)

Phonetic determinant of kandi 'beads' and kaṇḍ 'furnace' is the tusk glyph, which is read khaṇḍ 'ivory'; rebus: kaṇḍ = altar, furnace (Santali) kaṇḍ = altar, furnace (Santali)

**लोहकारकन्दुः** f. a blacksmith's smelting furnace (Grierson Kashmiri lex.) payĕn-kō̃da **पयन्-कोँद / परिपाककन्दुः** f. a kiln (a potter's, a lime-kiln, and brick-kiln, or the like); a furnace (for smelting) ]. kāndavika = a baker; kandu = an iron plate or pan for baking cakes etc. (Ka.lex.) jaṇḍ khaṇḍ = ivory (Jat.ki) khaṇḍi_ = ivory in rough (Jat.ki_); gaṭī = piece of elephant's tusk (S.)

Ka. kaṇḍi, kiṇḍi, gaṇḍi chink, hole, opening. Tu. kaṇḍi, khaṇḍi, gaṇḍi hole, opening, window; kaṇḍeriyuni to make a cut. Te. gaṇḍi, gaṇḍika hole, orifice, breach, gap, lane (DEDR 1176). kandhi = a lump, a piece (Santali.lex.)

Ta. kaṇ eye, aperture, orifice, star of a peacock's tail. Ma. kaṇ, kaṇṇu eye, nipple, star in peacock's tail, bud. Ko. kaṇ eye. To. koṇ eye, loop in string. Ka. kaṇ eye, small hole, orifice. Koḍ. kaṇṇï id. Te. kanu, kannu eye, small hole, orifice, mesh of net, eye in peacock's feather. Kol. kan (pl. kanḍl) eye, small hole in ground, cave. Ga. (Oll.) kaṇa (pl. kaṇul) hole; (S.) kanu (pl. kankul)eye. Go. (Tr.) kan (pl. kank) id.; (A.) kaṛ (pl. kaṛk) id. Konḍa kaṇ id. Pe. kaṇga (pl. -ŋ, kaṇku) id. Manḍ. kan (pl. -ke) id. Kui kanu (pl. kan-ga), (K.) kanu (pl. kaṛka) id. Kuwi (F.) kannū (pl. kar&nangle;ka), (S.) kannu (pl. kanka), (Su. P. Isr.) kanu (pl. kaṇka) id. (DEDR 1159a). Pa. kanḍp- (kanḍt-) to look for, seek. Ga. (Oll.) kanḍp- (kanḍt-) to search. Ta. kāṇ (kāṇp-, kaṇṭ-) to see, consider, investigate, appear, become visible; n. sight, beauty Te. kanu (allomorph kān-), kāncu to see (DEDR 1443)

B. kan ' eye of corn, particle ', kanā ' piece of dust, cummin seed ', kanī ' atom, particle '; Or.kaṇa, ṇā ' particle of dust, eye of seed, atom ', kaṇi ' particle of grain '; OAw. kana ' drop (of dew) ' M. kaṇ m. ' grain, atom, corn ', kaṇī f. ' hard core of grain, pupil of eye, broken bit ', kaṇẽ n. ' very small particle ' (CDIAL 2661)

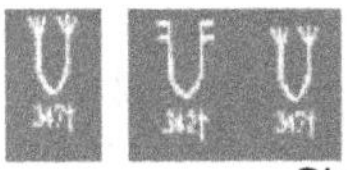

Sign 347 is a ligature of a wide-mouthed, rimless pot and a pair of 'sprout, paddy-plant' glyphs. kolom'sprout'; kolom = cutting, graft; to graft, engraft, prune; kolma hoṛo = a variety of the paddy plant (Desi)(Santali.) kolmo 'rice plant' (Mu.) Rebus: kolami 'furnace,smithy' (Te.) Since a pair of 'sprout.rice-plant' glyphs are used, the pair connotes : dula 'pair'; Rebus: dul 'cast (metal)(Santali) This pair is ligatured to: baṭhu m. 'large pot in which grain is parched (S.) Rebus: baṭa = a kind of iron (G.) bhaṭa 'furnace' (G.) baṭa = kiln (Santali).

Vikalpa: Ta. akai (-v-, -nt-) to flourish, sprout; (-pp-, -tt-) to sprout, rise; to raise; akaippu rising, elevation. Ma. aka germ, bud, shoot; akekka to bud; ava bud, esp. the fruit-like sprout of Artocarpus; avekka to sprout. Ka. age seedling, shoot from the root of a plant or tree, sprout. Koḍ. age paddy seedling. Tu. agge the shoot of a branch. Kur. akhuā seed-bud, sprout, shoot; akrārnā to germinate, shoot, sprout. (DEDR 15) Rebus: agasāle 'goldsmithy' (Te.)

Sign 342: kaṇḍ kanka 'rim of jar'; Rebus: karṇaka 'scribe'; kaṇḍ 'furnace, fire-altar'. Thus the ligatured sign is decoded: kaṇḍ karṇaka 'furnace scribe

Thus, the pair os signs 347 + 342 is decoded: dul kolmo baṭa kaṇḍ kanka 'casting smithy (iron) furnace scribe'.

Allographs:

Many circumscribed signs occur as the left-most glyph and comparable to the 'rim of jar' sign 342 in position. Similarly, the 'arrow' sign terminates 184 epigraphs (read from right to left) – in a total of 227 arrow-sign occurrences

kaṇḍa kanka, 'rim of jar' (Santali); kaṇḍa 'arrow' (Skt.)

kaṇḍa 'fire-altar (Santali); kan 'copper' (Ta.)

*hāṇḍa ' pot ', haṇḍikā -- f. ' earthen pot ' Subh. [Cf. hāḍikā -- f. ' id. ' Kathārṇ. and *haḍappha -- . -- Connexion, if any, with bhāṇḍa -- 1 not clear. -- LM 427 compares Hsüan -- Tsang's utakia -- hanch'a (= *udakahāṇḍa), but this may be < *udaka -- bhāṇḍa -- ]S. haṇḍī f. ' pot ' (← Center?), L. hāṇḍī f. ' cooking pot '; P. hā̃ḍā m. ' large cooking pot '; hā̃ḍī f. ' smaller do. '; WPah.bhal. hāṇḍi f. ' receptacle for oil in an oilmill ', khaś. heṇḍū ' kettle ', rudh. haṇḍū, marm. huṇḍū; Ku. hāno, hā̃ḍo m. ' large earthen pot, head, brains ', hānī, hā̃ḍī ' small pot '; N. hā̃ṛi ' earthen cooking pot ' (whence hā̃ṛe ' mumps ' believed to be cured by rubbing on pot -- black), A. hāri; B. hā̃ṛā, °ṛi ' cooking pot ', hā̃ṛal ' hole, pit ' (semant. cf. kuṇḍá -- 1); Or. haṇḍā,°ḍi ' pot ', haṇḍalā ' big brass pot '; Bi. hā̃ṛā ' cavity in a sugar -- mill ', (Patna) haṇḍā, hā̃ṛhā ' large copper vessel for boiling rice in '; Bhoj. hā̃ṛī, hā̃ṛiyā ' earthen pot '; Aw.lakh. hā̃ṛī ' vessel '; H. hā̃ḍ, hā̃ḍā m. ' large cooking pot of earth or metal ', hā̃ḍī, hā̃ṛī, hā̃ḍiyā, hā̃ṛiyā f. ' earthen cooking pot '; G. hā̃ḍɔ m. ' large pot ', hā̃ḍī, hā̃ḍlī f., hā̃ḍlū, hā̃llū n. ' pot '; M. haṇḍā m. ' open -- mouthed metal vessel ', hā̃ḍī, haṇḍī f. ' small pot of earth or metal ', haṇḍē n. ' general term for pot '; -- ext. -- kk -- : Ku. hankiyā ' potter, mumps ' (see N. above). *hāṇḍavāha -- .Addenda: *hāṇḍa -- :WPah.kc. haṇḍko m. ' pot ', A. also hā̃ri ' pot ' AFD 225, 234. (CDIAL 14050)

kaṇḍ is pot; kan-ka in Sanskrit is karṇaka 'ear or rim of jar'. kaṇḍ also means 'fire-altar'.

kárṇa— m. 'ear, handle of a vessel' RV., 'end, tip (?)' RV. ii 34, 3. [Cf. *kāra—6] Pa. kaṇṇa— m. 'ear, angle, tip'; Pk. kaṇṇa—, aḍaya- m. 'ear', Gy. as. pal. eur. kan m., Ash. (Trumpp) karna NTS ii 261, Niṅg. kõmacr;, Woṭ. kanΘ, Tir. kana; Paš. kan, kaṇ(ḍ)— 'orifice of ear' IIFL iii 3, 93; Shum. kõmacr;ṛ 'ear', Woṭ. kan m., Kal. (LSI) kuṛõmacr;, rumb. kuŕũ, urt. kŕã (< *kaṇ), Bshk. kan, Tor. k *l ṇ, Kand. kōṇi, Mai. kaṇa, ky. kān, Phal. kāṇ, Sh. gil. kọn pl. kọní m. (→ Ḍ kon pl. k *l ṇa), koh. kuṇ, pales. kuāṇΘ, K. kan m., kash. pog. ḍoḍ. kann, S. kanu m., L. kann m., awāṇ. khet. kan, P. WPah. bhad. bhal. cam. kann m., Ku. gng. N. kān; A. kāṇ 'ear, rim of vessel, edge of river'; B. kāṇ 'ear', Or. kāna, Mth. Bhoj. Aw. lakh. H. kān m., OMarw. kāna m., G. M. kān m., Ko. kānu m., Si. kaṇa, kana. — As adverb and postposition (ápi kárṇē 'from behind' RV., karṇē 'aside' Kālid.): Pa. kaṇṇē 'at one's ear, in a whisper'; Wg. ken 'to' NTS ii 279; Tir. kõ; 'on' AO xii 181 with (?); Paš. kan 'to'; K. kåni with abl. 'at, near, through', kani with abl. or dat. 'on', kun with dat. 'toward'; S. kani 'near', kanā̃ 'from'; L. kan 'toward', kannū̃ 'from', kanne 'with', khet. kan, P. ḍog. kanē 'with, near'; WPah. bhal. k *l ṇ, ṇi, k e ṇ, ṇi with obl. 'with, near', kiṇ, ṇiā̃, k *l ṇiā̃, k e ṇ with obl. 'from'; Ku. kan 'to, for'; N. kana 'for, to, with'; H. kane, ni, kan with ke 'near'; OMarw. kanai 'near', kanā̃ sā 'from near', kã̄nī̃ 'towards'; G. kan e 'beside'. Addenda: kárṇa—: S.kcch. kann m. 'ear', WPah.kṭg. (kc.) kān, poet. kanṛu m. 'ear', kṭg. kanni f. 'pounding—hole in barn floor'; J. kā'n m. 'ear', Garh. kān; Md. kan— in kan—fat 'ear' (CDIAL 2830)

kárṇaka m. ' projection on the side of a vessel, handle ' ŚBr. [kárṇa -- ]Pa. kaṇṇaka -- ' having ears or corners '; Wg. kaṇə ' ear -- ring ' NTS xvii 266; S. kano m. ' rim, border '; P. kannā m. ' obtuse angle of a kite ' (→ H.kannā m. ' edge, rim, handle '); N. kānu ' end of a rope for supporting a burden '; B. kāṇā ' brim of a cup ', G. kānɔ m.; M. kānā m. ' touch -- hole of a gun (CDIAL 2831)

करण [ karaṇa ] m (Popular form of कर्ण S amongst artisans. ) The hypotenuse of a triangle, or diagonal of a quadrangular figure (Marathi)

*கர்ணம்²* karṇam, n. < karaṇa. 1. Village accountantship; *கிராமக்கணக்குவேலை.* 2. Village accountant; *கிராமக்கணக்கன்.*

காரணவன் kāraṇavaṉ, n. < id. 1. Accountant; கணக்கன். சுந்தரபாண்டியநல்லூர்க் காரணவரோம் (S. I. I. v, 105). 2. Head of a family; குடும்பத்தலைவன். Nāñ. *காரணிக்கன்* kāraṇikkaṉ, n. < id. Accountant; *கணக்கன்.* (Insc.)*காரணிக்கஜோடி* kāraṇikka-jōṭi, n. < id. +. Quit-rent paid by the accountant; *கணக் கன் செலுத்தும் வரி.* (I.M.P. Tj. 1302.)(Tamil)

*காரணிகன்* kāraṇikaṉ, n. < id. Judge; arbitrator, umpire; *நியாயமத்தியஸ்தன். நமக்கோர் காரணிகனைத் தரல்வேண்டும்* (*இறை.* 1, *உரை*).

kāraṇika m. ' teacher ' MBh., ' judge ' Pañcat. [kā- raṇa ]Pa. usu -- kāraṇika -- m. ' arrow -- maker '; Pk. kāraṇiya -- m. ' teacher of Nyāya '; S. kāriṇī m. ' guardian, heir '; N. kārani ' abettor in crime '; M.kārṇī m. ' prime minister, supercargo of a ship ', kul -- karṇī m. ' village accountant '. (CDIAL 3058). karṇadhāra m. ' helmsman ' Suśr. Pa. kaṇṇadhāra -- m. ' helmsman '; Pk. kaṇṇahāra -- m. ' helmsman, sailor '; H. kanahār m. ' helmsman, fisherman '. (CDIAL 2836).

karanikamu. Clerkship: the office of a Karanam or clerk. (Telugu)

कारकुनी [ kārakunī ] f (कारकून) The office or business of Kárkún. 2 Remuneration to a Kárkún for service rendered. 3 The profits or fees (of Kárkúns) on services done, articles bought &c. 4 Any extra cess laid to pay Kárkún-service. 5 fig. Economizing; careful and thrifty management. कारकुनी [ kārakunī ] a (कारकून) Relating to Kárkún--mode of writing &c. कारकुन [ kārakuna ] m ( P A factor, agent, or business-man.) A clerk, scribe, writer. सवा हात लेखणीचा का0 A term of ironical commendation for a clerk.देशकुळकरण [ dēśakuḷakaraṇa ] n The office of देशकुळकरणी.

देशकुळकरणी [ dēśakuḷakaraṇī ] m An hereditary officer of a Mahál. He frames the general account from the accounts of the several Khots and Kulkarṇís of the villages within the Mahál; the district-accountant.गांवकुळकरणी [ gāmvakuḷakaraṇī ] m The hereditary village-accountant: in contrad. from देशकुळकरणी District accountant. नाडकरणी [ nāḍakaraṇī ] m An hereditary district-accountant. नारकरणी [ nārakaraṇī ] m An hereditary district accountant. (Marathi)

Vikalpa: khanaka m. one who digs , digger , excavator MBh. iii , 640 R. ; a miner L. ; a house-breaker , thief L. ; a rat L. ; N. of a friend of Vidura MBh. i , 5798 f. ; (%{I}) f. a female digger or excavator Pāṇ. 3-1 , 145 Pat. ; iv , 1 , 41 Ka1s3.

***ஆலை³* ālai, n. < šālā. 1. Apartment, hall; *சாலை. ஆலைசேர் வேள்வி* (*தேவா.* 844. 7). 2. Elephant stable or stall; *யானைக்கூடம். களிறு சேர்ந் தல்கிய வழுங்க லாலை* (*புறநா.* 220, 3).*ஆலைக்குழி* ālai-k-kuḻi, n. < *ஆலை¹* +. Receptacle for the juice underneath a sugar-cane press; *கரும்பாலையிற் சாறேற்கும் அடிக்கலம்.* ஆலைத்தொட்டி* ālai-t-toṭṭi, n. < id. +. Cauldron for boiling sugar-cane juice; *கருப்பஞ் சாறு காய்ச்சும் சால்.ஆலைபாய்-தல்* ālai-pāy-, v. intr. < id. +. 1. To work a sugar-cane mill; *ஆலையாட்டுதல். ஆலைபாயோதை* (*சேதுபு. நாட்டு.* 93). 2. To move, toss, as a ship; *அலைவுறுதல்.* (R.) 3. To be undecided, vacillating; *மனஞ் சுழலுதல்.*

*நெஞ்ச மாலைபாய்ந் துள்ள மழிகின்றேன்* (*அருட்பா,*) Vikalpa: sal 'splinter'; rebus: workshop (sal) '

குடி¹-த்தல் kuṭi-, 11 v. tr. cf. kuḍ. [K. kuḍi, M. kuṭi.] 1. [T. kuḍucu.] To drink, as from a cup, from the breast; பருகுதல். கடலைவற்றக் குடித்திடுகின்ற செவ்வேற் கூற்றம் (கந்தபு. தாரக. 183). 3232 kuṭī— f. 'hut' MBh., ṭikā— f. Divyāv., ṭīkā— f. Hariv. [Some cmpds. have ṭa(ka)—: ← Drav. EWA i 222 with lit.: cf.KŌṭA—3] Pa. kuṭī—, ṭikā— f. 'single—roomed hut'; Pk.kuḍī— f., ḍaya— n. 'hut'; Gy. pal. kúri 'house, tent, room', as. kuri, guri 'tent' JGLS New Ser. ii 329; Sh. kúi 'village, country'; WPah.jaun. kūṛo house'; Ku. kuṛī, ṛo 'house, building', ghar—kuṛī house and land', gng. kuṛ 'house'; N. kur'nest or hiding place of fish', kuri 'burrow, hole for small animals', kaṭ—kuro 'small shed for storing wood'; B. kuṛiyā'small thatched hut'; Or. kuṛī, ṛiā 'hut'; H. kuṛī f. 'fireplace'; M. kuḍī f. 'hut'; Si. kiḷiya 'hut, small house'. WPah.kṭg. krvṛı f. 'granary (for corn after threshing)'; Garh. kuṛu 'house'; — B. phonet. kũṛ (CDIAL 3232) kuṭumba— n. 'household' ChUp. 2. kuṭumbaka— m. Daś. 1. Pa. kuṭumba—, ṭimba— n. 'family, riches'; Pk.kuḍuṁba—, ḍaṁba— n. 'family', S. kuṛmu m., Ku. gng.kũm; H. kuṛum—codī f. 'incest'. 2. P. kunbā m. 'kindred, caste, tribe'; WPah. jaun. kuṇbā 'family'; A. kurmā, f. āni 'a connexion by mar- riage'; H. kuṛmā, kumbā, kunbā m. 'family, caste, tribe'. (CDIAL 3233) குடி&sup4; kuṭi, n. cf. kuṭi. [M. kuṭi.] 1. Ryot; குடியானவன். கூடு கெழீஇய குடிவயினான் (பொருந. 182). 2. Tenants; குடியிருப்போர். 3. Subjects, citizens; ஆட்சிக்குட்பட்ட பிரசைகள். மன்னவன் கோனோக்கி வாழுங் குடி (குறள், 542). 4. Family; குடும்பம். ஒருகுடிப்பிறந்த பல்லோருள்ளும் (புறநா. 183). 5. Lineage, descent; கோத்திரம். (பிங்.) 6. Caste, race; குலம். (பிங்.) 7. House, home, mansion; வீடு. சிறுகுடி கலக்கி (கந்தபு. ஆற்று. 12). 8. Town, village; ஊர். குன்றகச்சிறுகுடிக் கிளை யுடன் மகிழ்ந்து (திருமுரு. 196). 9. [T. K. kuṭi.] Abode, residence; வாழ்விடம். அடியாருள்ளத் தன்பு மீதூரக் குடியாக்கொண்ட (திருவாச. 2, 8). Ta. kuṭi (-pp-, -tt-) to drink, inhale; n. drinking, beverage,drunkenness; kuṭiyan̠ drunkard. Ma. kuṭi drinking, water drunk after meals, soaking; kuṭikka to drink, swallow; kuṭippikka to give to drink, soak; kuṭiyan drunkard. Ko. kuṛy- (kuṛc-) to drink (only in: uc kuṛy- to drink urine, i.e. to be humbled). To. kuḍt- (only 2nd stem) to drink (in song; < Badaga or Ta.). Ka. kuḍi to drink, inhale; n. drinking; kuḍisu to cause to drink; kuḍika, kuḍaka drinker, drunkard; kuḍita, kuḍata drinking, a draught; kuḍu, kuḍiyuvike drinking. Koḍ. kuḍi- (kuḍip-, kuḍic-) to drink. Tu. kuḍcuni to drink excessively, swallow liquor; kuḍcel, kuḍicel; drunkenness; kuḍcele, kuḍicele drunkard. Te. kuḍucu to eat, suck, drink, enjoy, suffer;kuḍupu to feed, suckle, cause to eat, enjoy, or suffer; n. eating, food, enjoying, suffering; kuḍupari one who eats, enjoys, or suffers; kuḍi right, right-hand;kuḍiti the washings of rice, split pulse, etc., used as a drink for cattle. Cf. 1658 Ko. guṛakn. / Cf. Skt. kuṭī- intoxicating liquor. (DEDR 1654) Ta. kuṭi house, abode, home, family, lineage, town, tenants; kuṭikai hut made of leaves, temple; kuṭical hut; kuṭicai, kuṭiñai small hut, cottage;kuṭimai family, lineage, allegiance (as of subjects to their sovereign), servitude; kuṭiy-āḷ tenant; kuṭiyilār tenants; kuṭil hut, shed, abode; kuṭaṅkar hut, cottage; kaṭumpu relations. Ma. kuṭi house, hut, family, wife, tribe; kuṭima the body of landholders, tenantry; kuṭiyan slaves (e.g. in Coorg); kuṭiyāninhabitant, subject, tenant; kuṭiññil hut, thatch; kuṭil hut, outhouse near palace for menials. Ko. kurjl shed, bathroom of Kota house; kuṛm family; kuḍḷ front room of house; kuṛḷ hut; guṛy temple. To. kwïṣ shed for small calves; kuṣ room (in dairy or house); kuḍṣ outer room of dairy, in: kuḍṣ waṣ fireplace in outer room of lowest grade of dairies (cf. 2857), kuḍṣ moṇy bell(s) in outer section of ti· dairy, used on non-sacred buffaloes (cf. 4672); kuṛy Hindu temple; ? kwïḍy a family of children. Ka. kuḍiya, kuḍu śūdra, farmer; guḍi house, temple; guḍil, guḍalu, guḍisalu, guḍasalu, guḍasala, etc. hut with a thatched roof. Koḍ. kuḍi family of servants living in one hut; kuḍië man of toddy-tapper caste. Tu. guḍi small pagoda or shrine; guḍisal;, guḍisil;, guḍsil;, guḍicil; hut, shed. Te. koṭika hamlet; guḍi temple; guḍise hut, cottage, hovel. Kol. (SR) guḍī temple. Pa. guḍi temple, village resthouse. Ga. (Oll.) guḍi temple. Go. (Ko.) kuṛma hut, outhouse; (Ma.) kurma menstruation; (Grigson) kurma lon menstruation hut (Voc. 782, 800); (SR.) guḍi, (Mu.) guḍḍi, (S. Ko.) guṛi temple; guḍḍī (Ph.) temple, (Tr.) tomb (Voc. 1113). Kui guḍi central room of house, living room. / Cf. Skt. kū˘ṭa-, kuṭi-, kū˘ṭī- (whence Ga. (P.) kuṛe hut; Kui kūṛi hut made of boughs, etc.; Kur. kuṛyā small shed or outhouse; Malt. kuṛya hut in the fields; Br. kuḍ(ḍ)ī hut, small house, wife), kuṭīkā-, kuṭīra-, kuṭuṅgaka-, kuṭīcaka-, koṭa- hut; kuṭumba- household (whence Ta. Ma. kuṭumpam id.; Ko. kuṛmb [? also kuṛm above]; To. kwïḍb, kwïḍbïl [-ïl fromwïkïl, s.v. 925 Ta. okkal]; Ka., Koḍ., Tu. kuṭumba; Tu. kuḍuma; Te. kuṭumbamu; ? Kui kumbu house [balance word of iḍu, see s.v. 494 Ta. il]). See Turner, CDIAL, no.

3232, kuṭī-, no. 3493, kōṭa-, no. 3233, kuṭumba-, for most of the Skt. forms; Burrow, BSOAS 11.137. (DEDR 1655)

ālai 'workshop' (Ta.) **ஆலை*[3] ālai, n. < šālā. 1. Apartment, hall; *சாலை. ஆலைசேர் வேள்வி* (*தேவா.* 844. 7). 2. Elephant stable or stall; *யானைக்கூடம். களிறு சேர்ந் தல்கிய வழுங்க லாலை* (*புறநா.* 220, 3).*ஆலைக்குழி* ālai-k-kuḻi, n. < *ஆலை*[1] +. Receptacle for the juice underneath a sugar-cane press; *கரும்பாலையிற் சாறேற்கும் அடிக்கலம்.***ஆலைத்தொட்டி* ālai-t-toṭṭi, n. < id. +. Cauldron for boiling sugar-cane juice; *கருப்பஞ் சாறு காய்ச்சும் சால்.ஆலைபாய்-தல்* ālai-pāy-, v. intr. < id. +. 1. To work a sugar-cane mill; *ஆலையாட்டுதல். ஆலைபாயோதை* (*சேதுபு. நாட்டு.*)

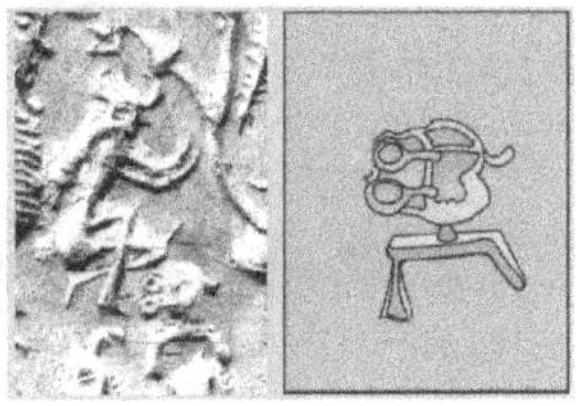

merḍgo = rimless vessels (Santali) Rebus: meḍ 'iron' (Ho.)

bārṇe, bāraṇe = an offering of food to a demon; a meal after fasting, a breakfast (Tu.) barada, barda, birada = a vow (G.lex.) Rebus: baran, bharat (5 copper, 4 zinc and 1 tin)(P.B.) karadamu present to a superior (Te.) kareṭum = an annual offering and present to a godess or to an evil spirit (G.) karavṛtti (Skt.) Rebus; kharādī 'turner' (G.) saman: = to offer an offering, to place in front of; front, to front or face (Santali) Rebus: samr.obica, stones containing gold (Mundari.lex.) cf. soma (ṛgveda) samanom = an obsolete name for gold (Santali). kharādī 'turner' (G.) कातारी or कांतारी [ kātārī or kāntārī ] m (कातणें) A turner. (Marathi) karaḍo, karāḍī 'a goldsmith's tool' (G.)

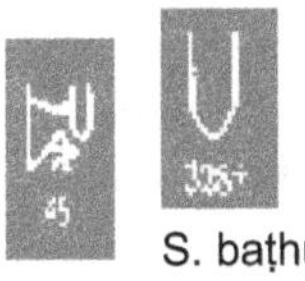

S. baṭhu m. 'large pot in which grain is parched, Rebus; bhaṭṭhā m. 'kiln' (P.) baṭa = a kind of iron (G.)

bhaṭa 'furnace' (G.) baṭa = kiln (Santali); baṭa = a kind of iron (G.) bhaṭṭha -- m.n. ' gridiron (Pkt.) baṭhu large cooking fire' baṭhī f. 'distilling furnace'; L. bhaṭṭh m. 'grain— parcher's oven', bhaṭṭhī f. 'kiln, distillery', awāṇ. bhaṭh; P. bhaṭṭh m., ṭhī f. 'furnace', bhaṭṭhā m. 'kiln'; S. bhaṭṭhī keṇī 'distil (spirits)'. (CDIAL 9656)

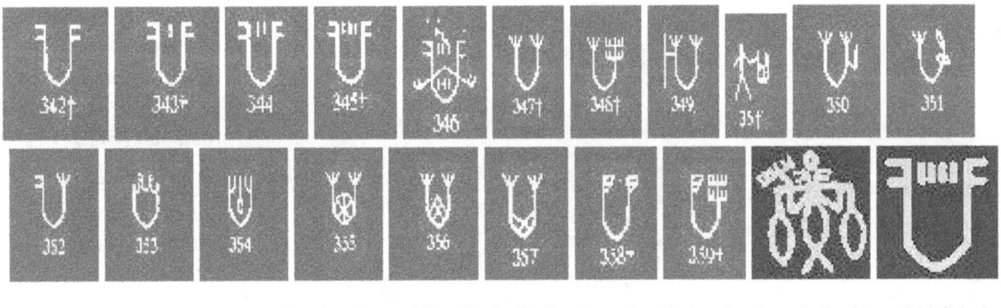

Allographs of a duplicated 'leaf' glyph, ligatured with 'crab-claws' glyph and U ('rimless pot') glyph – shown on one copper tablet [After Parpola, 1994, fig. 13.15] seems to be a comparable rebus reading of the archer shown on another copper tablet. The archer shown on one copper tablet seems to be a synonym of a ligatured complex glyph -- the 'leave's ligatured with crab and 'U' glyph on another copper tablet since the inscription on the obverse of each of the tablets is identical. [cf. Parpola, 1994, fig. 13.13] This ligatured complex glyph appears on two seals- one from Harappa and another from Lothal. Leaves ligatured with crab is a sign which occurs on these seals and with similar sign sequences. [cf. Parpola, 1994, fig. 13.12]

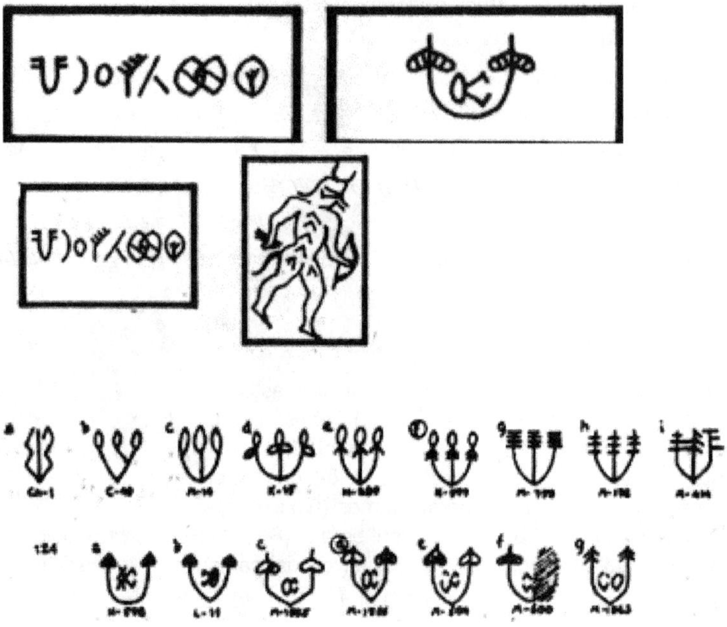

Glyph: 'archer': kamāṭhiyo = archer; kāmaṭhum = a bow; kāmaḍ, kāmaḍum = a chip of bamboo (G.) kāmaṭhiyo a bowman; an archer (Skt.lex.) Rebus: kammaṭi a coiner (Ka.); kampaṭṭam coinage, coin, mint (Ta.) kammaṭa = mint, gold furnace (Te.)

Allographs (graphemes):

kamḍa, khamḍa 'copulation' (Santali)

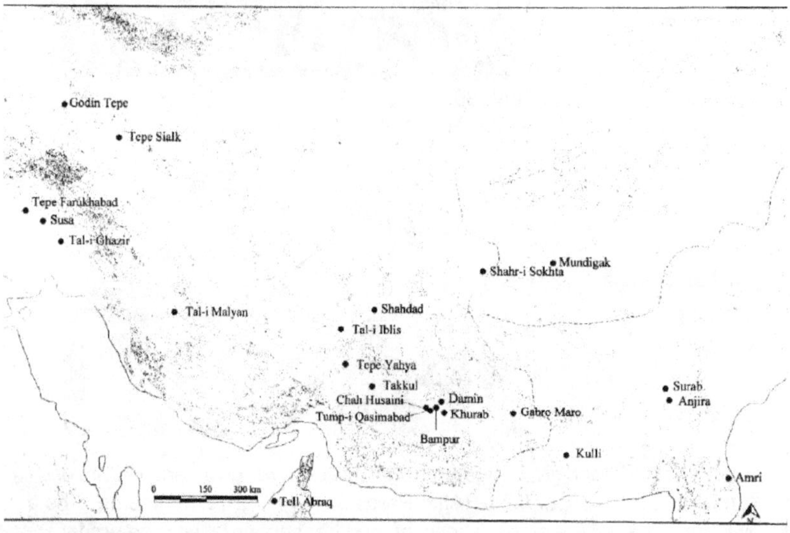


kamaṭha crab (Skt.)

kamaṛkom = fig leaf (Santali.lex.) kamarmaṛā (Has.), kamaṛkom (Nag.); the petiole or stalk of a leaf (Mundari.lex.) kamat.ha = fig leaf, religiosa (Skt.)

Glyptic art and glyptic writing in contact areas of Indus script hieroglyphs

What started as glyptic art to represent reality transformed into glyptic writing systems in Mesopotamian cylinder seals or Elam tablets (and inscriptions on other artefacts) and in Indus Script (on seals and other artefacts) to establish and sustain trade contacts to announce, describe and market new products of the Bronze Age artisans emerging out of the chalcolithic era.

Lamberg-Karlovsky who excavated the Elamite site of Tepe-Yahya records a seal with Indus script:

Fig Fig A.1 Map of the Indo-Iranian borders illustrating the principal sites (e.g. Amri, Tepe Yahya, Tell Abraq, Susa).

10.63 Stamp seal impression on plain red ware sherd of Tepe Yahya with Harappan inscription. (See other parallel glyphs – Fig. 10.62, 10.64, 10.66 discussed in this note) firmly establishing the site as the mid-point contact area in Persian Gulf sites (e.g. Tell Abraq). Objects with Indus script hieroglyphs had also been discovered in Mesopotamian civilization area (Elamite site of Susa and other sites).

Glyptic art tradition of Mesopotamia and Elam has been well-documents and the meanings/significance of glyphs explained in the writings of savants like Edith Porada, Henri Frankfort, Beatrice Teissier and Amiet. This note suggests that the glyptic art tradition evidenced on many tablets and cylinder seals of the Mesopotamian civilization area has to be re-evaluated as complementary to the writing systems which developed both in Mesopotamia (cuneiform, proto-elamite and elamite writing systems) and in Indus script (hieroglyphs). "Susa... profound affinity between the Elamite people who migrated to Anshan and Susa and the Dilmunite people... Elam proper corresponded to the plateau of Fars with its capital at Anshan. We think, however that it probably extended further north into the Bakhtiari Mountains... likely that the chlorite and serpentine vases reached Susa by sea... From the victory proclamations of the kings of Akkad we also learn that the city of Anshan had been re-established, as the capital of a revitalised political ally: Elam itself... the import by Ur and Eshnunna of inscribed objects typical of the Harappan culture provides the first reliable chronological evidence. [C.J. Gadd, Seals of ancient Indian style found at Ur, *Proceedings of the British Academy, XVIII*, 1932; Henry Frankfort, Tell Asmar, Khafaje and Khorsabad, *OIC*, 16, 1933, p. 50, fig. 22). It is certainly possible that writing developed in India before this time, but we have no real proof. Now Susa had received evidence of this same civilisation, admittedly not all dating from the Akkadian period, but apparently spanning all the closing years of the third millennium (L. Delaporte, *Musee du Louvre. Catalogues des Cylindres Orientaux...*, vol. I, 1920, pl. 25(15), S.29. P. Amiet, Glyptique susienne, *MDAI*, 43, 1972, vol. II, pl. 153, no. 1643)...The finds of object with Indus script had served the purpose of validating the chronology and dating of Indus Civilization (Meluhha).

Now, there is sufficient justification to go beyond this chronological affirmation to understanding the exchanges of glyptic traditions between two contemporaneous contact areas – Mesopotamia and Indus. A good starting point is the discovery of a storage pot in Susa (Elam) with an Indus script hieroglyph: fish.

Susa pot showing the interaction areas of Meluhha, Magan, Dilmun and Mesopotamia (After Maurizio Tosi, 2010). This storage jar has a FISH glyph inscribed on the pot. This pot contained metal artefacts. See the two slides of Maurizio Tosi (2010). The slides were presented by Prof. Maurizio Tosi (2010: The middle Asian intercultural space and the Indus civilization: a comparative perspective for a definition of diversity) in the international conference held in Delhi between 25 to 27 November 2010) http://www.vifindia.org/sites/default/files/Abstract_22_11_10.pdf "There is a solid archaeological evidence that trade and exchanges took place among all this regions and the Indus plains during the whole of the formative period." The 'fish' glyphic is a glyph of the civilization denoting ayo, ayas 'metal' of the Indian *sprachbund* or Indian linguistic area. Fish + crocodile is read as: ayakāra 'metal smith' (Pali).

...B. Buchanan has published a tablet dating from the reign of Gungunum of Larsa, in the twentieth century BC, which carries the impression of such a stamp seal. (B.Buchanan, *Studies in honor of Benno Landsberger*, Chicago, 1965, p. 204, s.). The date so revealed has been wholly confirmed by the impression of a stamp seal from the same group, fig. 85, found on a Susa tablet of the same period. (P. Amiet, Antiquites du Desert de Lut, *RA*, 68, 1974, p. 109, fig. 16. Maurice Lambert, *RA*, 70, 1976, p. 71-72). It is in fact, a receipt of the kind in use at the beginning of the Isin-Larsa period, and mentions a certain Milhi-El, son of Tem-Enzag, who, from the name of his god, must be a Dilmunite. In these circumstances we may wonder if this document had not been drawn up at Dilmun and sent to Susa, after sealing with a local stamp seal. This seal is decorated with six tightly-packed, crouching animals, characterised by their vague shapes, with legs tucked under their bodies, huge heads and necks sometimes striped obliquely. The impression of another seal of similar type, fig. 86, depicts in the center a throned figure who seems to dominate the animals, continuing a tradition of which examples are known at the end of the Ubaid period in Assyria... Fig. 87 to 89 are Dilmun-type seals found at Susa. The boss is semi-spherical and decorated with a band across the center and four incised circles. [Pierre Amiet, Susa and the Dilmun Culture, pp. 262-268].

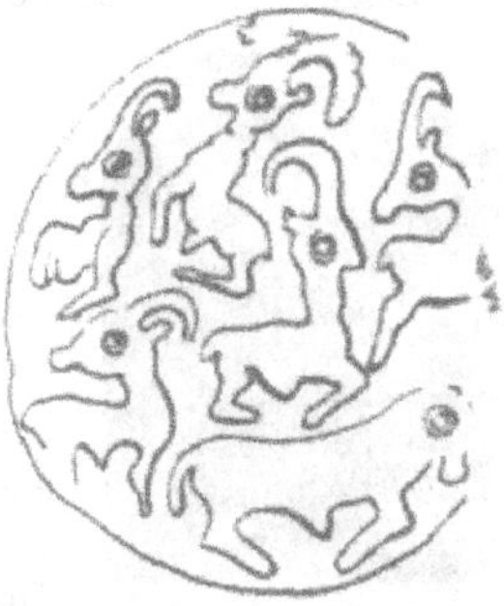

seal impressionl Louvre
MDAI, 43, no. 240

Susa Fig.85; Susa, tablet: seal impression, Louvre Sb 11221

Susa, sealing:

Fig. 86;

Fig. 87;

Susa, stamp seal
from the Gulf, Louvre,
MDAI, 43, No. 1716; depicts two goat-antelopes
crouching head to tail, inside and outside an oval. Incised eyes are saucer-shaped.

Fig. 88; Susa, stamp seal from the Gulf, Teheran museum, MDAI, 43, no. 1717; an animal tamer wearing a skirt and rasping with one hand a goat-antelope with its head turned back and with its feet bound; with the other hand, the person holds a large object which looks like an architectural feature or shield.

Fig. 89; Susa, stamp seal from the Gulf, Teheran Museum, MDAI, 43, no. 1718; a person, naked and thin, has a stylised head shaped like a narrow arch with indentations to mark the nose and mouth.
Animals have bound feet and surround a square object on which the person stands.

Fig.90; Susa, cylinder seal from the Gulf, Louvre, MDAI, 43, no. 2021; made of steatite; a person with a horned tiara, wearing an unevenly chequered robe; the person is attended by a naked man and alongside are two tamers grasping a pair of crossed animals.

Fig. 91; Susa, cylinder seal from the Gulf, Teheran Museum, MDAI, 43, no. 1975; steatite; three figures with stylised heads in the form of notched arches, wearing boldly chequered skirts; one is seated; the other two stand with backs turned, hold an enormous feathered arrow, and one of them extends a hand towards a stylised goat-antelope.

Fig. 92; Susa, stamp seal made of bitumen compound, Louvre, MDAI, 43, no. 1726; a tamer with three heavily hatched animals

Fig. 93; Susa stamp seal made of bitumen compound, Louvre, MDAI, 43, no. 1720

Fig. 94; Susa, stamp seal from a butimen compound, Louvre, MDAI, 43, no. 1726

Fig. 95; Susa, stamp seal of bitumen compound, Louvre, MDAI, 43, no. 1725; a woman shown full-face is squatting with legs apart, possibly on a stool. (A similar image of a woman with legs spread outoccurs on an Indus tablet).

See also: Beatrice Teissier, *Ancient Near Eastern Cylinder Seals: From the Marcopoli Collection*, Berkeley, University of California Press, 1984.
http://www.hindunet.org/hindu_history/sarasvati/lapis/lapis_lazuli.htm People called MAR-TU

The Proto-Elamite Settlement at Tepe Yaḥyā

C. C. Lamberg-Karlovsky

Iran

Vol. 9, (1971), pp. 87-96

Lamberg-Karlovsky, C. C., 2001, *Excavations at Tepe Yahya, Iran, 1967-1975: the third millennium*, Cambridge, Mass.: Peabody Museum of Archaeology and Ethnology, Harvard University.

Lamberg-Karlovsky, C. C., 1979, *Excavations at Tepe Yahya, Iran 1967-1969: progress report 1*, Bulletin (American School of Prehistoric Research) ; no. 27, Cambridge, Mass.: Peabody Museam, (Jointly with The Asia Institute of Pahlavi University).

PLATE XXXVII

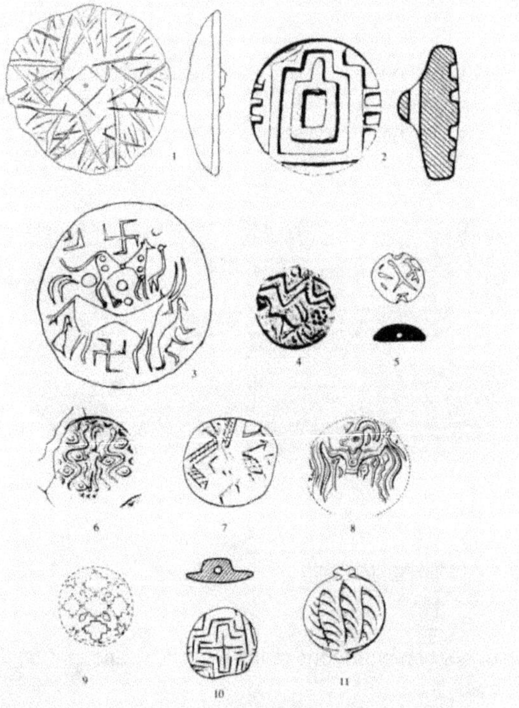

Drawings of Late Chalcolithic seal designs.

Plate XXXVII. Drawings of Late Chalcolithic seal designs.

Of the seals found by M.-J. Steve in his excavations of the terrace of Susa I (Steve and Gasche, pl. 37) and drawn by Amiet (Plate XXXVII/1; 1973b, pl. II/25) the large one with a complicated cross-shaped design corresponds to seals from Tall-i Bakun. One of the latter (shown in Plate XXXVI/16) was based on the same scheme as the one from Susa. The scheme is a combination of a cross with two opposed equilateral triangles overlaying each other. It is sketched in simplified form on a deformed lenticular tablet from the Acropole of Susa dated in the Proto-Elamite period (Amiet, 1971, p. 228, fig. 71/7). This may suggest that the design had a specific meaning.

The large size of that stamp is related to the large stamps found by Geneviève Dollfus at Djaffarabad (Jaʿfarābād), an example of which is shown in Plate XXXVII/2 (Dollfus,1971, p. 58, fig. 23/2; idem, 1973, p. 5 fig. 3/2), with markings that suggest some type of general meaning accepted in the community in which these objects were made and employed.

Figured designs on Late Chalcolithic seals. The number of figured designs on Chalcolithic seals is small in comparison with the geometric ones. To the same period as the large seals just discussed, however, Susa I, belongs a stamp seal (Plate XXXVII/3; Amiet, 1972, no. 143), which shows a bovine animal with a long-legged feline above it and a dog at the side; the rest of the field is filled with swastika designs. The body of the bovine animal is stylized in two triangles with incurving sides, corresponding to the stylization of horned animals on Susa pottery, for example, the great beaker, frequently reproduced (Amiet, 1966, p. 41 fig. 13).

A seal of unparalleled style with two animals comes from level 27 of the Acropole at Susa. It shows a leaping feline above a goat facing in the opposite direction (Plate XXXVII/4; Amiet, 1971, pl. XXII/7). A perhaps slightly later low hemispheroid from Seh Gabi (Plate XXXVII/5; Henrickson, pl. I/D) shows two figures that cannot be determined from the photo graphs, but two animals are frequently found, often back to back or head to tail.

The next phase, later by two levels at Susa, has a more clearly discernible subject, a goat-headed demon restraining serpents, found in level 25 of the Acropole (Plate XXXVII/6; Amiet, 1971, pl. XXII/6). The sealing is related by Amiet (1971, p. 220) to the numerous representations of such figures on stamp seals (see Barnett). One of these figures on stamp seals was excavated in Lorestān (Plate XXXVII/7; Ghirshman 1935, pl. 38/36). In view of the fact that such goat-headed demons were also found at Tepe Gawra (Tobler, pls. CLXIII/81, CLXIV/94-96) and Tell Asmar in Mesopotamia (Frankfort,

1935, p. 29 fig. 30), the figure obviously had a wide distribution beyond Lorestān. The most elaborate representations of the goat-headed figure, however, are those on sealings from Susa (Plate XXXVII/8; Amiet, in a level called Susa B by Le Breton, pp. 101-04).

The goat demon is particularly associated with ser pents, which may represent the principal inimical force in these representations. The combination of horned animal and serpent is a motif that greatly outnumbered representations of a horned animal and feline, which became more common at a later date. A function of the seals as amulets against snakebite should also be considered.

Various Late Chalcolithic stamp-seal designs. Elabo rate ornamental designs were found among the seal designs of the intermediate layer B at Susa; they were anchored in level 25 of the Acropole by one such design (Plate XXXVII/9; Amiet, 1973b, pl. II bottom).

A simple cross on a button seal (Plate XXXVII/10, with strongly convex sealing surface) was also found in level 25 of the Acropole and indicates the Late Chalcolithic date of that frequent motif.

A new feature in the shape of stamp seals was noted in the collars at the suspension holes of the example in Plate XXXVII/11, found in level 23 of the Acropole (Amiet, 1971, pl. XXII/10). The design, consisting of rows of curving lines, resembles some devices for decorating other Late Chalcolithic stamps.
Plate XXXVIII. Drawings of ancient seal impressions from the Susa II period (1-6, 8) and modern impressions of Proto-Elamite cylinders (9, 10).
Plate XXXIX. Susa II seal impressions.
Plate XL. Ancient and modern (1, 4) cylinder-seal impressions, Proto-Elamite period to Early Dynastic III. "The second example (Plate XL/4; Amiett, 1980b, no. 537) comes from the old excavations, but it is shown here because it is the earliest example of goats flanking a tree, one of the most enduring motifs of the ancient Near East. The different plants in the design also demonstrate the love of plants that characterizes Persian art through the ages."

Fig 4.6 Stone stamp seal

PLATE XXXIX
Susa II seal impressions

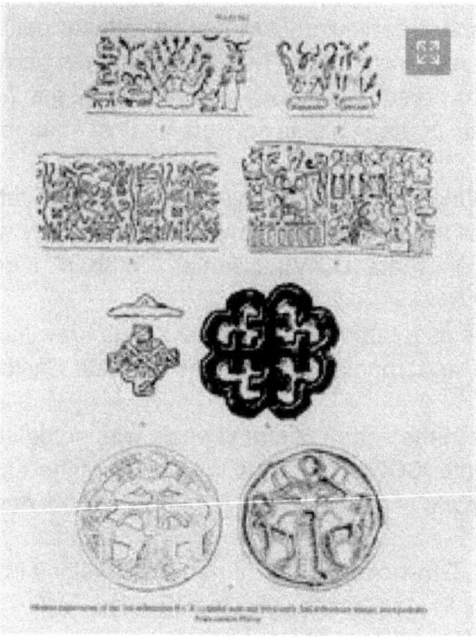

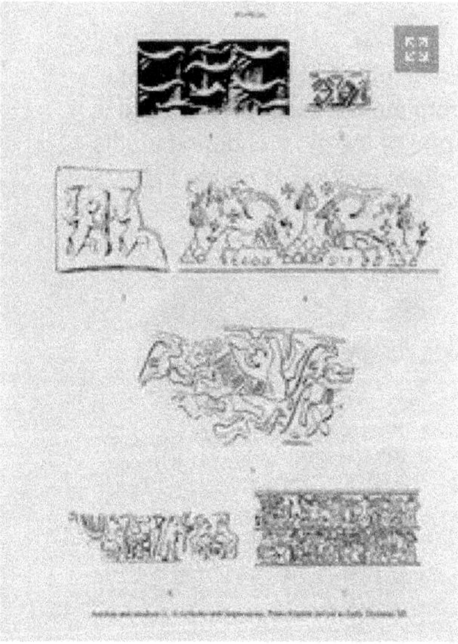

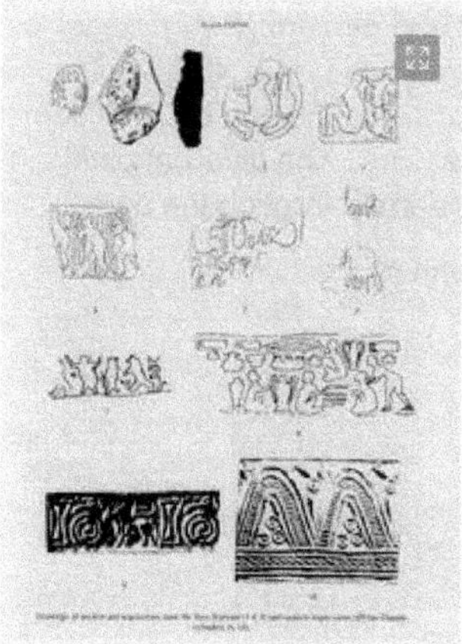

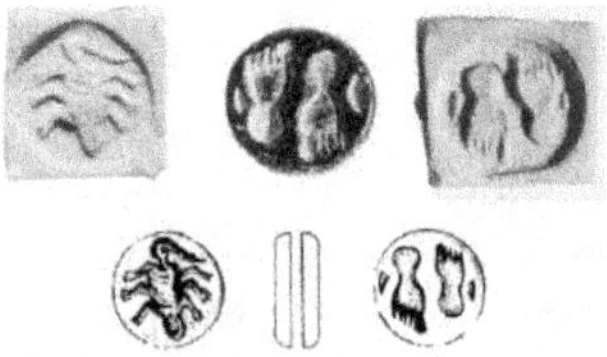

Fig. 5-15 Disk seal Double-sided steatite stamp seal with opposing footprints and six-legged creature on opposite sides.

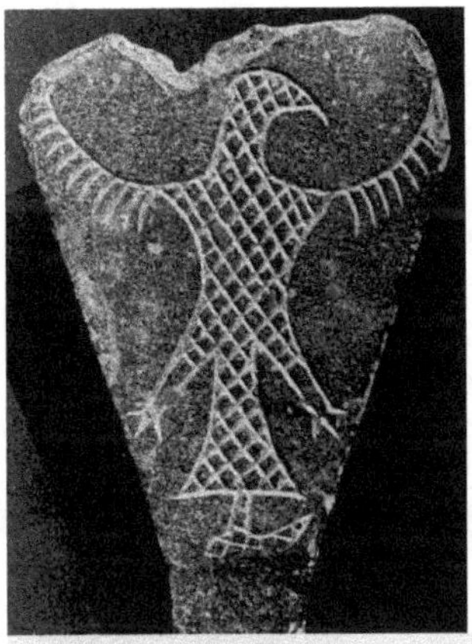

Fig. 9-6 Two sides of ceremonial chlorate axe hed with incised design of an eagle or bird from the chlorite-rich level of the Teye Yaha Period IVB workshop.

Figure 9.11 Two sides of Tepe Yahya ('weight'?) fragment apparently reused as door socket during IVB times. One side depicts palms, and the other has a representation of a humped bull with a scorpion set above its back.

Fig. 9-12. Plaque of 'weight?' fragment from Agrab in the Diyala Valley with a humped bull and scorpion design similar to figure 9.11.

Fig 10.27 Classic style cylinder seal reconstructed from seven fragments. Two rampant caprids against a stepped platform surmounted by tree with third caprid and four-sided crosses (after Potts: Figs. 13-15, pls 17-19, 25).

Fig 10.57 Stmp seal with human-headed lion (?) with head turned back and tail raised (after Lamberg-Karlovsky 1971).

Fig. 10.59 Copper or bronze compartmented stamp seal with animal in profile with scalloped body patterning (after Lamberg-Karlovsky 1970).

Fig. 10.62 Stamp seal impression on sherd of two overlapping impressions of seal with head of horned caprid.

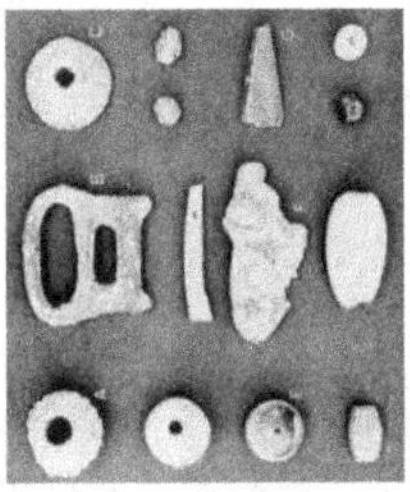

Fig. 10.64 Stamp seal impression on clay bullae with humanoid figure with raised arms.

Fig 10.66 Steatite stamp seal made from four-sided perforated bead with images of a scorpion, palm tree, fish, and two stars.

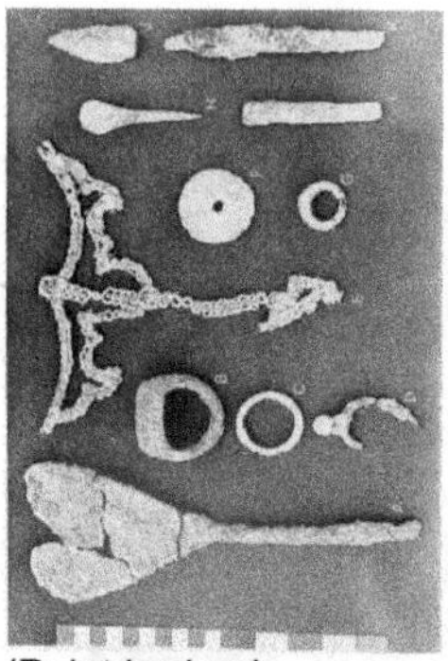

Lamberg-Karlovsky, C. C., 1979, *Excavations at Tepe Yahya, Iran 1967-1969: progress report 1*, Bulletin (American School of Prehistoric Research) ; no. 27, Cambridge, Mass.: Peabody Museam, (Jointly with The Asia Institute of Pahlavi University).

Period VI 5000 BCE; Period VC 3800 BCE; Period IVB 2800 BCE; Period III 1000 BCE; Period II 400 BCE; Period I Partho-sassanian 300 CE.

Plate 7 Small finds, metal, Period I A1-1 Copper-bronze spoon; B A3 copper-bronze finger ring, undecorated; C A3E-2 Bone ring; D E Copper-bronze ring with pearl (?); E A1E copper-bronze thread chain; F A3 lead spindle whorl; G A4E gold earring; H A2-4 copper-bronze awl; I A2-4 copper-bronze rod; J A2 copper-bronze socketed trilobate arrowpoint; K A2 copper-bronze needle (Point broken)

Plate 8 Miscellaneous small finds, Period I A A2 faience bed; B A3E copper-bronze belt buckle; C A3E steatite bead; D A four surface beads; E A2 agate bead; F A4 animal, with rear attachment; G A3 carnelian pendant bead (perforated); H A3 four beds: steatite, shell, blue-glass and shell

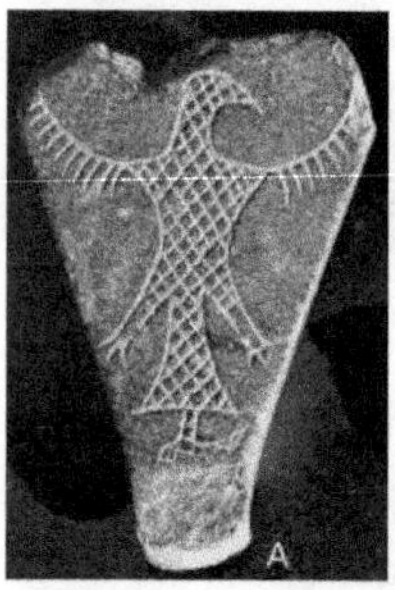


Plate 19A steatite: shaft-hole axe with incised eagles (identical) on both sides of the blade.

Reading svastika hieroglyph as zinc, zinc retort distillation furnace

A metallurgical marvel to isolate and capture the eigth metal discovered with the invention by a stroke of genius, a brilliant zinc retort distillation furnace, which led to an astonishing enquiry in Indian alchemical traditions -- see the photograph of the retorts arrayed, displayed in an ancient mining site of Zawar, Rajasthan -- it's alchemy because copper could be made to shine like gold as aara-ku_t.a adding zinc to create the brass alloy) and svastika glyph (which occurs over 50 times on the Sarasvati epigraphs -- so-called Indus script). The svastika hieroglyph represents zinc, a zinc retort distillation furnace. The array of zinc retort distillation units displayed is comparable to the array of four or five 'svastika' glyphs which appear as Sarasvati hieroglyphs on Indus script inscriptions.

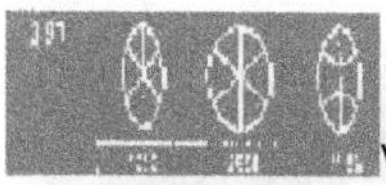
V391

V393

Sign 286 seems to ligature sign 267 and sign 391; Sign 355 seems to ligature sign 347 and sign 391 (Sign 391 depicts the opening in the nave or hub of wheel and also six spokes: arā).

A ligature occurs on a Mohenjo-daro seal, m0712:

m0712  1091 Note Sign391 ligatured on the animal's neck. meḍa 'neck' (Telugu). Rebus: meḍ 'iron' (Ho.) The artisan is a turner of copper and iron metals.

era, eraka = nave of wheel (Ka.); rebus: era, eraka 'copper' (Ka.) The glyph, 'nave of circle with six spokes': arā 'spokes'; eraka 'nave of wheel'; arā 'iron'; eraka 'copper'; kūṭa 'summit of mountain'; kūṭa 'mixing, alloy'. In historical times, brass gets called *pittaḷa* which has an expanded semantic homonym: *pittalāṭṭam* See also uploaded my ebook on Indian alchemy. [http://www.scribd.com/doc/2268545/Soma1]No wonder, the viśvakarma of Bharatam were able to create the wootz steel, the pancaloha murti-s from Swamimalai and also the Sanchi (now Delhi) iron pillar, apart from a hieroglyph, *śrivatsa*, adorning a torana..

Zinc retort distillation furnaces, to add to copper to create the alloy, brass – corrosion-resistant, strong alloy, a fore-runner of the industrial revolution. Ancient zinc smelting site, Zawar mines, south of Udaipur.

http://www.indogold.com.au/assets/images/photos/album/C7.jpg See lexemes: bakayantra 'crane-instrument'; name of a particular retort ; ka_cabakayantra 'a glass retort' (Skt.) The cognate kancu, kamsya indicates the possibility of such a retort having been used to create distillates of metals using a retort furnace. Tiryakpa_tana 'a kind of process applied esp. to mercury'; tiryakpa_tin 'falling obliquely on (loc.) (S'is.X.40); tiryaksu_tra 'a cross-line'; tiryakks.ipta 'placed obliquely' (Skt.) The prefix tiryak- may be derived from: S. *ṭrimaṇu* 'to ooze', *ṭrimiṇo* 'leaky', *ṭrimṭrimi* f. 'dripping'; L. *trimmaṇ* 'to drop, distil, leak', *trimmo* f. 'leaking, distillation'. (CDIAL 6039). āgrayaṇī— f. 'oblation of first fruits' KātyŚr., *āgrayaṇá*— 'the first soma libation at the Agniṣṭoma sacrifice' VS.A. *āgani* 'first distilled, strong' (CDIAL 1052). s'ucy 'to distil'; s'cut 'to cause to drop or flow , shed S'Br.' Pa_n. 7-4 , 61 Sch. Dha_tup. iii , 4 Dha_tup. xv , 6. a_su 'to distil' (RV 9.108.7) gad. 'to distil or drop, run as a liquid' (Dha_tup. 19.15); gad.ayati 'to cover, hide' (Dha_tup. 35,84).

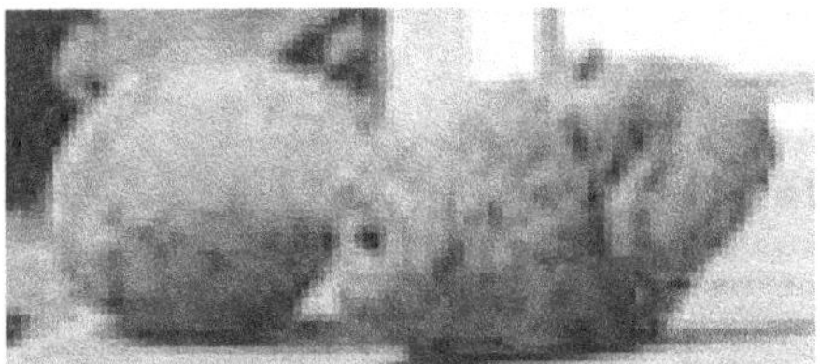

Zinc retort. Ancient smelting site mear Zawar mines, Rajasthan. Compare the retor distillation units shown at Zawar (in the above picture) with the following schematic of *tiryakpatana yantra* for distillation of zinc (*Rasaratnasamuccaya*).

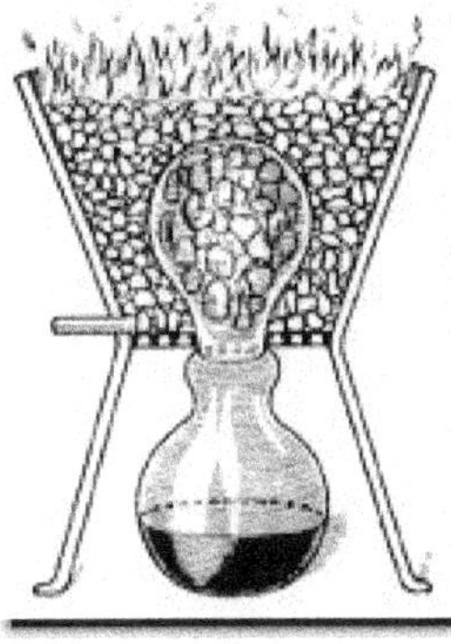

[quote] In the Rasaratnasamuchhaya a very famous Indian text on alchemy composed in 13AD, mentions many ancient Indian (pre christian era) alchemists like Nagarjuna, Govinda. It also mentions many ancient types of instruments, furnaces, bellows, retorts for extracting the metals from the ores and smelting. The Tirakpatana yantram(distillation by descending machine) was used for distillation purposes. It also mentions an ancient zinc production factory at Zawar(Rajahstan; located 24° 21' N; 73° 41'E ) and situated about 40km of Udaipur. In the early 1980's it was excavated and studied by the British Museum, MS university and Hindustan Zick limited. Zinc smelting was done in small cylindrical retorts (about 30 cm long and 10 cm in diameter) and the vapour was distilled from the charged retorts by placing them in the furnace in a vertically inverted position. The furnaces were found in two parts consisting of a zinc vapour condensation chamber at the bottom and a furnace chamber at the top.

These are separated by a perforated terracotta plate measuring 65 X 65 X 20cm. As many as 36 charged retorts were arranged inverted vertically on the perforated plate. From the condensation funnel tubes, luted with retorts, which were inserted through the perforated plate, zinc vapour was collected in vessels in the lower chamber and condensed.

Svastikā symbol used in historical periods

EC515. India, Ujjain, Sunga Province, ca 150-75BCE, AE Square Karshapana. Floral device and stylized man/2 swastika symbols, cf. MACW4625-4627.http://www.ancient-art.com/images/ec515.jpg

Sri lanka ancient cast coins, of copper-lead (association of the svastika with a tree glyph or an elephant glyph can be traced back to the evidence from Sarasvati epigraphs (Indus script inscriptions):

Obverse : A six branched tree within enclosure of six compartments in two rows of three each.
Reverse : A Railed *svastika* revolving to right (clockwise).

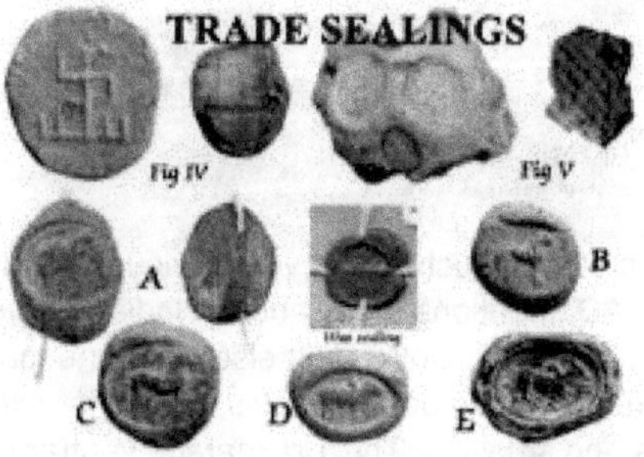


*http://www.lakdiva.org/coins/ancient/tree06c_rsvastika.html*

http://www.lakdiva.org/coins/ancient/tree08c_lsvastika.html

http://www.lakdiva.org/coins/ruhuna1/tree12c_rsvastika_bg.html

Ancient clay stamp seals and sealings have reportedly been found in Sri Lanka.

Glyptic art themes which parallel the Sarasvati hieroglyphs are found on early punch-marked coins (Dilip Rajgor, 2001, Punch-marked coins of early Historic India, California, Reesha Books International) and on Pallava coins (R. Krishnamurthy, 2004, The Pallava Coins, Chennai, Garnet Publishers). Some of these themes are:

Ancient coins of Bharat with svastikas, normal and ogee (After Figs. 231 to 234 in Thomas Wilson, opcit). The coins were found by Cunningham at Behat near Shaharanpur. E. Thomas assigns them to about 330 BCE. (Edward Thomas, *Jour. Royal Asiatic Soc. (new series),* I, p. 175). The svastika sign does not appear in Indo-Bactrian (ca. 300 to 126 BCE), Indo-Sassanian (from 200 to 636 CE) or later Hindu or Mohammedan coins. The sign of svastika becomes an integral part of the temple architectural tradition and becomes a sacred symbol of the Hindu, Bauddha and Jaina traditions.

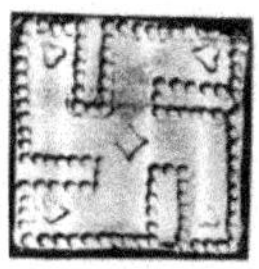

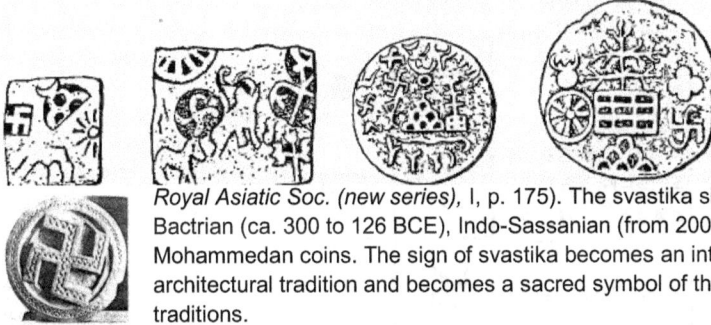

Stone toilet tray, Sirkap, Taxila, Stratum II (pl. g = No. 246, Marshall);

Gold amulet, Svastika_, 1st cent. CE, Sirkap, Taxila (Pl. 191, No. 85, Marshall).

Copper seal, svastika_, Sirkap, Taxila, stratum II, legend indistinct, pl. 55 no. 27, Marshall).

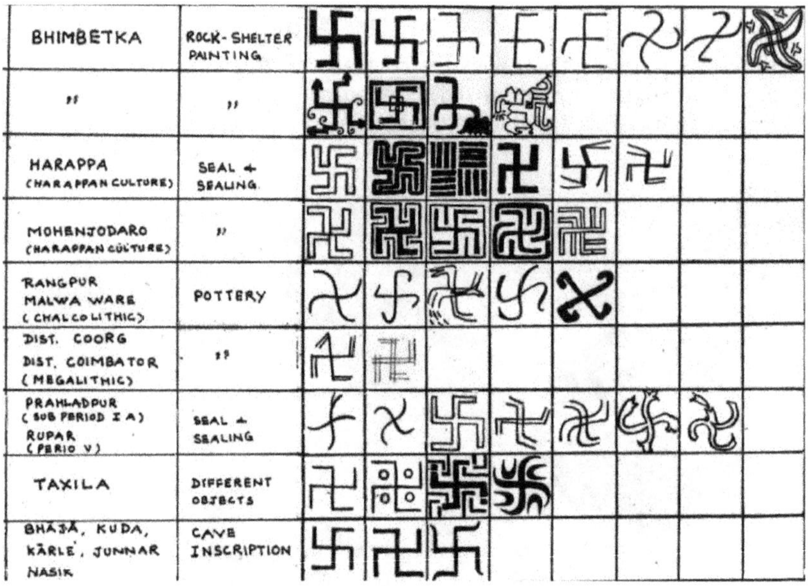


[Pl. 27, Svastika_ symbol: distribution in cultural periods]

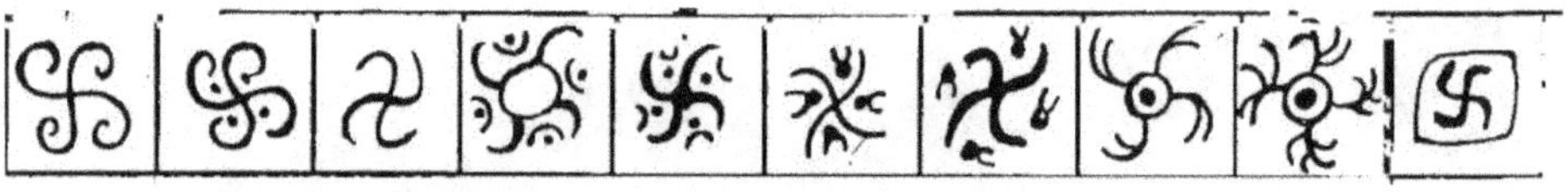

[Pl. 28, A, Ramnagar, Lotapur, Mamdar, Singavaran: Punch-marked coins]

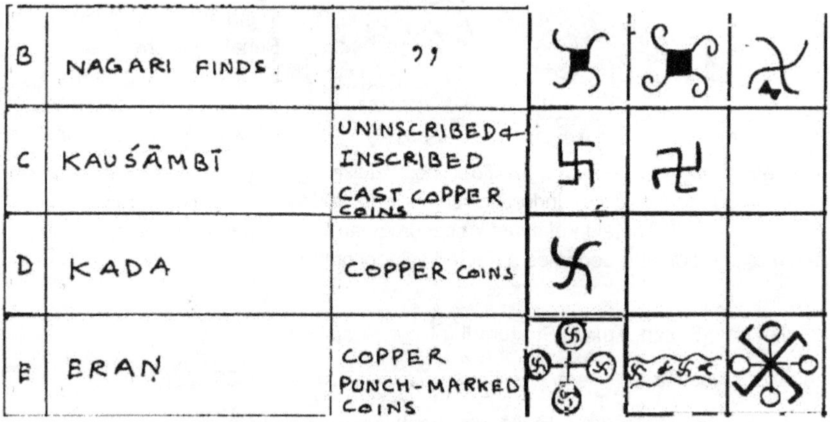


[Pl. 28, B to E: svastika_ symbol on punch-marked/cast copper coins]

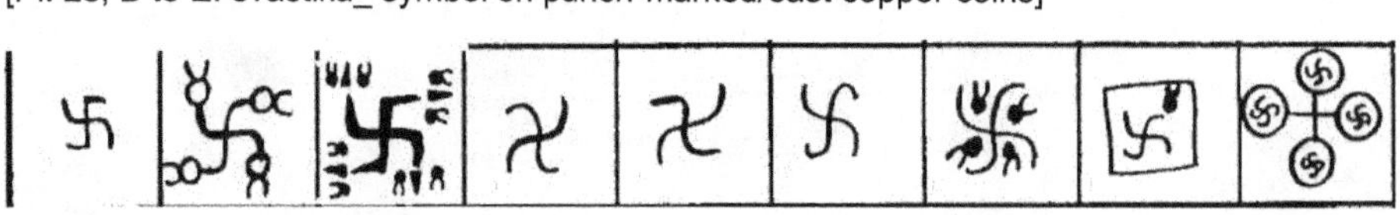

[Pl.28, F: Ujjayini, copper coins with svastika_ symbol]

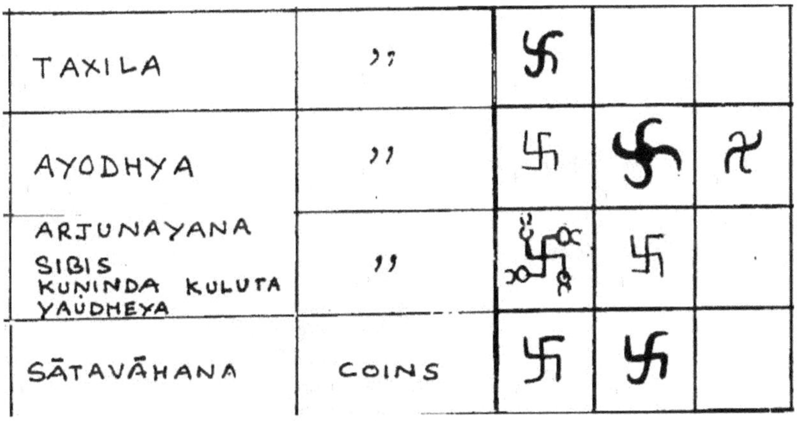


[Pl. 28, G to J, Taxila, Ayodhya, Arjunayana, Sibis, Kuṇinda, Kuluta, yaudheya, śātavāhana coins: Svastika symbol]

Standing male, dotted circles, portable furnace, Tree and Svastika, Elephant and Svastika glyphs on Srilanka punch-marked coins

Svastika

The finds of Pallava coins at Dvaravati of Thailand also attest to the continuing maritime tradition which began with the Sarasvati civilization.

High quality zinc alloys and zinc sheets have been found in ancient India. At Pratkashe, two copper objects containing 25.86 and 17.75% ink has been found in 2000BC. In the prehistoric Harappan civilisation copper bronze artefacts to 6% zinc were found.

About 20 miles north of Rawalpindi of modern Pakistan, brass objects(two bangles, one vase and pot) dated to around 300BC contained 34.34% of zinc. A chariot found in the lost city of Dwarika (4000-6000BCE) contained 10.68% zinc. Similarly, scores of brass items of items of Buddha, coins and caskets had some 17-25% zinc.

In fact an entire roll of sheet zinc at Agora in Athens in 300-400BC was found. And the Greeks were not producing zinc, and as we have ample evidence that it was produced in India, it can only be assumed they obtained these sheets from India. [unquote]

http://www.abovetopsecret.com/forum/thread111071/pg7

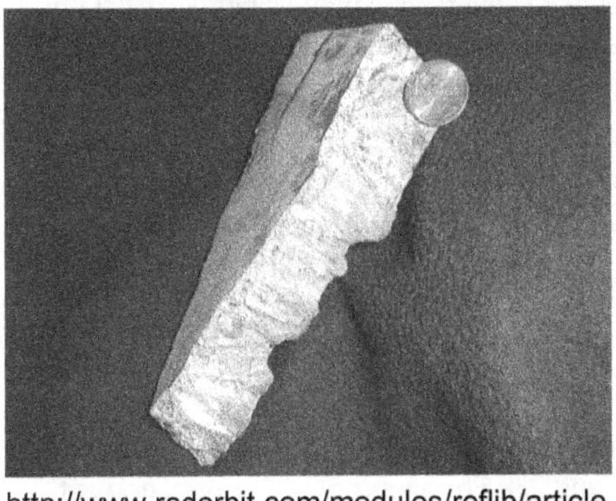

"Zinc alloys have been used for centuries, as brass goods dating to 1000-1400 BC have been found in Palestine and zinc objects with 87% zinc have been found in prehistoric Transylvania…the Hindus were aware of the existence of zinc as a metal separate from the seven known to the ancients."

http://www.redorbit.com/modules/reflib/article_images/28_66bc72775f3eb8353bc01ba3c861703a.jpg

Brass was used in Lothal and Atranjikhera in the 3rd and 2nd millennium BCE. "Among the old workings for zinc, the Zawar complex of Rajasthan in Western India is the most famous. Impressively abundant traces of old workings extend all over the 25 km mining belt and go down to a depth of 90 m below surface. It is claimed that the Zawar miners went up to depths exceeding 150m. The miners perhaps used wooden ladders, scaffolds and launders to drain water in the mines. The wooden samples of two such mines each at Zawar and at Mochina have been dated by $^{14}C$. These dates certainly suggest that in the second half of first millennium BCE extensive mining and smelting of lead-zinc ores were done in western India and perhaps the metal was supplied for various regions for coins and other objects. The earliest dates we have for zinc distillation are from a white heap, which is of the 12th century AD." http://www.infinityfoundation.com/mandala/t_pr/t_pr_khara_zinc_frameset.htm

KTM Hegde and Ericson, J.E., 1985, Ancient Indian Copper Smelting Furnaces, in: *Furnaces and Smelting Technology in Antiquity*, ed. P.T. Craddock, Occasional Paper No. 48, British Museum, London, pp. 59-67: The survey covered six ancient copper ore mining and smelting sites in the Aravalli (Arbuda) hills extending over a thousand kms.: Khetri and Kho Dariba in NE, Kankaria and Piplawas in the Central part and Ambaji in SW.. A large majority of mine-pits measure 7-8 metres in dia. and 3-4 metres deep showing evidence of fire-treating of the host rocks on the mine walls to widen rock joints. The evidene indicated probable mining in the chalcolithic period. Timber supports recovered from a gallery at a depth of 120 metres at Rajpura-Dariba mines in Udaipur District were radio-carbon dated to 3120+_ 160 years before the present (1987). This correlates with the zinc-containing copper artefacts of Atran~jikhera."The Arthasastra describes the production of zinc. The Rasaratnakara by Nagarjuna describes the production of brass and zinc. There are references of medicinal uses of zinc in the Charaka Samhita (300 BC). The Rasa Ratna Samuccaya (800 AD) explains the existence of two types of ores for zinc metal, one of which is ideal for metal extraction while the other is used for medicinal purpose. It also describes two methods of zinc distillation." see: Craddock, P.T. *et al.*, Zinc production in medieval India, World Archaeology, vol.15, no.2, Industrial Archaeology, 1983.

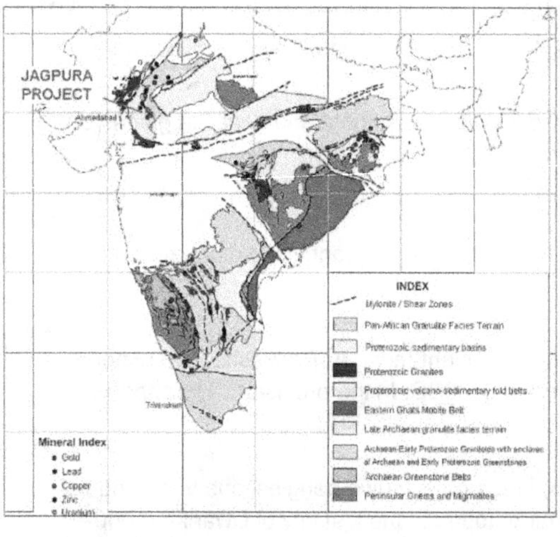


http://en.wikipedia.org/wiki/History_of_metallurgy_in_the_Indian_subcontinent

"An ingenious method was devised of downward distillation of the zinc vapour formed after smelting zinc ore using specifically designed retorts with condensers and furnaces, so that the smelted zinc vapour could be drastically cooled down to get a melt that could solidify to zinc metal." http://www.tf.uni-kiel.de/matwis/amat/def_en/articles/metallurg_heritage_india/metallurgical_heritage_india.html

"Lead isotope analyses undertaken by the author on a zinc ingot with a 4th century Deccan Brahmi inscription (previously exhibited in Science Museum, London, courtesy Nigel Seeley) corroborated a likely Andhra Deccan provenance, making it one of the earliest known surviving examples of metallic zinc in the world." (Srinivasan, S. 1998. "Highlights of ancient south Indian metallurgy-technical evidence for the early use of high-tin bronzes, high-carbon steel, metallic zinc, smelting of bronze and cast images, *Proceedings of the Fourth International Conference on the Beginning of the Use of Metals and Alloy (BUMA-IV)*, pp. 79-84. Matsue: Japan Institute of Metals). http://www.indianscience.org/projects/t_pr_srinibook2.shtml

The Aravallies Belt in Rajasthan is host to a number of major base metal deposits, including the world class, open pit deposit of Rampur Agucha (62 Mt @ 13% Zn and 2% Pb resource). The Khetri deposit in Western Rajasthan contains 24 Mt @ 1.2% Cu and 1.5g/t Au. http://www.indogold.com.au/rajasthan_mineralresources.htm

Geological map of India showing gold, lead, copper, zinc, uranium mineral locations. http://www.indogold.com.au/fig_1.htm

The early meaning of svastika as a glyph

This note reviews the evidence of the use of svastika as a glyph throughout the ancient world for over 3 millennia. The conclusion is that it connotes an object, a mineral – zinc (maybe, in its zinc oxide form called calamine). Brass was an alloy of copper and zinc and was known even before zinc was sublimated and discovered; by melting copper with calamine, brass which was a relatively easy material to cast (at a melting point of about 900 degrees C) with a yellow color comparable to the color of gold was produced. This decipherment is consistent with the occurrence of svastika glyph in the following contexts:

1. together with an endless-knot glyph (mer.ed 'iron'; rebus: mer.hao 'twisted');
2. together with the glyphs of a tiger looking back and an elephant [(kol krammara 'alloy smith'; rebus: kol 'tiger', krammara 'turning back'); (ib 'iron'; rebus: ibha 'elephant')]
3. together with a drummer glyph
4. Syracuse coin showing Arethusa at the center of a svastika
5. together with ducks in a Cyprus artifact (shown in Annex 1)
6. spearhead from Germany (shown in Annex 1)

Depiction of four or five svastika glyphs is an indication of the number of parts of zinc mixed with, say, eight parts of copper to create different types of hard or soft brasses (high brass has 35% zinc; low brass has 20% zinc), including arsenical brasses or lead brasses. They are also combined with iron, silicon and manganese to increase wear and tear resistance. An alloy called Corinthian brass, an alloy of gold, silver and copper, was known in ancient times. (In later technological developments, zinc is used to galvanize steel to prevent corrosion). "Before the discovery of zinc metal in India (made by the distillation route) sometime during the fifth-fourth century BC, brass could be made, as in Lothal and Atranjikhera, only by the cementation route in which one of the following was smelted along with copper ore : zinc ore, sphalerite concentrate or the roasted product, philosopher's wool or zinc oxide. The traditions of making philosopher's wool and cementation brass could have persisted even after the discovery of the distillation process of making zinc... the distillation route of making zinc and alloying this with molten copper was the only way of making high-zinc (more than 28%) brass, such as the 4th century BC Taxila vase (34.34% zinc)" (Arun Kumar Biswas, Zinc and related alloys, http://metalrg.iisc.ernet.in/~wootz/heritage/zn.html

"References to Zinc and brass are found in the lost text Philippica or Theopompus (4th century BC), quoted in Strabo's Geography (XIII, 56): "There is a stone near Andreida (north west Anatolia) which yields Iron when burnt. After being treated in a furnace with a certain earth it yields droplets of false silver. This added to copper, forms the so-called mixture, which some call oreichalkos." This pertains probably to the process of downward distillation of zinc ("droplets of false silver") and its subsequent mixing with Copper to make brass oreichalkos (arakuta in Kautilya's Arthasastra) described in detail in the post-Christian era Sanskrit texts." http://www.vanderkrogt.net/elements/elem/zn.html Caraka Samhita has references to medicinal uses of zinc(300 BCE).

A remarkable account of the use of svastika in ancient periods and conclusion that the glyph connoted an object is provided in: Thomas Wilson, 1896, *The Svastika_. The earliest known symbol, and its migrations; with observations on the migration of certain industries in prehistoric times,* Washington DC, The Smithsonian Institution, US National Museum, Washington DC.

Elsewhere, the entire corpus of Sarasvati hieroglyphs (Indus script epigraphs) has been deciphered as related to the repertoire of a smith and smithy. Consistent with this decipherment, the early meaning of svastika as a glyph is presented as a hieroglyph, read rebus: satva, 'zinc' (Pkt.) satavu, satuvu, sattu = pewter, zinc (Ka.) dosta = zinc (Santali) jasta = zinc (Hindi) jasada, yasada, yasadyaka, yasatva = zinc (Jaina Pali). Homonyms to denote the glyph are: sathiya_ (H.), sa_thiyo (G.); satthia, sotthia (Pkt.) = svastika_ sign.

Many hieroglyphs (including svastika and endless-knot motifs) become metaphors of wealth as shown in the use on ashtamangala necklace and on archways hoisted with s'rivatsa glyph. (Details provided in notes on decipherment of Sarasvati hieroglyphs). Svasti which is derivable as su + asti in Sanskrit grammar is explained as a metaphor for 'welfare, auspiciousness' by the depiction of the glyph on temple doors, during the historical periods. The rationale for using the glyph to connote welfare is that zinc as an additive to create an alloy of copper called brass, produced a metal which was 'as good as gold', that precious metal called soma 'electrum'.

That zinc – represented by the hieroglyph, svastika -- was a traded commodity together with other minerals is apparent from the finds of epigraphs containing Sarasvati hieroglyphs at locations such as Altyn Depe. Swat, Seistan.

The burden of this account is that this 'object' was in fact, zinc, a commodity traded and used for alloying with copper, to create brass. This alloy has alchemical overtones as discussed in Kalyanaraman, 2006, *Indian Alchemy: Soma in the Veda*, Delhi, Munshiram Manoharlal.

Svastika, the earliest known symbol

An interesting point is that some scholars agree that the model for the symbol of svastika_ must have been an object, known and useful throughout the ancient world. [Thomas Wilson, 1896, *The Svastika_. The earliest known symbol, and its migrations; with observations on the migration of certain industries in prehistoric times,* Washington DC, The Smithsonian Institution, US National Museum, Washington DC]. See notes at Annex 1 (Svastika and Endless-knot motifs) The annex also shows the picture of a special furnace for making bangles. The lid is stamped with a glyph, apparently before firing.

Our hypothesis is that the traders with their seals, and people who travelled in Swat and Seistan, in search of minerals, were the bronze-age smiths and lapidaries of Meluhha.

Association of svastika with endless-knot motif on epigraphs

m1356

m443At
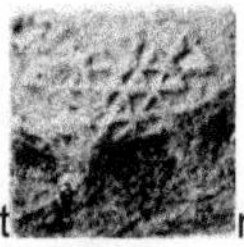
m443Bt The svastika glyph is associated with endless-knot glyph; the endless-knot glyph appears on a copper plate epigraph, indicating that both glyphs may connote the products made by metal-workers or equipment/processes involved in metal-work. mer.hao = v.a.m. entwine itself; wind round, wrap round roll up; mar.hna_ cover, encase (H) (Santali.lex.Bodding) Rebus: m ẽ mẽṛhẽt = iron (Santali)

The seals m443 and m1356 show the endless knot motif together with the svastikā glyph. The semantics connoted: meṛha, 'twisted; leader, merchant's clerk, meḍh'; svastikā, 'caravan'; the Sumer cylinder seal impression showing a chariot-rider and a caravan, by adding the endless knot motif as a semantic determinant is a depiction of a merchants' caravan, meḍh svastikā.

This interpretation is suggested because the deśī phonemes for svastikā are: suvatthi, sotthi = well-being (Pali)(CDIAL 13913). sāthiyo = auspicious mark painted on the front of a house (G.)(CDIAL 13917). svastikā is the emblem of the seventh deified teacher of the present era (Jainism)(G.lex.)

The symbol or the word, 'svasti' becomes an invocatory message on many epigraphs of the historical periods in Bha_rata.

Terracotta stamp seal, Taxila, c. 1st cent. CE. [After Parpola, 1994, fig. 4.6]

Mcmohan cylinder seal with six signs, found in 'Swat and Seistan', unrolled photographically and the unbroken stamp-end of the seal; positive impression of the cylinder showing Harappan inscriptions

(Robert Knox, 1994, A new Indus Valley Cylinder Seal, pp. 375-378 in: *South Asian Archaeology* 1993, Vol. I, Helsinki) The triangle motif is similar to the motif shown on M-443B.

"The Seistan findspot of this seal is of great interest. Evidence exists for the movement of Indus commodities, and, therefore, Indus commercial activities in the direction of western Asia and, in return, from there to the Indus world.Evidence for the Harappan penetration of Seistan and farther to southeastern Iran is scanty but includes at least one other Indus inscription from an impression of a sherd discovered at Tepe Yahya, period IV A (c. 2200 BC) (Lamberg- Karlovsky and Tosi 1973: pl. 137)" (Knox, p. 377).

Paul Amiet suggests an Iranian origin for the svastika motif. [Paul Amiet, 1961, *La glyptique Mesopotamienne Archaique,* Paris]

Two seals found at Altyn-depe (Excavation 9 and 7) found in the shrine and in the 'elite quarter'. V.M. Masson, Seals of a Proto-Indian Type from Altyn-depe, pp. 149-162; V.M. Masson, Urban Centers of Early Class Society, pp. 135-148; I.N. Khlopin, The Early bronze age cemetery in Parkhai II: The first two seasons of excavations, 1977-78, pp. 3-34 in: Philip L. Kohl (ed.), 1981, *The Bronze Age Civilization in Central Asia*, Armonk, NY, ME Sharpe, Inc. "The discovery in Altyn-Depe of a proto-Indian seal with two signs deserves special mention. V.M. Masson pointed out, that what the seal depicted was a pictogram and not just a representation of animals. In his opinion this means that some of the ancient residents of Altyn-Depe were able to read this text."(G. Bongard-Levin, 1989, Archaeological Finds in Central Asia throw light on Ancient India, Jagdish Vibhakar and Usha Gard (Eds.), *Glimpses of Ancient India through Soviet Eyes*, Delhi, Sundeep Prakashan).

Text 4500 (Incised miniature tablet; not illustrated).

Thus, a svastika appears together with an elephant or a tiger.The 'svastika' is a pictorial and also a sign

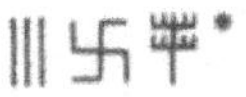

Svastikā: A marker of Bronze-age civilization in Bha_rata; its significance in the context of bronze-working in Bhārata with parallel imageries of Cyprus

meṛha = twisted, crumpled, as a horn (Santali.lex.) meli, melika = a turn, a twist, a loop, entanglement; meliyu, melivad.u, meligonu = to get twisted or entwined (Te.lex.) [Note the endless knot motif].

The seals m443 and m1356 show the endless knot motif together with the svastikā glyph. The Sumer cylinder seal impression showing a chariot-rider and a caravan, by adding the endless knot motif (figure shown in a later section) as a semantic determinant is a depiction of iron and zinc: med.h, satthiya .

Sign 148 Glyph:

There are over 50 inscribed objects with just the svastika_ pictorial motif.

In the Punjab, the mixed alloys were generally called, bharat (5 copper, 4 zinc and 1 tin). In Bengal, an alloy called bharan or toul was created by adding some brass or zinc into pure bronze. Sometimes lead was added to make it soft.

Arethusa and svastikā

Svastikā is a dominant glyph among the epigraphs of Sarasvati Civilization. Over 50 inscribed objects depict this glyph.

That the head of Arethusa is imprinted on a tin ingot and on a Greek coin in the middle of a svastikā glyph is a pointer to the decoding of the true meaning of svastikā glyph. The morpheme which occurs in Kannada may hold a key to this decoding: satavu, satuvu, sattu = pewter, zinc (Ka.) dosta = zinc (Santali) jasta = zinc (Hindi) jasada, yasada, yasadyaka, yasatva = zinc (Jaina Pali) ruhi-tutiya (Urdu) tuttha (*Arthaśāstra*) totamu, tutenag (Te.) oriechalkos (Gk.)

Homonyms are: sathiyā(H.), sāthiyo (G.); satthia, sotthia (Pkt.) = svastikā sign cf. svastika 'meeting of four roads' (Sk.) svastika the meeting of four roads; the crossing of the arms, making a sign like the cross (Skt.lex.) canti the cross roads, junction of three or more roads (Tirumuru. 225); cantikkarai junction where several roads meet (Ta.lex.)

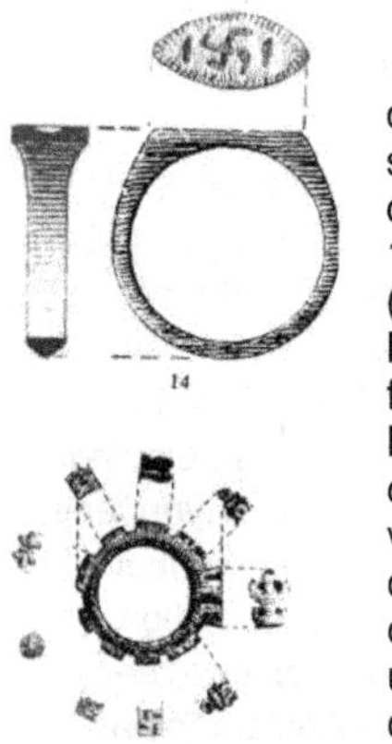


A copper additive, 'tin or arsenic or zinc' creates the alloy bronze/brass.

In early cementation processes roasted zinc ore (oxide) was mixed with copper fragments and charcoal (reducing agent) and the mixture was heated in a sealed crucible upto 1000 degrees C. The zinc vapour dissolved to yield a quality of brass. Examples of brass have been found in Lothal and Atranjikhera (6.28 to 16.2 % zinc) dated to c. 3rd and 2nd millennia BCE respectively. Carbon 14 dates (uncalibrated) for the Zawar mines of Rajasthan (40 kms. south of Udaipur) are PRL 932, 430+100 BCE and BM 2381, 380+ 50 BCE. Mining of lead zinc ores are found in the old workings at Rajpura-Dariba (375 BCE) and Rampura-Agucha (370 BCE) . At Prakashe, a Chalcolithic site (2nd millennium BCE) in Deccan, two copper objects each containing 25.86 and 17.75 percent zinc have been found. A vase found at Bhir mound (3rd cen. BCE), Taxila contained 34.34% zinc. A part of chariot in submerged Dwarka assayed 10.68% zinc (unknown date); many copper coins and many bronze images of historical periods contain upto 25% zinc. Silver used in many punch-marked coins was obtained from Zawar mines which yielded copper, zinc, lead and silver.

On coins from Syracuse the head of Arethusa was often portrayed (ca. 500 BCE). This girls' head has often a net in her hair and is usually surrounded by fish.

Arethusa coin from Syracuse, 4th cent. BCE Arethusa is a water divinity, as shown by the four fish circling around; she wears a diadem of beads.

Arethusa on a Greek coin [c. 510-490 BCE] The coin shows the image of Arethusa in the middle of a svastika_ glyph. Arethusa, a nymph known in several different parts of Greece, usually the Pelopponnese and Sicily. She was one of the Nereids. The river-god Alpheus fell madly in love with her, but she fled to Sicily. There she was changed into a fountain (the Fonte Aretusa, in Syracuse) by Artemis. Apheus made his way beneath the sea, and united his waters with those of Arethusa.

Svastika, a traded commodity – zinc

The svastika glyph connotes a countable object as seen from the number of glyphs shown on inscribed objects, On h165 seal, there are 4 svastika signs; this leads to the surmise that the svastika represents a countable *object.*

Copper finger ring, Sirkap, Taxila, Stratum I, (Pl. 197, No. 24, Marshall); a total of nine symbols are inlaid on the ring including svastikā, vajra, cakra, triratna, śrīvatsa, Pl. XXII.

Vajra and cakra are weapons. It is likely that svastikā is also a weapon or tool: śakti (flag) staff, spear (MBh.); satti = knife, dagger (Pali); satti = a kind of weapon (Pkt.); sāt = sword, spear (CDIAL 12251). It can be demonstrated that the 'śrīvatsa' glyph is a derivative from a composite glyph of two fishes.

Svastikā connotes satva, sattu 'zinc, pewter'; endless-knot connotes meṛed 'iron'. (Rebus: sattiya 'svastika glyph'; meṛhao 'twisted')

Endless-knot motif appears on the following objects:

1. Rojdi. Ax-head or knife of copper, 17.4 cm. long (After Possehl and Raval 1989: 162, fig. 77

2. Cylinder seal impression. Sumer (ca. 2500 BCE). After Amiet 1980a: pl. 108, no. 1435

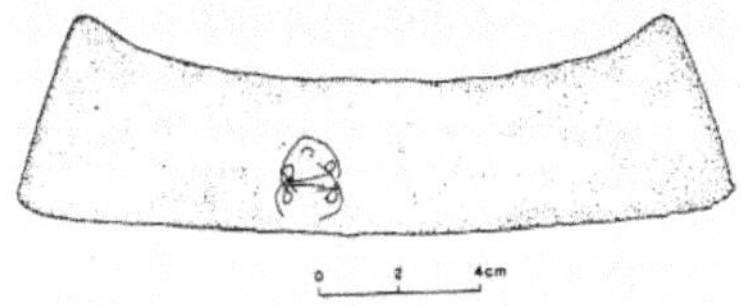

3. Early Dynastic seal. Lagash.
Early Dynastic seal, depicting an endless knot motif facing the turned face (krem-) of a battling tiger (kol-kamar, smelter-smith); Lagash. [After Amiet, 1980, pl. 83: no. 1099]

The endless-knot glyph and the signs may be read as:

Alternatives:

Alternative: Substantive: *mēṛhēt* 'iron'; *mēṛhēt icena* 'the iron is rusty'; *ispat mēṛhēt* 'steel', *dul mēṛhēt* 'cast iron'; *mēṛhēt khaṇḍa* 'iron implements' (Santali) *meḍ.* (Ho.)(Santali.lex.Bodding) *meṛed, mṛed, mṛd* iron; enga meṛed soft iron; *sanḍi meṛed* hard iron; *ispāt meṛed* steel; *dul meṛed* cast iron; *i meṛed* rusty iron, also the iron of which weights are cast; *bica meṛed* iron extracted from stone ore; *bali meṛed* iron extracted from sand ore (Mu.lex.)

kacc iron, iron blade (Go.)(DEDR 1096). karṣi furrowing (Skt.); kārṣi ploughing (VS.); karṣū furrow, trench (śBr.); kṣī plough iron (Pr.); kaṣi mattock, hoe (Paś.); kaṣi spade, pickaxe (Shum.); khaṣī small hoe (Dm.)(CDIAL 2909). kṛṣika, kuśika, kuśi, kuśira a ploughshare (Skt.Ka.)(Ka.lex.) keṣa plough (Pas'.)(CDIAL 3444). kiś plough (Kho.)(CDIAL 3455). ks.e plough iron (Pr.)(CDIAL 2809). Mattock, hoe: kaṣi mattock, hoe (Paś.); Spade, pickaxe: kaṣi spade, pickaxe (Shum.); karṣi furrowing (Skt.); karṣū furrow, trench (śBr.)(CDIAL 2909)

keccu the knot which is formed by twisting; to join the end of two threads by twisting them with the fingers (Ka.); kerci a knot (Tu.)(DEDR 1965).

granthi = knot (RV. 9.97.18); gāṇṭha (H.); granthin = twined together (RV 10.95.6); granth = to tie together (Vedic lex.)

L051a Seal. granthi = honey-comb (Pāṇini 4.3.116, Vārtt.); cf. Nir. 1.20; granthi = knot of a cord, knot tied in the end of a garment for keeping money (Pañcat.); a knot tied closely and therefore difficult to be undone, difficulty, doubt (Ch.Up.); granthila = knotted, knotty; grath = to be crooked (Dha_tup. 2.35); granthi = crookedness (Skt.lex.)

gaṇṭlu (pl.), gaṇṭi = hole bored in ears for ear-rings (Te.lex.)

brahma granthi = a sort of knot holding together the ends of dwija's sacred thread; gan.t.u = a knot (Te.lex.) grathanā = tying, binding, ensnaring; grathita = strung, tied (RV 9.97.18; śBr. 11) (Skt.lex.)

kranta = the meeting place of cross-roads; a lane; a hole (Te.lex.)

A remarkable demonstration of

(1) the continuity of the motif of endless knot in the Indian civilization from ca. 3rd millennium BC upto the 17th cent. AD.and even today, in South India; and

(2) the parallel use of the motif of the endless knot in Mesopotamian civilization ca. 3rd millennium BC.

grantha = a book or composition in prose or verse; a code; grantha lipi = one of the various characters used in writ (Ka.lex.)

kṛta = injured, killed; kṛti = hurt, hurting, injuring; a kind of weapon, sort of knife or dagger (RV 1.163.3) (Skt.lex.)

krandukayyamu = tumultuous mob fight (Te.lex.)

krandadiṣṭi = having roaring speed or moving with a great noise, said of Vāyu (RV 10.100.2); kranda = a cry, neighing (AV 11.2.22); a cry, calling out (AV 11.2.2 and 4.2) krandanu = roaring (RV 7.42.1); krandya = neighing (TBr. 2.7.7.1, parjanya krandya); krandana = crier; crying out; mutual daring or defiance, challenging (Skt.lex.). khaṛ = a call to cattle (Santali.lex.) khaṭ khaṭ = with a swish, thud, as of a horse's hoofs (Santali.lex.) kharajru = quick in motion (RV 10.106.7)(Vedic.lex.) kranditamu, krandanamu = cry, lamentation; krandillu = to sound, to resound (Te.lex.)

kratha = name of a race always named with the Kais'ikas and belonging to the yādava people; name of an Asura (MB h. 2.585; Skt.lex.)

kranta = the betrothal presents taken to the bride from the bridegroom's house (Te.lex.) grantha = giving, dāna; bhāgi, vibhāga (Ka.lex.)

grantha = wealth, property (Ka.lex.)

Inscribed objects containing the 'endless knot'

Glyph: The endless knot = krānta, gāṇṭha (Hindi) [cf, Lagash. Early Dynastic Seal with a variant of the endless knot. After Amiet 1980a: pl. 83, no. 1099.]

Substantive: krānta = invading, attacking (Skt.lex.) In the Tantra tradition, Bhāratavars.a is divided into three parts called krānta-s: viṣṇu-krānta, ratha-krānta, aśva-krānta each part having 64 tantra-s attached.

Land east of the Vindhya ranges, extending upto Jāva is Viṣṇu-krānta; the region north of Vindhya including mahācīna is aśva-krānta and the rest of the nation is aśva-krānta.

krandas = battle-cry, army (RV 10.121.6) yam krandasī avasā tastabhāne 'dyāvāpṛthivyau' (Vedic.lex.) krath = to hurt, kill (Dhātup. 19,39; caus. krāthayati, to hurt, injure, destroy (with gen. of the person hurt, Pāṇini. ii, 3.56, Dhātup. 34.19); krathana = cutting through (as with an ax); slaughter, killing (Skt.lex.) krathana = killing, slaughter (Ka.lex.) gaṇṭu = to cut, to wound; a wound, hurt; gaṇṭi = a wound (Te.lex.)

krandas = n. battle-cry; du. two contending armies shouting defiance [heaven and earth: Sāyaṇa]
*yam krandasī sṛlatayat ī vihvayete pare vara ubhayā amitrāh*
*samānam cid ratham ātasthivalatasā nānā havete sa janāsa indrah*

RV 2.012.08 Whom (two hosts), calling and mutually encountering, call upon; whom both adversaries, high and low, (appeal to); whom two (charioteers), standing in the same car, severally invoke; he, men, is Indra. [Whom (two hosts): yam krandasī sanyatī vihvayete = whom, crying aloud, encountering (two), invoke; the substantive is supplied: rodasī, heaven and earth; or, dve sene, two armies; whom (two charioteers): here also a substantive is supplied: rathinau, two charioteers; or Agni and Indra].

*śūro vā śūram vanate śar res tanūrucā taruṣi yat kṛṇvaite*
*toke vā goṣu tanaye yad apsu vikrandasī urvarāsu bravaite*

RV 6.025.04 The hero, (favoured by you), assuredly slays the (hostile) hero by his bodily prowess, when, both excelling in personal strength, they strive together in conflict, or when, clamorous, they dispute for (the sake of) sons, of grandson, of cattle, of water, of land.

*yam krandasī avasā tastabhāne abhy aikṣetām manasā rejamāne*
*yatrādhi sūra udito vibhāti kasmai devāya haviṣ ā vidhema*

RV 10.121.06 Whom heaven and earth established by his protection, and shining brightly, regarded with their mind, in whom the risen sun shines forth -- let us offer worship with an oblation to the divine Ka.

The importance of the glyph denoting svastika may be seen from the composition in m0488 tablet in bas relief. It occupies the center of the field and is flanked by an elephant and a tiger looking back:

m0488Atm0488Btm0488Ct

2802 Prism: Tablet in bas-relief. Side b: Text +One-horned bull + standard. Side a: From R.: a

composite animal; a person seated on a tree

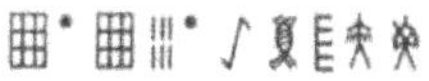

with a tiger below looking up at the person; a svastika within a square border; an elephant (Composite animal has the body of a ram, horns of a zebu, trunk of an elephant, hindlegs of a tiger and an upraised serpent-like tail). Side c: From R.: a horned person standing between two branches of a pipal tree; a ram; a horned person kneeling in adoration; a low pedestal with some offerings.

Glyph: 'cobra's hood': paṭam , *n.* < *phaṭa*. 1. Cobra's hood (CDIAL 9040). Rebus: 'sharpness of iron': padm (obl. Padt-) temper of iron (Ko.)(DEDR 3907).

On side B of a tablet (h177), kneeling person is shown in prayer in front of a standing person under an arch decorated with a toran.a of ficus leaves.

maṇḍa = a branch; a twig (Te.lex.)

maṇḍi = kneeling position (Te.lex.) mandil, mandir = temple (Santali) māḍa = shrine of a demon (Tu.); māḍia = house (Pkt.); māḷa a sort of pavilion (Pali); māḷikai = temple (Ta.)(DEDR 4796).

maṇḍiga = an earthen dish (Te.lex.) maṇḍe = a large earthen vessel (Tu.lex.) maṇḍi earthen pan, a covering dish (Konḍa); cooking pot (Pe.); brass bowl (Kui); basin, plate (Kuwi)(DEDR 4678). maṇḍe = head (Kod.)(DEDR 4682).

maṇḍā = warehouse, workshop (Kon.lex.)

Glyph: *sal* a gregarious forest tree, *shorea robusta*; *kambra* a kind of tree (Santali)

Substantive: *sal* workshop (Santali)

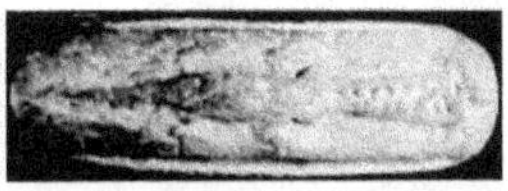

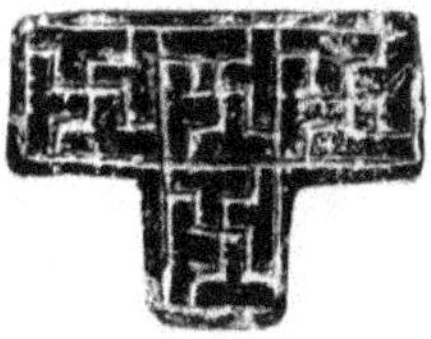
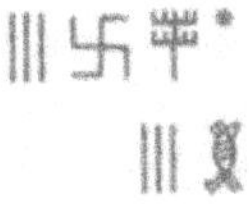

m0482Atm0482Bt 1620 Pict-65: Gharial (or lizard), sometimes with a fish held in its jaw and/or surrounded by a school of fish.

h1654500 On h182 tablet, there are 5 svastika signs; on h165 seal, there are 4 svastika signs; this leads to the surmise that the svastika represents a countable *object.* Ponea 'four' (Santali); rebus: pon 'gold' (Ta.); sathiya 'svastika glyph'; rebus: sattva, jasada 'zinc' (Ka.Skt.H.) mõṛe 'five (count)' (Santali); rebus: maṇḍua 'booth, shed' (Santali)

On tablet m0482, the svastika follows the glyph of a tree branch '*aduru*'; hence the two signs may be read as: *aduru* 'metal' + *satthiya* 'knife, dagger' (*śakti* –Skt.) swadhiti (RV.AV.) sathiyā (H.) knife, dagger, sathiā, satthaka = knife (Pkt.Ka.)

m1225A m1225B.1311 Cube seal with perforation through the breadth of the seal Pict-118: svastikā , generally within a square or rectangular border.

m1389t Rahman-dheri150

m0507At m0507Bt 3350

m0508Atm0508Bt 3352

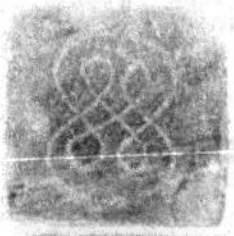

http://kalyan97.googlepages.com/svastika1.doc

http://kalyan97.googlepages.com/svastika2.doc

http://kalyan97.googlepages.com/annex1asvastika.doc

http://kalyan97.googlepages.com/annex1bsvastika.doc

http://kalyan97.googlepages.com/Annex2aSvastikaseals.doc

http://kalyan97.googlepages.com/Annex2bSvastikaseals.doc

Rao finds the svastika motif more common in Mesopotamia than in the Sarasvati civilization. Paul Amiet suggests an Iranian origin for the svastika motif. [Paul Amiet, 1961, *La glyptique Mesopotamienne Archaique,* Paris]

Yaudheya coin. Godess Sas.t.hi on reverse. S.an.mukha with lance on obverse. Lucknow State ...vati Sindhu inscriptions is echoed in the glyphs of a svastikā ...*ismatics Society of India*, Vol. V, Pt.I, June 1943) This is ...śakti, spear, saṣṭi = six, satthika = auspicious symbol. The ...n.

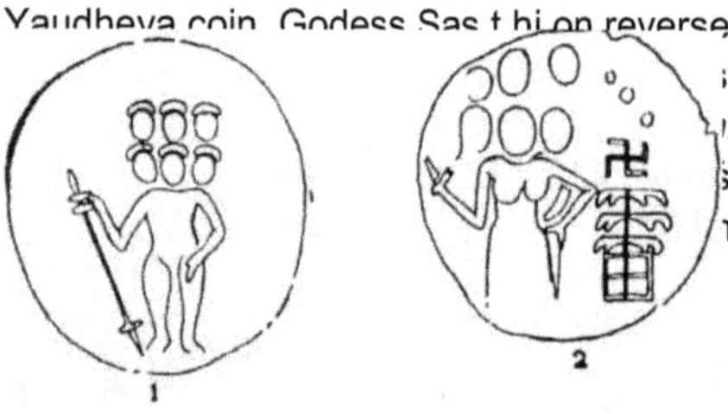

Godess śaṣṭhi. Mathura, 2nd cent. Mottled red sandstone 67.8 X 34.5 cm (MIK I 5924). "The godess lifts her right hand in a gesture of salutation that is typical of the Kushana period. The hand is slightly turned inwards, towards the body (vyāvṛtta-mudra). Her left arm, which bends outward, rests on her hip. She wears a broad girdle, a thin band around the waist, and aa sash over the shoulders and arms. her jewellery comprises earrings, a braod necklace, and bangles... on the large nimbus, which occupies the entire upper half of the stele, five more female figures are seen, which seem to emanate from the main figure. Each of the secondary figures have both arms lifted, perhaps in an expression of joy. They hold certain objects in their hands which are difficult to identify... the large size of the present stele suggests that it was meant for a temple..." (Heino Kottkamp, Exhibit 26 in: Saryu Doshi, ed., 1998, *Treasures of Indian Art: Germany's tribute to India's cultural heritage*, Delhi, National Museum, p.33).

Sattva 'svastika glyph'; rebus: jasta, yasada, sattva 'zinc' *mõṛẽ* 'five (count)'. Rebus 1: Md. *moḍenī*' massages, mixes '. (CDIAL 9890) Pa. *mōdanā* -- f. ' blending (?)(CDIAL 10356). Rebus 2: *maṇḍua* 'booth, shed'

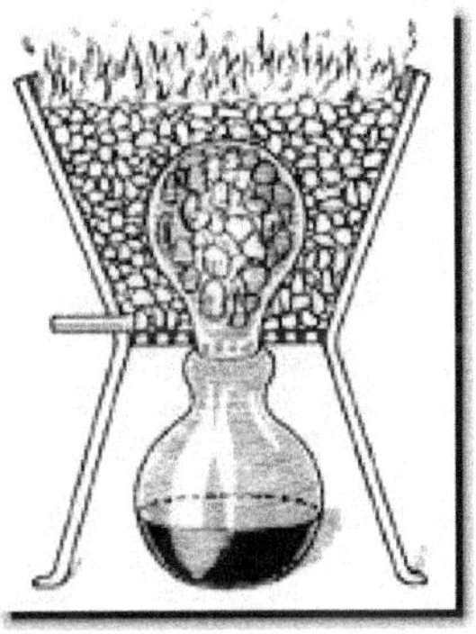

The hieroglyph showing five svastika: zinc-shed or zinc-granary.

Discovering the 8th metal A history of Zinc
Fathi Habashi

*History of Zinc*

Centuries before zinc was discovered in the metallic form, its ores were used for making brass and zinc compounds were used for healing wounds and sore eyes. Although the word brass frequently occurs in the Old Testament, there is little evidence that an alloy of zinc and copper was known in early times. The word translated "brass" might equally well be rendered bronze or copper, both of which were in common use.

*Figure1: Schematic representation of the Indian method for producing zinc.*

In the latter part of the thirteenth century, Marco Polo described the manufacture of zinc oxide in Persia and how the Persians prepared tutia (a solution of zinc vitriol) for healing sore eyes.

The Roman writer Strabo (66 B.C. - 24 A.D.) mentioned in his writings that only the Cyprian ore contained "the cadmian stones, copper vitriol, and tutty," that is to say, the constituents from which brass can be made. It is believed that the Romans first made brass in the time of Augustus (20 B.C. to 14 A.D.) by heating a mixture of powdered calamine, charcoal and granules of copper. Roman writers observed that coins made from orichalcum were undistinguished from gold.

Zinc in India

The production of metallic zinc was described in the Hindu book Rasarnava which was written around 1200 A.D. The fourteenth century Hindu work Rasaratnassamuchchaya describes how the new "tin-like" metal was made by indirectly heating calamine with organic matter in a covered crucible fitted with a condenser. Zinc vapour was evolved and the vapour was air cooled in the condenser located below the refractory crucible (Figure 1). By 1374, the Hindus had recognized that zinc was a new metal, the eighth known to man at that time, and a limited amount of commercial zinc production was underway. At Zawar, in Rajasthan, great heaps of small retorts bear testimony to extensive zinc production from the twelfth to the sixteenth centuries. The tubular retorts are about 25 cm long and 15 cm in diameter with walls about 1 cm thick. A small diameter tube was sealed onto the open end and the zinc vapours likely condensed in this. The retorts were closely spaced in a furnace which was probably heated with charcoal fanned by bellows. Both zinc metal and zinc oxide were produced. Zinc was used to make brass whereas the oxide was used medicinally. Over 130,000 tons of residue remain at Zawar and this represents the extraction of the equivalent of 1,000,000 tons of metallic zinc and zinc oxide.

Zinc in China

*Figure 2: The Chinese learned about zinc production sometime around 1600 A.D.*

From India, zinc manufacture moved to China where it developed as an industry to supply the needs of brass manufacture. The Chinese apparently learned about zinc production sometime around 1600 A.D. An encyclopedia issued in the latter half of the sixteenth century makes no mention of zinc, but the book Tien-kong-kai-ou published early in the 17th century related a procedure for zinc manufacture. Calamine ore, mixed with powdered charcoal, was placed in clay jars and heated to evolve zinc vapour. The crucibles are piled up in a pyramid with lump coal between them (Figure 2), and, after being brought to redness, are cooled and broken. The metal is found in the center in the form of a round regulus. Zinc production expanded and metal began to be exported.

Zinc in Europe

*Figure 3: Albertus Magnus described the production of brass.*

Albertus Magnus (Figure 3) (ca. 1248) described how either calamine or furnace tutty might be used to colour copper gold. He suggested that a more golden lustre might be obtained by sprinkling crushed glass on top of the mixture in the crucible to form a slag which would help prevent the escape of the zinc vapour; in other words, increase the zinc content of the brass.

Biringuccio (ca. 1540) has the next most complete description of brass making. He described how either calamine or furnace tutty could be mixed with broken up pieces of copper and sprinkled with a layer of powdered glass, then heated in a closed crucible for 24 hours.

*Figure 4: Georgius Agricola (1490-1555) observed in 1546 that a metal called "zincum" was being produced in Silesia.*

Agricola (Figure 4) in 1546 reported that a white metal was condensed and scraped off the walls of the furnace when Rammelsberg ore was smelted in the Harz Mountains to obtain lead and silver to which he gave the name "contrefey" because it was used to imitate gold. This often consisted to metallic zinc, although he did not recognize it as such. He observed, furthermore, that a similar metal called "zincum" was being produced under similar circumstances in Silesia by the local people. Paracelsus (1493-1541) (Figure 5) was the first European to state clearly that "zincum" was a new metal and that it had properties distinct from other known metals.

*Figure 5: Paracelsus (1493-1541) was the first European to state clearly that "zincum" was a new metal.*

Thus, by about 1600, European scientists were aware of the existence of zinc. All the metal they had examined, however, had likely been imported from the East by Portuguese, Dutch and Arab traders. However, there was a profusion of names quite unrelated to the local names for zinc ores. These included tutenag (derived from the Persian tutiya, calamine,which became the English tutty, zinc oxide) and spelter (likely from the similar coloured lead-tin alloy, pewter, or the Dutch equivalent, spiauter or Indian tin which the British scientist Robert Boyle latinised to speltrum in 1690 from which originates spelter, the commercial term for zinc. The word tutia, an old name for zinc oxide, is derived from a Persian word that means smoke and refers to the fact that zinc oxide is evolved as white smoke when zinc ores are roasted with charcoal.

In Renaissance times, latten (or laten, laton, lattyn) became the common English word for brass, akin to the French laiton (= brass) and Italian latta (= sheet brass), and probably based on the Latin latte or lathe (= sheet). The origins of the German word for brass, Messing, may be related to the Latin massa (= lump of metal). The modern English brass may be related to the French braser (= braze or solder). The word "zinc" may be derived from the Persian word sing meaning stone. In Arabic, zinc is known as kharseen, i.e. Khar from Al-Ghar = mine, seen from Al-Seen = China, hence kharseen, the metal from

Chinese mines. The spelter trade with the East flourished throughout the seventeenth and first half of the eighteenth centuries, although there seem to be no records concerning the tonnages involved.

*Figure 6: Andreas Marggraf (1709-1782) fully described the production of zinc from calamine.*

In an extensive research "On the method of extracting zinc from its true mineral, calamine", Andreas Marggraf (Figure 6) in 1746 reduced calamine from Poland, England, Breslau and Hungary with carbon in closed retorts and obtained metallic zinc from all of them. He described his method in detail, thereby establishing the basic theory of zinc production. Marggraf also showed that the lead ores from Rammelsberg contained zinc and that zinc can be prepared from sphalerite. Marggraf was probably unaware that in 1742, the Swedish chemist Anton von Swab (1703-1768) had distilled zinc from calamine and that, two years later, he had even prepared it from blende. Since the vapors rose to the top of the alembic before passing into the receiver, this process was called distillation per ascendum. In 1752 Swab and another Swedish chemist Axel Fredrik Cronstedt (1722-1765) developed at government expense the use of Swedish zinc ores for the manufacture of brass, to avoid the necessity of importing calamine.

The knowledge of deliberate zinc smelting in a retort was acquired by an Englishman on a visit to China just prior to 1740. A vertical retort procedure was developed by William Champion (1709-1789) and by 1743 a zinc smelter had been established at Bristol in the United Kingdom. A charge of calamine and carbon was sealed into a clay crucible having a hole in the bottom. This was luted onto an iron tube extending below the crucible furnace into a cool chamber below. The closed end of the iron tube sat in a tub of water and it was here that the metallic zinc was collected (Figure 7). The distillation took a total of about 70 hours to yield 400 kg of metal from all 6 crucibles positioned in the furnace. An annual production rate of 200 tons has been suggested for the works at that time.

*Figure 7: William Champion's zinc smelting furnace.*

This type of apparatus continued to be employed until 1851 although it was fuel inefficient, consuming 24 tons of coal for every ton of spelter produced. In 1758, William's brother, John, patented the calcination of zinc sulfide to oxide for use in the retort process, thereby laying the foundation for the commercial zinc practice which continued well into the twentieth century. The English zinc industry was concentrated in Bristol and Swansea.

The Welsh process was a batch operation which required withdrawing the crucible and retort after each cycle. It was labour intensive and fuel inefficient. A major technological improvement came with the development of the German process by Johann Ruberg (1751-1807) who built the first zinc smelting works in Wessola in Upper Silesia in 1798 which used the horizontal retort process developed by him. The principal advantage of this technique is that the retorts were fixed horizontally into the furnace allowing them to be charged and discharged without cooling. By placing the retorts in large banks, fuel efficiency was greatly increased. The raw material initially used was zinc galmei (calamine), a by-product of lead and silver production. Later, it became possible to produce zinc directly from smithsonite, an easily smelted ore. This was shortly followed by the use of zinc blende, which had first to be converted into the oxide by roasting. After this development, other smelting works were soon erected in Silesia near the deposits, in the areas around Liège in Belgium, in Aachen, in the Rhineland and Ruhr regions in Germany.

The first Belgian plant was built by Jean-Jacques Daniel Dony (1759-1819) in 1805 and also used horizontal retorts but of slightly different design. A larger plant was built in 1810. This was the predecessor of the Societé de la Vieille Montagne which a few years later became the largest zinc producing company in the world.

Zinc production in the United States started in 1850 using the Belgium process and soon became the largest in the world. In 1907, world production was 737,500 tons of which the USA contributed 31%, Germany 28%, Belgium 21%, United Kingdom 8%, and all other countries 12%.

The excellent resistance of zinc towards atmospheric corrosion soon led to its use in sheet production. The possibility of rolling zinc at 100-150¡C was discovered as early as 1805 and the first rolling mill was built in Belgium in 1812. More such mills were built in Silesia from 1821 onwards. Hot-dip galvanizing, the oldest anticorrosion process, was introduced in 1836 in France. This became possible on an industrial scale only after the development of effective processes for cleaning iron and steel surfaces. At first, only small workpieces were zinc coated. Continuous hot-dip galvanizing of semi-finished products and wire came later. In the United States, the rich ore deposits led to rapid growth in zinc production in 1840, so that by 1907, Germany, which had for long been the world's leading producer of zinc, was left behind.

Zinc was produced for about 500 years from its oxide ores which are far less abundant than the sulfides, before the sulfides became the major source of supply. The technology of zinc production changed gradually during the centuries towards a more pyrometallurgical route. However, this tendency underwent a radical change during World War I when the roasting-leaching-electrowinning process was introduced and in the 1980's, when pressure leaching-electrowinning offered another practical route to zinc production.

Fathi Habashi is Professor of Extractive Metallurgy at the Department of Mining and Metallurgy, Université Laval, Québec Cty, Canada G1K 7P4.

http://www.initiative-zink.de/309.htm

Thomas Wilson, [curator, Department of Prehistoric Anthropology], notes: "(svastika_) is characterized by straight bars of equal thickness throughout, and cross each other at right angles, making four arms of equal size, length and style." While not finding definitive clues as to its time or place of origin, Wilson concludes that the svastika_ was perhaps the first symbol to be made with 'a definite intention' and a continuous or consecutive meaning, the knowledge of which passed from person to person.

The view that the symbol may perhaps have represented a known object, is echoed by Ashley and Butts. H.J.D Ashley wrote: "In the first instance probably the svastika_ may have represented the course of the sun in the heavens revolving normally from left to right." (1925, The Swastika: A study, *The Quest*, January 1925). Edward Butts noted: "…It is evident that the svastika_ figure is only emblematic of what it originally was, from the fact that it must have been a more useful device and of very necessary application to have forced itself into the needs of so many widely distributed localities." [1901, *Statement No.1: The Swastika*, Kansas City, Franklin Hudson Publishing Co.]

Friedrich Max Mueller characterized the symbol with its hooks facing left-ward as suavastika, but there is no corroboration for such a lexeme. Wilson analyzed the occurrence of the symbol on artifacts – from funeral urns to spears – and attempted a classification by physical and symbolic properties to fathom some logic as to why the symbol has been prevalent in so many cultures for so long. It is difficult to surmise that the sign was just ornamental; it had some specific symbolic importance.

Troy. Svastika_ with four birds. [Compare the two ducks shown with the symbol in Cyprus. Source: Dr. Henry Schliemann, 1885, *Tiryns: the prehistorical palace of the kings of Tiryns*, New York, Charles Scribner's Sons]. "According to the migration theory (as opposed to the coincidence theory), the svastika_'s earliest known habitat is a wide territory beginning at the valley of the river Indus in India and extending westward across Persia and Asia Minor to Hissarlik (where the remains of ancient Troy were found) on the shore of the Hellespont…W. Norman Brown contented (1933, The Swastika: The study of the Nazi claims of its Aryan Origin, Emerson Books) that 'for combined age, frequency, and perfect execution, the examples from the Indus Valley are the most interesting.'..Brown noted that the svastika_ was among India's 'first civilized remains, as early as 2500 BCE, possibly 3000 BCE, and appears in forms perfectly developed, in contrast with slightly older but primitive and less perfect forms found farther westward.' More important, Brown concluded that it existed in India before the arrival of the Aryans. 'Like other symbols which the Aryans of India used on coins and stone sculpture, it came to them from non-Aryan predecessors. It was a simple minutia of the spoils the victors had taken from those they had vanquished.'..The svastika_ was also discovered in the early 1930s in explorations of the ancient civilization in Baluchistan (in Central Asia)...The next chronological stratuth' (as Brown calls it) for the svastika_ appears at Hissarlik, the site of Homer's Troy, and many older cities that had risen and perished before it...According to Brown (and contrary to Schliemann's assertion), it was at Hissarlik or elsewhere in Asia Minor that the Indo-Europeans may for the first time have met the svastika_, but this is only a supposition." (Steven Heller, 2000, *The Swastika: symbol beyond redemption?* New York, Allworth Press, pp. 28-33).

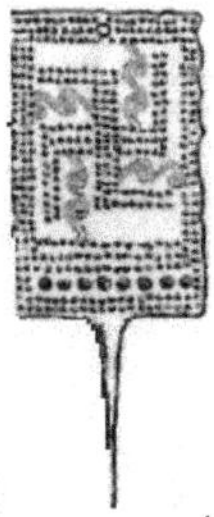

W. Norman Brown who refuted the claim of Indo-European origins of the svastika_ was emphatic that the people who first used the symbol were the 'Japhetic' and the Indus Valley Peoples. "Whatever these various peoples were, they were not Indo-Europeans; and the Indo-Europeans, as far as our evidence indicates, did not know the svastika_ until a thousand years after the

time of its earliest preserved specimens." He further adds: "Egypt seems to have been without it (svastika_) until very late, when Greece had arisen. Ancient Assyria and Palestine, as far as I know, were also without it... Although by 2000 BCE it extended across to the Hellespont, it passed to the north of the great Semitic territory and missed that people. The jews did not use it. Early Christianity seems not to have known it. The Christians used the svastika_ only after their religion was well established in Europe."

Many bronze articles with svastika_ sign; Dates: Unknown [Source: Thomas Wilson, *Report of National Museum*, 1894]. Celts who were proficient bronze- and gold-workers also used the svastika_ motif.

Bronze pin-head from the Caucasus

Marks of three svastika_ on black pottery from Caucasus

Fragment of bronze ceinture from Necropolis of Koban, Caucasus

Bronze pin from Bavaria

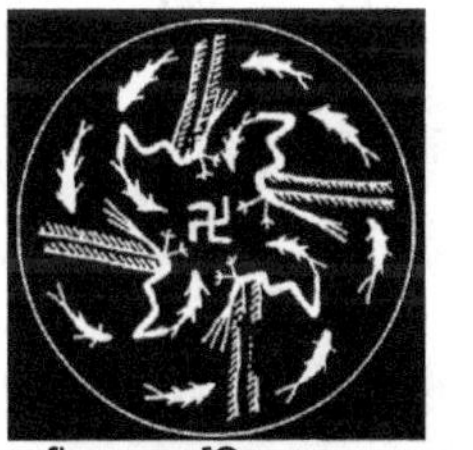

Footprints of the Feet of the Buddha; note the svastika_ just below the fingers. [Source: Alexander Cunningham, 1962, *The Stupa of Bharhut: a Buddhist monument*, Varanasi, Indological Book House].

Cypriot artifact with svastika_. Note the symbol on the stylized, flower-like wheel of the chariot.

Ireland. Triskelion on carved wood.

Cypriot artifact with svastikā flanked by two ducks.

Cypriot artifact with svastika_ on the shoulder of the warrior holding a bull model in his left hand; his hind-part is the hind-part of a bull?

The picture on the left shows a large runic stone bearing an inscription concerning the dead man it commemorates, three interlocked drinking horns, and a sinistroverse meandroid swastika. It was found at Snoldelev, Denmark.

Iron spearhead showing runic inscriptions and two closed meandroid swastikas, one of them destroverse, and the other one sinistroverse.

Found at Brest-Litovsk, Russia, probably of Gothic origin, and dated from approximately the third, the fourth, or perhaps even the fifth century B. C.

Swastikas, mostly in its sinistroverse form, but also in its destroverse form, are currently found in weapons.

http://www.intelinet.org/swastika/swasti09.htm

Coin from Crete ca. 1000 BCE.

Samara (near Baghdad) 5000 BCE. (Fish and svastika glyphs)

Greek pottery 700 BCE. Two tigers (jackals?) and two peacocks facing each other. Svastika glyphs shown all around. The lady with outstretched hands wears a skirt with fish glyph on it. (kolli 'fish'; kola 'woman'). Head of a bull (?) atop the tiger on the left.

http://www.heathenworld.com/swastika/

Shipwreck, Greek pottery, Ischia Museum / VIII century BC (Fish and svastika glyphs)

Minoan writing,
(Crete) / XIV century BC (Svastika within circles is shown on row 2 and row 4).

Altar, Pyrenees (South of France) /I Century BC (The altar shows a svastika and a fish – both are Sarasvati hieroglyphs.)

http://pagesperso-orange.fr/archeometrie/swastika.htm

 h613A  h613C  4259 Endless-knot motif?

 Chanhu-daro49A  Chanhu-daro49B

 Chanhu-daro50A  Chanhu-daro50B

 m1457Act  m1457Bct  2904 Copper tablet [4 out of 4 are copper tablets]

 m0457At 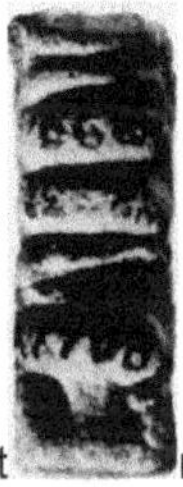 m0457Bt  m0457Et [Frequency 13]

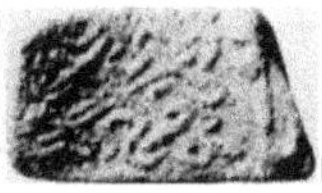 m0458At  m0458Bt 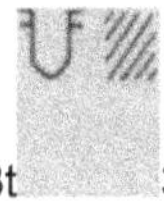 3227

 m0459At  m0459Bt  3225

 m0460At  m0460Bt  3228

m0461At m0461Bt 2806 Pict-73: Alternative 1. Serpent (?) entwined around a pillar with capital (?); motif carved in high-relief.

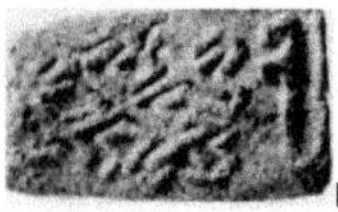m0462At m0462Bt 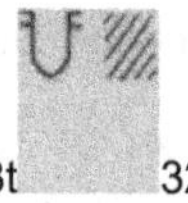3215

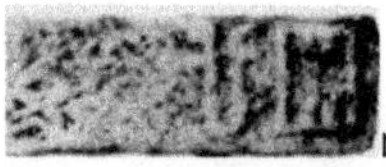m0463At m0463Bt 2813

Four-crosses motif on a Mohenjo-daro tablet M-463 is comparable to the same motif which appears painted on a potsherd of Malwa ware from Navdatoli, Maharashtra, c. 1700-1400 BCE. [After H.D.Sankalia, SB Deo and ZD Ansari, 1971, *Chalcolithic Navdatoli: the excavations at Navdatoli, 1957-59*. Poona: 216f., fig. 87: D 585 (sherd 8355 I A 13/5; After Paropla, 1994, p.55, fig. 4.4).

Alternatives:

kōlam = form (Ta.Ma.) Rebus: kol 'metal'

kaṇḍa kanka 'rim of pot'; rebus: kaṇḍ 'altar, furnace' + kan- 'copper' or, kaṇḍ 'stone (ore) metal'.

Alternatively, the endless-knot motif which follows the pair of signs (following Text 2813, for example) may be read as:

mẽṛhẽt = iron (Santali)

The entwined stones around a pillar or an entwined snake glyph:

meṛhao = v.a.m. entwine itself; wind round, wrap round roll up; maṛhnā cover, encase (H) (Santali.lex.Bodding) [Note: the endless-knot motif may be a rebus representation of this semant. 'entwine itself']. meḍhā = curl, snarl, twist or tangle in cord or thread (M.); meli, melika = a turn, a twist, a loop, entanglement; meliyu, melivaḍu, meligonu = to get twisted or entwined (Te.lex.) merhao = twist (Mun.d.ari)

meḍi = sound, roar (TS 5.7.8.1); methis.t.ha = worthy of hearing (TBr. 2.7.6)(Vedic.lex.) mleccha = a man speaking any language but Sam.skr.ta and not conforming to brahmanical institutions; a kirāta, s'abara or pulinda etc.; mleccharene koḍava koḍagaru…koḍava kon:garu (Ka.lex.) mlaskati = to snap with tongue (Slovan)(Vedic.lex.) mlech = speak indistinctly (Skt.); mlecchati speaks indistinctly (S'Br.) brichun, pp. bryuchu = to weep and lament, cry as a child for something wanted or as motherless child (K.)(CDIAL 10384). milakkha, milakkhu non-aryan (Pali); malak savage; malaki-dū a Vaddā woman (Si.); milāca wild man of the woods, non-aryan (Pali); maladu wild, savage (Si.); mīcuth, mīcatas habit or life of an outcaste (K.)(CDIAL 10390). mleccha = non-aryan (*śathapathabrāhmaṇa*); malecha, milicha, meccha, miccha = barbarian (Pkt.); mī~ch, mī~cas non-hindu (K.); milech, malech Moslem, unclean outcaste, wretch (P.); melech dirty (WPah.); mech a Tibeto-Burman tribe (B.); milidu, milindu wild, savage (Si.)(CDIAL 10389).

Alternative : doṇṭho 'knot'; rebus: dhoṇḍ 'stone-cutter'

Glyph: *doṇṭho, dhoṇṭho, dhoṇṭo* a knot (Santali)

*dhoṇḍ.-phoḍo* [M. *dhoṇḍā*, a stone] a stone-cutter, a stone-mason; *dhoṇḍjhoḍo* [M. *dhoṇḍā* a stone + *jhoḍavum*] a stone-cutter; a stone-mason; *dhoṇḍo* a stone; a blockhead; a stupid person (G.)

Considering that on the cylinder seal impression from Sumer the motif of 'endless-knot' is shown together with a chariot accompanied by persons carrying weapons and also a dog, the entire glyptic could be related to a hunting expedition. This is consistent with the other part of the cylinder seal on the top register depicting a boat journey, also accompanied by a person carrying a spear. Thus, the 'endless-knot' as a glyph should be related to semant. 'attack' or 'killing'.

The association of the 'endless-knot' glyph with the 'svastika' glyph points to both the glyphs as related to the description of a weapon.

 h182A   h182B 4

306Tablet in bas-relief

h182a Pict-107: Drummer and a tiger. h182b Five svastika signs alternating right- and left-handed.  har609 terracotta tablet, bas-relief [The drummer is also shown on h182B tablet with a comparable epigraph and five svastika glyphs alternating right- and left-handed arms. [Lexeme : *mõṛẽ* = five (Santali. lex.)]

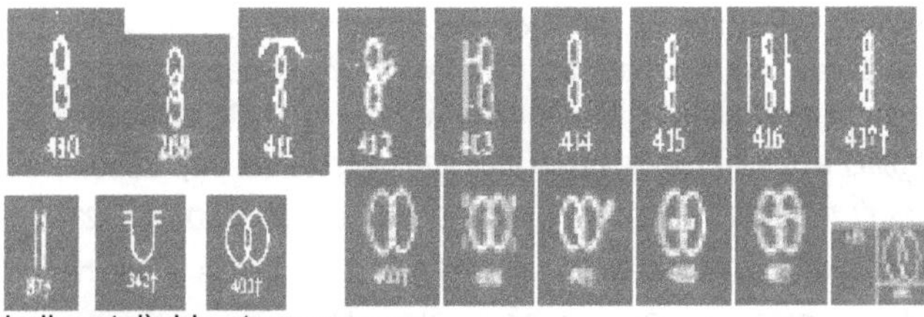  m1406B  Rebus message: alloying (mixing) zinc (sattiya). Casting (metal, iron, bronze, bell-metal); big stone mason

G. kā̃sā m. pl. ' cymbals ' (CDIAL 2576). Ko. kā̃śẽ n. ' bronze '; H. kās, kā̃sā m. ' bell -- metal ', G. kā̃sũ n., M. kā̃sẽ (CDIAL 2987). Vikalpa: sangaḍa 'bangles' (Pali). Rebus: sangāta 'association, guild' (Skt.)

Glyph: 'rim of jar'. kaṇḍ kanka. Rebus: kaṇḍ kanka 'stone (ore) metal furnace account (scribe)'.

Glyph: 'two long linear strokes': ib 'two'. Rebus: ib 'iron' (Santali) Vikalpa: Glyph: A pair of linear strokes (two long linear strokes) Vikalpa: dula 'pair'. Rebus: dul 'cast (metal)(Santali)

kaḍī a chain; a hook; a link (G.); kaḍum a bracelet, a ring (G.) Rebus: kaḍiyo [Hem. Des. kaḍaio = Skt. sthapati a mason] a bricklayer; a mason; kaḍiyaṇa, kaḍiyeṇa a woman of the bricklayer caste; a wife of a bricklayer (G.)

Glyph: *ḍhol* 'a drum beaten on one end by a stick and on the other by the hand' (Santali); *ḍhol* 'drum' (Nahali); *dhol* (Kurku); *ḍhol* (Hi.) *dhol* a drum (G.)(CDIAL 5608)

Rebus: dul 'to cast in a mould'; dul *mẽṛhẽt, dul meṛeḍ, dul; koṭe meṛeḍ* 'forged iron' (Santali) WPah.kṭg. (kc.) *ḍhṑl* m. ' stone ', kṭg. *ḍhòḷṭɔ* m. ' big stone or boulder ', *ḍhòḷṭu* ' small id. ' Him.I 87.(CDIAL 5536).

Graphemes: డోలు [ ḍōlu ] ḍōlu. [Tel.] n. A drum.ḍollu. [Tel.] v. n. To fall, to roll over. పడు, పొరలు. డొలుచు [ ḍolucu ] or ḍoluṭsu. [Tel.] v. n. To tumble head over heels as dancing girls do (Telugu) Mth. Bhoj. Aw. lakh. Marw. G. M. *ḍhol* m. *ḍhōlayati ' makes fall '(CDIAL 5608).

Vikalpa: *maṇḍao* 'to occupy a new house, to take up one's residence'; *maṇḍhwa, maṇḍua, maṇḍwa* 'a temporary shed or booth erected on the occasion of a marriage'; *maṇḍom* 'a raised platform or scaffold'; *mãṛom* 'a platform, used to keep straw on, or from which to watch crops' (Santali) *mandar* 'the headman of a village'; *maṇḍwari* 'the Marwari caste of hindus' *Ko.* manḏ Toda mund (i.e. village); burning place for dry funeral; mandm (*obl.* mandt-) meeting. *To.* moḏ (*obl.* moṟt-) locus of tribal activity, including village with dairy, dairy apart from village, and funeral place; patrilineal clan. *Ka.* mandu hamlet of the Todas on the Nilagiri. *Koḍ.* mandï village green; *Ta.* maṉṟu hall of assembly, golden hall of Chidambaram, court of justice, arbitration court, cow-stall, herd of cows, raised platform under a tree for village meetings, center of a garden, junction of four roads or streets (DEDR 4777).

Glyph: *mõṛẽ* 'five' (Munda etyma)

Glyphic element: 'vaulting'

Steatite stamp seal with a water-buffalo and leapers.Seal: Mohenjo-daro, Harappan, ca. 2600 – 1900 BCE. National Museum, New Delhi, 147.

m0312 Persons vaulting over a water-buffalo. Rebus: sāl 'shed, workshop' (B.)(CDIAL 12414) sal 'place, as in dancing place'; kamar sal 'a smithy'; paura sal 'a liquor shop'; paṭhsal 'a school house'; ak sal 'a place where sugarcane is pressed'; kaṭ sal 'a carpenter or joiner's workshop'; lagṛẽ sal 'a place where the lagṛẽ dance is danced'; piarsalare kamarko salakata 'blacksmiths have opened a smithy in Piarsala'; dare baṭareko salakata 'they have set up a forge under a tree'. *சாலை*[1] cālai, n. < šālā. Sacrificial hall; *யாகசாலை. திருத்திய சாலை புக் கனன்* (*கம்பரா. திருவவ.* 84). School; *பள்ளிக் கூடம். கறையறு கல்விகற்குங் காமர்சாலையும்* (*குசே லோ. குசே. வைகுந்.* 23). Cow shed; *பசுக்கொட்டில். ஆத்துறுசாலைதோறும்* (*கம்பரா. ஊர்தேடு.* 101). Large public hall; *பெரிய பொதுமண்டபம்.* Loc. Royal palace; *அரசன் அரண்மனை.* (*பிங்.*). House, mansion; *வீடு. விதுரன்சாலைக் கரும்புது விருந்தாமருந்தே* (*அழகர்கல.* 5). Sālā (f.) [cv. Vedic śālā, cp. Gr. kali/a hut, Lat. cella cell, Ohg. halla, E. hall] a large (covered & enclosed) hall, large room, house; shed, stable etc., as seen fr. foll. examples: aggi˚ a hall with a fire Vin i.25, 49=ii.210; āsana˚ hall with seats DhA ii.65; udapāna˚ a shed over the well Vin i.139; ii.122; upaṭṭhāna˚ á service hall Vin i.49, 139; ii.153, 208, 210; S ii.280;v.321; J i.160; kaṭhina˚ a hall for the kaṭhina Vin ii.117. kīḷa playhouse J vi.332; kutūhala˚ a common room D i.179= Siv.398. kumbhakāra potter's hall DhA i.39; gilāna˚ sick room, hospital S iv.210; Vism 259; jantāghāra˚ (large) bath room Vin i.140; ii.122; dāna˚ a hall for donations J i.262; dvāra˚ hall with doors M i.382; ii.66; pāniya˚ a water -- room Vinii.153; bhatta˚ refectory Vism 72; yañña˚ hall of sacrifice PugA 233; rajana˚ dyeing workshop Vism 65; ratha˚ car shed DhA iii.121; hatthi˚ an elephant stable Vin i.277, 345; ii.194; Ji.187. (Pali) śā´lā f. ' shed, stable, house ' AV., śālám adv. ' at home ' ŚBr., śālikā -- f. ' house, shop ' lex.Pa. Pk. sālā -- f. ' shed, stable, large open -- sided hall, house ', Pk. sāla -- n. ' house '; Ash. sal ' cattleshed ', Wg. šāl, Kt. šål, Dm. šâl; Paš.weg. sāl, ar. šol ' cattleshed on summer pasture '; Kho. šal ' cattleshed ', šeli ' goatpen '; K. hal f. ' hall, house '; L. sālh f. ' house with thatched roof '; A. xāl, xāli ' house, workshop, factory '; B. sāl ' shed, workshop '; Or.sāḷa ' shed, stable '; Bi. sār f. ' cowshed '; H. sāl f. ' hall, house, school ', sār f. ' cowshed '; M. sāḷ f. ' workshop, school '; Si. sal -- a, ha ' hall, market -- hall '.upaśāla -- , *pariśālā -- Add., *pratiśālā -- , *praśālā -- ; aśvaśālā -- , āpānaśālā -- , *kaṇikaśālā -- , karmaśālā -- , *karmāraśālā -- , *kōlhuśālā -- , *khaṇḍuśālā -- , *gāvaśāla -- , gōśālā -- , cathuśāla -- , candraśālā -- , citraśālā -- , chā´ttriśālā -- , jyōtiḥśālā -- , dānaśālā -- , *dhānyaśālā -- , *nayaśālā -- , nayaśālin -- , *nītiśālā -- , paṇyaśālā -- , parṇaśālā -- , *pituḥśālā -- , *prapāśālā -- , bhāṇḍaśālā -- , *bhusaśālā -- , *bhrāṣṭraśālikā

-- , *yantraśālā -- , lēkhaśālā -- , *lōhaśālā -- , *vaidyaśālā -- , *śvaśuraśālā -- , hastiśālā -- .Addenda: śā´lā -- : †*āhanaśālā -- , †dharmaśālā -- . (CDIAL 12414)

sal 'house, as in school house; shop, as in workshop (Santali)

baṭi trs. To overturn, to overset or ovethrow; to turn or throw from a foundation or foothold (Santali) baṭi to turn on the ground to any extent, or roll; uaurbaṭi, to upset or overthrow by shoving or pushing; mabaṭi to overturn by cutting, to fell trees; baṭi-n rflx. v., to lay oneself down; ba-p-aṭi repr. V., to throw each other; baṭi-o to be overturned, overthrown; ba-n-at.i vrb.n., the extent of the overturning, falling down or rolling; baṭi-n rlfx.v., to lie down; baṭi-aṛagu to bring or send down a slope by rolling; baṭi bar.a to roll again and again or here and there; baṭi-bur to turn over by rolling (Mundari) Rebus: baṭi, bhaṭi 'furnace' (H.)

m1202 seal.

The inscription on one side of 2-sided tablet h771 read rebus: kā̃sē bronze '; *khaḍu* 'stone nodule, metal'. *dul* 'cast' *lb* 'iron'. *khātī* 'wheelwright'. Side 2: *kaṇḍa bhaṭi* 'stone (ore) metal furnace'. [Glyphic elements: kā̃sā m. pl. 'cymbals'; khaḍū 'squirrel'; dula 'pair'; ib 'two'.]

h419

Nindowari damb seal. Enlargement of the part of the text on Nindowari seal.  Moulded Harappa tablet h771At  h771Bt

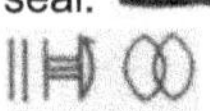

 4678 The 'squirrel' glyph variants seen on Harappa tablet, Harappa seal and Nandowari damb seal -- are normalised as Sign 187 for purposes of concordance list (Mahadevan).

Squirrel glyph on h419. खडी [ khaḍī ] A squirrel. खडू [ khaḍū ] *f* खडूळ *f* A squirrel. Rebus: *khaḍu, kaṇ* 'stone/nodule (metal)' *khātī* 'wheelwright'. గణము [ gaṇemu ] *gaṇemu*. [Tel.] n. Frippery. Ornaments, trappings, horns, &c., worn by maskers. వేషధారులు ధరించే లక్కసొమ్ము.

Allograph: 'bier': khaḍū1 m. ' bier ' lex. 2. khaṭṭi -- m. lex. [Cf. kháṭvā -- ]1. B. *khaṛu* ' bier '.2. B. *khāṭi* ' bier ', Or. *khāṭa*. (CDIAL 3785). Rebus: H. *khātī* m. ' member of a caste of wheelwrights '; kṣattṛ́ m. ' carver, distributor ' RV., ' attendant, door- keeper ' AV., ' charioteer ' VS. (CDIAL 3647). Vikalpa: glyph: 'squirrel': tsāni, tsānye 'squirrel' (Kon.) rebus: śannī a small workshop (WPah) caṇila squirrel (To.).

Vikalpa (alternative reading): sega 'a species of squirrel' (Santali) Koḍ. aṇekoṭṭï id. Tu. caṇil, canil, taṇil, (B-K. also) aṇil id. (DEDR 2315). Rebus: śannī (WPah.) may denote a small shed (?workshop): Woṭ. šen ' roof ', Bshk. šan, Phal. šān (AO xviii 251, followed by Buddruss Woṭ 126, < śar(a)ṇa -- ); WPah. (Joshi) śannī f. ' small room in a house to keep sheep in '.(CDIAL 12326). The duplicated grapheme may thus be decoded as: dul sannī 'casting workshop (small shed or workshop).'

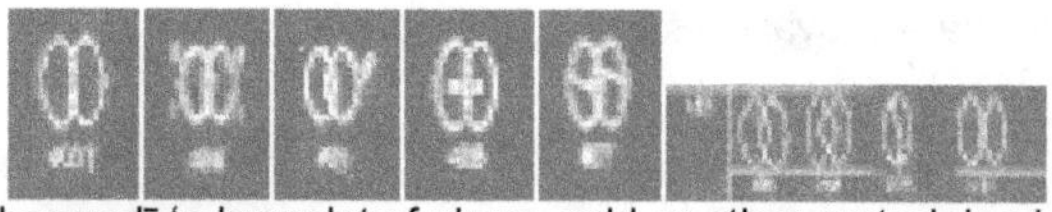

bangaḍī 'a bracelet of glass, gold or other material, a bangle worn on the wrist by women (G.) Rebus: bangala 'a goldsmith's portable furnace' (Te.)

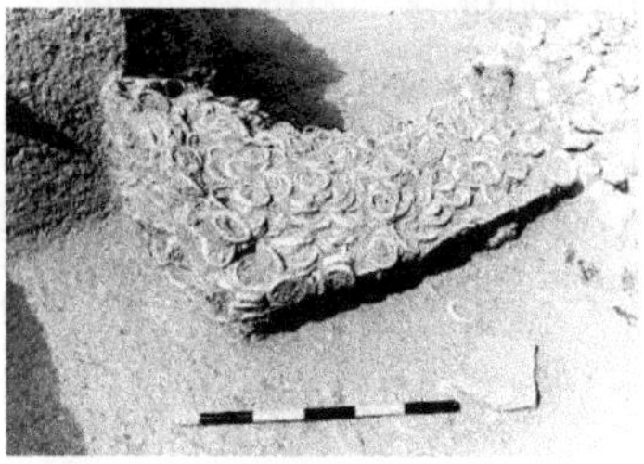

Gola dhoro, Gujarat. Unfinished shell circlets with grinding stone in front. The gloss sẽkhā (Bengali) may denote such shell circlets produced as bracelets. shẽkh शेँख् (Kashmiri) Rebus: sekra 'a hindu caste who work in brass and bell metal' (Santali) Hence, the pair of glyphs can together read: bangaḍī 'a bracelet of glass, gold or other material (G.) Rebus: bangala 'a goldsmith's portable furnace' (Te.)

pãeṛẽ = overflow channel of a tank (Santali).

Rebus: articles of joint family (pãeṛẽ) (Santali).

The text 4306:

Glyph: *cuṛi* a bracelet,  a bangle (Santali)

Glyph: millstone: san:ghaṭi = a millstone, that crushes (Ka.)

Rebus: cūḷai, 'kiln' (Ta.) culli = a fireplace (Ka.)

Rebus: saghaḍī = furnace (G.)

Elephant hieroglyph: *ibbo*, 'merchant' (*deśī nāmamālā)* ib 'iron'. *ibha, karibha* 'elephant'. *karbaṇa* 'iron'.

Cylinder seal impression: Rhinoceros, elephant, lizard (gharial?).Tell Asmar (Eshnunna), Iraq. IM 14674; glazed steatite; Frankfort, 1955, No. 642; Collon, 1987, Fig. 610.

Indus 'elephant' seal from Gonur Tepe (compiled from images supplied by Maurizio Tosi, Gregory L Possehl and Viktor Sarianidi). Posted in Expedition, Vol. 49, No. 1, 2007

The first glyph from the right on the seal impression seems to combine some glyphic elements of the following glyphs (text signs):

Halbi 'iron' 8132).

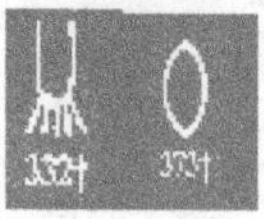

*mendī* eyelashes (DEDR 4864). Rebus: *meḍ* (Ho.) *pāso* 'die'. M. *pās* f. ' silver ingot (CDIAL S. *baṭhu* large cooking fire; P. *bhaṭṭh* m., °*ṭhī* f. ' furnace ' (CDIAL 9656) baṭa = kiln (Santali); baṭa = a kind of iron (G.) The combination of glyphic elements on the the first glyph -- *pās meḍ* -- of Gonur Tepe seal may therefore connote a type of kiln and/or metallurgical process for , metal (iron, silver) ingots, polished. [Ligaturing with 'four or five slanted strokes may connote 'polished (metal)' – semantics as in *baṭa* 'a kind of iron' (G.)].

m1702a (Glyphic comparable to the Gonur Tepe glyph?) dula 'pair'. Rebus: dul 'cast (metal)'. Cast and polished (ingot)?

Glyph: 'winged insect': *Ma.* pōnta a great fly. *Kol.* potte any winged insect, bee; surunt potte bee. *Nk.* potte large flying insect. *Pa.* (S.) potta large insect. / Cf. Skt. puttikā- a kind of bee (*Car. S.* I.27.243, Comm.: piṅgalā makṣikā mahatyaḥ puttikāḥ); pauttika- the honey from such bees. (DEDR 4518).

Rebus: 'glass beads or jeweller's polishing stone': Pk. *pottī*-- f. ' glass '; S. *pūti* f. ' glass bead ', P. *pot* f.; N. *pote* ' long straight bar of jewelry '; B. *pot* ' glass bead ', *puti, pūti* ' small bead '; Or. *puti* ' necklace of small glass beads '; H. *pot* m. ' glass bead ', G. M.*pot* f.; -- Bi. *pot* ' jeweller's polishing stone ' (CDIAL 8403).

Glyph: 'burn at the bottom of vessel': *Ka.* pottu to be kindled, catch fire, flame; be burnt (as rice, etc., at the bottom of the vessel), be boiled or baked too much; *n.* flaming; pottige flaming, flame. Rebus: 'to burn': *Ta.* pottu (potti-) to light (as a fire). *Kurub. (LSB* 1.12) potte a torch of leaves. *Ko.* pot- (poty-) to light (as a fire); pot torch made of a bundle of thin sticks. *Tu.* pottuni to burn (*intr.*); pottāvuni, pottāḍruni to light, kindle, burn; potta hot, burning; potturuni, potruni to kindle, set fire, incite to a quarrel. *Go.* (A. Y.) pot-, (Tr.) pattānā, (Ch.) patt-, (Mu.) pat-/patt-, (Ma.) pot- to burn, blaze; (Tr. Ph.) pacānā to make a bright light; (SR.) potusānā to light (*Voc.* 2384). (DEDR 4517).

Rebus readings of other glyphs (the 'iron (metal) merchant' lists his metallurgical repertoire/workshop (smithy/forge) facilities: Glyph: ibha, karibha 'elephant'. Rebus ibbo 'merchant'; karba 'iron'. Ib 'iron'. glyph: sal 'splinter'. Rebus: sal 'workshop'. Glyph: aya 'fish'. Rebus: ayas 'metal'. *aḍaren, ḍaren* 'lid,cover' (Santali) Rebus: aduru 'native metal' (Ka.) G. *kāmṭhiyɔ* m. ' archer ' (CDIAL 2760). kammaṭi a coiner (Ka.). ranku 'liquid measure'. Rebus ranku 'tin' (Santali) kolmo 'rice plant'. Rebus: Kolami 'smithy/forge' (Telugu). Glyph: 'rim of jar'. Rebus: *kaṇḍa kanka* 'stone (ore) metal furnace account (scribe)'.

The seal inscription is decoded: iron merchant; iron, silver ingot kiln (smelter); coiner (mint) workshop; native metal, metal, tin smithy/forge; stone (ore) metal furnace account (scribe).

B.B. Lal, 2007, Let not the 19th century paradigms continue to haunt us! - Inaugural address delivered at the 19th Intl. conf. on South Asian archaeology, held at Univ. of Bologna, Ravenna, italy on July 2-6, 2007. This inaugural address by BB Lal concludes that the Bactria-Margiana Archaeological Complex (BMAC) exemplified by the artifacts found at Gonur Tepe should not lead a researcher to conclude that Aryan migration occurred through BMAC en route to India!

Lal's notes from the concluding part of the address: (Begin quote) Have we not in the past explained the occurrence of some items of a given culture-complex in another complex by means of trade / exchange / casual gift or a similar mechanism: for example, the occurrence of Harappan seals, etched carnelian beads, etc. in Mesopotamia, Iran and even Central Asia by trade and not by migration of the Harappan population? Then why invoke the migration of the BMAC people to explain the presence of some seals / seal-impressions, etc. at stray Indian sites?

In the context of the debate whether the ¡Rigvedic people were indigenous or invaders / immigrants from outside, the evidence of two sister disciplines, namely human biology and human genetics, must also be brought into the picture.

After a thorough examination of the relevant human skeletons, Hemphill and his colleagues (1991) categorically pronounced: "As for the question of biological continuity within the Indus Valley, two discontinuities appear to exist. The first occurs between 6000 and 4500 BC ... and the second occurs at some point after 800 BC." In other words, there was no entry of a new set of people between 4500 and 800 BCE, much less of Aryan invaders / immigrants !

In recent years a great deal of genetic research has been carried out which too throws valuable light on this issue; and I quote here Sanghamitra Sahoo, et al. (2006: 843-48): "The sharing of some Y-chromosomal haplogroups between Indian and Central Asian populations is most parsimoniously explained by a deep, common ancestry between the two regions, with the diffusion of some Indian-specific lineages northward. The Y-chromosomal data consistently suggest a largely South Asian origin for Indian caste communities and therefore argue against any major influx, from regions north and west of India, of people associated either with the development of agriculture or the spread of the Indo-Aryan language family."

Scholars have already abandoned (though after much dithering) the 'Aryan Invasion' theory. Is it not high time to rethink and shelve the newly hugged-to-the-chest 'Bactria-Margiana Immigration' thesis as well? (End quote)

Text of Indus inscription on Mohenjo-daro copper tablet m527 (obverse: elephant in front of trough) m527 Mohenjo-daro copper tablet.

ibha 'elephant' (Skt.); rebus: ib 'iron' (Santali) karibha 'elephant' (Skt.); rebus: karb 'iron' (Ka.) Two semantic clusters point to glosses meaning 'iron'. One cluster relates to karba and cognates in Indian linguistic area. The second cluster relates to ib and cognates in Inddian linguistic area. Both are relatable to homonyms (and related graphemes) of elephant. The rebus words for elephant are: karin, karabha and ibha.

An allograph is ficus religiosa: karibha -- m. ' Ficus religiosa (?) [Semantics of ficus religiosa may be relatable to homonyms used to denote both the sacred tree and rebus gloss: loa, ficus (Santali); loh 'metal' (Skt.)]

karba 'iron' (Ka.)(DEDR 1278) as in ajirda karba 'iron' (Ka.) kari, karu 'black' (Ma.)(DEDR 1278) karbura 'gold' (Ka.) karbon 'black gold, iron' (Ka.) kabbiṇa 'iron' (Ka.) karum pon 'iron' (Ta.); kabin 'iron' (Ko.)(DEDR 1278)

Ib 'iron' (Santali) [cf. Toda gloss below: ib 'needle'.] Ta. Irumpu iron, instrument, weapon. a. irumpu,irimpu iron. Ko. ibid. To. Ib needle. Koḍ. Irïmbï iron. Te. Inumu id. Kol. (Kin.) inum (pl. inmul) iron, sword. Kui (Friend-Pereira) rumba vaḍi ironstone (for vaḍi, see 5285). (DEDR 486)

Mohenjo-daro. Elephant glyph shown on two copper tablets. karabha 'young elephant; karin elephant; ibha id. (Skt.)

Griffin, Baluchistan (Provenance unknown); ficus leaves, tiger, with a wing, ligatured to an eagle. The ligature on the Nal pot ca 2800 BCE (Baluchisan: first settlement in southeastern Baluchistan was in the 4th millennium BCE) is extraordinary: an eagle's head is ligatured to the body of a tiger. In BMAC area, the 'eagle' is a recurrent motif on seals. Ute Franke-Vogt: "Different pottery styles link this area also to central and northern Balochistan, and after about 2900/2800 BCE to southern Sindh where, at this time, the Indus Civilization took shape. The Nal pottery with its particular geometric and figurative patterns painted in blue, yellow, red and turquoise after firing is among the earliest and most dominanstyles in the south."

Lentoid seal with a griffin, ca. 1450–1400 B.C.;Late Minoan II Minoan; Greece, Crete Agate; H. 1 1/16 in. (2.7 cm), W. 1 1/16 (2.7 cm), Diam. ½ in. (1.2 cm) It is engraved with an image of a crouching griffin, a powerful mythical creature with the head and wings of a bird and the body of a lion. "This Minoan seal is lentoid, which describes its shape when viewed in profile. It is engraved with an image of a crouching griffin, a powerful mythical creature with the head and wings of a bird and the body of a lion. Before literacy became widespread, such seals served for identification or to mark ownership. While the first seals may have been made of organic materials that have perished, the earliest surviving examples are of clay. Later, in the Early Minoan period, various easily worked materials such as ivory, bone, shell, and soft stones, including serpentine and steatite, were adopted. In the Middle and Late Minoan periods, harder stones such as rock crystal, hematite, jasper, agate, and chalcedony gained favor. The general dating of seals is correlated with that of the palaces that were the centers of culture on Crete. The apogee of Minoan gem engraving occurred during the time of the second palaces, between about 1600 and 1450 B.C., when semiprecious stones such as agate were engraved with consummately rendered figural subjects, particularly animals."

m1390Bt Text 2868 Pict-74: Bird in flight.m0451A,B Text3235 h166A,B Harappa Seal; Vats 1940, II: Pl. XCI.255.http://www.metmuseum.org

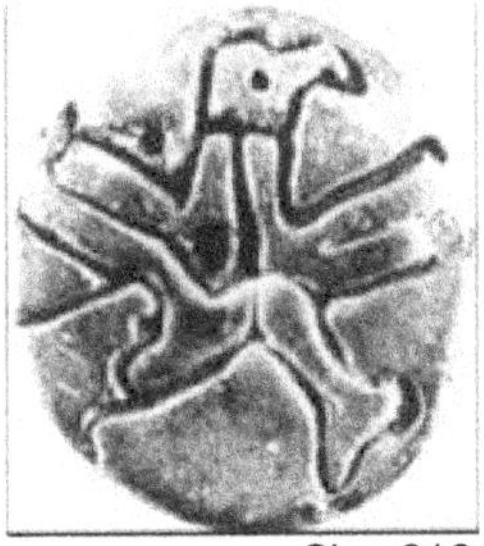

Bird-in-flight Mohenjo-daro tablet (m1390) with Indus script inscription (Text 2868)

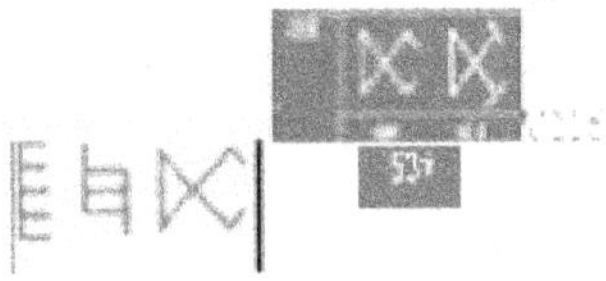

Sign 216 and variants. ḍato = claws of crab (Santali) ḍato 'claws or pincers (chelae) of crabs'; ḍaṭom, ḍiṭom to seize with the claws or pincers, as crabs, scorpions; ḍaṭkop = to pinch, nip (only of crabs) (Santali) Rebus: dhātu = mineral (Skt.)

Vikalpa: Ta. koṭiṟu pincers. Ma. koṭil tongs. Ko. koṛ hook of tongs. / Cf. Skt. (P. 4.4.18) kuṭilikā- smith's tongs.(DEDR 2052). ulai-k-kuṟaṭu smith's tongs (Ta.)

Vikalpa: erā 'claws'; Rebus: era (Skt.) Rebus: kammaṭa = coiner, mint (Ta.) Vikalpa: sannī, Rebus: sāna 'grindstone' (Te.)

'copper'. Vikalpa: kamaṭha crab portable furnace (Te.) kampaṭṭam sannhī = pincers, smith's vice (P.)

Peg 'khuṇṭa'; rebus: kūṭa 'workshop' khũṭi = pin (M.) kuṭi= smelter furnace (Santali) koṇḍu मूलिकादिघर्षणवस्तु m. a washerman's dressing iron (El. kunḍh); a scraper or grater for grating radishes, or the like; usually ° -- , the second member being the article to be grated, as in the following: -- kȧnḍi-mujü घर्षिता मूलिका f. grated radish, but mujĕ-konḍu, a radish-grater (cf. mujü). (Kashmiri) *khuṭṭa1 ' peg, post '. 2. *khuṇṭa -- 1. [Same as *khuṭṭa -- 2? -- See also kṣōḍa -- .]1. Ku. khuṭī ' peg '; N. khuṭnu ' to stitch ' (der. *khuṭ ' pin ' as khilnu from khil s.v. khī´la -- ); Mth. khuṭā ' peg, post '; H. khūṭā m. ' peg, stump '; Marw. khuṭī f. ' peg '; M. khuṭā m. ' post '.2. Pk. khuṁṭa -- , khoṁṭaya -- m. ' peg, post '; Dm. kuṇḍa ' peg for fastening yoke to plough -- pole '; L. khũḍī f. ' drum -- stick '; P. khuṇḍ, ḍā m. ' peg, stump '; WPah. rudh. khuṇḍ ' tethering peg or post '; A. khūṭā ' post ', ṭi ' peg '; B. khũṭā, ṭi ' wooden post, stake, pin, wedge '; Or. khuṇṭa, ṭā' pillar, post '; Bi. (with -- ḍa -- ) khũṭrā, rī ' posts about one foot high rising from body of cart '; H. khũṭā m. ' stump, log ', ṭī f. ' small peg ' (→ P.khũṭā m., ṭī f. ' stake, peg '); G. khũṭ f. ' landmark ', khũṭɔ m., ṭī f. ' peg ', ṭũ n. ' stump ', ṭiyũ n. ' upright support in frame of wagon ', khũṭrũn. ' half -- burnt piece of fuel '; M. khũṭ m. ' stump of tree, pile in river, grume on teat ' (semant. cf. kīla -- 1 s.v. *khila -- 2), khũṭā m. ' stake ', ṭī f. ' wooden pin ', khũṭaḷṇẽ ' to dibble '.Addenda: *khuṭṭa -- 1. 2. *khuṇṭa -- 1: WPah.kṭg. khv́ndɔ ' pole for fencing or piling grass round ' (Him.I 35 nd poss. wrong for ṇḍ); J. khuṇḍā m. ' peg to fasten cattle to '. (CDIAL 3893) Vikalpa: pacar = a wedge driven ino a wooden pin, wedge etc. to tighten it (Santali.lex.) pasra = a smithy, place where a black-smith works, to work as a blacksmith; kamar pasra = a smithy; pasrao lagao akata se ban:? Has the blacksmith begun to work? pasraedae = the blacksmith is at his work (Santali.lex.)

The ligatured Sign 382 is decoded as: dul mũhã kharādī 'cast bronze ingot turner'. kharedo = a currycomb (G.) Rebus: kharādī ' turner' (G.)

Vikalpa: kāmsako, kāmsiyo = a large sized comb (G.) Rebus: kaṁsa= bronze (Te.) kãsāri 'pewterer' (Bengali) kāsārī; H. kasārī m. ' maker of brass pots' (Or.) Rebus: kaṁsá1 m. ' metal cup ' AV., m.n. ' bell -- metal ' Pat. as in S., but would in Pa. Pk. and most NIA. lggs. collide with kā´ṁsya -- to which L. P. testify and under which the remaining forms for the metal are listed. 2. *kaṁsikā -- .1. Pa. kaṁsa -- m. ' bronze dish '; S. kañjho m. ' bellmetal '; A. kãh ' gong '; Or. kāsā ' big pot of bell -- metal '; OMarw. kāso (= kã -- ?) m. ' bell -- metal tray for food, food '; G. kãsā m. pl. ' cymbals '; -- perh. Woṭ. kasṓṭ m. ' metal pot ' Buddruss Woṭ 109. 2. Pk. kaṁsiā -- f. ' a kind of musical instrument '; A. kãhi ' bell -- metal dish '; G. kãśī f. ' bell -- metal cymbal ',kãśiyɔ m. ' open bellmetal pan ' kā´ṁsya -- ; -- *kaṁsāvatī -- ? Addenda: kaṁsá -- 1: A. kãh also ' gong ' or < kā´ṁsya – (CDIAL 2576). kāṁsya ' made of bell -- metal ' KātyŚr., n. ' bell -- metal ' Yājñ., ' cup of bell -- metal ' MBh., aka -- n. ' bell -- metal '. 2. *kāṁsiya -- .[kaṁsá -- 1] 1. Pa. kaṁsa -- m. (?) ' bronze ', Pk. kaṁsa - - , kāsa -- n. ' bell -- metal, drinking vessel, cymbal '; L. (Jukes) kãjā adj. ' of metal ', awāṇ. kāsā ' jar ' (← E with -- s-- , not ñj); N. kãso ' bronze, pewter, white metal ', kas -- kuṭ ' metal alloy '; A. kãh ' bell -- metal ', B. kãsā, Or. kāsā, Bi. kãsā; Bhoj. kãs ' bell -- metal ',kãsā ' base metal '; H. kās, kãsā m. ' bell -- metal ', G. kãsũ n., M. kãsẽ n.; Ko. kãśẽ n. ' bronze '; Si. kasa ' bell -- metal '. 2. L. kãihã m. ' bell -- metal ', P. kãssī, kãsī f., H. kãsī f.*kāṁsyakara -- , kāṁsyakāra -- , *kāṁsyakuṇḍikā -- , kāṁsyatāla -- , *kāṁsyabhāṇḍa -- .Addenda: kāṁsya -- : A. kãh also ' gong ', or < kaṁsá -- . (CDIAL 2987).*kāṁsyakara ' worker in bell -- metal '. [See next: kāṁsya -- , kará -- 1] L. awāṇ. kasērā ' metal worker ', P. kaserā m. ' worker in pewter ' (both ← E with -- s -- ); N. kasero ' maker of brass pots '; Bi. H. kaserā m. ' worker in pewter '. (CDIAL 2988). kāṁsyakāra m. ' worker in bell -- metal or brass ' Yājñ. com., kaṁsakāra -- m. BrahmavP. [kā´ṁsya -- , kāra -- 1] N. kasār ' maker of brass pots '; A. kãhār ' worker in bell -- metal '; B. kãsāri ' pewterer, brazier, coppersmith ', Or. kāsārī; H. kasārī m. ' maker of brass pots '; G.kāsārɔ, kas m. ' coppersmith '; M. kãsār, kās m. ' worker in white metal ', kāsārḍā m. ' contemptuous term for the same '. (CDIAL 2989).

The eagle on Mohenjo-daro tablet reads: *pajhar*, which connotes (rebus): *pasra* 'smithy, forge'. The inscription on Mohenjo-daro tablet m1390 reads: dhatu kuta 'mineral workshop'; the comb, kharedo is read rebus: kharadi, 'maker of brass pots'. These are rebus readings based on the Indian linguistic area.

It would thus appear that the user of Indus script hieroglyphs on the Gonur Tepe inscriptions – showing eagle hieroglyphs, wings of falcon (seals/seal impressions) is describing the nature of metalworking he or she is engaged in. It would also appear that the explanations of the narratives in Rigveda and in Mesopotamian hieroglyphs (cf. Apkallu) are echoes of these metalworking activities of Indus artisans (smiths and mine-workers).
Electrum is believed to have been used in coins circa 600 BC in Lydia under the reign of Alyattes II.

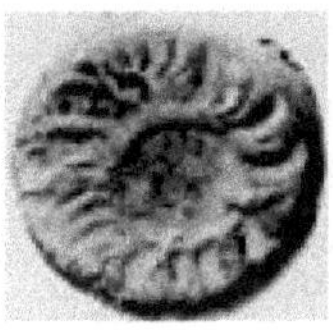

Early 6th century BC Lydian electrum coin (one-third stater denomination). KINGS of Lydia. Uncertain King. Early 6th century BC. EL Third Stater - Trite (4.71 gm). Head of roaring lion right, sun with multiple rays on forehead / Double incuse punch. In Lydia, electrum was minted into 4.7-gram coins, each valued at 1/3 stater (meaning "standard"). Three of these coins (with a weight of about 14.1 grams, almost half an ounce) totaled one stater, about one month's pay for a soldier. To complement the stater, fractions were made: the trite (third), the hekte (sixth), and so forth, including 1/24 of a stater, and even down to 1/48th and 1/96th of a stater. The 1/96 stater was only about 0.14 to 0.15 grams. Larger denominations, such as a one stater coin, were minted as well.

An image of the obverse of a Lydian coin made of electrum

The 'wart' on the nose of the tiger.

Is it intended to depict rays of the sun?
M428b The 'rays of the sun' glyph of this Mohenjo-daro seal also recurs on early punch-marked coins of India. Rebus reading: arka 'sun'; agasāle 'goldsmithy' (Ka.) erka = ekke (Tbh. of arka) aka (Tbh. of arka) copper (metal); crystal (Ka.lex.) cf. eruvai = copper (Ta.lex.) eraka, er-aka = any metal infusion (Ka.Tu.); erako molten cast (Tu.lex.) Rebus: eraka = copper (Ka.) eruvai = copper (Ta.); ere - a dark-red colour (Ka.)(DEDR 817). eraka, era, er-a = syn. erka, copper, weapons (Ka.)

Or, does the 'wart' glyph connote a polar star? If so, the lexeme could be: mēḍha 'The polar star' (Marathi). Does it make a rebus reading of Medes? "The original source for different words used to call the Median people, their language and homeland is a directly transmitted Old Iranian geographical name which is attested as the Old Persian "Māda-" (sing. masc.).The meaning of this word is not precisely established. The linguist W. Skalmowski proposes a relation with the proto-Indoeuropean word "med(h)-" meaning "central, suited in the middle" by referring to Old Indic "madhya-" and Old Iranic "maidiia-" both carrying the same meaning." Cf. Diakonoff, I. M. (1985), "Media", *The Cambridge History of Iran*, 2 (Edited by Ilya Gershevitch ed.), Cambridge, England: Cambridge University Press, pp. 36–148. http://en.wikipedia.org/wiki/Medes

It is remarkable that the Indian linguistic area attests the following lexeme for sun: aru m. ' sun ' lex. Kho. yor Morgenstierne NTS ii 276 with ? <-> Whence y -- ? (CDIAL 612)

Aramaic aryaa 'l' aryeh 'lion'. A Northwest Semitic root *ryh 'lion'. (Kaplan, 1957-58, The lion in the Hebrew bible). Akkadian aleru. von Soden points out that Akkadian eru is also attested as aru. Akkadian a/eru 'eagle'.

Akkadian aru/eru may be equivalent of the Hebrew 'rh 'eagle'. The concise dictionary of Akkadian (Jeremy A. Black, 2000) notes: eru, aru, also ru 'eagle'. Bab. also vulture?
aru 'granary, storehouse' OA, jB lex. aru(m) 'warrior'.

Altyn-Depe and Meluhha interaction area in Middle Asia

-- Decoding Indus script seals of Altyn-Depe

What Possehl calls the Middle Asian Interaction sphere (*Expedition*, Vol. 49, Number 1, UPenn Museum), extended west of Rakhigarhi upto Altyn Depe in Turkmenistan. “Cuneiform documents also inform us that some people in Mesopotamia called themselves ‘Son of Meluhha’, and there are references to Meluhhan villages and granaries. We even have the personal cylinder seal of Shu-ilishu, a translator of the Meluhhan language (*Expedition* 48 (1): 42-43)...First, beginning in the $4^{th}$ millennium BCE, the people of southern Central Asia shared a pottery style called ‘Quetta ware’ with the people of Baluchistan far to the south. Along with female figurines and occasional compartmented seals, this style of pottery persisted until the early centuries of the $2^{nd}$ millennium BCE, suggesting long-term interaction north and wouth...at Altyn Depe in Turkmenistan, the Soviets found two provincial style Indus seals, along with much ivory (presumably from elephants), which was also apparently from India. Their discoveries were all found in correct chronological sequence dating to the second half of the $3^{rd}$ millennium BCE, indicating that Altyn Depe was contemporary with the Indus cities. Furthermore, this also provided evidence for Middle Asian interaction stretching north to the Oxus civilization which, in a second phase beginning about 2200 BCE, occupied inland river delta oases such as Margiana...Since the 1960s excavations on the Iranian Plateau at such places as Tepe Yahya, Shahr-i-Sokhta, Shahdad, and Jiroft have also added to the corpus of finds linking the Indus civilization with the BMAC (Bactria-Margiana Archaeological Complex) and Mesopotamia.”

Namazga V and Altyndepe were in contact with the Late Harappan culture (ca. 2000-1600 BC)

Altyndepe (Алтын-Депе, the Turkmen for "Golden Hill") is a Bronze Age(BMAC) site in Turkmenistan, near Aşgabat, inhabited in the 3rd to 2nd millennia BC, abandoned around 1600 BC.

Interaction area of Sarasvati (Indus) civilization in Central Asia

Altyn Depe, Turkmenistan 60.43E, 36.85N

“Altyn Depe is a major Bronze Age center (third and second millennia BC) in Turkmenistan, overlooking the Tedzen delta. It lies at the foot of the Köpet Dag, a range of mountains marking the northern border of Iran. The site itself is watered, not by the major river (the Harirud) which feeds the Tedzen delta, but by smaller rivers descending from the mountains. For its general location and context, its position is marked on the far right of image.

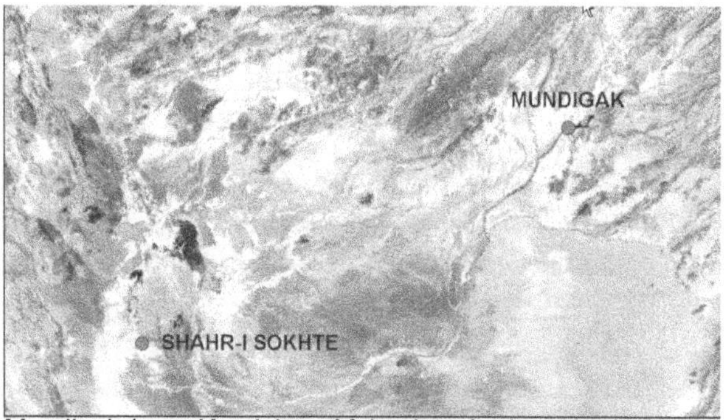


“The site occupied a pivotal position at the junction of routes: along the foot of the Köpet Dag, southward to Afghanistan, and eastward via the oasis stepping-stones along what was to become the Silk Road.

“Altyn Depe ('Gold hill') is the largest of a small cluster of settlements in an embayment in from of the mountains, where several streams emerge.”

Relative locations of Shahr-i Sokhte and Mundigak (near Kandahar, Afghanistan), along the Helmand river. Settlement clusters either along the edges of the mountains, or in the river-delta which forms an oasis of settled life.

Landsat image, 30m resolution, circa 1990, with Band 7 displayed as red, Band 4 as green and Band 2 as blue. Landsat TM imagery provided by NASA.

http://www.archatlas.dept.shef.ac.uk/SitesFromSatellites/sites.php?name=sha-i-sok&view=c&ge=no

“The rich mineral resources of the highland rim of the Fertile Crescent were a latent precondition for the formation of a complex trading system: a "periphery" waiting for a "core". The growth of temple-centers in the unusual conditions of lowland Mesopotamia and southwest Iran, with their relatively dense concentrations of farming population supported by irrigation agriculture, created an organised body of potential consumers in the middle of a network of contacts reaching into the surrounding highlands. The Tigris and Euphrates provided arteries of transport as well as water for irrigation. During the fourth millennium the combination of a powerful ideology with a labour-force capable of manufacturing textiles, milk-products and alcoholic drinks from their domesticated plants and livestock, provided the basis for a process of expansion which mobilised the products of surrounding areas and initiated an explosive process of urban growth in the later fourth millennium BC. In the second half of the millennium, colonial settlements were founded at nodal points in upper Mesopotamia, giving access to Anatolia, the Caucasus, and the Levant. Coastal connections brought this growing network into contact with Egypt, stimulating a period of accelerated changes and the formation of a second "alluvial civilisation" along the Nile.

“After 3200 BC there was a notable expansion on the Persian plateau, and an extension of contacts down the Gulf. The "colonial" enterprise in the north was replaced by an expansion of indigenous trading networks, which reached beyond Anatolia to the steppes and the Aegean. Egyptians founded their own colonial settlements in the southern Levant. Then, towards the end of the third millennium, the Indus valley joined the trio of "alluvial civilisations", and much of the traffic formerly crossing the Persian plateau was carried down the Indus and along the Gulf (including lazurite from new sources in Badakhshan, initially tapped by Indus colonies.) After 2000 BC there was a major expansion of population and trading activity on the steppes and the Danube corridor, partly stimulated by the spread of new metalworking technologies in the outer hinterlands of the urban core region. After 1700 BC, the Indus valley and the Gulf network collapsed, while expansion in the east Mediterranean continued. Between 1600 and 1400 BC a major maritime trading network developed, integrating the coastlands from Egypt and the Levant to Anatolia and the Aegean, where large sailing-ships plied a circular route. Links to Italy stimulated the formation of contacts across the Alps, and the formation of a new Amber route which replaced the earlier Danube axis. Latitudinal routes across the steppes continued to extend, bringing wheeled vehicles to China (hitherto ignorant of the wheel) in the late Shang period.

“This brief summary ends with the climax of Bronze Age development, before the radical changes which took place at the end of the second millennium, leading to widespread retraction and reorganisation, and also to the development and spread of ironworking. The larger scale of demographic growth and urban development in the first millennium BC, which saw expansion both in the Mediterranean basin and the Ganges valley and in the intervening area where the first large land-empires developed, demands a larger scale of treatment which is impossible here. Nevertheless the systematic mapping of urban centers and trade networks is as illuminating for this larger world as it is for the early stages of urban expansion represented here.”

Sherratt, Andrew (2004), 'Trade Routes: the Growth of Global Trade', ArchAtlas, January 2008, Edition 3, http://www.archatlas.org/Trade/Trade.php, Accessed: 10 December 2009

What language did the settlers of Altyn-Depe speak?

It is hypothesized that the settlers of Altyn-Depe spoke mleccha (Meluhhan).

Alexander Lubotsky argues for a pre-indo-european substratum.

“Study of loanwords can be a powerful tool for determining prehistoric cultural contacts and migrations, but this instrument is used very differently in various disciplines. For instance, loanword studies are fully accepted in Uralic linguistics, whereas Indo-Europeanists are often reluctant to acknowledge foreign origin for words attested in Indo-European languages. The reason is obvious: in Uralic, we know the source of borrowings (Indo-Iranian, Germanic, Baltic), but the source of possible Indo-European loans is usually unknown. And still, it is a matter of great importance to distinguish between inherited lexicon and borrowings, even if the donor language cannot be determined...In my paper, I shall apply this methodology to the Indo-Iranian lexicon in search of loanwords which have entered Proto-Indo-Iranian before its split into two branches. As a basis for my study I use the list, gleaned from Mayrhofer's EWAia, of all Sanskrit etyma which have Iranian correspondences, but lack clear cognates outside Indo-Iranian...I use the term “substratum” for any donor language, without implying sociological differences in its status, so that “substratum” may refer to an adstratum or even superstratum. It is possible that Proto-Indo-Iranian borrowed words from more than one language and had thusmore than one substratum...Proto-Indo-Iranian for a long time remained a dialectal unity, possibly even up to the moment when the Indo-Aryans crossed the Hindukush mountain range and lost contact with the Iranians...The phonological and morphological features of Indo-Iranian loanwords are strikingly similar to those which are characteristic of *Sanskrit* loanwords, i.e. words which are only attested in Sanskrit and which must have entered the language after the Indo-Aryans had crossed Hindukush. The structure of Sanskrit loanwords has been discussed by Kuiper 1991...The phonological and morphological similarity of loanwords in Proto-Indo-Iranian and in Sanskrit has important consequences. First of all, it indicates that, to put it carefully, a substratum of Indo-Iranian and a substratum of Indo-Aryan represent the same language, or, at any rate, two dialects of the same language. In order to account for this fact, we are bound to assume that the language of the original population of the towns of Central Asia, where Indo-Iranians must have arrived in the second millennium BCE, on the one hand, and the language spoken in Punjab, the homeland of the Indo-Aryans, on the other, were intimately related...Another consequence is that the Indo-Iranians must still have formed a kind of unity during their stay in Central Asia, albeit perhaps dialectally diversified. Judging by the later spread of the Indo-Aryans – to the south-west in the case of the Mitanni kingdom and to the south-east during their move to Punjab –, they were situated to the south of the Iranians, forming the vanguard, so to speak, of the Indo-Iranian movement. Accordingly, the Indo-Aryans were presumably the first who came in contact with foreign tribes and sometimes "passed on" loanwords to the Iranians...The urban civilization of Central Asia has enriched the Indo-Iranian lexicon with building and irrigation terminology, with terms for clothing and hair-do, and for some artifacts. It is tempting to suggest that the word **gadA-* \`club, mace' refers to the characteristic mace-heads of stone and bronze abundantly found in the towns of the so-called "Bactria-Margian Archaeological Complex". Also *\*uAcI-* \`axe, pointed knife' may be identified with shaft-hole axes and axe-adzes of this culture."

(Lubotsky, A., 1999, *Early Contacts between Uralic and Indo-European: Linguistic and Archaeological Considerations. Papers presented at an international symposium held at the Tvärminne Research Station of the University of Helsinki 8-10 January 1999.* (Mémoires de la Société Finno-ougrienne 242.) Chr. Carpelan,A. Parpola, P. Koskikallio (eds.). Helsinki 2001, 301-317). http://www.ieed.nl/lubotsky/pdf/Indo-Iranian%20substratum.pdf

From the list of some 120 Indo-Iranian isolates appended by Lubotsky, it is clear that most words do NOT have IE cognates but have Sanskrit, Old Avestan, Middle and Modern Persian cognates. These substratum words of proto-Indo-Iranian point to the settlement of speakers from Sarasvati civilization area in the Middle Asian Interaction Sphere, extending upto Altyn-Depe on the southern banks of the Caspian Sea.

This substantiates BB Lal's view that Baudhayana Shrauta Sutra reference to migrations out of (Sarasvati) civilization area were westwards to Gandhara, Parshu and Aratta. http://sites.google.com/site/kalyan97/vedic-people Did some vedic people emigrate westwards, out of India?)

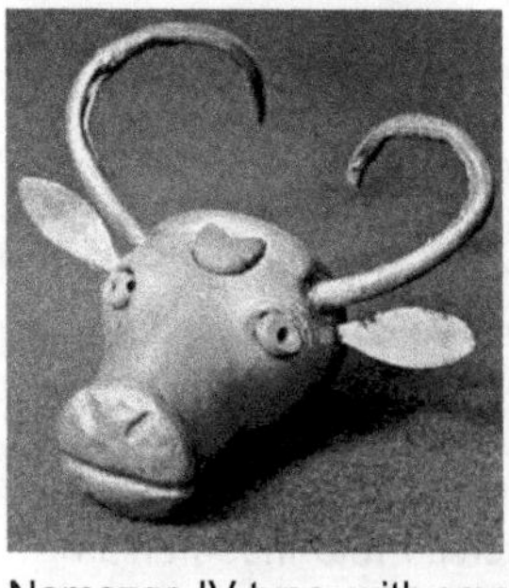

Archaeological evidence of Altyn-Depe

Altyn-Depe is a Neolithic settlement extending into the bronze age in south Turkmenistan near village Miana. The settlement covered an area of 25 hectares and with a total stratification thickness of 30 m. (including 8m. deep stratum with human habitation). Strata of the Neolithic period (5th millennium BCE) have yielded bone and copper artifacts. Settlements of 4th millennium BCE show female figures with painted necklaces and ornaments. Early 3rd millennium BCE, the settlement had an unbaked brick wall 1.5 to 2m. thick, with brick kilns and an oval hearth sanctuary in the center of a house. Mid-34d millennium BCE shows a complex of Namazga IV type, with small temple buildings with rectangular hearths (podia). By end 3rd millennium and early 2nd millennium BCE (Namazga V type), the urban Altyn-Depe has artisans' quarters with 62 two-tiered kilns, beads and seals, four-stepped ziggurats, storerooms and a priest's tomb with gold heads of a wolf and a bull and other tombs with silver ornaments, precious stones, seals, female terracotta statuettes with plaited hair. Stone vessels, hafted bronze and copper daggers with flat blades, tabbed silver and bronze seals with pictographs of animals (goats, eagles, panthers, a three-headed composite animal) were discovered. One quarter of a 'nobility' had a seal with two signs of Indus script. It is possible that the underlying speech of the writings on seals refer to the bronze-age settlers of Altyn-Depe. Exhaustion of the soil and climatic changes might have led to the abandonment of the settlement and consequent migrations to Mugrab, Southern Uzbekistan (Sappali) an

d northern Afghanistan (Dashli). (cf. *Encyclopaedia Iranica*). Namazga III-V periods are dated ca. 3200-. 2000 BCE.

Golden bull's head (H7.5cm), horns made of silver wire covered with gold foil. On the forehead and in the eyes are turquoise inlays (excavation #7, priest's tomb, room #7)

http://en.wikipedia.org/wiki/Bactria–Margiana_Archaeological_Complex

From the publishers' blurb of Altyn-Depe (University Museum Monographs, No. 55) by V. M. Masson and Henry N. Michael (1988) : "The excavations at the Bronze Age site of Altyn-Depe in southwest Soviet Central Asia (Turkmenistan) have revealed an urban community dating to the Middle Bronze Age. The region of Turkmenistan forms a natural crossroads between Eastern Iran and Central Asia, and between Siberia and southern Russia and the Indus Valley. Altyn-Depe was important not only for its development as a cultural center in its own right but as a link between the various Bronze Age cultures of Eurasia."

From the Foreword by Gregory Possehl: "Altyn-Depe, and the discovery of the Turkmenian Bronze Age civilization, filled the remaining blank in the ancient 'Middle Asian' interaction sphere. The urbanization of Turkmenia, best exemplified by Altyn-Depe, brought to closure the third millennium system that had been hinted at with Harappan seals in Mesopotamia and other 'stray' finds of uncertain origin on the Iranian plateau..." (p.xiii)

Bronze artefacts found in Parkhai cemetery II: double-edged knives, small fragments and spiral-headed pins; the pins of different sizes had spirals no fewer than four lops; six spiral-headed pins are known from the northern foothills of Kopet Dagh; one came from Kysyl Arvant and dated to Namazga IV period; all identical to the Parkhai examples and considered an import from the Sumbar Valley; the remainder---two from the southern mound at Anau, two from Namazga-depe and one from Shor-depe -- had small loops twisted only 1.5-2 times. They were found in Namazga V levels from cemeteries in northern Afghanistan and Tajikistan. Slightly twisted spiral-head pins from Mundigat (periods IV, I-IV, 3) and multi-looped spiral-headed pins from Tepe Hissar (period IIB), which are identical to those from Parkhai II, are also related to this period; the dates of Parkhai finds are ca. middle of the third millennium B.C.

V.M. Masson, Seals of a Proto-Indian Type from Altyn-depe, pp. 149-162; V.M. Masson, Urban Centers of Early Class Society, pp. 135-148; I.N. Khlopin, The Early bronze age cemetery in Parkhai II: The first two seasons of excavations, 1977-78, pp. 3-34 in: Philip L. Kohl (ed.), 1981, The Bronze Age Civilization in Central Asia, Armonk, NY, ME Sharpe, Inc.

Bactria; cosmetic flacon, fig. 1.2 and fig. 1.6 (V.Sarianidi, p. 646); there is an exact replica of the flacon with a chequered body and distinctive base, fig. 1.6 at Chanhu-daro (Mackay 1943: pl. LXXIII 39). Similar falcons have been found in Luristan.

"It transpired that in the 2nd millennium BC there existed in the territory of ancient Bactria a highly-developed, largely original culture of the ancient-oriental type. A close, or rather identical culture spread at that time through the southern regions of central Asia, particularly in Margiana, which gave grounds for singlign out a special Bactrian-Margian Archaeological Complex (BMAC). The basic features of this complex are: the coexistence of non-fortified settlements and of rectangular fortresses with round corner turrets. The latter belonged to individual families or clans... Occurring in sufficient quantities, along with stone and flint tools and wapons, are copper and bronze ones. These are sickles, knives, adzes, awls, razors, daggers, massive spearheads, battle axes; of the ornaments there are mirrors, toilet pins, cosmetic falcons, bracelets, ear-rings, rings... At present we may regard as an established fact the existence of an Iranian-Turkmenian metallurgical province where, beginning from the turn of the 5th and 4th millennia BC, uni-typical wares take shape and exist for a long time. There is every ground to assume the dissemination from it of metal-works (celts, daggers, pins) and specific forms of earthenware (stemmed vases, saucers, etc.) in the eastern direction down to the vally of the Indus, by way of exchange, trade and cultural contacts. This period embraces the existence of the Harappan civilization and does not presuppose the arrival of any new tribes. This is strikingly proved by the Harappa culture itself, which demonstrates a continuous line of development without any invasions from outside... We shall merely remark that southwestern Iran and possibly Caucasus emerge as a zone where numerous metal articles come to be produced (mid- 2nd millennium BC), while Iranian Khorassan is doubtlessly the main venue for their penetration into the souther areas of central Asia, Bactria and possibly the valley of the Indus river."(Viktor I. Sarianidi, 1979, New Finds in Bactria and Indo-Iranian Connections, pp. 643-659, in: *South Asian Archaeology 1977*, Naples).

"The Southern Complex...The centrally located room 48 was fairly large, contained a platform hearth, and was probably a living room. The equally large room 49 had a hearth next to a wall; in the hearth copper slag and a maul for breaking up the ore were found. Aside from these, the excavations yielded a piece of fused copper ore in a sort of clay crucible, and an unfinished stone seal. Similar assemblages of finds elsewhere indicate that this unit was a place of manufacture for various craftsmen and not of potters only...

The major burial, 60, was that of an adult, apparently a woman...The unique find in this burial was a silver seal (Plate XVII, item 12). It represented a fantastic, three-headed being, with a torso of a feline beast of prey; the three heads were that of a bird of prey and two reptiles (snakes or lizards). The other burial (59) was of a male adolescent. The complex magical symbolism (the two statuettes held in the

hand, and the seal representing a fantastic being), leads to the preliminary conclusion that burial 60 is that of a priestess...An important component of the Altyn-Depe assemblages are artifacts which have been called seals. It is possible that at the same time they were kept as amulets or other sacred objects. These artifacts have a flat surface worked with a pattern of high rlief, and evidently they were meant to provide impressions since on the obverse side they are provided with a looped handle for that purpose and also for suspension. In a number of burials the seals were positioned about the hip bones; apparently they were carried on a belt. Impressions of seals are rare at Altyn-Depe and, generally speaking, they are represented only on fragments of fired clay (Plate XVI, item 13). At other sites of this period, particularly at Shahr-I Sokhta, the impressions are very numerous and varied (Tosi 1969: figs. 277-292). The seals could have been used to stamp various things under the jurisdiction of a community or family. As an ethnographic parallel we mention the case of a wooden seal from Afghanistan representing a six-rayed rosette in an oval, which was used to stamp produce (Vavilov and Bukinich 1959: p. 188, fig. 89). Technically, the seals are made in two ways. Seals of bronze mixed with low quality silver are the most widespread; they have high relief and were cast with the lost wax process. Stone seals with ornamentation made by drilling small holes close together to form lines (Plate XVI, item 17; Plate XVII, items 1 and 4) are more rare...All seals may be divided into two large groups: zoomorphic (or representing zoomorphic motifs) and geometric...From Altyn-Depe we have seals representing a goat (Plate XVII, item 14); a hooved anikal, probably a ram (Plate XXIV, item 9); a feline beast of prey (Plate XVII, item 10); and a fantastic three-hded dragon with the body of a feline beast of prey, one head of a bird of prey, and two heads of a reptile, perhaps of a snake (Plate XVII, item 12). Another syncretic form is seen on a seal representing a four-legged animal with a beak and with talons on its paws (Plate XVII, item 8). A seal representing an eagle with outspread wings was found at Namazga-Depe (Masson and Sarianidi 1972: pl. 47), and a seal with a goat was found at the small site of Shor-Depe (Massimov 1978b). At Altyn-Depe a seal with a bird with spread wings was also found, but its head was heavily corroded (Plate XVII, item 13). Examples of the second subgroup contain images in the form of a snake coiled inside a half-moon. One such seal was a terracotta seal (Plate XVII, item 3), and another was metallic and had an appendage incorporating a cross (Plate XVII, item 15). The geometric seals...Those in the form of a cross are most frequent and comprise about half of the metallic seals at Altyn-Depe (Plate XVI, items 1-8, 10, and 14)...In the center of the crosslike seals we often find a supplementary figure: an oval, square or small cross...On one large oval seal four double circles surround a griangle. In two other similar seals a triangle (Plate XXIX, item 8) and a multi-rayed star respectively ((Plate XXIX, item 10) were incorporated.Employing an oval as the compositional center, four-rayed and five-rayed (Plate XVI, item 9) seals were formed...Two seals have the form of a stepped pyramid (Plate XXIX, item 5), and the third had pyramids united at their apices (Plate XVI, item 12). As already implied, the majority of the seals are semantically linked to the symbols of the Eneolithic painted ceramics of southern Turkmenistan (Fig. 26) (Masson 1967d, 1970d)...it is particularly important that at Altyn-Depe objects were found which undoubtedly were carried there from the Indus valley. For instance, artifacts of elephant ivory were found at three points...This is emphasized by the finds of nearly rectangular seals of the Harappan type one with a swastika in the already-mentioned priest's burial...and the other with two symbols of prto-Indic writing... (Plate XXII, items 1a and 1b)." (pp.35-36, p.40, pp. 89-90, p.93).

Finds at Atlyn-depe: ivory sticks and gaming pieces (?) obtained from Sarasvati Sindhu civilization; similar objects with dotted circles found in Mohenjo-daro and Harappa. (Masson, VM, 1988, *Altyn-depe*, UPenn museum, p. 90)

Altyn-depe. Silver seal. Pictograph of ligatured animal with three heads.

Two seals found at Altyn-depe (Excavation 9 and 7) found in the shrine and in the 'elite quarter'.

The script on some of the Altyn-Depe seals and artifacts may be decoded in mleccha (Meluhhan), the substratum of proto-Indo-Iranian (cf. Lubotsky).

Silver seal with three heads of animals. The metal seal is difficult to interpret. But a parallel can be seen on many Indus script epigraphs showing such composite animals with three heads.

m1171

Bet Dwaraka 1

śankha seal. One-horned bull, short-horned bull looking

down and an antelope looking backward.

> Huntington notes: “There is a continuity of composite creatures demonstrable in Indic culture since Kot Diji ca. 4000 BCE” http://huntingtonarchive.osu.edu/Makara%20Site/makara/index.html
>
> Generally, the three animal heads relate to: bull, heifer and antelope (looking back). The silver seal of Altyn-Depe shows an animal head turned back.

Metalsmith guild working with ore, iron, copper:

krammara ‘turn back’ (Te.); rebus: kamar ‘smith’ (Santali) me~d.ha ‘antelope’ (Santali); rebus: meD ‘iron’ (Mu.)

*damra* = heifer, young bull, steer (G.); rebus:tambra = copper (Skt.)

bail ‘bull, ox’; bali ‘iron sand ore’ (Santali) ḍangra ‘bull’ (H.); adar ḍangra ‘zebu’ (Santali) d.hagara_m pl. the buttocks; the hips (G.lex.) ḍāṅgar ‘blacksmith’ (H.); d.ha~_gar., dha~_gar blacksmith; digger of wells (H.)

san:gaḍi = joined animals (M.) Rebus: (Interpreted as guild, family) sanghara ‘one's own house’ J v.222 (Pali). CDIAL 12858 Pa. *saṅghara* -- with one's own family (?); L. *sagghrā* accompanied by one's own family; H. *sā̃ghar* m. wife's son by former husband. sanghāḍo (G.) = cutting stone, gilding; san:gatarāśū = stone cutter (Te.) Thus, san:gha_ta is a composite product. Thus, when a standard device is shown in front of, say, a one-horned bull, the device, i.e. san:gad.a connotes a composite product, created or alloyed with cut stones (or minerals). The inscription on an inscribed object depicting such a device can, thus be interpreted as a list of 'composed (alloyed)' products. san:gha_r.iba_ to mix many materials, stir boiling curry, tie two cattle together and leave to graze (Or.) (CDIAL 12859,12860). to mix many materials, stir boiling curry, tie two cattle together and leave to graze (Or.) (CDIAL 12859,12860). Persian word سنگ seng meaning stone

aḍar ‘harrow’; rebus: aduru ‘native metal’ (Ka.) ayir = iron dust, any ore (Ma.) aduru = *gan.iyinda tegadu karagade iruva aduru* = ore taken from the mine and not subjected to melting in a furnace (Ka. Siddha_nti Subrahman.ya' S'astri's new interpretation

There are over 50 epigraphs showing the svastika glyph which can be read rebus: *svastika* pewter (Kannada); sattva ‘zinc’ (Ka.) jasta = zinc (Hindi) yasada (Jaina Pkt.) Old Persian Qxida? Zargun "زرگون" ‘gold-like’? Kashmiri. Grierson lex. zasath ज़स़््थ् or zasuth ज़सुथ् । त्रपु m. (sg. dat. zastas ज़स्तस्), zinc, spelter, pewter (cf. Hindī *jast*). jasti jasti ज&above;स्ति&below; । त्रपुधातुविशेषनिर्मितम् adj. c.g. made of zinc or pewter. jasth जस्थ । त्रपु m. (sg. dat. jastas जस्तस्), zinc, spelter; pewter. jastuvu जस्तुवु&below; । त्रपूद्भवः adj. (f. jastüvü जस्त&above;वू&below;), made of zinc or pewter. satavu, satuvu, sattu = pewter, zinc (Ka.) dosta = zinc (Santali) jasada, yasada, yasadyaka, yasatva = zinc (Jaina Pali) ruhi-tutiya (Urdu) tuttha (Arthas'a_stra) totamu, tutenag (Te.) oriechalkos (Gk.)

m1225A

m1225B.
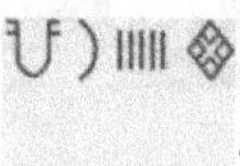
1311 m1225 cube seal with perforation through breadth.

Dotted circle shown on ivory sticks of Altyn-Depe can be compared with similar glyphs on Indus script artifacts.

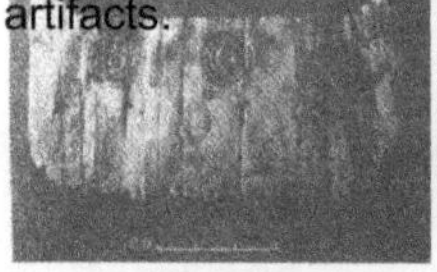

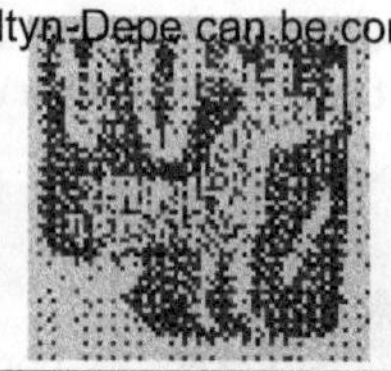

After Vats, Pl.CXIX,.No.6 An ivory comb fragment with one preserved tooth and ornamented with double incised circles

(3.8 in. long).

Kalibangan, Ivory comb with three dotted circles; Kalibangan, Period II; Thapar 1979, Pl.XXVII, in: *Ancient Cities of the Indus.*

*Ivory rod, ivory plaque with dotted circles. Mohenjo-daro. [Musee National De Arts Asiatiques Guimet, 1988-1989, Les cites oubliees de l'Indus Archeologie du Pakistan.]*

h1017ivorystick

Orthographically, the dotted circle is also a fish-eye or eye of an antelope. The eye is *kāṇ* rebus: *kāṇḍ* 'iron (stone) ore' as in *ayaskāṇḍa* 'excellent iron' (Pan.). It may also be rebus for *kaṇḍ* 'fire-altar'. *kaṇḍ* also denotes 'ivory'.

The gloss related to the dotted circle is thus, decoded rebus as *kāṇ*.

- kandhi = a lump, a piece (Santali.lex.) [The dotted circle thus connotes an ingot taken out of a kaṇḍ, furnace]. kāndavika = a baker; kandu = an iron plate or pan for baking cakes etc. (Ka.lex.)
- kaṇḍ = altar, furnace (Santali) लोहकारकन्दुः f. a blacksmith's smelting furnace (Grierson Kashmiri lex.) payĕn-kōda पयन्-कोंद । परिपाककन्दुः f. a kiln (a potter's, a lime-kiln, and brick-kiln, or the like); a furnace (for smelting) This yajn~a kuṇḍam can be denoted rebus, by perforated beads (kandi) or on ivory (khaṇḍ):
- kandi (pl. -l) beads, necklace (Pa.); kanti (pl. -l) bead, (pl.) necklace; kandit. bead (Ga.)(DEDR 1215). The three stringed beads depicted on the pictograph may perhaps be treated as a phonetic determinant of the substantive, the rimmed jar, the khaṇḍa kanka. khaṇḍa, xanro, sword or large sacrificial knife. kandil, kandi_l = a globe of glass, a lantern (Ka.lex.)
- jaṇḍ khaṇḍ = ivory (Jaṭkī) khaṇḍ ī = ivory in rough (Jaṭkī); gaṭī = piece of elephant's tusk (S.) [This semant. may explain why the dotted circle -- i.e., kandi, 'beads' -- is often depicted on ivory objects, such as ivory combs]. See also: khaṇḍiyo [cf. khaṇḍaṇī a tribute] tributary; paying a tribute to a superior king (G.lex.) [Note glyph of a kneeling adorant].
- Rebus: kaṇḍ 'stone (ore) metal' as in: *ayaskāṇḍa* 'excellent iron (metal)'. Allograph: Glyph: 'eye'.

m0008, m0021, h228B

Carved Ivory Standard in the middle

har501 Harappa 1990 and 1993. Standard device, model reconstructed after Mahadevan

? The dotted circles on the bottom portion of the device connote ghangar ghongor; rebus: kangar 'portable furnace'.

Pict-49 Uncertain animal with dotted circles on its body.

Obverse of steatite Dilmun stamp seal from Failaka Island (c. 2000 BCE). A human figure and a variety of animals – two

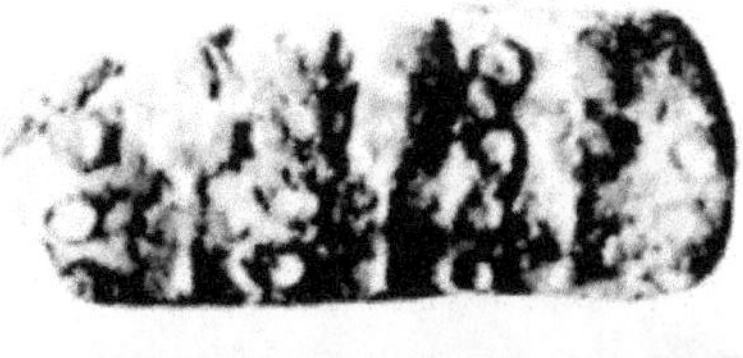

antelopes one with its head looking backward; possibly a scorpion at the feet of the human figure. A dotted circle is seen above one antelope and a vase in between the antelope and the human figure. Kuwait National Museum. French Archaeological Expedition in Kuwait. Several inscriptions at Failaka mention the Dilmunite god Enzak and his temple or Mesopotamian deities. [Remi Boucharlat, Archaeology and Artifacts of the Arabian Peninsula, in: Jack M. Sasson (ed.), Civilizations of the Ancient Near East, pp. 1335-1353].

urseal8Seal; BM 118704; U. 6020; Gadd PBA 18 (1932),. 9-10, pl. II, no.8; two figures carry between them a vase, and one presents a goat-like animal (not an antelope) which he holds by the neck.

Ropar 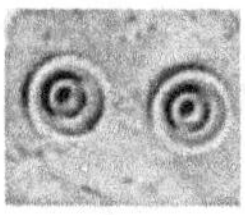 1,Text 9021 h128  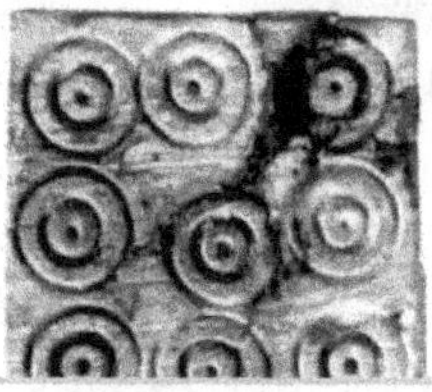

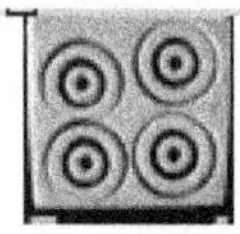
Slide 203 (Kenoyer, 2002). Steatite button seal Fired steatite button seal with four concentric circle designs from the Trench 54 area (H2000-4432/2174-3)

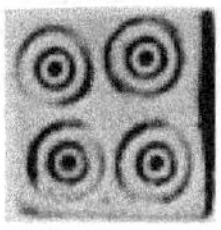  Kalibangan057 Kalibangan058 h855At h855Bt h855Ct

m1259 m1260 h974Ait h974Bit h974Cit

4592 h978Ait h978Bit  h978Cit 

5412 h888Abit 4466 h889Abit 5477

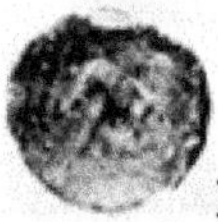 h832At  h832Bt Tablet in bas-relief h638 

h352A h352B  h352C4575 Pict-120: One or more dotted circles. [54 out of 67 objects on which this glyph occurs, are miniature tablets]
The text on top line occurs mainly on miniature tablets of Harappa over 46 times.

h353A h353B h353C 5416

h354A h354B h354C, 5499

h359a h359B h359C

h361A h361B h361C 5476

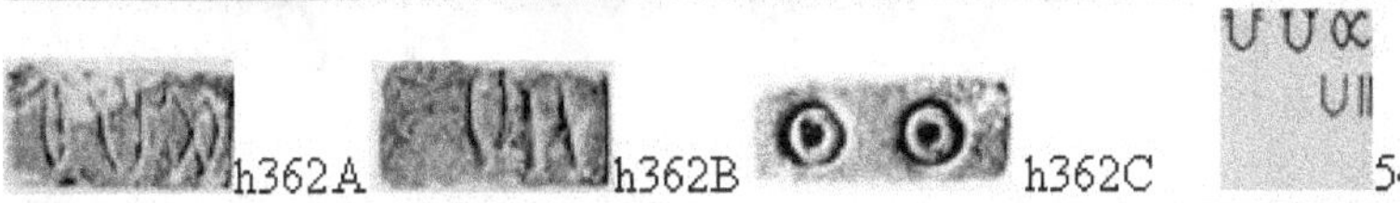
h362A h362B h362C 5466

h365A h365B h365C h365E

h367A h367B h367C h367E

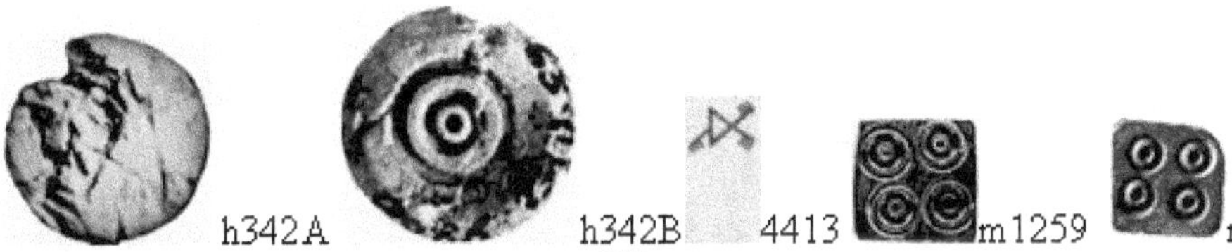
h342A h342B 4413 m1259 m1260

m0352A m0352C m0352D m0352E

m0352F m1654A ivory cube m1654B ivory cube

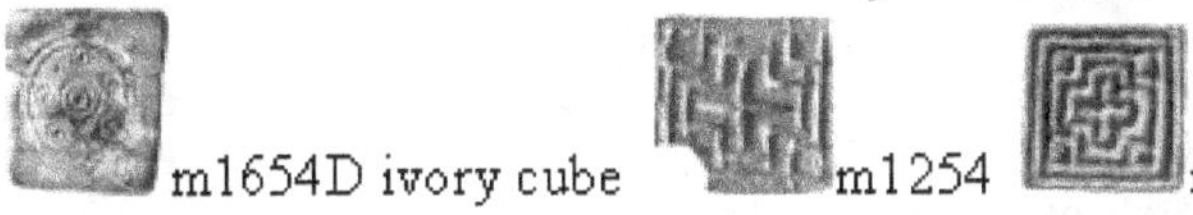
m1654D ivory cube m1254 m1255 Nausharo10 Slide 187 A faience button seal with geometric motif (H2000-4491/9999-34) was found on the surface of Mound AB at Harappa by one of the workmen.

[Harappa 2000 find].

m1256 m1257 m1258

After Vats, Pl.CXIX,.No.6 An ivory comb fragment with one preserved tooth and ornamented with double incised circles (3.8 in. long).

Kalibangan, Ivory comb with three dotted circles; Kalibangan, Period II; Thapar 1979, Pl.XXVII, in: Ancient Cities of the Indus.

Ivory rod, ivory plaque with dotted circles. Mohenjo-daro. [Musee National De Arts Asiatiques Guimet, 1988-1989, Les cites oubliees de l'Indus Archeologie du Pakistan.]

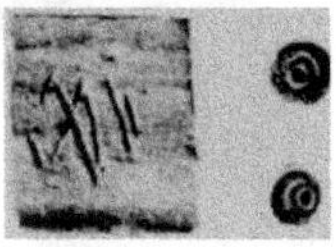

h1017ivorystick

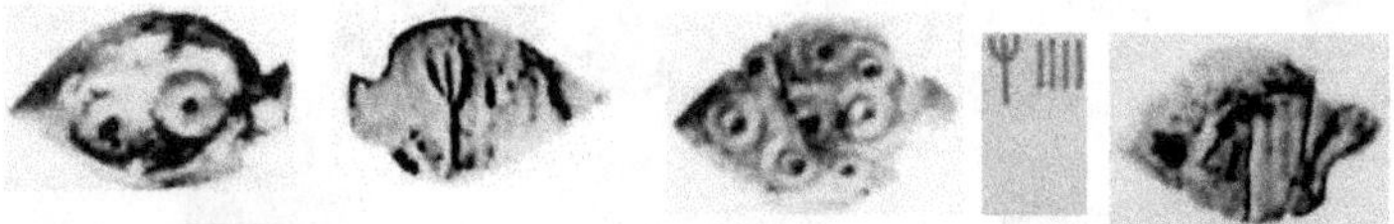

Wild tulip motif. A motif that occurs on southeast Iranian cylinder seals and on Persian Gulf seals. 1st row: Bactrian artifacts; 2nd row: a comb from the Gulf area and late trans-Elamite seals [After Marie-Helene Pottier, 1984, Materiel funeraire de la Bactriane meridionale de l'age du bronze, Recherche sur les Civilizations, Memoire 36, Paris, fig. 21; Sarianidi, V.I., 1986, Le complexe culturel de Togolok 21 en Margiane, Arts Asiatiques 41: fig. 6,21; Potts, 1994, fig. 53,8; Amiet, 1986, fig. 132].

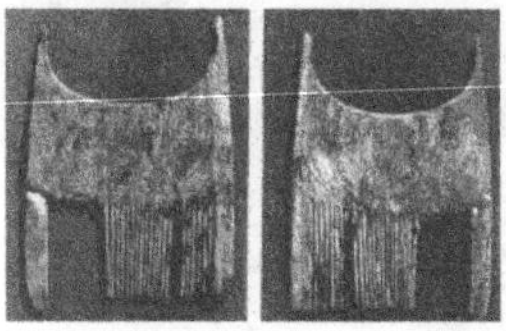

The ivory comb found at Tell Abraq measures 11 X 8.2 X .4 cm. Both sides of the comb bear identical, incised decoration in the form of two long-stemmed flowers with crenate or dentate leaves, flanking three dotted circles arranged in a triangular pattern. Bone and ivory combs with dotted-circle decoration are well-known in the Harappan area (e.g. at Chanhu-daro and Mohenjo-daro), but none of the Harappan combs bear the distinctive floral motif of the Tell Abraq comb. These flowers are identified as tulips, perhaps Mountain tulip or Boeotian tulip (both of which grow in Afghanistan) which have an undulate leaf. There is a possibility that the comb is an import from Bactria, perhaps transmitted through Meluhha to the Oman Peninsula site of Tell Abraq.

Ivory comb with Mountain Tulip motif and dotted circles. TA 1649 Tell Abraq. [D.T. Potts, South and Central Asian elements at Tell Abraq (Emirate of Umm al-Qaiwain, United Arab Emirates), c. 2200 BC—AD 400, in Asko Parpola and Petteri Koskikallio, South Asian Archaeology 1993: , pp. 615-666] h337, h338 Texts 4417, 4426 (Dotted circles on leaf-shaped tablets) Tell Abraq comb and axe with epigraph After Fig. 7Holly Pittman, 1984, Art of the Bronze Age: Southeastern Iran, Western Central Asia, and the Indus Valley, New York, The Metropolitan Museum of Art, pp. 29-30].

kaṇḍ kanka = rim of jar; rebus: kan- 'copper' (Ta.), kaṇḍ 'furnace' (Santali) kaṇḍ 'stone (ore) metal'. *Ga.* (Oll.) kanḍ, stone, (S.) kanḍu (*pl.* kanḍkil) id. (DEDR 1298).

The rim of a jar is kaṇḍ kan-ka (Santali).

Daimabad seal (c. 1400 BCE). Frequency of occurrence of sign: 1395. kaṇḍ is pot; kan-ka in Sanskrit is

karṇaka 'ear or rim of jar'. kaṇḍ also means 'fire-altar'. Rebus1: kaṇḍ kan-ka lit. 'engraved account in stone. 'furnace account (scribe, engraver)' or 'stone (ore) metal account (scribe, engraver)'. Pk. *kaṁḍa* -- m. ' piece, fragment '; -- Deriv. Pk. *kaṁḍārēi* ' scrapes, engraves '; M. *kā̃ḍārṇẽ, karā̃ḍṇẽ* ' to gnaw ', *kā̃ḍārṇẽ* n. ' jeweller's hammer, barber's nail -- parer '. (CDIAL 2683) कंडारणें [ kaṇḍāraṇēṃ ] *n* An instrument of goldsmiths,--the iron spike which is hammered upon plates in reducing them to shape (Marathi) khanun खनुन् to engrave (Śiv. 414, 671, 176; Rām. 1583). (Kashmiri) *Ta.* karaṇṭu (karaṇṭi-) to paw (as a dog), gnaw (as a rat), scrape. *Ma.* karaṇṭuka to scrape the inside of metal vessels with a grating noise. (DEDR 1268).khanaka m. one who digs , digger , excavator MBh. iii , 640 R. ; a miner L. ; a house-breaker , thief L. ; a rat L. ; N. of a friend of Vidura

MBh. i , 5798 f. ; (%{I}) f. a female digger or excavator Pāṇ. 3-1 , 145 Pat. ; iv , 1 , 41 Ka1s3. kanka 'rim (of jar, kaṇḍ)' (Santali) kárṇa— m. 'ear, handle of a vessel' RV., 'end, tip (?)' RV. ii 34, 3. [Cf. *kāra—6] Pa. kaṇṇa— m. 'ear, angle, tip'; Pk. kaṇṇa—, °aḍaya- m. 'ear', Gy. as. pal. eur. kan m., Ash. (Trumpp) karna NTS ii 261, Niṅg. kõmacr;, Woṭ. kanƏ, Tir. kana; Paš. kan, kaṇ(ḍ)— 'orifice of ear' IIFL iii 3, 93; Shum. kõmacr;ṛ 'ear', Woṭ. kan m., Kal. (LSI) kuṛõmacr;, rumb. kuŕũ, urt. kŕã (< *kaṇ), Bshk. kan, Tor. k

*l ṇ, Kand. kōṇi, Mai. kaṇa, ky. kān, Phal. kāṇ, Sh. gil. kọn pl. kọní m. (→ Ḍ kon pl. k *l ṇa), koh. kuṇ, pales. kuāṇƏ, K. kan m., kash. pog. ḍoḍ. kann, S. kanu m., L. kann m., awāṇ. khet. kan, P. WPah. bhad. bhal. cam. kann m., Ku. gng. N. kān; A. kāṇ 'ear, rim of vessel, edge of river'; B. kāṇ 'ear', Or. kāna, Mth. Bhoj. Aw. lakh. H. kān m., OMarw. kāna m., G. M. kān m., Ko. kānu m., Si. kaṇa, kana. — As adverb and postposition (ápi kárṇē 'from behind' RV., karṇē 'aside' Kālid.): Pa. kaṇṇē 'at one's ear, in a whisper'; Wg. ken 'to' NTS ii 279; Tir. kõ; 'on' AO xii 181 with (?); Paš. kan 'to'; K. kảni with abl. 'at, near, through', kani with abl. or dat. 'on', kun with dat. 'toward'; S. kani 'near', kanã 'from'; L. kan 'toward', kannũ 'from', kanne 'with', khet. kan, P. ḍog. kanē 'with, near'; WPah. bhal. k *l ṇ, °ṇi, k e ṇ, °ṇi with obl. 'with, near', kiṇ, °ṇiã, k *l ṇiã, k e ṇ° with obl. 'from'; Ku. kan 'to, for'; N. kana 'for, to, with'; H. kane, °ni, kan with ke 'near'; OMarw. kanai 'near', kanã sā 'from near', kãnī 'towards'; G. kan e 'beside'. Addenda: kárṇa—: S.kcch. kann m. 'ear', WPah.kṭg. (kc.) kān, poet. kanṛu m. 'ear', kṭg. kanni f. 'pounding—hole in barn floor'; J. kā'n m. 'ear', Garh. kān; Md. kan— in kan—fat 'ear' (CDIAL 2830). The Sohgaura copper plate (4th cent. BCE) refers to a pair of kos.t.ha_ga_ra (dva_ra kot.t.haka); the two storehouses described as tri-garbha (i.e. having three rooms) are illustrated on line 1. (Fleet, JRAS, 1907). The illustrations indicate that the three rooms are in three storeys, with supporting pillars clearly seen. The inscription refers to the junction of three highways named Manavati, in two villages called Dasilimita and Usagama. The storehouses were made at this junction for the goods of people using the highways, which are indicated in line 3 by mentioning the three places to and from which they led. One of the names give is recognized by Fleet as Chanchu. (Fleet, JRAS, 63, 1894 proceedings, 86, plate, IA 25. 262; cf. Sohgaura copper plate/B.M. Barua. The Indian Historical Quarterly, ed. Narendra Nath Law. Reprint. 41)

Punchmarked coin. Fifth sign from left is a rimmed, short-necked jar (Sign 342, Daimabad seal, which has the most-frequent, 1,395 occurrences on epigraphs).

khundha 3902 *khundha ' humpbacked '. [Cf. the ' hump ' group s.v. kubjá -- and the ' defective ' group s.v. kuṇṭha -- ]G. *khũdhi* f. ' hump on the back ', *khũdhũ* ' humpbacked

kuṇḍī = crooked buffalo horns (L.) khuṇḍa 3901 *khuṇḍa ' defective '. [See list s.v. kuṇṭha -- ] L. *khuṇḍā* ' blunt, crooked -- horned '; P. *khuṇḍī* ' crooked -- horned '; N. *khũṛo* ' blunt ', H. *khuṇḍā.*

kuṇḍī = chief of village. kuṇḍi-a = village headman; leader of a village (Pkt.lex.) I.e. śreṇi jeṭṭha chief of metal-worker guild.

Dotted circle, rebus: pasra 'smithy'; kaṇḍ 'fire-altar'

pāslo = a nugget of gold or silver having the form of a die (G.) Rebus: pasra 'smithy' (Santali)

kandhi = a lump, a piece (Santali.lex.) [The dotted circle thus connotes an ingot taken out of a kaṇḍ, furnace]. kāndavika = a baker; kandu = an iron plate or pan for baking cakes etc. (Ka.lex.)

kaṇḍ = altar, furnace (Santali) लोहकारकन्दुः f. a blacksmith's smelting furnace (Grierson Kashmiri lex.)

payĕn-kõda पयन्-कोँद । परिपाककन्दुः f. a kiln (a potter's, a lime-kiln, and brick-kiln, or the like); a furnace (for smelting) This yajn~a kuṇḍam can be denoted rebus, by perforated beads (kandi) or on ivory (khaṇḍ):

kandi (pl. -l) beads, necklace (Pa.); kanti (pl. -l) bead, (pl.) necklace; kandit. bead (Ga.)(DEDR 1215). The three stringed beads depicted on the pictograph may perhaps be treated as a phonetic determinant of the substantive, the rimmed jar, the khaṇḍa kanka. khaṇḍa, xanro, sword or large sacrificial knife. kandil, kandi_l = a globe of glass, a lantern (Ka.lex.)

jaṇḍ khaṇḍ = ivory (Jat.ki) khaṇḍī = ivory in rough (Jat.ki_); gaṭī = piece of elephant's tusk (S.) [This semant. may explain why the dotted circle -- i.e., kandi, 'beads' -- is often depicted on ivory objects, such as ivory combs]. See also: khaṇḍiyo [cf. khaṇḍaṇī a tribute] tributary; paying a tribute to a superior king (G.lex.) [Note glyph of a kneeling adorant]

Glyph: khan:ghar, ghan:ghar, ghan:ghar gon:ghor 'full of holes' (Santali)

Substantive: kan:gar 'portable furnace' (K.)

``^eye":So. mO'OD/ mAD `eye'.Go. man ~ mu: ~ ma:(V) `eye'.Gu. mo: `eye'.Re. m'o: `eye'.Kh. mO'D ~ mO~'D `eye'.Ju. e-mor `eye'.Sa. mE~'d `eye'.Ma. mE'd `eye'.Mu. mE'd ~ mE~'d `eye'.Ho me'd `eye'.Bj. me'd `eye'.Bh. mE'd `eye'.Dh. mE~'d `eye'.Kw. mE~'d `eye'.Ku. met `eye'. !i.e. me~d(HJP).@(V250)

``^iron":Sa. mE~R~hE~'d `iron'. ! mE~RhE~d(M).Ma. mErhE'd `iron'.Mu. mERE'd `iron'. ~ mE~R~E~'d `iron'. ! mENhEd(M).Ho meD `iron'.Bj. merhd(Hunter) `iron'.

KW mENhEd @(V168,M080)

గాడి [ gāḍi ] *gāḍi.* [Tel.] n. A drinking trough or manager, a ditch, a groove. గాడినుయ్యి a well that is provided with a trough for watering cattle. గాడిపొయ్యి a kitchen range, being a trench containing fire under a line of places for pots.

গণীভূত [ gaṇībhūta ] a belonging to a race or tribe, racial, tribal, belonging to a genus, generic; belonging to a community, communal; belonging to a party.

Marathi: खड्या [ khaḍyā ] *m* The name of a very large red seafish.Kashmiri: gāḍ गाड् । मीनः f. a fish (K.Pr. 14, 38, 63, 14, 15, 168, 258; H. i, 8, 9). Regarding the fish of Kashmīr, see El. s.v. *gáḍ.* --āparüñü -- निरुत्तरीकरणम् (प्रतिहननम्), f.inf. to feed fish into a person's mouth; met. to confound a person in argument; to defeat a person in a scolding match, to render him speechless by giving him abuse so foul that he is at a loss to invent anything fouler in reply. -- raṭüñü -- रट&above;ञ्ू&below; f.inf. to fish (El.). -- raṭanwôlu -- n.ag. m. (f.raṭanwājĕñ रटन्ॗवाज्यञ्), a fisherman (El.). gāḍa-bāha gāḍa-bāha गाड-बाह । मत्स्यधूमौषधम् m. fishsteam, a diet of fish combined with the application of the steam and juice of cooked fish, employed as a remedy in cases of impotence and the like. -bata -बत । बलिदानविशेषः m. N. of an offering of cooked fish and rice, usually made in the month of Pŏh (Skt. *Pauṣa* = December-January) to the *Vāstupuruṣa,* or personified archetype of a house worshipped as a deity; cf. dāyĕth-gāḍa, s.v. dāyuth. -dĕgulu -द्यगुलु&below; । मत्स्योखाभेदः m. an earthenware vessel used for cooking a spiced stew of fish previously fried in oil. Cf. -tövü, bel. -güñü -ग&above;ञ्ू&below; । मत्स्यखण्डः f. a piece or slice of fish, cooked or uncooked, sliced fish as a dish (K.Pr. 25, *-gani*). -gañĕ khārañĕ -गञ खारञ । अतिताडनम् f. pl. inf. to raise bits of fish; met. to cudgel or whip the naked body so as to raise weals (considered to resemble fishes in shape). -hönzü -हा&above;न्ज़ू&below; । मत्स्यवधाजीवी m. (f. -hānzañ - हान्ज़ञ्), a fish boatman, a man who lives by netting fish, a fisherman. The f. is a woman who lives by selling fish so caught (Gr.M.). -kāh -काह् । तिथिविशेषः f. (sg. dat. -köshü -का&above;शू&below;), the eleventh lunar day of the dark half of the month of Phāgun (Skt. *Phālguna* = February-March), on which offerings of fish are made to the böravs (*bhairavas*) in preparation for the Śivarātri festival culminating on the ensuing thirteenth lunar day of the dark half of the same month (cf. börav). -khŏḍ - ख्वड् । मत्स्यगर्तः m. a hollow flooded in the rainy season and filled with fish. When the water dries off the fish remain behind and are caught. -khôru -ख्वोरु&below; । काण्डोलविशेषः m. the outer basket-work of akā̆gürü, or portable brazier, of which the inner earthenware receptacle for burning fuel has been broken, and which is commonly used as a fish-basket; see khôru 1. -khāv -ख्राव् । पक्षिविशेषः m. fish-eater, a kind of fish-eating bird, described as small, of a dark colour, and possessing a long beak. -kala -कल । मत्स्यशिरः m. the head of a fish; a person with a head shaped like that of a fish. -kan -कन् । मीनकर्णास्थि m. the ear-bone of a fish, i.e. the flat bones at the side of the head of a large fish, supposed to cover the ears. These are used in the manufacture of little boxes or the like. -konḍu - क&above;ण्डु&below; । मत्स्यास्थि m. a fish-bone. -kåndi-dôvu -कण्डि;<-> दोवु; । चित्रल्परज्जुविशेषः m. a kind of embroidery resembling the backbone of a fish, herring-boning. -kanañĕ -क्ॅनञ । गृहे गृहे निन्दाख्यापनम, वाग्युद्धविधानम् f. pl. inf. to sell fish; met. to go about from house to house uttering scandalous tales against a person; to engage in a verbal quarrel, to use Billingsgate. -krāy -क्राय् । मत्स्यपाककटाहः f. large iron pan for frying fish. -lĕji -ल्य&above;जि&below;or -lĕ˘jü -ल्य&above;जू&below; । मत्स्योखा f. an earthen pot for cooking fish; such a pot full of cooked fish. -lüṭü -लटू; । मत्स्यपुच्छभागः f. the tail end of a fish. -pakhash -पख्ॅश् । मत्स्यपक्षः m. the fin of a fish. -parmāna -पर्मान । मत्स्यमानप्रस्थः m. a stone or iron weight for weighing fish (usually heavier than similar weights used for other purposes). -shĕhalun -शहलुन् । मत्स्यदुर्गन्धः m. the smell of unwashed fish; genl. a fishy smell. -shikār -शिकार् m. fishing (W. 114). -ṭhyupu ठिपु&below; । मत्स्यधानी m. a kind of deep basket made of withies, built like a cage, in which fish are kept. -ṭĕpun -ट्यपुन् । मत्स्यान्तरङ्गसमूहः m. (sg. dat. -ṭĕpanas - ट्यपनस्), fish-guts. - । मत्स्यजीर्षम् f. a pan in which pieces of fish are fried before making them into a stew. Cf. -dĕgulu ab. -wörü -वा&above;रू&below; । लघुनौका f. a fishing-boat; genl. a small boat used as tender to a larger one.

DEDR 1160 *Ta.* kaṇ joint in bamboo or cane; kaṇu joint of bamboo, cane, etc., knuckle, joint of the spine, vertebra; kaṇu-kkai wrist;kaṇu-kkāl ankle. *Ma.* kaṇ, kaṇu, kaṇṇu, kaṇpu joint in knot or cane; kaṇavu node of bamboo, cane, etc.; kaṇakkai, kaṇaṅkai wrist; kaṇakkāl, kaṇaṅkāl ankle; kaṇippu articulation of limbs. *Ko.* kaṇ joint of bamboo. *To.* koṇ joint of bamboo or cane. *Ka.* kaṇ joint in reeds, sticks, etc.; gaṇalu knuckle of the fingers, joint or knot of any cane; gaṇike knot or joint. *Te.* kanu, kannu joint in cane or reed; kaṇupu, gaṇupu joint, knot, node (of bamboo, sugar-cane, etc.); (*VPK*) ganupu (ganapu, genapu, genupu), kanupu, kannu, gani, ganike, gane, ganne, gunupu = gaṇupu. *Kol.* (Kin.) gana knot in tree. *Nk.* khan joint in bamboo. *Go.* (Ko.) gana, gana-kay wrist (*Voc.* 1039). *Kur.* xann place on bamboo or cane where side shoot was cut away. *Br.* xan knot in wood. 1946 Ta. keṇṭai ankle. Ma. keṇippu joint, articulation. Ka. giṇṇu, geṇṇu knot, joint, as of sugar-cane, finger, etc.;gaṇṭu knot of cord, joint of reed, bamboo, cane, joint or articulation of body. Koḍ. gïṇṇï joint in wrist or fingers, knot in sugar-cane; ka·lï-gïṇṇï ankle. Tu. gaṇṭu knot in string, ankle, knot or joint of reed or cane. Te.gaṇṭu, (VPK) gaṇṭa a knot. Nk. kanḍe joint in bamboo. Cf. 1160 Ta. kaṇ joint. / Cf. Skt. gaṇḍa- joint; Turner,CDIAL, no. 3998 (also *gēṇḍa-).

Annex

Eye stones

Achaemenid era "eye stones" were found in January 2008 at Parsa, made of agate that Professor Callieri said were used either as the eyes of stone statues or as amulets to ward off the evil eye.

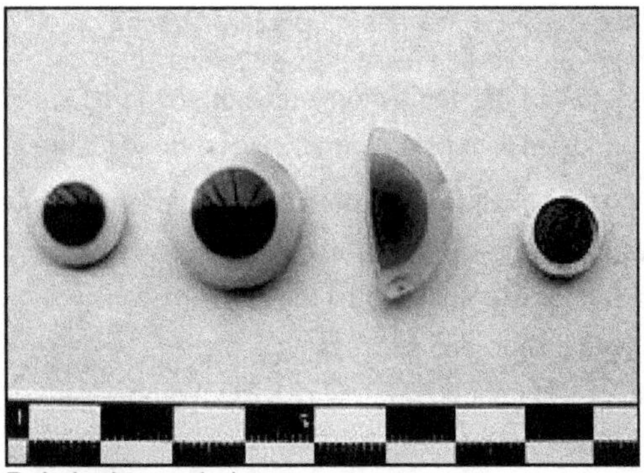

Achaemenid era "eye stones" used either as the eyes of statues or as amulets to repel the evil eye have been discovered by the Iranian-Italian joint archaeological team during their latest excavation at the ancient town of Parsa near Persepolis.

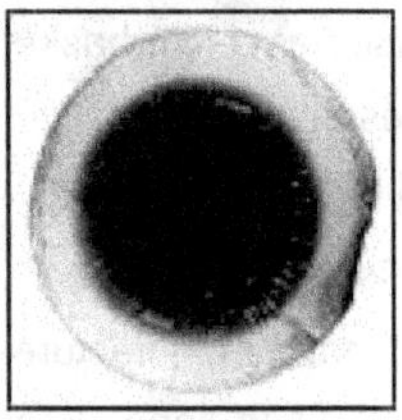

Eye Stone Amulet of Nebuchadnezzar II (604–562 B.C.)
Amulet
Mesopotamia, Neo-
Babylonian period
(ca. 1000–539 B.C.)
Agate Diameter: 38.4 mm The Morgan Library
and Museum, NY

Inscribed: *To Marduk his lord, Nebuchadnezzar, king of Babylon, son of Nabopalassar, gave [this] for his life.*

“It is now generally argued that when texts refer to ‘fish eyes’ as items in the Gulf trade c. 2000 BCE (Oppenheim, A.L.,1978, Assyrian dictionary: 663 n. 185) they mean not pearls, as was formerly argued, but rather banded agate beads cut to look like the eyes of fishes. It is also possible that Turkey provided some agate. Agate ranks with lapis lazuli and cornelian as the most popular gemstones in Mesopotamia, most commonly appearing as amulets, beads and pendants.” (Moorely, Peter Roger Stuart, 1999, Ancient Mesopotamian materials and industries: the archaeological evidence,OUP, p.99)

Ur III text, UET V 292, refers to ships of Dilmun bringing luxury goods, such as ivory, timber, gold, copper, lapis lazuli, and ‘fish eyes’, to the cities in southern Mesopotamia. Tosi notes that ‘it seems increasingly likely that the Indus civilization contributed more to oceanic sea craft than any of the other proto-urban civilizations of the Middle East…The early efficiency of this transmaritime network greatly impressed the memory of the agricultural civilizations of Mesopotamia and Egypt that remained marginal to it.’ Ur III texts (2062-2028 BCE) also refer to a ‘Meluhhan village’, in Lagash territory, perhaps acculturated people from Meluhha. [(Oppenheim 1954; Bass 1972, 14; Alster 1983, 44; Tosi 1986, 107; Parpola et al. 1977, 152,157. During Caspers (1984) suggests that Sumerians were also residing in trading communities in Meluhha.loc. Cit.Makela, Tommi Tapani, 2002, Ships and ship-building in Mesopotamia (ca. 3000-2000 BCE), MA Thesis,Texas A&M Univ.]

http://nautarch.tamu.edu/pdf-files/Makela-MA2002.pdf

"The addresses on fragments of clay at Tello prove that sealings were employed on bundles despatched from city to city (L.W. King: A history of Sumer and Akkad, 1910, pp. 236-7)...

Tilmun, Telmun, Dilmun, the land of the famous red stone

“Documents of the Larsa period in Ur were on tablets. Volume UET V includes texts which deal with Ur as the port of entry for copper into Mesopotamia during the time of the Dynasty of Larsa. The copper was imported by boat from Telmun. (Tilmun is associated with the famous red stone, of which Gudea speaks repeatedly as being imported from Meluhha.) "This 'Telmun-trade' was in the hands of seafaring merchants--called alik Telmun-- who worked hand in hand with enterprising capitalists in Ur to take garments to the island in order to buy large quantities of copper there... In our period-- that of the fifth to seventh king of the Dynasty of Larsa-- the island exported not only copper in ingots but also copper objects, beads of precious stones, and-- most of all-- ivory... Travels to Telmun are repeatedly mentioned in a group of tablets whih come patently from the archives of the temple of the goddess Ningal and list votive offerngs, incoming tithe, etc. The contexts suggest that returning sailors were wont to offer the deity in gratitude a share of their goods. In UET V 526 we read of a small amount of gold, copper and copper utensils characterized as 'tithe of the goddess Ningal from an expedition to Telmun and (from) single persons having gone (there) on their own', during the first 3 months of the year. UET V 292... listing of merchandise is more extensie; besides 'red' gold, copper, lapiz lazuli in lumps, various stone beads, ivory-inlaid tables, et., we find also 'fish-eyes'--perhaps pearls. (The meaing 'pearl' for IGI.HA has been proposed by R.C. Thompson (1936y: 53, n2) on the basis of UET V... The appearance of rather numerous references to IGI.HA in Ur and especialy in connection with imports from Tilmun must be considered an argument in favor of an interpretation which is not based on philological evidence. The lack of archaeological proof for the use of pearls is of course an important arguent against the identification but its value is somewhat diminished when one considers that no ivory object has been found in Ur although the texts report on ivory as raw material as well as on ivory objects.) ... UET 78, recording ivory combs, eye-paint and certain kinds of wood, not to mention designations which we fail to understand... UET V 367: '2 mina of silver (the value of): 5 gur of oil (and of) 30 garments for an expedition to Telmun to buy (there) copper, (as the) capital for a partnership, L. and N. have borrowed from U. After safe termination of the voyage, he (the creditor) will not recognize commercial losses (incurred by the debtor); they (the debtors) hae agree to satisfy U (the creditor) with 4 mina of copper for each shel of silver as a just (price(?)].'.. babtum must denote some kind of customs or dues imposed on the merchants by the city administration... all extant Old and Neo-Babylonian contracts on partnership reserve for the tamkarum not only the invested capital (plus interest) but also an equal share of the profit yielded by the business venture... The complex legal relationship between the investing and the travelling merchant has created a number of loan types of which at least two are mentioned in the Code of Hammurabi. One of them uses the characteric termtadmiqtu. We encounter this word in the paragraphs 102-103 of the Code and in a few documents of that period... UET V 428: '5 shekels of silver as a tadmiqtu-loan PN1 has borrowed from PN2. He will return the silver at a moment (yet) to be determined (?) (This) he has sworn by the life of the king.' The specific designation of the loans as tadmiqtu 'favor, kindness' (in Sumerian: KA.sa 'friendly word') should not, in spite of the obvious etymology of these terms in both languages, induce us to presume that this business transaction was not as completely under the sway of the laws of economic life as any other loan... As to the main object of the Telmun trade, the copper (termed URUDU), we obtain most of the evidence from the letters (UET V 22,29, 71 and 81) addressed to a certain Ea-na_s.ir, a travelling merchant and importer of Telmun copper. The metal came in large quantities (UET V 796 mentions more than 13,000 minaz of copper according to the weight standard of Telmun) and often in ingots termed gubarum which weighed up to 4 talents each (UET V 678). The ingots are sometimes qualified as damqu (UET V 22,81) as is also the copper itself (UET V 20 wariam la damqam, but wariam dummuqam in UET V 5 and 6). The quoted passages do not entitle us to speak of refining of copper, because Ea-na_s.ir was not a coppersmith but a merchant and because the meaning of damqum as well as dummuqum as 'good (in quality)' is borned out by such letter passages as UET V 5:28 or 22: 10-13 ('show him 15 ingots so that he may select 6 damqu ingots' ... UET V 81, lines 33-39: 'I myself gave on account of you 19 talents of copper to the palace and S'umi-abum gave (likewise) 18 talents of copper, apart from the sealed document which we both handed over to the temple of Shamash.'... Ea-na_s.ir is supposed to have imported a large copper kettle (UET V 5:25)... UET V 428: '1 mina of...silver, 1/2 mina of... silver to buy (precious stones), 'fish-eyes' and other merchandise on an expedition to Telmun, PN2 has borrowed from PN1...'... ivory as raw material (UET V 546) as well as finished ivory objects have been imported from Telmun. Among the latter we find exactly the same objects which we know so well from the dowry inventories, etc. of the Amarna letters: ivory combs (UET V 292, 678), breast plates (UET V 279), boxes (UET V 795), inlaid pieces of furniture (UET 292) and spoons (UET V 795)... Southern Mesopotamia had to rely exclusively upon ivory imported from the East, to be exact: via Telmun... we have from Mohenjo-daro actual ivory combs... UET V 82 refers to the karum as a locality in which business accounts have been settled, which in Old-Babylonian practice is normally done in the temple of Shamash... A certain Lu-En-li_l-la_ is said in UET III 1689 (Ibbi-Sin, 4th year) to have received large amounts of garments and wool from the storehouse of the temple of Nanna in order to buy copper in Makkan (nig.s'am.marudu Ma.gan ki, literally: equivalent for buying copper in M.)... When Sargon of Agade proudly proclaims (Legrain 1923: 208f., col. v-vi) that ships from or destined for Meluhha, Makkan and Telmun were moored in the harbor which was situated outside of his capital, this obviously proves the existence of flourishing commercial relations with the East... We even know the name of a person, a native of 'Great-Makkan' i.e. Ur-Nammu (UET III 1193). In the period, Makkan-- 'the country of mines' seems to have been the only importer of copper... After the collapse of the Dynasty of Ur, Telmun replaces Makkan in the Eastern trade of the city... Telmun, as against Makkan, seems never to have completely lost contact with Mesopotamia... Telmun had lost contact with the mining centers of Makkan and with those regions which supplied it with stone and timber, etc. some time between the fall of the Dynasty of Larsa and the decline of power of the Hammurabi Dynasty... It turned again into an island famous only for its agricultural products, its sweet water, etc. Copper, precious stones, and rare woods have now to come to Southern Mesopotamia either over the mountain ranges and from the West along the river routes... Sometime in the second half of the 2nd millennium B.C., Telmun seems to have come in closer contact with the rulers of Southern Babylonia (Goetze 1952)... We are fortunate indeed to have three letters at our disposal, two written by Assurbanipal's general Bel-ibni mentioning Hundaru, king of Telmun, and one written by Assurbanipal and addressed to Hundaru. The details of the dealings of the king of Telmun in his fight for survival are of little interest in the present context, far more revealing is the mention of metal (bronze), precious woods and 'kohl' i.e. eye-paint in these letters. We read of great amounts of kohl, 26 talent of bronze, numerous copper and bronze objects, of sticks of precious wood as part of the booty taken from Telmun, while another speaks of the tribute of Telmun mentioning, at the same time, bronze, perfumes and likewise 'sticks' of precious wood offered by merchants from Bit-Naialu... a passage of the inscription KAH 122 of Sennacherib which describes the tools of the crew of corvee-workers sent from Telmun to Babylon to assist the Assyrian king to tear down the city. Their tools are characterized as follows: 'bronze spades and bronze pikes, tools which are the (characteristic) product of their (native) country.' Thus, it becomes evident that Telmun has again access to the copper mines of Makkan, to the spices, perfumes and rare woods of the East... Assurbanipal's inscription in the temple of Ishtar in Niniveh mentions another island-- beyond Telmun--: '[x-y]-i-lum, king of the [ ]-people who resides in Hazmani which is an island alongside Telmun' whose messengers had to travel a long way across the sea and overland to Assyria. "(A.Leo Oppenheim, The Seafaring Merchants of Ur, *Journal of the American Oriental Society*, Vol. 74, 1954, pp. 6-17).

R.A. Donkin notes: "From the earliest times, the eye has exercised a peculiar fascination for man. Eye-divinities and eye-beads prized as amulets have been widely reported. Comparisons between the pearl and a fish's eye date from Androsthenes's report (ca. 324 BCE), as preserved by Arthenaeus – 'sometimes, [the pearl]…is silvery, sometimes perfectly white, resembling the eye of a fish.' In Theophrastus's De Lapidibus (ca. 315 BCE), we are told that 'the dimensions of the pearl are those of a fish's eye of large size,' an observation repeated by Clement of Alexandria who lived around the turn of the second century AD. Ancient Indian sources extend the comparison. 'On certain pearls, there are marks like the eye of a fish and these are hence called minaaksha (lit. 'the eye of a fish').' In Varahamihira's Brhatsamhita (ca. AD 550) we find: 'The pearl coming from dolphins resembles a fish's eye…' Chinese accounts, too, incorporate the same idea, compounded of observation and mythology: 'Fish pearls are in the eye' (eleventh century). Powdered pearls were used for disorders of the eye on the ground that they were 'shaped like the eye'. Pearls supposedly from whales, sharks and other 'great fish' have already been mentioned. A putative connection with the eyes of fish in particular is hardly surprising. The 'swans with eyes of pearl' in Somadeva's Kathasaritsagara (com. 1070) is unusual. All form part of a larger literature in which a variety of precious and semi-precious stones are associated with or named after the eyes of animals. The suggestion that 'fish-eyes' (IGI.HA, IGI-KU6), imported through Ur, may have been pearls has been advanced by a number of scholars. 'Fish-eyes' were among a number of valuable commodities (gold, copper, lapis lazuli, stone beads) offered in thanksgiving at the temple of the Sumerian goddess Ningal at Ur by seafaring merchants who had returned safely from Dilmun and perhaps further afield. Elsewhere they are said to have been bought in Dilmun. Whether 'fish-eyes' differed from 'fish-eye stones' (NA4 IGI.HA, NA4 IGI-KU6) and from simply 'eye-stones' is not entirely clear. The latter are included among goods imported from Meluhha (NA4 IGI-ME-LUH-HA)ca. 1816-1810 BCE and ca. 1600-1570 BCE. Any pearls from Meluhha – probably coastal Baluchistan-Sind – would have been generally inferior to those from Dilmun itself. It has been strongly argued that 'fish-eyes', 'fish-eye stones' and 'eye-stones' in Old Babylonian and Akkadian texts were not in fact pearls, but rather (a) etched cornelian beads, imported from India and/or (b) pebbles of banded agate, cut to resemble closely a black/brown pupil and white cornea. The nearest source of good agate is in northwest India, which would accord with supplies obtained from Meluhha. 'Eye-stones' of agate were undoubtedly treasured: some were inscribed and used as amulets, others have been found in votive deposits. Perhaps pearls were at times included among 'fish-eyes,' if not 'fish-eye stones'. More likely, however, the word for 'pearl' is among the 'more than 800 terms in the lexical lists of stones and gems [that] remain to be identified.'" (Donkin, R.A., 1998, Beyond price: pearls and pearl-fishing: origins to the age of discoveries, Philadelphia, American Philosophical Society, Memoir Volume 224, pp.49-50)Full text at http://tinyurl.com/y9zpb5n

Note 109. For Sumerian words, see Delitzch, 1914: pp.18-19 (igi, eye), 125 (ku, fish), 195 (na, stone); and cf. Chicago Assyrian Dictionary I/J: 1960: pp.45 (iga), 153-158 (Akk. i_nu), N(2), 1980: p.340 (k), 'fish-eye stones'.

Note 110. A.L. Oppenheim, 1954: pp.7-8; Leemans, 1960b: pp.24 f. (IGI-KU6). Followed by Kramer, 1963a: p.113, 1963b: p.283; Bibby, 1970: pp.189, 191-192: Ratnagar, 1981: pp.23-24,79, 188; M. Rice, 1985: p.181.

Note 111. A.L. Oppenheim, 1954: p.11; Leemans, 1960b: p.37 (NA4 IGI-KU6, 'fish-eye stones').

Note 112. Leemans, 1968: p.222 ('pearls from Meluhha'. Falkenstein (1963: pp.10-11 [12]) has 'augenformigen Perlen aus Meluhha'. (lit. shaped eyes beads from Meluhha).

Note 113. Unger, 1931: p. 277 (Agumkakrime II).

Note 114. During Caspers, 1983: pp.46-49, 1987: pp.72-76. Cornelian beads have been found in Mesopotamia from Early Dynastic IIIa to Ur III (H. Crawford, 1991: p.146).

Note 115. Howard-Carter, 1986: pp.305-310. On 'eye-stones' or 'eye-beads' of agate, onyx and sardonyx, see E.F. Schmidt, 1939: pp.74 (and pl. 54), 75 (Persepolis); H.C. Beck, 1941: pp.5-7 (Taxila): Stronach, 1963: p.4 (Pasargadae); W.G. Lambert, 1969: pp. 65-71 (Mesopotamia).

116. Howard-Carter, 1986: p.309 n.36.

Susa-Meluhha interactions

http://bharatkalyan97.blogspot.com/2011/11/mohenjo-daro-stupa-great-bath-modeled.htmlThis blogpost notes that the ziggurat shown on the Sit-Shamshi bronze compares with a ziggurat which might have existed in the Stupa mound of Mohenjo-daro (lit. mound of the dead), indicating the veneration of ancestors in Susa and Meluhha in contemporaneous times.

This post has also documented that an Elamite statuette showed a person (king?) carrying an antelope on his hands, the same way a Meluhhan carried an antelope on his hands (as shown on a cylinder seal). Department des Antiquites Orienteles, Musee du Louvre, Paris.'Based on cuneiform documents from Mesopotamia we know that there was at least one Meluhhan village in Akkad at that time, with people called 'Son of Meluhha' living there. The cuneiform inscription (ca. 2020 BCE) says that the cylinder seal belonged to Shu-ilishu, who was a translator of the Meluhhan language. "The presence in Akkad of a translator of the Meluhhan language suggests that he may have been literate and could read the undeciphered Indus script. This in turn suggests that there may be bilingual Akkadian/Meluhhan tablets somewhere in Mesopotamia. Although such documents may not exist, Shu-ilishu's cylinder seal offers a glimmer of hope for the future in unraveling the mystery of the Indus script." (Gregory L. Possehl,Shu-ilishu's cylinder seal, Expedition, Vol. 48, Number 1, pp. 42-43).http://www.penn.museum/documents/publications/expedition/PDFs/48-1/What%20in%20the%20World.pdf

Antelope carried by the Meluhhan is a hieroglyph: mlekh 'goat' (Br.); mṛeka (Te.); mēṭam (Ta.); meṣam (Skt.) Thus, the goat conveys the message that the carrier is a Meluhha speaker. A phonetic determinant.mṛreka, mlekh 'goat'; Rebus: melukkha Br. mēl̤h 'goat'. మేక [ mēka ] mēka. [Tel.] n. A goat.

మేకపిల్ల a kid. మేకవన్నెపులి a tiger of the color of a goat. i.e., a wolf in sheep's clothing. పెంటిమేక a she-goat. మేకపోతు a he-goat. పిల్లలుమేకలుగలవారము I am the head of a large family containing many individuals of both sexes. The Indians goat has excrescences like teats on the neck: as these are useless, వాడు వట్టిమేక మెడచన్ను denotes He is a mere useless burden or appendage. మేకతిండి meka-tinḍi. n. That which feeds on goats, i.e., a wolf, తోడేలు, మేకము [borrowed by Skt. from Tel.] n. Same as మేక.

See: Ka. mēke she-goat; mē the bleating of sheep or goats. Te. mẽka, mēka goat. Kol. me·ke id. Nk. mēke id. Pa. mēva, (S.) mēya she-goat. Ga. (Oll.) mēge, (S.) mēge goat. Go. (M) mekā, (Ko.) mēka id. ? Kur. mēxnā (mīxyas) to call, call after loudly, hail. Malt. méqe to bleat. [Te. mr̤ēka (so correct) is of unknown meaning. Br. mēl̤h is without etymology; see MBE 1980a.] / Cf. Skt. (lex.) meka- goat (Monier-Williams lex.) (DEDR 5087) meluh.h.a !

mlekh 'goat' (Br.); meḷh 'goat' (Br. mr̤eka (Te.); mēṭam (Ta.); meṣam (Skt.) Te. mr̤eka (DEDR 5087)

Rebus: meṛha, meḍhi 'merchant's clerk; (G.)

Rebus: mḗdha m. ' sacrificial oblation ' RV. mēdha -- m. ' sacrifice ' (Pa.) (CDIAL 10327).

Semantics of Kannada lexeme, *mēku* 'superiority, rivalry' (a vikalpa rebus reading which may explain the use of the goat-glyph carried by an elamite 'superior'). cf. mahīyas ' greater, very great ' ŚvetUp. [mah -- ]Pk. mahia -- ' great '; OG. mahīāṁ gen. pl. m. ' superior '.(CDIAL 9976) máhas1 n. ' greatness, glory ' RV., ' splendour, light ' Inscr. [máh -- ] Pa. maha -- n.m. ' greatness '; -- Si. maha ' light, brilliance ' (ES 66) ← Sk.?(CDIAL 9936)Maha (m. & nt.) [fr. mah, see mahati & cp. Vedic nt. mahas] 1. worthiness, venerableness Miln 357. -- 2. a (religious) festival (in honour of a Saint, as an act of worship) Mhvs 33, 26 (vihārassa mahamhi, loc.); VvA 170 (thūpe ca mahe kate), 200 (id.). mahā° a great festival Mhvs 5, 94. bodhi° festival of the Bo tree J iv.229. vihāra° festival held on the building of a monastery J i.94; VvA 188. hatthi° a festival called the elephant f. J iv.95. (Pali)மகம்¹ makam, n. < makha. 1. Sacrifice; யாகம். மகந்தான் செய்து வழிவந்தார் (திருவாச. 21, 3). 2. Sacrificial offering or food oblation; பலி. (யாழ். அக.) 3. Happiness; இன்பம். (யாழ். அக.) 4. Light, brilliance; பிரபை. (யாழ். அக.) 5. Festival; விழவு. (யாழ். அக.)máhas2 n. ' delight in praise ' VS., ' festival, worship ' Pañcar., ' sacrifice ' lex., mahá -- m. ' festival, sacrifice ' MBh. [In later MIA. collides with makhá -- m. ' sacrifice ' ŚBr. -- √maṁh?] Pa. maha -- n.m. ' festival '; Pk. maha -- m. ' festival, sacrifice '; OG. maha ' festival '; Si. maha ' sacrifice '.(CDIAL 9937). cf. makh मख् । कुठारः m. (sg. dat. makas मकस्), an axe (Gr.Gr. 39; Gr.M.; K.Pr. 144; Śiv. 13, 1573, 1856); met. in comp. indicating violence, as in daga-makh, lit. an axe with a blow; hence, ultimate recourse to force (p. 193b, l.(Kashmiri)

Shu-ilishu's cylinder seal. Department des Antiquites Orienteles, Musee du Louvre, Paris.

Example of water-carrier glyph as Indus script. Seal impression, Ur (Upenn; U.16747)

Another blogpost was about decoding Indus Script Susa cylinder seal: Susa-Indus interaction areas This cylinder sealshowed a bull and trough together with Indus script glyphs [water-carrier glyph decoded rebus as *kuṭhi* 'smelter furnace' (Santali)] A pair of glyphs flank the water-carrier. It is read as the polar star मेढ [*mēḍha*](Marathi) Rebus: *meḍ* 'iron' (Ho.) dula 'pair' (Kashmiri); rebus: dul 'cast (metal)'(Santali) Thus, the glyphic is decoded as *dul meḍ kuṭhi* 'iron (cast metal) smelter furnace'.

měď (copper)(Czech) mid' (copper, cuprum, orichalc)(Ukrainian) med' (copper, cuprum, Cu), mednyy (copper, cupreous, brassy, brazen, brass), omednyat' (copper, coppering), sul'fatmedi (Copper), politseyskiy (policeman, constable, peeler, policemen, redcap), pokryvat' med'yu (copper), payal'nik (soldering iron, copper, soldering pen, soldering-iron), mednyy kotel (copper), medno-krasnyy (copper), mednaya moneta (copper). медь (copper, cuprum, Cu), медный (copper, cupreous, brassy, brazen, brass), омеднять (copper, coppering), Сульфатмеди (Copper), полицейский (policeman, constable, peeler, policemen, redcap), покрывать медью (copper), паяльник (soldering iron, copper, soldering pen, soldering-iron), медный котел (copper), медно-красный (copper), медная монета (copper).(Russian)

Decoding fish and ligatured-fish glyphs of Indus script (S. Kalyanaraman, November 2011) in the context of a Susa pot showing a fish glyph and containing metal artefacts, the fish glyph [*aya*'fish'(Santali)] was decoded as *aya* 'metal, iron' (G.) Comparable to the ligatured-fish glyphs discussed in this blogpost are the ligatures found on a basin of Susa decorated with goat-fish figures (discussed below).

While a composite comparable glyph (Goat + fish) of the Uruk trough type has not been identified in the corpus of Indus inscriptions,there are seals which show fish glyph together with antelope glyph; fish glyph together with composite bull + heifer glyph.

Harappa seal (h350B); Harappa seal (h330)

Seal. National Museum: 135.

The rebus readings of the hieroglyphs are: mēḍha 'antelope'; rebus: meḍ 'iron' (Ho.) koḍiyum 'heifer'; rebus: koḍ 'artisan's workshop'. aya 'fish'; rebus: aya 'cast metal' (G.).

A Susa ritual basin dated to ca. 12th or 13th century BCE depicts goat and fish ligatured into a 'fabulous' or 'composite' animal representation, clearly intended to connote the underlying hieroglyphic meaning.

Deification of glyphs: When did it happen?

At what point in time, the glyphic representations denoting native metal or cast metal artefacts and which were used to authenticate trade transactions of the civilization, using Indus script inscriptions, were deified can only be conjectured. This shift from use in trade to use in cultural/religious contexts may have occurred -- in the interaction areas such as Susa and Meluhha -- between 19th and 13th centuries BCE (i.e. between the time when the continued use of Indus Script glyphs is attested, say, 19th century BCE and the time when the same glyphs or cognate glyphic representations were deified, say, 13th century BCE).

This conjecture has a semantic basis in mleccha (meluhha) -- the underlying Indus language. A remarkable evidence is provided by a lexeme in Kota. The lexeme is: *kole.l* 'smithy, temple' (Kota) kwala·l Kota smithy (Toda)*kol* 'working in iron, blacksmith (Tamil)(DEDR 2133)Ta. kol working in iron, blacksmith; kollaṉ blacksmith. Ma. kollan blacksmith, artificer. Ko. kole·l smithy, temple in Kota village. To. kwala·l Kota smithy. Ka. kolime, kolume, kulame, kulime, kulume, kulme fire-pit, furnace; (Bell.; U.P.U.) konimi blacksmith; (Gowda) kolla id. Koḍ. kollë blacksmith. Te. kolimi furnace. Go. (SR.) kollusānā to mend implements; (Ph.) kolstānā, kulsānā to forge; (Tr.) kōlstānā to repair (of ploughshares); (SR.) kolmi smithy (Voc. 948). Kuwi (F.) kolhali to forge. (DEDR 2133).

kula कुल (Monier-Williams lexicon): (with शाक्तs) N. of शक्ति and of the rites observed in her worship (cf. कौल); m. the chief of a corporation or guild.

There are semantic intimations that the early meaning of *kula* could be: principal, chief (as in the use of the compound *kula-giri* denoting chief mountain) and hence kwale.l as 'temple': குலம்*kulam* Temple; கோயில். நீலவனக் குலமனந்தம் (இரகு. நகர. 46). குலமுதல் *kula-mutal*Family god; குலதெய்வம். மலையுறைகடவுள் குலமுதல் வழுத்தி (ஐங்குறு. 259).குலகிரி kula-kiri , n. < id. +. Chief mountain ranges in Jambū-dvīpa. See அஷ்டகுல பர்வதம். (பிங்.) *kularājadhānī* 'chief residence' (Skt. Monier-Williams lexicon)

*devakula* temple J ii.411; ñāti -- kula (my) home Vv 3710 (: pitugehaŋ sandhāya VvA 171). (Pali) dēvakula n. ' temple ' ŚāṅkhGṛ., °likā -- f. ' small temple ' Pañcad. [dēvá -- 1, kúla -- ] Pk. dēvaüla -- , dēvala -- , dēula -- n., dēvaüliyā -- , dēuliā -- f.; Ku. dyol ' temple ', dyoli ' small temple dedicated to a goddess '; A. daul, dâl ' temple ', B. deul, Or. deuḷa, dauḷa; H. dewal m. ' temple ', °lī f. ' small shrine '; G. devaḷ n. ' temple ', M. devaḷ, deūḷ n., Si. devola, °vela; <-> X dēvālaya -- : N. deurāli ' place of worship ' < *deulālī.(CDIAL 2524). dēvakulika m. ' temple attendant ' lex. [dēvakula -- ]Pk. dēulia -- m. ' temple attendant ', A. dewalīyā, B. deuliyā, Or. deuḷiā.(CDIAL 6426).*daivakula ' belonging to the temple '. [dēvakula -- ]A. dewal ' a brahman priest living on offerings made at a temple '. -- Rather < or ← dēvala -- , °laka -- m. ' hawker of idols ' Pāṇ.com. (' dēvakōṣōpajīvin -- ' Kull.)(CDIAL 6570). An artifact produced in a smithy becomes a deified representation in the attributes of divinities represented in a temple because the smithy itself is perceived as a temple. The creativity of the smith or artisan finds a parallel in divine creation or the cosmic dance traditions of Indian linguistic area. The Susa ritual basin with the ligatured goat and fish can be interpreted in the context of deification of pictorial representations as detailed in the embedded note and also in the write-up presented about the artifact in the Louvre Museum The composite glyphic of goat-fish on the Susa ritual basin can be compared with the more comprehensive composition glyphic which is exemplified by the inscription on m0302.

Mohenjo-daro seal (m0302).

The composite animal glyph is one example to show that rebus method has to be applied to every glyphic element in the writing system.

This image is also interpreted in corpora (e.g. Mahadevan's Corpus of Indus script) as: body of a ram, horns of a bison, trunk of elephant, hindlegs of a tiger and an upraised serpent-like tail.

m0301 Mohenjo-daro seal shows a comparable 'composite animal' glyphic composition.

The glyphic elements of the composite animal shown together with the glyphs of fish, fish ligatured with lid, arrow (on Seal m0302) are:

--ram or sheep (forelegs denote a bovine)
--neck-band, ring
--*bos indicus* (zebu)(the high horns denote a *bos indicus*)
--elephant (the elephant's trunk ligatured to human face)
--tiger (hind legs denote a tiger)
--serpent (tail denotes a serpent)
--human face

All these glyphic elements are decoded rebus:

*meḍho* a ram, a sheep (G.)(CDIAL 10120);
*kaḍum* 'neck-band, ring'
*adar ḍangra* 'zebu'
*ibha* 'elephant' (Skt.); rebus: ib 'iron' (Ko.)
*kolo* 'jackal' (Kon.)

Glyph: 'cobra's hood': paṭam , *n.* < *phaṭa*. 1. Cobra's hood (CDIAL 9040). Rebus: 'sharpness of iron': padm (obl. Padt-) temper of iron (Ko.)(DEDR 3907). patam 'sharpness, as of the edge of a knife' (Ta.) Vikalpa: *moṇḍ* the tail of a serpent (Santali) Rebus: Md. moḍenī ' massages, mixes '. Kal.rumb. moṇḍ -- ' to thresh ', urt. maṇḍ -- ' to soften ' (CDIAL 9890) Thus, the ligature of the serpent as a tail of the composite animal glyph is decoded as: polished metal (artifact).

*mūhe* 'face' (Santali); mleccha-mukha (Skt.) = milakkhu 'copper' (Pali)

கோடு kōṭu : •நடுநிலை நீங்குகை. கோடிறீக் கூற் றம் (நாலடி, 5). 3. [K. kōḍu.] Tusk; யானை பன்றிகளின் தந்தம். மத்த யானையின் கோடும் (தேவா. 39, 1). 4. Horn; விலங்கின் கொம்பு. கோட்டிடை யாடினை கூத்து (திவ். இயற். திருவிருத். 21).
Ta. kōṭu (in cpds. kōṭṭu-) horn, tusk, branch of tree, cluster, bunch, coil of hair, line, diagram, bank of stream or pool; kuvaṭu branch of a tree; kōṭṭāṉ, kōṭṭuvāṉ rock horned-owl (cf. 1657 Ta. kuṭiñai). Ko. kṛ (obl. kṭ-) horns (one horn is kob), half of hair on each side of parting, side in game, log, section of bamboo used as fuel, line marked out. To. kwṛ (obl. kwṭ-) horn, branch, path across stream in thicket. Ka. kōḍu horn, tusk, branch of a tree; kōṟ horn. Tu. kōḍů, kōḍu horn. Te. kōḍu rivulet, branch of a river. Pa. kōḍ (pl. kōḍul) horn (DEDR 2200)

*meḍ* 'iron' (Ho.)
*khāḍ* 'trench, firepit'
*aduru* 'native metal' (Ka.) *ḍhangar* 'blacksmith' (H.)
*kol* 'furnace, forge' (Kuwi) *kol* 'alloy of five metals, pancaloha' (Ta.)
*mẽṛhẽt, meḍ* 'iron' (Mu.Ho.)
*mūhā mẽṛhẽt* = iron smelted by the Kolhes and formed into an equilateral lump a little pointed at each of four ends (Santali)
*koḍ* = the place where artisans work (G.)

Orthographically, the glytic compositions add on the characteristic short tail as a hieroglyph (on both ligatured signs and on pictorial motifs)

*xolā* = tail (Kur.); qoli id. (Malt.)(DEDr 2135). Rebus: *kol* 'pañcalōha' (Ta.)கொல் kol, n. 1. Iron; இரும்பு. மின் வெள்ளி பொன் கொல்லெனச் சொல்லும் (தக்கயாகப். 550). 2. Metal; உலோகம். (நாமதீப. 318.) கொல்லன் kollaṉ, n. < T. golla. Custodian of treasure; கஜானாக்காரன். (P. T. L.) கொல்லிச்சி kollicci, n. Fem. of கொல்லன். Woman of the blacksmith caste; கொல்லச் சாதிப் பெண். (யாழ். அக.) The gloss kollicci is notable. It clearly evidences that kol was a blacksmith. *kola* 'blacksmith' (Ka.); Koḍ. *kollë* blacksmith (DEDR 2133). Vikalpa: *dumba* दुम्ब or (El.) *duma* दुम । पशुपुच्छः m. the tail of an animal. (Kashmiri) Rebus:*ḍōmba* ?Gypsy (CDIAL 5570).

In the following examples many inscribed objects are decoded. For some glyphs which can be orthographically interpreted with some variationsin identification, vikalpa (alternative) rebus readings are also provided.

Inscriptions in Indus and Indus-related characters on Gulf Type seals as seen on the impression. The numbers refer to seal numbers in Table 1. Note the general abundance of 'twins' signs, especially at the beginning of the sequences.

Indus writing: professional guild calling cards

--(including decoding of Indus script epigraphs of Chanhujo-daro and 19 other sites)

From a review of the decoded Indus script epigraphs from 42 sites, one semantic category is seen to explain the entire range of texts: smithy guild artisans' work.

Indus writing can be described as corpus of inscriptions of professional guild calling cards.

This is consistent with the cultural tradition attested in the historical periods of the contributions made shreni (guilds), and institutions such as gana, samgha, nigama, jati in socio-economic organization.

Indus writing thus describes the corporate life of ancient India with particular reference to the smith guilds who created mineral and metal artefacts and traded them over an extensive interaction area of the civilization.

Hisorical periods attest the contributions made by shreni and other institutions to the nation. (cf. Jolly, Julius, 1896, *Reicht und Sitte: Einschliesslich der einheimischen Litteratur*, Strassburg, KJ Trubner) The decoded epigraphs are consistent with the texts of early historical periods referred to as Hindu law or dharmashastras.

The unique social organization of śreṇi (corporate guilds) continues into the historical periods of India and attested by punch-marked coins of mints, Rampurva copper bolt, Sohgaura copper plate using Indus script glyphs and by copper plate- and stone-inscriptions of contributions made by shreni to promoting cultural life in India. The seeds of this tradition were seen to have been laid in the days of Sarasvati-Sindhu civilization which produced over 3800 Indus script epigraphs.

The commonly occurring glyphs have the same reading on all these and hence are not repeated.

Decoding Gulf type seals

Detailed by Steffen Terp Laursen (2010) as the westward transmission of Indus valley sealing technology: origin and development of 'Gulf type' seal and other administrative technologies in early Dilmun, ca. 2100-2000 BCE (Published in *Arabian Archaeology and Epigraphy* 2010: vol. 21: 96–134).

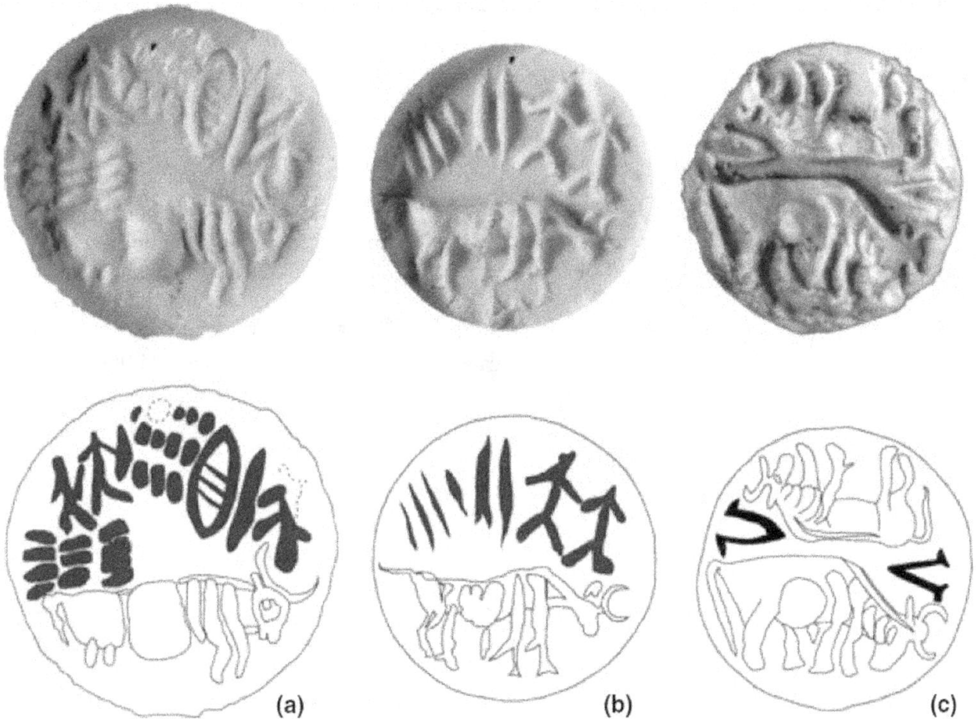


Impressions and drawings of Gulf Type seals with Indus text and bull motif found in Early Dilmun burial mounds on Bahrain: a. Table 1. no. 10; b. Table 1. no. 11; c. Table 1 no. 56. (Scale: 150%).

The characteristic Indus type writing system on these three seals is evidenced by the following hieroglyphs:

- Short-horned bull ḍangur m. 'bullock', rebus: ḍāṅro 'blacksmith' (N.)
- Pair of bodies (persons) meḍ "body ' (Mu.) Rebus: meḍ 'iron' (Ho.) dula 'pair' (Kashmiri; rebus: dul meṛeḍ cast iron (Mundari. Santali)

  dol 'likeness, picture, form' [e.g., two tigers, two bulls, sign-pair.] Kashmiri. dula दुल । युग्मम् m. a pair, a couple, esp. of two similar things (Rām. 966). Rebus: dul meṛeḍ cast iron (Mundari. Santali) dul 'to cast metal in a mould' (Santali) pasra meṛed, pasāra meṛed = syn. of koṭe meṛed = forged iron, in contrast to dul meṛed, cast iron (Mundari.lex.)]

- Pair of bulls ḍangur m. 'bullock', rebus: ḍāṅro 'blacksmith' (N.) dula 'pair' (Kashmiri; rebus: dul meṛeḍ cast iron (Mundari. Santali) Thus a pair of bulls is read rebus : dul ḍāṅro 'casting (metal) blacksmith'.

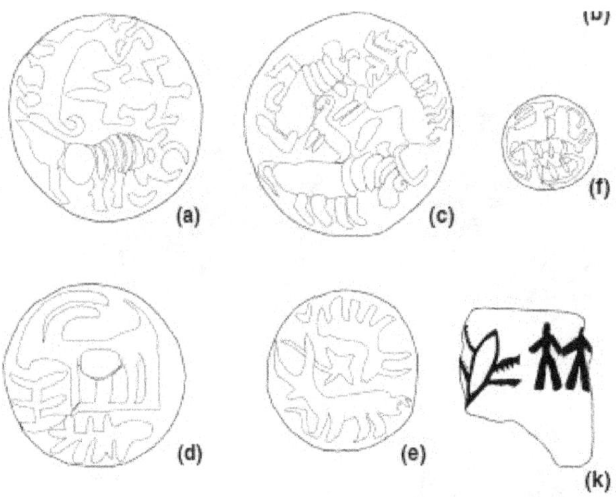


Pair of 'rim-of-jar' glyphs dula 'pair' (Kashmiri; rebus: dul meṛeḍ cast iron (Mundari. Santali) kan-ka 'rim of jar' (Santali), rebus karṇaka 'scribe' (Te.) Thus a pair of 'rim-of-jar' glyphs is read rebus: dul kan-ka 'casting (metal) scribe'.

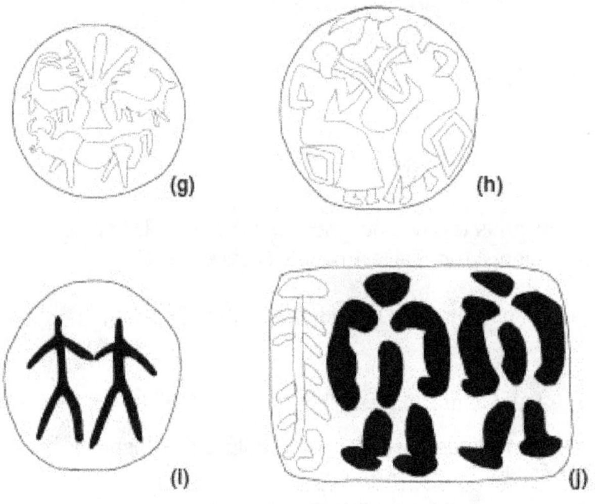


a. An example of a seal with Indus-inspired bull without inscription (Table 1 no. 108) illustrated as an impression drawing (scale 1:1). Note the crescent-shaped 'manger' unparalleled in uninscribed seals; b. impression drawing of a cylinder seal from Ur with a humped bull and a 'bale of fodder' (not to scale) (Gadd 1932: pl. I/6), courtesy of Gregory L. Possehl; c. an example of a seal with Indus-inspired bull without inscription (Table 1 no. 57) illustrated as an impression drawing (scale 1:1); d–f. examples of Gulf Type seals from Bahrain in the 'local' style illustrated as impressions (scale 1:1); d (Table 1 no. 114) depicts two palm branches below a quadruped. e (Table 1 no. 32) depicts two quadrupeds and a pair of crescents while in the centre a 'comet' or 'shooting star' can be identified by its long tail; f (Table 1 no. 53) depicts a scorpion below a pair of quadrupeds; g is a unique example of a Gulf Type seal with Mesopotamian styled 'vulture' above a bull in profile; h is a Gulf Type seal depicting the classic 'two men drinking scene' (Table 1 no. 62), illustrated as an impression drawing (scale 1:1); i is from Kalba site K4 with a possible pseudo-'twins' sign (scale 1:1), after Cleuziou 2003: fig.6/2; j is from Ra's al-Jinz RJ-2 also with a possible pseudo-'twins' sign (scale 1:1), after Cleuziou 2003: fig. 6/1.; k is a fragment of a 'cylinder seal' from Mohenjo-Daro with a 'twins' sign and another undistinguishable sign (scale 1:1), after Shah & Parpola 1991: 179, M-1370.

Typical glyph in these seals is 'pair of bodies (persons)' Pair of bodies (persons) meḍ 'body ' (Mu.) Rebus: meḍ 'iron' (Ho.) dula 'pair' (Kashmiri. This paired glyph is read rebus:: dul meṛeḍ cast iron (Mundari. Santali)

2.

23.

22.

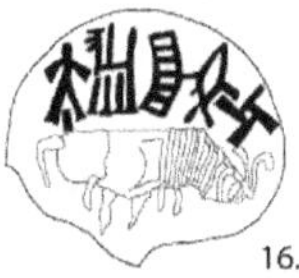
16.

21.

26.

20.

25.

17.

27.

7.

8.

11.

9.

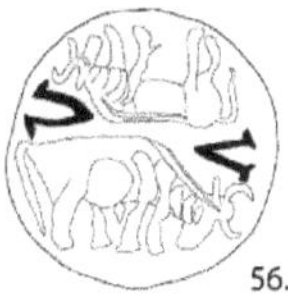
56.

6.

18.

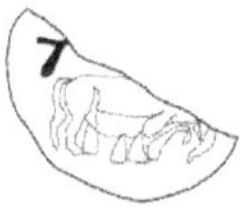
19.

24.

13.

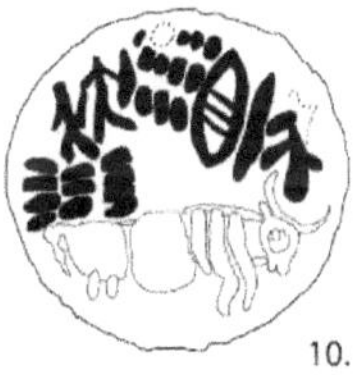
10.

12.

28.

15.

14.

Fig. 11.

Glyph: rim of jar. *kaṇḍakanka.* Rebus: 'furnace stone ore account scribe'

Glyph: heifer + standard device. *koḍ* 'horn'. Rebus: *koḍ* 'artisan's workshop'. *kōda* 'heifer'. Rebus: *kūdār 'turner'. sangaḍa* 'lathe, furnace'. Rebus: *samgara* 'living in the same house, guild'. Hence, smith guild.

Seal. Lakhian jo daro.  Sign 124

badhi 'to ligature, to bandage, to splice, to join by successive rolls of a ligature' (Santali) batā bamboo slips (Kur.); bate = thin slips of bamboo (Malt.)(DEDR 3917). Rebus: baḍhi = worker in wood and metal (Santali) baṛae = blacksmith (Ash.)

Decoding glyphs of entwined tigers and related inscriptions

m0295 Seal. Mohenjodaro. Four entwined tigers, plus text with five glyphs.

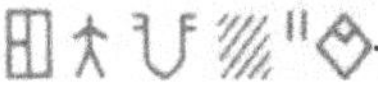 Text 1386.

A motif of entwined tigers (perhaps four) appears on the obverse of two tablets: m441 and m1395. The reverse of these tablets m441 and m1395 contain the motif which is comparable to the motifs shown on m439a, m440, m1393, m1394 tablets. The motif has a crocodile surrounded by: a pair of bulls on the top register, a rhinoceros and a monkey looking back on the middle register and an elephant and a tiger looking back on the bottom register.

| | | |
|---|---|---|
|  m1393 |  m1394 |  m1395a, b |
|  m439 |  m440a |  m441a,b |

The hieroglyphs – and related semantics -- contained in these seven inscriptions are identified in lexemes from Indian linguistic area:

Four entwined tigers: gaṇḍa 'four', kol 'tigers', sā̃gaḍa 'jointed animals'. Rebus: kaṇḍa (furnace), kol (iron, metal), sā̃gāḍo 'lathe'. Vikalpa: pon, ponea 'four'; rebus: pon (gold). Semant. (decrypted): gold, metal turner (i.e. goldsmith, metalsmith).

Other glyphs: krammaru 'looking back', kara 'crocodile', ibha 'elephant', kuṭhāru 'monkey', baḍhia 'castrated boar', two bulls 'dul ḍaṅgar'. Rebus: कर्मार karmāra (artisan-smith), khar (blacksmith-artisan), ib 'iron', baḍhi 'worker both in iron and wood', kuṭhāru 'armourer, scribe', ib ḍhaṅgar 'iron-smith'. Semant. (decrypted): furnace scribe, ironsmith, carpenter-cum-smith, blacksmith artisan, armourer.

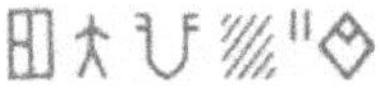

Inscription on m0295: Semant. (decrypted) iron-turner, iron-smelter, furnace scribe, iron, smithy

Glyphic elements read rebus:

kuṭi 'bent' (rebus: kuṭhi 'smelter'), kōṇṭu 'angle' (rebus: kūdār 'turner'), ib 'two' (rebus: ib 'iron'), kaṇḍ kanka 'rim of jar' (rebus: kaṇḍ 'furnace', karṇaka 'scribe'), mēd, mẽd 'body' (rebus: meḍ 'iron')

kole.l 'smithy' (rebus: kole.l 'temple')

Lexemes of Indian linguistic area

Semant. 'Looking back' (tiger, monkey). krammaru. [Tel.] v. n. To turn, return, go back. (Telugu) krəm back'(Kho.)(CDIAL 3145) Kho. krəm ' back ' NTS ii 262 with (?) (CDIAL 3145)[Cf. Ir. *kamaka -- or *kamraka -- ' back ' in Shgh. čůmč ' back ', Sar. čomǰ EVSh 26] (CDIAL 2776) cf. Sang. kamak ' back ', Shgh. čomǰ (< *kamak G.M.) ' back of an animal ', Yghn. kama ' neck ' (CDIAL 14356). kár, kăr 'neck' (Kashmiri) Kal. gřä ' neck '; Kho. goḷ ' front of neck, throat '. gala m. ' throat, neck ' MBh. (CDIAL 4070) Rebus: khār, khar 'blacksmith' (Kashmiri) kôru 2 कोरु । अशोभनाङ्गः adj. (f. körü 2 कारू; for 1, see s.v.), one-eyed (= kônu 4, q.v.) (L.V. 2); crooked limbed, deformed (of a person). (Kashmiri)

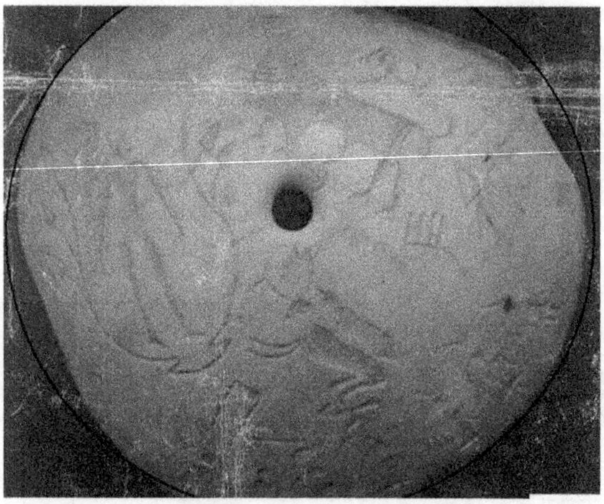

Rebus:कर्मार [Monier-Williams, p. 259,3] [L=45505]' *m.* an artisan , mechanic , artificer, a blacksmith &c RV._x , 72 , 2 AV._iii , 5 , 6 VS._Mn._iv , 215 &c 'kammāra [Vedic karmāra] a smith, a worker in metals, a goldsmith. (Pali) •karmārakula 'smithy' (Pa.) Generally D ii.126, A v.263; a silversmith Sn 962= Dh 239; J i.223; a goldsmith J iii.281; v.282. The smiths in old India do not seem to be divided into black -- , gold -- and silver -- smiths, but seem to have been able to work equally well in iron, gold, and silver, as can be seen e. g. from J iii.282 and VvA 250, where the smith is the maker of a needle. They were constituted into a guild, and some of them were well -- to -- do as appears from what is said of Cunda at D ii.126; owing to their usefulness they were held in great esteem by the people and king alike J iii.281.--kula a smithy M i.25

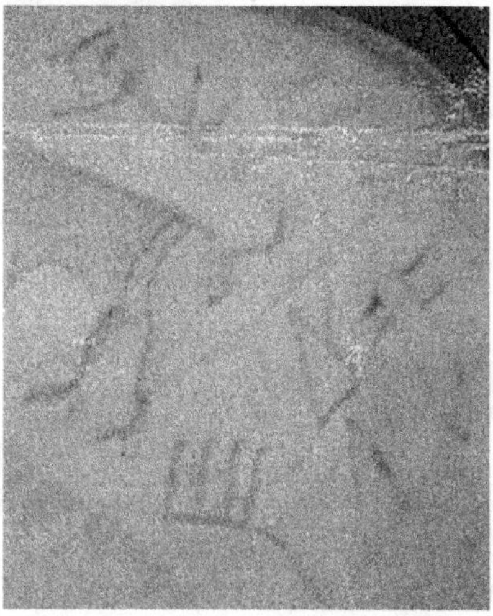

Glyphics on a Sumerian circular seal

Source: (provenance has to be verified further) http://www.indoeurohome.com/indussumerstars.html

The glyphics on this circular object are comparable to the glyphics on m0442, h-97, m1186. [For m1186 see page 51 Indus Script Cipher (2010)]

The glyphics are:

On top left of the circular object:

Kneeling adorant with horns

Horned person with scarf as pigtail standing within a pipal-tree vessel

Seven persons wearing skirts, with scarfs as pigtails and twig on heads close to

kole·l smithy, temple in Kota village. (Ko.) kol working in iron, blacksmith (Ta.)(DEDR 2133) kollan̠ blacksmith. Ma. kollan blacksmith, artificer. To. kwala·l Kota smithy. Ka. kolime, kolume, kulame, kulime, kulume, kulme fire-pit, furnace; (Bell.; U.P.U.) konimi blacksmith; (Gowda) kola id. Koḍ. Kollë blacksmith. Te. kolimi furnace. Go. (SR.) kollusānā to mend implements; (Ph.) kolstānā, kulsānā to forge; (Tr.) kōlstānā to repair (of ploughshares); (SR.) kolmi smithy (Voc. 948). Kuwi (F.) kolhali to forge. (DEDR 2133)

On top right of the circular object:

Variants of three glyphics:

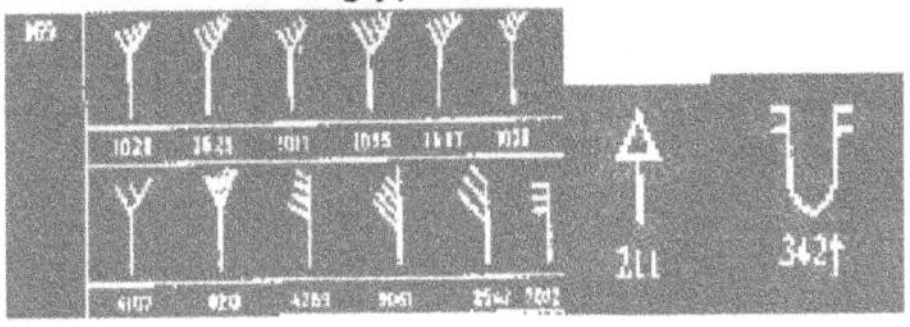

kammaṭa = mint, gold furnace (Te.)

kolom = cutting, graft; to graft, engraft, prune; kolma hoṛo = a variety of the paddy plant (Desi)(Santali.)

kaṇḍa 'arrow' (Skt.)

kanka 'rim of jar' (Santali)

All these glyphs can be read with homonyms:

Kolami 'forge, smithy'

kaṇḍa 'excellent quantity of iron'

kanka 'scribe'

On scarfs as pigtails and seven robed persons, see Indus Script Cipher:

dhaṭu m. (also dhaṭhu) m. 'scarf' (WPah.) (CDIAL 6707) Rebus: dhatu 'minerals' (Santali)

kūdī, kūṭī 'bunch of twigs' (Skt.) Rebus: kuṭhi 'smelter furnace' (Santali) Thus seven robed persons with twigs on head: seven smelter furnaces.

Decoding select glyphs of Indus script

Agreeing with Mahadevan and Parpola on their use of the rebus method but disagreeing on 1. the religious overtones they see in the inscriptions and glyphs and 2. assignment of grammatical morph and phonetic values glyphs, alternative straight-forward rebus decoding of the select glyphs is presented, without indulging in special pleading, but using glosses of the Indian linguistic area which semantically cluster into repertoire -- products and skills of artisans and thus justifies the use of inscriptions directly in a trading context without suggesting occurrence of any names of people, places or deities.

Text on m0290. The inscription can be decoded rebus as: kanṭ pot kuro kharādī 'stone ore bead furnace, silver, turner' (Glyphs: pot 'calf of hind leg'; khuru 'wild ass'; khareḍo = a currycomb) Glyptic context (pictorial motif): tiger + trough: kolimi ḍhangar 'forge, smith'. If the reading for the 'wild ass' glyph is *khar*, the rebus is: *khar* 'blacksmith' (Kashmiri).

khuru 'wild ass' (Kashmiri) kuro silver (Kol.Nk.Go.)(DEDR 1782).

Long-linear stroke + wild ass. khuru 'wild ass' (Kashmiri) Rebus: khura silver (Nk.); kuruku whiteness'; kuru brilliancy (Ta.); kuro silver (Kol.Nk.Go.) (DEDR 1782). koḍa 'one'(Santali); koḍ 'workshop' (G.)

Thus, the seal is decoded rebus: khuru koḍa 'wild-ass, one'; rebus: khura k oḍ 'silver workshop'

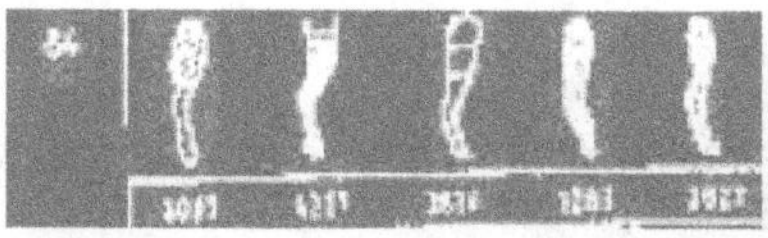

m022, Text 1194 Text of inscription:
Glyphs: kū̃dār 'turner'. *kaṇḍ 'stone ore'. gaṇṭa* = bat (Te.lex.) rebus: *kaṇḍ* 'fire-altar, furnace' (Santali) Reading: stone ore turner with furnace.

Ko. *kaṇṭ-po·t* 'flesh of hind thigh of animal (DEDR 1175). Pe. pota calf of leg. Manḍ. pata id. Kui pota id. ? (DEDR 4513) Rebus: 1. *kaṇḍ* 'stone ore' 2. pot 'glass bead' (H.); putti 'small bead' (B.)(CDIAL 8403). Glyph: pot 'thigh' (Ko.); rebus: pot 'glass bead' (H.)

Vikalpa (alternative) 1: Pa. *jaṅghā* -- f., Pk. *jaṁghā* -- f.; Gy. eur. *čang*, pl. *°ga* f. ' thigh, knee ' (CDIAL 5082). *jangaḍiyo* 'military guard who accompanies treasure into the treasury'; san:ghāḍiyo, a worker on a lathe (G.) Vikalpa 2: ḍhagaraam 'thigh' (G.); ḍhangar 'smith' (H.)

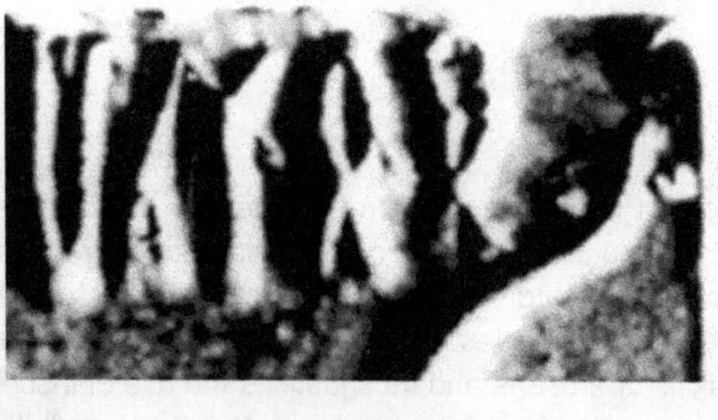
Glyph of 'hind leg' in a modern impression of seal Mohenjo-daro 0071Sequence of glyphs: 'hind leg' + 'fish' on Mohenjo-daro seal m1690 (taken fom a photograph of a modern impression).

Ko. kaṇṭ-po·t flesh of hind thigh of animal; kaṇṭ-ka·l calf of leg. Ka. kaṇḍa flesh, meat. Koḍ. kaṇḍa piece or lump of meat. Te. kaṇḍa id., flesh.Nk. khaṇḍe piece, piece of flesh. Ga. (S.3) kaṇḍa muscle (< Te.). Go. (Tr.) khānḍum (pl.

khānḍk), (Ch.) khānḍ, khānḍum, (Ph.) khānḍk flesh; (SR.)khānḍum id., mutton (Voc. 1001). Konḍa kaṇḍa meat, flesh, muscle. Kuwi (Isr.) kaṇḍa piece. / Probably < Skt. khaṇḍa- (Turner, CDIAL, no. 3792) with development of meaning: piece > piece of flesh > flesh. (DEDR 1175) khaṇḍá ' broken, crippled ' VarBr̥S., ' having gaps or chasms ' Suśr., m.n. ' fragment ' R., ḍaka -- 1 ' having no nails ' lex., ḍikā -- f. Pān. [Cf. ' defective ' words listed s.v. baṇḍá -- . -- √khaṇḍ] Pa. khaṇḍa -- ' broken (usu. of teeth) ', m.n. ' piece ', ḍikā -- f. ' broken bit, stick '; Pk. khaṁḍa -- m.n., ḍiā -- f. ' piece '; Gy. SEeur. xaļi ' a little ', gr. xandí, xanrík ' a little ', xarno ' humble, low ', rum. boh. xarno ' short ', it. xarnišeró ' judge, magistrate ' (< ' small -- headed, stupid ') (CDIAL 3792)

Pk. pottī -- f. ' glass '; S. pūti f. ' glass bead ', P. pot f.; N. pote ' long straight bar of jewelry '; B. pot ' glass bead ', puti, pũti ' small bead '; Or. puti ' necklace of small glass beads '; H. pot m. ' glass bead ', G. M. pot f.; -- Bi. pot ' jeweller's polishing stone '(CDIAL 8403)

Body glyph with upraised arm

M1224d,e two sides of a seal Pa. pot upper part of back; pottel back; adv. behind. Ga. (Oll.) poṭ, poṭṭel, (S.3) poṭṭu back. (DEDR 4514) Rebus: pot 'glass bead' (H.); putti 'small bead' (B.)(CDIAL 8403). [Person ligatured to the back of a bovine on m1224; the person is lifting up his arm.]

Pk. pottī -- f. ' glass '; S. pūti f. ' glass bead ', P. pot f.; N. pote ' long straight bar of jewelry '; B. pot ' glass bead ', puti, pũti ' small bead '; Or. puti ' necklace of small glass beads '; H. pot m. ' glass bead ', G. M. pot f.; -- Bi. pot ' jeweller's polishing stone '(CDIAL 8403)

Vikalpa: ḍhagarām pl. the buttocks; the hips (G.lex.) Rebus: *ḍhãgar*, *ḍhãgar* blacksmith; digger of wells (H.)

Person lifting up his hand med. 'body'; rebus: meḍ 'iron' 94) er-aka 'upraised arm' (Ta.); rebus: eraka = copper (Ka.) The body is ligatured to the back of a bovine: pot 'back' (Pa.); rebus: pot 'glass bead' (H.)The glyph of a body with right-hand raised and ligatured to the back of a bovine is read rebus: kuḍi eraka 'upraised right arm'; rebus: kuṭhi eraka 'copper-furnace'. The body is horned: koḍ 'horns'; rebus: koḍ 'workshop' (Kuwi.G.) Thus, the glyptic composition is decoded rebus: meḍ pot kuḍi eraka koḍ 'iron, bead, copper furnace workshop'.

Glyphs with ligatured tail

Sign 224

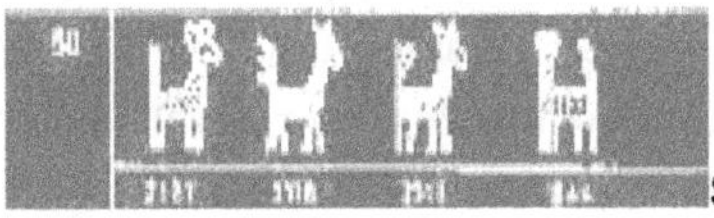

Sign 50 (Variantts)

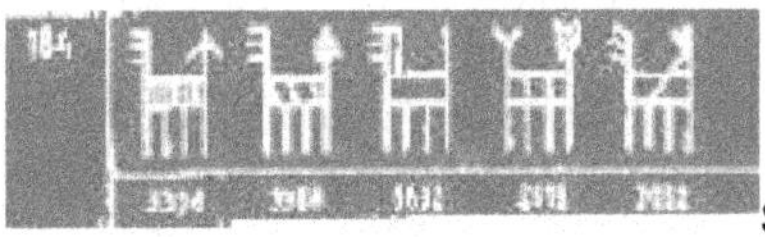

Sign 184 (Variants)

m0516B

Copper tablet  Text 3398

c023

Pict-88

Pict-37

m0271

h286B

xolā = tail (Kur.); qoli id. (Malt.)(DEDr 2135). Rebus: kol 'pañcalōha' (Ta.)கொல் kol, n. 1. Iron; இரும்பு. மின் வெள்ளி பொன் கொல்லெனச் சொல்லும் (தக்கயாகப். 550). 2. Metal; உலோகம். (நாமதீப. 318.) கொல்லன் kollaṉ, n. < T. golla. Custodian of treasure; கஜானாக்காரன். (P. T. L.) கொல்லிச்சி kollicci, n. Fem. of கொல்லன். Woman of the blacksmith caste; கொல்லச் சாதிப் பெண். (யாழ். அக.) The gloss kollicci is notable. It clearly evidences that kol was a blacksmith. kola 'blacksmith' (Ka.); Koḍ. kollë blacksmith (DEDR 2133). Vikalpa: dumba दुम्ब or (El.) duma दुम । पशुपुच्छः m. the tail of an animal. (Kashmiri) Rebus: ḍōmba ?Gypsy (CDIAL 5570).

Ta. kol working in iron, blacksmith; kollaṉ blacksmith. Ma. kollan blacksmith, artificer.Ko. kole·l smithy, temple in Kota village. To. kwala·l Kota smithy. Ka. kolime, kolume, kulame, kulime, kulume, kulme fire-pit, furnace; (Bell.; U.P.U.) konimi blacksmith; (Gowda) kola id. Koḍ. Kollë blacksmith. Te. kolimi furnace. Go. (SR.) kollusānā to mend implements; (Ph.) kolstānā, kulsānā to forge; (Tr.) kōlstānā to repair (of ploughshares); (SR.) kolmi smithy (Voc. 948). Kuwi F.) kolhali to forge (DEDR 2133). [kolimi] kolimi. n. A pit. A fire pit or furnace. mudga kolimi a smelting forge (Telugu) கொல்லுலை kol-l-ulai, n. < id. +. Black-smith's forge; கொல்லனுலை. கொல்லுலைக் கூடத் தினால் (குமர. பிர. நீதிநெறி. 14) உலை³ ulai, n. < உலை²-. [K. ole, M. ula.] 1. Smith's forge or furnace; கொல்லனுலை. கொல்ல னுலையூதுந் தீயேபோல் (நாலடி, 298). 2. Fireplace for cooking, oven; நெருப்புள்ள அடுப் பு. (W.) 3. Pot of water set over the fire for boiling rice; சோறு சமைத்தற்காகக் கொதிக்க வைக்கும் நீர். உலைப்பெய் தடுவதுபோலுந் துயர் (நாலடி, 114). 4. Flurry, excitement, agitation; மன நடுக்கம். உலைதருமலின மொன்ற தொழித்திடுஞ் சுத்த மொன்றே (ஞானவா. வைரா. 26) (Tamil). ulai < cullī f. ' fireplace ' Mn. [← Drav. EWA i 396 with lit.] Pa. cullī -- f., Pk. cullī̆ -- , (Deśīn.) ullī -- f., Ḍ. čila f., K. ċōl f., S. culhi f., ho m., L. cullh, pl. hī̃ f., cullhā m., P. culh m., cullhī f., hā m., Ku. N. culi, lo, B. cullī, culā, cullā, Or. cullī, culā, Bi. Mth. cūlh, hī, hā, Mth., Bhoj. cūlhi, H. cūlhī f., hā m., G. cūl, culī, culṛī f., cūlɔ m., M. ċūl f., ċulā, llā, lvā m.*culliyasi -- , *cullīkarttāra -- , *cullīdhāna -- , *cullīdhāra -- ; *ācullī -- ; *ēkkacullī -- .Addenda: cullī -- : WPah.kṭg. (kc.) ċūl (obl. -- i) f. ' fireplace, oven ', J. culi f., Brj. cūlho m. (CDIAL 4879) kolime, kolume, kulame, kulime, kulume, kulme fire-pit, furnace (Ka.); kolimi furnace (Te.); pit (Te.); kolame a very deep pit (Tu.); kulume kanda_ya a tax on blacksmiths (Ka.)

*dumbha ' tail '. [Only Kal. attests an aspirate: poss. all NIA. forms, and cert. those of Dard. with l -- , are ← Ir., Av. duma -- , Pahl. dumbak, Pers. dum(b), Psht.ləm EVP 36. But, besides Kal., some derivatives, e.g. s.v. *dumbhaśa -- , suggest possibility of orig. IA. form]Gy. eur.Dumo m. ' back, shoulder '; Wg. dumä́ŕ, tumtä́ ' tail ', Kt. dəmŕéi, Pr. lümū̃, dəmū́ (← Kt. Rep1 47), Paš.gul. dum(b), nir. dumā́ (← Pers. IIFL iii 3, 55), ar. līm, Shum. līmə, Gaw. limoṭá, Kal. dh*lmŕẽi, Kho. rūm, K. dumba m.; L. dumb m.

' ear of millet '; P. dumb, dumm m. ' tail ', N. dum, Or. duma, Mth. dom, H. dumb, dum f., G. dum f.; M. dumālā m. ' hind part '. (CDIAL 6419) Rebus: ḍōmba m. ' man of low caste living by singing and music ' Kathās., ḍōma -- m. lex., ḍōmbinī -- f. [Connected with Mu. words for ' drum ' PMWS 87, EWA i 464 with lit.] Pk. ḍoṁba -- , ḍuṁba -- , ḍoṁbilaya -- m.; Gy. eur. rom m. ' man, husband ', romni f. ' woman, wife ', SEeur. ịom ' aGypsy ', pal. dōm ' a Nuri Gypsy ', arm. as. (Boša) lom ' a Gypsy ', pers. damini ' woman '; Ḍ. ḍōm (pl. ma) ' a Ḍom '; Paš. ḍōmb ' barber '; Kho. (Lor.) ḍom ' musician, bandsman '; Sh. ḍom ' a Ḍom ', K. ḍūmb, ḍūm m., ḍūmbiñ f.; S. ḏūmu m., ḍūmṛī f. ' caste of wandering musicians ', L. ḍūm m., ḍūmṇī f., (Ju.) ḏom m., ḍomṇī, ḍomṛī f., mult. ḍōm m.,ḍōmṇī f., awāṇ. naṭ -- ḍūm ' menials '; P. ḍūm, ḍomrā m., ḍūmṇī f. ' strolling musician ', ḍūmṇā m. ' a caste of basket -- maker '; WPah. ḍum ' a very low -- caste blackskinned fellow '; Ku. ḍūm m., ḍūmaṇ f. ' an aboriginal hill tribe '; N. ḍum ' a low caste '; A. ḍom m. ' fisherman ', ḍumini f.; B. ḍom, ḍam m. ' a Ḍom ', ḍumni f. (OB. ḍombī); Or. ḍoma m., aṇī f., ḍuma, aṇī, ḍamba, ḍama, aṇī ' a low caste who weave baskets and sound drums '; Bhoj. ḍōm ' a low caste of musicians H.ḍomb, ḍom, ḍomṛā, ḍumār m., ḍomnī f., OMarw. ḍūma m., ḍūmaṛī f., M. ḍōb, ḍom m. -- Deriv. Gy. wel. romanō adj. (f. nī) ' Gypsy ' romanō rai m. ' Gypsy gentleman ', nī čib f. ' Gypsy language '.*ḍōmbakuṭaka -- , *ḍōmbadhāna -- .Addenda: ḍōmba -- : Gy.eur. rom m., romni f. esp. ' Gypsy man or woman '; WPah.kṭg. ḍōm m. ' member of a low caste of musicians ', ḍv̄m m.; Garh. ḍom ' an untouchable '. (CDIAL 5570).

Duplicate epigraphs

Duplicate tablets found in Harappa (HARP) recently have been explained as tallies to account for categories of artifacts from miners/smithy/forge to be consolidated in a furnace account scribe record of a seal and a seal impression thereafter on the trade load.

Though the corpus is limited, it is surprising that there is a substantial number of duplicate inscriptions; this has become apparent from the recent report of excavations at Harappa (1993 to 1995 seasons). Obviously, the inscriptions do not represent not 'names' of owners. The inscriptions could simply be 'functions' performed by or the 'professional title' of the person who carried the inscribed object on his wrist (or as a pendant attached to a necklace) or the list of objects he/she was invoicing for trade (as bill of lading) or to list possessions of property items listed). In Indian cultural continuum from Indus civilization, the use of copper plate inscriptions served the purpose of recording property transactions, listing possessions of property items.

This hypothesis gets re-inforced by (1) the finds of inscriptions on copper tablets (again, with many duplicates – all apparently made by a metal-worker and hence may relate to metal objects produced, say, in an armoury); and (2) the presence of over 200 inscribed objects with no sign (only pictorial motif) or just one or two signs. [The signs could hardly have been alphabets or syllables since there are not many 'names' attested in the historical periods with just one or two syllables.]

Allographs

> An allograph is a variant shape of a glyph or a combination of glyphs (as in ligatures) that can represent one gloss. An example in English are f and gh which can represent the phoneme /f/. There are allographs within the set of glyphs rendered as pictorial motifs and as signs of Indus script. The presence of allographs may explain the occurrence of over 500 glyphs.

Decoding_Indus_script epigraphs of 42 sites

http://tinyurl.com/yaz57va

(1) Gumla, Jhukar, Pirak, Qala'at el-Bahrain, Pabumath, Nippur, Lohumjo-daro, Luristan, Hulas, Hajar

(2) Gharo Bhiro (Nuhato), Djoka (Umma), Rojdi, Tepe Yahya, Amri, Altyn Tepe, Tello, Tarkhanewala-dera, Shortugai, Bakkar Buthi, Failaka, Hissam-dheri

(3) Chanhujo-daro, Khirasara, Kish, Susa, Nindowari-damb, Chandigarh, Ropar, Ur, Desalpur, Rakhigarhi, Alamgirpur, Naru-Waro-Dharo, Ra's al-Junayz, Surkotada, Bala-kot, Nausharo, Kot-diji, Allahdino (Nel Bazaar), Dholavira, Banawali (& Unknown provenance)

The texts are from Mahadevan corpus followed by readings of texts taken from ICIT corpus which analyses 3831 epigraphs: http://caddy.bv.tu-berlin.de/indus/welcome.htm Qala'at el-Bahrain and Hajar epigraphs are not listed in Mahadevan corpus.

Each of these twenty sites have yielded between two to 21 epigraphs each.

The epigraphs are inscribed on pots or seals or tags. Some seals also have an animal glyph (for e.g. bull).

Bull glyph in the following epigraphs may be decoded as: *ḍhangra* 'bull'; rebus: *ḍhangar* 'blacksmith' (H.)

Composite animal glyph may be decoded as a metals repertoire of a smithy.

[ID Text and symbol/sign refereences are to http://caddy.bv.tu-berlin.de/indus/welcome.htm]

Chanhujo-daro

Chanhudaro41a

Chanhudaro42 Iron, alloy of five metals

Elephant, tiger, four dotted circles

ibha 'elephant'; rebus: ib 'iron' (Santali)

kola 'tiger'; rebus: kol 'alloy of five metals' (Ta.)

pon 'four'; rebus: pon 'metal' (Ta.)

*kāṇ* 'eye' ; rebus : *kāṇḍa* 'iron' (Skt.)

Chanhudaro43 Copper

*arka* 'rays of sun'; *arka* 'copper' (Ka.)

Chanhudaro46a

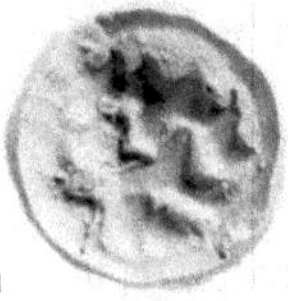
Chanhudaro46b

paṭa, 'hood of snake'. Rebus: padm 'sharp, tempered iron'

 Chanhudaro47 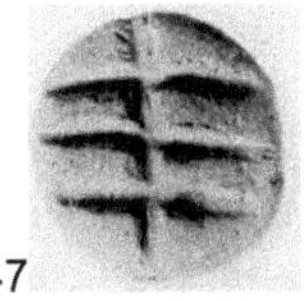 Chanhudaro 48 Smithy

*panǰā́r* 'ladder, stairs' (Bshk.)(CDIAL 7760) Rebus: *pasra* 'smithy' (Santali)

 Chanhudaro49A  Chanhudaro49B

 Chanhudaro50A  Chanhudaro50B Smithy

*ḍhompo* = knot on a string (Santali) *ḍhompo* = ingot (Santali)

Fig. 3 and 3a of Plate L. After Mackay, 1943. Pict-40  Ox-antelope with a long tail; a trough in front.  6121 Iron, mine-worker guild, scribe

*mẽḍha* 'antelope'; rebus: *meḍ* 'iron' (Mu.)

*loa* 'fig leaf' (Santali): Rebus: *lo* 'iron' (Assamese, Bengali); *loa* 'iron' (Gypsy) Glyph: *lo* = nine (Santali); *no* = nine (B.) *on-patu* = nine (Ta.)

 Chanhudaro14a 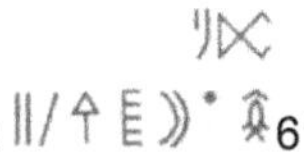 6108 Coppersmith guild, mint worker in wood and metal, native metal, cast nodule (ore)/stone, iron, fire-altar, smithy

kamaṭha crab (Skt.) Rebus: kammaṭa = portable furnace (Te.) kampaṭṭam coiner, mint (Ta.)

badhi 'to ligature, to bandage, to splice, to join by successive rolls of a ligature' (Santali) batā bamboo slips (Kur.); bate = thin slips of bamboo (Malt.)(DEDR 3917). Rebus: baḍhi = worker in wood and metal (Santali) baṛae = blacksmith (Ash.)

ad.aren 'lid'; Rebus: aduru 'native metal' (Santali) Hence, ayo adar 'iron native metal' (Maybe a reference to unsmelted mketeoric iron.)

dol 'likeness'; dul 'cast (metal)' (Santali) *khaḍā* 'circumscribe' (M.); Rebs: *khaḍā* 'nodule (ore), stone' (M.)

*kangha* (IL 1333) *kãgherā* comb-maker (H.) Rebus: kangar 'portable furnace' Rebus: kangar 1 कंगर् m. a large portable brazier (El.). kãgürü काँग्‌&above;रू&below; or kãgürü काँग&above;रू&below; or kãgar काँग्‌र्‌ I हसब्तिका f. (sg. dat. kãgrĕ काँग्र्य or kãgarĕ काँगर्य, abl. kãgri काँग्रि), the portable brazier, or *kāngrī,* much used in Kashmīr (K.Pr. *kángár,* 129, 131, 178; *káṅgrí,* 5, 128, 129). For particulars see El. s.v. *kángri;* L. 7, 25, *kangar;* and K.Pr. 129. The word is a fem. dim. of kang, q.v. (Gr.Gr. 37). kãgri-khŏphürü

*kāṇḍa* 'arrow' (Skt.); rebus: *kāṇḍa* 'iron' as in *ayaskāṇḍa* a 'excellent iron' (Pan.Skt.)

Glyph: *gaṇḍe* 'to place at a right angle to something else, cross, transverse'; *gaṇḍ gaṇḍ* 'across, at right angles, transversely' (Santali) [Note: A slanted line Lahṇḍa writing of accounts connotes a quarter; a straight line connotes 'one'.] Rebus: *kaṇḍ* 'fire-altar' (Santali)

*kolmo* 'three' (Mu.); rebus: *kolami* 'smithy' (Te.)

Chanhudaro18a  6216 Chanhudaro. Tablet. Obverse and reverse. Alligator and Fish. Fig. 33 and 33a. of Plate LII. After Mackay, 1943. Coppersmith guild, bronze workshop, artisan's workshop, mint

*kanac* 'corner' (Santali); Rebus: *kañcu* 'bronze' (Te.) s*al* stake, spike, splinter, thorn, difficulty (H.); Rebus: *sal* 'workshop' (Santali)

*koḍa* 'in arithmetic, one' (Santali); rebus: *koḍ.* 'artisan's workshop' (Kuwi)

kamaṭha crab (Skt.) Rebus: kammaṭa = portable furnace (Te.) kampaṭṭam coiner, mint (Ta.)

Chanhudaro Seal obverse and reverse. The oval sign of this Jhukar culture seal is comparable to other inscriptions. Fig. 1 and 1a of Plate L. After Mackay, 1943. Metal ingot, iron blacksmith

*mēḍha* 'antelope'; rebus: *meḍ* 'iron' (Mu.)

*krammara* 'turning back' (Te.); rebus: *kamar* 'blacksmith' (Santali)

ḍhālako = a large metal ingot (G.) ḍhālakī = a metal heated and poured into a mould; a solid piece of metal; an ingot (G.) ḍabu 'an iron spoon' (Santali) Rebus: ḍab, ḍhimba, ḍhompo 'lump (ingot?)'

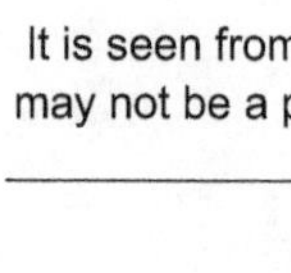
Chanhudaro26  6405 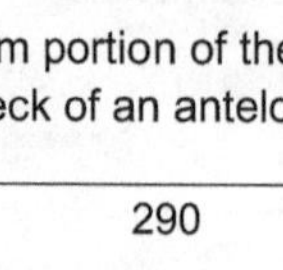 Chanhudaro28

It is seen from an enlargement of the bottom portion of the seal impression that the 'prostrate person' may not be a person but a ligature of the neck of an antelope with rings on its necks or of a post with ring-stones. The head of the 'person' is not shown. So, I would surmise that this is an artist's representation of an act of copulation (by an animal) + a ligatured neck of another bovine or alternatively, a pillar with ring-stones ligatured to the bottom portion of a body (perhaps of a cow, why not?). It is not uncommon in the artistic tradition to ligature bodies to the rump of, for example, a bull's posterior ligatured to a horned woman (Pict. 103 Mahadevan) or standing person with horns and bovine

features (hoofed legs and/or tail) -- Pict. 86-88 Mahadevan. ison (gaur) trampling a prostrate person (?) underneath. Impression of a seal from Chanhujodaro (Mackay 1943: pl. 51: 13). The prostrate 'person' is seen to have a very long neck, possibly with neck-rings, reminiscent of the rings depicted on the neck of the one-horned bull normally depicted in front of a standard device. Smithy guild, mine-worker, scribe, cast metal smithy, mint smithy

*kūṭamu* = summit of a mountain (Te.lex.) *kuṭṭāra* = a mountain (Skt.lex.) kudharamu = a mountain, a hill (Te.lex.) Rebus: *kūṭa* 'guild' (Ka.) kolmo 'three' (Mu.); rebus: kolimi 'smithy' (Te.)

kolmo 'paddy plant'; rebus: kolami 'smithy' (Te.Ka.); dol 'likeness'; rebus: dul 'cast' (i.e. smithy (for) casting metal)

kamaṭha crab (Skt.) Rebus: kammaṭa = portable furnace (Te.) kampaṭṭam coiner, mint (Ta.)

kolmo 'three' (Mu.); rebus: kolami 'smithy' (Te.)

Chanhudaro Seal obverse and reverse. 'water-carrier' and X glyphs Smelter furnace, mineral (ore)

*kuṭi* 'woman water carrier' (Te.); *kuṭhi* 'smelter furnace' (Santali)

*dāṭu* = cross over; daṭ- (da.ṭ-t-) to cross (Kol.)(DEDR 3158) Rebus: *dhātu* 'mineral'; dhatu = a mineral, metal (Santali)

ad.aren 'lid'; Rebus: aduru 'native metal' (Santali) Hence, ayo adar 'iron native metal' (Maybe a reference to unsmelted mketeoric iron.)

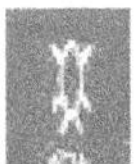

Sign 67 Vikalpa readings: keṇṭai carp (Ta.); *gaṇḍe* = a fish (Te.lex.) The glyphs of ligatured fin: *ceṭṭai* fin (Ta.); caṭṭupa wing (Te.)(DEDR 2764) Rebus, substantive: *kẽṛẽ* bell-metal, brass.

Sanghaṭṭa2 (?) bangle Sn 48 (˚yanta): thus Nd2 reading for ˚māna (ppr. med. of sanghaṭṭeti). Sanghaṭṭeti [saŋ+ghaṭṭeti] 1. to knock against Vin ii.208. -- 2. to sound, to ring Mhvs 21, 29 (˚aghaṭṭayi). -- 3 to knock together, to rub against each other J iv.98 (aŋsena aŋsaŋ samaghaṭṭayimha); Dāvs iii.87. -- 4. to provoke by scoffing, to make angry J vi.295 (paraŋ asanghaṭṭento, C. on asanghaṭṭa); VvA 139 (pres. pass. ˚ghaṭṭiyati). -- pp. sanghaṭ(ṭ)ita. Rebus: CDIAL 12858 *saṁghara ' living in the same house '. [Cf. *ságṛha*<-> ĀpŚr. -- ghara -- ]
Pa. *saṅghara* -- ' with one's own family (?) '; L. *sagghrā* ' accompanied by one's own family ';
H. *sā̃ghar* m. ' wife's son by former husband '.

bar, barea = two (Mu.); Rebus: *barī* = blacksmith, artisan (Ash.)(CDIAL 9464).

kolom = cutting, graft; to graft, engraft, prune; kolma hoṛo = a variety of the paddy plant (Desi)(Santali.) kolom 'three' (Mu.) Rebus: kolami 'furnace, smithy' (Te.)

Chanhudaro33a  6104  Misc. ID 1732 Stone ore, smelter-furnace mine-worker-scribe, iron guild mine-worker-scribe

The Sanskritization of Assamese bicā , deśī vachi is: vṛścika scorpion (RV); vicchika (Pali); vicchia, vim.chia (Pkt.); bich (Sh.); bichī (Ku.); bicā (A.); bichā (B.Or.); būch (Mth.); bīchī (Bhoj.Aw.H.); vīchī, vi~chī (G.); ucum (Pas'.); vichu~ (S.); vicchua, vim.chua (Pkt.); vichu~ (L.); bicchu~ (P.); bichu (Or.); bīchu (Mth.); bicchu~, bīchū (H.); vīchu (G.); viccu, viccua, vim.cua (Pkt.); byucu (K.); biccū (P.); biccū (WPah.); vīcū (M.); viccu, vim.cu (Kon.); bacchius large hornet (n.)(CDIAL 12081). Rebus: bica, bica-diri (Sad. bicā; Or. bicī) stone ore; meṛeḍ bica, stones containing iron; tambabica, copper-ore stones; samṛobica, stones containing gold (Mundari.lex.)

kuṭi = a slice, a bit, a small piece (Santali.lex.Bodding) Rebus: kuṭhi 'iron smelter furnace' (Santali) kuṭhī factory (A.)(CDIAL 3546) kan.d.a kanka 'rim of jar' (Santali) kan.d.a 'furnace, fire-altar' (Santali); khanaka 'miner' karNaka 'scribe' (Skt.)

ayo 'fish' (Mu.); ayas 'iron, metal' (Pan.Skt.)

अंकडा [aṅkaḍā] *m* (अंक S) Also अकडा *m* A hook or crook, a curved end gen. (M.) Rebus: अखाडा [ akhāḍā ] *m* ( H) A community, or the common place of residence or of assembly, of persons engaged in study or some particular pursuit; a college, a disputation-hall, a gymnasium, circus, arena. Hence, A club or clubroom; a stand of idlers, loungers, newsmongers, gossips, scamps. 2 An order of men. Ex. गोसाव्यांचे अठरा अखाडे आहेत.(M.)

Chanhudaro38A  Misc. ID 1742

ḍabu 'an iron spoon' (Santali) Rebus: ḍab, ḍhimba, ḍhompo 'lump (ingot?)', baṭa = wide-mouthed pot; Rebus: baṭa = kiln (Te.)

badhi 'worker in iiron and wood'.

ayo 'fish' (Mu.); rebus: ayas 'iron, metal' (Pan.Skt.)

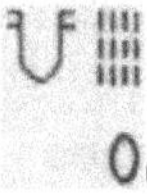6305  Pot ID 86

Śanku 'twelver'. Rebus: 'arrowhead'.

ḍhālako = a large metal ingot (G.) ḍhālakī = a metal heated and poured into a mould; a solid piece of metal; an ingot (G.)

Text 6304  Pot ID 110 Vikalpa: The Sanskritization of Assamese bicā , deśī vachi is: vṛścika scorpion (RV); vicchika (Pali); vicchia, vim.chia (Pkt.); bich (Sh.); bichī (Ku.); bicā (A.); bichā (B.Or.); būch (Mth.); bīchī (Bhoj.Aw.H.); vīchī, vi~chī (G.); ucum (Pas'.); vichu~ (S.); vicchua, vim.chua (Pkt.); vichu~ (L.); bicchu~ (P.); bichu (Or.); bīchu (Mth.); bicchu~, bīchū (H.); vīchu (G.); viccu, viccua, vim.cua (Pkt.); byucu (K.); biccū (P.); biccū (WPah.); vīcū (M.); viccu, vim.cu (Kon.); bacchius large hornet (n.)(CDIAL 12081). Rebus: bica, bica-diri (Sad. bicā; Or. bicī) stone ore; meṛeḍ bica, stones containing iron; tambabica, copper-ore stones; samṛobica, stones containing gold (Mundari.lex.)

Chanhujodaro39A1 Chanhudaro39A2

Rod ID 120 Guild, nodule (ore)/stone cast metal

khaḍā 'circumscribe' (M.); Rebs: khaḍā 'nodule (ore), stone' (M.) kolom 'three' (Mu.)

Chanhudaro23 6402 Goat-antelope with a short tail. The object in front of the goat-antelope is a double-axe.

Seal Mult. ID 110 Iron-merchant, mint, bronze, brass-bellmetal, workshop, iron smithy, nodule (ore)-stone-furnace, mint, ingot kiln

*mēḍha* 'antelope'; rebus: *meḍ* 'iron' (Mu.) *meḍh* 'merchant' (G.)

hako, ayo 'axe' (Mu.); rebus: ayas 'iron, metal' (Pan.Skt.)

kāmaṭhum = a bow; kāmaṭhiyo a bowman; an archer (Skt.lex.) Rebus: kammaṭa = portable furnace (Te.) kampaṭṭam coiner, mint (Ta.)

kanac 'corner' (Santali); Rebus: kañcu 'bronze' (Te.)

bharna = the name given to the woof by weavers; otor bharna = warp and weft (Santali.lex.) bharna = the woof, cross-thread in weaving (Santali); bharnī (H.) (Santali.Boding.lex.) Rebus: bhoron = a mixture of brass and bell metal (Santali.lex.) bharan = to spread or bring out from a kiln (P.lex.) bhāraṇ = to bring out from a kiln (G.) bāraṇiyo = one whose profession it is to sift ashes or dust in a goldsmith's workshop (G.lex.) bharant (lit. bearing) is used in the plural in Pañcavimśa Brāhmaṇa (18.10.8). Sāyaṇa interprets this as 'the warrior caste' (bhāatam – bharaṇam kurvatām kṣatriyāṇām). *Weber notes this as a reference to the Bharata-s. (*Indische Studien*, 10.28.n.2)

*sal* stake, spike, splinter, thorn, difficulty (H.); Rebus: *sal* 'workshop' (Santali)

loa 'fig leaf' (Santali): Rebus: lo 'iron' (Assamese, Bengali); loa 'iron' (Gypsy) Glyph: *lo* = nine (Santali); *no* = nine (B.) *on-patu* = nine (Ta.)

kolmo 'three'; rebus: kolami 'smithy, forge' (Te.)

khaṇḍ 'division'; rebus: kaṇḍ 'furnace' (Santali) khaḍā 'circumscribe' (M.); Rebs: khaḍā 'nodule (ore), stone' (M.)

kāmaṭhum = a bow; Rebus: kammaṭa = portable furnace (Te.) kampaṭṭam coiner, mint (Ta.)

ḍhālako = a large metal ingot (G.) ḍhālakī = a metal heated and poured into a mould; a solid piece of metal; an ingot (G.) ḍabu 'an iron spoon' (Santali) Rebus: ḍab, ḍhimba, ḍhompo 'lump (ingot?)', baṭa = wide-mouthed pot; Rebus: baṭa = kiln (Te.)

Chanhudaro32a  6123  Seal ID 114 Coppersmith guild, smithy, forge, portable furnace, furnace-smithy

kole.l = temple in Kota village (Ko.) Rebus : kole.l smithy (Ko.)

kolom = cutting, graft; to graft, engraft, prune; kolma hoṛo = a variety of the paddy plant (Desi)(Santali.) Rebus: kolami 'furnace, smithy' (Te.)

kangha (IL 1333) kãgherā comb-maker (H.) Rebus: kangar 'portable furnace' Rebus: kangar 1 कंगर् m. a large portable brazier (El.). kãgürü कॉंग्ःरु&above;रू&below; or kãgürü कॉंग&above;रू&below; or kãgar कॉंग्ःर्ः । हसब्तिका f. (sg. dat. kãgrĕ कॉंग्र्य or kãgarĕ कॉंगर्य, abl. kãgri कॉंग्रि), the portable brazier, or *kāngrī,* much used in Kashmīr (K.Pr. *kángár,* 129, 131, 178; *káṅgrí,* 5, 128, 129). For particulars see El. s.v. *kángri;* L. 7, 25, *kangar;* and K.Pr. 129. The word is a fem. dim. of kang, q.v. (Gr.Gr. 37). kãgri-khŏphürü

pajhar. = to sprout from a root (Santali) Rebus: pasra 'smithy' (Santali)

ganḍe 'to place at a right angle to something else, cross, transverse'; *ganḍ ganḍ* 'across, at right angles, transversely' (Santali) [Note: A slanted line Lahn.d.a writing of accounts connotes a quarter; a straight line connotes 'one'.]

  Seal ID 84 Copper molten cast workshop

eraka 'nave of wheel' (Ka.); Rebus: eraka, er-aka = any metal infusion (Ka.Tu.) *Tu.* eraka molten, cast (as metal); eraguni to melt (DEDR 866)

sal stake, spike, splinter, thorn, difficulty (H.); Rebus: sal 'workshop' (Santali)

Chanhudaro 8  6227  Seal Bull:i ID 96 Coppersmith guild brass-bellmetal, iron smelter mine-worker-scribe, iron hearth, nodule (ore) smithy, mine-worker-scribe

Glyph: *bāraṇum* [Hem. Des. *bār, dvār,* fr. Skt. *dvāra*] a door, a gate, an entrance; the court-yard in front of a house; *ba_r* a door (G.) Glyph: *bār* a courtyard in front of a house (G.) Rebus: *bharaṇa* = filling stuff, filling material (Ka.M.lex.) *bhoron* = a mixture of brass and bell metal (Santali.lex.)

ayo 'fish' (Mu.); ayas 'iron, metal' (Pan.Skt.)

kuṭi = a slice, a bit, a small piece (Santali.lex.Bodding) Rebus: kuṭhi 'iron smelter furnace' (Santali) kut.hī factory (A.)(CDIAL 3546) *kaṇḍa kanka* 'rim of jar' (Santali) *kaṇḍa* 'furnace, fire-altar' (Santali); khanaka 'miner' karṇaka 'scribe' (Skt.)

bheḍa hako a species of fish (Santali) bedha cross-grained (Santali) Rebus: beḍa either of the sides of a hearth Thus, ayo bheḍa, this glyph connotes the hearth (beḍa) for ayas.

khaḍā 'circumscribe' (M.); Rebs: khaḍā 'nodule (ore), stone' (M.) kolmo 'paddy plant' (Santali); Rebus: kolimi 'smithy, forge' (Te.) kolom = cutting, graft; to graft, engraft, prune; kolma hoṛo = a variety of the paddy plant (Desi)(Santali.) kolom 'three' (Mu.) Rebus: kolami 'furnace, smithy' (Te.)

*kaṇḍ* .a 'furnace, fire-altar' (Santali); khanaka 'miner' *karṇaka* 'scribe' (Skt.)

Chanhudaro1a 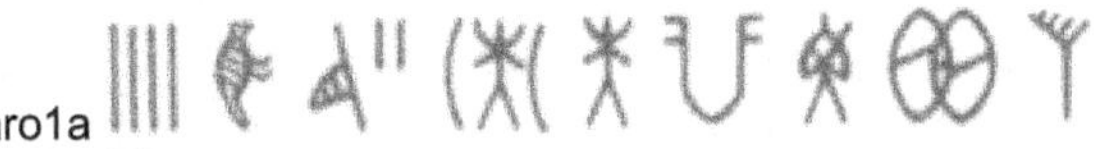 6125 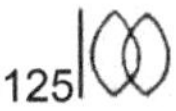

 ID89 Coppersmith guild, smithy guild, iron kiln, mine-w\orker-scribe, iron artisan's workshop, nodule (ore)/stone artisan's workshop, metal artisan's workshop, metal furnace

pajhar. = to sprout from a root (Santali) Rebus: pasra 'smithy' (Santali)

Sanghaṭṭa2 (?) bangle Sn 48 (˚yanta): thus Nd2 reading for ˚māna (ppr. med. of sanghaṭṭeti). Sanghaṭṭeti [saŋ+ghaṭṭeti] 1. to knock against Vin ii.208. -- 2. to sound, to ring Mhvs 21, 29 (˚aghaṭṭayi). -- 3 to knock together, to rub against each other J iv.98 (aŋsena aŋsaŋ samaghaṭṭayimha); Dāvs iii.87. -- 4. to provoke by scoffing, to make angry J vi.295 (paraŋ asanghaṭṭento, C. on asanghaṭṭa); VvA 139 (pres. pass. ˚ghaṭṭiyati). -- pp. sanghaṭ(ṭ)ita. Rebus: CDIAL 12858 *saṁghara ' living in the same house '. [Cf. *ságr̥ha*<-> ĀpŚr. -- ghara -- ]
Pa. *saṅghara* -- ' with one's own family (?) '; L. *sagghrā* ' accompanied by one's own family ';
H. *sā̃ghar* m. ' wife's son by former husband '.

 bhaṭa 'warrior'; bhaṭa 'six' (G.) Rebus: baṭa = kiln (Santali); baṭa = a kind of iron (G.)

baṭ.a 'quail'; rebus: baṭ.a 'furnace' (Santali)

Chanhudaro24a  6116   Seal ID 1702 Workshop, smelter-furnace-workshop, workshop-mint, smithy-forge, bronze, native metal smelter, artisan's workshop, blacksmith-merchant, iron fire-altar

kanac 'corner' (Santali); Rebus: kancu 'bronze' (Te.)

ad.aren 'lid'; rebus: aduru 'native metal' (Ka.)

kuṭi = a slice, a bit, a small piece (Santali.lex.Bodding) Rebus: kuṭhi 'iron smelter furnace' (Santali)

bar, barea = two (Mu.); Rebus: barī = blacksmith, artisan (Ash.)(CDIAL 9464).

sal stake, spike, splinter, thorn, difficulty (H.); Rebus: sal 'workshop' (Santali)

gan.d.a 'four' (Santali) kan.d.a 'fire-altar' (Santali); ayo 'fish' (Mu.); Rebus: ayas 'metal'; ayaska_n.d.a 'excellent iron' (Pan.)

sal stake, spike, splinter, thorn, difficulty (H.); Rebus: sal 'workshop' (Santali) bat.a = wide-mouthed pot; Rebus: bat.a = kiln (Te.); smelter (Santali)

sal stake, spike, splinter, thorn, difficulty (H.); Rebus: sal 'workshop' (Santali)

kāmaṭhum = a bow; ka_mad.i_, ka_mad.um = a chip of bamboo (G.) ka_maṭhiyo a bowman; an archer (Skt.lex.) Rebus: kammaṭa = portable furnace (Te.) kampaṭṭam coiner, mint (Ta

kolom = cutting, graft; to graft, engraft, prune; kolma hoṛo = a variety of the paddy plant (Desi)(Santali.) kolom 'three' (Mu.) Rebus: kolami 'furnace, smithy' (Te.)

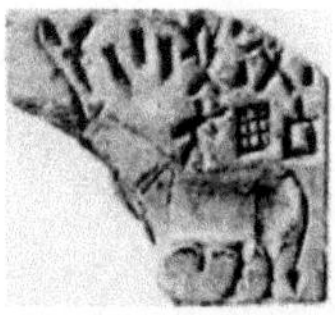 Chanhudaro 11 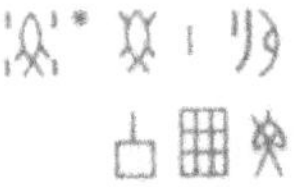 6220  Seal Bull: i:I ID 1707 Iron guild, coppersmith guild, guild of workers in wood and metal, bell-metal-brass smelter, smelter-furnace-fire-altar, kiln nodule (ore)-stone, tin

 Chanhudaro 6 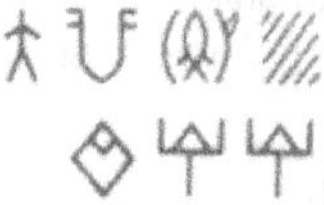 6205  Seal Bull:i:J ID 1705 Coppersmith guild, iron cast metal, bronze, artisan's workshop guild, artisan's workshop, workshop nodule (ore)/stone, iron guild, mine-worker-scribe, iron

 Chanhudaro29 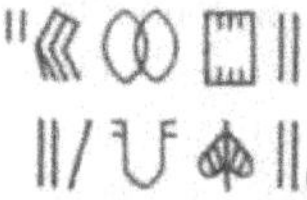 6403   Seal ID 1703 Smelter furnace, smithy, guild, brass-bellmetal-workshop, iron workshop, mine-worker, scribe, fire-altar-smithy

khaṇḍ 'division'; rebus: kaṇḍ 'furnace' (Santali) khaḍā 'circumscribe' (M.); Rebs: khaḍā 'nodule (ore), stone' (M.)

ranku 'liquid measure'; rebus: ranku 'tin' (Santali)

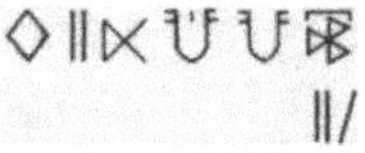 6113 Pict-98  Seal Bull: ii ID 1709 Coppersmith guild, nodule (ore)/stone-smithy guild mine-worker-scribe, mint smelter-furnace-mine-worker-scribe, blacksmith, bronze, fire-altar smithy

kamaḍha crab (Skt.) Rebus: kammaṭa = portable furnace (Te.) kampaṭṭam coiner, mint (Ta.) dol 'likeness' ; rebus : dul 'cast (metal)(Santali)

barea = two (Ka.); baṛea = blacksmith (Santali)

 Seal Bull: I ID 1710 Coppersmith guild, nodule (ore)/stone-guild, workshop bronze...

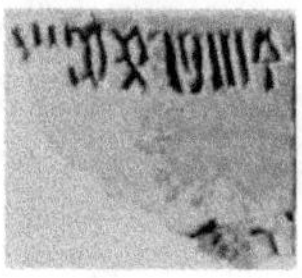 Chanhudaro 7  6207  Seal Bull ID 1711 Coppersmith guild...mint workshop bell-metal-brass, ingot kiln, smithy-forge-copper merchant, iron

 Chanhudaro12a  6231 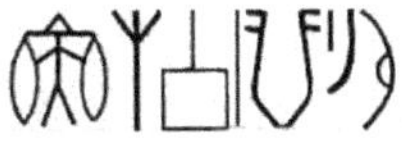 Seal Bull: I ID 1712 Coppersmith guild, iron guild, guild of workers in wood and metal, smelter-furnace-mine-worker-scribe, artisan's workshop, tin, iron-smelter-furnace-smithy

 Seal Bull: i ID 1714 Coppersmith guild, iron guild, guild of workers in wood and metal, artisan's workshop, tin fire-altar, smithy-forge-copper merchant, fire-altar-hearth guild

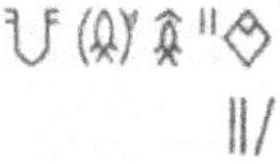

Chanhudaro. Seal impression. Fig. 35 of Plate LII. After Mackay, 1943.

6124 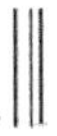  Seal Bull: I ID 1715

 Seal Bull:i ID 1713 Coppersmith guild, bronze workshop, jeweller's polishing stone native metal, nodule (ore)-stone-iron guild, mine-worker-scribe, blacksmith-artisan-merchant-workshop

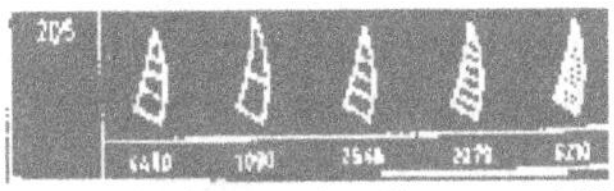

V205 Sign 205 and variants: pōtramu = snout of a hog; pōtri = a hog; a boar (Te.) Rebus: pot = jeweller's polishing stone (Bi.) Vikalpa: soṇḍ.a = a tusk, as of wild boar, elephant (Santali.lex.) sonda = a billhook, for cutting fire wood (Santali.lex.)

 Seal Bull:i ID 1716 Coppersmith guild, bronze artisan's workshop merchant, iron-bell-metal-brass, iron artisan's workshop.

 Seal Bull:I ID 1717 Coppersmith guild…brass-bell-metal workshop, blacksmith-artisan-merchant-guild, mine-worker-scribe

 Chanhudaro 5  6132  Sel Bull:i ID 1718 Coppersmith guild, smelter-furnace-mine-worker-scribe, brass-bell-metal, silver, iron, mine-worker- scribe

khur 'hoof' (M.); rebus: khura silver (Nk.); *kuruku* 'whiteness'; *kuru* brilliancy (Ta.); *kuro* silver (Kol.Nk.Go.)(DEDR 1782). koru = bar of metal (Ta.) *khud.do, khurdo* (Persian *khurdah*) small change in copper; *khurdiyo* a merchant who exchanges copper coins for silver (G.)

 Chanhudaro 9  6127  Seal Bull: i ID 1720 Coppersmith guild, bell-metal-brass, ingot kiln, copper-smithy-forge, nodule (ore) smithy, iron-hearth, smelter-furnace

 Seal Bull ID 1721 Coppersmith guild, bronze workshop, blacksmith-partisan-merchant, iron, iron-smelter-furnace, mine-worker-scribe

 Chanhudaro22a 6115   Seal Bull ID 1722 Blacksmith goldsmith-guild worker in wood and metal, nodule (ore)/stone-guild, smithy-forge, artisan's workshop; blacksmith-artisan-merchant, smithy-forge, guild

Vikalpa: baddī = ox (Nahali); baḍhi = worker in wood and metal (Santali) ḍāngrā = a wooden trough just enough to feed one animal. cf. iḍankaṛi = a measure of capacity, 20 iḍankaṛi make a par-r-a (Ma.lex.) ḍangā = small country boat, dug-out canoe (Or.); ḍõgā trough, canoe, ladle (H.)(CDIAL 5568). Rebus: ḍānro term of contempt for a blacksmith (N.) (CDIAL 5524) pattar 'trough'; pattar (Ta.), battuḍu (Te.) goldsmith guild (Ta.Te.)

 Seal Bull ID 1723 Iron guild, coppersmith guild, guild of workers in wood and metal, native metal, iron, casting metals in moulds

baraḍo = spine; backbone; the back; baraḍo thābaḍavo = lit. to strike on the backbone or back; hence, to encourage; baraḍo bhāre thato = lit. to have a painful backbone, i.e. to do something which will call for a severe beating (G.lex.) baraḍ, baraḍu = barren, childless; baranṭu = leanness (Tu.lex.) *maṇuk.o* a single vertebra of the back (G.) Rebus:bharatiyo = a caster of metals; a brazier; bharatar, bharatal, bharataḷ = moulded; an article made in a mould; bharata = casting metals in moulds; bharavum = to fill in; to put in; to pour into (G.lex.) bhart = a mixed metal of copper and lead; bhart-īyā = a barzier, worker in metal; bhat., bhrāṣṭra = oven, furnace (Skt.) bharata = a factitious metal compounded of copper, pewter, tin (M.)

 Seal Bull ID 1724 Coppersmith guild, native metal, bell-metal-brass, mine-worker-scribe, smelter-furnace, blacksmith-artisan-merchant-workshop

 Seal Bull ID 1725 Coppersmith guild, bell-metal-brass, ingot kiln, coppersmithy-forge-merchant, nodule (ore)/stone-artisan's workshop, iron

 Chanhudaro3 6230 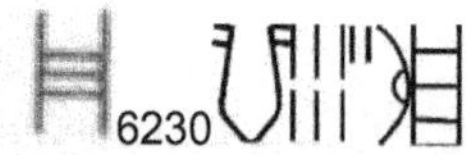 Seal Bull ID 1727 Coppersmith guild, smithy, nodule (ore)/ironstone workshop, cast-metal-furnace-smithy, mine-worker-scribe

 Chanhudaro4  6206  Seal Bull ID 1728 Coppersmith guild, bronze workshop, nodule (ore) smithy, native metal iron

 Seal Bull ID 1729 Coppersmith guild, ingot-mine-worker-scribe smithy, worker in wood and metal, blacksmith-artisan-merchant, iron

 Chanhudaro16a 6222  Seal Bull ID 1730 Iron guild,

coppersmith guild, smelter-furnace-mine-worker-scribe, smithy, iron sand ore

Standing crop: CDIAL 11425 valla m. ' a kind of wheat ' VarBr̥S., ' winnowing corn ' W. Pk. *valla* -- m. ' a kind of grain ', *vālā* -- f. ' a kind of grain, millet '; S. *vali* f. ' heap of reaped ears of corn ', L. *val*; Ku. *bāl* ' ear of corn ', *bālo,bālṛo* m. ' crops '; N. *bālo* ' ear of corn ', *bāli* ' cornfield, crops, harvest ' (whence *balyāunu* ' to pick off ears of corn '); Bi. *bāl* ' ear of wheat ', Mth. *bālī*; Aw.lakh. *bālī* ' ear of maize '; H. *bālī* f. ' spike of corn ', *bālū* m. ' beard of grain (esp. maize) '; OMarw. *bālī* f. ' standing crop '; G. *vāl* m. ' a kind of pulse '. Rebus: bali 'iron sand ore' (Santali)

 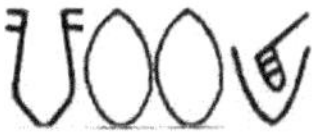 Seal Bull ID 73 Coppersmith guild, iron kiln, artisan's workshop, mine-worker-scribe, blacksmith-artisan-merchant-workshop

kōḍi a kind of flag, an image of garud.a, basava, or other demi-god set upon a long post before a temple; cf. gud.i, temple (Ka.lex.) Rebus: kod., 'artisan's workshop' (Kuwi)

Chanhudaro20 6210 Seal Bull ID 1731 Coppersmith guild, jeweller's polishing stone, nodule (ore)-stone-cast metal-workshop, smelter-furnace

Chanhudaro29 6403 ID 112 Blacksmith-artisan-merchant smithy-guild bell-metal-brass workshop; Blacksmith-artisan-merchant, iron, mine-worker-scribe, fire-altar smithy

 Seal ID 1734 Bronze workshop, bell-metal brass, smithy workshop, mine-worker-scribe

 Seal Bull ID 1735 Coppersmith guild, mint, mineral (ore) workshop, smelter-furnace-mine-worker-scribe, fire-altar smelter-furnace, mine-worker-scribe

 Seal Bull ID 1736 Coppersmith guild, bronze workshop, nodule (ore) smithy, iron-hearth, iron

 Seal Bull ID 1737 Coppersmith guild, silver workshop, blacksmith worker in metal and wood, nodule (ore) smelter-furnace, smithy

khur 'hoof' (M.); rebus: khura silver (Nk.); *kuruku* 'whiteness'; *kuru* brilliancy (Ta.); *kuro* silver (Kol.Nk.Go.)(DEDR 1782). koru = bar of metal (Ta.) *khud.do, khurdo* (Persian *khurdah*) small change in copper; *khurdiyo* a merchant who exchanges copper coins for silver (G.)

koḍa 'sluice'; Rebus: koḍ 'artisan's workshop (Kuwi)

 Seal Bull ID 1738 Coppersmith guild, bronze-workshop, blacksmith-artisan-merchant, caster of metal, mine-worker-scribe

 Chanhudaro15a 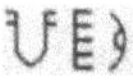 6213  Seal Bull ID 1739 Coppersmith guild, workshop nodule (ore)/stone/iron?, portable furnace

 Seal Bull ID 1740 Coppersmith guild, bronze workshop, workshop

Person kneeling under a tree facing a tiger. [*Chanhudaro Excavations*, Pl. LI, 18] 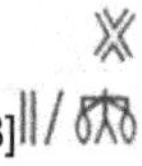 6118  Seal T-A-T ID 1743

Alloy of five metals, moltencast copper (*erako*), smelter-furnace, mineral (*dhatu*) smelter-furnace, fire-altar smithy

*dā̃ṭu* = cross over; daṭ- (da.ṭ-t-) to cross (Kol.)(DEDR 3158) Rebus: dhātu 'mineral'; rebus: dhatu = a mineral, metal (Santali)

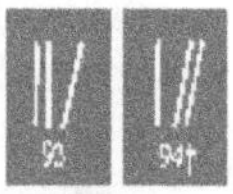

*gaṇḍe* 'to place at a right angle to something else, cross, transverse'; *gaṇḍ* gaṇḍ 'across, at right angles, transversely' (Santali) [Note: A slanted line Lahn.d.a writing of accounts connotes a quarter; a straight line connotes 'one'.] Rebus: kaṇḍa 'fire-altar' (Santali) *kāṇḍa* 'iron' as in *ayaskāṇḍa* 'excellent iron' (Pan.Skt.) kolmo 'three' (Mu.); rebus: kolimi 'smithy' (Te.)

This is a remarkable example of Indus script epigraphs where the pictorial motifs and signs coalesce to convey a message.

The tree glyph shown on this Chanhudaro seal is vividly depicted on a side of a Harappa tablet occupying the entire field:

Molded terracotta tablet showing a tree with branches; the stem emanates from a platform (ingot?). Harappa. (After JM Kenoyer/Courtesy Dept. of Archaeology and Museums, Govt. of Pakistan).

kuṭi, kuṭhi, kuṭa, kuṭha a tree (Kaus'.); kud.a tree (Pkt.); kuṛā tree; kaṛek tree, oak (Pas;.)(CDIAL 3228). kuṭha, kuṭa (Ka.), kudal (Go.) kudar. (Go.) kuṭha_ra, kuṭha, kuṭaka = a tree (Skt.lex.) kuṭ, kurun: = stump of a tree (Bond.a); khut. = id. (Or.) kuṭamu = a tree (Te.lex.)

Rebus: kuṭhi 'a furnace for smelting iron ore to smelt iron'; *kolheko kut.hieda* koles smelt iron (Santali) kuṭhi, kuṭi (Or.; Sad. koṭhi) (1) the smelting furnace of the blacksmith; kut.ire bica duljad.ko talkena, they were feeding the furnace with ore; (2) the name of ēkuṭi has been given to the fire which, in lac factories, warms the water bath for softening the lac so that it can be spread into sheets; to make a smelting furnace; kuṭhi-o of a smelting furnace, to be made; the smelting furnace of the blacksmith is made of mud, cone-shaped, 2' 6" dia. At the base and 1' 6" at the top. The hole in the centre, into which the mixture of charcoal and iron ore is poured, is about 6" to 7" in dia. At the base it has two holes, a smaller one into which the nozzle of the bellow is inserted, as seen in fig. 1, and a larger one on the opposite side through which the molten iron flows out into a cavity (Mundari.lex.) kuṭhi= a factory; lil kuṭhi= an indigo factory (H.kot.hi)(Santali.lex.Bodding) kuṭhī = an earthen furnace for smelting iron; make do., smelt iron; kolheko do kut.hi benaokate baliko dhukana, the Kolhes build an earthen furnace

and smelt iron-ore, blowing the bellows; tehen:ko kuṭhi yet kana, they are working (or building) the furnace to-day (H. koṭhī) (Santali.lex. Bodding) kuṭṭhita = hot, sweltering; molten (of tamba, cp. uttatta)(Pali.lex.) uttatta (ut + tapta) = heated, of metals: molten, refined; shining, splendid, pure (Pali.lex.) kuṭṭakam, kuṭṭukam = cauldron (Ma.); kuṭṭuva = big copper pot for heating water (Kod.)(DEDR 1668). gudga_ to blaze; gud.va flame (Man.d); gudva, gu_du_vwa, guduwa id. (Kuwi)(DEDR 1715). dāntar-kuṭha = fireplace (Sv.); kōti wooden vessel for mixing yeast (Sh.); kot.ha_ house with mud roof and walls, granary (P.); kuth ī factory (A.); koṭhā brick-built house (B.); kuṭhī bank, granary (B.); koṭho jar in which indigo is stored, warehouse (G.); koṭhī lare earthen jar, factory (G.); koṭhī granary, factory (M.)(CDIAL 3546). koṭho = a warehouse; a revenue office, in which dues are paid and collected; koṭhī a store-room; a factory (G.lex.) koḍ = the place where artisans work (G.lex.)

Water-carrier glyph shown on Chanhujo-daro seal is depicted vividly as a hieroglyph on a Gadd seal (Ur.): Seal impression, Ur (Upenn; U.16747); [After Edith Porada, 1971, Remarks on seals found in the Gulf States. *Artibus Asiae* 33 (4): 331-7: pl.9, fig.5]; Parpola, 1994, p. 183; water carrier with a skin (or pot?) hung on each end of the yoke across his shoulders and another one below the crook of his left arm; the vessel on the right end of his yoke is over a receptacle for the water; a star on either side of the head (denoting supernatural?). The two celestial objects depicted on either side of the water-carrier's head can be interpreted as a phonetic determinant: kōḷ 'planet'. The whole object is enclosed by 'parenthesis' marks. The parenthesis is perhaps a way of splitting of the ellipse (Hunter, G.R., *JRAS*, 1932, 476). An unmistakable example of an 'hieroglyphic' seal. enclosure signs of the field: Rebus: kol = metal (Ta.) Two kōḷ 'planets'; rebus: kuṭhi kol kin = two furnaces for metal vessels.

This is Sign 12 kuṭi = a woman water-carrier (Te.) kuṭi = to drink; drinking, beverage (Ta.); drinking, water drunk after meals (Ma.); kud.t- to drink (To.); kuḍi to drink; drinking (Ka.); kuḍi to drink (Kod.); kuḍi right, right hand (Te.); kuṭī intoxicating liquor (Skt.)(DEDR 1654).

kola, kolum = a jackal (G.) kolhuyo (Dh.Des.); kulho, kolhuo (Hem.Des.); kroṣṭṛ (Skt.) kul seren = the tiger's son, a species of lizard (Santali) kolo, kolea_ jackal (Kon.lex.) Jackal: kuṛi-nari jackal (Kur-r-ā. Tala. Vēṭan-valam. 13)(Ta.); id. (Ma.)(Ta.lex.) kul tiger; kul dander den of tiger; an.d.kul to become tiger; hudur. to growl as tiger; maran. d.at.kap kul a big-headed tiger (Santali.lex.) kōlupuli = a big, huge tiger, royal or Bengal tiger; kōlu = big, great, huge (Te.lex.) kula tiger; syn. of maran: kula, burukula, kamsikula, the striped royal tiger; syn. of maran: kula, laṛokula, the brown royal tiger without stripes; syn. of hur.in: kula, soncita, leopard: sin:kula = the lion; kindorkula, kinduakula = the panther; tagukula (lit. the shaggy tiger), the hyena; ḍurkula, a smaller feline animal, which when attacking a man bites him in the knee, probably a tiger-cat; kula-bin: collective noun for all dangerous animals; kulabin:-o to become infested by dangerous animals; kla (Khasi.Rongao) tiger (Mundari.lex.) kroṣṭṛ. = jackal (RV.); kroṣṭu = id. (Pa_.n.); kroṣṭṛ = crying (BhP.); koṭṭhu, koṭṭhuka, kotthu, kotthuka = jackal (Pali); koṭṭhu (Pkt.); koṭa (Si.); koṭiya = leopard (Si.); kōlhuya, kulha = jackal (Pkt.); kolhā, kolā jackal; adj. crafty (H.); kohlũ, kohlū jackal (G.); kolhā, kolā (M.)(CDIAL 3615). Fr. krus' = cry, call; krōśati cries out (RV)(CDIAL 3613). koṭho = a call, a messenger; koṭha invitation; koṭhaṇu = to send for (S.)(CDIAL 3614). koś to abuse, curse, blame (Gypsy); kosna_ to curse (H.); kosn.a_ (P.); akos' to abuse (Gypsy); kros'ati cries out (RV)(CDIAL 3612). krośa shout (VS); kuru_ voice, word (Pas'); kosā curse (H.)(CDIAL 3611). kuḷ = the tiger, filis tigris; kul en:ga = tigress; *kul seren* 'the 'tiger's song', a species of lizard (Santali)

Rebus: kol metal (Ta.) kol = pan~calo_kam (five metals) (Ta.lex.) kol = *pan~calo_kam* (five metals); kol metal (Ta.lex.) pan~caloha = a metallic alloy containing five metals: copper, brass, tin, lead and iron (Skt.); an alternative list of five metals: gold, silver, copper, tin (lead), and iron (dha_tu; Na_na_rtharatna_kara. 82; Man:gara_ja's Nighan.t.u. 498)(Ka.) *kol, kolhe*, 'the koles, an aboriginal tribe if iron smelters speaking a language akin to that of Santals' (Santali) kol = kollan-, kamma_l.an- (blacksmith or smith in general)(Ta.lex.) kollar = those who guard the treasure (Ta.lex.) cf. golla (Telugu) khol, kholi_ = a metal covering; a loose covering of metal or cloth (G.) [The semant.

expansions to kolla_puri or kolha_pur and also to 'kolla_ppan.t.i' a type of cart have to be investigated further].

kol 'working in iron, blacksmith (Ta.); *kollan-* blacksmith (Ta.); *kollan* blacksmith, artificer (Ma.)(DEDR 2133)

Obeisance, kneeling person

erugu = to bow, to salute or make obeisance (Te.) er-agu = obeisance (Ka.), ir_ai (Ta.) er-agisu = to bow, to be bent; to make obeisance to; to crouch; to come down; to alight (Ka.lex.) cf. arghas = respectful reception of a guest (by the offering of rice, du_rva grass, flowers or often only of water)(S'Br.14)(Skt.lex.) erugu = to bow, to salute or make obeisance (Te.)

Allographs (from epigraphs of Mohenjodaro):

m0478Bt erga = act of clearing jungle (Kui) [Note image showing two men carrying uprooted trees].

eraka, hero = a messenger; a spy (G.lex.) hēraka = spy (Skt.); ēra = to spy (Kui); er = to see (Malt.); hēru = spy (Pkt.); hēriu = spy (Kl.); hero (G.); heru~ spying (G.); herṇẽ to spy (M.); hernā (H.); herai (Oaw.)(CDIAL 14165). heriyām = prying, peeping; heravum = to spy (G.lex.) ere = to see, behold; erye to peep, spy (Malt.); her to look at or for (Pkt.); er uk- to play 'peeping tom' (Ko.); ēra spying, scouting (Kui); hēri kiyali to see (Kuwi); ērna_ (i_ryas) to see, look, lok for (Kur.)(DEDR 903).

m1431A The first sign of the text is a glyph depicting a kneeling person, in front of a leafless tree, making an offering, holding a rimless pot in his hands.

m0480At Sign 45  seems to be a kneeling adorant offering a pot (Sign 328 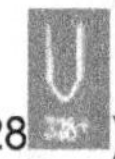) 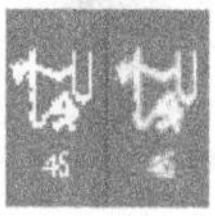 Signs 45/46 seem to ligature the pictorial of a kneeling-adorant with sign 328 

Rebus: eraka, er-aka any metal infusion (Ka.Tu.) eruvai 'copper' (Ta.); ere dark red (Ka.)(DEDR 446). erka = ekke (Tbh. of arka) aka (Tbh. of arka) copper (metal); crystal (Ka.lex.) Metal: akka, aka

(Tadbhava of arka) metal; akka metal (Te.) arka = copper (Skt.) erka = ekke (Tbh. of arka) aka (Tbh. of arka) copper (metal); crystal (Ka.lex.) erako molten cast (Tu.lex.) agasa_le, agasa_li, agasa_lava_d.u = a goldsmith (Te.lex.) erakaddu = any cast thng; erake hoyi = to pour meltted metal into a mould, to cast (Ka.); cf. arika = rice beer (Santali.lex.) er-e = to pour any liquids; to pour (Ka.); ir-u (Ta.Ma.); ira- i_i (Ta.); er-e = to cast, as metal; to overflow, to cover with water, to bathe (Ka.); er-e, ele = pouring; fitness for being poured(Ka.lex.) erako molten cast (Tu.lex.) eh-kam any weapon made of steel (Cu_t.a_.); eh-ku steel; eh-ku-pat.utal to melt, to soften (Cilap. 15, 210, Urai.)(Ta.lex.) eraka, era, era = syn. erka, copper, weapons (Ka.) erako_lu = the iron axle of a carriage (Ka.M.); cf. irasu (Ka.lex.) erako molten cast (Tu.lex.) eh-kam any weapon made of steel (Cu_t.a_.); eh-ku steel; eh-ku-pat.utal to melt, to soften (Cilap. 15, 210, Urai.)(Ta.lex.)

 6120  Seal Tiger 1744 Alloy of 5 metals, mineral (dhatu), worker in wood and metal, cast metal mint, mine-worker-scribe

kol 'tiger'; rebus: kol 'alloy of five metals' (Ta.)

  Seal ID 1746 Bronze, blacksmith-artisan-merchant, iron fire-altar

 Seal Bull ID 1747 Coppersmith guild, copper merchant, smithy

kolmo 'three' (Mu.); rebus: kolami 'smithy, forge' (Te.) tebra 'three' (Santali); ta(m)bra 'copper'; tibira 'merchant' (Akkadian)

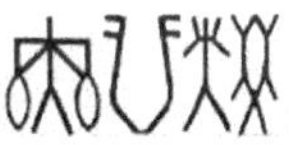 Seal Bull ID 1748 Coppersmith guild, iron workshop, smelter-mine-worker-scribe

Chanhudaro2  6128  Seal Bull ID 1749

Coppersmith guild, tin smithy, mine-worker-scribe

ranku 'liquid measure'; rebus: ranku 'tin' (Santali)

kolom = cutting, graft; to graft, engraft, prune; kolma hoṛo = a variety of the paddy plant (Desi)(Santali.) kolom 'three' (Mu.) Rebus: kolami 'furnace, smithy' (Te.)

Chanhudaro30  6111  Seal ID 1750 Furnace-smithy workshop, iron, cast molten metal blacksmith-artisan-copper merchant

kolom 'three' (Mu.) Rebus: kolami 'furnace, smithy' (Te.) sal stake, spike, splinter, thorn, difficulty (H.); Rebus: sal 'workshop' (Santali)

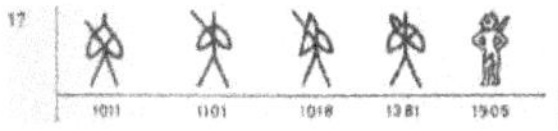 bhaṭa 'warrior'; bhaṭa 'six' (G.) Rebus: baṭa = kiln (Santali); baṭa = a kind of iron (G.)

bar, barea = two (Mu.); Rebus: barī = blacksmith, artisan (Ash.)(CDIAL 9464). barea 'merchant' (Santali) dol 'likeness' dul 'cast metal' (Mu.)

era, er-a = eraka = ?nave; erako_lu = the iron axle of a carriage (Ka.M.); cf. irasu (Ka.lex.) [Note Sign 391 and its ligatures Signs 392 and 393 may connote a spoked-wheel, nave of the wheel through which the axle passes; cf. ara_, spoke] eraka, era, er-a = syn. erka, copper, weapons. Rebus: er-r-a = red; eraka = copper (Ka.) erka = ekke (Tbh. of arka) aka (Tbh. of arka) copper (metal); crystal (Ka.lex.) agasa_le, agasa_li, agasa_lava_d.u = a goldsmith (Te.lex.) erka = ekke (Tbh. of arka) aka (Tbh. of arka) copper (metal); crystal (Ka.lex.) cf. eruvai = copper (Ta.lex.) eraka, er-aka = any metal infusion (Ka.Tu.); erako molten cast (Tu.lex.)

 Seal Bull ID 1755 Coppersmith guild, bronze workshop, portable furnace, mint

 Seal Bull ID 1756 Coppersmith guild, furnace-forge-smithy, artisan's workshop, iron smelter furnace

 Seal Bull ID 1757 Coppersmith guild, iron native metal, native metal, mine-worker-scribe

 Seal Bull ID 1758 Coppersmith guild, native metal…

Chanhudaro17a  6122  Seal Bull ID 1759 Coppersmith guild, iron, iron workshop, mine-worker-scribe

 Seal Bull ID 1761Coppersmith guild, kiln, mint

 Seal Bull ID 1762 Coppersmith guild, furnace, mine-worker-scribe

baṭa 'quail'; rebus: baṭa 'furnace' (Santali)

 Seal Bull ID 1763 Coppersmith guild, metal-smithy forge, mint, iron smelter furnace

gan.d.a 'four' (Santali) kan.d.a 'fire-altar' (Santali) Vikalpa: pon 'four' (Santali); pon 'metal' (Ta.) kolmo 'three'; rebus: kolami 'smithy, forge' (Te.)

kut.i 'woman water carrier' (Te.); kut.hi 'smelter furnace' (Santali)

ka_n.d.a 'arrow'; rebus: ka_n.d.a 'iron' (as in ayaska_n.d.a 'excellent iron') (Pan.Skt.)

 Seal Bull ID 1764 Coppersmith guild, iron, smithy

loa 'fig leaf' (Santali): Rebus: lo 'iron' (Assamese, Bengali); loa 'iron' (Gypsy) Glyph: *lo* = nine

(Santali); *no* = nine (B.) *on-patu* = nine (Ta.)

*panǰā́r* 'ladder, stairs' (Bshk.)(CDIAL 7760) Rebus: pasra 'smithy' (Santali)

 Seal Bull ID 1765 Coppersmith guild, nodule (ore), mineral ore

Chanhudaro21a  6209 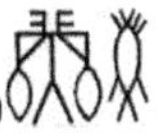 Seal Bull ID 3828
Coppersmith guild, iron, smelter-mine-worker-scribe

ad.ā 'circumscribe' (M.); Rebus: khad.ā 'nodule (ore), stone' (M.)

6233  Tablet Gavial ID 1706
Blacksmith, iron, nodule (ore) smithy, blacksmith-artisan-merchant, iron, iron kiln, iron-smelter-furnace-guild, smithy fire-altar

iṭankar 'crocodile' (Ta.); rebus: ḍhangar 'blacksmith' (H.)

ayo 'fish'; rebus: ayas 'iron, metal' (Pan.Skt.)

khad.ā 'circumscribe' (M.); Rebs: khad.ā 'nodule (ore), stone' (M.) kolmo 'paddy plant' (Santali); Rebus: kolimi 'smithy, forge' (Te.) kolom = cutting, graft; to graft, engraft, prune; kolma hoṛo = a variety of the paddy plant (Desi)(Santali.) kolom 'three' (Mu.) Rebus: kolami 'furnace, smithy' (Te.)

bar, barea = two (Mu.); Rebus: barī = blacksmith, artisan (Ash.)(CDIAL 9464). barea 'meerchant' (Santali)

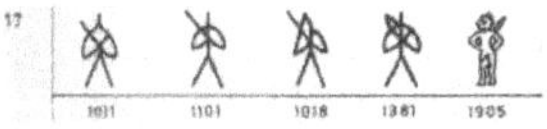 bhaṭa 'warrior'; bhaṭa 'six' (G.) Rebus: baṭa = kiln (Santali); baṭa = a kind of iron (G.)

kut.i = a slice, a bit, a small piece (Santali.lex.Bodding) Rebus: kut.hi 'iron smelter furnace' (Santali) kut.hī factory (A.)(CDIAL 3546) Sanghaṭṭa2 (?) bangle Sn 48 (˚yanta): thus Nd2 reading for ˚māna (ppr. med. of sanghaṭṭeti). Sanghaṭṭeti [saŋ+ghaṭṭeti] 1. to knock against Vin ii.208. -- 2. to sound, to ring Mhvs 21, 29 (˚aghaṭṭayi). -- 3 to knock together, to rub against each other J iv.98 (aŋsena aŋsaŋ samaghaṭṭayimha); Dāvs iii.87. -- 4. to provoke by scoffing, to make angry J vi.295 (paraŋ asanghaṭṭento, C. on asanghaṭṭa); VvA 139 (pres. pass. ˚ghaṭṭiyati). -- pp. sanghaṭ(ṭ)ita. Rebus: CDIAL 12858 *saṁghara ' living in the same house '. [Cf. *ságr̥ha*<-> ĀpŚr. -- ghara -- ]
Pa. *saṅghara* -- ' with one's own family (?) '; L. *sagghrā* ' accompanied by one's own family ';
H. *sā̃ghar* m. ' wife's son by former husband '.

kolom = cutting, graft; to graft, engraft, prune; kolma hor.o = a variety of the paddy plant (Desi)(Santali.) kolom 'three' (Mu.) Rebus: kolami 'furnace, smithy' (Te.)

  gan.d.e 'to place at a right angle to something else, cross, transverse'; *gan.d. gan.d.* 'across, at right angles, transversely' (Santali) [Note: A slanted line Lahn.d.a writing of accounts connotes a quarter; a straight line connotes 'one'.] Rebus: kan.d. 'fire-altar' (Santali)

Chanhudaro. Tablet. Fig. 34 of Plate LII. After Mackay, 1943.  623 
Tablet ID 1751

 Tablet ID 1752 Smelter furnace, ingot kiln, artisan's workshop

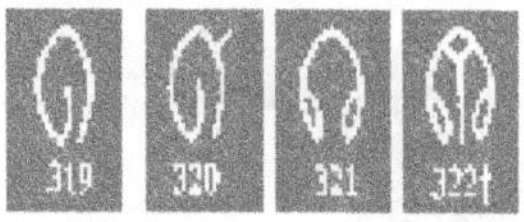 Orthography of Sign 319 is difficult to decode and interpret as a pictograph.

If the pattern is related to Sign 322, this sign's variants provide some clue  V322
Possibly, this is a stylized rendering of the water-carrier glyph which can be decoded:

kut.i 'woman water carrier' (Te.); kut.hi 'smelter furnace' (Santali)

d.hālako = a large metal ingot (G.) d.hālakī = a metal heated and poured into a mould; a solid piece of metal; an ingot (G.) d.abu 'an iron spoon' (Santali) Rebus: d.ab, d.himba, d.hompo 'lump (ingot?)', bat.a = wide-mouthed pot; Rebus: bat.a = kiln (Te.)

kod.a 'in arithmetic, one' (Santali); rebus: kod. 'artisan's workshop' (Kuwi)

Chanhudaro. Seal impression. Fig. 35 of Plate LII. After Mackay, 1943. 
6235  Tag ID 1760 Smithy fire-altar mine-worker-scribe

Unknown provenance

 (provenance) unkn01  unkn02 Svastika zinc

Sattva 'svastika glyp'; rebus: sattva, jasta 'zinc' (P.)

Seau l'nde. Musee des Arts Asiatique, Guimet, France Iron guild, iron kiln, bronze workshop...

ibha 'elephant' (Skt.) ; ib 'iron' (Santali)

sanghaṭṭa2 (?) bangle (Pali); rebus: samghara 'guild, community' (Skt.) sanghara 'living in the same house' (Pali)

 bhaṭa 'warrior'; bhaṭa 'six' (G.) Rebus: baṭa = kiln (Santali); baṭa = a kind of iron (G.)

kanac 'corner' (Santali); Rebus: kancu 'bronze' (Te.) sal stake, spike, splinter, thorn, difficulty (H.); Rebus: sal 'workshop' (Santali)

 Seal Bull ID 3785 Coppersmith guild, mint, mine-worker-scribe

अंकडा [aṅkaḍā] *m* (अंक S) Also अकडा *m* A hook or crook, a curved end gen. (M.) Rebus: अखाडा [ akhāḍā ] *m* ( H) A community, or the common place of residence or of assembly, of persons engaged in study or some particular pursuit; a college, a disputation-hall, a gymnasium, circus, arena. Hence, A club or clubroom; a stand of idlers, loungers, newsmongers, gossips, scamps. 2 An order of men. Ex. गोसाव्यांचे अठरा अखाडे आहेत.(M.)

kamaṭha crab (Skt.) Rebus: kammaṭa = portable furnace (Te.) kampaṭṭam coiner, mint (Ta.)

kan.d.a kanka 'rim of jar' (Santali) Rebus: kan.d.a 'furnace, fire-altar' (Santali); khanaka 'miner' karNaka 'scribe' (Skt.)

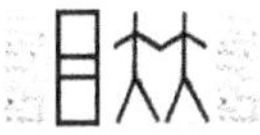 Seal Scene ID 3786 ...iron cast metal smithy..

med. 'body'; rebus: med. 'iron' (Mu.) dol 'likeness'; rebus: dul 'cast metal ' (Santali)

kole.l 'temple'; rebus: kole.l 'smithy' (Kota).

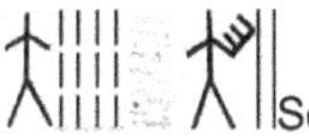Seal Mult. ID 3792 Blacksmith-artisan-merchant, iron portable furnace...iron, metal smithy forge

bar, barea = two (Mu.); Rebus: barī = blacksmith, artisan (Ash.)(CDIAL 9464). barea 'meerchant' (Santali)

med. 'body'; rebus: med. 'iron' (Mu.) kangha (IL 1333) ka~ghera_ comb-maker (H.) Rebus: kangar 'portable furnace' Rebus: kangar 1 कंगर् m. a large portable brazier (El.). kã̄gürü कॉँग्&above;रू&below; or kã̄gürü कॉँग&above;रू&below; or kã̄gar कॉँग्‌र्‌ I हसब्तिका f. (sg. dat. kã̄grĕ कॉँग्र्य or kã̄garĕ कॉँगर्य, abl. kã̄gri कॉँग्रि), the portable brazier, or *kāngrī,* much used in Kashmīr (K.Pr. *kángár,* 129, 131, 178; *káṅgrí,* 5, 128, 129). For particulars see El. s.v. *kángri;* L. 7, 25, *kangar;* and K.Pr. 129. The word is a fem. dim. of kang, q.v. (Gr.Gr. 37). kã̄gri-khŏphürü

gan.d.a 'four' (Santali) kan.d.a 'fire-altar' (Santali) Vikalpa: pon 'four' (Santali); pon 'metal' (Ta.) kolmo 'three'; rebus: kolami 'smithy, forge' (Te.)

med. 'body'; rebus: med. 'iron' (Mu.)

unkn03 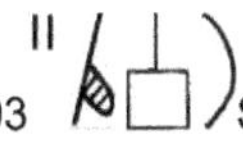Seal ID 3787 Nodule (ore)/stone, tin, artisan's workshop

khaḍā 'circumscribe' (M.); Rebs: khaḍā 'nodule (ore), stone' (M.)

ranku 'liquid measure'; rebus: ranku 'tin' (Santali)

 Seal Bull ID 3791 Coppersmith guild, moltencast copper, worker in wood and metal, bell-metal-brass, iron smelting furnace, artisan's workshop, mine

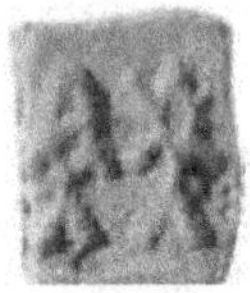

unkn06  Tablet ID 3788 Bell-metal-brass, iron hearth orker-scribe

unkn04  Tablet ID 3789 Moltencast copper workshop, iron hearth, mint

unkn05Aunkn05B  

Tablet ID 3790 Bronze workshop, building, kiln workshop, mine-worker-scribe

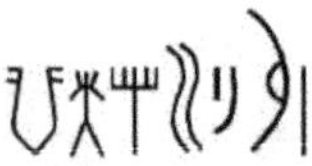 Seal 3891 Nodule (ore) iron guild, worker in wood and metal, ? , native metal, iron workshop, mine-worker-scribe

 Bull ID 3896 Coppersmith guild, moltencast copper workshop, native metal, nodule (ore) iron, mine-worker-scribe

Khirsara1a  Khirasra seal ID 3732 Mason, ingot kiln, tin smithy, blacksmith smithy, iron smelter furnace, nodule/ore stone furnace, brass-bellmetal kiln, native-metal-iron smelter

ḍabu 'an iron spoon' (Santali) Rebus: ḍab, ḍhimba, ḍhompo 'lump (ingot?)', bat.a = wide-mouthed pot; Rebus: bat.a = kiln (Te.)

ranku 'antelope'; rebus: ranku 'tin' (Santali)

*panǰắr* 'ladder, stairs' (Bshk.)(CDIAL 7760) Rebus: pasra 'smithy' (Santali)

badhi 'to ligature, to bandage, to splice, to join by successive rolls of a ligature' (Santali) batā bamboo slips (Kur.); bate = thin slips of bamboo (Malt.)(DEDR 3917). Rebus: baḍhi = worker in wood and metal (Santali) baṛae = blacksmith (Ash.)

kolmo 'three' (Mu.); rebus: kolimi 'smithy' (Te.)

khaṇḍ 'division'; rebus: kaṇḍ 'furnace' (Santali) khaḍā 'circumscribe' (M.); Rebs: khaḍā 'nodule (ore), stone' (M.)

bharna = the name given to the woof by weavers; otor bharna = warp and weft (Santali.lex.) bharna = the woof, cross-thread in weaving (Santali); bharni_ (H.) (Santali.Boding.lex.) Rebus: bhoron = a mixture of brass and bell metal (Santali.lex.) bharan = to spread or bring out from a kiln (P.lex.) bha_ran. = to bring out from a kiln (G.) ba_ran.iyo = one whose profession it is to sift ashes or dust in a goldsmith's workshop (G.lex.) bharant (lit. bearing) is used in the plural in Pan~cavim.s'a Bra_hman.a (18.10.8). Sa_yan.a interprets this as 'the warrior caste' (bharata_m – bharan.am kurvata_m ks.atriya_n.a_m). *Weber notes this as a reference to the Bharata-s. (*Indische Studien*, 10.28.n.2)

kuṭi = a slice, a bit, a small piece (Santali.lex.Bodding) Rebus: kuṭhi 'iron smelter furnace' (Santali)

ad.aren 'lid'; rebus: aduru 'native metal' (Ka.)

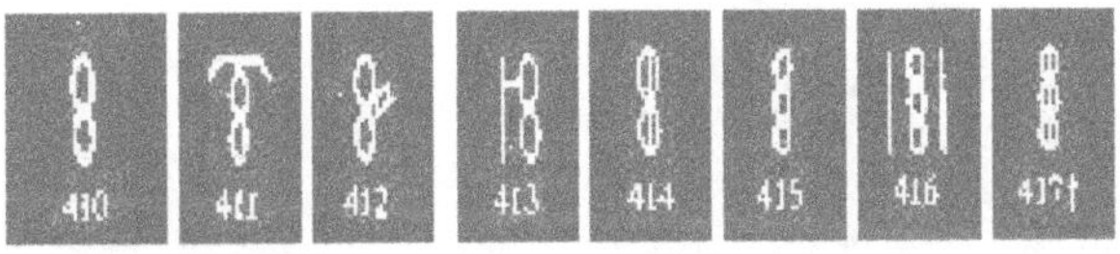
kad.i_ a chain; a hook; a link (G.); kad.iyo [Hem. Des. kad.a i o = Skt. sthapati a mason] a bricklayer; a mason; kad.iyan.a, kad.iyen.a a woman of the bricklayer caste; a wife of a bricklayer (G.)

 Khirsara2a  Khirasra seal ID 3733 Fire-altar (gold) smithy, artisan smith's workshop, mineworker, scribe

gaṇḍa set of four (Santali) kaṇḍa 'fire-altar' (Santali) Vikalpa: pon 'four' (Santali); pon 'metal' (Ta.)

kolmo 'three' (Mu.); rebus: kolimi 'smithy' (Te.)

koḍa 'sluice'; Rebus: koḍ 'artisan's workshop (Kuwi) Vikalpa: सांड [ sāṇḍa ] *f* (षद S) An outlet for superfluous water (as through a dam or mound); a sluice, a floodvent. सांडशी [ sāṇḍaśī ] *f* (Dim. of सांडस, or from H) A small kind of tongs or pincers.

kan.d.a kanka 'rim of jar' (Santali) kan.d.a 'furnace, fire-altar' (Santali); khanaka 'miner' karNaka 'scribe' (Skt.)

 9821 Kish Iron granary, mine-worker, scribe

कोष्ठ [ kōṣṭha ] *m* A granary. An apartment.

ayo 'fish'(Mu.); ayas 'iron' (Skt.)

kan.d.a kanka 'rim of jar' (Santali) kan.d.a 'furnace, fire-altar' (Santali); khanaka 'miner' karNaka 'scribe' (Skt.)

 9822 Kish Guild, native metal, worker in metal and wood, workshop, iron, tin, smithy, mine-worker, scribe

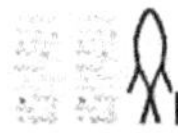 Kish seal Bull ID 3734

ad.ar 'harrow'; rebus: aduru 'native metal, unsmelted' (Ka.) dol 'likeness'; rebus: dul 'cast (metal)(Mu.) Doubling of harrow spikes thus connotes cast (native metal)

Sanghaṭṭa2 (?) bangle Sn 48 (˚yanta): thus Nd2 reading for ˚māna (ppr. med. of sanghaṭṭeti). Sanghaṭṭeti [saŋ+ghaṭṭeti] 1. to knock against Vin ii.208. -- 2. to sound, to ring Mhvs 21, 29 (˚aghaṭṭayi). -- 3 to knock together, to rub against each other J iv.98 (aŋsena aŋsaŋ samaghaṭṭayimha); Dāvs iii.87. -- 4. to provoke by scoffing, to make angry J vi.295 (paraŋ asanghaṭṭento, C. on asanghaṭṭa); VvA 139 (pres. pass. ˚ghaṭṭiyati). -- pp. sanghaṭ(ṭ)ita. Rebus: CDIAL 12858 *saṁghara ' living in the same house '. [Cf. *ságṛha*<-> ĀpŚr. -- ghara -- ]Pa. *saṅghara* -- ' with one's own family (?) '; L. *sagghrā* ' accompanied by one's own family '; H. *sā̃ghar* m. ' wife's son by former husband '.

badhi 'to ligature, to bandage, to splice, to join by successive rolls of a ligature' (Santali) batā bamboo slips (Kur.); bate = thin slips of bamboo (Malt.)(DEDR 3917). Rebus: baḍhi = worker in wood and metal (Santali) baṛae = blacksmith (Ash.)

koḍa 'sluice'; Rebus: koḍ 'artisan's workshop (Kuwi)

ayo 'fish'(Mu.); ayas 'iron' (Skt.)

ranku 'liquid measure'; rebus: ranku 'tin' (Santali)

kolom = cutting, graft; to graft, engraft, prune; kolma hoṛo = a variety of the paddy plant (Desi)(Santali.) kolom 'three' (Mu.) Rebus: kolami 'furnace, smithy' (Te.)

kan.d.a kanka 'rim of jar' (Santali) kan.d.a 'furnace, fire-altar' (Santali); khanaka 'miner' karNaka 'scribe' (Skt.)

Kish seal Bull ID3735 Iron…

ayo 'fish'(Mu.); ayas 'iron' (Skt.)

 Susa seal Bull ID 3779 … … iron smithy … …

med. 'body'; rebus: med. 'iron' (Mu.)

pajhaṛ = to sprout from a root (Santali) Rebus: pasra 'smithy' (Santali)

Susa, Iran; steatite cylinder seal . A bison with head lowered, feeding from a basin. A second bison figure is seen. Inscription on top. Louvre Sb 2425, Delaporte, 1920, s.299 and cf. T.24 from Tello, Iraq; Collon, 1987, Fig. 608.Musee du Louvre and Pierre and Maurice Chuzeville;

Legend: Indus script; bone. 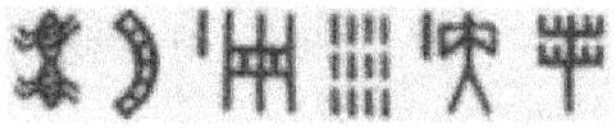

9801Susa

Susa seal Bull ID 3780 Blacksmith, granary, ore (worker) guild, bronze….fire-altar smithy workshop, (iron) smelter furnace, cast native metal

A spider. कोष्ठ [ kōṣṭha ] *m* A granary. An apartment.

khaḍā 'circumscribe' (M.); Rebs: khaḍā 'nodule (ore), stone' (M.) अंकडा [aṅkaḍā] *m* (अंक S)

Also अकडा *m* A hook or crook, a curved end gen. (M.) Rebus: अखाडा [ akhāḍā ] *m* ( H) A community, or the common place of residence or of assembly, of persons engaged in study or some particular pursuit; a college, a disputation-hall, a gymnasium, circus, arena. Hence, A club or clubroom; a stand of idlers, loungers, newsmongers, gossips, scamps. 2 An order of men. Ex. गोसाव्यांचे अठरा अखाडे आहेत.(M.)

kanac 'corner' (Santali); Rebus: kancu 'bronze' (Te.)

gan.d.a 'four' (Santali) kan.d.a 'fire-altar' (Santali); kolmo 'three' (Mu.); rebus: kolimi 'smithy' (Te.)

sal stake, spike, splinter, thorn, difficulty (H.); Rebus: sal 'workshop' (Santali)

kut.i 'woman water carrier' (Te.); kut.hi 'smelter furnace' (Santali)

ad.ar 'harrow'; rebus: aduru 'native metal, unsmelted' (Ka.) dol 'likeness'; rebus: dul 'cast (metal)(Mu.) Doubling of harrow spikes thus connotes cast (native metal)

Nindowari-damb01  Nindowari-damb Seal Bull ID 3756 Blacksmith, nodule/ore worker in wood and metal, furnace, casting smithy, mine-worker, scribe guild, granary, iron, bronze

खडी [ khaḍī ] *f* खटी S) खडू [ khaḍū ] *f* खडूळ *f* A squirrel; Rebus: (खडा) Pebbles or small stones: also stones broken up (as for a road) (i.e. nodules/ore stones)

badhi 'to ligature, to bandage, to splice, to join by successive rolls of a ligature' (Santali) batā bamboo slips (Kur.); bate = thin slips of bamboo (Malt.)(DEDR 3917). Rebus: baḍhi = worker in wood and metal (Santali) baṛae = blacksmith (Ash.)

bhaṭa 'six' (G.) bhaṭa 'furnace' (G.)

kolom = cutting, graft; to graft, engraft, prune; kolma hoṛo = a variety of the paddy plant (Desi)(Santali.) kolom 'three' (Mu.) Rebus: kolami 'furnace, smithy' (Te.) dol 'likeness'; rebus: dul 'cast (metal)(Mu.) Doubling of harrow spikes thus connotes cast (native metal)

kan.d.a kanka 'rim of jar' (Santali) kan.d.a 'furnace, fire-altar' (Santali); khanaka 'miner' karNaka 'scribe' (Skt.)

अंकडा [aṅkaḍā] *m* (अंक S) Also अकडा *m* A hook or crook, a curved end gen. (M.) Rebus: अखाडा [ akhāḍā ] *m* ( H) A community, or the common place of residence or of assembly, of persons engaged in study or some particular pursuit; a college, a disputation-hall, a gymnasium, circus, arena. Hence, A club or clubroom; a stand of idlers, loungers, newsmongers, gossips, scamps. 2 An order of men. Ex. गोसाव्यांचे अठरा अखाडे आहेत.(M.)

कोष्ठ [ kōṣṭha ] *m* A granary. An apartment.

ayo 'fish'(Mu.); ayas 'iron' (Skt.)

kanac 'corner' (Santali); Rebus: kancu 'bronze' (Te.)

Nindowari-damb02  Nindowari-damb Seal Bull ID 3757 Coppersmith guild, Iron stone ore, mint, portable furnace

sangad.a 'lathe, furnace' rebus: samghara 'guild' (i.e. living in same house) (Pali)

The Sanskritization of Assamese bicā , deśī vachi is: vṛścika scorpion (RV); vicchika (Pali); vicchia, vim.chia (Pkt.); bich (Sh.); bichī (Ku.); bicā (A.); bichā (B.Or.); būch (Mth.); bīchī (Bhoj.Aw.H.); vīchī, vi~chī (G.); ucum (Pas'.); vichu~ (S.); vicchua, vim.chua (Pkt.); vichu~ (L.); bicchu~ (P.); bichu (Or.); bīchu (Mth.); bicchu~, bīchū (H.); vīchu (G.); viccu, viccua, vim.cua (Pkt.); byucu (K.); biccū (P.); biccū (WPah.); vīcū (M.); viccu, vim.cu (Kon.); bacchius large hornet (n.)(CDIAL 12081). Rebus: bica, bica-diri (Sad. bicā; Or. bicī) stone ore; meṛeḍ bica, stones containing iron; tambabica, copper-ore stones; samṛobica, stones containing gold (Mundari.lex.)

kamaṭha crab (Skt.) Rebus: kammaṭa = portable furnace (Te.) kampaṭṭam coiner, mint (Ta.)

kangha (IL 1333) ka~ghera_ comb-maker (H.) Rebus: kangar ‘portable furnace’ Rebus: kangar 1 कंगर् m. a large portable brazier (El.). kãgürü काँग&above;रु&below; or kãgürü काँग&above;रु&below; or kãgar काँग्र् I हसब्तिका f. (sg. dat. kãgrĕ काँग्र्य or kãgarĕ काँगर्य, abl. kãgri काँग्रि), the portable brazier, or *kāngrī,* much used in Kashmīr (K.Pr. *kángár,* 129, 131, 178; *káṅgrí,* 5, 128, 129). For particulars see El. s.v. *kángri;* L. 7, 25, *kangar;* and K.Pr. 129. The word is a fem. dim. of kang, q.v. (Gr.Gr. 37). kãgri-khŏphürü

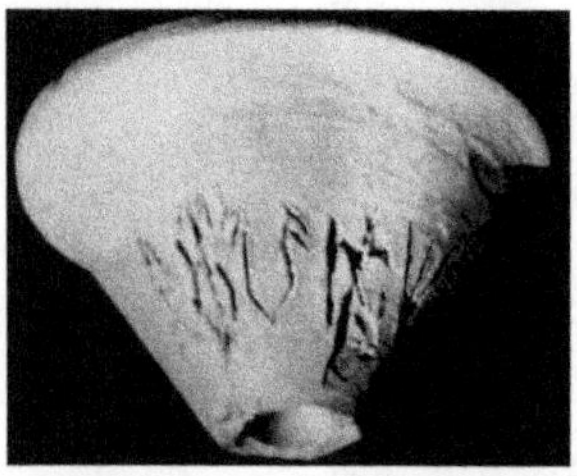

Chandigarh01  9101 
Chandigarh pot ID 3713 Ingot kiln, mint, mine-worker, scribe, mason, iron (worker)

ḍabu ‘an iron spoon’ (Santali) Rebus: ḍab, ḍhimba, ḍhompo ‘lump (ingot?)’, bat.a = wide-mouthed pot; Rebus: bat.a = kiln (Te.)

kamaṭha crab (Skt.) Rebus: kammaṭa = portable furnace (Te.) kampaṭṭam coiner, mint (Ta.)

kan.d.a kanka ‘rim of jar’ (Santali) kan.d.a ‘furnace, fire-altar’ (Santali); khanaka ‘miner’ karNaka ‘scribe’ (Skt.)

Chandigarh02  9102  Chandigarh pot ID 3714
Ingot kiln, fire-altar smithy, mine-worker, scribe

ḍabu ‘an iron spoon’ (Santali) Rebus: ḍab, ḍhimba, ḍhompo ‘lump (ingot?)’, bat.a = wide-mouthed pot; Rebus: bat.a = kiln (Te.)

gan.d.a ‘four’ (Santali) kan.d.a ‘fire-altar’ (Santali); kolmo ‘three’ (Mu.); rebus: kolimi ‘smithy’ (Te.)

kan.d.a kanka ‘rim of jar’ (Santali) kan.d.a ‘furnace, fire-altar’ (Santali); khanaka ‘miner’ karNaka ‘scribe’ (Skt.)

 9103  Chandigarh pot ID 3715 (Metalworker) Guild, jeweller’s polishing stone

sangad.a ‘lathe, furnace’ rebus: samghara ‘guild’ (i.e. living in same house) (Pali)

po_tramu = snout of a hog; po_tri = a hog; a boar (Te.) Rebus: pot = jeweller's polishing stone (Bi.)

 Ropar pot ID 3771 Smithy, iron, tin…

kolmo ‘three’ (Mu.); rebus: kolimi ‘smithy’ (Te.)

ayo ‘fish’(Mu.); ayas ‘iron’ (Skt.)

ranku ‘liquid measure’; rebus: ranku ‘tin’ (Santali

Rupar1A 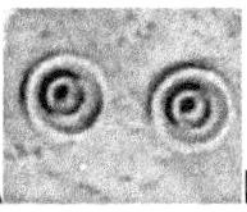Rupar1B  9021Ropar seal Bull ID 3769 Native metal, iron fire-altar, portable furnace

ad.ar 'harrow'; rebus: aduru 'native metal, unsmelted' (Ka.)

ayo 'fish' (Mu.); ayas 'metal, iron' (Pan. Skt.) gan.d.a 'four'; kan.d. 'fire-altar' (Santali)

kangha (IL 1333) ka~ghera_ comb- "comb"maker (H.) Rebus: kangar 'portable furnace' Rebus: kangar 1 कंगर् m. a large portable brazier (El.). kãgürü काँग्ॖ&above;रू&below; or kãgürü काँग&above;रू&below;

or kãgar काँग्ॖरॖ । हसब्तिका f. (sg. dat. kãgrĕ काँग्र्य or kãgarĕ काँगर्य, abl. kãgri काँग्रि), the portable brazier, or *kāngrī,* much used in Kashmīr (K.Pr. *kángár,* 129, 131, 178; *káṅgrí,* 5, 128, 129). For particulars see El. s.v. *kángri;* L. 7, 25, *kangar;* and K.Pr. 129. The word is a fem. dim. of kang, q.v. (Gr.Gr. 37). kãgri-khŏphürü

Dotted cicles: ka_n. 'eye'; ka_n.d. 'iron' as in ayaska_n.d.a 'excellent iron' (Pan. Skt.)

9022Ropar tag Bull ID 3770 Blacksmith, iron artisan (merchant), mine-worker, scribe, fire-altar smithy, workshop, mine-worker, scribe...smithy-guild, bell-metal/brass kiln

ayo 'fish'(Mu.); ayas 'iron' (Skt.)

bar, barea = two (Mu.); Rebus: barī = blacksmith, artisan (Ash.)(CDIAL 9464). barea 'merchant' (Santali)

kanac 'corner' (Santali); Rebus: kancu 'bronze' (Te.) gan.d.a 'four'; rebus: kan.d. 'furnace' (Santali)

gan.d.a 'four' (Santali) kan.d.a 'fire-altar' (Santali); kolmo 'three' (Mu.); rebus: kolimi 'smithy' (Te.)

koḍa 'sluice'; Rebus: koḍ 'artisan's workshop (Kuwi)

kan.d.a kanka 'rim of jar' (Santali) kan.d.a 'furnace, fire-altar' (Santali); khanaka 'miner' karNaka 'scribe' (Skt.)

ku_t.amu = summit of a mountain (Te.lex.) kut.t.ta_ra = a mountain (Skt.lex.) kudharamu = a mountain, a hill (Te.lex.) Rebus: ku_t.a 'guild' (Ka.) kolmo 'three' (Mu.); rebus: kolimi 'smithy' (Te.)

bharna = the name given to the woof by weavers; otor bharna = warp and weft (Santali.lex.) bharna = the woof, cross-thread in weaving (Santali); bharni_ (H.) (Santali.Boding.lex.) Rebus: bhoron = a mixture of brass and bell metal (Santali.lex.) bharan = to spread or bring out from a kiln (P.lex.) bha_ran. = to bring out from a kiln (G.) ba_ran.iyo = one whose profession it is to sift ashes or dust in a goldsmith's workshop (G.lex.) bharant (lit. bearing) is used in the plural in Pan~cavim.s'a Bra_hman.a (18.10.8). Sa_yan.a interprets this as 'the warrior caste' (bharata_m – bharan.am kurvata_m ks.atriya_n.a_m). *Weber notes this as a reference to the Bharata-s. (*Indische Studien*, 10.28.n.2)

urseal16  9846 UrSeal impression; BM 123208; found in the filling of a tomb-shaft (Second Dynasty of Ur). Dia. 2.3; ht. 1.5 cm.; Gadd, PBA 18 (1932), pp. 13-14, pl. III, no. 16; Buchanan, JAOS 74 (1954), p. 149.

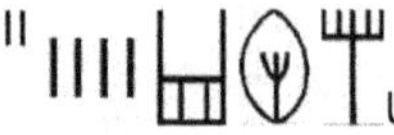 Ur Seal c Bull ID 3793 Blacksmith, native metal ore (nodule/stone) smithy, silver, smithy workshop

ad.ar 'harrow'; rebus: aduru 'native metal, unsmelted' (Ka.)

khaḍā 'circumscribe' (M.); Rebs: khaḍā 'nodule (ore), stone' (M.) kolmo 'paddy plant' (Santali); Rebus: kolimi 'smithy, forge' (Te.) kolom = cutting, graft; to graft, engraft, prune; kolma hoṛo = a variety of the paddy plant (Desi)(Santali.) kolom 'three' (Mu.) Rebus: kolami 'furnace, smithy' (Te.)

khur 'hoof' (M.); rebus: khura silver (Nk.); *kuruku* 'whiteness'; *kuru* brilliancy (Ta.); *kuro* silver (Kol.Nk.Go.)(DEDR 1782). koru = bar of metal (Ta.) *khud.do, khurdo* (Persian *khurdah*) small change in copper; *khurdiyo* a merchant who exchanges copper coins for silver (G.)

kolmo 'three' (Mu.); rebus: kolimi 'smithy' (Te.)

sal stake, spike, splinter, thorn, difficulty (H.); Rebus: sal 'workshop' (Santali)

urseal2  9832 Ur Seal; BM 122187; dia. 2.55; ht. 1.55 cm. Gadd PBA 18 (1932), pp. 6-7, pl. 1, no. 2

 Ur Seal c Bull ID 3794 Blacksmith guild, furnace, iron, tin, iron workshop

bat.a 'quail'; rebus: bat.a 'furnace' (Santali)

ayo 'fish'; rebus: ayas 'iron, metal' (Pan. Skt.)

Guild: khaḍā 'circumscribe' (M.); Rebs: khaḍā 'nodule (ore), stone' (M.) अंकडा [aṅkaḍā] *m* (अंक S) Also अकडा *m* A hook or crook, a curved end gen. (M.) Rebus: अखाडा [ akhāḍā ] *m* ( H) A community, or the common place of residence or of assembly, of persons engaged in study or some particular pursuit; a college, a disputation-hall, a gymnasium, circus, arena. Hence, A club or clubroom; a stand of idlers, loungers, newsmongers, gossips, scamps. 2 An order of men. Ex. गोसाव्यांचे अठरा अखाडे आहेत.(M.)

ranku 'antelope'; rebus: ranku 'tin' (Santali)

med. 'body'; rebus: med. 'iron' (Mu.) sal stake, spike, splinter, thorn, difficulty (H.); Rebus: sal 'workshop' (Santali)

urseal15 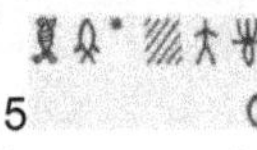 09845 Ur [The first sign looks like an animal with a long tail – as seen from the back and may have been the model for the orthography of Sign 51 as noted in Mahadevan corpus].  Ur Seal c Bull ID 3795 Blacksmith, ingot kiln, iron, metal, iron stone ore ḍhālako = a large metal ingot (G.) ḍhālakī = a metal heated and poured into a mould; a solid piece of metal; an ingot (G.) ḍabu 'an iron spoon' (Santali) Rebus: ḍab, ḍhimba, ḍhompo 'lump (ingot?)', bat.a = wide-mouthed pot; Rebus: bat.a = kiln (Te.)

med. 'body'; rebus: med. 'iron' (Mu.)

ayo 'fish'; rebus: ayas 'metal, iron' (Pan.Skt.)

The Sanskritization of Assamese bicā , deśī vachi is: vṛścika scorpion (RV); vicchika (Pali); vicchia, vim.chia (Pkt.); bich (Sh.); bichī (Ku.); bicā (A.); bichā (B.Or.); būch (Mth.); bīchī (Bhoj.Aw.H.); vīchī, vi~chī (G.); ucum (Pas'.); vichu~ (S.); vicchua, vim.chua (Pkt.); vichu~ (L.); bicchu~ (P.); bichu (Or.); bīchu (Mth.); bicchu~, bīchū (H.); vīchu (G.); viccu, viccua, vim.cua (Pkt.); byucu (K.); biccū (P.); biccū (WPah.); vīcū (M.); viccu, vim.cu (Kon.); bacchius large hornet (n.)(CDIAL 12081). Rebus: bica, bica-diri (Sad. bicā; Or. bicī) stone ore; meṛeḍ bica, stones containing iron; tambabica, copper-ore stones; samṛobica, stones containing gold (Mundari.lex.)

 Desalpur1a 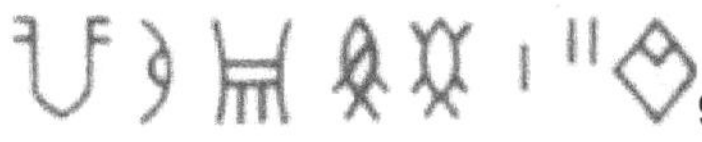 9071 
Desalpur seal ID 3717 Bronze workshop, smelter, iron casting, tin, iron, mine-worker, scribe

kanac 'corner' (Santali); Rebus: kancu 'bronze' (Te.)

sal stake, spike, splinter, thorn, difficulty (H.); Rebus: sal 'workshop' (Santali)

kuṭi = a slice, a bit, a small piece (Santali.lex.Bodding) Rebus: kuṭhi 'iron smelter furnace' (Santali)

ayo 'fish'; rebus: ayas 'metal, iron' (Pan.Skt.) dol 'likeness'; rebus: dul 'cast (metal)' (Santali)

ranku 'antelope'; rebus: ranku 'tin' (Santali)

koṇḍa-miṇḍi eyelid (Go.)(DEDR 4864). Rebus: meḍ 'iron' (Santali. Mundari)

kan.d.a kanka 'rim of jar' (Santali) kan.d.a 'furnace, fire-altar' (Santali); khanaka 'miner' karNaka 'scribe' (Skt.)

 Desalpur2 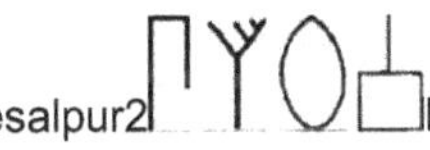 Desalpur seal ID 3718 Tin, nodule (ore) smithy, guild

ranku 'liquid measure'; rebus: ranku 'tin' (Santali)

khaḍā 'circumscribe' (M.); Rebs: khaḍā 'nodule (ore), stone' (M.)

pajhaṛ = to sprout from a root (Santali) Rebus: pasra 'smithy' (Santali)

अंकडा [aṅkaḍā] *m* (अंक S) Also अकडा *m* A hook or crook, a curved end gen. (M.) Rebus: अखाडा [ akhāḍā ] *m* ( H) A community, or the common place of residence or of assembly, of persons engaged in study or some particular pursuit; a college, a disputation-hall, a gymnasium, circus, arena. Hence, A club or clubroom; a stand of idlers, loungers, newsmongers, gossips, scamps. 2 An order of men. Ex. गोसाव्यांचे अठरा अखाडे आहेत.(M.)

Desalpur3  Desalpur tag ID 3719 Mine-worker, scribe, mint workshop, artisan-merchant, native metal smithy

kan.d.a kanka 'rim of jar' (Santali) kan.d.a 'furnace, fire-altar' (Santali); khanaka 'miner' karNaka 'scribe' (Skt.)

kāmaṭhum = a bow; ka_mad.i_, ka_mad.um = a chip of bamboo (G.) ka_maṭhiyo a bowman; an archer (Skt.lex.) Rebus: kammaṭa = portable furnace (Te.) kampaṭṭam coiner, mint (Ta.)

sal stake, spike, splinter, thorn, difficulty (H.); Rebus: sal 'workshop' (Santali)

bar, barea = two (Mu.); Rebus: barī = blacksmith, artisan (Ash.)(CDIAL 9464). barea 'merchant' (Santali)

ad.ar 'harrow'; rebus: aduru 'native metal, unsmelted' (Ka.) kolom = cutting, graft; to graft, engraft, prune; kolma hoṛo = a variety of the paddy plant (Desi)(Santali.) kolom 'three' (Mu.) Rebus: kolami 'furnace, smithy' (Te.)

Rakhigarhi 2

Rakhigarhi Seal ID 3766

Ingot kiln, mint, worker in metal and wood, casting metals in moulds, mint-smithy (pasra)

ḍabu 'an iron spoon' (Santali) Rebus: ḍab, ḍhimba, ḍhompo 'lump (ingot?)', bat.a = wide-mouthed pot; Rebus: bat.a = kiln (Te.)

kāmaṭhum = a bow; ka_mad.i_, ka_mad.um = a chip of bamboo (G.) ka_maṭhiyo a bowman; an archer (Skt.lex.) Rebus: kammaṭa = portable furnace (Te.) kampaṭṭam coiner, mint (Ta.)

badhi 'to ligature, to bandage, to splice, to join by successive rolls of a ligature' (Santali) batā bamboo slips (Kur.); bate = thin slips of bamboo (Malt.)(DEDR 3917). Rebus: baḍhi = worker in wood and metal (Santali) baṛae = blacksmith (Ash.)

baraḍo = spine; backbone; the back; baraḍo thābaḍavo = lit. to strike on the backbone or back; hence, to encourage; baraḍo bhāre thato = lit. to have a painful backbone, i.e. to do something which will call for a severe beating (G.lex.) baraḍ, baraḍu = barren, childless; baranṭu = leanness (Tu.lex.) *maṇuk.o* a single vertebra of the back (G.) Rebus:bharatiyo = a caster of metals; a brazier; bharatar, bharatal, bharataḷ = moulded; an article made in a mould; bharata = casting metals in moulds; bharavum = to fill in; to put in; to pour into (G.lex.) bhart = a mixed metal of copper and lead; bhart-īyā = a barzier, worker in metal; bhat., bhrāṣṭra = oven, furnace (Skt.) bharata = a factitious metal compounded of copper, pewter, tin (M.)

kan.d.a kanka 'rim of jar' (Santali) kan.d.a 'furnace, fire-altar' (Santali); khanaka 'miner' karNaka 'scribe' (Skt.)

kamaṭha crab (Skt.) Rebus: kammaṭa = portable furnace (Te.) kampaṭṭam coiner, mint (Ta.)

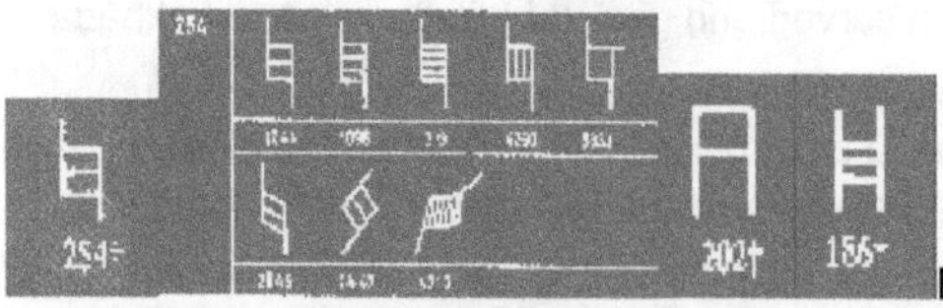

Parpola notes (1994, pp.103-104): "A comparative study of the allographs provides one important means of identifying the iconic meaning of even fairly abstract shapes...the (allograph) continuum)...Taken together, these signs can be understood as pictures of a single object, namely, 'steps, staircase or ladder'; taken individually, such a conclusion would hardly be possible."

*panǰắr* 'ladder, stairs' (Bshk.)(CDIAL 7760) Rebus: pasra 'smithy' (Santali)

Rakhigarhi 1  Rakhigarhi Seal Bull ID 3765 Coppersmith-guild, worker in wood and metal, iron smelter furnace, smithy, casting metal smithy, mine-worker, scribe

koṇḍa-miṇḍi eyelid (Go.)(DEDR 4864). Rebus: meḍ 'iron' (Santali. Mundari)

badhi 'to ligature, to bandage, to splice, to join by successive rolls of a ligature' (Santali) batā bamboo slips (Kur.); bate = thin slips of bamboo (Malt.)(DEDR 3917). Rebus: baḍhi = worker in wood and metal (Santali) baṛae = blacksmith (Ash.)

kuṭi = a slice, a bit, a small piece (Santali.lex.Bodding) Rebus: kuṭhi 'iron smelter furnace' (Santali) kuṭhī factory (A.)(CDIAL 3546) kan.d.a kanka 'rim of jar' (Santali) kan.d.a 'furnace, fire-altar' (Santali); khanaka 'miner' karNaka 'scribe' (Skt.)

kole.l = temple in Kota village (Ko.) Rebus : kole.l smithy (Ko.)

kolmo 'paddy plant'; rebus: kolami 'smithy' (Te.Ka.); dol 'likeness'; rebus: dul 'cast' (i.e. smithy (for) casting metal)

kan.d.a kanka 'rim of jar' (Santali) kan.d.a 'furnace, fire-altar' (Santali); khanaka 'miner' karNaka 'scribe' (Skt.)

Rakhigarhi 65  Rakhigarh tag Bull ID 3767 Same seal impression is repeated. Coppersmith guild, artisan-merchant, native metal iron

era, er-a = eraka = ?nave; erako_lu = the iron axle of a carriage (Ka.M.); cf. irasu (Ka.lex.) [Note Sign 391 and its ligatures Signs 392 and 393 may connote a spoked-wheel, nave of the wheel through which the axle passes; cf. ara_, spoke] eraka, era, er-a = syn. erka, copper, weapons. Rebus: er-r-a = red; eraka = copper (Ka.) erka = ekke (Tbh. of arka) aka (Tbh. of arka) copper (metal); crystal (Ka.lex.) agasa_le, agasa_li, agasa_lava_d.u = a goldsmith (Te.lex.) erka = ekke (Tbh. of arka) aka (Tbh. of arka) copper (metal); crystal (Ka.lex.) cf. eruvai = copper (Ta.lex.) eraka, er-aka = any metal infusion (Ka.Tu.); erako molten cast (Tu.lex.)

bar, barea = two (Mu.); Rebus: barī = blacksmith, artisan (Ash.)(CDIAL 9464). barea 'merchant' (Santali)

ad.ar 'harrow'; rebus: aduru 'native metal, unsmelted' (Ka.) med. 'body'; rebus: med. 'iron' (Mu.)

Alamgirpur Sharma) Late Harappan pottery, a three-legged chakala_(After YD

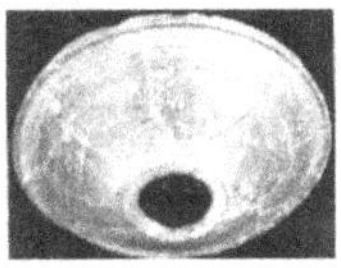

Alamgirpur Agr-1 a(2) graffiti

 9062

 9063Alamgirpur: Late Harappan pottery (After YD Sharma)

Alamgirpur2  Alamgirpur pot ID 3667  Alamgirpur pot ID 3668  Alamgirpur pot ID 3669
Smithy (pasra), fire-altar smithy

pajhaṛ = to sprout from a root (Santali) Rebus: pasra 'smithy' (Santali)

gan.d.a 'four' (Santali) kan.d.a 'fire-altar' (Santali); kolmo 'three' (Mu.); rebus: kolimi 'smithy' (Te.)

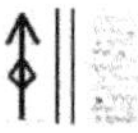 Naru-Waro-Dharo pot ID 3747 …Artisan-merchant iron

bar, barea = two (Mu.); Rebus: barī = blacksmith, artisan (Ash.)(CDIAL 9464). barea 'merchant' (Santali)

ka_n.d.a 'arrow' (Skt.); rebus: ka_n.d.a 'iron' as in ayaska_n.d.a 'excellent iron' (Pan.Skt.)

 Naru-Waro-Dharo pot ID 3748 Smithy, furnace…

kolom = cutting, graft; to graft, engraft, prune; kolma hoṛo = a variety of the paddy plant (Desi)(Santali.) Rebus: kolami 'furnace, smithy' (Te.)

 Naru-Waro-Dharo pot ID 3749 …Smelter furnace mine-worker, scribe…

kuṭi = a slice, a bit, a small piece (Santali.lex.Bodding) Rebus: kuṭhi 'iron smelter furnace' (Santali) kuṭhī factory (A.)(CDIAL 3546) kan.d.a kanka 'rim of jar' (Santali) kan.d.a 'furnace, fire-altar' (Santali); khanaka 'miner' karNaka 'scribe' (Skt.)

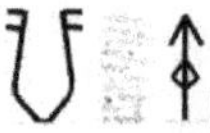 Ra's al-Junayz pot ID 3762 Iron...mine-worker, scribe

ka_n.d.a 'arrow' (Skt.); rebus: ka_n.d.a 'iron' as in ayaska_n.d.a 'excellent iron' (Pan.Skt.)

kan.d.a kanka 'rim of jar' (Santali) kan.d.a 'furnace, fire-altar' (Santali); khanaka 'miner' karNaka 'scribe' (Skt.)

copper seal.  Ra's al-Junayz pot ID 3763 Fire-altar, (gold) smithy

gan.d.a 'four' (Santali) kan.d.a 'fire-altar' (Santali) Vikalpa: pon 'four' (Santali); pon 'metal' (Ta.)

pajhaṛ = to sprout from a root (Santali) Rebus: pasra 'smithy' (Santali)

 Ra's al-Junayz pot ID 3764 ...Iron smithy, mine-worker, scribe

ayo 'fish'; rebus: ayas 'iron, metal' (Pan.Skt.)

kolmo 'three'; rebus: kolami 'smithy, forge' (Te.)

kan.d.a kanka 'rim of jar' (Santali) kan.d.a 'furnace, fire-altar' (Santali); khanaka 'miner' karNaka 'scribe' (Skt.)

Surkotada pot ID Surkotada pot ID 3776

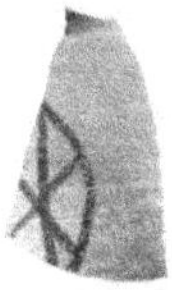

3775 Surkotada 4 9094 Surkotada 7. Molten cast copper

era, er-a = eraka = ?nave; erako_lu = the iron axle of a carriage (Ka.M.); cf. irasu (Ka.lex.) [Note Sign 391 and its ligatures Signs 392 and 393 may connote a spoked-wheel, nave of the wheel through which the axle passes; cf. ara_, spoke] eraka, era, er-a = syn. erka, copper, weapons. Rebus: er-r-a = red; eraka = copper (Ka.) erka = ekke (Tbh. of arka) aka (Tbh. of arka) copper (metal); crystal (Ka.lex.) agasa_le, agasa_li, agasa_lava_d.u = a goldsmith (Te.lex.) erka = ekke (Tbh. of arka) aka (Tbh. of arka) copper (metal); crystal (Ka.lex.) cf. eruvai = copper (Ta.lex.) eraka, er-aka = any metal infusion (Ka.Tu.); erako molten cast (Tu.lex.)

Surkotada 6 9095Surkotada pot ID 3777Surkotada3c

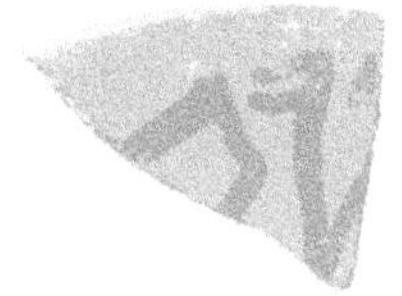

9093Surkotada pot ID 3778 Bronze smelter furnace mine-worker, scribe...

kanac 'corner' (Santali); Rebus: kancu 'bronze' (Te.)

kuṭi = a slice, a bit, a small piece (Santali.lex.Bodding) Rebus: kuṭhi 'iron smelter furnace' (Santali) kuṭhī factory (A.)(CDIAL 3546) kan.d.a kanka 'rim of jar' (Santali) kan.d.a 'furnace, fire-altar' (Santali); khanaka 'miner' karNaka 'scribe' (Skt.)

Surkotada1 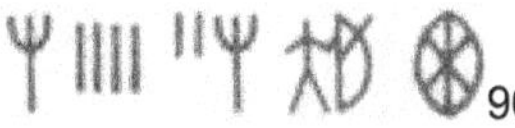9091Surkotada seal Bull ID 3779 Molten cast copper, mint, smithy workshop, fire-altar furnace-smithy

era, er-a = eraka = ?nave; erako_lu = the iron axle of a carriage (Ka.M.); cf. irasu (Ka.lex.) [Note Sign 391 and its ligatures Signs 392 and 393 may connote a spoked-wheel, nave of the wheel through which the axle passes; cf. ara_, spoke] eraka, era, er-a = syn. erka, copper, weapons. Rebus: er-r-a = red; eraka = copper (Ka.) erka = ekke (Tbh. of arka) aka (Tbh. of arka) copper (metal); crystal (Ka.lex.) agasa_le, agasa_li, agasa_lava_d.u = a goldsmith (Te.lex.) erka = ekke (Tbh. of arka) aka (Tbh. of arka) copper (metal); crystal (Ka.lex.) cf. eruvai = copper (Ta.lex.) eraka, er-aka = any metal infusion (Ka.Tu.); erako molten cast (Tu.lex.)

kamāt.hiyo = archer; kāmaṭhum = a bow; ka_mad.i_, ka_mad.um = a chip of bamboo (G.) ka_maṭhiyo a bowman; an archer (Skt.lex.) Rebus: kammaṭa = portable furnace (Te.) kampaṭṭam coiner, mint (Ta.)

kolom = cutting, graft; to graft, engraft, prune; kolma hoṛo = a variety of the paddy plant (Desi)(Santali.) Rebus: kolami 'furnace, smithy' (Te.)

sal stake, spike, splinter, thorn, difficulty (H.); Rebus: sal 'workshop' (Santali)

gan.d.a 'four' (Santali) kan.d.a 'fire-altar' (Santali) Vikalpa: pon 'four' (Santali); pon 'metal' (Ta.)

kolom = cutting, graft; to graft, engraft, prune; kolma hoṛo = a variety of the paddy plant (Desi)(Santali.) Rebus: kolami 'furnace, smithy' (Te.)

 Surkotada 2 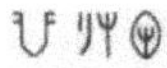 9092  Surkotada seal ID 3774 Nodule-stone ore smithy, furnace, worker in wood and metal, mine-worker, scribe

khaḍā 'circumscribe' (M.); Rebs: khaḍā 'nodule (ore), stone' (M.) kolmo 'paddy plant' (Santali); Rebus: kolimi 'smithy, forge' (Te.) kolom = cutting, graft; to graft, engraft, prune; kolma hoṛo = a variety of the paddy plant (Desi)(Santali.) kolom 'three' (Mu.) Rebus: kolami 'furnace, smithy' (Te.)

kolom = cutting, graft; to graft, engraft, prune; kolma hoṛo = a variety of the paddy plant (Desi)(Santali.) Rebus: kolami 'furnace, smithy' (Te.)

badhi 'to ligature, to bandage, to splice, to join by successive rolls of a ligature' (Santali) batā bamboo slips (Kur.); bate = thin slips of bamboo (Malt.)(DEDR 3917). Rebus: baḍhi = worker in wood and metal (Santali) baṛae = blacksmith (Ash.)

kan.d.a kanka 'rim of jar' (Santali) kan.d.a 'furnace, fire-altar' (Santali); khanaka 'miner' karNaka 'scribe' (Skt.)

Balakot 06 bangle Balakot 06C Balakot 06bangle 

Bala-kot Bangle ID 3690 Mint mine-worker, scribe

kamatha crab (Skt.) Rebus: kammat.a = portable furnace (Te.) kampat.t.am coiner, mint (Ta.)

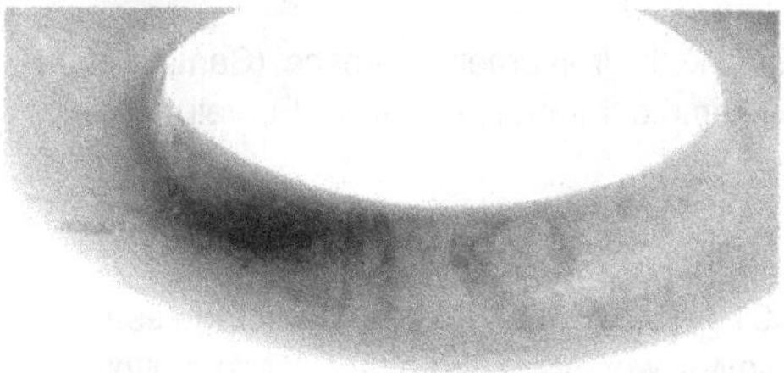

kan.d.a kanka 'rim of jar' (Santali) kan.d.a 'furnace, fire-altar' (Santali); khanaka 'miner' karNaka 'scribe' (Skt.)

 Balakot01 

Coppersmith guild, smithy, mint, forge, (iron) metal fire-altar

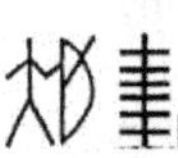 Bala-kot Seal Bull ID 3685 ingot kiln, brass-bellmetal workshop, smithy-

*panǰár* 'ladder, stairs' (Bshk.)(CDIAL 7760) Rebus: pasra 'smithy' (Santali)

kamāt.hiyo = archer; kāmaṭhum = a bow; ka_mad.i_, ka_mad.um = a chip of bamboo (G.) ka_maṭhiyo a bowman; an archer (Skt.lex.) Rebus: kammaṭa = portable furnace (Te.) kampaṭṭam coiner, mint (Ta.)

d.hālako = a large metal ingot (G.) d.hālakī = a metal heated and poured into a mould; a solid piece of metal; an ingot (G.) d.abu 'an iron spoon' (Santali) Rebus: d.ab, d.himba, d.hompo 'lump (ingot?)', bat.a = wide-mouthed pot; Rebus: bat.a = kiln (Te.)

bharna = the name given to the woof by weavers; otor bharna = warp and weft (Santali.lex.) bharna = the woof, cross-thread in weaving (Santali); bharni_ (H.) (Santali.Boding.lex.) Rebus: bhoron = a mixture of brass and bell metal (Santali.lex.) bharan = to spread or bring out from a kiln (P.lex.) bha_ran. = to bring out from a kiln (G.) ba_ran.iyo = one whose profession it is to sift ashes or dust in a goldsmith's workshop (G.lex.) bharant (lit. bearing) is used in the plural in Pan~cavim.s'a Bra_hman.a (18.10.8). Sa_yan.a interprets this as 'the warrior caste' (bharata_m – bharan.am kurvata_m ks.atriya_n.a_m). *Weber notes this as a reference to the Bharata-s. (*Indische Studien*, 10.28.n.2)

sal stake, spike, splinter, thorn, difficulty (H.); Rebus: sal 'workshop' (Santali)

kolmo 'three' (Mu.); Rebus: kolami 'furnace, smithy' (Te.)

gan.d.a 'four' (Santali) kan.d.a 'fire-altar' (Santali) ayo 'fish' (Mu.); rebus: ayas 'iron, metal' (Pan.Skt.)

Balakot 04  Bala-kot Seal Bull ID 3686 Coppersmith guild, smithy, brass-bellmetal, artisan's workshop, building manager, silver smithy

kole.l = temple in Kota village (Ko.) Rebus : kole.l smithy (Ko.)

 ko_d.i a kind of flag, an image of garud.a, basava, or other demi-god set upon a long post before a temple; cf. gud.i, temple (Ka.lex.) Rebus: kod., 'artisan's workshop' (Kuwi)

sal stake, spike, splinter, thorn, difficulty (H.); Rebus: sal 'workshop' (Santali)

kat.a = stride; rebus: *kat.* To build, manage (house) (Ka.); *kat.t.e* platform build under tree on village green (Ka.); *kat.t.ad.a* a building (Ka.); *kat.t.alme* building (Tu.); *kat.t.ad.amu* building (Te.); *ghat.t.a* quay, landing-place, bathing place (Skt.)(DEDR 1147)

khur 'hoof' (M.); rebus: khura silver (Nk.); *kuruku* 'whiteness'; *kuru* brilliancy (Ta.); *kuro* silver (Kol.Nk.Go.)(DEDR 1782). koru = bar of metal (Ta.) *khud.do, khurdo* (Persian *khurdah*) small change in copper; *khurdiyo* a merchant who exchanges copper coins for silver (G.)

kolom = cutting, graft; to graft, engraft, prune; kolma hoṛo = a variety of the paddy plant (Desi)(Santali.) Rebus: kolami 'furnace, smithy' (Te.)

Balakot 02  Bala-kot Seal Bull ID 3687 Coppersmith guild, ...Iron hearth...

loa 'fig leaf' (Santali): Rebus: lo 'iron' (Assamese, Bengali); loa 'iron' (Gypsy)

Glyph: *lo* = nine (Santali); *no* = nine (B.) *on-patu* = nine (Ta.)

ayo 'fish'; rebus:  ayas 'iron' (Pan.Skt.) bhed.a hako a species of fish (Santali) bedha cross-grained (Santali) Rebus: bed.a either of the sides of a hearth Thus, ayo bhed.a, this glyph connotes the hearth (bed.a) for ayas.

Balakot 03  Bala-kot Seal Bull ID 3688 Coppersmith guild, workshop brass-bell metal, mint, silver smithy

kole.l = temple in Kota village (Ko.) Rebus : kole.l smithy (Ko.)

bharna = the name given to the woof by weavers; otor bharna = warp and weft (Santali.lex.) bharna = the woof, cross-thread in weaving (Santali); bharni_ (H.) (Santali.Boding.lex.) Rebus: bhoron = a mixture of brass and bell metal (Santali.lex.) bharan = to spread or bring out from a kiln (P.lex.) bha_ran. = to bring out from a kiln (G.) ba_ran.iyo = one whose profession it is to sift ashes or dust in a goldsmith's workshop (G.lex.) bharant (lit. bearing) is used in the plural in Pan~cavim.s'a Bra_hman.a (18.10.8). Sa_yan.a interprets this as 'the warrior caste' (bharata_m – bharan.am kurvata_m ks.atriya_n.a_m). *Weber notes this as a reference to the Bharata-s. (*Indische Studien*, 10.28.n.2)

 ko_d.i = a kind of flag, an image of garud.a, basava, or other demi-god set upon a long post before a temple; cf. gud.i, temple (Ka.lex.) Rebus: kod., 'artisan's workshop' (Kuwi)

kamaṭha crab (Skt.) Rebus: kammaṭa = portable furnace (Te.) kampaṭṭam coiner, mint (Ta.)

khur 'hoof' (M.); rebus: khura silver (Nk.); *kuruku* 'whiteness'; *kuru* brilliancy (Ta.); *kuro* silver (Kol.Nk.Go.)(DEDR 1782). koru = bar of metal (Ta.) *khud.do, khurdo* (Persian *khurdah*) small change in copper; *khurdiyo* a merchant who exchanges copper coins for silver (G.)

kolom = cutting, graft; to graft, engraft, prune; kolma hoṛo = a variety of the paddy plant (Desi)(Santali.) Rebus: kolami 'furnace, smithy' (Te.)

Balakot 05 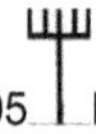 Bala-kot Seal Antelope ID 3689 Ironsmith, iron, native metal

ka_n.d.a 'arrow'; rebus: ka_n.d.a 'iron' (ayaska_n.d.a 'excellent iron')(Pan.Skt.)

ad.ar 'harrow'; rebus: aduru 'native metal, unsmelted' (Ka.)

me~d.ha 'antelope'; med. ;'iron' (Mu.)

 Nausharo01 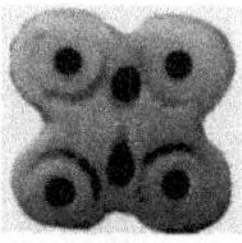 Nausharo02 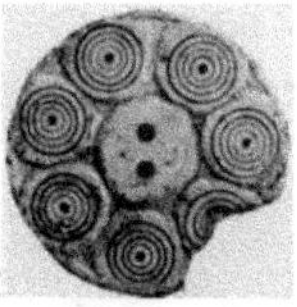 Nausharo03 Blacksmith, iron

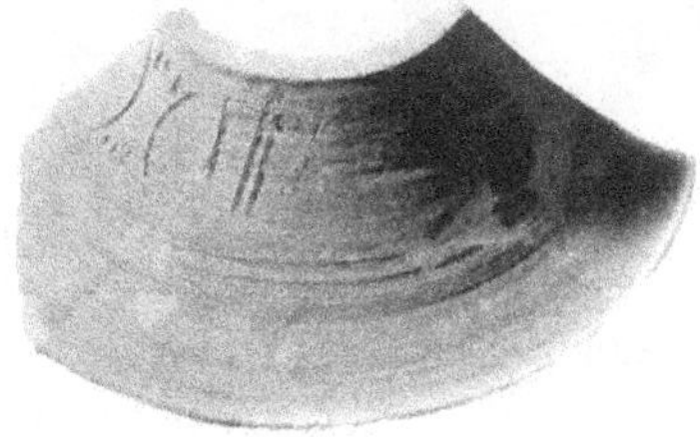

Nausharo04  Nausharo Pot ID 3750 Smelter furnace, cast metal smithy, nodule (ore)/stone

kut.i 'woman water carrier' (Te.); kut.hi 'smelter furnace' (Santali)

kolmo 'three' (Mu.); Rebus: kolami 'furnace, smithy' (Te.); dol 'likeness'; dul 'cast (metal)' (Santali) khad.ā 'circumscribe' (M.); Rebs: khad.ā 'nodule (ore), stone' (M.)

Nausharo05  Nausharo Seal Bull ID 3751 Coppersmith guild, molten cast copper workshop, smithy metal cast, forge, iron, mine-worker, scribe,

era, er-a = eraka = ?nave; erako_lu = the iron axle of a carriage (Ka.M.); cf. irasu (Ka.lex.) [Note Sign 391 and its ligatures Signs 392 and 393 may connote a spoked-wheel, nave of the wheel through which the axle passes; cf. ara_, spoke] eraka, era, er-a = syn. erka, copper, weapons. Rebus: er-r-a = red; eraka = copper (Ka.) erka = ekke (Tbh. of arka) aka (Tbh. of arka) copper (metal); crystal (Ka.lex.) agasa_le, agasa_li, agasa_lava_d.u = a goldsmith (Te.lex.) erka = ekke (Tbh. of arka) aka (Tbh. of arka) copper (metal); crystal (Ka.lex.) cf. eruvai = copper (Ta.lex.) eraka, er-aka = any metal infusion (Ka.Tu.); erako molten cast (Tu.lex.)

sal stake, spike, splinter, thorn, difficulty (H.); Rebus: sal 'workshop' (Santali)

kolmo 'three'; rebus: kolami 'smithy, forge' (Te.); dol 'likeness'; dul 'cast (metal)(Santali) ayo 'fish'; rebus: ayas 'iron ,metal' (Pan.Skt.)

kan.d.a kanka 'rim of jar' (Santali) kan.d.a 'furnace, fire-altar' (Santali); khanaka 'miner' karNaka 'scribe' (Skt.)

med. 'body'; rebus: med. 'iron' (Mu.)

Nausharo06  Nausharo Seal Bull ID 3752 Coppersmith guild, metal, worker in wood and metal, bell-metal, brass, iron

koṇḍa-miṇḍi eyelid (Go.)(DEDR 4864). Rebus: meḍ 'iron' (Santali. Mundari)

badhi 'to ligature, to bandage, to splice, to join by successive rolls of a ligature' (Santali) batā bamboo slips (Kur.); bate = thin slips of bamboo (Malt.)(DEDR 3917). Rebus: baḍhi = worker in wood and metal (Santali) baṛae = blacksmith (Ash.)

Sign 67 *ken.t.ai* carp (Ta.); gan.d.e = a fish (Te.lex.) The glyphs of ligatured fin: cet.t.ai fin (Ta.); cat.t.upa wing (Te.)(DEDR 2764) Rebus, substantive: ke~r.e~ bell-metal, brass (Santali).

ka_n.d.a 'arrow'; rebus: ka_n.d.a 'iron' (as in ayaska_n.d.a 'excellent iron') (Pan.Skt.)

era, er-a = eraka = ?nave; erako_lu = the iron axle of a carriage (Ka.M.); cf. irasu (Ka.lex.) [Note Sign 391 and its ligatures Signs 392 and 393 may connote a spoked-wheel, nave of the wheel through which the axle passes; cf. ara_, spoke] eraka, era, er-a = syn. erka, copper, weapons. Rebus: er-r-a = red; eraka = copper (Ka.) erka = ekke (Tbh. of arka) aka (Tbh. of arka) copper (metal); crystal (Ka.lex.) agasa_le, agasa_li, agasa_lava_d.u = a goldsmith (Te.lex.) erka = ekke (Tbh. of arka) aka (Tbh. of arka) copper (metal); crystal (Ka.lex.) cf. eruvai = copper (Ta.lex.) eraka, er-aka = any metal infusion (Ka.Tu.); erako molten cast (Tu.lex.)

sal stake, spike, splinter, thorn, difficulty (H.); Rebus: sal 'workshop' (Santali)

kolmo 'three'; rebus: kolami 'smithy, forge' (Te.)

kolom = cutting, graft; to graft, engraft, prune; kolma hoṛo = a variety of the paddy plant (Desi)(Santali.) Rebus: kolami 'furnace, smithy' (Te.)

Nausharo08  Nausharo Seal Bull ID 3754 Coppersmith guild, jeweller's polishing stone, smithy, mine-worker, scribe

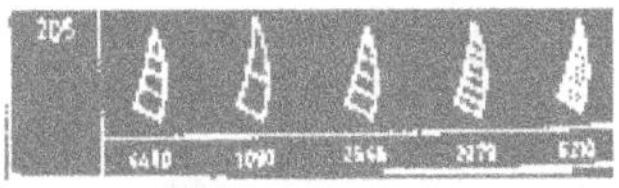

V205 Sign 205 and variants: po_tramu = snout of a hog; po_tri = a hog; a boar (Te.) Rebus: pot = jeweller's polishing stone (Bi.) Vikalpa: son.d.a = a tusk, as of wild boar, elephant (Santali.lex.) sonda = a billhook, for cutting fire wood (Santali.lex.)

kolmo 'three' (Mu.); rebus: kolami 'smithy,. Forge' (Te.)

kan.d.a kanka 'rim of jar' (Santali) kan.d.a 'furnace, fire-altar' (Santali); khanaka 'miner' karNaka 'scribe' (Skt.)

Nausharo Seal Other ID 3755 Nodule (ore)/stone workshop, jeweller's polishing stone, ingot kiln, brass-bellmetal smithy workshop…iron workshop, mine-worker, scribe kod.a ‘in arithmetic, one’ (Santali); rebus: kod. ‘artisan’s workshop’ (Kuwi) khad.ā ‘circumscribe’ (M.); Rebs: khad.ā ‘nodule (ore), stone’ (M.) kod. ‘horn’; kod. ‘artisan’s workshop’ (Kuwi)

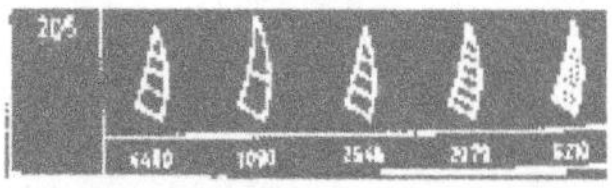
V205 Sign 205 and variants: po_tramu = snout of a hog; po_tri = a hog; a boar (Te.) Rebus: pot = jeweller's polishing stone (Bi.) Vikalpa: son.d.a = a tusk, as of wild boar, elephant (Santali.lex.) sonda = a billhook, for cutting fire wood (Santali.lex.)

d.hālako = a large metal ingot (G.) d.hālakī = a metal heated and poured into a mould; a solid piece of metal; an ingot (G.) ḍabu ‘an iron spoon’ (Santali) Rebus: d.ab, d.himba, d.hompo ‘lump (ingot?)’, bat.a = wide-mouthed pot; Rebus: bat.a = kiln (Te.)

bharna = the name given to the woof by weavers; otor bharna = warp and weft (Santali.lex.) bharna = the woof, cross-thread in weaving (Santali); bharni_ (H.) (Santali.Boding.lex.) Rebus: bhoron = a mixture of brass and bell metal (Santali.lex.) bharan = to spread or bring out from (P.lex.) bha_ran. = to bring out from a kiln (G.) ba_ran.iyo = one whose profession it is to sift ashes or dust in a goldsmith's workshop (G.lex.) bharant (lit. bearing) is used in the plural in Pan~cavim.s'a Bra_hman.a (18.10.8). Sa_yan.a interprets this as ‘the warrior caste’ (bharata_m – bharan.am kurvata_m ks.atriya_n.a_m). *Weber notes this as a reference to the Bharata-s. (*Indische Studien*, 10.28.n.2)

pajhaṛ = to sprout from a root (Santali) Rebus: pasra ‘smithy’ (Santali)

sal stake, spike, splinter, thorn, difficulty (H.); Rebus: sal ‘workshop’ (Santali)

kod.a ‘in arithmetic, one’ (Santali); rebus: kod. ‘artisan’s workshop’ (Kuwi) med. ‘body’; rebus: med. ‘iron’ (Mu.)

kan.d.a kanka ‘rim of jar’ (Santali) kan.d.a ‘furnace, fire-altar’ (Santali); khanaka ‘miner’ karNaka ‘scribe’ (Skt.)

9051 Kot-diji Kot-Diji Pot ID 3736 Smithy, iron smelter furnace, bronze,mine-worker, scribe, blacksmith, artisan, iron

Kolmo ‘three’; rebus: kolami ‘smithy,forge’ (Te.)

bat.a ‘pot’; bat.a ‘smelter’ (Santali) med. ‘body’; rebus: med. ‘iron’ (Mu.)

kanac ‘corner’ (Santali); rebus: kancu ‘bronze’ (Te.)

kut.i = a slice, a bit, a small piece (Santali.lex.Bodding) Rebus: kut.hi ‘iron smelter furnace’ (Santali) kut.hī factory (A.)(CDIAL 3546) kan.d.a kanka ‘rim of jar’ (Santali) kan.d.a ‘furnace, fire-altar’ (Santali); khanaka ‘miner’ karNaka ‘scribe’ (Skt.)

bar, barea = two (Mu.); Rebus: barī = blacksmith, artisan (Ash.)(CDIAL 9464).

ayo ‘fish’; rebus: ayas ‘iron, metal’ (Pan.Skt.)

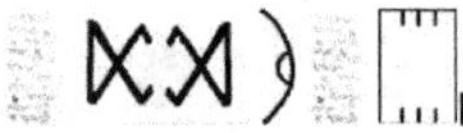Kot-Diji Pot ID 3737 Granary…iron, mint, metal casting…

कोष्ठ [ kōs.t.ha ] *m* A granary. An apartment.

kon.d.a-min.di eyelid (Go.)(DEDR 4864). Rebus: meḍ ‘iron’ (Santali. Mundari) kamad.ha crab (Skt.) Rebus: kammat.a = portable furnace (Te.) kampat.t.am coiner, mint (Ta.) dol 'likeness' ; rebus : dul 'cast (metal)(Santali)

Kot-Diji Pot ID 3738 Copper, iron, smithy, forge

eraka 'upraised arm' (Te.); eraka 'copper' (Te.) med. 'body'; rebus: med. 'iron' (Mu.)

Kolmo 'three' (Mu.); rebus: kolami 'smithy, forge' (Te.)

 Kot-Diji Pot ID 3739 ...Mine-worker, scribe

kan.d.a kanka 'rim of jar' (Santali) kan.d.a 'furnace, fire-altar' (Santali); khanaka 'miner' karNaka 'scribe' (Skt.)

 Kot-Diji Pot ID 3740 ...Mine-worker, scribe

kan.d.a kanka 'rim of jar' (Santali) kan.d.a 'furnace, fire-altar' (Santali); khanaka 'miner' karNaka 'scribe' (Skt.)

Kot-Diji Pot ID 3741 Smelter furnace

kut.i 'woman water carrier' (Te.); kut.hi 'smelter furnace' (Santali)

Kot-Diji Pot ID 3742 Coppersmithy forge

kolmo 'three' (Mu.); rebus: kolami 'smithy, forge' (Te.) tebra 'three' (Santali); ta(m)bra 'copper'; tibira 'merchant' (Akkadian)

 Kot-Diji Pot ID 3743 ...smelter-furnace workshop

bat.a 'pot'; rebus: bat.a 'smelter furnace'(Mu.)

sal stake, spike, splinter, thorn, difficulty (H.); Rebus: sal 'workshop' (Santali)

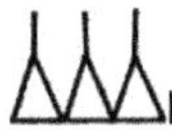Kot-Diji Pot ID 3744 Smithy guild

ku_t.amu = summit of a mountain (Te.lex.) kut.t.ta_ra = a mountain (Skt.lex.) kudharamu = a mountain, a hill (Te.lex.) Rebus: ku_t.a 'guild' (Ka.) kolmo 'three' (Mu.); rebus: kolimi 'smithy' (Te.)

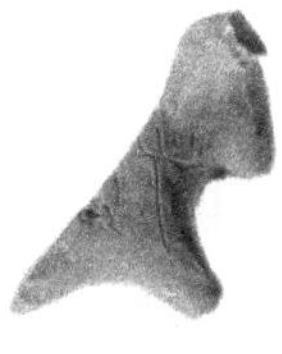

Allahdino (Nel Bazaar)11 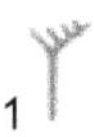 9061 Metal fire-altar, smithy gaṇḍa set of four (Santali) kaṇḍa 'fire-altar' (Santali) Vikalpa: pon 'four' (Santali); pon 'metal' (Ta.)

kolmo 'three' (Mu.); rebus: kolimi 'smithy' (Te.)

pajhaṛ = to sprout from a root (Santali) Rebus: pasra 'smithy' (Santali)

 Allahdino Misc. ID 368 Native metal...

ad.ar 'harrow'; rebus: aduru 'native metal, unsmelted' (Ka.)

Allahdino (Nel Bazaar)09  Allahdino Pot ID 3678 Metal (worker) guild, fire-altar…

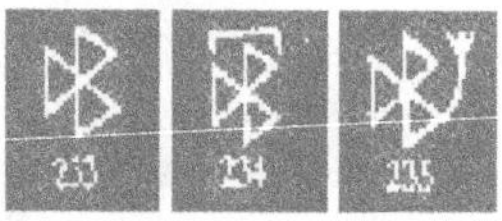


Sign 233 gets ligatured to create Signs 234 and 235 Sign 235 could be an allograph of mountain-summit glyph. ku_t.amu = summit of a mountain (Te.lex.) kut.t.ta_ra = a mountain (Skt.lex.) kudharamu = a mountain, a hill (Te.lex.) Rebus: ku_t.a 'guild' (Ka.) kolmo 'three' (Mu.); rebus: kolimi 'smithy' (Te.)

gan.d.a set of four (Santali) kan.d.a 'fire-altar' (Santali) Vikalpa: pon 'four' (Santali); pon 'metal' (Ta.)

 Allahdino Pot ID 3679 …iron

ayo 'fish'; rebus: ayas 'iron, metal' (Pan. Skt.)

Allahdino (Nel Bazaar)01  Allahdino Seal Bull ID 3670 Coppersmith guild,Tin, smithy, mine-worker, scribe

ranku 'liquid measure'; rebus: ranku 'tin' (Santali)

kolom = cutting, graft; to graft, engraft, prune; kolma hoṛo = a variety of the paddy plant (Desi)(Santali.) Rebus: kolami 'furnace, smithy' (Te.)

kan.d.a kanka 'rim of jar' (Santali) kan.d.a 'furnace, fire-altar' (Santali); khanaka 'miner' karNaka 'scribe' (Skt.)

Allahdino (Nel Bazaar)06  Allahdino Seal Bull ID 3671 Coppersmith guild, copper merchant, mint, smithy workshop

kolmo 'three' (Mu.); rebus: kolami 'smithy, forge' (Te.) tebra 'three' (Santali); ta(m)bra 'copper'; tibira 'merchant' (Akkadian) kamāt.hiyo = archer; kāmaṭhum = a bow; ka_mad.i_, ka_mad.um = a chip of bamboo (G.) ka_mat.hiyo a bowman; an archer (Skt.lex.) Rebus: kammat.a = portable furnace (Te.) kampat.t.am coiner, mint (Ta.)

kolom = cutting, graft; to graft, engraft, prune; kolma hoṛo = a variety of the paddy plant (Desi)(Santali.) Rebus: kolami 'furnace, smithy' (Te.)

ko_d.i a kind of flag, an image of garud.a, basava, or other demi-god set upon a long post before a temple; cf. gud.i, temple (Ka.lex.) Rebus: kod., 'artisan's workshop' (Kuwi)

Allahdino (Nel Bazaar)02 Allahdino Seal Bull ID 3672
Coppersmith guild, iron native metal, copper merchant, nodule (ore)/stone cast (metal), mine-worker, scribe

ad.aren 'lid'; Rebus: aduru 'native metal' (Santali) Hence, ayo adar 'iron native metal' (Maybe a reference to unsmelted mketeoric iron.)

d.hālako = a large metal ingot (G.) d.hālakī = a metal heated and poured into a mould; a solid piece of metal; an ingot (G.) ḍabu 'an iron spoon' (Santali) Rebus: d.ab, d.himba, d.hompo 'lump (ingot?)', bat.a = wide-mouthed pot; Rebus: bat.a = kiln (Te.)

kolmo 'three' (Mu.); rebus: kolami 'smithy, forge' (Te.) tebra 'three' (Santali); ta(m)bra 'copper'; tibira 'merchant' (Akkadian)

dol 'likeness'; dul 'cast (metal)' (Santali) khad.ā 'circumscribe' (M.); Rebs: khad.ā 'nodule (ore), stone' (M.)

kan.d.a kanka 'rim of jar' (Santali) kan.d.a 'furnace, fire-altar' (Santali); khanaka 'miner' karNaka 'scribe' (Skt.)

Allahdino (Nel Bazaar)03Allahdino Seal Bull ID 3673
Coppersmith guild, nodule (ore)/stone, iron smelter furnace, fire-altar, native metal iron guild, fire-altar smithy, mine-worker, scribe

अंकडा [aṅkaḍā] *m* (अंक S) Also अकडा *m* A hook or crook, a curved end gen. (M.) Rebus: अखाडा [ akhāḍā ] *m* ( H) A community, or the common place of residence or of assembly, of persons engaged in study or some particular pursuit; a college, a disputation-hall, a gymnasium, circus, arena. Hence, A club or clubroom; a stand of idlers, loungers, newsmongers, gossips, scamps. 2 An order of men. Ex. गोसाव्यांचे अठरा अखाडे आहेत.(M.) Rebs: khaḍā 'nodule (ore), stone' (M.)

kuṭi = a slice, a bit, a small piece (Santali.lex.Bodding) Rebus: kuṭhi 'iron smelter furnace' (Santali) kuṭhī factory (A.)(CDIAL 3546) kan.d.a kanka 'rim of jar' (Santali) kan.d.a 'furnace, fire-altar' (Santali); khanaka 'miner' karNaka 'scribe' (Skt.)

ad.aren 'lid'; Rebus: aduru 'native metal' (Santali) Hence, ayo adar 'iron native metal' (Maybe a reference to unsmelted mketeoric iron.)

ku_t.amu = summit of a mountain (Te.lex.) kut.t.ta_ra = a mountain (Skt.lex.) kudharamu = a mountain, a hill (Te.lex.) Rebus: ku_t.a 'guild' (Ka.)

gaṇḍa set of four (Santali) kaṇḍa 'fire-altar' (Santali) Vikalpa: pon 'four' (Santali); pon 'metal' (Ta.)

kolmo 'three' (Mu.); rebus: kolimi 'smithy' (Te.)

kan.d.a kanka 'rim of jar' (Santali) kan.d.a 'furnace, fire-altar' (Santali); khanaka 'miner' karNaka 'scribe' (Skt.)

Allahdino (Nel Bazaar)04 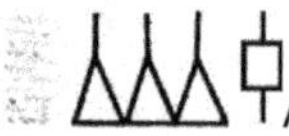Allahdino Seal Bull ID 3674 Coppersmith guild, tin, smithy-guild...

Ranku 'liquid measure'; rebus: ranku 'tin' (Santali)

ku_t.amu = summit of a mountain (Te.lex.) kut.t.ta_ra = a mountain (Skt.lex.) kudharamu = a mountain, a hill (Te.lex.) Rebus: ku_t.a 'guild' (Ka.) kolmo 'three' (Mu.); rebus: kolimi 'smithy' (Te.)

Allahdino (Nel Bazaar)05 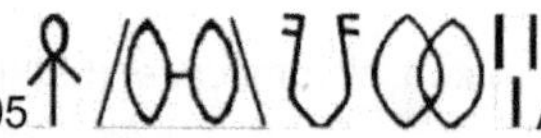Allahdino Seal Rhinoceros ID 3675 Guild of workers in iron and wood, iron-smelter workshop guild, mine-worker, scribe, metal ingot, iron

badhia 'castrated boar' (Santali) Rebus: bad.hi 'a caste who work both in iron and wood' (Santali) bar.ae = a blacksmith; bar.ae kudlam = a country made hoe, in contrast to cala_ni kudlam, an imported hoe; bar.ae mer.ed – country smelted iron; bar.ae muruk = the energy of a blacksmith (Mundari.lex.) bar.ae = bad.ae (Santali.lex.) bari_ = blacksmith, artisan (Ash.)(CDIAL 9464). The occurrence of bari_ in Ash. (CDIAL 9464) and bar.ae in Mundari and of vardhaka in Skt. point to the early phonetic form: bard.a; semantic: worker in iron and wood, artisan. Thus, it is suggested that the depiction of the backbone, barad.o is rebus for bard.a, artisan. barduga = a man of acquirements, a proficient man (Ka.)

sal stake, spike, splinter, thorn, difficulty (H.); Rebus: sal 'workshop' (Santali) kuṭi = a slice, a bit, a small piece (Santali.lex.Bodding) Rebus: kuṭhi 'iron smelter furnace' (Santali) kuṭhī factory (A.)(CDIAL 3546) Vikalpa: kolmo 'three' (Mu.); rebus: kolami 'smithy, forge' (Te.)

sanghat.t.a2 (?) bangle (Pali); rebus: samghara 'guild, community' (Skt.) sanghara 'living in the same house' (Pali)

kan.d.a kanka 'rim of jar' (Santali) kan.d.a 'furnace, fire-altar' (Santali); khanaka 'miner' karNaka 'scribe' (Skt.)

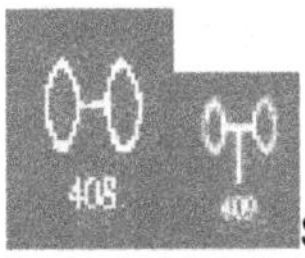

Sign 409: glyph: cart: gad.i 'cart' (Santali) Rebus : gat.t.i = ingot, as in: gat.t.i-ban:ga_ramu = gold ingot (Te.)

ka_n.d.a 'arrow'; rebus: ka_n.d.a 'iron' (as in ayaska_n.d.a 'excellent iron') (Pan.Skt.)

Notes: bari_ = blacksmith, artisan (Ash.)(CDIAL 9464). bar.ae = bad.ae (Santali.lex.) bar.ae = a blacksmith. "Although their physique, their language and their customs generally point to a Kolarian origin, they constitute a separate caste, which the Mundas consider as inferior to themselves, and the Baraes accept their position with good grace, the more so as no contempt is shown to them. ...In every Munda village of some size there is at least one family of Baraes...The ordinary village smith is versed in the arts of iron-smelting, welding and tempering, and in his smithy, which is generally under one of the fine old large trees that form the stereotyped feature of the Mundari village, are forged from start to finish, all the weapons and the instruments and implements the Mundas require. There are of course individuals who succeed better than others in the making of arrows and various kinds of hunting-axes and these attract customers from other villages... they dig the kut.i (smelting furnace), they prepare and lay the bamboo tubes through which the air is driven from the bellows to the bottom of the furnace, they re-arrange the furnace after the lump of molten metal has been removed from it, and then the smith starts transforming it into ploughshares, hoes, yoking hooks and rings, arrow-heads, hunting axes of various shapes and sizes, wood axes, knives, his own implements, ladles, neat little pincers to extract thorns from hands and feet, needles for sewing mats and even razors. Formerly, he was also forging swords...susun-kanda (dancing-sword)...If it appears too bold to attribute the invention of iron smelting and working to some of the aboriginal inhabitants of this, in many respects so richly blessed part of India (Chota Nagpur), it is certain that no land in the world is better qualified to push man to this invention. The excavations made recently (in 1915) by Mr. Sarat Chandra Roy, the author of the *Mundas and their Country* have shown conclusively, that it was inhabited by man in the stone age, the copper age and the early iron age. Baraes are also found in the villages of Jashpur, Barwai, Biru, Nowagarh, Kolebira and Bano from which the Mundas have been either driven out by the Hindus or crowded out by the Uraons. There they have adopted the Sadani dialect but retained their own social and religious customs. In the districts named above they are called lohar or loha_ra, but in Gangpur they go under the name of Kamar. These Kamars are animists like the Lohars, but they use tanned hides for their single bellows, which they work by bulling, like the blacksmiths in Europe. The Lohars say that is is on account of this that they do not intermarry or eat with them any more. Baraes, Kamars and Lohars must not be confounded with the Aryan blacksmiths also called Lohars. These latter differ not only in race from the first but also in their methods of working. The Aryan blacksmith does not smelt iron, and uses only the single-nozzled hand bellows. He is met with only in such Chota Nagpur villages, where colonies of Hindu or Mohammedan landlords, merchants, money-lenders and native policement require his services, especially to get their bullocks and horses shod...The account the Baraes, Lohars and Kamars generally give of themselves is as follows: they say that they descend from Asura and Asurain, i.e., Asur and his wife, and that they were originally of one and the same caste with the Mundas. In this the Mundas agree with them... If the iron smelters and workers of the legend really belonged to the Munda race then their trade and art must in the beginning have given them a prominent position, such as is held in some ancient races by smiths...Like the Mundas they formerly burnt their dead, the bones of those dying out of their original village were carried back to it in a small earthen vessel into which some pice were placed, and this was then dashed to pieces against a rock in a river...Like the Mundas they practise ancestor worship in practically the same forms. Like them they worship Sin:bon:ga, whom the Lohars call Bhagwan... They also worship Baranda Buru whom the Sadani-speaking lohars call Bar Pahari...bar.ae-ili = the rice beer which has been brewed by the whole village, one pot per house, in honour of the Barae, and is drunk with him, at the end of the year; bar.ae-kud.lam = a country-made hoe, bar.ae-mer.ed = country-smelted iron; in contrast to cala_ni mer.ed, imported iron; bar.ae-muruk = the energy of a blacksmith." (Mundari.lex., *Encyclopaedia Mundarica*, Vol. II, pp. 410-419).

bar.hi, bar.hi_-mistri_, bar.u_i_, bar.u_i_-mistri_ (Sad.H. barha_i_) = a professional carpenter. This class of artisans is not found in purely Munda villages because every Munda knows carpentry enough for all his own purposes; trs. caus., to make somebody become a professional carpenter; intr., to call someone a carpenter; cina ka_m koko bar.hi_akoa? What kind of artisans are called carpenters; bar.hi-n rflx. v., to train oneself for, or to undertake, the work of a professional carpenter; bar.hi_-o, v., to become a professional carpenter; bar.hi_ kami = the work, the proession of carpenter, carpentry; bar.hi_-mistri_ a professional carpenter (Mundari.lex.)

bad.ohi = a worker in wood, a village carpenter; bad.hor.ia = expert in working in wood; bad.hoe = a carpenter, worker in wood; bad.horia = adj. Who works in wood; (as a scolding to children who use a carpenter's implements) mischievous (Santali.lex.) ba_r. blade of a khukri (N.); badhri_, badha_ru_ knife with a heavy blade for reaping with (Bi.); ba_r.h, ba_r. = edge of knife (H.); va_d.h (G.); ba_r.h = book-binders papercutter (Bi.); brdha_n.u_ = to sheer sheep (WPah.)(CDIAL 11371). vardha a cutting (Skt.); vad.hu a cut (S.)(CDIAL 11372). vardh- = to cut (Skt.); vardhaka carpenter (R.); bardog, bardox axe (Kho.); wadok (Kal.); wa_t. axe (Wg.); wa_t.ak (Pas'.)(CDIAL 11374). bad.gi, bad.gya_ carpenter (Kon.lex.) bad.hi, bar.hi mistri, bad.hoe, bad.ohi, kat. bad.hoe carpenter (Santali.lex.) bad.agi, bad.a_yi, bad.iga, bad.igi, bad.ige, bad.igya_, bad.d.agi (Tadbhava of vardhaki) a carpenter; bad.agitana carpentry (Ka.lex.) Image: stick: bar.ga, bar.iya stick (Kuwi); bur.ga stick, club; badga walking stick (Kuwi); bar.ga, bad.ga, bad.d.e, bad.d.i, bar.iya, war.iya_ stick (Go.); bar.iya stick (Pa.); vat.i small cane or stick; vat.ippu iron rod (Ta.); vat.i stick, staff, club or armed brahmans, shaft, stroke; vat.ikka to strike; vat.ippikka to have the measure struck (Ma.); bad.i, bad.e, bod.i, bod.e to beat, strike, thrash, bang, pound; n. beating, blow, castration, a short thick stick, cudgel; bad.ike beating; bad.ige stick, staff, cudgel, hammer, mallet; bad.isu to cause to beat; bad.ukatana beating, etc.; ba_y bad.i to prevent one from speaking, silence one (Ka.); bad.i (bad.ip-, bad.ic-) to hammer, pound; ba.y bad.i- to bawl out (Kod..); bad.ipuni, bad.iyuni to strike, beat, thrash; bad.u stick, cudgel (Tu.); bad.ita, bad.iya, bad.e thick stick, cudgel (Te.); bed.ta club; bad.ya walking stick (Kol.); bad.iga big walking stick; bad.ga stick (Kond.a); bad.ge stick, staff (Pe.); bad.ga stick (Mand..); bad.ga_ cudgel, stick; bad.vin.e~ to bruise, beat (M.)(DEDR 5224). bharia a carrying stick (Santali.lex.) vad.aga_ a stick, staff (M.); bad.iko_l a staff for striking, beating or pounding; bad.i-man.i an instrument for levelling a surface by beating; bad.iho_ri a gelded young bull (Ka.)(Ka.lex.) vardhaka =in cmpd. = cutting (Skt.); ci_vara-vad.d.haka = tailor; vad.d.haki = carpenter, building mason; vad.d.hai_ = carpenter (Pkt.); vad.d.haia = shoemaker (Pkt.); ba_d.ho_i_ = carpenter (WPah.); ba_d.hi (WPah.); bar.hai, bar.ahi (N.); ba_rai (A.); ba_r.ai, ba_r.ui (B.); bar.hai_, bar.ha_i, ba_r.hoi (Or.); bar.ahi_ (Bi.); bar.hai_ (Bhoj.); va_d.ha_ya_ (M.); vad.u-va_ (Si.); vardhaki carpenter (MBh.); vad.d.haki carpenter, building mason (Pali)(CDIAL 11375). vad.hin.i_ cutting (S.); vardhana cutting, slaughter (Mn.)(CDIAL 11377). vad.d.ha_pe_ti cuts (moustache)(Pali); badhem I cut, shear (Kal.); so_r-berde_k custom of cutting an infant's original hair (Kho.); bad.n.o_ to cut, (K.); vad.han.u (S.); vad.d.han. to cut, reap (L.); ba_d.hna_ to cut, shear (H.)(CDIAL 11381). va_d.ho carpenter (S.); va_d.d.hi_, ba_d.d.hi_ (P.)(CDIAL 11568). bed.i_r sledgehammer (Kho.); bad.il (Gaw.); bad.i_r (Bshk.); bad.hi_r axe (Phal.); sledgehammer (Phal.)(CDIAL 11385).

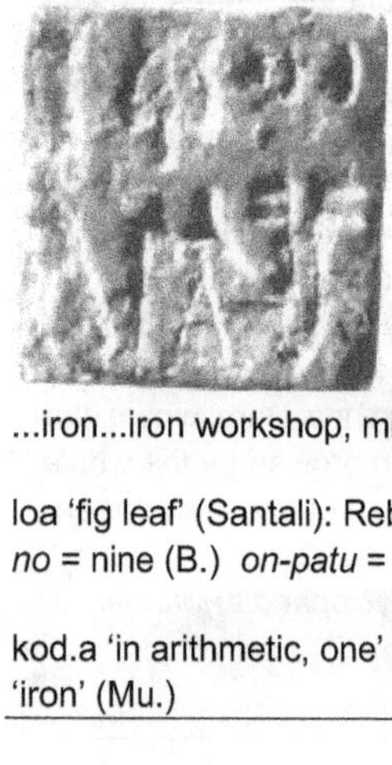

Allahdino (Nel Bazaar)07 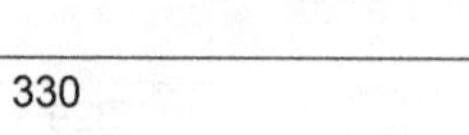 Allahdino Seal ID 3676

...iron...iron workshop, mine-worker, scribe

loa 'fig leaf' (Santali): Rebus: lo 'iron' (Assamese, Bengali); loa 'iron' (Gypsy) Glyph: *lo* = nine (Santali); *no* = nine (B.) *on-patu* = nine (Ta.)

kod.a 'in arithmetic, one' (Santali); rebus: kod. 'artisan's workshop' (Kuwi) med. 'body'; rebus: med. 'iron' (Mu.)

kan.d.a kanka 'rim of jar' (Santali) kan.d.a 'furnace, fire-altar' (Santali); khanaka 'miner' karNaka 'scribe' (Skt.)

Allahdino (Nel Bazaar)08 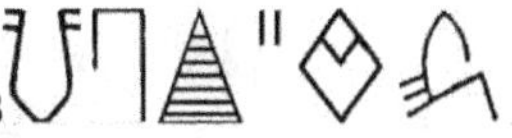 Allahdino Seal Elephant ID 3677 Iron guild, bronze workshop, metal guild, mine-worker, scribe

Ibha 'elephant'; rebus: ib 'iron' (Santali)

baraḍo = spine; backbone; the back; baraḍo thābaḍavo = lit. to strike on the backbone or back; hence, to encourage; baraḍo bhāre thato = lit. to have a painful backbone, i.e. to do something which will call for a severe beating (G.lex.) baraḍ, baraḍu = barren, childless; baranṭu = leanness (Tu.lex.) *maṇuk.o* a single vertebra of the back (G.) Rebus:bharatiyo = a caster of metals; a brazier; bharatar, bharatal, bharataḷ = moulded; an article made in a mould; bharata = casting metals in moulds; bharavum = to fill in; to put in; to pour into (G.lex.) bhart = a mixed metal of copper and lead; bhart-īyā = a barzier, worker in metal; bhat., bhrāṣṭra = oven, furnace (Skt.) bharata = a factitious metal compounded of copper, pewter, tin (M.)

kanac 'corner' (Santali); Rebus: kancu 'bronze' (Te.)

sal stake, spike, splinter, thorn, difficulty (H.); Rebus: sal 'workshop' (Santali)

ku_t.amu = summit of a mountain (Te.lex.) kut.t.ta_ra = a mountain (Skt.lex.) kudharamu = a mountain, a hill (Te.lex.) Rebus: ku_t.a 'guild' (Ka.)

अंकडा [aṅkaḍā] *m* (अंक S) Also अकडा *m* A hook or crook, a curved end gen. (M.) Rebus: अखाडा [ akhāḍā ] *m* ( H) A community, or the common place of residence or of assembly, of persons engaged in study or some particular pursuit; a college, a disputation-hall, a gymnasium, circus, arena. Hence, A club or clubroom; a stand of idlers, loungers, newsmongers, gossips, scamps. 2 An order of men. Ex. गोसाव्यांचे अठरा अखाडे आहेत.(M.)

kan.d.a kanka 'rim of jar' (Santali) kan.d.a 'furnace, fire-altar' (Santali); khanaka 'miner' karNaka 'scribe' (Skt.)

 Allahdino Seal ID 3680 Iron native metal, mine-worker, scribe

 ad.aren 'lid'; Rebus: aduru 'native metal' (Santali) Hence, ayo adar 'iron native metal' (Maybe a reference to unsmelted mketeoric iron.)

kan.d.a kanka 'rim of jar' (Santali) kan.d.a 'furnace, fire-altar' (Santali); khanaka 'miner' karNaka 'scribe' (Skt.)

Dholavira Sign-board mounted on a gateway.

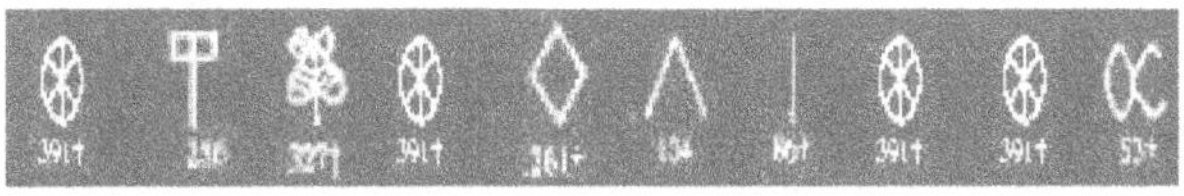

 Dholavira Misc. ID 3722

Message on Dholavira Signboard: metal services at a smithyDholavira Sign board mounted on gate to announce to seafarers: molten cast furnace, mint, moltencast copperwork, native-metalwork, iron-smelter workshop; metal-caster-mineral-smith

era = knave of wheel; rebus: era = copper; erako = molten cast (G.)

kund opening in the nave or hub of a wheel to admit the axle (Santali) kundam, kund a sacrificial fire-pit (Skt.)

khu~ṭi = pin (M.) kuṭi= furnace (Santali)

kamaḍha = ficus religiosa (Skt.); kamaṭa = portable furnace for melting precious metals (Te.); kampaṭṭam = mint (Ta.)

kana, kanac = corner (Santali); kan~cu = bronze (Te.) kan- copper work (Ta.)

aḍaren, ḍaren lid, cover (Santali) Rebus: aduru 'native metal' (Ka.)

kuṭi = a slice, a bit, a small piece (Santali.lex.Bodding) Rebus: kuṭhi 'iron smelter furnace' (Santali) kuṭhī factory (A.)(CDIAL 3546) Vikalpa: goṭ = one (Santali); goṭi = silver (G.) Vikalpa: kod.a 'in arithmetic, one' (Santali); rebus: kod. 'artisan's workshop' (Kuwi)

barea = two (Ka.); bar.ea = blacksmith (Santali)[A pair of glyphs showing nave of wheel, i.e. metal-caster-smith]

d.ato = claws of crab (Santali); dhātu = mineral (Skt.)

Vikalpa:

Nave of wheel: eraka; rebus: eraka, (copper) 'metal infusion'

Pair 'barea'; rebus: baṛea 'merchant' (vikalpa: dul 'cast metal'; dol 'likeness')

Claws of crab 'kamaṭha'; rebus: kampaṭṭam 'mint'

One 'met'; rebus: meḍ 'iron'

Lid 'aḍaren'; rebus: aduru 'native metal'

Fig leaf 'loa'; rebus: loh '(copper) metal'

Peg 'khuṇṭa'; rebus: kūṭa 'workshop'

· Dholavira sign-board on the Gateway of the citadel. Mounted on the façade of the gate, the sign-board would have commanded the entire cityscape.

· Each of the ten signs 37cm. high, is made of crystalline rock.

· The wooden plank is about 3 m. long.

· Bottom: Close up of the first three signs from left to right.

· The 'spoked-wheel' sign seems to be the divider of a three-part message.

Dholavira (Kotda) on Kadir island, Kutch, Gujarat; 10 signs inscription found near the western chamber of the northern gate of the citadel high mound (Bisht, 1991: 81, Pl. IX); each sign is 37 cm. high and 25 to 27 cm. wide and made of pieces of white crystalline rock; the signs were apparently inlaid in a wooden plank ca. 3 m. long; maybe, the plank was mounted on the facade of the gate to command the view of the entire cityscape. Ten signs are read from left to right. The 'spoked circle' sign seems to be the divider of the three-part message. (Bisht, R.S., 1991, Dholavira: a new horizon of the Indus Civilization. *Puratattva*, Bulletin of Indian Archaeological Society, 20: 81; now also Parpola 1994: 113).

 Dholavira 2a Dholavira Seal ID 3721 Bronze workshop...

kanac 'corner' (Santali); Rebus: kancu 'bronze' (Te.) sal stake, spike, splinter, thorn, difficulty (H.); Rebus: sal 'workshop' (Santali)

Dholavira Seal ID 3813 Ingot kiln, silver, iron smelter furnace, mine-worker, scribe

d.abu 'an iron spoon' (Santali) Rebus: d.ab, d.himba, d.hompo 'lump (ingot?)', bat.a = wide-mouthed pot; Rebus: bat.a = kiln (Te.)

khur 'hoof' (M.); rebus: khura silver (Nk.); *kuruku* 'whiteness'; *kuru* brilliancy (Ta.); *kuro* silver (Kol.Nk.Go.)(DEDR 1782). koru = bar of metal (Ta.) *khud.do, khurdo* (Persian *khurdah*) small change in copper; *khurdiyo* a merchant who exchanges copper coins for silver (G.)

loa 'fig leaf' (Santali): Rebus: lo 'iron' (Assamese, Bengali); loa 'iron' (Gypsy) Glyph: *lo* = nine (Santali); *no* = nine (B.) *on-patu* = nine (Ta.)

kut.i 'woman water carrier' (Te.); kut.hi 'smelter furnace' (Santali) kan.d.a kanka 'rim of jar' (Santali) kan.d.a 'furnace, fire-altar' (Santali); khanaka 'miner' karNaka 'scribe' (Skt.)

Dholavira Seal ID 3814 Tin smithy, nodule(ore)/stone blacksmith/artisan

ranku 'liquid measure'; rebus: ranku 'tin' (Santali)

pajhaṛ = to sprout from a root (Santali) Rebus: pasra 'smithy' (Santali)

khad.ā 'circumscribe' (M.); Rebs: khad.ā 'nodule (ore), stone' (M.)

bar, barea = two (Mu.); Rebus: barī = blacksmith, artisan (Ash.)(CDIAL 9464). barea 'merchant' (Santali)

Dholavira Seal ID 3815 Bronze workshop, cast (metal) furnace, smithy, forge

kanac 'corner' (Santali); Rebus: kancu 'bronze' (Te.) sal stake, spike, splinter, thorn, difficulty (H.); Rebus: sal 'workshop' (Santali)

kolmo 'three' (Mu.); Rebus: kolami 'furnace, smithy' (Te.); dol 'likeness'; rebus: dul 'cast (metal)' (Santali)

kolom = cutting, graft; to graft, engraft, prune; kolma hoṛo = a variety of the paddy plant (Desi)(Santali.) Rebus: kolami 'furnace, smithy' (Te.)

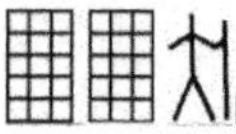Dholavira Seal ID 3816 Iron workshop, cast (metal) furnace

kod.a 'in arithmetic, one' (Santali); rebus: kod. 'artisan's workshop' (Kuwi) med. 'body'; rebus: med. 'iron' (Mu.)

khaṇḍ 'division'; rebus: kaṇḍ 'furnace' (Santali) dol 'likeness'; rebus: dul 'cast (metal)' (Santali)

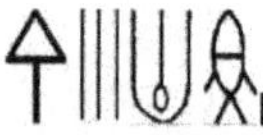Dholavira Seal ID 3817 Iron hearth, ingot furnace, copper-, iron-smithy

bhed.a hako a species of fish (Santali) bedha cross-grained (Santali) Rebus: bed.a either of the sides of a hearth Thus, ayo bhed.a, this glyph connotes the hearth (bed.a) for ayas.

ḍabu 'an iron spoon' (Santali) Rebus: ḍab, ḍhimba, ḍhompo 'lump (ingot?)', bat.a = wide-mouthed pot; Rebus: bat.a = kiln (Te.)

kolmo 'three' (Mu.); rebus: kolami 'smithy, forge' (Te.) tebra 'three' (Santali); ta(m)bra 'copper'; tibira 'merchant' (Akkadian)

ka_n.d.a 'arrow'; rebus: ka_n.d.a 'iron' (as in ayaska_n.d.a 'excellent iron') (Pan.Skt.)

Dholavira Seal ID 3818 Tin smithy, iron artisan's workshop, mine-worker, scribe

ranku 'liquid measure'; rebus: ranku 'tin' (Santali)

pajhaṛ = to sprout from a root (Santali) Rebus: pasra 'smithy' (Santali)

med. 'body'; rebus: med. 'iron'; kod. 'horn'; rebus: kod. 'artisan's workshop' (Kuwi)

kan.d.a kanka 'rim of jar' (Santali) kan.d.a 'furnace, fire-altar' (Santali); khanaka 'miner' karNaka 'scribe' (Skt.)

Dholavira1a  9121  Dholavira Seal Bull ID Coppersmith guild, bronze artisan's workshop, iron smelter furnace

kanac 'corner' (Santali); Rebus: kancu 'bronze' (Te.) sal stake, spike, splinter, thorn, difficulty (H.); Rebus: sal 'workshop' (Santali)

kod.a 'in arithmetic, one' (Santali); rebus: kod. 'artisan's workshop' (Kuwi)

loa 'fig leaf' (Santali): Rebus: lo 'iron' (Assamese, Bengali); loa 'iron' (Gypsy) Glyph: *lo* = nine (Santali); *no* = nine (B.) *on-patu* = nine (Ta.)

kut.i 'woman water carrier' (Te.); kut.hi 'smelter furnace' (Santali)

Dholavira Seal Bull ID 3805 Coppersmith guild, artisan-merchant, mint, smelter furnace

bar, barea = two (Mu.); Rebus: barī = blacksmith, artisan (Ash.)(CDIAL 9464). barea 'merchant' (Santali)

kamāt.hiyo = archer; kāmat.hum = a bow; ka_mad.i_, ka_mad.um = a chip of bamboo (G.) ka_mat.hiyo a bowman; an archer (Skt.lex.) Rebus: kammat.a = portable furnace (Te.) kampat.t.am coiner, mint (Ta.)

kut.i 'woman water carrier' (Te.); kut.hi 'smelter furnace' (Santali)

Dholavira Seal Bull ID 3806 Coppersmith guild, cast (metal) fire-altar workshop, smelter furnace, mine worker, scribe

gaṇḍa set of four (Santali) kaṇḍa 'fire-altar' (Santali) Vikalpa: pon 'four' (Santali); pon 'metal' (Ta.) dol 'likeness'; rebus: dul 'cast (metal)(Santali)

sal stake, spike, splinter, thorn, difficulty (H.); Rebus: sal 'workshop' (Santali)

kut.i 'woman water carrier' (Te.); kut.hi 'smelter furnace' (Santali) kan.d.a kanka 'rim of jar' (Santali) kan.d.a 'furnace, fire-altar' (Santali); khanaka 'miner' karNaka 'scribe' (Skt.)

Dholavira Seal Composite animal ID 3807 Metal smithy guild, iron-smelter workshop...mine-worker-scribe workshop, cast metal smithy, mine-worker-scribe; mine-worker-scribe workshop, cast metal mint

Composite animal: sangad.a 'joined animals'; samghara 'guild'; the animals denote metals. The parts of the following animals are used to create the composite animal glyph; these can be read rebus:

Elephant, rhinoceros, tiger, tiger looking back, heifer, antelope, bull, bos indicus (zebu):

Ibha, badhia, kol, krammara kol

damṛa, melh, bail, adar ḍangra

Iron (ib), carpenter(badhi), smithy (kol 'pancaloha'), alloy-smith (kol kamar)

tam(b)ra copper, milakkhu copper, bali (iron sand ore), native metal (aduru), ḍhangar 'smith'

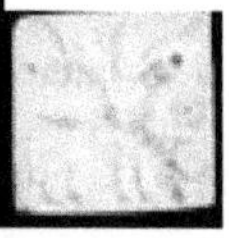 These seals with composite animals can be decoded: Blacksmith, iron sand ore, iron, copper

med. 'body'; rebus: med. 'iron' (Mu.)

damr.a 'heifer'; rebus: tam(b)ra 'copper' (Skt.)

bail 'ox'; rebus: bali 'iron sand ore' (Mu.)

me~d.ha 'antelope'; krammara 'looking back'; med. 'iron'; kamar 'blacksmith' (Santali)

sa sal stake, spike, splinter, thorn, difficulty (H.); Rebus: sal 'workshop' (Santali) kuṭi = a slice, a bit, a small piece (Santali.lex.Bodding) Rebus: kuṭhi 'iron smelter furnace' (Santali) kuṭhī factory (A.)(CDIAL 3546)

sa sal stake, spike, splinter, thorn, difficulty (H.); Rebus: sal 'workshop' (Santali) kan.d.a kanka 'rim of jar' (Santali) kan.d.a 'furnace, fire-altar' (Santali); khanaka 'miner' karNaka 'scribe' (Skt.)

kolmo 'paddy plant'; rebus: kolami 'smithy' (Te.Ka.); dol 'likeness'; rebus: dul 'cast' (i.e. smithy (for) casting metal)

kan.d.a kanka 'rim of jar' (Santali) kan.d.a 'furnace, fire-altar' (Santali); khanaka 'miner' karNaka 'scribe' (Skt.)

sa sal stake, spike, splinter, thorn, difficulty (H.); Rebus: sal 'workshop' (Santali) kan.d.a kanka 'rim of jar' (Santali) kan.d.a 'furnace, fire-altar' (Santali); khanaka 'miner' karNaka 'scribe' (Skt.)

kamaṭha crab (Skt.) Rebus: kammaṭa = portable furnace (Te.) kampaṭṭam coiner, mint (Ta.) dol 'likeness' ; rebus : dul 'cast (metal)(Santali)

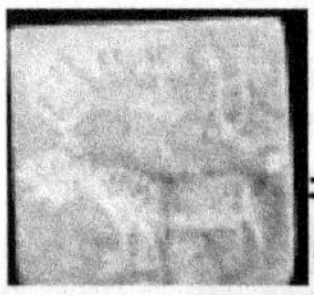 Dholavira Seal Tiger ID 3808 Smithy for alloy of five metals (kol), bronze workshop, cast native metal, mine-worker, scribe

kanac 'corner' (Santali); Rebus: kancu 'bronze' (Te.)

sal stake, spike, splinter, thorn, difficulty (H.); Rebus: sal 'workshop' (Santali)

ad.ar 'harrow'; rebus: aduru 'native metal, unsmelted' (Ka.) dol 'likeness'; rebus: dul 'cast (metal)(Mu.) Doubling of harrow spikes thus connotes cast (native metal)

kan.d.a kanka 'rim of jar' (Santali) kan.d.a 'furnace, fire-altar' (Santali); khanaka 'miner' karNaka 'scribe' (Skt.)

Dholavira Seal Bull ID 3809 Coppersmith guild, nodule (ore), metal ingot, iron smelter furnace

d.hālako = a large metal ingot (G.) d.hālakī = a metal heated and poured into a mould; a solid piece of metal; an ingot (G.) khad.ā 'circumscribe' (M.); Rebs: khad.ā 'nodule (ore), stone' (M.)

med. 'body'; rebus: med. 'iron' (Mu.) kuṭi = a slice, a bit, a small piece (Santali.lex.Bodding) Rebus: kuṭhi 'iron smelter furnace' (Santali)

Coppersmith guild, bell-metal-brass, iron (artisans) guild...

Sign 67 *ken.t.ai* carp (Ta.); gan.d.e = a fish (Te.lex.) The glyphs of ligatured fin: cet.t.ai fin (Ta.); cat.t.upa wing (Te.)(DEDR 2764) Rebus, substantive: ke~r.e~ bell-metal, brass.

ku_t.amu = summit of a mountain (Te.lex.) kut.t.ta_ra = a mountain (Skt.lex.) kudharamu = a mountain, a hill (Te.lex.) Rebus: ku_t.a 'guild' (Ka.) kolmo 'three' (Mu.); rebus: kolimi 'smithy' (Te.)

ayo 'fish'; rebus: ayas 'iron, metal' (Pan.Skt.)

kan.d.a kanka 'rim of jar' (Santali) kan.d.a 'furnace, fire-altar' (Santali); khanaka 'miner' karNaka 'scribe' (Skt.)

Coppersmithy guild, nodule (ore)-stone smithy workshop, bronze

khad.ā 'circumscribe' (M.); Rebs: khad.ā 'nodule (ore), stone' (M.)

kolmo 'paddy plant'; rebus: kolami 'smithy' (Te.Ka.);

ranku 'liquid measure'; rebus: ranku 'tin' (Santali)

sal stake, spike, splinter, thorn, difficulty (H.); Rebus: sal 'workshop' (Santali)

kanac 'corner' (Santali); Rebus: kancu 'bronze' (Te.)

Dholavira Seal Bull ID 3810 Coppersmith guild, bronze workshop, nodule (ore) smithy, cast native-metal, iron, smelter-furnace-bronze, mine-worker-scribe, smelter-furnace-fire-altar

sal stake, spike, splinter, thorn, difficulty (H.); Rebus: sal 'workshop' (Santali)

kanac 'corner' (Santali); Rebus: kañcu 'bronze' (Te.)

*khaḍā* 'circumscribe' (M.); Rebs: *khaḍā* 'nodule (ore), stone' (M.) kolmo 'paddy plant' (Santali); Rebus: kolimi 'smithy, forge' (Te.) kolom = cutting, graft; to graft, engraft, prune; kolma hor.o = a variety of the paddy plant (Desi)(Santali.) kolom 'three' (Mu.) Rebus: kolami 'furnace, smithy' (Te.)

*aḍar* 'harrow'; rebus: aduru 'native metal, unsmelted' (Ka.) dol 'likeness'; rebus: dul 'cast (metal)(Mu.) Doubling of harrow spikes thus connotes cast (native metal)

ayo 'fish'; rebus: ayas 'iron, metal' (Pan.Skt.)

*kuṭi* = a slice, a bit, a small piece (Santali.lex.Bodding) Rebus: *kuṭhi* 'iron smelter furnace' (Santali) kut.hī factory (A.)(CDIAL 3546)

kanac 'corner' (Santali); Rebus: kañcu 'bronze' (Te.)

*kaṇḍa kanka* 'rim of jar' (Santali) *kaṇḍ* 'furnace, fire-altar' (Santali); khanaka 'miner' karNaka 'scribe' (Skt.)

 gaṇṭavēṭa = batfowling, nightfowling wherein lights and lowbells are used; *gaṇṭa* = bat (Te.lex.) rebus: *kaṇḍ* 'fire-altar, furnace' (Santali)

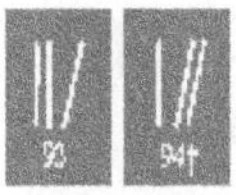 *gaṇḍe* 'to place at a right angle to something else, cross, transverse'; *gaṇḍ gaṇḍ.* 'across, at right angles, transversely' (Santali) [Note: A slanted line Lahṇḍa writing of accounts connotes a quarter; a straight line connotes 'one'.]

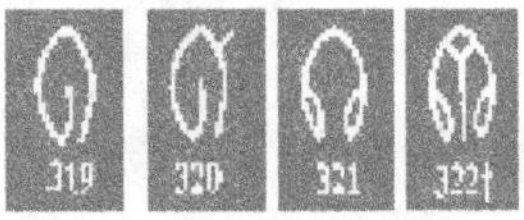 Orthography of Sign 319 is difficult to decode and interpret as a pictograph.

If the pattern is related to Sign 322, this sign's variants provide some clue  V322 Possibly, this is a stylized rendering of the water-carrier glyph which can be decoded:

*kuṭi* 'woman water carrier' (Te.); kuṭhi 'smelter furnace' (Santali)

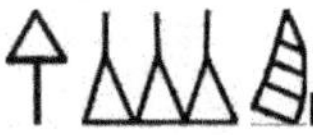Dholavira Seal Bull ID 3811 Coppersmith guild, smithy guild, iron

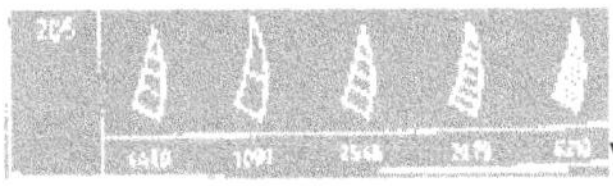V205 Sign 205 and variants: po_tramu = snout of a hog; po_tri = a hog; a boar (Te.) Rebus: pot = jeweller's polishing stone (Bi.) Vikalpa: son.d.a = a tusk, as of wild boar, elephant (Santali.lex.) sonda = a billhook, for cutting fire wood (Santali.lex.)

ku_t.amu = summit of a mountain (Te.lex.) kut.t.ta_ra = a mountain (Skt.lex.) kudharamu = a mountain, a hill (Te.lex.) Rebus: ku_t.a 'guild' (Ka.) kolmo 'three' (Mu.); rebus: kolimi 'smithy' (Te.)

ka_n.d.a 'arrow' (Skt.); rebus: ka_n.d.a 'iron' as in ayaska_n.d.a 'excellent iron' (Pan.Skt.)

Dholavira Seal ID 3812 Smithy guild, iron

ku_t.amu = summit of a mountain (Te.lex.) kut.t.ta_ra = a mountain (Skt.lex.) kudharamu = a mountain, a hill (Te.lex.) Rebus: ku_t.a 'guild' (Ka.) kolmo 'three' (Mu.); rebus: kolimi 'smithy' (Te.)

ka_n.d.a 'arrow' (Skt.); rebus: ka_n.d.a 'iron' as in ayaska_n.d.a 'excellent iron' (Pan.Skt.)

Dholavira Tablet Gavial ID 3822 Blacksmith, bronze-workshop, artisan's workshop, ingot kiln, portable furnace…

it.ankar 'crocodile' (Ta.); rebus: d.hangar 'blacksmith' (H.)

sal stake, spike, splinter, thorn, difficulty (H.); Rebus: sal 'workshop' (Santali)

kanac 'corner' (Santali); Rebus: kancu 'bronze' (Te.)

kod.a 'in arithmetic, one' (Santali); rebus: kod. 'artisan's workshop' (Kuwi) khad.ā 'circumscribe' (M.); Rebus: khad.ā 'nodule (ore), stone' (M.) kod. 'horn'; kod. 'artisan's workshop' (Kuwi)

d.hālako = a large metal ingot (G.) d.hālakī = a metal heated and poured into a mould; a solid piece of metal; an ingot (G.) d.abu 'an iron spoon' (Santali) Rebus: d.ab, d.himba, d.hompo 'lump (ingot?)', bat.a = wide-mouthed pot; Rebus: bat.a = kiln (Te.)

kangha (IL 1333) ka~ghera_ comb-maker (H.) Rebus: kangar 'portable furnace' Rebus: kangar 1 कंगर् m. a large portable brazier (El.). kẵgürü काँग्&above;रू&below; or kẵgürü काँग&above;रू&below; or kẵgar काँग्र् I हसब्तिका f. (sg. dat. kẵgrĕ काँग्र्य or kẵgarĕ काँगर्य, abl. kẵgri काँग्रि), the portable brazier, or *kāngrī,* much used in Kashmīr (K.Pr. *kángár,* 129, 131, 178; *káṅgrí,* 5, 128, 129). For particulars see El. s.v. *kángri;* L. 7, 25, *kangar;* and K.Pr. 129. The word is a fem. dim. of kang, q.v. (Gr.Gr. 37). kẵgri-khŏphürü

Dholavira tag ID 3821 Copper, iron merchant

kolmo 'three' (Mu.); rebus: kolami 'smithy, forge' (Te.) tebra 'three' (Santali); ta(m)bra 'copper'; tibira 'merchant' (Akkadian)

ka_n.d.a 'arrow' (Skt.); rebus: ka_n.d.a 'iron' as in ayaska_n.d.a 'excellent iron' (Pan.Skt.)

 Dholavira tag ID 3819 …iron, mine-worker, scribe

kan.d.a kanka 'rim of jar' (Santali) kan.d.a 'furnace, fire-altar' (Santali); khanaka 'miner' karNaka 'scribe' (Skt.)

med. 'bdy'; rebus: med. 'iron' (Mu.)

 Dholavira tag ID 3820 … mine-worker-scribe

kan.d.a kanka 'rim of jar' (Santali) kan.d.a 'furnace, fire-altar' (Santali); khanaka 'miner' karNaka 'scribe' (Skt.)

Banawali, Chanhudaro Indus script epigraphs

Banawali13a

Banawali16

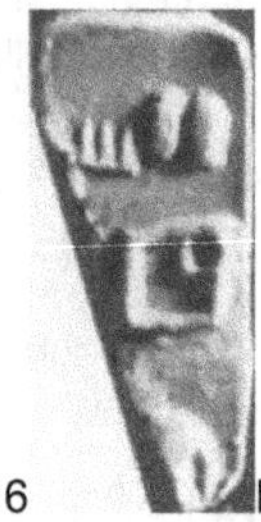
Banawali 18a

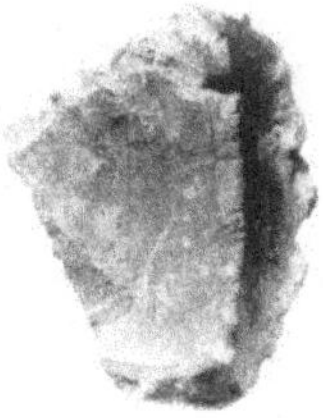
Banawali 14

Banawali2

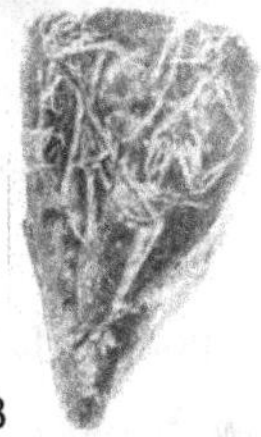
Banawali 23B

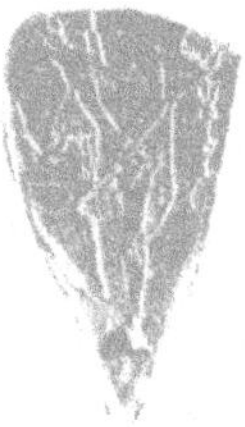
Banawali 26ª

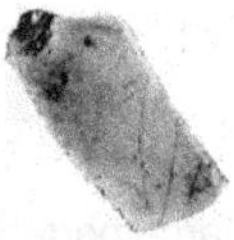
Banawali0026a

Banawali3

Banawali 6

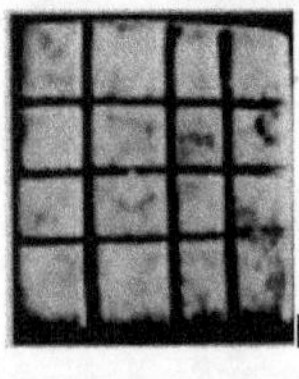
Banawali 20 Nodule (ore), stone

khaṇḍ 'division'; rebus: kaṇḍ 'furnace' (Santali) khaḍā 'circumscribe' (M.); Rebs: khaḍā 'nodule (ore), stone' (M.)

 Banawali Misc. ID 3707 Smelter artisan's workshop

bat.a 'pot'; bat.a 'smelter' (Mu.)

kod.a 'in arithmetic, one' (Santali); rebus: kod. 'artisan's workshop' (Kuwi)

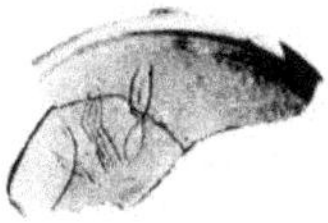 Banawali 28A  9221  Banawali Pot ID 3708 Ingot kiln brass-bellmetal smithy

d.hālako = a large metal ingot (G.) d.hālakī = a metal heated and poured into a mould; a solid piece of metal; an ingot (G.) ḍabu 'an iron spoon' (Santali) Rebus: d.ab, d.himba, d.hompo 'lump (ingot?)', bat.a = wide-mouthed pot; Rebus: bat.a = kiln (Te.)

bharna = the name given to the woof by weavers; otor bharna = warp and weft (Santali.lex.) bharna = the woof, cross-thread in weaving (Santali); bharni_ (H.) (Santali.Boding.lex.) Rebus: bhoron = a mixture of brass and bell metal (Santali.lex.) bharan = to spread or bring out from a kiln (P.lex.) bha_ran. = to bring out from a kiln (G.) ba_ran.iyo = one whose profession it is to sift ashes or dust in a goldsmith's workshop (G.lex.) bharant (lit. bearing) is used in the plural in Pan~cavim.s'a Bra_hman.a (18.10.8). Sa_yan.a interprets this as 'the warrior caste' (bharata_m – bharan.am kurvata_m ks.atriya_n.a_m). *Weber notes this as a reference to the Bharata-s. (*Indische Studien*, 10.28.n.2)

pajhar. = to sprout from a root (Santali) Rebus: pasra 'smithy' (Santali)

 Banawali Pot ID 3709 Smithy-forge mine-worker-scribe

kolmo 'three' (Mu.); rebus: kolami 'smithy, forge' (Te.) kan.d.a kanka 'rim of jar' (Santali) Rebus:

kan.d.a 'furnace, fire-altar' (Santali); khanaka 'miner' karNaka 'scribe' (Skt.)

 Banawali Pot ID 3710 Mine-worker, scribe

kan.d.a kanka 'rim of jar' (Santali) Rebus: kan.d.a 'furnace, fire-altar' (Santali); khanaka 'miner' karNaka 'scribe' (Skt.)

 Banawali Pot ID 3711 Fire-altar iron hearth

 bhed.a hako a species of fish (Santali) bedha cross-grained (Santali) Rebus: bed.a either of the sides of a hearth Thus, ayo bhed.a, this glyph connotes the hearth (bed.a) for ayas. gan.d.a 'four' (Santali) kan.d.a 'fire-altar' (Santali)

 Banawali Pot ID 3712 …Smelter

bat.a 'pot'; bat.a 'smelter' (Mu.)

Banawali 21a 9205Banawali Seal ID 3704 Ore, worker in wood and metal, smithy, fire-altar

dā~ṭu = cross over; daṭ- (da.ṭ-t-) to cross (Kol.)(DEDR 3158) Rebus: dhātu 'mineral'; dhatu = a mineral, metal (Santali)

badhi 'to ligature, to bandage, to splice, to join by successive rolls of a ligature' (Santali) batā bamboo slips (Kur.); bate = thin slips of bamboo (Malt.)(DEDR 3917). Rebus: baḍhi = worker in wood and metal (Santali) baṛae = blacksmith (Ash.)

gan.d.a 'four' (Santali) kan.d.a 'fire-altar' (Santali); kolmo 'three' (Mu.); rebus: kolimi 'smithy' (Te.)

kolmo 'three' (Mu.); rebus: kolami 'smithy, firge' (Te.)

gaṇḍa set of four (Santali) kaṇḍa 'fire-altar' (Santali) Vikalpa: pon 'four' (Santali); pon 'metal' (Ta.)

Banawali11 Alloy of five metals, native metal, iron

ad.ar 'harrow'; rebus: aduru 'native metal, unsmelted' (Ka.)

me~d.ha 'antelope'; rebus: med. 'iron' (Mu.) xola_ = tail (Kur.); qoli id. (Malt.)(DEDr 2135). [Note the short tail ligatured to antelope] rebus: kol 'alloy of five metals' (Ta.)

Banawali1Banawali Seal Bull ID 3691 Coppersmith guild mint, artisan's workshop, metal, mine-worker-scribe, iron

eraka 'nave of wheel' (Ka.); Rebus: eraka, er-aka = any metal infusion (Ka.Tu.) *Tu.* eraka molten, cast (as metal); eraguni to melt (DEDR 866) dol 'likeness'; rebus: dul 'cast metal' (Santali)

kamaṭha crab (Skt.) Rebus: kammaṭa = portable furnace (Te.) kampaṭṭam coiner, mint (Ta.)

ko_d.i a kind of flag, an image of garud.a, basava, or other demi-god set upon a long post before a temple; cf. gud.i, temple (Ka.lex.) Rebus: kod., 'artisan's workshop' (Kuwi)

sal stake, spike, splinter, thorn, difficulty (H.); Rebus: sal 'workshop' (Santali)

ayo 'fish'; rebus: ayas 'iron, metal' (Pan. Skt.)

kan.d.a kanka 'rim of jar' (Santali) Rebus: kan.d.a 'furnace, fire-altar' (Santali); khanaka 'miner' karNaka 'scribe' (Skt.)

med. 'body'; rebus: med. 'iron' (Mu.)

 Banawali 3  Banawali Seal Bull ID 3692 Coppersmith guild, iron workshop, blacksmith-merchant iron

ka_n.d.a 'arrow' (Skt.); rebus: ka_n.d.a 'iron' as in ayaska_n.d.a 'excellent iron' (Pan.Skt.)

sal stake, spike, splinter, thorn, difficulty (H.); Rebus: sal 'workshop' (Santali)

ayo 'fish'; rebus: ayas 'iron, metal' (Pan. Skt.)

bar, barea = two (Mu.); Rebus: barī = blacksmith, artisan (Ash.)(CDIAL 9464). barea 'meerchant' (Santali)

 Banawali 4  Banawali Seal Bull ID 3693 Iron smithy, mint, mine-worker-scribe

me~d.ha 'antelope' ; rebus : med.' Iron' (Mu.) kolmo 'paddy plant' (Santali); Rebus: kolimi 'smithy, forge' (Te.)

kamaṭha crab (Skt.) Rebus: kammaṭa = portable furnace (Te.) kampaṭṭam coiner, mint (Ta.)

kan.d.a kanka 'rim of jar' (Santali) Rebus: kan.d.a 'furnace, fire-altar' (Santali); khanaka 'miner' karNaka 'scribe' (Skt.)

Banawali 5  Banawali Seal Bull ID 3694 Iron bronze workshop

me~d.ha 'antelope' ; rebus : med.' Iron' (Mu.)

kanac 'corner' (Santali); Rebus: kancu 'bronze' (Te.) sal stake, spike, splinter, thorn, difficulty (H.); Rebus: sal 'workshop' (Santali)

 Banawali Seal Bull ID 3695 Iron bronze workshop

me~d.ha 'antelope' ; rebus : med.' Iron' (Mu.)

kanac 'corner' (Santali); Rebus: kancu 'bronze' (Te.) sal stake, spike, splinter, thorn, difficulty (H.); Rebus: sal 'workshop' (Santali)

 Banawali 8 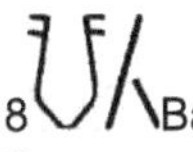 Banawali Seal Goat 4 ID 3696 Iron, alloy of five metals, builder, mine-worker-scribe

me~d.ha 'antelope' ; rebus : med.' Iron' (Mu.) xola_ = tail (Kur.); qoli id. (Malt.)(DEDr 2135). [Note the short tail ligatured to antelope] rebus: kol 'alloy of five metals' (Ta.)

kat.a = stride; rebus: *kat.* To build, manage (house) (Ka.); *kat.t.e* platform build under tree on village green (Ka.); *kat.t.ad.a* a building (Ka.); *kat.t.alme* building (Tu.); *kat.t.ad.amu* building (Te.); *ghat.t.a* quay, landing-place, bathing place (Skt.)(DEDR 1147).

kan.d.a kanka 'rim of jar' (Santali) Rebus: kan.d.a 'furnace, fire-altar' (Santali); khanaka 'miner' karNaka 'scribe' (Skt.)

 Banawali 9C  Banawali Seal Goat 3 ID 3697 Iron metal, alloy of five metals, fire-altar smithy

me~d.ha 'antelope' ; rebus : med.' Iron' (Mu.) xola_ = tail (Kur.); qoli id. (Malt.)(DEDr 2135). [Note the short tail ligatured to antelope] rebus: kol 'alloy of five metals' (Ta.)

gaṇḍa set of four (Santali) kaṇḍa 'fire-altar' (Santali) Vikalpa: pon 'four' (Santali); pon 'metal' (Ta.)

kolom = cutting, graft; to graft, engraft, prune; kolma hoṛo = a variety of the paddy plant (Desi)(Santali.) kolom 'three' (Mu.) Rebus: kolami 'furnace, smithy' (Te.)

Banawali10 9204 Banawali Seal Goat 3 ID 3698 Iron metal, alloy of five metals, smith workshop, forge workshop

me~d.ha 'antelope' ; rebus : med.' Iron' (Mu.) xola_ = tail (Kur.); qoli id. (Malt.)(DEDr 2135). [Note the short tail ligatured to antelope] rebus: kol 'alloy of five metals' (Ta.)

kolom = cutting, graft; to graft, engraft, prune; kolma hoṛo = a variety of the paddy plant (Desi)(Santali.) kolom 'three' (Mu.) Rebus: kolami 'furnace, smithy' (Te.)

sal stake, spike, splinter, thorn, difficulty (H.); Rebus: sal 'workshop' (Santali)

kolmo 'three'; rebus: kolami 'smithy, forge' (Te.)

sal stake, spike, splinter, thorn, difficulty (H.); Rebus: sal 'workshop' (Santali)

Banawali12  Banawali Seal Goat 2 ID 3699 Iron, alloy of five metals, metal smithy, forge workshop

me~d.ha 'antelope' ; rebus : med.' Iron' (Mu.) xola_ = tail (Kur.); qoli id. (Malt.)(DEDr 2135). [Note the short tail ligatured to antelope] rebus: kol 'alloy of five metals' (Ta.)

gaṇḍa set of four (Santali) kaṇḍa 'fire-altar' (Santali) Vikalpa: pon 'four' (Santali); pon 'metal' (Ta.)

kolmo 'three'; rebus: kolami 'smithy, forge' (Te.)

kolom = cutting, graft; to graft, engraft, prune; kolma hoṛo = a variety of the paddy plant (Desi)(Santali.) kolom 'three' (Mu.) Rebus: kolami 'furnace, smithy' (Te.)

Banawali15  9203 Banawali Seal Rhinoceros ID 3700 Worker in iron and wood, bronze workshop

badhia 'castrated boar' (Santali) Rebus: bad.hi 'a caste who work both in iron and wood' (Santali) bar.ae = a blacksmith; bar.ae kudlam = a country made hoe, in contrast to cala_ni kudlam, an imported hoe; bar.ae mer.ed – country smelted iron; bar.ae muruk = the energy of a blacksmith (Mundari.lex.) bar.ae = bad.ae (Santali.lex.) bari_ = blacksmith, artisan (Ash.)(CDIAL 9464). The occurrence of bari_ in Ash. (CDIAL 9464) and bar.ae in Mundari and of vardhaka in Skt. point to the early phonetic form: bard.a; semantic: worker in iron and wood, artisan. Thus, it is suggested that the depiction of the backbone, barad.o is rebus for bard.a, artisan. barduga = a man of acquirements, a proficient man (Ka.)

kanac 'corner' (Santali); Rebus: kancu 'bronze' (Te.) sal stake, spike, splinter, thorn, difficulty (H.); Rebus: sal 'workshop' (Santali)

Banawali 17 9201 Banawali Seal Htgr ID 3701 Workshop—alloy of five metals, iron, brass-bellmetal workshop, native metal iron fire-altar

kolo 'jackal' (Kon.); kola, kolum = a jackal (G.) kolhuyo (Dh.Des.); kulho, kolhuo (Hem.Des.); kros.t.r. (Skt.) kul seren = the tiger's son, a species of lizard (Santali) rebus: kol 'furnace, forge' (Kuwi) kol 'alloy of five metals, pancaloha' (Ta.) kod. 'horn'; kod. 'artisan's workshop' (Kuwi)

med. 'body'; rebus: med. 'iron' (Mu.)

bharna = the name given to the woof by weavers; otor bharna = warp and weft (Santali.lex.) bharna = the woof, cross-thread in weaving (Santali); bharni_ (H.) (Santali.Boding.lex.) Rebus: bhoron = a mixture of brass and bell metal (Santali.lex.) bharan = to spread or bring out from a kiln (P.lex.) bha_ran. = to bring out from a kiln (G.) ba_ran.iyo = one whose profession it is to sift ashes or dust in a goldsmith's workshop (G.lex.) bharant (lit. bearing) is used in the plural in Pan~cavim.s'a Bra_hman.a (18.10.8). Sa_yan.a interprets this as 'the warrior caste' (bharata_m – bharan.am kurvata_m ks.atriya_n.a_m). *Weber notes this as a reference to the Bharata-s. (*Indische Studien*, 10.28.n.2)

sal stake, spike, splinter, thorn, difficulty (H.); Rebus: sal 'workshop' (Santali)

ad.aren 'lid'; Rebus: aduru 'native metal' (Santali) Hence, ayo adar 'iron native metal' (Maybe a reference to unsmelted mketeoric iron.) gaṇḍa set of four (Santali) kaṇḍa 'fire-altar' (Santali) Vikalpa: pon 'four' (Santali); pon 'metal' (Ta.)

Banawali 7  Banawali Seal ID 3702 Tin alloy, bronze workshop

ran:gā 'buffalo'; ran:ga 'pewter or alloy of tin (ran:ku), lead (nāga) and antimony (an~jana)'(Santali)

kanac 'corner' (Santali); Rebus: kancu 'bronze' (Te.) sal stake, spike, splinter, thorn, difficulty (H.); Rebus: sal 'workshop' (Santali)

 Banawali19  Banawali Seal ID 3703 Nodule (ore) smithy, mine-worker-scribe

khad.ā 'circumscribe' (M.); Rebus: khad.ā 'nodule (ore), stone' (M.) kolmo 'paddy plant' (Santali); Rebus: kolimi 'smithy, forge' (Te.) kolom = cutting, graft; to graft, engraft, prune; kolma hoṛo = a variety of the paddy plant (Desi)(Santali.) kolom 'three' (Mu.) Rebus: kolami 'furnace, smithy' (Te.)

kan.d.a kanka 'rim of jar' (Santali) Rebus: kan.d.a 'furnace, fire-altar' (Santali); khanaka 'miner' karNaka 'scribe' (Skt.)

 Banawali 24t Text 9211  Banawali tablet ID 3706
Native metal, iron, nodule (ore)/stone mine-worker, scribe...iron (worker) guild

ad.aren 'lid'; rebus: aduru 'native metal' (Ka.)

loa 'fig leaf' (Santali): Rebus: lo 'iron' (Assamese, Bengali); loa 'iron' (Gypsy) Glyph: *lo* = nine (Santali); *no* = nine (B.) *on-patu* = nine (Ta.)

khad.ā 'circumscribe' (M.); Rebs: khad.ā 'nodule (ore), stone' (M.) kan.d.a kanka 'rim of jar' (Santali) Rebus: kan.d.a 'furnace, fire-altar' (Santali); khanaka 'miner' karNaka 'scribe' (Skt.)

med. 'body'; rebus: med. 'iron' (Mu.)

rebus: अंकडा [aṅkaḍā] *m* (अंक S) Also अकडा *m* A hook or crook, a curved end gen. (M.) Rebus: अखाडा [ akhāḍā ] *m* ( H) A community, or the common place of residence or of assembly, of persons engaged in study or some particular pursuit; a college, a disputation-hall, a gymnasium, circus, arena. Hence, A club or clubroom; a stand of idlers, loungers, newsmongers, gossips, scamps. 2 An order of men. Ex. गोसाव्यांचे अठरा अखाडे आहेत.(M.)

 bhaṭa 'warrior'; bhaṭa 'six' (G.) Rebus: baṭa = kiln (Santali); baṭa = a kind of iron (G.)

Banawali 23A  Banawali tag Mult. ID 3705 Coppersmith Ironsmith guild, copper furnace, iron

damr.a 'heifer'; rebus: tam(b)ra 'copper' (Skt.) me~d.ha 'antelope'; rebus: med. 'iron' (Mu.)

eraka 'upraised arm' (Te.); eraka 'copper' (Te.) gan.d.a 'hero'; rebus: kan.d. 'fire-altar, furnace' (Santali)

ayo 'fish'; rebus: ayas 'iron, metal' (Pan.Skt.)

Decoding Indus script epigraphs of small sites

-- (1) Gumla, Jhukar, Pirak, Qala'at el-Bahrain, Pabumath, Nippur, Lohumjo-daro, Luristan, Hulas, Hajar

(2) Gharo Bhiro (Nuhato), Djoka (Umma), Rojdi, Tepe Yahya, Amri, Altyn Tepe, Tello, Tarkhanewala-dera, Shortugai, Bakkar Buthi, Failaka, Hissam-dheri

The pictures of epigraphs are from Epigraphia Sarasvati. The texts are from Mahadevan corpus followed by readings of texts taken from ICIT corpus which analyses 3831 epigraphs: http://caddy.bv.tu-berlin.de/indus/welcome.htm Qala'at el-Bahrain and Hajar epigraphs are not listed in Mahadevan corpus.

Each of these twnty-two sites have yielded one epigraph each. Jhukar has yielded an additional epigraph showing only a pictorial glyph (elephant).

The epigraphs are inscribed on pots or seals. Some seals also have an animal glyph (for e.g. bull). Jhukar shows a seal with just the elephant glyph as an epigraph (without any signs).

Bull glyph in the following epigraphs may be decoded as: d.hangar 'bull'; rebus: d.hangar 'blacksmith' (H.)

Heifer glyph in the following epigraphs may be decoded as: damr.a 'heifer'; rebus: tam(b)ra 'copper' (Skt.)

[ID Text and symbol/sign refereences are to http://caddy.bv.tu-berlin.de/indus/welcome.htm]

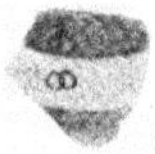 Gumla8a  Gumla pot ID 3726 Guild: Sanghaṭṭa2 (?) bangle Sn 48 (˚yanta): thus Nd2 reading for ˚māna (ppr. med. of sanghaṭṭeti). Sanghaṭṭeti [saŋ+ghaṭṭeti] 1. to knock against Vin ii.208. -- 2. to sound, to ring Mhvs 21, 29 (˚aghaṭṭayi). -- 3 to knock together, to rub against each other J iv.98 (aŋsena aŋsaŋ samaghaṭṭayimha); Dāvs iii.87. -- 4. to provoke by scoffing, to make angry J vi.295 (paraŋ asanghaṭṭento, C. on asanghaṭṭa); VvA 139 (pres. pass. ˚ghaṭṭiyati). -- pp. sanghaṭ(ṭ)ita. Rebus: CDIAL 12858 *saṁghara ' living in the same house '. [Cf. *sáĝr̥ha*<-> ĀpŚr. -- ghara -- ] Pa. *saṅghara* -- ' with one's own family (?) '; L. *sagghrā* ' accompanied by one's own family '; H. *sā̃ghar* m. ' wife's son by former husband '.

jhukar1 Iron ibha 'elephant' (Skt.); ib 'iron' (Santali)

jhukar2  9001  Jhukar seal ID 3731 Bronze-metal workshop, forge (smithy), mine-ore-stone/nodule, scribe

kanac 'corner' (Santali); Rebus: kancu 'bronze' (Te.) sal stake, spike, splinter, thorn, difficulty (H.); Rebus: sal 'workshop' (Santali) ayo 'fish' (Mu.); Rebus: ayas 'metal';

kanka 'rim of jar' (Santali); khaḍā 'circumscribe' (M.); Rebs: khaḍā 'nodule (ore), stone' (M.) kolmo 'paddy plant' (Santali); Rebus: kolimi 'smithy, forge' (Te.); karNaka (Skt.); Rebus: khanaka 'mineworker'; karNaka 'scribe' (Skt.);

Pirak1  Pirak seal Bull ID 3760 Smithy community, smelter, metal caster, mine-worker, scribe

pajhaṛ = to sprout from a root (Santali) Rebus: pasra 'smithy' (Santali)

अंकडा [aṅkaḍā] *m* (अंक S) Also अकडा *m* A hook or crook, a curved end gen. (M.) Rebus: अखाडा [ akhāḍā ] *m* ( H) A community, or the common place of residence or of assembly, of persons engaged in study or some particular pursuit; a college, a disputation-hall, a gymnasium, circus, arena. Hence, A club or clubroom; a stand of idlers, loungers, newsmongers, gossips, scamps. 2 An order of men. Ex. गोसाव्यांचे अठरा अखाडे आहेत.(M.)

kuṭi = a slice, a bit, a small piece (Santali.lex.Bodding) Rebus: kuṭhi 'iron smelter furnace' (Santali) kuṭhī factory (A.)(CDIAL 3546) kan.d.a kanka 'rim of jar' (Santali) kan.d.a 'furnace, fire-altar' (Santali)

baraḍo = spine; backbone; the back; baraḍo thābaḍavo = lit. to strike on the backbone or back; hence, to encourage; baraḍo bhāre thato = lit. to have a painful backbone, i.e. to do something which will call for a severe beating (G.lex.) baraḍ, baraḍu = barren, childless; baranṭu = leanness (Tu.lex.) *maṇuk.o* a single vertebra of the back (G.) Rebus:bharatiyo = a caster of metals; a brazier; bharatar, bharatal, bharataḷ = moulded; an article made in a mould; bharata = casting metals in moulds; bharavum = to fill in; to put in; to pour into (G.lex.) bhart = a mixed metal of copper and lead; bhart-īyā = a barzier, worker in metal; bhat., bhrāṣṭra = oven, furnace (Skt.) bharata = a factitious metal compounded of copper, pewter, tin (M.)

karNaka (Skt.); Rebus: khanaka 'mineworker'; karNaka 'scribe' (Skt.);

Qala'at el-Bahrain seal Bull ID 3761 Granary (of) wood-metal worker, smithy, iron(metal) smelter कोष्टी [ kōṣṭī ] *m* A caste or an individual of it. They are spinners and weavers. In occupation they agree with साळी, but in caste they differ. 2 *f* fig. A spider. कोष्ठ [ kōṣṭha ] *m* A granary. An apartment.

badhi 'to ligature, to bandage, to splice, to join by successive rolls of a ligature' (Santali) batā bamboo slips (Kur.); bate = thin slips of bamboo (Malt.)(DEDR 3917). Rebus: baḍhi = worker in wood and metal (Santali) baṛae = blacksmith (Ash.)

gan.d.a 'four' (Santali) kan.d.a 'fire-altar' (Santali); kolmo 'three' (Mu.); rebus: kolimi 'smithy' (Te.)

med. 'body'; rebus med.' Iron' (Mu.)

kut.i 'woman water carrier' (Te.); kut.hi 'smelter furnace' (Santali)

Pabumath  Pabumath seal Bull ID 3759 Smelter furnace, native metal iron, casting iron kuṭi = a slice, a bit, a small piece (Santali.lex.Bodding) Rebus: kuṭhi 'iron smelter furnace' (Santali) kuṭhī factory (A.)(CDIAL 3546) kan.d.a kanka 'rim of jar' (Santali) kan.d.a 'furnace, fire-altar' (Santali); khanaka 'miner' karNaka 'scribe' (Skt.)

Ad.ar 'harrow'; rebus: aduru 'native metal, unsmelted' (Ka.)

ayo 'fish' (Mu.); Rebus: ayas 'metal'; ayaska_n.d.a 'excellent iron' (Pan.)

dol 'likeness'; rebus: dul 'cast (metal)(Mu.) Doubling of harrow spikes thus connotes cast (native metal)

Nippur; ca. 13th cent. BC; white stone; zebu bull and two pictograms

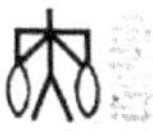 Nippur seal Bull ID 3758 Guild of smelters, furnace

kut.i 'woman water carrier' (Te.); kut.hi 'smelter furnace' (Santali)

अंकडा [aṅkaḍā] *m* (अंक S) Also अकडा *m* A hook or crook, a curved end gen. (M.) Rebus: अखाडा [ akhāḍā ] *m* ( H) A community, or the common place of residence or of assembly, of persons engaged in study or some particular pursuit; a college, a disputation-hall, a gymnasium, circus, arena. Hence, A club or clubroom; a stand of idlers, loungers, newsmongers, gossips, scamps. 2 An order of men. Ex. गोसाव्यांचे अठरा अखाडे आहेत.(M.) bat.a 'quail'; rebus bat.a 'furnace'(Mu.)

Lohumjodaro1a 9011

Lohumjo-daro seal Bull ID 3745 Blacksmith artisan workshop tin, iron, silver, native iron, furnace, casting smithy, mineworker scribe

kod.a 'in arithmetic, one' (Santali); rebus: kod. 'artisan's workshop' (Kuwi)

ranku 'liquid measure' (Santali) Rebus: ranku 'tin' (Santali)

ad.aren 'lid'; rebus: aduru 'native metal' (Ka.); ayo 'fish'(Mu.); ayas 'iron' (Skt.)

khur 'hoof' (M.); rebus: khura silver (Nk.); *kuruku* 'whiteness'; *kuru* brilliancy (Ta.); *kuro* silver (Kol.Nk.Go.)(DEDR 1782). koru = bar of metal (Ta.) *khud.do, khurdo* (Persian *khurdah*) small change in copper; *khurdiyo* a merchant who exchanges copper coins for silver (G.)

ad.aren 'lid'; rebus: aduru 'native metal' (Ka.) ligatured to med. 'body'; rebus: med. 'iron'(Mu.)

khaṇḍ 'division'; rebus: kaṇḍ 'furnace' (Santali)

kolmo 'paddy plant'; rebus: kolami 'smithy' (Te.Ka.); dol 'likeness'; rebus: dul 'cast' (i.e. smithy (for) casting metal)

kan.d.a kanka 'rim of jar' (Santali) kan.d.a 'furnace, fire-altar' (Santali); khanaka 'miner' karNaka 'scribe' (Skt.)

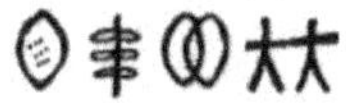

Louvre Museum; Luristan; unglazed, gray steatite; short-honed bull and 4 pictograms

Luristan seal Bull ID 3746 Blacksmith casting iron guild smithy, ore smithy

dol 'likeness'; dul 'cast' (Santali) dul mer.ed 'cast iron' (Mu.) med. 'body'; rebus: med. 'iron' (Santali)

sanghaṭṭa2 (?) bangle (Pali); rebus: samghara 'guild, community' (Skt.) sanghara 'living in the same house' (Pali)

*panǰár* 'ladder, stairs' (Bshk.)(CDIAL 7760) Rebus: pasra 'smithy' (Santali) khaḍā 'circumscribe' (M.); Rebs: khaḍā 'nodule (ore), stone' (M.) kolmo 'three' (Mu); Rebus: kolimi 'smithy, forge' (Te.)

hulas Hulas tag ID 3730 Tin smithy, mineworker, scribe

ranku 'liquid measure' (Santali); rebus: ranku 'tin' (Santali); p

pajhaṛ = to sprout from a root (Santali) Rebus: pasra 'smithy' (Santali)

kan.d.a kanka 'rim of jar' (Santali) kan.d.a 'furnace, fire-altar' (Santali); khanaka 'miner' karNaka 'scribe' (Skt.)

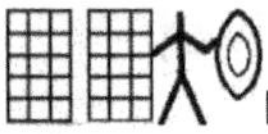Hajar tab ID 3727 Iron forge, casting metal

koṭṭa 'seed' (Ma.); rebus: koṭe 'forging (metal)(Mu.)

med. 'body'; rebus: med. 'iron' (Mu.)

dol 'likeness'; dul 'cast (metal)(Santali) khaṇḍ 'division'; rebus: kaṇḍ 'furnace' (Santali)

-- (2) Gharo Bhiro (Nuhato), Djoka (Umma), Rojdi, Tepe Yahya, Amri, Altyn Tepe, Tello, Tarkhanewala-dera, Shortugai, Bakkar Buthi, Failaka, Hissam-dheri

 Gharo Bhiro (Nuhato) 01Gharo Bhiro seal ID 3725 Ore (nodule/stone) workshop, furnace, mineworker, scribe

kod.a 'in arithmetic, one' (Santali); rebus: kod. 'artisan's workshop' (Kuwi) khaḍā 'circumscribe' (M.); Rebs: khaḍā 'nodule (ore), stone' (M.)

अंकडा [aṅkaḍā] *m* (अंक S) Also अकडा *m* A hook or crook, a curved end gen. (M.) Rebus: अखाडा [ akhāḍā ] *m* ( H) A community, or the common place of residence or of assembly, of persons engaged in study or some particular pursuit; a college, a disputation-hall, a gymnasium, circus, arena. Hence, A club or clubroom; a stand of idlers, loungers, newsmongers, gossips, scamps. 2 An order of men. Ex. गोसाव्यांचे अठरा अखाडे आहेत.(M.)

kan.d.a kanka 'rim of jar' (Santali) kan.d.a 'furnace, fire-altar' (Santali); khanaka 'miner' karNaka 'scribe' (Skt.)

9811Djoka (Umma) Tell Umma tag Bull ID 3782 Blacksmith Mint, cast (metal), smelter workshop, metal furnace, smithy

kamāt.hiyo = archer; kāmaṭhum = a bow; ka_mad.i_, ka_mad.um = a chip of bamboo (G.) ka_maṭhiyo a bowman; an archer (Skt.lex.) Rebus: kammaṭa = portable furnace (Te.) kampaṭṭam coiner, mint (Ta.)

ḍabu 'an iron spoon' (Santali) Rebus: ḍab, ḍhimba, ḍhompo 'lump (ingot?)', bat.a = wide-mouthed pot; Rebus: bat.a = kiln (Te.)

sal stake, spike, splinter, thorn, difficulty (H.); Rebus: sal 'workshop' (Santali) ayo 'fish' (Mu.); Rebus: ayas 'metal';

gaṇḍa set of four (Santali) kaṇḍa 'fire-altar' (Santali) Vikalpa: pon 'four' (Santali); pon 'metal' (Ta.)

kolom = cutting, graft; to graft, engraft, prune; kolma hoṛo = a variety of the paddy plant (Desi)(Santali.) kolom 'three' (Mu.) Rebus: kolami 'furnace, smithy' (Te.)

Rojdi 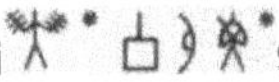 9041 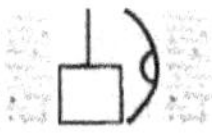 Rojdi pot ID 3768 ...Kiln, iron, tin pasra (smithy)...

 bhaṭa 'warrior'; bhaṭa 'six' (G.) Rebus: baṭa = kiln (Santali); baṭa = a kind of iron (G.)

koṇḍa-miṇdi eyelid (Go.)(DEDR 4864). Rebus: meḍ 'iron' (Santali. Mundari)

ranku 'liquid measure'; rebus: ranku 'tin' (Santali)

 glyph ligatured to man's body, held in either hand. *panǰā́r* 'ladder, stairs' (Bshk.)(CDIAL 7760) Rebus: pasra 'smithy' (Santali)

med. 'body'; rebus: med. 'iron' (Mu.)

 Tepe yahya pot ID 3784 Copper, iron workshop

Eraka 'upraised arm' (Te.); eraka 'copper' (Te.) med. 'body'; rebus: med. 'iron' (Mu.)

sal stake, spike, splinter, thorn, difficulty (H.); Rebus: sal 'workshop' (Santali)

 Amri pot ID 3683 Gold smithy

kolom = cutting, graft; to graft, engraft, prune; kolma hoṛo = a variety of the paddy plant (Desi)(Santali.) kolom 'three' (Mu.) Rebus: kolami 'furnace, smithy' (Te.)

gaṇḍa set of four (Santali) kaṇḍa 'fire-altar' (Santali) Vikalpa: pon 'four' (Santali); pon 'metal' (Ta.)

Amri06 Epigraph with only a pictorial motif: three headed composite animal: bull, heifer, antelope Copper-, iron-smith

d.angra 'bull'; rebus: d.hangar 'blacksmith' (H.)

damra. 'heifer'; rebus: tam(b)ra 'copper' (Skt.)

me~d.ha 'antelope'; rebus: med. 'iron' (Mu.)

 Altyn Tepe seal ID 3682 Native metal smithy

kolom = cutting, graft; to graft, engraft, prune; kolma hoṛo = a variety of the paddy plant (Desi)(Santali.) kolom 'three' (Mu.) Rebus: kolami 'furnace, smithy' (Te.)

ad.ar 'harrow'; rebus: aduru 'native metal, unsmelted' (Ka.)

[Pierre de talc. Louvre, AO 9036. P. Amiet, Bas-relliefs imaginaries de l'Orient ancien, Paris, 1973, p. 94, no. 274…ils proviendrait de Tello, l'ancienne Girsu, une des cites de l'Etat sumerien de Lagash. Musee National De Arts Asiatiques Guimet, 1988-1989, *Les cites oubliees de l'Indus Archeologie du Pakistan*.]

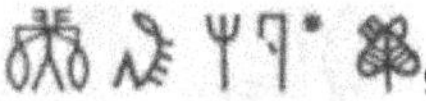9851 Telloh

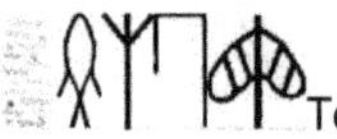Tello seal Tiger ID 3783 Iron (smelter) guild, iron smithy

loa 'fig leaf' (Santali): Rebus: lo 'iron' (Assamese, Bengali); loa 'iron' (Gypsy) Glyph: *lo* = nine (Santali); *no* = nine (B.) *on-patu* = nine (Ta.)

अंकडा [aṅkaḍā] *m* (अंक S) Also अकडा *m* A hook or crook, a curved end gen. (M.) Rebus: अखाडा [ akhāḍā ] *m* ( H) A community, or the common place of residence or of assembly, of persons engaged in study or some particular pursuit; a college, a disputation-hall, a gymnasium, circus, arena. Hence, A club or clubroom; a stand of idlers, loungers, newsmongers, gossips, scamps. 2 An order of men. Ex. गोसाव्यांचे अठरा अखाडे आहेत.(M.)

kolom = cutting, graft; to graft, engraft, prune; kolma hoṛo = a variety of the paddy plant (Desi)(Santali.) kolom 'three' (Mu.) Rebus: kolami 'furnace, smithy' (Te.)

ayo 'fish'(Mu.); ayas 'iron' (Skt.)

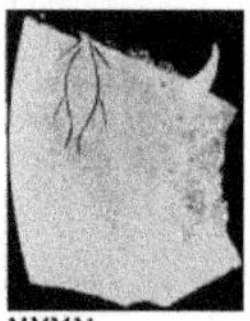

Tarkhanewala-dera 3 9031Tarkhanewala-dera pot ID 3781 Native metal iron

ad.aren 'lid'; rebus: aduru 'native metal' (Ka.); ayo 'fish'(Mu.); ayas 'iron' (Skt.)

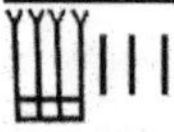Shortughai Seal Rhinoceros ID 3772 Smithy, iron sand ore

kolom 'three' (Mu.) Rebus: kolami 'furnace, smithy' (Te.)

Standing crop: CDIAL 11425 valla m. ' a kind of wheat ' VarBṛS., ' winnowing corn ' W.
Pk. *valla* -- m. ' a kind of grain ', *vālā* -- f. ' a kind of grain, millet '; S. *vali* f. ' heap of reaped ears of corn ', L. *val*; Ku. *bāl* ' ear of corn ', *bālo,bāḷro* m. ' crops '; N. *bālo* ' ear of corn ', *bāli* ' cornfield, crops, harvest ' (whence *balyāunu* ' to pick off ears of corn '); Bi. *bāl* ' ear of wheat ', Mth. *bālī*; Aw.lakh. *bālī* ' ear of maize '; H. *bālī* f. ' spike of corn ', *bālū* m. ' beard of grain (esp. maize) '; OMarw. *bālī* f. ' standing crop '; G.*vāl* m. ' a kind of pulse '. Rebus: bali 'iron sand ore' (Santali)

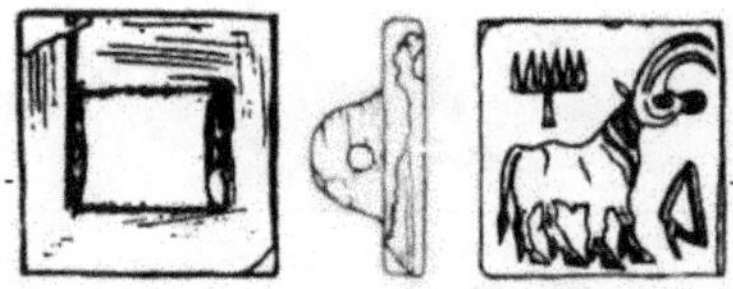

Seal from Shortugai incised with an antelope and two other pictographs. Native metal, iron

"...Shortugai in Oxus basin, on the Kokcha-Amu Darya doab, has revealed the existence of a Harappan colony for carrying out trade in lapis lazuli. Apart form typical Harappan pottery, a seal bearing the script has also been found to confirm the trading character of the colony." (Six decades of Indus Studies in: BB Lal and SP Gupta, eds., *Frontiers of the Indus Civilization*, Fig. .8, p. 9].

Ayo 'fish'; kaṇḍa 'arrow'; rebus: ayaskāṇḍa 'excellent iron' (Pan.)

ad.ar 'harrow'; rebus: aduru 'native metal, unsmelted' (Ka.)

me~d.ha 'antelope'; rebus: med. 'iron' (Mu.)

Bakkar Buthi pot ID 3684 Bronze workshop guild, blacksmith, smithy guild

kanac 'corner' (Santali); Rebus: kancu 'bronze' (Te.) sal stake, spike, splinter, thorn, difficulty (H.); Rebus: sal 'workshop' (Santali)

sanghaṭṭa2 (?) bangle (Pali); rebus: samghara 'guild, community' (Skt.) sanghara 'living in the same house' (Pali)

bar, barea = two (Mu.); Rebus: barī = blacksmith, artisan (Ash.)(CDIAL 9464).

Kolmo 'three'; rebus: kolami 'smithy'; sanghaṭṭa2 (?) bangle (Pali); rebus: samghara 'guild, community' (Skt.) sanghara 'living in the same house' (Pali)

pajhaṛ = to sprout from a root (Santali) Rebus:

pasra 'smithy' (Santali)

Textseal, impression, inscription; Failaka; brownish-grey unglazed steatite; Indus pictograms above a short-horned bull.

Failaka seal Bull ID 3723 ...Iron,bronze...ed. 'body'; rebus: med. 'iron' (Mu.)

kanac 'corner' (Santali); Rebus: kancu 'bronze' (Te.)

ayo 'fish'; ayas 'metal' (Skt.)

TextFailaka; unglazed steatite; an arc of four pictograms above the hindquarter of a bull.

Failaka seal ID 3724 Blacksmith iron ingot mint

med. 'body'; rebus med. 'iron' (Mu.)

ḍhālako = a large metal ingot (G.) ḍhālakī = a metal heated and poured into a mould; a solid piece of metal; an ingot (G.) ḍabu 'an iron spoon' (Santali) Rebus: ḍab, ḍhimba, ḍhompo 'lump (ingot?)', bat.a = wide-mouthed pot; Rebus: bat.a = kiln (Te.)

kuṭi = a slice, a bit, a small piece (Santali.lex.Bodding) Rebus: kuṭhi 'iron smelter furnace' (Santali)

kāmaṭhum = a bow; ka_mad.i_, ka_mad.um = a chip of bamboo (G.) ka_maṭhiyo a bowman; an archer (Skt.lex.) Rebus: kammaṭa = portable furnace (Te.) kampaṭṭam coiner, mint (Ta.)

Hissam-dheri pot ID 3728 Hissam-dheri pot ID 3729 Native metal iron smelter

kuṭi = a slice, a bit, a small piece (Santali.lex.Bodding) Rebus: kuṭhi 'iron smelter furnace' (Santali)

ad.aren 'lid'; rebus: aduru 'native metal' (Ka.)

Susa ritual basin decorated with goatfish figures, molluscs. Compared wlth śrivatsa depicted on*sāñci stūpa* and Mathura Lion Capital.

Explaining the glyphic of the 'mason, architect' shown next to *śrīvatsa* glyphic composition on Sanchi torana: This is an announcement of puja for prosperity of ariya sangha, ariya dhamma and is rendered using the Indian hieroglyphic tradition of an ancient writing system of Indian linguistic area, from the days of Sarasvati-Sindhu civilization.

Glyph: Vaḍḍhaki (& °ī) [cp. Epic & Class. Sk. vardhaki & vardha- kin; perhaps from vardh to cut: see vaddheti] a carpenter, builder, architect, mason. On their craft and guilds see Fick, *Sociale Gliederung* 181 sq.; Mrs. Rh. D. *Cambridge Hist. Ind.* i.206. -- The word is specially characteristic of the Jātakas and other popular (later) literature J i.32, 201, 247; ii.170; vi.332 sq., 432; Ap. 51; DhA i.269; iv.207; Vism 94; PvA 141; Mhbv 154. --iṭṭha° a stonemason Mhvs 35, 102; nagara° the city architect Miln 331, 345; brāhmaṇa° a brahmin carpenter J iv.207; mahā° chief carpenter, master builder Vism 463. In metaphor taṇhā the artificer lust DhA iii.128. (Pali) WPak.kṭg. *ōḍ* m. ' carpenter, name of a caste '; Garh. *oḍ* ' mason '.(CDIAL 2549). Pa. *vaḍḍhaki* -- m. ' carpenter, building mason '; Pk. *vaḍḍhaï* -- m. ' carpenter ', °*aïa* -- m. ' shoemaker '; WPah. jaun. *bāḍhōī* ' carpenter ', (Joshi) *bāḍhi* m., N. *baṛhaï*, *baṛahi*, A. *bārai*, B. *bāṛaï*, °*ṛui*, Or. *baṛhaï*, °*ṛhāi*, (Gaṛjād) *bāṛhoi*, Bi. *baṛahī*, Bhoj. H. *baṛhaī* m., M. *vāḍhāyā* m., Si. *vaḍu* -- *vā*. vardhaki -- : WPah.kṭg. *báḍḍhi* m. ' carpenter '; kṭg. *bəṛhe\i*, *báṛhi*, kc. *baṛhe* ← H. beside genuine *báḍḍhi* Him.I 135), J. *bāḍhi*, Garh.*baṛhai*, A. also *bāṛhai* AFD 94; Md. *vaḍīn*, *vaḍin* pl. (CDIAL 11375).

Rebus: Vaḍḍhati [Vedic vardhati, vṛdh, cp. Av. vərədaiti to increase. To this root belongs P. uddha "high up" (=Gr. orqo/s straight). Defd at Dhtp 109 simply as "vaḍḍhane"] primary meaning "to increase" (trs. & intrs.); hence: to keep on, to prosper, to multiply, to grow S i.15 to participate in, to practise, attend to, to serve (acc.) S ii.109 (tanhaŋ) (Pali)

Molluscs shown on Mathura Lion Capital together with two fishes in śrivatsa.

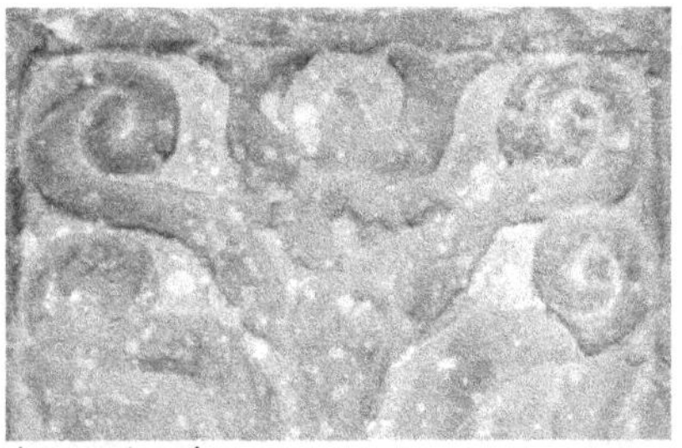

Note the pattern of molluscs on the Mathur panel which compares with Susa ritual basin glyphic. Photograph of a sculpture panel from Mathura, taken by Edmund William Smith in the 1880s-1890s. Mathura has extensive archaeological remains as it was a large and important city from the middle of the first millennium onwards. It rose to particular prominence under the Kushans as the town was their southern capital. The Buddhist, Brahmanical and Jain faiths all thrived at Mathura, and we find deities and motifs from all three represented in sculpture. In reference to this photograph in the list of photographic negatives, Bloch wrote that, "The technical name of such a panel was ayagapata [homage panel]." The tablet shows a representation of a stupa with a staircase leading up to a terrace which is surrounded by a railing similar of those of the stupas oBharhut and Sanchi. It appears from the inscription that the tablet is Jain. The piece is now in the Lucknow Museum.

Molluscs on Susa ritual basin compared with Molluscs on Sanchi Monument Stupa II Huntington Scan Number 0010873 (See more examples in: http://www.scribd.com/doc/13267649/Resources-Hieroglyphs-Ancient-Indian-Tradition)

Decoding some hieroglyphs of ancient Indian art tradition

To be read with:

1. Resources for decoding some hieroglyphs of ancient Indian art tradition at Begram, Khandagiri, Udayagiri, Kankali Tila, Bharhut, Sanchi and Mathura (pdf) http://www.scribd.com/doc/13267649/Resources-Hieroglyphs-Ancient-Indian-Tradition

2. Hieroglyphs of ancient Indian art tradition (ppt) http://www.scribd.com/doc/13268084/Hieroglyphs-of-Historical-Periods

This monograph is a continuation of the monograph decoding Indus Script.
http://sites.google.com/site/kalyan97/indus-script
Monograph http://www.scribd.com/doc/12752530/mlecchamlecchitavikalpa
Powerpoint presentation slides http://www.scribd.com/doc/12823723/Hieroglyphs

Hieroglyph is defined as a picture or symbol used in hieroglyphic writing: bartleby.com

Some hieroglyphs were used at a time (between ca. 6th to 2nd century BCE) in contexts wherein Kharoshthi and Brahmi scripts were also used. The hieroglyphs represented a legacy of an earlier, ancient writing system which dates back to the Sarasvati civilization (ca. 3rd millennium BCE). Remarkable examples of continuity in artistic tradition of using hieroglyphs are those of the svastika and tree hieroglyphs (cf. Khandagiri). Each of svastika and tree hieroglyphs occurs on scores of inscriptions of the civilization.

The continuity of the use of hieroglyphs on a) punch-marked coins and other ancient coinage of Hindusthan; b) Sohgaura copper plate inscription; c) inscriptions on a copper bolt of Rampurva Ashoka edict pillar has been presented in separate monographs.

Hieroglyphs as cultural metaphors

Indian hieroglyphs enshrined in ancient art traditions, starting from the days of Sarasvati hieroglyphs (of circa 3rd millennium BCE), are cultural metaphors, conveying through the underlying language, the abiding continuity of Hindu civilization.

Many hieroglyphs are combined motifs of unambiguous orthographic elements the meanings of which can be understood from mleccha glosses of the Indian vernacular, the *lingua franca* of Hindusthan.

An orthographic tradition unites the finds of exquisite artistic forms at Begram, Khandagiri, Udayagiri, Kankali Tila, Bharhut, Sanchi and Mathura. The most characteristic feature of this orthographic tradition is the use of 'ligaturing' technique to use hieroglyptic elements to compose artistic motifs.

An assemblage of ancient art history and language resources is provided in a separate document from which the glyptic elements have been taken and included in this note.

The objective of the assemblage of art history and language resources is to present variant representations of the hieroglyphs and glyptic elements, to help unravel the meanings of these hieroglyphs.

The glyphs are read as mlecchita vikalpa, i.e. alternative writing system representation of underlying mleccha *lingua franca* – mlecchita vikalpa which is a writing system tradition that dates back to the Sarasvati civilization of circa 3rd millennium BCE where the 'ligaturing' technique was evidenced in hundreds of inscriptions. See the monographs and epigraphica sarasvati at http://sites.google.com/site/kalyan97

Representation of the divine, paramātman

Veneration of hamsa in Bharhut:

Photograph of the upper panel of the left side of the Ajatachatru pillar excavated from the stupa at Bharhut, taken by Joseph David Beglar in 1874. This pillar would have stood close to the western gateway of the stupa complex, forming part of the entrance but also attached to the railing. The exact date that a stupa was first erected at this site is not known, however, by the time the railing was added in the latter half of the second century BCE, Bharhut had been established as a Buddhist place of worship for centuries. At this stage, the stupa complex consisted of a hemispherical dome, encircled by an inner and an outer railing or vedika. Evidence from inscriptions shows that the construction of the railing was funded by donors from all over India, therefore Bharhut was known and important, to people from a wide geographical area...

The hieroglyph of hamsa, 'swan' is the clearest representation of something held to be divine as apparent from the following glosses:

> Telugu. హంస [ haṃsa ] or **హంసము** *hamsa*. [Skt.] n. A swan. A certain fabulous bird supposed to be a swan. Also, a water-fowl, probably the Ruddy Shieldrake. శ్వేతగరుత్తువు. నీళ్లువిడిచి పాలుద్రాగే పక్షి. "రాజహంసలు గాని రాజహంసలుకారు." Vasu. pref. 62. The name of one of the vital airs. శారీరవాయువు, ఉచ్ఛ్వాసనిశ్వాసరూపమైన వాయువు. The Divine Spirit, పరమాత్మ.

Some hieroglyphs are common in the selected examples. The composite glyphs with unambiguously identifiable orthographic elements may be listed as follows (thumbnails) (sources for the glyphs and credits are provided in the resources document):

| | | | |
|---|---|---|---|
|  Begram |  Khandagiri |  Khandagiri |  Udayagiri |
|  Kankali Tila |  Kankali Tila |  Bharhut |  Bharhut |

| | |
|---|---|
| <br>Sanchi | <br>Mathura/Sanchi |

Decoding the glyphs (Glyphs and rebus meanings)

Garlands/buds/ties/girdle used on hieroglyphs:

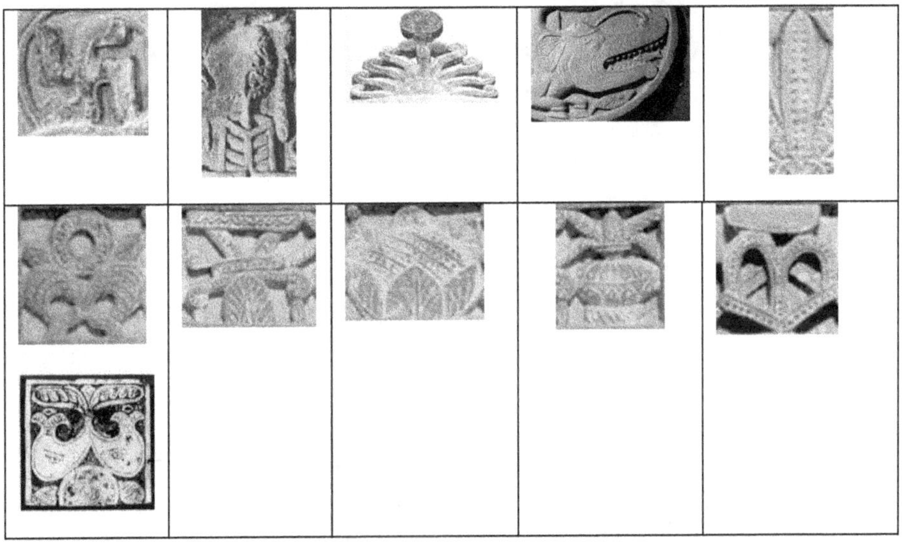

The glyph with the upturned 'fish-tails' mounted on a wheel is an object of worship in a temple as shown in the following sculptures of Bodh Gaya; the hieroglyph connotes, rebus: dhamma-cakka-puja, worship of dharma, dhamma:

Location Bodhgaya, Gaya, Bihar, India Date 2nd-1st century BC
ca 99-1 BCE Description Railing pillar

Location Bodhgaya, Gaya, Bihar, India Date 2nd-1st century BC
ca 99-1 BCE Description Railing pillars. Presently located at: Bodhgaya Museum View Overview Image Identification Accession No 38815

The continuity of the artistic tradition using such motifs is seen also on early punch-marked and cast coins of mints from Taxila to Srilanka:

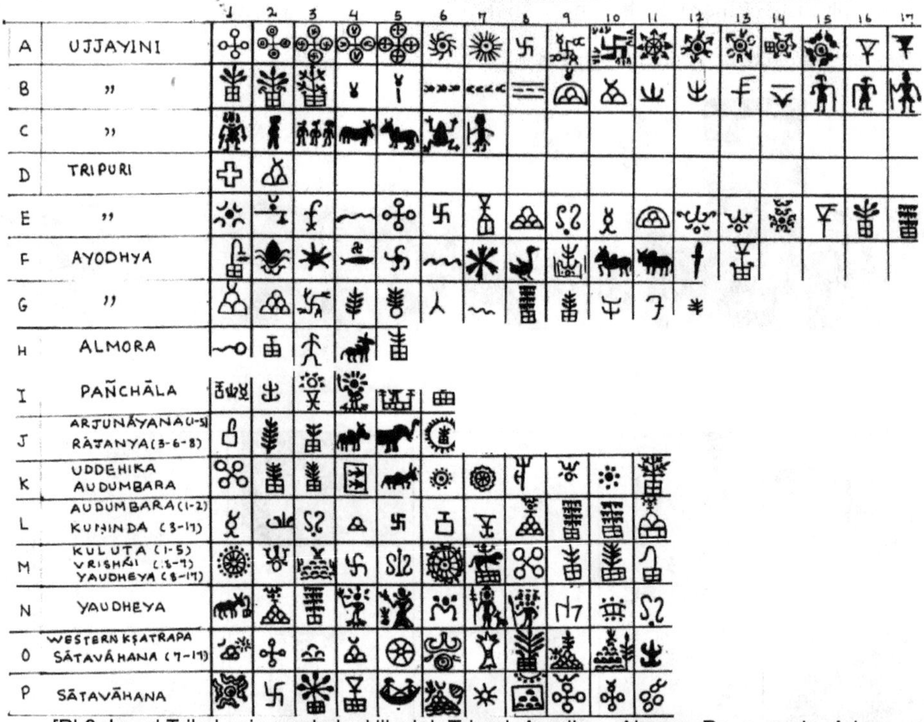


[Pl.8, Local Tribal coin symbols: Ujjayini, Tripuri, Ayodhya, Almore, Pa_n~ca_la, Arjuna_yana (1-3), Ra_janya (3,6,8), Uddehika, Audumbara, Kun.inda, Kuluta, Vr.s.n.i, Yaudheya, Ks.atrapa, S'a_tava_hana: Savita Sharma, 1990, *Early Indian Symbols: Numismatic evidence*, Delhi, Agam Kala Prakashan]]

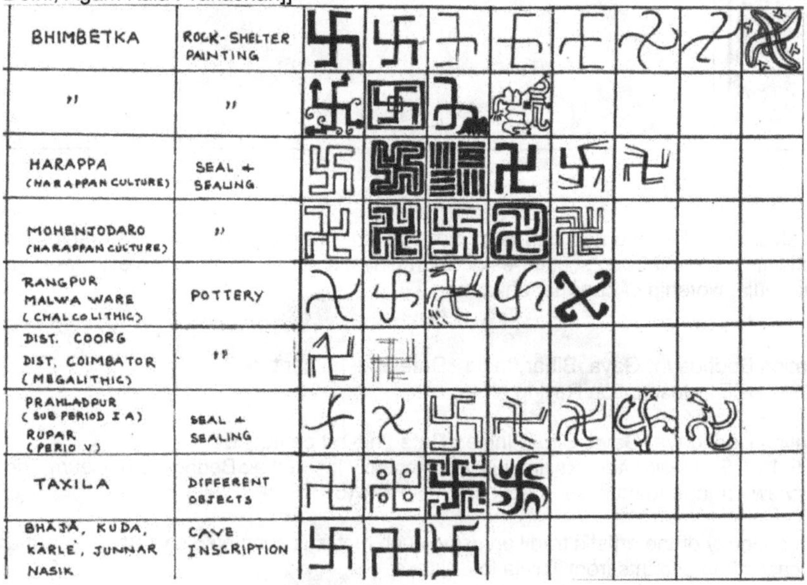


[Pl. 27, Svastika symbol: distribution in cultural periods: Savita Sharma, 1990, *Early Indian Symbols: Numismatic evidence*, Delhi, Agam Kala Prakashan]

svastika— '*auspicious', m. 'auspicious mark' R. [svastí—] Pa. *sotthika—*, *°iya—* 'auspicious'; Pk. *satthia—*, *sot°* m. 'auspicious mark'; H. *sathiyā*, *sati°* m. 'mystical mark of good luck'; G. *sāthiyɔ* m. 'auspicious mark painted on the front of a house'(CDIAL 13916)

sattvá— n. 'existence, reality' TS., 'true character' MBh. 2. n. (m. lex.) 'living being, creature' MBh. [sánt—] 1. Pk. *satta—* n. 'strength, essence'; K. *sath*, dat. *°tas* m. 'truth, essence'; S. *satu* m. 'courage'; P. *satt* m. 'truth'; Or. *satā* 'strength', H. *sattā* m.— H. *sat* m. 'essence', G. M. *sat* n. ← Sk. 2. Pa. Pk. *satta—* m. 'living being', Kharl. *satva*; Si. *sata* 'being, animal'. ஆரியசத்தை āriya-cattai , *n.* < *ārya- sattva.* (Buddh.) The noble truths of the Buddhas (CDIAL 13111).

kuṭa, *°ṭi* -- , *°ṭha* -- 3, *°ṭhi* -- m. ' tree ' lex., *°ṭaka* -- m. ' a kind of tree ' Kauś. (CDIAL 3228).

Ma. kuṭuma, kuṭumma narrow point (DEDR 2049).

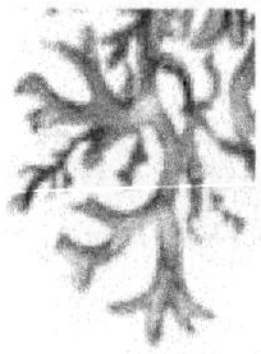

Coraline algae, coral seaweed.

Bouquet held in the gate-keeper's hand.

*Ka.* taḷavāra, taḷāra, talāri watchman, beadle. *Tu.* taḷavāre village watchman. *Te.* talāri watchman. / Cf. Skt. talāra(ka)-, talavarga- city guard (*Bṛhatkathākośa; Udayasundarīkathā* 75); Pkt. talāra- town watchman; Mar. taḷvār an officer of a village; tarāḷ a man of low caste whose duty it is to protect a village. (CDIAL 3129).

taravāri m. ' one -- edged sword ' Hcar., *taravālikā* -- f. lex., *talavāraṇa* -- n. W. Gy. pal. *tirwáli* ' sword ', *tirwárir* ' your sword '; Ash. *tarälī́* ' sword ', Wg. *tarwilī́*, *torṓlī́*; Bshk. *tarbḗl* f., pl. *°bāl*, Tor. (Biddulph) "*terbel*", K. *tarwār* f., S. *tarāri* f., P. *tarvār*, *talvār* f., WPah.bhal. *taruwā́r* f., Ku. *tarwār*, N. *tarwār*, *talwār*, A. *tarowāl*, B. *taroyāl*, Or. *tarudri*, *°ra*, *taruāḷa*, Mth. *taruāri*, Aw.lakh. *tarwāri*, H. *tarwār*, *talwār* f., G. M. *tarvār* f. -- Divergent forms in Kt. *tərwōč*, Pr. *trāž*, Or. *tarāṛi* (cf. Sant. *tarwaṛe*).Addenda: taravāri -- : WPah.kc. *tərār* f. (obl. -- *i*) ' sword ', J. *trār*, *trāḷ* f. (ktg. *təḷwār* f. ← H.?) (CDIAL 5706)

*Pa.* guḍi temple (DEDR 1655)
Pk. *paōlī́—* f. 'city gate, main street'; WPah. (Joshi) *prauḷ* m., *°ḷi* f., *pauḷ* m., *°ḷi* f. 'gateway of a chief', *proḷ* 'village ward'; H. *paul*, *pol* m. 'gate, courtyard, town quarter with its own gate' (CDIAL 8633).
Pkt. talāra- town watchman (CDIAL 3129).

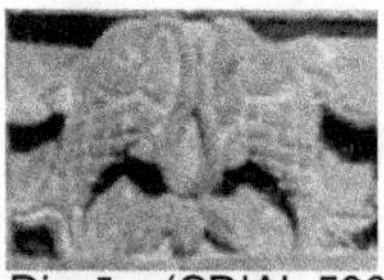

*Ta.* ayirai, acarai, acalai loach, sandy colour, *Cobitis thermalis*; ayilai a kind of fish (DEDR 191).

tū́la— 1 n. 'tuft of grass or reeds, panicle of flower or plant' AV., 'cotton' MBh., 'pencil' Divyāv. (CDIAL 5904)

Pali. Puppha-- āveḷā flower -- garland VvA 125. -- dāma a wreath or garland of fls. J i.397; dāma wreath, garland

Pali. dāma a bond, fetter, rope; chain; Telugu. దారము [ dāramu ]n. A thread, cord, string, rope. dāman rope RV. (CDIAL 6283).

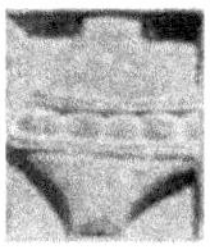

H. *dāwan* m. girdle (CDIAL 6283).

Other vatiant of the glyph on Jaina āyāgapaṭa of Kankali Tila, Manoharpura.

dol = likeness, picture, form (Santali) Marathi. तुला [ tulā ] *f* Equality, likeness, resemblance. Rebus: Ku. *dyol* 'temple', *dyoli* 'small temple dedicated to a goddess'; A. *dâl*, *daul*, H. *dewal* m. dēvakula— n. 'temple' ŚāṅkhGr̥., *°likā*— f. 'small temple' Pañcad. [dēvá—1, kúla—] Pk. *dēvaüla*—, *dēvala*—, *dēula*— n., *dēvaüliyā*—, *dēuliā*— f.; (CDIAL 6524)

Pali. ariya -- dhamma the national customs of the Aryans (= ariyānaŋ eso dhammo Nd1 71, 72) M i.1, 7, 135; A ii.69; v.145 sq., 241, 274; Sn 783; Dhs 1003. Pali. Ariya (adj. -- n.) [Vedic ārya, of uncertain etym. The other Pāli forms are ayira & ayya] 1. *(racial)* Aryan D ii.87. <-> 2. *(social)* noble, distinguished, of high birth. Ayyaka [demin. of ayya] grandfather, (so also BSk., e. g. M Vastu ii.426; iii.264) J iii.155; iv.146; vi.196; Pv i.84; Miln 284. ayyaka -- payyakā grandfather & great grandfather, forefathers, ancestors J i.2; PvA 107 Ayira (& Ayyira) (n. -- adj.) [Vedic ārya, Metathesis for ariya as diaeretic form of ārya, of which the contracted (assimilation) form is ayya. See also ariya] (n.) ariyan, nobleman, gentleman (opp. servant); (adj.) arīyan, well-born, belonging to the ruling race, noble, aristocratic, gentlemanly J v.257; Vv 396. -- puggala an (ethically) model person, Ps i.167; Vin v.117; ThA 206. -- magga the Aryan Path. -- vaŋsa the (fourfold) noble family, i. e. of recluses content with the 4 requisites D iii.224 = A ii.27 = Ps i.84 = Nd2 141; cp. A iii.146.

Dhp. *dharma*—, *dhama*—, Pk. *dhamma*— m.; OB. *dhāma* 'religious conduct' (CDIAL 6753).

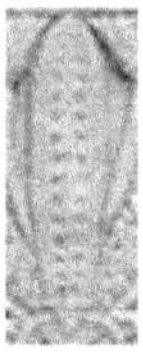

Mu. *kula* `tiger (*Felis_tigris*)'.

కోలాకు a long leaf. కోల [ kōla ] *kōla*. [Tel.] adj. Long. (DEDR 2237) కోలముఖము a long face.

*Ko.* el leaf. *To.* eṣ id. *Ka.* ele, ela id. *Koḍ.* elakaṇḍa id. *Tu.* elè, irè id. (497)
*Kur.* xolā tail. *Malt.* qoli id. (DEDR 2135)

*Ko.* kole·l temple in Kota village (also smithy) (DEDR 2133).

H. *pū̃ch* f. ' tail ', *pūchī* f. ' fish's tail ' WPah.kṭg. *punjhəṛ* m., poet. *punjhṭa* m. ' (big) tail ', kṭg. (kc.) (CDIAL 8249).

Pa. *pūjā* -- f. worship;

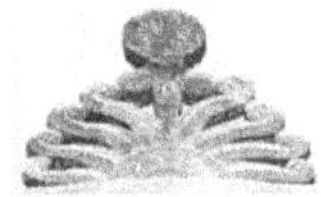

Kashmiri. a snail (L. 157, 464, *hāngi*). Bengali. शामुक [ śāmuka ] n the snail. Marathi. शंखिनी A sort of sea-snail; popularly गोगलगाय

Pali. Sanghāṭa [fr. saŋ+ghaṭeti, lit. "binding together"; on etym. see Kern, *Toev.* ii.68]

Pali. Sangha [fr. saŋ+hr̥; lit. "comprising." The quâsi pop. etym. at VvA 233 is "diṭṭhi -- sīla -- sāmaññena sanghāṭabhāvena sangha"] 1. multitude, assemblage Miln 403 (kāka˚); J i.52 (sakuṇa˚); Sn 589 (ñāti˚); 680 (deva˚)

Dhamma -- cakka the perfection or supreme harmony of righteousness (see details under cakka), always in phrase dhcakkaŋ pavatteti (of the Buddha) "to proclaim or inaugurate the perfect state or ideal of universal righteousness" Vin i.8=M i.171; Vin i.11; S i.191; iii.86; Sn 556, 693; Miln 20, 343; DhA i.4; VvA 165; PvA 2, 67 etc.; besides this also in simile at S i.33 of the car of righteousness
dhamma -- cakka (the wheel of the Doctrine, i. e. the symbol of conquering efficacy, or happiness implicated in the D.) and brahma -- c˚ the best wheel, the supreme instrument, the noblest quality. Both

with pavatteti to start & kcep up (like starting & guiding a carriage), to set rolling, to originate, to make universally known. dhamma˚ e. g. S i.191; A i.23, 101; ii.34, 120; iii.151; iv.313; Sn 556 sq.; 693; J iii.412; Ps ii.159 sq.; PvA 67

*kuṭi*- 'brows' (Santali) bhr̥kuṭi— f. 'frown' MBh., *bhrakuṭi*— Yaśast. [*bhr̥*— and *bhra*— (though the latter is given by Pāṇ. as the form of *bhrū́*— in cmpds.) were orig. independent of *bhrū́*— and may be of Austro—as. and Mu. origin (cf. esp. Sant. *kuṭi*- 'brows'); though later replaced in *bhrŭkuṭi*— MBh., Pa. *bhūkuṭi*—. — EWA ii 517 with lit.] (CDIAL 9575) Marathi. भृकुटी [ bhṛkuṭī ] *f* S Contraction of the brows; frowning or a frown: but, commonly, the brows or a brow. భ్రుకుటి [ bhrukuṭi ] , భృకుటి or భ్రూకుటి *bhrukuṭi*. [Skt.] n. A frown. కనుబొమ్మలువిరువడము, బొమముడి. భ్రూ [ bhrū ] *bhrū*. [Skt.] n. The eye-brow. కనుబొమ్మ. భ్రూభంగము or భ్రూవిక్షేపము moving the eyebrows as in winking. బొమముడి. "పరిహాసంబులు కన్నుసన్నలును భ్రూభంగంబులున్ నర్మముల్." T. iv. 13. టీ భ్రూభంగంబులున్, కనుబొమ్మసన్నలును. భ్రూకుటి Same as భ్రుకుటి. (q. v.)

Pali. Pamha (nt.) [the syncope form of pakhuma=Sk. pakṣman used in poetry and always expld in C. by pakhuma] eye -- lash, usually in cpd. aḷāra˚ having thick eyelashes, e. g. at J v.215; Vv 357; 6411; Pv iii.35 Pamukha2 (nt.) [identical with pamukha, lit. "in front of the face," i. e. frontside, front] 1. eyebrow (?) only in phrase alāra˚ with thick eyebrows or lashes J vi.503 (but expld by C. as "visāl' akkhigaṇḍa); PvA 189 (for aḷāra -- pamha Pv iii.35). Bengali. পেখম [ pēkhama ] n a peacock's plumage or tail esp. when expanded or spread out like a fan at the time of dancing.

*Tu.* guḍi small pagoda or shrine; *Te.* koṭika hamlet; guḍi temple; kuṛḷ hut; guṛy temple (Ko.) kuṛḷ hut; guṛy temple (*Ka.* )(DEDR 1655)

Marathi. प्रमुख [ pramukha ] *a* (S) Chief, main, principal: also best or most excellent. 2 In comp. Leading, taking the lead or head of. Ex. विष्णु प्रमुखदेव महादेवापासीं गेले.

Kashmiri. sang-sār संग्- -सार् । अवहारः (सामुद्रिकजन्तुविशेषः) m.(in Ksh.) public general abuse; a shark, a water-elephant, a Gangetic crocodile (the *ghaṛiyāl* of India).

mákara— 1 m. 'crocodile' VS. Pa. *makara*— m. 'sea—monster'; Pk. *magara*—, *mayara*- m. 'shark', Si. *muvarā*, *mōrā*, Md. *miyaru*. — NIA. forms with —*g*— (e.g. H. G. *magar* m. 'crocodile') or —*ṅg*- (S. *maṅgar—macho* m. 'whale', *maṅguro* m. 'a kind of sea fish' → Bal. *māngar* 'crocodile') are loans from Pk. or Sk. or directly from non—Aryan sources from which these came, e.g. Sant. *maṅgaṛ* 'crocodile'(CDIAL 9692).

Kashmiri. sang 2 संग् m. a stone (Rām. 199, 143, 1412; YZ. 557). Marathi. संगीन [ saṅgīna ] *a* ( P) Built or made of stone.

sang--sār संग्-सार् mengro should, thus, mean 'stone artisan'. [cf. kerri mangro 'workman' (Gypsy); kaulo mengro 'blacksmith'; thus, mangro, mengro in Gypsy connotes an artisan.] The makara composite glyph becomes the signature-tune of stone-work by the stone-artisan or śilpi, viśvakarma architect. It is notable that in Sarasvati hieroglyphs, the 'standard device' is: sangaḍa; rebus: sangatarāśu 'stone-cutter' or lapidary.The hieroglyph *ghaṛiyāl* from the set of Sarasvati hieroglyphs gets ligatured with the water-elephant sang-sār संग्- -सार् to create the abiding hieroglyph of the sculptors, stone-artisans, of ancient Hindusthan. Begram ivories and bone sculptures of are the products created by tanana mleccha – in the Sarasvati lapidary tradition continuum -- using artistic motifs which get replicated in sites such as Bharhut and Sanchi. The additional ligaturing element of the fish-tail, puccha is to connote, rebus, worship, puja. Sculptures for these artisans of yore was indeed worship of kalādevi Sarasvati.]

Coraline algae, coral seaweed. Bouquet held in the gate-keeper's hand ప్రవాళము [ pravāḷamu ] *pra-vāḷamu*. [Skt.] n. A coral, పగడము. A shoot, sprout, new leaf. pravāḍa— m.n. 'coral' BHSk., *pravāla*—2, *prabāla*— m.n. MBh. [← Drav., Tam. *pavaṛam* &c., DED 3295] Pa. *pavāḷa*—, °*āla*— m.n., Pk. *pavāla*— m. (CDIAL 8794).

Pk. *paōlī*— f. 'city gate, main street'; WPah. (Joshi) *prauḷ* m., °*ḷi* f., *pauḷ* m., °*ḷi* f. 'gateway of a chief', *proḷ* 'village ward'; H. *paul*, *pol* m. 'gate, courtyard, town quarter with its own gate' (CDIAL 8633).

maṅgalá— n. 'auspicious sign' (in cmpds.) RV (CDIAL 9706)

Pali. Sangha [fr. saŋ+hṛ; lit. "comprising." The quâsi pop. etym. at VvA 233 is "diṭṭhi -- sīla -- sāmaññena sanghāṭabhāvena sangha"] 1. multitude, assemblage Miln 403 (kāka˚); J i.52 (sakuṇa˚); Sn 589 (ñāti˚); 680 (deva˚) Sanghin (adj.) [fr. sangha] having a crowd (of followers), the head of an order D i.47, 116; S i.68; Miln 4; DA i 143. -- sanghâsanghī (pl.) in crowds, with crowds (redupl. cpd.!), with gaṇi -- bhūtā "crowd upon crowd" at D i.112, 128; ii.317; DA i.280.

mengro 'smith' (artisan?)[in: kaulo mengro 'blacksmith' (Gypsy)]

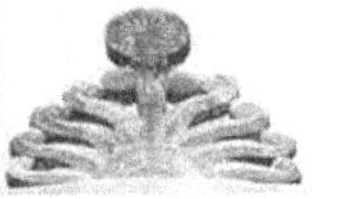

Dhamma -- cakka the perfection or supreme harmony of righteousness (see details under cakka), always in phrase dhcakkaŋ pavatteti (of the Buddha) "to proclaim or inaugurate the perfect state or ideal of universal righteousness" Vin i.8=M i.171; Vin i.11; S i.191; iii.86; Sn 556, 693; Miln 20, 343; DhA i.4; VvA 165; PvA 2, 67 etc.; besides this also in simile at S i.33 of the car of righteousness dhamma -- cakka (the wheel of the Doctrine, i. e. the symbol of conquering efficacy, or happiness implicated in the D.) and brahma -- c˚ the best wheel, the supreme instrument, the noblest quality. Both with pavatteti to start & kcep up (like starting & guiding a carriage), to set rolling, to originate, to make universally known. dhamma˚ e. g. S i.191; A i.23, 101; ii.34, 120; iii.151; iv.313; Sn 556 sq.; 693; J iii.412; Ps ii.159 sq.; PvA 67

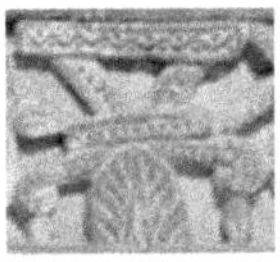

Pali. Medhi (f.) [Vedic methī pillar, post (to bind cattle to); BSk. medhi Divy 244; Prk. meḍhi Pischel *Gr.* § 221. See for etym. Walde, *Lat. Wtb.* s. v. meta] pillar, part of a stūpa [not in the Canon?]. M. *meḍ(h)*, *meḍhī* f., *meḍhā* m. 'post, forked stake'(CDIAL 10317).

mḗdha— m. 'sacrificial oblation' RV. Pa. *mēdha*— m. 'sacrifice'; Pa. *mejjha*— 'pure', Pk. *mejjha*—, *mijjha*— (CDIAL 10327).

paduma Paduma (nt.) [cp. Epic Sk. padma, not in RV.] the lotus Nelumbium speciosum. It is usually mentioned in two varieties, viz. ratta˚ and seta˚, i. e. red and white lotus, so at J v.37; SnA 125; as ratta˚ at VvA 191; PvA 157. The latter seems to be the more prominent variety; but paduma also includes the 3 other colours (blue, yellow, pink?), since it frequently has the designation of pañcavaṇṇa -- paduma (the 5 colours however are nowhere specified), e. g. at J i.222; v.337; vi.341; VvA 41. It is further classified as satapatta and sahassapatta -- p., viz. lotus with 100 & with 1,000 leaves: VvA 191. *பதுமம் patumam , n. < padma. 1. Lotus. See தாமரை. அறுவர் மற்றையோரும் . . . பயந்தோ ரென்ப பதுமத்துப்பாயல் (பரிபா. 5, 49). 2. See பதுமரேகை. (சங். அக.) 3. See பதுமபுராணம். பதுமமேலவன் புராணமாம் பிரமமே பதுமம் (கந்தபு. பாயி. 54). 4. See பதுமபீடம். இவர் எழுந்தருளி நின்ற . . . பதுமம் ஒன்று (S. I. I. ii, 135).*

One of the nine nidhi-s of Kubera. *பதுமம் patumam பதுமநிதி*

puṇṇaghaṭa

Puṇṇa [pp. of pṛ, Vedic pṛṇāti, Pass. pūryate, *pelē to fill; cp. Sk. prāṇa & pūrṇa=Av. pərəna; Lith. pílnas; Lat. plēnus; Goth fulls=E. full=Ger voll] full, seldom by itself (only passage so far pannarase puṇṇāya puṇṇamāya rattiyā D i.47=Sn p. 139). nor -- ˚ (only Sn 835 muttakarīsa˚), usually in cpds., and there mostly restricted to phrases relating to the full moon.
-- ghaṭa a full pitcher (for feeding the bhikkhus, as offering on festive days, cp. *J.P.T.S.* 1884) DhA i.147; KhA 118 (v. l. suvaṇṇaghaṭa); DA i.140 (˚paṭimaṇḍita ghara). Ghaṭa1 [Non -- Aryan?] a hollow vessel, a bowl, vase, pitcher. Used for holding water, as well as for other purposes, which are given under pānīya˚ paribhojana˚ vacca˚ at Vin i.157=352=M i.207. In the Vinaya freq. combd with kolamba, also a deep vessel: i.209, 213, 225, 286. -- As water -- pitcher: J i.52, 93 (puṇṇa˚), 166; VvA 118, 207, 244 (˚satena nhāto viya); PvA 66 (udaka˚), 179 (pānīya˚), 282. -- In general: S iv.196. For holding a light (in formula antoghaṭe padīpo viya upanissayo pajjalati) J i.235 (cp. kuṭa), PvA 38. Used as a drum J vi.277 (=kumbhathūna); as bhadda˚ Sdhp 319, 329.

Pa. *koṭṭha*— n. 'monk's cell, storeroom'; WPah.kṭg. *kóṭṭhi* f. 'house, quarters, temple treasury, name of a partic. temple', (CDIAL 3546)

WPah.kṭg. *krvṛi* f. 'granary (for corn after threshing)'; Garh. *kuṛu* 'house' kuṭī— f. 'hut' MBh., °*ṭikā*— f. Divyāv.(CDIAL 3232)
kuṛḷ hut; guṛy temple (Ko.) kuṛḷ hut; guṛy temple (*Ka.* ) *Tu.* guḍi small pagoda or shrine; *Te.* koṭika hamlet; guḍi temple (DEDR 1655)

Rebus readings of hieroglyphs of Begram, Khandagiri, Udayagiri, Kankali Tila, Bharhut Sanchi, Mathura

Now, we can read the following hieroglyphs and explain their meanings:

Begram

Plate 389 Triratna with eyes.Reference: Hackin, 1954, fig.195, no catalog N°.
Khandagiri

Khandagiri cave 3 (Ananta gumpha).Three motifs venerated. Cave 7 (Navamuni gumpha), Cave 8 (Baaraabhuji gumpha), Cave 9 (Mahavira gumpha), Cave 10 and Cave 11 (Lalaatendukesari gumpha) of Khandagiri represent tirthankara and their s'aasanadevis.

Khandagiri cave 3 (Ananta gumpha). A tree in a railing, under a canopy. A man stands with his hands folded, a woman is offering a lotus with a stalk. Is it the sacred jaina kevala tree?

Cave 9 (Manchapuri & Svargapuri) - cell on south, doorframe detail
Udayagiri-Khandagiri (Udaya.), cave Location Udayagiri-Khandagiri (Udaya.), Puri, Orissa, India Date 2nd-1st century BC

ca 50-25 BCE Description Cave 9 (Manchapuri & Svargapuri) Dotal, lower storey Stone, Jaina affiliation View Detail of the interior Image Identification Accession No 88214

http://dsal.uchicago.edu/images/aiis/images/large/ar_088214.jpg

Kankali Tila

Jain votive plaque. Ayagapata.
Mathura UP, Kankali Tila. Kushana (2nd c. CE). 65 x 57.5 cm.
J249 http://depts.washington.edu/silkroad/museums/delhi/earlynb.html

Top row hieroglyphs (From L. to R.)

Pali. ariya – dhamma. Ku. *dyol* 'temple' (CDIAL 6524).
*Pa.* guḍi temple; guṛy temple (*Ka.* ) (DEDR 1655)
Pali. Sangha ariya-dhamma
Pa. dhamma H. *dāwan* m. girdle (CDIAL 6283).

Bottom row hieroglyphs (From L. to R.)

P. *pūj* m. (dhamma) devotee (CDIAL 8319).
Padumanidhi one of nine treasures of Kubera (Ta.)
mĕdha— m. 'sacrificial oblation' RV.(CDIAL 10327).
puṇṇaghaṭa a full pitcher (for feeding the bhikkhus, as offering on festive days, cp. *J.P.T.S.* 1884)

The venerable person in the centre surrounded by the glyph: P. *pūj* m. (dhamma) devotee (CDIAL 8319).

Marathi. प्रमुख [ pramukha ] *a* (S) Chief, main, principal: also best or most excellent.

(Pk. *paōlī—* f. 'city gate, main street'; Pa. sangha dhammacakka Pa. dhamma).

Fragment of a Jaina stupa railing, Kankali Tila. Toranas adoring the stupa and with dharma symbols. Binay K. Behl notes: "In ancient times, the symbols and motifs of the art of all faiths in India were the same. This depiction is identical to the toranas of Buddhist stupas of early times".

http://www.flonnet.com/fl2420/stories/20071019505206400.htm

Bharhut

(Pk. *paōlī—* f. 'city gate, main street'; Pa. sangha dhammacakka *Parji.* guḍi temple (DEDR 1655)

Location Bharhut, Satna, Madhya Pradesh, India Date 2nd-1st century BC
ca 199-100 BCE Description Stupa, Great railing
Sandstone Standing figure, Status Architectural fragment
Presently located at: Calcutta, Indian Museum View Overview
Image Identification Accession No 68599 Sanchi Stupa 2, vedika., Northeast quadrant, inner face, north entrance, left pillar, south face, detail, sandstone

http://imagesvr.library.upenn.edu/a/aiis/thumb/311-14.JPG

Close-up of east gateway, finial on top architrave Bharhut

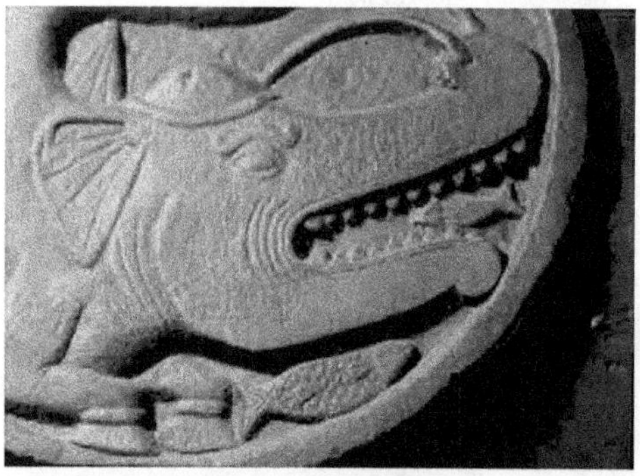

Bharhut. Makara. Location Bharhut, Satna, Madhya Pradesh, India Date 2nd-1st century BC ca 199-100 BCE Subject cross-bar medallion Description Stupa, Great railing Sandstone Standing figure, Status Architectural fragment Presently located at: Calcutta, Indian Museum View Overview Image Identification Accession No 34302

Bharhut. Makara. A coral emanates from the elephant trunk.
Site Name: Sanchi
Monument: Stupa II at Sanchi
Subject of Photo: detail from east face of west gate Makara also ligatured with fin/wings.

WPah. (Joshi) *prauḷ* m., city gate (CDIAL 8633).

maṅgalá— n. 'auspicious sign' (in cmpds.) RV (CDIAL 9706) mengro 'smith' (artisan?)[in: kaulo mengro 'blacksmith' (Gypsy)] cf. Kerri mangro 'workman' (Gypsy); thus, mangro, mengro in Gypsy connotes an artisan.

Pali. Sangha [fr. saŋ+hṛ; lit. "comprising." The quâsi pop. etym. at VvA 233 is "diṭṭhi -- sīla -- sāmaññena sanghāṭabhāvena sangha"] 1. multitude, assemblage Miln 403

Sanchi

P. *pūj* m. (dhamma) devotee (CDIAL 8319).
Marathi. प्रमुख [ pramukha ] *a* (S) Chief, main, principal: also best or most excellent.
*Parji.* guḍi temple (DEDR 1655)
Pali. dhamma -- cakka (the wheel of the Doctrine, i. e. the symbol of conquering efficacy, or happiness implicated in the D.)

Pennant of dharma glyph and wheel of dharma. Great Stupa (Stupa 1), eastern gateway, architrave, sandstone, detail of elephants on the architrave.
http://hdl.library.upenn.edu/1017/d/wheeler/mbwmp0100

Pennant of dharma glyph and wheel of dharma. Great Stupa (Stupa 1), eastern gateway, architrave, sandstone, detail of yakshi on the architrave

Sanchi Stupa 1, northern gateway., north side, architraves, sandstone.
http://hdl.library.upenn.edu/1017.2/A36-60

Pencil drawing by Frederick Charles Maisey of an ornament carved on the north gateway of great Stupa of Sanchi, taken from an album of 60 drawings dated 1847-1854.

The great Stupa of Sanchi, Stupa 1, is the finest example of monumental architecture of the Shunga era. Its core is believed to date from the reign of Ashoka in the 3rd century BC. The original brick stupa was one of the numerous stupas that Ashoka built in his kingdom to enshrine the bodily remains of the Buddha. In 150 BC the Stupa was enlarged and encased in stone and around 50 BC it was embellished with four monumental gates (*toranas*). These consist of square pillars supporting three curved architraves, completely covered with magnificent reliefs depicting *jatakas* (stories of Buddha's earlier incarnations) as well as stories from the historical Buddha and various auspicious symbols. This drawing represents what Maisey defined the 'disc-and-crescent symbol' which consists of a wheel (*chakra*), a solar symbol, surmounted by a trident (*trishula*), symbolising the 'three precious jewels' of Buddhism, Buddha, Dharma, Samgha.

http://ogimages.bl.uk/images/019/019WDZ000000546U00018B00%5BSVC1%5D.jpg
Site Name: Sanchi
Monument: Stupa II at Sanchi
Subject of Photo: foliate motif carved on section of a vedika pillar
Locator Info. of Photo: N gate, E (left) pillar of N vedika projection, N face
Photo Orientation: detail of bottom section
Dynasty/Period: Sunga
Date: ca. 100 BCE, 120 BCE - 80 BCE

Material: stone
Architecture: structural
Current Location: same as site location

Copyright Holder: Huntington, John C. and Susan L.
Scan Number: 0010991

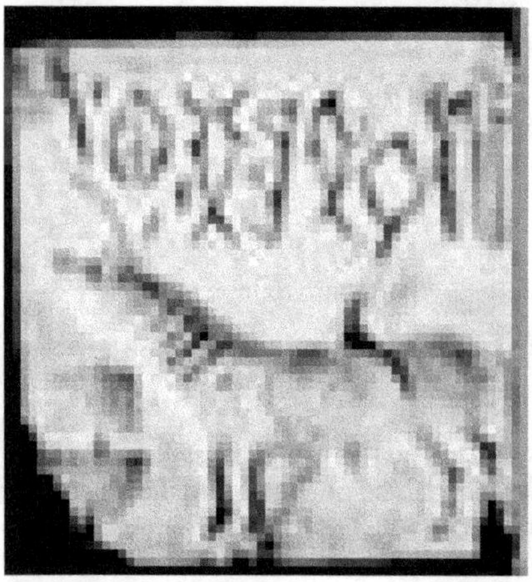

Mu. *kula* `tiger (*Felis_tigris*)'.

కోలాకు a long leaf. కోల [ kōla ] *kōla*. [Tel.] adj. Long. (DEDR 2237) కోలముఖము a long face.

*Ko.* el leaf. *To.* eṣ id. *Ka.* ele, ela id. *Koḍ.* elakaṇḍa id. *Tu.* elè, irè id. (497)
*Kur.* xolā tail. *Malt.* qoli id. (DEDR 2135)

*Ko.* kole·l temple in Kota village (also smithy) (DEDR 2133).

Mathura

Mathura lion capital (Now in British Museum).

Pali. Sangha [fr. saŋ+hṛ; lit. "comprising." The quâsi pop. etym. at VvA 233 is "diṭṭhi -- sīla -- sāmaññena sanghāṭabhāvena sangha"] 1. multitude, assemblage Miln 403
P. *pūj* m. (dhamma) devotee (CDIAL 8319).

Mu. *kula* `tiger (*Felis_tigris*)'. *Kur.* xolā tail. *Malt.* qoli id. (DEDR 2135)
*Ko.* kole·l temple in Kota village (DEDR 2133).

Sangham or sangiti are assemblies of monks. Magadhe-sangham, santi (sanci) sangham were Bauddha fraternities of Magadha (cf. Bhabra inscription, JASB, ix, 618: opening words: 'piyadasi-raja Magadha-sangham abhivad-manam cha' 'Piadasa Raja, unto the multitude assembled in Magadha saluting him, speaks (thus)'.) and Sanchi (cf. Sanchi pillar inscription, Pl. XIX, No. 177 carved on a pillar near the south gateway. Cunningham (p. 261) reads the highly mutilated inscription (with some help from James Prinsep's reading: *devanam(piya) magadhe (raja)..(a)bhi)vadena)nam chetiyagiri...tikhi-cha(dha)magiri..ikeya sangham. Bhokhati bhikkhunabhikhamavise dato nidu..ti sanam..chhava aund sasiel(ye)petariye. Ichhahime santi sangham samage milathitike siyati*. 'Devanamapiya, king of Magadha, offers his salutation to the community of Chaityagiri (and perhaps that of Dharmagiri also)...with a gift of food for the Bhikshus, much-emaciated (ks.aama read for Pali khama)(with their austerities?)...and prays that the Santi community may always be united.'). . (Alexander Cunningham, 1854, *The Bhilsa Topes or Buddhist monuments of Central India*, London, Smith Elder and Co.)

Kankali Tila. Photograph taken by Edmund William Smith in 1880s-90s of a Jain homage tablet. This tablet presents, in the bottom row, an alternative list of eight auspicious hieroglyphs (including the svastika hieroglyph).

## 3 INDUS OR PROTO-INDIC LANGUAGE

As a corollary to the decoding of the Indus script cipher, hermeneutic interpretation helps identify the *lingua franca* of the Indus age. Hermeneutics is the science of discovering new meanings and interpretations in 'all those situations in which we encounter meanings that are not immediately understandable but require interpretive effort' (Gadamer, Hans-Georg. 1976, *Philosophical Hermeneutics*, ed. and trans. by David E. Linge, Berkeley: University of California Press, xii). Such an interpretive effort has led to the decoding of most of Indian hieroglyphs as the repertoire of miners and metalsmiths of the civilization in a linguistic area. The ancient words read rebus can be traced in many Bharatiya (Indian) languages as borrowings from mleccha (Language X + proto-Munda). Such a gloss will provide further research leads to identify and define proto-Indic language of the bronze-age.

The *lingua franca* (or parole, spoken tongue) of Bharat circa 5000 years ago is hypothesized as a continuum of dialects, evolving in tandem with the cultural setting and technological innovations. Since the civilization which emerged on and was nurtured on the banks of Rivers Sarasvati and Sindhu continues into the historical periods in Bharat, the language spoken circa 5000 years Before Present can be reconstructed from substratum lexemes in languages of present-day Bharat and based on the lexical work done by philologists from the days of Yaska (circa $6^{th}$ century BCE) upto the discovery of Bangani in the $20^{th}$ century.

Mleccha is a word cognate with Pali Melukka which means copper. Mlecchita vikalpa mentioned by Vatsyayana as cryptography, may, therefore, be the work of metal workers and may be related to the writing system found on many copper tablets and inscribed weapons, apart from seals and tablets of the civilization.

Meluhha as a language and Indus script as a messaging system in contact/interaction areas are attested archaeologically and in epigraphia of indus script inscriptions. Corpora (plural of 'corpus') related to Meluhha as a language and Indus script epigraphia have become available, thanks to the dedicated work of many researchers.

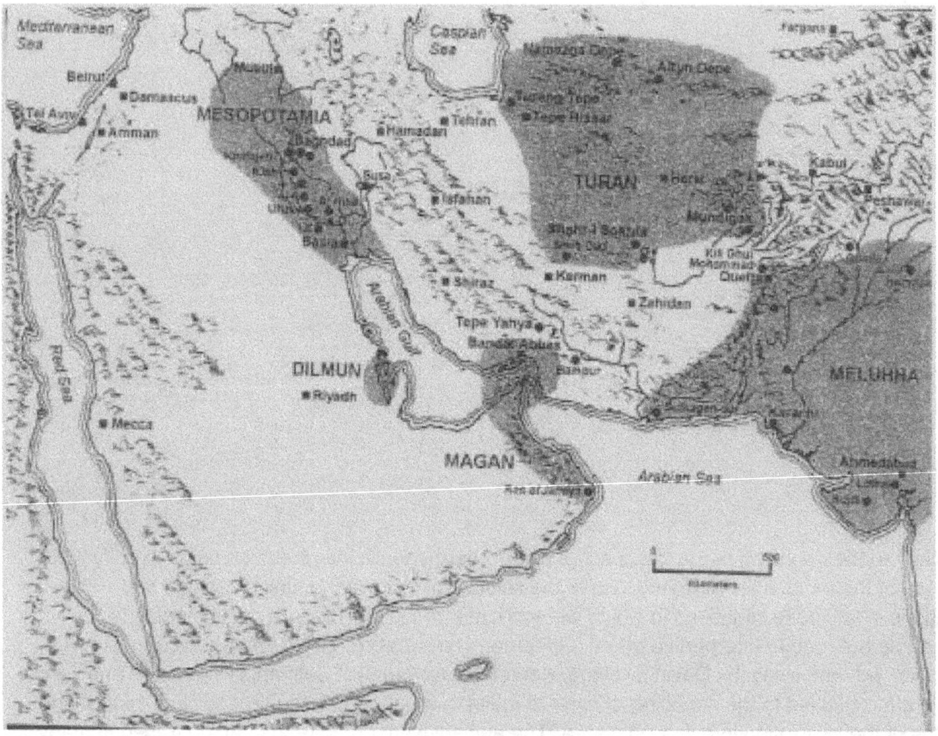


Western Asia showing Mesopotamia, Turan, Dilmun, Magan and Meluhha. See Steinkeller 1984,265,Fig. 2)

Language studies of the Indian linguistic area (Indian *sprachbund*) are suggested to continue the recent linguistic advances in methodology to identify substratum words in ancient languages (like those of Rigveda or Avesta or Sanskrit or Prakrits) and to construct isoglosses for Proto-Indo-Iranian or Proto-Indo-Aryan or Proto-Indian. Such studies will substantiate this decryption of Indus script that a combination of Proto-Munda, Proto-Dravidian, Prakrit, Language 'X' and Indo-Aryan language speakers wrote the inscriptions of Indus script to communicate the underlying mlechchha (meluhha) lingua franca of lapidary/metalworking artisan words.

Mleccha is a cognate of 'meluhha'. Mlecchitavikalpa is a term which occurs in Vatsyayana's vidyaasamuddes'a (objectives of learning) s'loka listing 64 arts: three of these arts related to language are: des'abhaashaa jnaana; akshara mushtika kathana; mlecchita vikalpa [trans. learning dialects of the linguistic area (des'a); messaging through use of fingers and wrists; cryptography (writing system)].

Mlecchitavikalpa means: alternative representation of language through writing. Mlecchita means 'made by mleccha'. Mleccha means 'copper workers'.

Thus, mlecchitavikalpa relates to the writing system invented by early metal-workers, mleccha (meluhha) of the Sarasvati linguistic area.

Evidence for mleccha spoken in India, prior to 8th century BCE

If mlecchita vikalpa occurred in *Kamaśāstra*, Mleccha could have been lingua franca prior to 8th century BCE, when Nandi transcribed the work (The work of Vātsyāyana uses the term, mlecchita vikalpa, to denote cipher writing of mleccha, lingua franca).

An early version of *Kamaśāstra* is pre-dates eighth century BCE. As Alain Danielou notes: "The predecessors of Vātsyāyana. The first formulation of the *Kamaśāstra*, or rules of love, is attributed to Nandi, Shiva's companion. During the eighth century BCE, Shvetaketu, son of Uddalaka, undertook the summary of Nandi's work.The date is known, since Uddalaki and Shvetaketu are the protagonists of the Brihat Aranyaka Upanishad and Chandogya Upanishad, which are usually dated to this period and contain important passages connected with erotic science. A man of letters called Babhru, together with his sons or disciples, known as the Babhravya, made an important written work, summarizing the too-vast work of Shvetaketu. The Babhravya came originally from Panchala, a region located between the Ganges and the Yamuna, to the south of present-day Delhi, but most probably lived in the city of Pataliputra, the great center of the kingdom of Chandragupta, which resisted Alexander's invasion in the fourth century and became the seat of the Ashoka empire a century later...The text of Suvarnanabha must date from the first century BCE, since it mentions a king of Kuntala (to the south of Pataliputra), named Shatakarni Shatavahana who reigned at this time and who killed his wife accidentally in the course of sadistic practices. On the other hand, Yashodhara, at the beginning of his commentary, attributes the origin of erotic science to Mallanaga, the 'prophet of the Asuras' (the ancient gods), meaning to prehistoric times. Nandi, Shiva's companion, is then said to have transcribed it for manking today. The attribution of the first name Mallanaga to Vatsyayana is due to the confusion of his role as editor of the Kama Sutra with that of the mythical creator of erotic science." (Alain Danielou, 1994, *The complete Kama Sutra*, Park Street Press, Rochester, Vermont, pp.3-4).

Richard Burton translates 'mlecchita vikalpa' as one of the 64 arts mentioned in Vatsyayana's Kamasutra as follows: "the art of understanding writing in cypher, and the writing of words in a peculiar way." Writing in cypher. Vikalpa is an alternative representation of language, in this case, spoken words expressed in writing (cypher). Two other language-related arts listed by Vatsyanana are: deshabhaashaa jnaanam and akshara mushtika kathanam (that is: knowledge of dialects of the land and story-telling using fingers and wrists, that is, hand-gestures and finger-gestures forming mudra-s). In this triad, it is logical to interpret mlecchita vikalpa as cypher writing made by mleccha. http://www.bharatadesam.com/literature/vatsyayana_kamasutras/vatsyayana_kamasutra_3.php

"In his commentary on the Kama-sutra, Yashodhara describes two kinds of mlecchita-vikalpa. One is called kautilyam in which the letter substitutions are based upon phonetic relations -- the vowels become consonants, for example. A simplification of this form is called durbodha. Another kind of secret writing is muladeviya. Its cipher alphabet consists merely of the reciprocal one with all other letters remaining unchanged. Muladeviya existed in both a spoken form -- as such it figures in Indian literature and is used by traders, with geographical variations -- and a written form, in which case it is called gudhalekhya." (David Kahn, *The Code-Breakers: The Story of Secret Writing*, New York, Macmillan, 1967, pp. 74-75)

Tamilla as a synonym of Milangka, Wilangka (Milakkha, mleccha, Pali)

"This is something about Pali on the northern Thai fringe, or about Sri Lanka in the Chiangmai valley: The term Lawa was used in reference to highland outsiders in Lanna and Shan States. Its longer form is Damilawa , and is said to derive from the Sanskrit Damila, the same term as informed the Buddhist Sri Lankan ethnic term Tamil for their non-Buddhist Others. The root of the term lay in Sinhalese chronicle accounts of the state and its dark-skinned enemies. Thus, along with the localization of Buddhism in mainland Southeast Asia came certain aspects of ethnic ranking and prejudice that contributed to rulers' ability to contextualize in universalistic terms their rule and the peoples that it excluded. Many Chiangmai chronicles used the term Tamilla for Lawa. Some used the term Milangka. Wilangka, a variant on that term, was used among Lawa in reference to their chief who lost out to the lowland

forces. Milangka is derived from Milakkha, the Pali language equivalent to the Sankrit Mleccha ("savages")." Leif Jonsson // Oct 17, 2008
http://rspas.anu.edu.au/rmap/newmandala/2008/09/30/pali/#comment-568304

Decrypting Indus script - what it means to the study of Indian civilization -- S. Kalyanaraman (2011)

Michael Witzel calls for a paradigm change in language studies:

[quote]...Large pockets of the Para-Munda Indus language, pre-munda substratum, of the newly arrived Dravidian as well as some remnants of the Gangetic Language "X" (a group of Hindi loan words whose origin is uncertain) must have survived as well... Instead of fighting the ghosts of the 19th and early 20th century, we should, in the 21st, look for the similarities or differences, for overlap or linkages, and for the obvious cultural changes that are visible both within the archaeological and the linguistic/textual record...

"...we should strive for a new paradigm of the early linguistic (and ethnic) situation of South Asia. Using the earliest available evidence, the loan words in the Rgveda (and a few words transmitted in Mesopotamian documents), we can establish the following spheres of influence. (The dates given below are, as always, very approximate).

• Before c. 1450 BCE
In the Greater Panjab, the prefixing Para-Mundic or Para-Austroasiatic Harappan language was spoken, along with a few hints of Masica's more eastern (Haryana/U.P.) "Language X"; the Central Asian substrate, brought into the Panjab by the oldest layer of gvedic, probably was of little consequence during the Harappan period.

• From c. 1450-1300 BCE
The Greater Panjab saw the first influx of Dravidian words, most likely from Sindh; the situation in Sindh and Baluchistan is less clear: a variety of the Para-Mundic Harappan was amalgamated with Munda influences from the east, with the immigrant(?) ProtoDravidian, and the immigrant early Old Indo-Aryan and in Baluchistan also some preIranian. Amalgamation of Indo-Aryan, Para-Munda and Dravidian elements in the Greater Panjab and in Haryana.

• After c. 1300 BCE
Continuing amalgamation, evidenced by increase of 'foreign' words in the late gveda. The trend continues in the post-RV texts (YV, AV Mantras and in later Vedic) with a continuing influx of the same types of vocabulary into the educated Vedic speech of the Brahmins. By this time, the increasing amount of textual materials allows to detail the existence of some other languages in the Greater Panjab or on its rim: Proto-Burushaski in the northwest, Tibeto-Burmese in the Himalayas and in Kosala, Dravidian in Sindh, Gujarat and Central
India, and predecessors of remnants language groups, now found in isolated pockets of the subcontinent.

"Because of the amalgamation of at least three groups (IA, Para-Munda, Drav.) we have to suppose a large degree of bilingualism (cf. Kuiper, A bilingual rsi, in press) and even trilingualism, and the forming of pidgins. While a Vedic pidgin was the lingua franca and used at home, proper Vedic Sanskrit was learnt 'in school' by members of the Ārya classes. Large pockets of the Para-Munda Indus language, of the newly arrived Dravidian as well as some remnants of the Gangetic Language "X" must have survived as well. [unquote]

http://www.people.fas.harvard.edu/~witzel/IndusLang.pdf

(Michael Witzel, 2006, Early loan words in western Central Asia, Indicators of substrate populations, migrations and trade relations, in: Victor H. Mair, 2006, *Contact and Exchange in the Ancient World*, University of Hawaii Press, p. 183).

In the context of the researches to locate the homeland of Aryans, Witzel notes: In retracing our steps to the beginning of this investigation, it may be asked what the evidence presented here teaches us. It is obvious that instead of looking, in the Avestan texts, for a "mythical homeland" of all Iranians (or evenof all Aryans/Indo-Iranians), we need to take the texts seriously, at their own word.

B.B. Lal calls for a paradigm change in deliberating on Aryan Invasion Theory in the context of Bactria-Margiana Archaeological Complex finds:

B.B. Lal, 2007, Let not the 19th century paradigms continue to haunt us! - Inaugural address delivered at the 19th Intl. conf. on South Asian archaeology, held at Univ. of Bologna, Ravenna, italy on July 2-6, 2007.

Georges-Jean Pinault, 2006, Further links between the Indo-Iranian substratum and the BMAC language in: Bertil Tikkanen & Heinrich Hettrich, eds., 2006, *Themes and tasks in old and middle Indo-Aryan linguistics*, Delhi, Motilal Banarsidass, pp. 167 to 196. "...we have Toch. A. *ancu 'iron', the basis of the derived adjective ancwaashi 'made of iron', to which corresponds Toch. B encuwo, with the parallel derived adjective encuwanne 'made of iron'...The two forms go back to CToch. oencuwoen-non.sg. *oencuwo, the final part of which is a regular product of IE *-on...This noun is deprived of any convincing IE etymology...The term Ved. ams'u-, Av . asu- goes back to a noun borrowed from some donor language of Central Asia, as confirmed by CToch. *oencuwoen-...the BMAC language would not belong to the Indo-European family; it does not seem to be related to Dravidian either...New identifications and reconstructions will certainly help to define more precisely the contours of the BMAC vocabulary in Indo-Iranian, as well as in Tocharian."(p.192)]

There is evidene from an Akkadian cylinder seal that the language of the civilization area was Meluhha (cognate: mleccha in Skt. Milakkhu in Pali).

The Meluhhan being introduced carries an antelope on his arm. Cylinder seal Impression. Akkadian. Inscription records that it belongs to 'S'u-ilis'u, Meluhha interpreter'. Musee du Louvre. Ao 22 310, Collection De Clercq.

'In a letter dated 16 May 1990, Dr. Dominique Collon comments on the iconography as follows: 'The seal depicts a seated figure, identifiable by her long hair as feminine and by her horned head-dress (chipped) as a deity. The flounced robe is also generally an indication of divinity. The child on her lap could be the owner of the seal but is more likely to be an attributor of the godess. The figures approaching the godess are probably the owner of the seal and his wife although it is possible that these are priestly figures. Several centuries later, in Old Babylonian times, it is the king who almost always carries the animal offering but he is probably seeking favourable omens and the deities he approaches are ther particularly connected with omens (see Collon 1986: III.37). On these later, Old Babylonian seals, the figure carrying a situla or bucket is generally a priest but here it is clearly a woman and there is nothing to indicate that she is a priestess of a queen. Both wear Akkadian dress and nothing distinguishes them as foreigners. The significance of the kneeling male figure and the pots behind is difficult to interpret: they could be an attribute of the godess, and the large pots on stands are used even today for water – perhaps an additional reference to the godess' fertility aspect. Among the seals illustrated by R.M. Boehmer (1965) seals 549 and 555 make clear that some sort of drink is involved. Boehmer's plate 47 shows that the scene belongs to a well-established iconographical group and was not specifically created for the Meluhha interpreter – indeed it was probably chosen from a range of ready-cut seals in a seal-cutter's workshop and the inscription was added. This would account for the fact that the figures overlap the inscription frame on both sides. Boehmer attributes the seal to Akkadisch III period – i.e. from Naramsin onwards." [cf. Parpola, 1994, fig. 8.4]

An Akkadian seal (after Powell, p. 390: *The Bronze Age Civilization of Central Asia*, New York, 1980) shows the translator of the Meluhhan (Sindhu Sarasvati) language (EME.BAL.ME.LUH.HA.KI) is received by a person of high rank and sitting by his lap. Another Meluhhan sitting by three jars makes a greeting gesture. Two persons enter: one carries an animal, the other a purse. British Museum tablet #79987 enumerates a 'man of Meluhha' named (...)-ibra in a list of foes of Naram-Sin, King of Akkad, ca. 2250 BCE. "During the second half of the 3rd millennium BC, textual sources frequently refer to trade with Dilmun, Magan and Meluhha. Dilmun is known to be the island of Bahrain, Magan is probably present-day Makran and the territory opposite it in Oman, while at this period it seems that Meluhha referred to the Indus Valley where the flourishing cities of Mohenjo Daro and Harappa have been excavated. The Indus Valley civilisation used square stamp seals but under the impetus of trade some cylinder seals appear and a Meluhhan interpreter used a typical Akkadian seal." (Collon, 1987).

An attempt to unravel the language spoken by the Meluhhan on this cylinder seal has been made, through a number of sources. Proceeding on the assumption that Meluhha as seen from Mesopotamia was the Sapta-Sindhu region of Bhārata, one such source is the compilation of a lexicon based on sememes from the ancient versions of present-day languages of Bhārata. Another source is the application of many lexemes from this lexicon using the rebus method to many glyphs of the inscribed objects from Meluhha of the period, ca. 2250 BCE.

It appears that the 'antelope' or 'ram' shown on the back of the Meluhhan is a homonym for a semantic determinant connoting the nature of his profession, the helper of a merchant. mr..eka 'goat' (Telugu); mlekh 'goat' (Brahui). He is from Meluhha, copper-region. [mlecchamukha 'copper' (Skt.); milakkhu 'copper' (Pali)]

Manu notes (10.45) the existence of a mleccha-speaking community among dasyu:

*mukhabāhuroopajjānām yā loke jātayo bahih*

*mlecchavācas' cāryavācas te sarve dasyuvah smṛtāh*

"All those people of the world which are excluded from the (community of) those born from the mouth, the arms, the thighs and the feet (of Brahman) are called Dasyu, whether they speak the language of the mleccha or that of the Arya." (Buhler). Alt. Mleccha dialect speakers and arya dialect speakers are all remembered as dasyu.

In Mahabharata, Pahlava, Shabara, Shaka, Yavana, Pundra, Kirata, Dramida, Simbhala, Barbara, Darada and Mleccha are collectively summed up as mleccha (1.165.35-37).

Manu 10.43-45 considered Coda, Dravida, Persian etc. as former kshatriya who sank to the level of shudra, whether they speak the language of the mleccha or the language of arya. Kane H.Dh. Vol. II, p. 383 gives the impression that these groups were bilingual, speaking both 'mleccha' language and 'arya' language.

A more reasonable interpretation is that mleccha is the ungrammatical lingua franca as distinct from grammatically correct, literary bhaashaa as proto-Sanskrit. Samskr.ta (refined speech) is distinguished from asura, pisaca, mleccha as dialects with incorrect pronunciation of Samskṛtam. For instance, *śatapatha brāhmaṇa* notes that the mleccha-speakers failed to articulate arava(h) correctly; they uttered 'helava helava'. (*te asura attavacasa he'alave he'alava* 3.2.1.23). One notes that the madhyandina-branch of the Satapathi Brahmins were occasionally indifferent to correct articulation; so that they got corrupt recitation as the mleccha did. http://www.koshur.org/Linguistic/8.html "Mleccha were those who cfould not pronounce Samskrta (vak) appropriately as prescribed in Svaravidhana of the grammatical treatises. Mostly the mleccha were the Kirata, the Savara, the Pulinda (Amarakosha, Sundravarga)." Akkadian maliku(m) means god, king, lord. This anecdote clearly notes mleccha as a grammatical entity, a language.

Jayaswal notes that mleccha was the Samskr.tam representation of Hebrew melekh meaning, 'king' and that the utterance: he lavah! he lavah! in the *śatapatha brāhmaṇa* was a specimen of mleccha speech; that this spech is cognate with Hebrew ēloāh (plural ēlohim) meaning, 'God' (Jayaswal, KP, 1914, 'Kleine Mitteilungen', Zeitschrift der Deutschen Morgenlandischen Gesellschraft,, vol. LXXII, p. 719). For the specimen of mleccha speech, an alternative explanation is provided in *Mahābhāṣya* with a variation, helayo helayo; Sāyaṇācārya notes that the speimen of asura/mleccha speech is a variant of he 'rayo, he 'raya meaning, 'O the (spiteful) enemies', explained by the asuras' inability to pronounce the sounds, - r- and –y-. (*Mahābhāṣya* 1.1.1; KC Chatterjee, 1957, *Patañjali's Mahābhāṣya*, Calcutta, pp. 10-11; Sāyaṇa on *śatapatha brāhmaṇa*, 3.2.1.23).] Another example of a substrate term: Sumerian tibira, tabira (Akkadian. LU2 URUDU-NAGAR =. "[person] copper-carpenter"); a word indicating borrowing from a substrate. In Pkt. tambira = copper. According to Gernot Wilhelm, the Hurrian version of tabira is: tab-li 'copper founder'; tab-iri 'the one who has cast (copper)'.

Asko and Simo Parpola claim that Meluhha is the origin of the Sanskrit mleccha. Asko Parpola and Simo Parpola, 1975, "On the relationship of the Sumerian toponym Meluhha and Sanskrit mleccha". *Studia Orientalia* 46: 205–238. Sargon of Akkad (c. 2200 BCE) had 'dismantled the cities, as far as the shore of the sea. At the wharf of Agade, he docked ships from Meluhha, ships from Magan.' Comparable words are: Sindhi milis, Panjabi malech, Pali milakkhu.

*śatapatha brāhmaṇa* 3.2.1.18-24 speaks of asuryā vāk. After the Asura were deprived of speech (vak) which was offered to fire for purification while reciting anushtubh, the asura shouting he'layo he'layo got defeated. No Brahmin should speak such mleccha (speech).

Linguistic Area as Language-community

Since 1956, there has been a paradigm shift in IE linguistics as applied to the area called 'India' using terms such as areal linguistics, *sprachbund*, linguistic area.

The credit for using the term 'linguistic area' goes to MB Emeneau, even though he used the term as a translation of '*sprachbund*' invented by HV Velton in 1943.

The term *sprachbund* was used in 1931 by Nikol Trubetzkoy and Roman Jakobson when they discussed the long-recognized linguistic areas such as the languages of the Caucasus or of the Balkans. The following works have been reviewed: *Language and Linguistic Area, Essays by Murray B. Emeneau*, (selected and introduced by Anwar S. Dil), 1980, Stanford University Press, California (which includes: Emeneau, MB, 1956, India as a linguistic area, in: Language, 32.3-16 Kuiper, FBJ, 1967, The genesis of a linguistic area, *Indo-Iranian Journal* 10: 81-102 Masica, Colin P., 1976, *Defining a linguistic area, South Asia*, Chicago, niversity of Chicago Press (Based on the author's thesis, 1971).

Linguistic areas are areas in which 'languages belonging to more than one family show traits in common which do not belong to the other members of (at least) one of the families'.The methodology used to recognize a linguistic area is a bifurcate one. First, a typological feature is established as pan-Indic and at the same time not extra-Indic. Second, the historical diffusion of features throughout the languages of the linguistic area are investigated through questions of lexical lists, phonology, syntactic, morphological and semantic development and sociolinguistic questions. (Emeneau, opcit., pp.1, 2). Emeneau recognizes that '...it is rarely possible to demonstration this (Indo-Aryan to Dravidian) direction (except for diffusion of lexical items).

Features investigated

In this investigation, a staggering list of features are involved. Some features listed by Colin Masica are as follows: (From Appendix A, Colin Masica, opcit., pp. 187-190)

Phonological

1. retroflex consonants, esp. stops
2. aspirated onsonants
3. nasalized vowels
4. affricatin opposition ta/ts
5. syllabic structure and phoneme distributions?
6. tendency to initial stress?

B. morphological

1. absence of prefixes
2. verbal prefixes
3. two stems in personal pronouns
4. same case morphemes added to singular and plural stems
5. dative in k-/g-
6. morphological causatives
7. anticausatives
8. negative conjugation
9. phonaesthetic forms a)repludicated; b) in –k
10. echo words

C. syntactic

1. conjunctive participle
2. quotative c.p. 'having said' a) w. phonaesthemes
3. agentive (quasi-ergative) construction, esp. 'impersonal' type
4. numeral classifiers
5. enclitic particle –api/-um; 'even/also/indefinite/and'
6. dative-subject construction
7. absence of verb have
8. word order features SOV, AN, GN, demN, Po, SMAdj, etc.
9. explicator compound verbs
10. recapitulation of final finite V by initial conjunctive ppl. in following sentence
11. relative participle

Based on an investigation of these features of languages of Bharat (of Indo-Aryan, Munda and Dravidian families), the conclusion drawn by Emeneau and Masica is that Bharat constitutes a linguistic area, as defined by Emeneau. FBJ Kuiper's paper, 'The genesis of a linguistic area' (1967, *Substratum influence on (Rig-vedic) Sanskrit? Studies in the Linguistic Sciences,* University of Illinois, 5, 76-125) was published in a 1974 volume 3 of International Journal of Dravidian Linguistics (ed. VI Subramoniam, Trivandrum) and was devoted to Contact and Convergence in South Asian

Languages. The volume also had a paper by Franklin C. Southworth, 'Linguistic stratigraphy of North India'. Kuiper investigated the existence of retroflex phonemes in Sanskrit, even in the earliest Vedic language in terms of bilingualism, the use of gerunds in the Rigveda and the use of iti as a marker found already in the Rigveda. This analysis of Kuiper should convince anyone that 'pre-indo-aryan' was not a 'language spoken in a vacuum' (p.86). Emeneau argues further that the sources for the borrowed traits could be Dravidian and not a lost language family; that the three traits noted by Kuiper are of the highest antiquity in the record. (Emeneau, opcit., p. 175).

A critique of South Asia as a linguistic area is Heinrich Hock (1975) who stretches himself to find Indo-European antecedents or parallels for some of the alleged areal features and points to Indo-Aryan to Dravidian direction of influence, to native Indo-Aryan developments uninfluenced by substratum contacts. "This is to downgrade the striking Indianization which Indo-Aryan has undergone, and in at least the case of retroflex consonants to find perverse a century and a half of scholarly endeavor." (Emeneau, opcit., p. 5). This is subdued but vehement denunciation of Hock's heroic effort at debunking 150 years of scholarship. Emeneau goes on to argue: "Hock's skepticism (88,114) as to 'whether Proto-Dravidian did in fact, as is generally assumed (at least implicitly), antedate the arrival of the Indo-Aryans' seems unjustified, based as it is on a rejection of the glottochronological method of relative dating – this is merely the negation of results based on a method which is otherwise dubious in its results, and no argument can be based on it. Another attempt, archaeological, to put a late date on Dravidian was, I argued, based in part on a prioristic linguistic arguments...The 2000-year record of Tamil in its present position and the certainty that Tamil is not equitable with Proto-Dravidian require an intervention of a long period between PDr. and Tamil, as is clear fom the tree-diagram now given for the Dravidian family (whatever the details of the diagram) – but of course the question is: 'how long a period?' " (Emeneau, opcit., fn.1, p. 14).

India and linguistics

"It was...the linguistics of India of more than two millennia ago that was the direct germinal origin of the linguistics of the Western world of today...the (collection of Vedic) texts has as their basic operative principle the revealed words themselves. They could bring their desired benefits only if the words were correctly enunciated; they could even harm their utterers if they were mishandled. How to achieve this correctness over the centuries in the face of relentlessly encroaching linguistic change? This problem which has engaged other communities as well, seems to have been better solved by the Hindus than by any others. They became very exact phoneticians at a time (was it the beginning of the first millennium BC, or was it a litter earlier or a little later?) when all other peoples either had made no advances in this direction or were only the most hopeless fumblers. It is thought that the phoneticians were actually responsible for the text of the Rigveda as we have it today. Their phonetic handbook (pra_tis'a_khya) to this Veda is warrant indeed that three millennia have produced only the most insignificant of changes in the text and the pronunciation of the text. But it was not only phonetics that had to be developed. Meanings were important, and the transmitters of the Veda composed lists of words (nighan.t.u) which served as partial glossaries to the Vedic text; as meanings became more difficult for later generations to be sure of, lists grew fuller and commentaries were added. Morphological and syntactic matters too were important in arriving at an understanding of the purport of the old texts, and that such matters received treatment is certain, even though none of the old treatises have survived...Intellectual thoroughness and an urge toward ratiocination, intellection, and learned classification for their own sakes should surely be recognize as characteristic of the Hindu higher culture. It has often been pointed out that the Hindu is spiritual, i.e. concerned with his soul and its relation to the universe, and that his philosophy is a means of salvation whereby his soul may be released from the bonds of the phenomenal and may attain to union with the spiritual element of the universe..Since, notoriously, philosophers cannot agree, a large number of philosophical substructures have emerged from the Indian thinking – monist, modified monist, dualist, and pluralist, theist and atheist, based on a soul and denying a soul, concentration on the substantiation of evidence and relatively neglectful of this... (the Hindus) became grammarians, it would seem, for grammar's sake...the language described by Pa_n.ini became India's literary language because of his description...Respiration and digestion are automatic but not learned, gesture and speech are automatic but the result of learning. Hindu culture was so much interested in all these things that techniques both of investigation and of manipulation were developed... This is essentially a raising of the subliminal to full consciousness. This too is the essence of the classical Hindu dance – a codification of the learned but subsconscious use of gesture, and addition to and elaboration of it...And surely the study of language is but another example of the raising to consciousness of an acquired but subliminal activity – for analysis of the activity and for normative manipulation of it...The only type of description that is adequate qua description, for any body of data, is one that attempts to identify all similarities that are to be found in the data, and to organize the similars into classes and those into more inclusive classes, and so on until the most inclusive classes of classes are found...The native medieval Greek and Latin phonology is immature and inept compared with the Hindu phonetic, phonemic, and morphophonemic analysis...One point of contrast may be made with Greek grammar; the Hindu analysis of relations between allomorphs in terms of gun.a and vr.ddhi is a prefiguring of the Indo-European ablaut system, taken as far as it could go, considering that Sanskrit had lost the qualitative ablaut and considering too that the Hindu grammarians did not know...any other Indo-European language with which to make comparisons. The Greek language, on the other hand, preserved both qualitative and quantitative ablaut relations in a remarkably transparent form, and yet the Greek grammarians, and those who followed them in the West until the nineteenth century, were unable to construct a system of relations comparable to that seen in Pāṇini." (Emeneau, opcit., pp. 19-20; emphasis added). If Emeneau and IE linguistics had pursued this inclusive definition of description -- to identify all similarities that are to be found in the data, and to organize the similars into classes – to a logical conclusion of the analysis of the features of bharatiya languages would have led to define

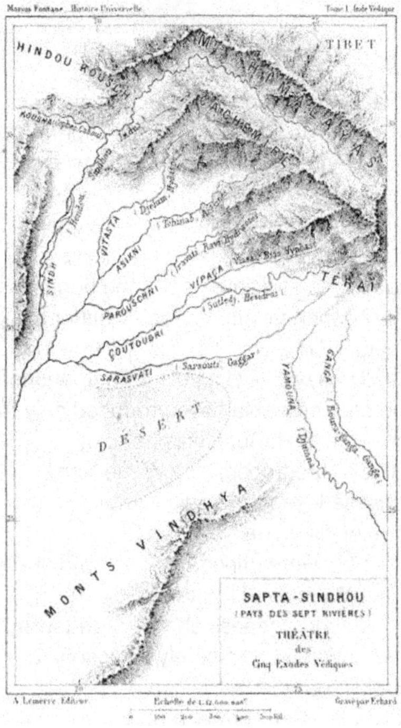


Prakrit as a language family of Bharat. But alas, it was not to be, because the linguistics had to carry the baggage, the received wisdom which had already straight-jacketed an IE family of languages (including of course, Vedic and Sanskrit, given the wealth of literature and the texts which were available to develop the discipline). Emeneau (p. 89) argues that in regard to retroflex (domal or cerebral) consonants which is a pan-indic feature, the later Indo-Aryan developments are due to a borrowing of indigenous speech habits through bilingualism, and "to the well-ground suspicion that even the early development of retroflexes from certain Indo-European consonant clusters results from the same historic cause. (This doctrine is held by, e.g. Jules Bloch, *Sanskrit et dravidien*, Bull. Soc. Ling. Paris 25.1-21 esp. 4-6 (1925); SM Katre, *Some problems of historical linguistics in Indo-Aryan,* Bombay, 1944, pp. 135 ff.; Gundert in 1869, *Ztsch. Deutsch. Morgenlandischen Ges.* 23.517 ff.") Prima facie, it should be clear from the Indian Lexicon which absorbs over 4000 of the etyma of Dravidian Etymological Dictionary and over 1000 words of Munda with concordant semantic clusters of Indo-Aryan (cf.http://www.hindunet.org/saraswati) that there was a virile culture that had developed on the Saptasindhu region (exemplified by the discovery of the Sarasvati Civilization, ca. 3500 to 1500 BCE), and that the nomadic looters and cattle-reivers if they ever came into the Saptasindhu region from elsewhere already found a high level of Hindu culture. IE linguistics was unduly focused on finding etymologies from the vocabularies of the Indo-European languages rather than understanding the substructure of languages which flourished and continue to the present day in the Saptasindhu region and larger Bharat. Even a cursory inspection of the glossaries will suggest at least some borrowings from Munda and Dravidian into Sanskrit or versions of Indo-Iranian. Emeneau notes that the Sanskrit etymological dictionary of Uhlenbeck (1898-99) and the Indo-European etymological dictionary of Walde and Pokorny (1930-32) completely ignore the work of Gundert (1869), Kittel (1872, 1894), and Caldwell (1856, 1875). Even the earliest Sanskrit texts show features which are historically un-Indo-European in their nature. (Emeneau, opcit., p. 110). "Vocabulary loans…They are in fact all merely 'suggestions'. Unfortunately, all areal etymologies are in the last analysis unprovable, are 'acts of faith' (as Meillet and Jules Bloch said of non-obvious etymologies in general), in contradistinction to the etymologies within a family which are probable through their conformity to phonetic correspondenced. The areal etymologies fit on a sliding scale of plausibility…it is always possible, e.g. to counter a suggestion of borrowing from one of the indigenous language families by suggesting that there has been borrowing in the other direction." (Emeneau, opcit. P. 177).

The most significant aspect of the work done so far related to linguistic areas is that "…it will not be neglected henceforth when the question is raised whether linguistic features, especially those of morphology and syntax, can diffuse across genetic boundaries… Certainly the end result of the borrowings is that the languages of the two families, Indo-Aryan and Dravidian, seem in many respects more akin to one another than Indo-Aryan to the other Indo-European languages." (Emeneau, opcit., pp. 119-120). Thus, after an analysis of Bharat as a linguistic area, a remarkable

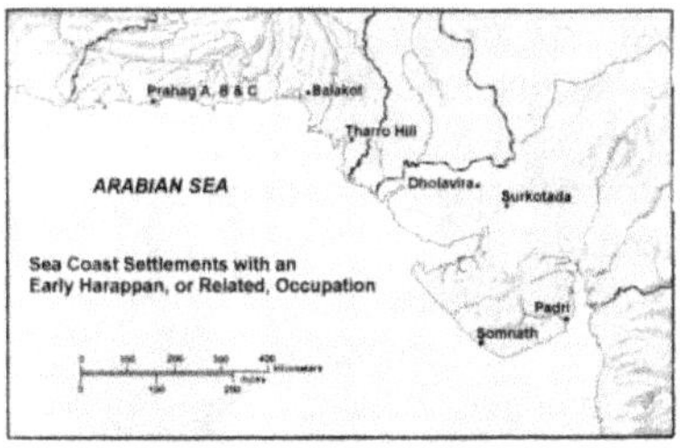


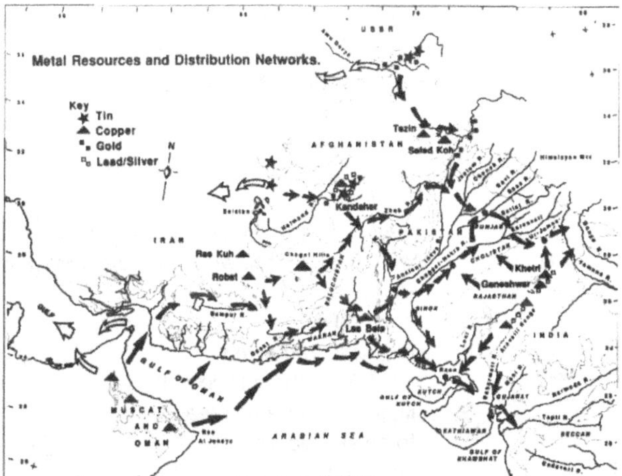


conclusion emerges: Bharatiya languages may be related or akin to one another. And thus, constituting a Prarkrit Family of languages of Bharat. If the areal features are treated isoglosses (e.g. retroflexes, non-finite verb forms such as gerunds, pronominal siffixes), lines encircling the languages which have the features may be drawn on a map. Such a linguistic areal feature line can itself become an isogloss for classifying language families. Pashto of Peshawar has many words of uncertain origin (so Morgenstierne) and is largely indianized in its phonetic system. Similarly, about 40 percent of the agricultural terms in Hindi cannot be traced to any known family and hence get assigned to 'Language X'.Language families

Map of Sapta Sindhu (Nation of Seven Rivers): Theatre of Pan~cajana_h,Five Peoples Marius Fontane, 1881, *Histoire Universelle, Inde Vedique* (de 1800 a 800 av. J.C.), Alphonse Lemerre, Editeur, Paris

Sea-faring meluhha Sarasvati merchants

Sea-faring early Sarasvati, Meluhha Culture, Map of Amri-Nal sea coast settlements "...inhabitants were well acquainted with the sea and its resources" (After Fig. 4.124 in G. Possehl, 1999, p. 618) How is a language family recognized? Many textbooks cite Greenberg's table of Language relationship of Major European languages (1957). The lexemes used are related to the semantics: one, two, three, head, ear, mouth, nose. (Hans Henrich Hock, 1991, *Principles of Historical Linguistics*, New York, Mouton de Gruyter, p. 10). It is from such rudimentary lexemes that families began to be recognized. It will be a tough call for an linguistics student to question the sanctity of these 'families' already categorized. The only hope is to come up with synonyms such as 'linguistic area' or '*sprachbund*'. An ancient bharatiya text records the nature of speech of at least some of the speakers in the following terms*: te 'surā āttavacaso he lavo he lava iti vadantah parābabhūvuh tatraināmapi vācamūduh upajijñāsyā sa mlecchastasmānna brāhmaṇao mlecchedasuryā haiṣā vāg* "The Asuras, deprived of (correct) speech, saying *he lavo, he lavah*, were defeated. This is the unintelligible speech which they uttered at that time. Who speaks thus is a mleccha. Therefore a brāhmaṇa should not speak like a mleccha, for that is the speech of the Asuras." (*śathapathabrāhmaṇa* 3.2.1.23-24) Conclusion about the IE 'linguistic doctrine' A linguistic area is a euphemism for a language family. The Indian linguistic area recognized in linguistic studies is in fact a recognition of the Prakrit Family in Bharat, exemplified by the language called mleccha, a Prakrit language. Emeneau who popularized the phrase, 'linguistic area' makes an honest admission of bias in the following terms:

"At some time in the second millennium BC, probably comparatively early in the millennium, a band or bands of speakers of an Indo-European language, later to be called Sanskrit, entered India over the northwest passes. This is our linguistic doctrine which has been held now for more than a century and a half. There seems to be no reason to distrust the arguments for it, in spite of the traditional Hindu ignorance of any such invasion, their doctrine that Sanskrit is 'the language of the god', and the somewhat chauvinistic clinging to the old tradition even today by some Indian scholars. Sanskrit, 'the language of the gods', I shall therefore assume to have been a language brought from the Near East or the Western world by the nomadic bands." (Emeneau, opcit., p. 85).This is the fundamental problem with IE linguistics which holds the entry of nomadic bands into Bharat as the 'linguistic doctrine'. With such a non-linguistic framework supporting the edifice of IE linguistics, one has reason to be skeptical of the integrity of the discipline itself.

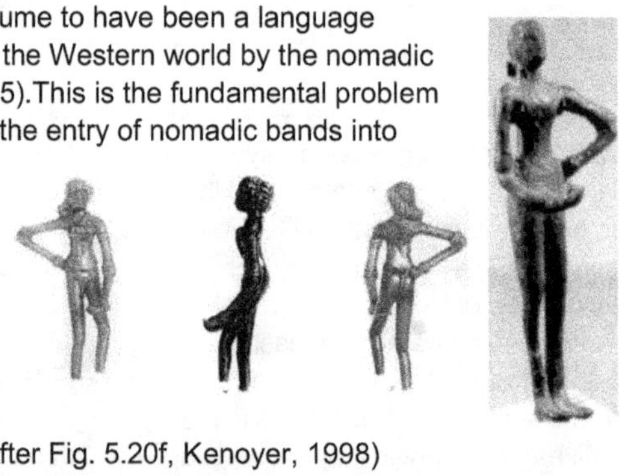

Map of Metal Resources and Distribution Networks (After Fig. 5.20f, Kenoyer, 1998)

A remarkable example of the continuity of the metallurgical tradition of Sarasvati civilization comes from a technique used to make bronze statues, a technique called *cire perdue* (lost-wax method). The bronze statue of a woman wearing bangles and holding a small bowl in her right hand, Mohenjo-daro (DK 12728; Mackay 1938: 274, pl. LXXIII, 9-11); was made using *cire perdue* (lost wax) method, a method used by vis'vakarma-s in Swa_mimalai to make bronze figurines of deities – vis'vakarma tradition lives on.

[Pl. 39, Tree symbol (often on a platform) on punch-marked coins; a symbol recurring on many tablets of SSVC].

[Pl. 2, N: Sahet-Mahet punch-marked coins symbols]

[Pl. 3, M,N: Singavaran punch-marked coin symbols]

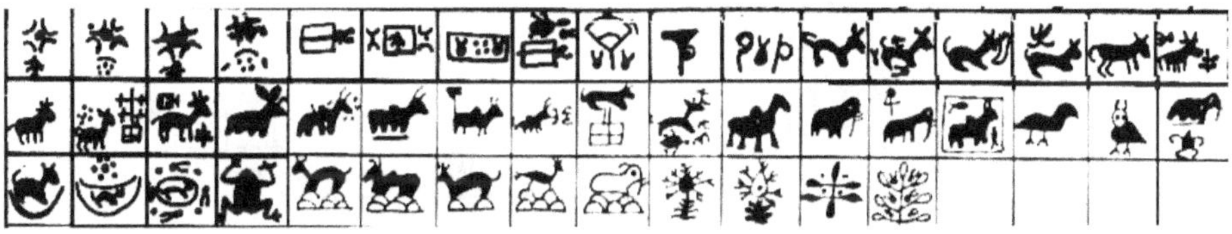

Pl. 5, A to C, Amaravati punch-marked coin symbols]

Pl. 5, D, Punch-marked copper coins, Madhipur]

[Pl. 5, E, Uninscribed cast coins]

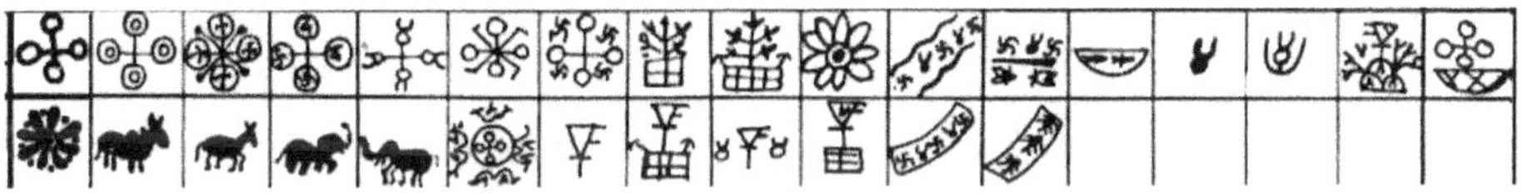

[Pl. 5, F, G, Eran punch-marked local coin symbols]

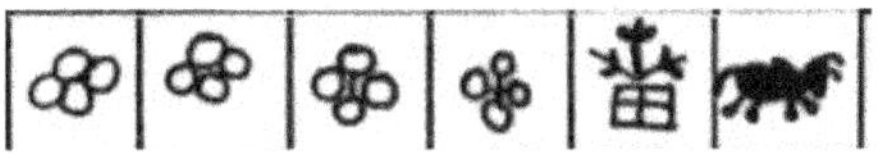

[Pl.5, J, Ahichhatra, punch-marked local coin symbols]

[Pl.5, K, Kada, punch-marked local coin symbols]

[Pl. 5, L, Kanauj, punch-marked local coin symbols]

[Pl. 5, M, Mathura, punch-marked local coin symbols]

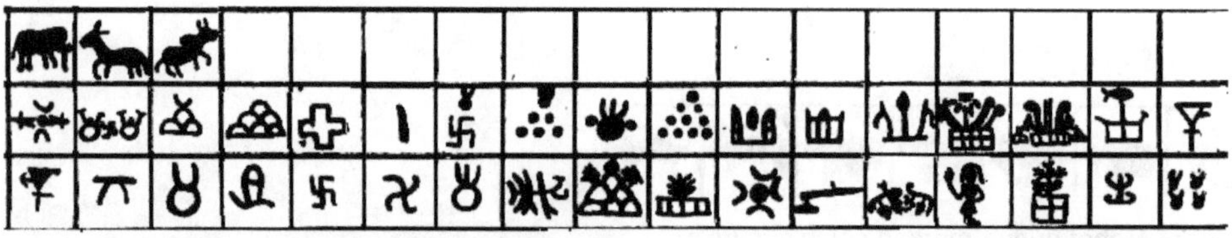

[Pl. 5, N, O, P, Taxila, punch-marked local coin symbols]

[Pl. 6, A, Shamiawala (Lucknow Museum) Uttara Pāñcāla Ahicchatra (Type I) punch-marked coin symbols]

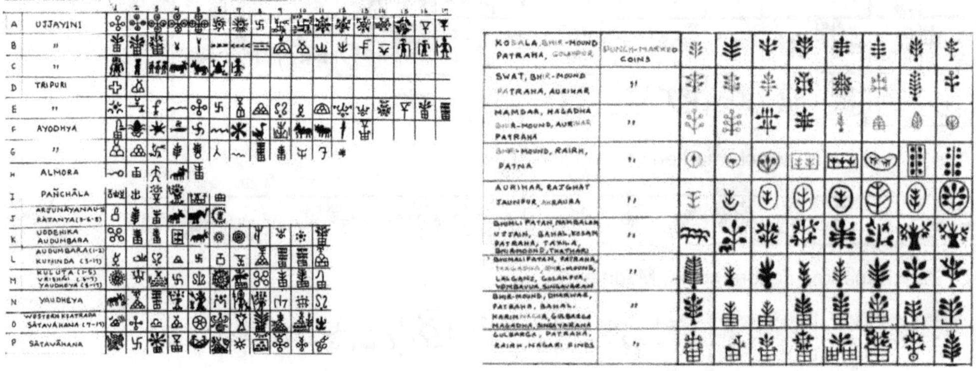


[Pl.8, Local Tribal coin symbols: Ujjayini, Tripuri, Ayodhya, Almore, Pāñcāla, Arjunāyana (1-3), Rājanya (3,6,8), Uddehika, Audumbara, Kuṇinda, Kuluta, V ṛ ṣṇi, Yaudheya, Kṣatrapa, śātavāhana]

Rakesh Tiwari, 2003, Origins of iron working in India: new evidence from the Central Ganga plain and Eastern Vindhyas, pp.536-545

http://www.antiquity.ac.uk/ProjGall/tewari/tewari.pdf

Tiwari notes: “Recent excavations in Uttar Pradesh have turned up iron artefacts, furnaces, tuyeres and slag inlayers radiocarbon dated between c. BC 1800 and 1000. This raises again the question of whetheriron working was brought in to India during supposed immigrations of the second millennium BC, or developed independently.” Thus circa 19th century BCE, when the Sarasvati river was in the throes of desiccation, there was emergence of iron age in Ganga river basin. The sites excavated were: Lohra Dewa, Raja Nal Ka Tila and Malhar

This twin phenomenon of the rise of the bronze age in Saptasindhu region and the iron age in Ganga river basin explain the find spots of punch-mark coin hoards.

(After *Punch-marked Coins* of Early Historic India, Dilip Rajgor, 2001)

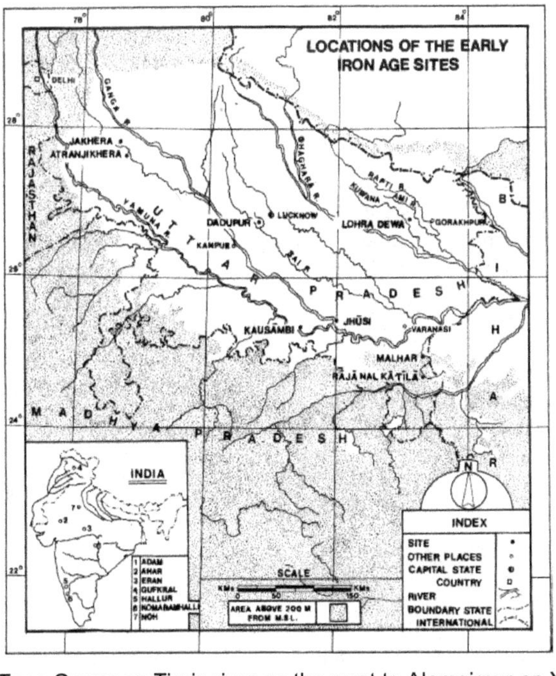


Over 45 sites where objects with epigraphs have been discovered – dated circa 3300 BCE to 1500 BCE. The sites extend from Tepe Gawra on Tigris river on the west to Alamgirpur on Yamuna river on the east; from Altin Tepe in the north -- east of Caspian Sea (south of Turkmenistan) to Maski on Krishna river on the south. (Map after Asko Parpola and Jagatpati Joshi, 1988, *Corpus of Indus Seals and Inscriptions, Volume 1*, Helsinki, Academia Scientiarum Fennica and Map 8 in: Jane R. McIntosh, 2002, *A Peaceful Realm – the Rise and Fall of the Indus Civilization*, New York, Westview Press).

Linguistic area: The clustering of the find sites around the Sarasvati Sindhu river basins and the coasts of Gulf of Khambat and Kutch point to Meluhha (mleccha) as the language underlying the epigraphs.

Proto-Bharatiya *Lingua Franca* or *parole* (spoken tongue)

There are hundreds of lexical isolates attested in 'Indo-Aryan' which are not found in other branches of Indo-European. These are clearly a substratum layer of Old Indic which was spoken by the people of Bharat on the Sarasvati-Sindhu river basins and on the coastal settlements of Sindhu sa_gara (Arabian Sea). Some of these people were called Meluhhan in Mesopotamian texts. The Austroasiatic components of this substratum have to be resolved further in the context of (1) ancestors of Brahui and Elamite; and (2) other Austroasiatic groups such as those in the Brahmaputra (Lohitya)-Meghna-Barak river basins and around the Bay of Bengal.

*Mleccha* (Skt.) is *milakkha or milakku* (Pali) to describe those who dwell on the outskirts of a village. (Shendge, Malati, 1977, *The civilized demons: the Harappans in Rigveda*, Abhinav Publications). A milakkhu is disconnected from va_c and does not speak Vedic; he spoke Prakrt. na a_rya_ mlecchanti bha_s.a_bhir ma_yaya_ na caranty uta: aryas (i.e., cultured people) do not speak with crude dialects like mlecchas, nor do they behave with duplicity (MBh. 2.53.8). a dear friend of Vidura who was a professional excavator is sent by Vidura to help the Pa_n.d.avas in confinement; this friend of Vidura has a conversation with Yudhisthira, the eldest Pa_n.d.ava: kr.s.n.apakse caturdasyàm ràtràv asya purocanah, bhavanasya tava dvàri pradàsyati hutàsanam, màtrà saha pradagdhavyàh pa_n.d.avàh purus.ars.abhàh, iti vyavasitam pàrtha dha_rtara_s.t.ra_sya me šrutam, kiñcic ca vidurenkoto mleccha-vàcàsi pa_n.d.ava, tyayà ca tat tathety uktam etad visvàsa ka_ran.am: on the fourteenth evening of the dark fortnight, Purocana will put fire in the door of your house. 'The Pandavas are leaders of the people, and they are to be burned to death with their mother.' This, Pa_rtha (Yudhis.t.ira), is the determined plan of Dhr.tara_s.t.ra's son, as I have heard it. When you were leaving the city, Vidura spoke a few words to you in the dialect of the mlecchas, and you replied to him, 'So be it'. I say this to gain your trust.(MBh. 1.135.4-6). This passage shows that there were two groups distinguished by dialects and ethnicity: Yudhis.t.ra and Vidura – and both could understand mleccha dialect – mleccha-vàcàsi.

Melakkha, ocean island-dwellers

According to the great epic, Mlecchas lived on islands: sa sarva_n mleccha nr.patin sa_gara dvi_pa va_sinah, aram a_ha_ryàm àsa ratna_ni vividha_ni ca, andana aguru vastra_n.i man.i muktam anuttamam, ka_ñcanam rajatam vajram vidrumam ca maha_ dhanam: (Bhima) arranged for all the mleccha kings, who dwell on the ocean islands, to bring varieties of gems, sandalwood, aloe, garments, and incomparable jewels and pearls, gold, silver, diamonds, and extremely valuable coral... great wealth. (MBh. 2.27.25-26).

Elsewhere in the Great Epic we read how Sahadeva, the youngest of the Pa_n.d.ava brothers, continued his march of conquest till he reached several islands in the sea (no doubt with the help of ships) and subjugated the Mleccha inhabitants thereof.(1)

Brahma_n.d.a 2.74.11, Brahma 13.152, Harivam.s'a 1841, Matsya 48.9, Va_yu 99.11, cf. also Vis.n.u 4.17.5, Bha_gavata 9.23.15, see Kirfel 1927: 522:

pracetasah putras'atam ra_ja_nah sarva eva te // mlecchara_s.t.ra_dhipa_h sarve udi_ci_m dis'am a_s'rita_h

which means, of course, not that these '100' kings conquered the 'northern countries' way beyond the Hindukus. or Himalayas, but that all these 100 kings, sons of praceta_s (a descendant of a 'druhyu'), kings of mleccha kingdoms, are 'adjacent' (a_s'rita) to the 'northern direction,' -- which since the Vedas and Pa_n.ini has signified Greater gandha_ra. Kirfel, W. Das Pura_n.a Pan~calaks.an.a. Bonn : K. Schroeder 1927.

Erythraen Sea and Meluhha

Fifth century BC Greek historian, Herodotus referred to the body of water which linked Africa, the Arabian Peninsula, Iran and the Indian subcontinent as the Erythraen sea. This sea includes the Red sea, the Gulf of Aden, Indian Ocean, Arabian Sea, Gulf of Oman and the Persian or Arabian Gulf.

"The land of Melukkha shall bring carnelian, desirable and precious, sissoo-wood from Magan, excellent mangroves, on big-ships!" said a statement in the Sumerian myth, *Enki and Ninkhursag* (cf. lines 1-9, trans. B. Alster). "In the late Early Dynastic period (about 2500), Ur-Nanshe, king of the Sumerian city-state Lagash, "had ships of Dilmun transport timber from foreign lands" to his capital (modern Tell al-Hiba), just as a later governor of Lagash, named Gudea, did in the mid-twenty-first century. In the early twenty-fourth century, Lugalbanda and Urukagina, two kings of Lagash, imported copper from Dilmun and paid for it with wool, silver, fat, and various milk and cereal products... That these (round stamp) seals were used in economic transactions is proven by the discovery of two important tablets bearing their impressions. One of these tablets was found at Susa, and dates to the first half of the second millennium. It is a receipt for goods, including ten minas of copper (about eleven pounds or five kilograms). The second tablet, in the Yale Babylonian Collection, is dated to the tenth year of Gungunum of Larsa (modern Tell Senkereh), that is, around 1925, and records a consignment of goods (wool, wheat, and sesame) prior to a trading voyage that almost certainly had Dilmun as its goal. Dilmun seals characteristically depict two men drinking what could be beer through straws, or two or three prancing gazelles...a merchant named Ea-nasir, who is identified as one of the a_lik Tilmun, or "Dilmun traders"... Ea-nasir paid for Dilmun copper with the textiles and silver that he received from the great Nanna-Ningal temple complex at Ur...The Mari texts contain several references to Dilmunite caravans...Melukkha was a source of wood (including a black wood thought to have been ebony), gold, ivory, and carnelian...Melukkha was accessible by sea...Sargon of Akkad...boasts that ships from Dilmun, Magan and Melukkha docked at the quay of his capital Akkad...While points of contact with other regions are attested, they can hardly have accounted for the strength and individuality of civilization in the subcontinent...Unmistakably Harappan cubical weights of banded chert (based on a unit of 13.63 grams) are known from a number of sites located around the perimeter of the Arabian GUlf, including Susa, Qalat al-Bahrain, Shimal (Ras al-Khaimah), and Tell Abraq (Umm al-Qaiwain)...an inscribed Harappan shard has been found at Ras al Junayz... Harappan pottery has been found at several sites throughout Oman and the United Arab Emirates...A "Melukkhan village" in the territory of the ancient city-state of Lagash, attested in the thirty-fourth year of the reign of Shulgi (2060), may have been a settlement of Harappans, if the identification with the civilization of the Indus Valley is correct...But...there is little evidence of a Sumerian, Akkadian, or Babylonian presence in the Indus Valley... That the language of Melukkha was unintelligble to an Akkadian or Sumerian speaker is clearly shown by the fact that, on his cylinder seal, the Akkadian functionary Shu-ilishu is identified as a "Melukkhan translator"...the word "Melukkha" appears occasionally as a personal name in cuneiform texts of the Old Akkadian and Ur III periods. "(Potts, D., 1995, Distant Shores: Ancient Near Eastern Trade, in: Jack M. Sasson (ed.), *Civilizations of the Ancient Near East*, Vol. I, pp. 1451-1463).

Mleccha trade was first mentioned by Sargon of Akkad (Mesopotamia 2370 BCE) who stated that boats from Dilmun, Magan and Meluhha came to the quay of Akkad (Hirsch, H., 1963, Die Inschriften der Konige Von Agade, Afo, 20, pp. 37-38; Leemans, W.F., 1960, Foreign Trade in the Old Babylonian Period, p. 164; Oppenheim, A.L., 1954, The seafaring merchants of Ur, *JAOS*, 74, pp. 6-17). The Mesopotamian imports from Meluhha were: woods, copper (ayas), gold, silver, carnelina, cotton. Gudea sent expeditions in 2200 BCE to Makkan and Meluhha in search of hard wood. Seal impression with the cotton cloth from Umma (Scheil, V., 1925, Un Nouvea Sceau Hindou Pseudo-Sumerian, RA, 22/3, pp. 55-56) and cotton cloth piece stuck to the base of a silver vase from Mohenjo-daro. (Wheeler, R.E.M., 1965, Indus Civilization) are indicative evidence.

Umma seal impression shows a Meluhha trader in Mesopotamia; there is no comparable evidence of a Mesopotamian trader in Meluhha. Babylonian and Greek names for cotton were: sind, sindon. This is an apparent reference to the cotton produced in the black cotton soils of Sind and Gujarat.

Euphrates River was a link in the maritime trade of the eastern Mediterranean with that of the Gulf and Meluhha beyond. The Sumerian 'colonies' on the northern bend of the Euphrates were the conduits to carry the culture of Uruk to Egypt and linked the head of the Gulf to the Egyptian Delta through the Syrian ports (Moorey, 1990). The famous bilingual inscription of Sargon of Akkad (ca. 2234-2279 BC) sets out in geographical order from south-east to north-west the trading posts: Meluhha, Magan, Dilmun, Mari, Yarmuti, and Ebla: that is, from the Indus to the Taurus -- the Indus which was also linked with central Asia through Afghanistan. (Hirsch 1963: 37-8).

Meluhha and interaction areas

Ubaid: ca. 5500-4000 BCE
Uruk ca. 4000-3000 BCE
Early Dynastic I: ca. 3000-2750 BCE
Early Dynastic II: ca. 2750-2600 BCE
Early Dynastic III: ca. 2600-2350 BCE
Akkadian (or Sargonic): ca. 2350-2000 BCE
Ur III: ca. 2100-2000

Isin-Larsa/Old Babylonian/Old Assyrian: ca. 2000-1600 BCE
Kassite/Mitannian/Middle Babylonian/Middle Assyrian: ca. 1600-1000 BCE
Neo-Assyrian: ca. 1000-612 BCE
Neo-Babylonian: ca. 612-539 BCE
Achaemenid Persian: ca. 539-330 BCE

Vratya

Mleccha-s could be related to the vratya-s of Magadha. Reference to Satvants of the Chambal valley may relate to the term, *satvata*, used in the *pan~cara_tra* tradition and *vra_tya-s* are associated with the people of Magadha.

"The literature is replete with the names of clans. The most powerful among them, commanding the greatest respect, was the Kuru-Pañcala, which incorporated the two families of Kuru and Puru (and the earlier Bharatas) and of which the Pañcala was a confederation of lesser-known tribes. They occupied the Upper Doab and the Kuruksetra region. In the north the Kamboja, Gandhara, and Madra groups predominated. In the middle Ganges Valley the neighbours and rivals of the Kuru-Pañcalas were the Kasi, Kosala, and Videha, who worked in close cooperation with each other. The Magadha, Anga, and Vanga peoples in the lower Ganges Valley and delta were outside the Aryan pale and regarded as mlecchas. Magadha (Patna and Gaya districts of Bihar) is also associated with the vratya people, who occupied an ambiguous position between the aryas and mlecchas. Other mleccha tribes frequently mentioned include the Satvants of the Chambal valley and, in the Vindhyan and northern Deccan region, the Andhra, Vidarbha, Nisadha, Pulinda, and Sabara. The location of all these tribes is of considerable historical interest, because they gave their names to the geographic area."

http://www.britanica.com/bcom/eb/article/9/0,5716,121169+2+111197,00.html

This leads to the formulation of two hypotheses:

A cooperative society and a continuous culture had existed right from the chalcolithic- age through the bronze-age to the historical periods on the Sarasvati-Sindhu doab and the rest of India.

Emergence of *lingua franca* in Bharat

A *lingua franca* had emerged in the doab ca. 3000 BCE with intense interaction and resultant cross-borrowings of lexemes of an expansive contact zone (from Tigris-Euphrates to Ganga, from the Caucus mountains to the Gulf of Khambat, from Kashmir to Kanya_kumari) constituting the Sarasvati-Sindhu doab and the rest of Bha_rata as an Bha_rati_ya Linguistic Area.

The assumption for establishing this concordance among lexemes removed in time, by over 1 millennium, is that the names of the arms and armour of the linguistic area, ca. 5500 BP continued, as parole, in the ancient languages of Bharat, by a hereditary tradition nurtured among the artisans (vis'vakarma) and warriors (ks.atriya) alike and by the literary tradition of *Dhanurveda Sam.hita_* and related texts.

The areal map of Austric (Austro-Asiatic languages) showing regions marked by Pinnow correlates with the bronze age settlements in Bharatam or what came to be known during the British colonial regime as 'Greater India'. The bronze age sites extend from Mehrgarh-Harappa (Meluhha) on the west to Kayatha-Navdatoli (Nahali) close to River Narmada to Koldihwa-Khairdih-Chirand on Ganga river basin to Mahisadal – Pandu Rajar Dhibi in Jharia mines close to Mundari area and into the east extending into Burma, Indonesia, Malaysia, Laos, Cambodia, Vietnam, Nicobar islands. A settlement of Inamgaon is shown on the banks of River Godavari.

This, together with the islands in Balochistan, Amri-Nal on the Makran coast and settlements in the Rann of Kutch and Gujarat , broadly corresponds to the Bharatiya Language Community of mleccha-speakers. Mleccha as island-dwellers !

Ca.2000 BC, there were movements of people in search of minerals and metals. From Meluhha, there were copper mining and smelting expeditions to Oman. At Namazga IV-V (Turkmenia), a number of alloys were experimented with. (Kohl, P., 1984, *Central Asia: palaeolithic beginnings to the Iron age,* Paris, Editions Recherchedes Civilisations, p. 113, 169; Harappan artefacts are found at Altyn-depe in the latest levels; the suggestion is that 'contact was strongest on the eve of the collapse of the site'). At Hissar were found arsenic-bronze, lead-bronze, lead, silver and gold. (Tepe Hissar III, 3rd millennium BCE.: a seal shows a four-spoke wheel). Jarrige reports the find of a vented furnace at Sibri. On the Baluchistan and Afghanistan border, Dales found 'miles of slag and furnaces' (Dales, G.F., 1973, Archaeological and Radioactive chronologies for protohistoric south Asia, in: *South Asian Archaeology*, N. Hammond ed., London, Duckworth, p. 167).

The resource base is verily the nidhi of bharatīya bhāṣā jñāna which can guide us to pursue studies in the evolutionary history related to every bharatiya language. It is apposite to record a tribute to the late Sudhibhushan Bhattacharya who initiated studies on Munda etymology , to the late Kuiper for his work on Nahali etymology and to the work of Norman Zide on Munda numerals. This was followed by Patricia J. Donegan and David Stampe, 2004, Munda Lexical Archive. See full bibliography at http://www.ling.hawaii.edu/faculty/stampe/AA/Munda/BIBLIO/biblio.authors

When the River Sarasvatī got desiccated between ca. 3900 and 3500 BP, many people of the River Basin moved into the Ganga-Yamuna doab and south of Gujarat to the Godavari River Basin and further south along the coast of Sindhu Sāgara (Arabian Sea) and also moved west of Gāndhāra in Afghanistan, resulting in the naming of a small river as Haraquaiti, in remembrance of River Sarasvatī. Similar instances of cherishing the legacy of River Sarasvatī are noticed in the naming of rivers near Puṣkar (Ajmer), and near Little Rann of Kutch (Siddhapura) also as Sarasvati. The mother who nourished the forefathers of many Bhāratīyas could not be forgotten. When a mother prays to river godesses, she invokes the names of Gangā, Yamunā, Sarasvatī; when she goes to a tīrthayātra and notices a san:gamam of two rivers, she learns from the folklore and folk traditions, that the san:gamam is triveṇi, the third river being the antahsalilā Sarasvatī (the Sarasvatī which flows underground). The sthala purāṇa of the Sarasvatī temple at Basara (Vyāsapura) on the banks of River Godavari (near Adilabad district, Andhra Pradesh) states that the pratimā of Sarasvatī was made by Vyāsa taking three muṣṭī (hand-fuls) of sand from the river bed. There is also a temple for Sarasvatī on the banks of Cauvery in Kūttanūr, near Swāmimalai (the pilgrimage center for ēraka Subrahmaṇya, Kārttikeya – ēraka, 'copper'!).

The formation of the hypotheses related to Indian linguistic area is a plea for unraveling further the as yet untold story of the formation of Bharatiya languages, as an exercise in general semantics.

Discovery Sites of Indus script inscriptions

Alamgirpur

Allahdino

Amri

Balakot

Banawali

Bet Dwaraka

Chandigarh

Chanhu-daro

Daimabad

Desalpur

Dholavira

Gharo Bhiro (Nuhato)

Gumla

Harappa

Hissam-dheri

Hulas

Jhukar

Kalibangan

Kalako-deray

Khirsara

Kot-diji

Lewandheri

Loebanr

Lohumjodaro

Lothal

Maski

Mehi

Mehrgarh

Mohenjo-daro

Nausharo

Nindowari-damb

Naro-Waro-dharo

Nippur

Pabumath

Prabhas Patan (Somnath)

Pirak

Rangpur

Rakhigarhi

Rahman-dheri

Rohira

Rojdi

Rupar

Saharanpur, Western Uttar Pradesh

Shahi-tump

Sibri-damb

Surkotada

Tarkhanewala-dera

Tarakai Qila

Tell Suleimah, Iraq

Tell Asmar (Eshnunna), Iraq

Ur

Many Indus script inscriptions are of 'Unknown Provenance' or categorized as 'Bulla-envelope, Adab, Sumer'; 'Proto-elamite glyptics' or 'other objects' or 'Shaft-hole axhead (Bactria-Margiana)'; 'Early Harappan bowl with 'fish' glyph'. Some are now found in the following museums, e.g.: National Museum, New Delhi; Museum Guimet, France; Proto-elamite glyptics; West Asia; Near East Ashmolean Museum, Oxford; Pierport Morgan Library, New York; Gulf states; Metropolitan Museum of Art, New York; Manuscripts in Schoyen Collection; Royal Ontario Museum; Burdin Fine Arts Exhibition; British Museum; Museum of Fine Arts (Boston, MA); Cambridge University Museum of Archaeology and Anthropology; Archaeological Museum of Gurukul, Jhajjar, Egmore Museum, Chennai.

Hieroglyphs and frequencies of occurrence on Sarasvati epigraphs

One-horned heifer with a pannier 1159 + 5 (with two horns)

| | |
|---|---|
| Standard device | 19 + ca. 1100 occurrences in front of the one-horned heifer |
| Shor-horned bull | 95 +2 (in opposition) |
| Zebu or Bra_hman.i bull | 54 |
| Buffalo | 14 |
| Elephant | 55 + 1 (horned) |
| Tiger (including tiger looking back) | 16 + 5 (horned) |
| Boar | 39 + 1 (in opposition) |
| Goat-antelope | 36 + 1 (flanking a tree) |
| Ox-antelope | 26 |
| Hare | 10 +1 (object shaped like hare) |
| Ligatured animal | 41 |
| Alligator | 49 |
| 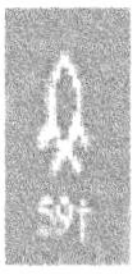 Fish | 14 (objects shaped like fish); fish also a sign |
| Frog | 1 |
| Serpent | 10 |
| Tree | 34 + 1 (leaves) |
| Dotted circle | 67 |
| Svastika | 23 |
| Endless-knot | 4 |
| Double-axe | 14 (inscribed objects shaped like axe) |
| Rimmed narrow-necked jar 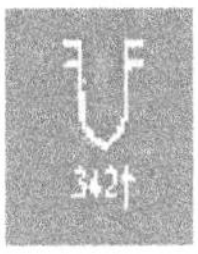 | 1395 |
| Fish signs 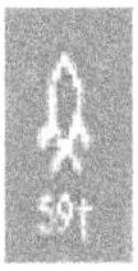 | 1241 |
| Leaf signs | 100 |

| | |
|---|---|
| Spoked wheel | 203 |

| | |
|---|---|
| Cart frame + wheels | 26 |
| Sprout (or, tree stylized) | 800 |
| Water-carrier | 220 |
| Scorpion | 106 |
| Claws (of crab) | 130 + 90 (shaped like pincers) |
| Arrow (spear) | 227 |
| Rimless, wide-mouthed pot | 350 |

**Figure 20: Positional Order of the "Fish" Signs**

(Fig. 20 in Michael Pieter Kovink, 2008, *The Indus script -- a positional-statistical approach*, USA,

Gilund Press, ISBN 978-0-6151-8239-1showing varieties of fish signs and positional sequencing on epigraphs.)

ken.t.a ‘fish’; ke~r.e~ brass or bell-metal

ayo, hako 'fish'; a~s = scales of fish (Santali); rebus: aya = iron (G.); ayah, ayas = metal (Skt.)

Fully hieroglyptic nature of the writing system (mlecchita vikalpa) is presented with examples of pictorial motifs and signs used on epigraphs and with intimations of continuing tradition of glyphs on punch-marked coin devices.

Hieroglyph sign list (Mahadevan + variants), Sign list of Tuomo Saarikivi and Bertil Tikkanen

Decoding the most frequently-occurring Sarasvati hieroglyphs in mlecchitavikalpa:

1.rim of jar and 2.pannier on one-horned heifer

Two glyphs of most frequent occurrence are: rim of jar and pannier on one-horned heifer. The rim (kanka) of jar connotes the fire-altar of a miner (khanaka). The pannier (kamarsaala) connotes the workshop of a smith (karmaarashaala). The heifer connotes tam(b)ra ‘copper’; hence, the composite glyph connotes coppersmith’s workshop.

Richard Burton translates 'mlecchita vikalpa' as one of the 64 arts mentioned in Vatsyayana's Kamasutra as follows: "the art of understanding writing in cypher, and the writing of words in a peculiar way." Writing in cypher. Vikalpa is an alternative representation of language, in this case, spoken words expressed in writing (cypher). Two other language-related arts listed by Vatsyanana are: deshabhaashaa jnaanam and akshara mushtika kathanam (that is: knowledge of dialects of the land and story-telling using fingers and wrists, that is, hand-gestures and finger-gestures forming mudra-s). In this triad, it is logical to interpret mlecchita vikalpa as cypher writing made by mleccha.

http://www.bharatadesam.com/literature/vatsyayana_kamasutras/vatsyayana_kamasutra_3.php

"In his commentary on the Kama-sutra, Yashodhara describes two kinds of mlecchita-vikalpa. One is called kautilyam in which the letter substitutions are based upon phonetic relations -- the vowels become consonants, for example. A simplification of this form is called durbodha. Another kind of secret writing is muladeviya. Its cipher alphabet consists merely of the reciprocal one with all other letters remaining unchanged. Muladeviya existed in both a spoken form -- as such it figures in Indian literature and is used by traders, with geographical variations -- and a written form, in which case it is called gudhalekhya." (David Kahn, _*The Code-Breakers: The Story of Secret Writing*_,New York, Macmillan, 1967, pp. 74-75)

Some mleccha words in Sarasvati hieroglyphs

> Bronze age trade and writing system of Meluhha (Mleccha) evidenced by tin ingots from the near vicinity of Haifa (For Bronze Age Trade Workshop in 5 ICAANE, April 5, 2006) including Appendix B Mahabharata reference to mleccha (with devanagari text and translation in English)

1 khanaka m. one who digs , digger , excavator MBh. iii , 640 R. ; a miner L. ; a house-breaker , thief L. ; a rat L. ; N. of a friend of Vidura MBh. i , 5798 f. ; (%{I}) f. a female digger or excavator Pa1n2. 3-1 , 145 Pat. ; iv , 1 , 41 Ka1s3.

2 khānaka mfn. ifc. one who digs or digs out Mn. viii , 260 (cf. %{kUpa-}) ; m. a house-breaker , thief

VarBr2S. lxxxix , 9 ; (%{ikA}) f. a ditch Gal.

கனி&sup5; kaṉi

, *n*. < *khani*. Mine; பொன்முதலியன எடுக்கும் சுரங்கம். கரைகனிப் பொருளும் (திருக்காளத். பு. 11, 22).P 838 Tamil lexicon

CDIAL 3810 khaná— 'digging' AV. [√khan] K. *khan* m. 'hole, hollow made in grain, breach in a river bank'; Ku. gng. *khaṇ* m. 'digging'; N. *khan—jot* 'tillage'.

CDIAL 3811 khánati 'digs' RV. 2. khānayati 'causes to dig' ŚāṅkhŚr. [√khan] 1. Pa. *khanati*, Pk. *khaṇaï*; Paš. lauṛ. *khan—*, ar. weg. *xan—* 'to pull out or off, flay', weg. also 'to dig'; K. *khanun*, 'to dig', S. *khaṇaṇu*, Ku. *khaṇṇo*, N. *khannu*, B. *khanā*; H. *khannā* 'to dig, scrape'; G. *khaṇvũkhaṇṇẽ*, Ko. *khaṇūka*. — Deriv. Pa. *khanāpēti* 'causes to be dug', N. *khanāunu*. — X *kṣuráti*: P. *khuṇṇā* 'to dig, carve, cut'; — X *kōtr— q.v. 2. Pa. *khānēti* 'causes to be dug', Pk. *khāṇia—*; Kho. (Lor.) *kh e neik, kan°* 'to dig', A. *khāniba*, M. *khāṇṇẽ*, Si. *kaninavā*, pret. *kännā*. — Deriv. Aś. shah. man. *khanapita—*, gir. kāl. *khānāpita—*, NiDoc. *khaṇavide*, A. *khanāiba*, OSi. absol. *kaṇavaya*. — Gy. pal. *kánărk̥ănăr* 'strips', eur. hung. *xan—*, gr. *xand-* (pret. *xanló* < *khānita—*) 'to dig' rather than < kháṇḍ- atē. — M. *khā̃dṇẽ* 'to dig' X *khōdd—? Addenda: khánati. 1. Garh. *khaṇnu* 'to dig'; Md. *konnanī*khānayati: A. also *khāndiba* 'to dig' (X *khōdd—?). 'to dig', M. 'plucks, tears', 'digs'. 2.

CDIAL 3812 khanana— n. 'act of digging' Bhartr̥. [√khan] Pa. *khaṇana—* n., Pk. *khaṇaṇa—* n., OSi. *kaṇanu*; - deriv. K. *khananāwun* 'to cause to be dug'.

CDIAL 3813 khaní— 'digging up' AV., f. 'mine' VarBr̥S. 2. X gúhā—1. [√khan] 1. Pk. *khaṇi—* f. 'mine'; NiDoc. *kheni* 'pit'; A. *khani* 'mine'; Or. *khaṇi* 'large pit for storing paddy', *khaṇā* 'large and deep pit, trench'; H. *khan* m. 'mine', *khanī* f. 'pit in which husked rice or other grain is kept'; M. *khaṇ* f. 'mine, quarry'. 2. Sh. (Lor.) *khōh, kho* 'cave, shelter of overhanging cliff'; P. *khoh* f. 'hole, cavern, pit'; OAw. *khoha* 'cave'; H. *khoh, kho, khau* f. 'hole, pit, cave'; G. *kho* f. 'cave'. *kūpakhani—.

CDIAL 3814 khanítra— n. 'digging tool' RV., *°trā—* f. R., *°trikā—* f. lex., *°traka—* n. 'small do.' Pañcat. [√khan] Pa. *khanittī—* f., Pk. *khaṇitta—* n.; N. *khanti* 'spud', A. *khanti*; B. *khantā* 'long—handled spade', *khuntikhurpā* < kṣurapra—); Or. *khaṇatā, °tī, khaṇantā, °tī* 'narrow spade'; Bi. *khantī* 'pointed iron instrument for tapping well—spring'; Mth. *khanatī* 'hoe'; Bhoj. *khantā* 'digging instrument'; H. *khantī* f. 'spud'; M. *khaṇtẽ* n. 'instrument for digging holes'. 'long- handled spud'

CDIAL 3873 khāni—, *°nī—* f. '*digging instrument'. 2. 'mine' lex. [For twofold meaning 'digging and result of digging' cf. *khaní—* and *khātra—*. — √khan] 1. Kho. *khen* 'mattock, hoe'. 2. Pk. *khāṇī̆—* f. 'mine'; Gy. as. *xani*, eur. sp. *xaní* f., boh. *xaníg* f., gr. *xaníng* f. 'well'; K. *khān* f. 'mine'; S. *khāṇi* f. 'mine, quarry, water in a pit'; L. *khāṇ* f. 'mine', P. *khāṇī* f., Ku. *khāṇ*, N. *khāni;* A. *khāni* 'quantity'; B. *khānī* 'mine'; Bi. *khān* 'cavity in oil or sugar mill', *maṭi—khān* 'clay pit'; Bhoj. Aw. lakh. *khāni* 'mine'; H. *khān* f. 'mine, quarry, abundance'; G. *khāṇi* , *°ṇī* f. 'mine, source', M. *khāṇ, °ṇī* f.; OSi. *kani* 'cave, cell', Si. *käna* 'bunch (of fruit), multitude'. — Kho. *ken* 'cave, hollow in cliff', Phal. *kēṇ* ← Ir.?

CDIAL 3874 khānya— 'anything being dug out' Pāṇ. [Cf. *khánya-* 'coming from excavations' TS. — √khan] Pk. *khaṇṇa—* 'fit for digging', n. 'ditch'; B. *khānā* 'pit, pond, ravine'.

The rim of a jar is kan.d. kan-ka (Santali). kan.d. is pot; kan-ka in Sanskrit is karn.aka 'ear or rim of jar'. Kan.d. also means 'fire-altar'.

kanka = rim of pot (Santali)

kan:ka = a metal (Pali); kan- = copper (Ta.) kanaka = gold; kanaka_dhyaks.a = superintendent of gold, treasurer (Skt.) kan-n-a_r, blacksmiths, coppersmiths (Ta.)

kan.d.a = a pot of certain shape and size (Santali) Rebus: kan.d. = altar, furnace (Santali) khan.d.a = instrument, implement, weapon; khan.d.a puruskedae, he stretched his arm grasping the sword as high as he could; khan.d.a bhan.d.a = implements of all kinds, arms of all sorts (Santali.lex.)

Fig. Daimabad seal showing rim of jar. This is glyph Sign No. 342 (Mahadevan corpus) -- the most frequently occurring glyph in the entire corpus of Sarasvati hieroglyphs.

The most freuqently occurring glyph among Sarasvati hieroglyphs is kan.d. kan-ka 'rim of jar' (the emphasis is on the rim). This denotes rebus: the fire-altar of a miner, mine-worker (khanaka). This becomes the only glyph on a Daimabad seal dated circa 14th century BCE.

Association and guild of smithy workshop turner, stone-carver, military guard

The next most freuquently-occurring glyph is the one-horned heifer (seen on 1159 epigraphs). The identifying feature of this glyph is the pannier which adorns it. See m1656 pectoral. On this petoral, the pannier is vividly displayed. The orthographic accent is on the waist-zone, the pannier. This is an orthographic feature unique to the one-horned heifer. It is a semantic rebus determinative of the artisan's workhop: *kammarsāla* 'pannier' (Telugu); rebus: *karmāraśāla* 'workshop of smith' (Skt.) It is possible that the depressions on the neck, shoulder, stomach and thigh regions of the heifer were filled with 'red pigment' emphasizing that each of these glyphic elements had a semantic determinative role in rebus readings: koḍiyum ‘rings on neck’; kammarsāla ‘pannier’; kothlo ‘bag’; jangha ‘thigh’. Each of these lexemes have definitive rebus readings consistent with the rebus reading of the glyphics of one-horn on the heifer and the glyphics of ‘lathe/portable furnace’ on the ‘standard device’ in front of the heifer. The glyphics of ‘water-overflow’ from the ‘rim’ of the ‘short-necked jar’ completes the semantic rendering by the *lo* ‘overflow’ Rebus: *loa* ‘copper’ *kaṇḍa kanka* ‘stone (ore) metal furnace account scribe’.

Thus, the functions assigned to the pectoral owner in the guild are clearly, semantically explained by the hieroglyphic composition of this extraordinary Indus script inscription on the pectoral. He is a military guard entrusted by the guild with the function of delivering copper/metal goods made by the artisans of workshops into the treasury. These are accounted for using the short-inscription tablets delivered with the goods by the artisans.

Sign 323. Together with a ‘pannier’ glyphic on the shoulder of the heifer, a remarkable glyph appears on the back (stomach) of the heifer: a bag. K. kŏthul, lu m. ‘ large bag or parcel ’ (CDIAL 3511) 3545 kṓṣṭha1 m. ‘ any one of the large viscera ’ MBh. [Same as kṓṣṭha -- 2? Cf. *kōttha -- ] Pa. *koṭṭha* -- m. ‘ stomach ’, Pk. *koṭṭha* -- , *kuṭ°* m.; L. (Shahpur) *koṭhī* f. ‘ heart, breast ’; P. *koṭṭhā, koṭhā* m. ‘ belly ’, G. *koṭhɔ* m., M. *koṭhā* m. (CDIAL 3545).Rebus: S. *koṭāru* m. ‘ district officer who watches crops, police officer ’ (CDIAL 3501). Cf. *kṓṣṭhaka* ‘treasury’ (Skt.); *kóṭṭhi* ‘temple treasury’ (WPah.); *koṭho* ‘warehouse’ (G.)(CDIAL 3546).

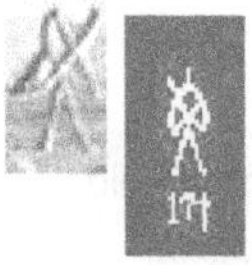

Glyph which appears on the inscription on a large Mohenjo-daro seal, m1203. This lends added emphasis on the possible use of ‘standard device’ glyphic composition to denote: *jangaḍiyo* ‘military guard who accompanies treasure into the treasury’; san:ghāḍiyo, a worker on a lathe (G.) With the ligature of glyphic element of Sign 323 (‘bag’), as a semantic determinant , the glyphic composition of Sign 17 reads: *koṭha jangaḍiyo* ‘treasury military guard’.

A semantic determinant for the rebus identification of the lexeme, *jangaḍiyo* , is the emphasis shown on the pectoral on the ‘thigh/hip’ of the heifer. jáṅghā f. ‘ shank (ankle to knee) ’ RV., *ratha -- jaṅghā* -- f. ‘ part of a chariot ’ lex.Pa. *jaṅghā* -- f., Pk. *jaṁghā* -- f.; Gy. eur. *čang*, pl. *°ga* f. ‘ thigh, knee ’; Paš. *ǰaṅā̃, āl -- ǰaṅgṓ* ‘ plough handle ’; Tor. *ǰāṅ* ‘ calf of leg ’; K.*zang* f. ‘ leg ’, S. *ǰaṅgha* f.; L. *jaṅgh*, (Ju.) *ǰāgh* f. ‘ leg (from hip down) ’; P. *jaṅgh* f. ‘ thigh ’; WPah. bhal. *jhaṅg* f. ‘ leg ’, bhad. *zhaṅg* f.; Ku.*jāṅ* f. ‘ thigh ’, gng. *ǰāṅaṛ*; N. *jā̃gh, jāṅ* ‘ hip, thigh ’; A. *zāṅ* ‘ leg ’; B. *jāṅ, jāṅi* ‘ thigh, leg ’; Or. *jaṅgha* ‘ thighs and hips ’, *°ghā* ‘ calf of leg ’; Mth. *jā̃gh* ‘ thigh ’, Bhoj. *jāṅh*, Aw. lakh. *jā̃gh;* H. *jā̃gh, jā̃g* f. ‘ thigh ’, *jā̃gar* m. ‘ thigh and leg ’; G. *jā̃g(h)* f. ‘ thigh ’, M. *jā̃g(h)* f., Ko. *jā̃ṅga*f.; Si. *daṅgaya* ‘ calf of leg ’. jáṅghā -- : S.kcch. *jaṅgh* f. ‘ thigh ’, Garh. *jā̃gru (CDIAL 5082).*

It is reasonable to infer that all seals and seal impressions which have these glyphic compositions – one-horned heifer + lathe/portable furnace are used by the military guard who delivers the products into the temple treasury. The products are collected using tablets to denote the products made by artisans of the guild and delivered on circular working platforms for preparation of bills of lading and stocking in the nearby warehouses. It appears that the seals and seal impressions are the functions of the scribe accountant for either preparing trade loads to be couriered to long-distance customers or for preparing account of products delivered by the guild workers into the guild treasury.

*kamar* a semi-hinduised caste of blacksmiths; kamari the work of a blacksmith, the money paid for blacksmith work; nunak ato reak in kamarieda I do the blacksmith work for so many villages (Santali) kārmāra = metalsmith who makes arrows etc. of metal (RV. 9.112.2*: jaratībhih oṣadhībhih parṇebhih śakunānām kārmāro aśmabhih dyubhih hiraṇyavantam icchatī*) kammar a, kammāra, kammagāra, karmāra, karmakāra, kammagāra, kambāra = one who does any business; an artisan, a mechanic; a blacksmith (Ka.) kammāḷa = an artisan, an artificer: a blacksmith, a goldsmith (Ta.Ka.); a goldsmith

(Ka.) kammara = the blacksmith or ironsmith caste; kammaramu = the blacksmith's work, working in iron, smithery; kammaravāḍu, kammari, kammarīḍu = a blacksmith, ironsmith; kammarikamu = a collective name for the people of the kamma caste (Te.) kammāṛasāle = the workshop of a blacksmith (Ka.); kamasālavāḍu = a blacksmith (Te.) kamarsārī smithy (Mth.) kambāṛike, kammāṛike = a blacksmith's business (Ka.Ma.)(Ka.lex.)(DEDR 1236). karmakāra = labourer (Pāṇini's *aṣṭādhāyī* : kārukarma = artisan's work (*Arthaśāstra*: 2.14.17); karmānta = a workshop or factory (*Arthaśāstra* : 2.12.18, 23 and 27, 2.17.17, 2.19.1, 2.23.10). kamaru to be singed, burnt or scorched (by the sun, by fire)(Ka.); kamaru, kamuru, kamalu (Te.); kamarike, kamarige = the state of being singed etc.; kamaru, kanaru, kamara, kamut.u, kavut.u, kavuru, gavulu = id. (Ka.) (Ka.lex.) kamar = a blacksmith; rana kamar, the ordinary blacksmith in the country (rana is their caste or tribal name); saloi kamar, a kind of blacksmith. Kamar kami mit bar hor.ko cet akata = a few Santals have learnt blacksmith work (Santali. Bodding). Kambru = a blacksmith; ale t.hen bar oṛak kambru menakkoa = two families of blacksmiths live with us; kambru t.hene sen akana = he has gone to the blacksmith (Santali.Bodding). karumaṉ, karumakaṉ blacksmith (Ta.lex.) kammam = kammiyar toḻil (i.e. work of kammiyar or kammāḷar: kaṉṉār, kollar, ciṟpar, taccar, taṭṭār); kammiyanūl = ciṟpanūl, i.e. book of sculpture (Ta.lex.) kammara = the blacksmith or ironsmith caste; kammaramu = the blacksmith's work, working in iron, smithery; kammaravāḍu, kammari, kammarīḍu = a blacksmith, ironsmith (Te.lex.) kammaṟa, kammagāṟa = blacksmith (Ka.lex.); kammāḷa = an artisan, an artificer; a blacksmith, a goldsmith (Ka.Ta.Ma.); a goldsmith (Ka.lex.) kammara = the blacksmith or ironsmith caste; kammaramu = the blacksmith's work, working in iron, smithery; kambāṟa = blacksmith; kambāṟike, kammāṟike = a blacksmith's business (Ka.lex.) kamār (Or. kamhār, toil) syn. of baṛae, blacksmith. This term seems to be applied especially to the blacksmiths of Gangpur, who, though of Munḍari race like the lohars of Biru, Barway and other Oraon parts, are considered outcasts by the latter because they use tanned hides for their bellows. (Mundari.lex.) kambru = a blacksmith. Ale t.hen bar or.ak kambru menakkoa = two families of blacksmiths live with us; kambru t.hene sen akana = he has gone to the blacksmith (Santali.lex.Bodding) kambru guru = the reputed original teacher of the ojhas, a mythical teacher of charms and incantations, as also of medicine. Acc. To one form of the Santal traditions the person who taught the women witchcraft was Kambru; acc. To another, it was Maran buru. It is not possible to decide whether there has been an old sage of this name; or whether it should be understood as a person from Kamrup; the Santal traditions may be understood both ways (Santali.lex.Bodding). kamar = a blacksmith, a semi-hinduized caste; kolhe kamar, a Kolhe blacksmith and iron-smelter; lohar kamar, a caste of blacksmiths that live more in conformity with Hindu caste rules (do not eat meat, do not drink beer; rare in the Santal country); rana kamar, the ordinary blacksmiths in the country (rana is their caste or tribal name); saloi kamar, a kind of blacksmith. Kamar kami mit bar hor.ko cet akata = a few Santals have learnt blacksmith work. The rule among the Santals is that a village (or several villages) keep a blacksmith who does all repairs to agricultural implements free of charge, but receives twenty seers of paddy and one winnowing-fan full of Indian corn cobs and two sheaves of pady for each plough; to make a ploughshare he is paid for the iron; to put teeth on a sickle he gets two seers of paddy, and he is also paid half a seer of rice from each house at the Sohrae. He is paid for whatever else he makes new; kara era, the wife of a blacksmith (Desi kamar; H. karmka_r; B. ka_ma_r); kamari = the work of a blacksmith, pay for such work (Santali.lex.) karmāruḍu a blacksmith, an artisan (Te.lex.) kamarsār ī smithy (Mth.); kamarsakyar (Bi.)(CDIAL 2899). 2104. Workshop: kamhala workshop (Si.); kammala smithy (Si.); kammasālā (Pkt.); karmaśālā workshop (MBh.)(CDIAL 2896). Blacksmith; labourer: karmāra blacksmith (RV.); kammāra worker in metal (Pali); kammāra, kammāraya blacksmith (Pkt.); kamār (A.); kāmār (B.); kamāra blacksmith, caste of non-Aryans, caste of fishermen (Or.); kamār blacksmith (Mth.); kamburā (Si.)(CDIAL 2898). karmakṛt performing work, skilful in work (AV.); one who has done any work (Pāṇ.); workman (Skt.); kambuḷa doing menial work (Si.)(CDIAL 2891). karmakāra doing work without wages (Kāś.); karmakāraka one who does any work (Pāṇ.); kammakāra hired labourer, workman (Pali); kammagāra servant (Pkt.); kammāriyā female servant or slave (Pkt.); kāmar slave (Sv.); kamārā servant (L.); kamāro slave (Ku.N.)(CDIAL 2888). karmakara workman, hired labourer (MBh.); kammakara (Pali); kammayara servant (Pkt.); kamerā hired labourer (H.); kamburanavā to serve as a menial or slave (Si.)(CDIAL 2887). karmakārāpayati causes to work as a servant (Skt.); kamārāiṇu to cause to work (S.)(CDIAL 2889). kārma active, laborious (Pāṇ.); kamma connected with work (Pkt.); ka_mu, ka_mo slave (K.); ka_mma~_, ka_ma_ farm servant (P.); kāmā, kāmo servant (WPah.)(CDIAL 3074). kārmika engaged in action, name of a partic. Buddhist sect (Ya_j.); Public officer: kāmā public officer (S.); servant (WPah.)(CDIAL 3076). Work: karman act, work (RV.); kamma (Pali); kramam., kramane, kamma (As'.); kama (NiDoc.Si.); kamman, kamma, kammā (Pkt.); kam work, esp. smith's work (Gypsy); gām (Shum.Gaw.Bshk.); kam (Wot..K.); krum (Kal.); korum (obl. kormo)(Kho.); kam work, thing, booty (Gypsy); kām (Mai.Tor.Ku.); id. (N.A.B.Mth.Bhoj. H.Marw.G.M.); keram (Sv.); krom (Sh.D..); kom (Sh.); komu (K.); kamu (S.); kamm (L.P.WPah.); kāma (Or.Konkan.i); kāmu (Aw.); kāũ an office, administration (G.); krem, kam, klem (Ash.); ṣlam (Ash.Wg.); kram (Dm.Tir.Phal.); lām, ṣam, kuṛūm, gām, plōm (Pas'.)(CDIAL 2892). Fatigue: śrama labour (RV.); fatigue (S'Br.AV.); sama fatigue (Pali); samam. energy (As'.); sama fatigue, effort (Pkt.); seũ worry (WPah.); mehe-ya, mēya work, service (Si.)(CDIAL 12683). sammati is weary (Pali); śramyati is tired (RV.); sammai (Pkt.); śamūna to become tired (D..); ṣomoiki, ṣomōnu (Sh.)(CDIAL 12693). santa tired (Pali); śranta wearied (RV.); samta (Pkt.); śāndṇu to tire (WPah.)(CDIAL 12692). Labourer: kāmaṭh, kāmīṭ. busy, diligent (M.); karmiṣṭha very active (Skt.)(CDIAL 2901). kamāṭhī, kameṭhī beating (P.)(CDIAL 2890). kāmāṭṭi labourer, one who works with a hoe, digger of earth (Ta.Ma.); kāmāṭi (Te.Ka.); kāmāṭe(Tu.); kāmāṭhi (M.)(Ta.lex.) kamaveti causes to work, works (NiDoc.); kammāvēi earns, works (Pkt.); kamā̃wun to work, earn, smelt (metal)(K.); kamāiṇu to work, earn, slaughter (S.); kamāvaṇ to work, earn (L.); kamāuṇā (P.); kumāṇa (WPah.); kamūṇo to work, cultivate (Ku.); kamāunu (N.); kāmāna to earn, shave (B.)[cf. kammai does barber's work (Pkt.); kramoīki to use, employ, spend (Sh.)(CDIAL 2894)]; kamāiba to work, earn (Or.); kamāeb to serve, weed (a field)(Mth.); kamāvai earns (OAw.); kamānā (H.); kamāvvũ to help to earn (G.); kamāvũ to earn (G.); kamāviṇ ē (M.)(CDIAL 2897).

kamarasāla = waist-zone, waist-band, belt (Te.) kammaru = the loins, the waist (Ka.Te.M.); kamara (H.); kammarubanda = a leather waist band, belt (Ka.H.) kammaru = a waistband, belt (Te.) kammariñcu = to cover (Te.) kamari = a woman's girdle (Te.) komor = the loins; komor kat.hi = an ornament made of shells, resembling the tail of a tortoise, tied round the waist and sticking out behind worn by men sometimes when dancing (Santali) kambra = a blanket (Santali) [Note the pannier tied as a waist band to the one-horned heifer.][Bartleby.com notes that the English word 'shawl' meaning 'a square or oblong piece of cloth worn as a covering for the head, neck, and shoulders' has th eymology: Persian *shāl*, ultimately from Sanskrit śāṭī, cloth, sari. Hence, kamarsaala in Telugu to refer to the pannier taken through the kamar 'loins'. ]

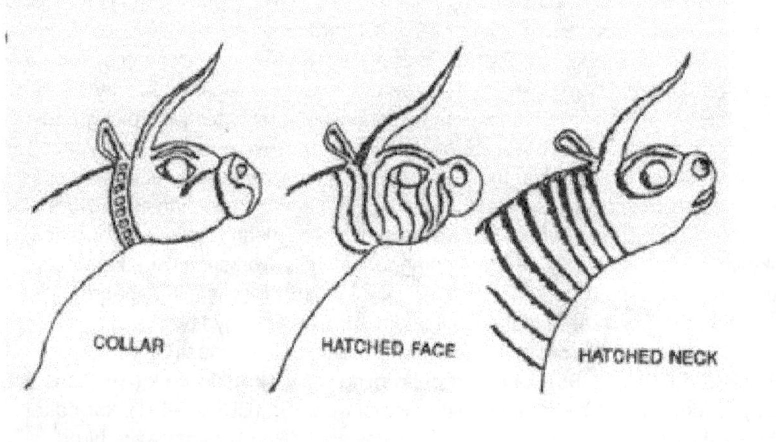


Vikalpa: damṛa m. a steer; a heifer; damkom = a bull calf (Santali)

Rebus: damṛi = copper; tamb(r)a = copper (Skt.); tamba = copper (Santali) *damṛi, dambṛi, daṭi* 'one-eighth of a pice (copper)'; dammid.i id. (Telugu) damr.i, dambr.i one eighth of a pice (Santali) damḍ ī, damḍo lowest copper coin (G.) tāmbaḍa copper plate; tāmbaḍī, tāmbaḍo a copper pot; tāmbum copper (G.)

The imagery on the pectoral m1656 shows overflowing (liquid) from the rim of the jar. The words which evoke this imagery are: eṟe = to pour any liquids; to pour (Ka.); iṟu (Ta.Ma.); ira- īi (Ta.); eṟe = to cast, as metal; to overflow, to cover with water, to bathe (Ka.); eṟe, ele = pouring; fitness for being poured(Ka.lex.) erako molten cast (Tu.lex.)

Rebus: eraka, eṟaka = any metal infusion (Ka.Tu.); urukku (Ta.); urukka melting; urukku what is melted; fused metal (Ma.); urukku (Ta.Ma.); eragu = to melt; molten state, fusion; erakaddu = any cast thng; erake hoyi = to pour meltted metal into a mould, to cast (Ka.)

The owner of the pectoral is a coppersmith with a workshop and professional in working with metal infusion or fused metal or cast metal.

Rings on neck of one-horned heifer. One horn is kod. Rings on neck are: kot.iyum.

Rebus: kot. 'artisan's workshop'.(Kuwi)

kūṭa 'horn'; rebus: kūṭam 'workshop' (Ta.) kūṭam is also connoted by a glyph: a 'summit of a mountain'.

*koṭiyum* [*koṭ, koṭī* neck] a wooden circle put round the neck of an animal (G.) [cf. the orthography of rings on the neck of one-horned young bull]. kōd.iya, kōḍe = young bull; kōḍelu = plump young bull; *kōḍe* = a. male as in: *kōḍe dūḍa* = bull calf; young, youthful (Te.lex.) *kōḍiya, kōḍe* young bull; adj. male (e.g., *kōḍe dūḍa* bull calf), young, youthful; *kōḍekā̃ḍu* a young man (Te.); *kōḍē* bull (Kol.); *khoṛe* male calf (Nk.); *kōḍi* cow; *kōṛe* young bullock (Konḍa); *kōḍi* cow (Pe.); *kūḍi* id. (Mand.); *kōḍi* id., ox (Kui); *kajja kōḍi* bull; *kōḍi* cow (Kuwi)(DEDR 2199). *koṛa* a boy, a young man (Santali) *gōnde* bull, ox (Ka.); *gōda* ox (Te.); *kondā* bull (Kol.); *kōnda* bullock (Kol.Nk.); bison (Pa.); *kōnde* cow (Ga.); *kōndē* bullock (Ga.); *kondā , konda* bullock, ox (Go.)(DEDR 2216).

ācāri koṭṭya = forge, kammārasāle (Tu.) kod. = place where artisans work (G.) *koṭḍī* a room (G.)

*koḍ* = place where artisans work (G.lex.) *koḍ* = a cow-pen; a cattlepen; a byre (G.lex.) goṛa = a cow-shed; a cattleshed; goṛa orak = byre (Santali.lex.) got.ho [Skt. koṣṭha the inner part] a warehouse; an earthen vessel in wich indigo is stored (G.lex.) koṭṭamu = a stable (Te.lex.)

*koḍ* = artisan's workshop (Kuwi)

*kōḍ* (pl. *kōḍul*) horn (Pa.); *kōṭu* (in cmpds. *kōṭṭu-*) horn (Ta.); ko.r. (obl. *koṭ-*) horns (one horn is kob), half of hair on each side of parting, side in game, line marked out (Ko.); kwiṛ (obl. *kwiṭ.-*) horn (To.); *kōḍ* horn (Ka.); *kōṟ* horn (Ka.); *kōḍu* horn (Tu.); *kōḍu* rivulet (Te.); *kōr* (pl. *kōrgul*) id. (Ga.); *kōr* (obl. *kōt-*, pl. *kōhk*) horn of cattle or wild animals (Go.); *kōr* (pl. *kōhk* ), *kōṛu* (pl. *kōhku*) horn (Go.); kogoo a horn (Go.); kōju (pl. kōska) horn, antler (Kui)(DEDR 2200). Tailless he-buffalo; ox with blunt horns: kūṟai that which is short; dwarf snake, calamaridae; kūṟai-k-kiṭā, kūṟai-k-kaṭā tailless he-buffalo (Ta.)(DEDR 1914). Image: horn: kūṭa any prominence: a horn (Ka.); *kōḍu, kōṟ* a horn of animals; a tusk (Ka.)(Ka.lex.) *kōṟ, kōḍu* a horn; *kōṟke, kōṟkil., kōṟkiḷim, kōṟge* id. (Ka.); *kōḍu* kut.t.u to strike or gore with the horn or with the tusk (Ka.); *kōḍu* a horn of animals; a tusk (Ka.); *kōḍu* -v ī sa the allowance of a vis of corn etc. for every bullock-load that comes into town etc.; *kuḍu* the state of being crooked, bent (Ka.); *koḍu* (Ma.)(Ka.lex.) kūṭa horn, bone of the forehead, prominence (Vedic); prominence, top (Pali.lex.) kūṭa a horn; an ox whose horns are broken; kūṇikā the horn of any animal (Skt.lex.) sin:ghin horn projecting in front (Santali.lex.); kūṭa bone of the forehead with its projections, the crown of the head; end, corner (Skt.lex.)

kūṭa = horn (RV 10.102.4; AV 8.8.16; AitBr. 6.24; S'Br. 3.8.1.15; JBr.1.49.9; 50.1 (JAOS, 19, 114). Rebus: *khūṭ* 'community, guild' (Mu.)

The entire composition of the heifer with a panier and a horn can be read rebus: Glyphic composition: *kōḍē* (heifer) *koḍiyum* (rings on neck) *kūṭa* (horn) Rebus: *kōda koḍ khūṭ kammarsāla* 'pannier' (Telugu); rebus: *karmāraśāla* 'workshop of smith' (Skt.) 'turner, smithy workshop, guild'. The composition animal is often shown in front of the 'standard' device which reads: *sā̃gaḍa* (lathe/portable furnace) Rebus: *sāngatarāsu* 'stone-cutter, stone-carver'. The two glyphic compositions together thus semantically read:

*kōda koḍ kammarsāla khūṭ sāngāta* 'association and guild of smithy workshop turner, stone-carver'. That a lapidary, carver, engraver,scribe is involved becomes emphatically denoted with a semantic determinant using a glyphic composition of 'rim of jar'. This composition of 'rim of short-necked jar' is used as frequently as the 'heifer-standard-device' composition glyph. This rim of jar glyphic composition connotes: *kaṇḍa kanka* "furnace, stone (ore) metal account (scribe)'.

The glyph 'horns' also represents 'hammer' and suffixed to *āra-* the metal, *āra kūṭa* 'brass':

kūṭamu = the summit of a mountain (Te.lex.)

*kollan-ulai-k-kūṭam* blacksmith's workshop, smithy (Ta.lex.) koll-ulai blacksmith's forge (*kollulaik kūṭattin-āl* : Kumara. Pira. Nītineṟi. 14)(Ta.lex.) *kampaṭṭa-k-kūṭam* mint (Ta.)

Rebus: *kūṭakamu* = mixture (Te.lex.)

*ārakūṭa* = brass (Skt.) *ārakūṭa* = arsenical copper [Arthas'a_stra].

*kūṭakamu* = mixture (Te.lex.)

[āṟa, aṟa = suffix to denote one who makes things: kammāṟa, uppāṟa = smith, salt-maker (Ka.); āṟṟu = to do, make (Ta.); āre, ārekāṟa, āreya = a Mahratta man (Ka.Te.)]

kūṭa m= a room (Ta.lex.)

Kuiper cites from Southworth the following examples of glosses, testifying to a 'strong foreign impact': kūṭa, 'house'; *kuṇḍa*, 'pot, vessel'; *ūrdara*, 'a measure for holding grain'; *apūpa*, 'cake'; *odana*, 'rice dish'; *karambha*, 'a kind of gruel'; *piṇḍa*, 'a lump of flesh'; *ulūkhala*, 'mortar'; *kārotara*, 'sieve, drainer'; *camris.,* 'ladle'; *kos'a*, 'cask, bucket'; *kṛśana*, 'pearl'; *kīnāśa, kīnāra,* 'ploughman'; *khilya*, 'waste piece of land'; *lān:gala*, 'plough'; *sīra*, 'plough'; *phāla*, 'ploughshare'; *tilvila*, 'fertile, rich'; *bīja*, 'seed'; *pippala*, 'berry of the ficus religiosa'; *mūla*, 'root'; *khala*, 'threshing floor'; *ṛbīsa*, 'volcanic cleft'; *kevaṭa*, 'cave, pit'; *kṛpṛta*, 'thick or firewood'; *śakaṭī ,* 'cart'; *āṇi*, 'linch-pin'; *vāṇi*, 'swingle tree'; *kuliśa*, 'axe'; kūṭa, 'mallet'.(cf. Southworth, F.C., 1979, Lexical evidence for early contacts between Indo-Aryan and Dravidian, in: M.M. Deshpande and P.E. Hook, eds., *Aryan and Non-Aryan in India*, Ann arbor, pp.191-233).

kūṭa, 'chief' kūṭa.a a house, dwelling (Skt.lex.) kauṭa living in one's own house, hence, independent, free; kauṭika-takṣa (opp. to grāma-takṣa) an independent carpenter, one who works at home on his own account and not for the village (Skt.lex.) grāma- kūṭa = village chief (Skt.lex.) kūṭaḍu = a stone cutter (Te.lex.)

Thus, the hieroglyph of a one-horned heifer, with a pannier, with rings on neck clearly connotes an artisan's workshop koḍ -- in this case, the coppersmith's karmāraśāla. The artisan could also be a village chief 'kūṭa'.

The other glyph which occurs as frequently as the one-horned heifer is the 'standard device' in front of the heifer. The standard device is also a hieroglyph, san:gad.a 'lathe'; rebus: furnace. The word san:gad.a can also be denoted by a glyph of combined animals. The bottom portion of the 'standard device' is sometimes depicted with 'dotted circles'. khangar ghongor 'full of holes'; (Santali) rebus: kangar 'portable furnace' (Kashmiri). This device also occurs by itself and as variants on 19 additional epigraphs, in one case held aloft like a banner in a procession which also includes the glyph of the one-horned heifer as one of the banners carried.

Orthography and rebus reading of Standard device (often shown in front of one-horned heifer on Sarasvati hieroglyph corpus)

m1203A m1203B1018 Note the gimlet precisely indicated on the standard device on m1203A, the sharp point is drilling into a disc-shaped bead].

san:ghāḍo, saghaḍī (G.) = firepan; saghaḍī, s'aghaḍi = a pot for holding fire (G.)[culā sagaḍī portable hearth (G.)] aguḍe = brazier (Tu.)

san:gaḍa, 'lathe, portable furnace'; rebus: battle; jangaḍiyo 'military guard who accompanies treasure into the treasury'; san:ghāḍiyo, a worker on a lathe (G.) The dotted circles on the bottom portion of the device connote ghangar ghongor; rebus: kangar 'portable furnace'.

Evidence for mleccha spoken in India, prior to 8th century BCE

If mlecchita vikalpa occurred in *Kamaśāstra*, Mleccha could have been lingua franca prior to 8th century BCE, when Nandi transcribed the work (The work of Vātsyāyana uses the term, *mlecchita vikalpa*, to denote cipher writing of mleccha, lingua franca).

An early version of *Kamaśāstra* pre-dates eighth century BCE. As Alain Danielou notes: "The predecessors of Vātsyāyana. The first formulation of the Kamashastra, or rules of love, is attributed to Nandi, Shiva's companion. During the eighth century BCE, Shvetaketu, son of Uddalaka, undertook the summary of Nandi's work.The date is known, since Uddalaki and Shvetaketu are the protagonists of the Brihat Aranyaka Upanishad and Chandogya Upanishad, which are usually dated to this period and contain important passages connected with erotic science. A man of letters called Babhru, together with his sons or disciples, known as the Babhravya, made an important written work, summarizing the too-vast work of Shvetaketu. The Babhravya came originally from Panchala, a region located between the Ganges and the Yamuna, to the south of present-day Delhi, but most probably lived in the city of Pataliputra, the great center of the kingdom of Chandragupta, which resisted Alexander's invasion in the fourth century and became the seat of the Ashoka empire a century later...The text of Suvarnanabha must date from the first century BCE, since it mentions a king of Kuntala (to the south of Pataliputra), named Shatakarni Shatavahana who reigned at this time and who killed his wife accidentally in the course of sadistic practices. On the other hand, Yashodhara, at the beginning of his commentary, attributes the origin of erotic science to Mallanaga, the 'prophet of the Asuras' (the ancient gods), meaning to prehistoric times. Nandi, Shiva's companion, is then said to have transcribed it for manking today. The attribution of the first name Mallanaga to Vatsyayana is due to the confusion of his role as editor of the Kama Sutra with that of the mythical creator of erotic science." (Alain Danielou, 1994, *The complete Kama Sutra*, Park Street Press, Rochester, Vermont, pp.3-4).

Tamilla as a synonym of Milangka, Wilangka (Milakkha, mleccha, Pali)

"This is something about Pali on the northern Thai fringe, or about Sri Lanka in the Chiangmai valley: The term Lawa was used in reference to highland outsiders in Lanna and Shan States. Its longer form is Damilawa , and is said to derive from the Sanskrit Damila, the same term as informed the Buddhist Sri Lankan ethnic term Tamil for their non-Buddhist Others. The root of the term lay in Sinhalese chronicle accounts of the state and its dark-skinned enemies. Thus, along with the localization of Buddhism in mainland Southeast Asia came certain aspects of ethnic ranking and prejudice that contributed to rulers' ability to contextualize in universalistic terms their rule and the peoples that it excluded. Many Chiangmai chronicles used the term Tamilla for Lawa. Some used the term Milangka. Wilangka, a variant on that term, was used among Lawa in reference to their chief who lost out to the lowland forces. Milangka is derived from Milakkha, the Pali language equivalent to the Sankrit Mleccha ("savages")." Leif Jonsson // Oct 17, 2008 http://rspas.anu.edu.au/rmap/newmandala/2008/09/30/pali/#comment-568304

I am thankful to Prof. Shrinivas Tilak for the following explanations.

At one stage, mleccha referred to an alien or an outsider. According to the Bhavishya Purana, it was King Shalivahana who demarcated Sindhurashtra as the land and nation of the Aryas that lay east of the Sindhu River effectively separating it from the land of the mlecchas on the west of the Sindhu River(sthapita tena maryada mleccharyanam prithak prithak. Sindhu sthanam iti jneyam rashtram aryasya ca uttamam. Mleccha sthanam param sindhoh kritam tena mahatmana (Pratisarga adhyaya 2).

Mimamsa, usually dismissed as the most orthodox school of Indian philosophy, nevertheless paid more attention to the mlecchas and unhesitantly lauded their accomplishments in secular matters than any other darshanas. For instance, commenting on Jaiminisutra (1:3.10), Shabara raised and discussed the problem whether the meaning of certain Vedic words like pica or nema (which were not common among the Aryas but well known among the mlechhas) should be derived from Sanskrit roots or from their actual usage among the mlechhas. He advocated the linguistic usages of the mlecchas in secular matters and encouraged their incorporation at the Prakrit (lokavani) level.

Kumarila (ca. 700), another great Mimasa philosopher, granted them a potentially superior competence in worldly and secular (laukika) matters. In his Tantravartttika he discusses the mlecchas at length and advises to engage with them in empirical transactions (drisharthavyavahara) and learn from them such secular professions and skills as agriculture, astrology, and drama. Acknowledging that the mlecchas were more qualified in fields like building houses, producing silk products, and making harnesses he credited them for providing appropriate terminology and words in these areas (I am wondering if Dr Kalyanraman's reference to and discussion of 'Mlecchita vikalpa' would be relevant here)? Kumarila also invited Indians to explore countries inhabited by the mlecchas (see Tantra Varttika # 150, 153 on Jaiminisutra 1:3.10).

Prabhakara, another leading exponent of the Mimamsa school, also rejected parochial attempts to (1) derive all mleccha words from Sanskrit roots and (2) construe their meanings `etymologically' regardless of their actual usage by the mlecchas (see Shabara and Kumarila on Jaiminisutra 1:3.10)(also Wilhelm Halbfass 1990: 179). As a result, there has been a long tradition of Sanskrit scholars who were diglossic (i.e., bilingual = dvaibhashika)(see Wilhelm Halbfass, India and Europe: An Essay in Philosophical Understanding, Delhi: Motilal Banarasidass, 1990:185).

Such an early positive perception of the mlecchas however changed over the centuries. Some of the reasons may be found in Bodhayana's Dharmasutras where he defined the mleccha as one who eats beef, records his disagreement repeatedly [assertively?], and is devoid of righteous behaviour (Gomamsa khadako yastu, viruddham bahu bhashate, sarvacara vihinasya mleccha iti abhidhiyate).

Mlecchitavikalpa is a term which occurs in Vatsyayana's vidyaasamuddes'a (objectives of learning) s'loka listing 64 arts: three of these arts related to language are: *des'abhaashaa jnaana; akshara mushtika kathana; mlecchita vikalpa* [trans. learning dialects of the linguistic area (des'a); messaging through use of fingers and wrists; cryptography (writing system)].

Mlecchitavikalpa means: alternative representation of language through writing. Mlecchita means 'made by mleccha'. Mleccha means 'copper workers'.

Thus, mlecchitavikalpa relates to the writing system invented by early metal-workers, mleccha (meluhha) of the Sarasvati linguistic area.

Early references to mleccha (meluhha) do indicate it as a dialect and NOT as a term referring to speakers or groups of people. The distinction between arya vaacas and mleccha vaacas is only in reference to, respectively, the grammatical or non-grammatical forms of the lingua franca.

That a term should have been coined to represent the writing system of mleccha language is also significant. That it was called mlecchita vikalpa and that a study of this cryptography was a prescribed art by Vatsyayana should make us pause and rethink the early 'meaning' of mleccha. The famous Mesopotamian cylinder seal (showing the meluhhan merchant carrying the antelope (read: ranku, tin; ranku, antelope) also refers to meluhha as a language (requiring an interpreter).

Whenever the Indian tradition came across new ideas and practices, they naturally tested the hermeneutical ingenuity of its thinkers and commentators to address them according to the known rules preserved in the tradition of Mimamsa.

Vikalpa has been one favoured strategy wherein one is invited to choose from one or the other of the alternatives if they seem to have about the same power or authority. Thus, Arjuna is offered the option of selecting any one or more of the three types of yogas taught in the Gita.

Badha, however, is recommended in a situation where it can be demonstrated that one idea or practice is more authoritative than the other. In that event, the injunction, idea or practice with the lesser authority is annulled allowing the one having greater authority to stand.

Samuccaya is the third available strategy according to which all the items enjoined by [conflicting] injunctions, ideas or practices are considered equally valid or obligatory. Any apparent conflict is then resolved by adjudicating the implicated views or practices to different times, authorities, or ages. This strategy is discernible in the concept advocating the joint deployment of knowledge and action(jnanakarmasamuccaya).

See Jaiminisutra 12:3.9-17; P.V. Kane History of Dharmashastra: Ancient & Medieval Religious & Civil Law 2:1326-30; Patrick Olivelle The Ashrama System: The History and Hermeneutics of a Religious Institution. New York: Oxford University Press, 1993.

The expression Mlecchita vikalpa suggests that the tradition opted for the vilakpa option (rather than the badha or samuccaya) when evaluating or assessing the ideas or practices (whether as language,art or professions)described as Mleccha.

Reverting to my interpretation of mlecchita-vikalpa.

Clearly, mleccha-speakers had the competence to work with technologies, say, of agriculture or metals. Hence, the following lexemes:

mlecchita {mlis.t.a} from mla_na `faded, withered'; hence, mlis.t.a `spoken indistinctly' Pa1n2. 7-2 , 18; mleccha `a person who lives by agriculture or by making weapons'

The compound mlecchita-vikalpa as one of the 64 arts is normally associated with representation of des'a bhaashaa in an alternative representation (vikalpa), say, a glyptic writing or pictorial writing system.

The triad of arts listed by Vatsyayana among the 64 arts are: akshara mushtika kathana, des'a bhaashaa jnaana, mlecchita vikalpa. All three relate to social communication methods.

I suggest that mlecchita vikalpa was the ONLY writing system related to des'a bhaashaa jnaana -- that is expression of language through writing. And, the invention of this writing system complemented the invention of alloying metals and also complemented the method of communication called akshra mushtika kathana (story-telling using fingers and wrist, also called mudra?). If there were alternative writing systems, wouldn't Vatsyayana have mentioned it?

I agree about the samuccaya strategy of absorbing inventions. Rasaratnasamuccaya is the title of an early work in chemistry (alchemy).

It is not mere coincidence that most of the Sarasvati hieroglyphs find their expression on 5 or 6 devices on early punch-marked coins of janapada-s including yaudheya.

It appears, therefore, that vikalpa is in the context of an option, an alternative method of representing spoken language.

Three of the 64 arts listed by Vatsyayana are:

- The art of understanding writing in cipher and the writing of words in a peculiar way (mlecchita vikalpa)
- The art of communicating through fingers and knuckles/wrists (mudra) (akshara mushtika kathanam)
- Knowledge of language and of the vernacular dialects (desha bhaashaa vijnaanam)

The work discovers some lexemes of the Meluhha language and tags them to epigraphs of Indus script, containing hieroglphs. A few 'rosetta stones' validate the decipherment.
Through the entire corpus of about 4,000 epigraphs is included the document, only one instance of a broken seal (chipped in a corner) is-used as reconstructed by Huntington. This is a seal which shows a face with tiger's mane ligatured to a person seated in a yogic posture and surrounded by a set of animals. Yes, there are many cracked pottery which also comtain epigraphs. Tigers's mane =cu_l.a; rebus: furnace. person seated in penance =*kamaḍha*; rebus: *kampaṭṭa* 'mint'. Face =mukha; rebus: *mũha* 'ingot'. In the contewt of Iranica, there is an Akkadian cylinded seal which shows aa Meluhhan merchant who required an interpreter. This indicates that Meluhhan was a non-Akkadian language. A substrate language has however been reconised from terms such as tibira 'merchant'; sanga 'priest'--words which have cognates in Bharatiya languages.

Muhly, the archaeo-metallurgist scholar notes that Meluhha supplied tin to Mesopotamia. The general identification of Meluhhu as Baloch region is concordant with early Amri-Nal culture in the Makran coast (south of Karachi). A cognate term Meluhha is Mleccha which is mentioned in ancient text such as Manusmruti and Mahabharata. In the Mahabharata, a miner named Khanaka speaks Mleccha. In Manusmruti, languages are classified as Mleccha vaacas and Arya vaacas ( that is, lingua franca and literary Sanskrit).

The objective of the work is to delineate the glosses of mleccha vaacas.

In addition to the Meluhhan shown on the Akkadian cylinder seal, there are three other objects with epigraphs: two tin ingots and one cylinder seal with pictographs. Rebus (Latin: 'by means of things') is a graphemic expression of the phonetic shape of a word or syllable.The two tin ingots contain glyphs which do not find any parallels in cretan but have concordant glyphs in Indus Script. These pictographic glyphs can be read rebus as related to tin (ran:ku; rebus: antelope ). On one cylinder seal, a tabernae montana plant is depicted as identifies by Potts. That tabaerna montana is called tagaraka in many Bharatiya (Indic) languages; read rebus: tagara, 'tin'.

Two tin ingots with Sarasvati epigraphs

Two other rosetta stones are the two late bronze age tin ingots from the harbor of Haifa, Israel contain glyphs used in epigraphs of Sarasvati civilization!

The picture of these two ingots was published by J.D. Muhly [New evidence for sources of and trade in bronze age tin, in: Alan D. Franklin, Jacqueline S. Olin, and Theodore A. Wertime, *The Search for Ancient Tin*, 1977, Seminar organized by Theodore A. Wertime and held at the Smithsonian Institution and the National Bureau of Standards, Washington, D.C., March 14-15, 1977]. Muhly notes:"A long-distance tin trade is not only feasible and possible, it was an absolute necessity. Sources of tin stone or cassiterite were few and far between, and a common source must have served many widely scattered matallurgical centers. This means that the tin would have been brought to a metallurgical center utilizing a nearby source of copper. That is, copper is likely to be a local product; the tin was almost always an import...The circumstances surrounding the discovery of these ingots are still rather confused, and our dating is based entirely upon the presence of engraves signs which seem to be in the Cypro-Minoan script, used on Cyprus and at Ugarit over the period 1500-1100 BCE. The ingots are made of a very pure tin, but what could they have to do with Cyprus? There is certainly no tin on Cyprus, so at best the ingots could have been transhipped from that island. How did they then find their way to Haifa? Are we dealing with a ship en route from Cyprus, perhaps to Egypt, which ran into trouble and sank off the coast of Haifa? If so, that certainly rules out Egypt as a source of tin. Ingots of tin are rare before Roman times and, in the eastern Mediterranean, unknown from any period. What the ingots do demonstrate is that metallic tin was in use during the Late Bronze Age...rather extensive use of metallic tin in the ancient eastern Mediterranean, which will probably come as a surprise to many people." (p.47)

We will demonstrate that the symbols incised on the ingots are not Cypro-Minoan symbols but Harappan pictographs.

 m-1336a  2515 (Mahadevan)

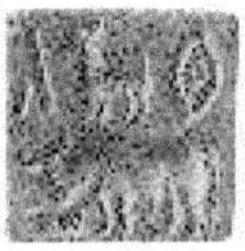

m-1097 (On this seal, the antelope appears in the middle of the inscription; it is apparently this pictograph that gets normalised as a 'sign', Sign 184 and variants].

m1341 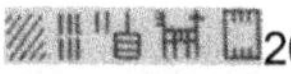2092 m0516At 

m0516Bt 3398  m0522At 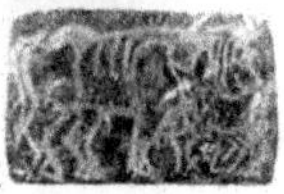 m0522Bt 3378

The sign pictographs are:

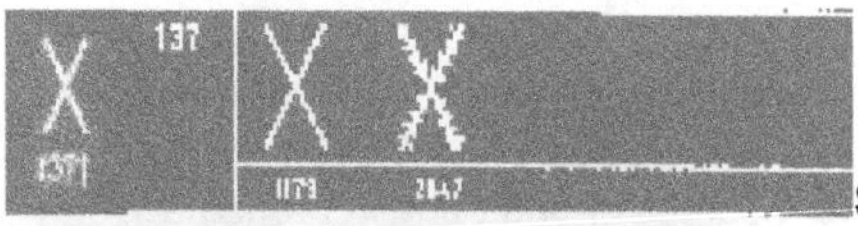Sign 137 and variants

Sign 142 and variants dā̃ṭu = cross over (Kol.)(DEDR 3158). Rebus: dhatu 'mineral' (Santali). Vikalpa: bāṭa 'road' (Telugu). Rebus: bhaṭa 'furnace' (Santali)

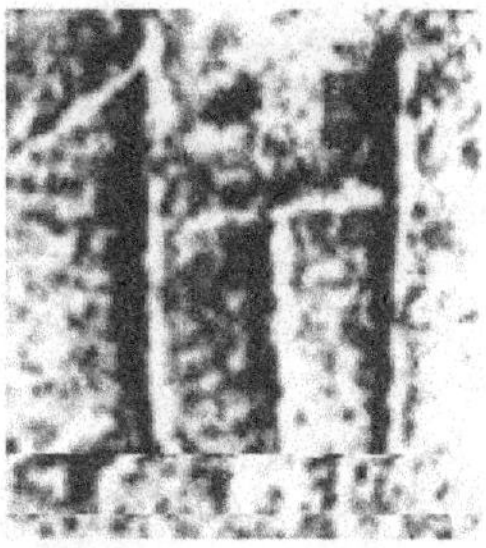 

Sign 249 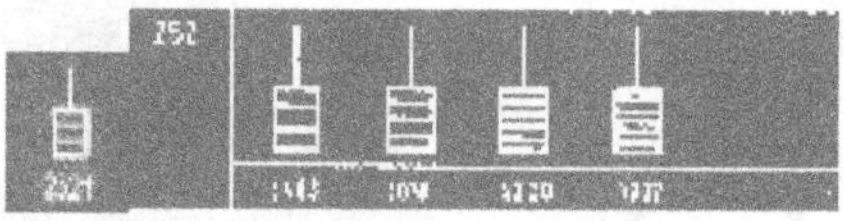
Sign 252 and variants

This pictograph clearly refers to an antelope as depicted on the Mohenjo-daro copper plate inscription: (m-516b shown).

Sign 182 is a stylized glyph denoting a ram or antelope: tagar (Skt.); rebus: takaram 'tin' (Ta.)

On each ingot, there are two signs as shown below:

[Let us refer to these signs as, 'antelope' and X]

  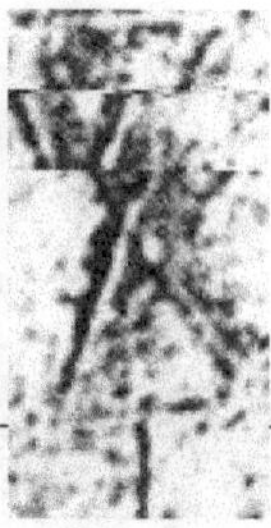

[Let us refer to these signs as, X and 'mould' or 'liquid measure'].

Liquid measure: ran:ku; rebus: ran:ku = tin; rebus: ran:ku = antelope. Thus both liquid measure glyph and antelope glyphs are graphonyms (graphically denoting the same rebus substantive: ran:ku, 'tin'. X glyph which is common to epigraphs on both the tin ingots may refer to an 'ingot' or a dha_tu 'mineral'. Only a smith had the competence to inscribe on metal ingots and slso on bronze tools/weapons, apart from copper plates. Many epigraphs have been found on such objects. The language mleccha is a Bharatiya language. Over 2000 lexemes include homonyms depicting pictographic glyphs (such as rhino, elephant, tiger etc.) and also substantive repertoire related to a mine or a smithy: furnace types , minerals, metals, alloys.

This identification of language lexemes and corresponding glyptic representation in pictographic writing is primised on the existqance of a linguistic area circa 2500 BCE. (A linguistic area is recognized as a region where languages absorb features from one another and make them their own). Thus, proto-versions of Tamil, Austtric, Munda, Prakrits, Sanskrit (and over 20 present-day languages in India) have hundreds of cognates, in particular, related to agriculturai terms and smithy terms and smithy terms, consistent with the maritime-riverine civilization along the Indian ocean Rim and with trade transactions with ANE. Muhly rightly notes the link between the emergence of the bronze age and the invention of a writing system. Rebus readings of almost all glyphs (pictorial motifs as well as signs) relate to mine workers' and metalsmiths' repertoire. http://sites.google.com/site/kalyan97

Indus economics, language and script: Chanhu-daro as Sheffield of ancient India

Chanhu-daro was called "Sheffield of ancient India," by Mackay, the excavator of the small Indus site.

This 'Sheffield' used Indus script to encode underlying Mleccha (Meluhha) speech.

The transition from Stone Age into Bronze Age resulted in stone-workers' and lapidaries' competence being complemented by 1) invention of metallurgical technique of alloying minerals to create hard metal and metal artefacts and 2) invention of Indus writing system. Both inventions of the artisans drew upon the repertoire of mleccha (Meluhha) language of Indian linguistic area to trade with their contact areas and to create a record of their economic transactions.

Many researchers have analyzed and documented economic facets, in particular, of the Indus civilization area and their insights support the decoding of inscriptions of the civilization, in the context of economic activities by Meluhhans, who are mleccha speakers of Indus language and users of Indus script. The areas investigated by researchers and scholars also cover, in an inter-disciplinary evaluation of archaeology, literature and language of ancient times, an extensive civilization area across the Persian Gulf and in maritime trade contact with Mesopotamia, detailing the material resources used for bead-making, manufacture of grinding stones, of copper plates/utensils/tools/weapons - many with inscriptions, agricultural products used/produced, metallurgy including alloying, casting, forging:

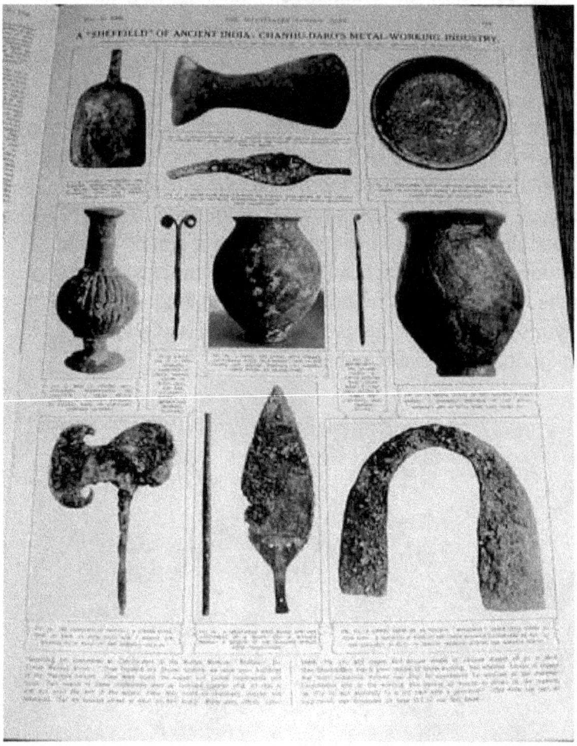
A "SHEFFIELD" OF ANCIENT INDIA: CHANHU-DARO'S METAL-WORKING INDUSTRY.

Slide351. Copper tablet (H2000-4498/9889-01) with raised script found in Trench 43.
Decoding the 'backbone' glyph on the copper tablet: kaśēru 'the backbone' (Bengali. Skt.); kaśēruka id. (Skt.) Rebus: kasērā ' metal worker ' (Lahnda)(CDIAL 2988, 2989) Vikalpa: riṛ 'ridge formed by the backbone' (Santali); rebus: rīti 'brass' (Skt.) A pair of glyphs 'ovals inlaid wih short-stroke' flanking the backbone glyph: 'pair' glyph: dula. Rebus: dul 'casting'. 'Oval' glyph: 'ingot'. Rebus: dhāḷako 'large ingot'. Thus, the eight copper tablets with raised script text message denotes: cast brass ingots, delivered by workers of the guild into the warehouse.

From the Illustrated London News - A "Sheffield of Ancient India: Chanhu-Daro's Metal Working Industry 10 x photos of copper knives, spears , razors, axes and dishes

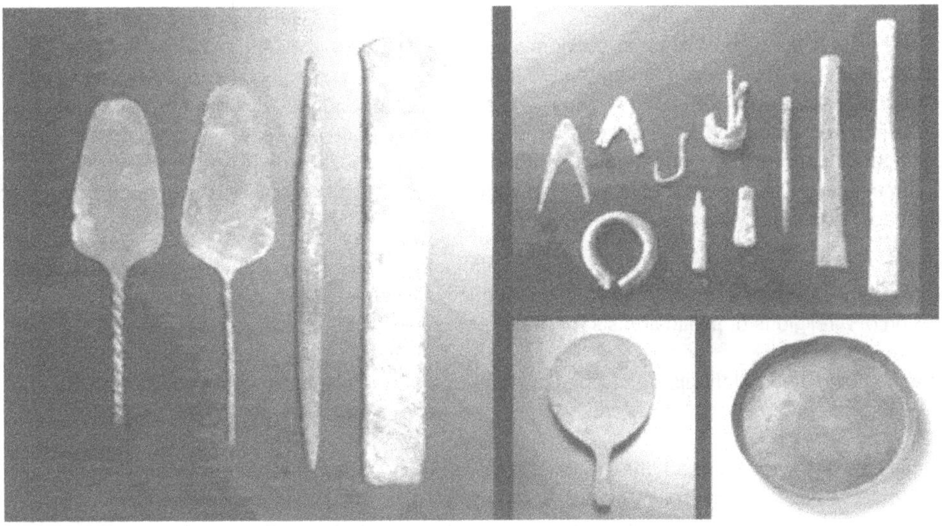

Harappans made knives, weapons, bowls and figures from bronze.

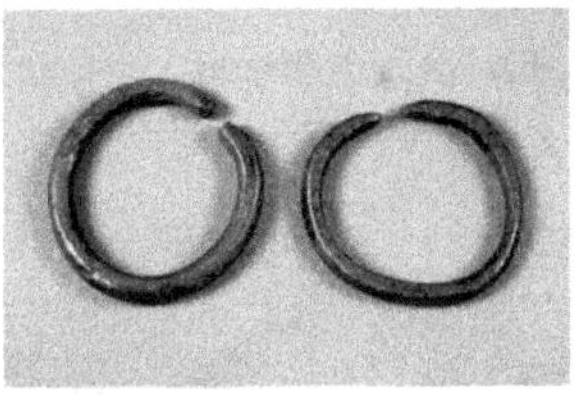

Slide 78. Bangles Two copper/bronze bangles, one from Harappa and the other from Mohenjo-daro. The bangles were made from a round hammered rod bent in a full circle. The space between the ends of the bangle would be pried apart to slip it over the wrist. Dimensions of left bangle: 6 cm diameter, 0.73 cm thickness Harappa National Museum, Karachi, HM 13 710 Dimensions of right bangle: 6.13 cm dia Mohenjo-daro, DK 3457a National Museum, Karachi, NMP 51.899, HM 13.809 Mackay 1938: 535, pl. CXXXVI, 60

Randall W Law, Jeffrey Rose, James Muhly, Colin Renfrew, Lamberg-Karlovsky, Massimo Vidale, Jonathan Mark Kenoyer, Dorian Fuller, Asko Parpola, Iravatham Mahadevan,Brajbasi Lal, SP Gupta, Shivaji Singh, Rajesh PN Rao, Nicholas Kazanas, PRS Moorey,Gregory L Possehl, IsMEO-Aachen University Mission, Harappa Archaeological Research Project, KS Valdiya, S. Kalyanaraman, Michel Danino, Maurizio Tosi.

The contribution of Randall W. Law co-authored with Prabhakar VN and Tejas Garge has been linked in the decoding of 1) a Mitathal seal with Indus script and underlying language and 2) glyphs of standard device, heifer and scarf used on the Indus inscriptions. The standard device, sangada, is shown as relatable, rebus, to stone-workers called sangataras. संगतराश lit. 'to collect stones, stone-cutter, mason.' संगतराश संज्ञा पुं० [फ़ा०] पत्थर काटने या गढ़नेवाला मजदूर । पत्थरकट । २. एक औजार जो पत्थर काटने के काम में आता है । (Dasa, Syamasundara. Hindi sabdasagara. Navina samskarana. 2nd ed. Kasi : Nagari Pracarini Sabha, 1965-1975.) पत्थर या लकडी पर नकाशी करनेवाला, संगतराश, 'mason'.

The cumulative conclusion drawn from these contributions is that the primacy of economic activities necessitated the invention and use of a writing system to convey messages using the language – lingua franca – of the civilization. This inference is consistent with the insight provided by James Muhly: invention of alloying tin with copper to create bronze alloy heralding the Bronze Age had to be linked with another invention: the writing system used in economic activities, in trade transactions, in particular.

The objects on which the Indus script is inscribed are part of the material artefacts discovered through archaeological excavations. It is, therefore, reasonable to evaluate the writing system on these inscribed objects in the context of other economic activities of the civilization – activities such as cultivation of rice, millet or maize (glyphs related to which had been used in the script), mining of mineral resources, lapidary crafts on precious- and semi-precious stones – turning the stones into beads used on necklaces and other ornaments, bones, ivory, stone-work related to ring-stones – used as architectural supports in buildings, grinding stones – used in households for grinding cereals or pulses into edible flour, metallurgical activities of alloying minerals into metals, casting and forging them into household utensils or artisan tools or weapons.

The challenge of decoding the writing system is, in effect, the challenge of identifying the words used by the people of the civilization engaged in such economic activities – without invoking an a priori assumption of a religious or political basis for the use of glyphs of the writing system.

It has been shown that a Mohenjo-daro tablet inscribed with three glyphs: standard device, heifer and scarf – decoded rebus related to the workshop of stone-workers and mineral-workers or miners.

As Randall Law has demonstrated, the stone work covered a variety of resources: grinding stone, chert, steatite, agate, vesuvianite-grossular, alabaster, and limestone. In addition to these resources, bone, ivory, copper, tin, arsenic, meteoric iron were also used to produce artefacts as archaeologically attested.

In what language and with what words did the creators of the urbanized civilization refer to these resources?

A clue is provided by the inscriptions already decoded in a known language in a known writing system: Mesopotamian cuneiform inscriptions.

USE OF STRUCTURAL RINGSTONES IN DHOLAVIRA (CA. 2500 B.C.)

Decryption of Indus script cipher of hieroglyphs of Indian linguistic area, announced in Indus Script Cipher – Hieroglyphs of Indian linguistic area(2010), avoids the pitfalls of many past decipherment claims. The work is premised on the Indian linguistic area and consistent with the principle of occam's razor, uses a simple rebus method to read all the glyphs – pictorial motifs with glyptic elements and signs with glyptic elements – as based on words of the Indus language from a repertoire of artisans' work attested archaeologically. The Indus language is independently delineated by the linguistic area' principle and a comparative Indian Lexicon provides the glosses for matching words with glyptic elements and identifying homonyms which render the message content of inscriptions. The set of glosses from the Indian linguistic area lead to a decipherment of the messages as representations of the repertoire of artisans – lapidaries, miners and smiths. The underlying language – for glosses which render the glyptic elements and concordant homonyms -- is not exclusive Munda or exclusive Sanskrit or exclusive Dravidian but the *lingua franca* which included *substrata* glosses from all three language families – with glosses borrowed from one another. Evidence for the decipherment comes from the cultural continuum including punch-marked coins and sculptural glyphs of the historical periods which continued to use the glyphs of Indus script. Evidence is also provided to

equate the Indus language with a language category called mleccha (cognate: meluhha) attested in Mesopotamian texts, in an archaeological context and attested in ancient Indian texts which point to mleccha as a language with shared super-set of glosses, as lingua franca clearly distinguishable from literary language – just as Prākṛtam is distinguishable from Sanskrit. Thus, mleccha is construed as the set of glosses shared in the Indian *sprachbund* in contact situations and the context of history of changes in phonetic forms and/or semantic expansions of glosses.

MS 2814
Royal inscription commemorating defeat of Oman and Indus Valley.
Sumer, 2100-1800 BC

Two Schoyen Indus seals have been decoded. The Schoyen collection of manuscripts included MS 2814, a cuneiform inscription. The royal inscription on the Sumerian clay tablet of 2100 to 1800 BCE, commemorates defeat of Magn, Melukkham, Elam (?) and Amurru – linking Oman and Indus Valley.

MS 2814. MS in Neo Sumerian and Old Babylonian on clay, Sumer, 2100-1800 BC, 1 tablet, 14,8x14,0x3,3 cm (originally ca. 16x14x3 cm), 3+3 columns, 103 lines in cuneiform script.

Commentary: The text was copied from a Sargonic royal inscription on a statue in the Ur III or early Old Babylonian period. Magan was at Oman and at the Iranian side of the Gulf. Meluhha or Melukham was the Indus Valley civilisation (ca. 2500-1800 BC). This is one of fairly few references to the Indus civilisation on tablets. The 3 best known references are: 1. Sargon of Akkad (2334-2279 BC) referring to ships from Meluhha, Magan and Dilmun; 2. Naram-Sin (2254-2218 BC) referring to rebels to his rule, listing the rebellious kings, including '(..)ibra, man of Melukha'; and 3. Gudea of Lagash (2144-2124 BC) referring to Meluhhans that came from their country and sold gold dust, carnelian, etc. There are further references in literary texts. After ca. 1760 BC Melukha is not mentioned any more. For Indus MSS in The Schøyen Collection, see MS 2645 (actually linking the Old Acadian and Indus civilisations), MSS 4602, 4617, 4619, 5059, 5061, 5062 and 5065. Exhibited: Tigris 25th anniversary exhibition. The Kon-Tiki Museum, Oslo, 30.1. - 15.9.2003.

Mesopotamian texts provide the context of ships from Meluhha, of Meluhhans coming from their country and selling gold dust, carnelian, ivory, pointing to maritime trade exchanges and contacts with the Indus civilization area.

A significant contribution by Jeffrey I. Rose (2010) relates to the importance of Arabo-Persian Gulf. Another is by Steffen Terp Laursen (2010) detailing the westward transmission of Indus valley sealing technology: origin and development of 'Gulf type' seal and other administrative technologies in early Dilmun, ca. 2100-2000 BCE (Published in *Arabian Archaeology and Epigraphy* 2010: vol. 21: 96–134). See Decoding in Indus Script Gulf Type Seals.

Based on these analyses, it is reasonable to hypothesise that the inscribed objects of the civilization were compositions of glyphs related to the artisans' economic activities.

Another remarkable insight relates to the presence of Meluhhan traders in the Persian Gulf region (which links Meluhha – Indus valley – with Mesopotamia). "Several tablets refer to a colony of acculturated Meluhhan traders in Lagash." (Parpola,

S., A. Parpola and R.H. Brunswig, 1977, The Meluhha village: evidence of acculturation of Harappan traders in late third millennium Mesopotamia? *Journal of the Economic and Social History of the Orient*, Vol. 20. No. 2: 129-65).

This article sees support for the identification of Meluhha with Indus civilization using mleccha as cognate of Meluhha. Mleccha were associated with Asuras mentioned in Vedic texts. Since Vedic texts had their locus on Sarasvati river valley, mleccha speakers should also have their locus on Sarasvati river valley.

An Akkadian cylinder seal bears the inscription su-i-li-su/eme-bal me-luh-ha-ki 'Su-ilisu, Meluhha interpreter'). This together with a reference to a Meluhhan ship establishes contact between Mesopotamia and Meluhha over sea-route, in Akkadian times. Inscriptions of Gudea of Lagadh (2143-2124 BCE) refer to 'the Meluhhans came up (or down) from their country' to supply wood and other raw materials for the construction of the main temple of Gudea's capital. Refernces to import of luxury items from Meluhha also occur in these inscriptions. [Edzard, AfO 22 (1968), 15 no. 15.33. Oppenheim Anc. Mes. (Chicago 1964) 355, argues that the title eme-bal designated its bearer as one who translated from his native into a foreign language.] Suilisu means 'he of his god'. The logographs are read: 'bearded (su) [man protected by] the hands (su) of the god or goddess (ili).'

Thus, the use of Indus glyphs on seals found in Persian Gulf including Lagash clearly relate to the Meluhhan's native language - Mleccha. An eme-bal might have interpreted these glyphs to Mesopotamian trade contacts. It is not necessary to assume that the Indus glyphs were adapted to represent some words or syllables of Sumerian or Akkadian language. The glyphs may simply have been read rebus in mleccha as was done for these glyphs on inscriptions of other objects inscribed found in the civilization area on such sites as Mohenjo-daro, Harappa, Chanhu-daro, Mitathal or Dholavira, Kalibangan or nearly 40 other seal discovery sites, with Indus script.

The Akkadian texts referring to Meluhhans also refers to mill staff (scribes, gate-keepers, reed-weavers, carpenters, maltsters, grinding-slab cutters, 'chair-bearers', boat towers, etc.) and mention grain delivery. Meluhhans in Lagash are clearly part of domestic Ur III society.

Consistent with the focus of Akkadian texts on mill staff, it is also possible that the Indus script glyphs found on Persian Gulf sites may also refer to the professions of Meluhhans (scribes, carpenters, stone or grinding-slab cutters, etc.)

Mleccha as a Sanskrit word should also have referred to Meluhhan traders in Lagash.

RV 10.125 is addressed to Vak, the almightly feminine divinity par excellence, who punished the impious. The Sanskrit word mleccha ('non-vedic stranger speaking indistinctly or corruptly') is connected with Meluhha and is attested in Satapatha Brahmana. Goddess Vak is expressly said to have belonged to the mlecchas:

> Satapatha Brahmana 3,2,1,18 to 25
>
> "Thereupon he ties a black deer's horn to the end (of his garment). Now the gods and the Asuras, both of them sprung from Prajapati, entered upon their fathe Prajapati's inheritance: the gods came in for the Mind and the Asuras for Speech. Thereby the gods came in for the sacrifice and Asuras for speech; the gods for yonder (heaven) and the Asuras for this (earth)."
>
> 19. The gods said to Yajna (the sacrifice). 'That Vak (speech) is a woman: beckon her, and she will certinly call thee to her.' Or it may be, he himself thought, 'That Vak is a woman: I will beckon her and she will certainly call me to her.' He accordingly beckoned her. She, however, at first disdained him from the distance: and hence a woman, when beckoned by a man, at first disdains him from the distance. he said, 'She has disdained me from the distance.'

23. The gods then cut her off from the Asuras; and having gained possession of her and enveloped her completely in fire, they offered her up as a holocaust, it being an offering of the gods. And in that they offered her with anushtubh verse, thereby they made her their own; and the Asuras, being deprived of speech, were undone, crying, 'He 'lavah! he 'lavah!' [According to Sayana, 'He 'lavo' stands for 'he 'rayo' (i.e. ho, the spiteful enemies)!' which the Asuras were unable to pronounce correctly. The Kanva text, however reads, te hattavako 'sura hailo haila ity etam ha vakam vadantah parababhuvuh (? i.e. He ila 'ho, speech.'] A third version of this passage seems to be referred to in the Mahabhashya (Kielh.), p.2.]

24. Such was the unintelligible speech which they then uttered, -- and he (who speaks thus) is a mlecha (barbarian). Hence let no Brahman speak barbarous language, since such is the speech of th Asuras. Thus alone he deprives his spiteful enemies of speech; and whosoever knows this, his enemies, being deprived of speech, are undone.

25. The Yajna (sacrifice) lusted after Vak (speech), thinking, 'May I pair with her!' He united with her.

Indus script discoveries outside Meluhha – mleccha artisan guild tokens have been decoted.

It is reasonable to assume that the economic principles of Sarasvati-Sindhu (Indus) civilization and facets of *dharma* would have found their echoes – as continuing legacies -- in ancient India which is a major part of the civilization area. In the Economic principles in Ancient India as noted by Nicholas Kazanas (2009), the use of vārt(t)ā in Sanskrit to connote economic activities, i.e. manufacture, trade etc., it is underscored that these activities were not divorced from ethics and religion. '...; in a Rgvedic hymn the girl Apāla speaks distinctly of her father's cultivated field. [Rgveda ® VIII, 33 5-6]. But such references show occupation and use, not ownership. Ownership, as we know it, would be shown indisputably only if there was mention of sale, exchange, or giving away of land. There are no such references in the Hymns. The head of a tribe or community or hamlet often gives away gifts – as in the hymn on Liberality (Dakṣiṇā, a RV X, 107) or the Vālakhilya hymns 7 & 8 (RV VIII, 55 & 56) etc. The gifts are gold and jewels, cattle, steeds, skins and the like...Thus dharma denotes religion and religious laws but also secular law and, at the same time, the duties, religious and civil, that a man ha to perform towards himself, his family, the State-officials, other members of the community, the priests and holy men, strangers, the environment and gods! It is all dharma, aspects of universal Natural law. (pp.11-12). In the post-vedic literature, in Baudhāyana, we find mention of a householder who lives by the mode called "ṣannivartanī", which is a kind of tenant farming. "He cultivates six nivartanas [a nivartana=6000 sq ft] of fallow land giving a share to the owner, or soliciting his permission (to keep the whole produce)."[III, 2, 2,. SBE XIV, p 288] ... Kauṭilya's Arthaśāstra presents both private property and royal property in land; there are also vast uninhabited tracts, wastes and jungles, which seem to belong to the State as a whole. These last are used for new settlements (śūnyaniveśa : settlement or occupation of vacant land). Such settlements (forms of colonization) are small or large villages from 100 to 500 families (grāma; II, 1,2). [R P Kangle's edition, Pt I, Univ Bombay, 1965] ... Bṛhaspatisūtra XIX, 26: "A privy, a fireplace, a pit or a receptacle for leavings of food and other (rubbish), must never be made very close to the house of another man" ...Specialized craftsmen, tradesmen and other occupations, formed guilds and developed their own professional codes. Many law-givers enjoin that these should be respected by the ruler. In fact Yājñavalkya ordains (I,361) that the king should compel such guilds to comply with their own rules. (pp. 8, 18-19, p 32). See also Ancient Hindu principles of social and economic management.

The decoding of the Seals m1118 and Kalibangan032 which use the glyphs: Zebu (bos Taurus indicus), fish, four-strokes, arrow read rebus in mleccha (Meluhhan) as a reference to a guild of artisans working with ayas kāṇḍa 'excellent quantity of iron' (Pāṇini) is consistent with the primacy of economic activities which resulted in the invention of a writing system, now referred to as Indus Script.

There are two words in Indian linguistic area which connote economics as a separate department or subject: artha, kāṇḍa Ayo 'fish' (Mu.) + kaṇḍa 'arrow' (Skt.) ayaskāṇḍa 'a quantity of iron, excellent iron'

(Pāṇ.gaṇ) aya = iron (G.); ayah, ayas = metal (Skt.) The inscriptions on seals m1118 and K032 (with zebu or bos Taurus indicus pictorial motif) have been decoded: aḍar

ḍhangar khuṭ 'native-metal-blacksmith community (guild)(making) excellent metal'. kuṭi, 'smelting furnace' (Mundari.lex.).kuṭhi, kuṭi (Or.; Sad. koṭhi) (1) the smelting furnace of the blacksmith; kuṭire bica duljaḍko talkena, they were feeding the furnace with ore; (2) the name of ēkuṭi has been given to the fire which, in lac factories, warms the water bath for softening the lac so that it can be spread into sheets; to make a smelting furnace; kut.hi-o of a smelting furnace, to be made; the smelting furnace of the blacksmith is made of mud, cone-shaped, 2' 6" dia. At the base and 1' 6" at the top. The hole in the center, into which the mixture of charcoal and iron ore is poured, is about 6" to 7" in dia. At the base it has two holes, a smaller one into which the nozzle of the bellow is inserted, as seen in fig. 1, and a larger one on the opposite side through which the molten iron flows out into a cavity (Mundari.lex.)

There are over 50 epigraphs of the civilization showing bos taurus indicus which is decoded as a hieroglyph denoting in mleccha a metal-smithy-guild (community, khu~t.) This reference to a community through a glyph is indicative of the early guild working in the civilization. This is a surmise that the early semantics of the word khu~t. may have related to such a group formation of metalsmiths and artisans.

khũṭ Brahmani bull (Kathiawar G.); khũṭro entire bull used for agriculture, not for breeding (G.)(CDIAL 3899). Rebus: khũṭ a community, sect, society, division, clique, schism, stock (Santali). Decoded rebus: khũṭ 'community' (perhaps, a guild).

khũṭro = entire bull; khũṭ= brāhman.i bull (G.) khuṇṭiyo = an uncastrated bull (Kathiawad. G.lex.) khũ_ṭaḍum a bullock (used in Jhālwāḍ)(G.) kuṇṭai = bull (Ta.lex.) cf. khũ_dhi hump on the back; khuī̃_dhũ hump-backed (G.)(CDIAL 3902).

kūṭa a house, dwelling (Skt.lex.) khũṭ = a community, sect, society, division, clique, schism, stock; khũṭren peṛa kanako = they belong to the same stock (Santali) khũṭ Nag. khũṭ, kūṭ Has. (Or. khũṭ) either of the two branches of the village family.

It has been demonstrated that the lexeme kāṇḍa occurs on Indus script inscriptions as in: ayas kāṇḍa 'excellent quantity of iron' (Pāṇini).

अर्थ in RV._i-ix only *n.* aim , purpose (very often अर्थम् , अर्थेन , अर्थाय , and अर्थे ifc. or with gen. " for the sake of , on account of , in behalf of , for "); advantage , use , utility (generally named with काम and धर्म » त्रि-वर्ग ; used in wishing well to another dat. or gen. Pa1n2._2-3 , 73); substance , wealth , property , opulence , money; (hence in astron.) N. of the second mansion , the mansion of wealth (cf , धन) VarBr2S. affair , concern (Ved. often acc. /अर्थम् with √ इ , or गम् , to go to one's business , take up one's work RV._&c ); sense , meaning , notion (cf. अर्थ-शब्दौandअर्थात् s.v. below and वेदतत्त्वा*र्थ-विद्) (Monier-Williams Skt. Lexicon)

अर्थः [In some of its senses from अर्थ्; in others from ऋ-थन् Uṇ.2.4; अर्थते ह्यसौ अर्थिभिः Nir.] 1 Object, purpose, end and aim; wish, desire; ज्ञातार्थो ज्ञातसंबन्धः श्रोतुं श्रोता प्रवर्तते, सिद्ध°, °परिपन्थी Mu.5; °वशात् 5.8; स्मर्तव्योऽस्मि सत्यर्थे Dk.117 if it be necessary; Y.2.46; M.4.6; oft. used in this sense as the last member of compounds and translated by 'for', 'intended for', 'for the sake of', 'on account of', 'on behalf of', and used like an adj. to qualify nouns; अर्थेन तु नित्य- समासो विशेष्यनिघ्रता च Vārt.; सन्तानार्थाय विधये R.1.34; तां देवतापित्रतिथिक्रियार्थाम् (धेनुम्) 2.16; द्विजार्था यवागूः Sk.; यज्ञार्थात्कर्मणो$न्यत्र Bg.3.9. It mostly occurs in this sense as अर्थम्, अर्थे or अर्थाय and has an adverbial force; (*a*) किमर्थम् for what purpose, why; यदर्थम् for whom or which; वेलोपलक्षणार्थम् Ś.4; तद्दर्शनादभूच्छम्भोर्भूयान्दारार्थ- मादरः Ku.6.13; (*b*) परार्थे प्राज्ञ उत्सृजेत् H.1.41; ...that which can be perceived by the senses, an object of sense; इन्द्रिय° H.1.146; Ku.7.71; R.2.51; ...5 (*a*) An affair, business, matter, work; प्राक् प्रतिपन्नो$यमर्थो$- ङ्गराजाय Ve.3; अर्थो$यमर्थान्तरभाव्य एव Ku.3.18; अर्थो$र्था- नुबन्धी Dk.67; सङ्गीतार्थः Me.66 business of singing *i. e.* musical concert (apparatus of singing); सन्देशार्थाः Me. 5 matters of message, *i. e.* messages; (*b*) Interest, object; स्वार्थसाधनतत्परः Ms.4.196; द्वयमेवार्थसाधनम् R.1. 19;2.21; दुरापे$र्थे 1.72; सर्वार्थचिन्तकः Ms.7.121; मालविकायां न मे कश्चिदर्थः M.3 I have no interest in M. (*c*) Subject-matter, contents (as of letters &c.); त्वामवगतार्थं करिष्यति Mu.1 will acquaint you with the matter; उत्तरो$यं लेखार्थः *ibid.;* तेन हि अस्य गृहीतार्था भवामि V.2 if so I should know its contents; ननु परिगृहीतार्थो$- स्मि कृतो भवता V.5; तया भवतो$विनयमन्तरेण परिगृहीतार्था कृता देवी M.4 made acquainted with; त्वया गृहीतार्थया अत्रभवती कथं न वारिता 3; अगृहीतार्थे आवाम् Ś.6; इति पौरान् गृहीतार्थान् कृत्वा *ibid.* -6 Wealth, riches, property, money (said to be of 3 kinds : शुक्ल honestly got; शबल got by more or less doubtful means, and कृष्ण dishonestly got;) त्यागाय संभृतार्थानाम् R.1.7; धिगर्थाः कष्टसंश्रयाः Pt.1.163; अर्थानामर्जने दुःखम्*ibid.;* सस्यार्थास्तस्य मित्राणि1.3; तेषामर्थे नियुञ्जीत शूरान् दक्षान् कुलोद्गतान् Ms.7.62. -7 Attainment of riches or worldly prosperity, regarded as one of the four ends of human existence, the other three being धर्म, काम and मोक्ष; with अर्थ and काम, धर्म forms the well-known triad; cf. Ku.5.38; अप्यर्थकामौ तस्यास्तां धर्म एव मनीषिणः R.1.25. ... -अर्थिन् *a.* one who longs for or strives to get wealth or gain any object. अर्थार्थी जीवलोको$यम् । आर्तो जिज्ञासुरर्थार्थी Bg.7.16...शालिन् *a.* Wealthy. -शास्त्रम् 1 the science of wealth (political economy). -2 science of polity, political science, politics; अर्थशास्त्रविशारदं सुधन्वानमुपाध्यायम् Rām.2.1.14. Dk.12; इह खलु अर्थशास्त्रकारास्त्रिविधां सिद्धिमुपवर्णयन्ति Mu.3; °व्यवहारिन् one dealing with politics, a politician; Mu.5. -3 science giving precepts on general conduct, the science of practical life; Pt.1. -शौचम् purity or honesty in money-matters; सर्वेषां चैव शौचानामर्थशौचं परं स्मृतं Ms. 5.16. -श्री Great wealth. -संस्थानम् 1 accumulation of wealth. -2 treasury. -संग्रहः, -संचयःaccumulation or acquisition of wealth, treasure, property. कोशेनाश्रयणी- यत्वमिति तस्यार्थसंग्रहः R.17.6. कुदेशमासाद्य कुतो$र्थसंचयः H. -संग्रहः a book on Mīmāṁsā by Laugākṣi Bhāskara. (Apte Skt. Lexicon, pp. 223-224)

काण्डः kāṇḍḥ ण्डम् ṇḍam 1 A section, a part in general. -2 The portion of a plant from one knot to another. काण्डात्काण्ड- त्प्ररोहन्ती Mahānār.4.3. -3 A stem, stock, branch; लीलोत्खातमृणालकाण्डकवलच्छेदे U.3.16; Amaru.95; Ms. 1.46,48, Māl.3.34. -4 Any division of a work, such as a chapter of a book; as the seven Kāṇḍas of the Rām. -5 A separate department or sub- ject; *e. g.* कर्म° &c. -ऋषिः A class of sages including Jaimini. -6 A cluster, bundle, multitude. -7 An arrow. मनो दृष्टिगतं कृत्वा ततः काण्डं विसर्जयेत् Dhanur.3; Mb.5.155.7.-पृष्ठः 1 one of the military profession, a soldier; -ष्ठम् the bow of Karṇa &

Kāma. -भङ्गः, -भग्नम् a fracture of the bone or limbs. -वीणा the lute of a Chāṇḍāla. -सन्धिः a knot, joint (as of a plant). -स्पृष्टः one who lives by arms, a warrior, soldier. (Apte Skt. Lexicon, p. 555)

काण्ड *m.* (also) abundance, Vcar. काण्ड्/अ TS._Vii, any part or portion , section , chapter , division of a work or book (cf. त्रि-क्°) *mfn.* a separate department or subject (e.g. कर्म-काण्ड , the department of the वेदtreating of sacrificial rites Kas3._on Pan2._4-2 , 51) AV._TS._S3Br._R. *mfn.* a multitude , heap , quantity (ifc.) Pa1n2._4-2 , 51 Kas3. *mfn.* an arrow MBh._xiii , 265 Hit. (Monier-Williams Skt. Lexicon, p. 269)

4 INVENTION OF WRITING

Resolution of language problem in a *sprachbund*

The evidences presented of continued use of Indus script glyphs during the historical periods in India and in particular, on punch-marked coin symbols relate to a historical cultural continuum in India. This leads to a reasonable inference that the language of the writing system should be a language of the people, artisans, in particular, which continues to be used even today in India since language and culture are closely intertwined phenomena in a *sprachbund* (language union).

Duplicate seal impressions are one type of tablets. An evidence for the use of such tablets as category tallies of lapidary workshops is provided by the finds at Kanmer. (Source: http://www.antiquity.ac.uk/projgall/agrawal323/Antiquity, D.P. Agrawal et al, Redefining the Harappan hinterland, *Anquity*, Vol. 84, Issue 323, March 2010)

It is a category mistake to call these as 'seals'. These are three duplicate tablets created with seal impressions (glyphs: one-horned heifer, standard device, PLUS two text inscription glyphs (or 'signs' as written characters): one long linear stroke, ligatured glyph of body + 'harrow' glyph. There are perforations in the center of these duplicate seal impressions which are tablets and which contained identical inscriptions. It appears that three duplicates of seal impressions -- as tablets -- were created using the same seal. Perforations in the center would have been used to pass a string through the holes to constitute part of a bill of lading tagged to the packaged trade load.

Obverse of these tiny 2 cm. dia. tablets show some incised markings. It is unclear from the markings if they can be compared with any glyphs of the Indus script corpora. They may be 'personal' markings like 'potter's marks' – designating a particular artisan's workshop (working platform) or considering the short numerical strokes used, the glyphs may be counters (numbers or liquid or weight measures). More precise determination may be made if more evidences of such glyphs are discovered. Excavators surmise that the three tablets with different motifs on the obverse of the three tablets suggest different users/uses. They may be from different workshops of the same guild but as the other side of the tables showed, the product taken from three workshops is the same.

It is possible that the markings on the obverse of the three Kanmer tablets (as tallies) were markings using a form of *kharoṣṭī* proto-syllabary as follows, possibly indicting some quantitative measures of the products delivered to the furnace account scribe of turned (forged) native metal : *kharoṣṭī* numeral 'twenty' *kharoṣṭī* numeral 'two'. *kharoṣṭī* numeral 'one'. *kharoṣṭī* syllable (*ṭha-* for *ṭhakkura* 'blacksmith'?)

20 2 1

 ṭha

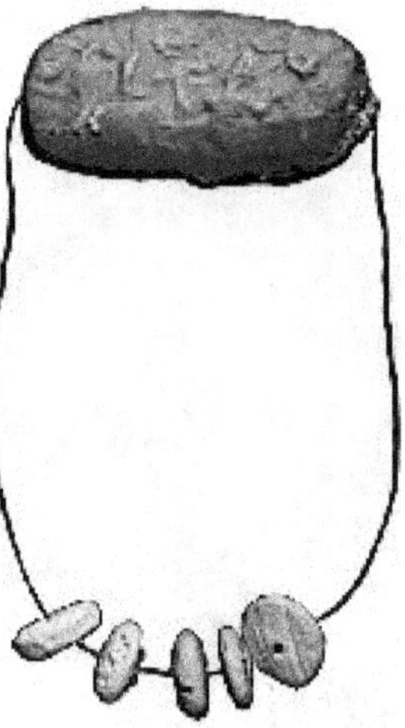

The practice of combining *kharoṣṭī* syllabary for names together with Indian hieroglyphs (from Indus script) for substantive messaging of the mint repertoire continues in the historical periods as evidenced by thousands of punch-marked coins starting from c. 600 BCE.

Decoding of the identical inscription on the three tablets of Kanmer.

Glyph: One long linear stroke. koḍa 'one' (Santali) Rebus: koḍ 'artisan's workshop' (Kuwi) Glyph: meḍ 'body' (Mu.) Rebus: meḍ 'iron' (Ho.) Ligatured glyph : aḍar 'harrow' Rebus: aduru 'native metal' (Kannada). Thus the glyphs can be read rebus. Glyph: koḍiyum 'heifer' (G.) Rebus: koḍ 'workshop (Kuwi) Glyph: sangaḍa 'lathe' (Marathi) Rebus 1: Rebus 2: sangaḍa 'association' (guild). Rebus 2: sangatarāsu 'stone cutter' (Telugu). The output of the lapidaries is thus described by the three tablets: *aduru meḍ sangaḍa koḍ* 'iron, native metal guild workshop'.

Conjecturing a parallel with Sumer bulla envelope system

The three perforated tablets (seal impressions) of Kanmer might have been strung together and the account compiled by the guild scribe to prepare a bill of lading. It is also possible that a seal impression on a bulla might have authenticated the bill of lading together with the three tablets (seal impressions) of Kanmer.

The hole on the following tablets may also have been strung together to create a bill of lading:

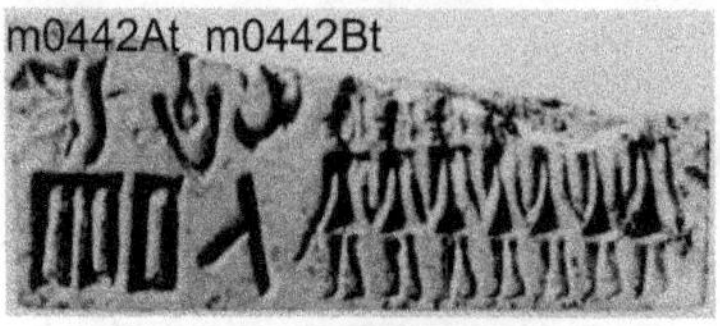


Mohenjo-daro, excavation number HR 4161, now in the National Museum of India, New Delhi. A seal from Mohenjo-daro, excavation number DK 6847 (m1186A), now in the National Museum of Pakistan, Karachi. Department of Archaeology and Museums, Government of Pakistan.

?Pleiades clustered in the context of other Indus script glyphs h097 Text 4251 h097 Pict-95: Seven robed figures (with stylized twigs on their head and pig-tails) standing in a row.

A group of six or seven women wearing twigs may not represent Pleiades, bagaḷā). The groups of such glyphs occur on four inscribed objects of Indus writing. (See four pictorial compositions on: m1186A, h097, m0442At m0442Bt). Glyph (seven women): bahula_ = Pleiades (Skt.)bagaḷā = name of a certain godess (Te.) bagaḷā ,bagaḷe, vagalā (Ka.); baka , bagaḷlā , vagaḷā (Te.) bakkula = a demon, uttering horrible cries, a form assumed by the Yakkha Ajakalāpaka, to terrify the Buddha (Pali.lex.) bahulā f. pl. the Pleiades VarBṛS., likā -- f. pl. lex. [bahulá -- ] Kal. bahul the Pleiades , Kho. ból, (Lor.) boul, bolh, Sh. (Lor.) b*lle (CDIAL 9195) bahulegal. = the Pleiades or Kṛittikā-s (Ka.lex.) bahula_ (VarBr.S.); bahul (Kal.) six presiding female deities: vahulā the six presiding female deities of the

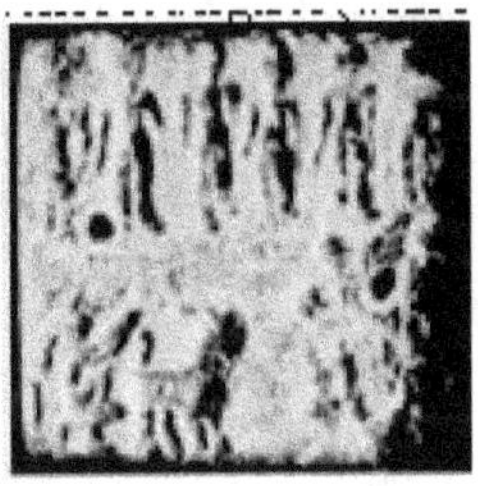
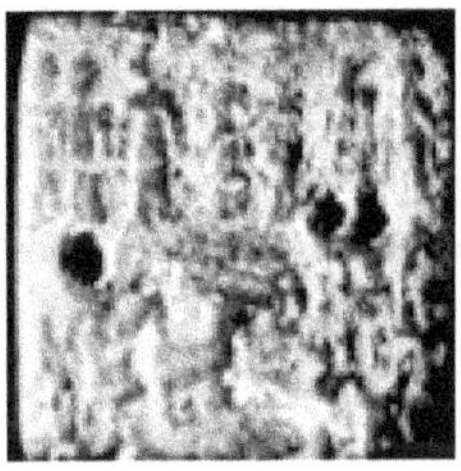

Pleiades (Skt.); vākulai id. (Ta.)(Ta.lex.) Pleiades: bahulikā pl. pleiades; bahula born under the pleiades; the pleiades (Skt.lex.) bahule, bahulegal. the pleiades or kr.ttikās (Ka.)(Ka.lex.) Image: female deities of the pleiades: vākulēyan- < va_kulēya Skanda (Ta.lex.) *பாகுளி* pākuḷi, n. perh. bāhulī. Full moon in the month of Puraṭṭāci; *புரட்டாசி மாதத்துப் பௌர்ணமி. அதைப் பாகுளி யென்று* (*விநாயகபு.* 37, 81).

Glyph (twig on head on seven women): adaru 'twig'; rebus: aduru 'native metal'. Thus, the seven women ligatured with twigs on their heads can be read as: bahulā + adaru; rebus: bangala 'goldsmith's portable furnace' + aduru 'native metal'.

bāhulēya Kārttikēya, son of S'iva; bāhula the month kārttika (Skt.Ka.)(Ka.lex.) *வாகுலை* vākulai, n. < Vahulā. The six presiding female deities of the Pleiades. Rebus: bagalo = an Arabian merchant vessel (G.lex.) bagala = an Arab boat of a particular description (Ka.); bagalā (M.); bagarige, bagarage = a kind of vessel (Ka.) bagalo = an Arabian merchant vessel (G.lex.) cf. m1429 seal.

bāhuḷyamu. [Skt. from బహుళము.] n. Abundance.

Vikalpa: Rebus: bhāgaḷiyo = a bazaar shopkeeper (G.lex) bakāḷa (Ka.); baāla = a shopkeeper with contemptuous implications (M.)(Ka.lex.) bakāl = [Ar. bakkāl, a greengrocer fr. bakcū, vegetable] a petty shopkeeper; a ānia (so called in contempt); bakālu = fresh vegetables (G.lex.)

Vikalpa: ban:gala = n. An oven. కుంపటి. kumpaṭi = an:gāra śakaṭī = a chafing dish a portable stove, a goldsmith's portable furnace (Te.lex.) cf. ban:garu, ban:garamu = gold (Te.lex.)

Slide 142. Moulded tablets from Trench 11 Harappa (Kenoyer); m1186; m488C adorant with 'scarf'; markhor in front, with rings (or neck-bands) on neck.

Glyph: 'rings on neck': koṭiyum = a wooden circle put round the neck of an animal; koṭ = neck (G.) Vikalpa: kaḍum 'neck-band, ring'; rebus: khāḍ 'trench, firepit' (G.) Vikalpa: khaḍḍā f. hole, mine, cave (CDIAL 3790) kanduka, kandaka ditch, trench (Tu.); kandakamu id. (Te.); kanda trench made as a fireplace during weddings (Konda); kanda small trench for fireplace (Kui); kandri a pit (Malt)(DEDR 1214) khaḍḍa— 'hole, pit'. [Cf. *gaḍḍa— and list s.v. kartá—1] Pk. khaḍḍā— f. 'hole, mine, cave', ḍaga— m. 'one who digs a hole', ḍōlaya— m. 'hole'; Bshk. (Biddulph) "kād" (= khaḍ?) 'valley'; K. khŏḍ m. 'pit', khŏḍü f. 'small pit', khoḍu m. 'vulva'; S. khaḍa f. 'pit'; L. khaḍḍ f. 'pit, cavern, ravine'; P. khaḍḍ f. 'pit, ravine', ḍī f. 'hole for a weaver's feet' (→ Ku. khaḍḍ, N. khaḍ; H. khaḍ, khaḍḍā m. 'pit, low ground, notch'; Or. khāḍi 'edge of a deep pit'; M. khaḍḍā m. 'rough hole, pit'); WPah. khaś. khaḍḍā 'stream'; N. khāṛo 'pit, bog', khāṛi 'creek', khāṛal 'hole (in ground or stone)'. — Altern. < *khāḍa—: Gy. gr. xar f. 'hole'; Ku. khāṛ 'pit'; B. khāṛī 'creek, inlet', khāṛal 'pit, ditch'; H. khāṛī f. 'creek, inlet', khaṛ—har, al m. 'hole'; Marw. khāṛo m. 'hole'; M. khāḍ f. 'hole, creek', ḍā m. 'hole', ḍī f. 'creek, inlet'. 3863 khā́tra— n. 'hole' HPariś., 'pond, spade' Uṇ. [√khan] Pk. khatta— n. 'hole, manure', aya— m. 'one who digs in a field'; S. khāṭru m. 'mine made by burglars', ṭro m. 'fissure, pit, gutter made by rain'; P. khāt m. 'pit, manure', khāttā m. 'grain pit', ludh. khattā m. (→ H. khattā m., khatiyā f.); N. khāt 'heap (of stones, wood or corn)'; B. khāt, khātṛū 'pit, pond'; Or. khāta 'pit', tā 'artificial pond'; Bi. khātā 'hole, gutter, grain pit, notch (on beam and yoke of plough)', khattā 'grain pit, boundary ditch'; Mth. khātā, khattā 'hole, ditch'; H. khāt m. 'ditch, well', f. 'manure', khātā m. 'grain pit'; G. khātar n. 'housebreaking, house sweeping, manure', khātriyū̃ n. 'tool used in housebreaking' (→ M. khātar f. 'hole in a wall', khātrā m. 'hole, manure', khātryā m. 'housebreaker'); M. khā̆t n.m. 'manure' (deriv. khatāviṇẽ 'to manure', khāterẽ n. 'muck pit'). — Un- expl. ṭ in L. khāṭvā̃ m. 'excavated pond', khāṭī f. 'digging to clear or excavate a canal' (~ S. khātī f. 'id.', but khāṭyāro m. 'one employed to measure canal work') and khaṭṭaṇ 'to dig'. (CDIAL 3790) •gaḍa— 1 m. 'ditch' lex. [Cf. *gaḍḍa—1 and list s.v. kartá—1] Pk. gaḍa— n. 'hole'; Paš. gaṛu 'dike'; Kho. (Lor.) gōḷ 'hole, small dry ravine'; A. garā 'high bank'; B. gaṛ 'ditch, hole in a husking machine'; Or. gaṛa 'ditch, moat'; M. gaḷ f. 'hole in the game of marbles'. 3981 *gaḍḍa— 1 'hole, pit'. [G. < *garda—? — Cf. *gaḍḍ—1 and list s.v. kartá—1] Pk. gaḍḍa— m. 'hole'; WPah. bhal. cur. gaḍḍ f., paṅ. gaḍḍṛī, pāḍ. gaḍōṛ 'river, stream'; N. gaṛ—tir 'bank of a river'; A. gārā 'deep hole'; B. gāṛ, ṛā 'hollow, pit'; Or. gāṛa 'hole, cave', gāṛiā 'pond'; Mth. gāṛi 'piercing'; H. gāṛā m. 'hole'; G. garāḍ, ḍɔ m. 'pit, ditch' (< *graḍḍa— < *garda—?); Si. gaḍaya 'ditch'. — Cf. S. giḍi f. 'hole in the ground for fire during Muharram'. — X khānĭ̄—: K. gān m. 'underground room'; S. (LM 323) gāṇ f. 'mine, hole for keeping water'; L. gāṇ m. 'small embanked field within a field to keep water in'; G. gāṇ f. 'mine, cellar'; M. gāṇ f. 'cavity containing water on a raised piece of land' WPah.kṭg. gāṛ 'hole (e.g. after a knot in wood)'. (CDIAL 3947) 3860 *khāḍa— 'a hollow'. [Cf. *khaḍḍa— and list s.v. kartá—1] S. khāṛī f. 'gulf, creek'; P. khāṛ 'level country at the foot of a mountain', ṛī f. 'deep watercourse, creek'; Bi. khāṛī 'creek, inlet'; G. khāṛi , ṛī f., ṛɔ m. 'hole'. — Altern. < *khaḍḍa—: Gy. gr. xar f. 'hole'; Ku. khāṛ 'pit'; B. khāṛī 'creek, inlet', khāṛal 'pit, ditch'; H. khāṛī 'creek, inlet', khaṛ—har, al m. 'hole'; Marw. khāṛo m. 'hole'; M. khāḍ f. 'hole, creek', ḍā m. 'hole', ḍī f. 'creek, inlet'.

Glyph: 'neck-band': kaḍum 'neck-band, ring' kaḍī a chain; a hook; a link (G.); kaḍum a bracelet, a ring (G.) Rebus: kaḍiyo [Hem. Des. kaḍaio = Skt. sthapati a mason] a bricklayer; a mason; kaḍiyaṇa, kaḍiyeṇa a woman of the bricklayer caste; a wife of a bricklayer (G.)

[The decoration on the neck of the 'ram' glyph is comparable to the rings on the neck of a heifer or on the neck of a composite animal.]

m0302

miṇḍāl 'markhor' (Tōrwālī) meḍho a ram, a sheep (G.)(CDIAL 10120); rebus: mẽṛhet, meḍ 'iron' (Mu.Ho.)

m1186A, Text 2430 Composition: horned person with a pigtail standing between the branches of a pipal on a creeper; a low pedestal with offerings (? Bowl with two ladles?);a horned person kneeling in adoration;a ram with short tail and curling horns; a row of seven robed figures, with twigs on their pigtails.

- bhaṭa 'six'; rebus: bhaṭa 'furnace'
- eae 'seven' (Santali); rebus: eh-ku 'steel' (Ta.)

adaru 'twig'; rebus: aduru 'native, unsmelted metal'. kola 'woman'; rebus: kol 'working in iron' (Ta.) Thus the group of women (six or seven) may connote: pl. kole.l rebus: 'smithy, temple' (Ko.)(DEDR 2133). Six women with twigs: adaru kol bhaṭa 'native metal, iron furnace'; seven women with twigs: adaru kol eh-ku 'native metal, iron, steel'.

A group of six or seven persons constitute unique glyphs. Each of the six or seven glyphs is ligatured

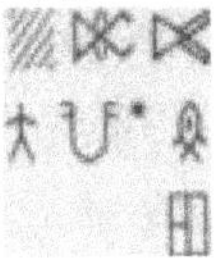

with a twig on the head and a scarf as a hair-dress. The other glyphs associated with the Pleiades, in the four pictorial compositions are:

- Human face ligatured to a ram with neck-bands
- Kneeling adorant with horns and scarf as pigtail
- Standing person (horns, twig as head-dress, scarf as pigtail) within a pot ligatured with leaves
- Temple (smithy?) glyph (third line of signs)
- Dotted fish, rim of jar, body (person)
- Pincers, claws (ligatured to ingots) ḍhālako Sign 274; rebus: 'a large metal ingot (G.)'
- Spoon in a rimless pot (Second sign on line 1, text 4251)

()The first sign from right on line 1 of Inscribed text 4251 and connotes 'cast bronze'; it is a glyptic formed of a pair of brackets (): kuṭila 'bent'; rebus: kuṭila, katthīl = bronze (8 parts copper and 2 parts tin) [cf. āra-kūṭa, 'brass' (Skt.) (CDIAL 3230) kuṭi— in cmpd. 'curve' (Skt.)(CDIAL 3231).

kuṭika— 'bent' MBh. [√kuṭ 1] Ext. in H. kuṛuk f. 'coil of string or rope'; M. kuḍċā m. 'palm contracted and hollowed', kuḍapṇē 'to curl over, crisp, contract'. CDIAL 3231 kuṭilá— 'bent, crooked' KātyŚr., aka— Pañcat., n. 'a partic. plant' lex. [√kuṭ 1] Pa. kuṭila— 'bent', n. 'bend'; Pk. kuḍila— 'crooked', illa— 'humpbacked', illaya— 'bent' DEDR 2054 Ta. koṭu curved, bent, crooked; koṭumai crookedness, obliquity; koṭukki hooked bar for fastening doors, clasp of an ornament. A pair of curved lines: dol 'likeness, picture, form' [e.g., two tigers, two bulls, sign-pair.] Kashmiri. dula दुल I युग्मम् m. a pair, a couple, esp. of two similar things (Rām. 966). Rebus: dul meṛeḍ cast iron (Mundari. Santali) dul 'to cast metal in a mould' (Santali) pasra meṛed, pasāra meṛed = syn. of koṭe meṛed = forged iron, in contrast to dul meṛed, cast iron (Mundari.lex.)

Thus, dul kuṭila 'cast bronze'.

Allograph: 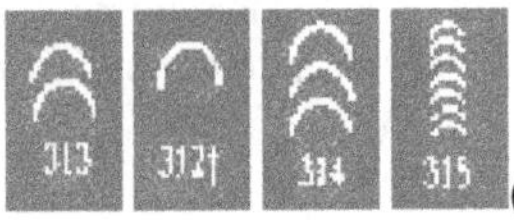 ( ) kuṭila = bent, crooked. The number of such 'arched' glyphs connote the proportions of tin alloyed with copper.

Vikalpa: Ta. kulavu (kulavi-) to bend, curve; n. bend, curve. Kuiklōnga (klōngi-) to be contracted, drawn in, bent up; klōpka(< klōk-p-; klōkt-) to contract, draw up, depress. Kur.xolkhnā, xolxnā to cause one to bend the head;xolkhrnā, xolxrnā to bend the head, bow, stoop. Malt. qolġrubelow, beneath, underneath; kolge to curve, bend; kolgro bent, curved. DEN 29 (Pfeiffer for Kur. Malt.) (DEDR 2136) *kōla4 ' curved, crooked '. [Cf. kaula -- m. ' worshipper of Śakti according to left -- hand ritual ', khōla -- 3 ' lame ' s.v. khōra -- 1. Prob. < *kaura -- (IE. *qou -- lo -- cf. WP i 371?) in Khot. kūra -- ' crooked ' BSOS ix 72 and poss. Sk. kōra -- m. ' movable joint ' Suśr.] Ash. kṓlə ' curved, crooked '; Dm. kōla ' crooked ', Tir. kṓolə; Paš. kōlā´ ' curved, crooked ', Shum. kolā´ṇṭa; Kho. koli ' crooked ', (Lor.) also ' lefthand, left '; Bshk. kōl ' crooked ', Tor. kōl (Grierson Tor 161 < kuṭila -- : rejected by Morgenstierne AO xii 181), Phal. kūulo; Sh. kōlụ̄ ' curved, crooked '. (CDIAL 3533).

(Skt.Rasaratna samuccaya, 5.205) Rebus: kuṭila, katthīl = bronze (8 parts copper and 2 parts tin) [cf. āra-kūṭa, 'brass' (Skt.) Vikalpa: खोंद [ khōnda ] *n* A hump (on the back): also a protuberance or an incurvation (of a wall, a hedge, a road). Rebus: koḍ 'workshop' (Kuwi)

Allograph

kuṭi— in cmpd. 'curve', kuṭika— 'bent' MBh. (CDIAL 3231); rebus: kuṭhi 'smelter' (Santali) [Shape of oval is consistent with the traditiojn of Koles to form equilateral lumps pointed at each end of ingots: mūh metal ingot (Santali) mūhā̃ = the quantity of iron produced at one time in a native smelting furnace of the Kolhes; iron produced by the Kolhes and formed like a four-cornered piece a little pointed at each end; mūhā me~r.he~t = iron smelted by the Kolhes and formed into an equilateral lump a little pointed at each end; kolhe tehen me~r.he~tko mūhā akata = the Kolhes have to-day produced pig iron (Santali.lex.) kaula mengro 'blacksmith' (Gypsy) paired: dul 'likeness'; dul 'cast (metal)']

This is an example of bulla in clay. MS 4523 Schoyen collection. Bulla for holding a string of complex counting tokens concerning a transaction.

Bulla for holding a string of complex counting tokens concerning a transaction

Bulla in clay, Syria/Sumer/Highland Iran, ca. 3500-3200 BC, 1 oblong bulla, diam. 2,5x6,5 cm, rollsealed with a line of animals walking left or 2 men standing with arms raised, pierced for holding a string of counting tokens.

*Commentary:* The bulla originally locked the ends of a string with a number of complex counting tokens attached to it, representing 1 transaction. The string with the tokens was hanging outside the bulla like a necklace. If the string had, say, 5 disk type tokens representing types of textiles, this number could not be tampered with without breaking the seal. The tokens could also be entirely enclosed in the center of the bulla, see MSS 4631, 4632 and 4638. Tokens were used for accounting purposes in the Near East from the Neolithic period ca. 8000 BC until ca. 3200 BC, when they were superseded by counting tablets and pictographic tablets. Some of the earliest tablets have actual tokens impressed into the clay to form numbers and pictographs, and some of the pictographs were illustrations of tokens, see 4551. (Source: http://www.schoyencollection.com/math.html)

Now, it can be reasonably inferred why the 'rim of jar' glyph occurs with such high frequency on Indus script inscriptions (as shown on this seal – fourth glyph from right on top line above the one-horned heifer -- from Mohenjo-daro. National Museum, New Delhi).

The 'rim of jar' glyph connoted *kaṇḍ kanka* 'furnace account (scribe)'. The other glyphic composition which occurs with high frequency are the glyphic pair: 'one-horned heifer' glyph in front of 'standard device' glyph. *sangaḍa koḍ* 'stone-cutter artisan's workshop'. The lapidary had graduated into a smithy worker in the bronze age and needed Indus script inscriptions to account for processing, collating, and dispatching trade loads to trade contacts in interaction areas. The scribe created a seal to account for contributions by artisans of the guild as a record of product descriptions sorted, grouped and delivered into the treasury.

*"From the beginnings in about 30,000 BCE, the evolution of information processing in the prehistoric Near East proceeded in three major phases, each dealing with data of increasing specificity. First, during the Middle and late Upper Paleolithic, ca. 30,000 – 12,000 BCE, tallies referred to one unit of an unspecified item. Second, in the early Neolithic, ca. 8000 BCE, the tokens indicated a precise unit of a particular good. With the invention of writing, which took place in the urban period, ca. 3100 BCE, it was possible to record and communicate the name of the sponsor/recipient of the merchandise, formerly indicated by seals…The events that followed the invention of tokens can be reconstructed as follows: ca. 3700-2000 BCE: A second stage was reached when groups of tokens representing particular transactions were enclosed in envelopes to be kep in archives. Some envelopes bore on the outside the impression of the tokens held inside. Such markings on envelopes were the turning point between tokens and writing. Ca. 3500-3100 BCE (starting in Uruk VI-V): Tablets displaying impressed markings in the shape of tokens superseded the envelopes. Ca. 3100-3000 BCE (starting in Uruk Iva): Pictographic script traced with a stylus on clay tablets marked the true takeoff of writing. The tokens dwindled…The tokens were mundane counters dealing with food and other basic commodities of life, but they played a major role in the societies that adopted them. They were used to manage goods and they affected the economy; they were an instrument of power and they created new social patterns; they were employed for data manipulation and they changed a mode of thought. Above all, the tokens were a counting and record-keeping device and were the watershed of mathematics and*

*communication."* (Denise Schmandt-Besserat, 1996, *How writing came about*, University of Texas Press, p.99, p. 125).

Goods which counted were basic necessities such as: animals (lamb, sheep, ewe, cow, dog); foods (bread, oil, food, sweet (honey?), beer, sheep's milk); textiles (textile, wool, type of garment or cloth, fleece, rope, type of mat or rug); commodities (perfume, metal, bracelet, ring, bed); service (make, build).

'Hollow tablet', Nuzi, Iraq. Courtesy Ernest Lacheman. A hollow egg-shaped tablet discovered in Nuzi, northern Iraq, recorded a cuneiform inscription and belonged to the family archive of a sheep owner named Puhisenni. The same transaction wa also recorded on a normal tablet. The excavators found that the hollow tablet held 49 counters, which corresponded to the list of animals detailed in the the cuneiform inscription which read:

21 ewes that lamb

6 female lambs

8 full grown male sheep

4 male lambs

6 she-goats that kid

1 he-goat

3 female kids

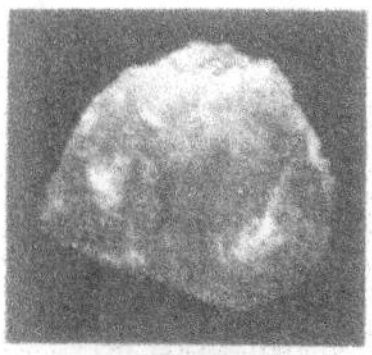

M-2131 A

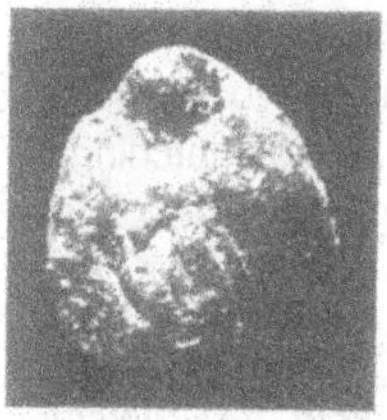

M-2131 B

The seal of Ziqarru, the shepherd. (A. Leo Oppenheim, On an operational device in Mesopotamian Bureaucracy, Journal of Near Eastern Studies 18 (1959): 121-128). It is clear that the counters (Akkadian, abnu, pl. abnati, 'stone' – each stone representing each animal of a flock) were used for accounting. These abnati were deposited, transferred or removed to keep track of changes in the shepherds or pasture, when animals were shorn etc. Thus, tokens and envelopes (bullae) served the purpose of archaic accounting.

Only one object from Mohenjo-daro comes close to being a bulla. Photograph from ASI: Sindh series Photo archive of ASI, Janpath, New Delhi. Si. 5:6639, 5:6640. Recorded in the corpora as m-2131 (Parpola et al. Corpus, Vol. 3, Part 1, p. 131). Rattle? Bulla? There are no records recording the provenance of this object and if the glyph inscribed on the bulla (rattle?) can in anyway be related to any glyph of Indus script.

The following excerpt from CDLI provides a precise account of the contributions made in developing early writing systems using tokens and bullae at Uruk (Warka).

[quote] Uruk (modern Warka)

IntroductionThe site of Uruk, modern Warka, is located in southern Iraq about 35 kilometers east of the modern course of the Euphrates river. Settlement at the site began in the Ubaid period (5$^{th}$ millennium BC). In the Uruk period (4000-3000 BC) the site was the largest in Mesopotamia at 100 hectares. Uruk continued to grow in the Early Dynastic period (2900-2350 BC), reaching a size of about 400 hectares. After the end of the Early Dynastic period, the city declined in size and significance until the Ur III period (2100-2000 BC), when the ruling dynasty pursued new building projects in the Eanna precinct. It is to this period that the massive ziggurat still visible today dates. Uruk declined again after the Ur III period, and was resettled in the Neo-Assyrian (883-612 BC) and Neo-Babylonian periods (612-539 BC).

Occupation continued at Uruk in the Achaemenid, Seleucid, and Parthian periods. Settlement at Uruk finally came to an end during the Sassanian period (224-633 AD).

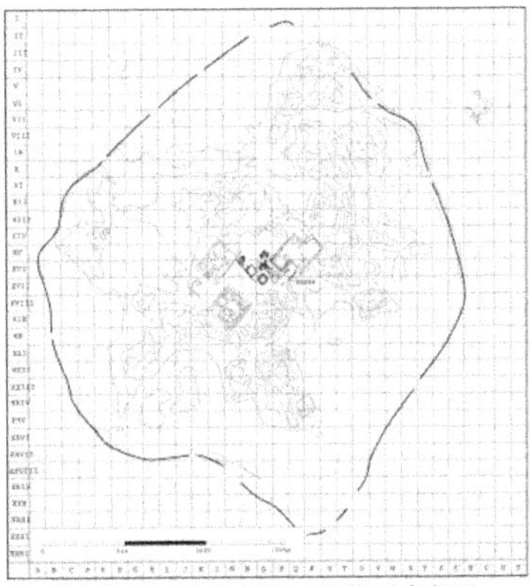

*Plan of Uruk, showing excavations in the Eanna precinct (from England 1998)*

History of Excavation

W. K. Loftus was the first archaeologist to visit Uruk in 1850 and 1854. During his excavations, he uncovered several small items, including a numerical tablet, and prepared a map of the site. R. Koldewey and W. Andrae, who would later excavate Babylon and Assur, each visited the site in the early years of the 20$^{th}$ century. It wasn't until 1912 that large scale excavations began under J. Jordan. After only one season of work, however WW I put an abrupt halt to work at Uruk. Jordan returned to the site in 1928, with A. Falkenstein serving as epigrapher. Jordon's excavation set a precedent by concentrating primarily in the Eanna district of the site, the main religious complex in the center of Uruk. When Jordan became Director of Antiquities in Baghdad in 1931, German excavations continued under A. Nöldeke, E. Heinrich, and H. J. Lenzen until WW II forced a halt in 1939. Lenzen continued to direct excavations for the German Archaeological Institute after the war from 1953 to 1967. He was succeed by H. J. Schmidt until 1977, and R. M. Boehmer after 1980. The 39 campaigns of German excavations came to a halt in 1989 and in 2001, a team lls des by M. van Ess returned to Uruk to begin mapping the site using subsurface magnetometry.

The Eanna Precinct in the Late Uruk Period

The Late Uruk period (3600-3200 BC) saw an explosion of Mesopotamian cultural development. Construction activities expanded, writing developed, pottery technology advanced, and great works of monumental art were produced. At Uruk, levels VIII to IV correspond to the Late Uruk period, though the greatest achievements are apparent in levels V and IV. The most prominent area of Uruk during the Uruk period was the sacred Eanna ("House of Heaven") precinct dedicated to the goddess Inanna. Excavations there uncovered several monumental cult, administrative, and other public buildings, each rebuilt and reused over several occupation phases.

*Uruk V*

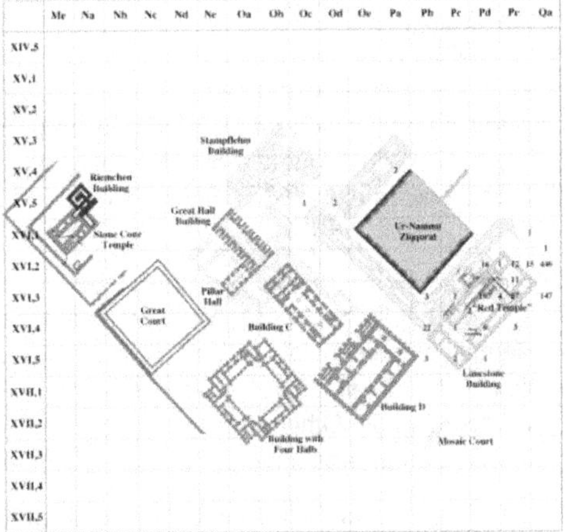


*Plan of the Eanna Precinct (from England, 1998)*

Uruk temples continued the architectural tradition of the preceding Ubaid period. Tripartite temple plans (i.e., a long central hall with rows of smaller rooms on either side) and niched and buttressed facades were characteristic of the earliest levels of the Uruk period. In Level V, the Limestone Temple, so called because the wall foundations (and possibly the entire building) were constructed of large slabs of limestone quarried from a site 80km from Uruk on the west side of the Euphrates, exhibited both of these classical Mesopotamian features.

Outside of the Eanna precinct, the earliest phases of the White Temple dedicated to the god Anu also probably date to the end of Level V. The niched and buttressed walls of the White Temple were covered with white gypsum plaster. The whole building was set upon a platform 13 meters high, a clear precursor to the ziggurat (a temple set on top of several stacked platforms) that would become so ubiquitous in later periods of Mesopotamian history.

*Uruk Ivb*

In this level, the sacred precinct was entered from the south through the Mosaic Court. This building and its columns were made of small mud bricks, which were then faced with a layer of mud plaster. Red, white, or black baked clay cones were then pushed into the mud plaster walls, creating colorful geometric patterns along the pillars and walls.

To the southwest of the Mosaic Court, the Square Building had a large square courtyard with a long rectangular hall on each side. Both the interior courtyard and exterior facade of the building had the niching characteristic of Uruk temples, but the plan of the building was unique, and its function is not certain.

Northwest of the Mosaic Court, several buildings with tripartite plans may have been temples. Three other buildings may have been the residences of the officials in charge of the temples in the Eanna precinct.

The Stone Cone Mosaic Temple was constructed to the west, apart from the complex of temples and ceremonial buildings attached to the Mosaic Court. A buttressed wall surrounded the tripartite temple building, and the temple itself was decorated with colored stone cones which formed geometric patterns on the walls in the same fashion as the Mosaic Court.

*Uruk Iva*

In level Iva, the new buildings were constructed over the level Ivb Eanna complex. The large Temple D (80x50 meters) stood on the filled-in courtyard of the building below it. Slightly smaller, Temple C lay to the northwest of Temple D, and exhibited a clear tripartite plan. Northwest of this building, the Pillared Hall was decorated with another stone cone mosaic. Just west of the Pillared Hall, the Great Court may have been a sunken area surrounded by benches.

Above the Stone Cone Mosaic Temple of Level Ivb, and odd building named theRiemchengebäude was constructed. It was given its name by the excavators because of the 'riemchen' bricks characteristic of Late Uruk architecture. These are small compact bricks with a square section. The building consisted of a long corridor surrounding a central chamber with a separate room to the southeast. The function of the building is unclear, but it may have been the site of a religious ritual.

The City Wall
In the Early Dynastic I period in the first half of the third millennium BC, the citizens of Uruk probably first contructed the 9km long mud brick wall that enclosed the city. Although it has not been thoroughly excavated, this early date for the construction of the wall is inferred based on evidence from a cylinder seal impression. Throughout the history of occupation of the city, the wall underwent many repairs, the last of which dates to the 18h century BC.

The Development of Writing in the Uruk Period
Among the other technological advances that the Uruk period witnessed was the advent of pictographic representations on clay tablets and the development in stages of written language. From the Eanna complex of Uruk itself, nearly 5000 tablets from this earliest phase of writing were excavated primarily from rubbish dumps. Other more complete tablets from the same period have been found at sites in both in the northern and southern extents of southern Mesopotamia (see also proto-cuneiform).

These archaic tablets were used to fill in pits left by the Ils des the Uruk IV buildings in order to build foundations for level III buildings. The tablets themselves, therefore, must date to a period prior to level III. The earliest phases of writing then dates to Uruk level IV, and more specifically, it probably dates to the latest subphase of that level, Iva. A second phase of writing is dated to Uruk level III, also called the

Jemdet Nasr period because a large number of texts from this date were found at the site of Jemdet Nasr, just south of modern day Baghdad.

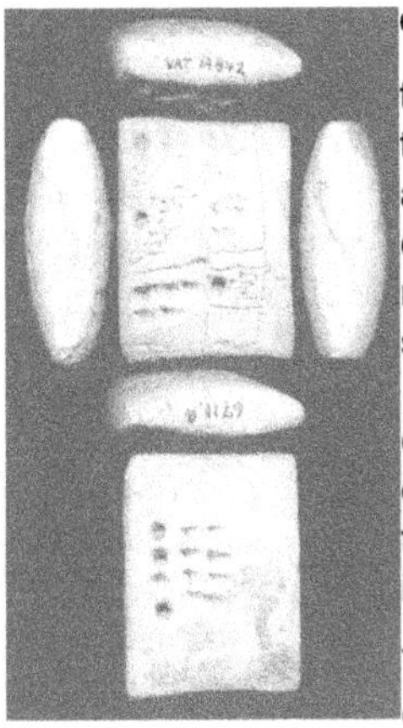

Although the first written tablets that appear in the Uruk IV period are quite underdeveloped in relation to the fully formed cuneiform systems of later periods, they did not appear spontaneously. Precursors to the Uruk tablets took the form of clay "tokens" sealed in "bullae" and clay tablets impressed with numerical notations. Tokens were simply lumps of clay fashioned into standardized shapes. Each shape represented a numerical unit (i.e., 1 or 10, etc.), and some may have represented a type of object (i.e., sheep or cloth). Often tokens were encased in bullae, hollow clay balls that were officially sealed by means of an incised cylinder seal which, when rolled over the surface of the bullae would leave a unique impression.

The second precursor to Uruk IV writing were simple clay tablets, sometimes with cylinder seal impressions, with rounded impressions representing numbers. These are very difficult to date and to interpret, as the shape of the impressions and the units of counting do not always correspond to what is know about counting systems in later periods.

In the Uruk IV phase, written documents come in three varieties:

Clay "tags" with incised drawings that probably corresponded to the person receiving or selling the item(s) to which the tag was attached.

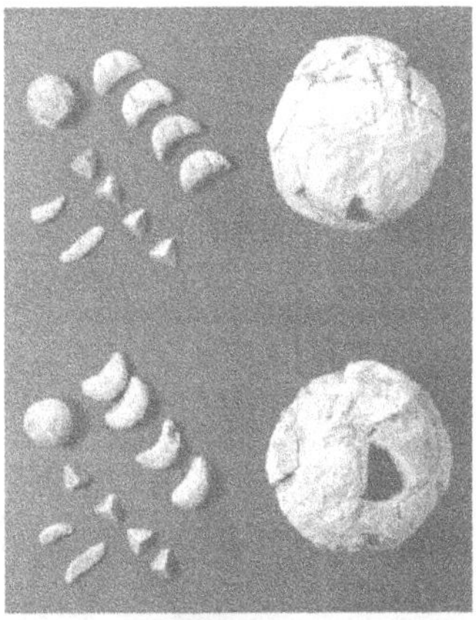

(2) Small tablets that combine impressed rounded numerical signs with incised pictographs representing objects or personal names.

(3) Larger tablets divided into sections, each containing impressions of numerical signs and incised pictographs representing objects or personal names. Sometimes, the numerical signs are added together and the total is incised on the back of the tablet.

In the Jemdet Nasr period, the majority of the texts fall into the third category, lists of numbers and associated commodities. A new category of texts also develops during the Jemdet Nasr period, though they may be a continuation of a type which has not been discovered in Uruk IV contexts. This lexical category continues into the following periods.

It is important to note that the purpose of all of these early forms of writing, including the Uruk IV and Jemdet Nasr period texts, along with their precursors, was to record economic transactions. Writing itself developed out of a need to remember exchanges of large numbers of goods among the inhabitants of those cities whose population had increased throughout the

Uruk period so that face-to-face contact was no longer the norm. It was a tool of economic administration, not a means to record literature, history, or sacred ideas.

It took several centuries for the written language to develop so that it could represent the complexities of grammar and syntax. The earliest signs used in the Uruk texts, which were either pictographic representations of objects, symbols representing deities, abstract images, or numerical signs, eventually developed into the more abstract cuneiform signs characterized by horizontal and vertical wedges. In the Uruk IV and Jemdet Nasr phases, signs represented concepts or nouns, and perhaps simple verbs, but there is no grammatical relationship between those ideas represented on the texts. Sometimes signs were combined to form ideas related to both signs (such as the sign for disbursement which combines the sign for head with the sign for ration), and other times signs were combined to form words that sounded like those signs. In this way, signs which originally had a pictographically assigned meaning became associated with abstract concepts that sounded similar. For example, the Sumerian word for “life” is pronounced “til,” and the word for “arrow” is pronounced “ti.” In writing, the same sign, TI, is used for both ideas presumably because it is easier to draw an arrow than it is to draw the more abstract notion of life.

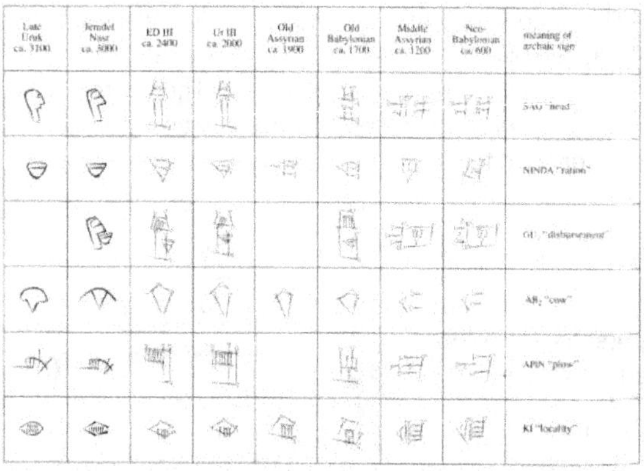
Late Uruk ca. 3100
Jemdet Nasr ca. 3000
ED III ca. 2400
Ur III ca. 2000
Old Assyrian ca. 1900
Old Babylonian ca. 1700
Middle Assyrian ca. 1200
Neo-Babylonian ca. 600
meaning of archaic sign
SAG "head"
NINDA "ration"
GU "disbursement"
AB₂ "cow"
APIN "plow"
KI "locality"

Later, the TI sign might be combined with other signs, whose sounds would act as the syllables that make up a longer word. Although it is generally agreed that the language represented on the archaic texts is Sumerian, it is only once the syllabic function of the signs was applied that language could truly be represented in a permanent medium.

The form of the signs also changed over time. Originally, pictographs were incised in clay using a sharp stylus. By the Jemdet Nasr phase, the sharp stylus was replaced by an angled stylus with a triangular tip. The result of pushing a stylus of this shape into wet clay is a wedge with a triangular shaped “head” and a long straight “tail.” The shape of these wedges provide the name we use for the writing system of Mesopotamia, “cuneiform,” Latin for wedge-shaped. As the use of the triangular stylus continued, the signs themselves became more and more abstracted into combinations of horizontal and vertical wedges that no longer bore much resemblance to their original forms. The range of sign forms used also decreased as the number of similar-looking signs reduced. <br>

The Spread of Uruk Culture
The name Uruk is also applied to the archaeological period corresponding to the fourth millennium BC (Uruk levels VIII-Iva). Not only did the written documents appear in this period, but the Uruk period also saw the rise of the first cities, monumental art and complex political structures. Prior to the Uruk period, maps of settlement in southern Mesopotamia show several sites of a small size, mostly under 10 hectares (0.1 km$^2$). These sites are evenly distributed over the landscape, and some may have been economic or religious centers. At the start of the Uruk period, the number and size of sites increased dramatically. Uruk itself swelled to 70 hectares (0.7 km$^2$). The reasons for such an extraordinary change are unclear. There may have been a sudden influx of

*Cylinder seal and impression showing ruler on a boat with icons symbolizing the goddess Inanna (ADFU 1, Plate 17).*

new population groups or favorable changes in climate, but the trend continued into the Late Uruk period. By the end of the Uruk period, the site of Uruk occupied about 100 hectares (1 $km^2$), and more than half of the settled area of southern Mesopotamia was located in its vicinity.

The rapid increase in the size of the settled area of Uruk meant that new developments in the social structure of society were inevitable. The archaic texts, cylinder seals and monumental art all provide information about these changes. In the cylinder seals and seal impressions on tablets of levels IV and III, a bearded figure wearing a netted skirt and hat appears in religious, agricultural, or military scenes. This figure is generally understood to represent the ruler of Uruk, whose role as priest, provider, and protector is emphasized. The same figure also appears on the Lion Hunt Stela, a basalt stone monument which shows him attacking lions with a spear and with a bow and arrow. On the Warka Vase, an alabaster vessel over a meter tall, he is depicted in relief presenting an offering to Inanna. Below him runs a row of naked servants or priests carry offerings, and below them is a row of domestic animals and a row of plants growing from a river. The remarkable vessel clearly shows the shared view of a social hierarchy, at the bottom of which were the plants an animals that sustained society, and at the top of which were the ruler and the god, who managed and distributed those staples. The Uruk period marks the first instance when these roles were expressed in figurative art, and this type of royal propaganda is a theme that continues in the millennia of Near Eastern history that follow.

The types of artifacts found in Uruk levels V-Iva have been found at sites from the same period throughout the entire Near East. The most easily recognizable identifier of this period is the lls de-rim bowl, a crude, handmade, mass-produced ceramic type with a distinctive rim. This type of pottery has been found in fourth millennium sites in southwest Iran, Syria, Turkey, and Egypt. Other aspects of Uruk culture, such as the tripartite temple plan and niched and buttressed facades of the Eanna precinct buildings are found in northern and southern Mesopotamian contexts. Cylinder seals of a type that was developed in Uruk also spread throughout the Near East. The convergence of these artifact classes at sites outside of Uruk has prompted theories of the expansion of Uruk political control over Mesopotamia by the establishment of merchant colonies north and east of Uruk itself. Now archaeologists recognize the unique cultural development of northern Mesopotamia that can be seen at sites alongside or in place of Uruk culture, which suggests that the methods by which Uruk influence expanded are much more complicated than originally thought. There is no doubt, however, that the Uruk period, which saw innovations including writing, the cylinder seal, the plow, and wheeled vehicles constituted a crucial phase in the history of the Near East.

References

*Ausgrabungen der Deutschen Forschungsgemeinschaft in Uruk-Warka*. Berlin: Mann. 17 volumes. 1946-2001

*Ausgrabungen in Uruk-Warka, Endberichte*. Mainz: Philipp von Zabern GmbH. 25 volumes. 1987-2003.

Boehmer, R. M. Uruk-Warka In *Oxford Encyclopedia of Archaeology in the Near East,* vol. 5, 294-298. New York: Oxford University, 1997.

Crawford, H. *Sumer and the Sumerians.* Cambridge: Cambridge, 1991.

Englund, R. K. Texts From the Late Uruk Period In *Mesopotamien 1: Späturuk-Zeit und Frühdynastische Zeit. OBO* 160, 15-233. Freiburg and Göttingen: Universitätsverlag and Vandenhoeck & Ruprecht, 1998.

Nissen, H., P. Damerow, and R. K. Englund. *Archaic Bookkeeping: Writing and Techniques of Economic Administration in the Ancient Near East.* P. Larsen, trans. Chicago: University of Chicago, 1993

Postgate, J. N. *Early Mesopotamia: Society and Economy at the Dawn of History.* London: Routledge, 1992.

Roaf, M. *The Cultural Atlas of Mesopotamia and the Ancient Near East.* Oxford and New York: Facts on File, 1990.[unquote]

c. 3500 BCE, a parallel accounting system and hieroglyphic writing system was developing in Meluhha (Indus valley civilization). There re indications that Meluhha was a contact area with Uruk (Warka).

FIGURE 3.4 COMPARISON OF SIGN FREQUENCIES FROM THREE ANCIENT SCRIPTS (DEMEROW 1989, AND DAHL 2005).

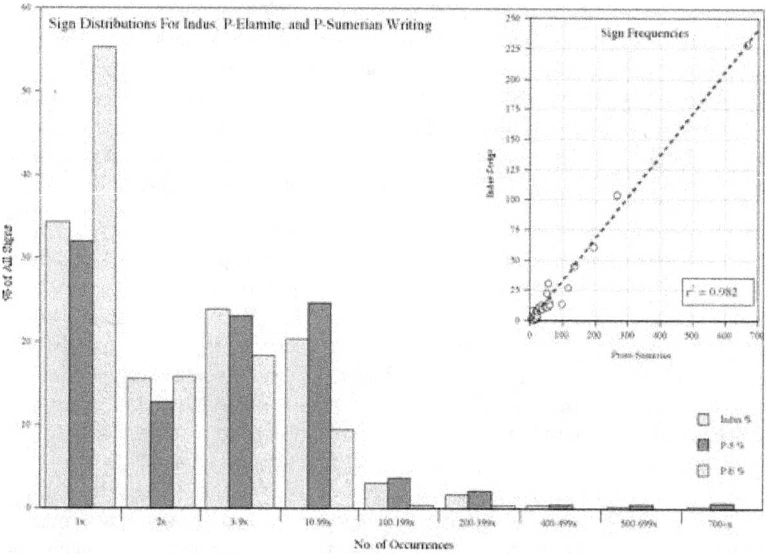


This graph provides a comparison of sign frequencies from Indus, Proto-Elamite and Proto-Sumerian writing.

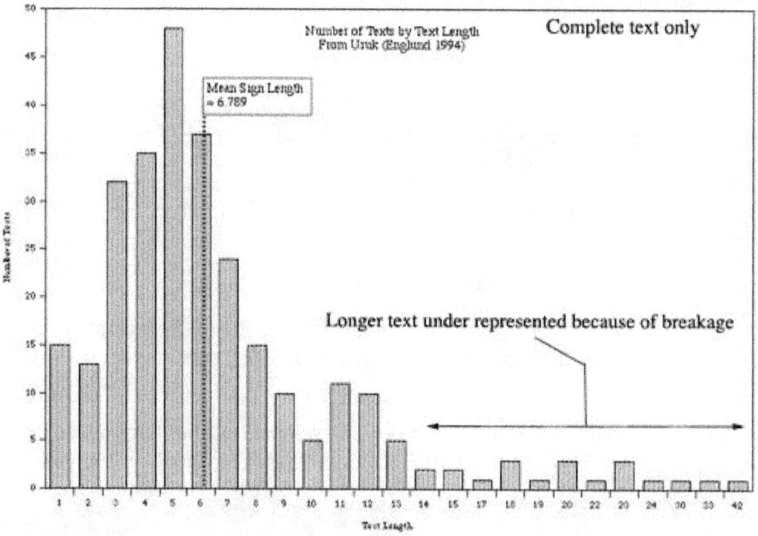

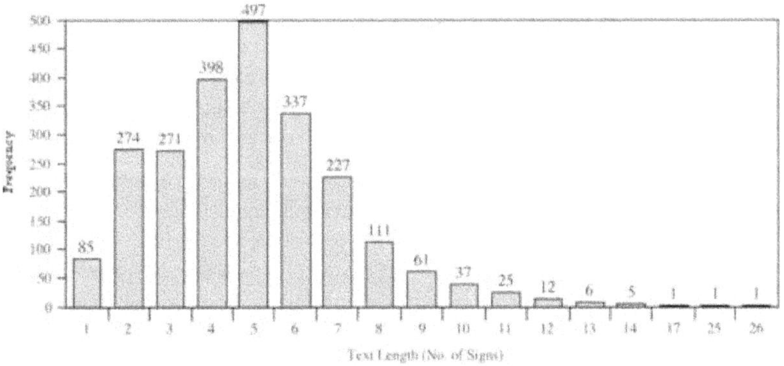


These graphs prepared by Bryan Wells show that mean text length of Proto-Elamite (Uruk) script was 7 signs , compared with Indus script's 5 signs.

Peter Damerow discusses "The Origins of Writing as a Problem of Historical Epistemology," in *Cuneiform Digital Library Journal* (*CDLJ*) 2006: 1.

It is likely that hieroglyphic writing systems of Proto-Elamite, Proto-Sumerian and Indus writing systems evolved independently to code the unique characteristics of languages represented dealing in lists and category descriptions related to property, inventory, economic administration or corporate (guild) management and not necessarily sentences and narrative texts of cultural traditions. In one case, token impressions on bullae may have been replaced by inscribed glyphs (as proto-writing) and in another, categorization might have been achieved by using duplicate tablets (as evidenced by the HARP findings of multiples of inscribed tablets) to compile important information needed for bills of lading (achieved by using seal impressions).

This work on *Indian hieroglyphs* seeks to demonstrate that pictographic representation and writing evolved together to represent semantics of language, to meet the trade/economic imperative of administering the guild transactions of the bronze age in the cultural context of Indian linguistic area. The most significant finding of this work is that almost all glyphs (both pictorial motifs/field symbols and text sign glyphs) of Indus script are readable rebus – and hence, meanings documented precisely — in Mleccha/Meluhha language of Indian linguistic area.

A revolutionary change had occurred in the patterns of social organization with the arrival of the bronze age. Apart from products made of stone, terracotta, wood, bone, ivory and *turbinella pyrum*, new materials (mineral resources, sand and stone ores) were located, mined, obtained and new processes such as smelting and forging were invented to work – in guild corporate forms — on metals, ingots, alloys, forging, turning, smithy, use of anvils and various types of furnaces.

Archaic accounting of tokens and bullae (together with tablets creating seal impressions) would have required an enormous expansion adding to the list of goods and types of transactions necessitated by the bronze age production and trade activities. Accounting for these varieties of transactions would have necessitated either the invention of writing like the syllabic cuneiform or the Indus script using hieroglyphs. A store-keeping record by categories, a bill of lading was also required when trade goods were stored in warehouses and couriered (by trade caravans) across long distances. The invention of Indian hieroglyphs served these requirements necessitated by the arrival of the bronze age. Writing was necessary not only to write names (as shown in cuneiform texts), but also to describe traded commodities such as industrial products -- grinding stones, minerals, metal alloys, metal ingots, tools/weapons, and jewellery of *turbinella pyrum*, gold or silver or semi-precious stones brought out of the lapidaries' or smiths' or miners' work-sites, workshops or warehouses.

Use of hieroglyphs for tablets was a revolution in the mode of thought of early inventors of the bronze age. Using the rebus method of the type used on Narmer palette, use of hieroglyphs together with their rebus rendering provided the facility for accounting for a large number of types of transactions (mining, smelting, ingot-making, forging, turning) and conveying the trade loads to trade agents across

a vast area extending from Rakhigarhi in the east to Altyn-tepe in the northwest, using caravans and from Daimabad in the southwest to Susa in the northwest, navigating the Persian Gulf using the famed Meluhhan boats.

The hieroglyphs also required improvisation. A series of hieroglyphic ligatures were created to communicate messages involving multiple transaction types. For example, when a bronze-age smith's role had to be described, three hieroglyphs were ligatured to communicate that the smith was also a merchant and a turner (with a forge/workshop). Bet Dwaraka 1 śankha (*turbinella pyrum*) seal. One-horned bull, short-horned bull looking down and an antelope looking backward. The message is complete. It is a calling card of a merchant-blacksmith-turner workshop. A professional has arrived on the civilizational arena.

Kalibangan 043 Seal. Body of ox shown with three heads: of a one-horned heifer (looking forward), of antelope (looking backward), and a short-horned bison (looking downward).

Bison*: ḍangrar* 'bull'; rebus: *ḍāṅgar* 'blacksmith' (H.)

One-horned heifer: *koḍiyum* 'heifer *kundār* turner (A.); *khōṇḍā, khōṇḍī , kothḷɔ*

Glyph: खोंड [khōṇḍa] *m* A young bull, a bullcalf (Marathi). Rebus: खोट [ khōṭa ] *f* A mass of metal (unwrought or of old metal melted down); an ingot or wedge.

खोंडा [khōṇḍā] m A कांबळा of which one end is formed into a cowl or hood. खोंडी [khōṇḍī] f An outspread shovelform sack (as formed temporarily out of a कांबळा, to hold or fend off grain, chaff &c. (Marathi) khŏdrang, khudrang ख्वद्‌रंग adj. c.g. self-coloured; as subst. m. N. of a kind of blanket having the natural colour of the wool (L. 37). khudürü और्णशाटकविशेषः f. a kind of coarse woollen blanket. (Kashmiri) Pa. kotthalī -- f. ' sack (?) '; Pk. kotthala -- m. ' bag, grainstore ' (kōha -- m. ' bag ' < *kōtha?); K. kŏthul, lu m. ' large bag or parcel ', kothüjü f. ' small do. '; S. kothirī f. ' bag '; Ku. kuthlo ' large bag, sack '; B. kūthlī ' satchel, wallet '; Or. kuthaḷi, thuḷi, kothaḷi, thiḷi ' wallet, pouch '; H. kothlā m. ' bag, sack, stomach (see *kōttha -- ) ', lī f. ' purse '; G.kothḷɔ m. ' large bag ', ḷī f. ' purse, scrotum '; M. kothḷā m. ' large sack, chamber of stomach (= peṭā ċā k) ', ḷẽ n. ' sack ', ḷī f. ' small sack '; -- X gōṇī´ -- : S. g̠othirī f. ' bag ', L. gutthlā m.(CDIAL 3511) Ta. kaṇṭāḷam travelling sack placed on a bullock, pack-saddle. Ka. kanṭale, kaṇṭāḷa, kaṇṭāḷe, kaṇṭle double bag carried across a beast. Te. kaṇṭalamu, kaṇṭlamubullock-load consisting of two bags filled with goods. / Cf. Mar. kaṇṭhāḷī a bag having opening in the middle (DEDR 1174) gōṇī´ f. ' sack ' Pāṇ., gōṇikā -- f. ' blanket ' BHS ii 215. [← Drav. EWA i 345 with lit.]Pa. gōṇa -- saṁthata -- ' covered with a woollen rug ', gōṇaka -- m. ' woollen rug with a long fleece '; NiDoc. goni ' sack '; Gy. pal. gŏni ' bag, purse ', eur. gono m. ' sack '; Ash.gō˜ ' carpet ', Wg. gřóī, gřẽ, Dm. gūni; Paš. gōnī ' saddlebag '; K.ʿguna f. ' pair of large saddlebags usu. of goat's hair for carrying grain '; S. g̠uṇī f. ' coarse sackcloth '; L. g̠ūṇī˜f. ' sack '; P. gūṇ f. ' hair cloth, hempen sacking ', gūṇī f. ' sack '; B. gun ' sacking '; Or. goṇī ' sackcloth, sack, corn measure, ragged garment '; Bi. gon ' grain sack '; H. gon f. ' sack '; G. gū˘ṇi f. ' sacking, sack '; M. goṇ f. ' sack ', ṇī f. ' sackcloth ', ṇā m. ' large grain sack '.Addenda: gōṇī´ -- : WPah.kṭg. gv̄ṇ f. (obl. -- i) ' sack for corn '; <-> Md. (RTMV1) gōni ' sack ' ← Ind. (CDIAL 4275) gōṇamu. [Tel. of Tam. కోమణము.] n. A waist cloth or modesty piece. [ gōṇi ] gōṇi. [Skt.] n. A sack, sackcloth. a sackful. [Tel.] gōtamu. [Tel.] n. A sack, a bag. (Telugu)

Rebus 1: kōṭṭapāla m. ' commander of a fort ' Pañcat. [kōṭṭa -- 1, pāla -- ] Pk. *koṭṭavāla* -- , *kuṭ*° m. ' police officer '; K. *kuṭawāl* m. ' captain of a fort, chief of police, city magistrate '; S. *koṭāru* m. ' district officer who watches crops, police officer '; L. *kuṭvāl* m. ' a kind of village constable '; WPah. bhal. *kuṭwāl* m. ' hon. title of a Ṭhakkur '; B. *koṭāl* ' watchman, constable ' (ODBL 329 < **kōṣṭhapāla* -- ); Or. *kaṭuāḷa* ' town policeman '; H. *koṭwār*, °*wāl* m. ' police officer ' (→ L. *koṭvāl* m., S. *koṭvālu*m.), G. *koṭvāḷ* m. (CDIAL 3501).

Rebus 2: B. kõdā 'to turn in a lathe'; Or. kŭnda 'lathe', kūdibā, kūd 'to turn' (→ Drav. Kur. kūd 'lathe') (CDIAL 3295) Rebus 2: koḍ 'artisan's workshop' (Kuwi)

Antelope: *meḷh* 'goat' (Br.) Rebus: *meṛha, meḍhi* 'merchant's clerk; (G.)

To indicate a particular type of bronze-age product, the shape of the product itself had to be used on inscriptions. For example, on a Chanhu-daro seal, a double-axe is shown as a pictograph.

Chanhu-daro 023 Seal.

Sometimes, the hieroglyph had to be painted on the container which was used to transport the goods as in the case of Susa pot with metal artifacts which was painted with 'fish' hieroglyph.

Susa pot, from Meluhha, with metal artifacts.

Some ligatures were orthographic abstractions. One example is shown on Sign glyphs : That

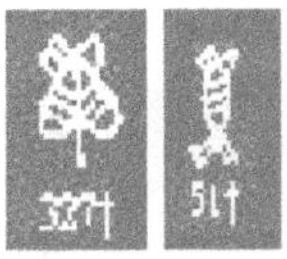

the ligature is unique is clear from the fact tht it occurs only on two glyphs [Signs 52 and 327 of inscription texts: One is a *loha-kāra* (metalsmith). The other is a *cunda-kāra* (ivory turner)].

Glyph: *loa* = a species of fig tree, ficus glomerata, the fruit of ficus glomerata (Santali) Rebus: *lo* 'iron' (Assamese, Bengali); *loa* 'iron' (Gypsy) *lauha* = made of copper or iron (Gr.S'r.); metal, iron (Skt.) *loha-kāra* a metal worker, coppersmith, blacksmith Miln 331 (Pali)

Glyph of musk-rat: *Ta. cuṇṭaṉ* grey musk shrew; cuṇṭ-eli, (Koll.) *cuṇṭān* mouse, *Mus urbanus*; cūṟaṉ grey musk shrew; mūñ-cūṟu musk-rat,*Sorex indicus. Ma.* cuṇṭ-eli mouse, musk-rat. *Ka.* suṇḍa, suṇḍ-ili, suṇḍil-ili, soṇḍ-ili, soṇḍil-ili, cuñc-ili musk-rat. *Koḍ.* Ciṇḍ-elihouse-mouse, field-mouse. *Tu.* Suṇḍ-eli musk-rat. *Te.* cuncu mouse, musk-rat; cunc-eluka, cuṇḍ-eluka mouse; cūr-eluka species of mouse *Kol* (Kin.) cinḍrag musk-rat. *Go.* (Mu. Ma.) cūci musk-rat (*Voc.* 1353); (Ma.) cuṭṭi-eli, (Mu.) cuṭi, cuṭiyal small rat (*Voc.*1344); (Ph.) coṭe mouse (*Voc* 1368). *Konḍa* (BB) susuki musk-rat. *Kur.* coṭṭō mouse. For eli, etc., see 833 Ta. Eli. Cf. 2664 Ta. cuṇṭu; the shrews seem to be differentiated from rats and mice by the length of the snout. / Cf. Skt. *śuṇḍi-mūṣikā-*, gandha-śuṇḍinī-(Burrow, *Kratylos* 15.56), cuñcu-mūṣikā-, chucchūndura-, cucundarī-; Turner, *CDIAL*, no. 5053. Cf. also Skt. Tuṭuma- mouse, rat. For similar words in Munda languages, see Pinnow, p. 95 (Santali cũnd musk-rat, etc.), and Emeneau, *JAOS* 82.109.(DEDR 2661) cunda an artist who works in ivory J vi.261 (Com: dantakāra); Miln 331. *cundakāra* a turner J vi.339 (Pali)

The superscript ligatures can also be read as suffixes: - *kāra* 'artisan'. *kāruvu* = mechanic, artisan, Viśvakarma, the celestial artisan (Te.); kāruvu [Skt.] n. An artist, artificer. An agent . One is a *loha-kāra* (metalsmith). The other is a *cunda-kāra* (ivory turner).

## 5 SMITHY AS A TEMPLE, SMITHY OF NATIONS

*"Man's development and the growth of civilizations have depended, in the main, on progress in a few activities – the discovery of fire, domestication of animals, the division of labor; but, above all, in the evolution of means to receive, to communicate, and to record his knowledge, and especially in the development of phonetic writing."* (Colin Cherry, 1957, *On human communication*, New York, John Wiley and Sons, p.31).

In historical periods, together with the use of syllabic scripts, the Indian hieroglyphs provided the identification devices on punch-marked coins.

Harosheth Hagoyim (Hebrew: חרושת הגויים, lit. Smithy of the Nations). It is lso spelled: Harosheth ha Gojim. The phrase in the Bible is Harosheth (pronounced khar-o-sheth) of the gentiles, of the nations. One can only offer conjectures on what is meant by the phrase, 'of the nations'. Maybe, it connotes the widespread presence of smithy in almost every ancient village settlement during the bronze- and iron-ages and in some settlements, producing metallic war-chariots. Judges 4:16 reads: *"Now Barak chased the chariots and the army all the way to Harosheth Hagoyim. Sisera's whole army died by the edge of the sword; not even one survived!"*

Cognate *kharoṣṭī* used in early Gandhara manuscripts and on early punch-marked coins together with Indian hieroglyphs should also, semantically, be lit. smithy of nations, following the tradition of Indian hieroglyphs in Indian linguistic area (*sprachbund*). This *sprachbund* could be as close as one can get to the ancient smithy of nations.

I suggest that just as Indian hieroglyphs as invention of writing were deployed by smith guilds, and used in trade transactions, starting from c. 3500 BCE, *kharoṣṭī* as an advancement in writing systems using syllabic characters should also have been developed by the followers and legatees of the smith guild traditions, in Indian linguistic area, ca. 6th century BCE. *kharoṣṭī* writing system was patterned after Aramaic which also was perhaps influenced by Harosheth Hagoyim. This is an area for further researches in evolution of writing systems across an extensive interaction area involving long distance trade contacts and even settlements of Meluhhans in Mesopotamia and other regions (such as Anatolia, Bactria, Elam, Persian Gulf – Dilmun, Magan), in what is now termed the Ancient Near East.

An Indus Seal from the excavation of the Salut Early Bronze Age tower

The remarkable findings reported on December 22, 2011, from Salut, Oman are consistent with the central thesis of *Indus Script Cipher*. The writing in Indus Script is of artisan ancestors of Harosheth, (cognate *kharoṣṭī*) tradition. It was harosheth hagoyim, a smithy of nations, indeed.

Location of Wādī Salūt, Oman (in relation to Indian civilization area).Latitude. 23.0444444°, Longitude. 57.6472222°

An Indus Seal from the excavation of the Salut Early Bronze Age tower

A stone seal, to be considered an import from Indus Valley, has been found during the last archaeological campaign in Salut.

Reading of the inscription of text:

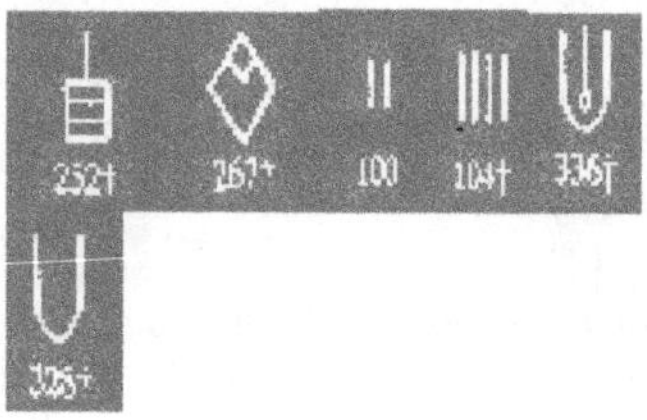


Field symbol: Ox with a trough (?) in front. This was a stone seal with a perforated boss and was perhaps tied to a trade load from Meluhha.

Glyphic elements read rebus: Blacksmith guild; Native metal + tin + turned metalwork from furnace.

ran:ku = liquid measure (Santali) Rebus: ran:ku = tin (Santali)

kōnṭa corner (Nk.); Tu. kōṇṭu angle, corner (Tu.); Rebus: kõdā 'to turn in a lathe' (B.)

Glyph: dāmṛa, damrā ' young bull (A.)(CDIAL 6184). Glyph: *ḍaṅgara1 ' cattle '. 2. *daṅgara -- . [Same as ḍaṅ- gara -- 2 s.v. *ḍagga -- 2 as a pejorative term for cattle] 1. K. ḍangur m. ' bullock ', L. ḍaṅgur, (Ju.) ḏãgar m. ' horned cattle '; P. ḍaṅgar m. ' cattle ', Or. ḍaṅgara; Bi. ḍā̃gar ' old worn -- out beast, dead cattle ', dhūr ḍā̃gar ' cattle in general '; Bhoj. ḍā̃ṅgar ' cattle '; H. ḍā̃gar, ḍā̃grā m. ' horned cattle '.2. H. dā̃gar m. = prec. (CDIAL 5526) Rebus: ḍhangar 'blacksmith' (H.)

Glyph: sal stake, spike, splinter, thorn, difficulty (H.); sal 'workshop' (Santali) Vikalpa: aṭar 'a splinter' (Ma.) aṭaruka 'to burst, crack, sli off,fly open; aṭarcca ' splitting, a crack'; aṭarttuka 'to split, tear off, open (an oyster) (Ma.); aḍaruni 'to crack' (Tu.) (DEDR 66) Rebus: aduru 'native, unsmelted metal' (Kannada)

gaṇḍa 'four' (Santali); rebus: kaṇḍ fire-altar, furnace' (Santali) Vikalpa: ponea 'four' (Santali); rebus: pon 'gold' (Ta.)

ḍabu 'an iron spoon' (Santali) Vikalpa: Kol. (SR.) gāṭe spoon (DEDR 1267). Rebus: Ta. kaṭai (-v-, -nt-) to churn, turn in lathe, mash to pulp (as vegetables with the bowl of a ladle); kaṭaical polishing, enamelling, turned work in wood; kaṭaiccal turning on a lathe, that which is turned on a lathe. கடைசற்பட்டரை kaṭaicaṟ-paṭṭarai , n. < id. +. Turner's shop; கடைசல்வேலைசெய்யுஞ் சாலை. Loc. Glyph: S. baṭhu m. 'large pot in which grain is parched, Rebus; bhaṭṭhā m. 'kiln' (P.) baṭa = a kind of iron (G.) Vikalpa: meṛgo = rimless vessels (Santali) bhaṭa 'furnace' (G.) baṭa = kiln (Santali); baṭa = a kind of iron (G.) bhaṭṭha -- m.n. ' gridiron (Pkt.) baṭhu large cooking fire' baṭhī f. 'distilling furnace'; L. bhaṭṭh m. 'grain—parcher's oven', bhaṭṭhī f. 'kiln, distillery', awāṇ. bhaṭh; P. bhaṭṭh m., ṭhī f. 'furnace', bhaṭṭhā m. 'kiln'; S. bhaṭṭhī keṇī 'distil (spirits)'. (CDIAL 9656) Rebus: ḍab, ḍhimba, ḍhompo 'lump (ingot?)' (Mu.) Rebus: baṭa = a kind of iron (G.) bhaṭa 'furnace' (G.) pattar 'trough' (Ta.) पात्र pātra,

(I.) s. Vessel, cup, plate; receptacle. [lw. Sk. Id.] (Nepali) pātramu A utensil, ఉపకరణము. Hardware. Metal vessels. (Telugu) Rebus paṭṭar-ai community; guild as of workmen (Ta.); pātharī 'precious stone' (OMarw.) (CDIAL 8857) Patthara [cp. late Sk. prastara. The ord. meaning of Sk. pr. is "stramentum"] 1. stone, rock S i.32. -- 2. stoneware Miln 2. (Pali) Pa. Pk. patthara -- m. ' stone ', S. patharu m., L. (Ju.) pathar m., khet. patthar, P. patthar m. (→ forms of Bi. Mth. Bhoj. H. G. below with atth or ath), WPah.jaun. pātthar; Ku. pāthar m. ' slates, stones ', gng. pāth*Ir ' flat stone '; A. B. pāthar ' stone ', Or. pathara; Bi. pāthar, patthar, patthal ' hailstone '; Mth. pāthar, pathal ' stone ', Bhoj. pathal, Aw.lakh. pāthar, H. pāthar, patthar, pathar, patthal m., G. patthar, pathrɔ m.; M. pāthar f. ' flat stone '; Ko. phāttaru ' stone '; Si. patura ' chip, fragment '; -- S. pathirī f. ' stone in the bladder '; P. pathrī f. ' small stone '; Ku. patharī ' stone cup '; B. pāthri ' stone in the bladder, tartar on teeth '; Or. pathurī ' stoneware '; H. patthrī f. ' grit ', G. pathrī f. *prastarapaṭṭa -- , *prastaramr̥ttikā -- , *prastarāsa -- .Addenda: prastará -- : WPah.kṭg. pátthər m. ' stone, rock '; pəthreuṇõ ' to stone '; J. pāthar m. ' stone '; OMarw. pātharī ' precious stone '. (CDIAL 8857) From one of the higher hills of the large ditch encircling the EBA tower currently excavated by IMTO some 300 m to the north-west of salut, came one stone stamp seal which, by virtue of its iconography, shape and incised inscription, can be considered a genuine (Greater) Indus Valley import. The seal shows a bull, facing right and standing in front of a rectangular feature, possibly an altar or maybe just a manger. Above this scene, stands a line of Indus alphabetical signs. The quality of the glyptic and the close resemblance with specimen coming from Indus Valley sites, seem to indicate that the seal is an original Indus import, rather than an imitation. Such characteristic square stamp seals marked the transition from Early Harappan to Mature Harappan, together with the appearance of the Indus script. This transition is dated around 2500 BC, a date after which various artefacts related to the Indus civilization started to be found in the Near East, from Mesopotamia to Iran, to Failaka and Bahrein. Among the few Bronze Age seals discovered so far in Oman, only two could be compared to the one from Salut EBA tower. One is a stamp seal found in Ras al-Jinz, also bearing Indus signs but made of a copper/bronze, and the other is a stone stamp seal from a tomb in Bisyah, with no inscription. Their overall shape and motifs induce to regard them as well as genuine imports, though in the case of metal seals, only very few examples are known from the Greater Indus Valley, thus leaving some doubts about a possible local production.http://arabiantica.humnet.unipi.it/index.php?id=715&tx_ttnews%5Btt_news%5D=68&tx_ttnews%5BbackPid%5D=711&cHash=2fe7666e8c

The 2005 campaign at Salut, Oman - Università degli Studi di Pisa

Redazione Archaeogate, 01-06-2005

Two areas were chosen for excavation on February/March 2005: trench 1, in the north-west corner of the upper part of the hill, and trench 2, across the 'lower structure' located at the eastern foothill of the mound. In addition, we made a survey along the ancient falaj system.

Trench 1
The excavation confirms the determinate constructional phases of 2004B sounding.

-1st construction phase. The corridor-like (room 1a), along the fortress defence wall, presents three small compartments with wide openings constructed in its western part, and on the opposite side it ends with a mud-bricks staircase, showing the presence of two-storage structures at this phase.

-2nd construction phase. Significant renovations of the lay-out and general organization of the site were undertaken: the outer defence wall was significantly enlarged, and a monumental mud-brick platform, delimited from the east by a well done stone wall, was constructed. The platform was used as foundation for a mud-brick building (Building1) which was mainly composed of a sub-rectangular room (7.2X9.3 m) supported once by six pillars; it presents a stone pavement of four low steps on the south corner, and two premises (room 2 and room 3) adjoining to its south-eastern corner.

-3rd construction phase. The top layer revealed horizontal surfaces, floors, pits (postholes) and remains of stone foundations of circular structures (2.5-3.0 m in diameter), a sort of dwelling, belonging to the mediaeval re-occupation of the site.

The foundation of Salut goes back to the Early Iron Age period (late 2nd millennia) and the site was occupied till at least the 9th- early 8th centuries BC, as it shown by the preliminary analyses of the materials and by the radiocarbon dates from different strata. The Building 1 recalls the monumental architecture of the 'pillared-halls' of some Iron Age sites in the U.A.E (Rumeilah, Qarn Bint Saud, Bithna, Muweilah); the set of finds represents votive objects (bronze snakes, miniature axe, bronze vessel), personal ornaments (rings, beads, pendant. pin) and tools (razors, hoe, awls, needles). Particularly interesting are several pottery sherds with applied decoration of snakes, whereas fragments of soft-stone vessels and several leaf-shaped, triangular and lanceolate arrowheads are characteristic materials of Iron Age assemblage.

Trench 2

The preserved height of the outer wall, which is round curved, is about 2.5 m. The construction technique, identical to that of the northern defence wall of the fortress, proves the contemporaneity of both walls.

The falaj

The falaj is an irrigation system through which underground water is directed by means canals to fields. The falaj of Salut (north-west and north of the fortress) belongs to 'shallow falaj' type, which tapped water from shallow water table as alluvional fans or wadi's bed; it was typical of Iron Age II (1100/1000-600 BC).

http://www.archaeogate.org/vicino_oriente/article/453/1/the-2005-campaign-at-salut-oman-universita-degli-studi.html

The room 1a

The pillared room, Building 1

A niche in the wall M26

The falaj: open channel

The 2004 campaign at Salut, Oman - Università degli Studi di Pisa
Redazione Archaeogate, 13-01-2005
The Survey
On March/April 2004 thirteen topographical Units (UT) have been determinated, on the base of the structures evidence and on the large amount of pottery scattered around. The surveyed area, which includes the hill of Salut and the closely surrounding plain, was 15000 square metres.

The most part of structures was located on the top of the hill, where the existence of a defence wall was indicated on the surface by rows of medium size squared sandstone slabs. A lower semicircular structure, made by the same building technique, adjoins the eastern slope of the hill. Isolated circular structures, made from roughly stones and stone slabs, lay on the west side of the top. Probably collapsed houses, large circular structures made of squared sandstone blocks (most probably pertinent to a third millennium context), an Islamic cemetery, the presence of irrigation system (falaj) and remains of a building (according to local reports are the ruin of an ancient mosque), testifying an intense peopling during different times.
The preliminary analyses of the collected surface materials, mainly pottery, confirmed the existence of medieval occupations divided into: Early Islamic (VIII-X centuries), Middle Islamic (XI-XIV centuries) and Late Islamic (XVI century to modern times); on the other hand, the presence of surface materials as bronze arrowheads and distinct types of pottery vessels, indicate an earlier occupation, dated to the late 2nd millennium BC.

The sounding

The excavation of October 2004 allowed us to determinate four constructional phases.
The first results of radiocarbon dating show that the foundation of the site must be dated close the late 2nd – first half of the 1st millennia BC (Early Iron Age period on Omani Peninsula). The large amount of pottery materials comes from layers of second and third construction phase, comprising diagnostic sherds as spouted-jars and carinate bowls, but also soft-stone decorated vessels, terracotta animal figurines and one triangular-shaped arrowhead.

http://www.archaeogate.org/vicino_oriente/article/451/1/the-2004-campaign-at-salut-oman-universita-degli-studi.html

The fortification wall

The main test-sounding

Terracotta camel figurine

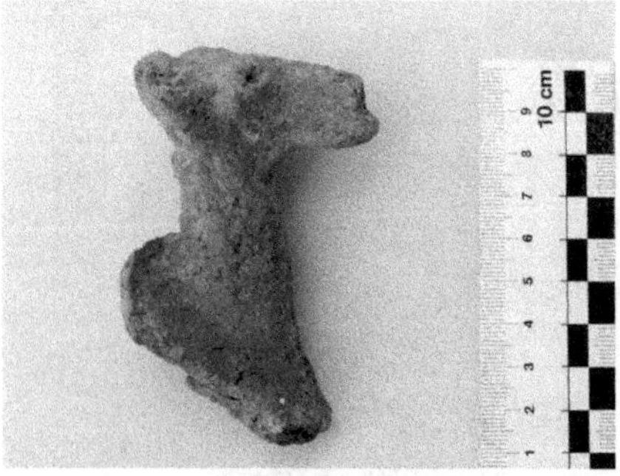

Fragment of soft-stone vessel

Saudi. The archaeological mission to Salut (Oman)

Floor tiles depicting a serpent (Salut) Salut is a fortified settlement dating to the Iron Age (1300-800 BC), located at the western foot of the Hajar mountain range, Bissiyah region, northern Oman.

Since 2004, imtoo (Italian Mission to Oman), under the guidance of prof. Avanzini, operates the site and its surroundings. The ruins of the fort are located on a rocky outcrop about 20 meters high, the center of an ancient oasis, where a mighty walls built of large stone blocks irregularly circular draws a profile.

This is a settlement in monumental character, perhaps the destination of the Templars, as confirmed by the objects that are not found in everyday use. Many depictions of snakes, both in bronze clay, seem, in fact attributable to a kind of worship and respect are materials from sites located in the UAE. The results of the excavations and general news on the site, on land and on research activities carried

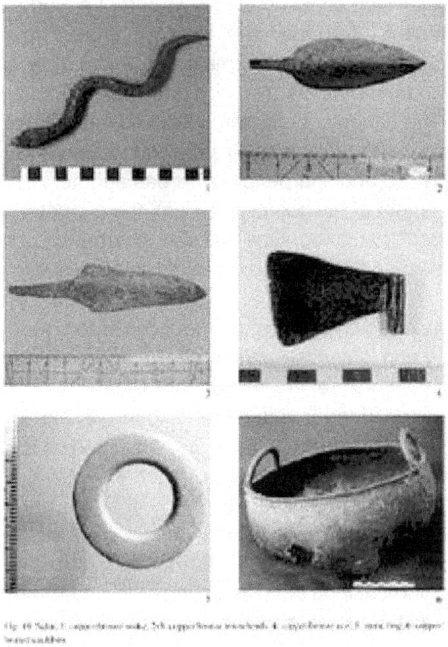

out by imtoo and its partners are available on the portal Saudi Ancient, from which you can download the pdf documents with the results of individual campaigns. Through an on-line, searchable by assigning a password You can also access to all information relating to the excavation.
http://sta.humnet.unipi.it/index.php?id=126
Archaeology report on Salut_ Oman _2004-5_

Fig. 19. Salut 1: copper/bronze snake; 2-3: copper/bronze arrowheads; 4: copper/bronze axe; 5: stone ring; 6: copper/bronze cauldron

Metal objects

The metal assemblage is represented by different kinds of tools and weapons, vessels, personal ornaments and decorations, and objects having a possible votive function. The majority of pieces were made from copper or bronze (analyses of the alloy have not yet been carried out which is why we denote pieces as copper/bronze), but the presence of fragments of several iron objects should be specially mentioned. It is well known that "until the middle of the 1st millennium B.C., the metal mostly used in the so-called "Iron Age" Omani cultures was bronze"[22] , and the finds of objects made from iron are extremely rare [23] . It seems that here, too, Salut is an exceptional site among the contemporary monuments of the Omani Peninsula.

Weapons and tools. Altogether twenty one complete (18 pieces) and fragmented copper/bronze arrowheads were found in different strata of the top periods of occupation of the site and/or on its surface. All belong to the category of the tanged arrowheads or arrowheads with the stem. Following the general typology proposed by P. Lombard [24] , they were divided into three types: leaf-shaped, triangular, and lanceolate arrowheads...

Two complete copper/bronze razors with straight backs and slightly rounded sharpened edges, probably used to scrape leather, were found in the top layers of the site. One of the pieces could be classified as a razor with tang handle, and the other as the razor with flat handle which is the continuation of the blade. The length of these razors is 3.3 and 4.3 cm. Quite a number of fragments of copper/bronze tools in the shape of pointed rods, rounded or quadrangular in section, were found in different layers of the top period of the site. Unfortunately, in the majority of cases it is not possible to specify precisely what all the pieces are. Probably, some of them might belong to needles, while others to pins, awls or other kind of similar tools and/or personal ornaments (see also below). Two almost complete needles (Pl. 11: 5) according to their sizes, were most probably used for sewing leather. The

length of complete needles is 7.0 and 27.0 cm. and the diameter of section is 0.4 and 0.5 cm...
A few fragments of knives were found in the top layers of the site and there are two almost complete pieces. One is a blade of a knife made from iron. It has a straight back, a pointed tip (the other end is broken) and one sharpened edge; the section is triangular. The length of the piece is 6.6 cm; its maximum thickness 0.7 cm. Another piece is made from copper or bronze, and has a rather thin double-sided blade, a rhomboidal section, and a pointed tip (the other end is broken). The object was folded. The proposed length of the object is 7.5 cm and its thickness 0.3 cm.
An object, which could be the lower part of a blade with broken tip of an iron double-sided dagger, was found in the US1 on the top of the monumental mud-brick platform. The blade is rhomboidal in section, and has pointed midrib. The maximum width of blade is 5.6 cm; its maximum thickness 2.4 cm. One more fragment of blade also of a double-sided iron dagger, together with fragments of iron tanged handle and a piece of rod, was found on the US3floor in the 'pillared hall'.
A complete copper/bronze chisel was made from a rounded rod. One end of the tool, slightly banded, was flattened and sharpened, whereas another end bore traces of hammering on its top surface (Pl.11: 6). The length of the object is 3.4 cm, the diameter of the rod 0.5 cm. Another chisel was made from a flat copper/bronze rod. One end was sharpened, and another one broken. The length of object is 3.2 cm and its section 0.3x0.6 cm. A similar object, but slightly bigger in size, is known from Rumeilah [28]
.

A complete tool made from copper/bronze rod quadrangular in section was found in the top strata of the site. One end is pointed and another rounded: it was probably used as an awl. The length of the object is 9.3 cm; the size of the section 2.6-3.2x2.6-3.2 cm. A fragment of a probably similar tool made from rectangular copper/bronze rod was found on the US23floor in room 2 of Building I. Both ends are broken. The length of the piece is 4.4 cm and its section 2.2x2.8 cm. A fragment of iron rod, rectangular in section, with a pointed end, could be also interpreted as part of an awl. The length of the object is 3.9 cm and its section 4.5x5.3 cm.
Vessels. A complete copper/bronze cauldron was found inside the oven discovered immediately to the SE limits of Building I (Fig. 19: 6; Pl. 11: 9). It has a hemispherical body with flat, slightly convex base and two vertical loop handles fixed at the upper part of the body. The rim was folded and flattened on the top, and elaborated on the exterior with a wide groove. The handles, oval in section, were fixed to the body by four rivets fixing to both the external and internal surfaces of the body two parallel thin rectangular plaques obtained by hammering the lower parts of each handle.
The cauldron was hammered from a single piece of metal. Traces of secondary burning on the exterior as well as the place where it was found indicate a probable utilitarian purpose of the object.
The diameter of the rim is 31.0 cm, the diameter of base 22.0 cm and the height of the vessel 20.0 cm. The maximum height of the handles above the rim is 5.5 cm, the maximum width of the handles is 12.0 cm and the diameter of the rounded section of the handles is 1.2 cm.
Two bronze bowls from the grave in Bydia (Emirate of Fujairah), dated close to the beginning of 2nd millennium BC, have single vertical handles similar to the cauldron from Salut [29]. Unfortunately, their sizes are too small for a direct comparison. Two bronze vessels, a cauldron and a large bowl, are known from Iron Age graves in Israel. Their size as well as their rounded vertical loop handles with similar technical details of the fittings could be taken as good parallels for the cauldron from Salut [30] .
A small copper/bronze conical lid of a miniature vessel was found on the US23floor in the room 2 of Building I. It has a shallow oval cavity on the internal surface. The diameter of lid is 3.1 cm and the height 1.8 cm.
Personal ornaments and decorations. A number of copper/bronze finds could be classified as personal ornaments. These are rings with rounded open ends, probably used as fingerings, and few banded wires used, probably, as clasps. Rings with pointed opened ends may be earrings. The same function is suggested for a ring fragment with an elaborate pendant which was somehow attached to it. A small bell-shaped pendant with circular hook on the top is of particular interest. A small hemispherical bead, made from gold foil and slightly dented in many parts, was found on the US23floor in room 2 of Building I. The diameter of finger rings is 2.1-2.5 cm; the diameter of complete earrings is 1.7 and 2.3 cm; the diameter of the golden bead is 0.6 cm. Fragments of rounded or flattened copper/bronze rods,

sometimes with one end pointed and the other decorated with grooves, could be identified as parts of pins. The diameter of the rods is 2.3-3.5 cm.
Fragments of at least two copper/bronze mirrors in the form of discs were found in the top strata of the site. There are remains of a handle attachment on one of the fragments: two small holes (a rivet preserved in one of the holes) near the edge of the disc.
Many objects, identified below as copper/bronze plaques, were found in the top strata of the site, scattered around above the US23 floor in the eastern part of room 2 of Building I. Some are rather small, thin rectangular pieces with two holes on the edges, while others, with slightly rounded ends, have the third additional hole in the center with, in some cases, the rivets for fixing still preserved. The size of the complete rectangular plaques is 0.8-1.0x2.4-2.6 and 1.1x3.6 cm, the diameter of the holes 0.2-0.3 cm and the length of the rivets 1.2-1.3 cm. A trapezoidal plaque with folded edges was probably once attached to the tip of a leather belt. Its size is 0.6-1.5x1.9 cm. There are also a number of hemispherical or convex/concave plaques with edges slightly pleated for attachment. The diameter of the hemispherical plaques is 1.8- 2.6 cm. They were most probably used for decorating leather belts or perhaps other kind of dresses, but we also suggest the different function of the rectangular pieces for restoring wooden and/or clay objects (vessels?).
Among the hemispherical plaques there are two of particular interest. Their external top surfaces were decorated with dots punctuated from the inside. We are in full agreement with Lombard's proposal about the use of a similar plaque from Rumeilah as the metal base of a quiver, made in perishable material; the arrows would have been slotted, inside the quiver, in this base with cavities/holes [31] . The diameters of the plaques with dots are 2.3 and 2.6 cm.
Votive objects. The following pieces were identified as votive objects. A complete copper/bronze 'plaque' in the form of snake with a banded body, triangular head and pointed tail was found on the top surface of the monumental mud-brick platform, immediately SE of the 'pillared hall' (Fig. 19: 1; Pl. 11: 8). The top surface of the body was richly decorated with tiny punctuated dots, and the eyes were shown as slightly bigger punctuated dots. The length of the 'plaque' is 16.9 cm, the width 1.3 (head), 1.0 (body) and 0.3 (tip of tail) cm and the thickness 0.5 cm.
A fragment of another similar 'plaque' was also found: the first band of the body and the rhomboidal head are preserved. Identical 'plaques' are known from the so-called "Mound of Serpents" at al-Qusais [32] . The presence of such objects in the form of snakes as well as appliqué snake decoration on the pottery vessels probably testify to the existence of a specific cult widespread in the south-eastern Arabia (including Salut) during the Iron Age period [33].
A miniature copper/bronze axe was found in the top strata of the site (Fig.19: 4). Its shape is trapezoidal with a tubular shafted handle; the edge of the blade is sharpened. The piece was made by hammering. The length of the blade is 4.0 cm, the width 1.5 and 3.6 cm, its thickness 0.25 cm, the length of shaft 2.2 cm and its diameter 0.6 cm. Several non-utilitarian bronze axes, different in shapefrom the Salut piece, are known from an Iron Age grave context in Al-Qusais, Hili 8, Qarn Bint Sa'ud and from Rumeilah [34].
A massive copper/bronze object was found on the US3 floor in the room with pillars. Despite the very poor state of conservation, it is reminiscent of a sort of finial of a wooden (?) object (standard?) with a hemispherical base and a V-shaped antenna-like projection at the top terminating with something similar to camel's heads. The proposed diameter of the base is 12.0 cm and the height of the object is about 8.4 cm. Some comparisons for the object, although quite remote, could be found in Luristan bronzes and in the antiquities from Scythian mound burials ('kurgans')...
Read on...

http://arabiantica.humnet.unipi.it/fileadmin/Arabian_Files/pdf/EVO_XXVIII.pdf

Indian hieroglyphs as metaphors of divinity

Abiding traditions of Indian hieroglyphs in Indian iconography can be mentioned as a continuum from the traditions of the Indian linguistic area (language union or *sprachbund*).

What was achieved in the writing system called Indus script using ligatures was also expressed in the art traditions of Indian iconography adding attributes to divine metaphors represented in *pratimā* (a picture, statue, figure, image, likeness,symbol).

The metaphors conveyed by attributes associated with the *pratimā* were surcharged with meaning, अर्थ *artha*, drawn from the linguistic repertoire of the *sprachbund*. Thus, most hieroglyphs in Indian tradition are not mere abstract, 'nameless' symbols which required elaborate hermeneutical or theological elucidations, but directly relatable to *lingua franca*, spoken words, of Indian linguistic area and the material artifacts handled in cultural interactions.

For example, the śankha (conch, *turbinella pyrum*) is an abiding sacred metaphor. In an archaeological context, śankha bangles and ornaments made of śankha were found in a burial of a woman in Nausharo dated to c. 6500 BCE. Even today, an industry thrives in the Gulf of Mannar, near Ramasetu, producing śankha worth an annual Rs. 25 crores, most of which is exported to Bengal and Orissa to make śankha bangles which are worn by brides as a sacred marriage badge. Same association of sacredness gets associated with *svastikā* or *pūrṇakumbha* (jar filled with sacred waters) or *ficus religiosa* – all examples of Indian hieroglyphs from Indus script traditions.

Semantics of the lexeme अर्थ are instructive and relate both to 'meaning' in language and to 'material wealth' in life activities or affairs of people: ' aim , purpose (very often अर्थम् , अर्थेन , अर्थाय , and अर्थे ifc. or with gen. " for the sake of , on account of , in behalf of , for "); object of the senses VarBrS; substance , wealth , property , opulence , money; अर्थम् with √ इ , or गम् , to go to one's business , take up one's work; sense , meaning , notion (cf. अर्थ-शब्दौandअर्थात् s.v. below and वेदतत्त्वा*र्थ-विद्)'.

Angkor Wat

Suvarnabhumi Airport

Churning of the ocean depicted in the bas-relief from Angkor Wat in Cambodia and Suvarnabhumi Airport in Bangkok, Thailand, shows Vishnu in the centre, his turtle Avatar Kurma below, asurasand devas to left and right.

Somaskanda Siva. Nayak Palace Art Museum, Thanjavur. TN, INDIA. A Deciption of Somaskanda with a dancing Skanda (Lord Murugan) in the middle of Uma and Siva. Siva carries an antelope, not unlike

the antelope carried on the Shu-ilishu Akkadian cylinder seal or by Elamite

royalty. Is this a memory of the Indian alchemical tradition of alchemy transmuting copper into gold? Cf. *Indian Alchemy – Soma in the Veda* (S. Kalyanaraman, 2004, Delhi, Munshiram Manoharlal)

Trimurti. Ardhanārīśvara. Elephant caves (c. 5th cent.)

Coin of Maues depicting Balarama, 1st century BCE.

Balarama, holding mace and conch on a Maurya coin (lower right), 3rd-2nd century CE. British Museum.

An iron-ore bearing mountain called kudremukh in Karnataka, referred to as hayamukha in Valmiki *Rāmāyaṇa*. It is so-called because it resembles a horse face.

Vyasa narrating the Mahabharata to Ganesha, his scribe, Angkor Wat.

Ganesha dancing on his mouse, 11th century, Bengal, *musée d'art asiatique de Berlin*.

Reproduction of the Two Sets of Line Drawings (Manuscripts 4.331 and 1.1314)
Manuscript 4.331
Manuscript 1.1314

An example from *Pratiṣṭhālakṣaṇasārasa*

*Muccaya.* More examples may be seen at
http://www.docstoc.com/docs/97739151/Pratiṣṭhālakṣaṇasārasamuccaya

प्रतिष्ठालक्षणसारसमुच्चय The oldest known manuscript is dated 1174 CE and preserved in the National Archives, Kathmandu. The text, *Pratiṣṭhālakṣaṇasārasamuccaya*, details the construction and installation of *linga*s (pratimā = *f.* an image , likeness , symbol RV.; *f.* a picture , statue , figure , idol Mn.Hariv.Ragh.) according to *āgama*s and is tentatively dated to later part of the eleventh century.

प्राणप्रतिष्ठा *f.* the ceremony of putting life into an idol by the recitation of certain मन्त्रs, consecration of an image or idol, RTL.7 (Monier-Williams, p. 1330). प्रति-ष्ठा ( √स्था) *P. A1.* -तिष्ठति , °ते to stand , stay , abide , dwell RV. the performance of any ceremony or of any solemn act , consecration or dedication (of a monument or of an idol or of a temple &c ; cf. प्रा*ण-प्र्°) , settling or endowment of a daughter , completion of a vow , any ceremony for obtaining supernatural and magical powers Var._Katha1s._ Rajat._Pur. (Monier-Williams, p. 671) The consecration of an idol or image; चलाचलेति द्विविधा प्रतिष्ठा जीवमन्दिरम् Bhāg.11.27.13; cf. प्राणप्रतिष्ठा. लक्षण *n.* (ifc. *f*(आ).) a mark , sign , symbol , token , characteristic , attribute , quality (ifc. = " marked or characterized by " , " possessed of ") Mn._MBh. (Monier-Williams, p.892) लिङ्गम् [लिङ्ग्-अच्] 1 A mark, sign, token, an emblem, a badge, symbol, distinguishing mark, character- istic; यतिपार्थिवलिङ्गधारिणौ R.8.16; अथवा प्रावृषेण्यैरेव लिङ्गै- र्मम राजोपचारः संप्रति V.4; मुनिर्दोहदलिङ्गदर्शी 14.71; Ms.1. 3;8.25,252.

Divinities in Indian linguistic area get depicted to recollect narratives of Dharma-Dhamma traditions, from ancient texts like the *Rigveda*, other vedic texts including Brāhmaṇas, Itihāsa (*Mahābhārata, Rāmāyaṇa*), *Purāṇas* and *Jātakas*.

It is possible that many survivals of hieroglyphic tradition can be found in such representations to denote metaphors of divinity. Many attributes get ligatured to *pratimā* (divine images) and convey meanings of sacredness of the divine attributes to the worshippers. Indian iconography is a veritable storehouse of the received collective memory of *bhāratm janam (*a phrase used by *Vi*śvāmitra in the *Ṛgveda* to refer to the people of India), a memory that dates back to the days of Indian hieroglyphs exemplified in Indus script inscriptions.

Semantics of the lexeme kole.l in Kota are instructive. The lexeme connotes both a smithy and a temple. This semantic concordance explains why traditions evolved deifying the hieroglyphs of Indus script: e.g. svastika, antelope, two fishes. In the Indian tradition, many divinities are shown carrying multiple weapons in multiple hands. The weapons are products of a smithy. The artificer was venerated as viśvakarma, personification of the creator of artifacts of the world.

*Koḍ.* Kollë blacksmith. *Te.* Kolimi furnace. *Go.* (SR.) kollusānā to mend implements; (Ph.) kolstānā, kulsānā to forge; (Tr.) kōlstānā to repair (of ploughshares); (SR.) kolmi smithy (*Voc.* 948). *Kuwi* (F.) kolhali to forge; *Ta.* Kol working in iron, blacksmith; kollaṉ blacksmith. *Ma.* Kollan blacksmith, artificer. *Ko.* Kole·l smithy, temple in Kota village. *To.* Kwala·l Kota smithy. *Ka.* Kolime, kolume, kulame, kulime, kulume, kulme fire-pit, furnace; (Bell.; U.P.U.) konimiblacksmith (Gowda) (DEDR 2133).

kole.l = smithy, temple in Kota village (Ko.) *Ko.* Kuṛjl shed, bathroom of Kota house; kuṛm family; kuḍḷ front room of house; kuṛḷ hut; guṛy temple. *To.* Kwïṣshed for small calves; kuṣ room (in dairy or house); kuḍṣ outer room of dairy, in: kuḍṣ waṣ̱ fireplace in outer room of lowest grade of dairies (cf. 2857), kuḍṣ moṇy bell(s) in outer section of ti· dairy, used on non-sacred buffaloes (cf. 4672); kuṛy Hindu temple; ? kwïḏya family of children. (DEDR 1655). Kuṭī f. ' hut '

MBh., °*ṭikā* — f. Divyāv., °*ṭīkā* — f. Hariv. [Some cmpds. Have °*ṭa*(*ka*) -- : ← Drav. EWA i 222 with lit.: cf.kōṭa — 3] Pa. *kuṭī* -- , °*ṭikā* — f. ' single — roomed hut '; Pk. *Kuḍī* — f., °*ḍaya* — n. ' hut '; Gy. Pal. *Kúri* ' house, tent, room ', as. *Kuri, guri* ' tent ' JGLS New Ser. Ii 329; Sh. *Kúi* ' village, country '; Wpah. Jaun. *Kūṛo* ' house '; Ku. *Kuṛī*, °*ṛo* ' house, building ', *ghar* — *kuṛī* ' house and land ', gng. *Kuṛ* ' house '; N. *kur* ' nest or hiding place of fish ', *kuri* ' burrow, hole for small animals ', *kaṭ* -- *kuro* ' small shed for storing wood '; B. *kuṛiyā* ' small thatched hut '; Or. *Kuṛī*, °*ṛiā* ' hut '; H. *kuṛī* f. ' fireplace '; M. *kuḍī* f. ' hut '; Si. *Kiḷiya* ' hut, small house '.(CDIAL 3232).

Śrīvatsa on āyāgapaṭṭa-s of Manoharpura.

Śrīvatsa symbol variants found at Kankalitila, Mathura,late1st cent.BCE: Jaina āyāgapaṭṭa-s; in these five specimen, a fish is shown in the middle apparently tied with two molluscs on either side; apparently, this ligatured pictorial formed the basis for the evolution of the Śrīvatsa symbol almost looking like a stylized trident. (After Pl. 30 C in: Savita Sharma, 1990, *Early Indian Symbols, Numismatic Evidence*, Delhi, Agam Kala Prakashan; cf. Shah, U.P., 1975, Aspects of Jain Art and Architecture, p. 77).

The hieroglyph composition of fish tied to a pair of can be read rebus: ayira 'fish'; dhama 'tie'; hangi 'snail'; pair 'dul'; Rebus: arya, ayira 'noble'; dhama 'global ethic': ayira dhama; ayira sangha 'community'; dol 'picture,form'. Thus, the composition connotes the message: ariya dhamma, ariya sangha. When the scribe had to depict a grapheme which sounded close to the word, 'dhamma', the artisan chose the form of a tied up up – tied to a fish, ayir; rebus: ayira, arya. The sthapati shown carries a mallet: Glyph: kūṭa, 'mallet'. Rebus: kūṭa 'chief (of guild)'. Glyph: *daḷa* 'petals (on circle)'. Rebus: *daḷa* 'guild'. The entire composition is *ayira dhamma sangha daḷa; arya kūṭa* 'Guild-community (practicing) ariya dhamma'.

This dhamma composition using a hieroglyph finds its expression onn the Sanchi stupa.

An Ils des symbol is depicted at sāñci stūpa (Smith, VA, Jaina Stupa, p. 15, Pl. VII, L. Buhler, Epigraphica Indica II, pp. 200, 313; Agrawala, VS, Guide to Lucknow Museum, p. 4). See many variants presented and discussed in a monograph.

The use of 'fish' glyphs (ayir 'fish') can be explained as rebus representations of the nobility associated in Jaina tradition with the word ayira (metath. Arya) 'noble person'.

Pali: Ayira (& Ayyira) (n. — adj.) [Vedic ārya, Metathesis for ariya as diaeretic form of ārya, of which the contracted (assimilation) form is ayya. See also ariya]

(n.) ariyan, nobleman, gentleman (opp. servant); (adj.) arīyan, well-born, belonging to the ruling race, noble, aristocratic, gentlemanly J v.257; Vv 396. -- f. ayirā lady, mistress (of a servant) J ii.349 (v. l. oyyakā); voc. ayire my lady J v.138 Ariya (adj. -- n.) [Vedic ārya, of uncertain etym. The other Pāli forms are ayira & ayya] 1. (racial) Aryan D ii.87. <-> 2. (social) noble, distinguished, of high birth. -- 3.(ethical) in accord with the customs and ideals of the Aryan clans, held in esteem by Aryans, generally approved. Hence: right, good, ideal. [The early Buddhists had no such ideas as we cover with the words Buddhist and Indian. Ariya does not exactly mean either. But it often comes very near to what they would have considered the best in each]. -- (adj.): D i.70 = (˚ena sīlakkhandhena samannāgata fitted out with our standard morality); iii.64 (cakkavatti -- vatta), 246 (diṭṭhi); M i.139 (pannaddhaja); ii.103 (ariyāya jātiyā jāto, become of the Aryan lineage); S ii.273 (tuṇhībhāva); iv.250 (vaddhi), 287 (dhamma); v.82 (bojjhangā), 166 (satipaṭṭhānā), 222 (vimutti), 228 (ñāṇa), 255 (iddhipādā), 421 (maggo), 435 (saccāni), 467 (paññā -- cakkhu); A i.71 (parisā); ii.36 (ñāya); iii.451 (ñāṇa); iv.153 (tuṇhībhāva); v.206 (sīlakkhandha); It 35 (paññā), 47 (bhikkhu sammaddaso); Sn 177 (patha = aṭṭhangiko maggo SnA 216); Dh 236 (bhūmi), 270; Ps ii.212 (iddhi). -- alamariya fully or thoroughly good D i.163 = iii.82 = A iv.363; nâlamariya not at all good, object, ignoble ibid. -- (m.) Vin i.197 (na ramati pāpe); D i.37 = (yaŋ taŋ ariyā ācikkhanti upekkhako satimā etc.: see 3rd. jhāna), 245;iii.111 (˚ānaŋ anupavādaka one who defames the noble); M i.17, 280 (sottiyo ariyo arahaŋ); S i.225 (˚ānaŋ upavādaka); ii.123 (id.); iv.53 (˚assa vinayo), 95 (id.); A i.256 (˚ānaŋ upavādaka); iii.19, 252 (id.); iv.145 (dele! see arīhatatta); v.68, 145 sq., 200, 317; It 21, 108; Dh 22, 164, 207; J iii.354 = Miln 230; M i.7, i35 (ariyānaŋ adassāvin: "not recognising the Noble Ones") PvA 26, 146; DhA ii.99; Sdhp 444 (˚ānaŋ vaŋsa). <-> anariya (adj. & n.) not Ariyan, ignoble, undignified, low, common, uncultured Ai.81; Sn 664 (= asappurisa SnA 479; DhsA 353); J ii.281 (= dussīla pāpadhamma C.); v.48 (˚rūpa shameless), 87; DhA iv.3. -- See also ñāṇa, magga, sacca, sāvaka. -- âvakāsa appearing noble J v.87. -- uposatha the ideal feast day (as one of 3) A i.205 sq., 212. -- kanta loved by the Best D iii.227. -- gaṇā (pl.) troops of worthies J vi.50 (= brāhmaṇa -- gaṇā, te kira tāda ariyâcārā ahesuŋ, tena te evam āha C.). -- garahin casting blame on the righteous Sn 660. -- citta a noble heart. -- traja a true descendant of the Noble ones Dpvs v.92. -- dasa having the ideal (or best) belief It 93 = 94. -- dhana sublime treasure; always as sattavidha˚ sevenfold, viz. saddhā˚, sīla˚, hiri˚, ottappa˚, suta˚, cāga˚, paññā˚ "faith, a moral life, modesty, fear of evil, learning, self -- denial, wisdom" ThA 240; VvA 113; DA ii.34. -- dhamma the national customs of the Aryans (= ariyānaŋ eso dhammo Nd1 71, 72) M i.1, 7, 135; A ii.69; v.145 sq., 241, 274; Sn 783; Dhs 1003. -- puggala an (ethically) model person, Ps i.167; Vinv.117; ThA 206. -- magga the Aryan Path. -- vaŋsa the (fourfold) noble family, i. e. of recluses content with the 4 requisites D iii.224 = A ii.27 = Ps i.84 = Nd2 141; cp. A iii.146. -- vattin leading a noble life, of good conduct J iii.443. -- vatā at Th 1, 334 should be read ˚vattā (nom. sg. of vattar, vac) "speaking noble words": -- vāsa the most excellent state of mind, habitual disposition, constant practice. Ten such at D iii.269, 291 = A v.29 (Passage recommended to all Buddhists by Asoka in the Bhabra Edict). -- vihāra the best practice S v.326. -- vohāra noble or honorable practice. They are four, abstinence from lying, from slander, from harsh language, from frivolous talk. They are otherwise known as the 4 vacī -- kammantā & represent sīla nos. 4 -- 7. See D iii.232; A ii.246; Vin v.125. -- sangha the communion of the Nobles ones PvA 1. -- sacca, a standard truth, an established fact, D i.189, ii.90, 304 sq.; iii 277; M i.62, 184; iii.248; S v.415 sq. = Vin i.10, 230. It 17; Sn 229, 230, 267; Dh 190; DhA iii.246; KhA 81, 151, 185, 187; ThA 178, 282, 291; VvA 73. -- sāvaka a disciple of the noble ones (= ariyānaŋ santike sutattā a. SnA 166). M i.8,

46, 91, 181, 323; ii.262; iii.134, 228, 272; It 75; Sn 90; Miln 339; DhA i.5, (opp. putthujjana). -- sīlin of unblemished conduct, practising virtue D i.115 (= sīlaŋ ariyaŋ uttamaŋ parisuddhaŋ DA i.286); M ii.167. When the commentators, many centuries afterwards, began to write Pali in S. India & Ceylon, far from the ancient seat of the Aryan clans, the racial sense of the wordariya was scarcely, if at all, present to their minds. Dhammapāla especially was probably a non -- Aryan, and certainly lived in a Dravidian environment. The then current similar popular etmologies of ariya and arahant (cp. next article) also assisted the confusion in their minds. They sometimes therefore erroneously identify the two words and explain Aryans as meaning Arahants (DhA i.230; SnA 537; PvA 60). In other ways also they misrepresented the old texts by ignoring the racial force of the word. Thus at J v.48 the text, speaking of a hunter belonging to one of the aboriginal tribes, calls him anariya -- rūpa. The C. explains this as "shameless", but what the text has, is simply that he looked like a non -- Aryan. (cp ' frank ' in English).

The glyphs on the aṣṭamangala hāara also appear with some variations in Jaina āyāgapaṭṭa-s. See for example: Manoharpura. Āyāgapaṭṭa-. Kusana 50 to 299 CE. Red Sandstone. National Museum, New Delhi. (Scan no. 0053014)

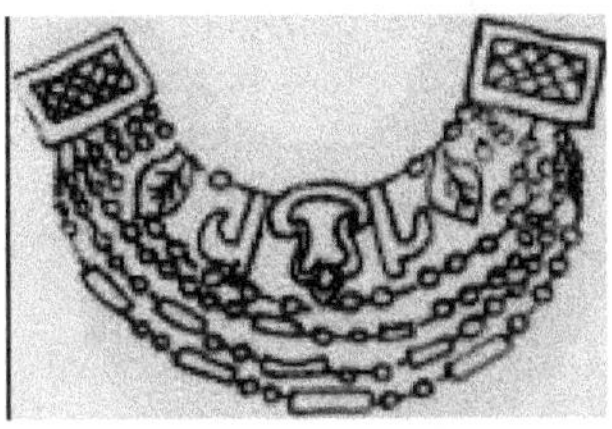

Weapons worn on the Maṅgalasūtra — or protective necklaces — parallels the tradition of aṣṭamaṅgala (eight symbols of welfare) . Chanda Yakṣi (c. 200 BCE, Indian Museum, Calcutta) ear-ring a seven-string necklace; the drawing shows lower three pearl strings consisting of flat stones or cylindrical beads; the upper row has symbols including:

lls leaf, elephant goad, śrivatsa (which is the middle glyph)

[Cunningham, Bharhut, pl. L.7] ] [After Figs. 232 and Pl. XI in:

Dr.Mohini Verma, 989, Dress and Ornaments in Ancient India: The Maurya and S'un:ga Periods, Varanasi, Indological Book House, p. 24.] A figure on a mithuna plaque from Ahicchatra isinterpreted: 'There are three additional symbols woven in her long necklace, namely a dagger on the left, a puppet (śrivatsa in the center) and on the right, a vajra with a pointed angle prongs.' These symbols also occur on a terracotta of Mathura. [VS Agrawa, a Terracotta figurines ofAhichchatra, Dist. Bareilly, UP, Ancient India, No. 4, pl. XXXII, 2; VS Agrawala, Mathura Terracottas, JUPHS, Vol. IX, fig.6,0,2,3).

Necklaces with a number of pendants aṣṭamaṅgalaka hāra depicted on a pillar of a gateway (toraṇa) at the stūpa of Sanchi, Central India, 1st century BCE. [After VS Agrawala, 1969,The deeds of Harsha (being a cultural study of Bāṇa's Harṣacarita, ed. By PK Agrawala, Varanasi: fig. 62] The hāra or necklace shows a pair of fish signs together with a number of motifs indicating weapons (cakra, paraśu, aṅkuś a), including a device that parallels the standard device normally shown in many inscribed objects of Sarasvati civilization in front of the one-horned bull. (cf. Marshall, J. and Foucher, The Monuments of Sanchi, 3 vols., Callcutta, 1936, repr.1982, pl. 27).

The first necklace has eleven and the second one has thirteen pendants (cf. V.S. Agrawala, 1977, Bhāratīya Kalā, Varanasi, p. 169); he notes the eleven pendants as: sun, śukra, padmasara, aṅkuśa, vaijayanti, paṅkaja, mīna-mithuna, śrīvatsa, paraśu, darpaṇa and kamala. "The axe (paraśu) and aṅkuśa pendants are common at sites of north India and some of their finest specimens from Kausambi are in the collection of Dr.MC Dikshit of Nagpur." (Dhavalikar, M.K., 1965, Sanchi: A cultural Study, Poona, p. 44;loc.cit. Dr.Mohini Verma, 1989, Dress and Ornaments in Ancient India: The Mauryaand śuṅga Periods, Varanasi, Indological Book House, p. 125).• Note that one of the pendants looks like the 'device' normally found in front of the onehornedbull, the saṅgaḍa, portable brazier and lathe (also meaning. Rebus, battle).• On the second hāra, clock-wise, after iṇaikkayal or mīnayugala (twin fish), and axe, thependant looks like a tree or a bunch of coral? [tukir = coral, pavaṟam; vaicayanti =tukir-koṭi, i.e. creeper containing coral; thus a sign interpreted as a maṅgala sign, i.e. vaijayanti may be connoted by this Tamil phrase: tukir- koṭi, i.e. a bunch of corals on a creeper. In Skt., vaijayanti can be interpreted as an attribute of victory].

[Pl. 33, Nandipāda-Triratna at: Bhimbetka, Sanchi, Sarnath and Mathura] śrivatsa symbol [with its hundreds of stylized variants, depicted on Pl. 29 to 32] occurs in Bogazkoi (Central Anatolia) dated ca. 6th to 14th cent. BCE on inscriptions.

The link with ayir 'iron' is explicit in the use of ayir in reference to a marriage badge of a woman, asin:

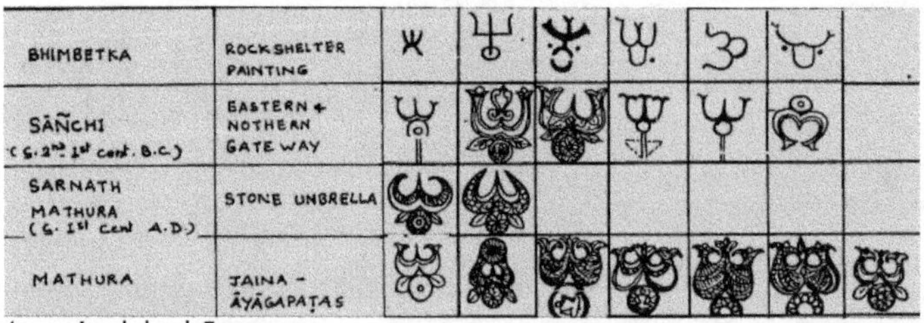


aṣṭamaṅgalaka hāra

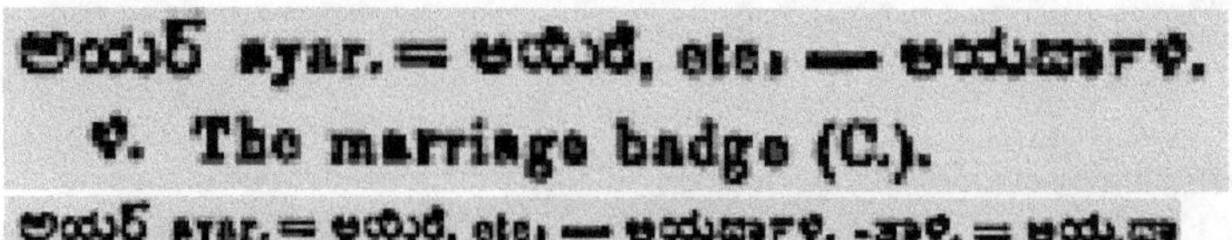


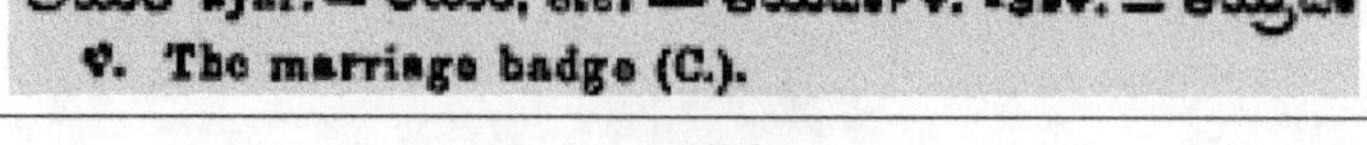

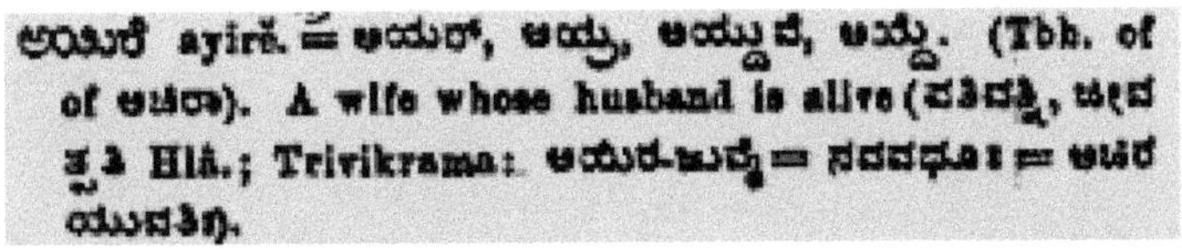
ಅಯಿರೆ ayirĕ = [illegible]. (Tbh. of of [illegible]). A wife whose husband is alive ([illegible], [illegible] Hlâ.; Trivikrama: [illegible] = [illegible] = [illegible]).

The glyphs ligatured to compose the makara may be seen from a Bharhut panel (ca. 100 BCE).

Glyph components are: snout of a crocodile, elephant trunk, head and forequarters of an elephant, body of a snake, curved-in  lls  de, and fins and tail of a fish. (Indian Museum, Calcutta)

Khandagiri caves (2nd cent. BCE). In the religious cults, ashtamangalass are eight glyphs which stand for good luck, auspiciousness, prosperity or are marks of enlightenment. In Jaina tradition, they become standardized only from about the 4th cent. CE. A. Cave 3 (Ananta gumpha), certain jaina motifs are depicted; nandipada, it is the same as triratna of Bauddha. B. Cave 3 (Ananta gumpha); a tree under a canopy enclosed within a railing. (Yuvraj Kerishan, 1996, *The Buddha image: its origin and development*, Bharatiya Vidya Bhavan, p. 24).

## 6 LEGACY OF INDIAN HIEROGLYPHS

Continuum legacy of Indus script glyphs on punch-marked coins

The association of auspiciousness with the glyphs shown on sculptures of Khandagiri caves, is comparable to the association of smithy with a temple in two glosses of Indian linguistic area:

Ko. Kole·l smithy, temple in Kota village. To. Kwala·l Kota smithy. (DEDR 2133).

This extraordinary and cultural phenomenon of equating a smithy with a temple, perhaps unique to the Indian linguistic area, may explain the sacredness associated with glyphs used on thousands of punch-marked coins which came from mints of all parts of India, treating the glyphs as hieroglyphs.

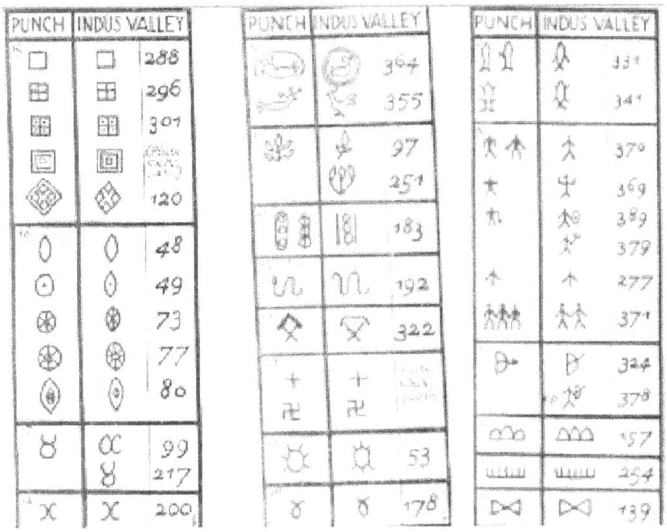


*Comparison of Punch and Indus Valley Writing*

Most of the symbols employed on ancient coins are traceable to Indus script glyphswhich are composed of pictorial motifs and unambiguous glyptic signs. That these glyphs on punch-marked coins which came  out of the mints  demonstrates the continuing legacy of the writing system of artisans who created Indus script.

Cast bronze coin.Mauryan empire. 3rd cent. BCE

British Museum: Silver kārṣāpaṇa of the Mauryan empire. More examples at (1) and (2). Source: C.J. Brown, 1922, *The coins of India, The Heritage of India Series*, Association Press, Calcutta.

Map of coin hoards of punch-marked coins after D. Rajgor.

CL Fabri and Thapliyal found lls des between Indus script glyphs and the glyphs on punch-marked coins. (Fabri, CL, 1935, JRAS, pp. 307-318 and Thapliyal, KK in: Studies in Ancient Indian Seals found that many Indian seals from the 3rd cent. BCE to 7th lls. CE portrayed animals, with an inscription above the animal (just as in the case of the Indus seals).

W. Theobald, 1890, Notes on some of the symbols found on the punch-marked coins of Hindustan, and on their relationship to the archaic symbolism of other races and distant lands, Journal of the Asiatic Society of Bengal, Bombay Branch (JASB), Part 1. History , Literature etc., Nos. III & IV, 1890, pp. 181 to 268; W. Theobald, 1901, A revision of the symbols on the 'Karshapana' Coinage,described in Vol. LIX,JASB, 1890, Part I, No. 3, and Descriptions of many additional symbols, *Journal of the Asiatic Society of Bengal,* Bombay Branch (*JASB*), No. 2, 1901 (Read December, 1899).

Plates VIII to XI of Theobald, 1890 listing symbols on punch-marked coins:

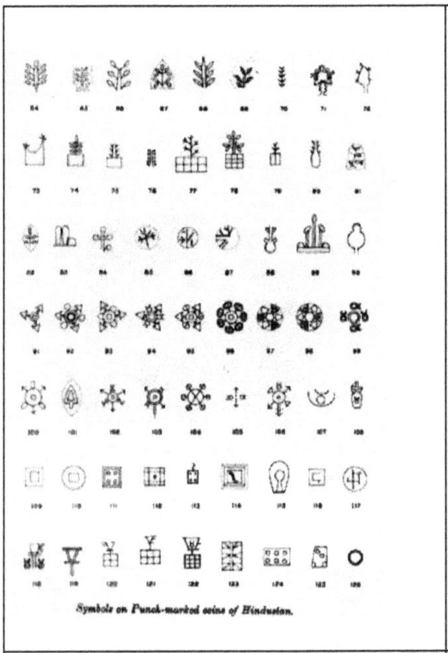


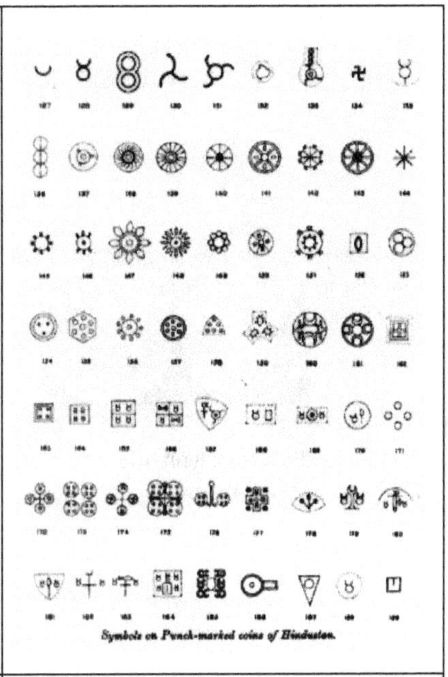


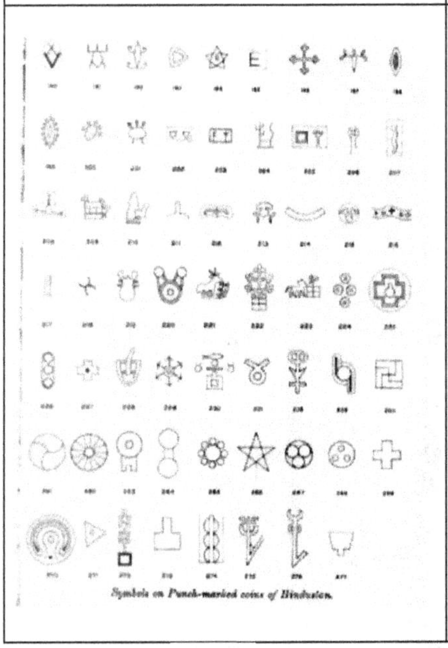


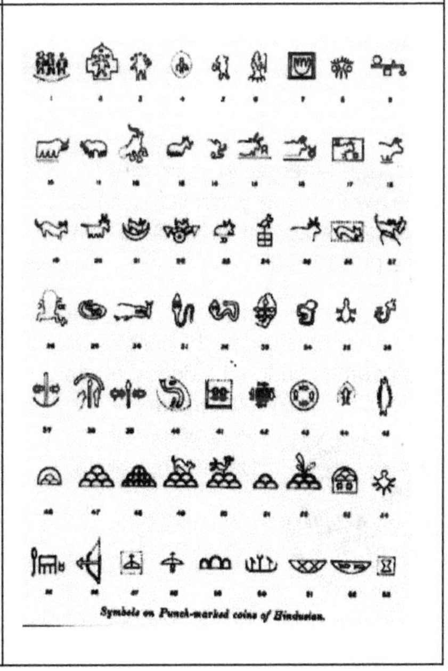

30

Glyph 30 shown by Theobald compares with the glyph on a Harappa tablet.

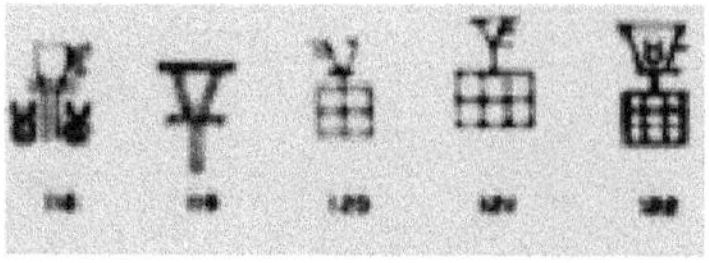

Theobald identifies glyphs 118 to 122 on punch-marked which are similar to the standard devic of Indus script. (After Fig. 7.32, Kenoyer, 1998).

Theobald identifies glyph 136 on punch-marked coins which is similar to the one shown on m1406 (Mohenjo-daro tablet).

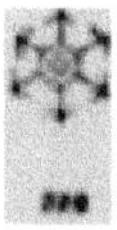

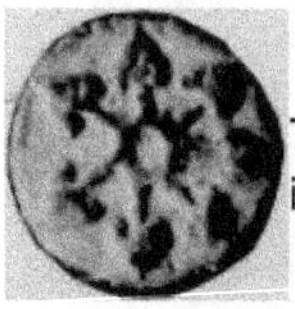

Theobald identifies glyph 138 which is similar to the glyph on an Indus script inscription on m0428 seal.

Theobald identifies glyph 209 which is similar to the glyph on Harappa seal h243.

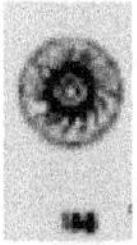

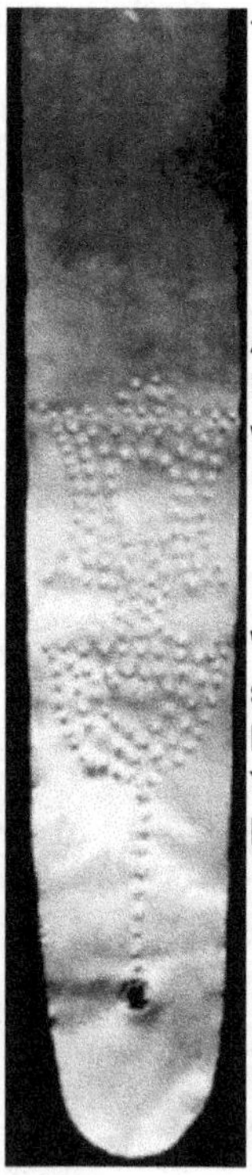

Taxila coin. Anonymous. Period of 170 BCE. AV quarter stater (2.34 gms). left. Taxila symbol before fish-like symbol crescents. Bopeerachchi –SNG ANS – MIG BMC India pl. 11.

Agathokles, ca. 185 to Humped bull standing with pellet and 163 (Pushkalavati);

Yotamira, silver drachm. C. 2nd cent. CE. 16 mm. diademed bust right, dotted border, legend around (at Bh)Yotamirasa Parataraja (Of Bagareva, Parata

Weight: 3.72 gms. Dia. swastika right, brahmi Bagarevaputasa Yotamira, son of king).

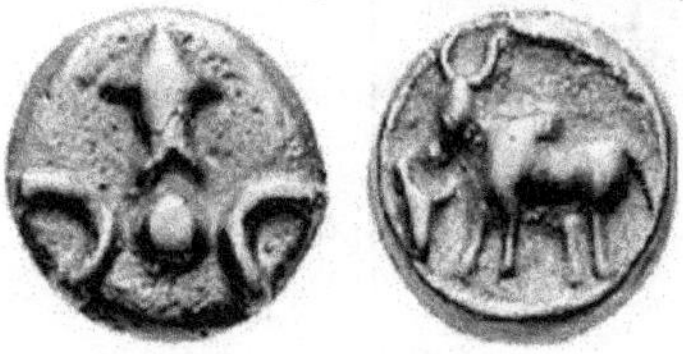

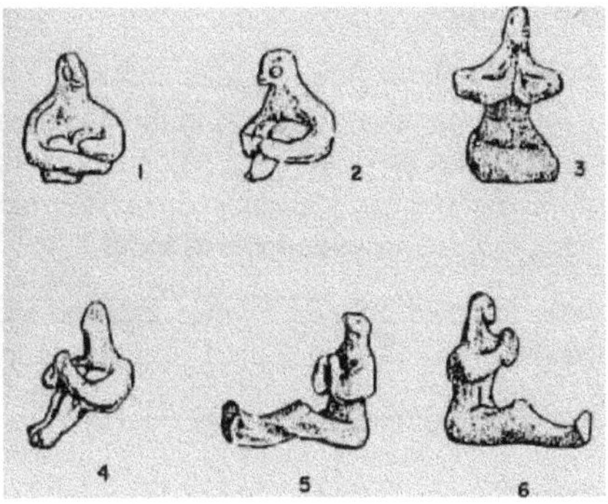


Terracotta toys show yogic asanas: 1-4, from Harappa; 5-6, from Mohenjo-daro.

Continued use of some glyphs of Indus script by artisans (smiths) during historical periods

Rampurva bull capital, 3rd cent. BCE

Rampurva bull capital was fixed to the Ashokan pillar using a copper bolt which had Indian hieroglyphs from Indus script. See Line 1 of Table showing four glyphs.

Rampurva pillar edict text:

- Thus saith king Priyadarsi, Beloved of the Gods. Twelve years after my coronation, records relating to Dharma were caused to be written by me for the first time for the welfare and happiness of the people, so that, without violation thereof, they might attain the growth of Dharma in various respects.

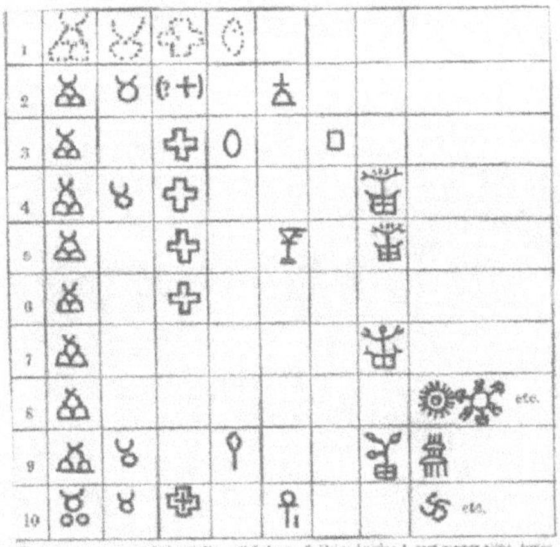

Fig. 2.—1, Rāmpurva bolt; 2, Kumrāhār base; 3, Patna bowls; 4, cast copper coins, types G, H, J, K; 5, ditto, type F; 6, ditto, type M; 7, ditto, type O; 8, debased silver punch marked coins; 9, Sohgaura plate; 10, Patna copper band.

- Thinking: "Only in this way the welfare and happiness of the people may be secured." I scrutinize as to how I may bring happiness to the people, no matter whether they are my relatives or residents of the neighborhood of my capital or of distant localities. And I act accordingly. In the same manner, I scrutinize in respect of all classes of people. Moreover, all the religious sects have been honored by me with various kinds of honors. But what I consider my principal duty is meeting the people of different sects personally.

- This record relating to Dharma has been caused to be written by me twenty-six years after my coronation.

Rampurva bull capital is a depiction of bos indicus comparable to the glyph on an Indus seal m1103.

A remarkable example is a 24 inch long and 12 inch dia. Copper bolt with an inscription of four glyhphs, used to bolt in the bull capital on an Ashokan pillar at Rampurva. See item 1 of the list of four glyphs used on this copper bolt. Similar use of Indus script glyphs occurs on nine other metal objects, pointing to the continued use of Indian hieroglyphs by metalsmiths of India.

A solid copper bolt (24 ½" in length and a circumference of 14" at the center and 12" at the ends), was found in the Rampurva Asoka Pillar near Nepal border.

The glyphs of the Indus script comparable to these inscribed metal objects are:

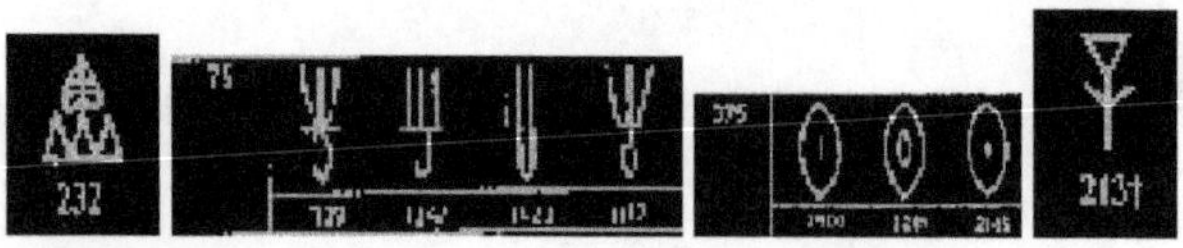

h188, h196, h291,

h630, h631

The + glyph may connote: M. अग्निकुंड [ agnikuṇḍa ] n (S) A hole in the ground, or an enclosed space on the surface, or a metal square-mouthed vessel, for receiving and preserving consecrated fire.

Sohgaura copper plate inscription (Item 9 of the table)

Sohgaura copper plate (Pre-Mauryan) Date? Pre-Mauryan, that is first millennium BCE

The line 1 of the inscription using Indus script glyphs details the repertoire of facilities provided to itinerant merchants/artisan guild caravans in the two koṣṭh āgāra (sheds/workshops/storerooms/ warehouses).

Hieroglyph 1 (from left): glyph: tree, rebus: smelting furnace

kuṭhi kuṭa, kuṭi, kuṭha a tree (Kaus'.); kuḍa tree (Pkt.); kuṛā tree; kaṛek tree, oak (Pas;.)(CDIAL 3228). Kuṭha, kuṭa (Ka.), kudal (Go.) kudar. (Go.) kuṭhāra, kuṭha, kuṭaka = a tree (Skt.lex.) kuṭ, kurun: = stump of a tree (Bond.a); khuṭ = id. (Or.) kuṭa, kuṭha = a tree (Ka.lex.) guṇḍra = a stump; khuṇṭut = a stump of a tree left in the ground (Santali.lex.) kuṭamu = a tree (Te.lex.) কুঁদ² [ kuṅda² ] n a stock or butt (of a gun); a stump or trunk (of a tree); a log (of wood); a lump (of sugar etc.). (Bengali) Rebus: kūdār 'turner' (B.)

কুঁদন, কোঁদন [ kuṅdana, kōṅdana ] n act of turning (a thing) on a lathe; act of carving; act of rushing forward to attack or beat; act of skip ping or frisking; act of bragging. (Bengali)কুঁদ [ kuṅda ] n a (turner's) lathe; a variety of multi-petalled jasmine.কুঁদ¹ [ kuṅda¹ ] v to turn (a thing) on a lathe, to shape by turning on a lathe; to carve; to rush forward to attack or beat; to skip, to frisk; to brag.

kuṭi, 'smelting furnace' (Mundari.lex.).kuṭhi, kuṭi (Or.; Sad. Koṭhi) (1) the smelting furnace of the blacksmith; kuṭire bica duljaḍko talkena, they were feeding the furnace with ore; (2) the name of ēkuṭi has been given to the fire which, in lac factories, warms the water bath for softening the lac so that it can be spread into sheets; to make a smelting furnace; kut.hi-o of a smelting furnace, to be made; the smelting furnace of the blacksmith is made of mud, cone-shaped, 2' 6" dia. At the base and 1' 6" at the top. The hole in the center, into which the mixture of charcoal and iron ore is poured, is about 6" to 7" in dia. At the base it has two holes, a smaller one into which the nozzle of the bellow is inserted, as seen in fig. 1, and a larger one on the opposite side through which the molten iron flows out into a cavity (Mundari.lex.)

Hieroglyph 3 glyph: spear rebus: furnace

śūla = spear (Skt.)

cuḷḷai = potter's kiln, furnace (Ta.); cūḷai furnace, kiln, funeral pile (Ta.); cuḷḷa potter's furnace; cūḷa brick kiln (Ma.); cullī fireplace (Skt.); cullī, ullī id. (Pkt.)(CDIAL 4879; DEDR 2709). Sulgao, salgao to light a fire; sen:gel, sokol fire (Santali.lex.) hollu, holu = fireplace (Kuwi); soḍu fireplace, stones set up as a fireplace (Mand.); ule furnace (Tu.)(DEDR 2857).

Hieroglyph 4 glyph: peak mounted by a rimless pot rebus: furnace

kūṭa = peak (Telugu)

baṭa = rimless pot (Kannada)

kūṭam = workshop (Tamil); baṭa = furnace (Santali) bhrāṣṭra = furnace (Skt.)

Hieroglyph 5 glyph: tree (as shown on hieroglyph 1) with a rim of a jar and a quail ligatured on the branches of tree.

kuṭi = tree; rebus: kuṭi = smelting furnace.

kaṇḍ kanka = rim of jar (Santali); kaṇḍ = fire-altar (Santali); kan = copper (Tamil)

baṭa = quail (Santali)

baṭa = furnace (Santali) bhrāṣṭra = furnace (Skt.)

Hieroglyph 2 and 6: koṣṭhāgāra, a pair of storehouses.

koṭṭamu, koṭṭama. [Tel.] n. A pent roofed chamber or house as distinguished from 'midde' which is flat-roofed. Pounding in a mortar. A stable for elephants or horses, or cattle A. i. 43. [ koṭṭāmu ] koṭṭāmu. [Tel.] n. A pent roofed house. [ koṭṭaruvu ] koṭṭaruvu. [Tel.] n. A barn, a grain store. [koṭāru], [Tel.] n. A store, a granary. A place to keep grain, salt, &c. కొఠారు [ koṭhāru ] Same as [ koṭhī ] koṭhī. [H.]

n. A bank. A mercantile house or firm (Telugu) kṓṣṭha2 n. ' pot ' Kauś., ' granary, storeroom ' MBh., ' inner apartment ' lex., aka -- n. ' treasury ', ikā f. ' pan ' Bhpr. [Cf. *kōttha -- , *kōtthala -- : same as prec.?] Pa. koṭṭha -- n. ' monk's cell, storeroom ', aka<-> n. ' storeroom '; Pk. koṭṭha -- , kuṭ, koṭṭhaya -- m. ' granary, storeroom '; Sv. dāntar -- kuṭha ' fire -- place '; Sh. (Lor.) kōti (ṭh?) ' wooden vessel for mixing yeast '; K. kōṭha m. ' granary ', kuṭhu m. ' room ', kuṭhü f. ' granary, storehouse '; S. koṭho m. ' large room ', ṭhī f. ' storeroom '; L. koṭhā m. ' hut, room, house ', ṭhī f. ' shop, brothel ', awāṇ. koṭhā ' house '; P. koṭṭhā, koṭhā m. ' house with mud roof and walls, granary ', koṭṭhī, koṭhī f. ' big well -- built house, house for married women to prostitute themselves in '; WPah. pāḍ. kuṭhī ' house '; Ku. koṭho ' large square house ', gng. kōṭhi ' room, building '; N. koṭho ' chamber ', ṭhi ' shop '; A. koṭhā, kōṭhā ' room ', kuṭhī ' factory '; B. koṭhā ' brick -- built house ', kuṭhī ' bank, granary '; Or. koṭhā ' brick -- built house ', ṭhī ' factory, granary '; Bi. koṭhī ' granary of straw or brushwood in the open '; Mth. koṭhī' grain -- chest '; OAw. koṭha 'storeroom '; H. koṭhā m. ' granary ', ṭhī f. ' granary, large house ', Marw. koṭho m. ' room '; G. koṭhɔ m. ' jar in which indigo is stored, warehouse ', ṭhī f. ' large earthen jar, factory '; M. koṭhā m. ' large granary ', ṭhī f. ' granary, factory '; Si. koṭa ' storehouse '. -- Ext. with -- ḍa -- : K. kūṭhürü f. ' small room '; L. koṭhṛī f. ' small side room '; P. koṭhṛī f. ' room, house '; Ku. koṭheṛī ' small room '; H. koṭhrī f. ' room, granary '; M. koṭhḍī f. ' room '; -- with -- ra -- : A. kuṭharī ' chamber ', B. kuṭhrī, Or. koṭhari; -- with -- lla -- : Sh. (Lor.) kotul (ṭh?) ' wattle and mud erection for storing grain '; H. koṭhlā m., lī f. ' room, granary '; G. koṭhlɔ m. ' wooden box ' kōṣṭhapāla -- , *kōṣṭharūpa -- , *kōṣṭhāṁśa -- , kōṣṭhāgāra -- ; *kajjalakōṣṭha -- , *duvārakōṣṭha-, *dēvakōṣṭha -- , dvārakōṣṭhaka -- .Addenda: kṓṣṭha -- 2: WPah.kṭg. kóṭṭhi f. ' house, quarters, temple treasury, name of a partic. temple ', J. koṭhā m. ' granary ', koṭhī f. ' granary, bungalow '; Garh. koṭhu ' house surrounded by a wall '; Md. koḍi ' frame ', <-> koři ' cage ' (X kōṭṭa -- ). -- with ext.: OP. koṭhārī f. ' crucible ', P. kuṭhālī f., H.kuṭhārī f.; -- Md. koṭari ' room '.(CDIAL 3546) kōṣṭhapāla m. ' storekeeper ' W. [kṓṣṭha -- 2, pāla -- ] M. koṭhvaḷā m. (CDIAL 3547) 3550 kōṣṭhāgāra n. ' storeroom, store ' Mn. [kṓṣṭha -- 2, agāra -- ] Pa. koṭṭhāgāra -- n. ' storehouse, granary '; Pk. koṭṭhāgāra -- , koṭṭhāra -- n. ' storehouse '; K. kuṭhār m. ' wooden granary ', WPah. bhal. kóṭhār m.; A. B. kuṭharī ' apartment ', Or. koṭhari; Aw. lakh. koṭhār ' zemindar's residence '; H. kuṭhiyār ' granary '; G. koṭhār m. ' granary, storehouse ', koṭhāriyũ n. ' small do. '; M. koṭhār n., koṭhārẽ n. ' large granary ', -- rī f. ' small one '; Si. koṭāra ' granary, store '.kōṣṭhāgārika -- .Addenda: kōṣṭhāgāra -- : WPah.kṭg. kəṭhā´r, kc. kuṭhār m. ' granary, storeroom ', J. kuṭhār, kṭhār m.; -- Md. kořāru ' storehouse ' ← Ind. (CDIAL 3550). kōṣṭhāgārika m. ' storekeeper ' BHSk. [Cf. kōṣṭhā- gārin -- m. ' wasp ' Suśr.: kōṣṭhāgāra -- ] Pa. koṭṭhāgārika -- m. ' storekeeper '; S. koṭhārī m. ' one who in a body of faqirs looks after the provision store '; Or. koṭhārī ' treasurer '; Bhoj. koṭhārī ' storekeeper ', H. kuṭhiyārī m. Addenda: kōṣṭhāgārika -- : G. koṭhārī m. ' storekeeper '. kōṣṭhin -- see kuṣṭhin -- Add2. (CDIAL 3552) Ta. koṭṭakai shed with sloping roofs, cow-stall; marriage pandal; koṭṭam cattle-shed; koṭṭil cow-stall, shed, hut; (STD) koṭambe feeding place for cattle. Ma. koṭṭil cowhouse, shed, workshop, house. Ka. koṭṭage, koṭige, koṭṭige stall or outhouse (esp. for cattle), barn, room. Koḍ. koṭṭï shed. Tu.koṭṭa hut or dwelling of Koragars; koṭya shed, stall. Te. koṭṭāmu stable for cattle or horses; koṭṭāyi thatched shed. Kol. (Kin.) koṛka, (SR.) korkācowshed; (Pat., p. 59) kontoḍi henhouse. Nk. khoṭa cowshed. Nk. (Ch.) koṛka id. Go. (Y.) koṭa, (Ko.) koṭam (pl. koṭak) id. (Voc. 880); (SR.) koṭka shed; (W. G. Mu. Ma.) koṛka, (Ph.) korka, kurka cowshed (Voc. 886); (Mu.) koṭorla, koṭorli shed for goats (Voc. 884). Malt. koṭa hamlet. / Influenced by Skt. goṣṭha-. (DEDR 2058) கொட்டகை koṭṭakai, n. < gōṣṭhaka. [T. koṭṭamu, K. koṭṭage, Tu. koṭya.] Shed with sloping roofs, cow-stall, marriage-pandal; பந்தல் விசேடம். கொட்டகைத் தூண்போற் காலிலங்க (குற்றா. குற. 84, 4). கொட்டம் koṭṭam, n. House; வீடு. ஒரு கொட்டம் ஒழிச்சுக் குடுத்துருங்கோ (எங்களூர், 47). கோட்டம்[2] kōṭṭam, n. < kōṣṭha. 1. Room, enclosure; அறை. சுடும ணோங்கிய நெடு நிலைக் கோட்டமும் (மணி. 6, 59). 2. Temple; கோயில். கோழிச் சேவற் கொடியோன் கோட்டமும் (சிலப். 14, 10).

koṭṭha (m. nt.) [Sk. koṣṭha abdomen, any cavity for holding food, cp. kuṣṭa groin, and also Gr. ku/tos cavity, ku/sdos pudendum muliebre, ku/stis bladder = E. cyst, chest; Lat. cunnus pudendum, Ger. hode testicle] anything hollow and closed in (Cp. gabbha for both meanings) as -- 1. the stomach or abdomen Miln 265, Vism 357; Sdhp 257. -- 2. a closet, a monk's cell, a storeroom, M i.332; Th 2, 283 (?)=ThA, 219; J ii.168. <-> 3. a sheath, in asi˚ Vin iv.171. -- aṭṭhi a stomach bone or bone of the abdomen Vism 254, 255. -- abbhantara the intestinal canal Miln 67; -- âgāra (nt.) storehouse, granary, treasury: in conn. with kosa (q. v.) in formula paripuṇṇa -- kosa -- koṭṭhâgāra (adj.) D i.134, expld at DA i.295 as threefold, viz. dhana˚ dhañña˚ vattha˚, treasury, granary, warehouse; PvA 126, 133; -- âgārika a storehouse -- keeper, one who hoards up wealth Vin i.209; DhA i.101; -- āsa [=koṭṭha +aŋsa] share, division, part; ˚koṭṭhāsa (adj.) divided into, consisting of. K. is a prose word only and in all Com. passages is used to explain bhāga: J i.254; 266; vi.368; Miln 324; DhA iv.; 108 (=pada), 154; PvA 58, 111, 205 (kāma˚=kāmaguṇā); VvA 62; anekena k˚ -- ena infinitely PvA 221. Koṭṭhaka1 (nt.) "a kind of koṭṭha," the stronghold over a gateway, used as a store -- room for various things, a chamber, treasury, granary Vin ii.153, 210; for the purpose of keeping water in it Vin ii.121=142; 220; treasury J i.230; ii.168; -- store -- room J ii.246; koṭthake pāturahosi appeared at the gateway, i. e. arrived at the mansion Vin i.291.; -- udaka -- k a bath -- room, bath cabinet Vin i.205 (cp. Bdhgh's expln at Vin. Texts ii.57); so also nahāna -- k˚ and piṭṭhi -- k˚, bath -- room behind a hermitage J iii.71; DhA ii.19; a gateway, Vin ii.77; usually in cpd. dvāra -- k˚ "door cavity," i. e. room over the gate: gharaŋ satta -- dvāra -- koṭṭhakapaṭimaṇḍitaŋ "a mansion adorned with seven gateways" J i.227=230, 290; VvA 322. dvāra -- koṭṭhakesu āsanāni paṭṭhapenti "they spread mats in the gateways" VvA 6; esp. with bahi: bahi -- dvārakoṭṭhakā nikkhāmetvā "leading him out in front of the gateway" A iv.206; ˚e thiṭa or nisinna standing or sitting in front of the gateway S i.77; M i.161, 382; A iii.30. -- bala -- k. a line of infantry J i.179. -- koṭṭhaka -- kamma or the occupation connected with a storehouse (or bathroom?) is mentioned as an example of a low occupation at Vin iv.6; Kern, Toev. s. v. "someone who sweeps away dirt." (Pali)

Thus the line 1 is a hieroglyphic representation of facilities provided to artisan guilds, itinerant metalsmiths at the tri-junction of three highways.

## 7 INDIAN LINGUISTIC AREA AS CULTURAL AREA

### Semantic clusters of *Indian Lexicon*

A contribution to general semantics is the *Indian Lexicon* which includes lists of many borrowings among and between languages. There are over 1240 semantic clusters included in the *Indian Lexicon* from over 25 languages which makes the work very large. Most of the lexical archive relate to the bronze-age cultural context and possible entries are relatable rebus to Indian hieroglyphs. Many are found to be attested as substratum lexemes only in a few languages such as Nahali, Kashmiri, Kannada or Telugu or lexical entries of Hemacandra's *deśī nāmamālā (Prākṛt)*; thus, many present-day Indian languages are rendered as dialects of an Indus language or proto-Indic *lingua franca* or gloss. This approach at semantic clustering into over 1240 groups, has resulted in clustering as many as over 3000 etymological entries of DEDR (Dravidian etyma) compared with cognate entries of CDIAL (Indo-Aryan etyma), together with thousands of lexemes of Santali, Mundarica and other languages of the Austro-Asiatic linguistic group, and, maybe, Language X.

There could be many opinions among linguists on semantic developments of a language. It is assumed that there were homophones in a Proto-Indic language which was the lingua franca of the Sarasvati-Sindhu civilization, ca. 2500 B.C.; this assumption, coupled with the Mesopotamian links, provides some hope for deciphering the inscriptions of the Sarasvati (Indus) Script.

The identification of a particular Indian language as the Indus language has presented some problems because of the received wisdom about grouping of language families in Indo-European linguistic analyses. Some claims of decipherment have assumed the language to be Tamil, of Dravidian language family; some have assumed the language to be Sanskrit, of Indo-Aryan language family. A resolution to these problems comes from a surprising source: Manu.

### Mleccha, Indus language of Indian linguistic area (*sprachbund*)

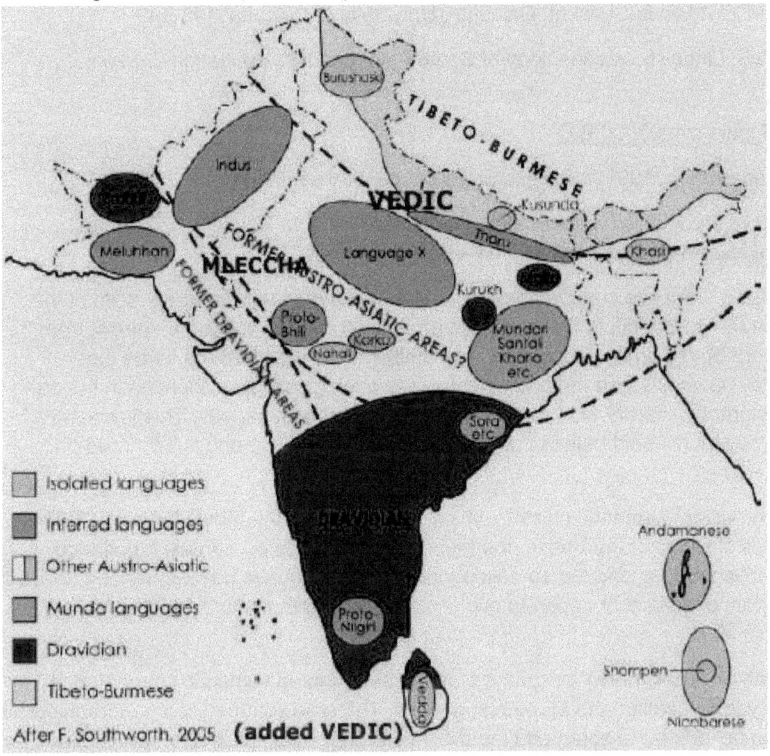


Indian linguistic area map, including mleccha and vedic (After F. Southworth, 2005; VEDIC AND MLECCHA added.) A language family, mleccha (?language X), is attested in the ancient literature of India. This is the lingua franca, the spoken version of the language of the civilization of about 5000 years ago, distinct from the grammatically correct version called Sanskrit represented in the vedic texts and other ancient literature. Ancient texts of India are replete with insights into formation and evolution of languages. Some examples are: Bharata's Natya Shastra, Patanjali's Mahabhashya, Hemacandra's Deśī nāmamālā, Nighanṭus, Panini's Aṣṭādhyayi, Tolkappiyam–Tamil grammar. The evidence which comes from Manu, dated to ca. 500 BCE. Manu (10.45) underscores the linguistic area: ārya vācas mleccha vācas te sarve dasyuvah smṛtāh [trans. "both ārya speakers and mleccha speakers (that is, both speakers of literary dialect and colloquial or vernacular dialect) are all remembered as dasyu"]. Dasyu is a general reference to people. Dasyu is cognate with dasa, which in Khotanese language means 'man'. It is also cognate with daha, a word which occurs in Persepolis inscription of Xerxes, a possible reference to people of Dahistan, a region east of Caspian sea. Strabo wrote :"Most of the scythians, beginning from the Caspian sea, are called Dahae Scythae, and those situated more towards the east Massagetae and Sacae." (Strabo, 11.8.1). Close to Caspian Sea is the site of Altyn-tepe which was an interaction area with Meluhha and where three Indus seals with inscriptions were found, including a silver seal showing a composite animal which can be called a signature glyph of Indus writing..

The identification of mleccha as the language of the Indus script writing system is consistent with the following theses which postulate an Indian linguistic area, that is an area of ancient times when various language-speakers interacted and absorbed language features from one another and made them their own: Emeneau, 1956; Kuiper, 1948; Masica, 1971; Przyludski, 1929; Southworth, 2005.

Emeneau, MB, 1956, India as a linguistic area, Language 32, 1956, 3-16.

Kuiper, FBJ, 1948, Proto-Munda words in Sanskrit, Amsterdam, 1948

1967, The genesis of a linguistic area, IIJ 10, 1967, 81-102

Masica, CP, 1971, Defining a Linguistic area. South Asia. Chicago: The University of Chicago Press.

Przyludski, J., 1929, Further notes on non-aryan loans in Indo-Aryan in: Bagchi, P. C. (ed.), Pre-Aryan and Pre-Dravidian in Sanskrit. Calcutta : University of Calcutta: 145-149

Southworth, F., 2005, Linguistic archaeology of South Asia, London, Routledge-Curzon.

## Discovering the language of India circa 3000 B.C.

The *Indian Lexicon* (S. Kalyanaraman, 1998) is an exploration in general semantics.

The document is a comparative study of lexemes of all the languages of India (which may also be referred to, in a geographical/historical phrase, as the Indian linguistic area).

This lexicon seeks to establish a semantic concordance, across the languages or numraire facile of the Indian linguistic area: from Brahui to Santali to Bengali, from Kashmiri to Mundarica to Sinhalese, from Marathi to Hindi to Nepali, from Sindhi or Punjabi or Urdu to Tamil. A semantic structure binds the languages of India, which may have diverged morphologically or phonologically as evidenced in the oral tradition of Vedic texts, or epigraphy, literary works or lexicons of the historical periods. This lexicon, therefore, goes beyond, the commonly held belief of an Indo-European language and is anchored on proto-Indian sememes.

The work covers over 1240 groups of semantic clusters which span and bind the Indian languages. The basic finding is that thousands of terms of the Vedas, the Munda languages (e.g., Santali, Mundarica, Sora), the so-called Dravidian languages and the so-called Indo-Aryan languages have common roots. This belies the received wisdom of distinct or separate evolution, for example, the Dravidian or Munda and the Aryan languages.

The lexicon seeks to establish an areal 'Indian' language type, by establishing semantic concordance among the so-called Indo-Aryan, Dravidian and Munda languages. The area spanned is a geographical region bounded by the Indian ocean on the south and the mountain ranges which insulate it from other regions of the Asian continent on the north, east and west.

This lexicon is a tribute to the brilliant work done by etymologists and scholars of Indian linguistics, and to a number of scholars who have contributed to resolving the enigma of the Indus (Sarasvati-Sindhu) Script, of the *lingua franca* of the civilization and to the study of ancient Indian science and technology.

The author believes that the work can contribute to/strengthen the unifying elements of Indian common cultural heritage and the conclusions will counter divisive forces which occasionally hold sway. The author also realizes that language is an extraordinarily emotional issue and is subject to a variety of possible interpretations. Language evolution, itself, is also a philosophical problem par excellence.

The justification for this comparative lexicon of languages currently spoken by over a billion people of the world can be provided at a number of levels:

(1) to bring people closer to the ancient heritage of a Indian language family of which the extant Indian languages (Indo-Aryan, Dravidian and Munda language streams) are but dialectical forms;

(2) to generate further studies in the disciplines of (i) Indian archaeology, (ii) general semantics and comparative linguistics; (iii) design of fifth-generation computer systems; and

(3) to provide a basis for further studies in grammatical philosophy and neurosciences on the formation of semantic patterns or structures in the human brain — neurosciences related to the study of linguistic competence which seems to set apart the humans from other living beings.

The urgent warrant for this work is the difficulty faced by scholars in collating different lexicons and in obtaining classical works such as CDIAL (A Comparative Dictionary of Indo-Aryan Languages) even in eminent libraries.

In tracing the etyma (lit. truth in Greek) of the Indian languages, it is adequate, to start with, to indicate the word forms which can be traced into the mists of history.

Hypotheses on Indian vocabulary

The following hypotheses govern the semantic clustering attempted in this lexicon.

1. It is possible to re-construct a proto-Indian idiom or *lingua franca* of circa the centuries traversed by the Sarasvati-Sindhu doab civilization (c. 2500 to 1700 B.C.E).
2. India is a linguistic area nurtured in the cradle of the Sarasvati-Sindhu doab civilization.

The hypotheses contest two earlier linguistic assertions: (i) Sir William Jones's assertion in 1786 of an Indo-European linguistic family and (ii) Francis Whyte Ellis's assertion in 1816 of a southern Indian family of languages. These two assertions have resulted in two comparative or etymological lexicons of the so-called 'Indo-Aryan' and 'Dravidian' languages. This apparent isolation between the two language families is rejected. The exclusion or isolation of the so-called Austro-Asiatic or Munda (or Kherwāri) languages is also rejected. Instead, it is proposed that there was a proto-Indian linguistic area (c. 2500 B.C.E) which included speakers of these three language groups interacting culturally in the civilizational domain. The underlying assumption is that the so-called Dravidian, Munda and Aryan languages can be traced to an ancient Indian proto-version of Indua language or proto-Indic by establishing the unifying elements, and identifying the substrata in semantic terms. This echoes Pope's observations made in a different context: '... that between the languages of Southern India and those of the Aryan family there are many deeply seated and radical affinities; that the differences between the Dravidian tongues and the Aryan are not so great as between the Celtic (for instance) and the Sanskrit; and that, by consequence, the doctrine that the place of the Dravidian dialects is rather with the Aryan than with the Turanian family of languages is still capable of defence... the resemblances (appeared) most frequently in the more uncultivated Dravidian dialects... the identity (was) most striking in the names of instruments, places, and acts connected with a simple life...' (G.U.Pope, Indian Antiquary; loc. Cit. R. Swaminatha Aiyar, Dravidian Theories, 1922-23, repr., Delhi, Motilal Banarsidass, 1987, pp.11-12).

Methodology and limitations of the work

The methodology to test the hypotheses will be based on the design of a vocabulary super-set (in semantic terms). The governing principle of this lexicon is that phonetic and grammatical laws are subordinate to semantic laws within a language family. Cognates do not have to be concordant in phonetic and morphological forms; cognates have to be concordant in phonetic and semantic forms to suggest linguistic affinity among dialects of a language family. To quote, Tolkāppiyam, "ellāc collum porul. Kuṟittaṉavē" (Tol. Col. Peya. 1), i.e. all words are semantic indicators.

The compounded forms of *sememes* of the *lingua franca* of the Sarasvati-Sindhu doab civilization have been reconstructed from the following sources:

(a) lexical entries of Indian languages found in the comparative, etymological lexicons: CDIAL (A Comparative Dictionary of Indo-Aryan Languages) and DEDR (A Dravidian Etymological Lexicon); etymological groups (as semantic super-sets) culled from lists of ancient verb forms such as those found in the dhātupāṭha, Niruktam, Whitney's lexicon and Vedic lexicon;

(b) lists of ancient noun forms, such as materia medica found in nighaṇṭu's and medical works, annotated with insights from botanical works, pharmacopoeia and works on pharmacognosy ;

(c) epigraphical records of many languages of the region which mainly record economic transactions; and

(d) language lexicons of Indian languages.

This lexicon is organized primarily on a comparative basis and secondarily on a historical basis (and not on a genealogical basis, i.e. not trying to trace the changes in phonetic forms of a sememe). Given the limitations of this organization, it has not been considered essential in this lexicon, to reformulate the old Indian phonetic form with an *. This is an area for further investigations in historical linguistics.

The vocabulary is presented in groups of etyma taken from CDIAL, DEDR, Tamil and other language lexicons of Dravidian, Aryan and Munda languages. The etymological groups are put together as semantic cognates and it will be left for future research work to determine the nature of the interactions (or what linguists call, using a pecuniary term: 'borrowing') between and among the languages which constituted the proto-Indian linguistic area. The results of the research are restricted to the identification, in a comparative lexicon, of comparative *sememes* and morphemes, including many allomorphs (i.e. two or more forms of a morpheme). An attempt to conjecture or decipher the possible*proto-Indian* 'phonetic' forms will require further studies and research work. The results of these studies will help for e.g. (1) to eliminate duplicate semantic clusters included in this lexicon and (2) to re-group the clusters in a true syllabic sequence.

For 'alphabetical` indexing or 'areal` (i.e. by geographical regions) sequencing, Turner's A Comparative Dictionary of Indo-Aryan Languages (CDIAL), Burrow and Emeneau's A Dravidian Etymological Lexicon (DEDR), Pali, Sanskrit, Kannada, Tamil, Munda, Santali and other lexicons of Indian languages are unsurpassed sources. DEDR solves the problem of sequencing by using Tamil morphemes as the reference base for the entire group in Tamil syllabic order. In effect, the vocabulary of this lexicon, include many CDIAL and DEDR entries as sub-sets and constitute a semantic index to both CDIAL and DEDR which will continue to provide the basic references to areal etyma.

The primary justification for choosing a simple sequencing based on a limited number of initial vowels/consonants and consonantal combinations (with intervening vowels or nasals) is that each semantic cluster can be treated as a distinct monograph which may provide material for further study of the Indian language family in which there has apparently been an extraordinary semantic affinity between and among related languages.

One substantive problem in organizing the semantic clusters was the problem of 'alphabetical' or 'syllabic' sequencing. It has been difficult to follow a strict alphabetical ordering in this work. This is due to the author's inability to pin down the ancient 'phonetics' of a sememe or to construct a proto-Indian form. This limitation has resulted in some duplication of terms in more than one semantic cluster. The idiosyncratic sequencing is due to the limits of knowledge of the author; the result has been a number of semantic clusters included in the lexicon containing phonetic forms which may not always correspond with the etymological grouping.

Samuel Johnson refers to a lexicographer as an harmless drudge. What a pleasant and glorious drudge! An etymologist is also a drudge but may provoke, hopefully lively, constructive, linguistic disputes among the proponents of dialects of a language family, on issues such as 'true inheritance' or 'great antiquity'! The disputes (or positive creative tensions), may also draw inspiration and guidance from the past linguistic studies of great scholars who have provided valuable insights into the phonological, grammatical and lexical aspects of a proto-Indian language family.

An English semantic index has been included. The index is composed of (i) English meanings, and (ii) flora (names of botanical species in Latin terms), plants and products of plants (in English and vernacular terms which have entered the English lexicon). As in DEDR, no attempt has been made to state the equivalence of Latin flora terms; DEDR entries in a group of etyma record the equivalence found in Hooker at the end of the numbered etymological group.

The index is primarily based on the elegantly designed index of A Dravidian Etymological Lexicon (DEDR). To quote from DEDR: (p.773) "This is an index of the more important meanings recorded for words in the Dravidian languages. No attempt has been made to list all the English meanings given in the entries, since such a procedure would have swollen this index beyond all reason. In fact, in any attempt to keep it within bounds, usually only one of a group of synonyms or near-synonyms has been listed: e.g. *resemble* is listed, but not *similar* and *like*... The derivational system of English words, since it does not coincide with that of Dravidian, has in general been ignored..."

Organization of the work

The dominance of economic activities in the lives of ancient Indians will be apparent from the semantic clusters compiled in this lexicon. Semantic clusters include words expressing cognate 'thoughts'.

The ancient economic court was dominated by plant products such as fragrances, incenses and exudations which were highly valued and in great demand. For example, the ancient Egyptian civilization records trans-continental expeditions to pw'nt (or punt) in search of such plant products which may be designated as Kubera's nava-nidhi or nine treasures of Kubera, in the yakṣa tradition of great antiquity.

The inclusion of names of many plants and plant products in the lexicon, has a strong justification in terms of ancient life-styles. The etyma related to plants have been elaborated with cross-references on therapeutic effects described in works dealing with the subject of pharmacognosy and, in some instances, the references in pharmacopoeia of various countries have also been provided.

Plants and plant products (gums, gum-resins, fragrances, incenses, plant exudations, bark, in particular) had an extraordinary place in the cultural processes of ancient civilizations (particularly in the Indian linguistic area, in the ancient Egyptian civilization and in the Biblical areas), including for example, the depiction of the so-called nine treasures of Kubera, all of which may relate to plant products. (i) The existence of many nighan.t.us principally devoted to lls des medica of the ancient medical systems and (ii) the archaeological finds of vihāras such as the Ajanta and Ellora caves which might have been used by medicine-men and to stock plant products justify further studies on the economic importance of plant products in cultural history.

Vedic soma was comparable in economic importance to the plants and plant products. In an extraordinary process described eloquently in Vedic chants, soma was purchased, and went through a process kept secret from the seller. Soma was washed in water *(yad-adbhih pariṣicyase mṛjyamāno gabhastyoh-* : RV. Ix.65.6), then pounded either with stone or in a mortar (RV. 1.83.6; RV. 1.28.4); it had amśu(RV. Ix.67.28); it yielded andhas, rasa, pitu, pīyūṣa or amṛta; it was filtered through a strainer (*antah- pavitra āhitah-* : RV. Ix.12.5). It was not 'drunk' by mortals. Soma was the product of an activity using intense fire, and involving the participation of the entire household for days and nights. Soma was wealth.

The dawn of urbanization and transition from agrarian economy to an economy dominated by artisans, are vividly reconstructed from the archaeological finds of the Sarasvati-Sindhu doab civilization which may also be called the Sarasvati-Sindhu civilization. A pen picture with exquisite photographs is provided in the Age of God-Kings:

"About 2500 BCE, a people of unknown origin started constructing a series of cities as remarkable as any the world had yet seen. Artisans set to work, trade flourished and a system of writing evolved. At its apogee, the Indus (Sarasvati-Sindhu) civilization encompassed nearly 1.3 million square kilometers; its boundaries stretched from the foothills of the Himalayas to the Arabian Sea and from the Ganges watershed to the Gulf of Bombay, just to the north of what is now Bombay. It was the largest cultural domain of its era... This people also perfected the art of casting objects in bronze, a breakthrough in technology that ranks among humankind's greatest early achievements... The pictographic script of the Indus (Sarasvati-Sindhu) people has not yet been successfully deciphered. The Southeast Asian rice farmers seem not to have developed a system of writing... the Indus (Sarasvati-Sindhu) people... built grand cities, centers of production and trade... One of these cities... Harappa (Sarasvati-Sindhu)... around 2300 BC, Harappa (Sarasvati-Sindhu) was home to 35,000 people... Another great city took shape 550 kilometers to the south, on the lower Indus (Sarasvati-Sindhu)... Mohenjo-Daro — 'Hill of the Dead' in Sindhi... Two gateways provided access through the wall. Within the citadel were assembly halls, administrative offices and a number of residences for various officials and functionaries. Only an enormous collective effort could have created these two great urban centers of the Indus (Sarasvati-Sindhu) culture... The huge complexes at Mohenjo-Daro and Harappa (Sarasvati-Sindhu) that are believed to be municipal granaries covered thousand upon thousand of square meters. They had raised brick floors... and strong, timbered roofs to protect against the weather. The apparent threshing areas nearby were paved in brick and included circular pits where workers pounded the kernels with wooden staves to remove the husks from the grain... The harvest was probably a state monopoly, and the granaries served, in effect, as state treasuries... They were the world's first people to grow cotton and to weave its fibre into textiles... Trading posts were established far beyond the valley's fringes. The Indus (Sarasvati-Sindhu) people founded a settlement at Sutkagen Dor, west of Baluchistan and within reach of the Persian Gulf. To the south of the valley, a large seaport took shape at Lothal on the Gulf of Cambay... From Lothal, high-prowed, double-ended sailing vessels carried the gold, gems and timber products of southern India along the coast to the Sarasvati-Sindhu doab and beyond. The richest trade route from the valley lay to the west, through the Persian Gulf to Mesopotamia. Starting about 2350 BC, traffic with the urban centers of Sumer and Akkad expanded to become a prime source of revenue... Merchants used sets of cubical stone weights that never varied in value throughout the Indus (Sarasvati-Sindhu) region. The basic unit was 16, equal to 14 grams. The larger weights were multiples of 16 — 32,64,128, and so on up to 12,800 (11 kilograms); the smaller ones were all fractions of 16... The Indus (Sarasvati-Sindhu) merchants, like their Sumerian counterparts, developed a method of record keeping and used carved stone seals to stamp their property. Every mercantile family had its own device, and probably every important citizen did also. More than 2,000 examples have been found in the Indus (Sarasvati-Sindhu) cities, and others have turned up in Mesopotamia, left there by overseas traders... One popular motif appears to have been a unicorn sniffing at an incense burner. The unicorn is probably a bull in profile, so that one horn hides the other. But why the creature has been offered incense is a puzzlement. In a seal from Mohenjo-Daro, both the unicorn and the incense brazier are being carried aloft in some kind of procession... the Indus (Sarasvati-Sindhu) tongue is lost in antiquity and none of the signs (on seals) corresponds to any used by the Egyptians or Sumerians. The seal inscriptions are brief — one or two lines... The Indus (Sarasvati-Sindhu) people left no surviving histories, no religious texts, no literary epics... (Harappa (Sarasvati-Sindhu)n merchants used the seals as a kind of trademark impressing them on clay tags to label their goods)... after each catastrophe (earthquake or flood), the citizens picked up their lives again. Some sections of Mohenjo-Daro were rebuilt as many as eight times. In each reconstruction, the architects re-created the previous construction virtually brick for brick... Sometime during the nineteenth century BC, however, the Indus (Sarasvati-Sindhu) cities began to slip into permanent decline... Scribes in Mesopotamia recorded rich shipments from the Sarasvati-Sindhu doab until around 1800 BCE, when they suddenly ceased... The urban heritage was passed on to the east... somber notes of Harappa (Sarasvati-Sindhu)n ideology would continue to reverberate through the coming centuries." (The Age of God-kings, 3000-1500 B.C.E, Amsterdam, Time-Life Books, 1991, pp. 129-141).

Archaeology and Language

One approach suggested by Colin Renfrew is a correlation, however hypothetically, of language changes with demographic and social changes recorded by archaeology. Decipherment of the script is important to bring the civilization within the bounds of history, and to establish that the civilization should not remain categorized as 'prehistoric'. For, 'pre-historic' would mean 'prior to the use of writing.' (cf. Colin Renfrew, Archaeology and Language: the Puzzle of Indo-European Origins, Penguin Books, 1987, p.2). If this lexicon has established that the Indian language family had closely related members, it should be reasonable to hypothesize that the Indus (Sarasvati-Sindhu) Script was related to an ancient language which evolved as one or more dialects of this language, though there is no direct evidence to prove precisely which language was spoken between 2500 to 1700 B.C.E. in the region traversed by this civilization.

"... (Archaeology) is beginning to interest itself in the ideology of early communities: their religions, the way they expressed rank, status and group identity. The question of language is important here... modern linguistics and current processual archaeology offer the opportunity for a new synthesis... (Sarasvati-Sindhu doab Civilization) was a literate civilization... some four hundred signs were found, fifty-three of them used commonly... this suggests that it must be a mixed hieroglyphic and syllabic script rather than a pure syllabic script like Minoan Linear B... not enough (signs) for a true pictographic script like that of the Egyptian hieroglyphs or the Chinese script... are the Sarasvati-Sindhu doab sealstone inscriptions in an early form of Indo-European?... there is no inherent reason why the people of the Sarasvati-Sindhu doab Civilization should not already have been speaking an Indo-European language, the ancestor of the Rigveda... Hypothesis A, then, would carry the history of the Indo-European languages in north India and Iran back to the early bronze-age period in those areas... (Hypothesis B) outlines an alternative... which accepts the likelihood of local farming origins... (and) a process of lite dominance... by well-organized and mobile tribal groups, with a chiefdom organization... while we cannot expect to find direct evidence in the archaeological record for a specific prehistoric language or language group, we can indeed study processes or demographic and social change. It is these processes of change which we may seek, however hypothetically, to correlate with language change in those areas... it is perfectly possible that the languages used in the Sarasvati-Sindhu doab civilization as early as 3000 BCE were already Indo-European... We are talking here of simple peasant farmers, with a restricted range of domestic plants and animals and a limited range of crafts. These may generally have included weaving and pottery-making and other farming skills, but theirs were egalitarian societies... 'segmentary societies,' laying stress on the almost autonomous nature of individual village or neighborhood communities. Naturally there were links and marriage exchanges between these... three issues now remain that we should look at: language origins, language dispersals, and the relationship between archaeology and linguistic studies... " (Colin Renfrew, op cit., pp. 5,7, 183-185, 190-191, 197, 205, 264. 271, 273).

One approach to study *changes* in languages is to cluster the dialects of a language together. Such a clustering is attempted in this lexicon. These clusters provide the basis for further studies to correlate the *changes* in languages with the socio-economic changes established through archaeology.

Language and Script

An attempt to link the Indus (Sarasvati-Sindhu) Script to the Indian etyma, is a search for Indian linguistic roots. It is, in effect, a search for words which are 'as old as time`.

Many scripts of the current Indian languages are syllabic in structure. It is notable that Tamil, in particular, utilizes a remarkably compact alphabet (syllabary derived via grantha forms from the *Brāhmī* script); for example, the script symbol for the syllable, ka connotes a phonetic spectrum of ka, kha, ga and gha. The use of a limited number of script symbols for syllables is perhaps an indication that, even if the phoneme (for a given morpheme) had a ka, kha, ga or gha, the semantic content remained unaltered. This extraordinary economy (yet, diversity) in script form is, therefore, an indication that for effective linguistic communication of a message, phonetic formants are subordinate to the semantic structure of morphemes.

Many ancient scripts were evolved on the principle of 'ideographs', i.e. depicting a word as an image (logo, on a seal, for example) using a homophone (i.e. a similar sounding word). The importance of 'images' in formulating 'meaning' (in neuronal structures) or for designing 'scripts', is paralleled by a distinct semantic structural feature of Santali language in which words are not uniquely marked for specific functions such as noun or verb but most stems of words are multifunctional. There is no grammatical gender for nouns which may be lexically marked (using for example, *herel* for male; *maejiu* for female). There are no formal marks for grammatical class, a word can perform various functions: as noun, as adjective or as verb. In Santali, every stem or root (sememe) is potentially a verb. Qualifiers can be constructed by simply adding —n for e.g. *kaḍawan hoṛ* 'a man who has buffaloes'. (George L. Campbell, Compendium of the World's Languages, Routledge, London, 1991, p. 1199). "In Santali, any word may (in theory at least) be used as a verb simply by adding *a*, which is the verbal sign, and other signs to signify tense, mood etc. The *a* alone signifies the general or future tense in the active voice — used to make general statements, or statements referring to the future... The verb generally comes at the end of a sentence or phrase... (Santali language) consists of root-words and various infixes, suffixes and particles, joined together or agglutinated in such a way as to form phrases and sentences... dalgot'kedeae... dal the root word, meaning to strike or striking; got' an adverbial particle giving the sense of quickly or suddenly; ked the sign ket', denoting the past tense of the active voice, modified to ked… e … signifying an animate object — him, or her… a the verbal sign, showing that the idea of striking is used verbally; e the short form of the 3rd personal pronoun, singular… denoting the subject — he, or she." (R.M. Macphail, An Introduction to Santali, 1953, p.2). Taking into account, this historical factor which governed the evolution of alphabets and the important part played by 'root word' in Santali (a member of the ancient Indian family of languages) this lexicon attempts to identify 'sememes' and also provide an aid to epigraphists or scholars interested in deciphering the Indus (Sarasvati-Sindhu) script. For this purpose (and based on the assumption that the Indus (Sarasvati-Sindhu) script may be related to the Indian language family), many semantic clusters in this lexicon include, what are titled as, 'image' words, i.e. word forms which could have been represented graphically, as in the symbols and signs used in the as-yet undeciphered Indus (Sarasvati-Sindhu) script. Such 'image' clusters are sequenced close to the other substantive clusters which are related to life-activities of ancient civilizations as evidenced by archaeological finds and artifacts. The titles provided to many semantic clusters with the prefix 'image' refer to a number of images provided by the pictographs and signs of the seals and tablets containing Indus (Sarasvati-Sindhu) script. Such pictographs and signs will be clustered to aid those interested in deciphering the script. At this stage of the author's knowledge, it has not been possible to include some thoughts on 'alternative interpretations' of these 'ideographs' of the Indus (Sarasvati-Sindhu) script. This work, *Indian Hieroglyphs*, is presented providing an approach to breaking the deadlock of the decipherment problem. A start can be made assuming that each pictograph is a homonym (i.e. an image of a similar sounding 'substantive' word). Many 'substantives' are indeed based on the economic activities of an evolving civilization.

'Rosetta Stone' of the Script: Umma seal

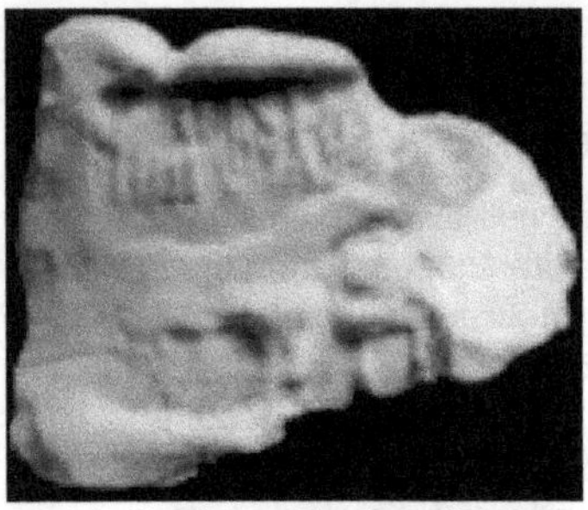

Seal Impression of an Indus 'one-horned heifer + standard device' seal thought to come from Tell Umma (Djoka). Text of inscription (9811).

Gadd 1 from Ur. Image of bison. Seal impression and reverse of

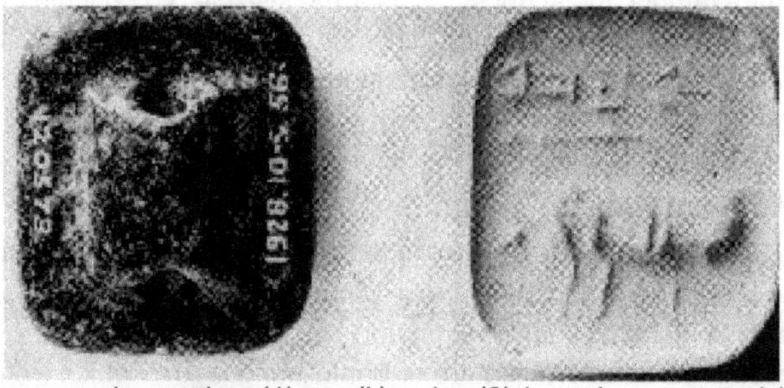

Ur seal (with pierced lug handle) from (U.7683; BM 120573); image of bison and cuneiform inscription; length 2.7, width 2.4, ht. 1.1 cm. cf. Gadd, PBA 18 (1932), pp. 5-6, pl. I, no.1; Mitchell 1986: 280-1 no.7 and fig. 111; Parpola, 1994, p. 131: signs may be read as (1) *sag(k)* or *ka,* (2) *ku* or *lu* or *ma*, and (3) *zi* or *ba (4)?*. SAG.KU(?).IGI.X or SAG.KU(?).P(AD)(?) The commonest value: *sag-ku-zi* A rebus reading can be hypothesized as a possible trade contact: sag (Akkadian), 'head'; कुसितः, कुसी (सि) द 1 An inhabited country. -2 One who lives on usury (Sanskrit).

On the problem of the Indus (Sarasvati-Sindhu) Script, it is important to refer to one message on a sealing from Umma, since no bilingual script messages have so far been found: "…an imprint of (Indus (Sarasvati-Sindhu)) seal upon the fragment of a clay label from a bale of cloth had also been published by Father Scheil (Revue d'Assyriologie, Vol. 22: 56), and this was said to come from the site of Umma, the neighbor city of Lagash…No.1. First among the seals discovered at Ur (in 1923) is the unique object …in the British Museum…On the face stands, below, the figure of a bull with head bent down…the inscription…is in archaic cuneiform writing…of a period before 2500 B.C. There are three signs and very probably traces of a fourth, almost obliterated; the three preserved are themselves scratchy and rather worn, though not ill-formed. Hence their reading is doubtful—the choices are, for the first SAG(K) or KA, for the second KU or possibly LU, while the third is almost certainly S'I, and the fourth, it existed at all, is quite uncertain...using the commonest values of the signs, sak-ku-s'i—(with possible loss of something at the end) may be pronounced the best provisional reading...It does not, at least, seem to be any Sumerian or Akkadian name...(the seal is) probably, a product of some place under the influence both of Indus (Sarasvati-Sindhu) and of the Sumerian civilizations." (Gadd, 1932, pp.3-32.)

Hunter noted that three round seals with Harappa (Sarasvati-Sindhu)n characters found in Mesopotamia may not be in Harappan (Sarasvati-Sindhu) language since there were marked differences in the sequence of letters. (Hunter, 1932, p.469.) Analogously, an Indus (Sarasvati-Sindhu)-type seal (squarish with a perforated button on the ridged back) with cuneiform characters may be surmised to relate to a non-Harappa (Sarasvati-Sindhu) language. The non-Harappa (Sarasvati-Sindhu)n origin is surmised for a glazed steatite cylinder seal found at Tell Asmar, which shows an Indus (Sarasvati-Sindhu) motif: procession of an elephant, a rhinoceros and a crocodile. (Frankfort, 1933, pp.50-53; Asthana, 1979, p.40.) Ur III texts indicate the need for interpreters to translate the Meluhhan language. Alternatively, the cuneiform characters were meant to be used by a Meluhhan settler in Umma for trade transactions with the Akkadian literate groups.

These are tentative interpretations which will have to be further validated by an evaluation of the entire (though, very limited — only about six thousand -- sample of messages without committing what Gilbert Ryle calls a 'category mistake.' An approach to a resolution of the decipherment problem has been attempted in *Indus Script Cipher* (S. Kalyanaraman, 2010), using, mainly, the semantic and image clusters of the Indian lexicon. The present work is a sequel to this book and provides a set of examples of Indian hieroglyphs starting with the invention of rebus writing from c. 3500 BCE, almost coterminu with the invention of Egyptian hieroglyphs of Nar-mer palette, c. 3300 BCE.

Semantics and Poets' search for the supreme language

To aid researchers in linguistics and neuro-scientists interested in the study of brain functions related to linguistic competence, some principal sememes of ancient speech are listed in separate annexes of this lexicon. This is consistent with the principal focus of this lexicon which is to: cluster together word forms with comparable semantic content and establish the essential semantic unity among the Indian languages. In this process of semantic clustering, attention is paid to concordant phonetic forms.

In evaluating the development of pronunciation and sense of words of the languages of the Indian linguistic area, an effort has been made to avoid duplicating the functions of lexicography. The focus is on 'meaning' of words, extensions of meaning and on phonetic transforms cognate with the basic words.

Lexicographers have attempted to define the phonetic structure of a morpheme in a language, with care and integrity, given the constraints of the phonetic symbols used for the script of the chosen language. This lexicon proceeds on the assumption that the language lexicons which are its source books, are based on painstaking social surveys and provide a commonly accepted form (i.e. through social contract) of the phonetic variants of various dialects of any one language. Since the focus is on semantics, the author has exercised a degree of freedom to coalesce the phonetic variations and as necessary, repeated some etyma in more than one semantic cluster. Speakers of every language and poets, in particular, of every language do possess enormous degrees of freedom for verbal creativity to anchor life experiences, but subject to the social contract on *sememes* or the 'meaning' of morphemes used in inter-personal verbal or written communication.

Take for instance, the rules of Sanskrit language, codified by the linguistic genius, Pāṇini and obeyed through literary media for over a millennium. Pāṇini's phonological and morphological canons are hypostatized (attributed real identities to a concept) aphorisms. Pāṇini was held in such awe that later linguists would not refer to what Pāṇini 'says' but use the verb 'paśyati' referring to his aphorisms [i.e. referring to what Pāṇini 'sees', as a ṛṣi or seer]. Pāṇini opposes the *bhāṣā*, defined by him in an archaic chandah- (cf. S. Lvi, J.A., 1891, II, p. 549; *Memoires de la Societe de Linguistic de Paris*, XVI, p.278-279; loc. Cit. Bloch, *The Formation of the Marāṭhī Language*, 1914, p.3). "... in the enumeration of Bharata (XVII, 48): *māgadhyavantijā prācyāsūryasenyardhamāgadhī bāhlīkā dākṣiṇātyā ca sapta bhāṣāh- prakīrtitāh-*"six out of seven are geographically determinable and three out of these four (*māgadhī, śaurasenī, Mahārāṣṭrī*) are mentioned by Vararuci. Later on Daṇḍin adds to these three *Lāṭī* 'and similar other ones' (*Kāvyādarśa*, I,35)... Later on Vararuci situates the Paiśācī on the same level as the three great Prākṛts with a geographical name... the language of braj is used for the cycle of kṛṣṇa, that of Bundelkhand for that of ālhā-ūdal, that of Avadha for that of Rāma and generally speaking for the Epic... No region of India has imposed its language on the entire country... within each dialect there is a large quantity of words or series of words which have had a history independent of the dialects where they have been found in use. This history, which can be established with some difficulty even in the case of well-known languages as those of Europe, is altogether impossible, at least provisionally, in India... " (Bloch, op cit., pp. 11-12; p.45). In making bold to attempt this 'impossible' task through semantics, one dominant structural characteristic of the Indian language family can be noted with confidence: the use of 'echo words' identified as such in this lexicon. (Pāṇini calls such words āmreḍita or repeated : Bk. VIII. Ch. 1.2). The tendency to repeat words or with fine initial consonantal variations is a characteristic that runs across the entire family of languages, a characteristic that was also noted by Vararuci. The ancient linguists tried to delineate this 'refined' language as the 'perfect' language (whether divinely inspired *smṛti* 'remembered' or *śruti* 'heard'); yet, the spoken word was governed by the inexorable laws of neurosciences and social contract — as evidenced by the Prākṛts (original or natural forms) which did not obey these 'rules' of the grammarian though adored by the linguists. The Prākṛts (including Pali) continued to diverge from the 'perfection' of Sanskrit and were socio-linguistically accepted in Sanskrit drama in the early centuries of the Christian era, though not spoken by gods or heroes in the dramas, but only by the proletariat! Women sang in *Mahārāṣṭrī* Prākṛt, spoke in *śaurasenī* Prākṛt and people in the lower rungs of the social ladder spoke *māgadhī* Prākṛt. Many Prākṛts were written in *kharoṣṭī* script. Buddha (c. sixth century B.C.E.) perhaps preached in *ardhamāgadhī* Prākṛt (Pali), written in *brāhmī* script. *Muṇḍāri* and *Santāli* (grouped as Kherwari or Austro-Asiatic) perhaps coexisted with the Indo-European or the so-called Dravidian linguistic presence in India. The Indian language family also includes Gypsy (Romany; gypsy ~~ Egyptian; ethonym: roma). Gypsies popularly believed to have come from Egypt, emigrated from India towards the end of the first millennium C.E. via Iran into Anatolia, South Russia, and the Balkans, to reach western Europe by the fifteenth century, Britain by the sixteenth; via Iran, Syria and the Mediterranean into north Africa and the Iberian peninsula. (George L. Campbell, Compendium of the World's Languages, Routledge, London, 1991, p.1164).

Yāska (6th-4th c. B.C.E), Pa_n.ini (5th c. B.C.), Kātyāyana (3rd c. B.C.E), Patañjali (c. 150 B.C.E) have laid the foundations of Sanskrit etymology and grammar. The s ū tras of Pāṇini analyze Sanskrit into a system of roots, stems and suffixes. Kātyāyana's vārttikas explain, criticize and supplement these rules. Patañjalii's bhāṣya explains the rules of Pāṇini and Kātyāyana and is often severely critical of the latter. Kaiyaṭa commends Patañjali of the three since he has observed more numbers of actual forms : (II.4.26) *munidvayāc ca bhāṣyakārah- pramāṇataram adhikalakṣyadarśitvāt* : the author of the commentary (i.e. Patañjali) has greater authority than the other two sages because he has observed more linguistic usage. Grammatical rules were formulated, perhaps, for the benefit of 'immigrants' or as teaching aids to students of a language. In this process of delineating grammatical rules, the phonetic and morphological structures of each of the Indian languages were codified and frozen as 'rules' of the language. (cf. the example of Tolkāppiyam for Tamil or *aṣṭādhāyī* for Sanskrit). Pāṇini also called Gonadrīya/ Gonikāputra) is perhaps the oldest grammarian of the world. His *aṣṭādhāyī* (lit. 8 chapters with 3,996 mnemonic sūtras) and later critical evaluation/defence by Patañjali (also called, Dākṣīputra in his Mahābhāṣya or Great Prose Work) countering Kātyāyana's criticism in the Vārttikās (explanatory tracts of words) are unsurpassed ancient linguistic explorations into the etyma of and rules governing the Sanskrit language. Pāṇini traces with stunning precision and scholarly excellence, the individual phonetic and morphological changes throughout the language which may be called a language that spanned both Vedic and Classical Sanskrit. (For a good survey of works on

Pāṇini cf. George Cardona, *Pāṇini: A Survey of Research*, 1976; for an excellent reader on the Sanskrit grammarians, cf. Staal, J.F. (ed.), A Reader on the Sanskrit Grammarians, Cambridge, M.I.T. Press, 1972). It would be inappropriate to call *Pāṇini's* Sanskrit brahminical or Aryan; for he notes (Ch. VI, 62,58) that there were non-Aryan speakers as well! The contributions made by ancient Indian linguists are echoes of the oral tradition of *padapāṭha-s* (i.e. the word texts which give every word of the samhitā free from euphonic combinations and analyze compounds into their component morphemes) of the Vedic chants which are as old as civilization itself. There are other linguistic tracts, in particular in the so-called Dravidian family of languages and in the so-called Austro-Asiatic family of languages (exemplified in India by Mundarica and Santali languages), which preserve the echoes of the ancient speech which sustained ancient civilizations such as the Sarasvati-Sindhu doab civilization.

Yāska is perhaps the first etymologist of the world. His Niruktam treats etymology as a complement of grammar (*tad idam vidyā-sthānam vyākaraṇasya kārtsnyam* : N. i.15) and is a principal aid to understanding Vedic texts. According to Yāska, grammatical rules are not universal; too much importance should not be attached to the grammatical form because, the complex formations (vṛttayah-) have many exceptions; he is a bold etymologist who derives iṣṭi (sacrifice) from yaj (to sacrifice) based on the meanings of words in the context of their use. His principal rule in general semantics is direct: 'If their meanings are the same, their etymologies should be the same, if the meanings are different, the etymologies should also be different (N. ii.7); 'words are used to designate objects with regard to everyday affairs in the world, on account of their comprehensiveness and minuteness (N. i.2)[Durga, the commentator, explains 'comprehensiveness' as a psychological process (manifest and unmanifest states of consciousness) to apprehend meaning through the instrumentality of the spoken word; the process is elaborated: manifest consciousness is expressed through an effort of exhalation of breath, modification of speech-organs to produce the word; the word pervades the unmanifest consciousness of the hearer, makes it manifest and the meaning is apprehended. Durga also comments on the term 'minuteness': movements of hands and the winking of the eyes etc. are also comprehensive; they will express the meaning and in this manner there will be no need to study grammar and the Vedic texts! But these are not minute, i.e. these communication modes are not definitive (or accurate) and are not economical in the effort in production.] Yāska notes the four word-classes, noun, verb, preposition and particle and adds: ... śākaṭāyana holds that nouns are derived from verbs. This, too, is the doctrine of the etymologists. 'Not at all,' says Gargya and some of the grammarians, 'but only those, the accent and grammatical form of which are regular and which are accompanied by an explanatory radical modification.' Those (nouns), such as cow, horse, man, elephant etc. are conventional (terms, and hence are underivable)(Ni. 1.12). Pāṇini combines particles (avyaya, 195 in number) and prepositions into one category, nipāta (Bk. I, Ch. IV, 56). According to Yāska, particles are of three types: (i) of comparison (upama), (ii) of adding or putting together of the senses or ideas (karmopasamgraha or semantic sub-clusters), (iii) of expletives which do not express any meaning (kam, īm, id, u and iva). Yāska notes that the verb has 'becoming' as its fundamental notion; and that the noun has 'being' as its fundamental notion and recalls that according to Audumbarāyaṇa speech is permanent in the organs only. This statement of Audumbarāyaṇa is fundamental in understanding the neural bases of linguistic competence.

Tamil (a primary member of the so-called Dravidian languages) is an ancient language. This lexicon contains a number of references from Tamil works, acknowledging the antiquity of the language and its importance as a dominant member of the Indian linguistic area. Similar references are provided from Vedic texts in many etyma groups. The rich ancient Tamil literature (which dates back to the San:gam age of c. the first millennium C.E.) includes Tolkāppiyam (?c. 5th century CE), a grammar and socio-linguistic tract; the fifth-century work, Tiruvaḷḷuvar's Tirukkuraḷ, śaiva religious works such as Tiruvācakam and Tirumantiram; existential expositions such as Puṟanāṉūru, Akanāṉūru (400 poems each on social and family lives); Pattuppāṭṭu (ten songs) and Eṭṭuttokai (eight anthologies) delineating love and war as facets of life. To quote Caldwell who relates a study of this language to the comparative grammatical structures of a family of the so-called Dravidian languages: "Does there not seem to be reason for regarding the Dravidian family of languages, not only as a link of connection between the Indo-European and Scythian groups, but — in some particulars, especially in relation to the pronouns —

as the best surviving representative of a period in the history of human speech older than the Indo-European stage, older than the Scythian and older than the separation of the one from the other... The orientalists who supposed the Dravidian languages to be derived from Sanskrit were not aware of the existence of uncultivated languages of the Dravidian family, in which Sanskrit words are not at all, or but very rarely, employed... Another evidence consists in the extraordinary copiousness of the Tamil vocabulary, and the number and variety of the grammatical forms of Shen-Tamil. The Shen-Tamil grammar is a crowded museum of obsolete forms, cast-off inflexions, and curious anomalies... It is a different question whether some of the Dravidian forms and roots may not have formed a portion of the linguistic inheritance, which appears to have descended to the earliest Dravidian from the fathers of the human race." (Caldwell's Comparative Grammar of the Dravidian Family of Languages, p.x, p.45, p.82). In Tolkāppiyam, Tamil does include the so-called vaṭacol (or northern words): *vaṭacoṟ kiḷavi vaṭaleḻut torī eṟuttoṭu puṇarnta collākumme* : Tol. Col. 395, i.e. 'northern' words are those words which shed their scripts and are adapted; this is distinguished from 'dialectical' words (*centamiḻ ... ticai-c-coṟ kiḷavi*) in vogue in the twelve territories of the Tamil land with regional variations and two other kinds of words: iyaṟ-col, tiri-col (primitives and derivatives) used in poetry (ceyyuḷ).

This lexicon establishes the possibility of tracing the etyma for both the agglutinative and inflexional types of languages. The inflexional languages such as Sanskrit and languages influenced significantly by Sanskrit show a myriad morphological variants. Unlike CDIAL which breaks out the inflexional variants under 'head words' based on assumed 'root words' with an *, the *Indian Lexicon* clusters the variants under semantic clusters. [Thus, for example, vij (move suddenly) can be clustered with vēga speed and vīj or vyaj 'fan' and vizun 'to sift, winnow' (K.) As far as practicable, only words listed in the language lexicons are included in the semantic clusters of this lexicon, without making any attempt to derive the ancient phonetic form of the Indic sememe or a proto-Indian reconstruction of a morpheme with an *.] This lexicon, as does R.L. Turner's A Comparative Dictionary of Indo-Aryan languages (CDIAL), includes a number of words from the Vedic texts, attesting to the great antiquity of many semantic clusters which are also concordant with the archaeological artifacts unearthed from the Sarasvati-Sindhu doab civilization and other Indian archaeological explorations. An early attempt to trace the 'sememes' was made in works such as the *Dhātupāṭha* for Sanskrit and in the brilliant work of the Vedic scholars of the nineteenth and twentieth centuries (following the tradition of Sāyaṇa in the ṛgveda bhāṣyabhūmikā of an earlier century) who have successfully established the semantic contents of the Vedic texts, proving Yāska right: "Vedic stanzas are significant, because (their) words are identical (with those of the spoken language)..." (Nirukta 1.16). Sāyaṇa makes a similar comment in his preface to the ṛgveda: *vākyārtho lokavedayoraviśiṣṭah-* (the meaning of expressions of the Vedic Sanskrit and of the popular speech is not different) and also notes: '*abhidhānērthavādah-* there is a figurative description in such expressions... this is very frequently employed in poetical compositions. For instance, a river is described as having a pair of cakravāka birds for her breasts, a row of swans for her teeth, a kāsa plant for her garment, and moss for her hair. Similarly, the Vedic texts invoking inanimate objects should be construed as implying praise...' It can be hypothesized that soma was a similar 'figurative description'.

## Grammatical philosophy

Some leads are available to explore further the concept of 'meaning' in philosophical and linguistic terms. "homo foneticus indicus was no mere cross-sectioned larynx sited under an empty cranium... on the contrary, the whole man, belly, heart and head, produced voice" (J.E.B. Gray 1959, "An Analysis of Nambudiri R.gvedic Recitation and the Nature of the Vedic Accent", Bulletin of the School of Oriental and African Studies 22, pp. 499-530) A word points to an external object, as a semantic indicator; it also refers to the intention of the speaker. One technical term is 'artha' which may be a synonym of 'meaning'. "For the grammarian, 'artha' does not mean the external reality but whatever the word brings to the mind. Artha does not mean vastvarttha but śabdārtha, not reality, but, the meaning of words. Individual words bring something to the mind and the sentence as a whole also brings something to the mind. But these things are included in the expression 'śabdārtha'. Grammar studies both these things in order to evolve notions which will explain the forms of the language. Grammar is satisfied if these notions conform to what we understand from words, no matter whether they conform to reality or not. Grammar does not look at reality directly in the face. As Helārāja puts it: *śabdapramāṇakānām. hi śabda eva hi yathārtham abhidhatte tathaiva tasyābhidhānam upapannam; na tu vastumukhaprakṣatayā* : for to those whose authority is the word, the word designates what it corresponds to, and its designation is accordingly appropriate; but it is not for looking reality directly in the face (Helārāja on *Vākyapadīya* III. Sam.. verse 66)... Thus while explaining the different conceptions of Time mentioned by Bharttr.hari in the Ka_lasamuddes'a such as that it is an entity which exists apart from the mind or that it is a mere construction of the human mind, Helārāja says that Bharttṛhari is not really concerned with what time is philosophically, but that he is anxious to examine and analyze that something which is responsible for our putting the Sanskrit verb in different tenses as in abhūt (was), asti (is) and bhaviṣyat (will be). That something may not be able to stand close philosophical scrutiny, but if it serves the purpose of explaining the different tenses, one would have to accept it (Helārāja on *Vākyapadīya*. III. Kā. 58). Similarly in the kriyāsamuddeśa, the question is: What is action? The answer given by Bharttṛhari on the basis of the Bhāṣya passages is that it is a process, something having parts arranged in a temporal sequence. It is not directly perceptible, but it is to be inferred... These parts may be further subdivided and the smaller parts will also be actions. There will come a time when the part cannot be further sub-divided. It cannot then be called action at all. Only that can be called action which has parts arranged in a temporal sequence. After having clearly explained all this, Helārāja adds that for grammarians the real question is not whether an action has actually parts or not, but whether the verb presents it as such. The answer is that verbs do present action, however momentary, in nature, as something having parts which cannot co-exist but are arranged in a temporal sequence. And Vaiyākaraṇas go by what the words present to us. (Helārāja on *Vākyapadīya*. III. Kri. 10)." (Subramania Iyer, K.A., "The Point of View of the Vaiyākaraṇas", Journal of Oriental Research, 18, pp.84-96, 1948).

Vyāḍi (Sarvadarśana-samgraha, Bibliographica Indica, pp. 140-4) notes that since letters by themselves cannot convey meaning, a unifying factor can be hypothesized; the factor (sphoṭa) which is all-pervading and exists independent of letters. Sphoṭa is the idea which bursts out or flashes on the mind when a sound is uttered, the impression produced on the mind at hearing a sound: *budhair vaiyākaraṇah- pradhāna bhūta sphoṭa rūpavyan:gyajakasya śabdasya dhviniriti vyavahārah kṛtah* (*Kāvyaprakāśa*. 1; it is also the eternal sound recognized by the Mīmāmsakas or inquirers (Skt. Lex.) It connotes the relationship between sounds and meaningful words. Sphuṭati śate'rtho' sma_d iti sphoṭo vācaka iti yāvat (Koṇḍabhaṭṭa, *Vyākaraṇa-bhūṣaṇa* (Bombay, 1915, p. 236); Nāgeśabhaṭṭa, *Sphoṭavāda* (Adyar Library, 1946), p.5). Mādhava,*Sarvadarśanasamgraha* (ed. Abhyankar, p. 300), gives the double explanation that the sphoṭa is revealed by the letters, and itself reveals the meaning: *sphuṭyate vyajyate varṇair iti sphoṭo varṇābhivyangyah-, sphuṭati sphuṭī bhavaty asmād artha iti sphoṭo' rthapratyāyakah-*. "The sphoṭa then is simply the linguistic sign in its aspect of meaning-bearer (*bedeutungstrager*). The termsphoṭa occurs first in the *Mahābhāṣya*, Nāges'a ascribed the doctrine to Sphoṭāyana, who is quoted by Pāṇini (vi.1.123) on a point of morphology... the sphoṭa (the unchanging substratum) is the word, the sound is merely an attribute of the word. How? Like a drum-beat. When a drum is struck, one drum-beat may travel twenty feet, another thirty, another forty. But the sphoṭa is of precisely such and such a size, the increase in length is caused by the sound... Patajañli's sphoṭa (except in so far as it is for him the meaning-bearer) is really comparable to Bharttṛhari's prākṛta-dhvani. The commentators, being acquainted with the later theory, naturally point out that the speed of utterance belongs to the vaikṛta-dhvani... Bharttṛhari (*Vākya-padīya* i.44 : *dvāv upādānaśabdeṣu śabdau śabdavido viduh- eko nimittam. śabdānām aparo'rthe prayujyate* : in meaningful language, linguists recognize two (entites which can be called) words: one is the underlying cause of words, the other is attached to the meaning..."

"The Nyāya philosophers... held that the meaning of a word was presented to the mind by the last sound, aided by the memory-impression of the preceding sounds... *Vākya-padīya* i. 75-8: *sphoṭasyābhinnakālasya dhvanikānupātinah-grahaṇopādhibhedena vṛttibhedam pracakṣte;*

*svabhāvabhedān nityatve hrasva-d ī rgha-plutādiṣu prākṛtasya dhvaneh- kālah- s'abdasyety upacaryate; śabdasya grahaṇe hetuḥ prākṛto dhvanir iṣyate sthitibhedanimittatvaṃ vaikṛtaḥ pratipadyate śabdasyordhvam abhivyakter vṛttibhedaṃ tu vaikṛtāḥ dhvanayaḥ samupohante sphoṭātmā tair na bhidyate* : According to the differences in the specific cause of its comprehension (in individual instances), men attribute differences in speed of utterance (vṛtti) to the sphoṭa which is not divided in time, and merely reflects the time of the sound. Similarly, in the case of the short, long, and prolate vowels—since, on the view that these are permanent, they are intrinsically distinct—it is the time-pattern of the primary sound which is metaphorically attributed to the word (the sphoṭa) itself. The 'primary sound' (prākṛta-dhvani) is defined as the cause of the perception of the letters (phonemes), the 'secondary sound' (vaikṛta-dhvani, literally 'modified') is the causal factor underlying differences of diction. But it is only after the word has been revealed that the secondary sounds are presented to the mind as differences of diction; hence (a fortiori) the essential nature of the sphoṭa is not disrupted by these... Mādhava's statement : *varṇātirikto varṇābhivyan:gyo' rthapratyāyako nityah- śabdah- sphoṭa iti tadvido vadanti* may be translated as 'the abiding word which is the conveyor of the meaning... is called the sphoṭa by the grammarians'..." (Brough, John "Theories of General Linguistics in the Sanskrit Grammarians", Transactions of the Philological Society, pp. 27-46, 1951).

Just as sphoṭa (the unchanging substratum or the abiding word which is the conveyor of meaning) explains the impression produced on the mind when a sound is heard, a similar concept can explain the recollection in the mind of a sound similar to the sound heard but with a different meaing. When a person views an Indus script hieroglyph the sounds related to both the glyphic and the rebus cognate sound are impressed on the mind. Thus the glyph bursts out or flashes on the mind with two meanings: one meaning relates to the glyphic itself and the other meaning relates to the rebus, similar sounding sound. In the context of the hieroglyphic writing system, both meanings together constitute the sphoṭa, the unchanging substratum or the word which conveys both 1) a glyphic meaning and 2) a rebus meaning.

The padapāṭha-s break down the samhitā into its constituent words.

Yāska's Nirukta studies the meaning of some of such words. Thus the phonetics of a word and its meaning are integral components of Vedic studies. Vārttika defines a grammatical sentence as eka-tiṇie, possessing one verb. (*Vākyapadīya* ii.3). "The Bhāṭṭa school (of the later Mīmāmsa) on the whole seems to preserve the more primitive attitude. According to them words have in themselves meanings, and as the words are uttered in a sentence, each word performs its task of expressing its meaning, and the sentence is the summation of these meanings. The Prābhākara school, on the other hand, held the more sophisticated theory that the individual words did not express any meaning until they were united together into a sentence. This was upheld by an appeal to the method whereby a child learns its own mother tongue.

They pointed out that it was by hearing sentences 'fetch the cow', 'fetch the horse', and so forth, that the child came gradually to understand that the animal which he saw on each several occasion was, in fact, either a cow or a horse and that the action performed by his elders was the act of fetching. These two views were named respectively abhihitānvaya-vāda and anvitābhidhāna-vāda, terms which are troublesome to translate by concise English expressions. Roughly speaking, the first is the theory that the sentence is 'a series of expressed word-meanings', and the second is that the sentence is 'the expressed meaning of a series (of words)' ... At the beginning of the second book of the *Vākyapadīya*, Bharttṛhari gives a list of definitions and quasi-definitions of a sentence. Five of these are grouped by the commentator under the traditional Mīmāmsa designations. Thus the view that the sentence is a unified collection (samghāta) and the view that it is an ordered series are aspects of the abhihitānvaya-vāda; while the other three belong to the anvitābhidhāna-vāda. These are, that the sentence is defined by a verbal expression (ākhyāta-s'abda) or by the first word (padamādyam) or by all the words taken separately with the feature of mutual requirement or expectancy superadded (pṛthak sarvapadam. Sṛkānkṣam). All these views, of course, imply the feature of expectancy, and the first and second are to be explained with reference to this feature, since the verb or the first word is only what it is in view of its ties with the other words in its own sentence. All these theories are adversely criticized by Bharttṛhari...

The occurrence of homophones in a language has always provided grammarians with an interesting problem... Bharttṛhari gives a list of such factors, of which the most important are vākya, sentence-context, and prakaraṇa, situational context... historical and comparative studies frequently enable us to glean from texts in related languages useful hints towards this understanding (of meaning)... In the end the utmost that can be said of the meaning of a sentence according to Bharttṛhari is that it is grasped by an instantaneous flash of insight (pratibhā) (*Vākyapadīya*, ii.119,145)... And when we have understood a sentence, we cannot explain to another the nature of this understanding. (*Vākyapadīya*, ii.146: *idam. tad iti sānyeṣam anṣkhyeyṣ kathamcana : pratyātmavṛttisiddhā kartrāpi na nirūpyate* : This (pratibhā) cannot in any way be explained to others in terms such as 'it is this'; its existence is ratified only in the individual's experience of it, and he himself cannot describe it)." (Brough, John, "Some Indian Theories of Meaning", Transactions of the Philological Society, 1953, pp. 161-176).

There is no supreme language; all languages are personal and social experiences of a community.

Yet, every language is governed by an extraordinary phonetic repertoire orchestrated by 'neuronal laws' of the human brain.

The neuronal structures in which verbal creativity is embedded are the common substratum; they are language-neutral. This means, that irrespective of the language used by a speaker, or the language heard by a listener, the neurons and neuronal networks pulsate, governed by the as-yet undefined semantic laws of neurosciences. Man can create poetry; if the poem has to convey meaning to the audience, the poet has to abandon his search for the 'perfect' language and bow to the superior wisdom of the common parlance which is, in effect, the linguistic social contract for which words are but social memory-markers, or '*numeraire facile*.' The private memory-markers in the private language of a speaker's or listener's brain are the product of his life-history which can be 'emotionally' or 'neuronally' experienced.

No scientific technique is relevant, no language is adequate and no poet is competent to communicate the emotions of the 'private language' of the brain.

List of languages covered and abbreviations in the *Indian Lexicon*

Indo-Aryan semantic clusters

A. Assamese
al. Alashai dialect of Pashai
amg. Ardhamāgadhī Prakrit
Ap. Apabhraṁśa
Ar. Arabic
Ār. Aryan, i.e. Indo-iranian
ar. Areti dialect of Pashai
Aram. Aramaic
Arm. Armenian
arm. Armenian dialect of Gypsy
as. Asiatic dialects of Gypsy
Aś. Aśokan, i.e. the language of the Inscriptions of Aśoka
Ash. Ashkun (Aṣkū̃ — Kaf.)
Austro-as. Austro-asiatic
Av. Avestan (Iranian)
Aw. Awadhī
awāṇ. Awāṇkārī dialect of Lahndā
B. Bengali (Baṅglā)
Bal. Balūčī (Iranian)
bāṅg. Bāṅgarū dialect of Western Hindī
Bashg. Bashgalī (Kaf.)
bh. Bairāṭ Bhābrū Minor Rock Edict of Aśoka
bhad. Bhadrawāhī dialect of West Pahāṛī
bhal. Bhalesī dialect of West Pahāṛī
bhaṭ. Bhaṭèālī sub-dialect of Ḍogrī dialect of Panjābī
bhiḍ. Bhiḍlàī sub-dialect of Bhadrawāhī dialect of West Pahāṛī
Bhoj. Bhojpurī
BHSk. Buddhist Hybrid Sanskrit
Bi. Bihārī
bir. Birir dialect of Kalasha
boh. Bohemian dialect of European Gypsy
Brah. Brāhūī (Dravidian)
Brj. Brajbhāṣā
bro. Brokpā dialect of Shina
Bshk. Bashkarīk (Dard.)
bul. Bulgarian dialect of European Gypsy
Bur. Burushaski
cam. Cameāḷī dialect of West Pahāṛī
Chil. Chilīs (Dard.)
chil. Chilasi dialect of Shina or of Pashai
cur. Curāhī dialect of West Pahāṛī
Ḍ. Ḍumāki
dar. Darrai-i Nūr dialect of

Pashai
Dard. Dardic
dh. Dhauli Rock Inscription of Aśoka
Dhp. Gāndhārī or Northwest Prakrit (as recorded in the Dharmapada ed. J. Brough, Oxford 1962)
Dm. Dameli (Damɛ̃ḍī´ — Kaf.-Dard.)
ḍoḍ. Ḍoḍī (Sirājī of Ḍoḍā), a dialect of Kashmiri in Jammu
ḍog. Ḍogrī dialect of Panjābī
dr. Drās dialect of Shina
Drav. Dravidian
Eng. English
eng. English dialect of European Gypsy
eur. European (Gypsy)
Fr. French
G. Gujarātī
Ga. Gadba (Dravidian)
Garh. Gaṛhwālī
Gau. Gauro (Dard.)
gav. Gavīmaṭh Inscription of Aśoka
Gaw. Gawar-Bati (Dard.)
germ. German dialect of European Gypsy
ghis. Ghisāḍī dialect of wandering blacksmiths in Gujarat
gil. Gilgitī dialect of Shina
gir. Girnār Rock Inscription of Aśoka
Gk. Greek
Gmb. Gambīrī (Kaf.)
gng. Gaṅgoī dialect of Kumaunī
Goth. Gothic
gr. Greek dialect of European Gypsy
gul. Gulbahārī dialect of Pashai
gur. Gurēsī dialect of Shina
Gy. Gypsy or Romani
H. Hindī
hal. Halabī dialect of Marāṭhī
haz. Hazara Hindkī dialect of Lahndā
h.rudh. High Rudhārī sub-dialect of Khaśālī dialect of West Pahāṛī
hung. Hungarian dialect of European Gypsy
IA. Indo-aryan
IE. Indo-european
Ind. Indo-aryan of India proper excluding Kafiri and Dardic
Indo-ir. Indo-iranian or Aryan
Ir. Iranian
ish. Ishpi dialect of Pashai
Ishk. Ishkāshmī (Iranian)
isk. Iskeni dialect of Pashai
it. Italian dialect of European Gypsy
jau. Jaugaḍa Rock Inscription of Aśoka
jaun. Jaunsārī dialect of West Pahāṛī
jij. Jijelut dialect of Shina
jmag. Jaina Māgadhī Prakrit
jmh. Jaina Mahārāṣṭrī Prakrit
[page xiv]
jt. Jāṭū sub-dialect of Bāṅgarū dialect of Western Hindī
jub. North Jubbal dialect of West Pahāṛī
K. Kashmiri (Kāśmīrī)
kach. Kāchṛī dialect of Lahndā
Kaf. Kafiri
Kal. Kalasha (Kaláṣa — Dard.)
kāl. Kālsī Rock Inscription of Aśoka
Kamd. See Kmd.
Kan. Kanarese (Kannaḍa — Dravidian)
Kand. Kandia (Dard.)
kar. Karači (Transcaucasian) dialect of Asiatic Gypsy
kash. Or kiś. Kashṭawāṛī dialect of Kashmiri
Kaṭ. Kaṭārqalā (Dard.)
kāṭh. Kāṭhiyāvāḍi dialect of Gujarātī
kb. Kauśāmbī Pillar Edict of Aśoka
kc. Kocī dialect of West Pahāṛī
kcch. Kacchī dialect of Sindhī
kch. Kachur-i Sala dialect of Pashai
kgr. Or kng. Kāṅgrā sub-dialect of Ḍogrī dialect of Panjābī
Kharl. MIA. Forms occurring in Corpus Inscriptionum Indicarum Vol. II Pt. 1
khas. Khasa dialect of Kumaunī
khaś. Khaśālī dialect of West Pahāṛī
khet. Khetrānī dialect of Lahndā
Kho. Khowār (Dard.)
Khot. Khotanese (Iranian)
kiś. See kash.
kiūth. Kiūthalī dialect of West Pahāṛī
Kmd. Or Kamd. Kāmdeshi (Kaf.), Kāmdesh dialect of Kati
kṇḍ. Kaṇḍak dialect of Pashai
kng. See kgr.
Ko. Koṅkaṇī
Koh. Kohistānī (Dard.)
koh. Kohistānī dialect of Shina
Kol. Kōlāmī (Dravidian)
kōl. Kōlā dialect of Shina
kq. Kauśāmbī (Queen's Edict) Inscription of Aśoka
Kt. Kati or Katei (Kaf.)
Ku. Kumaunī
Kur. Kurukẖ (Dravidian)
kuṛ. Kuṛaṅgali dialect of Pashai
Kurd. Kurdish (Iranian)
kurd. Kurdari dialect of Pashai
ky. Kanyawālī dialect of Maiyã̄
L. Lahndā
la. Lāṛī dialect of Sindhī
lagh. Laghmani dialect of Pashai
lakh. Lakhīmpurī dialect of

Awadhī
Lat. Latin
laur̥. Laur̥owānī dialect of Pashai
Lith. Lithuanian
l.rudh. Low Rudhārī sub-dialect of Khaśālī dialect of West Pahāṛī
ludh. Ludhiānī dialect of Panjābī
M. Marāṭhī
mag. Magahī dialect of Bihārī
Mai. Maiyā̃ (Dard.)
Mal. Malayāḷam (Dravidian)
Māl. Or Malw. Mālwāī
mald. See Md.
Malw. See Māl.
man. Mānsehrā Rock Inscription of Aśoka
marm. Marmatī sub-dialect of Khaśālī dialect of West Pahāṛī
Marw. Mārwāṛī
Md. Or mald. Maldivian dialect of Sinhalese
mg. Māgadhī Prakrit
mh. Mahārāsṭrī Prakrit
MIA. Middle Indo-aryan
mi. Delhi Mīrat Pillar Edict of Aśoka
mid.rudh. Middle Rudhārī sub-dialect of Khaśālī dialect of West Pahāṛī
Mj. Munǰī (Iranian)
Mth. Maithilī
mth. Mathiā (Lauṛiyā-Nandangaṛh) Inscription of Aśoka
Mu. Muṇḍā
mult. Multānī dialect of Lahndā
N. Nepāli
New. Newārī
ng. Nāgārjunī Cave Inscription of Aśoka
NIA. New (modern) Indo-aryan
NiDoc. Language of '*Kharoṣṭī* Inscriptions discovered by Sir Aurel Stein in Chinese Turkestan' edited by A. M. Boyer, E. J. Rapson, and E. Senart
nig. Niglīvā Inscription of Aśoka
nij. Nijelami (Neẓəlā'm) dialect of Pashai
Niṅg. Niṅgalāmī (Dard.)
nir. Nirlāmī dialect of Pashai
Nk. Naiki (Dravidian)
norw. Norwegian dialect of European Gypsy
OHG. Old High German
Opruss. Old Prussian
Or. Oṛiyā
Orm. Ōrmuṛī' (Iranian)
Oslav. Old Slavonic
Oss. Ossetic (Iranian)
P. Panjābī (Pañjābī)
Pa. Pali
pach. See pch.
pāḍ. Pāḍarī sub-dialect of Bhadrawāhī dialect of West Pahāṛī
Pah. Pahāṛī
Pahl. Pahlavi (Iranian)
paiś. Paiśācī Prakrit
pal. Palestinian dialect of Asiatic Gypsy of the Nawar
pales. Palesī dialect of Shina
paṅ. Paṅgwāḷī dialect of West Pahāṛī
Par. Parachi (Parāčī — Iranian)
Parth. Parthian (Iranian)
Paš. Pashai (Pašaī — Dard.)
paṭ. Paṭṭanī dialect of Gujarātī
pch. Or pach. Pachaghani dialect of Pashai
Pers. Persian (Iranian)
pers. Persian dialect of Asiatic Gypsy
Phal. Phalūṛa (Dard.)
Pk. Prakrit
pog. Pŏgulī dialect of Kashmiri
pol. Polish dialect of European Gypsy
poṭh. Poṭhwārī dialect of Lahndā
pow. Pōwādhī dialect of Panjābī
Pr. Prasun (Kaf.)
Prj. Parji (Dravidian)
Psht. Pashto (Iranian)
pun. Punchī dialect of Lahndā
punl. Puniali dialect of Shina
rām. Rāmbanī dialect of Kashmiri in Jammu
rdh. Radhia (Lauṛiyā Ararāj) Pillar Edict of Aśoka
Rj. Rājasthānī
roḍ. Roḍiyā dialect of Sinhalese
roh. Rohruī dialect of West Pahāṛī
rp. Rāmpurvā Rock Edict of Aśoka
ru. Rūpnāth Inscription of Aśoka
rudh. Rudhārī sub-dialect of Khaśālī dialect of West Pahāṛī
[page xv]
rum. Rumanian dialect of European Gypsy
rumb. Rumbūr dialect of Kalasha
rus. Russian dialect of European Gypsy
Russ. Russian
S. Sindhī
ś. Śaurasenī Prakrit
sah. Sahasrām Inscription of Aśoka
Sang. Sanglechi (Saṅlēčī — Iranian)
Sant. Santālī (Muṇḍā)
Sar. Sarīkolī (Iranian)
Seeur. South-east European dialects of Gypsy
śeu. Śeuṭī sub-dialect of Khaśālī dialect of West Pahāṛī
Sh. Shina (Ṣiṇā — Dard.)
shah. Shāhbāzgaṛhī Rock Inscription of Aśoka
sham. Shamakaṭ dialect of Pashai
she. Shewa dialect of Pashai
Shgh. Shughnī (Iranian)
Shum. Shumashti (Šumāštī

— Dard.)
shut. Shutuli dialect of Pashai
Si. Sinhalese
Sik. Sikalgārī (Mixed Gypsy Language: LSI xi 167)
sir. Sirājī dialect of West Pahāṛī
sirm. Sirmaurī dialect of West Pahāṛī
Sk. Sanskrit
sn. Sārnāth Inscription of Aśoka
snj. Sanjan dialect of Pashai
sod. Sŏdōcī dialect of West Pahāṛī
Sogd. Sogdian (Iranian)
sop. Bombay-Sopārā Inscription of Aśoka
sp. Spanish dialect of European Gypsy
srk. Sirāikī dialect of Sindhī
suk. Suketī dialect of West Pahāṛī
Sv. Savi (Dard.)
Tam. Tamil (Dravidian)
Tel. Telugu (Dravidian)
Tib. Tibetan
Tir. Tirāhī (Dard.)
Toch. Tocharian
top. Delhi-Tōprā Pillar Edict of Aśoka
Tor. Tōrwālī (Dard.)
Tu. Tuḷu (Dravidian)
Turk. Turkish
urt. Urtsun dialect of Kalasha
uzb. Uzbini dialect of Pashai
vrāc. Vrācaḍa Apabhraṁśa
waz. Waziri dialect of Pashto
weg. Wegali dialect of Pashai
wel. Welsh dialect of European Gypsy
Werch. Werchikwār or Wershikwār (Yasin dialect of Burushaski)
Wg. Waigalī or Wai-alā (Kaf.)
Wkh. Wakhi (Iranian)
Woṭ. Woṭapūrī (language of Woṭapūr and Kaṭārqalā — Dard.)
Wpah. West Pahāṛī
Yazgh. Yazghulami (Iranian)
Yghn. Yaghnobi (Iranian)
Yid. Yidgha (Iranian)

Dravidian semantic clusters

ĀlKu. = Ālu Kuṟumba

Bel. = Belari

Br. = Brahui

Dr. = Dravidian

Ga. = Gadba

Go. = Gondi

Ir. = Iruḷa

Ka. = Kannaḍa

Ko. = Kota

Koḍ. = Koḍagu (Coorg)

ol. = Kolami

Kor. = Koraga

Kur. = Kuṛux (Kurukẖ)

Kurub. = Beṭṭa Kuruba

Ma. = Malayalam

Malt. = Malto

Manḍ. = Manḍa

NIA = New Indo-Aryan

Nk. = Naikṛi

Nk. (Ch.) = Naiki of Chanda

Ota. = Old Tamil

Pa. = Parji

PālKu. = Pālu Kuṟumba

PDr. = proto-Dravidian

Pe. = Pengo

Ta. = Tamil

Te. = Telugu

To. = Toda

Tu. = Tulu

Munda semantic clusters

Ga. Gatai

Go. Gorum

Gu. Gutob

Ho

Ju. Juang

Kh. Kharia

Kher. Kherwarian

Kol. Kolami

Kw. Korwa

Mu. Mundari

Nahali

Sa. Santali

Sora

A note is appended which recounts Prof. Emeneau's postulation of an Indian Linguistic Area, together with some briefs on the key dates related to the desiccation of the Sarasvati River.(Note on Key dates of the Sarasvati River and the Indian Linguistic Area) This provides the underpinnings for a hypothesis that many entries in this *Indian Lexicon* are likely to provide the phonemes which were current for a millennium, starting circa 3000 B.C. This hypothesis will be tested by an attempt to decipher the inscriptions of the civilization which sustained the Indian Linguistic Area.

The semantic sequence provided in the Indian Lexicon is like a meta-index of meanings (provided in English, using synonyms or near-synonyms of basic English words), while trying to separate English homonyms or near-homonyms. Botanical names (primarily Latin) have been used after Hooker to index flora, though some entries are also sequenced in the context of sememes related to cultural processes, for e.g. 'food'.

The meta index consists of 1242 semantic clusters; it is a veritable compendium of the cultural categories, life-aspirations and knowledge systems sought to be represented through the lexemes of the Bharatiya or Indic Linguistic Area. The range of semantic clusters encompassing the entire gamut of life-experiences related to natural phenomena and the environment involving flora and fauna point to an essential semantic unity among Bharatiya languages (languages of India or Indic languages) which evolved out of a riverine-maritime civilization engaged in creating a Metals Age, emerging out of a lithic age life-and-social-activity.

The basic finding is that in this Bharatiya or Indic Linguistic Area, the proto-versions of words of the present-day languages of India (Tamil, Prakrit, Munda families) have concordant etyma in these 1242 semantic meta clusters – from butter to vermillion --, pointing to the cultural interactions which resulted in the creation of what may be called the Bharatiya Linguistic Area. The approximate dates of the creation of the Bharatiya Linguistic Area becomes evident after the decipherment of the script and inscriptions of the Sarasvati civilization (from circa 6500 BCE to 1900 BCE) using these semantic clusters related to the semantic category of the lexical repertoire of metallurgy, minerals, metals, smith, smithy, furnaces and skill sets of people who were sea-faring merchants from Meluhha (Bharat).

Semantic clusters in Indian Lexicon (1242 English words and Botanical species Latin)

Economic Court: Flora and Products from Flora

Birds

Insects

Fauna

Animate phenomena: birth, body, sensory perceptions and actions

Visual phenomen, forms and shapes

Numeration and Mensuration

Economic Court: Natural phenomena, Earth formations, Products of earth (excluding flora clustered in a distinct category)

Building, infrastructure

Work, skills, products of labour and workers (fire-worker, potter/ smith/ lapidary, weaver, farmer, soldier)

Weapons and tools

Language fields

Kinship

Social formations

Economic Court: Flora and Products from Flora

butter curdle flesh flour food grain honey liquor mahua molasses oil oilcake rice spice sugar supper tobacco wheat

bark cloth cotton drug flax fragrance fringe garland harvest granary glue hemp indigo itch kunda lac log medicine mouldy ointment peel poison pulp pungent raw reed resin root sandal scent seed sheaf sheath skein sow stick straw thorn thresh tip-cat

apple asparagus balsam bamboo banana barley basil basket betel bud camphor cardamom cashew celery chaff clearingnut clove bush cork coconut coffee creeper cucumber cumin ebony date fenugreek forest flower fruit garden garlic ginger gooseberry gourd hibiscus jackfruit jalap jujube leadwort leaf linseed lotus mango mushroom mustard palm orpiment pepper pericarp petal pomegranate raspberry saffron sago sprout tree tuber turmeric wax wood-apple

abies abrus acacia acalypha acampe acanthus achyranthes aconitum acorus adenanthera aegle aeschynomena aeschynomene agaricus agathotes agati ageratum aglaia aguilaria ailantus alangium aloe alosanthes alpinia amarantus albizzia amomum andropogon anethum anodendron anogeissus anthocephalus anthriscus antiaris areca aristolochia arka artemisia artocarpus arum atlantia averrhoea azima balanites barleria barringtonia basella bassia bauhinia berberis betula bixa blyxa bombax boswellia bryonia buchanania butea caesalpinia caesaria cajanus calamus calophyllum canarium cannabis canthium capparis carallia cardiospermum careya carissa carthamus carum caryota cassia cassytha cedrela cedrus celastrus celosia celtis cerbera ceropegia ceratonia chenopodium cicer cichorium cinnabar cinnamomum cinnamon citrus clarion cleistanthus clerodendrum clitoria coccinia cocculus colocasia colosanthes convolvulus cordia coriandrum costum costus cratraeva crocus crotalaria croton cucumis curculigo curcuma cyperus dalbergia datura desmodium dichrostachys dillenia dioscorea diospyros dodonea dolichos eclipta elaeocarpus elettaria eleusine ericybe erythrina erythroxylon eugenia eugenis euphorbia excoecaria feronia ferula ficus frankincense flacourtia garcinia galangal gamboge gardenia gaultheria gendarussa gentiana gloria gmelina grewia grislea gymnema gynandropsis gyrocarpus heliotropium hemidesmus hiptage holcus hopea hydnocarpus ichnocarpus ilex indigofera ipomoea jasminum juniper justicia kaempferia lagenaria lagerstroemia laurus lepidum leucas ligusticum linum lobellia lodhra luffa luvunga macaranga mangifera marsilia melastoma meliosma memecyclon mentha mesua millingtonia mimusops momordica moringa morus mucuna myrica myristica myrobalan myrtus nardostachys nauclea nelumbium nerium nyctanthes nymphaea ochlandra ochre ocimum odina olea ophioxylon oryza palmyra pandanus panicum papaver pavetta pavonia phaseolus phoenix phyllanthus physalis pimpinella pinus piper plumbago pogostemon polygala polygonum premna prunus psidium pterocarpus pterospermum pouzolzia prosopis quercus randia raphanus rauwofia rhizophora ricinus rottleria rubia rumex saccharum sal salicornia salvadora salvinia sandoricum santalum sapindus sarcostemma saussurea schleichera scirpus semecarpus sesamum sesbana sesbania shorea sinapis solanum soymida sphaeranthus spinachia sterculia stereospermum strobilanthes strychnos swertia symplocos syzygium tabernaemontana tamarindus tectona tephrosia terminalia thespesia tinospora tribulus tragia trapa trema trichosanthes trigonella trophis unquis utrica vaccinium veronia vitex vulpes wrightia xylia zizyphus

Birds

bird bluejay cock crane crow cuckoo dove duck eagle feather gizzard crest hawk heron kingfisher myna nest owl parrot pheasant quail robin shrike skylark snipe sparrow teal weaver-bird

Insects

bat beehive caterpillar chameleon cockroach crab frog insect lizard mosquito scorpion snake spider

Fauna

animal antelope, goat, deer, markhor, ram alligator bear buffalo bull camel dog elephant fish hare herd horn horse ivory lair lion lowing mongoose monkey musk-deer octopus pony porpoise rat rhinoceros shoal squirrel tail tiger tortoise yak yak-tail

Animate phenomena: birth, body, sensory perceptions and actions

abortion age amazed anger anus arrive ask attack back bald bathe behind beard beat beg being belly bile birth bite blink blood blow body boil bone breath bristle butt buttock care cheek chest chignon chin climb come copulate creep cross cry cut dance death decay doubt dream dumb dwarf echo elbow end excrement eye faeces fall fat finger fist flee fly frolic front funeral genus give gore groan hair hand hatch head heel hear heart herpes hiccup hide hit hunt hurt idle intoxicate invite itch jaundice joint juggler jump kick lame laugh lift leap leg lip listen liver look male mane meet mole mouth movement muscle nail navel neck nerve noise nose numb old penis perish phlegm plague pour pregnant pudendum pull pus push put raise rattle recite reply repress restrain rinse roar roll run rush scab scar scatter seize senses separate serve silence sing sink sit shoulder shrink slander slap sleep speak splash spleen split sprain squeeze stammer standing stay stirring stop strength suck surprise swallow sweep swell swing syllable take tame taste throb throw tired toe trunk tumour turning turn-back tusk twist udder urine vault vomit vulva waist walk woman word wrinkle young

Visual phenomena, forms and shapes

ball beauty bend bit black braid brown bubble chequered circle colour crack curve dense dot endless entangled extremity fitting flow fork full green heap hole hollow hump incline invert knob knot leak left line long loose middle ooze red slack slant small square straight stripe white

Numeration and Mensuration

account agreement audit average balance (scales) banker big broad center cheap coin collect collection contain counting deficient divide eight finger five four half high increase joint knot lightness load mark marked market marking numeration one remainder six seven ten two three twelve twenty measure weight zero

Economic Court: Natural phenomena, Earth formations, Products of earth (excluding flora clustered in a distinct category)

barren basin borax brass bright bronze burst clay cloud cold collyrium crystal darkness dawn desert dew dry extinguish fire frost gem glitter gold (including soma) goods earth hail heat hill island lapislazuli lightning moon mud night north ocean ore pearl planet pleiades rain rainbow river ruby sand salt sediment shell silk silver sky smoke soap solstice south star stone sun tank tin thunder water wave wet wind zodiac

Building, infrastructure

| |
|---|
| arch brick bridge building bund cave chisel chop churn corner door drain fence fencing ford fort house kitchen lattice loft parapet pillar rafter roof shelf space stable wall wattle way (path, road) |

Work, skills, products of labour and workers (fire-worker, potter/ smith/ lapidary, weaver, farmer, soldier)

[The lexemes related to weapons and tools are so vivid and distinctive that the entire group has been clustered together to provide an overview of the skills developed which are reflected in semantic expansions related to weapon types and to wielding them. Thus, the clusters in the following list (e.g. awl, axe, bow, goad, razor, saw, sickle) are only to be treated as 'tool' samplers of a Metals Age, emerging out of a lithic age.]

Weapons and Tools

| |
|---|
| awl axe bow goad razor saw sickle assembly amulet army axle badge bead bed bellows blanket boat bolt bore bracelet brazier break broken butcher camp cart carve censer cloak comb commonwealth convey crucible cymbals deliver dent depart dice distill drill drive drum edge embark engrave enter entreat erect fan fasten fatigue fear fell ferry filter fire flag flute forge fry furnace furrow glove gong groove guard guild hammer indra jacket join kill kiln kubera labour ladder ladle lamp land landless lathe leash leather lid lever loom lute manger mill mirror mould necklace net occupation oil-press ornament pannier patrol perforate pin plait plough pole pot potsherd potter pressed produce profession pure purity raft rope screen seat sew shackle script sling (bearing/ carrying) snare soldier spike spinner (weaver) spy stake stampsteam stirrup stool stopper store tablet trap treasury trough uproot vessel warrior wash water-lift well well-digger wheel whip winnow write |

Language fields

| | |
|---|---|
| grammar (Etymology, linguistics, grammar, particles, prepositions, adverbs) | arab tamil telugu<br>become near next now only other that there thus time until<br>augment consonant name no prefix riddle sign signature yes |

Kinship

| |
|---|
| ancestor bride brother companion family father friend gentleman girl lead love marriage mistress mother self single sister wife |

Social formations

| |
|---|
| abuse ambush auction authenticbard bawd brahma bravo buy chief class commend confidence conflict confusion cruel country court dedicate deity demon disgrace doctrine evil exile faith festival fop fraud free freedom game get gift goblin good gratitude guilt hindu honour idol justice law learn lease lend life load loan malice manner market meditate memorial mercy miser mystic oppose painting penalty place play please pledge pomp poor post power prank pride principal procession protect regularity regulation rich rob rogue royal rule sacrifice safety salutation scheme sell send shame sindhu stupid support surplus tax teacher temple terror theft tomb town trade tribe unruly useless value violence virtuous vow wager wicked win witness worship |

Other semantic clusters (including cognisance and lexemes which may indicate semantic expansion and may span many other semantic clusters; e.g. 'mix' cluster may relate to animate and inanimate clusters) adhere begin blocked bold bundle clean clever close coax commence dangle deceit defeat deliberate desire detached dip dirty disgust dull enclose endure false forget hard inferior know mark marked marking mass means medley mix narrow neat need new notch opportunity outside overflow part particle paste pit pitfall ponder purpose quick quit ready remember rise rot rough rub ruin section shade shake similar slow strip thin think trace tranquil trouble truth unripe upper vermillion

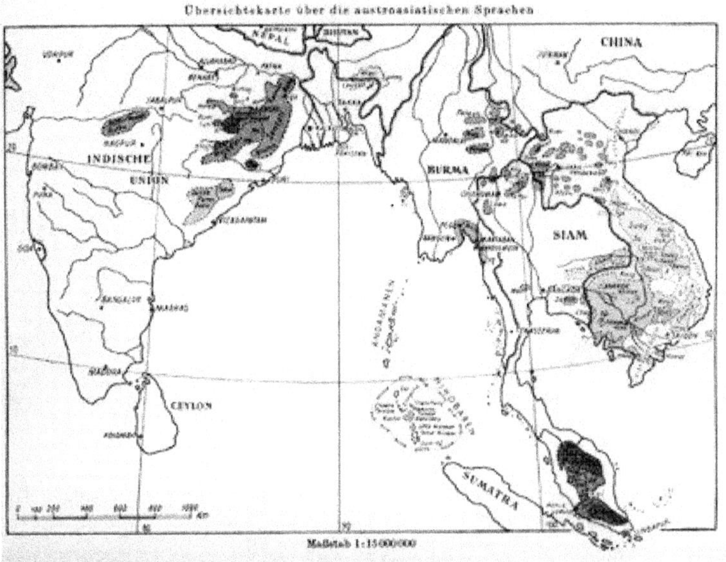


Pinnow's map of Austro-AsiaticLanguage speakers correlates with bronze age sites. http://www.ling.hawaii.edu/faculty/stampe/aa.html See http://kalyan97.googlepages.com/mleccha1.pdf The areal map of Austric (Austro-Asiatic languages) showing regions marked by Pinnow correlates with the bronze age settlements in Bharatam or what came to be known during the British colonial regime as 'Greater India'. The bronze age sites extend from Mehrgarh-Harappa (Meluhha) on the west to Kayatha-Navdatoli (Nahali) close to River Narmada to Koldihwa- Khairdih-Chirand on Ganga river basin to Mahisadal – Pandu Rajar Dhibi in Jharia mines close to Mundari area and into the east extending into Burma, Indonesia, Malaysia, Laos, Cambodia, Vietnam, Nicobar islands. A settlement of Inamgaon is shown on the banks of River Godavari.

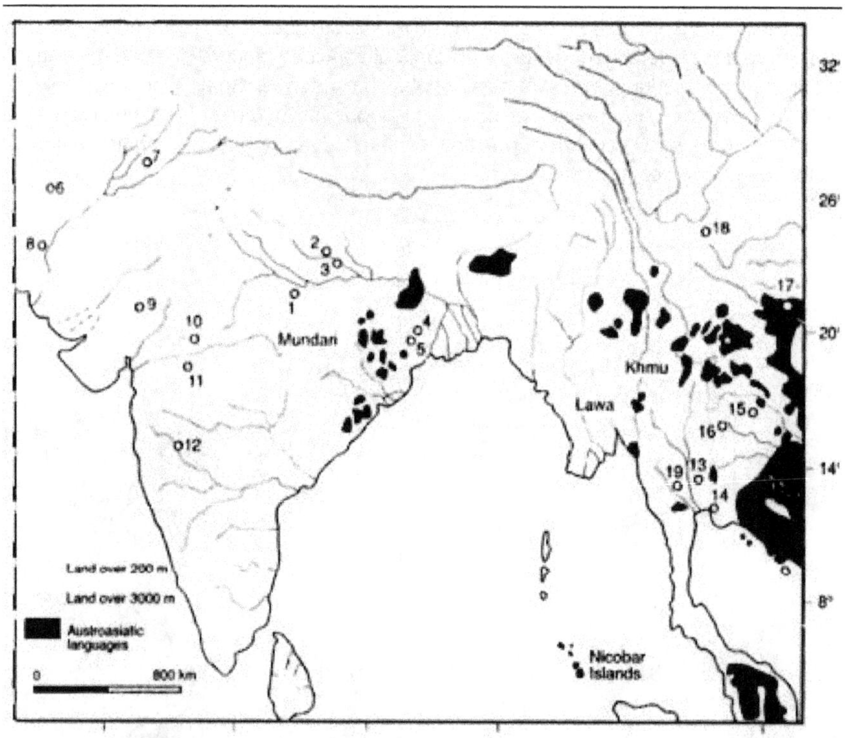


Bronze Age sites of eastern India and neighbouring areas: 1. Koldihwa; 2.Khairdih; 3. Chirand; 4. Mahisadal; 5. Pandu Rajar Dhibi; 6.Mehrgarh; 7. Harappa;8. Mohenjo-daro; 9.Ahar; 10. Kayatha; 11.Navdatoli; 12.Inamgaon; 13. Non PaWai; 14. Nong Nor;15. Ban Na Di andBan Chiang; 16. NonNok Tha; 17. Thanh Den; 18. Shizhaishan; 19. Ban Don Ta Phet [After Fig. 8.1 in: Charles Higham, 1996, The Bronze Age of Southeast Asia, Cambridge University Press].

Evidence related to proto-Indian or proto-Indic or Indus language

A proto-Indic language is attested in ancient Indian texts. For example, Manusmṛti refers to two languages, both of dasyu (daha): ārya vācas, mleccha vācas. *mukhabāhū rupajjānām yā loke jātayo bahih mlecchavācas'cāryav ācas te sarve dasyuvah smṛtāh* Trans. 'All those people in this world who are excluded from those born from the mouth, the arms, the thighs and the feet (of Brahma) are called Dasyus, whether they speak the language of the mleccha-s or that of the ārya-s.' (Manu 10.45)] This distinction between *lingua franca* and literary version of the language, is elaborated by Patañjali as a reference to 1) grammatically correct literary language and 2) ungrammatical, colloquial speech (*deśī*).

Ancient text of Panini also refers to two languages in *śikṣā*: Sanskrit and Prākṛt. Prof Avinash Sathaye provides a textual reference on the earliest occurrence of the word, 'Sanskrit' :

*triṣaṣṭiścatuh ṣaṣṭirvā varṇāh ṣambhumate matāh* |

*prākṛite samskṛte cāpi svayam proktā svayambhuvā || (pāṇini's śikṣā)*

Trans. There are considered to be 63 or 64 varṇā-s in the school (mata) of shambhu. In Prakrit and Sanskrit by swayambhu (manu, Brahma), himself, these varṇā-s were stated.

This demonstrates that pāṇini knew both samskṛta and prākṛita as established languages. (Personal communication, 27 June 2010 with Prof. Shrinivas Tilak.)

Chapter 17 of Bharatamuni's *Nāṭyaśāstra* is a beautiful discourse about Sanskrit and Prakrit and the usage of *lingua franca* by actors/narrators in dramatic performances. Besides, Raja Shekhara, Kalidasa, Shudraka have also used the word Sanskrit for the literary language. (Personal communication from Prof. TP Verma, 7 May 2010). *Nāṭyaśāstra* XVII.29-30: *dvividhā jātibhāṣāca prayoge samudāhṛtā mlecchaśabdopacārā ca bhāratam varṣam aśritā* 'The jātibhāṣā (common language), prescribed for use (on the stage) has various forms. It contains words of mleccha origin and is spoken in Bhāratavarṣa only...' Vātstyāyana refers to mlecchita vikalpa (cipher writing of mleccha) Vātstyāyana's Kamasutra lists (out of 64 arts) three arts related to language:

- *deśa bhāṣā jñānam* (knowledge of dialects)
- *mlecchita vikalpa* (cryptography used by mleccha) [cf. mleccha-mukha 'copper' (Skt.); the suffix –mukha is a reflex of mūh 'ingot' (Mu.)
- *akṣara muṣṭika kathanam* (messaging through wrist-finger gestures)

Thus, semantically, mlecchita vikalpa as a writing system relates to cryptography (perhaps, hieroglyphic writing) and to the work of artisans (smiths). I suggest that this is a reference to Indian hieroglyphs.

It is not a mere coincidence that early writing attested during historical periods was on metal punch-marked coins, copper plates, two-feet long copper bolt used on an Aśokan pillar at Rampurva, Sohoura copper plate, two pure tingots found in a shipwreck in Haifa, and even on the Delhi iron pillar clearly pointing to the smiths as those artisans who had the competence to use a writing system. In reference to Rampurva copper-bolt: "Here then these signs occur upon an object which must have been made by craftsmen working for Asoka or one of his predessors." (F.R. Allchin, 1959, Upon the contextual significance of certain groups of ancient signs, *Bulletin of the School of Oriental and African Studies*, London.)

*Mahābhārata* also attests to mleccha used in a conversation with Vidura. *Śatapatha Brāhmaṇa* refers to mleccha as language (with pronunciation variants) and also provides an example of such mleccha pronunciation by asuras. A Pali text, *Uttarādhyayana Sūtra* 10.16 notes: *ladhdhaṇa vimānusattaṇṇam āriattam puṇrāvi dullaham bahave dasyū milakkhuyā*; trans. 'though one be born as a man, it is rare chance to be an ārya, for many are the dasyu and milakkhu'. Milakkhu and dasyu constitute the majority, they are the many. Dasyu are milakkhu (mleccha speakers). Dasyu are also ārya vācas (Manu 10.45), that is, speakers of Sanskrit. Both ārya vācas and mleccha vācas are dasyu [cognate *dahyu, dańha, daha* (Khotanese)], people, in general. दाशः 1 A fisherman; इयं च सज्जा नौश्चेति दाशाः प्राञ्ज-लयो$ब्रुवन् Rām.7.46.32; Ms.8.48,49;1.34. दासः 'a fisherman' (Apte. Lexicon) Such people are referred to in Rgveda by Viśvāmitra as 'Bhāratam janam.' Mahābhārata alludes to 'thousands of mlecchas', a numerical superiority equaled by their valour and courage in battle which enhances the invincibility of Pandava (MBh. 7.69.30; 95.36).

Excerpt from Encyclopaedia Iranica article on cognate *dahyu* country (often with reference to the people inhabiting it): DAHYU (OIr. *dahyu-*), attested in Avestan *daxiiu-*, *dańhu-* "country" (often with reference to the people inhabiting it; cf. *AirWb.*, cot. 706; Hoffmann, pp. 599-600 n. 14; idem and Narten, pp. 54-55) and in Old Persian *dahyu-* "country, province" (pl. "nations"; Gershevitch, p. 160). The term is likely to be connected with Old Indian *dásyu* "enemy" (of the Aryans), which acquired the meaning of "demon, enemy of the gods" (Mayrhofer, *Dictionary* II, pp. 28-29). Because of the Indo-Iranian parallel, the word may be traced back to the root *das-*, from which a term denoting a large collectivity of men and women could have been derived. Such traces can be found in Iranian languages: for instance, in the ethnonym Dahae (q.v., i) "men" (cf. Av. ethnic name [fem. adj.] *dāhī*, from *dåńha-*; *AirWb.*, col. 744; Gk. Dáai, etc.), in Old Persian *dahā* "the Daha people" (Brandenstein and Mayrhofer, pp. 113-14), and in Khotanese *daha* "man, male" (Bailey, *Dictionary*, p. 155).

In Avestan the term did not have the same technical meaning as in Old Persian. Avestan *daxiiu-*, *dańhu-* refers to the largest unit in the vertical social organization. See, for example, Avestan $x^{v}$*aētu-*

(in the Gathas) "next of kin group" and *nmāna*-"house," corresponding to Old Persian *taumā*- "family"; Avestan *vīs*- "village," corresponding to Avestan *vərəzəna*- "clan"; Avestan *zantu*- "district"; and Avestan*daxiiu*-, *dańhu*- (Benveniste, 1932; idem, 1938, pp. 6, 13; Thieme, pp. 79ff.; Frye, p. 52; Boyce, *Zoroastrianism* I, p. 13; Schwartz, p. 649; Gnoli, pp. 15ff.). The connection *daxiiu*, *dańhu*- and *arya*- "Aryans" is very common to indicate the Aryan lands and peoples, in some instances in the plural: *airiiå daŋhāuuō,airiianąm daxiiunąm*, *airiiābiiō daŋhubiiō*. In *Yašt* 13.125 and 13.127 five countries (*daxiiu*-) are mentioned, though their identification is unknown or uncertain; in the same *Yašt* (13.143-44) the countries of other peoples are added to those of the Aryans: *tūiriia*, *sairima*, *sāinu*, *dāha*.

In Achaemenid inscriptions Old Persian *dahyu*- means "satrapy" (on the problems relative to the different lists of *dahyāva* [pl.], cf. Leuze; Junge; Walser, pp. 27ff.; Herzfeld, pp. 228-29; Herrenschmidt, pp. 53ff.; Calmeyer, 1982, pp. 105ff.; idem, 1983, pp. 141ff.) and "district" (e.g., Nisāya in Media; DB 1.58; Kent, *Old Persian*, p. 118). The technical connotation of Old Persian *dahyu* is certain and is confirmed—despite some doubts expressed by George Cameron but refuted by Ilya Gershevitch—by the loanword *da-a-yau-iš* in Elamite. On the basis of the hypothetical reconstruction of twelve "districts" and twenty-nine "satrapies," it has been suggested that the formal identification of the Old Persian numeral 41 with the ideogram *DH*, sometimes used for *dahyu* (Kent, *Old Persian*, pp. 18-19), can be explained by the fact that there were exactly forty-one *dahyāva* when the sign *DH*was created (Mancini).

From the meaning of Old Persian *dahyu* as "limited territory" come Middle Persian and Pahlavi *deh* "country, land, village," written with the ideogram *MTA* (*Frahang ī Pahlawīg* 2.3, p. 117; cf. Syr. *mātā*), and Manichean Middle Persian *dyh*(MacKenzie, p. 26). At times the Avestan use is reflected in Pahlavi *deh*, but already in Middle Persian the meaning "village" is well documented; it appears again in Persian *deh*.

*Bibliography*:

E. Benveniste, "Les classes sociales dans la tradition avestique," *JA* 221, 1932, pp. 117-34.

Idem, *Les Mages dans l'ancien Iran*, Paris, 1938.

W. Brandenstein and M. Mayrhofer, *Handbuch des Altpersischen*, Wiesbaden, 1964.

P. Calmeyer, "Zur Genese altiranischer Motive. Die "Statistische Landcharte des Perserreiches,"" *AMI* 15, 1982, pp. 105-87; 16, 1983, pp. 141-222.

G. G. Cameron, "The Persian Satrapies and Related Matters," *JNES* 32, 1973, pp. 47-56.

R. N. Frye, *The Heritage of Persia*, London, 1962.

I. Gershevitch, "The Alloglottography of Old Persian," *TPS*, 1979, pp. 114-90.

G. Gnoli, *The Idea of Iran. An Essay on Its Origin*, Rome, 1989.

C. Herrenschmidt, "Désignation de l'empire et concepts politiques de Darius I d'après ses inscriptions en vieux perse," *Stud. Ir.* 5, 1976, pp. 17-58.

E. Herzfeld, *The Persian Empire. Studies in Geography and Ethnography of the Ancient Near East*, ed. G. Walser, Wiesbaden, 1968.

K. Hoffmann, *Aufsätze zur Indoiranistik* II, Wiesbaden, 1976.

Idem and J. Narten, *Der sasanidische Archetypus*, Wiesbaden, 1989.

J. Junge, "Satrapie und Natio. Reichsverwaltung und Reichspolitik im Staate Dareios' I," *Klio* 34, 1941, pp. 1-55.

O. Leuze, *Die Satrapieneinteilung in Syrien und im Zweistromlande von 520-320*, Halle, 1935.

D. N. MacKenzie, *A Concise Pahlavi Dictionary*, Oxford, 1971.

M. Mancini, "Ant. pers. *dahyu-*, il segno "DH" e il problema degli ideogrammi nel cuneiforme achemenide," *Studi e Saggi Linguistici* 24, 1984, pp. 241-70.

M. Schwartz, "The Old Eastern Iranian World View According to the Avesta,"*Camb. Hist. Iran* II, 1985, pp. 640-63.

P. Thieme, *Mitra and Aryaman*, New Haven, Conn., 1957.

G. Walser, *Die Völkerschaften auf den Reliefs von Persepolis*, Berlin, 1966.

(Gherardo Gnoli)

Originally Published: December 15, 1993

Last Updated: November 11, 2011

This article is available in print.
Vol. VI, Fasc. 6, p. 590

That Pali uses the term 'milakkhu' is significant (cf. *Uttarādhyayana Sūtra* 10.16) and reinforces the concordance between 'mleccha' and 'milakkhu' (a pronunciation variant) and links the language with 'meluhha' as a reference to a language in Mesopotamian texts and in the cylinder seal of Shu-ilishu. [Possehl, Gregory, 2006, Shu-ilishu's cylinder seal, Expedition, Vol. 48, No. 1 http://www.penn.museum/documents/publications/expedition/PDFs/48-1/What%20in%20the%20World.pdf] This seal shows a sea-faring Meluhha merchant who needed a translator to translate meluhha speech into Akkadian. The translator's name was Shu-ilishu as recorded in cuneiform script on the seal. This evidence rules out Akkadian as the Indus or Meluhha language and justifies the search for the proto-Indian speech from the region of the Sarasvati river basin which accounts for 80% (about 2000) archaeological sites of the civilization, including sites which have yielded inscribed objects such as Lothal, Dwaraka, Kanmer, Dholavira, Surkotada, Kalibangan, Farmana, Bhirrana, Kunal, Banawali, Chandigarh, Rupar, Rakhigarhi. The language-speakers in this basin are likely to have retained cultural memories of Indus language which can be gleaned from the semantic clusters of glosses of the ancient versions of their current *lingua franca* available in comparative lexicons and nighanṭu-s.

Evidence from Valmiki Rāmāyaṇa

Slokas 5.30.16 to 21 in the 29th sarga of Sundara Kandam, provide an episode of Hanuman introspecting on the language in which he should speak to Sita. This evidence refers to two dialects: Sanskrit and mānuṣam vākyam (lit. jāti bhāṣā). In this narrative mānuṣam vākyam (spoken dialect) is distinguished from Sanskrit of a Brahmin (or, grammatically correct and well-prouncedd Sanskrit used in yajña-s).

*1. "antaramtvaha māsādya rākṣasīnam iha sthitah"*

*2. "śanairāśvāsaiṣyāmi santāpa bahulām imām"*

(Staying here itself and getting hold of an opportunity even in the midst of the female-demons (when they are in attentive), I shall slowly console Sita who is very much in distress. )
*3. "aham hi atitanuścaiva vānara śca viśeṣata"*

*4. "vācam ca udāhariṣyāmi mānuṣīm iha samskṛtām"*
(However, I am very small in stature, particularly as a monkey and can speak now Sanskrit, the human language too.)
*5. "yadi vācam pradāsyami dwijātiriva samskṛtām"*
*6. "rāvaṇam manyamānā mām sītā bhītā bhavi ṣyati"*

*7. vānarasya viśeṣena kathamsyādabibhāṣaṇam*
(If I use Sanskrit language like a lls de, Sita will get frightened, thinking that Rāva ṇ a has come disguised as a monkey. Especially, how can a monkey speak it?)
*8. "avaśyameva vaktavyam mānuṣam vākyam arthavat"*

*9. "mayā śāntvayitum śakyā"*

*10. "nānyathā iyam aninditā"*
(Certainly, meaningful words of a human being are to be spoken by me. Otherwise, the virtuous Sita cannot be consoled.)
*11. "sā iyam ālokya me rūpam jānakī bhāṣitam tathā ||*

*rakṣobhih trāsitaa pūrvam bhuūah trūsam gamiṣyati |"*

(Looking at my figure and the language, Seetha who was already frightened previously by the demons, will get frightened again.) [Translation based on http://www.valmikiramayan.net/sundara/sarga30/sundara_30_frame.htm See: Narayana Iyengar, 1938, Vanmeegarum Thamizhum; http://tashindu.blogspot.com/2006_12_01_archive.html In this work, Narayana Iyengar cites that the commentator interpret mānuṣam vākyam as the language spoken in Kosala.]

Evidence from Śatapatha Brāhmaṇa for *mleccha vācas*

An extraordinary narrative account from Śatapatha Brāhmaṇa is cited in full to provide the context of the yagna in which vaak (speech personified as woman) is referred to the importance of grammatical speech in yagna performance and this grammatical, intelligible speech is distinguished from mlecccha, unintelligible speech. The example of the usage of phrase 'he 'lavo is explained by Sayana as a pronunciation variant of: 'he 'rayo. i.e. 'ho, the spiteful (enemies)!' This grammatically correct phrase, the Asuras were unable to pronounce correctly, notes Sayana. The ŚB text and translation are cited in full because of the early evidence provided of the mleccha speech (exemplifying what is referred to Indian language studies as 'ralayo rabhedhah'; the transformed use of 'la' where the syllable 'ra' was intended. This is the clearest evidence of a proto-Indian language which had dialectical variants in the usage by asuras and devas (i.e. those who do not perform yagna and those who perform yagna using vaak, speech.) This is comparable to mleccha vācas and ārya vācas differentiation by Manu. The text of ŚB 3.2.1.22-28 and translation are as follows:

*yoṣā vā iyaṃ vāgyadenaṃ na yuvitehaiva mā tiṣṭhantamabhyehīti brūhi tām tu na āgatām pratiprabrūtāditi sā hainaṃ tadeva tiṣṭhantamabhyeyāya tasmādu strī pumāṃsaṃ saṃskṛte tiṣṭhantamabhyaiti tāṃ haibhya āgatām pratiprovāceyaṃ vā āgāditi tāṃ devāḥ |*

*asurebhyo 'ntarāyaṃstāṃ svīkṛtyāgnāveva parigṛhya sarvahutamajuhavurāhutirhi devānāṃ sa yāmevāmūmanuṣṭubhājuhavustadevaināṃ taddevāḥ svyakurvata te 'surā āttavacaso he 'lavo he 'lava iti vadantaḥ parābabhūvuḥ atraitāmapi vācamūduḥ |*

*upajijñāsyāṃ sa mlecastasmānna brāhmaṇo mlecedasuryā haiṣā vā natevaiṣa dviṣatāṃ sapatnānāmādatte vācaṃ te 'syāttavacasaḥ parābhavanti ya evametadveda o 'yaṃ yajño vācamabhidadhyau |*

*mithunyenayā syāmiti tāṃ saṃbabhūva indro ha vā īkṣāṃ cakre |*

*mahadvā ito 'bhvaṃ janiṣyate yajñasya ca mithunādvācaśca yanmā tannābhibhavediti sa indra eva garbho bhūtvaitanmithunam praviveśa sa ha saṃvatsare jāyamāna īkṣāṃ cakre |*

*mahāvīryā vā iyaṃ yoniryā māmadīdharata yadvai meto mahadevābhvaṃ nānuprajāyeta yanmā tannābhibhavediti tām pratiparāmṛśyaveṣṭyācinat |*

*tāṃ yajñasya śīrṣanpratyadadhādyajño hi kṛṣṇaḥ sa yaḥ sa yajñastatkṛṣṇājinaṃ yo sā yoniḥ sā kṛṣṇaviṣāṇātha yadenāmindra āveṣṭyācinattasmādāveṣṭiteva sa yathaivāta indro 'jāyata garbho bhūtvaitasmānmithunādevamevaiṣo 'to jāyate garbho bhūtvaitasmānmithunāt tāṃ vā uttānāmiva badhnāti |*

Translation: 22.The gods reflected, 'That Vaak being a woman, we must take care lest she should allure him. – Say to her, "Come hither to make me where I stand!" and report to us her having come.' She then went up to where he was standing. Hence a woman goes to a man who stays in a well-trimmed (house). He reported to them her having come, saying, 'She has indeed come.' 23. The gods then cut her off from the Asuras; and having gained possession of her and enveloped her completely in fire, they offered her up as a holocaust, it being an offering of the gods. (78) And in that they offered her with an anushtubh verse, thereby they made her their own; and the Asuras being deprived of speech, were undone, crying, 'He 'lavah! He 'lavah!' (79) 24. Such was the unintelligible speech which they then uttered, -- and he (who speaks thus) is a Mlekkha (barbarian). Hence let no Brahman speak barbarous language, since such is the speech of the Asuras. Thus alone he deprives his spiteful enemies of speech; and whosoever knows this, his enemies, being deprived of speech, are undone. 25. That Yajna (sacrifice) lusted after Vaak (speech [80]), thinking, 'May I pair with her!' He united with her. 26. Indra then thought within himself, 'Surely a great monster will spring from this union of Yagna and Vaak: [I must take care] lest it should get the better of me.' Indra himself then became an embryo and entered into that union. 27. Now when he was born after a year's time, he thought within himself, 'Verily of great vigour is this womb which has contained me: [I must take care] that no great monster shall be born from it after me, lest it should get the better of me!' 28. Having seized and pressed it tightly, he tore it off and put it on the head of Yagna (sacrifice [81]); for the black (antelope) is the sacrifice: the black deer skin is the same as that sacrifice, and the black deer's horn is the same as that womb. And because it was by pressing it tightly together that Indra tore out (the womb), therefore it (the horn) is bound tightly (to the end of the garment); and as Indra, having become an embryo, sprang from that union, so is he (the sacrifice), after becoming an embryo, born from that union (of the skin and the horn). (ŚB 3.2.1.23-25). (fn 78) According to Sayana, 'he 'lavo' stands for 'he 'rayo' (i.e. ho, the spiteful (enemies)!' which the Asuras were unable to pronounce correctly. The Kaanva text, however, reads te hātavāko 'su hailo haila ity etām ha vācam vadantah parābabhūvuh (? i.e. he p. 32 ilaa, 'ho, speech'.) A third version of this passage seems to be referred to in the Mahā bhāṣya (Kielh.), p.2. (p.38). (fn 79) Compare the corresponding legend about Yagna and Dakṣiṇā (priests' fee), (Taitt. S. VI.1.3.6. (p.38) (fn 79) 'Yagnasya sīrṣan'; one would expect 'kṛṣṇa(sāra)sya sīrṣan.' The Taitt.S. reads 'tām mṛgeṣu ny adadhāt.' (p.38) (fn81) In the Kanva text 'atah (therewith)' refers to the head of the sacrifice, -- sa yak khirasta upasprisaty ato vā enām etad agre pravisan pravisaty ato vā agre gāyamāno gāyate tasmāk khirasta upasprisati. (p.39)(cf. śatapatha Brāhmaṇa vol. 2 of 5, tr. By Julius Eggeling, 1885, in SBE Part 12; fn 78-81).

Mesopotamian texts refer to a language called meluhha (which required an Akkadian translator); this meluhha is cognate with mleccha. Seafaring meluhhan merchants used the script in trade transactions; artisans created metal artifacts, lapidary artificats of terracotta, ivory for trade. Glosses of the proto-Indic or Indus language are used to read rebus the Indus script inscriptions. The glyphs of the script include both pictorial motifs and signs and both categories of glyphs are read rebus. As a first step in delineating the Indus language, an Indian lexicon provides a resource, compiled semantically cluster over 1240 groups of glosses from ancient Indian languages as a proto-Indic substrate dictionary. See http://www.scribd.com/doc/2232617/lexicon linked at http://sites.google.com/site/kalyan97/indus-writing

"The word *meluh.h.a* is of special interest. It occurs as a verb in a different form (mlecha-) in Vedic only in ŚB 3.2.1, an eastern text of N. Bihar where it indicates 'to speak in barbarian fashion'. But it has a form closer to Meluh.h.a in Middle Indian (MIA): Pali, the church language of S. Buddhism which originated as a western N. Indian dialect (roughly, between Mathura, Gujarat and the Vindhya) has milakkha, milakkhu. Other forms, closer to ŚB mleccha are found in MIA *mliccha > Sindhi milis, Panjabi milech, malech, Kashmiri bri.c.hun 'weep, lament' (< *mrech-, with the common r/l interchange of IA), W. Pahari mel+c.h 'dirty'. It seems that, just as in other cases mentioned above, the original local form *m(e)luh. (i.e. m(e)lukh in IA pronunciation, cf. E. Iranian bAxdhl 'Bactria' > AV *bahli-ka, balhi-ka) was preserved only in the South (Gujarat? >Pali), while the North (Panjab, Kashmir, even ŚB and Bengal) has *mlecch. The sound shift from-h.h.-/-kh- > -cch- is unexplained; it may have been modeled on similar correspondences in MIA (Skt. Akṣi 'eye' _ MIA akkhi, acchi; ks.Etra '_eld' _ MIA khetta, chetta, etc.) The meaning of Mleccha must have evolved from 'self-designation' > 'name of foreigners', cf. those of the Franks > Arab farinjl 'foreigner.' Its introduction into Vedic must have begun in Meluh.h.a, in Baluchistan-Sindh, and have been transmitted for a long time in a non-literary level of IA as a nickname, before surfacing in E. North India in Middle/Late Vedic as Mleccha. (Pali milāca is influenced by a `tribal' name, Piśā ca, as is Sindhi milindu, milidu by Pulinda; the word has been further `abbreviated' by avoiding the difficult cluster ml- : Prākṛt mecha, miccha, Kashmiri m ī c(h), Bengali mech (a Tib.-Burm tribe) and perhaps Pashai mece if not < *mēcca `defective' (Turner, CDIAL 10389. | Parpola 1994: 174 has attempted a Dravidian explanation. He understands Meluh.h. a (var. Melah.h.a) as Drav. *Mēlakam [mēlaxam] `high country' (= Baluchistan) (=Ta-milakam) and points to Neo-Assyr. Baluh.h.u `galbanum', sinda `wood from Sindh'. He traces mlech, milakkha back to *mleks. , which is seen as agreeing, with central Drav. Metathesis with *mlēxa = mēlaxa-m. Kuiper 1991:24 indicates not infrequent elision of (Dravid.) —a- when taken over into Skt. | Shafer 1954 has a Tib-Burm. Etymology *mltse; Southworth 1990: 223 reconstructs Pdrav. 2 *muzi/mizi `say, speak, utter', DEDR 4989, tamil `Tamil' < `own speech'.)" [Witzel, Michael, 1999, Substrate Languages in Old Indo-Aryan (Rgvedic, Middle and Late Vedic, *Electronic Journal of Vedic Studies* (EJVS) 5-1 (1999) pp.1-67. http://www.ejvs.laurasianacademy.com/ejvs0501/ejvs0501article.pdf]

Note: Coining a term, "Para-Munda", denoting a hypothetical language related but not ancestral to modern Munda languages, the author goes on to identify it as "Harappan", the language of the Harappan civilization. The author later recounts this and posits that Harappan were illiterate and takes the glyphs of the script to be symbols without any basis in any underlying language.[cf. Steve Farmer, Richard Sproat, and Michael Witzel, 2005, The Collapse of the Indus-Script Thesis: The Myth of a Literate Harappan Civilization, EJVS 11-2 Dec. 13, 2005.]

ṛgveda (ṛca 3.53.12) uses the term, *'bhāratam janam'*, which can be interpreted as 'bhārata folk'. The ṛṣi of the sūkta is viśvāmitra gāthina. India was called Bhāratavarṣa after the king Bhārata. (Vāyu 33, 51-2; Bd. 2,14,60-2; lin:ga 1,47,20,24; Viṣṇu 2,1,28,32).

*Ya ime rodasī ubhe aham indram atuṣṭavam*

*viśvāmitrasya rakṣati brahmedam bhāratam janam*

3.053.12 I have made Indra glorified by these two, heaven and earth, and this prayer of viśvāmitra protects the people of Bhārata. [Made Indra glorified: indram atuṣṭavam — the verb is the third preterite of the casual, I have caused to be praised; it may mean: I praise Indra, abiding between heaven and earth, i.e. in the firmament].

The evidence is remarkable that almost every single glyph or glyptic element of the Indus script can be read rebus using the repertoire of artisans (lapidaries working with precious shell, ivory, stones and terracotta, mine-workers, metal-smiths working with a variety of minerals, furnaces and other tools) who created the inscribed objects and used many of them to authenticate their trade transactions. Many of the inscribed objects are seen to be calling cards of the professional artisans, listing their professional skills and repertoire.

The identification of glosses from the present-day languages of India on Sarasvati river basin is justified by the continuation of culture evidenced by many artifacts evidencing civilization continuum from the Vedic Sarasvati River basin, since language and culture are intertwined, continuing legacies:

Huntington notes [http://huntingtonarchive.osu.edu/Makara%20Site/makara]: "There is a continuity of composite creatures demonstrable in Indic culture since Kot Diji ca. 4000 BCE."

Mriga (pair of deer or antelope) in Buddha sculptures compare with Harappan period prototype of a pair of ibexes on the platform below a seated yogin. http://tinyurl.com/gonsh

Continued use of śankha (turbinella pyrum) bangles which tradition began 6500 BCE at Nausharo;

Continued wearing of sindhur at the parting of the hair by married ladies as evidenced by two terracotta toys painted black on the hair, painted golden on the jewelry and painted red to show sindhur at the parting of the hair;

Finds of shivalinga in situ in a worshipful state in Harappa (a metaphor of Mt. Kailas summit where Maheśvara is in tapas, according to Hindu tradition);

Terracotta toys of Harappa and Mohenjo-daro showing Namaste postures and yogasana postures;

Three-ring ear-cleaning device

Legacy of architectural forms

Legacy of puşkariṇi in front of mandirams; as in front of Mohenjo-daro stupa

Legacy of metallurgy and the writing system on punch-marked coins

Legacy of continued use of cire perdue technique for making utsava bera (bronze murti)

Legacy: Engraved celt tool of Sembiyan-kandiyur with Sarasvati hieroglyphs: calling-card of an artisan

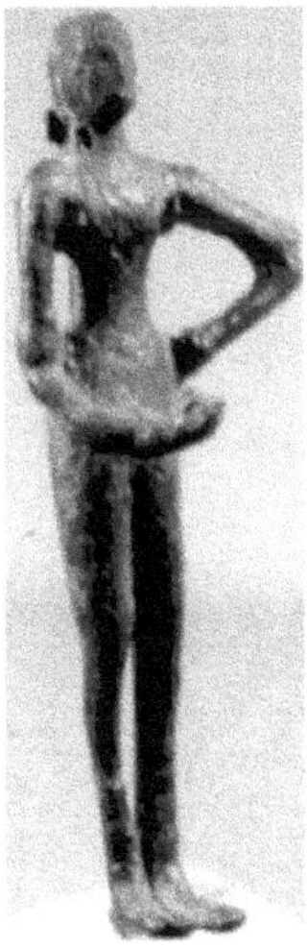

Legacy of acharya wearing uttariyam (shawl) leaving right-shoulder bare

Form of addressing a person respectfully as: arya, ayya (Ravana is also referred to as arya in the Great Epic Rāmāyaṇa)

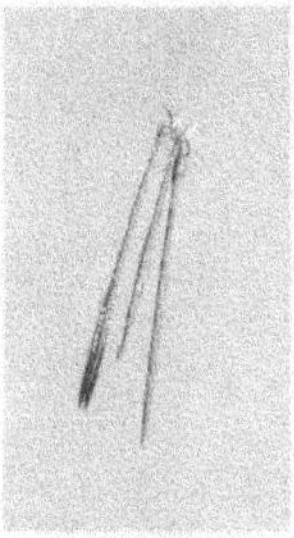

Fig. 4.11 Harappa: A three-in-one toiletry gadget, copper, Mature Harappan

Fig. 4.12 A modern three-in-one toiletry gadget, copper

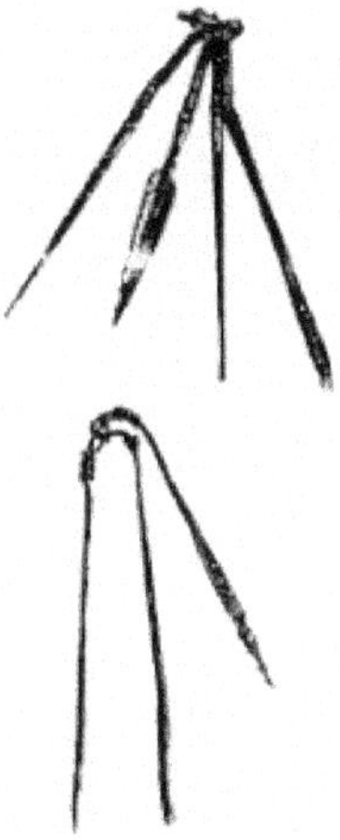

Plate X [c] Lingam in situ in Trench Ai (MS Vats, 1940, Excavations at Harappa, Vol. II, Calcutta) Lingam, grey sandstone in situ, Harappa, Trench Ai, Mound F, Pl. X (c) (After Vats). "In an earthenware jar, No. 12414, recovered from Mound F, Trench IV, Square I… in this jar, six lingams were found along with some tiny pieces of shell, a unicorn seal, an oblong grey sandstone block with polished surface, five stone pestles, a stone palette, and a block of chalcedony…" (Vats, MS, 1940, Excavations at Harappa, Delhi, p. 370).

Continued use of cire perdue technique of bronze-casting. Bronze murti: cire perdue technique used today in Swamimalai to make bronze utsavabera (idols carried in procession). Eraka Subrahmanya is the presiding divinity in Swamimalai. Eraka! Copper.Devices on punch-marked coins comparable to Sarasvati hieroglyphs.

Toilet gadgets: Ur and Harappa After Woolley 1934, Vats 1941

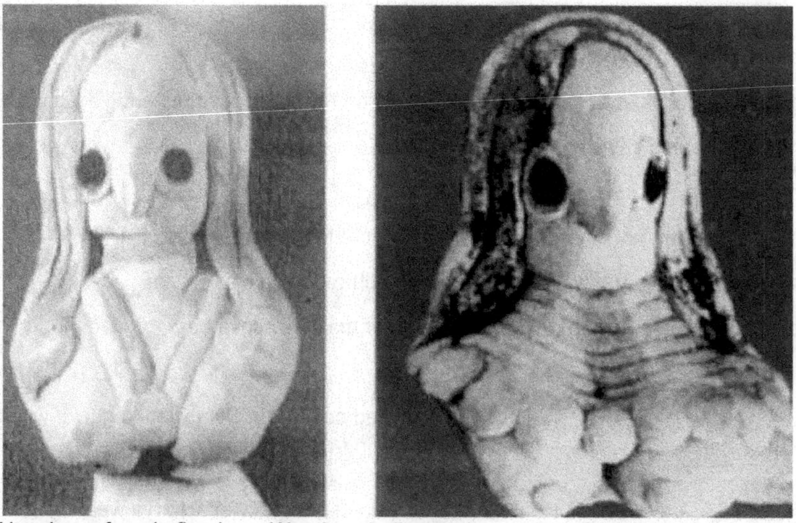

Nausharo: female figurines. Wearing sindhur at the parting of the hair. Hair painted black, ornaments golden and sindhur red. Period 1B, 2800 – 2600 BCE. 11.6 x 30.9 cm.[After Fig. 2.19, Kenoyer, 1998].

S'ankha artifacts: Wide bangle made from a single conch shell and carved with a chevron motif, Harappa; marine shell, Turbinella pyrum (After Fig. 7.44, Kenoyer, 1998) National Museum, Karachi. 54.3554. HM 13828. Seal, Bet Dwaraka 20 x 18 mm of conch shell. Seven shell bangles from burial of

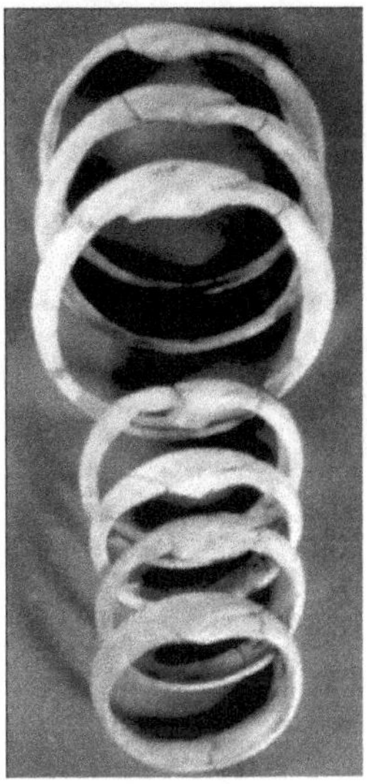

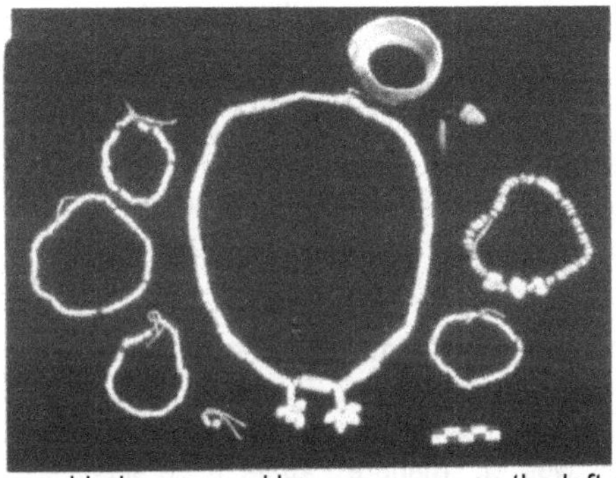

an elderly woman, Harappa; worn on the left arm; three on the upper arm and four on the forearm; 6.3 X 5.7 cm to 8x9 cm marine shell, Turbinella pyrum (After Fig. 7.43, Kenoyer, 1998) Harappa museum. H87-635 to 637; 676 to 679. Modern lady from Kutch, wearing shell-bangles.

6500 BCE. Date of the woman's burial with ornaments including a wide bangle of shankha.

Mehergarh. Burial ornaments made of shell and stone disc beads, and turbinella pyrum (sacred conch, s'an:kha) bangle, Tomb MR3T.21, Mehrgarh, Period 1A, ca. 6500 BCE. The nearest source for this shell is Makran coast near Karachi, 500 km. South. [After Fig. 2.10 in Kenoyer, 1998]. S'ankha wide bangle and other ornaments, c. 6500 BCE (burial of a woman at Nausharo). Glyph: 'shell-cutter's saw'

Some miniature tablets with Indus inscriptions are shaped like a shell-cutter's saw shown in the photograph of a bangle-maker from Bengal, cutting *turbinella pyrum.* Shapes of some text glyphs also resemble the shell-cutter's saw:

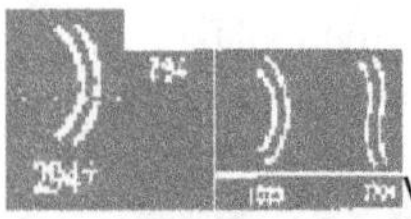 V294 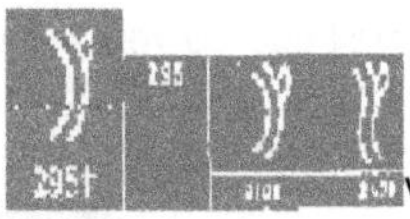 V295 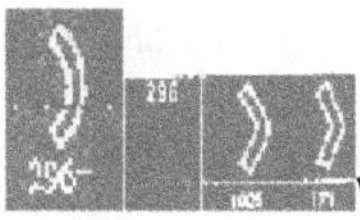 V296 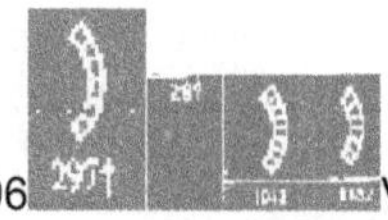 V297

Glyphic: 'spinner': H. *kātī* f. ' woman who spins thread '; -- Or. *kātiā* ' spinner ' with *ã* from verb *kā̃tibā* (CDIAL 2861). *Ta.* katir spinner's spindle. *Ma.* katir id. *Ka.* kadir, kadaru, kaduru id. *Tu.* kadůrů, kadirů, kadrů id. *Te.* kaduru id. *Ga.* (S.3) kadur an instrument used to spin threads from cotton. (DEDR 1195).

Glyph: 'ear of corn': *Ta.* katir ear of grain, spear of grass. *Ma.* katir ear, spike of corn; katirkka to shoot into ears; katirppu a sprout, shoot. *Ka.* kadir spike of corn, ear. *Koḍ.* kadï ear (of paddy, wheat, etc.). *Tu.* kadirů ear of corn; kadpu ear of ripened corn. (DEDR 1194). Cf. kaṇiśa n. ' ear of corn ' Kād., v.l. *kaṇisa* -- , *kaniśa* -- . [káṇa -- ] Pk. *kaṇisa* -- n. ' ear of corn, spike of corn ',
G. *kaṇas, kaṇsū̃, kaśṇū̃* (< **kasiṇū̃*), *karśaṇ* (with unexpl. *r*), *kaṇaslū̃* n. ' ear of corn ', M. *kaṇīs,°ṇas* n., *kaṇśī* f. (CDIAL 2667). Cf. kaṇēra -- see karṇikāra. Rebus: kā'ṁsya ' made of bell -- metal ' KātyŚr., n. ' bell -- metal ' Yājñ., ' cup of bell -- metal ' MBh., *°aka* -- n. ' bell -- metal '. 2. *kāṁsiya -- . [kaṁsá -- 1] 1. Pa. *kaṁsa* -- m. (?) ' bronze ', Pk. *kaṁsa* -- , *kāsa* -- n. ' bell -- metal, drinking vessel, cymbal '; L. (Jukes) *kā̃jā* adj. ' of metal ', awāṇ. *kāsā* ' jar ' (← E with -- *s* -- , not *ñj*); N. *kā̃so* ' bronze, pewter, white metal ', *kas* -- *kuṭ* ' metal alloy '; A. *kā̃h* ' bell -- metal ', B. *kā̃sā*, Or. *kāsā*, Bi.*kā̃sā*; Bhoj. *kā̃s* ' bell -- metal ', *kā̃sā* ' base metal '; H. *kās, kā̃sā* m. ' bell -- metal ', G. *kā̃sū̃* n., M. *kā̃sẽ* n.; Ko. *kā̃śẽ* n. ' bronze '; Si. *kasa* ' bell -- metal '. (CDIAL 2987). kāṁsyakāra m. ' worker in bell -- metal or brass ' Yājñ. com., *kaṁsakāra* -- m. BrahmavP. [kā'ṁsya -- , kāra -- 1]
N. *kasār* ' maker of brass pots '; A. *kāhār* ' worker in bell -- metal '; B. *kā̃sāri* ' pewterer, brazier, coppersmith ', Or. *kāsārī*; H. *kasārī* m. ' maker of brass pots '; G. *kāsārɔ, kas°* m. ' coppersmith '; M. *kā̃sār, kās°* m. ' worker in white metal ', *kāsārḍā* m. ' contemptuous term for the same '.(CDIAL 2989).

Glyphic: 'hole': 3863 khā'tra n. ' hole ' HPariś., Pk. *khatta* -- n. ' hole', *°aya* -- m. ' one who digs in a field '; S. *khāṭru* m. ' mine made by burglars ', *°ṭro* m. ' fissure, pit, gutter made by rain '; P. *khāt* m. ' pit, manure ', *khāttā* m. 'grain pit', ludh. *khattā* m. Bi. *khātā* ' hole, gutter, grain pit, notch (on beam and yoke of plough) ', Mth. *khātā, khattā* ' hole, ditch '; H. *khāt* m. ' ditch, well ', f. ' manure ', *khātā* m. ' grain pit '; G. *khātar* n. ' housebreaking, house sweeping, manure ', *khātriyū̃* n. ' tool used in housebreaking ' (→ M. *khātar* f. ' hole in a wall ', *khātrā* m. ' hole, manure '(CDIAL 3863).

*Rebus: 'charioteer, wheelwright':* kṣattṛ̥' m. ' carver, distributor ' RV., ' attendant, door- keeper ' AV., ' charioteer ' VS., ' son of a female slave ' lex. [√kṣad]
Pa. *khattar* -- m. ' attendant, charioteer '; S. *khaṭrī* m. ' washerman, dyer '; H. *khātī* m. ' member of a caste of wheelwrights '; G. *khātrī* m. ' do. of Hindu weavers '.(CDIAL 3647). 3649 kṣatríya ' ruling ' RV., m. ' one of the ruling order ' AV. [kṣatrá -- ]
Pa. *khattiya* -- m. ' member of the Kṣatriya caste ', *°yā<->* f., Pk. *khattia* -- m., *°ti* -- m.f., *°tiṇī* -- , *°tiyāṇī* -- f., L. *khattrī* m., *°rāṇī* f., P. *khattrīm*.; Si. *käti* ' warrior '.(CDIAL 3649).M. *khāṭī* f. ' digging to clear or excavate a canal ' (~ S. *khātī* f. ' id. ', but *khāṭyāro* m. ' one employed to measure canal work ') and *khaṭṭaṇ* ' to dig '.(CDIAL 3863).

[Cf. Av. *karəta* -- , °*ti* -- ' knife ': √kr̥t1]B. *kāti* ' shell -- cutter's saw ', *kātān* ' large sacrificial knife '; Or. *katā* ' small billhook ', *kātī* ' knife '; Bi. Mth. *kāt* ' brazier's cutters '; H. *kāt* m. ' shears for shearing sheep, cock's spur ', °*tā* m. ' knife for cutting bamboos ', (*kattā* m. ' small curved sword ', *kattī* f. ' knife ', *kaṭṭī* f. ' small sword ' ← EP.); G. *kātū̃* n. ' knife ', °*tī* f. ' knife, saw '; M. *kātī* f. ' cleaver '. kārti (CDIAL 2853) [Cf. Bal. *kārč* < **kārti* -- , Pahl. *kārt* < **kārti* -- or °*ta* -- . For the series kr̥tí -- 2: *karta -- 3 or °*ti* -- : *kārti -- cf. Gk. kardi/a: Goth. *haírtō*: Gk. kh=r and Sk. *hŕ̥d* -- : *hā´rdi.* -- √kr̥t1] Ash. *kāṭa* f. ' knife ', Kt. *kṭå*, Wg. *kaṭā´*; S. *kātī* f. ' large knife or dagger ', °*tu* m. ' large knife, tool for cutting edges of books '; L. mult. khet. *kātī* f. ' knife '; WPah. bhal. *kāt*, pl. °*tā̃* f. ' shears for shearing sheep '; Si. *kätta*, pl. *käti* ' billhook ' (early loan with *t*, not *ṭ*).(CDIAL 3069). *Ta.* katti knife, cutting instrument, razor, sword, sickle. *Ma.* katti knife. *Ko.* katy billhook knife; kati·r- (katrc-; < katy-tayr, katy-tarc-) to cut; kaṇkeyt, kaṇki·t sickle (for kaṇ, see 1166). *To.* kaṇ koty dagger-shaped knife burned with corpse (cf. 1166). *Ka.* katti knife, razor, sword. *Koḍ.* katti knife. *Tu.* katti, katte id. *Te.* katti knife, razor, sword. *Go.* (Ch.) katti cock's spur; (Elwin) kāti the knife attached to the cock's foot (*Voc.* 490). ?(DEDR 1204).

S'ankha, *turbinella pyrum* a signature tune of Hindu civilization and traditions of Jaina and Bauddham; a species which occurs only in Indian Ocean coastline. Śankha kr̥śāna (a phrase used in Rigveda, Atharvaveda) – śankha bowman, śankha cutter (who uses a bow like sword or saw to cut the śankha). A continuing, 8500 year-old industry. At Tiruchendur (kīṛakkarai, Gulf of Mannar), WB Handicrafts Dev. Corpn. Has an office; annual turnover of śankha obtained: Rs. 50 crores. [Source for the pictures showing use of bow to cut śankha: http://www.princelystates.com/ArchivedFeatures/fa-03-03d.shtml]

There are about 500 glyphs or glyptic elements of Indus script; it is significant that almost all the unambiguously identifiable glyphs can be read rebus consistently in a smithy artisan's workshop setting.

The composite animal glyph is one example to show that rebus method has to be applied to every glyptic element in the writing system. How does one explain a person seated on a leaf-less tree branch? The entire composition is a set of hieroglyphs.

So it is with the rim of a short-necked jar. The focus of the orthography is on the rim; karṇaka, kanaka; rebus: writer. See another example of a face ligatured to a markhor. The key is the face. This face is the rosetta stone proving it as a hieroglyph to be read rebus. So is the water-carrier a hieroglyph (as noted by Gadd). She is kuṭi 'water-carrier' (Telugu). Rebus: kuṭhi 'smelter furnace'. This object can also be denoted by pudendum muliebre. So is the glyph showing copulation scene: kamaḍha. This gloss can also be denoted by a person seated in penance. Kamaḍha 'penance' (Pkt.) Rebus: kampaṭṭam 'coiner, mint'.

Indian linguistic area or Indian *sprachbund*

The glyphs of Indus script have been read rebus using homonymous glosses of the linguistic area or Indian *sprachbund* using over 1000 glosses of this substrate dictionary. This means that most of the glosses in one or more of present-day Indian languages will be assumed to retain the memories of the Indus language. Homonyms of the set of such glosses define the underlying language of Indus script depicted on over 6000 inscribed objects of the corpus of Indus inscriptions.

Many rearchers have reached a consensus that ancient India constituted a linguistic area (cf.Southworth; Emeneau; Masica, CP 1993; Kuiper, FBJ 1967, Indo-Iranian Journal 10: 81-102), that is, an area wherein specific language-speakers absorbed features from other languages and made the features their own. To delineate such a linguistic area and the glosses that might have been used in that area, the glosses are chosen from all Indian languages. Indian language glosses are compared because there is evidence for cultural continuum of the civilization which produced the objects inscribed with Indus script. (cf. Sarasvati.The glosses are semantically-phonetically clustered together in an Indian lexicon which is a veritable substrate dictionary of the linguistic area. The assumption is that one or more languages of this lexicon could hold the legacy of the words used by the authors of the civilization who also invented the writing system. Ancient texts from India confirm this linguistic area.

It is unlikely that Akkadian was a possible underlying language because a cuneiform cylinder seal with an Akkadian inscription, showing a seafaring Meluhhan merchant (carrying an antelope) required an interpreter, Shu-ilishu, confirming that the Meluhhan's language was not Akkadian. There is substantial agreement among scholars pointing to the Indian civilization area as a linguistic area.

I suggest that Meluhha mentioned in Mesopotamian texts of 3rd-2nd millennium BCE is a language of this linguistic area. That meluhha and mleccha are cognate and that mleccha is attested as a mleccha vācas (mleccha speech) distinguished from arya vācas (arya speech) indicates that the linguistic area had a colloquial, ungrammatical mleccha speech – *lingua franca* and a grammatically correct arya speech – literary language. The substrate glosses of the Indian lexicon are thus reasonably assumed to be the glosses of mleccha vācas, the speech of the artisans who produced the artifacts and the inscribed objects with the writing system. This assumption is further reinforced by the fact that about 80% of archaeological sites of the civilization are found on the banks of Vedic River Sarasvati leading some scholars to rename the Indus Valley civilization as Sarasvati-Sindhu civilization.

In this context, the following monumental work by Sylvan Levi, Jules Bloch and Jean Przyluski published in the 1920's continues to be relevant, even today, despite some advances in studies related to formation of Indian languages and the archaeological perspectives of and evidences from the civilization.

Przyluski notes the principal forms of the words signifying 'man' and 'woman' in the Munda languages:

Man: hor, hōrol, harr, hõr, haṛa, hoṛ, koro

Woman: kūṛī, ērā, koṛi, kol

Comparing 'son' and 'daughter' in Santali:

Son = kora hapan; daughter = kuri hapan

"…a root kur, kor is differentiated in the Munda languages for signifying: man, woman, girl and boy. That in some cases this root has taken a relatively abstract sense is proved by Santali koḍa, koṛa, which signify 'one' as in the expression 'koḍa ke koḍa' 'each single one'. Thus one can easily understand that the same root has served the purpose of designating the individual not as an indivisible unity but as a numerical whole…Thus we can explain the analogy between the root kur, kor 'man' the number 20 in Munda kūṛī kūṛī , koḍī and the number 10 in Austro-Asiatic family ko, se-kūr, skall, gal." (ibid., pp. 28-30).

Homonym: कोल [ kōla ] *n* An income, or goods and chattels, or produce of fields &c. seized and sequestered (in payment of a debt). *V* धरून ठेव, सोड. 2 *f* The hole dug at the game of विटीदांडू, at marbles &c. कोलणें [ kōlaṇēm̤ ] *v c* To strike the विटी in the hole कोली with the bat or दांडू. (In the game of विटीदांडू) 2 To cast off from one's self upon another (a work). Ex. पैका मागावयास लागलों म्हणजे बाप लेंकावर कोल- तो लेंक बापावर कोलतो. 3 To cast aside, reject, disallow, flout, scout. कोलून मारणें To kick up the heels of; to trip up: also to turn over (from one side to the other). किरकोळी [ kirakōḷī ] *f* (किरकोळ) A heap of miscellaneous articles.

An old Munda word, kol means 'man'. S. K. Chatterjee called the Munda family of languages as Kol, as the word, according to him, is (in the Sanskrit-Prākṛt form Kolia) an early Aryan modification of an old Munda word meaning 'man'. [Chatterjee, SK, The study of kol, *Calcutta Review*, 1923, p. 455.] Przyluski accepts this explanation. [Przyluski, Non-aryan loans in Indo-Aryan, in: Bagchi, PC, *Pre-aryan and pre-dravidian,* pp.28-29 http://www.scribd.com/doc/33670494/preearyanandpredr035083mbp ]

Skanda Purana refers to kol as a mleccha community. (Hindu *śabdasagara*).

kolhe, 'the koles, are an aboriginal tribe of iron smelters speaking a language akin to that of Santals' (Santali) kōla m. name of a degraded tribe Hariv. Pk. Kōla — m.; B. kol name of a Muṇḍā tribe (CDIAL 3532). A Bengali lexeme confirms this: কোল[1] [ kōla[1] ] an aboriginal tribe of India; a member of this tribe. (Bengali) That in an early form of Indian linguistic area, kol means 'man' gets substantiated by a Nahali and Assamese glosses: kola 'woman'. See also: Wpah. Khaś.kuṛi, cur. kuḷī, cam. kŏḷā ' boy ', Sant. Muṇḍari koṛa ' boy ', kuṛi ' girl ', Ho koa, kui, Kūrkū kōn, kōnjē). Prob. separate from RV. kṟtā -- ' girl ' H. W. Bailey TPS 1955, 65; K. kūrü f. ' young girl ', kash. kōṛī, ram. kuṛhī; L. kuṛā m. ' bridegroom ', kuṛī f. ' girl, virgin, bride ', awāṇ. kuṛī f. ' woman '; P. kuṛī f. ' girl, daughter ', (CDIAL 3295). कारकोळी or ळ्या [ kārakōḷī or ḷyā ] a Relating to the country कार- कोळ--a tribe of Bráhmans (Marathi) —हरिवंश में **कोल** राज्य का नाम दक्षिण के पांडय और केरल के साथ आया है । पर बौद्ध ग्रंथों में कोल राज्य कपिलवस्तु के पूर्व रोहिणी नदी के उस पार बतलाया गया है । शुद्धौदन और सिद्धार्थ दोनों का विवाह इसी वंश में हुआ था । इस कोल वंश के विषय में बौद्धों मे ऐसा प्रसिद्ध कि इक्ष्वाकुवंश के चार पुरुष अपनी कोढ़िन बहन को हिमालय के अंचल में ले गए और उसे एक गुफा में बंद कर आए । कुछ दिनों के उपरांत काशी का एक कोढ़ी राजा भी उसी स्थान पर पहुँचा और काली मिर्च (कौल) खाकर अच्छा हो गया । राजा ने एक दिन देखा कि एक सिंह उस गुफा के द्वार पर रखे हुए पत्थर को हटाना चाहता है । राजा ने सिंह को मारा और गुहा से उसे कन्या का उद्धार करके उसका कुष्ट रोग छुड़ा दिया । उन्ही दोनों के संयोग से कौल वंश की उत्पत्ति हुई । स्कंद पुराण के हिमवत् खंड लिखा में है कि कोल एक म्लेच्छ जाति थी जो हिमालय में शिकार करती हुई घूमा करती थी । १२. एक जगली जाति । उ०—बन हित कोल किरात किसोरी । रची बिरंचि विषय सूख भोरी ।—मानस २ ।६० । **विशेष**—ब्रह्मवैवर्त पुराण में कोंल को लेट पुरुष और तीवर स्त्री से उत्पन्न एक वर्णसंकर जाति लिखा है । स्कंदपुराण में इसे म्लेच्छ जाति लिखा है । पद्मपुराण में लिखा है कि जब पवन, पल्लव, कोलि, सर्प आदि सगर के भय से वशिष्ठ की शरण में आए, तब उन्होंने उनका सिर आदि मुँड़ाकर उन्हें केवल संस्कारभ्रष्ट कर दिया । आजकल जो कोल नाम की एक जंगली जाति है, वह आर्यों से स्वतत्र एक आदिम जाति जान पड़ती है, और छोटा नागपुर से लेकर मिरजापुर के जंगलों तक फैली हुई है । (Hindi *śabdasagara*)

Mleccha and Bharatiya languages

Mleccha was substratum language of bharatiyo (casters of metal) many of whom lived in dvīpa (land between two rivers –Sindhu and Sarasvati -- or islands on Gulf of Kutch, Gulf of Khambat, Makran coast and along the Persian Gulf region of Meluhha).

Mleccha were bharatiya (Indians) of Indian linguistic area

According to Matsya Purāṇa (10.7), King Veṇa was the ancestor of the mleccha; according to Mahābhārata (MB. 12.59, 101-3), King Veṇa was a progenitor of the Niṣāda dwelling in the Vindhya mountains. Nirukta 3.8 includes Niṣāda among the five peoples mentioned in the ṛgveda 10.53.4, citing Aupamanyava; the five peoples are: brāhmaṇa, kṣatriya, vaiśya, śūdra and Niṣāda. Niṣāda gotra is mentioned in the gaṇapāṭha of Pāṇini (Aṣṭādhyāyī 4.1.100). Niṣāda were mleccha. It should be noted that Pāṇini associated yavana with the Kāmboja (Pāṇini, *Gaṇapāṭha*, 178 on 2.1.72).

Mullaippāṭṭu (59-66) (composed by kāvirippūmpāṭṭinattuppon vāṇigaṇār mahanārṇ.appūḍanār) are part of Pattuppāṭṭu, ten Tamil verses of Sangam literature; these refer to a chief of Tamil warriors whose battle-field tent was built by Yavana and guarded by mleccha who spoke only through gestures. (JV Chelliah, 1946, *Pattuppāṭṭu; ten Tamil idylls, translated into English verse*, South India Saiva Siddhanta Works Publishing Society, p. 91).

Mahābhārata notes that the Pāṇḍava army was protected by mleccha, among other people (Kāmboja , śaka, Khasa, Salwa, Matsya, Kuru, Mleccha, Pulinda, Draviḍa, Andhra and Kāñci) (MBh. V.158.20). Sūta laments the misfortune of the Kaurava-s: 'When the Nārāyaṇa-s have been killed, as also the Gopāla-s, those troops that were invincible in battle, and many thousands of mleccha-s, what can it be but Destiny?' (MBh. IX.2.36: *Nārāyaṇā hatāyatra Gopālā yuddhadurmahāh mlecchāśca bahusāhasrāh kim anyad bhāgadheyatah*?)

Nahali, Meluhhan, Language 'X'

On the banks of River Narmada are found speakers of Nahali, the so-called language isolate with words from Indo-Aryan, Dravidian and Munda – which together constitute the indic language substratum of a linguistic area, ca. 3300 BCE on the banks of Rivers Sarasvati and Sindhu – a region referred to as Meluhha in Mesopotamian cuneiform records; hence the language of the inscribed objects can rightly be called Meluhhan or Mleccha, a language which Vidura and Yudhiṣṭhira knew (as stated in the Great Epic, Mahābhārata).

Elsewhere in the Great Epic we read how Sahadeva, the youngest of the Pāṇḍava brothers, continued his march of conquest till he reached several islands in the sea (no doubt with the help of ships) and subjugated the Mleccha inhabitants thereof. Brahmāṇḍa 2.74.11, Brahma 13.152, Harivaṁśa 1841, Matsya 48.9, Vāyu 99.11, cf. also Viṣṇu 4.17.5, Bhāgavata 9.23.15, see Kirfel 1927: 522: *pracetasah putraśatam rājānah sarva eva te // mleccharāṣṭrādhipāh sarve udīcīm diśam āśritāh* which means, of course, not that these '100' kings conquered the 'northern countries' way beyond the Hindukuṣ or Himalayas, but that all these 100 kings, sons of pracetās (a descendant of a 'druhyu'), kings of mleccha kingdoms, are 'adjacent' (āśrita) to the 'northern direction,' — which since the Vedas and Pāṇini has signified Greater gandhāra. (Kirfel, W. Das *Purāṇa Pañcalakṣaṇa*.1927.Bonn : K. Schroeder.) This can be construed as a reference to a migration of the sons of Pracetas towards the northern direction to become kings of the mleccha states. The son of Yayati's third son, Druhyu, was Babhru, whose son and grandsons were Setu, Arabdha, Gandhara, Dharma, Dhṛta, Durmada and Praceta. It is notable that Pracetas is related to Dharma and Dhṛta, who are the principal characters of the Great Epic, the Mahābhārata. It should be noted that a group of people frequently mentioned in the Great Epic are the mleccha, an apparent designation of a group within the country, with Bhāratam janam (Bhārata people). This is substantiated by the fact that Bhagadatta, the king of Pragjyotiṣa is referred to as mleccha and he is also said to have ruled over two yavana kings (2.13).

Melakkha, island-dwellers, lapidaries

According to the great epic, Mlecchas lived on islands: "*sa sarvān mleccha nṛpatin sāgara dvīpa vāsinah, aram āhāryàm àsa ratnāni vividhāni ca, andana aguru vastrāṇi maṇi muktam anuttamam, kāñcanam rajatam vajram vidrumam ca mahādhanam*: (Bhima) arranged for all the mleccha kings, who dwell on the ocean islands, to bring varieties of gems, sandalwood, aloe, garments, and incomparable jewels and pearls, gold, silver, diamonds, and extremely valuable coral… great wealth." (MBh. 2.27.25-27). The reference to gems, pearls and corals evokes the semi-precious and precious stones, such as carnelian and agate, of Gujarat traded with Mesopotamian civilization. According to Sumerian records from the Agade Period (Sargon, 2373-2247 BC), Sumerian merchants traded with people from (at least) three named foreign places: Dilmun (now identified as the island of Bahrain in the Persian Gulf); Magan (a port on the coastline between the head of the Persian Gulf and the mouth of the Sindhu river); and Meluhha. Mentions of trade with Meluhha become freqùent in Ur III period (2168-2062 BCE) and Larsa dynasty (2062- 1770 BCE). To the end of the Sarasvati Civilization period, the trade declines dramatically attesting to Meluhha being the Sarasvati Civilization. By Ur III Period, Meluhhan workers residing in Sumeria had Sumerian names, leading to a comment: '…three hundred years after the earliest textually documented contact between Meluhha and Mesopotamia, the references to a distinctly foreign commercial people have been replaced by an ethnic component of Ur III society' This is an economic presence of Meluhhan traders maintaining their own village for a considerable span of time.(Parpola, Simo, Asko Parpola, and Robert H. Brunswig, Jr., 1977, "TheMeluhha Village — Evidence of Acculturation of Harappan Traders in Late Third Millenium Mesopotamia?", *Journal of the Economic and Social History of the Orient*, Volume 20, Part II.)

The epic also refers to the pāṇḍava Sahadeva's conquest of several islands in the sea with mleccha inhabitants.

A reference also to the salty marshes of Rann of Kutch in Gujarat (and also, perhaps, the Makran coast, south of Karachi), may also be surmised, where settlements and fortifications such as Amri Nal, Allahdino, Dholavira (Kotda) Sur-kota-da, and Kanmer have been excavated – close to the Sarasvati River Basin as the River traversed towards the Arabian ocean. *Kathāsaritsāgara* (tr. CH Tawney, 1880, Calcutta; rep. New Delhi, 1991), I, p. 151 associates mleccha with Sind. Mleccha kings paid tributes of sandalwood, aloe, cloth, gems, pearls, blankets, gold, silver and valuable corals.

Nakula conquered western parts of Bhāratavarṣa teeming with mleccha (MBh.V.49.26: *yah pratīcīm diśam cakre vaśe mlecchagaṇāyutām sa tatra nakulo yoddhā citrayodhī vyavasthitah*). Bṛhatsamhitā XIV.21 refers to lawless mleccha who inhabited the west: *nirmaryādā mlecchā ye paścimadiksthit āsteca*. A Buddhist chronicle, *āryaManjuśrī Mūlakalpa* [ed. Ganapati Śāstri, II, p. 274] associates pratyanta (contiguous)with mlecchadeśa in western Bhāratavarṣa: *paścimām diśīm āsṛtya rājāno mriyate tadā ye 'pi pratyantavāsinyo mlecchataskarajīvinah.* (trans. 'Then (under a certain astrological combination) the kings who go to the west die; also inhabitants of pratyanta live like the mlecchas and taskara.')

Where the black-antelope roams, along the sea-coast: mleccha areas Blackbuck (Antelope cervicapra) http://www.suwanneeriverranch.com/photos/BlackBuckBody.jpg

This metaphor defines the region fit for yajna. This metaphor also explains the movements of mleccha, such as kamboja-yavana, pārada-pallava along the Indian Ocean Rim as sea-faring merchants from Meluhha. This parallels the hindu-bauddha continuum exemplified by the Mathura lion capital with śrivatsa and Angkor Wat (Nagara vātika) as the largest Viṣṇu mandiram in the world, together with celebration of Bauddham in many parts of central, eastern and southeastern Asian continent. Mleccha were at no stage described in any text as people belonging to one ethnic, religious or linguistic group. This self-imposed restriction evidenced by all writers of the early Indian cultural tradition – Veda, Bauddha, Jaina alike – is of fundamental significance in understanding that mleccha constituted the core of the people on the banks of Rivers Sarasvati and Sindhu and were the principal architects, artisans, workers, and people, in general, of the Sarasvati-Sindhu Civilization throughout its stages of evolution through phases in modes of production – pastoral, agricultural, industrial – and interactions with neighbors, trading in surplus food products and artefacts generated and sharing cultural attributes/characteristics.

Various terms are used to describe mleccha social groups and communities: *pratyantadeś'a* (*Arthaśāstra* VII.10.16), *paccantimā janapada* (*Vinaya Piṭaka* V.13.12, vol. I, p. 197), *aṭavi, aṭavika* (DC Sircar, *Selected Inscriptions*, vol. I, 'Thirteenth Rock Edict Shābhāzgaṛhī, text line 7, p.37; 'Khoh Copper Plate Inscription of Saimkshobha', text line 8; *Arthaśāstra* VII.10.16; VII.4.43: *mlecchaṭavi* who were considered a threat to the state; *Arthaśāstra* IX.2.18-20 mentions *aṭavibala*, troops from forests as one of six types of troops at the disposal of a ruler). Some mleccha lived in border areas and forests, e.g. *pratyanta nṛpatibhir* (frontier kings: JF Fleet, CII, vol. II, 'Allahabad Posthumous Pillar Inscription of Samudragupta, text line 22, p. 116) cf. Arthaśāstra– a 4th century BCE text — I.12.21; VII.14.27; XIV.1.2; *mleccha jāti* are: *bheda,kirāta, śabara, pulinda*: *Amarakośa* II.10.20, a fifth century CE text).

In many Persian inscriptions Yauna, Gandhāra and Saka occur together. [For e.g., DC Sircar, *Selected Inscriptions*, no.2 'Persepolis Inscription on Dārayavahuṣ (Darius c. 522-486 BCE),' lines 12-13, 18, p.7; no. 5, 'Perseplis Inscription of Khshayārshā (Xerxes c. 486-465)', lines 23, 25-6, p. 12]. Thus, *yavana* may be a reference to people settled in the northwest Bhāratavarṣa (India).

There are references to Mleccha (that is, *śaka, Yavana, Kamboja, Pahlava*) in Bāla Kāṇḍa of the *Valmiki Rāmāyaṇa* (1.54.21-23; 1.55.2-3). *Taih asit samvrita bhūmih śakaih-Yavana miśritaih || 1.54-21 || taih taih Yavana-Kamboja barbarah ca akulii kritaah || 1-54-23 || tasya humkaarato jātah Kamboja ravi sannibhah | udhasah tu atha sanjatah Pahlavah śastra panayah || 1-55-2|| yoni deśāt ca Yavanah śakri deśāt śakah tathā | roma kupeṣ u Mlecchah ca Haritah sa Kiratakah || 1-55-3 ||.Kāmboja Yavanān caiva śakān paṭṭaṇāni ca | Anvīkṣya Varadān caiva Himavantam vicinvatha || 12 ||* — (*Rāmāyaṇa* 4.43.12)

The Yavanas here refer to the Bactrian Yavanas (in western Oxus country), and the Sakas here refer to the Sakas of Sogdiana/Jaxartes and beyond. The Vardas are the same as Paradas (*Hindu Polity*, 1978, p 124, Dr K. P. Jayswal; *Goegraphical Data in Early Purana*, 1972, p 165, 55 fn, Dr M. R.Singh). The Paradas were located on river Sailoda in Sinkiang (MBh II.51.12; II.52.13; VI.87.7 etc) and probably as far as upper reaches of river Oxus and Jaxartes (Op cit, p 159-60, Dr M. R.Singh).

Vanaparva of Mahābhārata notes: "......Mlechha (barbaric) kings of the śaka-s, Yavanas, Kambojas, Bahlikas etc shall rule the earth (i.e India) un-rightously in Kaliyuga..." *viparīte tadā loke purvarūpān kṣayasya tat || 34 || bahavo mechchha r\ājānah pṛthivyām manujādhipa | mithyanuśāsinah pāpa mṛ ṣavadaparāṇah || 35 || āndrah śakah Pulindaśca Yavanaśca narādhipāh | Kamboja Bahlikah śudrastathābhīra narottama* || 36|| MBH 3/188/34-36). Anushasanaparava of Mahābhārata affirms that Mathura, was under the joint military control of the Yavanas and the Kambojas (12/102/5). *Tathā Yavana Kambojā Mathurām abhitaś ca ye ete niyuddhakuśalā dākshiinātyāsicarminah*. Mahābhārata speaks of the Yavanas, Kambojas, Darunas etc as the fierce mleccha from Uttarapatha : *uttaraścāpare mlechchha jana bharatasattama. || 63 || Yavanashcha sa Kamboja Daruna mlechchha jatayah. | — (MBH 6.11.63-64) They are referred to as papakritah (sinful): uttara pathajanmanah kirtayishyami tanapi. | Yauna Kamboja Gandharah Kirata barbaraih saha. || 43 || ete pāpakṛtāstatra caranti prṛthivīmimām. | śvakakabalagridhraṇān sadharmaṇo narādhipa. || 44 ||* — (MBh 12/207/43-44) http://en.wikipedia.org/wiki/Invasion_of_India_by_Scythian_Tribes#Establishment_of_Mlechcha_Kingdoms_in_Northern_India

Yavana are descendants of Turvaśu, one of the four sons of Yayāti. The sons were to rule over people such as Yavana, Bhoja and Yādava (MBh. 1.80.23-4; Matsya Purāṇa 34.29-30). Yavana, descendants of Turvaśu are noted as meat-eaters, sinful and hence, anārya. [MBh. trans. PC Roy, vol. I, p. 179] These people were brought over the sea safely by Indra (RV 6.20.12). In the Mahābhārata, sons of Anu are noted as mleccha. ṛgveda notes that Yadu and Turvaśa are dāsa (RV 10.62.10):

*sanema te vasā navya indra pra pūrava stavanta enā yajnaih*

*sapta yat purah śarma śāradīr dadruiśa dhan dāsīh purukutsāya śikṣan*

*tvam vrdha indraprvyarja bhūr varivasyann uśane kāvyāya*

*parā navavāstvam anudeyam mahe pitre dadātha svam napātam*

*tvam dhunir indra dhunimtrṇor āpah sīrā na sravantīh*

*pra yat samudram ati śūra parśi pāraya turvaśam yadum svasti*

RV 6.020.10 (Favoured) by your proection, Indra, we solicit new (wealth); by this adoration men glorify you at sacrifices, for that you have shattered with your bolt the seven cities of śarat, killing the opponents (of sacred rites), killing the opponents (of sacred rites), and giving (their spoils) to Purukutsa. [Men: puravah = manuṣyah; śarat = name of an asura].

RV 6.020.11 Desirous of opulence, you, Indra, have been an ancient benefactor of Us'anas, the son of Kavi; having slain Navavāstva, you have given back his own grandson, who was (fit) to be restored o the grandfather.

RV 6.020.12 You, Indra, who make (your enemies) tremble, have caused the waters, detained by Dhuni, to flow like rushing rivers; so, hero, when, having crossed the ocean, you have reached the shore, you have brought over in safety Turvas'a and Yadu. [*samudram atipraparṣi* = samudram atikramya pratirṇo bhavasi = when you are crossed, having traversed the ocean, you have brought across Turvaśa and Yadu, both standing on the future shore, *samudrapāretiṣṭhantau apārayah*].

Nandana, another commentator of *Mānava Dharma śāstra*. X.45, defines *āryavāc as samskṛtavāc*. Thus, according to Medhātithi, neither habitation nor mleccha speech is the ground for regarding groups as Dasyus, but it is because of their particular names Barbara etc., that they are so regarded. These people were brought over the sea safely by Indra, as noted by this ṛca. This ṛca also notes that Yadu and Turvaśa (are) dāsa; and that Turvaśu is a son of Yayāti. The sons of Yayāti were to rule over people such as Yavana, Bhoja and Yādava. Turvaśu and Yadu crossed the oceans to come into Bhāratavarṣa. In this ṛca., 'samudra' can be interpreted only as an ocean. The ocean crossed by Indra, may be not too far from Sindhu. Sindhu is a 'natural ocean frontier' in ṛgveda. Given the activities of the Meluhha along the Makran Coast (300 km. south of Mehergarh, in the neighbourhood of Karachi), Gulf of Kutch and Gulf of Khambat, (evidence? *Turbinella pyrum* —śankha-bangle found in a woman's grave in Mehergarh, dated to c. 6500 BCE, yes 7th millennium BCE; the type of shell found nowhere else in the world excepting the coastline of Sindhu sāgara upto to the Gulf of Mannar).

The ocean referred to may be the ocean in the Gulf of Kutch and was situated with a number of dvīpas. In places north of Lamgham district, i.e. north bank of river Kabul, near Peshawar were regions known as Mi-li-ku, the frontier of the mleccha lands. [S. Beal, 1973, *The Life of Hiuen Tsiang*, New Delhi, p 57; cf. NL Dey, *Geographical Dictionary of India*, p. 113 for an identification of Lamgham (Lampakā) 20 miles north-west of Jalalabad.] *Harivamśa* 85.18-19 locates the mleccha in the Himalayan region and mleccha are listed with yavana, *śaka, darada, pārada, tuṣāra, khaśa* and *pahlava* in north and north-west Bhāratavarṣa: *sa viv ṛddho yad ā rāj ā yavan ānām mah ābalāh tata enam nṛpā mlecch āh sams'rity ānuyayaus tad ā śakās tuṣār ā daradāh pāradās tan:gaṇāh khasśāh pahlavāh śataśaścānye mlecch ā haimavat ās tathā. Matsya Purāṇa* 144.51-58 provides a list. Pracetā had a hundred sons all of whom ruled in mleccha regions in the north. [Matsya Purāṇa 148.8-9; Bhāgavata Purāṇa IX.23.16.] Bhīṣma Parvan of Mahābhārata notes that mleccha jāti people lived in Yavana, Kāmboa, Dāruṇā regions and are listed together with several other peoples of the northern and north-western parts of Bhāratavarṣa (MBh. VI.10.63-66: *uttarāścāpare mlecchā janā bharatasattama yavanāśca śaka, kāmbojā dārun.ā mlecchajātayah*). In *Rāmāyaṇa* IV.42.10, Sugrīva is asked to search for Sītā in the northern lands of mleccha, pulinda, sūrasena, praṣalā, bhārata, kuru, madraka, kamboja and yavana before proceeding to Himavat: *tatra mlecchān pulindāmśūrasen āmś tathaiva ca prasthalān bharatāmścaiva kurūmsśca saha madraih*. Mlecchas came from the valley adjoining the Himalaya. [Rājataranginī , VII. 2762-64.]

When Sagara, son of Bāhu, was prevented from destroying śaka, Yavana, Kāmboa, Pārada and Pāhlava after he recovered his kingdom, Vasiṣṭha, the family priest of Sagara, absolved these people of their duties but Sagara commanded the Yavana to shave the upper half of their heads, the Pārada to wear long hair and Pahlava to let their beards grow. Sagara also absolved them of their duty to offer yajna to agni and to study the Veda. [Vāyu Purāṇa 88.122. 136- 43; Brahmāṇḍa Purāṇa 3.48.43-49; 63.119-34.] This is how these Yavana, Pārada and Pahlava also became mleccha. [Viṣṇu Purāṇa 4.3.38-41.] The implication is that prior to Sagara's command, these kṣatriya communities did respect Vasiṣṭha as their priest, studied the Veda and performed yajna. [Harivamśa 10.41-45.] Śaka who were designated as kings of mleccha jāti by Bhaṭṭa Utpala (10th century) in his commentary on Bṛhatsamhitā, were defeated by Candragupta II. That the mleccha were also adored as ṛṣi is clear from the verse of *Bṛhatsamhitā* 2.15: *mlecchā hi yavanās teṣu samyak śāstram kadam sthitam ṛṣivat te 'pi pūjyante kim punar daivavid dvijāh* (The yavana are mleccha, among them this science is duly established; therefore, even they (although mleccha) are honoured as ṛṣi; how much more (praise is due to an) astrologer who is a brāhmaṇa'). *Bṛhatsamhitā* 14.21 confirms that the yavana, śaka and pahlava lived on the west. Similarly, Konow notes that Sai-wang (Saka King) mentioned in Chinese accounts should be interpreted as Saka Muruṇḍa and the territory he occupied as Kāpiśa. [Sten Konow, *CII*, vol. II, pp. xx ff; Sten Konow, EI, no. 20 'Taxila Inscription of the Year 136', vol. XIV, pp. 291-2.] Śaka migrated to Bhāratavarṣa through Arachosia via the Bolan Pass into the lower Sindhu, a region called Indo_Scythia by Greek geographers and called śaka-dvīpa in Bhāratiya texts. [EJ Rapson, ed., 1922,*Cambridge History of India* , vol. I, Ancient India, Cambridge, p. 564.] Another view expressed by Thomas is that the migration was through Sindh and the valley of the Sindhu River. [FW Thomas, 'Sakastana', JRAS, 1906, p. 216.] Kalhaṇa notes that Jalauka, a son of Aśoka took possession of Kāśmīra, advanced as far as Kanauj, after crushing a horse of mleccha. [Rājataranginī, 1.107-8.] Greek invasions occurred later, during the reign of Puṣyamitra śunga (c. 185-150 BCE). The regions inhabited by the 'milakkha' could be the Vindhyan region. The term, 'mleccha' of which 'milakkha' is a variant, could as well have denoted the indigenous people (Nahali?) or of Bhāratavarṣa who had lived on the Sarasvati River basin and who moved towards other parts of Bhāratavarṣa after the gradual desiccation of the river, over a millennium, between c. 2500 and 1500 BCE. Medhātithi, commenting on the verse of Manu, defines a language as mleccha : *asad avidyam ān\ārthās ādhu śabdatayā vāk mleccha ucyate yathā śabarāṇām kirātānām anyeyām va antyānām*: Medhātithi on *Mānava Dharmaśāstra* X.45 – 'Language is called mleccha because it consists of words that have no meaning or have the wrong meaning or are wrong in form. To this class belong the languages of such low-born tribes as the śabara-s, Kirāta and so forth...'... He further proceeds to explain that āryavāc is refined speech and the language of the inhabitants of āryāvarta, but only of those who belong to the four varṇa-s. The others are called Dasyus.: ibid. – *āryavāca āryāvartam vāsinas te cāturvarṇy ādanyajātīyatvena prasiddhas tadā dasyava ucyante* 'Arya (refined) language is the language of the inhabitants of āryāvarta. Those persons being other than the four varṇa-s are called Dasyus.'

In Dhammapada's commentary on Petuvathu, Dwaraka is associated with Kamboja as its Capital or its important city.[ The Buddhist Concepts of Spirits, p 81, Dr B. C. Law.] See evidence below:

"*Yasa asthaya gachham Kambojam dhanharika/ ayam kamdado yakkho iyam yakham nayamasai// iyam yakkham gahetvan sadhuken pasham ya/ yanam aaropyatvaan khippam gaccham Davarkān iti* " [Buddhist Text *Khudak Nikaya* (P.T.S)]

Mleccha who came to the Rājasūya also included those from forest and frontier areas (MBh. III. 48.19:*sāgarān ūpagāmścaiva ye ca paṭṭaṇavāsinah simhal ān barbarān mlecchān ye ca jān:galavāsinah*). Bhīmasena proceeded east towards Lohitya (Brahmaputra) and had conquered several mleccha people who bestowed on him wealth of various kinds (MBh. II.27.23-24: *suhmānāmādhipam caiva ye ca sāgaravāsinah sarvān mlecchagaṇāmścaiva vijigye bharatarṣabhah evam bahu vidhān deśān vijitya pavanātmajah vasu tebhya upādya lauhityam agad balī.* [NL Dey, *Geographical Dictionary*, p. 115.]

Celebrations at the Kalinga capital of Duryodhana were attended by preceptors and mleccha kings from the south and east of Bhārata (MBh. XII.4.8: *ete cānye ca bahavo dakṣinām diśām āśritah mlecchā āryāśca rāj ānah prācyodicyāśca bhārata*).

Bhāgadatta, the great warrior of Prāgjyotiṣa accompanied by mleccha people inhabiting marshy regions of the sea- coast (*sāgarānūpavāsibhih*), attends the Rājasūya of Yudhiṣṭhira (MBh. II.31.9-10: *prāgjyotiṣaśca nṛpatir bhagadatto mahāyaśāh saha sarvais tathā mlecchaih sāgarānūpavāsibhih*). This is perhaps a reference ot the marshy coastline of Bengal. *Amarakośa* II, Bhūmivarga – 6: pratyanto mlecchade śah syāt; Sarvānanda in his commentary, ṭīkāsarvasva, elaborates that mleccha deśa denotes regions without proper conduct such as Kāmarūpa: *bhāratavarṣasyāntadeśah śiṣṭācārā rahitah kāmarūpādih mlecchadeśāh* [Nāmalingānuśāsana, with commentary ṭīkāsarvasva, of Sarvānanda (ed. Ganapati śāstri)]; he also cites Manu that where four varṇa-s are not established that region is mlecchadeśa. A contemporary of Harṣavardhana was Bhāskaravarman of Kāmarūpa; this king was supplanted by another dynasty founded by śālastambha who was known as a mleccha overlord. [SK Chatterji, 1950, Kirāta-jana-kṛti --The Indo-Mongoloids: Their contributions to the and culture of India, Journal of Royal Asiatic Society of Bengal, Vol. XVI, pp.143-253.]

Meluhha, Mleccha areas: Sarasvati River Basin and Coastal Regions of Gujarat, Baluchistan

Meluhha referred to in Sumerian and old Akkadian texts refers to an area in Sarasvati Civilization; Asko and Simo Parpola add: '...probably, including NW India with Gujarat as well as eastern Baluchistan'.[ WF Leemans, Foreign Trade in the Old Babylonian Period, 1960; 'Trade Relations on Babylonia', Journal of Economic and Social History of the Orient, vol. III, 1960, p.30 ff. 'Old Babylonian Letters and Economic History', Journal of Economic and Social History of the Orient, vol. XI, 1968, pp. 215-26; J. Hansam, 'A Periplus of Magan and Meluhha', Bulletin of the School of Oriental and African Studies, vol. 36, pt. III, 1973, pp. 554-83. Asko and Simo Parpola, 'On the Relationship of the Sumerian Toponym Meluhha and Sanskrit Mleccha', Studia Orientalia,vol. 46, 1975, pp. 205-38.]

Imports from Meluhha into Mesopotamia included the following commodities which were found in north-western and western Bhāratavarṣa: copper, silver, gold, carnelian, ivory, uśu wood (ebony), and another wood which is translated as 'sea wood' – perhaps mangrove wood on the coasts of Sind ad Baluchistan. [J. Hansman, 'A Periplus of Magan and Meluhha', Bulletin of the School of Oriental and African Studies, vol. 36, pt. III, 1973, pp. 560.] The Ur texts specifically refer to 'seafaring country of Meluhha" and hence, Leemans' thesis that Meluhha was the west coast (modern state of Gujarat) of Bhārata. The Lothal dockyard had fallen into disuse by c.1800 BCE, a date when the trade between Mesopotamia and Meluhha also ended. [WF Leemans, 'Old Babylonian Letters and Economic History', Journal of Economic and Social History of the Orient, vol. XI, 1968, pp. 215-26. P. Aalto, 1971, 'Marginal Notes on the Meluhha Problem,' Professor KA Nilakanta Sastri Felicitation Volume, Madras, pp. 222-23.] In Leemans' view, Gujarat was the last bulwark of the (Indus or Sarasvati) Civilization. Records refer to Meluhhan ships docking at Sumer. There were Meluhhans in various Sumerian cities; there was also a Meluhhan town or district at one city. The Sumerian records indicate a large volume of trade; according to a Sumerian tablet, one shipment from Meluhha contained 5,900 kg of copper (13,000 lbs, or 6 ½ tons)! The bulk of this trade was done through Dilmun, not directly with Meluhha. In our view, the formative stages of the Civilization also had their locus in the coastal areas – in particular, the Gulf of Khambat, Gulf of Kutch and Makran coast, as evidenced by the wide shell-bangle, dated to c. 6500 BCE, made of turbinella pyrum or śankha, found in Mehergarh, 300 miles north of the Makran coast.

Evidence exists for trade in shells found uniquely in the region, in particular, a shell called xancus pyrum: See: Xancus Pyrum and trade routes emanating from the subcontinent. "Silvio Durante's study (1979) of marine shells from India and their appearance in the archaeological record in such distant sites as Tepe Yahya and Shahr-i Sokhta in Iran, as well as in the Indus Valley, sheds light on the ancient trading routes of certain types of shells which are specifically and exclusively found along the Indian coastline proper. Following Phil Kohl's arguments, where shells were traded, so culture, technology, religion, etc. must have followed.[ Kohl, Phil L., 1979, "The 'World Economy' of West Asia in the Third Millenium BC." In South Asian Archaeology 1977, Naples. Durante, Silvio, 1979, "Marine Shells from Balakot, Shahr-I-Sokhta and Tepe Yahya: Their Significance for Trade Technology in Ancient Indo-Iran." In South Asian Archaeology 1977, Naples.] "Durante primarily discusses the marine shell Xancus pyrum and the fact that it was traded whole and intact, then worked or reworked at its destination site, perhaps then moving on to other locations. The importance of this specific shell is that 'Xancus Pyrum has a very limited geographic distribution and thus has almost the same significance in the field of shells as that of lapis lazuli in the context of mineral resources as regards the determination of the possible routes along which a locally unavailable raw material is transported from a well-defined place of origin to the place where it is processed and, as also in the case of Xancus Pyrum, consumed' (Durante 1979:340). Durante also interestingly points out that as the shells were traded as a raw resource for later working, the trade phenomena of 'increasingly high degrees of product finishing in order to add a surplus value to the goods' (Durante 1979:340) does not exist. Perhaps, as these shells crossed so many cultural hands, they were left un-worked in order for the final owner or consumer to work the raw material into a style and usage specific to their region. Durante offers four possible trade routes from their gathering zone along the west and northwest Indian coast to destinations west: sea route direct to the Iranian coastal area; sea route to Sutkagen-dor and Sotka-koh on the Makran coast, then overland westwards; overland through the Indus plain and then through the Makran interior to Sistan; overland through the Indus Valley and then through the Gomal Valley to Sistan. "Thus we now have hard evidence for trade and cultural exchange, plus traceable routes for objects emanating from the farthest south eastern reaches of the Harappan cultural sphere to destinations far west of the Indus. There can be no doubt that the Harappans were part of multiple trading networks involving their immediately peripheral neighbors and others far beyond... "To facilitate the obtainment of the sought-after goods, sites were located in such far flung locations as Sutkagen-dor in Makran as a source for ocean materials such as shell and for the site's proximity to Persian Gulf trade routes; Bala Kot in eastern Makran, which, like Sutkagen-dor, was a source for ocean materials and access to Persian Gulf trade routes; Lothal in Gujarat, India, which is usually considered the 'gateway to the east;' Shortugai in Badakhshan, Afghanistan, for its proximity to the lapis mines..." [Chris JD Kostman, The Indus Valley Civilization: in search of those elusive centers and peripheries; Originally published in JAGNES, the Journal of the Association of Graduates in Near Eastern Studies. http://www.adventurecorps.com/centperiph.html]

Like Nahali (Nahari > Nagari) on banks of River Tapati, mleccha is a language-composite of Indo-Aryan, Dravidian and Munda linguistic area circa 5000 years Before Present on Sarasvati-Indus River Basins; all proto-versions of present-day languages of Bharat are a dialectical continuum from this linguistic area (Further researches and identification of isoglosses are called for).

It is possible to derive the underlying language of Indus script of the Indus civilization using the insights provided by areal linguistics pointing to an Indian *sprachbund*. Based on the reality of this underlying *sprachbund*, a substrate dictionary has been compiled with over 1240 semantic clusters. These clusters include about 4000 etyma with cognates in Indo-Aryan (CDIAL), Dravidian (DEDR) and Munda (Santali, Mundarica) language groups. That about 4000 of the 5200 dravidian etyma in Dravidian Etymological Dictionary (DEDR) get so clustered also substantiates the Indian *sprachbund*.

*Indian Lexicon* (Kalyanaraman, 1992) http://www.scribd.com/doc/2232617/lexicon lists cognate lexemes of 25+ ancient languages of Bharat; including about 4,000 of the 5,200 etyma of Dravidian Etymological Dictionary and hundreds of Munda lexemes. Most of the semantic clusters of this lexicon are a veritable substrate lexicon of the Indus language or proto-Indic.

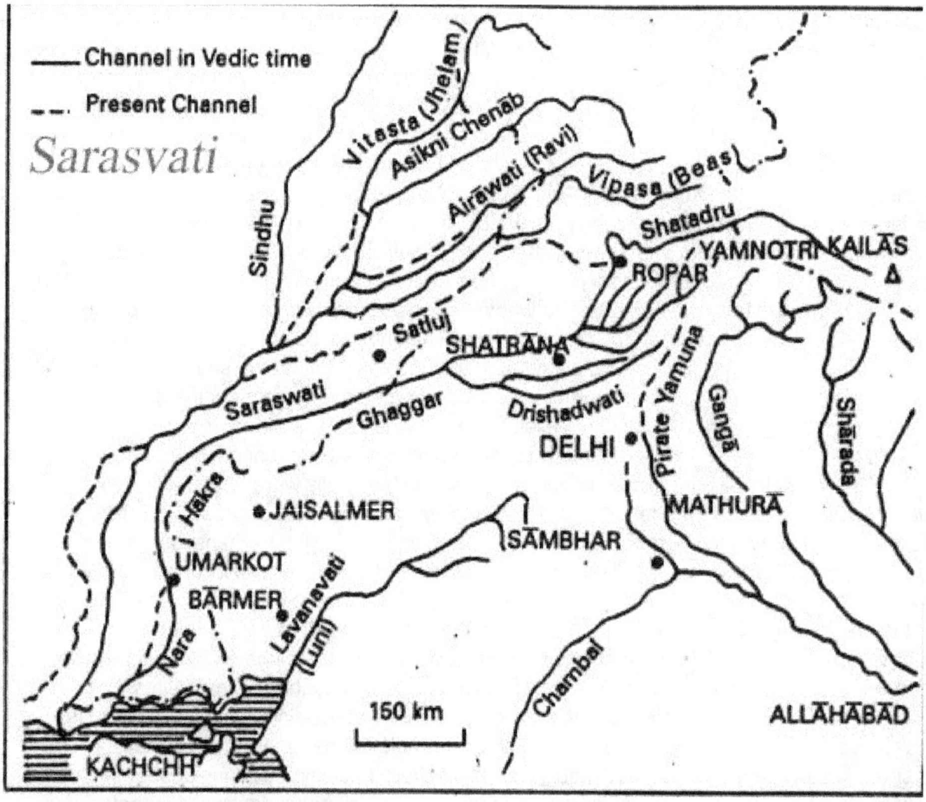


The map drawn by Prof. KS Valdiya shows Vedic River Sarasvati and diversion of Yamuna into Ganga and of Sutlej into Sindhu, ca. 1900 BCE, thus desiccating the glacial flows. (Valdiya, K. S., 1996, *Resonance*,1, pp.19-28.) Sarasvati civilization with over 2000 archaeological sites (that is, 80% of a total of about 2,600 sites of the civilization) on the Sarasvati River Basin in India, is a civilization continuum.

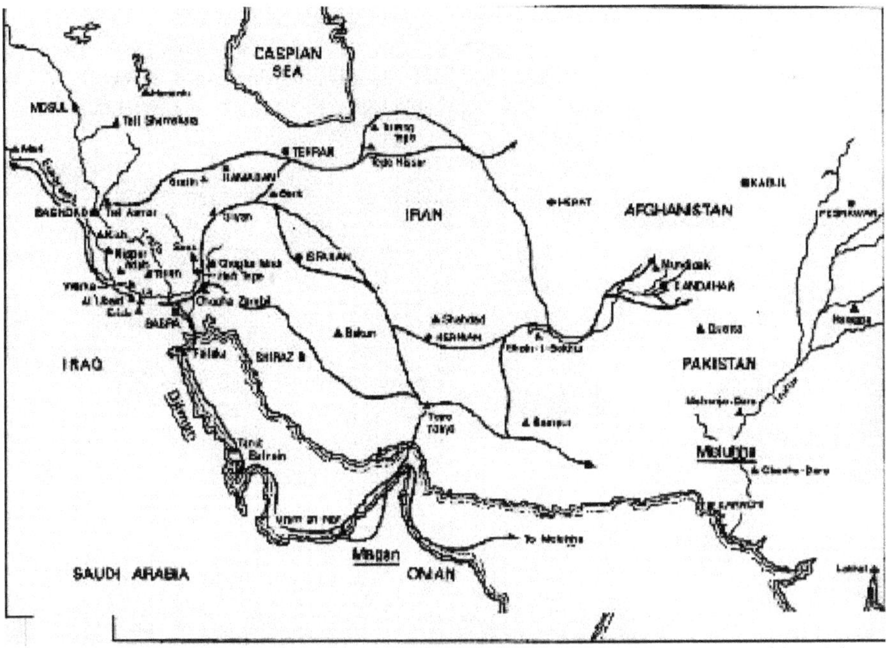


Interaction areas. After Fig. 2 in P.R.S. Moorey, 1994, *Ancient Mesopotamian Materials and Industries*, Oxford, Clarendon Press. [After Fig. 2 in P.R.S. Moorey, 1994, Ancient Mesopotamian Materials and Industries, Oxford, Clarendon Press.]

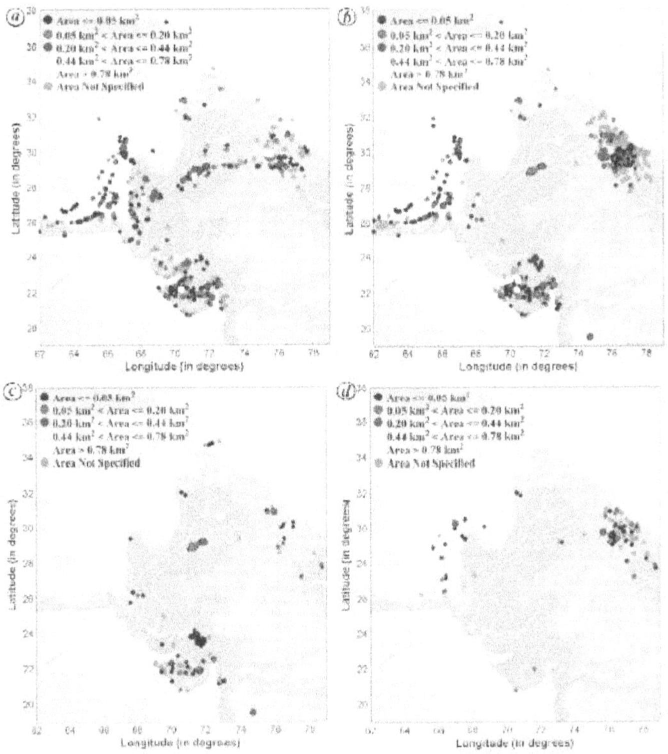

Plots of the distribution of archaeological sites in the greater Indus valley at (a) 2500 BCE; (b) 1900 BCE; (c) 1500 BCE; (d) 1000 BCE. Sites are color coded by area according to the legend. Large area sites are emphasized by increasing their symbol size. Source for the archaeological sites distribution maps: Current Science, Vol. 98, No. 6, 25 March 2010, pp 846-852; Spatio-temporal analysis of the

Indus urbanization Kavita Gangal, M. N. Vahia and R. Adhikari
http://www.ias.ac.in/currsci/25mar2010/846.pdf

Sarasvarti river basin and Gujarat have about 2000 (80%) of archaeological sites of the civilization.

The principal interaction areas were within Meluhha and in the regions identified as Turan towards the Caspian Sea, Magan, Dilmun and Mesopotamian cultural zones across the Persian Gulf and the Tigris-Euphrates doab.

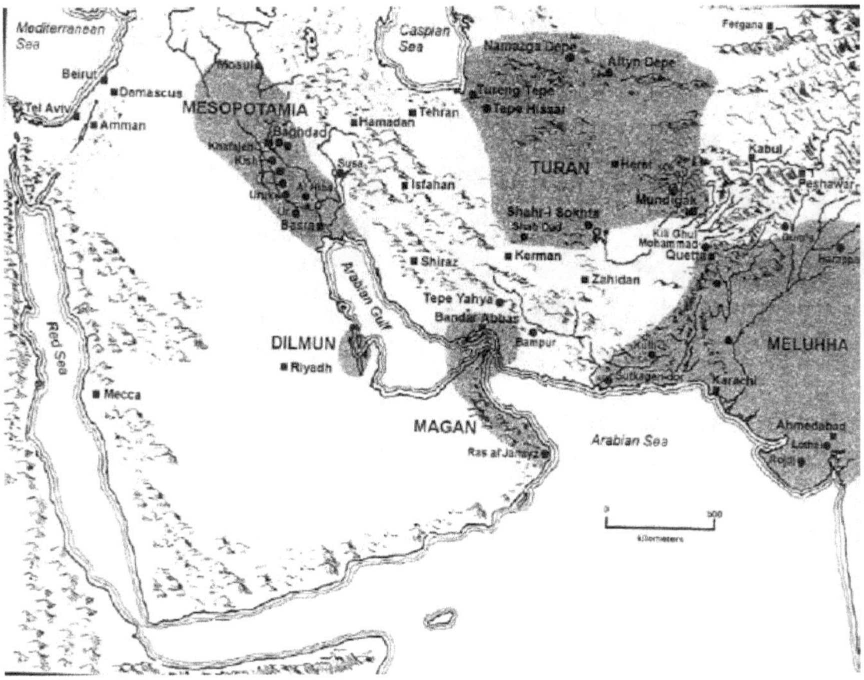


Western Asia showing Mesopotamia, Turan, Dilmun, Meluhha. Source: Magan and Meluhha See Steinkeller 1984, 265.

Over 45 sites where objects with epigraphs have been discovered

Tanana mleccha

A Jaina text, Avasyaka Churani notes that ivory trade was managed by mleccha, who also traveled from Uttaravaha to Dakshinapatha.[ Jain, 1984, Life in Ancient India as Described in the Jain Canon and Commentaries (6th century BC - 17th century AD, p. 150.] Guttila Jataka (ca.4th cent.) makes reference to itinerant ivory workers/traders journeying from Varanasi to Ujjain. [Cowell, 1973, Jatakas Book II, p. 172 ff.] The phrase, *tanana mleccha* may be related to: (i) tah'nai, 'engraver' mleccha; or (ii) tana, 'of (mleccha) lineage'. 1. See Kuwi. Tah'nai 'to engrave' in DEDR and Bsh. Then, thon, 'small axe' in CDIAL: DEDR 3146 *Go.* (Tr.) tarcana , (Mu.) tarc- to scrape; (Ma.) tarsk- id., plane; (D.) task-, (Mu.) tarsk-/tarisk- to level, scrape (*Voc.*1670).

Sea-faring merchants/artisans of Meluhha

Akkadian. Cylinder seal Impression. Inscription records that it belongs to 'S'u-ilis'u, Meluhha interpreter', i.e., translator of the Meluhhan language (EME.BAL.ME.LUH.HA.KI) The Meluhhan being introduced carries an goat on his arm. Musee du Louvre. Ao 22 310, Collection De Clercq 3rd millennium BCE. The Meluhhan is accompanied by a lady carrying a kamaṇḍalu.

Since he needed an interpreter, it is reasonably inferred that Meluhhan did not speak Akkadian.

Antelope carried by the Meluhhan is a hieroglyph: mlekh 'goat' (Br.); mṛeka (Te.); mēṭam (Ta.); meṣam (Skt.) Thus, the goat conveys the message that the carrier is a Meluhha speaker. A phonetic determinant.mrṛeka, mlekh 'goat'; Rebus: melukkha Br. Mēlh 'goat'. Te. Mṛeka (DEDR 5087) meluh.h.a !

"While Prof. Thomson maintained that a Munda influence has probably been at play in fixing the principle regulating the inflexion of nouns in Indo-Aryan vernaculars, such influence appeared to be unimportant to Prof. Sten Konow... Prof. Przyluski in his papers, translated here, have tried to explain a certain number of words of the Sanskrit vocabulary as fairly ancient loans from the Austro-Asiatic family of languages. He has in this opened up a new line of enquiry. Prof. Jules Bloch in his article on Sanskrit and Dravidian, also translated in this volume, has the position of those who stand exclusively for Dravidian influence and has proved that the question of the Munda substratum in Indo-Aryan cannot be overlooked...In 1923, Prof. Levi, in a fundamental article on *Pre-Aryen et Pre-Dravidian dans Vinde* tried to show that some geographical names of ancient India like Kosala-Tosala, Anga-Vanga, Kalinga-Trilinga, Utkala-Mekala and Pulinda-Kulinda, ethnic names which go by pairs, can be explained by the morphological system of the Austro-Asiatic languages. Names like Accha-Vaccha, Takkola-Kakkola belong to the same category. He concluded his long study with the following observation, " We must know whether the legends, the religion and the philosophical thought of India do not owe anything to this past. India has been too exclusively examined from the Indo-European standpoint. It ought to be remembered that India is a great maritime country... the movement which carried the Indian colonization towards the Far East... was far from inaugurating a new route...Adventurers, traffickers and missionaries profited by the technical progress of navigation and followed under better conditions of comfort and efficiency, the way traced from time immemorial, by the mariners of another race, whom Aryan or Aryanised India despised as savages." In 1926, Przyluski tried to explain the name of an ancient people of the Punjab, the Udumbara, in a similar way and affiliate it to the Austro-Asiatic group. (cf. *Journal Asiatique*, 1926, 1, pp. 1-25, Un ancien peuple du Pendjab — les Udumbaras: only a portion of this article containing linguistic discussions has been translated in the Appendix of this book.) In another article, the same scholar discussed some names of Indian towns in the geography of Ptolemy and tried to explain them by Austro-Asiatic forms...Dr. J. H. Hutton, in an interesting lecture on the Stone Age Cult of Assam delivered in the Indian Museum at Calcutta in 1928, while dealing with some prehistoric monoliths of Dimapur, near Manipur, says that " the method of erection of these monoliths is very important, as it throws some light on the erection of prehistoric monoliths in other parts of the world. Assam and Madagascar are the only remaining parts of the world where the practice of erecting rough stones still continues....The origin of this stone cult is uncertain, but it appears that it is to be mainly imputed to the Mon-Khmer intrusion from the east In his opinion the erection of these monoliths takes the form of the lingam and yoni. He thinks that the Tantrik form of worship, so prevalent in Assam, is probably due to " the incorporation into Hinduism of a fertility cult which preceded it as .the religion of the country. The dolmens possibly suggest distribution from South India, but if so, the probable course was across the Bay of Bengal and then back again westward from further Asia. Possibly the origin was from Indonesia whence apparently the use of supari (areca nut) spread to India as well as the Pacific." (From the Introduction by PC Bagchi and SK Chatterjee, 1 May 1929).

On 'Sanskrit and Dravidian', comments by Jules Bloch: "There is, therefore, nothing to justify the assertion that Indo-Aryan cerebrals are of indigenous origin. The local pronunciation has rendered the development of this class possible ; and in this sense the action of the substratum is undeniable. But it is necessary at once to insist upon the fact that the Munda languages have dentals and cerebrals just like Dravidian, and nothing, therefore, stands in the way of attributing theoretically the origin of the Sanskrit pronunciation to the action of a substratum of either Munda or some other language connected with it, if not of a fourth linguistic family still unknown...A curious fact that might be noted here is the continuous character of the Sanskrit sentences, which has given rise to the rules of sandhi, because Tamil and Canarese admit a rigorous sandhi in writing, But the same languages in their spoken form ignore it; Gondi and Kurukh also ignore it. In so far as these literary languages admit this tandhi, it is certainly due to the influence of Sanskrit ; and even in Sanskrit it is probable that the use of the rules in question has very much surpassed in extension the real use ; Aśoka ignores them absolutely. There is, therefore, no clear phonetic proof of the action of Dravidian on Indo-European, at any rate, in ancient times...The facts of a substratum result from the unconscious blending of two systems existing amongst the same people ; the loan results from a willing effort to add elements taken from outside to the mass of the vocabulary. The loan proves the contact of the two languages and not the substitution of the one by the other. On the other hand it is often difficult to say in what sense the borrowing is made between two given languages and to make sure that it has not been made by each of the two languages from a third one, known or unknown... Perhaps the principal interest for ourselves in the study of ancient loans (and it would be necessary to try both ways since Dravidian has borrowed much from Aryan) would be to form an idea of prehistoric Dravidian ; because even those Dravidian languages which have a past are only attested in a definite way, for the first time, a few centuries after the Christian Era. Moreover the complications we have met with, suggest that Dravidian like Sanskrit may have taken loans of vocabulary from Munda, which must be at least as ancient as Dravidian in India." (pp. 40-59).

Kuiper notes: " ...a very considerable amount (say some 40%) of the New Indo-Aryan vocabulary is borrowed from Munda, either via Sanskrit (and Prākṛt), or via Prākṛt alone, or directly from Munda; wide-branched and seemingly native, word-families of South Dravidian are of Proto-Munda origin; in Vedic and later Sanskrit, the words adopted have often been Aryanized, resp. Sanskritized. "In view of the intensive interrelations between Dravidian, Munda and Aryan dating from pre-Vedic times even individual etymological questions will often have to be approached from a Pan-Indic point of view if their study is to be fruitful. It is hoped that this work may be helpful to arrive at this all-embracing view of the Indian languages, which is the final goal of these studies." F.B.J. Kuiper, 1948, Proto-Munda Words in Sanskrit, Amsterdam, Verhandeling der Koninklijke Nederlandsche Akademie Van Wetenschappen, Afd. Letterkunde, Nieuwe Reeks Deel Li, No. 3, 1948, p.9
http://www.scribd.com/doc/12238039/mundalexemesinSanskrit

Emeneau notes: "In fact, promising as it has seemed to assume Dravidian membership for the Harappa language, it is not the only possibility. Professor W. Norman Brown has pointed out (The United States and India and Pakistan, 131-132, Cambridge, Harvard University Press, 1953) that Northwest India, i.e. the Indus Valley and adjoining parts of India, has during most of its history had Near Eastern elements in its political and cultural make-up at least as prominently as it had true Indian elements of the Gangetic and Southern types. [M.B.Emeneau, India as a Linguistic Area [Lang. 32, 1956, 3-16; LICS, 196, 642-51; repr. In Collected papers: Dravidian Linguistics Ethnology and Folktales, Annamalai Nagar, Annamalai University, 1967, pp. 171-186.] The passage is so important that it is quoted in full: 'More ominous yet was another consideration. Partition now would reproduce an ancient, recurring, and sinister incompatibility between Northwest and the rest of the subcontinent, which, but for a few brief periods of uneasy cohabitation, had kept them politically apart or hostile and had rendered the subcontinent defensively weak. When an intrusive people came through the passes and established itself there, it was at first spiritually closer to the relatives it had left behind than to any group already in India. Not until it had been separated from those relatives for a fairly long period and had succeeded in pushing eastward would I loosen the external ties. In period after period this seems to have been true. In the third millennium B.C. the Harappa culture in the Indus Valley was partly similar to contemporary western Asian civilizations and partly to later historic Indian culture of the Ganges Valley. In the latter part of the next millennium the earliest Aryans, living in the Punjab and composing the hymns of the Rig Veda, were apparently more like their linguistic and religious kinsmen, the Iranians, than like their eastern Indian contemporaries. In the middle of the next millennium the Persian Achaemenians for two centuries held the Northwest as satrapies. After Alexander had invaded India (327/6-325 B.C.) and Hellenism had arise, the Northwest too was Hellenized, and once more was partly Indian and partly western. And after Islam entered India, the Northwest again was associated with Persia, Bokhara, Central Asia, rather than with India, and considered itself Islamic first and Indian second. The periods during which the Punjab has been culturally assimilated to the rest of northern India are ew if any at all. Periods of political assimilation are almost as few; perhaps a part of the fourth and third centuries B.C. under the Mauryas; possibly a brief period under the Indo-Greek king menander in the second century B.C.; another brief period under the Muslim kingdom of Delhi in the last quarter of the twelfth century A.D.; a long one under the great Mughals in the sixteenth and seventeenth centuries A.D.; a century under the British, 1849-1947.'

"Though this refers to cultural and political factors, it is a warning that we must not leap to linguistic conclusions hastily. The early, but probably centuries-long condition in which Sanskrit, a close ally of languages of Iran, was restricted to the northwest (though it was not the only language there) and the rest of India was not Sanskritic in speech, may well have been mirrored earlier by a period when some other language invader from the Near East-a relative of Sumerian or of Elamitic or what not-was spoken and written in the Indus Valley-perhaps that of invaders and conquerors-while the indigenous population spoke another language-perhaps one of the Dravidian stock, or perhaps one of the Munda stock, which is now represented only by a handful of languages in the backwoods of Central India.

"On leaving this highly speculative question, we can move on to an examination of the Sanskrit records, and we find in them linguistic evidence of contacts between the Sanskrit-speaking invaders and the other linguistic groups within India...the early days of Indo-European scholarship were without benefit of the spectacular archaeological discoveries that were later to be made in the Mediterranean area, Mesopotamia and the Indus Valley... This assumption (that IE languages were urbanized bearers of a high civilization) led in the long run to another block-the methodological tendency of the end of the nineteenth and the beginning of the twentieth century to attempt to find Indo-European etymologies for the greatest possible portion of the vocabularies of the Indo-European languages, even though the object could only be achieved by flights of phonological and semantic fancy... very few scholars attempted to identify borrowings from Dravidian into Sanskrit...The Sanskrit etymological dictionary of Uhlenbrck (1898-1899) and the Indo-European etymological dictionary of Walde and Pokorny (1930-1932) completely ignore the work of Gundert (1869), Kittel (1872, 1894), and Caldwell (1856,1875)... It is clear that not all of Burrow's suggested borrowings will stand the test even of his own principles...'India' and 'Indian' will be used in what follows for the subcontinent, ignoring the political division into the Republic of India and Pakistan, and, when necessary, including Ceylong also... the northern boundary of Dravidian is and has been for a long time retreating south before the expansion of Indo-Aryan... We know in fact from the study of the non-Indo-European element in the Sanskrit lexicon that at the time of the earliest Sanskrit records, the R.gveda, when Sanskrit speakers were localized no further east than the Panjab, there were already a few Dravidian words current in Sanskrit. This involves a localization of Dravidian speech in this area no lather than three millennia ago. It also of course means much bilingualism and gradual abandonment of Dravidian speech in favor of IndoAryan over a long period and a great area-a process for which we have only the most lls d of evidence in detail. Similar relationships must have existed between Indo-Aryan and Munda and between Dravidian and Munda, but it is still almost impossible to be sure of either of these in detail... The Dravidian languages all have many Indo-Aryan items, borrowed at all periods from Sanskrit, Middle Indo-Aryan and Modern Indo-Aryan. The Munda languages likewise have much Indo-Aryan material, chiefly, so far as we know now, borrowed rom Modern Indo-Aryan, thogh this of course lls des items that are Sanskrit in form, since Modern Indo-Aryan borrows from Sanskrit very considerably. That Indo-Aryan has borrowed from

Dravidian has also become clear. T. Burrow, The Sanskrit Language, 379-88 (1955), gives a sampling and a statement of the chronology involved. It is noteworthy that this influence was spent by the end of the pre-Christian era, a precious indication for the linguistic history of North India: Dravidian speech must have practically ceased to exist in the Ganges valley by this period... Most of the languages of India, of no matter which major family, have a set of retroflex, cerebral, or domal consonants in contrast with dentals. The retroflexes include stops and nasal certainly, also in some languages sibilants, lateral, tremulant, and even others. Indo-Aryan, Dravidian, Munda and even the far northern Burushaski, form a practically solid bloc characterized by this phonological feature... Even our earliest Sanskrit records already show phonemes of this class, which are, on the whole, unknown elsewhere in the Indo-European field, and which are certainly not Proto-Indo-European. In Sanskrit many of the occurrences of retroflexes are conditioned; others are explained historically as reflexes of certain Indo-European consonants and consonant clusters. But, in fact, in Dravidian it is a matter of the utmost certainty that retroflexes in contrast with dentals are Proto-Dravidian in origin, not the result of conditioning circumstances... it is clear already that echo-words are a pan-Indic trait and that Indo-Aryan probably received it from non-Indo-Aryan (for it is not Indo-European)... The use of classifiers can be added to those other linguistic traits previously discussed, which establish India as one linguistic area ('an area which includes languages belonging to more than one family but showing traits in common which are found not to belong to the other members of (at least) one of the families') for historical study. The evidence is at least as clear-cut as in any part of the world... Some of the features presented here are, it seems to me, as 'profound' as we could wish to find... Certainly the end result of the borrowings is that the languages of the two families, Indo-Aryan and Dravidian, seem in many respects more akin to one another than Indo-Aryan does to the other Indo-European languages. (We must not, however, neglect Bloch's final remark and his reasons therefor: *'Ainsi donc, si profondes qu'aient ete les influences locales, Ils n'ont pas conduit l'aryen de l;inde... a se differencier fortement des autres langues indo-europeennes.'*)" M.B.Emeneau, Linguistic Prehistory of India PAPS98 (1954). 282-92; Tamil Culture 5 (1956). 30-55; repr. In Collected papers: Dravidian Linguistics Ethnology and Folktales, Annamalai Nagar, Annamalai University, 1967, pp. 155-171.

The profundity of these observations by Emeneau and Bloch will be tested through clusters of lexemes of an *Indian Lexicon*, which relate to the archaeological finds of the civilization.

Tamil and all other Dravidian languages have been influenced by Sanskrit language and literature. Swaminatha Iyer [Swaminatha Iyer, 1975, Dravidian Theories, Madras, Madras Law Journal Office] posits a genetic relationship between Tamil and Sanskrit. He cites GU Pope to aver that several Indo-European languages are linguistically farther away from Sanskrit than Dravidian. He cites examples of Tamil and Sanskrit forms of some glosses: hair: mayir, s'mas'ru; mouth: vāya, vā c; ear: s śevi, śrava; hear: kēḷ keṇ (Tulu), karṇa; walk: śel, car; mother: āyi, yāy (Paiśāci). Evaluating this work, Edwin Bryant and Laurie Patton note: "It is still more simple and sound to assume that the words which need a date of contact of the fourth millennium BCE on linguistic grounds as loan words in Dravidian might be words originally inherited in Dravidian from the Proto-speech which was the common ancestor of both Dravidian and Indo-Aryan...It will be simpler to explain the situation if both Indo-Aryan and Dravidian are traced to a common language family. In vocables they show significant agreement. In phonology and morphology the linguistic structures agree significantly. It requires a thorough comparative study of the two language families to conduct a fuller study. " Bryant, Edwin and Laurie L. Patton, 2005, The Indo-Aryan controversy: evidence and inference in Indian history, Routledge, p.197.

The influence of Vedic culture is profoundly evidenced in early sangam texts. *K. V. Sarma*, 1983, "Spread of Vedic Culture in Ancient. South India" in The *Adyar* Library *Bulletin*, *1983*, 43:1.

Proto-Munda continuity and Language X

Sources of OIA agricultural vocabulary based on Masica (1979)

Percentage

- IE/Iir 40%
- Drav 13%
- Munda 11%
- Other 2%
- Unknown 34%
- Total 100%

Hence, a Language X is postulated; Language 'X' to explain a large number of agriculture-related words with no IE cognates: Colin Masica, 1991, Indo-Aryan Languages, Cambridge Univ. Press

Since there is cultural continuity in India from the days of Sarasvati civilization, it is possible to reconstruct Language X by identifying isoglosses in the linguistic area.

Contributions of the following language/archaeology scholars have followed up on these insights of Sylvan Levi, Jules Bloch and Jean Przyluski published over 90 years ago: Emeneau, MB, Kuiper, FBJ, Masica, CP, Southworth F. [Emeneau, MB, 1956, India as a linguistic area, in: Language, 32.3-16
•Kuiper, FBJ, 1967, The genesis of a linguistic area, Indo-Iranian Journal 10: 81-102
•Masica, Colin P., 1976, Defining a linguistic area, South Asia, Chicago, University of Chicago Press •Franklin Southworth, 2005, Linguistic Archaeology of South Asia, Routledge Curzon]

Resemblances between two or more languages (whether typological or in vocabulary) can be due to genetic relation (descent from a common ancestor language), or due to borrowing at some time in the past between languages that were not necessarily genetically related. When little or no direct documentation of ancestor languages is available, determining whether a similarity is genetic or areal can be difficult.

A *sprachbund* (also known as a linguistic area, convergence area or diffusion area), is a group of languages that have become similar in some features because of geographical proximity. http://en.wikipedia.org/wiki/Areal_feature

Note: This area can be called speakers of 'mleccha, meluhha' or mleccha vācas according to Manusmṛti (lingua franca of the artisans). Manusmṛti distinguishes two spoken language-groups: mleccha vācas and arya vaacas (that is, spoken dialect distinguished from grammatically correct glosses).

"A *Sprachbund*...in German, plural "Sprachbünde" IPA, from the German word for "language union", also known as a linguistic area, convergence area, or diffusion area, is a group of languages that have become similar in some way because of geographical proximity and language contact. They may be genetically unrelated, or only distantly related. Where genetic affiliations are unclear, the *sprachbund* characteristics might give a false appearance of relatedness...In a classic 1956 paper titled "India as a Linguistic Area", Murray Emeneau [Emeneau, Murray. 1956. India as a Lingusitic Area. "Langauge" 32: 3-16. http://en.academic.ru/dic.nsf/enwiki/1113093] laid the groundwork for the general acceptance of the concept of a *Sprachbund*. In the paper, Emeneau observed that the subcontinent's Dravidian and Indo-Aryan languages shared a number of features that were not inherited from a common source, but were areal features, the result of diffusion during sustained contact." Common features of a group of languages in a *Sprachbund* are called 'areal features'. In linguistics, an areal feature is any typological feature shared by languages within the same geographical area. An example refers to retroflex consonants in the Burushaski {Berger, H. Die Burushaski-Sprache von Hunza und Nagar. Vols. I-III. Wiesbaden: Harrassowitz 1988 ] [Tikkanen (2005)]}, Nuristani [G.Morgenstierne, Irano-Dardica. Wiesbaden 1973], Dravidian, Munda and Indo-Aryan language families of the Indian subcontinent. *The Munda Languages*. Edited by Gregory D. S. Anderson. London and New York: Routledge (Routledge Language Family Series), 2008.

Notes on Indian linguistic area: pre-aryan,pre-Munda and pre-dravidian in India

It will be a hasty claim to make that Old Tamil or Proto-Munda or Santali or Prakṛt or Pali or any other specific language of the Indian linguistic area, by itself (to the exclusion of other languages in contact), explains the language of the Indus civilization. In this context, the work by Sylvan Levi, Jules Bloch and Jean Przyluski published in the 1920's (cited elsewhere) continues to be relevant, even today, despite some advances in studies related to formation of Indian languages and the archaeological perspectives of and evidences from the civilization.

Some glyphs of the script are yet to be decoded. Tentative readings of such glyphs yet to be validated by the cipher code key of Indus script are detailed (including decipherment of inscriptions from scores of small sites) at http://sites.google.com/site/kalyan97/induswriting If the glyphs are unambiguously identified and read in archaeological context and the context of other glyphs of the inscription itself, it will be possible to decipher them. For this purpose, some graphemes (which have homonyms and can be read rebus) are provided from the Indian Lexicon of the Indian linguistic area.

Graphemes:

kol 'the name of a bird, the Indian cuckoo' (Santali)

kolo 'a large jungle climber, dioscorea doemonum (Santali)

kulai 'a hare' (Santali)

Grapheme: Ta. kōl stick, staff, branch, arrow. Ma. kōl staff, rod, stick, arrow. Ko. kl stick, story of funeral car. To. kwṣ stick.Ka. kōl, kōlu stick, staff, arrow. Koḍ. Klī stick. Tu. kōlů, kōlustick, staff. Te. kōla id., arrow; long, oblong; kōlana elongatedness, elongation; kōlani elongated. Kol. (SR.) kolā, (Kin.) kōla stick. Nk. (Ch.) kōl pestle. Pa. kōl shaft of arrow.Go. (A.) kōla id.; kōlā (Tr.) a thin twig or stick, esp. for kindling a fire, (W. Ph.) stick, rod, a blade of grass, straw; (G. Mu. Ma. Ko.) kōla handle of plough, sickle, knife, etc. ( Voc.988); (ASu.) kōlā stick, arrow, slate-pencil; (LuS.) kola the handle of an implement. Konḍa kōl big wooden pestle. Pe. kōlpestle. Manḍ. kūl id. Kui kōḍu (pl. kōṭka) id. Kuwi (F.)kōlū (pl. kōlka), (S. Su.) kōlu (pl. kōlka) id. Cf. 2240 Ta.kōlam (Tu. Te. Go.). / Cf. OMar. (Master) kōla stick. (DEDR 2237). कोलदंडा or कोलदांडा [ kōladaṇḍā or kōladāṇḍā ] m A stick or bar fastened to the neck of a surly dog. (Marathi)

kola [ kōla ] f. The bandicoot rat, mus malibaricos (Rajasthani)

Graphemes: డోలు [ ḍōlu ] ḍōlu. [Tel.] n. A drum.

ḍollu. [Tel.] v. n. To fall, to roll over. పడు, పొరలు. డొలుచు [ ḍolucu ] or ḍoluṭsu. [Tel.] v. n. To tumble head over heels as dancing girls do (Telugu)

maṇḍa = a branch; a twig; a twig with leaves on it (Te.lex.)

maṇḍhwa, maṇḍua, maṇḍwa 'a temporary shed or booth erected on the occasion of a marriage' (Santali) maṇḍā = warehouse, workshop (Kon.lex.)

maṇḍā = warehouse, workshop (Kon.lex.)

*khōla2 ' cavity, hollow '. 2. *khōlla -- 2. 3. *khōḍa -- . 4. *khōra -- 2. [Cf. Par. khur ' cave ' IIFL i 265]1. Paš. gul. khōl ' ravine '; P. khol f. ' cavity, hollow '; WPah. cur. khoḷ ' stream '; N. kholo ' small river, valley '; Bi. khol, li ' trough in which the share lies when fixed in body of plough '; H. khol, laṛ m. ' cavity, cave '; -- A. kholiba ' to hollow out ', kholni ' mortice '; Or. khoḷibā ' to dig '. -- X kōṭará -- q.v.2. Pk. kholla -- n. ' hollow '; L. kholā ' hollow '; Or. khola ' cave '; G. khol f. ' hollowness '; M. khol ' deep '.3. Kho. (Lor.) khōḷ ' cave, hollow under rock '; P. khoṛ f. ' cavity, hollow '; -- A. khor ' cavity, hole ' or < *khōra -- 2.4. Gy. arm. xor ' deep, hollow, depth ', eur. xor ' deep, depth ', wel. xorō ' deep '; Sh. (Lor.) kōr ' cave '; L. khorī ' enclosure '; P. khorā ' empty '; N. khor ' enclosure, trap ', ro ' crack in skin of foot ', ri ' small pocket of leaves '; A. khor ' cave ' (or < *khōḍa -- ); B. khor ' sore in foot -- andmouth disease '; H. khorm. ' cave ', f. ' cavity ', rā m. ' pit, cave '; M. khor m. ' glen '. Addenda: *khōla -- 2. 3. khōḍa -- :

WPah.kṭg. khv́ṛ m. ' lowest storey of house where cattle are kept (often dug into the hillside) ' (but cf. P. kuṛ, kgr. kuṛh f. ' enclosure for cattle ' Him.I 35); -- perh. also khv́ṛ ' dung, manure '. (CDIAL 3943)

khōll ' to open '. 2. *khull -- ' to be open '.1. Gy. pal. kṓlăr ' loosens ', eur. wel. xulav -- ' to comb out (hair), part, divide '; K. khōlun ' to open ', S. kholaṇu, L. awāṇ. khōluṇ; P. kholhṇā ' to open, loose '; WPah. rudh. kholl -- ' to open '; Ku. gng. khoe ' releases '; N. kholnu ' to open ', B. kholā, khulā, Or. kholibā, Mth. Aw. lakh. khōlab, H. kholnā, Marw. kholṇo, G. kholvũ; M. kholṇẽ ' to deepen (a well) '.2. S. khulaṇu intr. ' to open ', L. awāṇ. khullaṇ ' to be open ', P. khullhṇā, WPah. cam. khulhṇā, Ku. khulṇo, N. khulnu, B. khulā, H. khulnā, G. khulvũ, M.khulṇẽ; -- OMarw. khulo adj. ' open '.*utkhōll -- , *niṣkhōll -- .Addenda: *khōll -- . 1. S.kcch. kholṇū ' to open '; WPah.kṭg. (kc.) khólṇõ.2. *khull -- : WPah.kṭg. khúlṇõ ' to be opened ', khullɔ ' spacious, wide '; J. khulā ' loosened '.(CDIAL 3945)

*Indus Script Cipher*, together with the substrates of the *Indian Lexicon*, provide the framework for further studies in evolution of general semantics, identification of isogloss bundles and history of changes in languages in the Indian linguistic area which continues to be a cultural continuum for over eight millennia, from the days the Indus civilization produced an artifact of a wide *turbinella pyrum* bangle dated to c. 6500 BCE from a woman's burial in Nausharo.

Further researches

In addition to studies in the evolution of and historical contacts among Indian languages, further researches are also needed in an archaeological context. Karl Menninger cites a remarkable instance. In the Indian tradition, finger signals were used to settle the price for a trade transaction. Finger gestures were a numeric cipher!

A pearl merchant of South India settling price for a pearl using finger gestures under a handkerchief. Cited in Karl Menninger, 1969, *Number words and number symbols: a cultural history of numbers*, MIT Press, p.212. http://tinyurl.com/26ze95s

Further work on the nature of the contacts between Indian artisans and their trade associates, say, in Meluhhan settlements in the Persian Gulf region, may unravel the the nature of long-distance contacts. Could it be that the Indus language and writing were Indus Artisans' cryptographic messaging system for specifications of artifacts made in and exported from Meluhha?

## 8 CONCLUSIONS: ARCHAEOLOGY AND LANGUAGE

Many scholars, starting with Jean-François Champollion (1790-1832) worked on Egyptian hieroglyphs and deciphered them thanks to the key: Rosetta Stone, a stela found in Egypt in 1799 by soldiers from Napoleon's army. Henry Creswicke Rawlinson, Edward Hincks, Julius Oppert and William H. Fox Talbot returned translations of cuneiform writing that broadly agreed with each other. Denise Schmandt-Besserat's *How writing came about* (1996) records the transition from tallies and bullae to cuneiform writing using the tallies for categorizing property items. Egyptian hieroglyphs were logo-syllabic, while cuneiform writing was syllabic.

Indian hieroglyphs presented in this book records the stage which took writing beyond categorization using tallies and related the glyphs to language.

Invention of Indus script (Indian hieroglyphs) was almost at the same time as the invention of Egyptian hieroglyphs – dated to c. 3300 BCE. The unique feature of Indian hieroglyphs is that pictographs (glyphs) representing semantics of Indian linguistic area were themselves combined creating ligatures to communicate composite messages, particularly about the economics of production and administration of trade activities of the civilization.

The first scholar to recognize cryptography in the writing system was Vātsyāyana (c. 1st to 6th cent.) who wrote a treatise on 64 arts including an art called *mlecchita-vikalpa* (lit. 'an alternative representation -- in cryptography or cipher -- of *mleccha vācas* or meluhha speech'). He was also author of *Nyāya sūtra bhāṣya,* the first commentary on Gotama's *Nyāya Sūtra*. The art of *mlecchita-vikalpa* (or writing system) is related to Indian hieroglyphs represented on Indus script inscriptions. Indian hieroglyphic tradition continued into the historical periods with the use of many symbols taken from the same set of glyphs of Indus script corpora on two pure tingots discovered in a shipwreck in Haifa, Rampurva copper bolt inscription on an Asoka pillar, on Sohgaura copper plate (c. 6th century BCE pre-Mauryan period) and on tens of thousands of punch-marked and cast coins all over the vast interaction area stretching from Altyn-Tepe (close to Caspian Sea) to Rakhigarhi (close to Delhi) spanning ancient Iran and Bactria-Margiana Archaeological Complex, Sindhu-Sarasvati-Yamuna river basins, and from Susa (Mesopotamia) to Daimabad (Maharashtra) across the Persian Gulf. While the Indian hieroglyphs were designed for and suited the needs of descriptive compilations of bills of lading or economic transactions, two alphabetic-syllabic scripts were used for preparing texts: kharoṣṭī and *brāhmī.* Kharoṣṭī is cognate with Harosheth in Harosheth-Hagoyim (lit. 'smithy of nations'), a site which yielded a 3000-year old bronze tablet –carved with the face of a woman -- used as a chariot linchpin. The kharoṣṭī and *brāhmī* scripts were also used for trade transactions together with the Indian hieroglyphs as evidenced by ancient coins using these two scripts for 'names' and using Indian hieroglyphs to describe details of economic wealth items in the repertoire of mints which produced the coins.

Of the two syllabic scripts kharoṣṭī and *brāhmī*, the latter script spread into many parts of Asia (Frits Staal, 2006, Sanskrit Studies Central Journal. *Journal of the Sanskrit Studies Center*, Silpakorn University, 2 (2006) 193-200).

The Vedic System of the Sounds of Language.

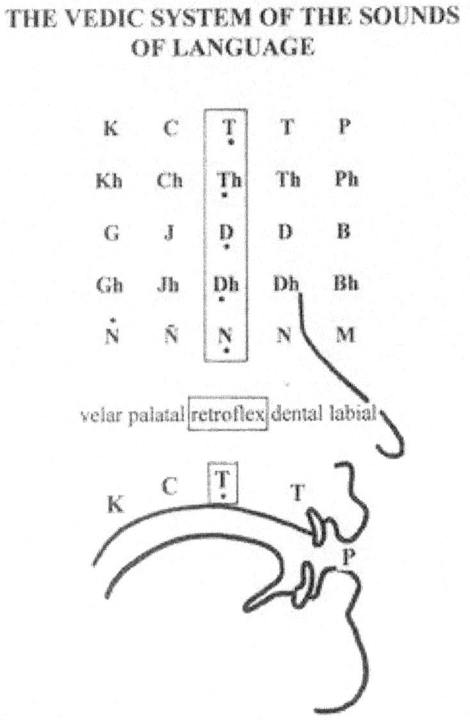


" The Vedic system of the sounds of language exhibits and embodies what is nowadays called phonetics, but is close to phonology which studies features of those same sounds as parts of a system. The system exhibits what I refer to as the sound pattern of Vedic, Sanskrit or language. I do not imply that it is the same for all languages, but most of the sounds of human speech may be accommodated in some such scheme. During the Late Vedic period, the Vedic scheme was expounded in the śikṣâ, the Prātiśākhya and other compositions...(The figure) shows at a glance that the Indian system together with the shapes of its syllables is confined to South and Southeast Asia. The Indian system without the shapes was adopted and adapted in Central Asia, Korea and Japan. Occasional uses of the system are found in China and in Southwest Asia or the Near East... I start this brief overview with a mystery: the script of Kharoshthi, probably the earliest Indic script, which was used in northwest India and spread to Central Asia from about the fourth century BCE to the third century CE. The order of syllables starts with *a ra pa ca na la da ba èa ṣa* . . . That order is unexplained and the script is called *Arapacana* after the first five syllables. It possesses clearly Indic features: each syllable ends in a short *–a* and diacritic signs are added when that short *–a* is replaced by another vowel. The order of vowels, however, is not Indic but Aramaic: *a e i o u* and not *a i u e o*. That order is also adopted by diacritics attached to consonants from top to bottom when changing a into *e, i, o* and *u*. The other early Indic script is Brahmi. It is the paradigm of the Vedic system. It influenced, directly or indirectly, via Pallava or other medieval Indian scripts, all the scripts of South and Southeast Asia that include (again in *alphabetic* order) Balinese, Bengali, Burmese, Devanagari, Grantha, Gujrati, Gupta, Gurmukhi, Kannada, Khmer, Lao, Malayalam, Nepali, Oriya, Pallava, Sinhala, Tamil, Telugu and Thai...The numbers of South, Southeast and Central Asian scripts that adopted the Indic order is large. An attractive estimate occurs in the tenth chapter of the *Lalitavistara*, called *Lipiśâlâsaṃdarśanaparivarta*, "the revolution of displays of the mansions of writing." It lists 64 different scripts that were mastered by the Bodhisattva. The title of the chapter is reminiscent of the Buddha's own *dharmacakrapravartana*. It emphasizes instructively that the carriers of the sound pattern of Sanskrit to other Asian regions were not only Indian Brahmans but also, and in increasing numbers, Buddhist monks. It is explained at least in part by the geographical facts with which I started: the discovery of the sound pattern of language by Vedic reciters occurred close in place and time to the areas where early Buddhism flourished. It was a feature of civilization that Buddhists carried across Asia...those Asian writing systems are applications of a theory of language, just as airplanes are applications of the laws of aerodynamics... If the sound pattern of Sanskrit had also reached the Near East and Europe, there would not be so many clumsy alphabets around and the modern world would have the benefit of rational and practical Indic syllabaries in addition to rational and practical Indic numerals."

Indian Scripts of Asia

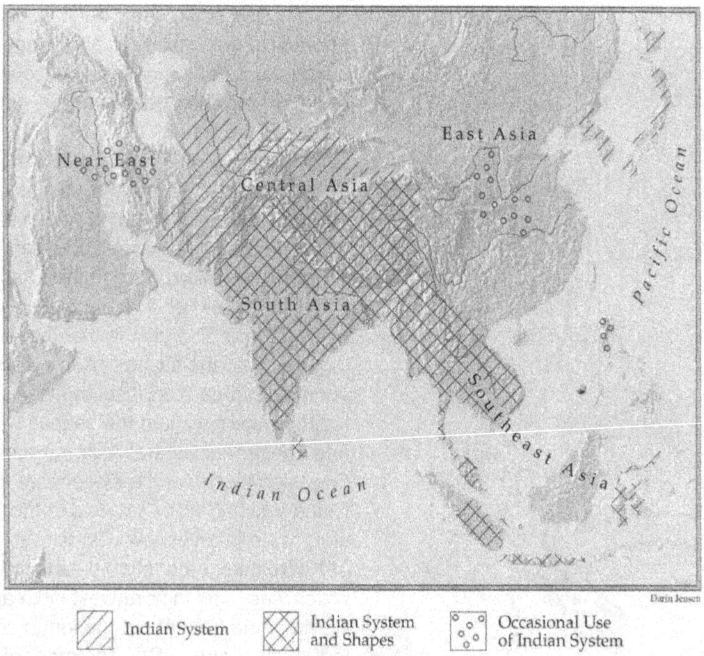


Indic scripts of Asia.

The author gratefully acknowledges the contributions made by Asko Parpola and Iravatham Mahadevan, Harappa Archaeological Research Project, in particular – and other compilers of Corpora of Indus script inscriptions – and owes a deep debt of gratitude to hundreds of scholars (including Gregory Possehl, Massimo Vidale, Lyle Campbell, Denise Schmandt-Besserat, Andrew Lawler) who have provided insights into the structure, form and purpose of the writing system, contact areas and the underlying linguistic area.

Decoding Indus script hieroglyphs which appear with Brahmi-*kharoṣṭī* inscriptions

Suniti Kumar Chatterjee had noted that *kharoṣṭī* is a Sanskrit formation, meaning 'art of writing' derived from the Hebrew Harosheth. (See appended notes from Wikipedia on 'Harosheth hagoyim').

Harosheth (Hebrew) may be relatable to the word: *kharoṣṭī* as the script used by smiths who made iron war-chariots armed with scythes. Harosheth (workmanship) "of the Gentiles" so called from the mixed races that inhabited it --a city in the north of the land of Canaan, supposed to have stood on the west coast of the lake Merom from which the Jordan issues forth in one unbroken stream. The name in the Hebrew is Harosheth ha Gojim, i.e., "the smithy of the nations;" probably, as is supposed, so called because here Jabin's iron war-chariots, armed with scythes, were made. It is identified with el-Harithiyeh.http://topicalbible.org/h/harosheth.htm

In the context of a report (2000) on the finds of 174 Kuninda coins in Pandola village, Indus hieroglyphs which appear together with inscriptions in Brahmi-Kharoshthi scripts on some Pulinda (Kuninda) coins can be explained.

This is a continuation of the following posts:
http://bharatkalyan97.blogspot.com/2011/11/syena-orthography.html
http://bharatkalyan97.blogspot.com/2011/11/assyrian-goat-fish-on-seal-interaction.html
http://bharatkalyan97.blogspot.com/2011/11/susa-ritual-basin-decorated-with.html
http://bharatkalyan97.blogspot.com/2011/11/sit-shamshi-bronze-glyphics-compared.html
http://bharatkalyan97.blogspot.com/2011/11/decoding-longest-inscription-of-indus.html
http://bharatkalyan97.blogspot.com/2011/11/decoding-indus-scipt-susa-cylinder-seal.html
http://bharatkalyan97.blogspot.com/2011/11/decoding-fish-and-ligatured-fish-glyphs.html
Also summarised in: Indus Script cipher - Hieroglyphs of Indian linguistic area (2010)

Brahmi-Kharoshthi scripts were used to denote names. Indus script glyphs were used to denote the repertoire of the metalsmiths' guild as a continuum of the Indus tradition which led to the kole.l 'smithy' interpreted as kole.l 'temple' (Kota language). This transition from smithy to cultural metaphors is also evidenced on Susa ritual basin, on Sit-Shamshi bronze and on the iconography of simurgh (*śyena* - Vedic) in Sasanian times (Iran).

On early punch-marked coins, inscriptions using Kharoshthi script were mirrored (transcribed) by the use of inscriptions in Greek or inscriptions in Brahmi script.

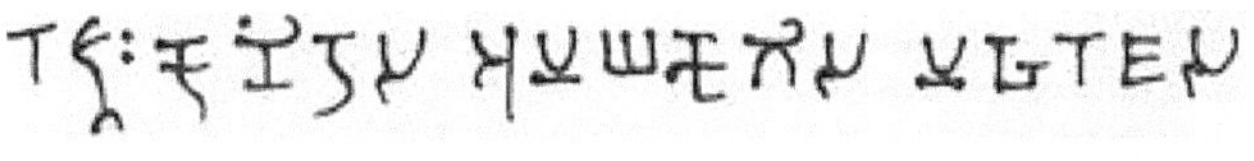

Brahmi script inscription on Kuninda coin (Obverse)

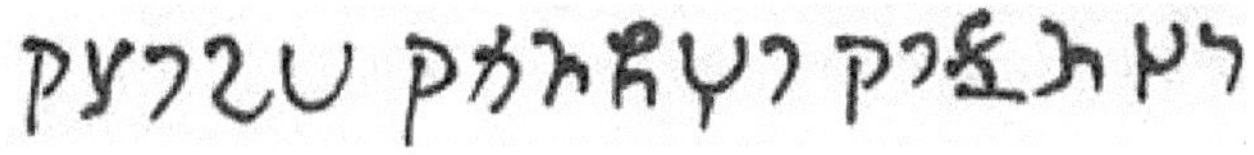

Kharoshthi script inscription on Kuninda coin (Reverse)

The reading of the two transcriptions (Brahmi and Kharoshthi) is the same:
Rana Kunindasa Amoghabhutisa maharajasa (trans. 'Great King Amoghabhuti, of the Kunindas).

Why were Brahmi and Kharoshthi inscriptions used together with Indus Script hieroglyphs? I suggest that the Brahmi and Kharoshthi inscriptions were used to precisely represent syllabically the legend on the coin referring to the king whose mint issued the coin. That is, Brahmi and Klharoshthi scripts were deployed to denote information about the name of the king and his title.

Indus script hieroglyphs were used to denote the principal repertoire of smiths/mints in the Indus script tradition -- using the hieroglyphs in the context of economic/trade transactions. It has been noted that kole.l was not only a smithy but also a temple and hence, many hieroglyphs of Indus script continued to be used not only in the Indian linguistic area but also in Susa (Elam), Mesopotamia, Iran and Persian Gulf states to represent the technical details of the minerals/metals/alloys/furnaces/smelters used by the artisans as professional calling cards. The Indus script hieroglyphs consisted of pictorial glyphs and also glyphs categorised in corpora as 'signs'. The hieroglypghs were not syllabic but morphemic connoting lexemes (i.e. words with meanings in meluhha/mleccha Indus language of the Indian linguistic area).

Indus script glyphs used on Kuninda coins and their decoding are:

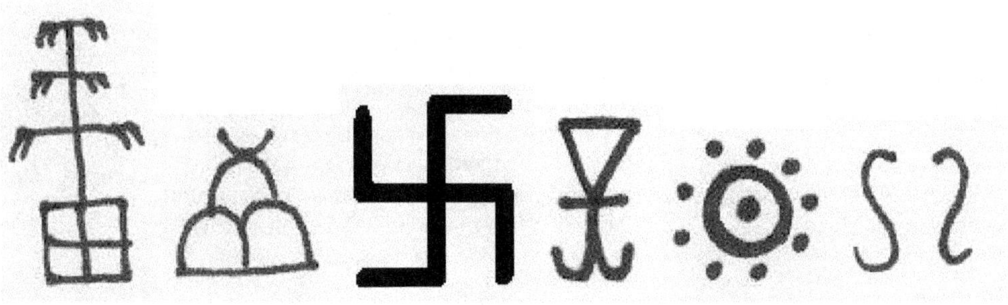

Tree-on-railing: kōṭu branch of tree; Rebus: koḍ 'workshop' (Kuwi) koṭe 'forge' (Santali) Kui (K.) koḍi hoe. (DEDR 2064)

Mountain/Summit: Ta. mēṭai artificial mound Ma. mēṭa raised place / Cf. Skt. (lex.) meṭa- whitewashed storied house; Pkt. meḍaya- id. (DEDR 4796b) Rebus: med. 'iron' (Mu.) koṭe meṛed = forged iron, in contrast to dul meṛed, cast iron (Mundari.lex.)

Svastika: sathiyā (H.), sāthiyo (G.); satthia, sotthia (Pkt.) Rebus: svastika pewter (Kannada)

Standard: san:gaḍa, 'lathe, portable furnace'; Rebus: sanghāḍo (G.) cutting stone, gilding (G.)

Dotted circle: pāso 'die' (orthography: dotted circle). Rebus: pāśo = a silver ingot; pāśātāṇiyo = one who draws silver into a wire (G.) pāslo = a nugget of gold or silver having the form of a die (G.)

Vikalpa: Circle (denoting hole): vēdha m. ' hitting the mark ' MBh., ' penetration, hole ' VarBṛS. [√vyadh] Pa. vēdha -- m. ' prick, wound '; Pk. vēha -- m. ' boring, hole ', P. veh, beh m., H. beh m., G. veh m.*CDIAL 12108) vēdhya ' to be pierced (of a vein) ' Car., n. ' mark for shooting at ' MārkP. [√vyadh] Pk. vejjha -- ' to be pierced '; OAw. bejha m. ' butt for archers ', H. bejhā m.; OM. vejha m. ' hole, opening ', M. veǰ, vejẽ n. ' eye (of needle), bore (in gem)'.(CDIAL 12110). Allograph: vēṭhaka -- ' surrounding ' (Pali); Pk. vēḍha -- m. ' wrap '; S. veṛhu m. ' encircling ';L. veṛh, vehṛ m. ' fencing, enclosure in jungle with a hedge, (Ju.) blockade ', veṛhā, vehṛā m. ' courtyard, (Ju.) enclosure containing many houses '; P. veṛhā, be° m. ' enclosure, courtyard '; Ku. beṛo ' circle or band (of people) '; vēṣṭá m. ' band, noose ' Kauś., ' enclosure ' lex., °aka- m. ' fence ', n. ' turban ' lex. [√vēṣṭ]M. veṭh, vēṭh, veṭ, vēṭ m.f. ' roll, turn of a rope '; Si. veṭya ' enclosure '; -- Pa. sīsa -- vēṭha -- m. ' head -- wrap '.(CDIAL 12130).

On the coin, a woman (kola 'woman'; rebus: kula 'guild') is holding up a flower (garland?) or a rope.

circa 1340-1300 BC. Technical information:Stele of Untash-Napirisha, king of Anshan and Susa. circa 1340-1300 BC Susa, Iran Sandstone H. 2.62 m; L. 0.8 m Jacques de Morgan excavations, Susa
Sb 12 Near Eastern Antiquities Ekta (slide) RMN 99DE23519 + drawing

Stele of Untash-Napirisha, king of Anshan and Susa

A rope is held by Untash-Napirisha, king of Anshan and Susa from a sculptural fragment found at Susa. See: http://bharatkalyan97.blogspot.com/2011/11/susa-ritual-basin-decorated-with.html

I suggest that the rope held by Untash is an orthographic representation of dhama 'rope'; rebus: dhamma 'law'. (Denoting the king as an upholder of dhamma).

dā´man1 ' rope ' RV. 2. *dāmana -- , dāmanī -- f. ' long rope to which calves are tethered ' Hariv. 3. *dāmara -- .[*dāmara -- is der. fr. n/r n. stem. -- √dā2]1. Pa. dāma -- , inst. °mēna n. ' rope, fetter, garland ', Pk. dāma -- n.; Wg. dām ' rope, thread, bandage '; Tir. dām ' rope '; Paš.lauṛ.dām ' thick thread ', gul. dūm ' net snare ' (IIFL iii 3, 54 ← Ind. or Pers.); Shum. dām ' rope '; Sh.gil. (Lor.) dōmo ' twine, short bit of goat's hair cord ', gur. dōm m. ' thread ' (→ Ḍ. dōṅ ' thread '); K. gu -- dômu m. ' cow's tethering rope '; P. dā̃u, dāvā̃ m. ' hobble for a horse '; WPah.bhad. daū n. ' rope to tie cattle ', bhal. daõ m., jaun. dā̃w; A. dāmā ' peg to tie a buffalo -- calf to '; B. dām, dāmā ' cord '; Or. duā̃ ' tether ', dāī ' long tether to which many beasts are tied '; H. dām m.f. ' rope, string, fetter ', dāmā m. ' id., garland '; G.dām n. ' tether ', M. dāvẽ n.; Si. dama ' chain, rope ', (SigGr) dam ' garland '. -- Ext. in Paš.dar. damaṭā´, °ṭī´, nir. weg. damaṭék ' rope ', Shum. ḍamaṭik, Woṭ. damṓṛ m., Sv. dåmoṛī´; -- with -- ll -- : N. dāmlo ' tether for cow ', dā̃wali, dāūli, dāmli ' bird -- trap of string ', dā̃wal, dāmal ' coeval ' (< ' tied together '?); M. dā̃vlī f. ' small tie -- rope '.2. Pk. dāvaṇa -- n., dāmaṇī -- f. ' tethering rope '; S. ḏāvaṇu, ḏāṇu m. ' forefeet shackles ', ḏāviṇī, ḏāṇī f. ' guard to support nose -- ring '; L. ḍā̃vaṇ m., ḍā̃vaṇī, ḍāuṇī (Ju. ḏ -- ) f. ' hobble ', dāuṇī f. ' strip at foot of bed, triple cord of silk worn by women on head ', awāṇ. dāvuṇ ' picket rope '; P. dāuṇ, dauṇ, ludh. daun f. m. ' string for bedstead, hobble for horse ', dāuṇī f. ' gold ornament worn on woman's forehead '; Ku. dauṇo m., °ṇī f. ' peg for tying cattle to ', gng. dɔ̃ṛ ' place for keeping cattle, bedding for cattle '; A. dan ' long cord on which a net or screen is stretched, thong ', danā ' bridle '; B. dāmni ' rope '; Or. daaṇa ' string at the fringe of a casting net on which pebbles are strung ', dāuṇi ' rope for tying bullocks together when threshing '; H. dāwan m. ' girdle ', dāwanī f. ' rope ', dā̃wanī f. ' a woman's orna<-> ment '; G. dāmaṇ, ḍā° n. ' tether, hobble ', dāmṇū n. ' thin rope, string ', dāmṇī f. ' rope, woman's head -- ornament '; M. dāvaṇ f. ' picket -- rope '. -- Words denoting the act of driving animals to tread out corn are poss. nomina actionis from *dāmayati2.
3. L. ḍāvarāvaṇ, (Ju.) ḏā̃v° ' to hobble '; A. dāmri ' long rope for tying several buffalo -- calves together ', Or. daūrā, daürā ' rope '; Bi. daūrī ' rope to which threshing bullocks are tied, the act of treading out the grain ', Mth. dā̃mar, daūraṛ ' rope to which the bullocks are tied '; H. dā̃wrī f. ' id., rope, string ', dāwrī f. ' the act of driving bullocks round to tread out the corn '. (CDIAL 6283)

Allograph: dharmaṇa1 m. ' species of snake ' lex.P. dhāmaṇ m. ' a non -- poisonous snake ', N. dhāman; Or. dhāmaṇā̆, ḍhā° ' the snake Zamenis mucosus '; H. dhāman, °min,dhāwan m. ' a large harmless snake ', G. dhāmaṇi f.; M. dhāmaṇ, °mīṇ f. ' species of coluber '.

Addenda: dharmaṇa -- 1 m. ' species of snake ', 6756 dharmaṇa -- 2 m. ' species of Grewia tree ' properly dhānvana -- ' living or growing in desert land ' Kām. (cf. dhanvanyà -- AV., dhanvaja -- Suśr., dhānva -- Car.), ' *species of snake and Grewia tree ' (cf.dhanvana -- m. ' kind of animal ' VarBṛS., ' species of Grewia ' lex., dhānvana -- ' made of its wood ' ŚāṅkhŚr.); -- dharmaṇa -- id. ← MIA. (T. Burrow JRAS 1967 42) (CDIAL 6755)

Rebus: dhárma m. ' what is established, law, duty, right ' AV. [dhárman -- n. RV. -- √dhṛ] Pa. dhamma -- m. (rarely n.), Aś.shah. man. dhrama -- , gir. kāl. &c. dhaṁma -- ; NiDoc. dhaṁa ' employment in the royal administration '; Dhp. dharma -- , dhama -- , Pk. dhamma -- m.; OB. dhāma ' religious conduct '; H. kāmdhām ' work, business '; OSi. dama ' religion ' (Si. daham ← Pa.) (CDIAL 6753)

Antelope: Glyph: miṇḍāl markhor (Tor.wali) meḍho a ram, a sheep (G.)(CDIAL 10120) Rebus: meḍ iron (Ho.) meṛed-bica = iron stone ore, in contrast to bali-bica, iron sand ore (Mu.lex.)Hem. Des. meḍhi = Skt. vaṇik-sahāya: a merchant's clerk, fr. Skt. mahita praised, great fr. mahto praise, to make great] a schoolmaster; an accountant; a clerk; a writer (G.lex.)Vikalpa: mlekh 'antelope'(Br.); milakkhu 'copper' (Pali)

Glyph on Kuninda coin.

Glyph of Indus script. Sign 241 (Indus script, Mahadevan corpus)

•ran:ku = liquid measure (Santali) •ran:ku a species of deer; ran:kuka (Skt.)(CDIAL 10559). See middle glyph on copper plates m0522 & m0516 Rebus: ran:ku = tin (Santali)

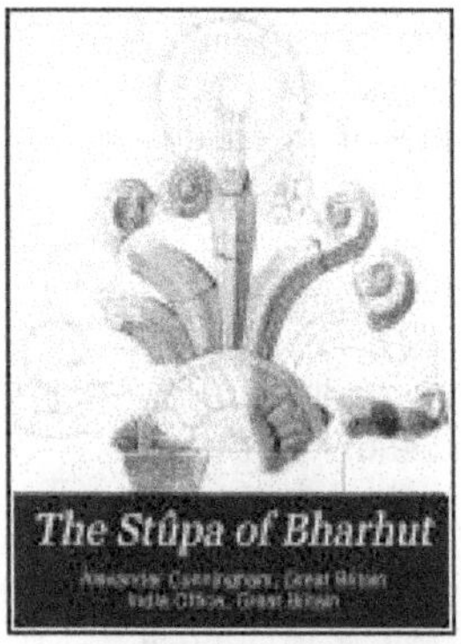


Cover page of the book: The stûpa of Bharhut: a Buddhist monument ornamented with numerous sculptures illustrative of Buddhist legend and history in the third century B.C. by Alexander Cunningham, 1879. The cover page shows the mollusc glyph on top of the stupa, denoting sangha.

Mollusc: hangi 'snail'; hŏgiñ हाँ&above;गिञ् । शुक्तिः f. a pearl-oyster shell (Śiv. 1551, 1755; Rām. 1142); the shell of any aquatic mollusc (cf. kŏla-hŏgiñ, s.v. kŏl 2); ? a snail (L. 157, 464, hāngi)(Kashmiri) rebus: sangi 'caravan of pilgrims' (G.)

A pair of tails of a pair of fishes: aya 'fish' (Munda); rebus: aya 'metal' (G.); dula 'pair, likeness'

(Kashmiri); Rebus: dul 'casting (metal)' (Santali) Thus, a pair of fishes read rebus: dul aya 'cast metal'.

dumba दुम्ब or (El.) duma दुम I पशुपुच्छः m. the tail of an animal. (Kashmiri) dumbha ' tail '. [Only Kal. attests an aspirate: poss. all NIA. forms, and cert. those of Dard. with l -- , are ← Ir., Av. duma -- , Pahl. dumbak, Pers. dum(b), Psht.ləm EVP 36. But, besides Kal., some derivatives, e.g. s.v. *dumbhaśa -- , suggest possibility of orig. IA. form]Gy. eur.Dumo m. ' back, shoulder '; Wg. dumä'ŕ, tumtä' ' tail ', Kt. dəmŕəi, Pr. lümṳ̄, dəmū' (← Kt. Rep1 47), Paš.gul. dum(b), nir. dumā' (← Pers. IIFL iii 3, 55), ar. līm, Shum. līmə, Gaw. limoṭá, Kal. dh*lmŕẽi, Kho. rūm, K. dumba m.; L. dumb m. ' ear of millet '; P. dumb, dumm m. ' tail ', N. dum, Or. duma, Mth. dom, H. dumb, dum f., G. dum f.; M. dumālā m. ' hind part '. (CDIAL 6419) Rebus: ḍōmba m. ' man of low caste living by singing and music ' Kathās., ḍōma -- m. lex., ḍōmbinī -- f. [Connected with Mu. words for ' drum ' PMWS 87, EWA i 464 with lit.] Pk. ḍoṁba -- , ḍuṁba -- , ḍoṁbilaya -- m.; Gy. eur. rom m. ' man, husband ', romni f. ' woman, wife ', SEeur. ịom ' aGypsy ', pal. dōm ' a Nuri Gypsy ', arm. as. (Boša) lom ' a Gypsy ', pers. damini ' woman '; Ḍ. ḍōm (pl. ma) ' a Ḍom '; Paš. ḍōmb ' barber '; Kho. (Lor.) ḍom ' musician, bandsman '; Sh. ḍom ' a Ḍom ', K. ḍūmb, ḍūm m., ḍūmbiñ f.; S. ḏūmu m., ḍūmṛī f. ' caste of wandering musicians ', L. ḍūm m., ḍūmṇī f., (Ju.) ḏom m., ḏomṇī, ḍomṛī f., mult. ḍōm m.,ḍōmṇī f., awāṇ. naṭ -- ḍūm ' menials '; P. ḍūm, ḍomrā m., ḍūmṇī f. ' strolling musician ', ḍūmṇā m. ' a caste of basket -- maker '; WPah. ḍum ' a very low -- caste blackskinned fellow '; Ku. ḍūm m., ḍūmaṇ f. ' an aboriginal hill tribe '; N. ḍum ' a low caste '; A. ḍom m. ' fisherman ', ḍumini f.; B. ḍom, ḍam m. ' a Ḍom ', ḍumni f. (OB. ḍombī); Or. ḍoma m., aṇī f., ḍuma, aṇī, ḍamba, ḍama, aṇī ' a low caste who weave baskets and sound drums '; Bhoj. ḍōm ' a low caste of musicians H.ḍomb, ḍom, ḍomṛā, ḍumār m., ḍomnī f., OMarw. ḍūma m., ḍūmaṛī f., M. ḍõb, ḍom m. -- Deriv. Gy. wel. romanō adj. (f. nī) ' Gypsy ' romanō rai m. ' Gypsy gentleman ', nī čib f. ' Gypsy language '.*ḍōmbakuṭaka -- , *ḍōmbadhāna -- .Addenda: ḍōmba -- : Gy.eur. rom m., romni f. esp. ' Gypsy man or woman '; WPah.kṭg. ḍōm m. ' member of a low caste of musicians ', ḍv̄m m.; Garh. ḍom ' an untouchable '. (CDIAL 5570).

Rebus (ingot): ḍab, ḍhimba, ḍhompo 'lump (ingot?)', clot, make a lump or clot, coagulate, fuse, melt together (Santali) Thus, the composition of two fish-tails and a circle may denote dul aya ḍhompo 'cast metal ingot'.

Vikalpa Rebus: ḍōmba ?Gypsy(CDIAL 5570). Gypsy are renowned as itinerant smiths?

This W-type glyph on the top register above the summit of the mountain pictorial is a representation of the glyphic shown on Sanchi stupa (referred to in later literature as śrivatsa), but a clear representation of two fish tails ligatured with molluscs to connote: *aya sanga* 'fish mollusc'; rebus: 'metal guild'. This phrase can also be read in a cultural context as a reference to artisan's guild or pilgrims' guild (sanga meaning 'caravan of pilgrims'(G.) or a guild of ariya (as on Jaina ayagapattas).

A lucid account (and transcriptions) of the inscriptions using Kharoshthi and Brahmi scripts is presented in: http://www.ancientcoins.ca/kuninda/kuninda.htm

"The land of Kuninda (also called Kulinda) stretched along the foothills of the Himalayas eastwards from the borders of Audumbara (c. 150-100 BCE) temporarily independent of the Punjab area in the Pathankot region of the Beas river valley to the borders of Nepal. See the photos of 1) a magnificent specimen of a 'Kuninda coin' minted by Raja Amoghabhuti (late 2nd century BCE) of the small tribal State of Kuninda and of the two pages showing 2) the Kharoshti and 3) Brahmi scripts to better understand the coin. Obverse:3 Deer facing female divinity, holding flowers. There are 2 snake-like symbols above the deer. The Brahmi legend reads from left to right: 'Rajna Kunindasa Amoghabhutisa Maharajasa'. Reverse:3 Shows a Buddhist Stupa in the center flanked by a tree on the right and ancillary symbols - tamga and swastika on the left. The Kharoshti script reads from right to left: 'Rana Kunidasa Amoghabhutisa Maharajasa'. Apart from archaeological clay tablets and articles found in the diggings and (more than 1000 known) inscriptions, numismatists have also contributed significantly to a better understanding of ancient genealogy, to the correction of improper dating attributed to events gone past and to calculating the era. Birch-bark (called bhoja-patra) was a primary writing material along with palm-leaf in India. Its use diminished in the Moghal period when paper replaced it as a writing material, but it still has a sacred status in India today. Birch bark was mentioned as a writing material by the Greek historian, Q. Curtius (c. 115 BCE), noting its wide use by the Hindus during Alexander's invasion. Early extant manuscripts date back to the 2nd and 3rd centuries, written in the Kharoshti script. Fragments survive from a range of time periods, and the material is described throughout Indian literature." (Appended essay on Kharoshti script by Sam Kerr)http://www.cais-soas.com/CAIS/Languages/kharoshti_script.htm

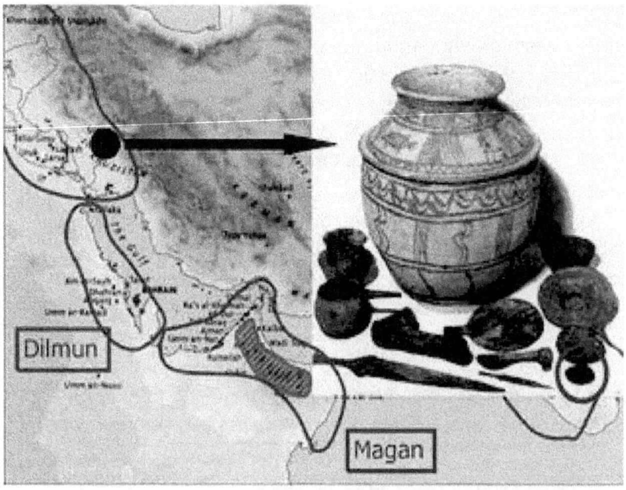


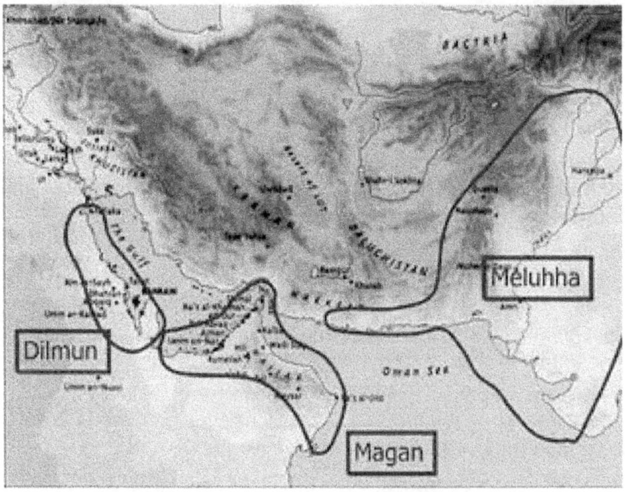


Indus Script was used in the context of trade. This is evidenced by the 'fish' glyph inscribed on a pot which contained metal artifacts. This pot was found in Susa (reported by Prof. Maurizio Tosi: context of interactions between Meluhha and Susa).

A sample of Kuninda coins found in Shimla district.

June 3, 2000,
Chandigarh, India

Kuninda coins found

From Hari Chauhan

SHIMLA: A hoard of 174 Kuninda coins have been found in Pandoa village in Shimla district. This hoard comprising 40 silver and 134 copper coins has been acquired by the State museum here.

The Kunindas were dominant in Himachal Pradesh for a long time. They are mentioned in epics and puranas. In the Mahabharata they are known to have been defeated by Arjuna. In the Vishnu Purana the Kuninda territory has been named specifically as Kulindopatyaka foothills. Varahamehra also places them somewhere in the Himalayan region.

On the basis of literary sources Cunningham has identified the ancient Kulindas with the present day Kunets of Kulu and Shimla. Ptolemy believed the origin of Kuninda in the country irrigated by the river Ganga, Yamuna, Sutlej and Beas.

Incidentally most of the Kuninda coins have been found in places associated with these rivers e.g. Kashipur, Kumaon, Saharnpur, Garhwal, Haryana and Punjab. In Himachal, Kuninda coins have been found at Tappa-Mewa in Hamirpur district, Jawalamukhi and Kangra. A hoard of coins was discovered at Chakker in the Balh valley. With the study of these coins and the knowledge of the places from where the discoveries were made one can conclude that this Kuninda tribe ruled this region from 1st century B.C. to 3rd century A.D.

The Kuninda issued two types of coins. One type was issued about 1st century B.C. and the other about three centuries later. The present hoard was issued during the 1st century B.C. and bears the name Amogbhuti.

The obverse of the coin is in Brahmi and reverse in Khroshti. The obverse has a deer on the right and Lakshmi is facing it. On the reverse a five- arched hill surmounted by Nandipada, on the right a tree in the railing and on the left two swastik and Inderdhwaja. At the bottom is a wavy line representing a river.

http://www.tribuneindia.com/2000/20000603/himachal.htm#1

Pulinda have been recognized as a group of people in ancient texts, for e.g.: "kirāta-hūnāndhra-pulinda-pulkaśā ābhīra-śumbhā yavanā khasādayaḥ" (Bhagavatam 2.4.18).

"The protected states and tribes brought in this way within the circle of Buddhist influence included Kambojas, who lived among the mountains either of Tibet or of the Hindu Kush; various Himalayan nations; the Gandharas and Yavanas of the Kabul valley and regions still farther west; the Bhojas, Pulindas, and Pitenikas dwelling among the hills of the Vindhya range and Western Ghats; and the Andhra kingdom between the Krishna and Godavari rivers. (Note: Pitenikas, uncertain; Bhojas, probably in Berar (Ilichpur, see Collins on *Dasakumaracharita*, and *Bomb. Gaz.* (1896), vol. I, pt. ii, p. 27); Pulindas among the Vindhya hills near the Narmada (ibid., p. 138). But the term Pulinda was used vaguely, and sometimes meant Himalayan tribes." (loc. Cit. JRAS, 1908, p. 315; Vincent A. Smith, 1999 (Repr.), *The early history of India*, Atlantic Publishers & Dist., p. 184.

Pulinda is mentioned in the context of other peoples such as aśmaka:

pulinda aśmaka jīmuta nar rāṣtra nivāsinah:
karnata kamboja ghata dakṣinapathvāsinah: — (Garuda Purana 1/15/13). Sathianathaiyer opines that

Pulindas of Asoka's inscriptions should be identified with the Kurumbas of Tondamandalam. (Sathianathaiyer, 1944, *Studies in the Ancient History of Thondamandalam*, Preface, p. i)http://www.archive.org/stream/studiesintheanci035060mbp/studiesintheanci035060mbp_djvu.txt

Mahabharata states that the Andhhas, Pulindas, Sakas, Kambojas, Yavanas, Valhikas, Aurnikas and Abhiras etc will become rulers in Kaliyuga and will rule the earth (India) un-righteously(MBh., Vanaparva, 3.187.28-30). In the context of Yudhistira's Rajasuya Kambojas, Vairamas, Paradas, Pulindas, Tungas, Kiratas, Pragjyotisha, Yavanas, Aushmikas, Nishadas, Romikas, Vrishnis, Harahunas, Chinas, Sakas, Sudras, Abhiras, Nipas, Valhikas, Tukharas, Kankas, etc. are mentioned. (Mahabharata 2.50-1.seqq). "Mahabharata (XIII, 33.20-23; XIII, 35, 17-18), lists the Sakas, Yavanas, Kambojas, Dravidas, Kalingas, Pulindas, Usinaras, Kolisarpas, Mekalas, Sudras, Mahishakas, Latas, Kiratas, Paundrakas, Daradas etc as the Vrishalas/degraded Kshatriyas (See also: Comprehensive History of India, 1957, p 190, K. A. N. Sastri)."
http://en.wikipedia.org/wiki/Mahajanapadas

The embedded document includes: W. Theobald, 1890, Notes on some of the symbols found on the punch-marked coins of Hindustan, and on their relationship to the archaic symbolism of other races and distant lands, JASB, Part 1,History, Literature etc., Nos. III and IV, 1890, pp. 181 to 268, Plates VIII to XI.

http://www.docstoc.com/docs/12434184/Indus-script-glyphs-on-coins

Indus script glyphs on coins

Kharoshti Script
A brief essay

By: Sam Kerr

The Kharoshti language was introduced into Gandhara - Afghanistan and the North-west frontiers of India during the early part of the 5th century BCE as a result of Achaemenian conquests eastwards4.

The language and script, it seems, became refined with time but it was ultimately overtaken by the much older language of the region, Brahmi and it became extinct by about the middle (c. 300-350 CE) of the Sassanian Dynasty (which lasted c.224 to 641 CE). It certainly differed from all other Indic scripts in that it retained the Semitic characteristic of being written from right to left. After all it was derived from its north Semitic parent, Aramaic, like Pahlavi was. Yet it retained the distinct Indian ways - in the use of the consonants, double consonants and the vowels.

Kuninda coin composite
Obverse: Brahmi script
Reverse: Kharoshti script

Sanskrit in Brahmi script slowly gave place to Prakrit in Devnagari script. As Brahmi progressed into the Devnagari group of Indic languages the Kharoshti script gradually died out about c. 305-325 CE. There was some overlap of the scripts on coins as Satraps vied with the suzerain Kings and usurped their Satrapy as an autonomous kingdom.

The coins showing the Greek divinities5 - Zeus (holding a thunderbolt and/or a sceptre), Hercules (usually holding a club and/or lion skin), Nike (usually winged, City divinity holding cornucopia), Artemis drawing arrow from bow, Helios (Sun), Selene (Moon) and the Indo-Iranian divinities: Mozao Oaho or Mazdaonho (Ahura Mazda), Athasho (Fire), Bago (Bhaga), Miiro/ Mioro (Sun/Mithra), Ardoksho (Earth), Orlango (Verethaghna), Saorhora (Sherewar, Mao (Moon), Apto/Appo (Waters), Vado (Wind), Pharro (Aura /Khwarena), Manaobago (Vohu Manah), Boddo (Buddha), sometimes a humped Indian bull or an elephant or the two-humped Bactrian camel on the reverse......etc were slowly replaced by the standing Shiva (holding a trident or a club) in front of a bull, Parvati (consort of Shiva) seated on a lion, Lakshmi (representing wealth) seated or standing on a lotus, Peacock motif.....etc. The coins were minted mainly in Balkh, Merv, Herat, Pushkalavati (near modern Kabul), Takhshashilla (modern Taxila), Baamiyan, Jammu....etc.

Kharoshti script and changes of regimes in Gandhara and and surrounding regions

Graeco-Bactrian Period: (c. 250-174 BCE)

See: Bactrian documents from ancient Afghanistan by Nicholas Sims-Williams.

See: DOCUMENTS ÉPIGRAPHIQUES KOUCHANS by Gérard Fussman (Bulletin de l'École Française d'Extrême Orient, Paris, LXI, 1974, 1-66)

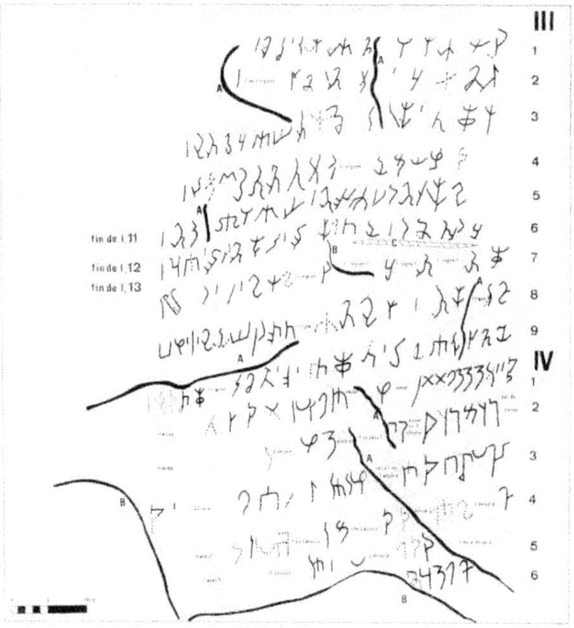


Fac-similé de DN III et de DN IV. A : rebord d'une écaille qui s'est détachée avant la gravure de l'inscription. B : rebord d'une écaille qui s'est détachée après la gravure de l'inscription. C : martelage (?) ancien (?).

Inscription DN IV (Pl. V, fig. 17-21). *kharoṣṭī* script in Dasht-e Nawur. See also the use of Greek script.

Mollusc glyphics on sculptures at Ai-khanum. Comparable to the glyphs on Mathura capital, Sanchi stupa etc. to denote, rebus, the 'sangha'. Molluscs are also used in the Indus script glyphics. For e.g. on a copper tablet showing head of a one-horned heifer' ligatured with 'octopus' like mollusc glyphic.
See: http://www.docstoc.com/docs/13650614/citadel

The history begins circa 250 BCE when the Indo-Greeks in Bactria revolted against their Seleucid masters and formed an autonomous empire free from the suzerainty of an overlord. It was led by Diodotus I (c. 250-230 BCE) with his son, Diodotus II (c. 250-230 BCE) usurped the Eastern Satraps, Sughda and Margiana from the Suzerain King Seleucus I Nikator (ruled c.313-281 BCE), who was himself assassinated. The Graeco-Bactrians had only the Greek legend on both sides of their coins. The Kharoshti script on coins was not in use during this period, which ended in 174 BCE.

Indo-Greek (Yonas, word for Ionians) Period: (c.174 BCE-10 CE)

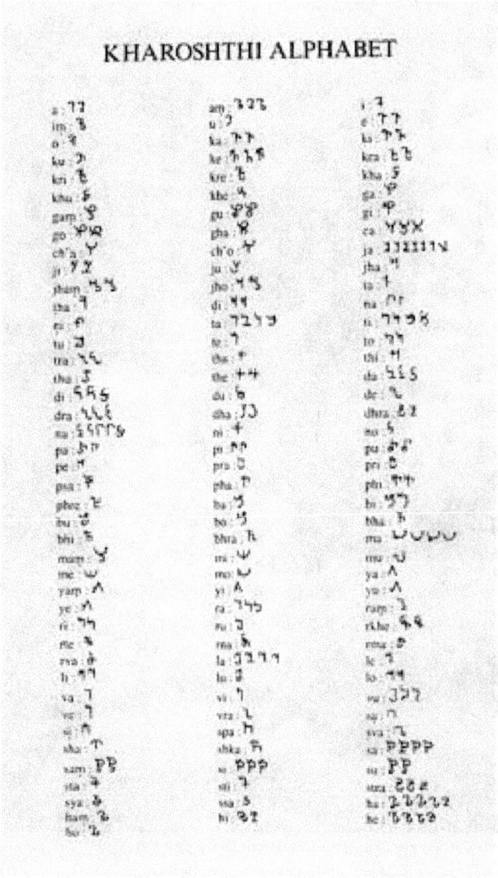


Kharosti Alphabet

Commencing with Apollodotus I (c.174-165 BCE) and ending with Strato II (ruled with Strato III c. 25 BCE -10 CE in North Afghanistan) coins were minted with the Greek legend on the obverse and the Kharoshti script on the reverse.

Demetrius (at first associated with his father c.205-190 BCE and then by himself c.190-166 BCE) ruling further east and in Arachosia (South Afghanistan) also minted bilingual coins, with Kharoshti on the Reverse (MAHARAJaSa APaRaJITaSa DEMETRIYaSa) and Greek on the Obverse (Invincible King Demetrius). This could have occurred only if Kharoshti was then a common spoken language among a large population in these regions. The script on the coins was Kharoshti throughout the Indo-Greek period.

Indo-Scythian Period: (c.10 CE-130 CE) 3
The Indo-Scythians were a branch of the Sakas from central Asia. Overlapping the Indo-Greeks they had initially settled in the west Afghan plateau of Drangiana, calling it 'Sakastan'. About 10 CE the Indo-Scythian King Rajuvula, a minor Satrap in Mathura defeated and dethroned Strato III. Around 80 CE they moved eastwards to overtake South Afghanistan. In previous times the Indo-Scythian king Maues had already occupied Gandhara and Taxila (improperly dated around 80 BCE), but his kingdom disintegrated upon his death and the Indo-Greeks had prospered again for a while, as suggested by the coinage of kings Apollodotus II (c.110-80 BCE) and Hippostratos (c.90-60 BCE), until the Saka King

Azes I permanently established Indo-Scythian rule in the northwest in 60 BCE. They too minted coins with the Greek legend on the obverse and the Kharoshti script on the reverse of their coins.

The Yueh-chi / Yuehzhi (Kushans from western China) Period: (c.135-350 BCE)

The Yueh-chi were a nomadic confederation of five tribes that originally lived near the border of China. They came from the Tarim Basin region, which is a part of what is now Gansu and Xinjiang provinces. They encountered severe problems with the Hsiung-nu (White Huns; later called Hephthalites) in the years 176-160 B.C. After suffering two major defeats by the Huns, the Yueh-chi decided to move west and then south. Their decision to migrate affected the course of history. When they moved south, some Turkic tribes went with them. The Turkic people had also encountered problems with the Huns. They moved into an area north of the Oxus in what is now Kazakhstan and Uzbekistan and displaced a branch of the Scythians called the Sakas. By about 135 B.C., the Yue-chi and their Turkic allies had reached Bactria, a region that included parts of North West Afghanistan and Tajikistan. Greek dynasties of the Seleucids and Greco-Bactrians had ruled it for a long time. The Yueh-chi were able to eventually gain control of Bactria. They had driven out the last nomadic Indo-Greek king, Heliocles I (c. 135-110 BCE).

The later Kushans called themselves the Kushano-Sassanians 230-271 CE and Kushanshahs 271-350 CE. Depending on the affiliation to the Sassanians or Kushans their coins had only the Pahlavi or Greek script. They thrived roughly up to the middle of the Sassanian rule (about 350 CE). The Nahapana Satraps of the Sassanian era, who ruled in India as far south as Kutch, Gujarat and Saurashtra, however, had coins minted with trilingual scripts - Greek, Brahmi and Kharoshti.

On their coins Kushan kings used Greek language legends combined with Pali legends (in *kharoṣṭī* script). A few years after the reign of Kaniska, kushan language legends in an adapted Greek script --- adding letter Þ to denote the sound 'sh' as in Kushan), was used together with Greek legends (Greek script) and Pali legends (*kharoṣṭī* script).

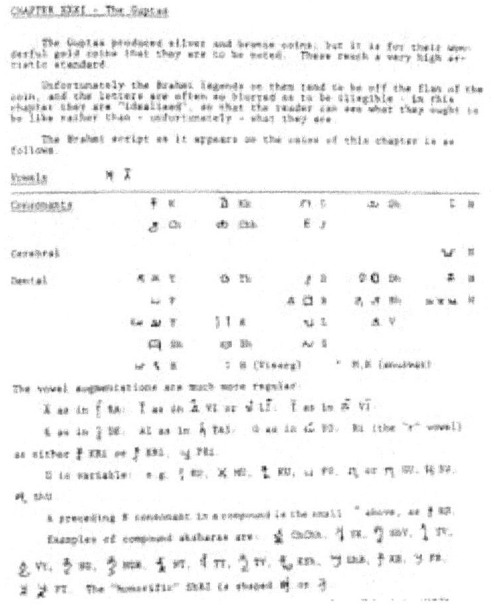
CHAPTER XXXI - The Guptas

The Guptas produced silver and bronze coins, but it is for their wonderful gold coins that they are to be noted. These reach a very high artistic standard.

Unfortunately the Brahmi legends on them tend to be off the flan of the coin, and the letters are often so blurred as to be illegible - in this chapter they are "idealised", so that the reader can see what they ought to be like rather than - unfortunately - what they are.

The Brahmi script as it appears on the coins of this chapter is as follows.

Kharosti Script

There was also a short rule of the Indo-Parthians in a limited region (c. 78-124 CE). Both groups minted coins with the Greek legend on the obverse and the Kharoshti script on the reverse of their coins. This second wave of 'Indo-Parthians' moved eastwards into the Kabul Valley and present Pakistan c. 20 CE led by 'Gondophores' taking over from the Kushan King, Kujula Kadophises. Gondophores has been mentioned in the manuscripts "Actae Thomae" as the 'King, Guduphara' who had met Saint Thomas, the Apostle on his journey to South India. Christianity had been established in India 500 years before the early Christian Portuguese missionaries c.1522 came with their dreams of the colonializing of India. The missionaries were surprised at seeing huts and buildings with a cross atop in the Malabar coastal region of the present State of Kerala. The region was recaptured from the Indo-Parthians by the Kushans, possibly by Soter Megas c.45-90 CE. The Kharoshti script was no longer seen on any of the coins. It was replaced by the Brahmi script, which was now written and read from left to right (although, it seems from an isolated document that the earliest Brahmi script 3rd Century BCE was written from right to left). He was succeeded by Kadophises II 120 CE.

By the time of Kanishka I, the greatest of the Kushan kings (the exact dates of his 23-27 years of rule are under dispute) his kingdom included Kashmir, Khotan and Kashgar and Yarkand The last three were Chinese dependencies in the Tarim Basin, modern Xinjiang. His vast kingdom extended from Bukhara in the west to Sarnath in India, with Peshawar as the Capital) the coins in the Brahmi script showed the images and/or inscriptions of Boddo (Buddha), (Oisho) Shiva holding a trident near a bull (Nandi), Mihira/Miira (Mithra), Athro (Atar), Varahran (Verethragna), Mao (Moon), Appo (Water), Aodo (Vata). The appearance of the Avestan divinities was attributed to the fact that the Sassanian King, Hormazd II (303-309 CE) had earlier married the daughter of a Kushan king in Gandhara.

Thereafter, Ardochso (Lakshmi), the consort of Vishnu remained a standard diety and was absorbed into the first Gupta Empire of Chandra Gupta (305-325 CE). His grandfather, Shrigupta (c 270-290 CE) ruling as 'Maharaja' of a small principality was the real founder of the Gupta Dynasty. Then, all traces of the Iranian influence have been found absent from the coins.

With regular revolts against the suzerain King there was some overlap of dynasties as kingdoms were lost and regained for short periods. Some tribal States - the Audumbara and the Kuninda (c. 150-100 BCE), used Kharoshti on one side of their coins and Brahmi on the other side. Indeed, the Audumbara tribal kings Dharagosa and Rudravarma were credited as being the first to introduce the Brahmi script on one side with the Kharoshti script on the other side of their coins. The neighbouring States soon followed. Most Kuninda coins have been found in hoards north of a line between Ambala and Saharanpur. There were also some even with trilingual inscriptions - Greek, Brahmi and Kharoshti. The Kuninda Kings followed the practice.

The land of Kuninda (also called Kulinda) stretched along the foothills of the Himalayas eastwards from the borders of Audumbara (c. 150-100 BCE) temporarily independent of the Punjab area in the Pathankot region of the Beas river valley to the borders of Nepal. See the photos of 1) a magnificent specimen of a 'Kuninda coin' minted by Raja Amoghabhuti (late 2nd century BCE) of the small tribal State of Kuninda and of the two pages showing 2) the Kharoshti and 3) Brahmi scripts to better understand the coin. Obverse:3 Deer facing female divinity, holding flowers. There are 2 snake-like symbols above the deer. The Brahmi legend reads from left to right: 'Rajna Kunindasa Amoghabhutisa Maharajasa'. Reverse:3 Shows a Buddhist Stupa in the center flanked by a tree on the right and ancillary symbols - tamga and swastika on the left. The Kharoshti script reads from right to left: 'Rana Kunidasa Amoghabhutisa Maharajasa'.

Apart from archaeological clay tablets and articles found in the diggings and (more than 1000 known) inscriptions, numismatists have also contributed significantly to a better understanding of ancient genealogy, to the correction of improper dating attributed to events gone past and to calculating the era. Birch-bark (called bhoja-patra) was a primary writing material along with palm-leaf in India. Its use diminished in the Moghal period when paper replaced it as a writing material, but it still has a sacred status in India today. Birch bark was mentioned as a writing material by the Greek historian, Q. Curtius (c. 115 BCE), noting its wide use by the Hindus during Alexander's invasion. Early extant manuscripts date back to the 2nd and 3rd centuries, written in the Kharoshti script. Fragments survive from a range of time periods, and the material is described throughout Indian literature.

Recently, an ancient Buddhist settlement, belonging to second and third century CE, has been discovered in Badgam district of Central Kashmir2. The tiles unearthed from the site area are in various shapes. They bear swastika motifs and the Kharoshti script, which was popular in Kashmir in the early centuries of the Common Era and ceased its popularity in circa fourth century. The presence of the Kharoshti numerals and swastika motif revealed the date of the site to be between second and third century CE. Measuring 36 cm x 40 cm, the Kharoshti numerical on the tiles were clearly stamped to maintain the order of tiles in the layout.

Palm leaf manuscripts1 were probably in use as early as the 2nd century, but no extant leaves survive earlier than the 10th century. Because palm-leaf is still used today in India for certain religious writings, much is known about the manufacture and treatment of the material. In 1998 an early manuscript of about the 5th century written in the Kharoshti script was found in the Bhaamiyan cave region near the Afghanistan city of Hadda. Microscopic examination revealed the pages were, in fact, laminated layers of very thin Birch-bark.

Birch-bark (bhoja-patra)1 manuscripts were literally the ancient database of Buddhism in India. In the 1930's, the Musee Guimet in Paris had acquired bundles of birch-bark found at Baamiyan in Afghanistan. The inner bark of the birch tree was used for writing. After being peeled off the tree, the bark was dried. Oil was then applied over it and it was polished. Layers were joined together by a natural gum. Finally, it was cut to a suitable size and kept in between wooden covers. The ink used for writing on birch bark was 'Indian black', a carbon ink. It was prepared by burning almond shells to charcoal, which was then boiled with cow's urine. This ink had a special brilliance and was indelible.

References:

1. ExpressIndia -Indian Express Newspapers (Bombay) Ltd., 1999

2. Mitchiner, Michael, The ancient and Classical World (600 BC-AD 650), Oriental Coins and their values, Hawkins Publications, London, 1978.

3. Plant, Richard J., Greek, Semitic, Asiatic coins and how to read them, Scorpion Publishers, Amherst, New York, 1979.

4. Sylloge Nummorum Graecorum, Graeco-Bactrian and Indo-Greek Coins, The collection of the American Numismatic Society, New York 1998.

http://www.cais-soas.com/CAIS/Languages/kharoshti_script.htm

See: Brahmi script on Indus civilization coins - the last nail on the coffin of the Aryan invasion theory - with a note on the survey of Prithudak by Birendr K. Jha

See: Richard Salomon, 1998, *Indian Epigraphy* (OUP) "This book provides a general survey of all the inscriptional material in the Sanskrit, Prakrit, and modern Indo-Aryan languages, including donative, dedicatory, panegyric, ritual, and literary texts carved on stone, metal, and other materials. This material comprises many thousands of documents dating from a range of more than two millennia, found in India

and the neighboring nations of South Asia, as well as in many parts of Southeast, central, and East Asia. The inscriptions are written, for the most part, in the Brahmi and Kharosthi scripts and their many varieties and derivatives.
Inscriptional materials are of particular importance for the study of the Indian world, constituting the most detailed and accurate historical and chronological data for nearly all aspects of traditional Indian culture in ancient and medieval times. Richard Salomon surveys the entire corpus of Indo-Aryan inscriptions in terms of their contents, languages, scripts, and historical and cultural significance. He presents this material in such a way as to make it useful not only to Indologists but also non-specialists, including persons working in other aspects of Indian or South Asian studies, as well as scholars of epigraphy and ancient history and culture in other regions of the world."

Indian Epigraphy from Kara-tepe in Old Termez: Problems of Decipherment andInterpretation by V. V. VertogradovaReview by: Richard Salomon in: *Journal of the American Oriental Society*, Vol. 117, No. 2 (Apr. - Jun., 1997), pp. 406-408 http://www.jstor.org/stable/605533 (embedded)

"The Buddhist cave monastery site of Kara-tepe at Old Termez in southern Uzbekistan, together with the closely adjoining site of Fayaz-tepe, provides one of the most important sources of information on the spread of Buddhism during the kuṣāṇa period...According to the author (p.5), more than 150 inscriptions in Indian scripts (*kharoṣṭī* and *brāhmī*) and languages (Prākrit and Sanskrit or hyubrid Sanskrit) were found at Kara-tepe, as well as 35 at Fayaz-tepe...referring to a trilingual inscription to be published in the next volume of Kara-tepe series...These inscriptions, according to Vertogradova's analysis (pp. 11-14), comprise two main types: donative records, almost always written in *kharoṣṭī* script, and possession records marking the inscribed vessels as the property of a particular monk, mostly written in *brāhmī*. The latter category also includes five biscript (*brāhmī* and *kharoṣṭī* or *brāhmī* and Bactrin) and one triscript (*brāhmī*, *kharoṣṭī* and Bactrian) inscription. Donative inscriptions on pottery are well attested in inscriptions from various parts of (traditional) India and Afghanistan (pp. 8-9), especially from the Gandhāra region. Inscriptions marking ownership are less common, but some examples have been recognized, notably at Salihundam in Andhra Pradesh. (See Oskar von Hinuber, 'Inscribed vessels from Buddhist Monasteries in Termez and Salihundam', *Pakistan Archaeology* 26 (1991): 120-24). In the present collection wee have some specimens of complete inscriptions, which have been in the past quite rare, as most of the previously published examples were only fragments, often very small, of the full records. Thus both the abundance of new materials from Kara-tepe and their relatively good condition make them a particularly important source for the study of Buddhist institutions of the kuṣāṇa era."(ibid., p. 406)

These insights of Richard Salomon provide the basis for a hypothesis which gets validated by theIndus script cipher: that the Indus script glyphs did NOT represent donative records NOR did they denote ownership of property items; but, that Indus script glyphs denoted technical information on minerals/metals/alloys/stones worked on by artisans to create artefacts of the civilization.

Indus script was used to describe the technical repertoire and materials with which the artisans worked.

Further validation of this hypothesis comes from the occurrence of tri-script legends on early coins as those of Kuninda (Pulinda) which contain legends deploying Indus script hieroglyphs, *brāhmī* and *kharoṣṭī* scripts.

ASI on treasure hunt, searches Andhra Buddhist ruins

Salihundam, Kotturu sites of Srikakulam Dist., Andhra Pradesh point to their possible maritime links across the Indian Ocean, with Sumatra and Khmer, as Bauddham traditions spread -- in an extensive stretch from Bactria to many nations of the Indian Ocean Community south into Sri Lanka and east upto Thailand.

*-tepe* suffix denoting some BMAC/Central Asia sites can be compared with *dibba* in Telugu; and hence the reference to hillocks of Salihundam as *dibbalu* 'mounds':

Ta. tippai mound, elevated ground; that which is bulky. Ko. tip rubbish heap. Ka. tippe heap, hillock, dunghill; dibba, dibbu eminence, hillock; tevar(u), tevari rising ground, hillock. Tu. tippè heap, pile, hill; tuppè stack, heap of corn or rice. Te. tippa hill, hillock, rock, mountain, heap, mound, small island; dibba hillock, mound, heap. Pa. ḍippa heap; ḍibba mound. Ga. (S.3) dibbe hillock, mound. Go. (Mu.) dippa highland for cultivation, forest field (Voc. 1865); (M.) dībe heap (Voc. 1869). Kui ḍepa rising ground, high land, lower slopes of a hill, shore, earth platform, veranda, dais. Kuwi (S.) debbe hill; bā'ali dibba sandhill. Kur. ḍippā mound, hillock. Malt. tube a heap of filth or sweepings (DEDR 3239).

Tuesday, 21 December 2010 06:12

The Archaeological Survey of India is on a "treasure hunt" in the nondescript Kotturu village of Visakhapatnam district searching Buddhist ruins for priceless artefacts, inscriptions and ancient gold and silver coins.

Kotturu is one of the six new archaeological sites selected by the Central government for excavations that are likely to throw a deep insight into the lifestyles of people dating back to second century BC. The ASI will dig up "mounds" in and around Kotturu that have so far been the target of vandals seeking treasure trove.

The Central government has decided to go in for a thorough excavation of the "mounds" in Kotturu after archaeologists discovered stone inscriptions containing Telugu words in Brahmi script about 2,200 years old. Earlier excavations at the site brought out 107 gold coins, silver coins, pearls, diamonds and gems stored in a small vessel. The vessel was hidden in a rectangular container.

According to officials at the ASI office in Hyderabad, the excavations on Buddhist "mounds" will also throw more light on the language spoken by Buddhist monks and local people in those times. A rock edict in Brahmi script contained the words, "Tambayya Danam" which in Telugu means "donated by Tambayya".

Tambayya was believed to be a Telugu noble who had donated gold ornaments and precious stones to Buddhist monks towards charity. Tambayya's donation includes 21 silver and gold flowers and two gold containers. Ever since the discovery of the rock edict, the interest of archaeologists and linguistics has gone up on the "mounds" in Kotturu. The edict has pushed the age of Telugu language by at least 800 years. Earlier, Telugu was thought to be evolved around the sixth. The latest evidence now shows that Telugu is as old as 2,200 years.

Like Sanskrit, Tamil and Kannada, the literature of Telugu has been in vogue for over 1,500 years. Some archaeologists have been arguing that Telugu is more than 2,000 years old. The first Telugu words can be observed in Ikshavakula inscriptions. Nagarjuna Hill inscriptions of 250 AD contain Telugu words. But the Kotturu inscriptions have come in as the first-ever "solid evidence" to prove that Telugu was spoken even before the start of the common era.

The Kotturu "mounds" are similar in structure to the internationally famous "Salihundam", a Buddhist site in Srikakulam district. Salihundam is an ancient settlement containing a mahastupa, votive stupas, chaityas, platforms and viharas. Here, the inscriptions date back to the second century AD. The Kotturu "mounds" are 400 years older than the Salihundam and archaeologists expect more "surprises" during the excavations.

Kotturu and surrounding areas as also the ancient sites along the river Krishna in Krishna and Godavari districts had played an important role in the spread of Buddhism from India to Sumatra, China and other countries in the Far East.

The "mounds" are known as "Dhana Dibbalu" (mounds of treasure) in local parlance. There are Chaitya Grihas or halls of worship built of brick. Similar ruins are also found in Andhra Pradesh at places like Guntapalli near Vijayawada, Nagarjunakonda and Amaravathi in Guntur district. But these mounds are 100 years older than the Kotturu mounds.

Along with Kotturu mounds, the ASI has taken up excavations at ancient sites in Chaturbhuj Nala (Mandsaur district) and Gondarmau (Bhopal district) in Madhya Pradesh, Aragarh (Puri district) in Orissa and Sanauli, Baghpat and Latiya (Ghazipur district) in Uttar Pradesh.

The other oldest Telugu inscription is from 633 AD. The Telugu literature begins with an 11th-century translation of the Sanskrit classic Mahabharata. Telugu words appear in the Maharashtri Prakrit anthology of poems (the Gathasaptashathi) collected by the first century BC Satavahana King Hala.

Telugu speakers were probably the oldest peoples inhabiting the land between Krishna and Godavari. ASI officials hope that the Kotturu findings are likely to give a historical look to the Telugu language and the traditions and culture of the Telugu-speaking people.
By: Syed Akbar
The Asian Age April 27, 2006
Last Updated ( Tuesday, 21 December 2010 06:12 )

About Salihundam.

Salihundam (18°28'; 84°3'), Dt Srikakulam, 7 km w. of Kalingapatna, with remains of a Buddhist *saṅghārāma* that flourished continuously from *c.* 3rd century B.C. to *c.* 8th century A.D. on the summit of a low hill. It was excavated A.L. Longhurst (*ASI—AR 1919-20*, p. 35), when structural remains of *stūpas*, *vihāras* and Tantric Buddhist images like Mārīci, Tārā, etc., were found. Excavation by the writer in 1954 (*IAR 1953-4*, p. 11) has revealed three phases of occupation. The Early Phase (3rd-2nd century B.C. to 1st century A.D.), marked by a few brick platforms and some irregular lines of brick associated with a punch-marked coin [3.1] and the Megalithic Black-and red Ware [11.15.3], besides other plain wares, was followed by the Middle Phase (1st-2nd century to 3rd-4th century A.D.), in which most of the monuments including the *mahā-caitya*, two smaller *stūpas*, two circular *caitya-gṛhas* housing stucco figures of Buddha, two such others with *stūpas* and several *vihāras*, all brick-built and provided with stone-paved approaches, came into existence. The material equipment comprised notably dishes of the Rouletted Ware [11.21], sprinklers of the Red Polished Ware [11.23] dull-red lamps, flat-based bowls with flaring sides, dishes and lids with flanged waist, terracotta arecanut-shaped beads and reel-shaped ear ornaments, inscribed conches (one mentioning the ancient name a *Sālipāsaka*), Sātavāhana coin, a Puri-Kushan coin, terracotta objects like seals, caparisoned horses and plaques with Buddha figures.

The Late Phase (*c*. 4th-5th century to 7th-8th century) witnesses the construction of only a few votive *stūpas*, some random-rubble revetments and a pillared *maṇḍapa* built of material drawn from the earlier structures. Plain dull ware, wedge-shaped and moulded bricks, flat tiles, terracotta finials, beads of crystal and terracotta, stone images of Tantric Buddhist deities and six stone inscriptions of the 7th-8th century are the notable associated items of this phase. These three phases roughly mark the shifting of sectarian predominance of Hinayāna, Mahāyāna and Vajrayāna.

Salihundam was generally exposed to cultural influences from n. and s. as revealed from the material equipment displaying similarities with those from sites like ARIKAMDU, BRAHMAPURI, NAGARJUNAKONDA, SISUPALGARH, TRIPURI and HASTINAPURA. But the solidly constructed *stūpas* without *āyaka* platforms or sculptured casing slabs show the greater influence of the n. tradition than that of the Andhra region. The stucco figures of Buddha are reminiscent of Gandhāra features. A remarkable feature of the site is the occurrence at all levels of a number of inscribed potsherds providing names of persons, places, etc., and some with drawings

of *vihāra* plans.

Subrahmanyam, R., 1964, *Salihundam, a Buddhist Site in Andhra Pradesh*, Hyderabad.—R. SUBRAHMANYAM

A. Ghosh, 1989, An encyclopedia of Indian archaeology, EJ BRILL, p.386.
See: http://www.hindu.com/fline/fl2605/stories/20090313260511800.htm

śakti statue, Salihundam.

ıaraman

Comparable to Sit-Shamshi bronze are the stupa in relation to rectangular structures in Salihundam stupa site. (Photo by Binoy K. Behl)

See Photo gallery.

Salihundam. The mains stupa made of wedge shaped bricks around a central hollow shaft with stone faced base survives in parts.

"Salihundam is a village and panchayat in Gara Mandal of Srikakulam district in Andhra Pradesh, India. It is a famous Buddhist Remnants site situated on the south bank of River Vamsadhara at a distance of 5 kilometers west of Kalingapatnam and 18 kilometers from Srikakulam town. It was known as “Salivatika” (meaning rice emporium). But many called it "Salyapetika" (meaning box of bones or relics). There are a number of Buddhist stupas and a huge monastic complex on a hillock amidst scenic surroundings. The site was first discovered by Gidugu Venkata Rama Murthy in 1919. During excavations relic caskets, four stupas, a Chaityagriha, structural emples and a number of sculptures reflecting the three phases of Buddhism - Theravada, Mahayana and Vajrayana were found dating back to about 2nd century BC to 12th century AD. The statues of 'Tara' and Marichi were discovered at this site and from here Buddhism spread to Sumatra and other far-eastern countries through River Vamsadhara and Kalingapatnam Port."
http://en.wikipedia.org/wiki/Salihundam

"Statue of Tara". The British Museum. Found between Trincomalee and Batticaloa, Sri Lanka, AD 700-750

Indian Epigraphy from Kara-tepe in Old Termez: Problems of Decipherment and Interpretation by V. V. VertogradovaReview by: Richard Salomon (1997)

Kara-Tepe monastery, (in) Old Termiz, Surxondaryo Viloyati, UZ

A Buddhist cave monastery close to the banks of the Amu-Darya - Bradley et al. (2007:248-249)

"Hinayana was widespread in Tokharistan; according to Hsüan-tsang" - Melikian-Chirvani (n.d.)
Termiz - "The main sights lurk northwest of the city on the road to Qarshi. Driving out here you'll notice various piles of rubble in the cotton fields of what used to be Termiz (and is now known as Old Termiz). These are Buddhist ruins, levelled by Jenghiz Khan along with the rest of Old Termiz in 1220. Today archaeologists are busy trying to recerse some of the damage at Fayouz-Tepe, a 3rd-century AD Buddhist monastery complex 9km west of the bus station. Discovered only in 1968, in recent years it's been restored and partly rebuilt with support from Unesco. The modern-looking teapot dome protects the monastery's original stupa. Looking south-west from here the remains of Kara-Tepe, a Buddhist

cave monastery, are visible on the banks of the Amu-Darya."

Bradley et al. (2007:248-249)

[2] The remains of Bactrian Buddhist monasteries have been found near Termez in southern Uzbekistan at Kara Tepe, Fayas Tepe and Dalverzin Tepe,

http://www.berzinarchives.com/web/en/archives/study/islam/historical_interaction/overviews/hist_sketch_west_turkistan.html

Brahmi inscriptions of Kara-tepe "mention a sangha, vihara [monastery] or school." p. 118 (Litvinskii et al. 1996:118)

Kara Tepe

Kara Tepe is the name of a natural hill made up by cemented sands, located not far from Old Termez. It consists of three complexes: Northern, Western and Southern. Unique ancient Indian inscriptions, clay statues of Buddhas and Boddhisattvas are today displayed in Termez and Tashkent museums.

http://www.wbcet.com/index.php?option=com_content&task=view&id=24&Itemid=44

Kara – tepa

Karatepa is a Buddhist place of worship built on three hills situated in the north-west part of Old Termez.

It includes a number of temples and monasteries that appeared in the beginning of the 2nd century A.D. The architecture of Karatepa is characterized by a combination of caves made of pahsa and unbaked brick.

Interiors of the shrines were decorated with topical and ornamental paintings on stucco plaster and sculptures made of loess and clay. In the architectural decor marble-like limestone and carved stucco were widely used.

During the Kushan period, as witness dedicatory inscriptions on ceramics, the Buddhist center in Karatepa (or part of it) could have had the name of Khadevakavihara, or King's Monastery (according to V.V. Vertogradova). Thanks to support from the Kushan administration, the Karatepa center achieved the peak of flourishing in the 2nd-3rd centuries. In the 4th-5th centuires a considerable part of the shrines stopped functioning. During that period caves were used as burial places, and entranceways were usually bricked up. However, it is highly probable that some shrines, or at least their surface parts continued to exist as Buddhist places of worship till the 6th century. In the 9th-12th centuires hermits called "sufi" settled in semi-destroyed caves.

The walls of Karatepa caves still carry numerous grafitti drawings and visitors inscriptions (Bactrian, Middle Persian, Brahmi, Soghdian, Syrian (?), Arabic), made both when the Buddhist center was functioning and in the period of its decline when caves were still accessible.

http://www.eastlinetour.com/uzbekistan/termez/history/karatepa.html

"While Begram was the summer capital, Kara-tepe presents a group of caves, stupas and monasteries [...] The Buddhist complex of Kara-tepe was also deserted at some moment when the Kushano-Sasanians occupied it, but the discovery of Kushano-Sasanian coints and later construction provides evidence of its subsequent continuity as a reliogious center." Dani and Litvinsky (1999:111)

Input by: tmciolek, Aug 28, 2009
http://monastic-asia.wikidot.com/kara-tepe

See: Dialogue October-December, 2004, Volume 6 No. 2 Historical and Cultural Relations between Kazakhstan, Central Asia and India from Ancient times to the beginning of the XX century Dr. M. Kh. Abuseitova

Nomads and the shaping of Central Asia: from the early Iron Age to the Kushan Period by Claude Rapin (2007) http://claude.rapin.free.fr/1BiblioTextesGeogrPDF/Rapin_Nomads2.pdf

Nomads and the shaping of Central Asia: from the early Iron Age to the Kushan Period by Claude Rapin (2007)

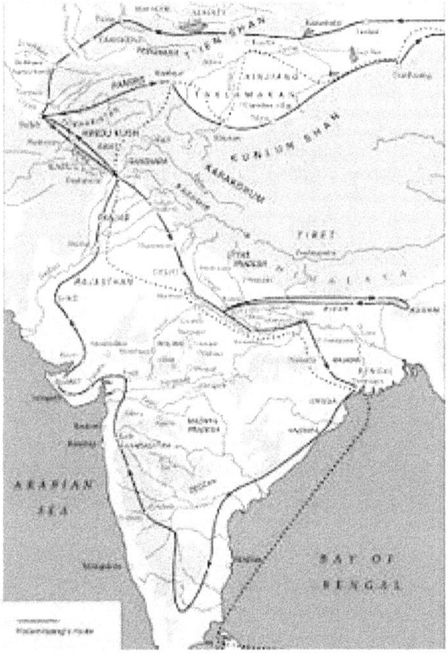


Location of Termez on Huang-Tsang's route.

"It is also important to point out the differences between the wording of the Kharoshthi and Brahmi inscriptions of Kara-tepe. Most of the Kharoshthi inscriptions are based on a traditional formula indicating the donor, the gift, the recipient, almost resembling n incantation formula. However, the Brahmi inscriptions, even though a dedication, mention a sangha, vihara (monastery) or school. They are focused on the donor and his attributes. others again serve as indicattions of the individual use of a vessel." (Vorobyova-Desyatovskaya, 1983, p. 24)

"The comparison of Indian inscriptions on the terriroty of Central Asia with those from India and Afghanistan shows that as a rule they were worded according to a general pattern. The palaeography of the Kara-tepe nd Gayaz-tepe inscriptions confirms the presence of a standard scribal tradition for the entire Kushan territory." (Vertogradova, 1984, p. 167; Vorobyova-Desyatovskaya, 1983, pp. 51-2).

Vertogradova, VV, 1984, Notes on the Indian inscriptions from Kara-Tepe. Summaries of papers presented by Soviet scholars to the VIth World Sanskrit Conference, 13-20 October 1984, Philadelphia, Pennsylvania, USA. Moscow.

Vorobyova-Desyatovskaya, MI 1983, Paryatniki pismom kharoshti i brakhmi iz Sovetoskoy Srdney Azii. In: Istoriya i kult/'tura Tsentralnoy Azii. Moscow.

See: http://bharatkalyan97.blogspot.com/2011/11/archaeology-capital-of-kushan-empire.html

Hellenism in Bactria and India (Presence of Indus script glyphs)

W. W. Tarn., 1902, Notes on Hellenic Studies *Journal of Hellenic Studies*, Vol. 22 (1902), pages 268–293) (embedded).http://www.docstoc.com/docs/105326556/notesonhellenisminbactriaandindiatran

Bronze coin of Taxila, single die (Fig. 1, Tarn opcit.)

Bronze coin of Taxila, double die (Fig. 2, Tarn opcit.)

Bronze coin of Agathokles (Fig. 3, Tarn opcit.)

Bronze coin of Agathokles (Fig. 4, Tarn opcit.)

The use of Indus script glyphs on the coin of Agathokles (Fig. 4) is a clear indication that together with Greek script, Indus script glyphs were also used (without any indication that these glyphs were a transcription of the Greek legend). Both examples of the coins of Agathokles indicate the use of Greek script,and Kharoshthi script; Greek script and Indus script glyphs.

Tran notes: "...it is possible that this square coinage was minted at Taxila in the existing mint...before the time of Maues, i.e. fairly early, this town was either independent or autonomous...Of the square coins of Agathokles, one (Fig. 3) bears on the reverse a 'maneless lion,' on the obverse of a nautch girl; the other (Fig. 4) obv. a stupa and a star, rev. a tree within a rail. The latter coin, of course, as has been noticed, can only have been struck to meet the susceptibilities of Buddhist subjects; but no one seems to have thought it necessary to consider whether their susceptibilities would have been equally pleased by a dancing girl...the 'maneless lion' of Fig. 3...is in realithy the attempt of the semi-Greek artist at a tiger...The dancing girl then would have to be connected with Buddhism in some way, and may perhaps be a reference to another well known Buddha story, his temptation by the Apsarases or nymphs, as Cunningham conjectured for the dancing girls of the Mathura sculptures...Iranian traders or settlements were probably numerous in that region. It appears to me that this Iranian element, which must have furnished considerable assistance to the second invasion of India by Demetrios and his successors, has also left a trace of itself on the coins in the star over Agathokles's stupa." (Tran, opcit., p. 276).

A rebus explantion has been offered for the hieroglyph of the 'dancing girl' using mleccha/meluhha language and rebus principle for this and other hieroglyphs of the script used on the coins.

meṭṭu 'dance step'; rebus: meḍ 'iron' (Ho.)

And, so for the other Indus script glyphs.

meṭṭu 'mound'; rebus: meḍ 'iron' (Ho.)

kuṭi 'tree'; rebus: kuṭhi 'smelter' (Santali)

ibha 'elephant; rebus: ib 'iron' (Santali)

kola 'tiger'; rebus: kol 'iron' (Tamil); kollan 'smith' (Tamil)

Nine ingots (next to the mound) on Fig. 1: lo, no 'nine'; rebus: loa 'copper' (Santali); loha 'copper' (Skt.)

satthia 'symbol of svastika'; rebus: sathiya 'pewter' (Kannada).

Mound with a semicircle on summit may indicate 'summit': डगर [ ḍagara ] f A slope or ascent (as of a river's bank, of a small hill). 2 unc An eminence, a mount, a little hill डांग [ ḍāṅga ] m n ( H Peak or summit of a hill.) (Marathi).ṭākuro = hill top (N.); ṭāngī = hill, stony country (Or.); ṭān:gara = rocky hilly land (Or.); ḍān:gā = hill, dry upland (B.); ḍā~g = mountain-ridge (H.)(CDIAL 5476). Rebus: ḍhaṅgar 'blacksmith' (H.)

Thus all the Indus script glyphs are relatable to the repertoire of a meluhha (mleccha) mint with artisans of Indian linguistic area, which issued the coins.

The use of Greek/*kharoṣṭī* scripts together with Indus script glyphs can thus be explained. Greek/*kharoṣṭī* scripts were used to transcribe name of the issuing ruler (in this case, Agathokles). Indus script glyphs were used to provide specifications of the materials handled in the mint: minerals, metals, alloys, ingots and furnaces/smelters.

notesonhellenisminbactriaandindiatran

*kharoṣṭī* script:

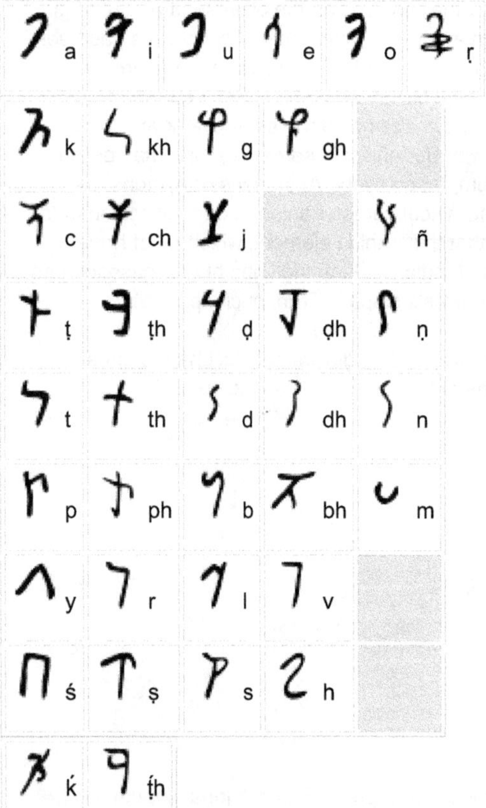


http://en.wikipedia.org/wiki/Kharosthi

A silver tetradrachm of the Indo-Greek king Philoxenus (100-95 BCE), with front legend in Greek and reverse legend in the *Kharoṣṭī* script.

Coin of Gurgamoya, king of Khotan. Khotan, 1st century CE. Obverse: Kharoshthi legend "Of the great king of kings, king of Khotan, Gurgamoya. Reverse: Chinese legend: "Twenty-four grain copper coin."

Image: Metropolitan Museum of Art, Art Resource, NY. The legend on the gold coin of King Kanishka: "King of kings, kanishka, of kushana." Greek script is used. Underlying language is Kushan. Greek legacy persisted there long after Hellenistic states disappeared from the region.

Gold coin of Kanishka I (late issue, c. 150 AD). Kanishka standing, clad in heavy Kushan coat and long boots, flames emanating from shoulders, holding standard in his left hand, and making a sacrifice over an altar. Bactrian legend in Greek script (with the addition of the Kushan Þ "sh" letter): ÞAONANOÞAO KANHÞKI KOÞANO ("Shaonanoshao Kanishki Koshano"): "King of Kings, Kanishka the Kushan". British Museum.

Gold coin of Kanishka I with a representation of the Buddha (c.120 AD).
Obv: Kanishka standing.., clad in heavy Kushan coat and long boots, flames emanating from shoulders, holding standard in his left hand, and making a sacrifice over an altar. Kushan-language legend in Greek script (with the addition of the Kushan Þ "sh" letter): ÞAONANOÞAO KANHÞKI KOÞANO ("Shaonanoshao Kanishki Koshano"): "King of Kings, Kanishka the Kushan".
Rev: Standing Buddha in Hellenistic style, forming the gesture of "no fear" (abhaya mudra) with his right hand, and holding a pleat of his robe in his left hand. Legend in Greek script: ΒΟΔΔΟ "Boddo", for the Buddha. Kanishka monogram (tamgha) to the right.

Coin of Kanishka with the Bodhisattva Maitreya -- with legend ΜΕΤΡΑΓΟ ΒΟΔΔΟ in Greek to read: "Metrago Boddo" [Maitreya 'friend' (Skt.Pali)]

A coin of Apollodotus I (r. c.180-160 BCE); the inscription on the left face is in Greek, and on the right is in the Indic Kharoshthi script

Source: http://www.vcoins.com/ancient/parscoins/store/viewItem.asp?idProduct=2245&large=1 (downloaded May 2006)

"Bactrian Kings: Apollodotos I, 160-150 BC. AE Hemiobol (9.51 gm; 22 mm)."

This very Indic square drachma of Apollodotus's features not only Kharoshthi script, but an Indic elephant and zebu as well

Source:
http://www.vcoins.com/ancient/mediterraneancoins/store/viewItem.asp?idProduct=2227&large=1 (downloaded Nov. 2006)

"Kings of Baktria Apollodotos C.180/174-165/160, Square AR Drachm (2.40 gm.) . "Basileus Apollodotoi Suthros," Indian elephant standing right, K in exergue / "Maharajasa Apaladatasa Tradarasa" in Karosthi, Zebu bull standing right."

Zebu (bos indicus) is an Indus script hieroglyph read rebus in mleccha/meluhha: adar ḍangar 'zebu'; rebus: aduru ḍangar 'native metal smith'. khũṭ Brahmani bull (Kathiawar G.); khũṭro entire bull used for agriculture, not for breeding (G.)(CDIAL 3899). Decoded rebus: khũṭ 'community' (perhaps, a guild). Cf. Santali gloss: khũṭ a community, sect, society, division, clique, schism, stock (Santali). Clearly, the two sides of the coin seeks to depict a guild of iron workers in the region reigned by Apollodotus. ibha

'elephant'; rebus: ib 'iron' (Santali)

A coin of Eukratides (r. c.170-145) that uses both Greek (left) and the local Kharoshthi script (right)

Source: http://www.vcoins.com/ancient/beastcoins/store/viewItem.asp?idProduct=6279&large=1 (downloaded Oct.. 2006)

"Eukratides, AE Quadruple Unit (Indian Standard), 171-135 BC, Bactrian Kingdom. BASILEWS-MEGALOU-EUKRATIDOU Obv.: Helmeted bust right. Rev.: Karosthi legend above and beneath. The Dioskouroi on horseback prancing right, each holding spear and palm. Monogram | E across fields. 21mm, 8.15g ."

Another example of Eukratides's Greek-and-Kharoshthi coins

Source: http://www.vcoins.com/ancient/sphinx/store/viewItem.asp?idProduct=3410&large=1 (downloaded Apr. 2006)

"Baktria, Eukratides, king of Bactria and India, c.B.C. 171-135; AE(square) 9.42 grms 24 x 25 mm Bust right of the king diad. And helmeted. Rv., the Dioscuri right, Kharosthi inscription."

A Greek-Kharoshthi coin minted by Strato I (r. c.120-110 BCE)

Source: http://www.vcoins.com/ancient/sphinx/store/viewItem.asp?idProduct=4002&large=1 (downloaded Oct. 2006)

"Indo-Greek Kings: Strato I 130-110 BC. AE Hemi-obol (7.96 grams). Bust of Herakles right, club over shoulder / Nike walking right, holding wreath and palm; monogram before; control mark sigma = Pushkalavati workshop."

Source:http://www.columbia.edu/itc/mealac/pritchett/00routesdata/bce_199_100/indogreekcoins/indogreekcoins.html

A Greek-Kharoshthi coin of Antialkides (r.c.115-95 BCE), the king whose ambassador erected the famous "Pillar of Heliodorus" near Sanchi

Source: http://www.vcoins.com/ancient/ritter/store/viewItem.asp?idProduct=972&large=1 (downloaded June 2006)

" BAKTRIA AND INDIA, Antialkidas, Drachm. Draped bust r., wearing helmet / Zeus enthroned l., holding Nike, before elephant.."

Somewhere along in here came the brief reign of Philoxenos, with his own Greek/Kharoshthi coins

Source: http://www.vcoins.com/ancient/yorkcoins/store/viewitem.asp?idProduct=3302 (downloaded Dec. 2007)

"Indo-Greek Kingdom, Philoxenos (c.100-95 B.C.), Silver Square Drachm, 2.44g., Indian standard; diademed and draped bust right, BASILEWS D NIKHTOU FILOXENOU; rev., helmeted king right on horseback; monogram before."

A coin of Apollodotos II (r. c.75-70 BCE) continues the Greek and Kharoshthi combination

Source: http://www.vcoins.com/ancient/parscoins/store/viewItem.asp?idProduct=2373&large=1 (downloaded May 2006)

"Apollodotos II 110-80 BC. AE Dichalkon (3.62 gm; 19 mm). Apollo standing right, holding arrow / Tripod; monogram to left and right. Mint. Taxila."

A coin of Hermaios (r.c.40-1 BCE), the last Indo-Greek king, with its Greek and Kharoshthi legends

Source:
http://www.vcoins.com/ancient/forumancientcoins/store/viewItem.asp?idProduct=4532&large=1 (downloaded Nov. 2006)

"Indo-Greek Kingdom, Hermaios, c. 40 - 1 B.C. Silver drachm, 1.774g, 16.1mm; obverse BASILEWS EWTHROS ERMAOIU, draped and diademed bust right; reverse, Karosthi legend around, Zeus enthroned slightly left, right hand extended, scepter in left, monograms left and right."

Another example of Demetrios's elephant coins

Source: http://www.vcoins.com/ancient/inclinatioroma/store/viewItem.asp?idProduct=1996&large=0 (downloaded Aug. 2006)

"GREEK KINGS of BAKTRIA: DEMETRIOS I. Circa 200-185 BC. Æ Triple Unit (28.19, 10.4 gm). Head of Indian elephant right, trunk raised, wearing bell / large caduceus, monogram in inner left field, legend to right and left."

Harosheth Hagoyim

From Wikipedia, the free encyclopedia

The *Defeat of Sisera* by Luca Giordano shows Sisera in battle.

*The Mother of Sisera looked out a Window* by Albert Joseph Moore.

Harosheth Hagoyim (Hebrew: חרושת הגויים, lit. *Smithy of the Nations*) is a fortress described in the Book of Judges as the fortress or cavalry base of Sisera, commander of the army of "Jabin, King of Canaan.[1]

Sisera is described as having had nine hundred iron chariots with which he fought the Israelites.[2] In Judges 5, the mother of Sisera is poignantly described looking from a window, presumably in Harosheth Hagoyim, and asking *"Why is his chariot so long in coming? Why is the clatter of his chariots delayed?"* when he does not return from the battle where his army was defeated by the Israelites, and he was killed by the Biblical heroine Yael.[3]

Archaeologists Oren Cohen and Adam Zertal of the University of Haifa propose that the site of El-ahwat, between Katzir-Harishand Nahal Iron, is the site of Harosheth Hagoyim.[4][5]

The site was excavated from 1993-2000 by teams from the University of Haifa and the University of Cagliari in Sardinia. The dig was headed by Professor Zertal.[5] The dig revealed a fortified place dating to the Late Bronze Age and early Iron Age (13th-12th centuries BCE). The style of the fortifications, walls, passageways in the walls and rounded huts is very different from Canaanite cities of the era, leading Zertal to propose that the site may have been occupied by the Shardana, one of the Sea-People who invaded the Levant in the Late Bronze Age.[5] Zertal based his 2010 Hebrew language *Sisera's Secret, A Journey following the Sea-Peoples and the Song of Deborah*, (Dvir, Tel Aviv) on this theory.[

CHARIOT LINCHPIN

Among the more intriguing objects uncovered by the dig is a small, round, bronze relief measuring about 2 cm. in diameter and 5 mm. thick. The bronze shows the "face of a woman wearing a cap and earrings shaped as chariot wheels." It was found inside a structure identified by the archaeological team as a the "Governor's House". It is clear that the bronze was once the finial or end of an "elongated object" from which it had been broken off in antiquity.[5]

It has now been identified as a linchpin from the wheel of a war chariot belonging to a high-ranking personage.[5] It would have appeared on the side of a chariot in much the position as a modern hubcap.

Professor Zertal explained the significance of the discovery, "This identification enhances the historical and archaeological value of the site and proves that chariots belonging to high-ranking individuals were found there. It provides support for the possibility, which has not yet been definitively established, that this was Sisera's city of residence and that it was from there that the chariots set out on their way to the battle against the Israelite tribes, located between the ancient sites of Taanach and Megiddo."[5]

REFERENCES

^ Judges 4^ Judges 4:3^ Judges 5:28^ [a b] Siegel-Itzkovich, Judy (July 2, 2010). "Long time archaeological riddle solved, Canaanite general was based in Wadi Ara". Jerusalem Post. ^ [a b c d e f] "Archaeological Mystery Solved". University of Haifa. July 1, 2010. http://en.wikipedia.org/wiki/Harosheth_Haggoyim

The occurrence of glyphs of a buffalo and a ficus religiosa motif on this cylinder seal impression are too vivid to be brushed away as mere coincidences. There WAS interaction among the neighboring civilization areas as bronze-age trade blossomed and created the framework for an industrial revolution. As hieroglyphs were absorbed the way the languages in the Indian linguistic area absorbed from one another linguistic features and made them their own, it is not unlikely that the underlyings sounds of speech related to such common hieroglyphs should relate to substrata words of contact areas or explained by the attested presence of Meluhhan colonies or settlements in areas inhabited by non-Meluhhan speakers. It is possible that lexemes of Meluhha are also attested in the as yet undeciphered Proto-Elamite writing system. This is a speculative statement and needs further investigation, but the Uruk (Warka) vase with its hieroglyphs comparable to Indian hieroglyphs. The identification of a few substratum Meluhha words in Sumerian – is a pointer to this possibility of Meluhhan presence and influence:

Professional names:simug `blacksmith' and tibira `copper smith';
Agricultural terms: engar `farmer', apin `plow' and absin `furrow';
Craftsmen: nangar `carpenter', agab `leather worker'; and
Religious terms: sanga `priest'.

Many hieroglyphs on Mesopotamian and other Ancient Near East cylinder seals may relate to such words.

Cuneiform has been successfully decoded.

A significant conclusion of this book is that Indian language union dates back to the period when Indus script was used. About 1000 lexemes of Meluhha (mleccha) have been identified and explained in the context of ciphertext of Indian hieroglyphs.

These substratum glosses are the foundation for further studies in the evolution of languages and linguistic features absorbed from one another, in Indian language union (sprachbund).

An inlay panel of the Great Lyre found in the King's grave of Ur. The head, face and horns are gold foil wrapped over a wooden form. The hair and beard are lapis lazuli, as are the eyes, inlaid into shell. The front panel is shell inlaid in bitumen. Note the dagger tucked in the waist belt of the jackal in the second register.

**Unfinished tasks**

Deciphering

1) the hieroglyphs on many Ancient Near East cylinder seals/artifacts such as the Great Lyre; 2) Proto-Elamite writing system; and

studying the evolution of languages – *deśa bhāṣā jñānam* -- in Indian language union (*sprachbund* or Indian linguistic area) are unfinished tasks in the history of Harosheth Hagoyim, the smithy of nations.

9 REFEFERENCES

Concordance lists for epigraphs

An outstanding contribution to the study of the script problem is the publication of the Corpus of Indus Seals and Inscriptions (CISI) Three volumes have been published so far:

*Corpus of Indus Seals and Inscriptions, 1. Collections in India, Helsinki,* 1987 (eds. Jagat Pati Joshi and Asko Parpola)

*Corpus of Indus Seals and Inscriptions, 2. Collections in Pakistan, Helsinki,* 1991 (eds. Sayid Ghulam Mustafa Shah and Asko Parpola)

*Corpus of Indus Seals and Inscriptions, 3. 1 Supplement to Mohenjo-daro and Harappa*, 2010 (eds. Asko Parpola, B.M. Pande and Petteri Koskikallio) in collaboration with Richard H. Meadow and Jonathan Mark Kenoyer. (Annales Academiae Scientiarum Fennicae, B. 239-241.) Helsinki: Suomalainen Tiedeakatemia.

These volumes in which Asko Parpola is the co-author constitute the photographic corpus. The CISI contains all the seals including those without any inscriptions, for e.g. those with the geometrical motif called the 'svastika'. Parpola's initial corpus (1973) included a total number of 3204 texts. After compiling the pictorial corpus, Parpola notes that there are approximately 3700 legible inscriptions (including 1400 duplicate inscriptions, i.e. with repeated texts). Both the concordances of Parpola and Mahadevan complement each other because of the sort sequence adopted. Parpola's concordance was sorted according to the sign following the indexed sign. Mahadevan's concordance was sorted according to the sign preceding the indexed sign. The latter sort ordering helps in delineating signs which occur in final position. With the publication of CISI Vol. 3, Part 1, the total number of inscriptions from Mohenjo-daro totals 2134 and from Harappa totals 2589; thus, these two sites alone accounting for 4,723 bring the overall total number of inscriptions to over 6,000 from all sites (even after excluding comparable inscriptions on 'Persian Gulf type' circular seals from the total count).

Compendia of the efforts made since the discovery by Gen. Alexander Cunningham, in 1875, of the first known Indus seal (British Museum 1892-12-10, 1), to decipher the script appear in the following references:

Indian linguistic area (*sprachbund* or language union)

A number of concordances and sign lists have been compiled, by many scholars, for the 'Indus' script and some references also discuss the decipherment problem:

Dani, A.H., *Indian Palaeography*, 1963, Pls. I-II

Gadd and Smith, *Mohenjo-daro and the Indus Civilization*, London,1931,, vol. III, Pls. CXIX-CXXIX

Hunter, G.R., *JRAS*, 1932, pp. 491-503

Hunter, G.R., *Scripts of Harappa and Mohenjo-daro*, 1934, pp. 203-10

*Langdon,* Mohenjo-daro and the Indus Civilization*, London, 1931, vol. II, pp. 434-55*
Koskenniemi, Kimmo and Asko Parpola, *Corpus of texts in the Indus script,* Helsinki, 1979; *A concordance to the texts in the Indus script*, Helsinki, 1982

Mahadevan, I., *The Indus Script: Texts, concordance and tables*, Delhi, 1977, pp. 32-35

Parpola et al., *Materials for the study of the Indus script, I: A concordance to the Indus Inscriptions*, 1973, pp. xxii-xxvi

Vats, *Excavations at Harappa*, Calcutta, 1940, vol. II, Pls. CV-CXVI

http://www.scribd.com/doc/2232464/epigraphica (ebook)

DEDR Dravidian Etymological Dictionary

CDIAL Comparative Dictionary of Indo-Aryan Languages

Boas, Franz. 1917. Introduction. International Journal of American Linguistics. (Reprinted: Boas, Franz. 1940.

Race, language, and culture, 199-210. New York: The Free Press.)

1920. The classification of American languages. American Anthropologist 22.367-76. (Reprinted: Boas, Franz. 1940. Race, language, and culture, 211-8. New York: The Free Press.

1929. The classification of American Indian languages. Language 5.1-7

Campbell, 1997,.American Indian languages: the historical linguistics of Native America. Oxford: Oxford University Press, 62-6

Campbell, Lyle, 2006 Areal linguistics: a closer scrutiny. In: Linguistic Areas: Convergence in Historical and Typological Perspective, ed.by Yaron Matras April McMahon, and Nigel Vincent, 1-31.Houndmills, Basingstoke, Hampshire: Palgrave Macmillan

Campbell, Lyle, 2006, Areal linguistics. In: Keith Brown (ed.), 2006, Encylopaedia of Languages and Linguistics, 2nd edn., Oxford, Elsevier, pp. 454-460

Campbell, Lyle, and Marianne Mithun. 1979. North American Indian historical linguistics in current perspective. The Languages of Native America: an Historical and Comparative Assessment, ed. by L. Campbell and Marianne Mithun, 3-69. Austin: University of Texas Press

Dales, George F., Jr. 1967, South Asia's earliest writing – still undeciphered, Expedition 9 (2): 30-37

Darnell, Regna and Joel Sherzer. 1971. Areal linguistic studies in North America: a historical perspective.

International Journal of American Linguistics 37.20-8

Durante, Silvio, 1979,"Marine Shells from Balakot, Shahr-i Sokhta and Tepe Yahya: Their Significance for Trade Technology in Ancient Indo-Iran." In South Asian Archaeology 1977, Naples.

Emeneau, MB, 1956, India as a linguistic area, Language 32, 1956, 3-16.

Farmer, Steve, Richard Sproat, and Michael Witzel, 2004, The collapse of the Indusscript thesis: The myth of a literate Harappan Civilization. Electronic Journal of Vedic Studies 11 (2): 19–57

Gould, S.J., 2003, I have landed. Splashes and reflections in natural history, London.

Hunter, G.R., 1934, Script of Harappa and Mohenjo-daro and its connection with other Scripts/G.R. Hunter.-London, p. 126

Jakobson, Roman, 1949 (1936), Sur la théorie des affinities phonologiques entre les langues. Actes du quatrieme congresinternational de linguists (tenu a Copenhague du 27 août 1 Septembre, 1936), 48-58.

(Reprinted, 1949, as an appendix to: Principes de phonologie, by N. S. Troubetzkoy, 351-65. Paris: Klincksieck.)

1944. Franz Boas' approach to language. International Journal of American Linguistics 10.188-95

Kalyanaraman, S., 1988, *Indus Script: A bibliography*, Manila.

Kalyanaraman, S., 1992, Indian Lexicon, an etymological dictionary of south Asian languages. http://www.scribd.com/doc/2232617/lexicon (ebook)

Kalyanaraman, S., 2008, Sarasvati—Vedic river and Hindu civilization, Chennai, Sarasvati Research and Education Trust (ISBN 978-81-901126-1-1) http://www.scribd.com/doc/7734436/Sarasvati-Book (ebook)

Kalyanaraman, S., 2010, Indus Script Cipher – Hieroglyphs of Indian linguistic area (ISBN 978-0982897102)

Kenoyer, J. M. 1997 Trade and technology of the Indus Valley: new insights from Harappa, Pakistan. World Archaeology 29(2): 262-280.

Kenoyer, J. M. and R. H. Meadow 1999 Harappa: New Discoveries on its origins and growth. Lahore Museum Bulletin XII(1): 1-12.

Kharakwal, J.S., Y.S. Rawat and Toshiki Osada, 2007, Kanmer: A Harappan site in Kachchh, Gujarat, India. PP. 21-137 in: Toshiki Osada (Ed.), Linguistics, archaeology and the human past. (Occasional papers 2.) Kyoto: Indus Project. Research Institute for Humanity and Nature.

Koskenniemi, Seppo, Asko Parpola and Simo Parpola, 1973, Materials for the study of the Indus script, I. A concordance to the Indus inscriptions, Annales Academiae Scientiaram Fennicae, Ser. B, Tom. 185. xxviii, 528, 55 pp. + errata sheet. Helsinki: [Academia Scientiarum Fennica]

Koskenniemi and Parpola, 1982, A Concordance to the Texts in the Indus Script. Helsinki: [University of Helsinki]. 201pp. Department of Asian and African Studies, University of Helsinki. Research Reports, No. 3., pp. 10-11.

Kuiper, FBJ, 1948, Proto-Munda words in Sanskrit, Amsterdam, 1948

1967, The genesis of a linguistic area, IIJ 10, 1967, 81-102

Lal, B.B., 2002, The Sarasvati flows on: The continuity of Indian culture. New Delhi: Aryan Books International.

Mahadevan, Iravatham, 1966, "Towards a grammar of the Indus texts: 'intelligible to the eye, if not to the ears', Tamil Civilization, Vol. 4, Nos. 3 and 4, Tanjore, 1966.

Mahadevan, Iravatham, 1977, The Indus script: texts, concordance and tables. (Memoirs of the Archaeological Survey of India, 77) New Delhi: Archaeological Survey of India.

Mahadevan, Iravatham, 1978, "Recent advances in the study of the Indus script", *Puratattva*, Vol. 9.)

Mahadevan, I., *What do we know about the Indus Script? Neti neti ('Not this nor that'),* Presidential Address, section 5, Indian History Congress, 49th Session, Dharwar, 2-4 November 1988, Madras.

Marshall, J. 1931. Mohenjo-daro and the Indus Civilization. Vol. I, II text, Vol. III plates. London: A. Probsthain

Masica, CP, 1971, Defining a Linguistic area. South Asia. Chicago: The University of Chicago Press.

Meadow, R. H., J. M. Kenoyer and R. P. Wright 1997 Harappa Archaeological Research Project: Harappa Excavations 1997, Report submitted to the Director General of Archaeology and Museums, Government of Pakistan, Karachi.

Meadow, Richard and Jonathan Mark Kenoyer, 1997, Excavations at Harappa 1994-1995: new perspectives on the Indus script, craft activities, and city organization, in: Raymond Allchin and Bridget Allchin, 1997, *South Asian Archaeology 1995*, Oxford and IBH Publishing, pp. 157-163.

Meadow, R. H., J. M. Kenoyer and R. P. Wright 1998 Harappa Archaeological Research Project: Harappa Excavations 1998, Report submitted to the Director General of Archaeology and Museums, Government of Pakistan, Karachi.

Meadow, R. H., J. M. Kenoyer and R. P. Wright 1999 Harappa Archaeological Research Project: Harappa Excavations 1999, Report submitted to the Director General of Archaeology and Museums, Government of Pakistan, Karachi.

Meadow, R. H., J. M. Kenoyer and R. P. Wright 2000 Harappa Archaeological Research Project: Harappa Excavations 2000, Report submitted to the Director General of Archaeology and Museums, Government of Pakistan, Karachi.

Meadow, R. H. and J. M. Kenoyer 2001 Harappa Excavations 1998-1999: New evidence for the development and manifestation of the Harappan phenomenon. In South Asian Archaeology 1999, edited by K. R. van Kooij and E. M. Raven, pp. in press. Leiden.

Mughal, M. R. 1990 Further Evidence of the Early Harappan Culture in the Greater Indus Valley: 1971-90. South Asian Studies 6: 175-200.

Mughal, M. R., F. Iqbal, M. A. K. Khan and M. Hassan 1996 Archaeological Sites and Monuments in Punjab: Preliminary report of Explorations: 1992-1996. Pakistan Archaeology 29: 1-474.

Parpola, Asko, 1994, Deciphering the Indus Script, Cambridge University Press, Cambridge, U.K. [Note: A comprehensive bibliography appears.]

Possehl, Gregory L., 1996, The Indus Age: The Writing System, Philadelphia: University of Pennsylvania Press.

Possehl, Gregory and Gullapalli, Praveena,1999, 'The Early Iron Age in South Asia'; in Vincent C. Piggott (ed.).The Archaeometallurgy of the Asian Old World; University Museum Monograph, MASCA Research Papers in Science and Archaeology, Volume 16; Pgs. 153-175; The University Museum, University of Pennsylvania; Philadelphia.

M. A. Probst, Alekseev, G. V., A. M. Kondratov, Y. V. Knorozov, I. K. Fedorova, and B. Y. Volchok, 1965, Preliminary report on the investigation of the Proto-Indian Texts. Academy of Sciences U.S.S.R., Soviet Institute of Scientific and Technical Information, Institute of Ethnography, Moscow

Przyludski, J., 1929, Further notes on non-aryan loans in Indo-Aryan in: Bagchi, P. C. (ed.), Pre-Aryan and Pre-Dravidian in Sanskrit. Calcutta : University of Calcutta: 145-149

Rajagopal, Sukumar, Priya Raju, and Sridhar Narayanan, 2009, Illiterate Indus?, Journal of Tamil Studies, December 2009 issue (#76), pp. 69-88, International Institute of Tamil Studies.

Southworth, F., 2005, Linguistic archaeology of South Asia, London, Routledge-Curzon.

Tewari, Rakesh, 2003, The origins of Iron-working in India: New evidence from the Central Ganga Plain and the Eastern Vindhyas, Antiquity, London http://www.antiquity.ac.uk/projgall/tewari298/tewari.pdf

Trubetzkoy 1939, Gedanken über das Indogermanenproblem Acta Linguistica 1.81-9

Vats, M.S., 1940, Excavations at Harappa, Being an Account of Archaeological Excavations at Harappa carried out between the Years 1920-1921 and 1933-34, Delhi, Archaeological Survey of India

Vidale, Massimo, 2007, The collapse melts down: A reply to Farmer, Sproat & Witzel. East and West 57 (1-4): 333-366. http://www.docstoc.com/docs/8916249/Indus-script-decoded-language----Massimo-Vidale.

Wells, Bryan, K., 2011, Epigraphic Approaches to Indus Writing, American School of Prehistoric Research Monographs, Oxbow Books, David Brown Book Co. ISBN:

9781842179949

Epigraphia Sarasvati

After corpora of Indus Script Epigraphs

Based on these resources and from the collections of inscribed objects held in many museums of the world, such as the Metropolitan Museum of Art, the corpus of Sarasvati epigraphs are prepared after lists of Sarasvati hieroglyphs from the corpora. Also included are texts of inscriptions, corresponding to the epigraphs inscribed on objects. The compilation is based mostly on published photographs in archaeological reports right from the days of Alexander Cunningham who ed a seal at Harappa in 1875, of Langdon at Mohenjo-daro (1931) and of Madhu Swarup Vats at Harappa (1940). The corpus includes objects collected in Bha_rata, Pakistan, other countries and the finds of the excavations at Harappa by Kenoyer and Meadow during the seasons 1994-1995 and 1999-2000.

Framework for decoding epigraphs of Sarasvati Sindhu Civilization

This is also intended to serve as a pictorial and text index to Mahadevan Concordance and to the two volumes published so far of pictorial corpus of Parpola et al.

Texts are indexed to the text numbers of Mahadevan concordance. The choice of this concordance is based on four factors: (a) the concordance is priced at a reasonable cost; (b) it is a true concordance for every sign of the corpus to facilitate an analysis of the frequency of occurrence of a sign and the context of other sign clusters/sequences in relation to a sign and for researchers to cross-check on the basic references for the inscribed objects; (c) the exquisite nature of orthography is notable and 'readings' are authentic, even for very difficult to read inscriptions; and (d) signs and variants of signs have been delineated with cross-references to selected text readings.

Mahadevan concordance excludes inscribed objects which do not contain 'texts'; for example, this concordance excludes about 50 seals inscribed with the 'svastika_' pictorial motif and a pectoral which contains the pictorial motif of a one-horned bull with a device in front and an over-flowing pot. Parpola concordance has been used to present such objects which also contain valuable orthographic data which may assist in decoding the inscriptions. Many broken objects are also contained in Parpola concordance which are useful, in many cases, to count the number of objects with specific 'field symbols', a count which also provides some valuable clues to support the decoding of the messages conveyed by the 'field symbols' which dominate the object space.

Cross-references to excavation numbers, publications, photographs and the museum numbers based on which these texts have been compiled are provided in Appendix V: List of Inscribed Objects (pages 818 to 829) in Iravatham Mahadevan, 1977, *The Indus Script: Texts, Concordance and Tables*, Memoirs of the Archaeological Survey of India No. 77, New Delhi, Archaeological Survey of India, Rs. 250. In most cases, these text numbers are matched with the inscribed objects after Asko Parpola concordance [Two volumes: Rs. 21,000: 1. Jagat Pati Joshi and Asko Parpola, eds., 1987, *Corpus of Indus Seals and Inscriptions: 1. Collections in India*, Memoirs of the Archaeological Survey of India No. 86, Helsinki, Suomalainen Tiedeakatemia; 2. Sayid Ghulam Mustafa Shah and Asko Parpola, eds., 1991, *Corpus of Indus Seals and Inscriptions: 2. Collections in Pakistan*, Memoirs of the Department of Archaeology and Museums, Govt. of Pakistan, Vol. 5, Helsinki, Suomalainen Tiedeakatemia]. *Memoir of ASI No. 96 Corpus of Indus Seals and Inscriptions, Vol. II* by Asko Parpola, B.M. Pande and Petterikoskikallio (containing copper tablets) is in press (December 2001).

The debt owed to Iravatham Mahadevan, Asko Parpola, Archaeological Survey of India, Department of Archaeology and Museums, Govt. of Pakistan and Finnish Academy for making this presentation possible is gratefully acknowledged. I am grateful to Iravatham Mahadevan who made available to me his annotated personal copy of a document which helped in collating the texts with the pictures of inscribed objects. [Kimmo Koskenniemi and Asko Parpola, 1980, Cross references to Mahadevan 1977 in: *Documentation and Duplicates of the Texts in the Indus Script, Helsinki*, pp. 26-32].

Four epigraphs from Bhirrana from ASI website http://asi.nic.in and five epigraphs from Bagasra (Gola Dhoro) reported by VH Sonawane in *Puratattva*, Number 41, 2011 have also been included.

Abbreviations and references to heiroglyphs and text transcripts

m-Mohenjo-daro

h-Harappa

ABCDE at the end of a reference number indicate side numbers of an inscribed object. Multiple seal impressions on the same object are numbered 1 to 4.

At the end of the reference number:

'a' sealing; 'bangle' inscription on bangle or bangle fragment; other objects: shell, ivory stick, ivory plaque, ivory cube, faience ornament, steatite ornament; 'ct' copper tablet; 'Pict-' Pictorial motifs ( 0 to 145) described as illustrations of field-symbols in Appendix III of Mahadevan corpus (pp. 793 to 813); 'it' inscribed tablet; 'si' seal impression; 't' tablet.

Illegible inscribed objects are excluded in the following tabulations. Many potsherds Rahmandheri and Nausharo are excluded since the 'signs' are considered to be potters' marks; only those inscriptions which appear to have parallels of field symbols or 'signs' in the corpus are included.

Pitfalls of normalising orthography of some glyphs

Parpola (1994) identifies 386 (+12?) signs (or graphemes) and their variant forms. Mahadevan (1977) identifies 419 graphemes; out of these 179 graphemes have variants totalling 641 forms. [See Sign List and Variants].

Parpola observes: "...the grapheme count might be as low as 350...The total range of signs once present in the Indus script is certain to have been greater than is observable now, for new signs have kept turning up in new inscriptions. The rate of discovery has been fairly low, though, and the new signs have more often been ligatures of two or more signs already known as separate graphemes than entirely new signs." (Parpola, 1994, p. 79)

As earlier discussed, many 'signs' are ligatures of two or more 'signs'.

In the process of normalizing the orthography of some glyphs to identify the core 'signs' of the script, some information is lost and at times, the process itself impedes the possibility of decoding the writing system. This can be demonstrated by (1) the 'identification' of a 'squirrel' glyph and (2) the failure to identify 'dotted circle' or 'stars' as glyphs.

It is, therefore, necessary to view the inscribed object as a composite message composed of glyphs: pictorial motifs and signs alike.

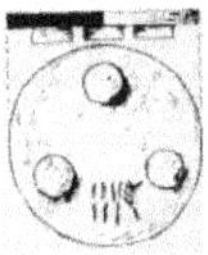

Alamgirpur Late Harappan pottery, a three-legged chakala_(After YD Sharma)

Alamgirpur Agr-1 a(2) graffiti

9062

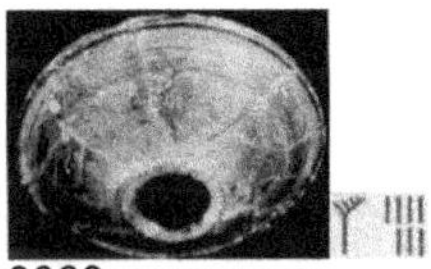

9063

Alamgirpur: Late Harappan pottery (After YD Sharma)

Alamgirpur2

Allahdino (Nel Bazaar)01

Allahdino (Nel Bazaar)02

Allahdino (Nel Bazaar)03

Allahdino (Nel Bazaar)04

Allahdino (Nel Bazaar)05

Allahdino (Nel Bazaar)06

Allahdino (Nel Bazaar)07

Allahdino (Nel Bazaar)08

Allahdino (Nel Bazaar)09

Allahdino (Nel Bazaar)11

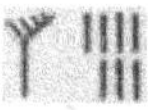9061

Amri

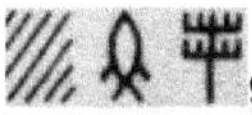9084

Amri

9085

Amri06

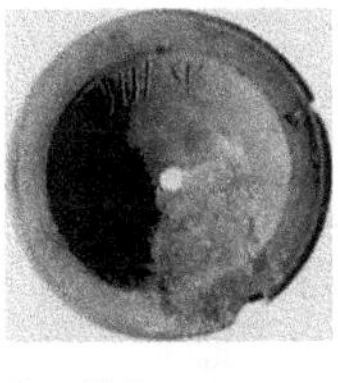

Amri07

Bagasra1 (Gola Dhoro)

Bagasra2 (Gola Dhoro)

Bagasra3 (Gola Dhoro)

Bagasra4 (Gola Dhoro)

Bagasra5 (Gola Dhoro)

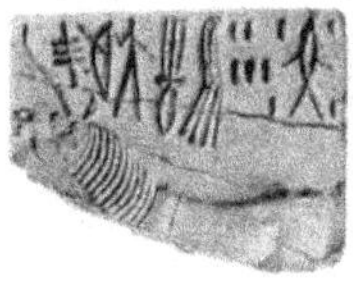

Balakot01

Balakot 02

Balakot 03

Balakot 04

Balakot 05

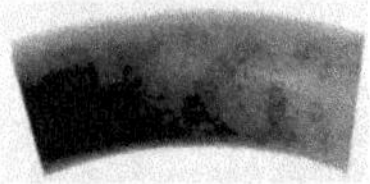
Balakot 06 bangle

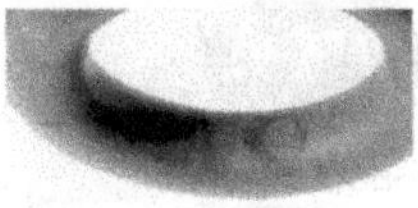
Balakot 06bangle

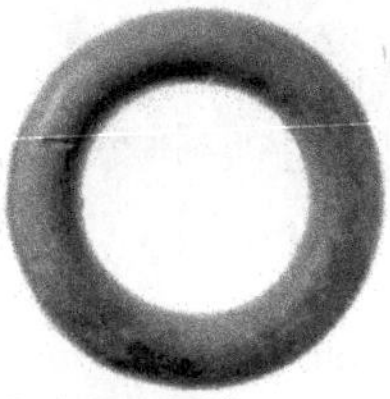
Balakot 06C

Banawali1

Banawali10
9204

Banawali11

Banawali12

Banawali13a

Banawali14

Banawali15 9203

Banawali16

Banawali 17

9201

Banawali 18a

Banawali19

Banawali2

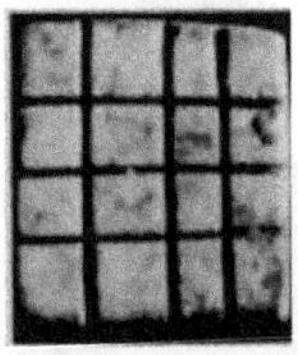
Banawali 20

Banawali 21a

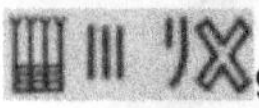9205

Banawali 23A

Banawali 23B

Banawali 24t

9211

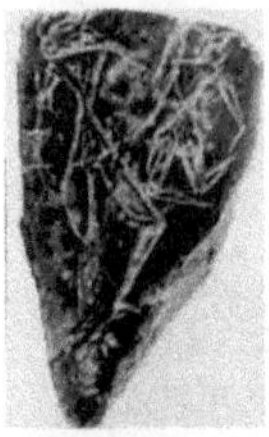
Banawali 26A

Banawali0026a

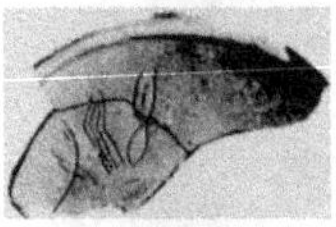
Banawali 28A

9221

Banawali 3

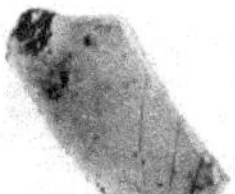
Banawali30

Banawali 4

Banawali 5

9203

Banawali 6

Banawali 7

Banawali 8

Banawali 9C

Bet Dwaraka 1

S'ankha seal. One-horned bull, short-horned bull looking down and an antelope looking backward.

Bhirrana1

Bhirrana2

Bhirrana3

Bhirrana4

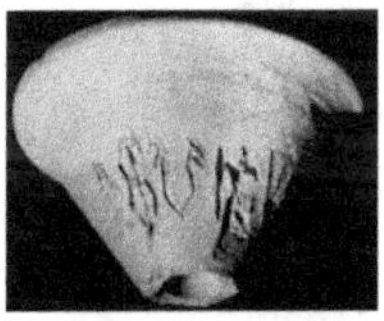

Chandigarh01

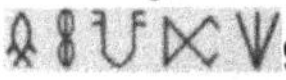9101

Chandigarh02

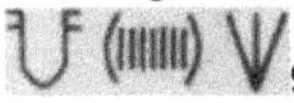9102

Chandigarh

9103

Chandigarh

9104

Chanhu-daro10

6129

Chanhu-daro 11

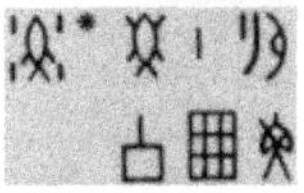6220

Chanhu-daro12a

6231

Chanhu-daro13

6221

Chanhu-daro14a

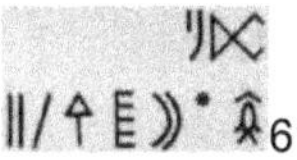6108

Chanhu-daro15a

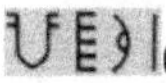6213

Chanhu-daro16a

6222

Chanhu-daro17a

6122

Chanhu-daro18a

6216

Chanhu-daro1a

6125

Chanhu-daro2

6128

Chanhu-daro20

6210

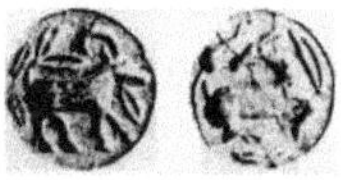

Chanhu-daro Seal obverse and reverse. The oval sign of this Jhukar culture seal is comparable to other inscriptions. Fig. 1

and 1a of Plate L. After Mackay, 1943.

Chanhu-daro21a

6209

Chanhu-daro22a

6115

Chanhu-daro23

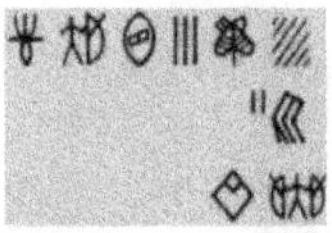

6402 Goat-antelope with a short tail.

The object in front of the goat-antelope is a double-axe.

Chanhu-daro24a

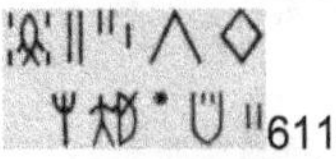
6116

Chanhu-daro25

Chanhu-daro26

6405

Chanhu-daro27

Chanhu-daro28

Chanhu-daro29

6403

Chanhu-daro3

6230

Chanhu-daro30

6111

Chanhu-daro32a

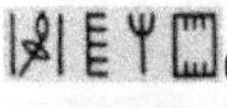
6123

Chanhu-daro33a

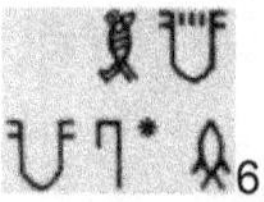
6104

Chanhu-daro. Tablet. Obverse and reverse. Alligator and Fish. Fig. 33 and 33a. of Plate LII. After Mackay, 1943.

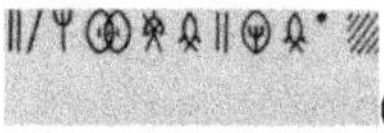
62

33 Pict-67: Gharial, sometimes with a fish held in its jaw and/or surrounded by a school of fish.

6303

6304

6301

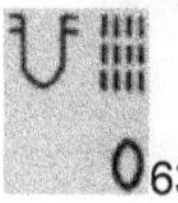
6305

6109

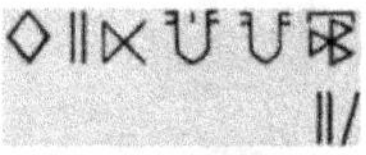

6112

6113 Pict-98

It is seen from an enlargement of the bottom portion of the seal impression that the 'prostrate person' may not be a person but a ligature of the neck of an antelope with rings on its necks or of a post with ring-stones. The head of the 'person' is not shown. So, I would surmise that this is an artist's representation of an act of copulation (by an animal) + a ligatured neck of another bovine or alternatively, a pillar with ring-stones ligatured to the bottom portion of a body. It is not uncommon in the artistic tradition to ligature bodies to the rump of, for example, a bull's posterior ligatured to a horned woman (Pict. 103 Mahadevan) or standing person with horns and bovine features (hoofed legs and/or tail) -- Pict. 86-88 Mahadevan.

Bison (gaur) trampling a prostrate person (?) underneath. Impression of a seal from Chanhujodaro (Mackay 1943: pl. 51: 13). The prostrate 'person' is seen to have a very long neck, possibly with neck-rings, reminiscent of the rings depicted on the neck of the one-horned bull normally depicted in front of a standard device.

6114 Pict-

108

Person kneeling under a tree facing a

tiger. [*Chanhu-daro Excavations*, Pl. LI,

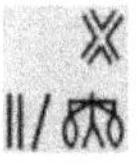

18] 6118

Chanhu-daro Seal obverse and reverse. The 'water-carrier' and X signs of this so-called Jhukar culture seal are comparable to other inscriptions. Fig. 3 and 3a of Plate L. After Mackay, 1943.

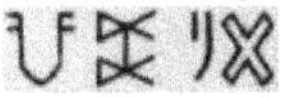

6120

Pict-40

Ox-antelope with a long tail; a trough in front.

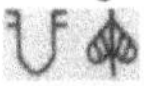

6121

Chanhu-daro. Seal impression. Fig. 35 of Plate LII. After Mackay, 1943.

6124

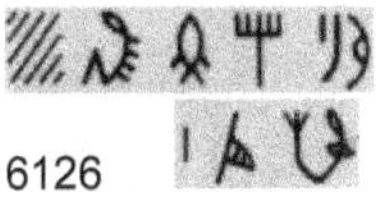

6126

6130

6131

6133

6201

6202

6203

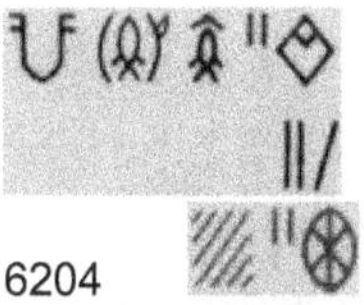

6204

6208

6211

6214

6215

6217

6218

6219

6223

6224

6225

6226

6228

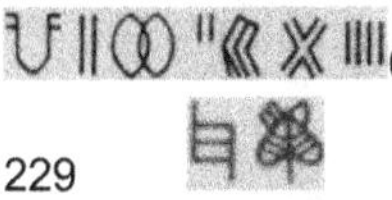

6

229

6232

Chanhu-daro. Tablet. Fig. 34 of Plate LII. After Mackay, 1943.

6234

Chanhu-daro. Seal impression. Fig. 35 of Plate LII. After Mackay, 1943.

6235

Chanhu-daro38A

Chanhujodaro

39A1

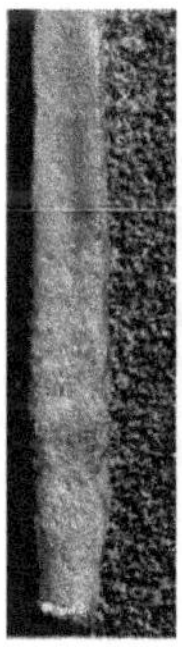

Chanhu-daro

39A2

Chanhu-daro4

6206

Chanhu-daro40A

63

06

Chanhu-daro40B

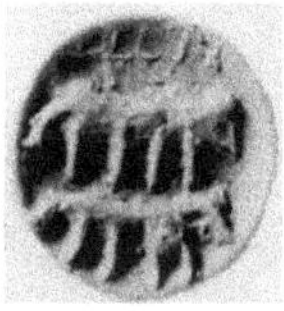

Chanhu-daro41a

Chanhu-daro42

Chanhu-daro43

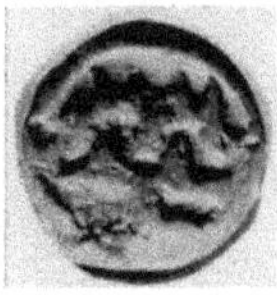

Chanhu-daro46a

Chanhu-daro46b

Chanhu-daro47

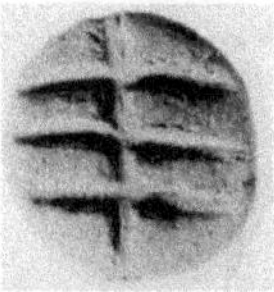
Chanhu-daro 48

Chanhu-daro49A

Chanhu-daro49B

Chanhu-daro 5

6132

Chanhu-daro50A

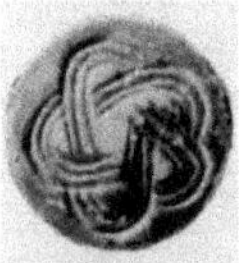
Chanhu-daro50B

Chanhu-daro 6

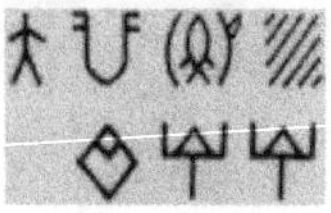
6205

Chanhu-daro 7

6207

Chanhu-daro 8

6227

Chanhu-daro 9

6127

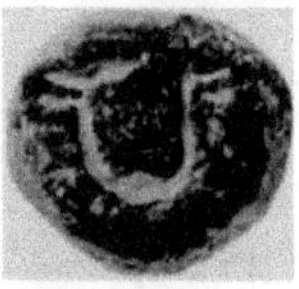
Daimabad1

Sign342

Daimabad 2a

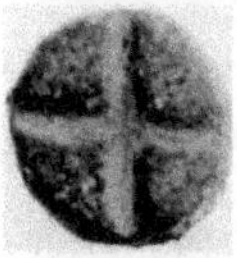
Daimabad 3A

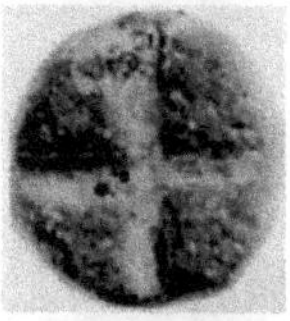
Daimabad 3B

Daimabad 4

Daimabad 5A

Daimabad 5B

Desalpur1a

9071

Desalpur2

Desalpur3

9073

Dholavira Sign-board mounted on a gateway.

Dholavira (Kotda) on Kadir island, Kutch, Gujarat; 10 signs inscription found near the western chamber of the northern gate of the citadel high mound (Bisht, 1991: 81, Pl. IX).

Dholavira: Seals (Courtesy ASI)

Dholavira1a

9121

Dholavira 2a

Gharo Bhiro (Nuhato) 01

Gumla10a

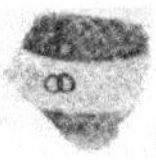

Gumla8a

h001a

4010

h002

4012

h003

4002

h004

4693

h005

4004

h006a

4006

h007

4008

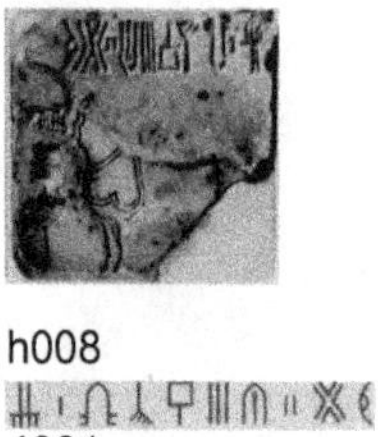

h008

4001

h009

4009

h010a

4003

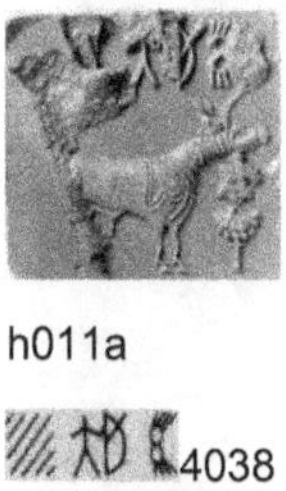

h011a

4038

h012

4005

h013

5055

h014

4106

h015

4053

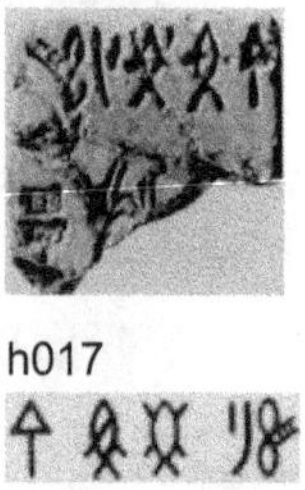

h017

4052

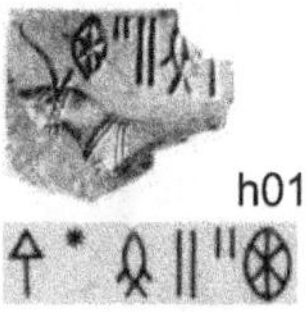

h018

4071

h019

4694

h020

4019

h021

4022

h022

4023

h023

4047

h024

4013

h025

4081

h026

4016

h027

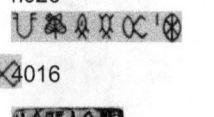

4017

h028

4040

h029

4042

h030

4049

h031

4103

h032 4018

h033

5059

h035

5083

h036

4113

h037 4031

h038

4029

h039

h040

4072

h041

4178

h042

4057

h043

4077

h044

4028

h045

4043

h046

4076

h047

4030

h048 4091

h049

4133

h050

4131

h051

4090

h052

4109

h053

5089

h054

4085

h055

4107

h056

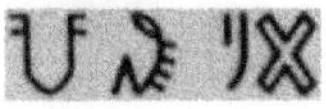
4110

h057

4086

h058

4105

h059

5120

h060

5119

h061

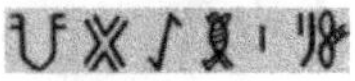
4118

h062

4128

h063

4142

h064

h065

4094

h066

4130

h067

4115

h068

4141

h069

4146

h070

4122

h071

5054

h072

4120

h073

4617 [An orthographic representation of a water-carrier].

h074

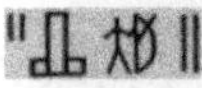
4135

h075

4161

h076

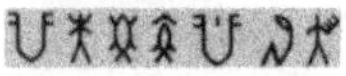
4241

h077

h078

4244

h079

5060

h080

4245

h081

5063

h082a

Text 4238

h08

3  4236

h084

h085

4232

h086

4233

h087

4240

h0

88 

4253

h0

89

090

227

h091

4230

h

092

4229

h093a

4231

h094 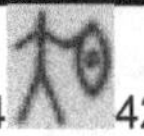 4246

h095

h096

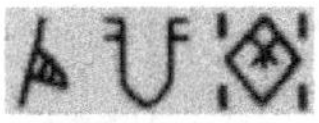

4249

h097 Pict-95: Seven robed figures (with pigtails, twigs)

4251

h098

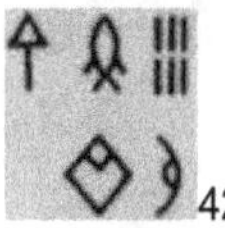
4256

Pict-122 Standard device which is normally in front of a one-horned bull.

h099

4223

h100

4258 One-horned bull.

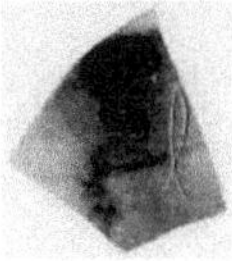
h1002

h1007

h101 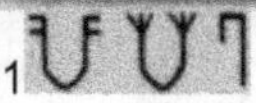

5069

h1010bangle

h1011cone 
5103

h1012cone

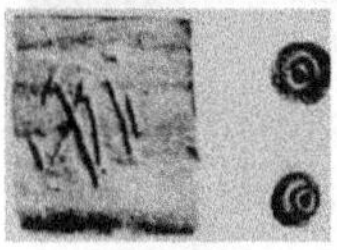
h1017ivorystick

 4561

h1018copperobject Head of one-horned bull ligatured with a four-pointed star-fish (Gangetic octopus?)

h102A

h102B

h102D

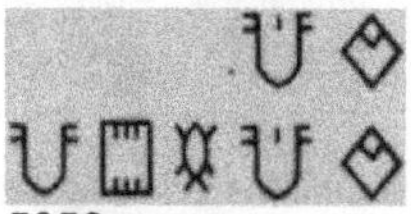
5056

h103

4254

h104

h105

h106

h107

h108

h109

h110

h111

h112

h113

h114

h115

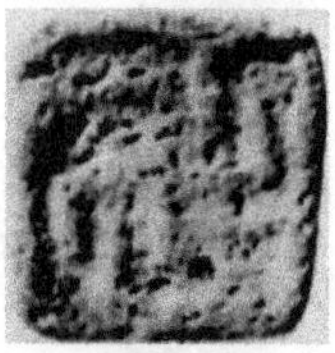
h116

h117

h118

h119

h130

5096

h131

4271

h128

h129A

h129E

h120

h121

h122

4269

h132

5052

h133

4261

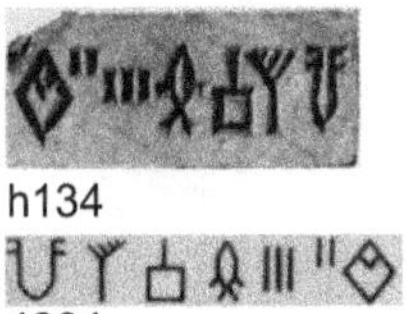

h134

4264

h135

4270

h136

4288

h137a

h123

h124

h125

5058

h138a

5072

h139

4267

h140

4268

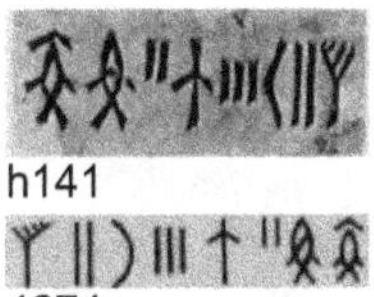

h141

4274

h142

4272

h143a

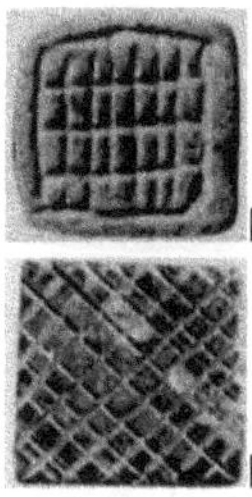

h126

h127

5101

h144

4280

h145

5067

h146

4628

h147

4629

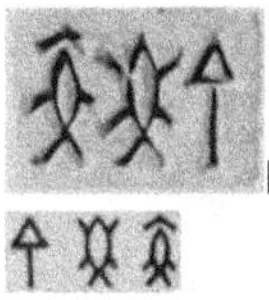

h148

4285

h149
4275

h150
4283

h151
5057

h152
5016

h153
4627

h154
4282

h155
4630

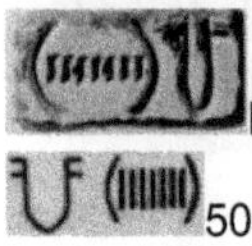
h156
5051

h157
4284

h158

4297

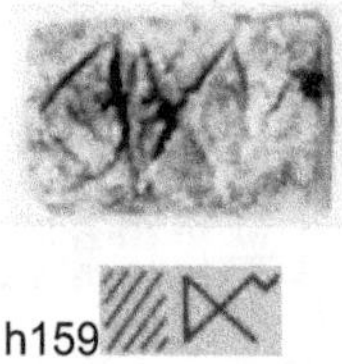
h159
4633

h160A

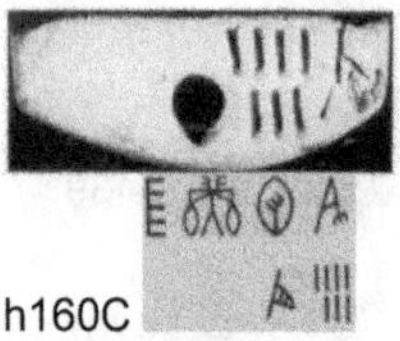
h160C
4276

h161

4262

h162

4294

h163

h164

5046

h165

h166A

h166B

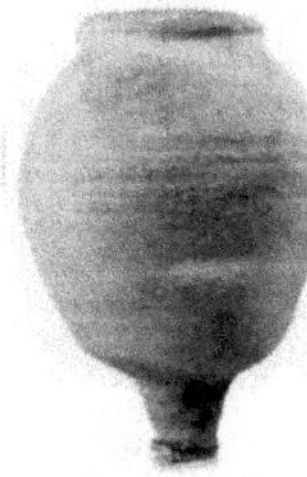
h167A

h167A2

5225

h168

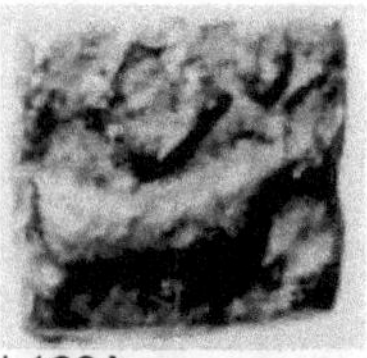
h169A

h169B

5298

h170A

h170B

4701

h171A

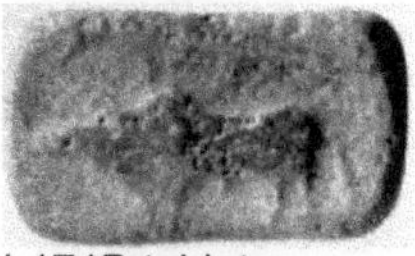
h171B tablet

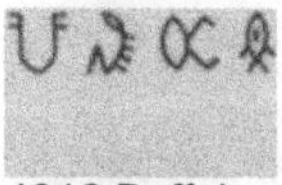
4312 Buffalo.

h172A

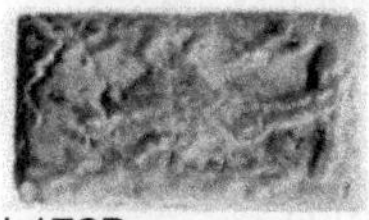
h172B

5305 Pict-66: Gharial, sometimes with a fish held in its jaw and/or surrounded by a school of fish.

h173A

h173B

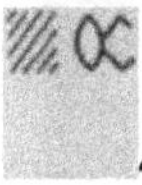

4333

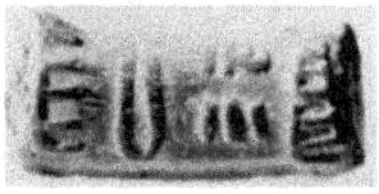

h174A

h174B

4338

h175A

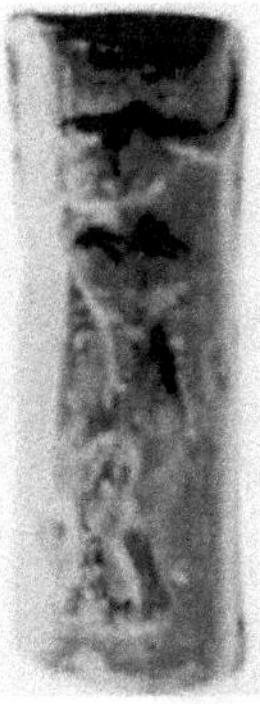

h175

B Pict-87

4319 Standing person with horns and bovine features (hoofed legs and/or tail).

h176A

h176B

h176bb

4303

Tablet in bas-relief h176a

Person standing at the centerbetween a two-tiered structure at R., and a short-horned bull (bison) standing near a trident-headed post at L. h176b

From R.—a tiger (?); a seated, pig-tailed person on a platform; flanked on either side by a person seated on a tree with a tiger, below, looking back. A hare (or goat?) is seen near the platform.

h177A

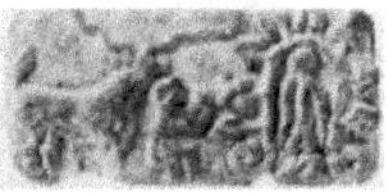

h177B

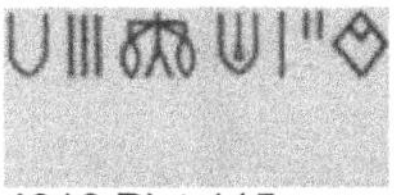

4316 Pict-115: From R.—a person standing under an ornamental arch; a kneeling adorant; a ram with long curving horns.

h178A

h178B

4318 Pict-84: Person wearing a diadem or tall head-dress (with twig?) standing within an arch or two pillars?

h179A

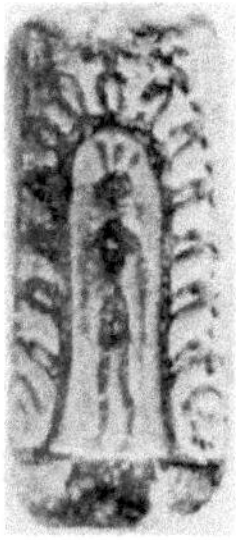

h179B

4307 Pict-83: Person wearing a diadem or tall head-dress standing within an ornamented arch; there are two stars on either side, at the bottom of the arch.

h180A

h180B

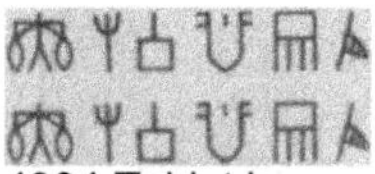

4304 Tablet in bas-relief h180a

Pict-106: Nude female figure upside down with thighs drawn apart and crab (?) issuing from her womb; two tigers standing face to face rearing on their hindlegs at L. h180b

Pict-92: Man armed with a sickle-shaped weapon on his right hand and a cakra (?) on his left hand, facing a seated woman with disheveled hair and upraised arms.

h181A

h181B

h182A

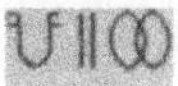

h182B

4306Tablet in bas-relief

h182a Pict-107: Drummer and a tiger.

h182b Five svastika signs alternating right- and left-handed.

h183A

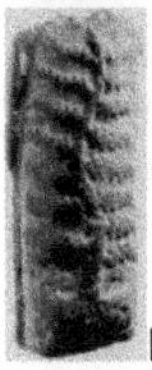

h183B

4327

h184A

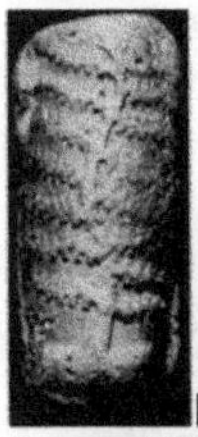

h184B

h185A

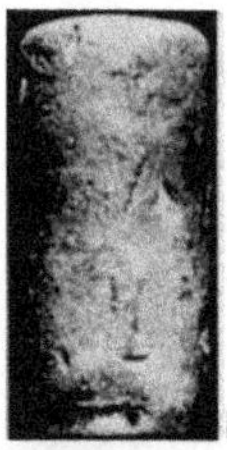

h185B

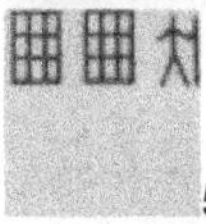

5279

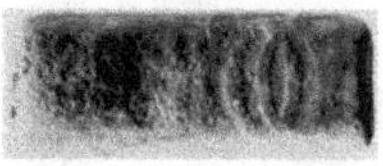

h186A

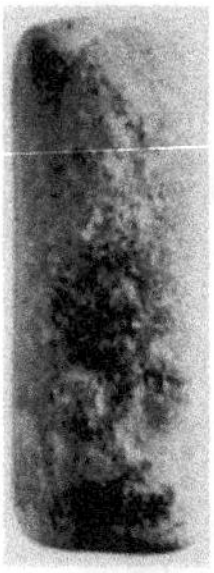

h186B

4329

h187A

h187B

5282

Pict-75: Tree, generally within a railing or on a platform.

h188A

h188B

4325

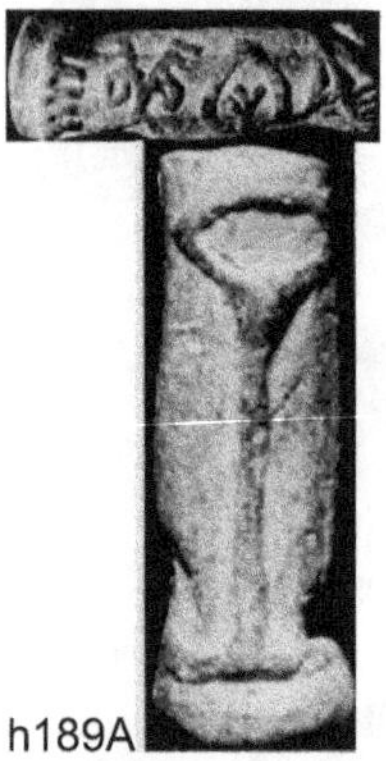

h189A

h189B

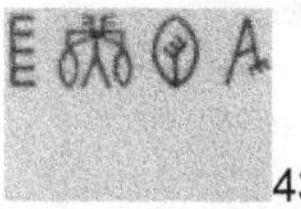

4341

Pict-126: Anchor?

h190A

h190B

4323

h191A

h191B

4332

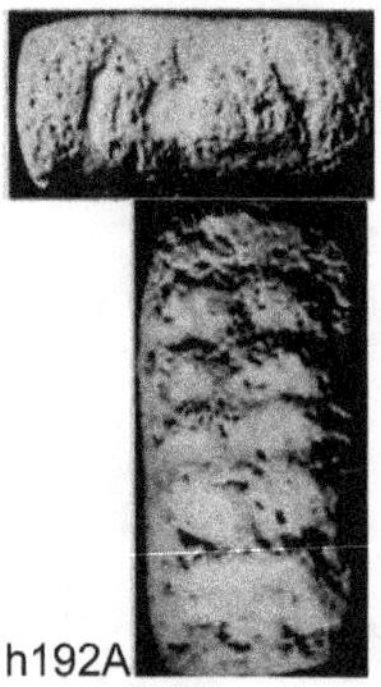

h192A

h192B

5340

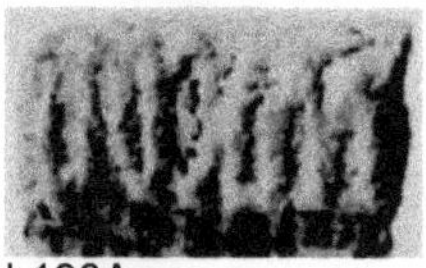

h193A

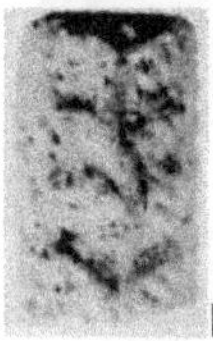

h193B

5332

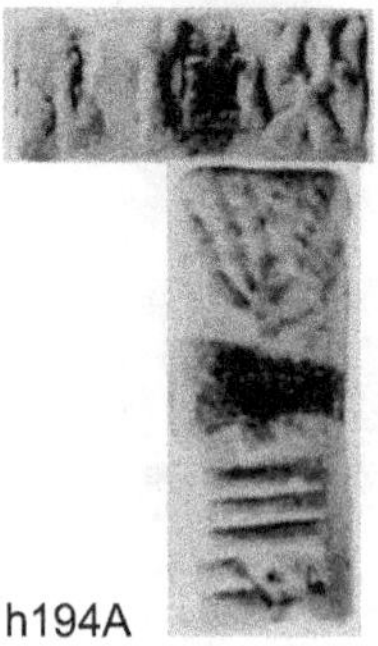

h194A

h194B

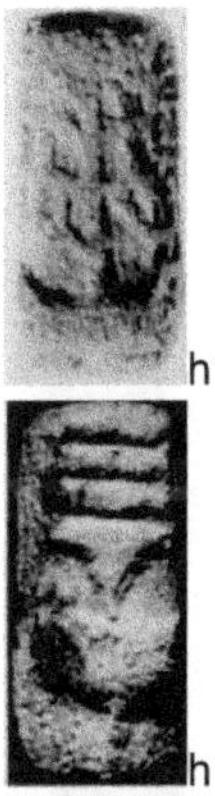
h195A
h195B

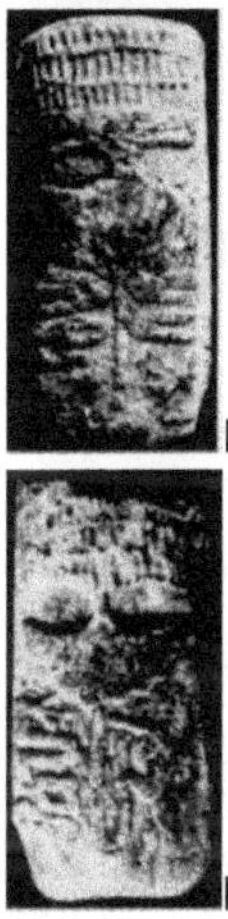
h196A
h196B

4309
Tablet in bas-relief h196b

Pict-91: Person carrying the standard. h196a The standard.

h197A
h197B

5333

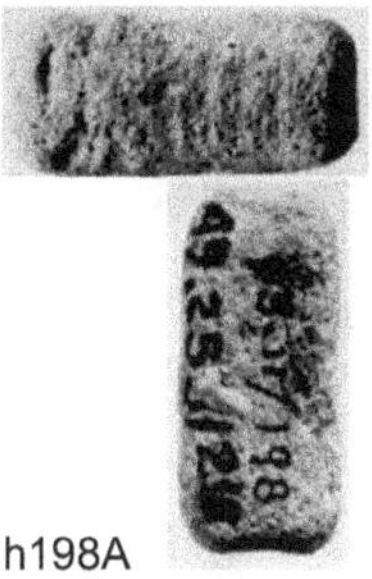
h198A

h198B 
5331

h199A
h199B

5252

h200A
h200B

4321

h201A

h201B

5289

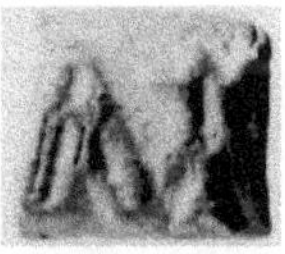
h202A

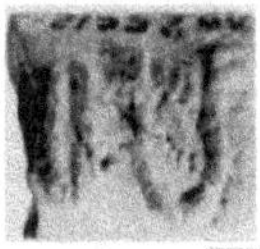

h202B
5334

h203A

5226

5236

h204A
h204B

5211

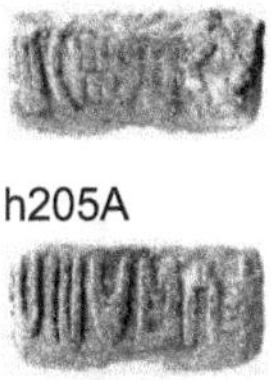
h205A
h205B

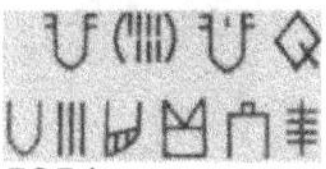
5254

h206A

h206B

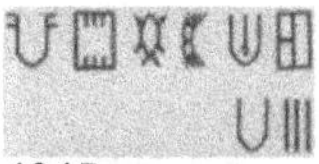
4345

h207A

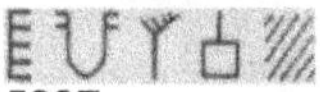
5297

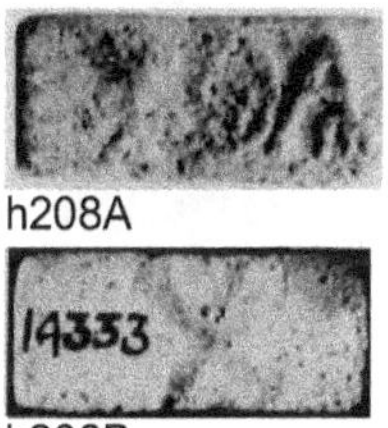
h208A
h208B

5296

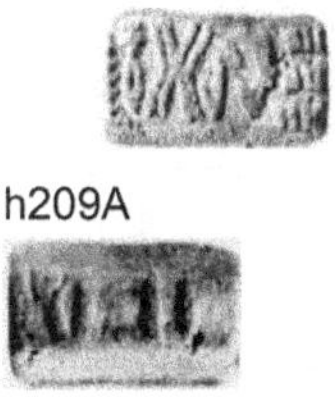
h209A
h209B

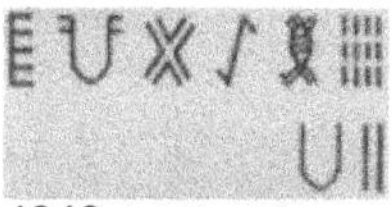
4348

h210A
h210B

4355

h211A

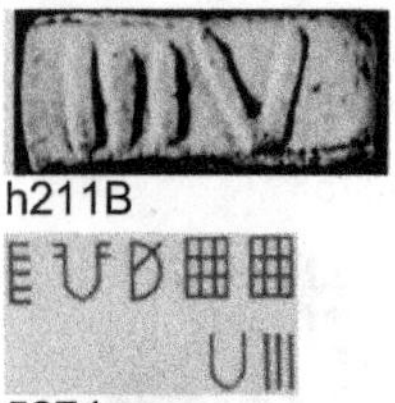
h211B
5274

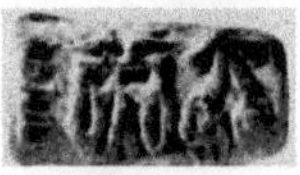
h212A

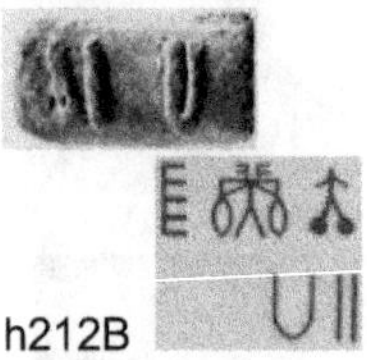
h212B
4357

h213A

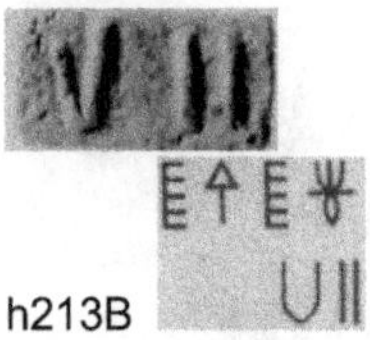
h213B
5270

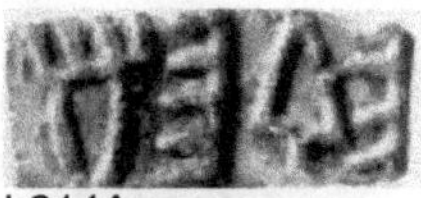
h214A

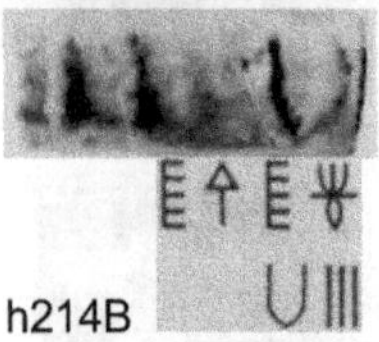
h214B
4684

h215A
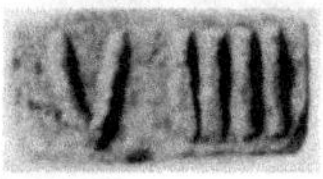
h215B

5271

h216A

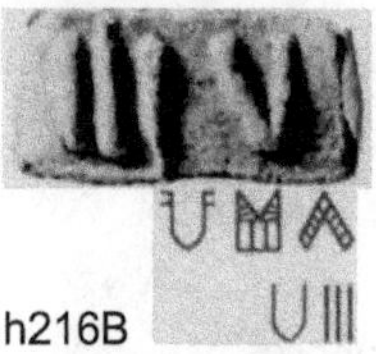
h216B
5335

h217A

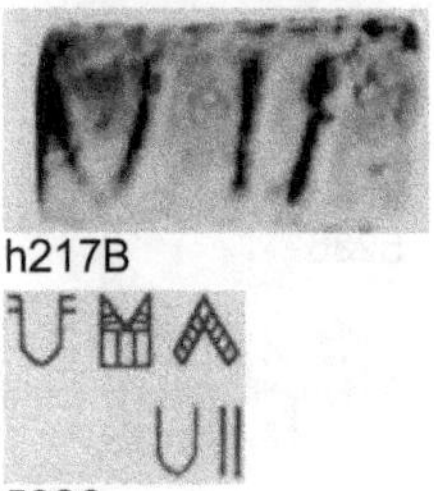
h217B
5336

h218A

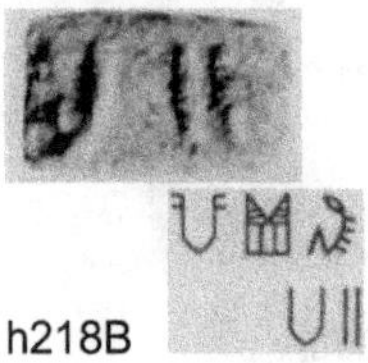
h218B
5293

h219A

h219B
5269

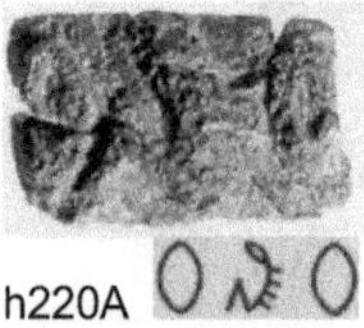
h220A
5267

h221A

h221B
5265

h222A

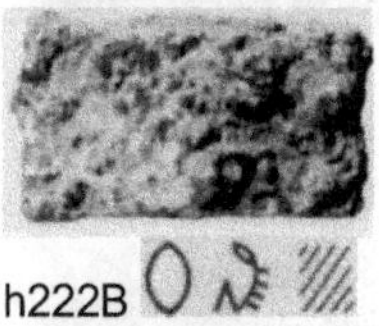
h222B
5339

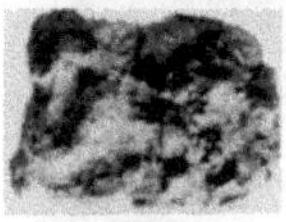
h223A

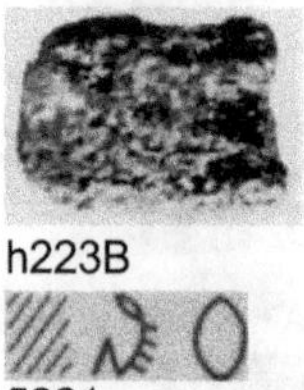
h223B
5221

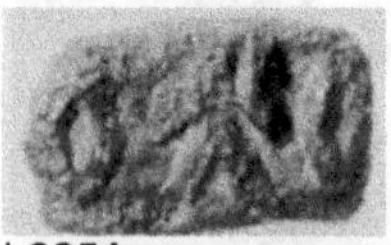
h225A

h226A

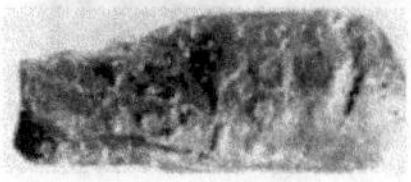

h226B
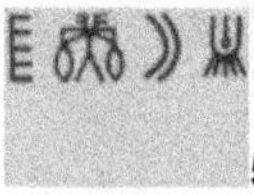
5243
Standard.

h227A

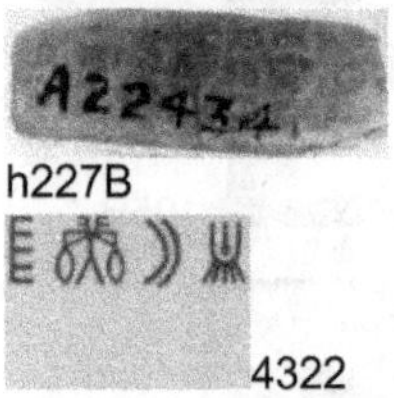
h227B
4322
Standard. Pict-123

Standard device which is normally in front of a one-horned bull. The device is flanked by columns of dotted circles.

h228A

h228B

5244 Standard.

h229A

h229B

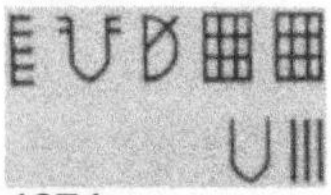
4674

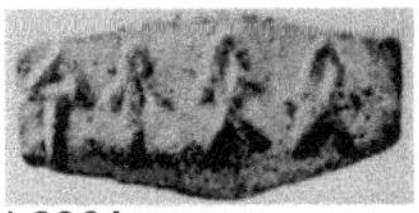
h230A

h230B

h231A

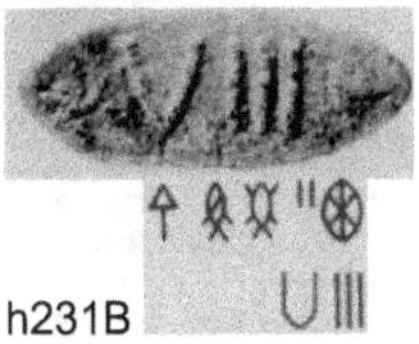
h231B
4673

h232A

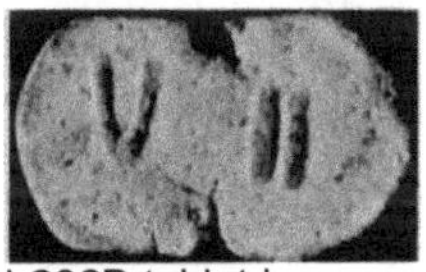
h232B tablet in bas relief

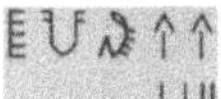
4368

Inscribed object in the shape of a double-axe.

h233A

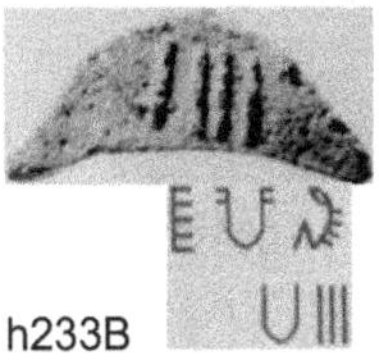
h233B

4387 Tablet in bas-relief. Sickle-shaped. Pict-131: Inscribed object in the shape of a crescent?

h234A

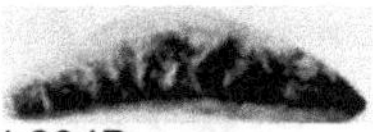
h234B

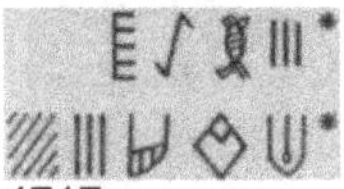
4717

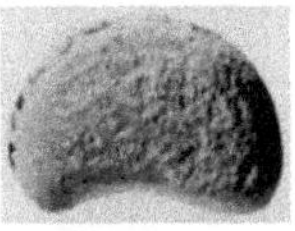
h235A

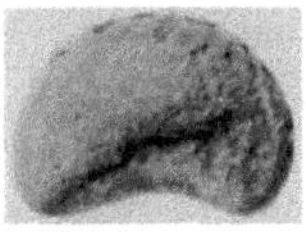
h235B

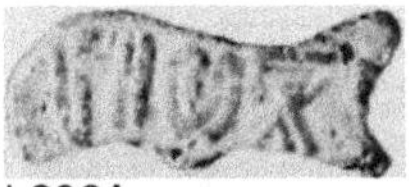
h236A

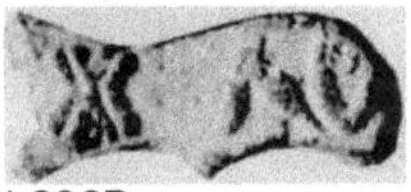
h236B

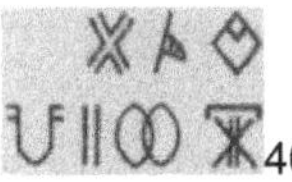
4658

Incised miniature tablet.
Object shaped like fish or sickle?
h825A h825B

h237A

h237B

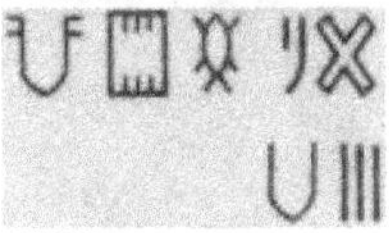
5337

h238A

h239A

h239B Tablet in bas relief

4386

h240

4657

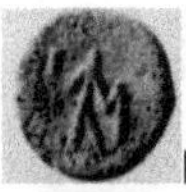
h241A

h241B

4663

Pict-69: Tortoise.

h242A

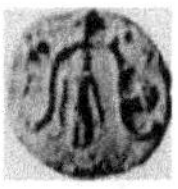
h242B

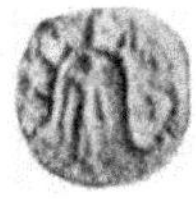
Pict-84

4317

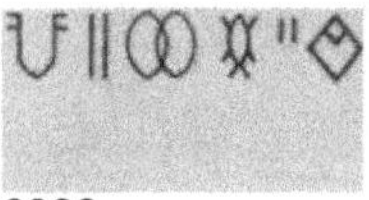
2863

h243A

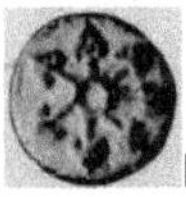
h243B

Tablet in bas-relief
Pict-78: Rosette of seven pipal (?) leaves.

4664

For See inscription: 4466

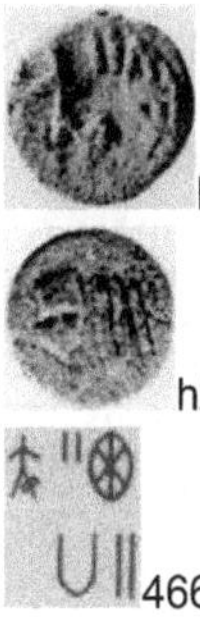
h244A
h244B
4665

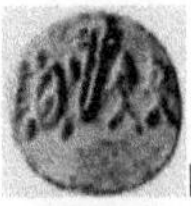
h245A

h245B

4702

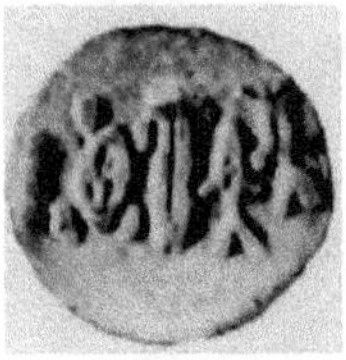
h246A

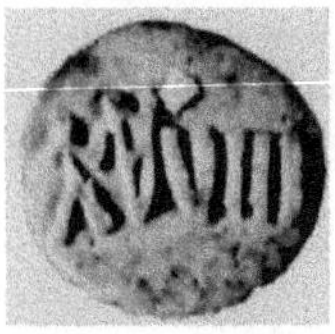
h246B

5283

h247A

h247B Tablet in bas-relief

4372

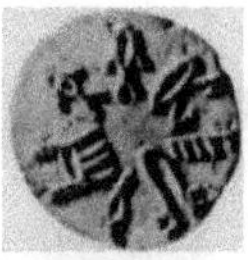
h248A

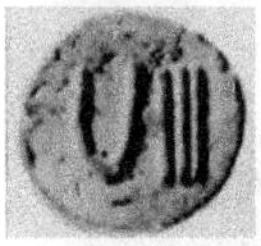
h248B Tablet in bas-relief

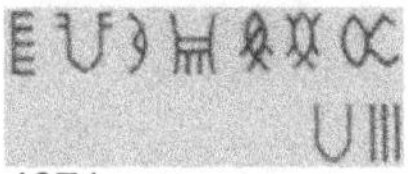
4371
See 3354.

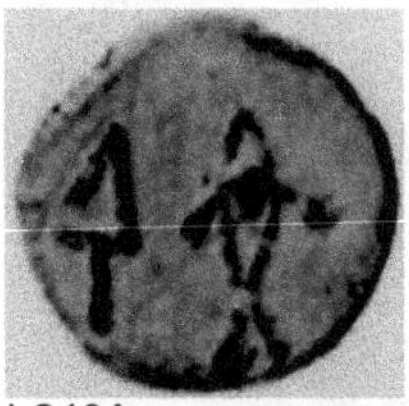
h249A

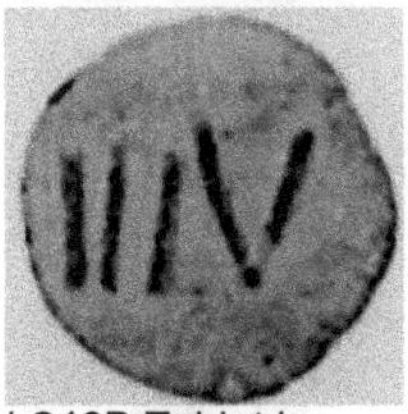
h249B Tablet in bas-relief

4374

h250A

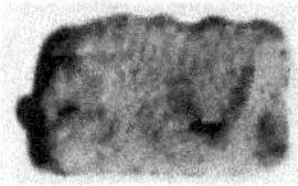
h250B

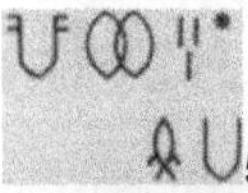
5250

h251A

h251B

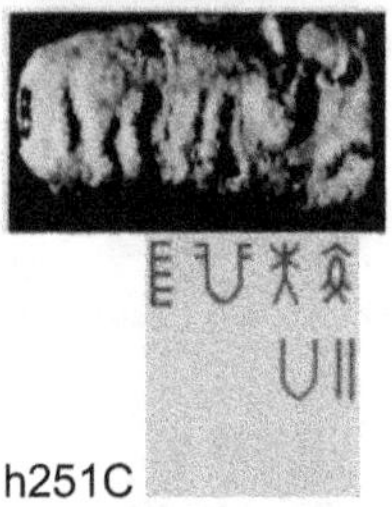
h251C
4342 Tablet in bas-relief. Prism. Bison (short-horned bull).

h252A

h252B

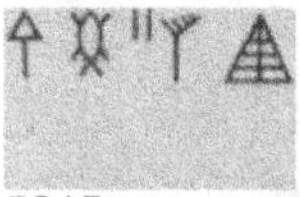
5215

h253A

h253B
5219

h254A

h254B

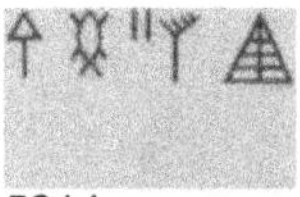
5214

h255A

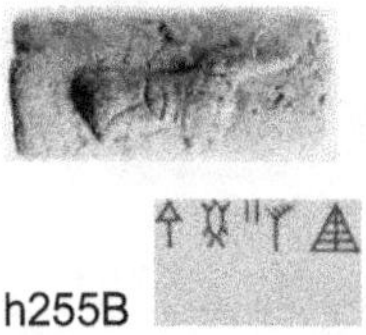
h255B
5208

h256A

h256B
5213

h257A

h257B

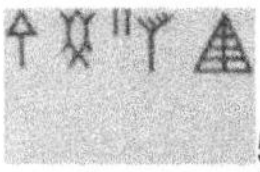
5216

h258A

h258B
5217

h259A

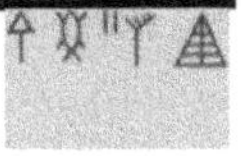

h259B
5218

h260A

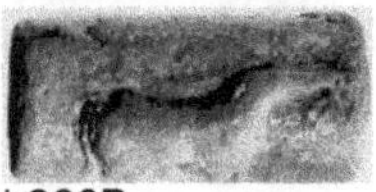

h260B

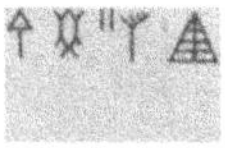

h261
5212

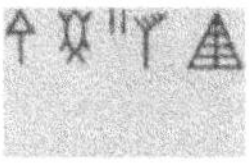

h262
5220

h270

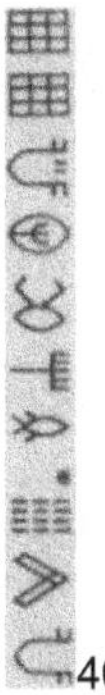

4014

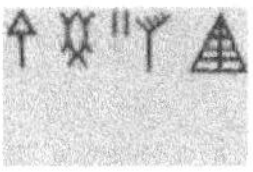

h263
5262

h264

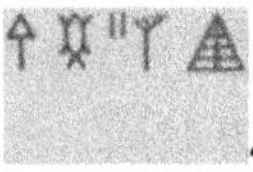

4315

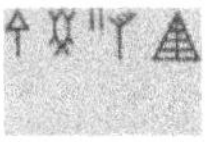

5207, 5208, 5209, 5210,
5212, 5213, 5214,5215, 5216, 5217, 5218,5219, 5220, 5262
Tablets in bas relief. The first sign looks like an arch around a pillar with ring-stones.
One-horned bull.
h252, h253, h255, h256, h257, h258, h259, h260,h261, h262, h263, h264, h265, h276, h277,

h271

4069

h272

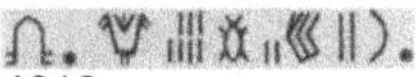

4619

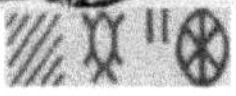

h273
4176

h859, h860, h861, h862,h863, h864, h865, h866,h867, h868, 869, 870

h266
4011

h267

4007

h274

h275

h276A

h276B

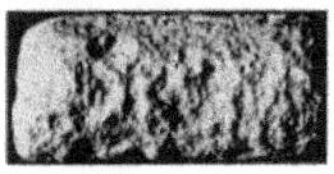

h277A

h268

4020

h269

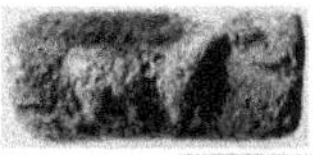
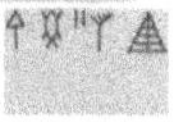

h277B
5207

h278A

h278B

h278C

5205

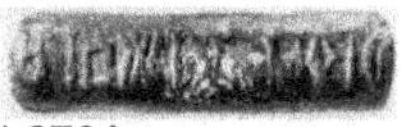

h279A

h279B

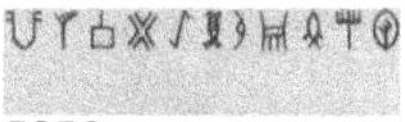

5256

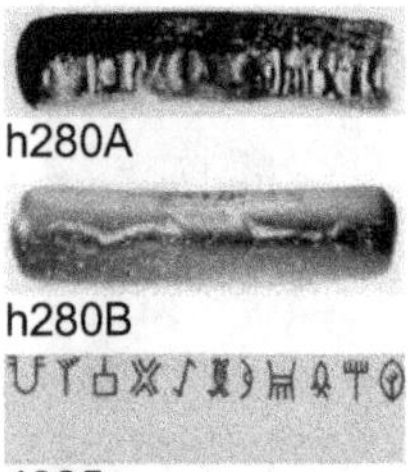
h280A
h280B
4335

h281A
h281B
4336

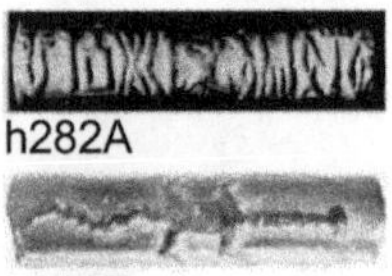
h282A
h282B

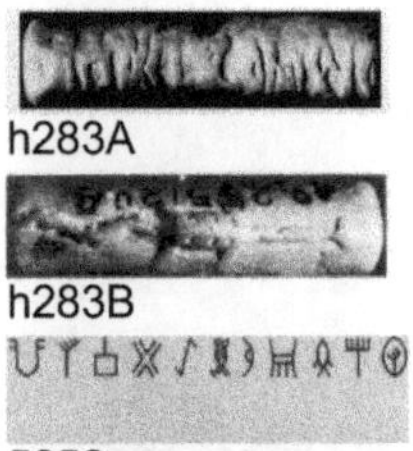
h283A
h283B
5253

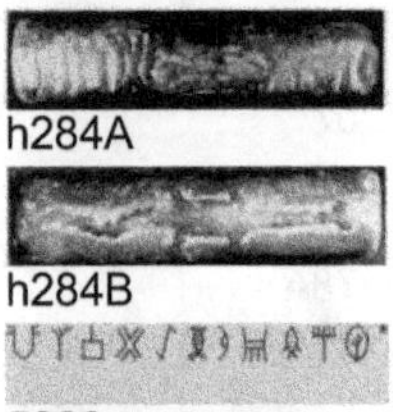
h284A
h284B
5229

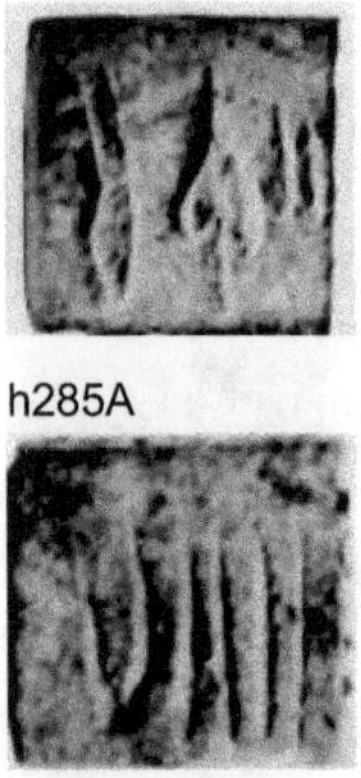
h285A
h285B

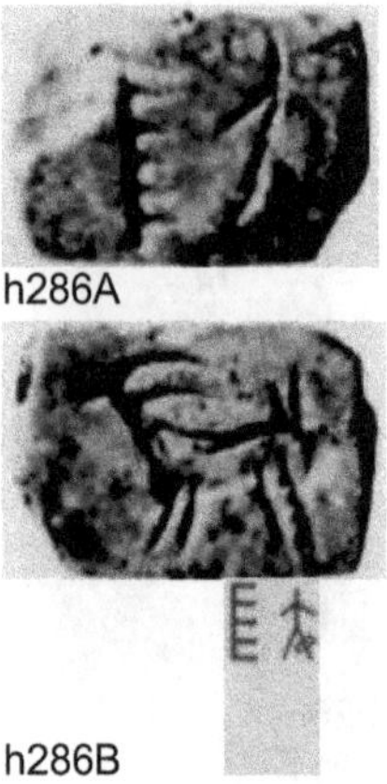
h286A
h286B
4429 Incised miniature tablet Goat-antelope with a short tail

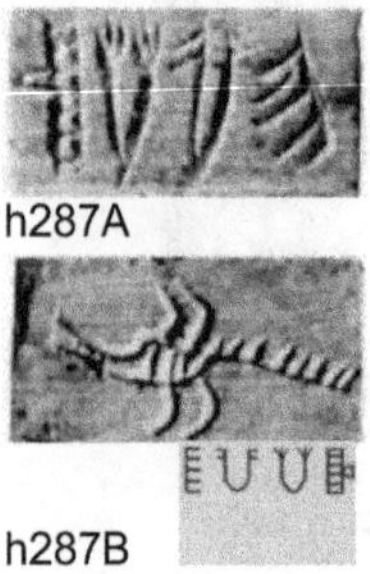
h287A
h287B
4430

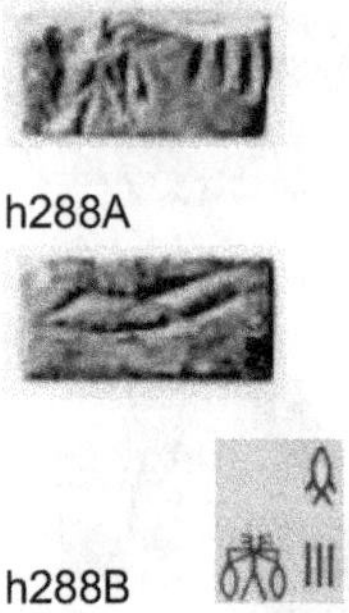
h288A
h288B
5463

h289A
h289B
5467

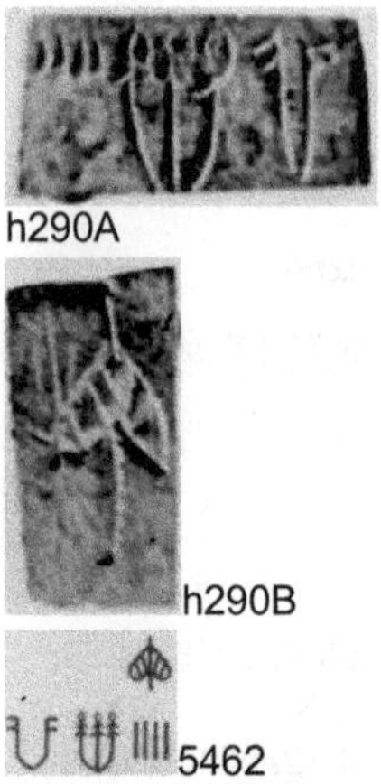
h290A
h290B
5462

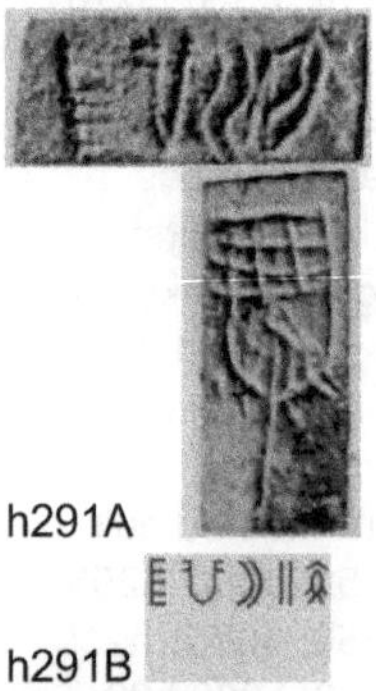
h291A
h291B
4440 Standard.

h292A
h292B
4443
Standard.

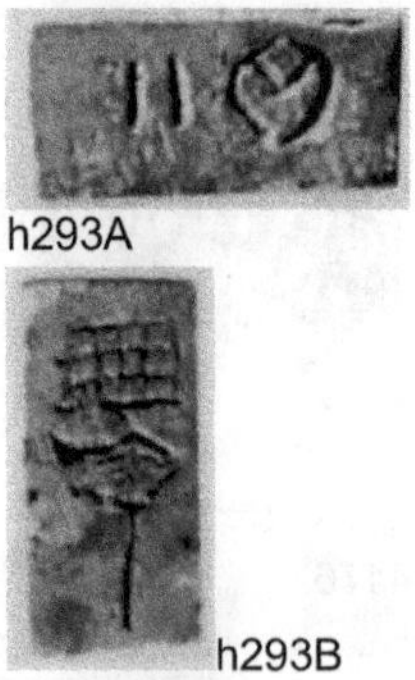
h293A
h293B

4441
Standard.

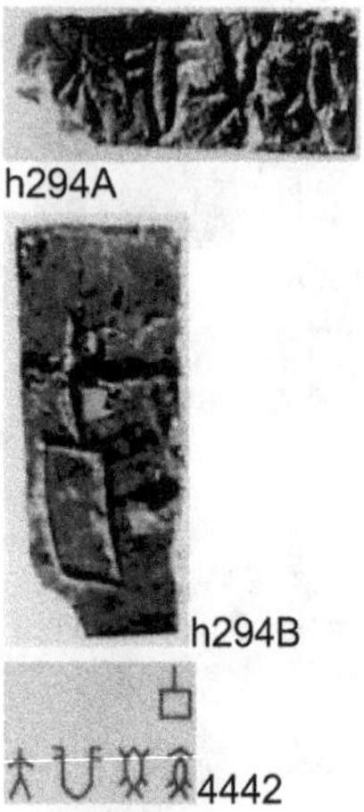
h294A
h294B
4442

h295A
h295B
4505

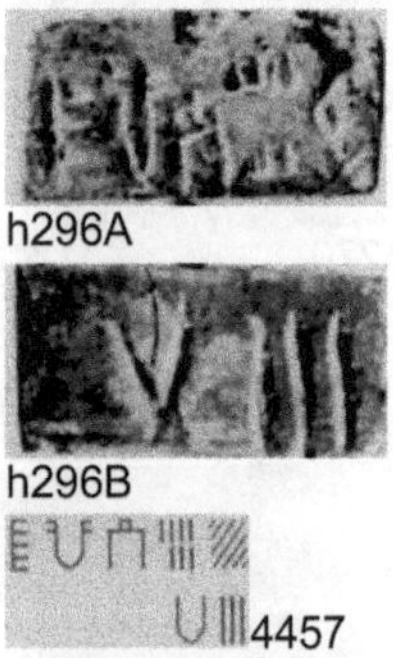
h296A
h296B
4457

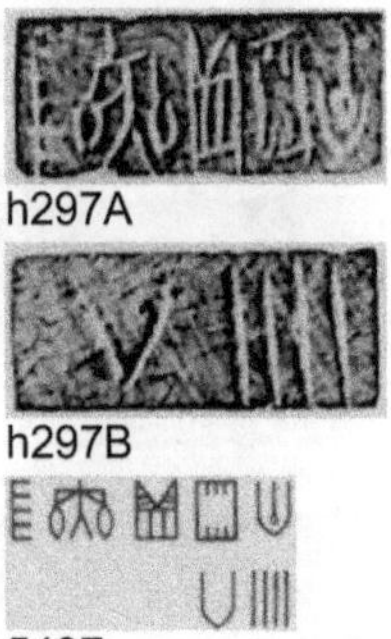
h297A
h297B
5497

h298A

h298B
5473

h299A

h299B
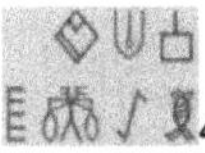
4478

h300A

h300B
4454

h301A

h301B
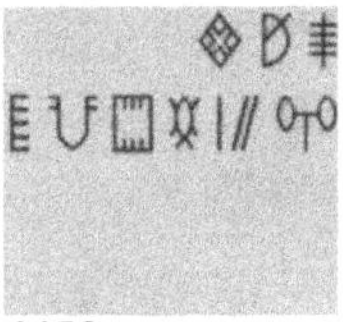
4450

h302A

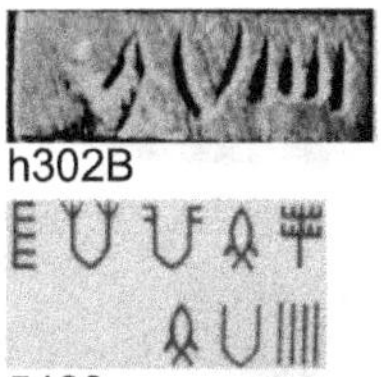
h302B
5460
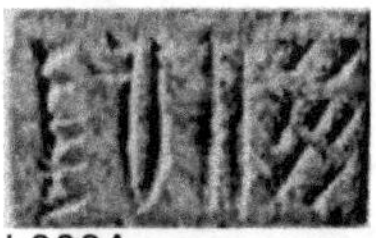
h303A
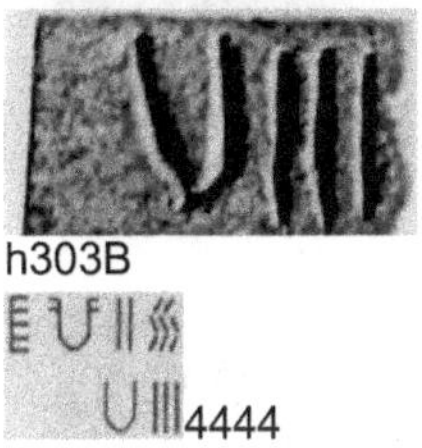
h303B
4444

h304A

h304B
5401
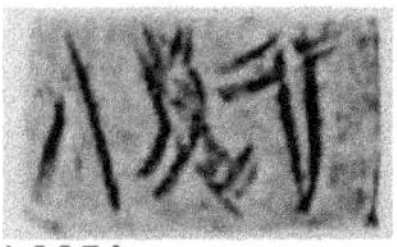
h305A

h305B Text 5460

h306A
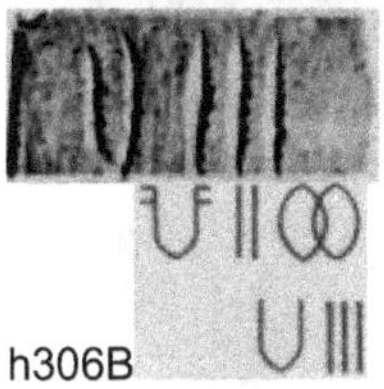
h306B
5474

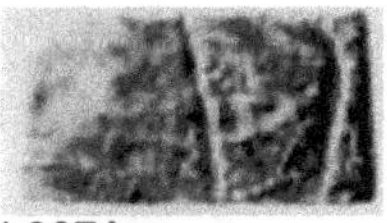
h307A

h307B

h308A
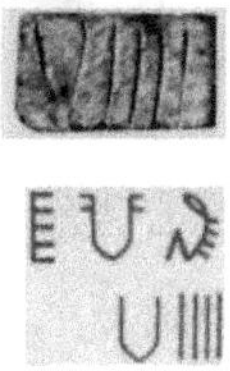
h308B
5427

h309A
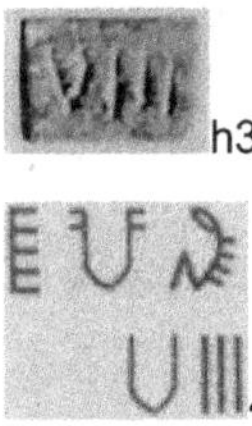
h309B
4403
4405, 4509, 4543, 5419, 5421, 5422, 5423, 5425, 5442, 5449

Incised miniature tablets h309, h311, h317, h932, h959, h935, h960

h310A
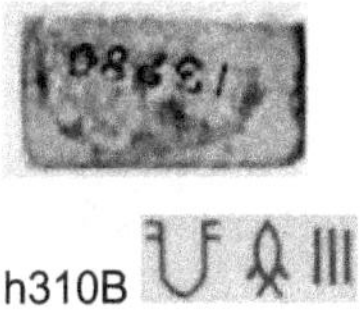
h310B
5475

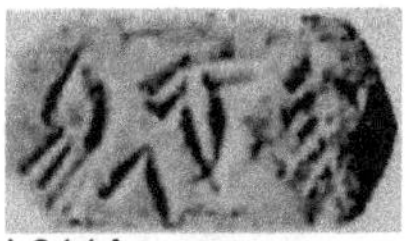
h311A
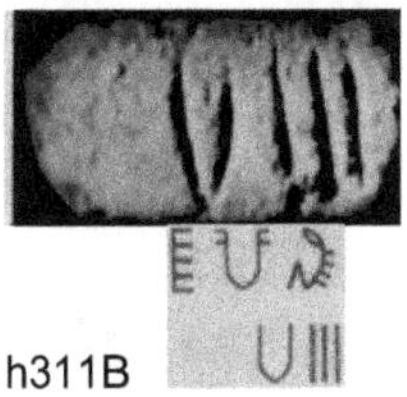
h311B
5421

h312B

h312Ac

5426

h313A

h313B
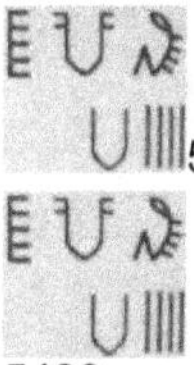
5432
5433

h314A
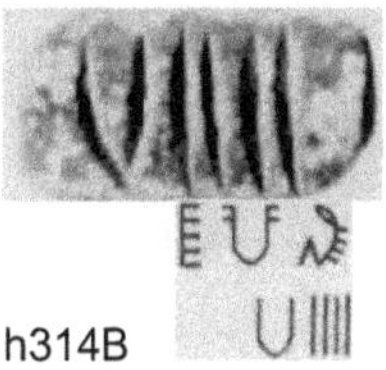
h314B
5447

h315A

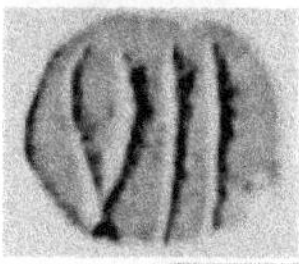

h315B

5464
h316A

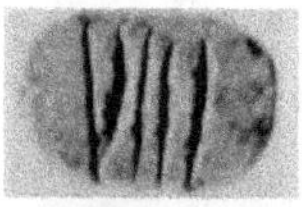
h316B

h317A

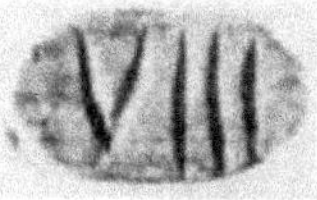

h317B
5442

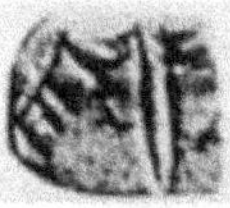
h318A

h318B
5451

h319A

h319B
4544

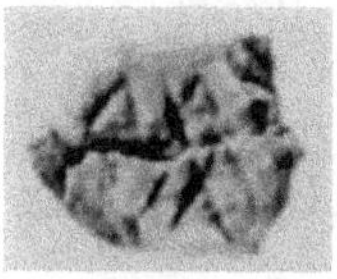
h320A

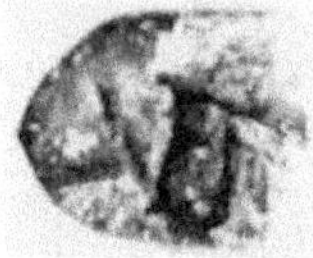

h320B
5450

h321A

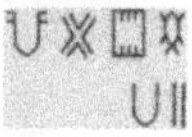
h321B
5402

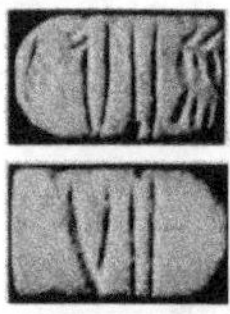
h322A
h322B

5498

h323A

h323B
4497

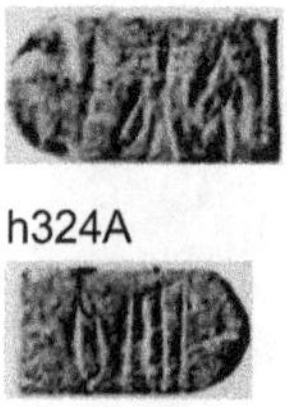
h324A

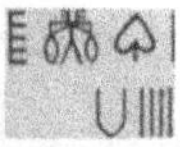
h324B
4484

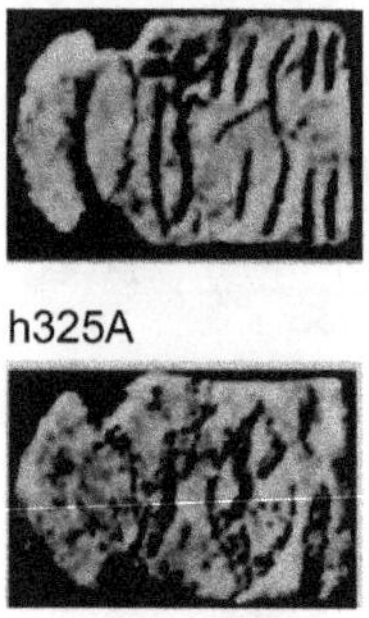
h325A
h325B

4416 Pict-130: Inscribed object in the shape of a writing tablet (?)

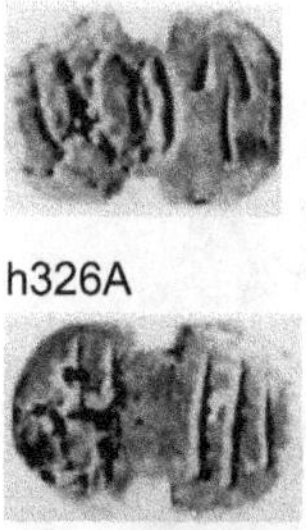
h326A

h326B
4564 Double-axe?

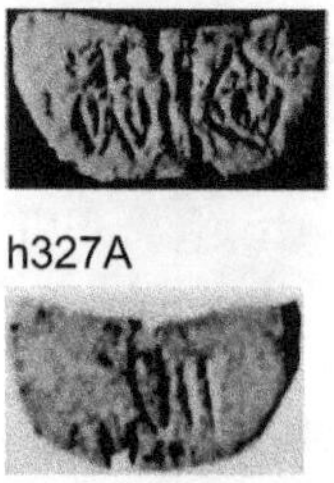
h327A

h327B

5472 5483
Shape of object: Blade of a weapon?

h328a

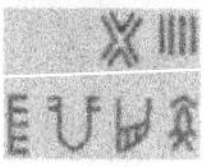
h328B
4415 Shape of object: Bladeof weapon?

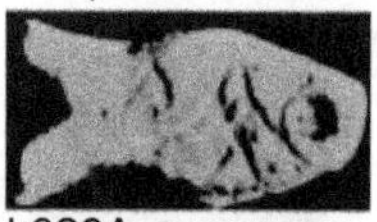
h329A

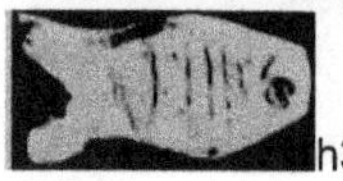
h3
29B

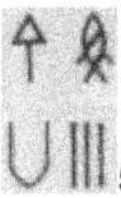
5496 Pict-68: Inscribed object in the shape of a fish.

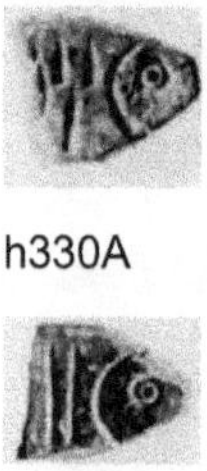
h330A

h330B 4560

h331A Incised miniature tablet.

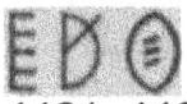
4421, 4422, 4423

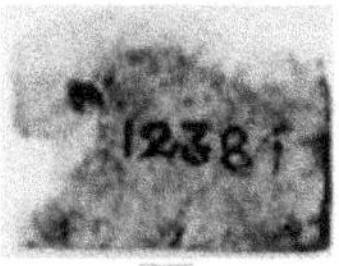
h332C 4885

h333A

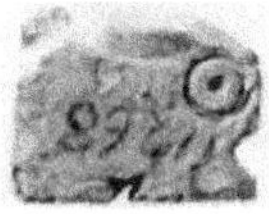
h333B

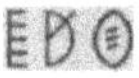 4421

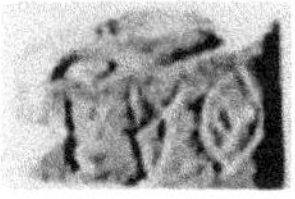
h334A

h334B 
4423

h335a

h335B 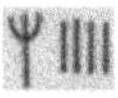
4425

h336A

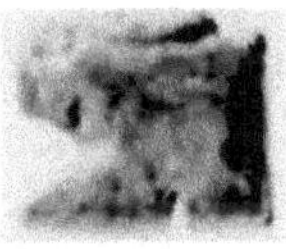
h336B

4424

h337A

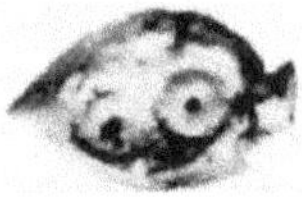

h337B
4417 Pict-79: shape of a leaf. Dotted circle on obverse.

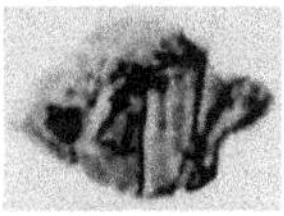
h338A

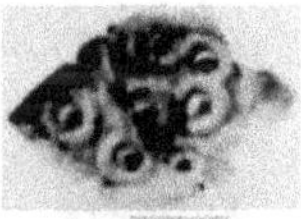

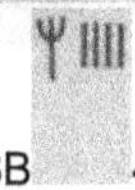
h338B 4426
Pict-39: Inscribed object in the shape of a tortoise (?) or leaf (?). Dotted circles on obverse.

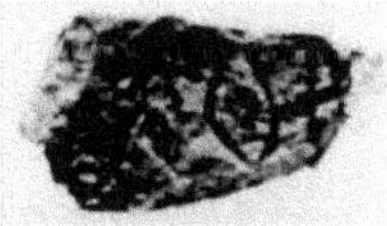
h339A

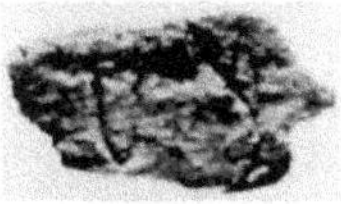
h339B

4559

h340A

h340B

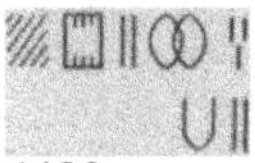
4420

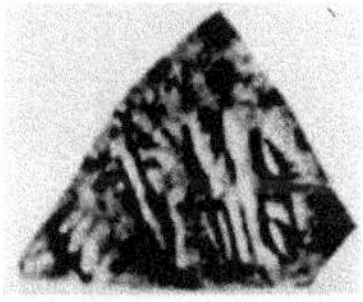
h341A

h341B

4419

h342A
h342B

4413

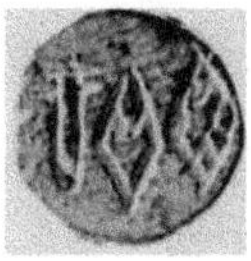
h343A

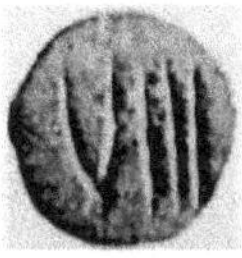

h343B
4549

h344A

h344B
4410

h345A

h345B
4550

h346A

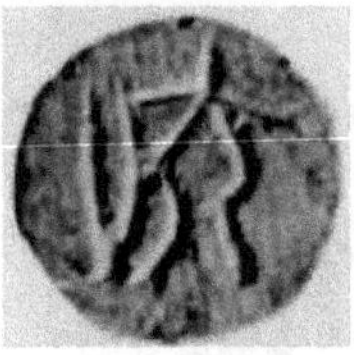

h346B Incised miniature tablet.

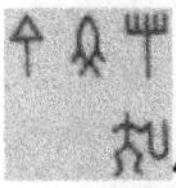
4412

h347A 4414

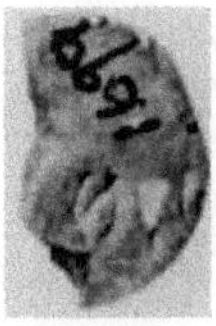

h348A

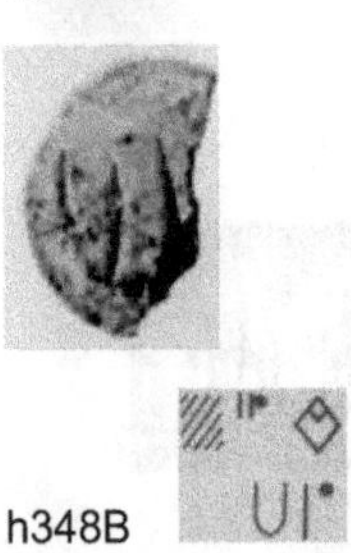

h348B
4552

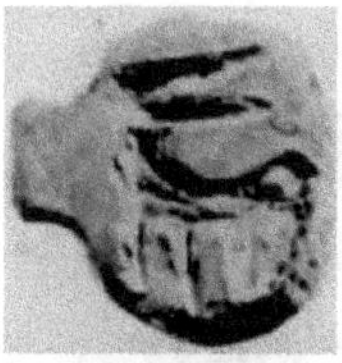

h349A

h349B

h350A

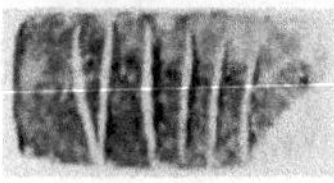

h350B

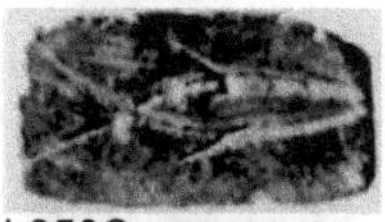

h350C

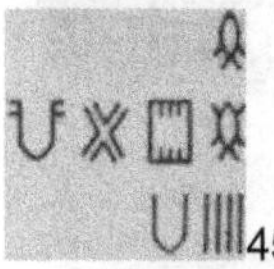
4576

h351A

h351B

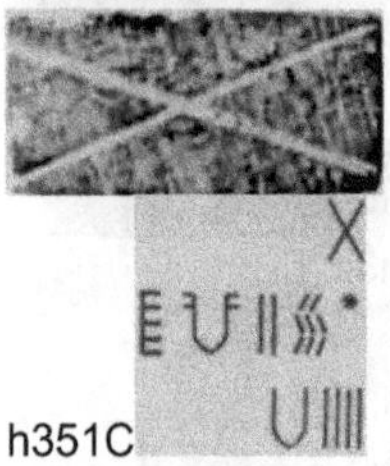

h351C
4581

h352A

h352B

h352C

4575 Pict-120: One or more dotted circles.

h353A

h353B

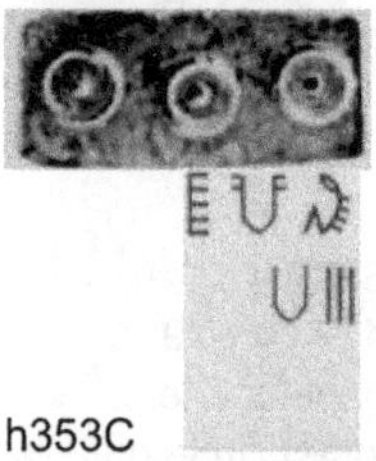

h353C
5416

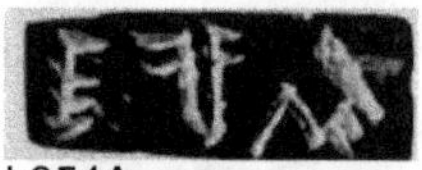

h354A

h354B

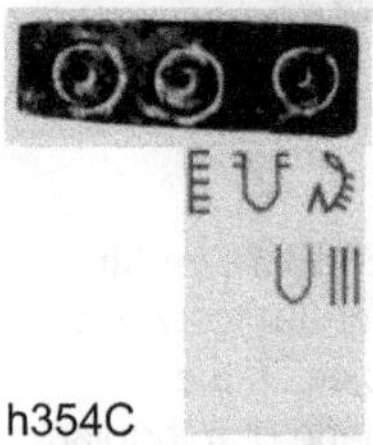

h354C
5499

h355A

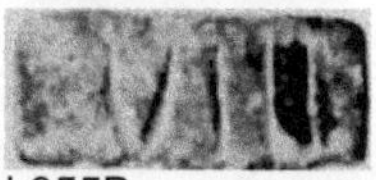

h355B

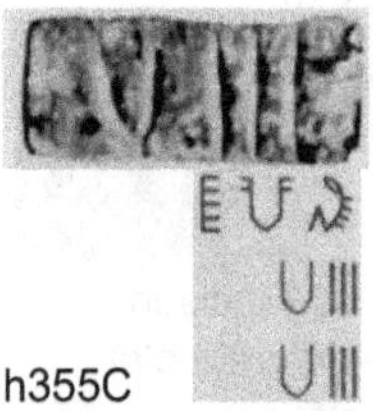

h355C
5413

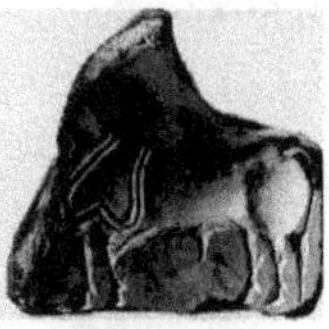

h356

h357

h358A

h358B

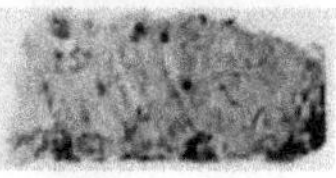

h358C

4579

h359a

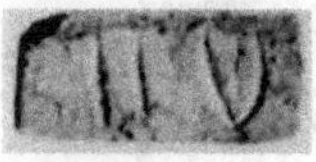

h359B

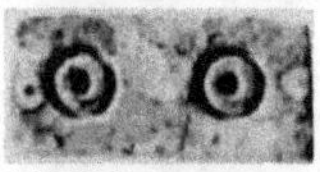

h359C

h360A

h360B

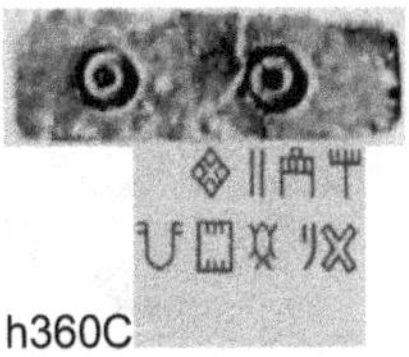

h360C
4584

h361A

h361B

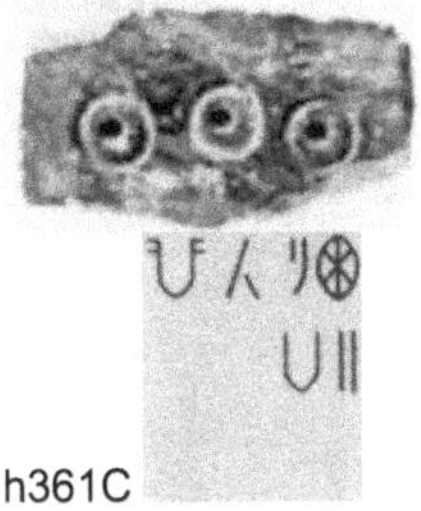

h361C
5476

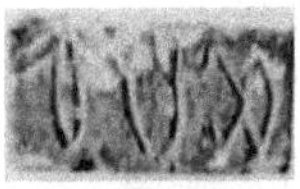

h362A

h362B

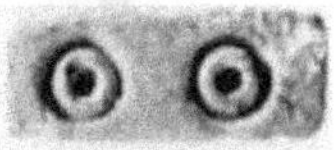

h362C

5466

h363A

h363B

h363C

h363E Pict-86

Pict-85
Standing person with horns and bovine features (hoofed legs and/or tail).

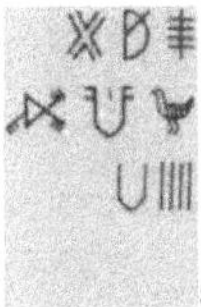

5471

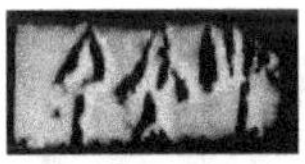

h364A

h364B

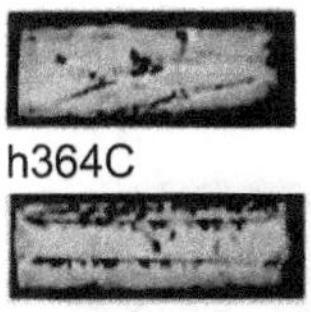

h364C

h364E
4635

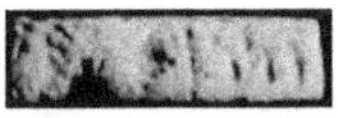

h365A

h365B

h365C

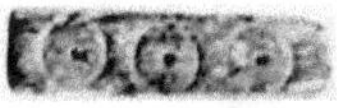

h365E

h366C

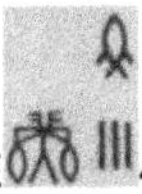

h366E 4590

h367A

h367B

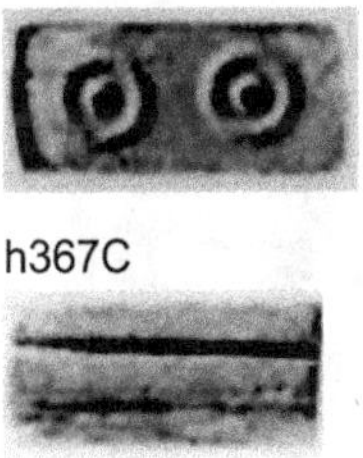

h367C

h367E 4401

h368a

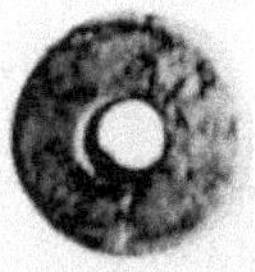

h368E

4409

h369a

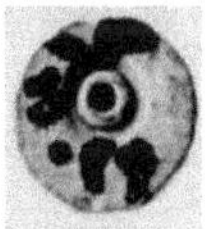

h369C

h369E

4718

h370A

h370A2

h371A

h371A2

h372A

h372A2

h374  4815

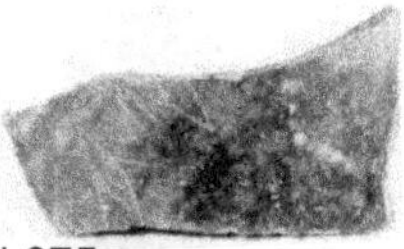

h375

4812

h377

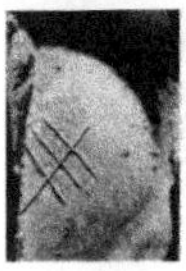

h378

h380 

4902 Bronze dagger

h381 

4901 Bronze dagger

h382

 4818

h383 (Not shown).

4021

h384

h385

4045

h386

4025

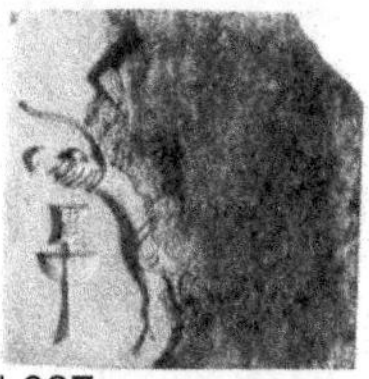

h387

h388

5062

h389

5090

h390

4024 [The second sign from right appears like a weaver's loom with three looped strings].

h391

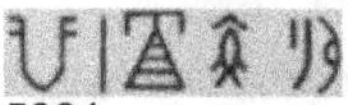

5064

h392a  4207

h393

h394a 

5003

h395a

h396

4027

h397

h398

h399

h400

h401

4168

h402

h403

h404

h405

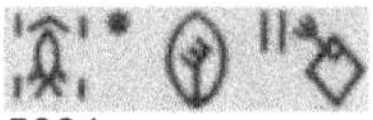

5091

h406  5034

h407 

4126

h408

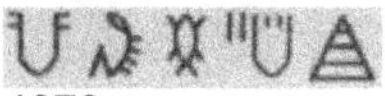

4079

h409

h410

4080

h411

 4078

h412

4036

h413

 4032

h414

h415

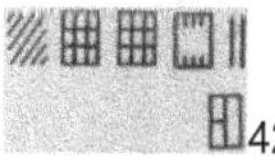 4204

h416 

4059

h417

4051

h418

h419

 5092

[  The first sign may be a squirrel as in Nindowaridamb 01 Seal].

h420

4614

h421

4026

h422
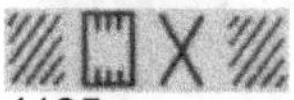
4185

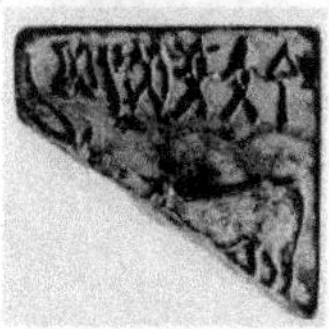
h423
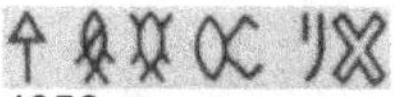
4056

h424

h425

h426

4153

h427

4217

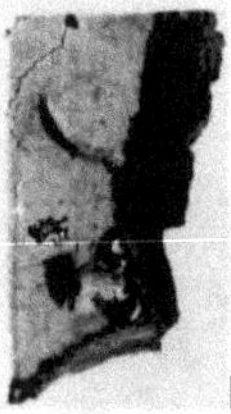
h428

h429

h430

h431

5068

h432

4616

h433

h434

h435

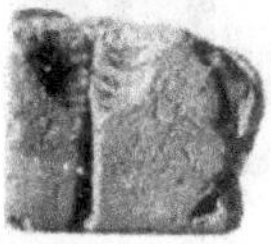
h436

h437

h438

h439

h440
4615

h441

4074

h442

4095

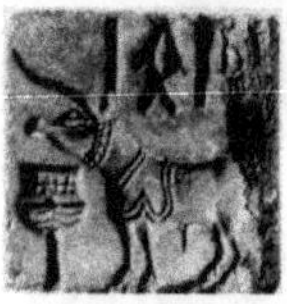
h443
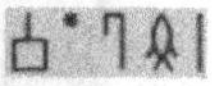
4121

h444

h445

5110

h446

4034

h447
4089

h448
4054

h449
4082

h450
4084

h451
4137

h452a
4124

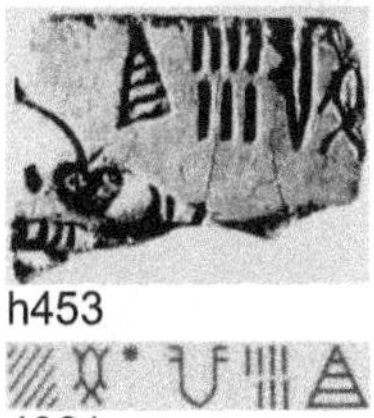
h453
4061

h454
4132

h455
4055

h456
4083

h457
5080

h458
4050

h459
4092

h460

h461
4037

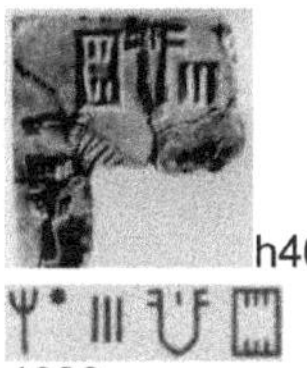
h462
4620

h463

h464a
4100

h465
4181

h466
4111

h467
4624

h468
4087

h469
4138

h470
4186

h471
4145

h472
4152

h473
4096

h474
4188

h475 4093

h476
4102

h477

h478
4088

h479
4099

h480 4180

h482 4208

h483

h484
4154

h485

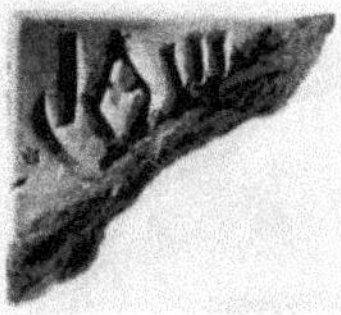
h486

h488
4198

h489
4189

h490

h492

h493

h494

h495

h497

h498

h499
5093

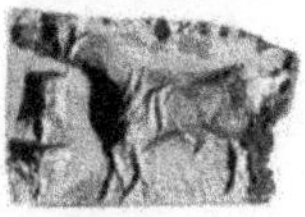
h500

h501
4112

h502
4143

h503
4129

h504
4183

h505 5094

h506
4097

h507 4159

h508

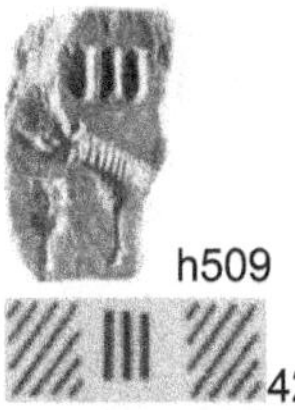
h509
4206

h510

4139

h511
4165

h512a
4618

h513
4163

h514

4116

h515
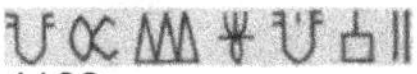
4162

Text  4166
h516a

h517

h518  4160

h519

4147

h520  4127

h521 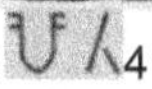 4155

h522

h523

5071

h524
4150

h525 
4149

h526

h527

h528

h529

h530 
4148 [May have to be arranged from right to left?]

h531

4172

h532

h533
4625

h534

h535

h536
h537
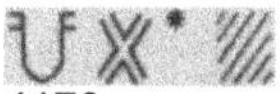
4170

h538
h539

h541

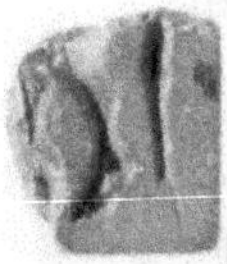
h542

h543
4177

h544
4144

h545
4622

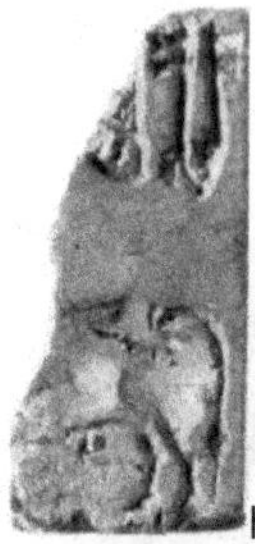
h546

4697

h547

h548

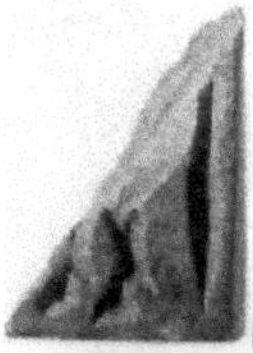
h549

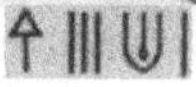
h550
4211

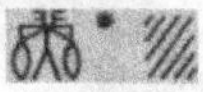
h551
4197

h552

h553

h554

h555

h556

h557

h558
4220

h559
4290

h561

h562

5066

h563
5065

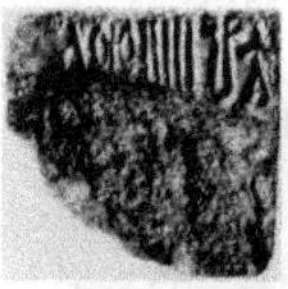
h565

4621

h566
4277

h567

h568

h569

4263

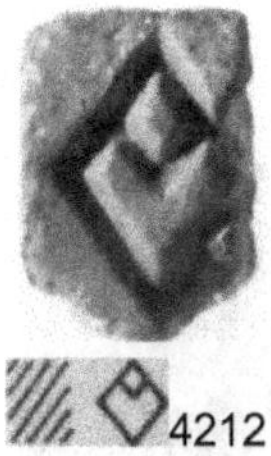
h570
4212

h571

h572
4695

h574
4696

h575

h576

h577
4243

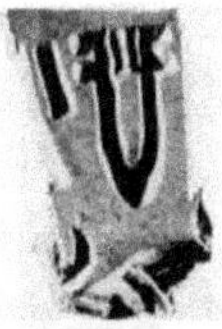
h578

h579

5109

h580

h581

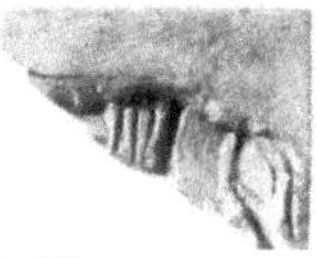
h582

h583

h584 4235
Bison.

h585

h586
4237

h587

h588

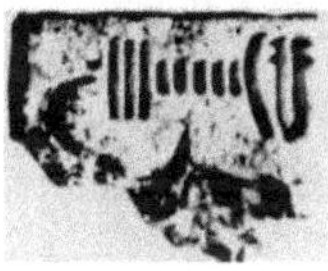
h589

4239

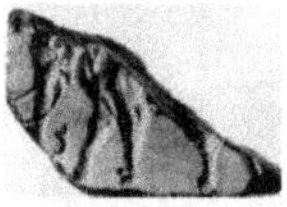
h590

h591

4228

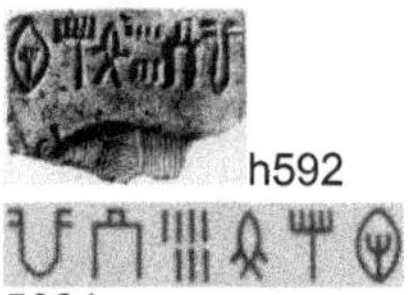
h592
5081

h593

4250 [Composite animal].

h594 [Composite animal].

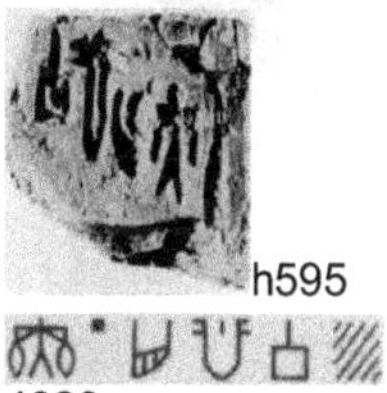
h595
4623

h596a
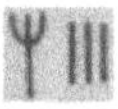
4382 [One-horned bull].

h597A

h597D

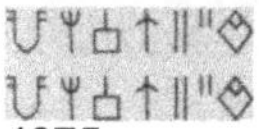
4075

h598A

h598D

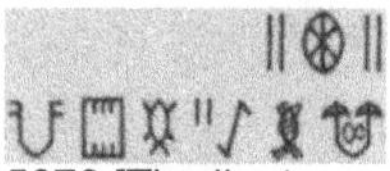

5073 [The ligature in-fixed on the last sign of the second line may be Sign

54 ]

h599A

h599D

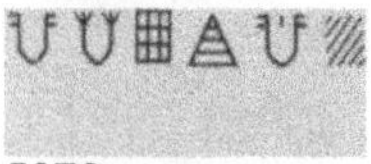

5076

h600

4156 [The last sign may be a

variant of Sign 51

]

h601

4044

h602a

4169

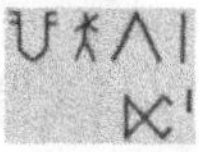

h603

4224

h604

h605

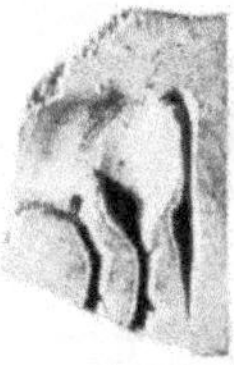

h606

4167

h608

4225

h609

4060

h610

4098

h611

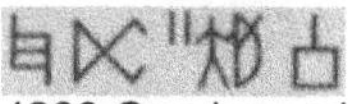

4260 One-horned bull.

h612A

h612B

h612D

4123

h613A

h613C

4259

Endless-knot motif?

h614

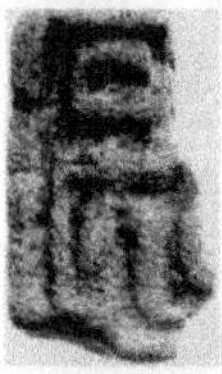

h616

h617

h618

h619

h620

h621

h622

h623

h624

h625

h626

h627

h628

h629

h630

h631

h632

h633

h634

h635

h636

h637

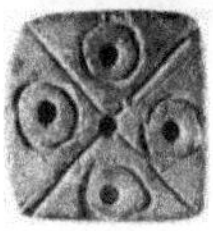
h638

h639
5061

h640

h641A

h641C
4698

h642
4266

h643
4273

h644 4299

h645
4265

h646
5108

h647
4291

h648

h649
4281

h650A

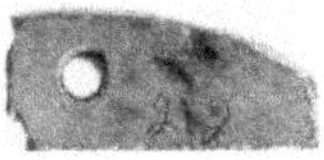

h650C

h651  4295

h652

h653 4301

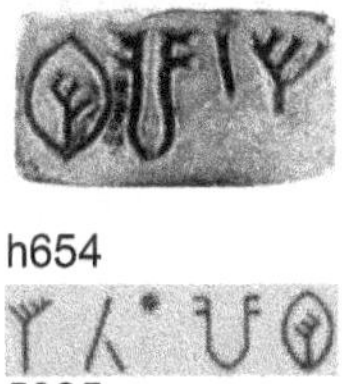
h654
5035

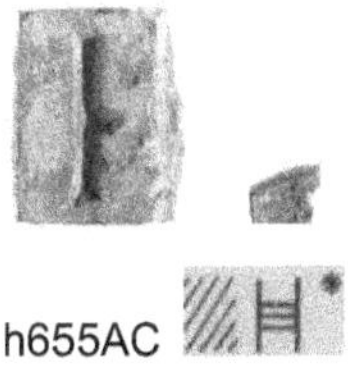
h655AC
4300

h656
4286

h657
4287

h658

4293

h659

5074

h660

5114

h661
4279
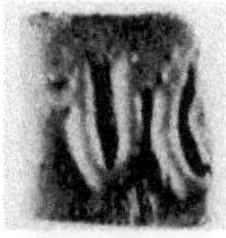
h662a

h663A
h663C
5006
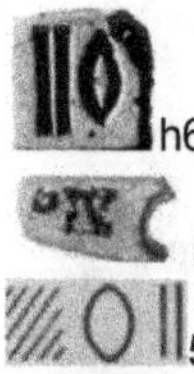
h664A
h664E
5010
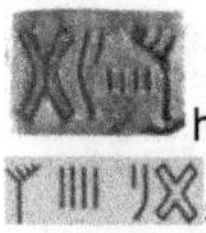
h665
5100

h666
4631

h667A

h667C

4634
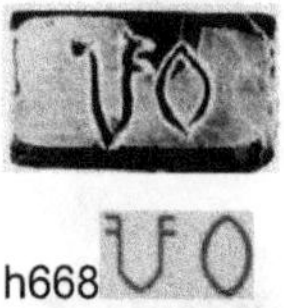
h668
5266

h669
4289

h670
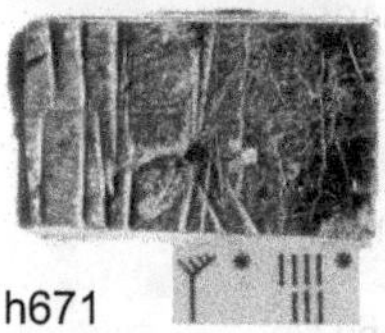
h671
4302

h679
4298

h680

5099

h681a

5105

h682

5078
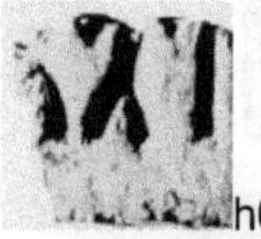
h683

h684
4632

h685

h686

h688A

h688F
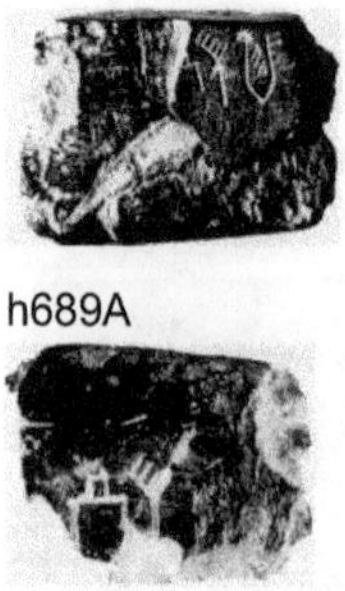
h689A

h689B
4222
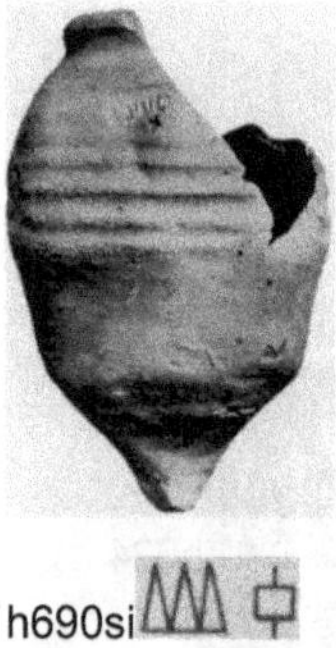
h690si
5304

h691A1si

h691A2si

h692A1si

h692A2si

h693t
4707

h694t

h695t

h696At

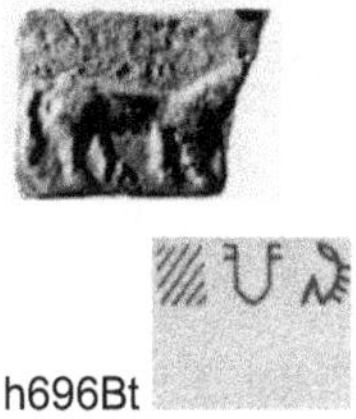

h696Bt
4677

h697At

h697Bt
4314

h698At

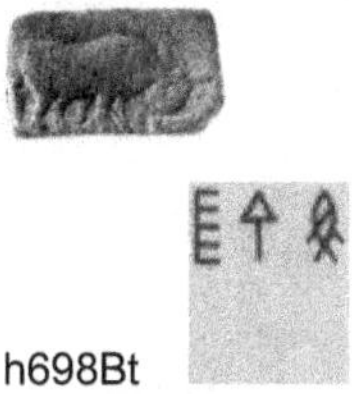

h698Bt
4659

h699At

h699Bt

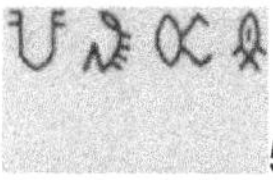

5288

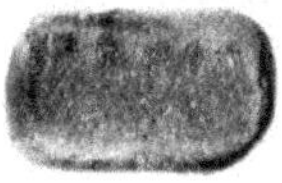

h700At

h700Bt

h701At

h701Bt

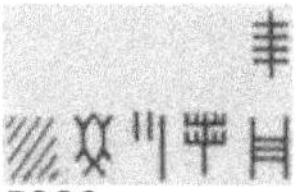

5329

h702At

h702Bt
4601

h703At

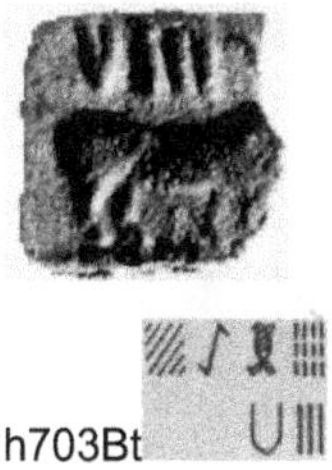

h703Bt
4595

h704At

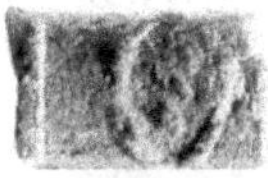

h704Bt

h705At

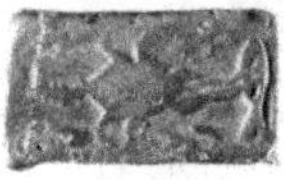

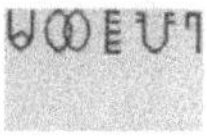

h705Bt
4337

h706At

h706Bt
4340

h707At

h707
4339

h708At

h708Bt
5280

h709 Text
5260

h710 Text
5249

h711

Text

4715

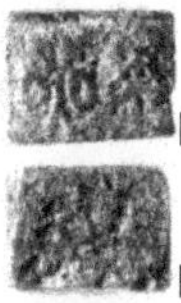

h713At

h713Bt

h714At

h714Bt
Standing person with horns and bovine features (hoofed legs and/or a tail) Icon of a person has bull's legs and a raised club.

h715At
h715Bt

5299

h716At

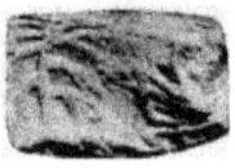

h716Bt

h717At

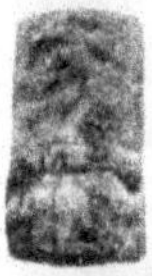
h717Bt

h718At

h718Bt

4328

h719At

h719Bt

4326

h720At

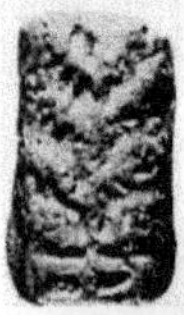
h720Bt

h722At

h722Bt

h723At

h723Bt

h724At

h724Bt

5255

h725At

h725Bt

h726At

h726Bt

h727At

h727Bt

h728At

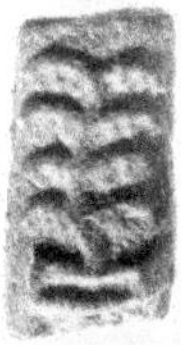
h728Bt

h729At

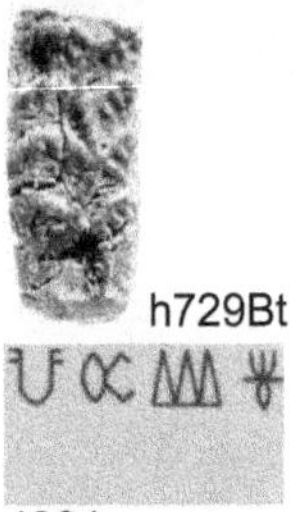
h729Bt

4331

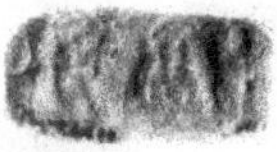
h730At

h730Bt

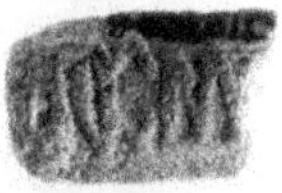
h731At

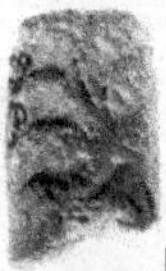
h731Bt

h732At

h732Bt

h733At

h733Bt

5222

h734At

h734Bt

5286

h735At

h735Bt

5310

h736At

h736Bt

h737At

h737Bt

h738At

h738Bt

h739At

h739Bt

h740At

h740Bt

h741At

h741Bt

5263

h742At

h742Bt

4320

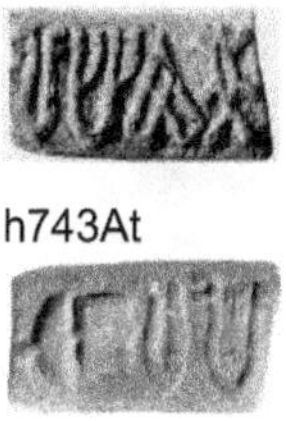

h743At

h743Bt

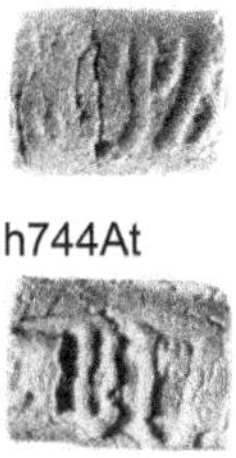

h744At

h744Bt

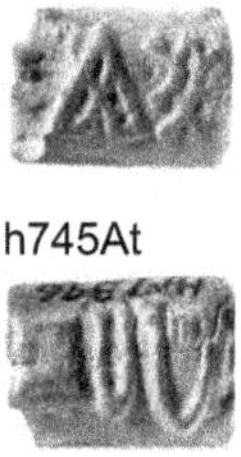

h745At

h745Bt

5257

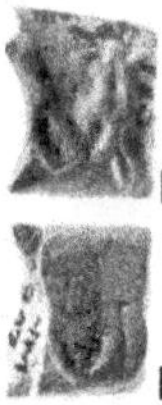

h746At

h746Bt

h747At

h747Bt

4656

h748At

4654

h749At

h750At

h751At

h752At

5275

h753At

5231

h754At

4716

h755At

5287

h756At

4669

h757At

4655

h758At

h759At

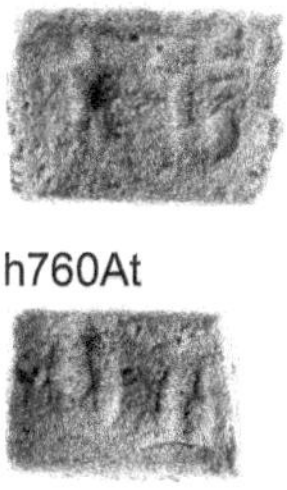

h760At

h760Bt

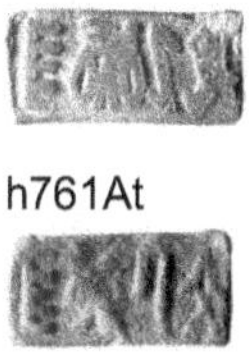

h761At

h761Bt

h762At

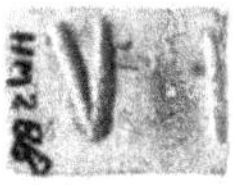

h762Bt Tablet in bas-relief.

4354

h763At

h763Bt

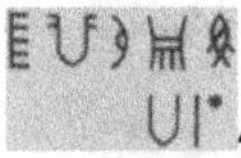
4661

h764At
h764Bt

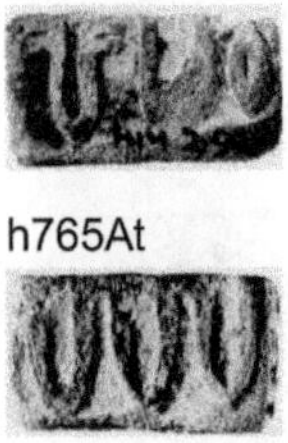
h765At

h765Bt
4653

h766At
h766Bt
4359

h767At

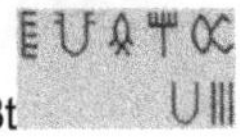
h767Bt
4352

h768At
h768Bt

4358

h769At
h769Bt

4667

h770At
h770Bt

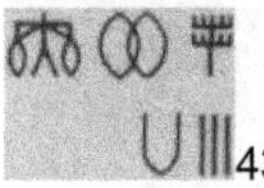
4353

h771At

h771Bt
4678 [The second sign on line 1 is a squirrel  ].

h772At
h772Bt

4660

h773At

h773Bt
4351

h774At
h774Bt

4672

h775At

h776At

h776Bt

4350

h777At

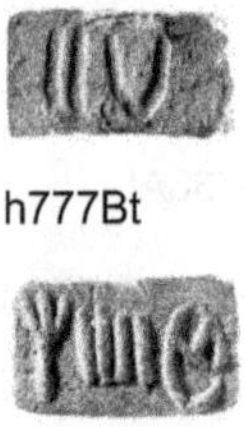
h777Bt

h778At

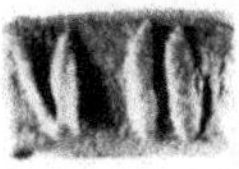

h778Bt
5322

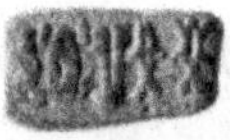

h779At

h779Bt

h780At

h780Bt
4361

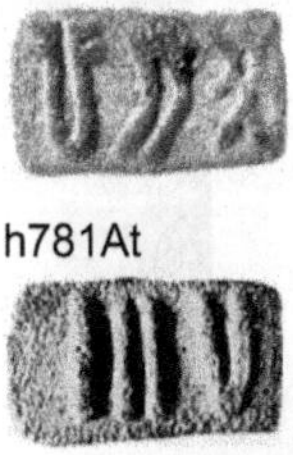
h781At

h781Bt
4670

h782At
h782Bt
5328

h783At
h783Bt

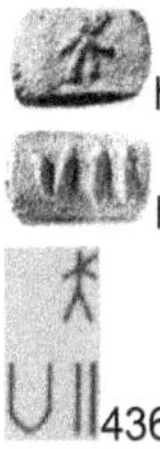
h784At
h784Bt
4364

h785At
h785Bt
4681

h786At
h786Bt
5320

h787At
h787Bt

h788At
h788Bt
4683

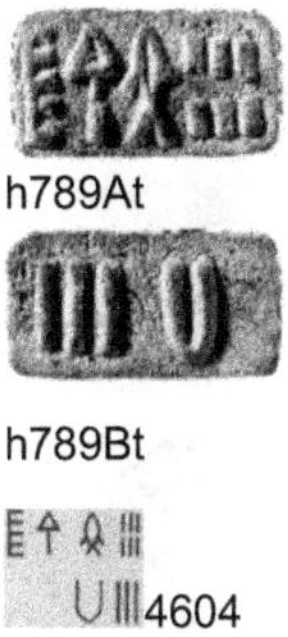
h789At
h789Bt
4604

h790At
h790Bt
4605

h791At
h791Bt
4676

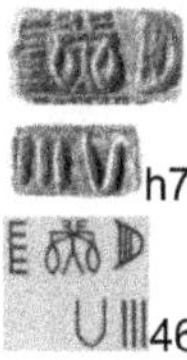
h792At
h792Bt
4692

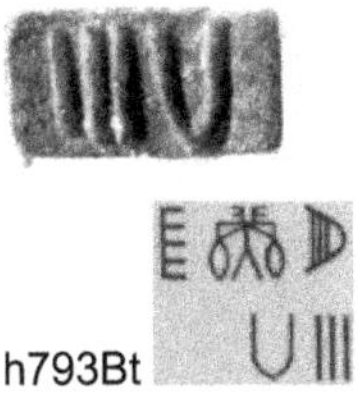
h793At
h793Bt
4680

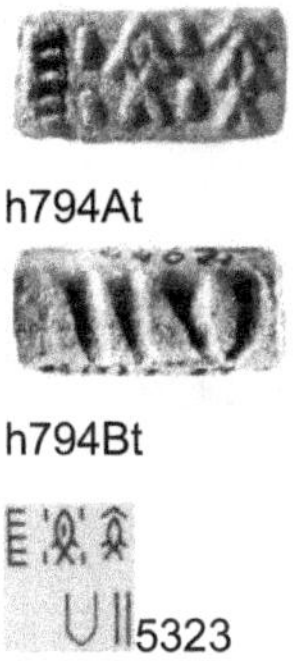
h794At
h794Bt
5323

h795At
h795Bt

h796At
h796Bt
5327

h797At
h797Bt
5281

h798At
h798Bt
4607

h799At
h799Bt
4603

h800At
h800Bt
4689

h801At
h801Bt

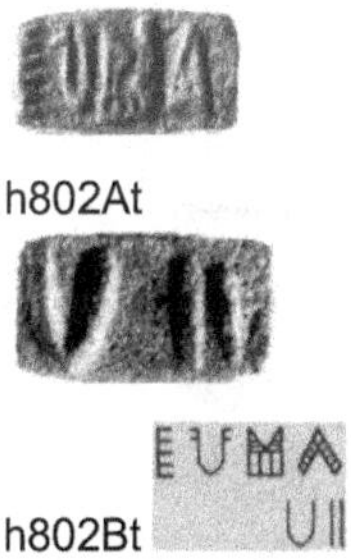
h802At
h802Bt
4679

h804At
5233

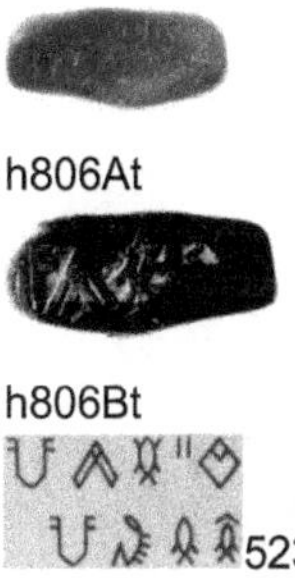
h806At
h806Bt
5237

h807At

h807Bt

4343

One-horned bull.

h808At

h808Bt

5238

h810At

4366

h811At

h811Bt

4349

h812At

h812Bt

4686

h813At

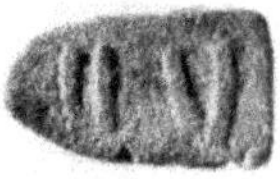

h813Bt

4682

h814At

h814Bt

4606

h815At

h815Bt

h816At

h816Bt

4602

h817At

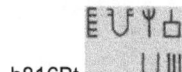

h817Bt Inscribed object in the shape of a double-axe.One or more dotted circles.

h818At

h818Bt Inscribed object in the shape of a double-axe.

4376

h819At

h819Bt Shape of object: Blade of a weapon?

5302

h820At

h820Bt

h821At

h821Bt Shape of object: axe.

h822At

h822Bt Shape of object: axe.

5319

h823At

h823Bt

4346

h824At

h824Bt

5278

h825At

h825Bt Shape of object: sickle?

5324

h827At

h827Bt Shape of object: axe?

h829At
h829Bt
5303

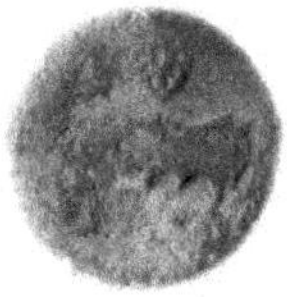
h830At

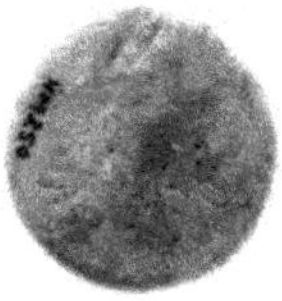
h830Bt Tablet in bas-relief. Bovid.

4311

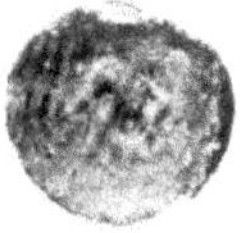
h832At

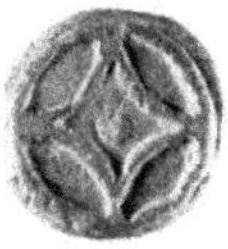
h832Bt Tablet in bas-relief
Pict-121: Lozenge within a circle with a dot in the center.

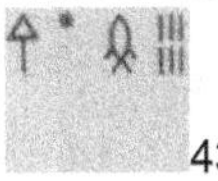
4377

h833At

h833Bt

4370

h834At

h834Bt

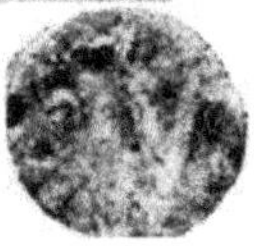
4666
h835Bt

h836At

h837At

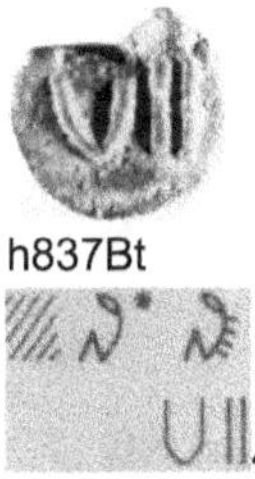
h837Bt
4381

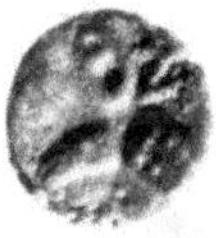

h838At
h838Bt

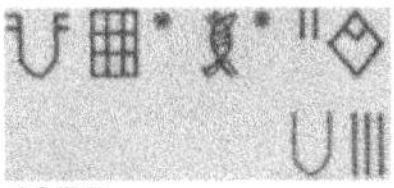
4375

h839At

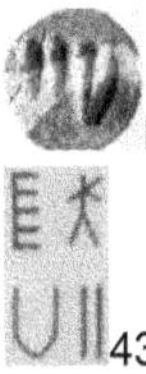
h839Bt
4378

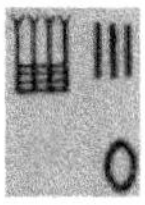
h840At
4380

h841At
4379

h842At

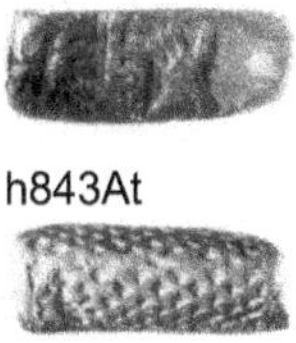
h843At
h843Ct

5326

h844At

h844Bt

h845At

h845Bt
h845Ct

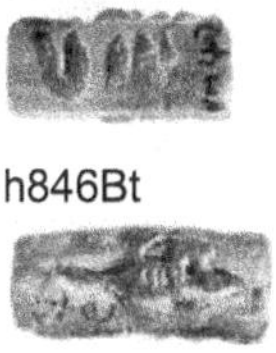
h846At
h846Bt

h846Ct

4641

h847At

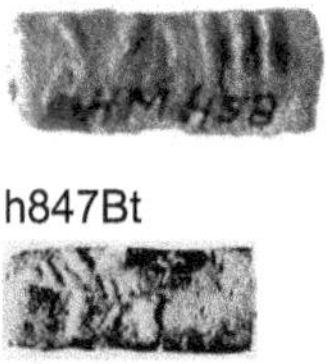
h847Bt
h847Ct

h848At
h848Bt

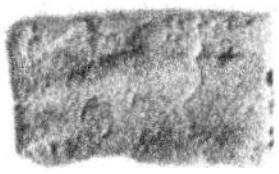

h848Ct
4597
h849At
h849Bt
h849Ct
4645
h850At
h850Bt
h850Ct
4642
h851At
h851Bt
h851Ct
h852At

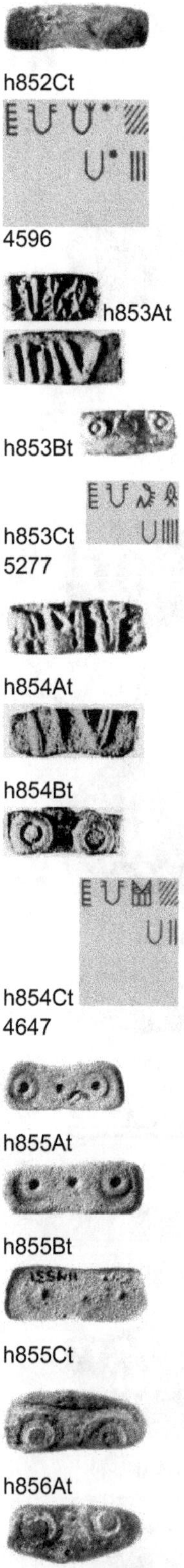
h852Bt
h852Ct
4596
h853At
h853Bt
h853Ct
5277
h854At
h854Bt
h854Ct
4647
h855At
h855Bt
h855Ct
h856At

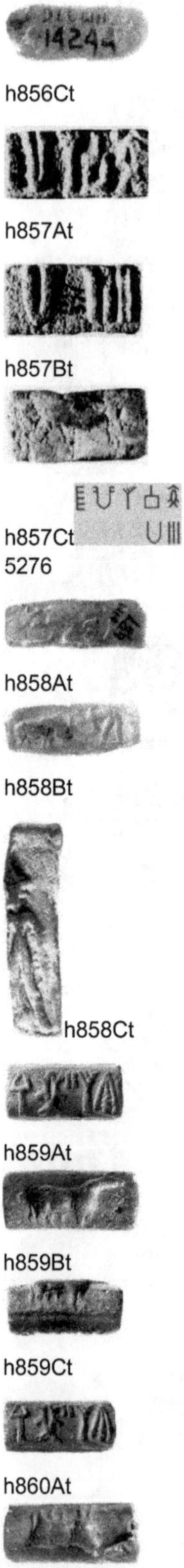
h856Bt
h856Ct
h857At
h857Bt
h857Ct
5276
h858At
h858Bt
h858Ct
h859At
h859Bt
h859Ct
h860At

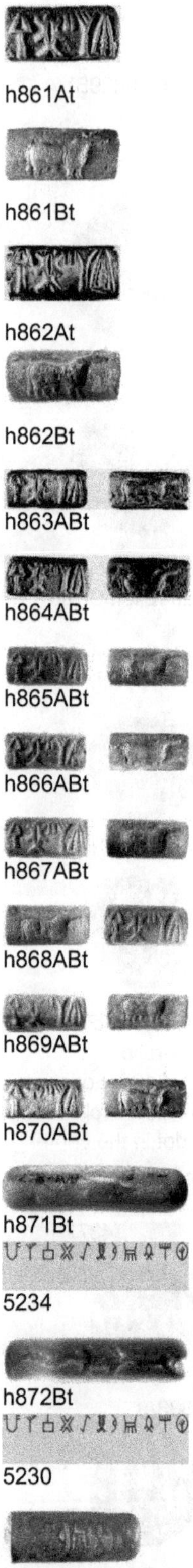
h860Bt
h861At
h861Bt
h862At
h862Bt
h863ABt
h864ABt
h865ABt
h866ABt
h867ABt
h868ABt
h869ABt
h870ABt
h871Bt
5234
h872Bt
5230

h873At

h873Bt

5227

h874At

h874Bt

4362

h875At

h875Bt

4651

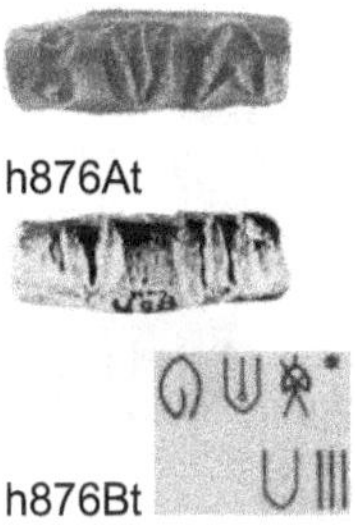

h876At

h876Bt

4675

h877At

h877Bt

4594

h878At

h878Bt

4687

h879Abit

h880ABit

4433

h881Abit

4434

h882Abit

4436

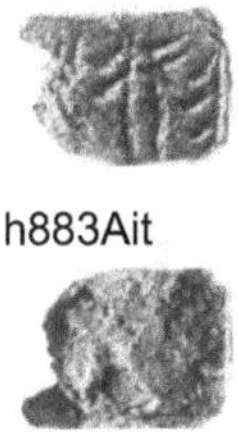

h883Ait

h883Bit

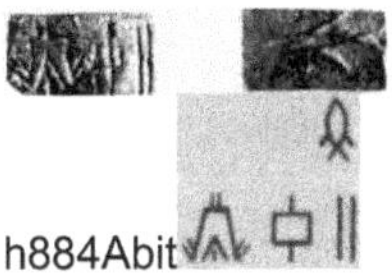

h884Abit

4437

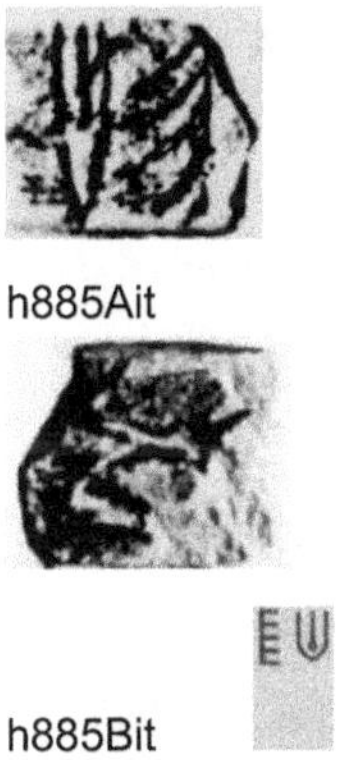

h885Ait

h885Bit

4530 Fish.

h887Ait

h887Bit

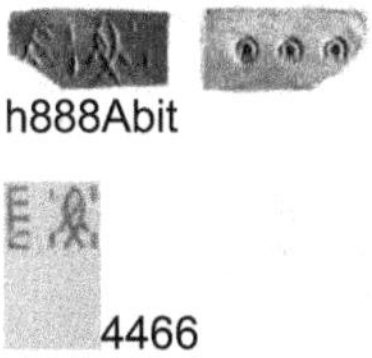

h888Abit

4466

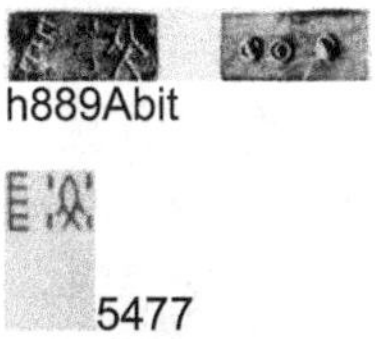

h889Abit

5477

h890ABit

4446

h891ABit

h892ABit

4451

h893Ait

h893Bit

4522

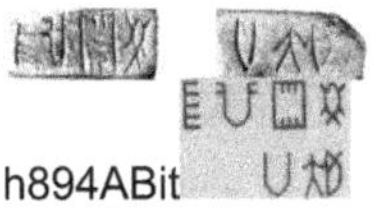

h894ABit

4487

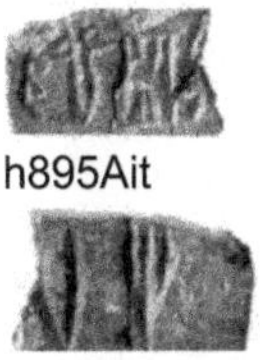

h895Ait

h895Bit

h896ABit

4480

h897ABit

h898ABit

4506

h899Ait

h899Bit

4471

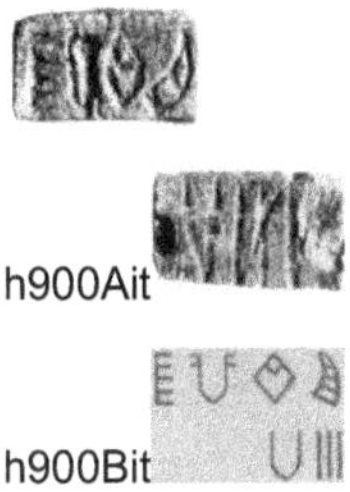

h900Ait

h900Bit

4455

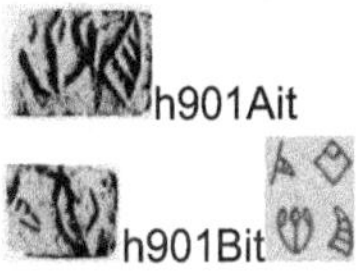

h901Ait

h901Bit

4460

h902Ait

h902Bit

4535

h903Ait

h903Bit

4485

h904Ait

h904Bit

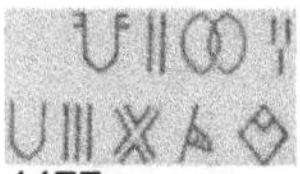

4477

h905ABit

4449

h906Ait

h906Bit

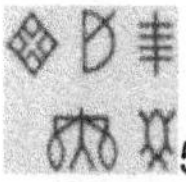

5494

h907Ait

h907Bit

4537 The second sign on h907Ait may be a ligatured fish?

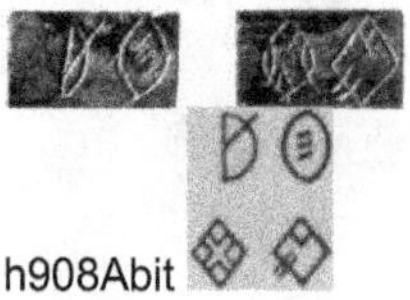

h908Abit
4488

h909ABit

5325

h910ABit

4470

h911Ait

h911Bit

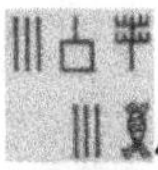

4486

h912Abit

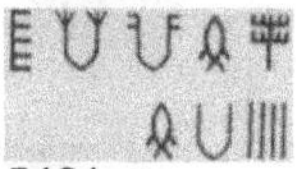

5461

h913Ait

h913Bit

h914Ait

h914Bit

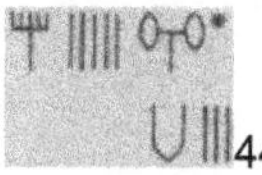

4483

h916Ait

h916Bit
4456

h917Ait

h917Bit
4472

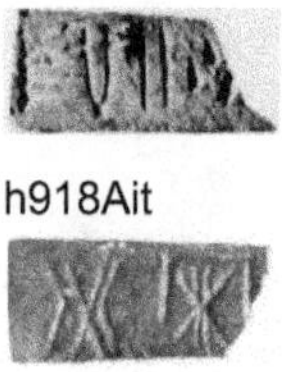

h918Ait

h918Bit

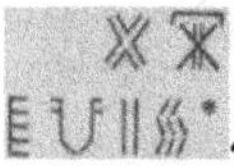

4481

h919Ait

h919Bit

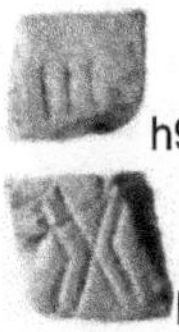

h920Ait

h920Bit

4527

h921ABit
4514

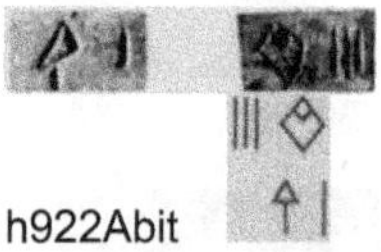

h922Abit
4518

h923Abit
4474

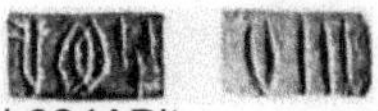

h924ABit

h925Abit
4512

h926Abit
4519

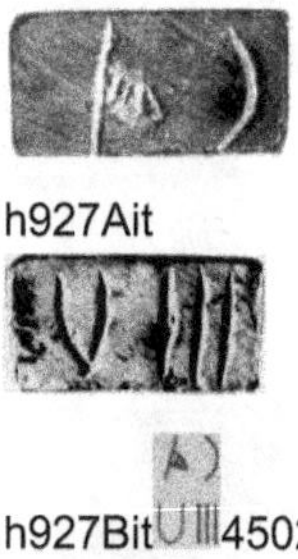

h927Ait

h927Bit 4502

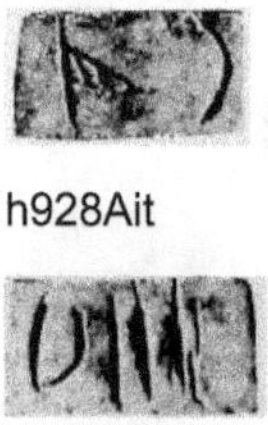

h928Ait

h928Bit

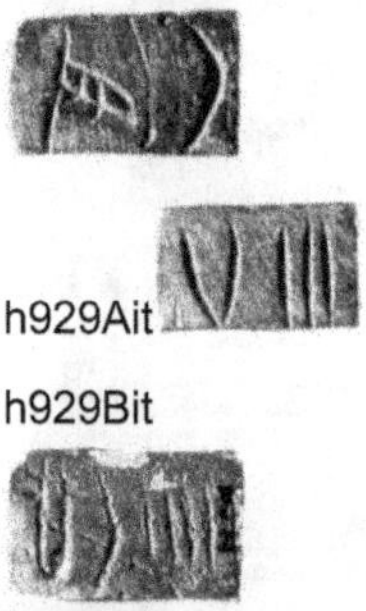

h929Ait

h929Bit

h930Ait

h930Bit

4520

h931Ait

h931Bit

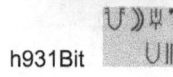

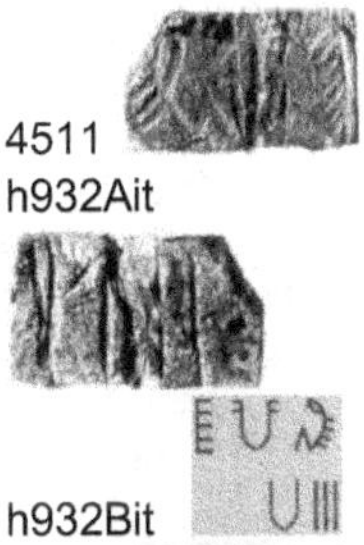
4511
h932Ait
h932Bit

4403
h933Ait
h933Bit

4516
h934Ait
h934Bit

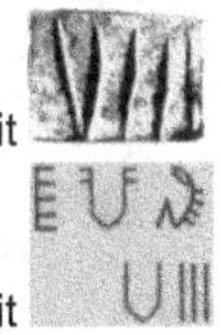
h935Ait
h935Bit
4509

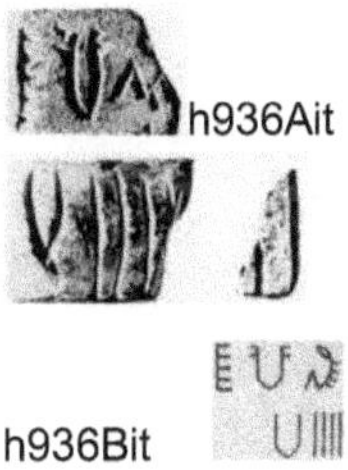
h936Ait
h936Bit
5405

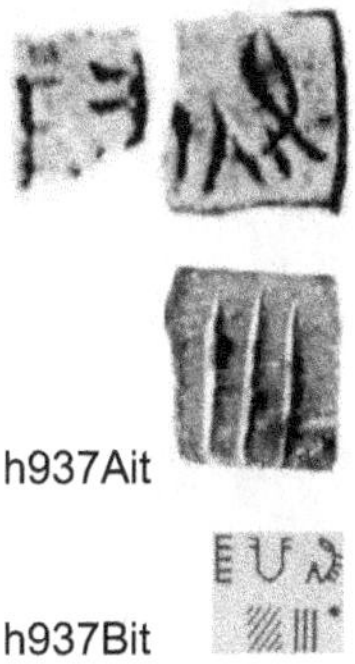
h937Ait
h937Bit
5458

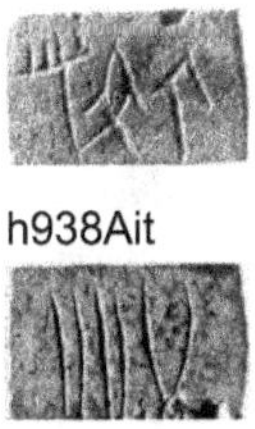
h938Ait
h938Bit

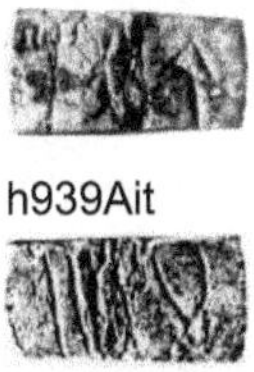
h939Ait
h939Bit

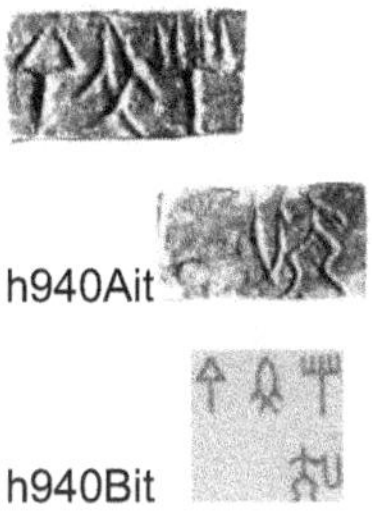
h940Ait
h940Bit
4453

h941Ait
h941Bit
4464

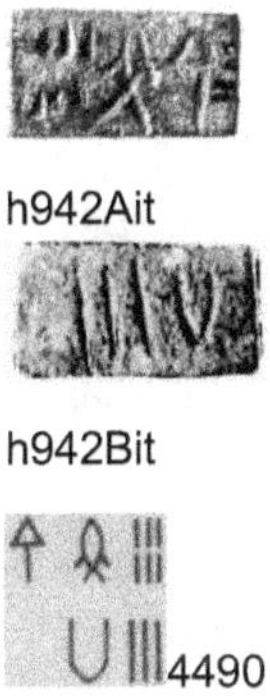
h942Ait
h942Bit
4490

h943Ait

h943Bit
4461

h944Ait
h944Bit
4475

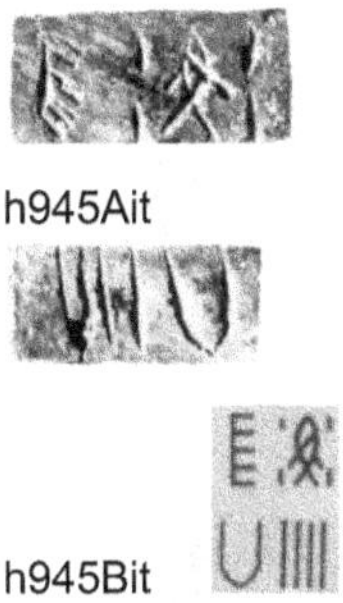
h945Ait
h945Bit
4503

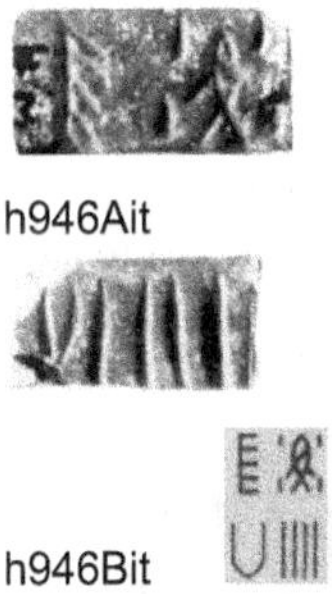
h946Ait
h946Bit
4501

h947Ait

h947Bit
4493

h948Abit
4489

h949Abit
4479

h950ABit
4463

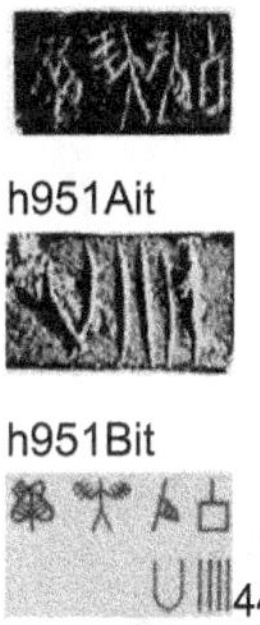
h951Ait
h951Bit
4498

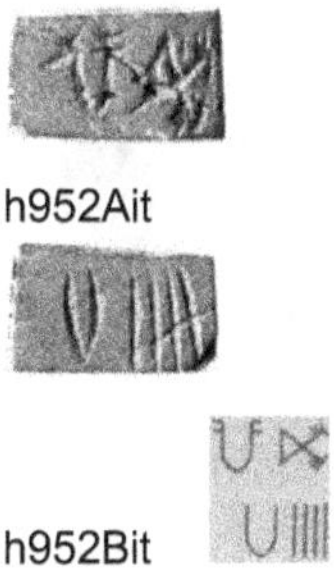
h952Ait
h952Bit
4469

h953Ait
h953Bit

h954Ait
4467

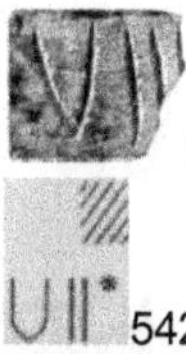

h955Bit

5429

h959Ait

h959Bit
4405

h960Ait

h960Bit

4543
h961Ait

h961Bit

5449
h962Ait

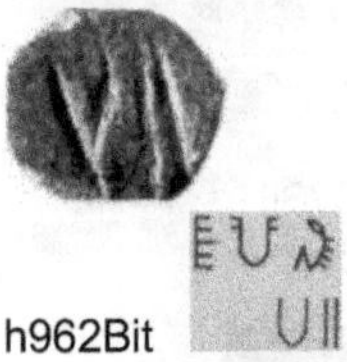

h962Bit

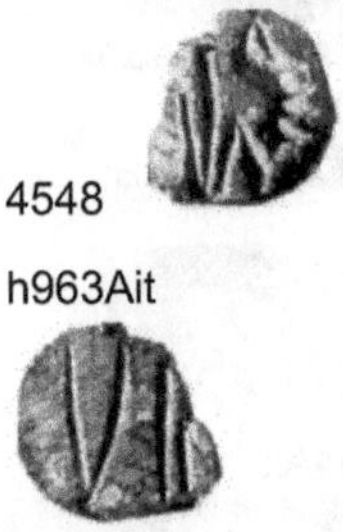

4548

h963Ait

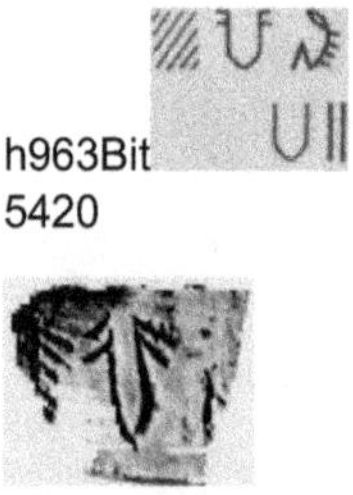

h963Bit
5420

h964Ait

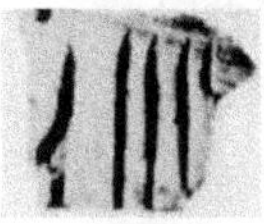

h964Bit
5456

h965Ait

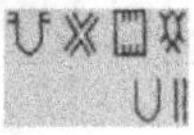

h965Bit
4562

h966Ait

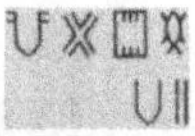

h966Bit
5479

h967Ait
4563

h968Ait

h968Bit

h969Ait

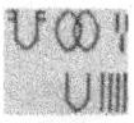

h969Bit
4555

h970Ait

h970Bit
4553

h971Ait

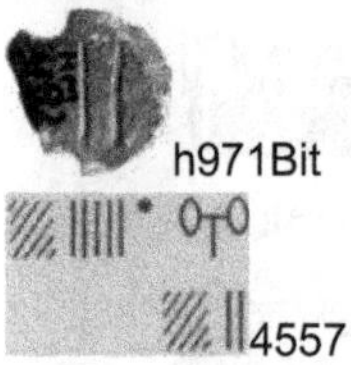

h971Bit

4557

Shape of object: double-axe?

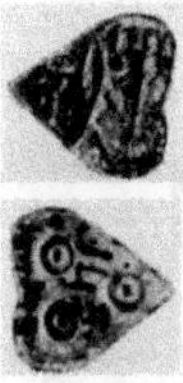

h972Ait

h972Bit

4418 Pict-128: Inscribed object in the shape of a leaf? Dotted circles on obverse.

h973Ait

h973Bit

4411

h974Ait

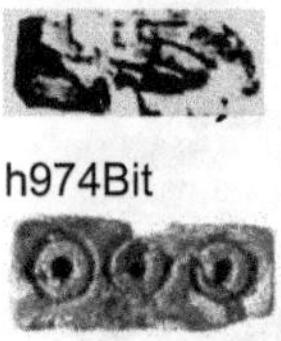

h974Bit

h974Cit
4592

h975Ait

h975Bit

h975Cit
4402

h976Ait

h976Bit

h976Cit

4588

h977Ait

h977Bit

h977Cit
4591

h978Ait

h978Bit

h978Cit
5412

h979Ait

h979Bit

h979Cit

h980Ait

h980Bit

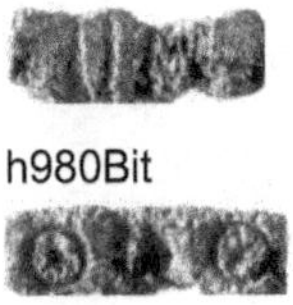

h980Cit

h981Ait

h981Bit

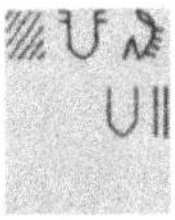

h981Cit
5415

h982Ait

h982Bit

h982Cit
m4574

h983Ait

h983Bit

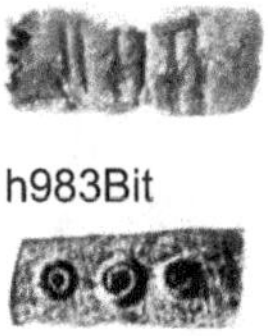

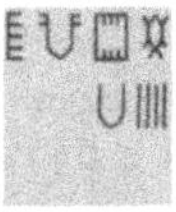

h983Cit
4582

h984Ait

h984Bit

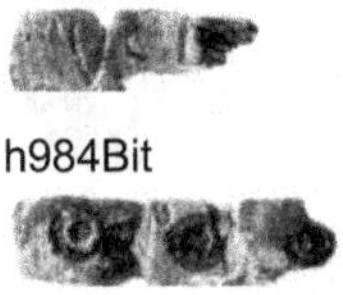

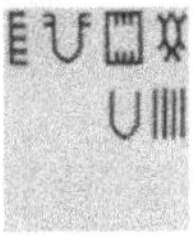

h984Cit
4587

h985Ait

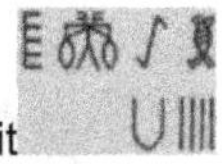

h985Bit
4577

h987Ait

h987Bit

h987Cit

4586

h988Ait

h988Bit

h
988B2it

h988Cit

h988Eit

4573

h990

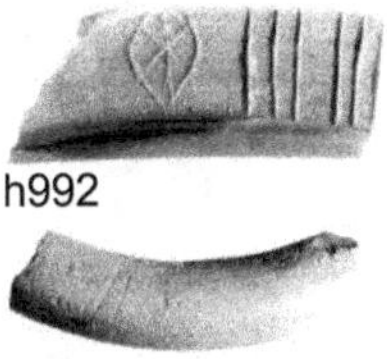

h992

h994

h1020

h1021

h1022

h1023

h1024

h1025a

h1027a

h1028

h1029a

h1030a

h1031

h1032a

h1033a

h1035

h1036

h1037

h1038

h1042a

h1043a

h1044a

h1045a

h1046

h1047a

h1048

h1049a

h1050

h1051

h1052

h1053a

h1056a

h1058a

h1059

h1064

h1065

h1066a

h1067a

h1068

h1071

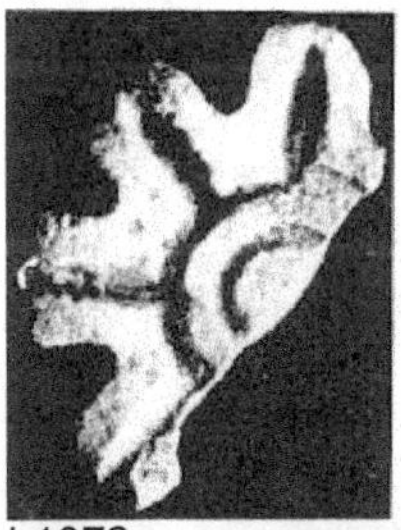
h1072

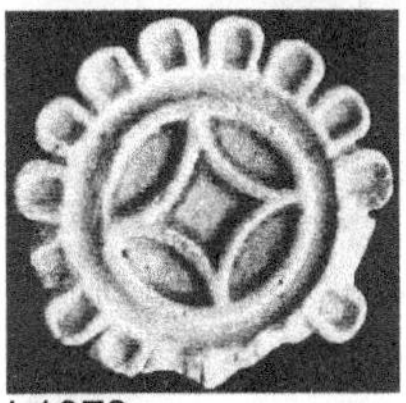
h1073

h1075

h1076

h1077

h1079a

h1080a

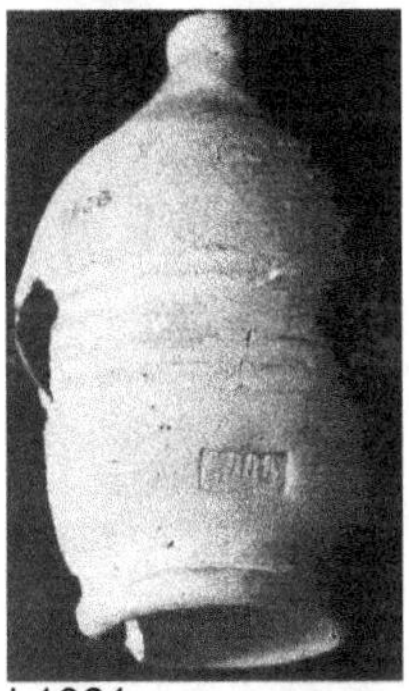
h1081

h1082

h1083

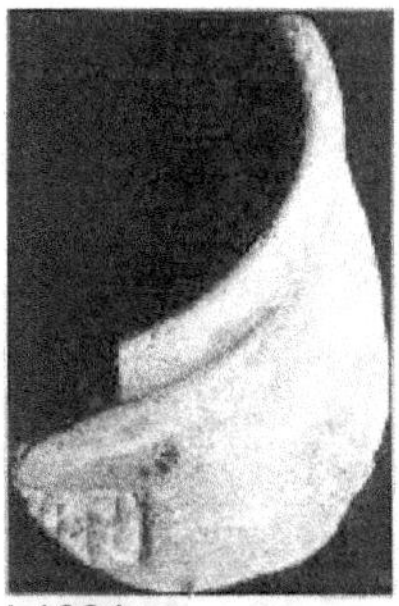
h1084

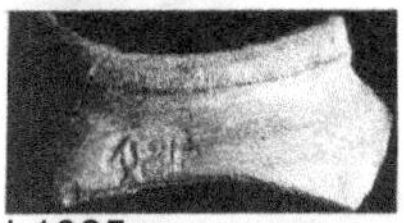
h1085

h1086

h1087

h1091

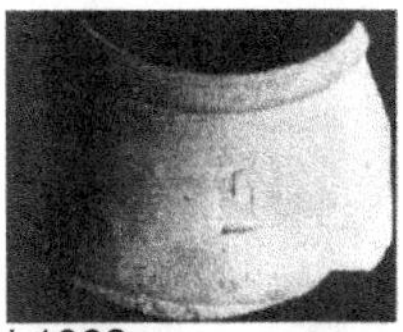
h1092

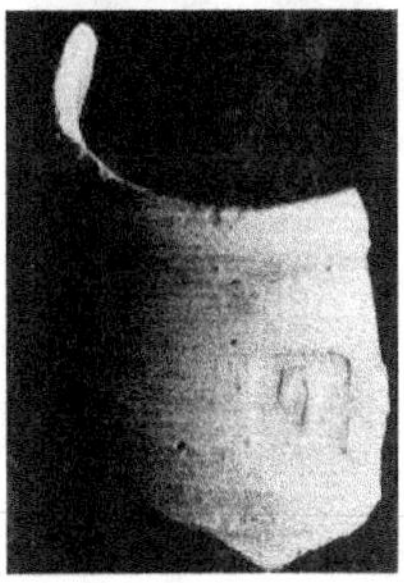

h1093

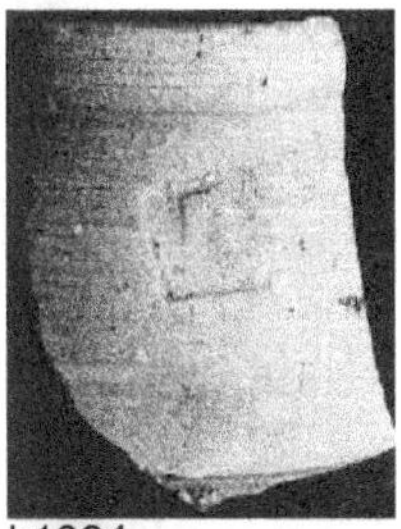
h1094

h1097

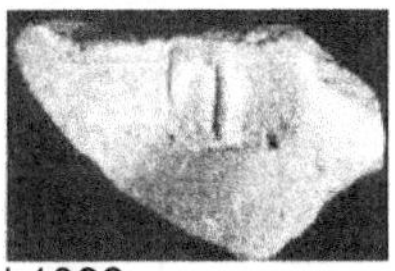
h1098

h1100A

h1100B

h1101A

h1101B

h1102A

h1102B

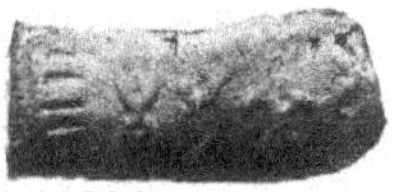
h1103A

h1103B

h1104A

h1104B

h1105A

h1105B

h1107A

h1107B

h1108A

h1108B

h1109A

h1109B

h1113A

h1113B

h1114B

h1115A

h1116A

h1116B

h1117A

h1121A

h1121B

h1122A

h1122B

h1123A

h1123B

h1124A

h1124B

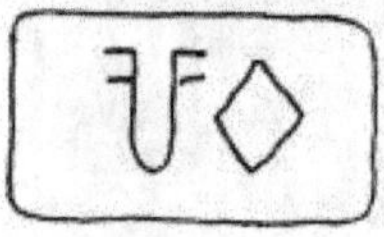
h1126A

h1126B

h1130A

h1130B

h1131A

h1131B

h1133A

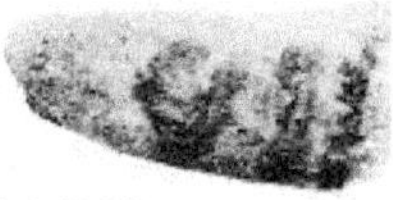

h1133B

h1134A

h1134B

h1137A

h1138A

h1138B

h1139A

h1139B

h1140A

h1140B

h1141A

h1141B

h1142A

h1142B

h1144A

h1144B

h1146A

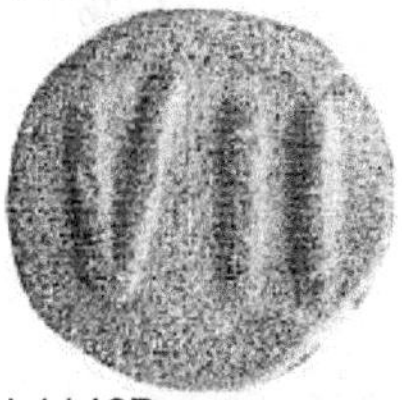

h1146B

h1148A

h1149A

h1150ABC

h1151A

h1151C

h1152A

h1152B

h1155A

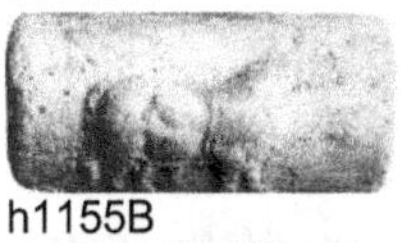

h1155B

h1158A

h1158B

h1159A

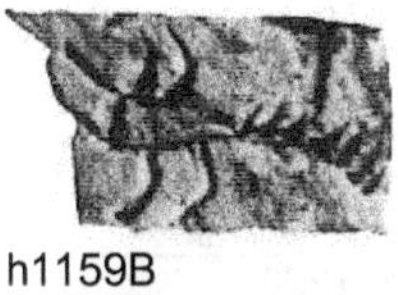

h1159B

h1160A

h1160B

h1165A

h1165B

h1166A

h1166B

h1178a

h1178b

h1181A

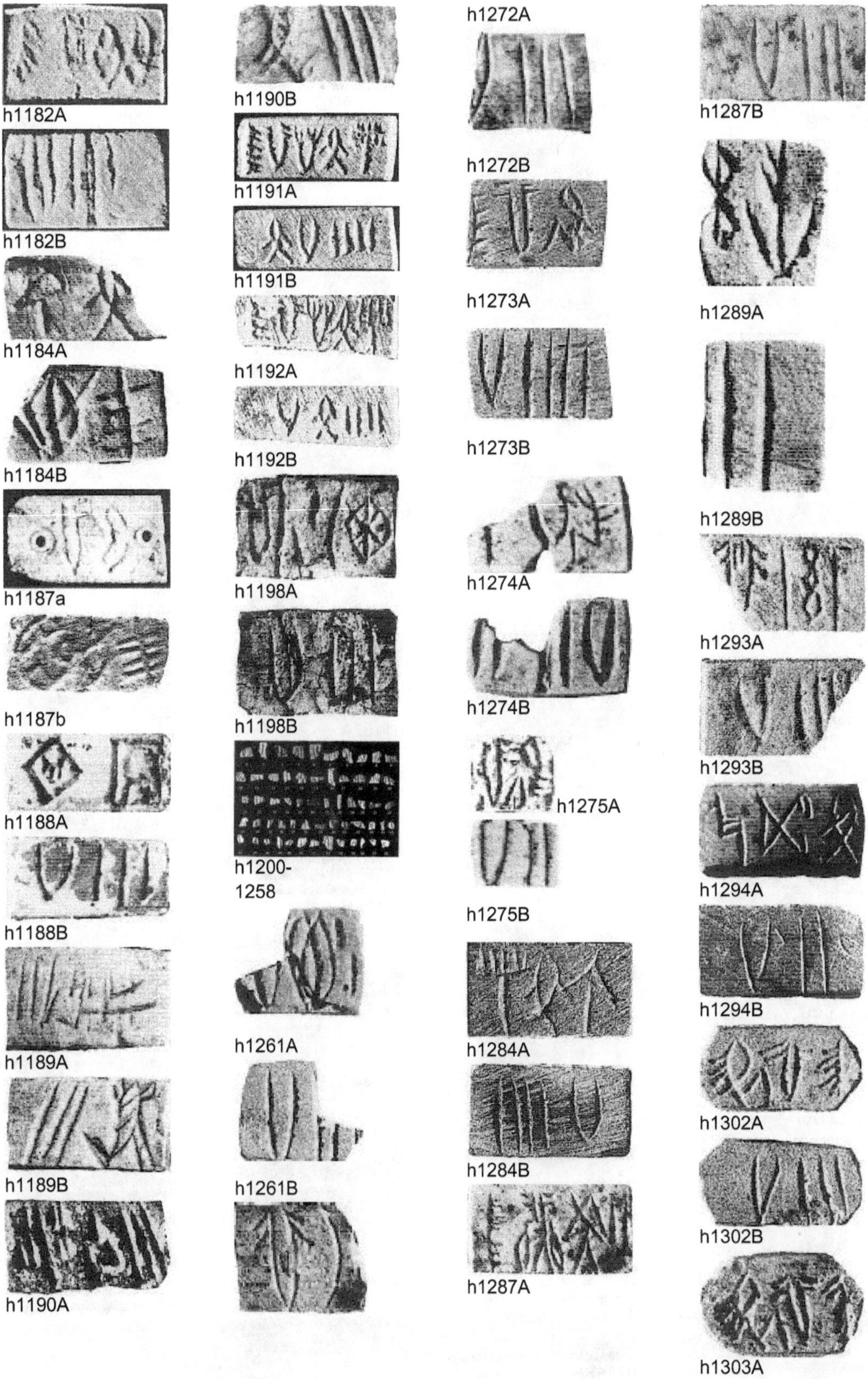

h1182A
h1182B
h1184A
h1184B
h1187a
h1187b
h1188A
h1188B
h1189A
h1189B
h1190A
h1190B
h1191A
h1191B
h1192A
h1192B
h1198A
h1198B
h1200-1258
h1261A
h1261B
h1272A
h1272B
h1273A
h1273B
h1274A
h1274B
h1275A
h1275B
h1284A
h1284B
h1287A
h1287B
h1289A
h1289B
h1293A
h1293B
h1294A
h1294B
h1302A
h1302B
h1303A

h1303B

h1304A

h1304B

h1308a

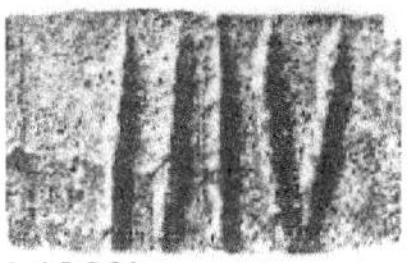
h1308b

h1309A

h1309B

h1313A

h1313B

h1319A

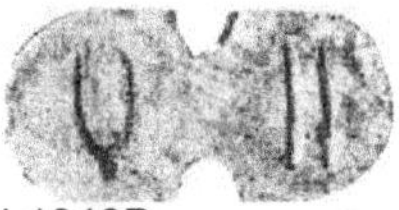
h1319B

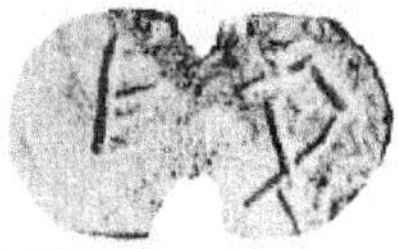
h1320A

h1320B

h1321A

h1321B

h1325A

h1325b

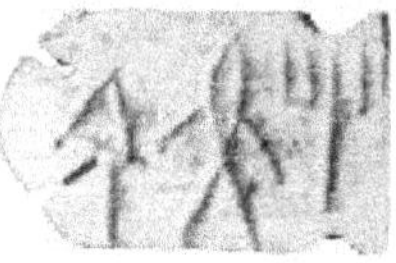
h1326A

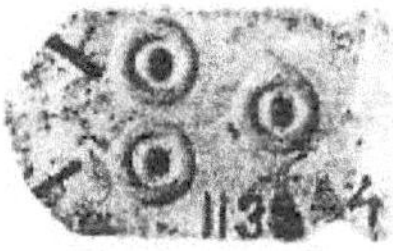
h1326B

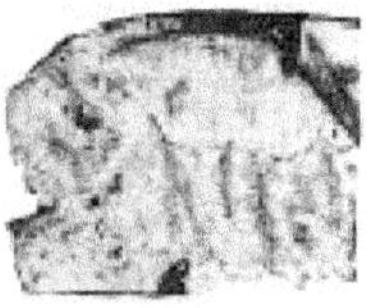
h1329A

h1329B

h1330A

h1330B

h1331A

h1331B

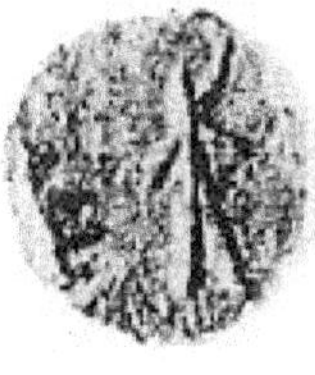
h1332A

h1332B

h1342A

h1342B

h1342C

h1344A

h1344B

h1345A

h1345B

h1345C

h1347A

h1347B

h1347C

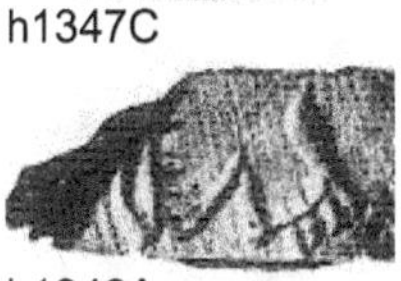
h1348A

h1348B

h1348C

h1350A

h1350B

h1350C

h1353a

h1353b

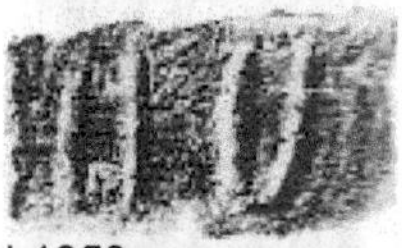
h1353c

h1354A

h1354B

h1354C

h1354D

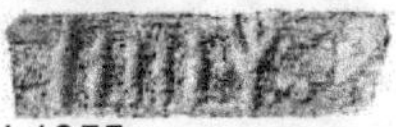
h1355a

h1355B

h1355c

h1355d

h1344C

h1357A

h1357b

h1366a

h1388A

h1392A

h1393A

h1394A

h1397A

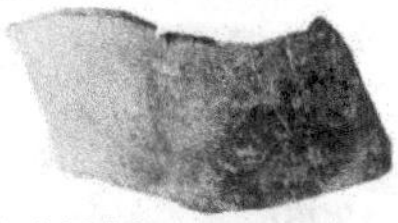
h1403A

h1404A

h1406A

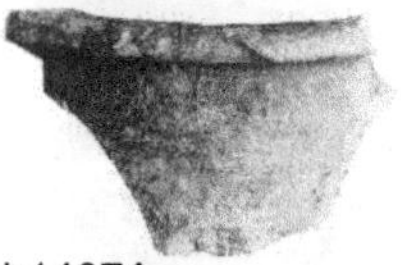
h1407A

h1408A

h1410A

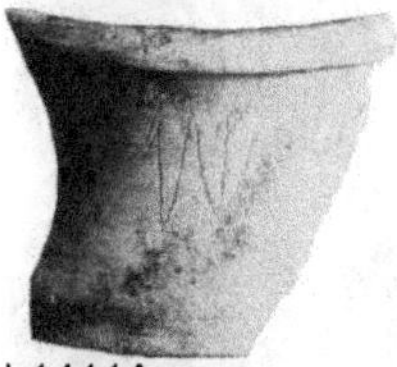
h1411A

h1412A

h1421A

h1422A

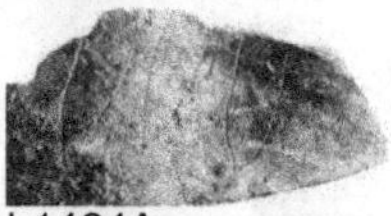
h1424A

h1431A

h1433A

h1434A

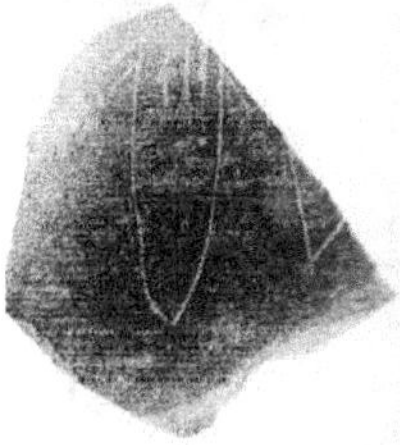

h1441A

h1444A

h1461A

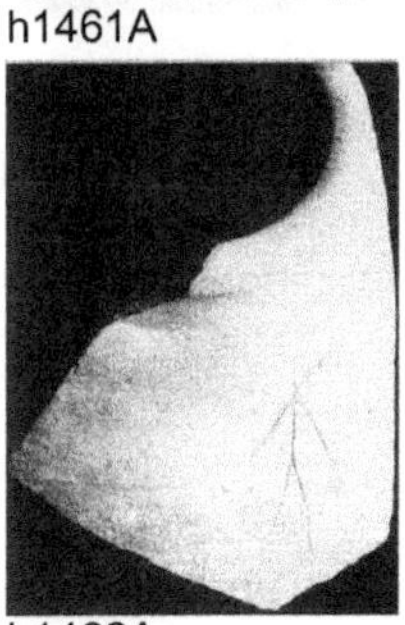

h1462A

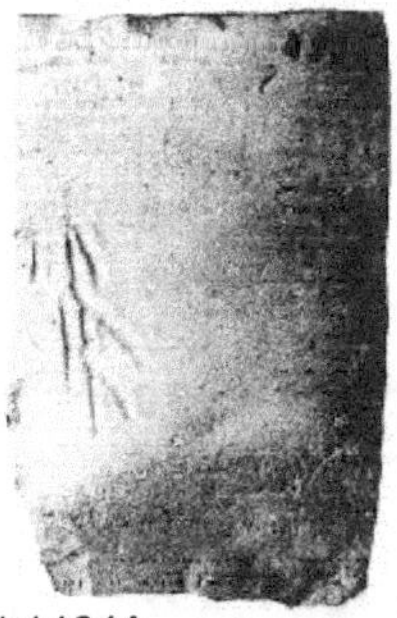

h1464A

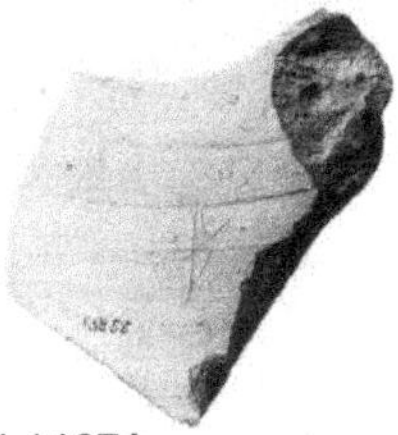

h1467A

h1468A

h1471A

h1481A

h1487A

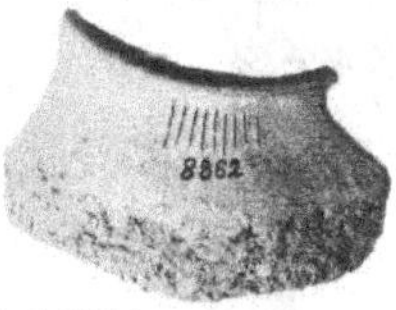


h1491A

h1501A

h1506A

h1507A

h1513A

h1516A

h1517A

h1518copperaxe

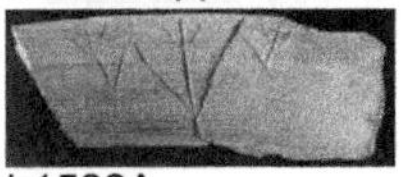

h1522A

h15533A

h1534A

h1535A

h1536A

h1537A

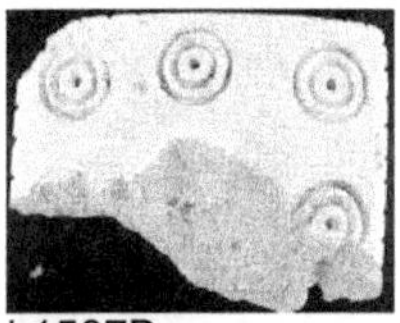

h1537B

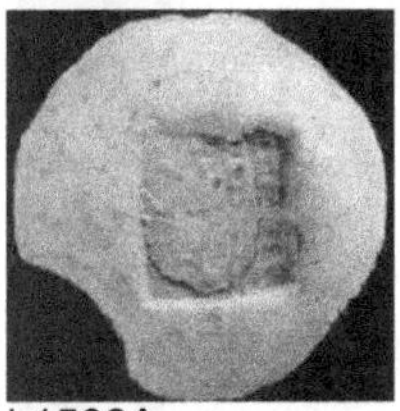

h1538A

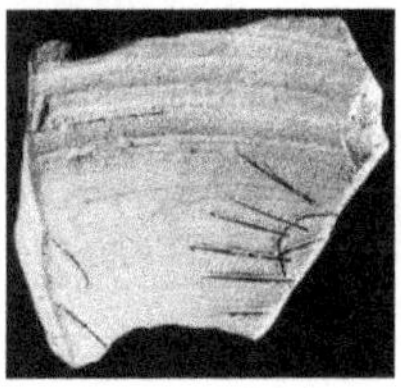

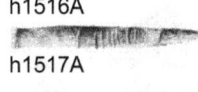

h1541A

h1544A

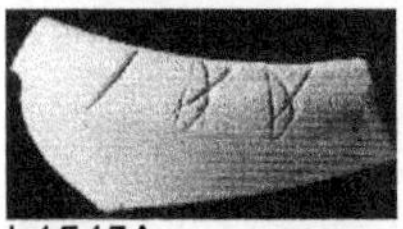

h1545A

h1547A

h1559A

h1586A

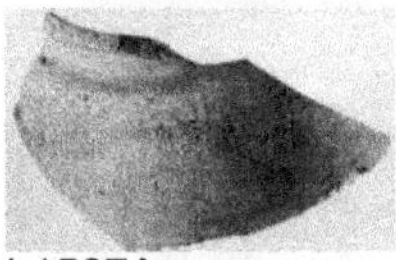

h1587A

h1657A

h1662A

h1663A

h1664A

h1666A

h1667A

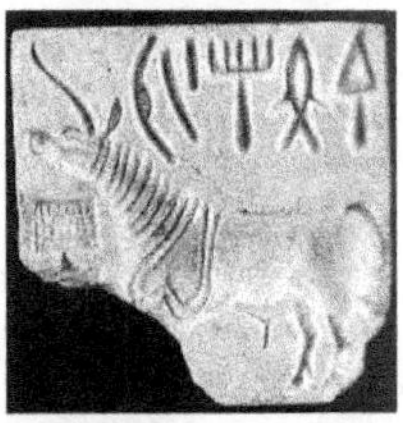

h1669A

h1670A

h1671A

h1672A

h1673A

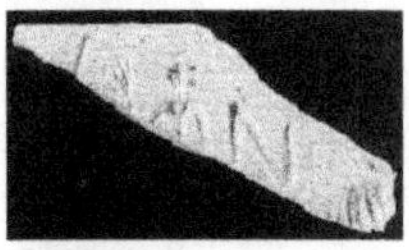

h1676A

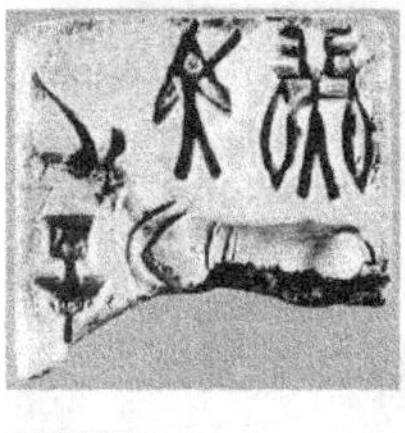

h1677A

h1678A

h1679A

h1680A

h1681A

h1682A

h1684A

h1685A

h1687A

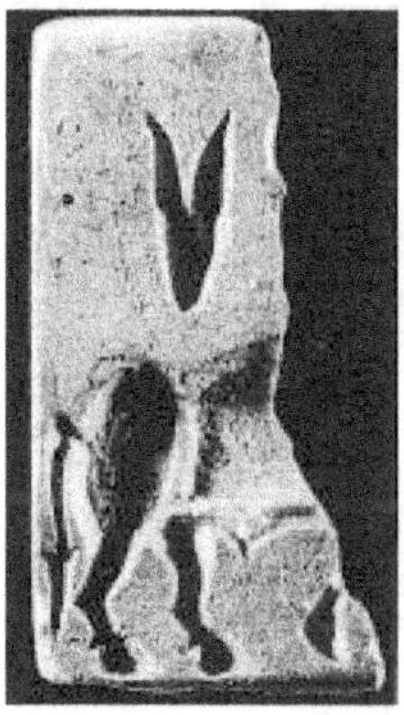

h1688A

h1690A

h1691A

h1692A

h1694A

h1695

h1696

h1697

h1698

h1699

h1700

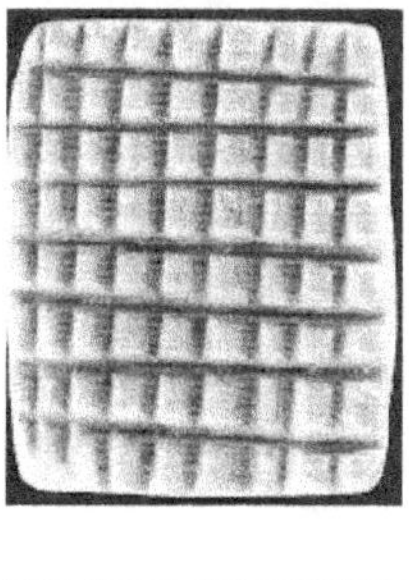

h1701

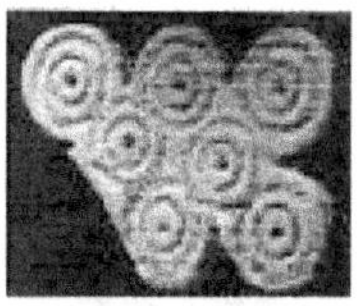

h1702

h1703

h1704

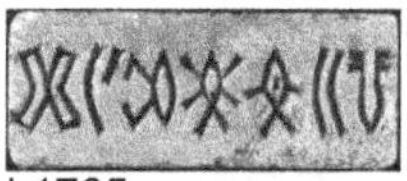

h1705

h1706

h1707

h1708

h1709

h1710

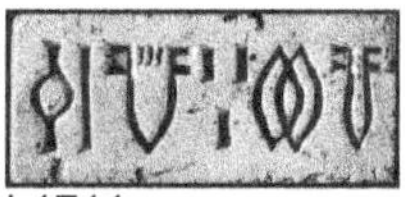

h1711

h1712

h1713

h1714

h1715

h1716

h1719A

h1719B

h1720A

h1720B

h1721A

h1721B

h1722A
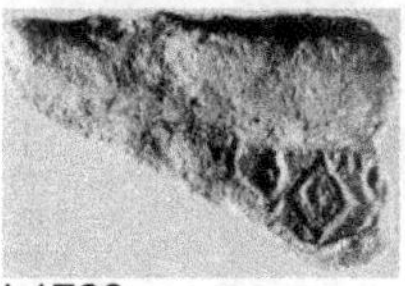
h1723

h1724

h1725A

h1726

h1727
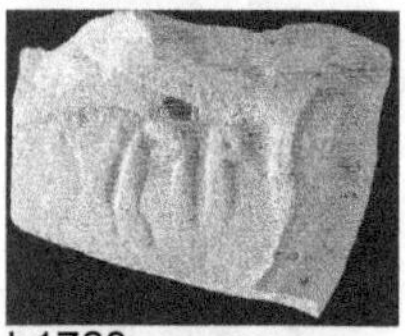
h1728
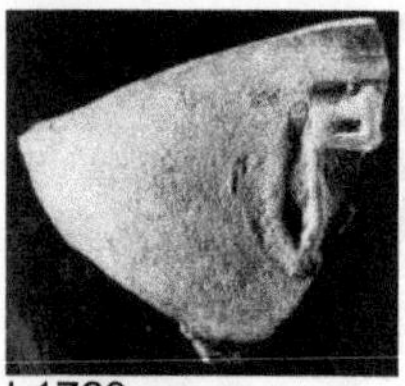
h1729

h1731

h1732
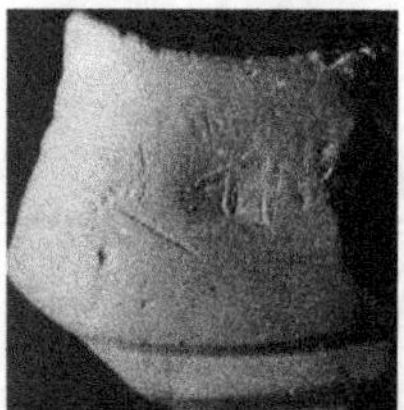
h1733

h1734

h1735

h1736

h1737

h1739

h1740

h1742

h1743

h1744
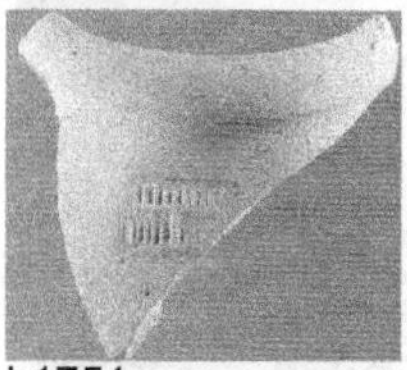
h1751
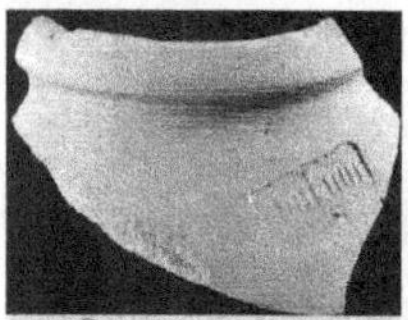
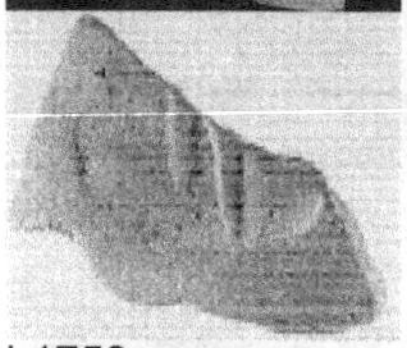
h1753

h1756

h1757

h1758

h1759

h1760

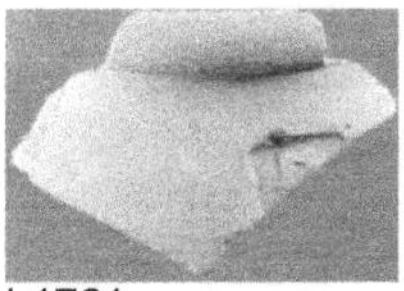
h1761

h1762

h1767A

h1767B

h1768A

h1768B

h1770A

h1770B

h1771A

h1771B

h1772A

h1772B

h1773A

h1773B

h1774A

h1774B

h1775A

h1775B

h1776A

h1776B

h1777A

h1777B

h1778A

h1778B

h1779A

h1779B

h1780A

h1780B

h1781A

h1781B

h1782A

h1783A

h1783B

h1785A

h1785B

h1786A

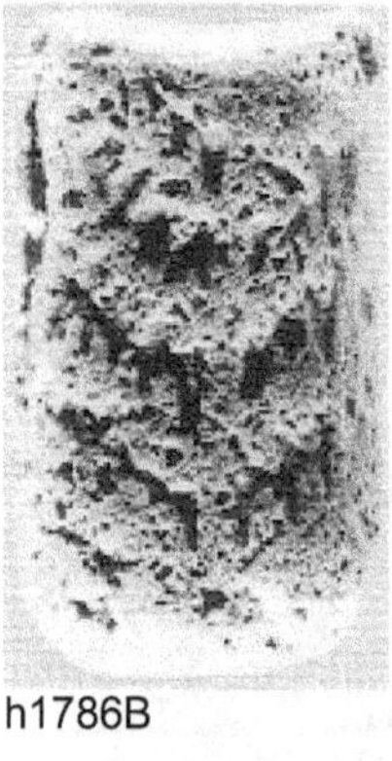
h1786B

h1787A

h1787B

h1788A

h1788B

h1791A

h1791B

h1792A
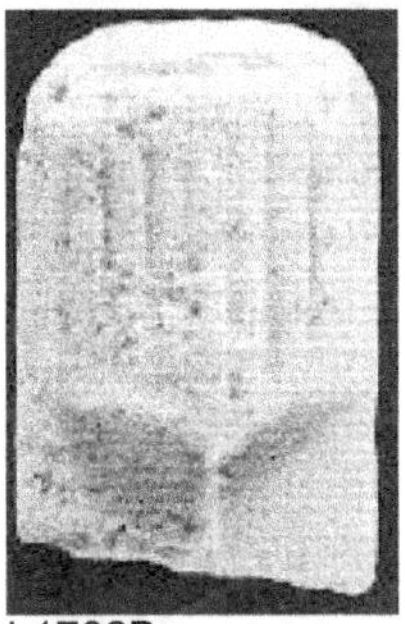
h1792B

h1793A

h1793B

h1796A

h1796B

h1797A

h1797B

h1799A

h1800A

h1800B

h1801A

h1801B

h1802A

h1802B

h1803A
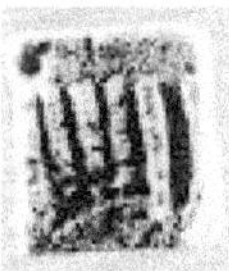

h1803B

h1804A

h1804B

h1805A
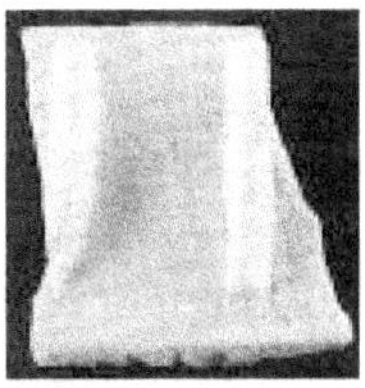
h1805B

h1806A

h1806B

h1807A

h1807B
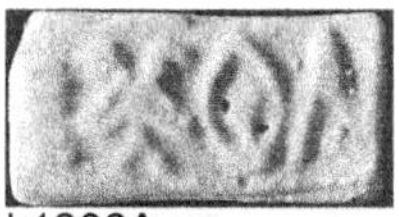
h1808A

h1809A

h1810A

h1810B

h1811A

h1811B

h1812A

h1812B

h1813A

h1813B

h1815A

h1815B

h1816A
h1816B
h1817A
h1817B
h1818A
h1818B
h1819A
h1819B
h1820A
h1820B
h1821A

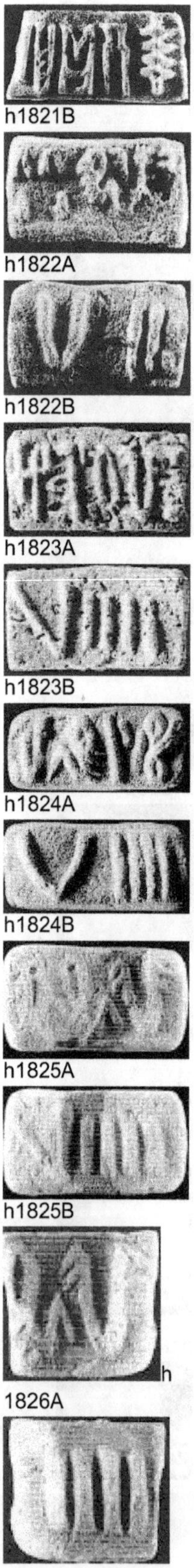

h1821B
h1822A
h1822B
h1823A
h1823B
h1824A
h1824B
h1825A
h1825B
h 1826A

h1826B

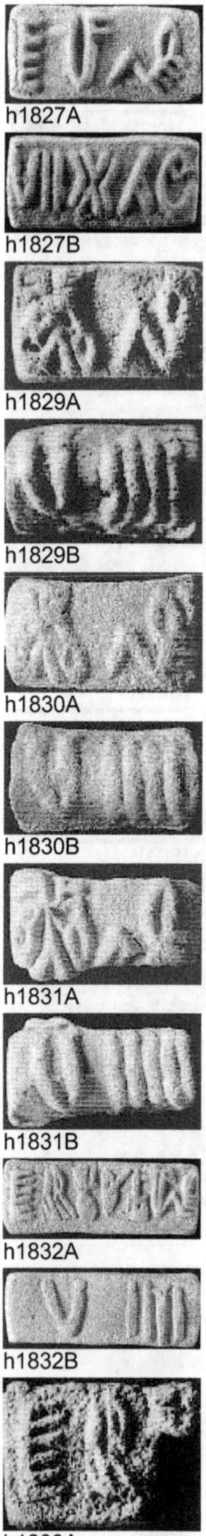

h1827A
h1827B
h1829A
h1829B
h1830A
h1830B
h1831A
h1831B
h1832A
h1832B
h1833A

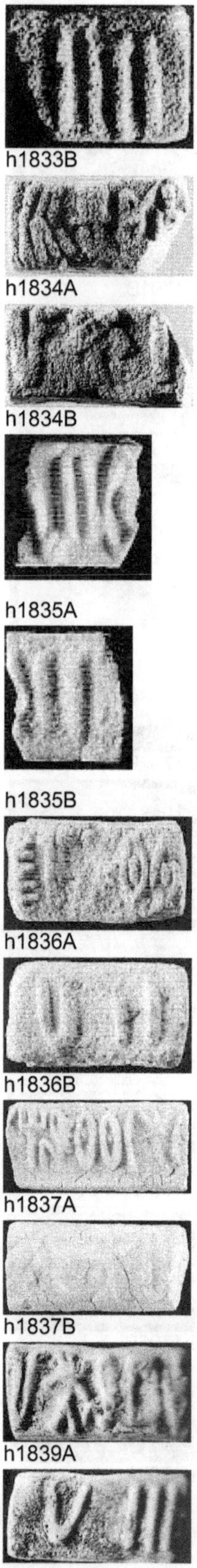

h1833B
h1834A
h1834B
h1835A
h1835B
h1836A
h1836B
h1837A
h1837B
h1839A

h1839B

h1840A

h1840B

h1841A

h1841B

h1842A
h1842B

h1843A

h1843B

h1844A

h1844B

h1845A

h1845B

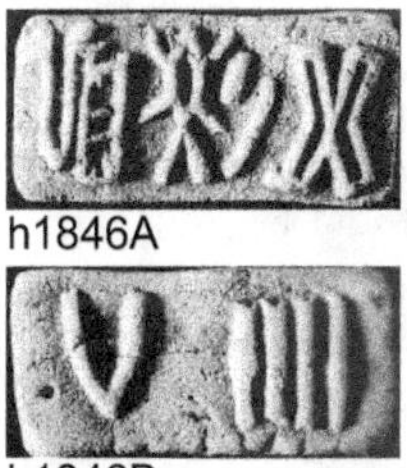
h1846A
h1846B

h1848A

h1848B

h1849A

h1849B

h1850A

h1850B

h1851A

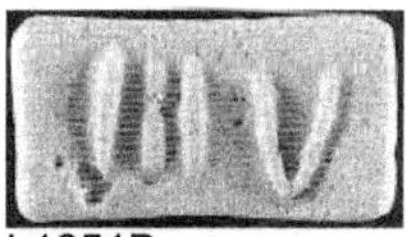
h1851B

h1853A

h1853B

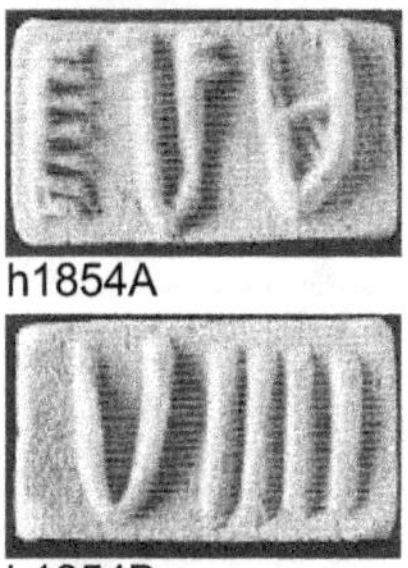
h1854A
h1854B

h1856A

h1856B

h1857A

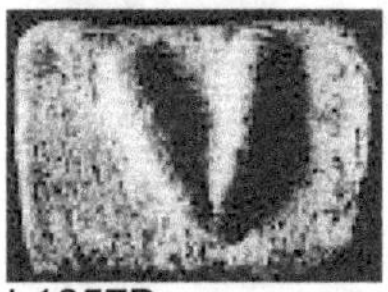
h1857B

h1858A

h1858B

h1859A

h1859B

h1860A

h1860B

h1861A

h1861B

h1862A

h1862B

h1863A

h1863B

h1864A

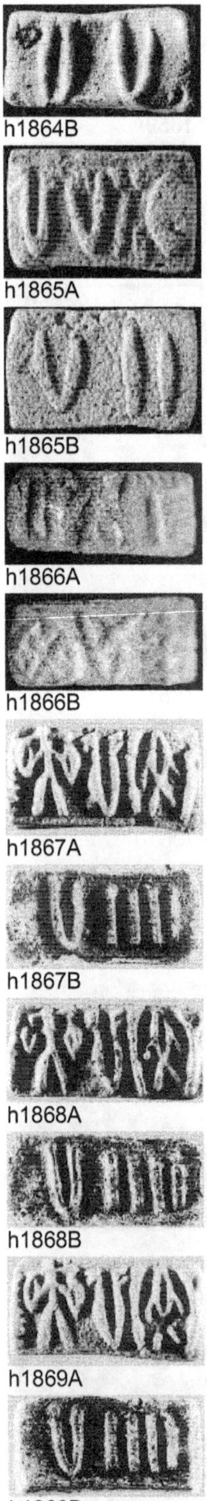

h1864B
h1865A
h1865B
h1866A
h1866B
h1867A
h1867B
h1868A
h1868B
h1869A
h1869B

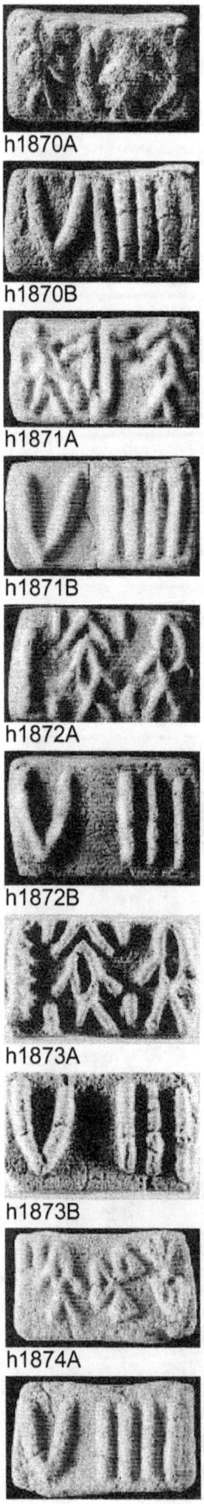

h1870A
h1870B
h1871A
h1871B
h1872A
h1872B
h1873A
h1873B
h1874A

h1874B

h1875A
h1875B
h1876A
h1876B
h1877A
h1877B
h1878A
h1878B

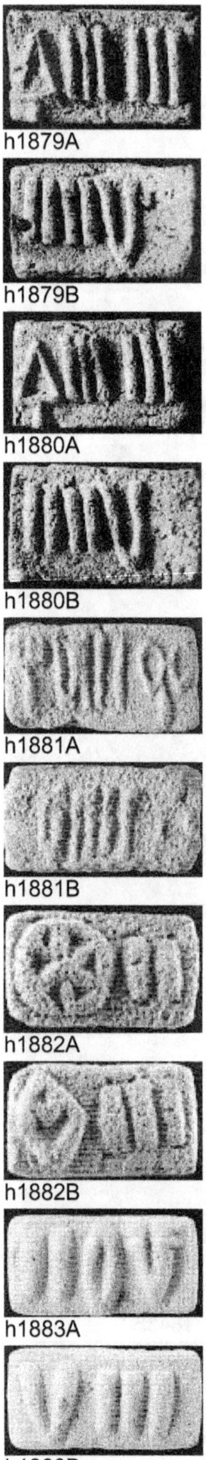

h1879A
h1879B
h1880A
h1880B
h1881A
h1881B
h1882A
h1882B
h1883A
h1883B

h1886A

h1886B

h1887A

h1887B

h1892A

h1892B

h1893A

h1893B

h1895A

h1895B

h1896A

h1896B

h1897A

h1897B

h1898A

h1898B

h1899A

h1899B

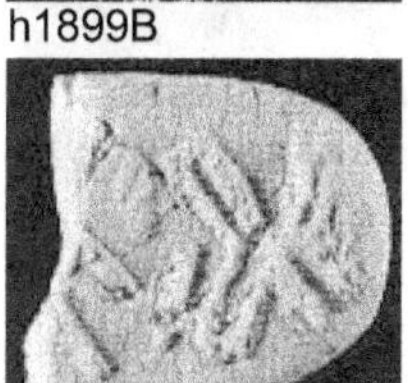
h1900A

h1900B

h1901A

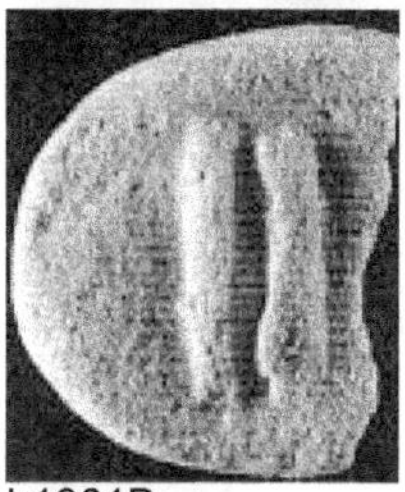
h1901B

h1902A

h1902B

h1903A

h1903B

h1904A

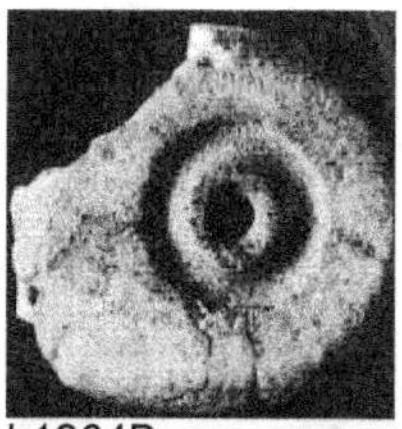
h1904B

h1905A

h1905B

h1906A

h1907A

h1907B

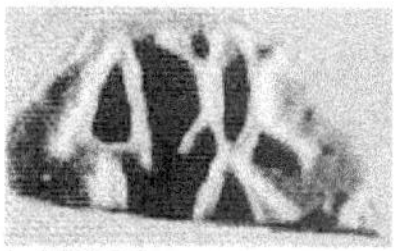
h1908A

h1908B

h1909A

h1909B

h1910A

h1910B

h1911A

h1911B

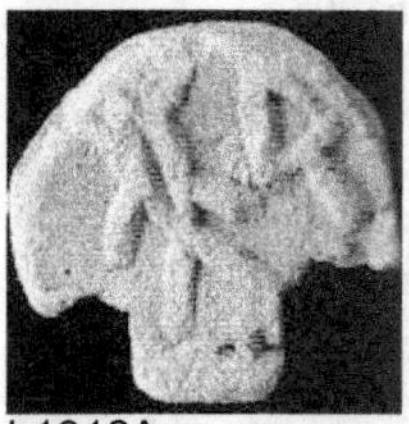

h1912A

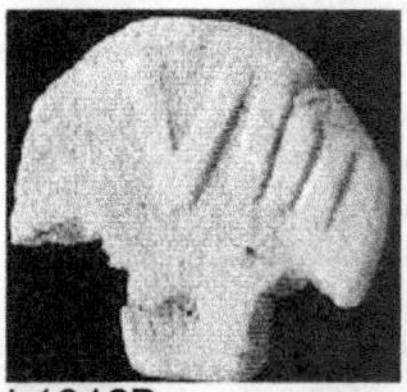

h1912B

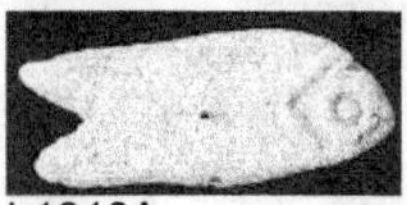

h1913A

h1913B

h1914A

h1914B

h1915A

h1915B

h1916A

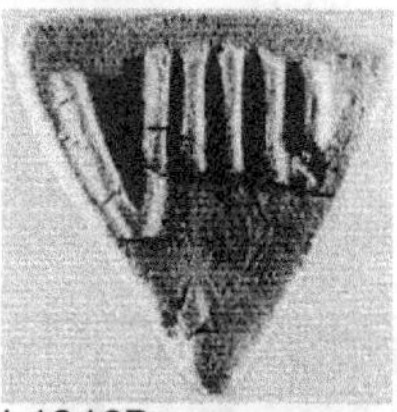

h1916B

h1917A

h1917B

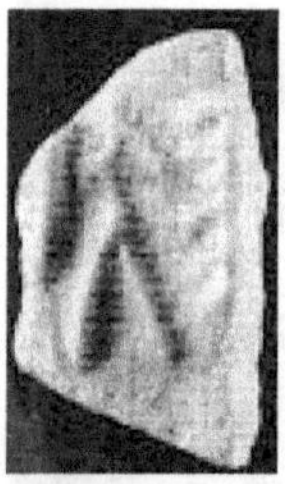

h1918A

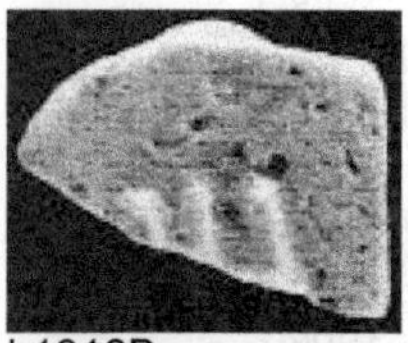

h1918B

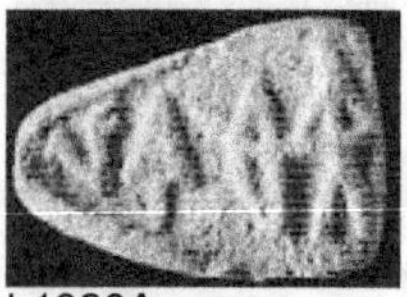

h1920A

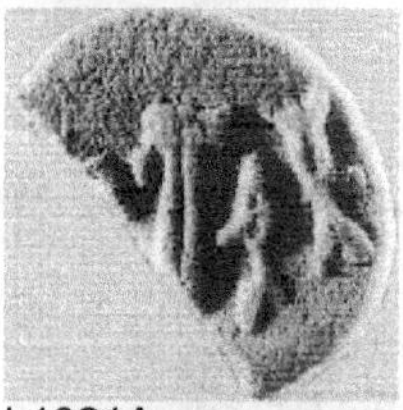

h1921A

h1921B

h1922A

h1922B

h1923A

h1923B

h1924A

h1924B

h1925A

h1925B

h1926A

h1927A
h1929A
h1929B
h1929C
h1930A
h1930B
h1930C
h1931A
h1931B
h1931C
h1932A

h1932B
h1932C
h1933A
h1933B
h1933C
h1934A
h1934B
h1934C
h1935A
h1935B
h1935C
h1936A
h1936B
h1936C

h1937A
h1937B
h1937C
h1938A
h1938B
h1938C
h1939A
h1939B
h1939C
h1940A
h1940B
h1940C

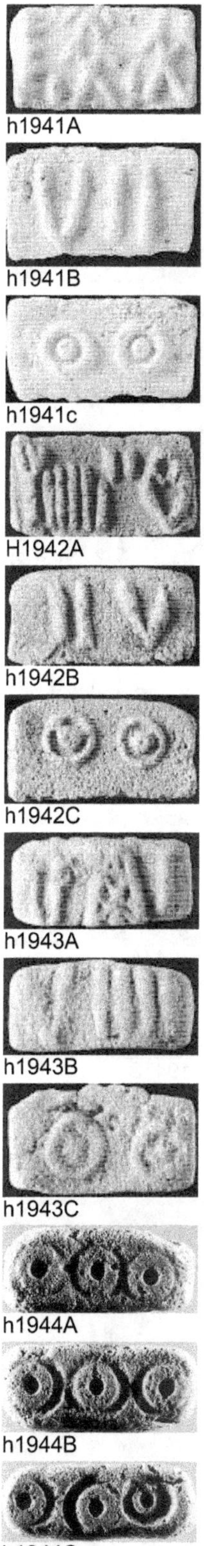

h1941A
h1941B
h1941c
H1942A
h1942B
h1942C
h1943A
h1943B
h1943C
h1944A
h1944B
h1944C

h1945A

h1945B

h1945C

h1946A

h1946B

h1946C

h1947A

h1947B

h1947C

h1950A

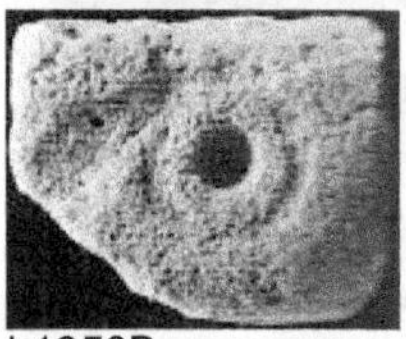
h1950B

h1950C

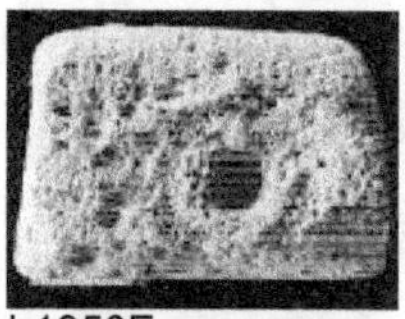
h1950E

h1951A

h1951B

h1953A

h1953B

h1955A

(bird+fish)

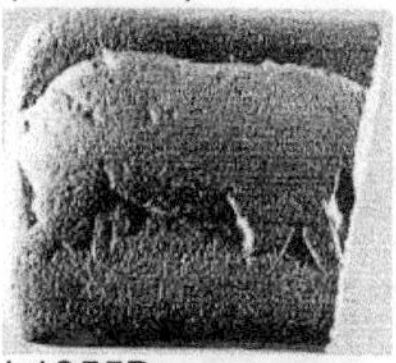
h1955B

h1958A

h1958B

h1959

h1961A

h1961B

h1962A

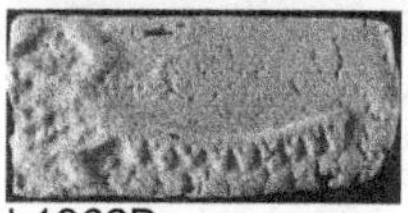
h1962B

h1963A

h1963B

h1964A

h1964B

h1966A

h1966B

h1967A

h1967B

h1968A

h1968B

h1969A

h1969B

h1970A

h1970B

h1971A

h1971B

h1972A

h1972B

h1973A

h1973B

h1974A

h1974B

h1975A

h1975B

h1976A

h1976B

h1977A

h1977B

h1978A

h1978B

h1979A

h1979B

h1980A

h1981B

h1981A

h1981B

h1985A

h1985B

h1987A

H1987B

h1988A, h1989A, h1990A

h1988B, h1989B, h1990B

h1991A

h1991B

h1992B

h1993A

h1993B

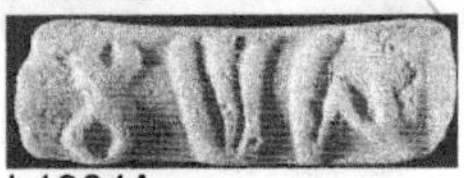

h1994A

h1994B

h1995A

h1995B

h1997A

h1997B

h1999A

h1999B

h2002A

h2003Ah

h2003B

h2005A

h2005B

h2006A

h2006B

h2010A

h2010B

h2012A

h2012B

h2013A

h2014A

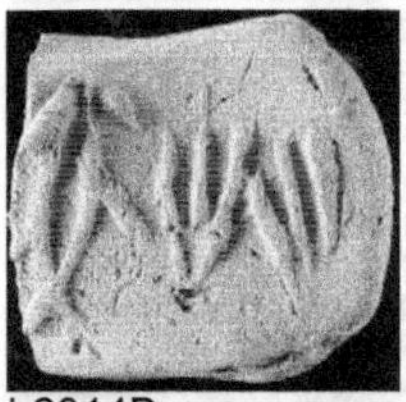

h2014B

h2015A

h2015B

h2016A

h2018A

h2018B

h2019A

h2019B

h2019C

h2020A

h2020C

h2021A

h2021B

h2021C

h2022A

h2022B

h2022C

h2023A

h2023B

h2023C

h2024A

h2024B

h2024C

h2025C

h2026A

h2026B

h2026C

h2026D

h2027A

h2027B

h2027C

h2027D

h2028A

h2028B

h2028C

h2028A

h2029A

h2029B

h2029C

h2029D

h2030A

h2030C

h2030D

h2031A

h2031B

h2031C

h2
031D

h2032B

h2032D

h2033A

h2033B

h2034A

h2034B

h2035A

h2035B

h2036A

h2036B

h2308A

h2038iB

h2039A

h2039B

h2040A

h2040B

h2041A

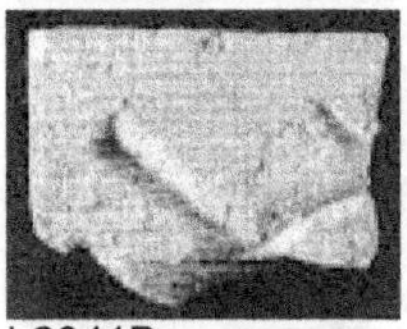

h2041B

h2043A

h2043B

h2044A

h2044B

h2045A

h2045B

h2046A

h2046B

h2047A

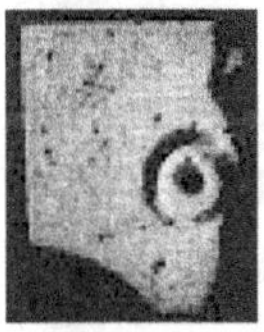

h2047B

h2048A

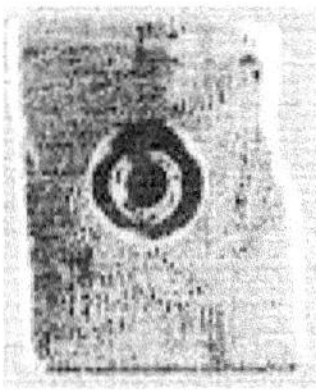

h2048B

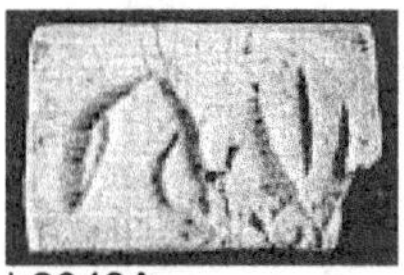

h2049A

h2049B

h2050A

h2050B

h2051A

h2052A

h2053A

h2054B

h2055A

h2055B

h2056A

h2056B

h2057A

h2057B

h2058A

h2058B

h2059A

h2059B

h2062A

h2062B

h2063A

h2063B

h2064A

h2064B

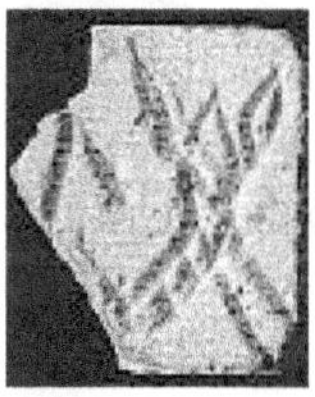

h2065A

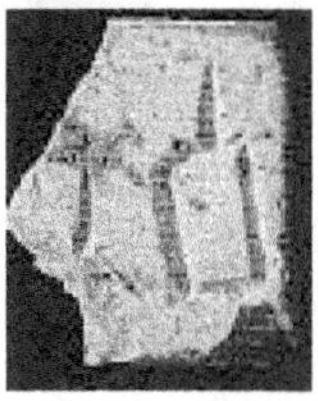

h2065B

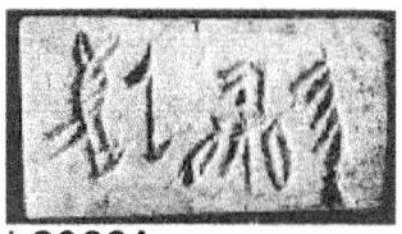

h2066A

h2066B

h2067A

h2067B

h2068A

h2068B

h2069A

h2069B

h2070A

h2070B

h2071A

h2071B

h2072A

h2072B

h2073A

h2073B

h2074A

h2074B

h2076A

h2082A

h2082B

h2083A

h2083B

h2084A

h2084B

h2085A

h2085B

h2086A

h2086B

h2089A

h2089B

h2090A

h2090B

h2091A

h2091B

h2092A

h2092B

h2093A

h2093B

h2094A

h2094B

h2095A

h2095B

h2096A

h2096B

h2097A

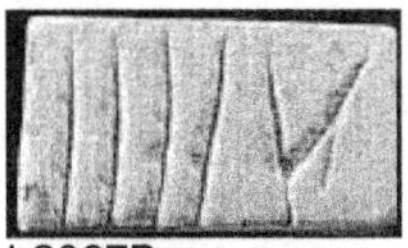

h2097B

h2098A

h2098B

h2099A

h2099B

h2102A

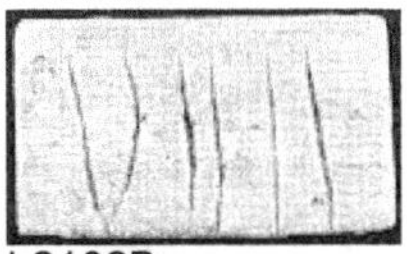

h2102B

h2104A

h2104B

h2105A

h2105B

h2106A

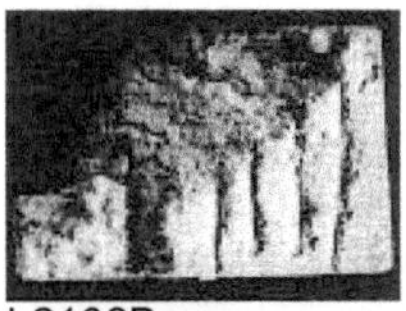

h2106B

h2107A

h2107B

h2108A

h2108B

h2109A1B2

h2109B1A2

h2110A

h2110B

h2111B

h2112A

h2112B

h2113A

h2113B

h2114A

h2114B

h2115A

h2115B

h2119A

h2119b
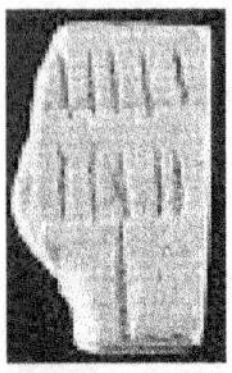
h2120A

h2120B

h2121A

h2121B

h2123A

h2123B
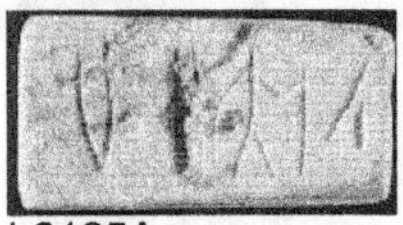
h2125A

h2125B

h2127A

h2127B

h2128A

h2128B

h2129A

h2129B

h2130A

h2130B

h2131A

h2131B

h2132A

h2132B

h2133A

h2133B

h2134A

h2134B

h2135A

h2136A

h2137A
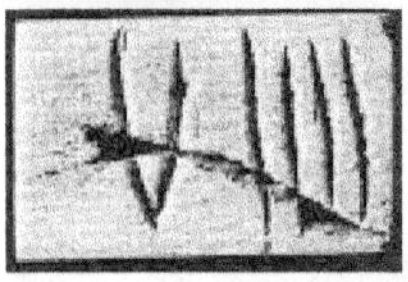

h2137B

h2138A

h2138B

h2139A

h2139B

h2140A

h2140B

h2141A

h2141B
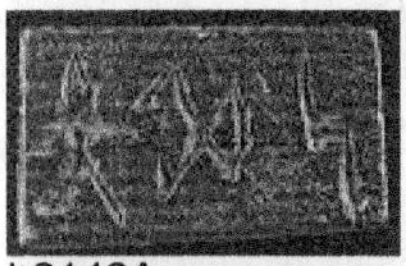
h2142A

h2142B

h2143A

h2143B

h2144A

h2144B

h2145A

h2145B

h2146A

h2146B

h2147A

h2147B

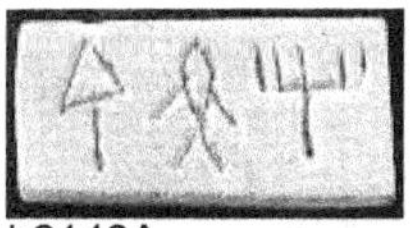
h2148A
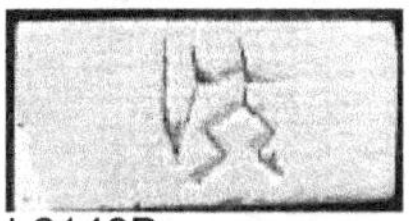
h2148B

h2149A

h2149B

h2150A

h2150B

h2151A

h2151B

h2152A

h2152B

h2153A

h2153B
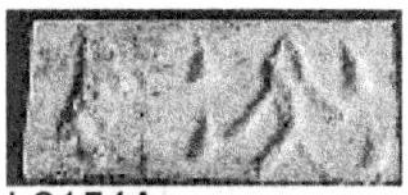
h2154A

h2154B

h2155A
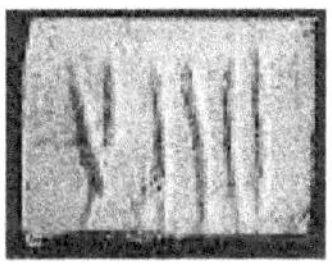
h2155B

h2156A

h2156B

h2158A
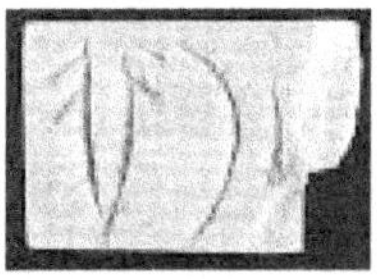
h2158B

h2159A

h2159B

h2160A

h2160B

h2173A

h2173B

h2174A

h2174B

h2175A

h2175B

h2176A

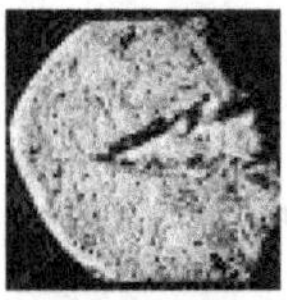

h2176B

h2177A

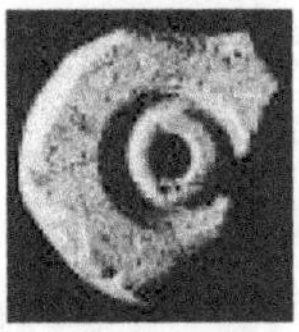

h2177B

h2178A

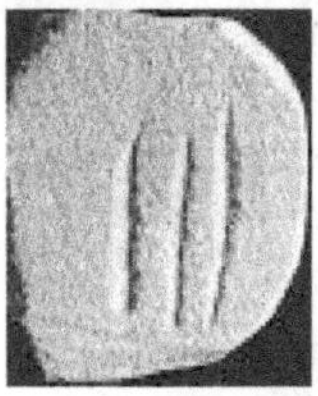

h2178B

h2180A

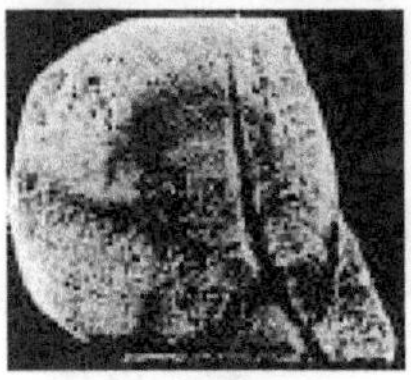

h2180B

h2181A

h2181B

h2182A

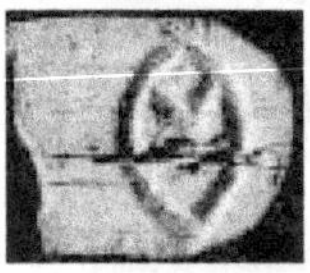

h2182B

h2183A

h2183B

h2184A

h2184B

h2185A

h2185B

h2186A

h2186B

h2187A

h2187B

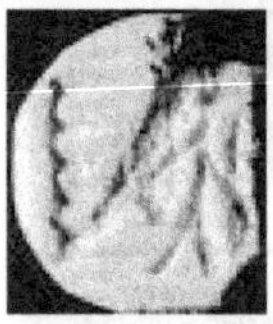

h2188A

h2188B

h2189A

h2189B

h2190A

h2190B

h2192A

h2192B

h2193A

h2193B

h2194A

h2194B

h2195A

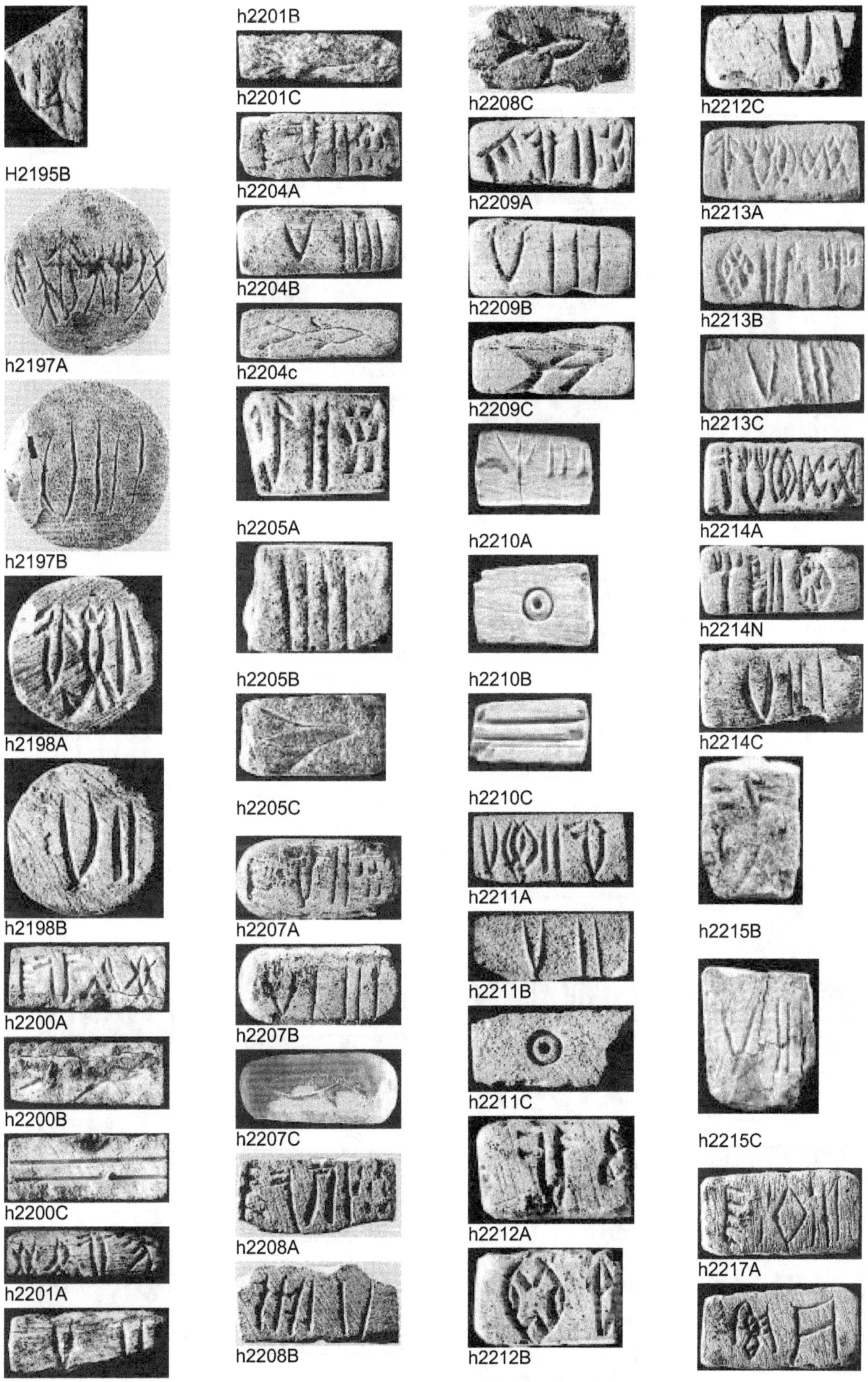

H2195B

h2197A

h2197B

h2198A

h2198B

h2200A

h2200B

h2200C

h2201A

h2201B

h2201C

h2204A

h2204B

h2204c

h2205A

h2205B

h2205C

h2207A

h2207B

h2207C

h2208A

h2208B

h2208C

h2209A

h2209B

h2209C

h2210A

h2210B

h2210C

h2211A

h2211B

h2211C

h2212A

h2212B

h2212C

h2213A

h2213B

h2213C

h2214A

h2214N

h2214C

h2215B

h2215C

h2217A

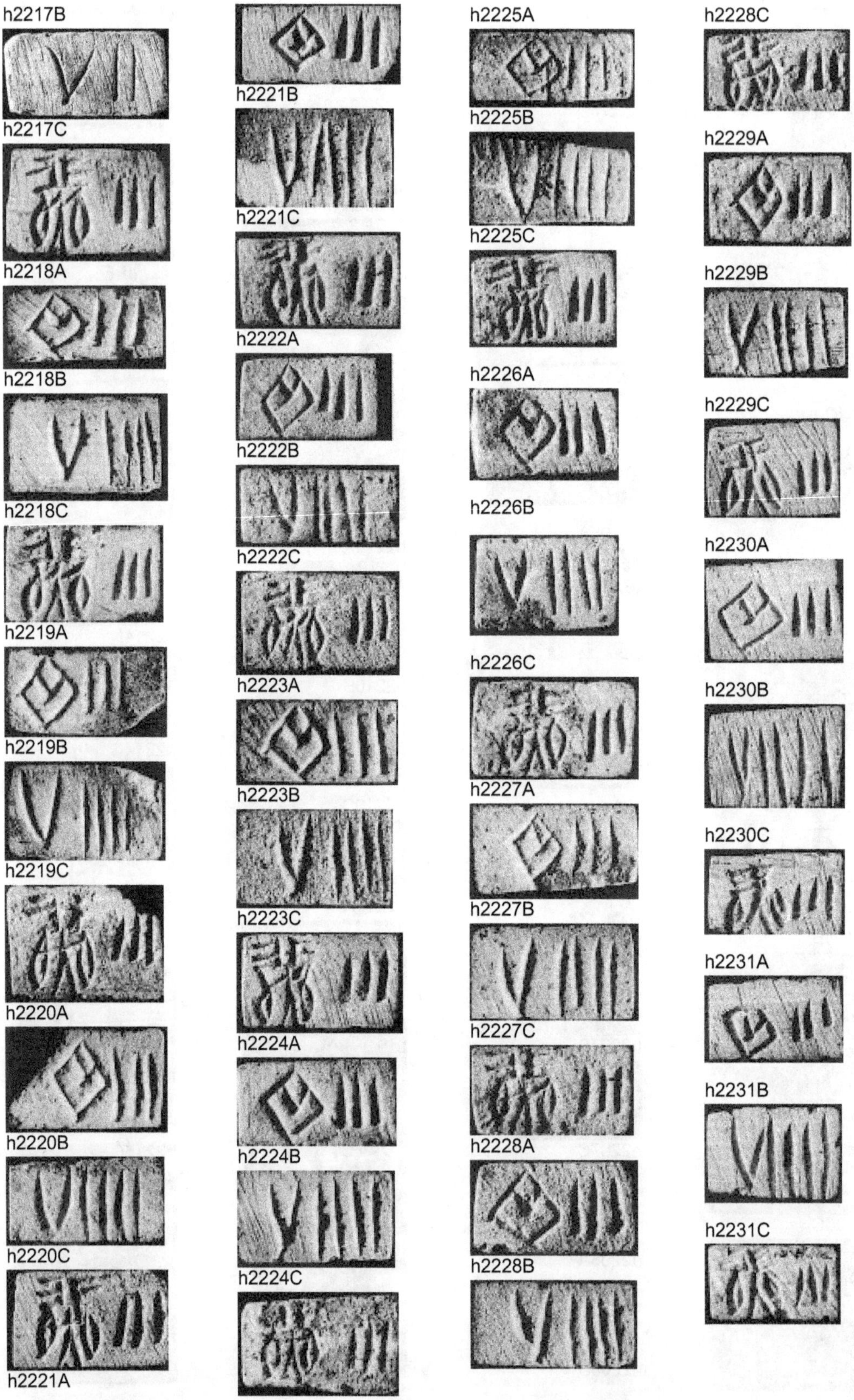
h2217B
h2217C
h2218A
h2218B
h2218C
h2219A
h2219B
h2219C
h2220A
h2220B
h2220C
h2221A
h2221B
h2221C
h2222A
h2222B
h2222C
h2223A
h2223B
h2223C
h2224A
h2224B
h2224C
h2225A
h2225B
h2225C
h2226A
h2226B
h2226C
h2227A
h2227B
h2227C
h2228A
h2228B
h2228C
h2229A
h2229B
h2229C
h2230A
h2230B
h2230C
h2231A
h2231B
h2231C

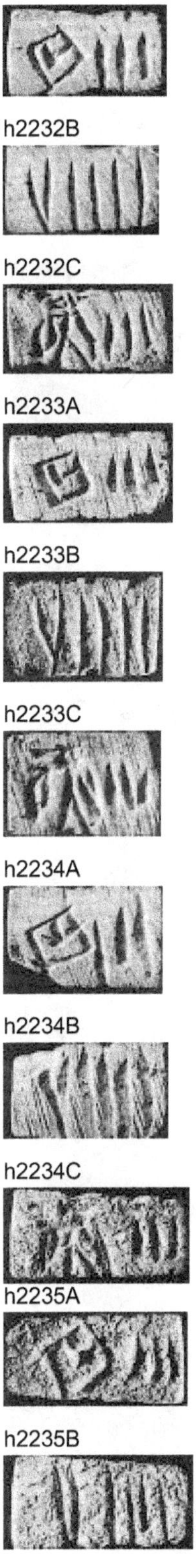

h2232A
h2232B
h2232C
h2233A
h2233B
h2233C
h2234A
h2234B
h2234C
h2235A
h2235B

h2235C
h2236A
h2236B
h2236C
h2237A
h2237B
h2237C
h2238A
h2238B
h2238C
h2240A
h2240B

h2240C
h2240E
h2241A
h2241B
h2241C
h2241E
h2243A
h2243B
h2244A
h2244B
h2244E
h2245A

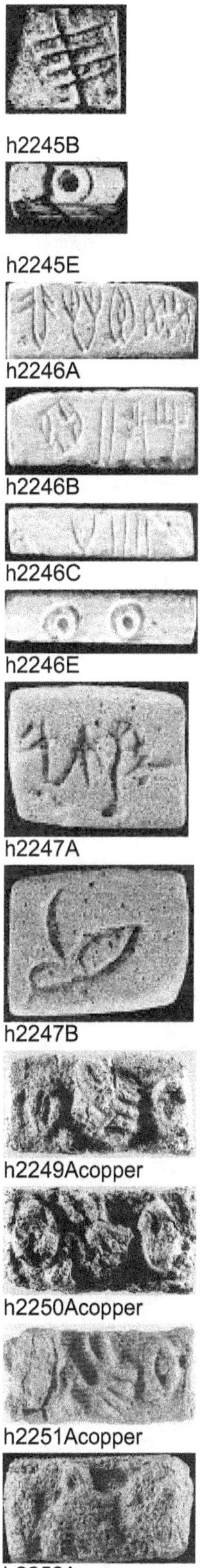

h2245B
h2245E
h2246A
h2246B
h2246C
h2246E
h2247A
h2247B
h2249Acopper
h2250Acopper
h2251Acopper
h2252Acopper

h2253Acopper

h2254Acopper

h2255Acopper

h2256Acopper

h2257Acopper

h2264A

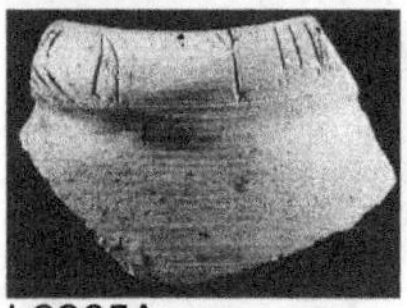
h2265A

h2270A

h2334A

h2339A

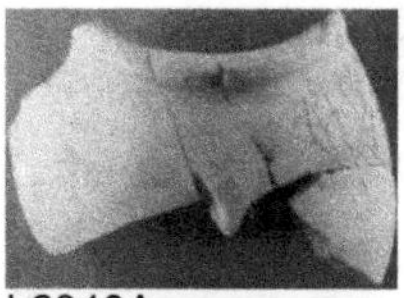
h2340A

h2341A

h2345A

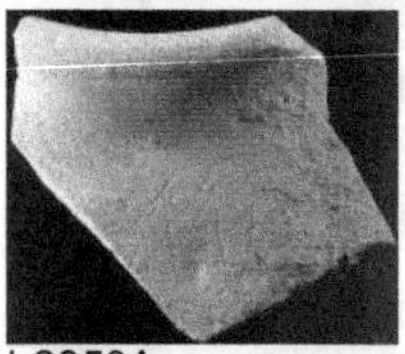
h2353A

h2354A

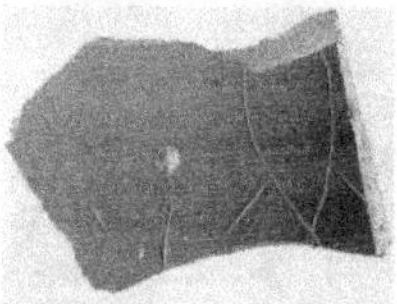
h2357A

h2358A

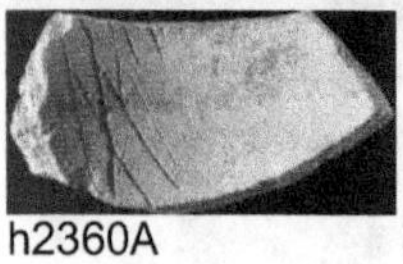
h2360A

h2367A

h2368A

h2373A

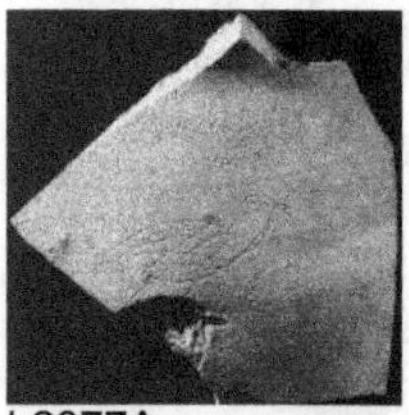
h2377A

h2380A

h2383A

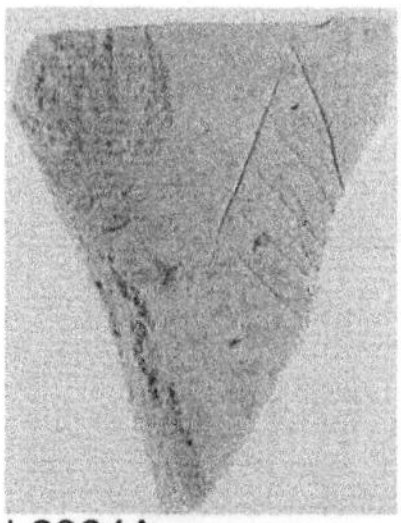
h2384A

h2390A

h2397A

j2398A

h2399A

h2400A

h2403A

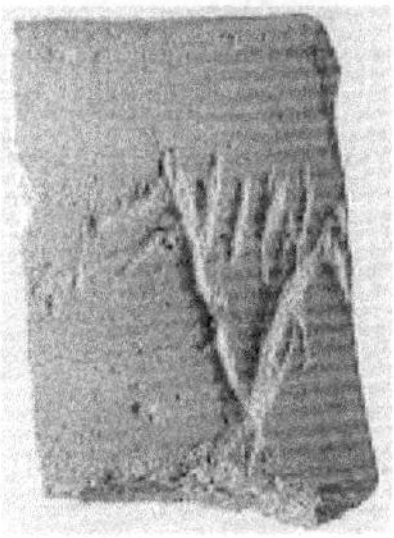
h2405A

h2548A

h2549A

h2586A

h2569Alead

h2570Abone

h2576Abangle

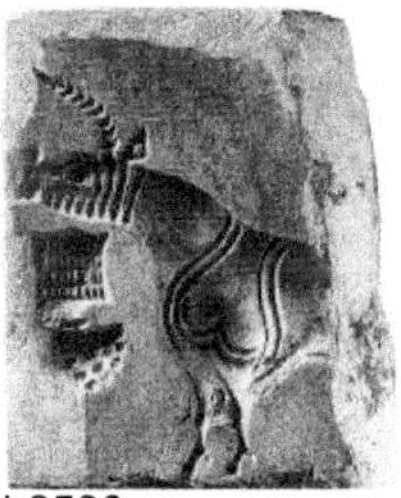
h2590

Harappa Texts (Either unmatched with inscribed objects or objects not illustrated)

4015

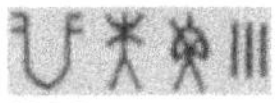
4033

4035

4046

4067

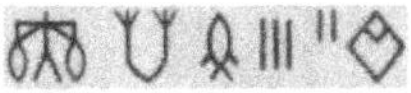
4073

4101

4108

4114

4117

4119

4134

4136

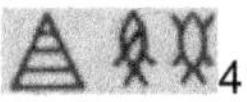
4140

4158

4164

4292

4296

4305

Pict-90: Standing person with horns and bovine features holding a staff or mace on his shoulder.

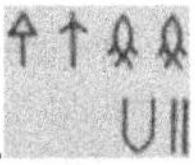

4324
4330

4334

Pict-63: Gharial, sometimes with a fish held in its jaw and/or surrounded by a school of fish.

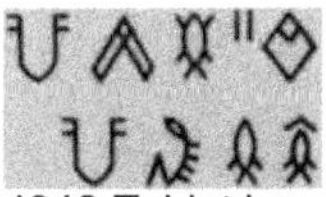
4343 Tablet in bas-relief One-horned bull

4344
4347

4356
4360
4363

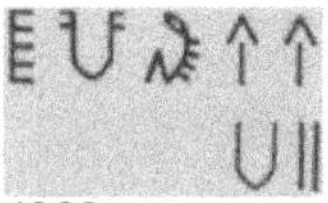
4369

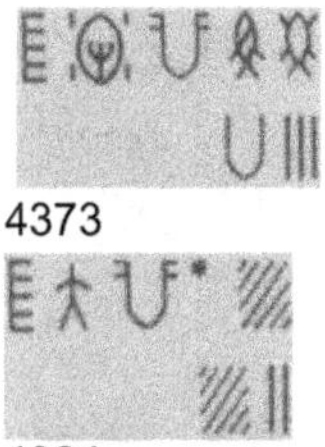
4373
4384

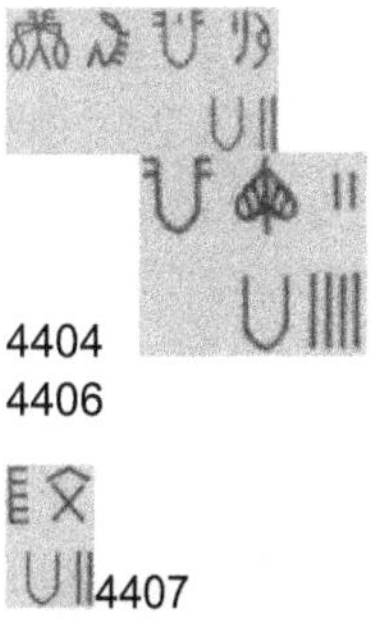
4404
4406
4407

Pict-129: Inscribed object in the shape of a double-

axe or double-shield?

4408

4422

4427

4428

4432

4435

4438

4439

4447

4448

4452

4458 4459

4462

4465

4468

4473

4476

Incised miniature tablet.

4491

4492

Incised miniature tablet.

4494

Incised miniature tablet.

4499

4500

4504 Incised miniature tablet.

4507

4508

4510

4517

4521

4523

4525

4528

4529

4532

Incised miniature tablet

4533

4534

Incised miniature tablet

4536

4538

4540

4545

4546

4547

4551

4554 4556

4566

4571

4572

4578

4580

4583

4585

4589

4593

4599

4610

4613

4633 4636

4637

4639

4643

4644

4646

4648

4649

4650 4652

4658

4668

4671

4685

4690

4691

4699

4700

4703

4704 4709

4710

4712

4713

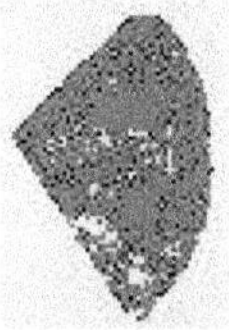

Pict-134: Motif on a pottery graffiti showing a rectangular enclosure with four marks within; the marks looks like X and V.

4714

4801

4802

4803

4804

4805

4806 4807

4808

4809

4810

4811

4813 4814

4816

4817

4819

4820

4821

4823

4824

4826

4827 4832

4833 4834

4835

4838

4839

4840

4841

4843 4844

4845

4846

4848

4849

4852

4853

4854 4856

4857

4861

4864

4865

4868

4871

4873 4874

4875 4876

4877

4878 4879

4880

4881

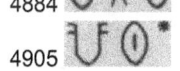

4884

4905

5001

5017

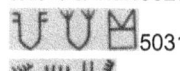

5023

5031

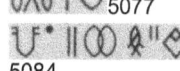

5070

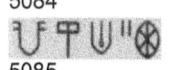

5077

5084

5085

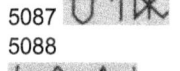

5086

5087

5088

5102

5104

5107

5115

5123

5124 5201

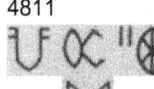

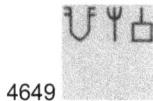

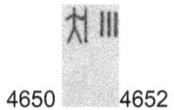

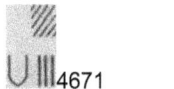

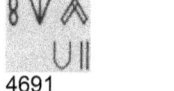

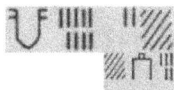

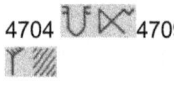

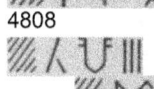

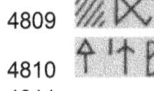

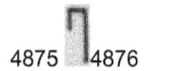

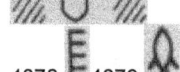

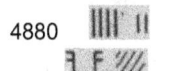

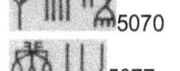

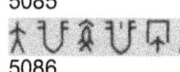

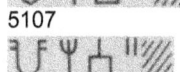

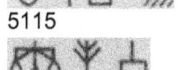

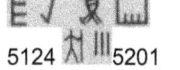

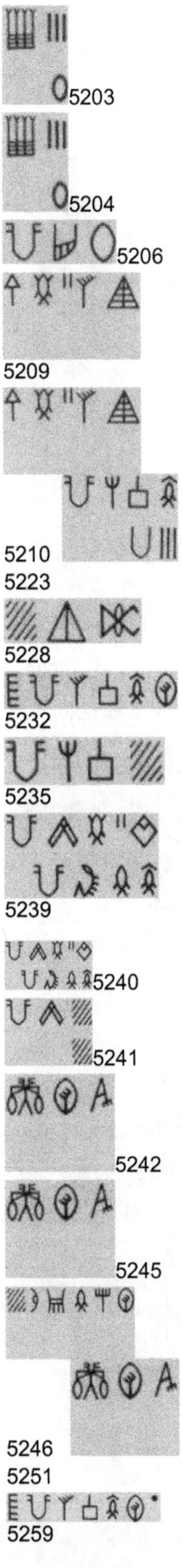

5203
5204
5206
5209
5210
5223
5228
5232
5235
5239
5240
5241
5242
5245
5246
5251
5259

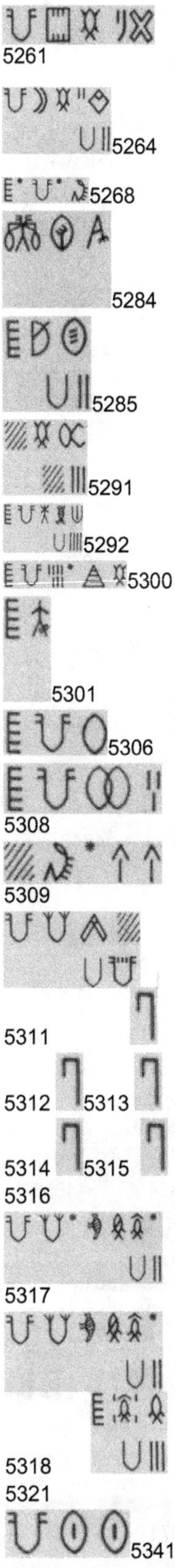

5261
5264
5268
5284
5285
5291
5292
5300
5301
5306
5308
5309
5311
5312
5313
5314
5315
5316
5317
5318
5321
5341

5403
5404
5406
5407
5408
5409
5410
5411
5414
5417
5418
5419
5422
5423

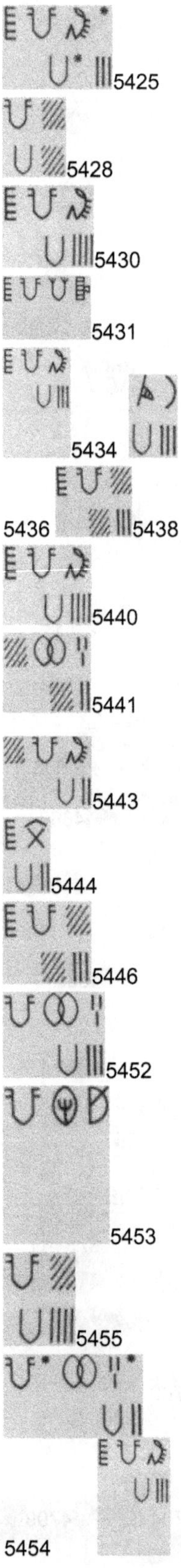

5425
5428
5430
5431
5434
5436
5438
5440
5441
5443
5444
5446
5452
5453
5455
5454

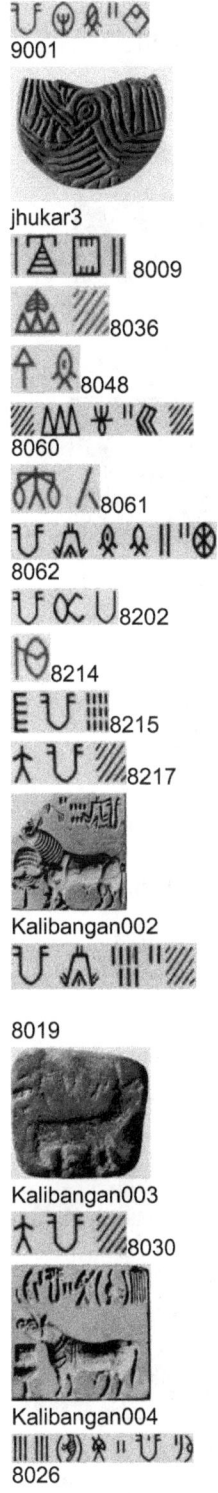

5457
5459
5469
5470
5478
5480
5481
5482
5484
5485
5486
5487
5488
5489
5490

5492
5495
5501 5504
5505
5506
5507
5508
5510
5511 5513
5514
5515
5516 5517
5518
5519
5601

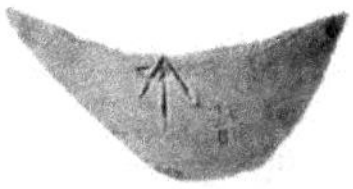
hd06

hulas

jhukar1
jhukar2

9001

jhukar3

8009
8036
8048
8060
8061
8062
8202
8214
8215
8217

Kalibangan002

8019

Kalibangan003

8030

Kalibangan004

8026

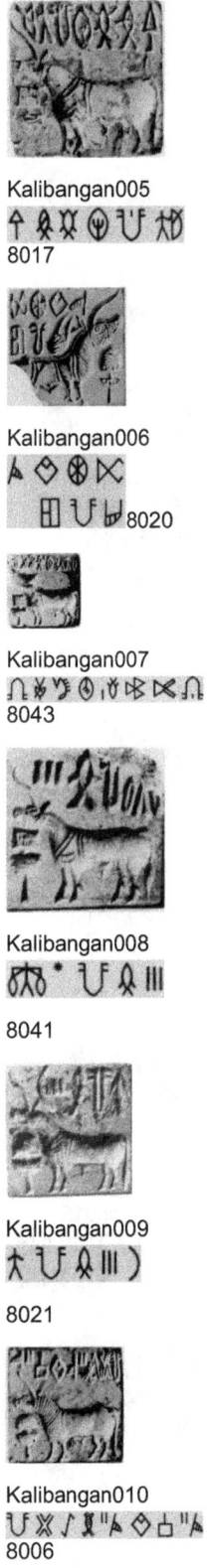

Kalibangan005

8017

Kalibangan006

8020

Kalibangan007

8043

Kalibangan008

8041

Kalibangan009

8021

Kalibangan010

8006

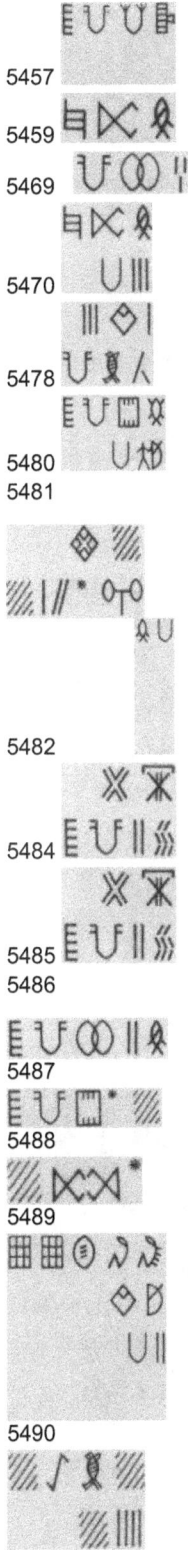

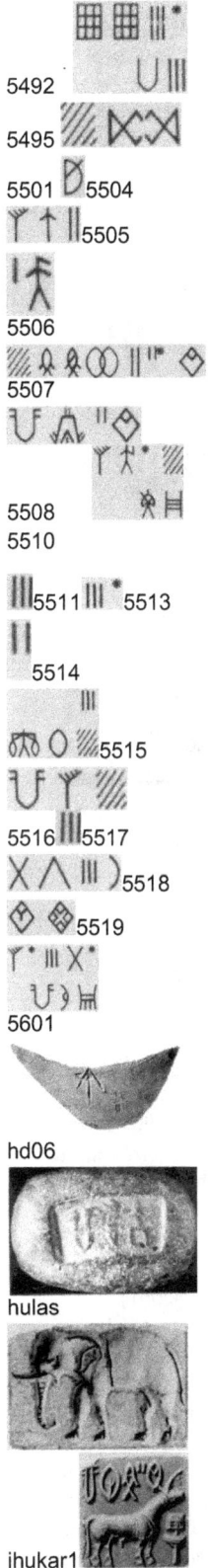

Kalibangan011

8034

Kalibangan012

Kalibangan013

8051

Kalibangan014

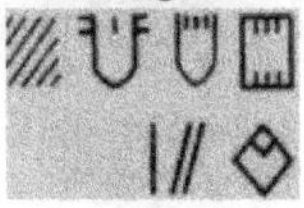

8012

Kalibangan015

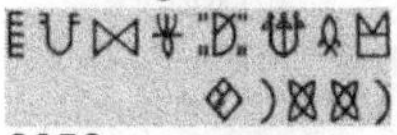

8056

Kalibangan016

8044

Kalibangan017

8027

Kalibangan018

8040

Kalibangan019

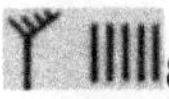

8058

Kalibangan020

8047

Kalibangan021

Kalibangan022

8008

Kalibangan023

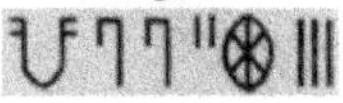

8029

Kalibangan024

Kalibangan025

8037

Kalibangan026

8071

Kalibangan027

8022

'Unicorn' with two horns! "Bull with two long horns (otherwise resembling the 'unicorn')", generally facing the standard. That it is the typical 'one-horned bull' is surmised from two ligatures: the pannier on the shoulder and the ring on the neck.

Kalibangan028

8038

Kalibangan029

8018

Kalibangan030

8002

Kalibangan031a

8007

Kalibangan032a

Kalibangan033

8025

Kalibangan034 
8052

Kalibangan035

Kalibangan036

Kalibangan037
 8042

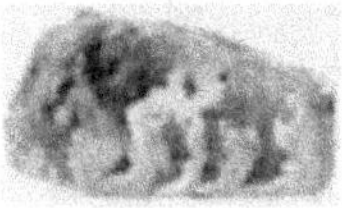

Kalibangan038

Kalibangan039
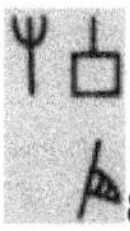 8011

Kalibangan040

8072

Kalibangan041

Kalibangan042a

Kalibangan043
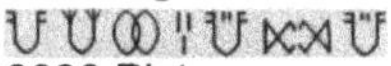
8039 Pict-59:Composite motif: body of an ox and three heads: of a one-horned bull (looking forward), of antelope (looking backward), and of short-horned bull (bison) (looking downward).

Kalibangan044
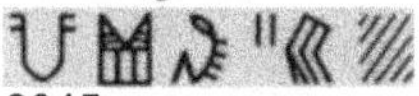
8045

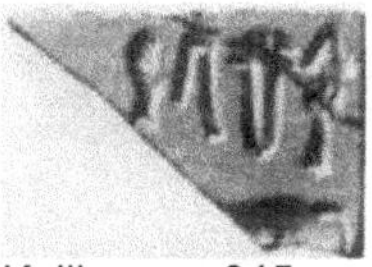

Kalibangan045

8054

Kalibangan046
 8053

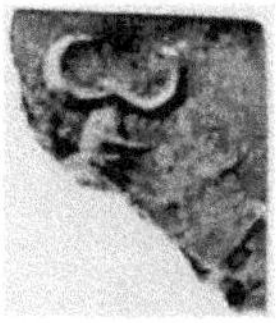

Kalibangan04
7

Kalibangan04
8

Kalibangan049
 8013

Kalibangan050c
 8031 Pict-53: Composition: body of a tiger, a human body with bangles on arm, a pig-tail, horns of an antelope crowned by a twig.

Kalibangan051
 8003

Kalibangan052
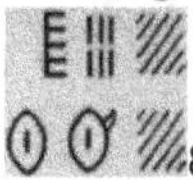 8015

Kalibangan053

Kalibangan054
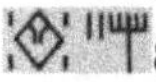 8033

Kalibangan055a
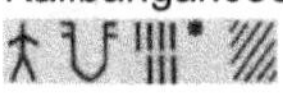
8035

Kalibangan056
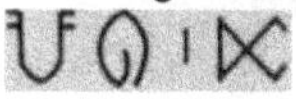
8004

Kalibangan057

Kalibangan058

Kalibangan059

8016

Kalibangan060

8059

Kalibangan061

8001

Kalibangan062

8023

Kalibangan063

8055

Kalibangan064

Kalibangan065a

Kalibangan065A6

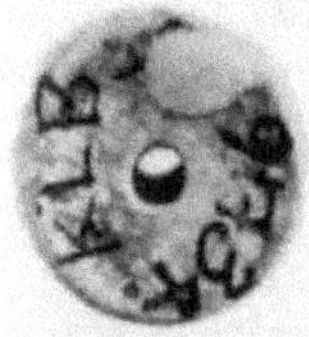
Kalibangan065E

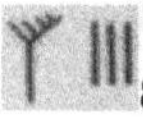
8024 Pict-104: Composition: A tree; a person with a composite body of a human (female?) in the upper half and body of a tiger in the lower half, having horns, and a trident-like head-dress, facing a group of three persons consisting of a woman (?) in the middle flanked by two men on either side throwing a spear at each other (fencing?) over her head.

Kalibangan066

8102

Kalibangan067

8121 Ox-antelope with a long tail; sometimes with a trough in front.

Kalibangan068A

Kalibangan068B

8117 [Is it a bird or an India River Otter? Could be a scorpion, a model for Signs 51

and 52 ? See variant in Text 9845 West Asia find]

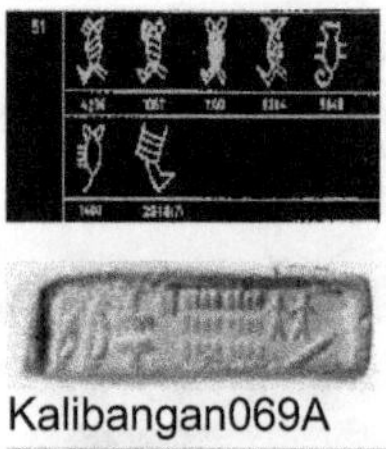
Kalibangan069A

8109

Kalibangan070A

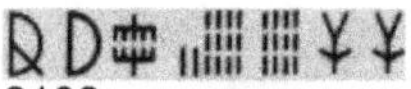
8108

Kalibangan071

8110

Kalibangan072

8111

Kalibangan073

8112

Kalibangan074

8115

Kalibangan075

8113

Kalibangan076A

Kalibangan076B

Kalibangan077A

Kalibangan077B

8118

Kalibangan078A

Kalibangan078B

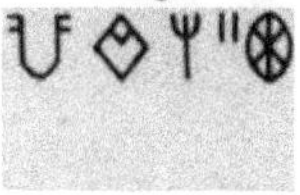

8104

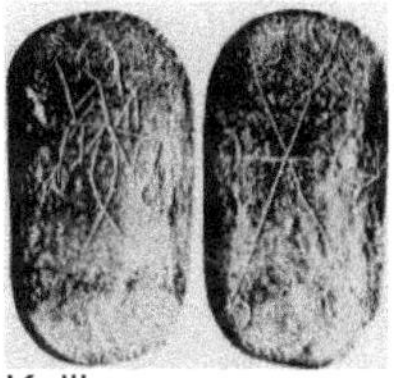

Kalibangan

079AB

Kalibangan080A

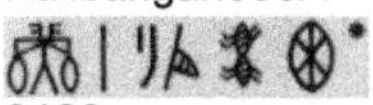

8120

Kalibangan081A

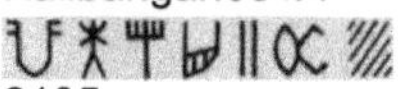

8105

Kalibangan082A

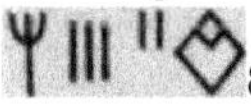
8122

Kalibangan

083A12

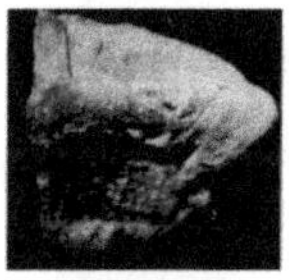

Kalibangan

084A12

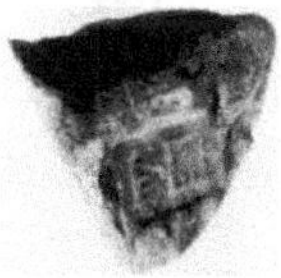

Kalibangan

084A2

8103

Kalibangan

085A12

Kalibangan085B

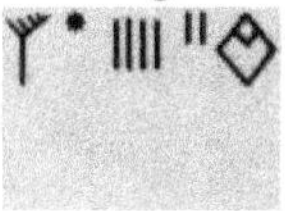

8106

Kalibangan086A1

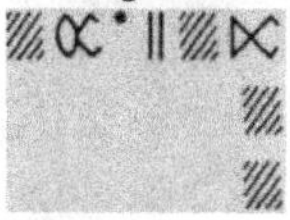
4

8114

Kalibangan087A1

2

8116

Kalibangan

088A14

Kalibangan088B

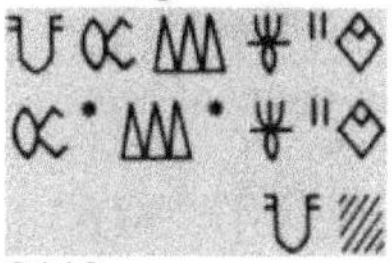

8119

Kalibangan089A1
4c

8101

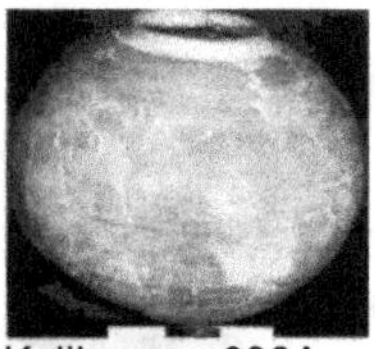

Kalibangan090A

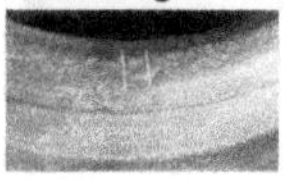

Kalibangan

090A1

Kalibangan

090A2

8202

Kalibangan091A

8212

Kalibangan092A

8210

Kalibangan093A

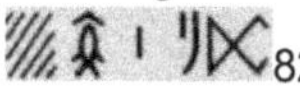
821
9

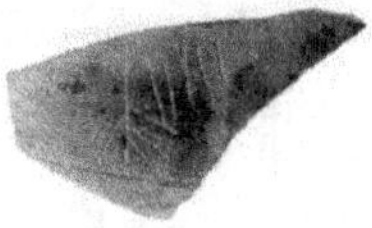
Kalibangan094A

Kalibangan095A

Kalibangan096c

8221

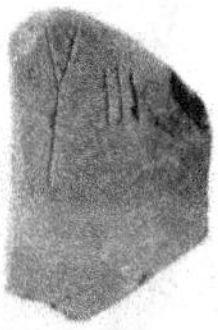
Kalibangan097A
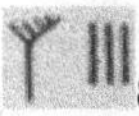
8213

Kalibangan098A
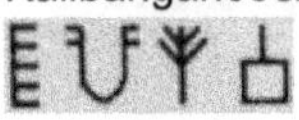
8201

Kalibangan099A
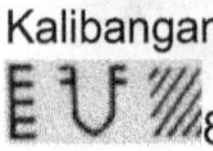
8208

Kalibangan100A

Kalibangan101A
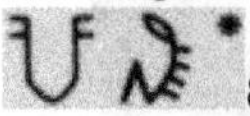
8205

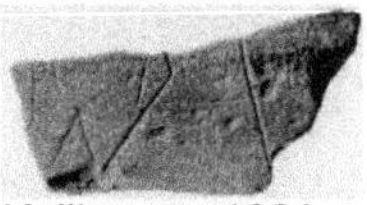
Kalibangan102A

8207

Kalibangan103A

8209

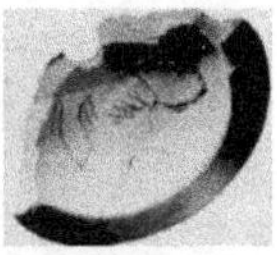
Kalibangan104A

8218

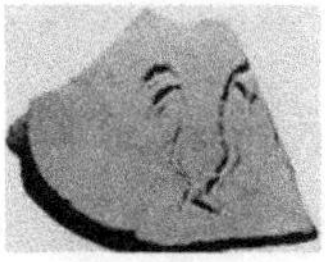
Kalibangan105A

8216

Kalibangan106A
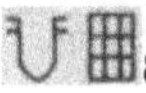
8204

Kalibangan107A

Kalibangan108A

8206

Kalibangan109A

Kalibangan110A
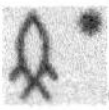
8211

Kalibangan111A

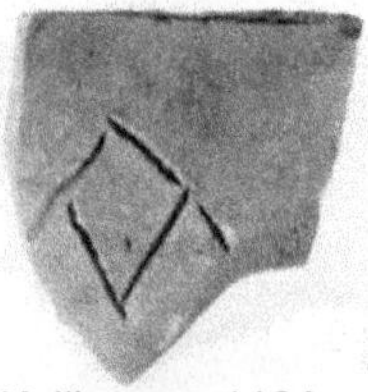
Kalibangan112A

Kalibangan118

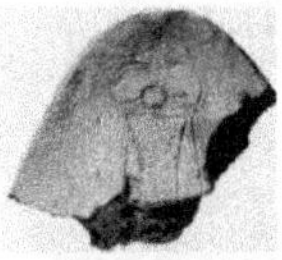
Kalibangan119A

Kalibangan119B

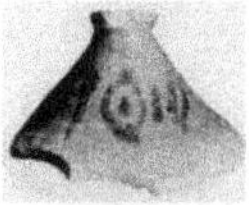
Kalibangan120A

8220

Kalibangan122B

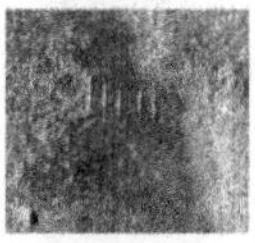
Kalibangan

122B2

Kalibangan

121A, B

8302

Kalibangan122A

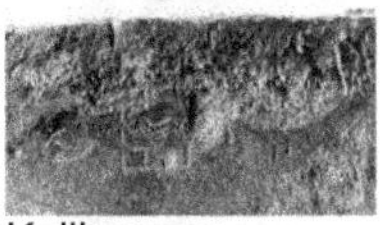

Kalibangan

122A2

8301

Kalako-deray 01

Kalako-deray 05

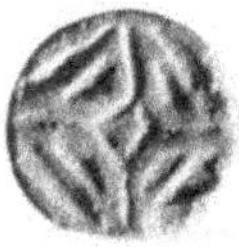

Kalako-deray 06

Kalako-deray 07

Kalako-deray 08

Kalakoderay10

Khirsara1a

Khirsara2a

9051 Kot-diji

Lewandheri01

Loebanr01

Lohumjodaro1a

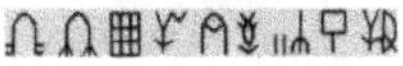

9011

Lothal001

7015

Lothal002

7031

Lothal003

Lothal004a

7080

Lothal005

7044

Lothal006a

7038

Lothal007a

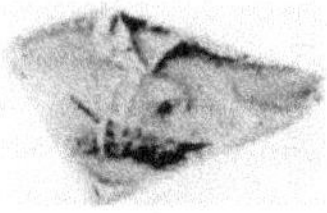

Lothal008a

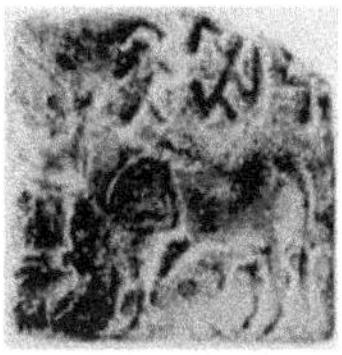

Lothal009

7022

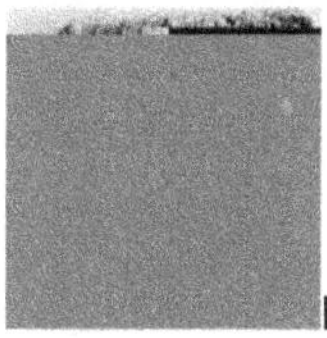

Lo

thal010

7009

Lothal011

7026

Lothal012a
7089

Lothal013
7050

Lothal014a
7094

Lothal015
7086

Lothal016
7002

Lothal017
7008

Lothal018
7096

Lothal019a
7092

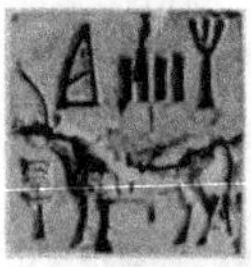

Lothal020
7078

Lothal021
7047

Lothal022a
7035

Lothal023a
7043

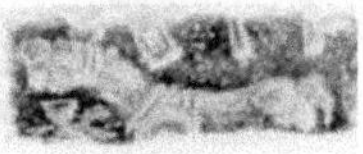

Lothal024

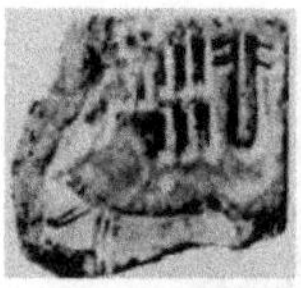

Lothal025
7104

Lothal026
7024

Lothal027
7036

Lothal028
7045

Lothal029
7005

Lothal030a

Lothal031
7076

Lothal032a

Lothal033a

Lothal035
7101

Lothal036a
7081

Lothal037
7034

Lothal038a
7053

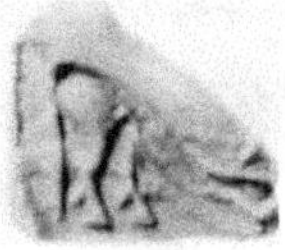

Lothal039
7102

Lothal040a

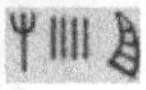

Lothal041

7066

Lothal042

Lothal043

7049

Lothal044

Lothal045

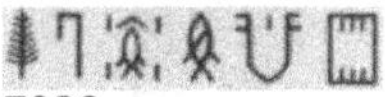

7028

Lothal046

7107

Lothal047a

7074

Lothal048

7025

Lothal049

Lothal050

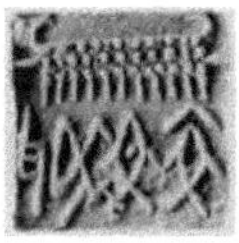

Lothal051a

7057 Pict-127: Upper register: a large device with a number of small circles in three rows with another row of short vertical lines below; the device is horned. A seed-drill? [Is this an orthographic model for

Sign 176?]

Lothal052 

7011

Lothal054a

7099

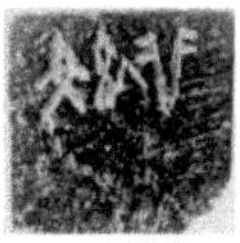

Lothal055

7106

Lothal056

7100

Lothal057

7095

Lothal058a

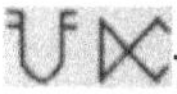7029

Lothal059

7097

Lothal060

7039

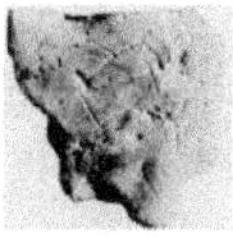

Lothal061

Lothal062

7054

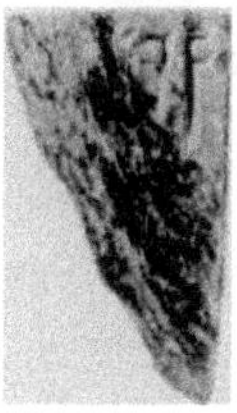

Lothal063

Lothal064

7030

Lothal065

7103

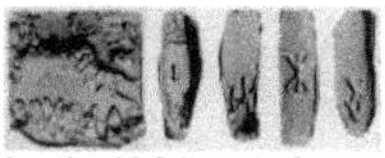

Lothal066acdef

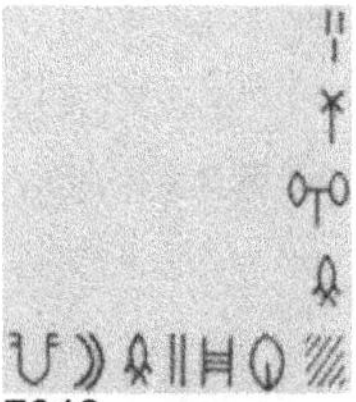

7048

Lothal068

7070

Lothal069

Lothal070

Lothal071

Lothal072

Lothal075

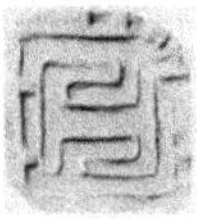

Lothal076a

Lothal077

Lothal078

7077

Lothal079

7063

Lothal080a

Lothal081

7093

Lothal082

7105

Lothal083

7068

Lothal084

7112

Lothal085

Lothal086

7007

Lothal087

7021

Lothal088

7017

Lothal089

7090

Lothal090

7032

Lothal091

7111

Lothal092

7062

Lothal093

7064

Lothal094a

7073

Lothal095

7042

Lothal096

7023

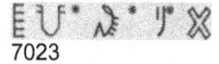

Lothal097

7072

Lothal098

7082

Lothal099

Lothal100a

Lothal100B

7055

Lothal101
7001

Lothal102
7040

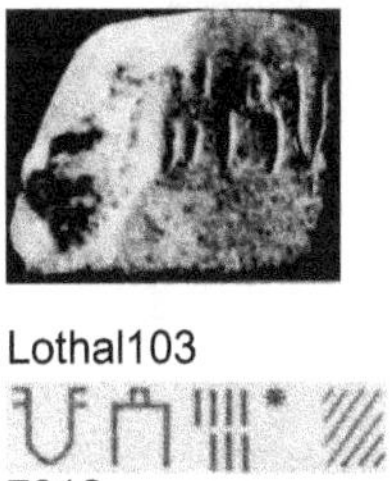
Lothal103
7018

Lothal104
7085

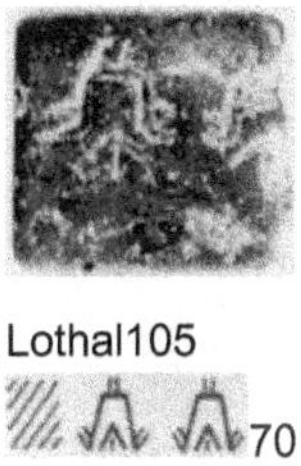
Lothal105
7016

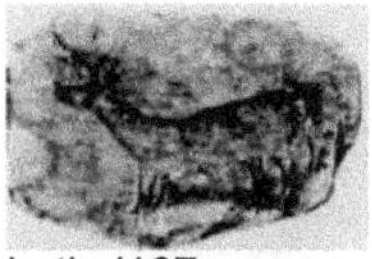
Lothal107

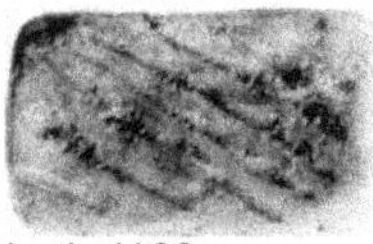
Lothal108

Lothal109a

7046

Lothal110
7006

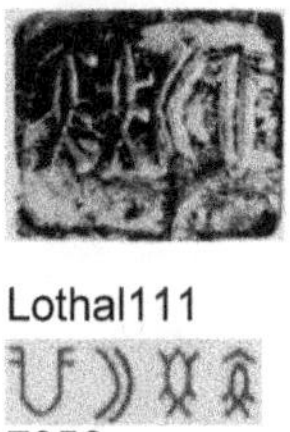
Lothal111
7056

Lothal112
7020

Lothal113a
7004

Lothal114a
7013

Lothal115
7065

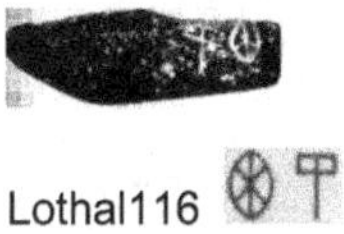
Lothal116
7027

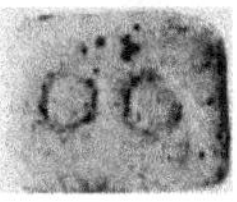

Lothal117 
7075

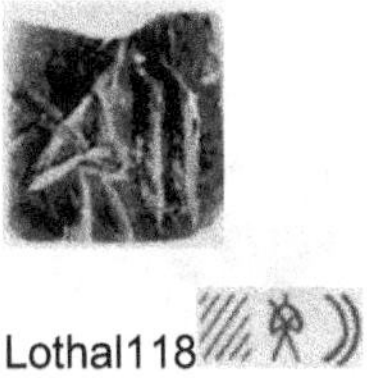
Lothal118
7019

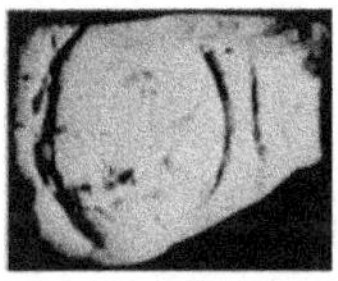
Lothal119

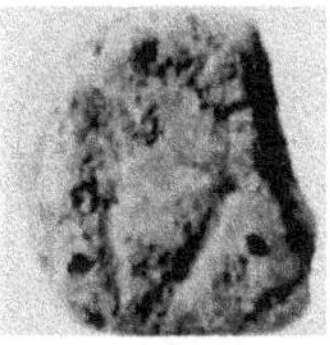
Lothal120

Lothal121

Lothal122
7069

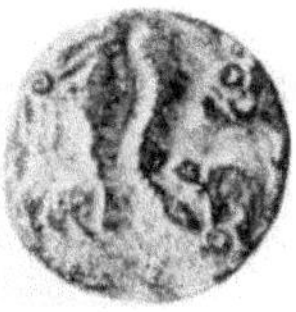
Lothal123A

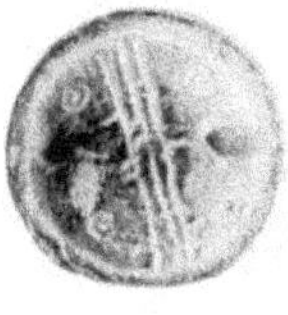
Lothal123B

Lothal124A
7224

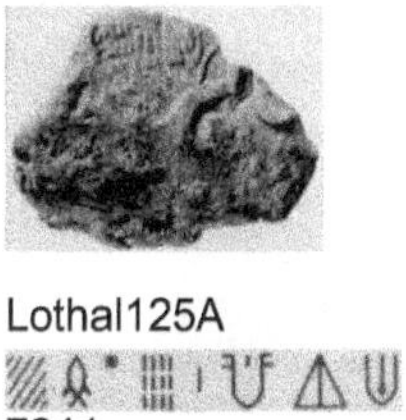
Lothal125A
7241

Lothal126A
7242

Lothal127A
7221

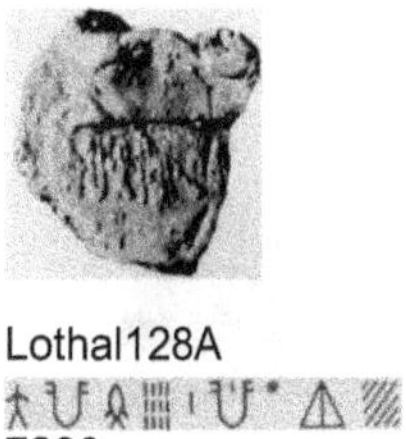
Lothal128A
7239

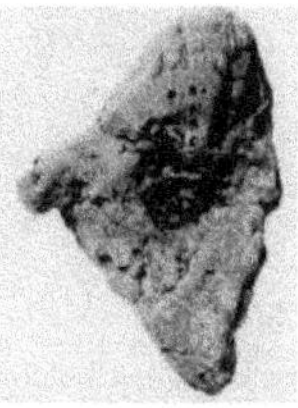
Lothal129A

Lothal130A

Lothal131A

7255

Lothal132A

7213

Lothal133A

7245

Lothal134A

7252

Lothal135A

7220

Lothal136A

7225

Lothal137A

7257

Lothal138A

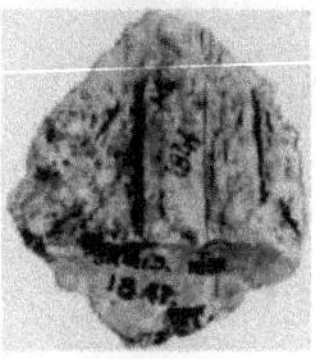

Lothal138B

7214

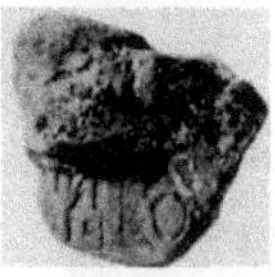

Lothal139A

7223

Lothal140A

7244

Lothal141A1

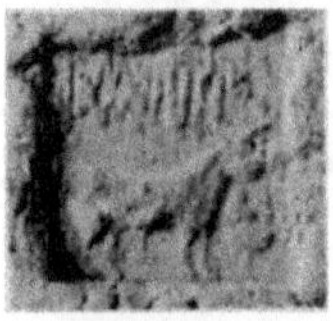

Lothal141A2

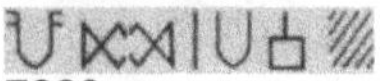

7280

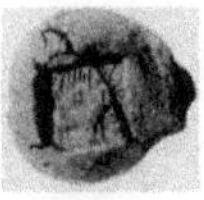

Lothal142A

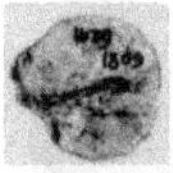

Lothal142B

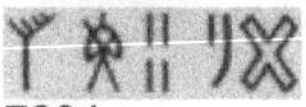

7204

Lothal143A

Lothal143B

7243

Lothal144A

7274

Lothal145A

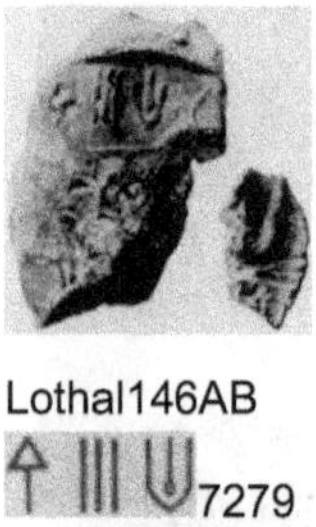

Lothal146AB

7279

Lothal147A

7260

Lothal148A

7270

Lothal149A

7272

Lothal150A

7268

Lothal151A

7266

Lothal152A

7222

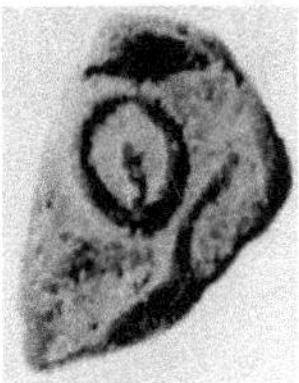
Lothal153A

7271

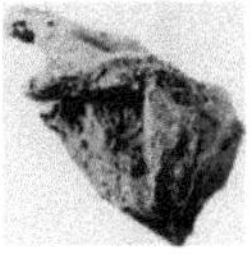
Lothal154A

Lothal155A

Lothal156A

Lothal157A

Lothal158A

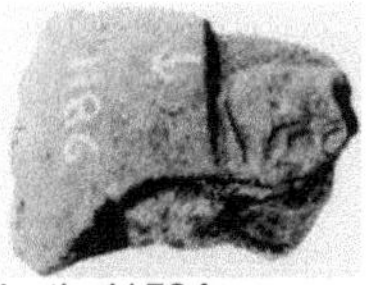
Lothal159A

Lothal160A

Lothal161A

7205

Lothal162A
Lothal162B

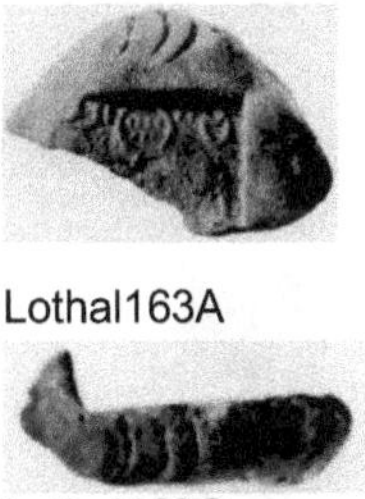
Lothal163A
Lothal163C

7228

Lothal164A

7230

Lothal165A

7203

Lothal166A

7206

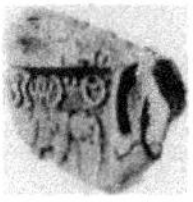
Lothal167A

7231

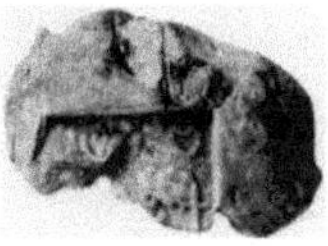
Lothal168A

7234

Lothal169A

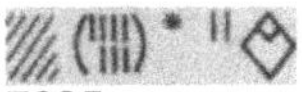
7235

Lothal170A

7229

Lothal171A

Lothal172A

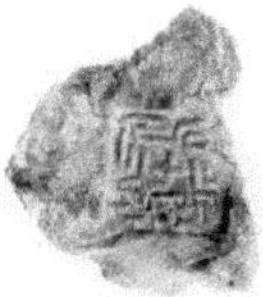
Lothal173A

Lothal174A

Lothal175A

Lothal176A
7216

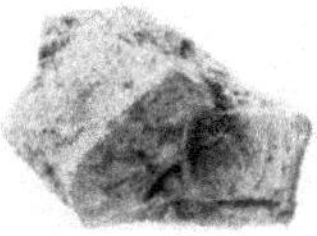
Lothal177A

7211

Lothal179A

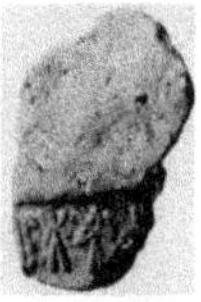

Lothal180A

7240

Lothal181A

7273

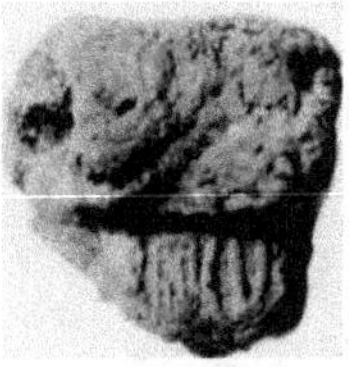

Lothal182A

7238

Lothal183A

Lothal184A

Lothal185A

Lothal186A

7259

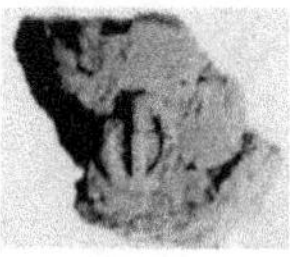

Lothal187A

7209

Lothal188A

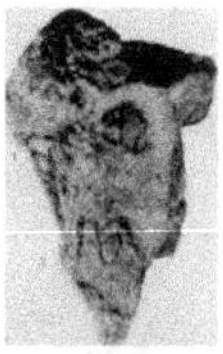

Lothal189A12

Lothal189A34

7217

Lothal190A13

7236

Lothal191A12

7249

Lothal192A12

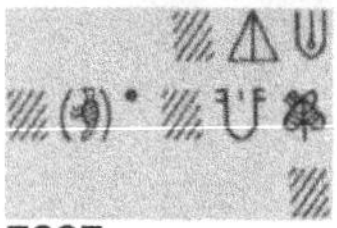

7227

Lothal193A12

Lothal193A3

7253

Lothal194A1

Lothal194A2

7251

Lothal195A12

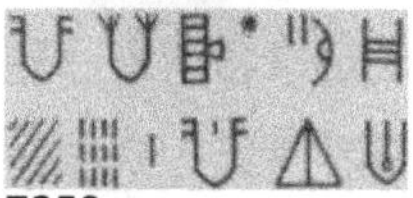

7258

Lothal196A12

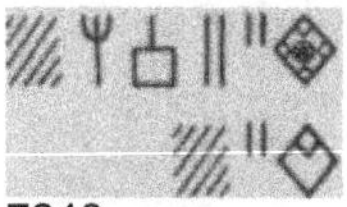

7248

Lothal197A12

7237

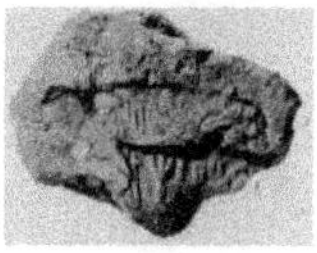

Lothal198A12

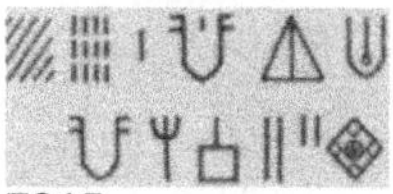

7215

Lothal199A12

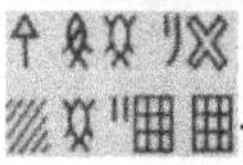

7247

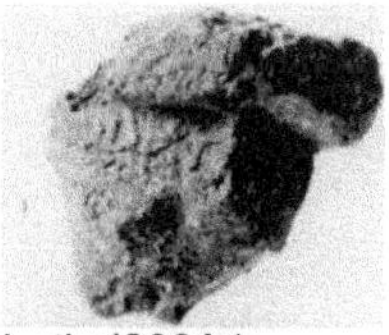

Lothal200A1

Lothal200A2

7219

Lothal201A12

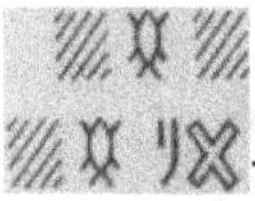
7263

Lothal202A12

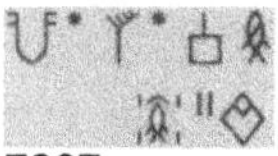
7267

Lothal203A12

7246

Lothal204A

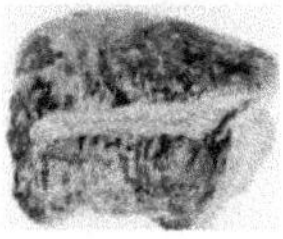

Lothal204F

7275

Lothal205A12

7218

Lothal206A12

7265

Lothal207A12

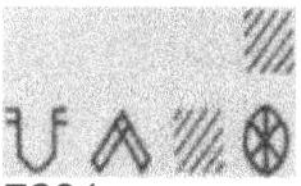
7281

Lothal208A12

Lothal209A12

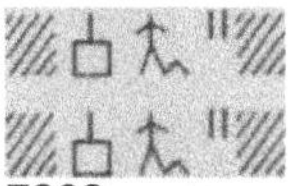
7262

Lothal210A12

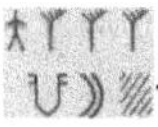
7201

Lothal211A13

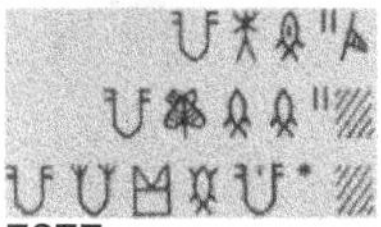
7277

Lothal212A12

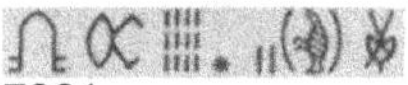
7261

Lothal213A2

7207

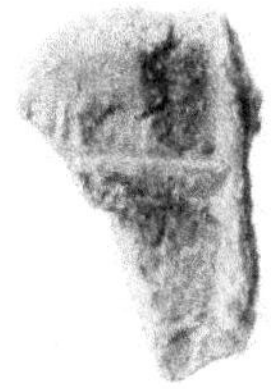

Lothal214A12

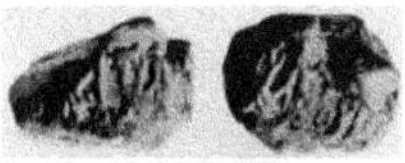

Lothal216D12

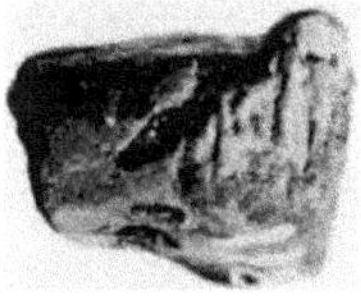

Lothal216E

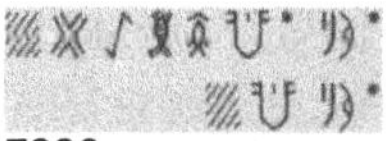
7283

Lothal217A

Lothal217B

Lothal218A

7202

Lothal219A

7282

Lothal220A

7278

Lothal221A

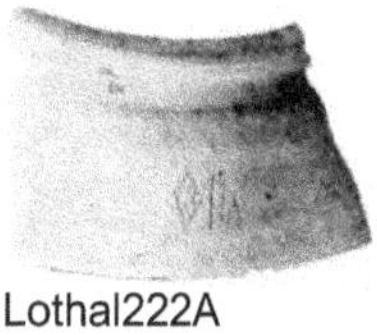

Lothal222A

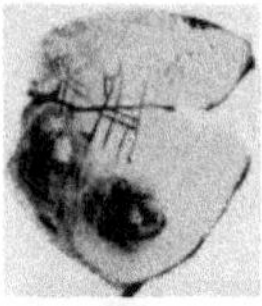

Lothal223A

Lothal224A

Lothal225A

Lothal227A

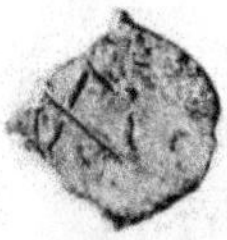

Lothal229A

Lothal230A

Lothal233A

Lothal246A

Lothal269A

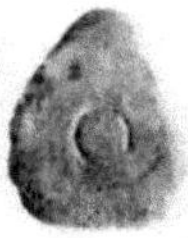

Lothal270A

Lothal272A

Lothal273A

7301

Lothal277A

Lothal280A

Lothal281A

7088

7098

7212

7232

7233

7269

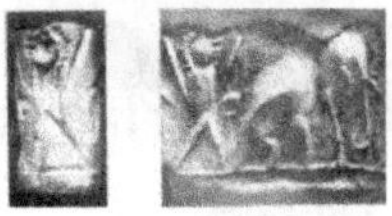

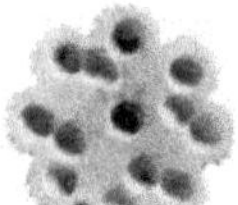

Maski

Mehi

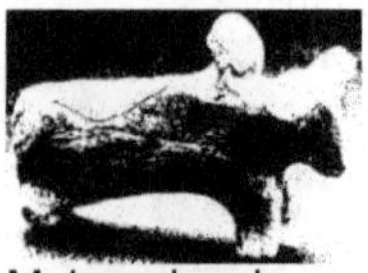

Mehrgarh zebu

Mehrgarh01

Mehrgarh04

Mehrgarh05

Mehrgarh08

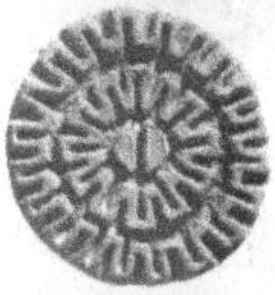

Mehrgarh10

Mehrgarh11

Mehrgarh12

Mehrgarh13

Mehrgarh14

Mehrgarh15

Mehrgarh16

Mehrgarh17

Mehrgarh18

m0001a

1067

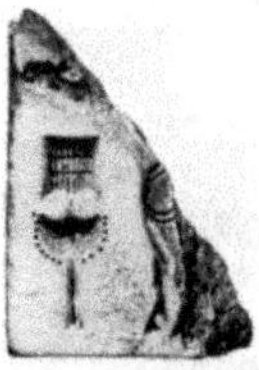

m0002a

m0003a

2225

m0004a
3109

m0005
2247

m0006a
2422

m0007
1011

m0008a
1038

m0009a
2616

m0010
1006

m0011

m0012
3031

m0013
1069

m0014
1022

m0015
2177

m0016a
1037

m0017
1035

m0018Ac
1548

m0019a
1085

m0020a
1054

m0021a
2103

m0022a
1023

m0023a
2398

m0024
2694

m0025
1056

m0026a

2074

m0027a

2084

m0028a

2178

m0029a

2033

m0030a

2396

m0031

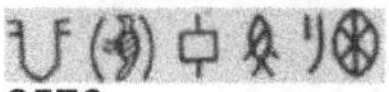

2576

m0032a

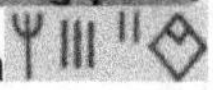

2180

m0033a

1042

m0034a

1058

m0035a

2333

m0036a

2455

m0037a

3103

m0039a

1544

m0040

1051

m0038a

1087

m0041

2271

m0042a

1096

m0043

2584

m0044a

3110

m0045a
1552

m0046a
3089

m0047a
1098

m0048a
1186

m0049a
1047

m0050a
1557

m0051a
1555

m0052a
1540

m0053a
2128

m0054
2307

m0055a
2511

m0056
2406

m0057a
2340

m0058a
2680

m0059a
1029

m0060a
2124

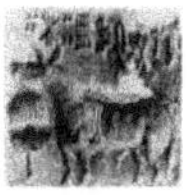

m0061

m0062
3112

m0063
3068

m0064
2524

m0065
2440

m0066AC
1052

m0067
2264

m0068
3108

m0069
1095

m0070
1048

m0071a
3083 [The second sign from left is an orthographic representation of the thigh of a bovid, perhaps a bull].

m0072a
2085

m0073
1046

m0074
2353

m0075
1019

m0076

m0077

3111

m0078
3118

m0079a
2083

m0080
2635

m0081a
1180

m0082
2451

m0083a
2267

m0084a
1108

m0085a
2365

m0086
2208

m0087
2148

m0088
1075

m0089
3116

m0090
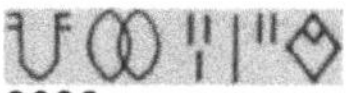
3039

m0091
2429

m0092
2407

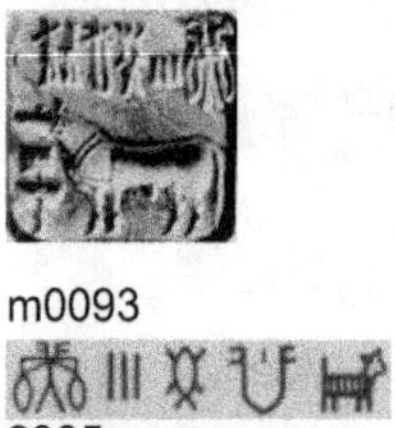
m0093
2305

m0094
2594

m0095
2657

m0096
2698

m0097

2549

m0098

2012

m0099

2475

m0100

1115

m0101

1537

m0102

1129

m0103

1076

m0104

2574

m0105

2337

m0106

2459

m0107

2593

m0108

1110

m0109

1151

m0110

2031

m0111

2029

m0112

2099

m0113

2115

m0114

2166

m0115

3087

m0116

2481

m0117

1105

m0118

1104

m0119a

2018

m0120a

1099

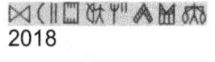

m0121a

1188

m0122a

2015

m0123a

2702

m0124

1120

m0125

m0126

2311

m0127

1119

m0128a

2284

m0129

2193

m0130a

2285

m0131

2263

m0132

2082

m0133a

2052

m0134

2187

m0135

1168

m0136

2233

m0137

2261

m0138

2381

m0139

2185

m0140

2563

m0141

2543

m0142

2630

m0143

2002

m0144

2048

m0145

1118

m0146

1100

m0147

3097

m0148

1245

m0149

1233

m0150

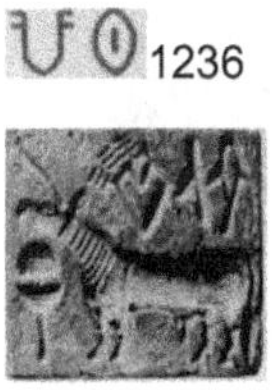

1236

m0151

2323

m0152

2102

m0153

2361

m0154

2373

m0155

1187

m0156

m0157

2022

m0158

2198

m0159

2355

m0160

2286

m0161

2088

m0162

2486

m0163

1543

m0164

2403

m0165

2687

m0166

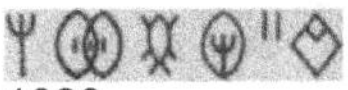

1080

m0167.

1297

m0168a [The second sign may be an orthographic variant for a thigh of a bovid?]

2442

m0169

1113

m0170

2237

m0171

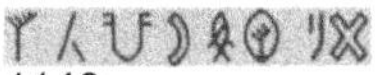

1149

m0172

1071

m0173
1161

m0174
1114

m0175
1291

m0176
1193

m0177

m0178
2354

m0179

m0180
2014

m0181
2490

m0182
2154

m0183
3113

m0184
2634

m0185

m0186
2161

m0187
2382

m0188
1287

m0189
1195

m0190
1205

m0191
1288

m0192
1206

m0193
2113

m0194
2254

m0195
2415

m0196
2474

m0197
2371

m0198
2363

m0199

2647

m0200

1148

m0201

2678

m0202

2625

m0203

1556

m0204

2623

m0205

1221

m0206

m0207

2458

m0208

2047

m0209

2375

m0210

2656

m0211

1214

m0212

2577

m0213

1150

m0214

2571

m0215

3081

m0216

3036

m0217

2087

m0218

2175

m0219

2433

m0220a

3093

m0221a

3164

m0222

1194

m0223

1167 [The sign in front of the one-horned bull may be Sign

162]

m0224

2215

m0225

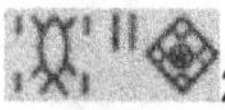2199

m0226
2152

m02272226

m0228 
2502

m0229

3075

m0230.
1295

m0231
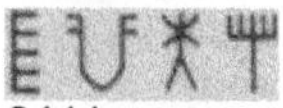
2444

m0232
2234 'Unicorn' with two horns! "Bull with two long horns (otherwise resembling the 'unicorn')", generally facing the standard. That it is the typical 'one-horned bull' is surmised from two ligatures: the pannier on the shoulder and the ring on the neck.

m0233

m0234.
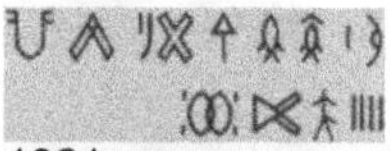
1321

m0235
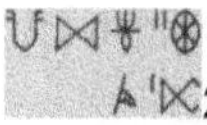2689

m0236

2123

m0237

m0238AC
2534

m0239

2238

m0240.

1324

m0241

1536

m0242
2216

m0243
2390

m0244
2399

m0245
2290

m0246.
1317

m0247
2298

m0248.

1310

m0249

2378

m0250.

1308

m0251

2370

m0252

2423

m0253

2701

m0254

2090

m0255

2409

[The second sign is diamond-shaped?]

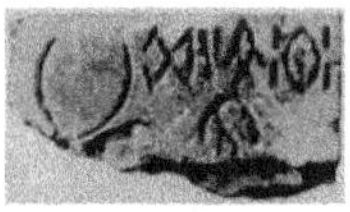

m0256

1332

m0257

2314

m0258a.

1340

m0259

2132

m0260

2567

m0261

2535

m0262 Zebu

2249

m0263

1336

m0264

2607

m0265

2155

m0266.

1306

m0267 Water-buffalo

2257

m0268 Water-buffalo

2445

m0269

2663

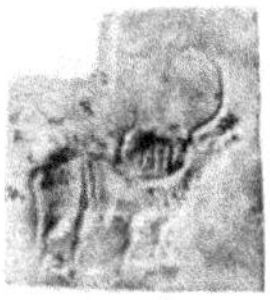

m0270

m0271 Goat-antelope with horns turned backwards and a short tail

m0272 Goat-antelope with horns bending backwards and neck turned backwards 2554

m0273 2673

m0274

1342

m0275

2131

m0276AC

3122

m0277

2309

m0278

2648

m0279

3060

m0280

1373

m0281

3115

m0282

2304

m0283

2127

m0284

2195

m0285

1367

m0286

2517

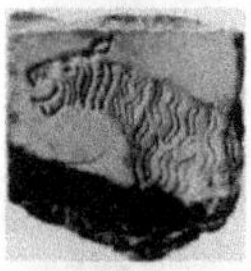

m0287

m0288

2518

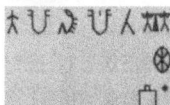

m0289

3121

m0290

2527

m0291 Tiger

3069

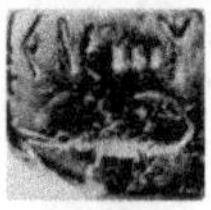

m0292 Gharial

1361

m0293 Gharial

1360

m0294 One-horned bull?; elephant

1376

m0295 Pict-61: Composite motif of three tigers joined together.

1386

m0296 Two heads of one-horned bulls with neck-rings, joined end to end (to a standard device with two rings coming out of the top part?), under a stylized pipal tree with nine leaves.

1387

m0297a Head of a one-horned bull attached to an undentified five-point symbol (octopus-like?)

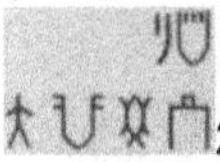2641

m0298

m0299 Composite animal with the body of a ram, horns of a bull, trunk of an elephant, hindlegs of a tiger and an upraise serpent-like tail.

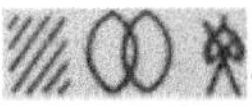1381

m0300 Pict51: Composite animal: human face, zebu's horns, elephant tusks and trunk, ram's forepart, unicorn's trunk and feet, tiger's hindpart and serpent-like tail.

2521

m0301 Composite motif: human face, body or forepart of a ram, body and front legs of a unicorn, horns of a zebul, trunk of an elephant, hindlegs of a tiger and an upraised serpent-like tail.

2258

m0302 Composite animal with the body of a ram, horns of a bull, trunk of an elephant, hindlegs of a tiger and an upraise serpent-like tail.

1380

m0303 Composite animal.

2411

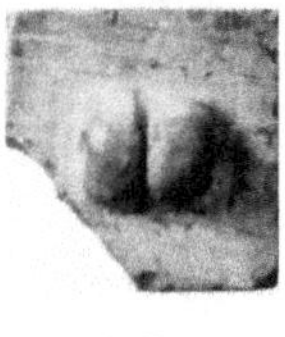

m0304B

m0304AC Pict-81: Person (with three visible faces) wearing bangles and armlets seated on a platform (with an antelope looking backwards) and surrounded by five animals: rhinoceros, buffalo, antelope, tiger and elephant.

2420

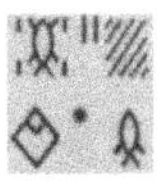

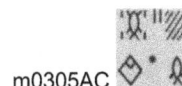

m0305AC 2235 Pict-80: Three-faced, horned person (with a three-leaved pipal branch on the crown with two stars on either side), wearing bangles and armlets.

m0306 Person grappling with two tigers standing on either side of him and rearing on their hindlegs.

2086

m0307 Person grappling with two tigers standing on either side of him and rearing on their hindlegs.

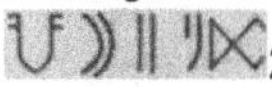2122

m0308AC Pict-105: Person grappling with two tigers standing on either side of him and rearing on their hindlegs.

2075 [The third sign from left may be a stylized 'standard device'?]

m0309 Pict-109: Person with hair-bun seated on a tree branch; a tiger looks at the person with its head turned backwards.

2522

m0310AC

1355

m0311 Pict-52: Composite motif: body of a tiger, a human body with bangles on arms, antelope horns, tree-branch and long pigtail.

2347

m0312 Persons vaulting over a water-buffalo.

m0313

2637

m0314

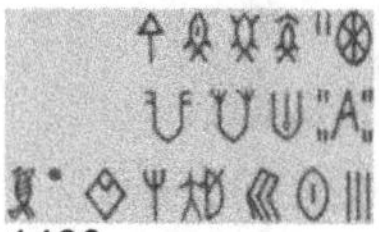

1400

m0315

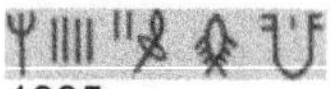

1395

m0316

2408

m0317silver

2016

Mohenjo-daro FEM, Pl. LXXXVIII, 316

2316

Mohenjo-daro MIC, Pl. CVI,93

1093

Mohenjo-daro. Copper seal. National Museum, New Delhi. [Source: Page 18, Fig. 8A in: Deo Prakash Sharma, 2000, *Harappan seals, sealings and copper tablets*, Delhi, National Museum].

m0318

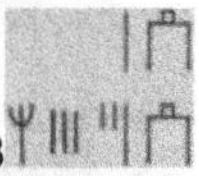

m0318B

2626

m0319

m0319C

2260

m0320

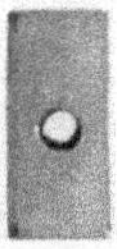

m0320D

2449

m0321

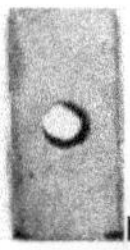

m0321D

2173

m0322

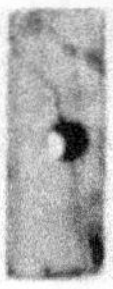

m0322D

1192

m0323

m0323D

1277

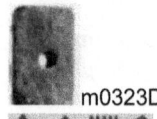

m0324A

m0324B

m0324D

1252

m0325A

m0325B

m0325F
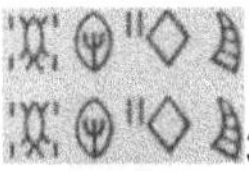
3106

m0326A

m0326B

m0326C

m0326D

m326E

m0326F
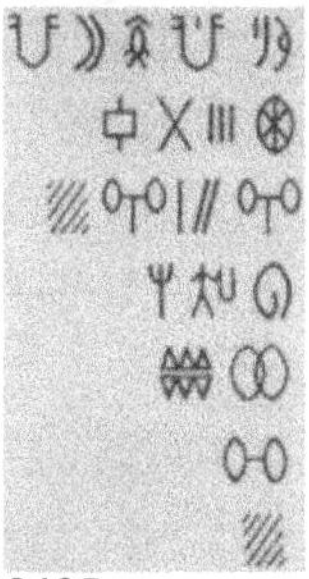
2405

m0327

2631

m0328
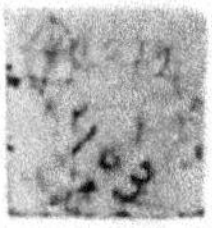
m0328B

2108

m0329

1477

m0330A

m0330B
Perforated through the narrow edge of a two-sided seal
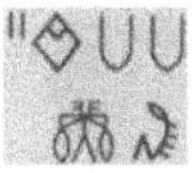
1475

m0331A
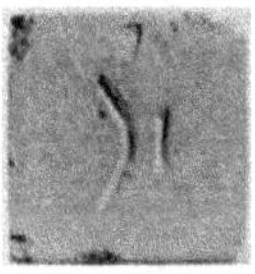
m0331B

m0331D

m0331F Cube seal

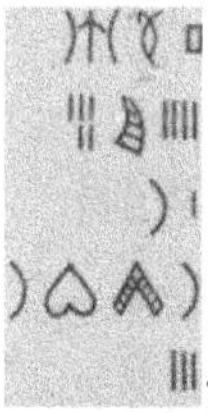
1471

m0332AC

m0333

m0334

m0335

m0336

m0337

m0338

m0339

m0340

m0341

m0342

m0343

m0344

m0345

m0346

m0347
m0348

m0349
m0350

m0351

m0352A

m0352C

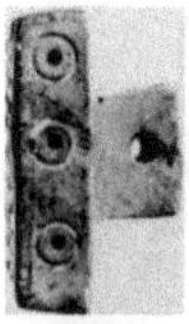
m0352D

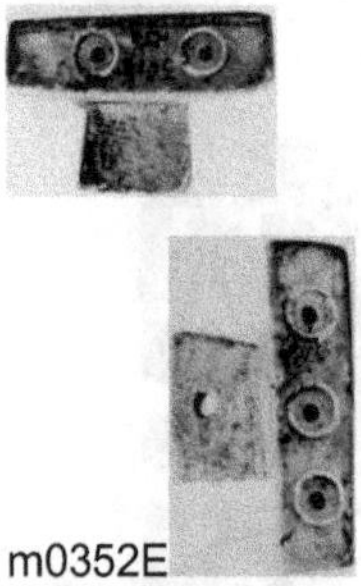
m0352E
m0352F

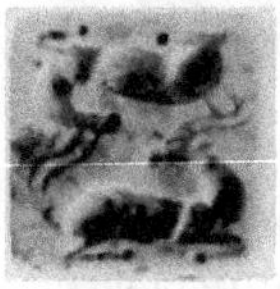
m0353

m0354

1403

m0356

1406

m0357

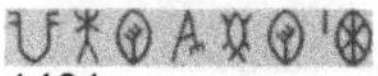
1401

m0358

m0355

2654

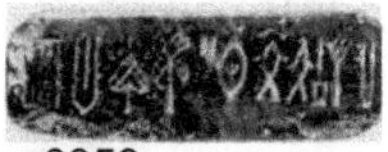
m0359

2325

m0369

2537

m0391

3107

2297

m0360

3102

m0361

2101

m0362

1466

m0363

1469

m0364

1465

m0365

2273

m0366

2077

m0367

2044

m0368

2336

m0370

2138

m0371

2461

m0372

1438

m0373

2043

m0374

2097

m0375

m375AC

m0376

1426

m0377

3120

m0378

1402

m0379

2159

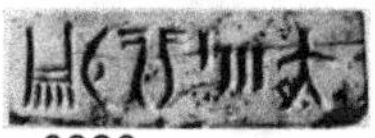
m0380

2470

m0381

2162

m382AC

1437

m0383

2240

m0384

2302

m0385

2387

m0386

1449

m0387

2041

m0388

2200

m0389

2397

m0390

1444

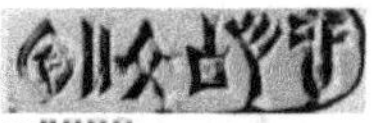
m0392

2046

m393AC

2120

m0394

2213

m0395

2183

m0396

1421

m0397

1415

m0398

2308

m399AC

1414

m0400

3088

m0401

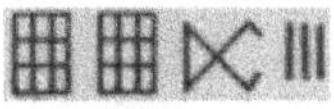

2346

m0402

2395

m0403

1410

m404AC

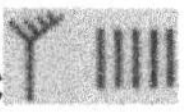

1422

m0405

2221

m0406

1399

m0407

2643

m0408

2100

m0409

2699

m0410 Pict-64: Gharial snatching, with its snout, the fin of a fish

2133

m0411

1431

m0412

1450

m0413

2319

m0414A

m0414B Seal with incision on obverse

2004

m0415a Bison

2500

m0416 Bison .

1309

m417AC Pict-62: Composition: six heads of animals: of unicorn, of short-horned bull (bison), of antelope, of tiger, and of two other uncertain animals) radiating outward from a hatched ring (or 'heart' design).

1383

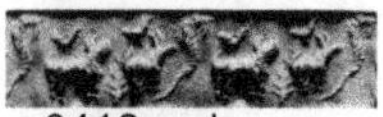

m0418acyl

m0419acyl

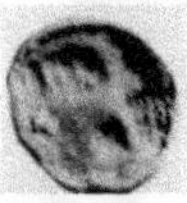

m0419dcyl

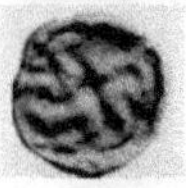

m0419fcyl

m0420A1si

m0420A2si

3236

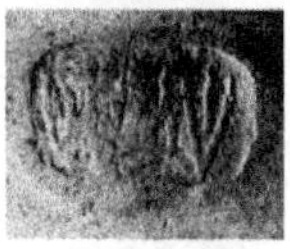

m0421A1si

m0421A2si

3237

m0422A1si

m0422A2si

m0423A1si

m0423A2si

3221

m0424A1si

m0424A2si

m0425A1si

m0425A2si

m0426Asi

m0426Bsi
2809

m0427t

1630

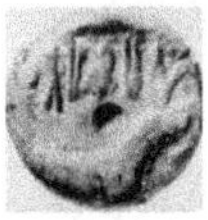

m0428At

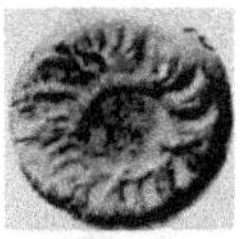

m0428Bt

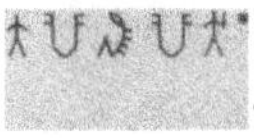

1607

Pict- 132: Radiating solar symbol.

m0429 Text 
2862

m0430At

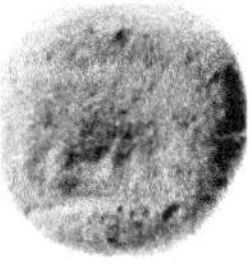

m0430Bt

2862

m0431At

m0431Bt

3239

m0432At

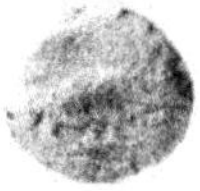

m0432Bt

1624

m0433At

m0433Bt

3233

m0434At

m0434Bt

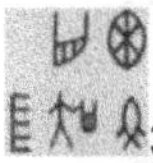

3248

m0435t

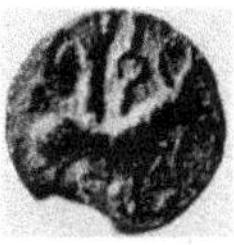

m0436At

m0436Bt

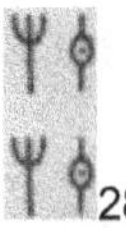

2804

m0437t

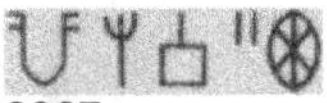

2867

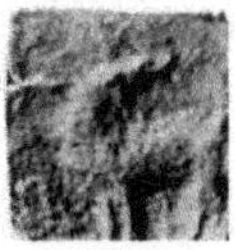

m0438atcopper

m0439t

m440AC

m0441At

m0441Bt

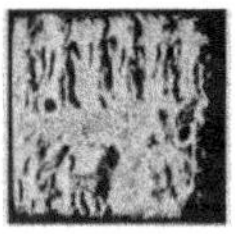

m0442At

m0442Bt

m443At

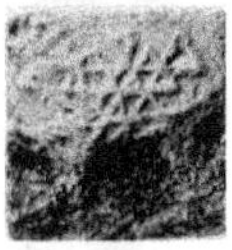

m443Bt

m444At
3223

m445Bt

m445AC

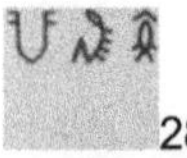
2821

m446At

m446Bt

2854

m447At

m447Bt

m448t

m449Bt

m449AC

2836

m450At

m450Bt

2864

m0451At

m0451Bt

3235

m0452At

m0452Bt

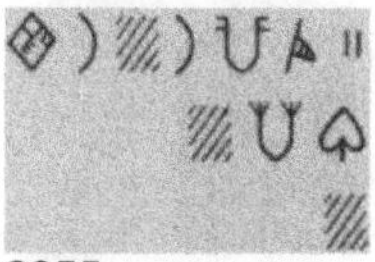
2855

m0453At

m453BC

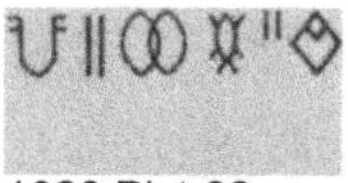
1629 Pict-82
Person seated on a pedestal flanked on either side by a kneeling adorant and a hooded serpent rearing up.

m0455At

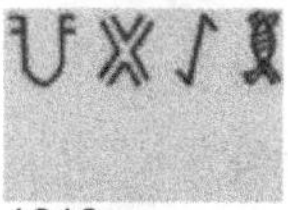
1619

m0456At

3219

m0457At
m0457Bt

m0457Et

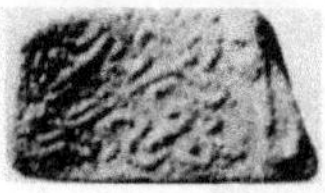

m0458At

m0458Bt

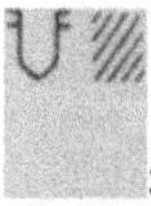
3227

m0459At
m0459Bt

3225

m0460At
m0460Bt

3228

m0461At

m0461Bt

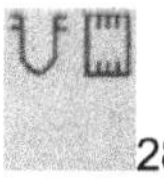

2806 Pict-73: Alternative 1. Serpent (?) entwined around a pillar with capital (?); motif carvd in high-relief. Alternative 2. Ring-stones around a pillar with coping stones in a building-structure as at Dholavira?

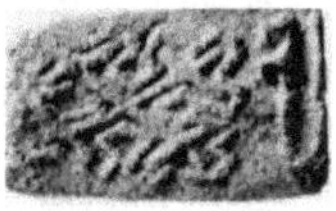

m0462At

m0462Bt

3215

m0463At

m0463Bt

2813

m0464At

m0464Bt

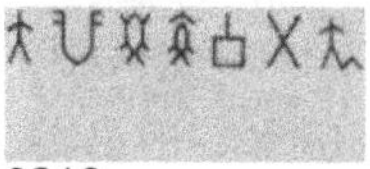

3216

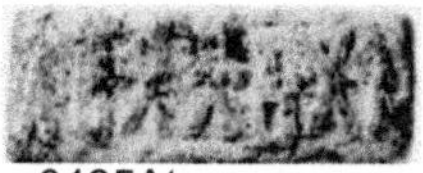

m0465At

m0465Bt

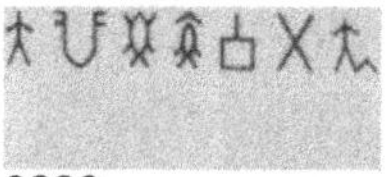

3220

m0466At

m0466Bt

m0467At

m0467Bt

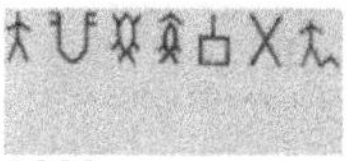

3209

m0468At

m0468Bt

3249

m0469At

m0469Bt

2830

m0470At

2810

m0471At

m0471Bt

3232

m0472At

1615

m0473At

2848

m0474At

3243

m0475Atcopper

3247

m0476At

m0476Ct

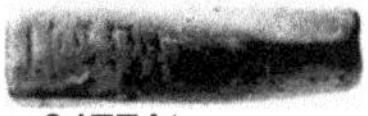

m0477At

m0477Bt

m0477Ct

2844

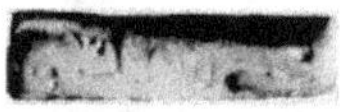

Two rhinoceroses, one at either end of the text (Pict-29).

m0478At

m0478Bt

m0479At

m0479Bt

3224

m0480At

m0480Bt Tablet in bas-relief. Side a: Tree Side b: Pict-111: From R.: A woman with outstretched arms flanked by two men holding uprooted trees in their hands; a person seated on a tree with a tiger below with its head turned backwards; a tall jar with a lid.

Is the pictorial of a tall jar the Sign 342 with a lid? Sign 45 seems to be a kneeling adorant offering a pot (Sign 328)

2815 Pict-77: Tree, generally within a railing or on a platform.

3230

m0481At

m0481Bt

m0481Ct

m0481Et

2846 Pict-41: Serpent, partly reclining on a low platform under a tree

m0482At

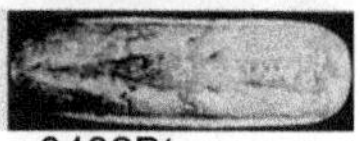
m0482Bt

1620 Pict-65: Gharial, sometimes with a fish held in its jaw and/or surrounded by a school of fish.

m0483At

m0483Bt

m0483Ct

m0483Et

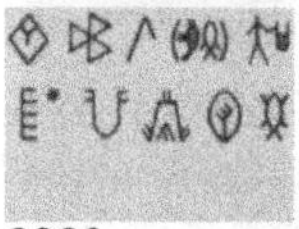
2866

Pict-145: Geometrical pattern.

m0484At

m0484Bt

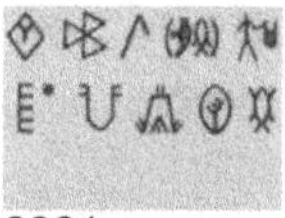
2861

m0486at

m0486bt

m0486ct

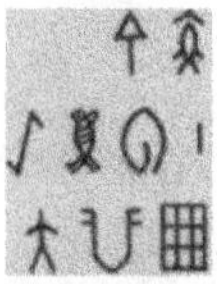
1625

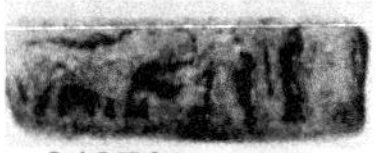
m0487At

m0487Bt

m0487Ct

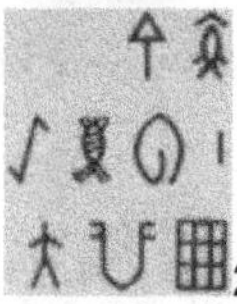
2852

m0488At

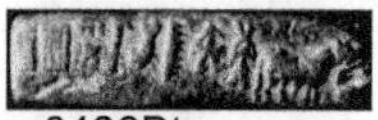
m0488Bt

m0488Ct

2802 Prism: Tablet in bas-relief. Side b: Text +One-horned bull + standard. Side a: From R.: a composite animal; a person seated on a tree with a tiger below looking up at the person; a svastika within a square border; an elephant (Composite animal has the body of a ram, horns of a zebu, trunk of an elephant, hindlegs of a tiger and an upraised serpent-like tail). Side c: From R.: a horned person standing between two branches of a pipal tree; a ram; a horned person kneeling in adoration; a low pedestal with some offerings.

m0489At

m0489Bt

m0489Ct

m0490At

m0490BCt

1605

m0491At

m0491BCt

1608 Pict-94: Four persons in a procession, each carrying a standard, one of which has the figure of a one-horned bull on top.

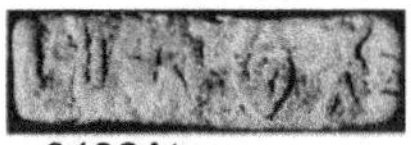

m0492At

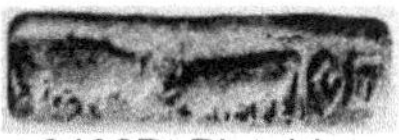

m0492Bt Pict-14: Two bisons standing face to face.

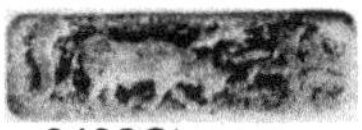

m0492Ct

2835 Pict-99: Person throwing a spear at a bison and placing one foot on the head of the bison; a hooded serpent at left.

m0493At

m0493Bt Pict-93: Three dancing figures in a row.

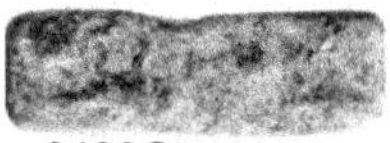

m0493Ct

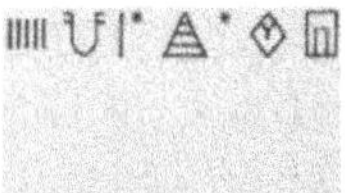

2843

m0494At

m0494BGt Prism Tablet in bas-relief.

1623

m0495At

m0495Bt

m0495gt

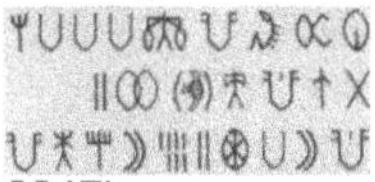

2847b

m0496At

m0496Bt

m0496Dt

m0497At

m0497Bt

m0498At

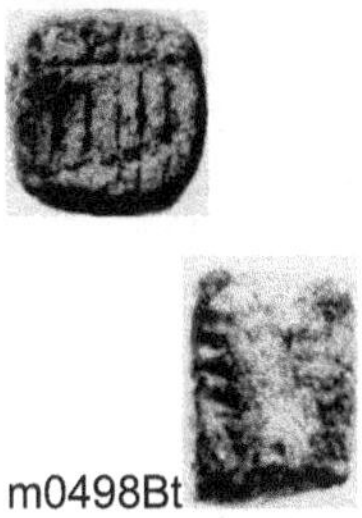

m0498Bt

m0498Dt

m0499At

m0500at

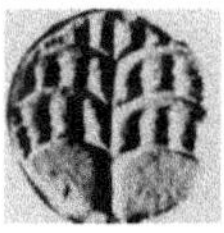

m0500bt

2604

Pict-76: Tree, generally within a railing or on a platform.

m0501At

m0501Bt

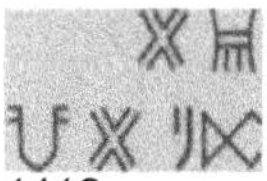

1412

m0502At

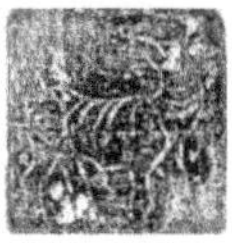

m0502Bt

3345

m0503 Text

3346

m0504At

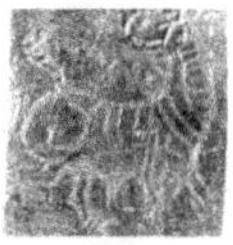

m0504Bt

3323

m0505At

m0505Bt

1702

m0507At

m0507Bt

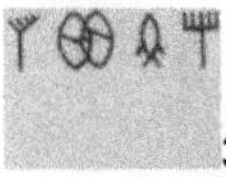

3350

m0508At

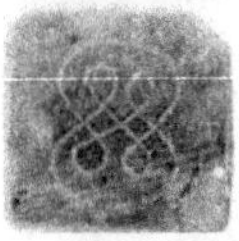

m0508Bt

3352

m0509At

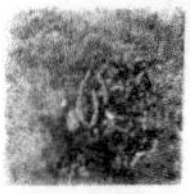

m0509Bt

3320

m0510At

m0510Bt

3319

m0511At

m0511Bt

2905

m0512At

m0512Bt

2906

m0513At

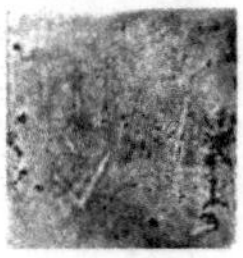

m0513Bt

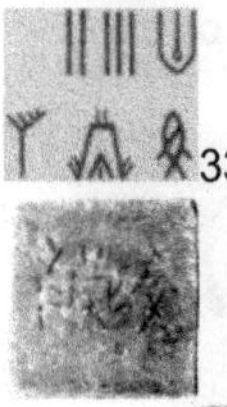

3364

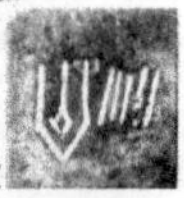

m0514At

m0514Bt

3302

m0515 Text

3335

m0516At

m0516Bt

3398

m0517At

m0517Bt

3334

m0519At

m0519Bt

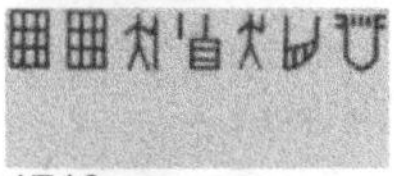

1710

m0520 At, Bt

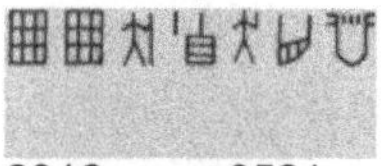

2916 m0521

3407

m0522At

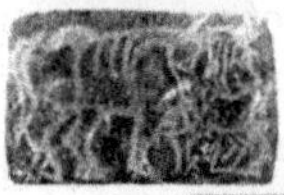

m0522Bt

3378

m0523At

m0523Bt

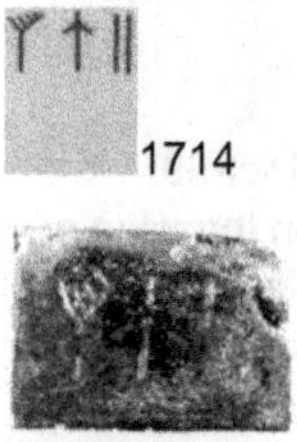

1714

m0524At

m0524Bt

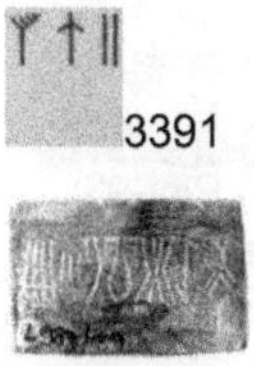

3391

m0525At

m0525Bt

1713 Buffalo

m0526At

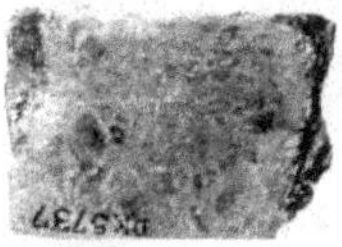

m0526Bt

3329

Buffalo

m0527At

m0527Bt

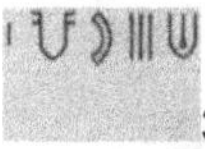

3336

m0528At

m0528Bt

3368

m0529At

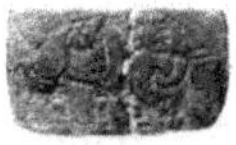

m0529Bt

3392

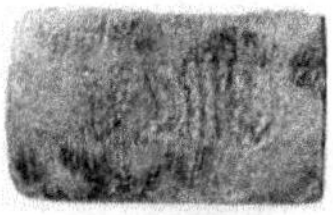

m0530At

m0530Bt

3356

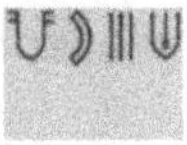

m0531At

m0531Bt

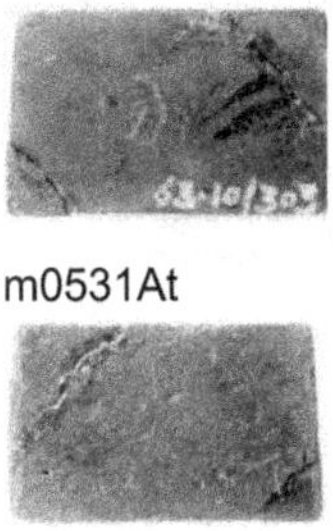

m0532At

m0532Bt

3349

m0534At

m0534Bt

3304

m0535At

m0535Bt

3355

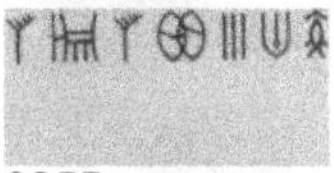

m0536At

m0536Bt

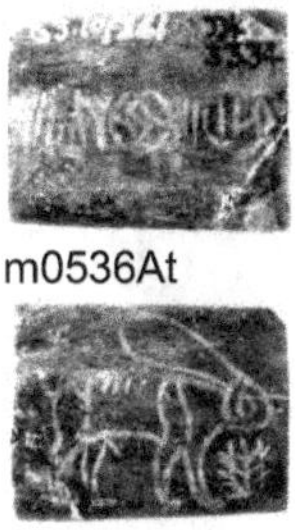

3312

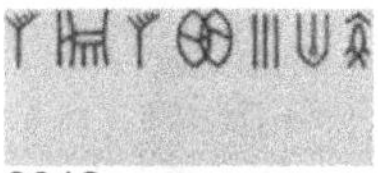

m0537At

m0537Bt

1705

m0538At

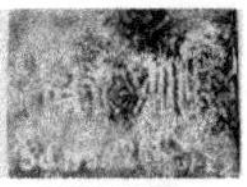

m0538Bt

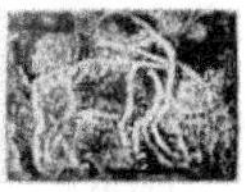

3384

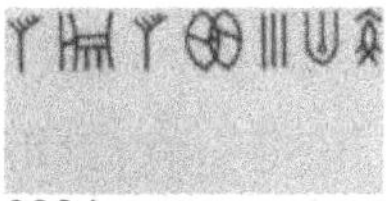

m0539At

m0539Bt

m540t

m0541At

m0541Bt

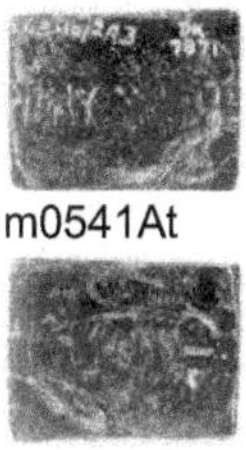

3331

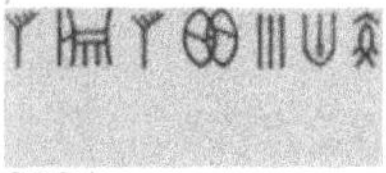

m0542At

m0542Bt

3326 Hare?

m0543At

m0543Bt

3363 [Note the 'heart' orthograph on the body of the antelope. This is comparable to

Sign 323 ]

m0544At

m0544Bt

3357

m0545At

m0545Bt

3301

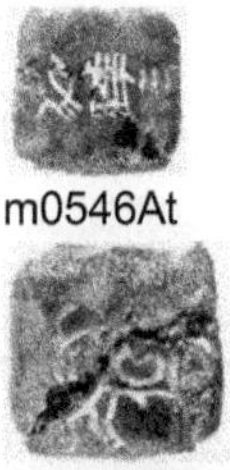

m0546At

m0546Bt

3383

m0547At

m0547Bt

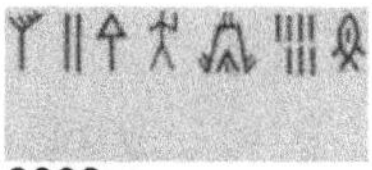

3303

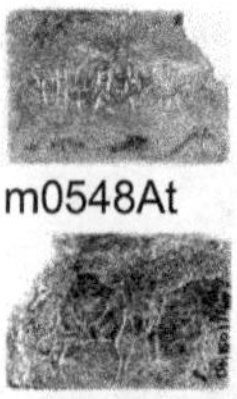

m0548At

m0548Bt

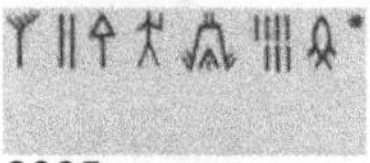

3305

m0549At

m0549Bt

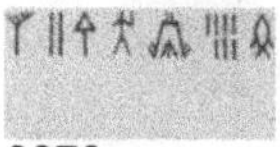

3373

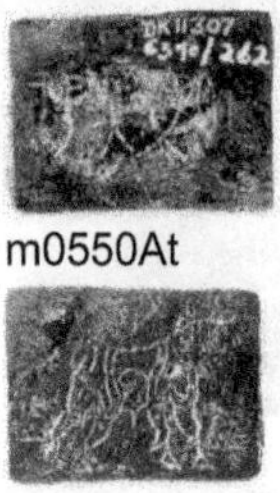

m0550At

m0550Bt

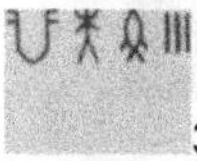

3351

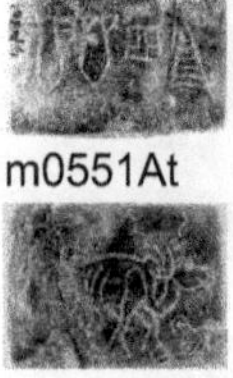

m0551At

m0551Bt

1708

Ox-antelope with long tail.

m0552At

m0552Bt

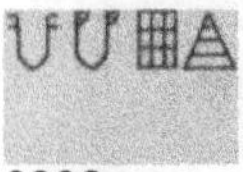

3306

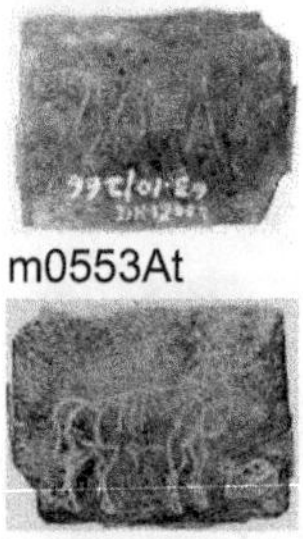

m0553At

m0553Bt

3353

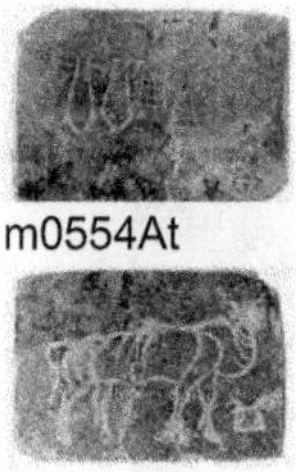

m0554At

m0554Bt

1712

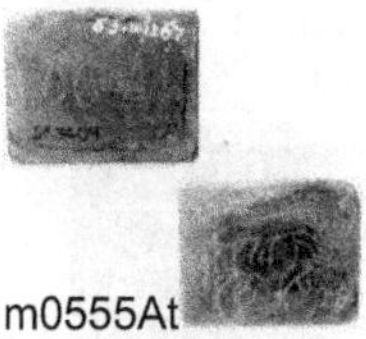

m0555At

m0555Bt

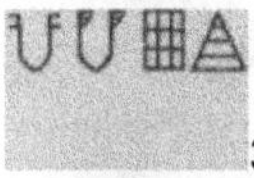

3314

m0556At

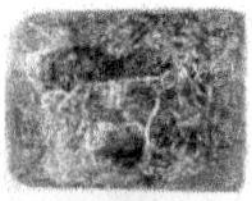

m0556Bt

3404

m0557At

m0557Bt

3341

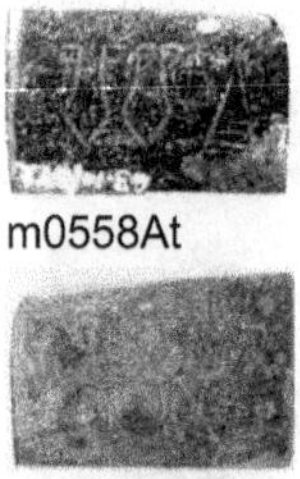

m0558At

m0558Bt

3342

m0559At

m0559Bt

2909

m0560At

m0560Bt

3386

m0561At
m0561Bt

3339

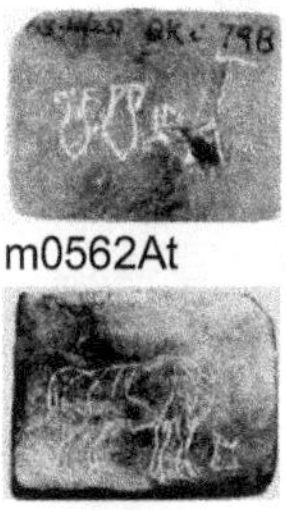
m0562At
m0562Bt

3361

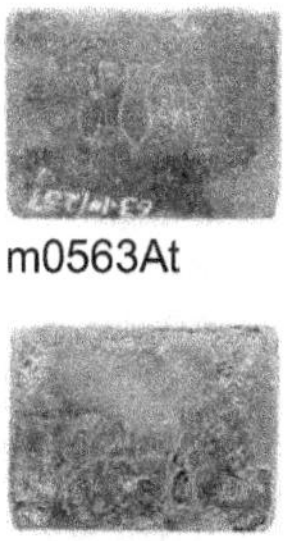
m0563At
m0563Bt

3379

m0564At
m0564Bt

3371

m0565At

m0565Bt

3403

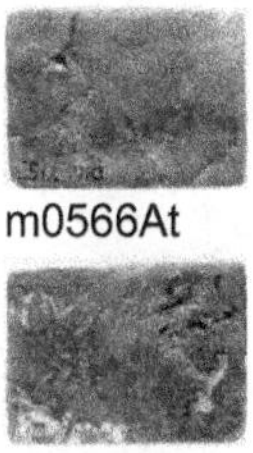
m0566At
m0566Bt

3359

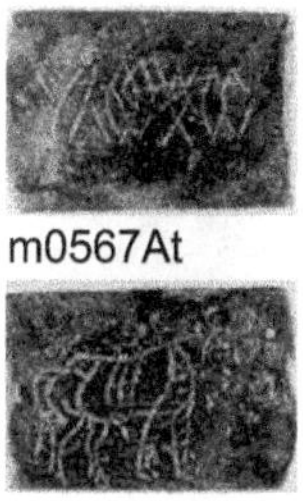
m0567At
m0567Bt

3322
Bison.

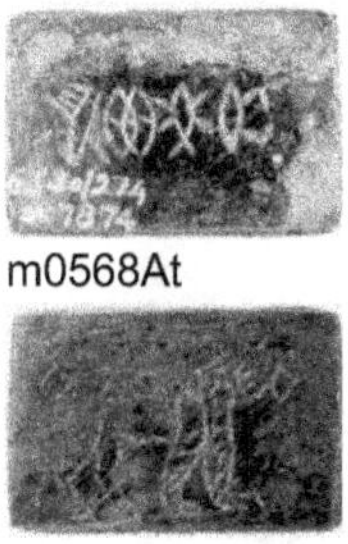
m0568At
m0568Bt

3332 Tiger.

m0569At

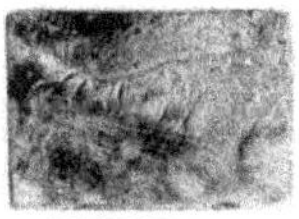
m0569Bt

3372

m0571At
m0571Bt

2913
Horned elephant. Almost similar to the composition: Body of a ram (with inlaid 'heart' sign), horns of a bull, trunk of an elephant, hindlegs of a tiger and an upraised serpent-like tail

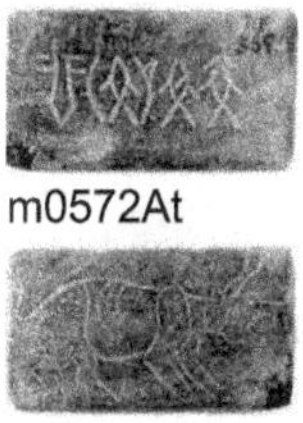
m0572At
m0572Bt

3317

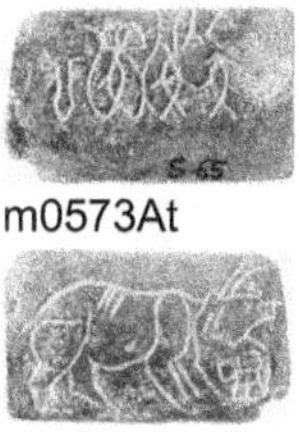
m0573At
m0573Bt
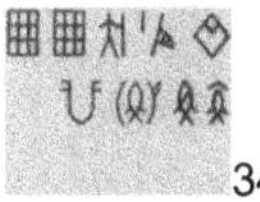
3415

m0574At
m0574Bt
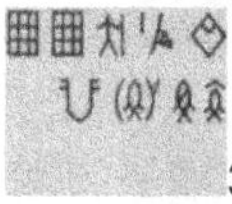
3318

m0575At
m0575Bt
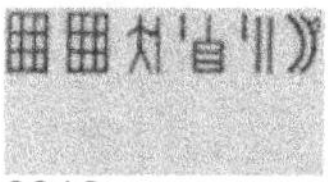
3316

m0576At
m0576Bt

3344

m0577At

m0577Bt

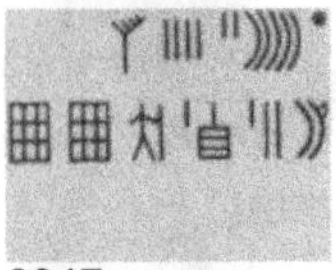
3347

m0578At

m0578Bt

2908

m0580At

m0580Bt

3321

m0581At

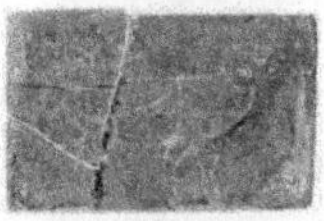
m0581Bt

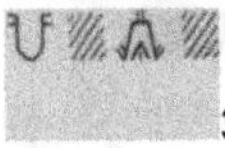
3340

2914

Pict-89: Standing person with horns and bovine features, holding a bow in one hand and an arrow or an uncertain object in the other.

m0582At

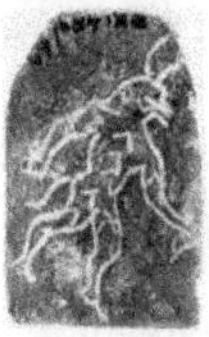
m0582Bt

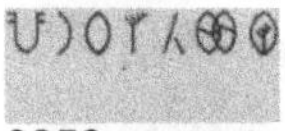
3358

m0583At

m0583Bt

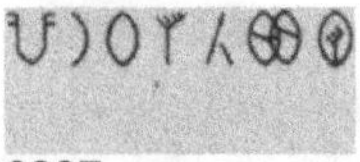
3387

m0584At

m0584Bt

m0585At

m0585Bt

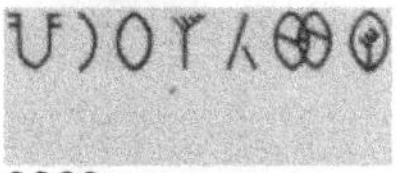
3369

m0586At

m0586Bt

3406

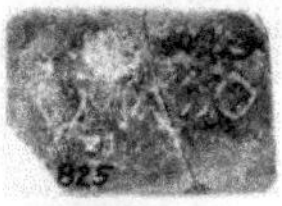
m0587At

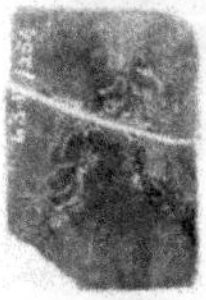
m0587Bt

3365 Horned Archer?

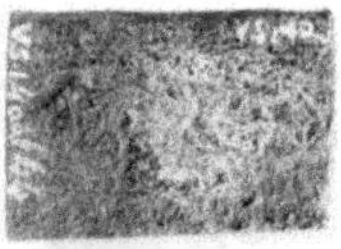
m0588At

m0588Bt Horned archer.

m0592At

m0592Bt

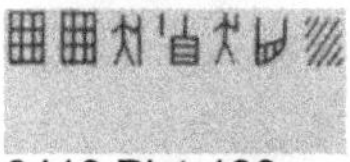
3413 Pict-133: Double-axe (?) without shaft. [The sign is comparable to the sign which appears on the text of a Chanhu-daro seal: Text 6402, Chanhu-daro Seal 23].

m0593At

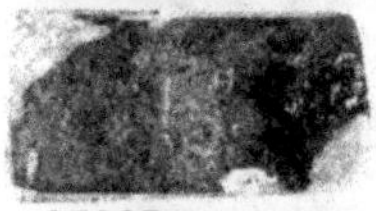
m0593Bt

3337

m0594At

m0594Bt

m0595A
m0595B

1010

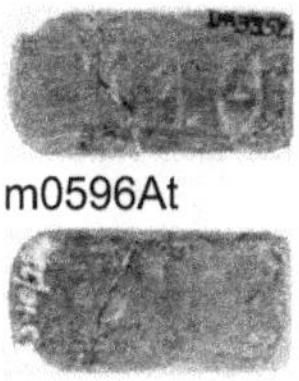
m0596At
m0596Bt

3313
m0598 Text
3410

m0599At
m0599Bt

3360

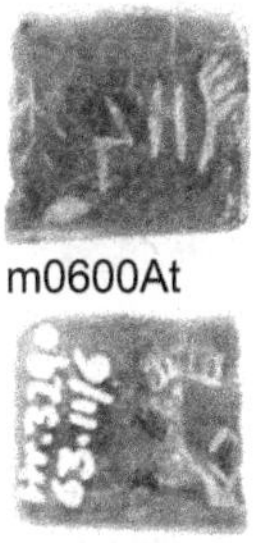
m0600At
m0600Bt

3375

m0601At
m0601Bt

m0602At
m0602Bt

3414

m0604At
m0604Bt

3315

m0605At
m0605Bt

2902

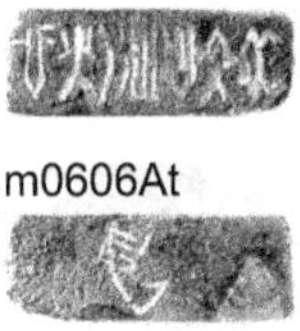
m0606At
m0606Bt

2918

m0608At

m0608Bt

m0614

1904

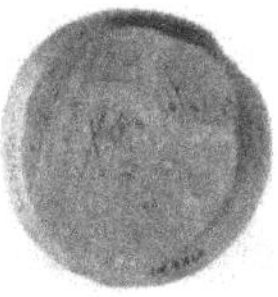
m0615

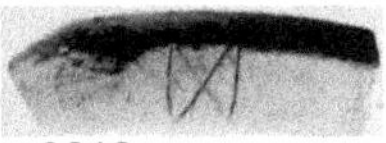
m0618

m0619

2939

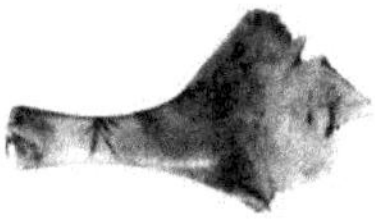
m0620

m0621

2367

m0622

m0623

m0624

1015

m0625
1027

m0626

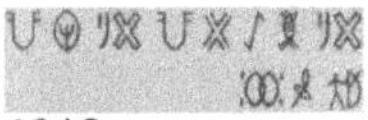
1012

m0627

1004

m0628

1033

m0629

m0630A

m0631

1008

m0632

1017

m0633

1016

m0634

2069

m0635a

m0636

2019

m0637

1034

m0638 One-horned bull

1404

m0639

m0640

m0641

m0642

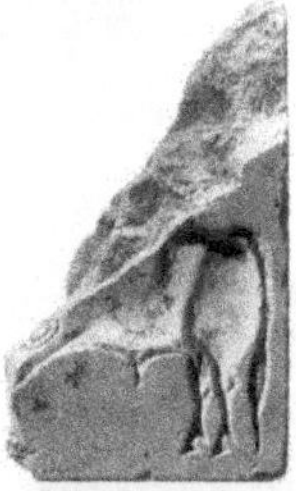
m0643

m0644

1553

m0645

m0646A1

m0646a12

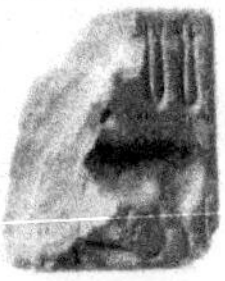
m0646A2

2653

m0647

1024

m0648

3104

m0649
2530

m0650
1032

m0651
2578

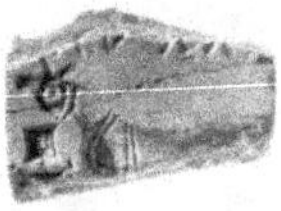
m0652

m0653
1057

m0654
2561

m0655
2098

m0656

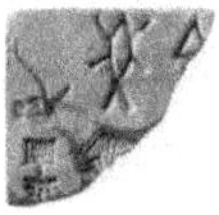
m0657

2026

m0658

1039

m0659

m0661

2207

m0662

1061

m0663

2597

m0664

2628

m0665

1139

m0666

2243

m0667

1111

m0668

2032

m0669

2686

m0670

1030

m0671

1021

m0672

1040

m0673

1025

m0674

1068

m0675

2197

m0676

m0677

m0678

1066

m0679

m0680A1

m0681

2182

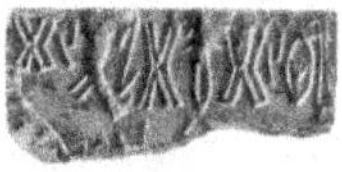
m0682

m0682A2

2690

m0683a

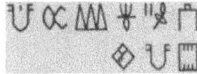

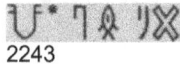

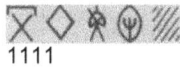

m0683A1

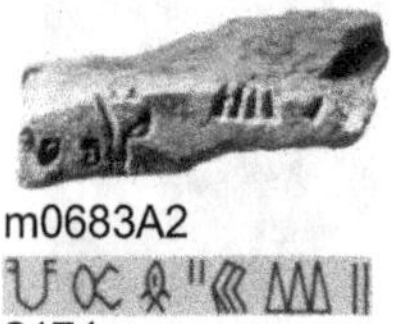

m0683A2

2174

m0684

m0685

1276

m0686

2324

m0687

m0688

m0689

m0690

m0691

m0692

1031

m0693

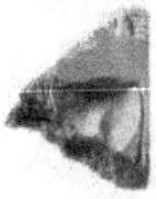

m0694

m0695

m0696

m0697

m0698

m0699

1050

m0700

m0701

1059

m0702

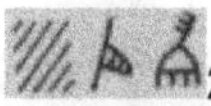

2206

m0703

2438

m0704

2351

m0705

2272

m0706

1097

m0707

m0708

2666

m0709

2071

m0710

3159

m0711

1166

m0712

1091

Note Sign391 ligatured on the animal's neck; this may be a logonym (i.e. two heiroglyphs – rings and spoked circle -- representing the same lexeme) for the rings on the neck?

m0713

2432

m0715

2681

m0716

2076

[Are there signs following these two signs?]

m0717

1078

m0714

2446

m0718

2209

m0719

2137

m0720

1082

m0721

1165

m0722

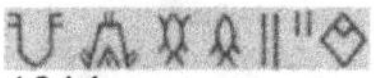
1014

m0723

2054

m0724

m0725

m0726

m0727a

m0727A1

m0727A2

2168

m0728

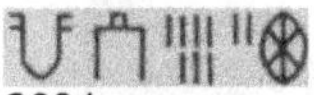
2691

m0729

1177

m0730

m0732

2674

m0733

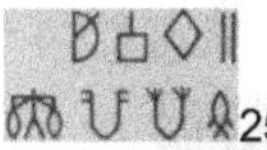
2519

m0734

1539

m0735

1060

m0736

2562

m0737

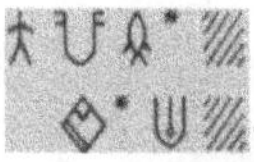
1112

m0738

2644

m0739

m0740

1090

m0741

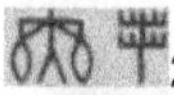
2421

m0742
2595

m0743

m0744

m0745

1175

m0746

1081

m0747

2471

m0748

1135

m0749

2008

m0750

2065

m0751

1102

m0752a

m0753a

m0753A1

m0753A2

2589

m0754

1145

m0755

m0756a

1028

m0757

2507

m0758a

2184

m0759 One-horned bull.

2384

m0760

m0761 One-horned bull.
1417

m0762a
2645

m0763

m0764

m0765

m0766

m0767

m0768
1176

m0769
2034

m0770a
1138

m0771
2676

m0772
2453

m0773

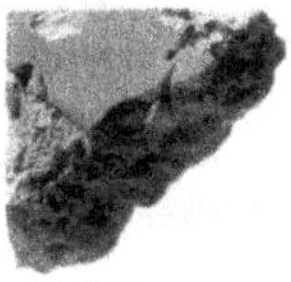
m0774

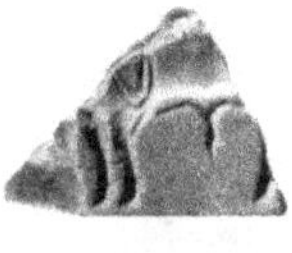
m0775

m0776
1146

m0777
2536

m0778
2425

m0779
2622

m0780
1178

m0781
2251

m0782
1122

m0783
1127

m0784
1128

m0785
1181

m0786
1107

m0787
2503

m0788

m0789

1185

m0790

m0791

m0792

2013

m0793

m0794

2067

m0795

1228

m0796

2105

m0797

m0798

1084

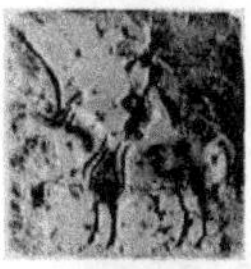
m0799 3015 or 3147

m0800

m0801
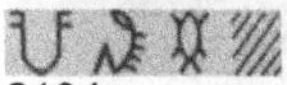
2104

m0802

1182

m0803
1131

m0804

2570

m0805

3041

m0806

m0807

2669

m0808

2146

m0809

2548

m0810
2364

m0811
2211

m0812
2629

m0813

m0814

2426

m0815
2555

m0816
2424

m0817
2435

m0818
1089

m0819
2081

m0820

m0821
1238

m0822
1249

m0823
1086

m0824
1164

m0825
1239

m0826

m0827
2513

m0828
2114

m0829

m0830
2274

m0831
2546

m0832

m0833
2281

m0834
2569b

m0835
2179

m0836

m0837
3085

m0838
2368

m0839
2476

m0840
2617

m0841

m0842

2704

m0843

m0844

1290

m0845

2202

m0846

1005

m0847
1156

m0848

2241

m0849

1121

m0850

2533

m0851

2660

m0852a

2413

m0853

2255

m0854

2501

m0855

2473

m0856

1211

m0857

2091

m0858a

2189

m0859

2063

m0860

m0861

1123

m0862

2253

m0863

2621 Is the 'stubble' ligatured glyph a variant of Sign 162  ?]

m0864

1240

m0865

1109

m0866

2646

m0867

m0868

3160

m0869

m0870

1160

m0871

m0872

m0873

1170

m0874

3092

m0875
1189

m0876

m0877

m0878

1092

m0879
2121

m0880

m0881

1242

m0882
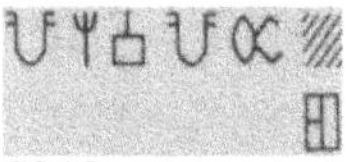
2312
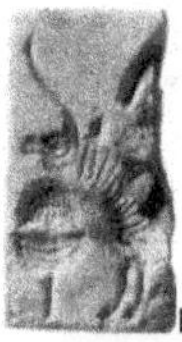
m0883

m0884
3158

m0885

m0886

3072

m0887a
1169

m0888

1155

m0889

1126

m0890

2117

m0891
1073

m0892
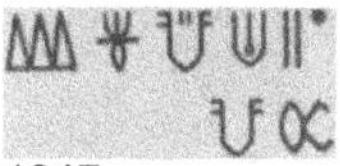
1247

m0893
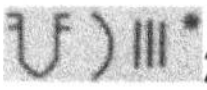
2659
One-horned bull.

m0894
2393

m0895

2262

m0896

2134

m0897

2545

m0898 2167

m0899

2242

m0900

2335

m0901

2276

m0902a

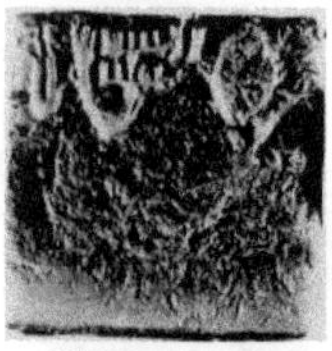

m0903a.

1294

m0904

m0905

m0906

m0907

2192

m0908

m0909

3028

m0910

m0911

m0914

2143

m0915

1218

m0916

1204

m0917

1224

m0918

m0919

2343

m0920

1219

m0921

m0922

1282

m0923

m0924

2591

m0925

1292

m0926

2219

m0927

1171

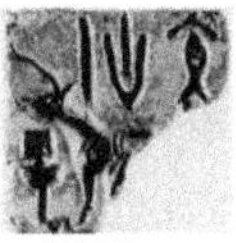
m0928

1202

m0929a

1144

m0930

3020

m0931
3091

m0932

3022

m0933

2160

m0934

1158

m0935

2144

m0936

1197

m0937

2066

m0938

2158

m0939a

2652

m0940a

2060

m0941

2256

m0942

1296

m0943

2282

m0944

2419

m0945

1208

m0946
2358

m0947

2404

m0948

2250

m0949A

m0949C

1271

Also, Sign 141

m0950a

1013

m0951

1263

m0952

2265

m0953
2582

m0954
1262

m0955
2547

m0956
1251

m0957
1026

m0958
2348

m0959
1147

m0960
1388

m0961
1163

m0962
3074

m0963
1232

m0964
2010

m0965
1222

m0966
2070

m0967
2460

m0968
2300

m0969
2239

m0970a
2116

m0971
1234

m0972a
2557

m0973a
2585

m0974a
2650

m0975
2295

m0976
1203

m0977
3152

m0978

m0979
2564

m0980
2317

m0981

m0982a

2021

m0983

m0984 1143

m0985

m0986a

2341

m0987a

1007

m0988

m0989

m0990

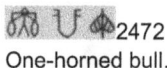

2472 One-horned bull.

m0991 2203

m0992

2464

m0993a

1267

m0994a

2165

m0995

m0996

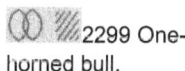

2299 One-horned bull.

m0997a 3105

m0998

2176

m0999

2452

m1000a

1487 One-horned bull.

m1001a

1283

m1002

m1003

1275

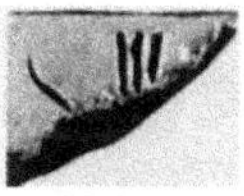
m1004

m1005

1001

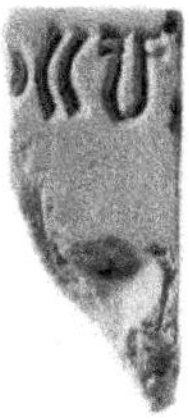
m1006

1499 Bovid.

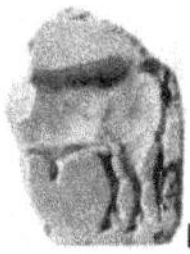
m1007

m1008

m1009

2627

m1010

2672 Bovid.

m1011

m1012

m1013

m1014 One-horned bull?

1397
m1015

m1016.

1348

m1017.

1300

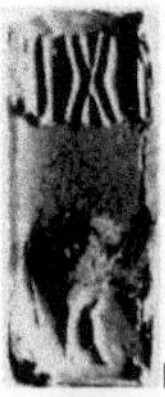
m1018a

2483

Bovid.

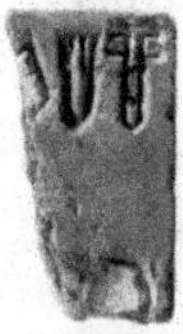
m1019.

1298

m1020
2496

m1021a.
1299

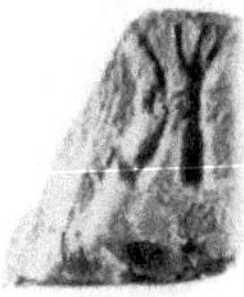
m1022

m1
023

m1024

m1025a

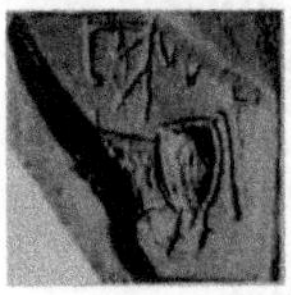
m1026a.

1307

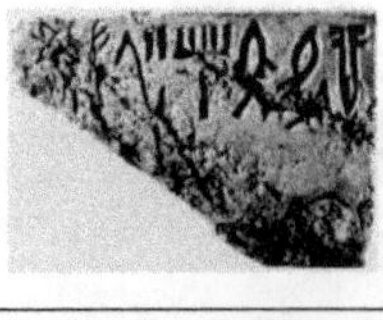

m1027

m1028
2671

Bovid.

m1029

1265

m1030 
3145

m1031

2053

m1032

2217

m1033

m1034
2467

m1036

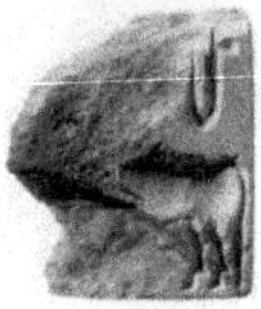
m1037

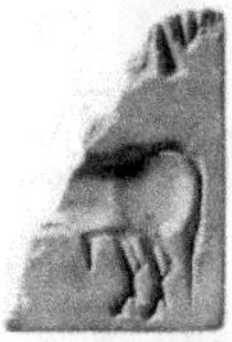
m1038

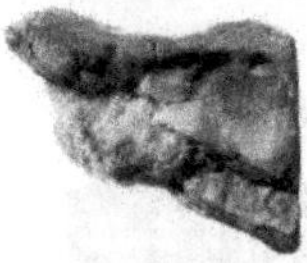
m1039

m1040

m1041

m1042

m1043

m1044a

1551

Bovid.

m1045

2447 Bovid.

m1046

3058

m1047

1281

m1048

m1049

3032

m1050 1196

m1051

m1052

3100

m1053

2163

m1054

2448

m1055

2529

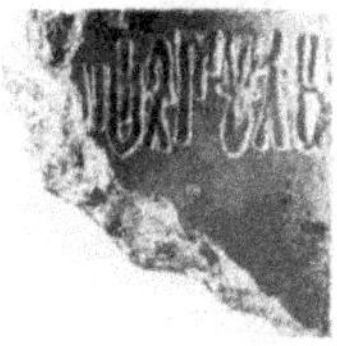
m1057

2566

m1058a

1392

m1059

m1060

1497

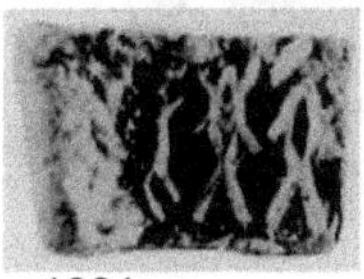
m1061a

1379

m1062

2089

m1063

2357

m1064

1492

m1065

2151

m1066

1547

m1067a

1496

m1068

m1069

1390

m1070

2040

m1071

1488

m1072a

1443

m1073

1489

m1074

m1075a

1479

m1076

m1077a

2359

m1078

m1079

2655

m1080

1542

m1081a

2129

m1082.

1349

m1083

m1084

1316 Bison.

m1085.

1322

m1086a

3070

m1087a.

1319

m1088

2268

m1089a.

1315

m1090

2675

m1091

m1092

1312

m1093

m1094

m1095

2495 Bison

m1096

2410

m1097

2313

m1098

1301

m1099

1313

m1100

2201 Bison

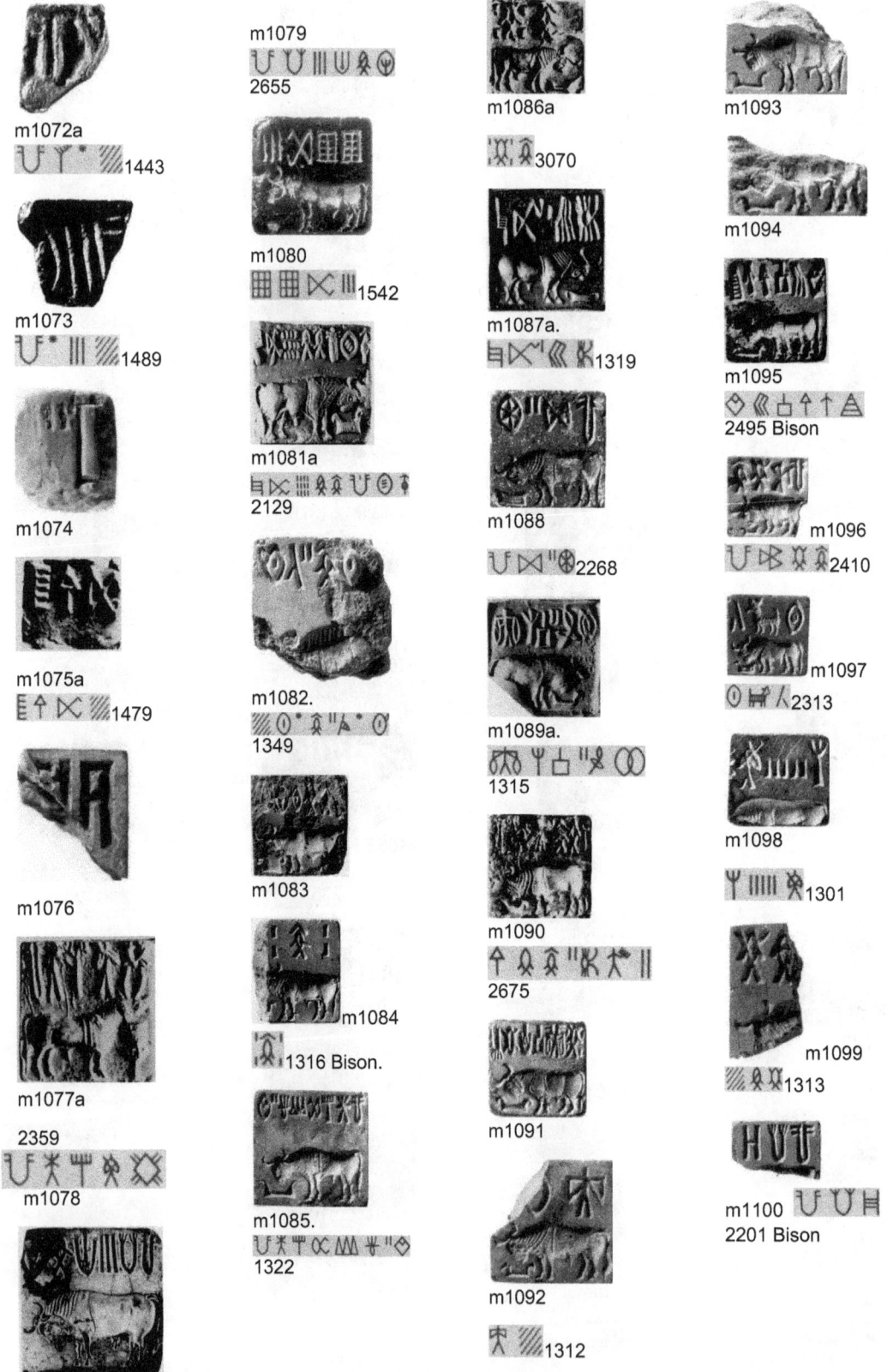

m1101
2431 Zebu.

m1102

m1103.
1337

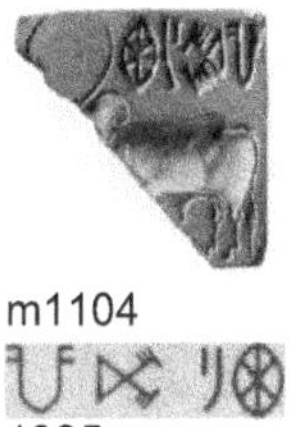
m1104
1335

m1105

m1106
2331
Zebu

m1107a
2306

m1108
1339

m1109
1327
Zebu

m1110
1334

m1111.
1333

m1112
2366
Zebu.

m1113
2441

m1114.
1331

m1115
1328 Zebu

m1116.
1329

m1117a
2615

m1118
3157

m1119
2463

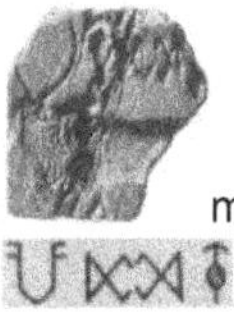
m1120
2362

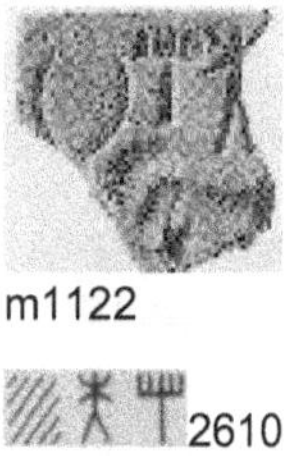
m1122
2610

m1126
2332

m1127
2696

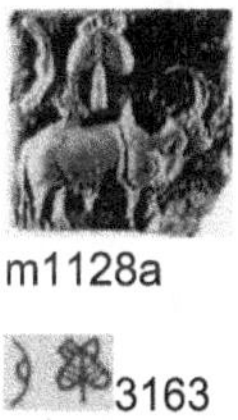
m1128a
3163

m1129a
1302
Markhor.

m1130

m1131

m1132

1545
Rhinoceros.

m1133

1343

m1134

2651

m1135

2140
Pict-50 Composite animal: features of an ox and a rhinoceros facing the standard device.

m1136

m1137

2531
Rhinoceros.

m1138.

1344

m1139.

1341

m1140a

2188 Rhinoceros.

m1141

2169

m1142

m1143

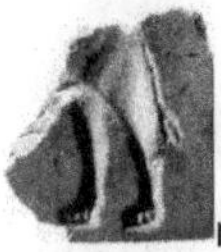
m1144

m1145

m146a

1374
Elephant

m1147

m1148

2590

m1149

1368
Elephant.

m1150

1534

m1151
1535

m1152

1369

m1154

1362 Elephant.

m1155

2573

m1156

1370

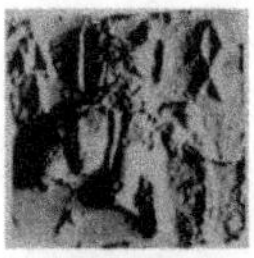
m1157a

2110

m158

m1159

2171

m1160

2057

m1161

2504

m1162

2058

m1163

2640

Tiger.

m1164

2665 Tiger.

m1165a

2064

m1166.

1351

m1167

2484

Tiger.

m1168

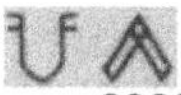
2360

Seal showing a horned tiger. Mohenjo-daro. (After Scala/Art Resource).

Tiger with long (zebu's) horns?

1385

Pict-49 Uncertain animal with dotted circles on its body.

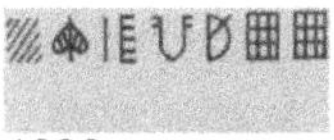
1626

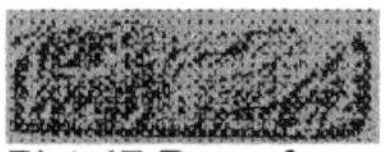
Pict-47 Row of uncertain animals in file.

m1169a

2024

Pict-58: Composite motif: body of an ox and three heads: of a one-horned bull (looking forward), of antelope (looking backward), and of short-horned bull (bison) (looking downward).

m1170a 

1382 Composite animal

m1171 Composite animal

m1172

m1173

1191

m1175a

2493

Composite animal: human face, zebu's horns, elephant tusks and trunk, ram's forepart, unicorn's trunk and feet, tiger's hindpart and serpent-like tail.

m1176

m1177

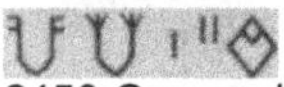
2450 Composite animal: human face, zebu's horns, elephant tusks and trunk, ram's forepart, unicorn's trunk and feet, tiger's hindpart and serpent-like tail.

m1178

2559

m1179

2606

Human-faced markhor with long wavy horns, with neck-bands and a short tail.

m1180a

1303
Human-faced markhor

m1181A

2222
Pict-80: Three-faced, horned person (with a three-leaved pipal branch on the crown), wearing bangles and armlets and seated on a hoofed platform

Padri . Head painted on storage jar from Padri, Gujarat (c. 2800 BCE). Details of body with multiple hands (?) Similar horned-heads painted on jars are found at Kot Diji, Burzhom and Kunal (c. 3rd millennium BCE). [Source: Page 21, Figs. 10A and B in: Deo Prakash Sharma, 2000, *Harappan seals, sealings and copper tablets*, Delhi, National Museum].

m1182a

m1183a

m1184

m1185

Pict-103 Horned (female with breasts hanging down?) person with a tail and bovine legs standing near a tree fisting a horned tiger rearing on its hindlegs.

1357

m1186A

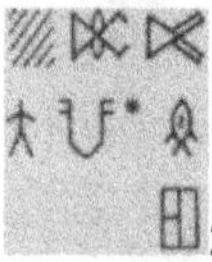
2430
Composition: horned person with a pigtail standing between the branches of a pipal tree; a low pedestal with offerings (? or human head?); a horned person kneeling in adoration; a ram with short tail and curling horns; a row of seven robed figures, with twigs on their pigtails.

m1187

m1188

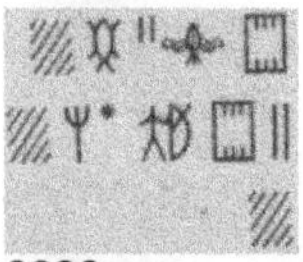
2228

m1189

1396

m1190

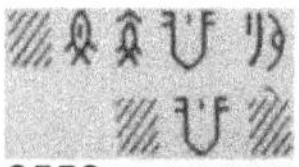
2558

m1191
1389

m1192

1495

m1193a

2401

m1194a

3066

m1195

2181

m1196

m1197

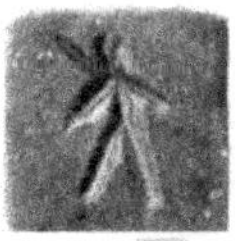

m1198  1482

Silver

m1199A 
2520

m1200A

m1200C

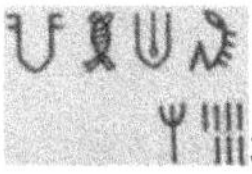 3078

m1201

m1202A

m1202C.

1325 Space on the side of the seal was used to inscribe a third line

m1203A

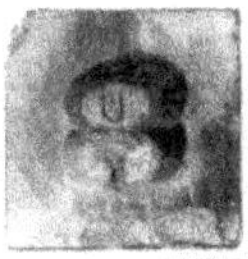

m1203B 
1018

m1204

 2095

m1205a

m1205c

m1205f

 1293 + Two signs on the sides of the seal.

m1206AE

m1206e1

m1206F

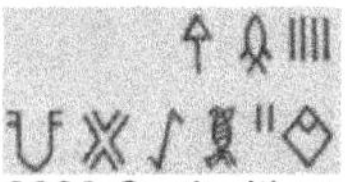

2229 Seal with a projecting knob containing the top three signs; m1206e is inscribed on the top edge of the lower indented frame which depicts the bison.

m1208

m1221

m1222

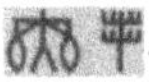 1268

m1223

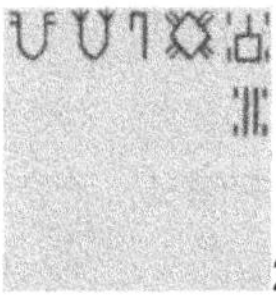

2045

Pict-40: Frog.

2565

Pict-37 Goat-antelope with a short tail

m1224A

m1224B

1224

m1224e

Pict-88

1227 Standing person with horns and bovine features (hoofed legs and/or tail).

m1225A
m1225B.

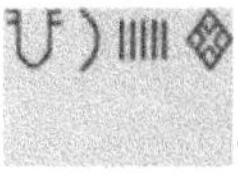

1311 Cube seal with perforation through the breadth of the seal Pict-118: svastika_, generally within a square or rectangular border.

m1226A.

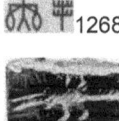

1326 Unfinished seal.

m1227

m1228a

1394

m1230a

1358

m1231

2321
Unfinished seal?

m1232a

2497
Unfinished seal

m1233A

m1233B

m1233cd
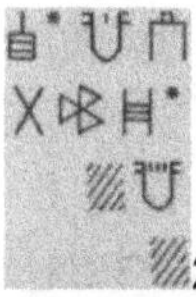
2352

m1234a

m1234b

m1234d

m1234e

m1235a

m1235bc

2394
Unfinished seal

m1236

1483
Unfinished seal?

m1239
m1240

m1241
m1242
m1243
m1244

m1245
m1246
m1247
m1248

m1249
m1250
m1251
m1252

m1253

m1254
m1255
m1256
m1257

m1258
m1259
m1260

m1261

m1262

2301

m1263

1391

m1264a

1405

m1265

2227

m1266

1470

m1267

1494

m1268

2288

m1269

m1270

1464

m1271

2603

m1272

m1273

2679

m1274

2106

m1275

3161

m1276

2428

m1277

m1278

2028

m1280a

1462

m1281

2266

m1282

m1283

m1284a

2477

m1285a

2204

m1286

1455

m1287

1454

m1288

3086

m1289

1452

m1290

1463

m1291a

2688

m1292

1461

m1293a

2388

m1294

2291

m1295

1458

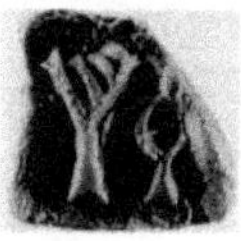

m1296a

3144

m1297

1445

m1298

3037

m1299a

1456

m1300

2350

m1301

m1302a

1432

m1303a

1398

m1304

1423

m1305

2289

m1306

1430

m1307

m1308

2697

m1309

2579

m1310

1418

m1311

2485

m1312

2318

m1313

2093

m1314a

1439

m1315

2345

m1316a

m1317

3095

m1318

1416

m1319

m1320

1447

m1321

1446

m1322a

3079

m1323

2006

m1324

2682

m1325

2118

m1326

3143

m1327

1408

m1328

2392

m1329A 

m1329C

2439

m1330

1409

m1331a

2303

m1332

m1333

1434

m1334a

2170

m1335a

2072

m1336a

2515

m1337

2055

m1338a

2020

m1339 2025

m1340 2369

m1341

2092

m1342a

1393

m1343

1433

m1344

2315

m1346a

m1349B

m1349A

m1350

2599

m1351

2142

m1353

1459

m1354a

1498

m1355a

2568

m1356

m1357

2356

m1358

m1359

2575

m1360

1442

m1361a

1474

m1362A

m1362C

2230

m1363

2372

m1364A

m1364C

2542

m1365A

m1365B

2658 Cricket, spider or prawn?

m1366

2094

m1367a

2661 Two bisons standing face-to-face

m1368

1460

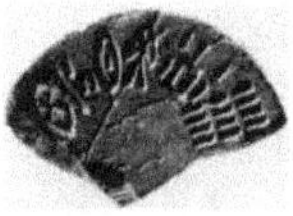

m1369

1478

m1370a

2509

Cylinder seal; tree branch

m1371A1

m1371A2

m1372A1

m1372A2

m1373A1

m1373A2

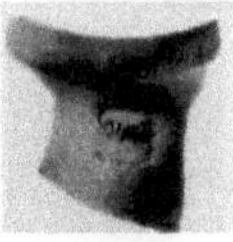

m1374A1

m1374A2

m1375A1

m1375A2

1560

Seal impression on pot

m1376A1

m1376A2

m1378A1

m1378A2

m1379A2

m1380A2

m1381A1

m1381A2

1559

Seal Impression on a pot

m1382A1

m1382A2 Seal impression on a potsherd

3244

m1383

m1384si

m1385A14

m1385A2

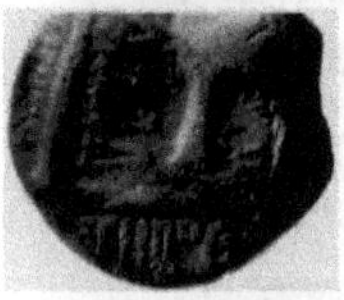

m1385A3

m1386si

m1387t

m1388t

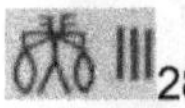2856

m1389t

m1390At

m1390Bt

2868 Pict-74: Bird in flight.

m1391t

2826

m1392t

2837

m1393t

m1394t

m1395At

m1395Bt

m1396t

m1397At

m1397Bt

m1398t

2807

m1400At

m1400B

2851

m1401t

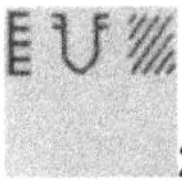2822

m1402At

m1402Bt

m1403At

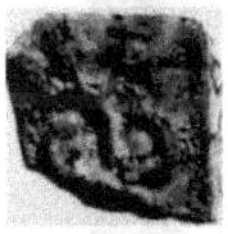

m1403Bt

m1405At Pict-97: Person standing at the center pointing with his right hand at a bison facing a trough, and with his left hand pointing to the

sign

Obverse: A tiger and a rhinoceros in file.

m1405Bt Pict-48 A tiger and a rhinoceros in file

2841

m1406At

m1406B 2827

Pict-102: Drummer and people vaulting over? An adorant?

m1407At

m1407Bt

m1408At

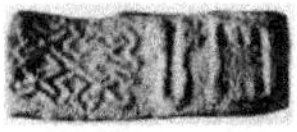

m1409At

m1409Bt

Serpent (?) entwined around a pillar with capital (?) or ring-stones stacked on a pillar?; the motif is carved in high relief on the reverse side of the inscribed object.

m1410At

m1410Bt

m1411At

m1411Bt

m1412At

m1412Bt

m1413At

m1413Bt

m1414At

m1414Bt

m1415At

m1415Bt

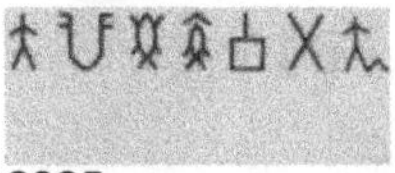

2825

m1416At

m1416Bt

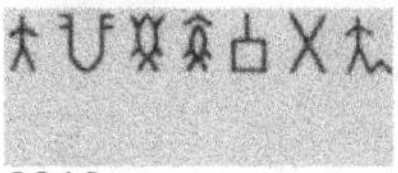

2818

m1417t

3242

m1418At

m1418Bt

m1419At

m1419Bt

2812

m1420At
2865

m1421At

m1421Bt

m1422At

2845

m1423At

m1423Bt Elephant shown on both sides of the tablet.

m1424Atc

m1424Btc

3234

m1425At

m1425Bt

m1427At

m1427Bt

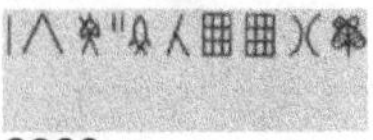

2860

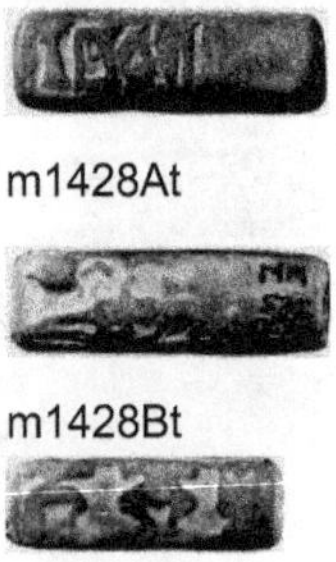

m1428At

m1428Bt

m1428Ct

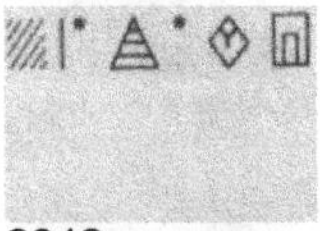

2842

m1426

1621

m1429At

m1429Bt Pict-125: Boat.

m1429Ct

3246 Gharial holding a fish in its jaws.

Pict-100

Person throwing a spear at a buffalo and placing one foot on the head of the buffalo.

2279

m1430Bt

m1430C

m1430At Pict-101: Person throwing a spear at a buffalo and placing one foot on its head; three persons standing near a tree at the center.

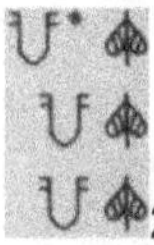

2819 Pict-60: Composite animal with the body of an ox and three heads [one each of one-horned bull (looking forward), antelope (looking backward) and bison (looking downwards)] at right; a goat standing on its hindlegs and browsing from a tree at the center.

m1431A

m1431B

m1431C

m1431E

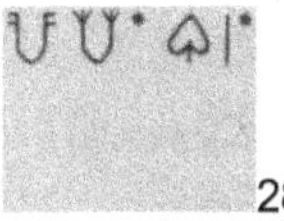

2805

Row of animals in file (a one-horned bull, an elephant and a rhinoceros from right); a gharial with a fish held in its jaw above the animals; a bird (?) at right. Pict-116: From R.—a person holding a vessel; a woman with a platter (?); a kneeling person with a staff in his hands facing the woman; a goat with its forelegs on a platform under a tree. [Or, two antelopes flanking a tree on a platform, with one antelope looking backwards?]

m1432At

m1432Bt

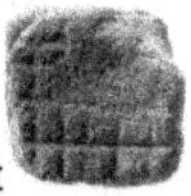

m1432Ct

m1433At

m1433Bt

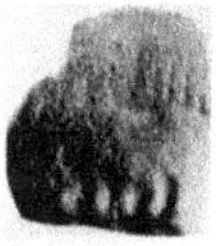

m1433Ct

m1436it

m1438it

m1439it

3132

m1440 it 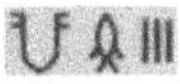

2374

m1441it

m1442it

m1443it

3213

m1444Ait

m1444Bit

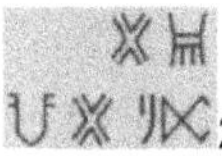

2339

m1445Ait

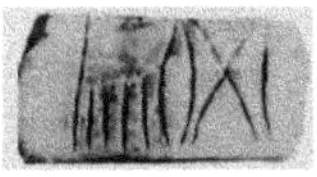

m1445Bit

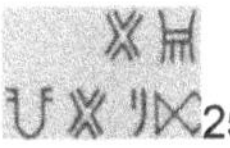

2505

m1447Ait

m1448Act

m1448Bct

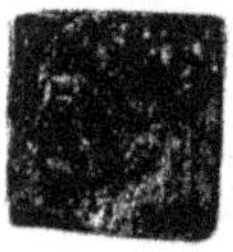

m1449Act

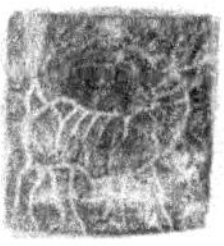

m1449Bct (obverse of inscription) Incised copper tablet (two sides) Markhor with head turned backwards

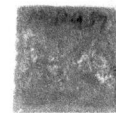

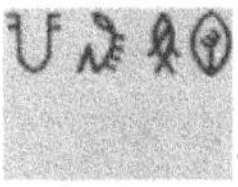

1801

m1450Act

m1450Bct

1701

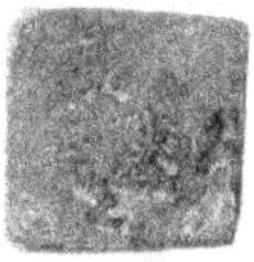

m1451Act

m1451Bct

m1452Act

m1452Bct

2912

m1453Act

m1453Bct

m1456Act

1805

m1457Act

m1457Bct

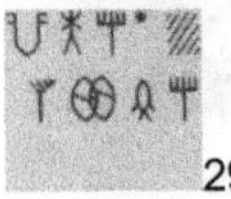
2904
Pict-124: Endless knot motif.

m1458Act

m1461Act

m1462Act

m1463ABct

2919

m1465Act
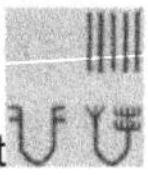
2921

m1470Act

m1472Bct

m1474Act

m1474Bct

m1475Act

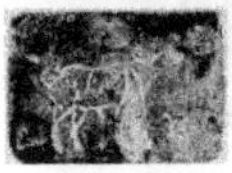
m1475Bct

m1476Bct

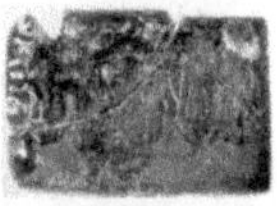
m1477Act

m1477Bct

m1482Act

m1482Bct

m1483Act

m1483Bct

m1484Act

m1484Bct

m1485Bct

m1486Act

m1486Bct

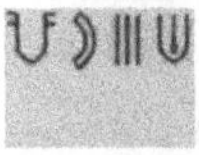
1711
Incised copper tablets.Elephant

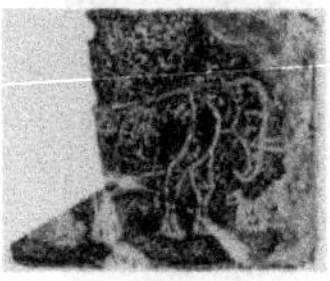
m1488Bct

m1491Act

m1491Bct

m1492Act

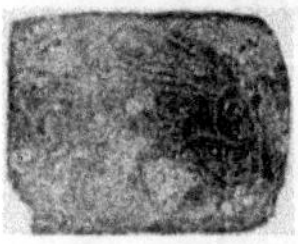
m1492Bct

m1493Bct

m1494

1706
Hare

Pict-42

m1497Act

m1498Act

m1498Bct

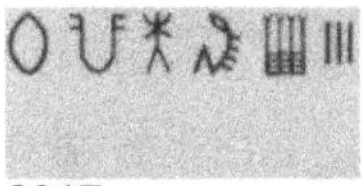
2917

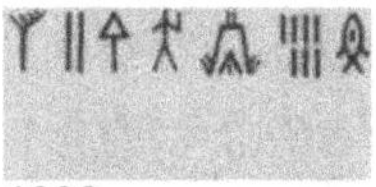
1803

Pict-30

1804

Pict-39 Ox-antelope with a long tail; a trough in front.

m1501Bct

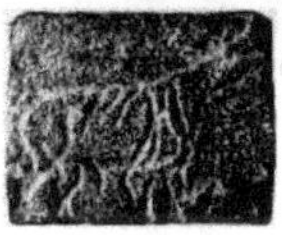
m1502Bct

m1503Act

m1503Bct

m1505Act

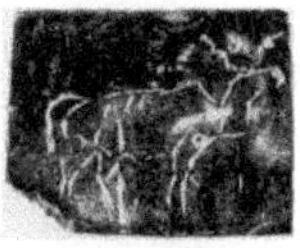
m1505Bct

m1506Act

m1506Bct

m1508Act

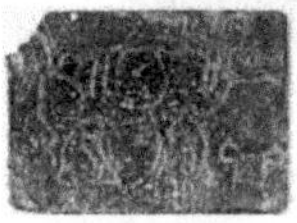
m1508Bct

1708

m1511Act

m1511Bct

m1512Act

m1512Bct

m1513

1712

m1514

1715

m1515Act

m1515Bct

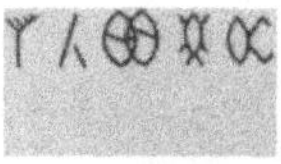
2910

m1516Act

m1516Bct

m1517Act

m1517Bct

m1518

1709

m1520Act

m1520Bct

2907

m1521Act

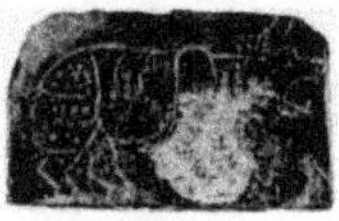

m1521Bct

m1522Act

m1522Bct

m1523Act

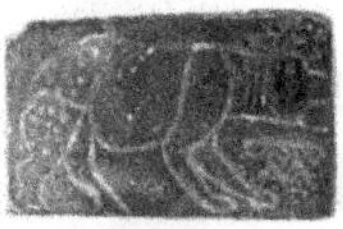

m1523Bct

m1524 

3396

m1528Act

m1529Act

2920

m1529Bct

m1532Act

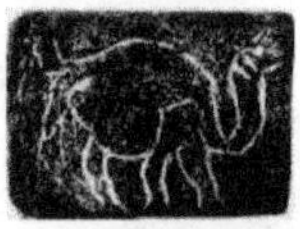

m1532Bct

m1534Act

m1534Bct

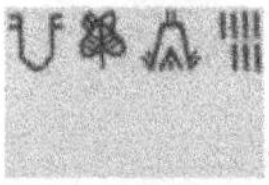

1703

Composition:

Two horned heads one at either end of the body. Note the dottings on the thighs which is a unique artistic feature of depicting a rhinoceros (the legs are like those of a rhinoceros?). The body apparently is a combination of two rhinoceroses with heads of two bulls attached on either end of the composite body.

m1535Act

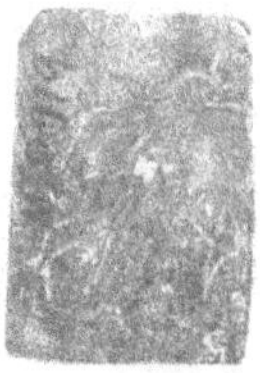

m1535Bct

m1540Act

m1540

m1547Act

1547Bct

m1548A

m1548Bct

m1549Act

m1549Bct

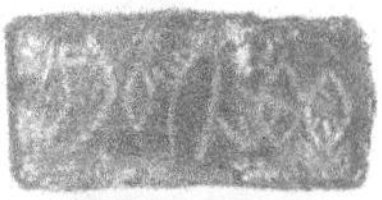

m1563Act

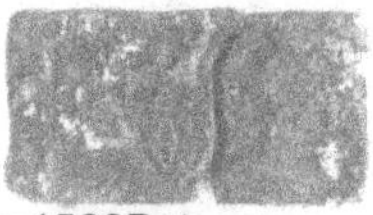

m1563Bct

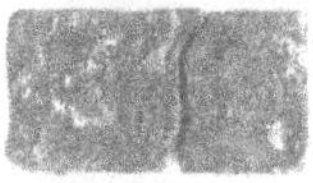

m1566Bct

m1568Act

m1568Bct

m1569 

3333

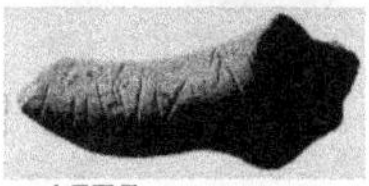

m1575

m1576

m1578 

3251

m1591

1592

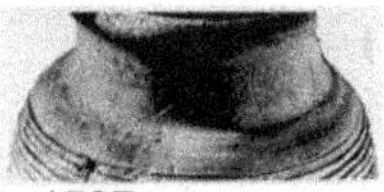
m1597

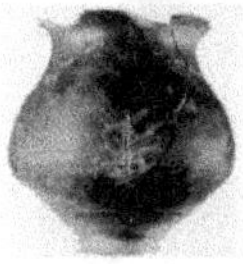
m1598

m1601

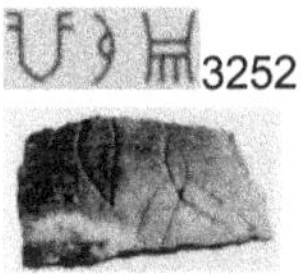
3252

m1603

m1609

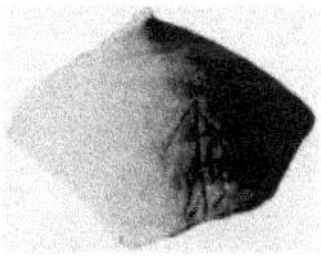
m1611

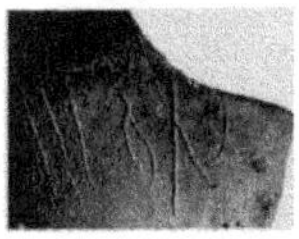
m1626

3245

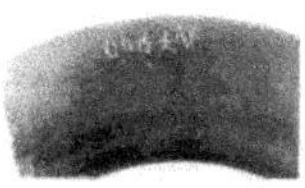
m1629bangle

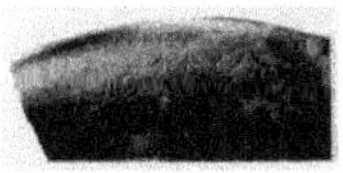
m1630bangle

m1631bangle

m1632bangle

m1633bangle

m1634bangle

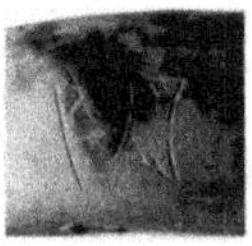
m1635bangle

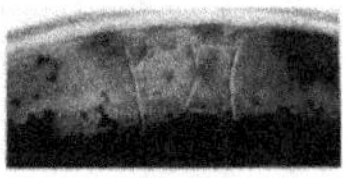
m1636bangle

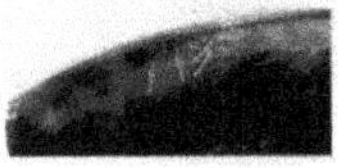
m1637bangle

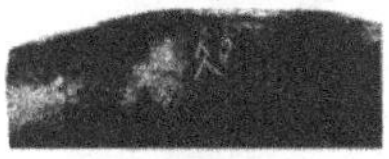
m1638bangle

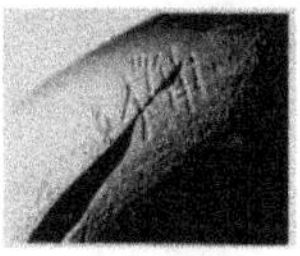
m1639bangle

m1640bangle

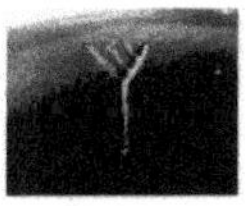
m1641bangle

m1643bangle

m1645bangle

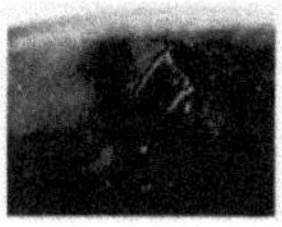
m1646bangle

m1647bangle

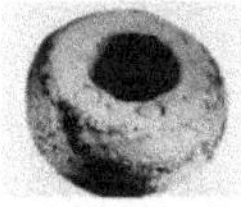
m1648shell

m1649Acone

m1649Bcone

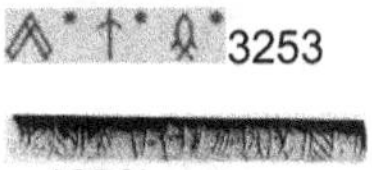
3253

m1650ivory stick

3505

Pict-144: Geometrical pattern.

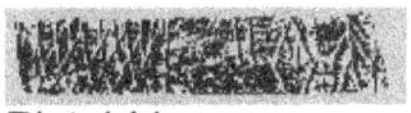
Pict-141: Geometrical pattern.

2942

Pict-142: Geometrical

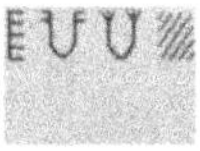
pattern.
2943 Ivory or bone rod

Pict-143: Geometrical pattern.Ivory stick

2948

Ivory rod, ivory plaque with dotted circles. Mohenjo-daro. [Musee National De Arts Asiatiques Guimet, 1988-1989, *Les cites oubliees de l'Indus Archeologie du Pakistan.*]

m1652A ivory stick

m1653 ivory plaque

1905

m1654A ivory cube

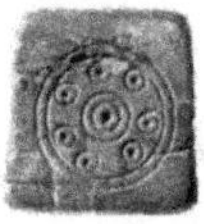
m1654B ivory cube

m1654D ivory cube

m1655faience ornament

m1656 steatite ornament

m1657A steatite

m1657B steatite

m1658AB etched bead

m1658 2952 Etched Bead

m1659 bangle

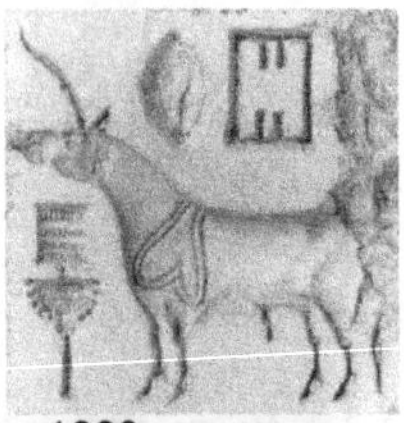
m1660

m1661a

m1662

m1663a

m1664a

m1665a

m1666a

m1667

m1668a

m1669a

m1670a

m1671a

m1672

m1673a

m1674a

m1675a

m1676a

m1677a

m1678a

m1679a

m1680a

m1681a

m1682a

m1683a

m1684a

m1685a

m1686a

m1687a

m1688a

m1689a

m1690a

m1691a

m1692a

m1693a

m1694a

m1695a

m1696a

m1697

m1698

m1699a

m1700a

m1701a

m1702a

m1703a

m17054

m1705a

m1706a

m1707a

m1708a

m1709a

m1710a

m1711a

m1712a

m1713a

m1714a

m1715a

m1716a

m1717a

m1718

m1719a

m1720

m1721

m1722a

m1723a

m1724a

m1725a

m1726a

m1727

m1728a

m1729a

m1730a

m1731a

m1732

m1733a

m1734

m1735

m1736a

m1737a

m1738

m1739a

m1740

m1741a

m1742

m1743

m17441

m1745a

m1746

m1747a

m1748

m1749a

m1750a

m1751a

m1752a

m1753a

m1754a

m1755a

m1756a

m1757a

m1758a

m1759a

m1760

m1761a

m1762a

m1763a

m1764a

m1765

m1766a

m1767

m1768a

m1769a

m1770a

m1771a

m1772a

m1773

m1774a

m1775a

m1776

m1777a

m1778

m1779a

m1780a

m1781a

m1782

m1783a

m1784a

m1785a

m1786a

m1787a

m1788a

m1789a

m1790a

m1791a

m1792a

m1793a

m1794

m1795a

m1796a

m1797

m1798a

m1799

m1800

m1801a

m1802

m1803a

m1804a

m1805a

m1806a

m1807a

m1808a

m1809a

m1810a

m1811a

m1812a

m1813a

m1814

m1815a

m1816a

m1817a

m1818

m1819

m1820

m1821a

m1822a

m1823

m1824a

m1825a

m1826

m1827

m1828a

m1829a

m1830

m1831a

m1832a

m1833a

m1834a

m1835a

m1836

m1837a

m1838a

m1839a

m1840

m1841a

m1842a

m1843a

m1844

m1845a

m1846a

m1847a

m1848

m1849

m1850a

m1851

m1852

m1853a

m1854a

m1855a

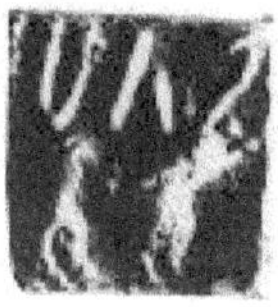

m1856a

m1857

m1858

m1860a

m1863a

m1864

m1865a

m1866

m1868a

m1869

m1872a

m1876a

m1877

m1878a

m1879a

m1880a

m1881

m1882

m1883

m1884a

m1885a

m1886a

m1887

m1888a

m1889

m1890

m1891a

m1892a

m1893

m1894

m1895a

m1896a

m1897

m1898a

m1899a

m1900a

m1901

m1092a

m1903a

m1904a

m1905a

m1906

m1907a

m1909

m1910

m1911a

m1912

m1912

m1913

m1914

m1915a

m1916a

m1917

m1918a

m1919

m1920a

m1921a

m1922a

m1923a

m1923c

m1923d

m1923e

m1927a

m1927b

m1928a

m1928b

m1930A

m1930B

m1931

m1932

m1933

m1934a

m1935

m1936

1937

m1938

m1939a

m1940

m1941a

m1942a

m1943a

m1944

m1945a

m1946

m1947a

m1948

m1950

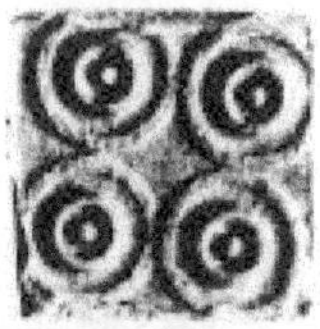

m1951a

m1953a

m1954a

m1955a

m1956a

m1957

m1958

m1959

m1960

m1961

m1962a

m1963a

m1964a

m1965a

m1966

m1967a

m1968A+C

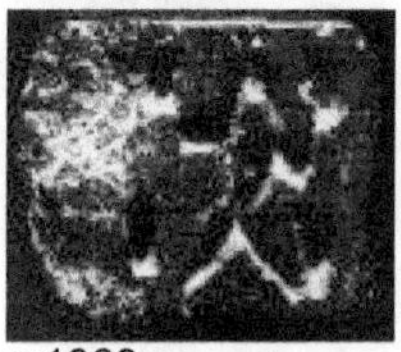

m1969

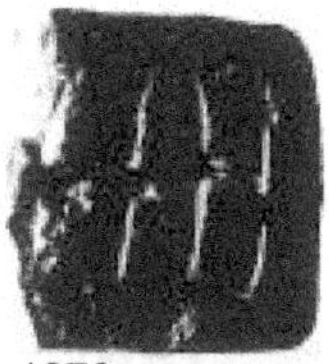
m1970

m1971a

m1972a

m1973a

m1974a

m1975a

m1976

m1977a

m1978a

m1979a

m1980
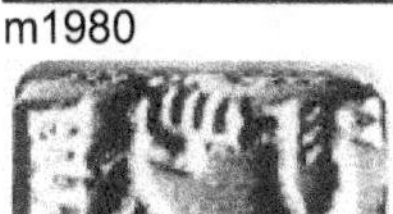
m1981a

m1982a

m1983a

m1984a

m1985a

m1986a

m1987a

m1988a

m1989a
m1989b

m1990a
m1990b

m1991a

m1992a

m1993a

m1994A

m1995A
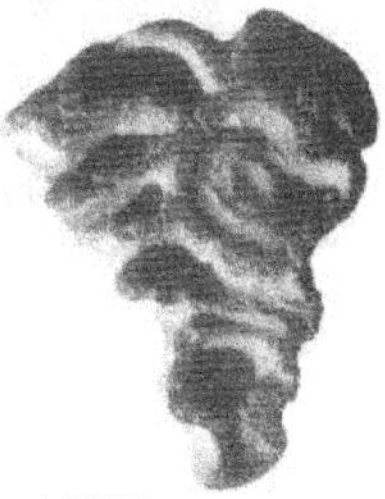
m1996A
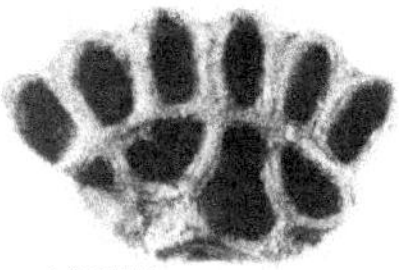
m1997A
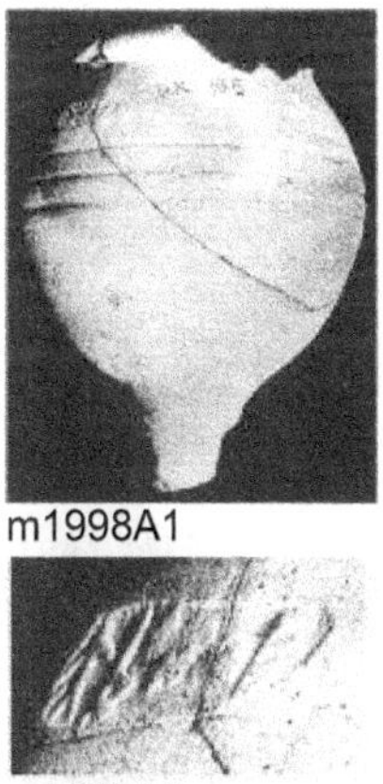
m1998A1
m1998A2

m1999A1

m1999A2
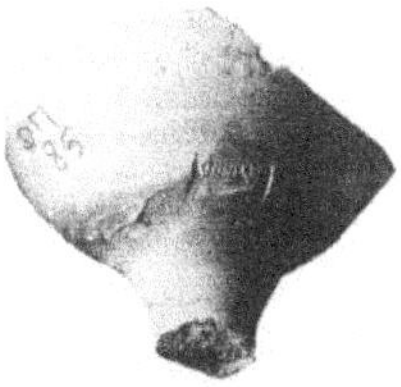
m2000A1

m2000A2
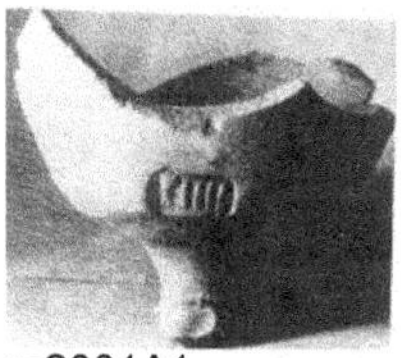
m2001A1

m2001A2
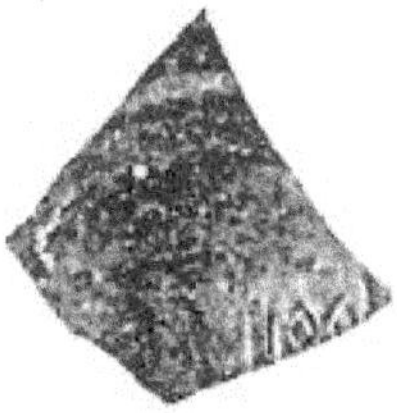
m2002

m2003

m2004

m2005

m2006

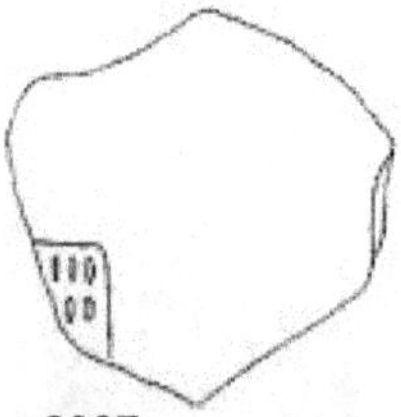
m2007

m2008

m2008B

m2009A

m2009B

m2010A

m2010AB

m2011A

m2012A

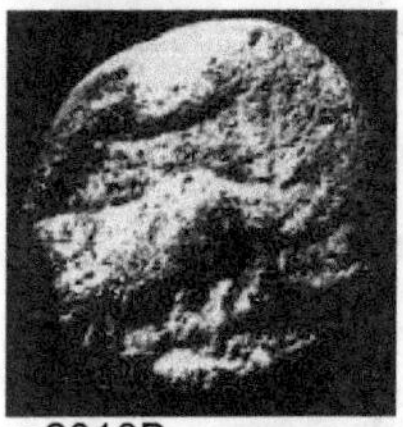
m2013B

m2014A

m2014B

m2015A

m2015B

m2016A

m2017A

m2017B

m2018A

m2018B

m2019A

m2019B

m2020A

m2020B

m2021A

m2021B

m2022A

m2024a

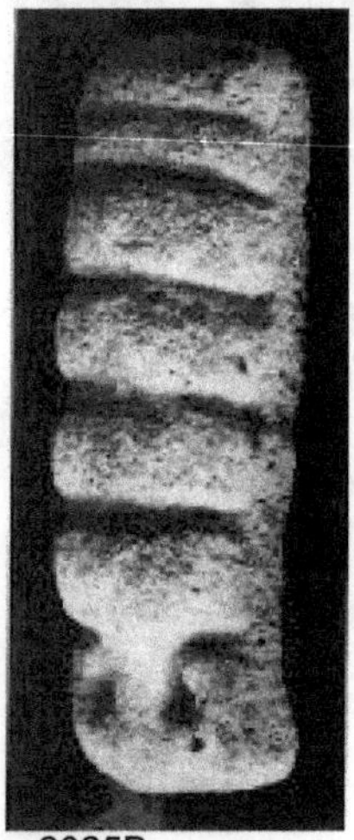
m2025B

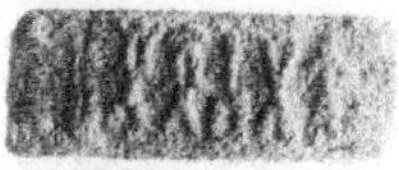
m2026A

m2026B

m2027A

m2027B

m2028A

m2028C

m2029A4

m2029B

m2029B1

m2030A

m2030B

m2032A

m2033A

m20333B

m2033C

m2034c

m2035A

m2035B

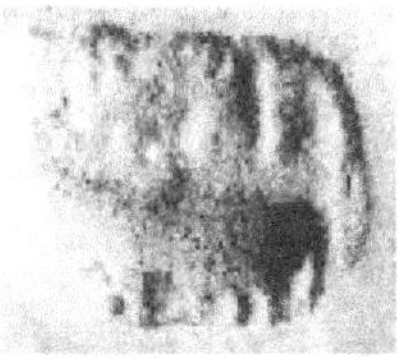
m2035d

m2036A

m2036F

m2037A

m2038F

m2039a

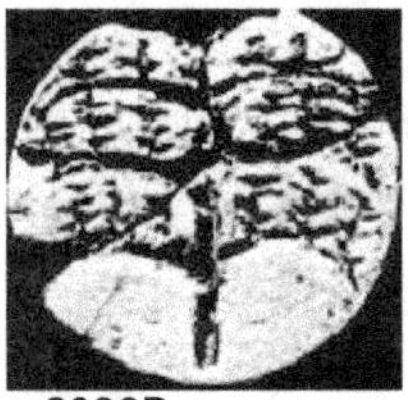
m2039B

m2040a

m2040b

m2041a

m2041b

m2042A

m2042B

m2044B

m2045A

m2045B

m2046A

m2046B

m2047A

m2047B

m2048A

m2048B

m2049A

m2049B

m2050A

m2050B

m2053A

m2053B

m2054A

m2054B

m2055A

m2059A

m2060A

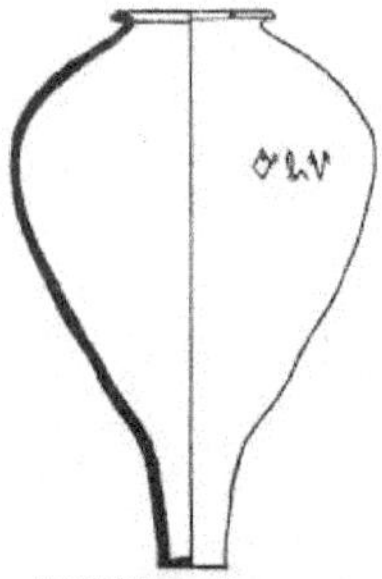
m2060A1+2

m2060b

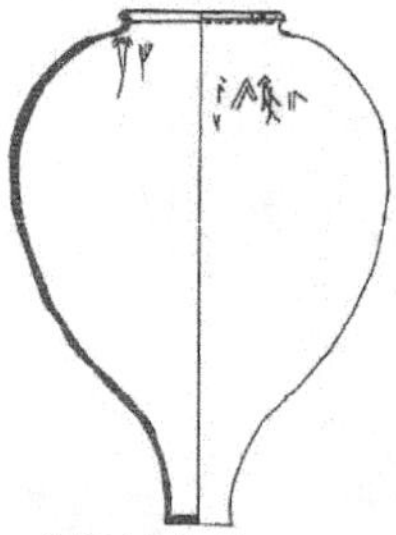
m2061A1+2

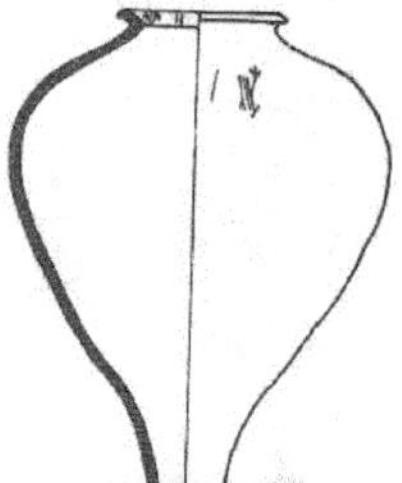
m2062A1+2

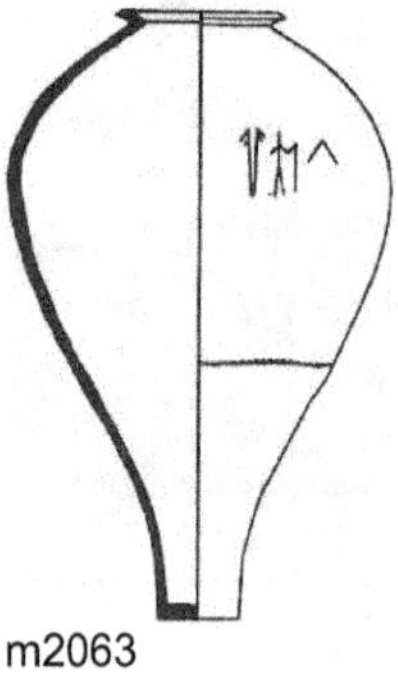
m2063

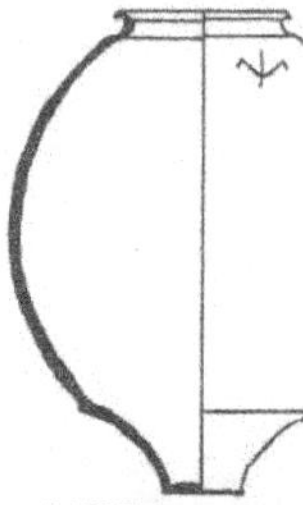
m2065

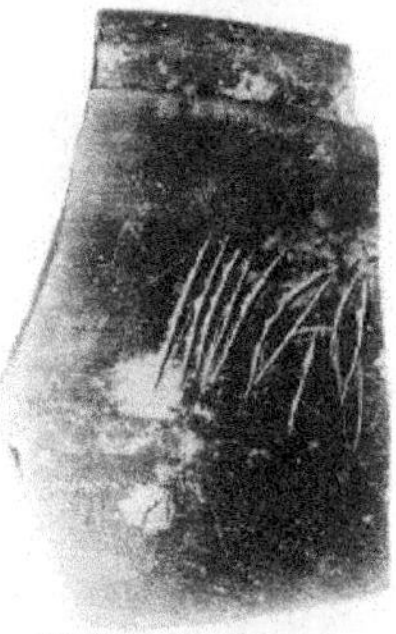
m2065

m2078

m2079

m2080

m2086

m2089A

m2089BC

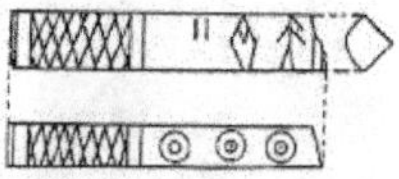
m2090

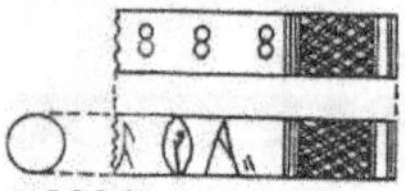
m2091

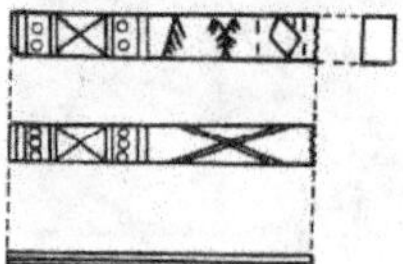
m2092

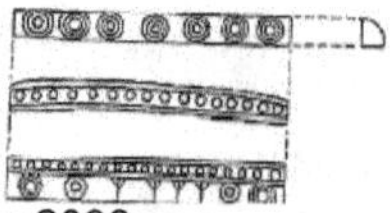
m2093

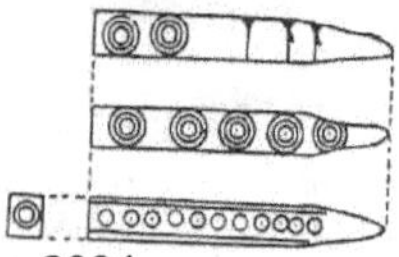
m2094

m2094A

m2095

m2096

m2097a

m2098a

m2099

m2102a

m2103a

m2104a

m2105

m2106D

m2107a

m2108a

m2109a

m2110

m2111

m2112a

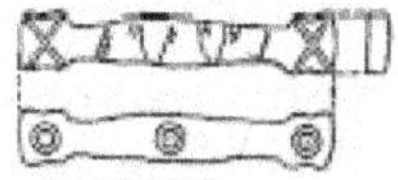
m2113ABD

m2114

m2115

m2116

m2118a

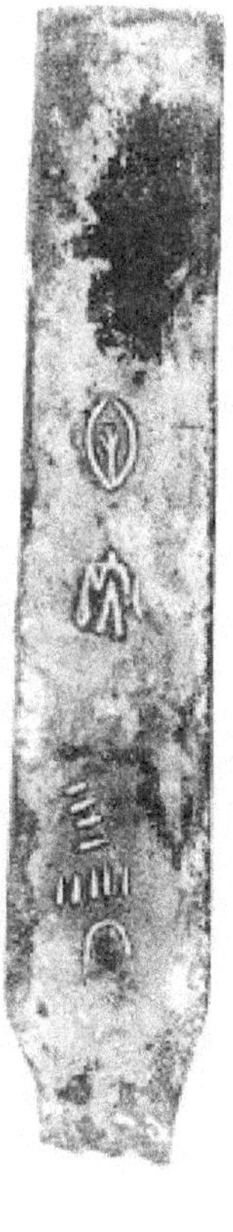

m2118B

m2121A

m2121B

m2123

m2124

m2125

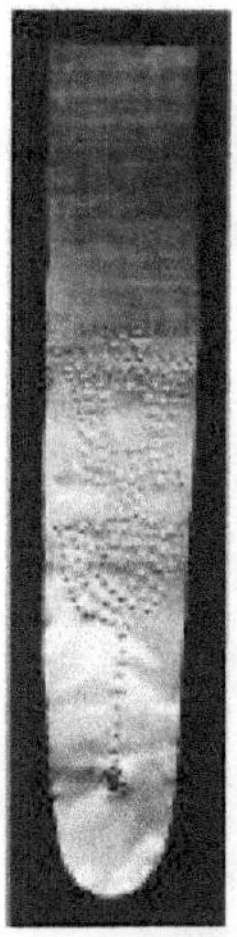

m2125A1

m2128A1

m2129A1

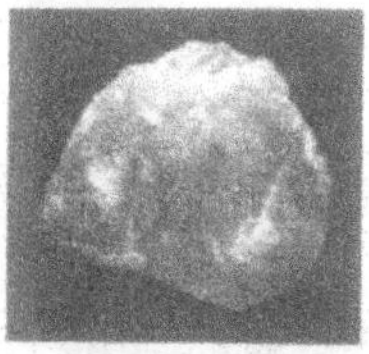

M-2131 A

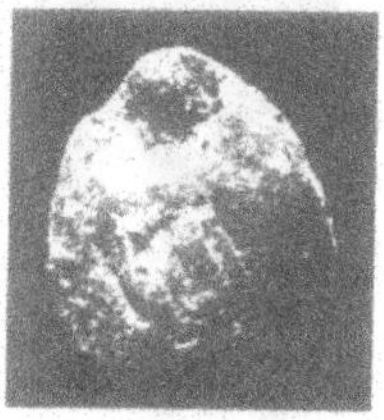

M-2131 B

Photograph from ASI: Sindh series Photo archive of ASI, Janpath, New Delhi. Si. 5:6639, 5:6640. Rattle? Bulla?

Mohenjo-daro Texts either not illustrated or not linked with inscribed objects:

1002

1003

1020

1036

1041

1043

1044

1045

1049

1053

1055

1065

1070

1072

1074

1077

1079

1083

1088

1094

1101

1103

1106

1116

1117

1125

1130

1429

m1651Aivory stick

m1651D

m1651F

2947

1132

1133

1134

1136

1137

1141

1142

1154

1157

1159

1162

1172

1173

1174

1179

1183

1190

1198

1199

1200

1201

1207

1209

1212

1213

1215

1217

1220

1225

1226

1229

1231

1235

1237

1243

1244

1246

1248

1253

1254
1255
1257
1260
1261
1266
1269
1270
1272
1273
1274
1278
1279
1285
1286
1289
1305
1314
1318
1320
1323
1330
zebu bull
1338
1345
1346
1347
1350
1365
1366
1372

1407
1411
1419
1420
1424
1425
1427
1435
1436
1441
1448
1451
1453
1457
1467
1468
1480
1484
1486
1490
1491
1527
1529
1530
1531
1532
1533
1538
1541

1549
1550
1554
1558
1561
1563
1602
1604
1609
1610
1611
1613
1616
1622
1628
1704
1707
1802
1806
1813
1902
1903
2005

2007
2023
2027
2035
2038
2039
2042
2049
2050
2051
2056
2061
2068
2073
2079
2080
2107
2109
2111
2112
2119
2125
2126
2130
2136
2139
2141
2145

2147
2153
2154
2157
2164
2186
2190
2191
2196
2205
2214
2220
2224
2231
2232
2236
2244
2246
2252
2269
2270
2275
2277
2278
2280
2283
2292
2293
2294
2296
2310
2322
2326
2327
2328
2334
2338
2342
2344
2349
2377
2379
2380
2385
2389
2402
2402
2414
2417
2418
2427
2434
2436
2437
2443
2456
2457
2465
2466
2468
2469
2478
2480
2482
2489
2491
2492
2498
2499
2506
2508
2512
2514
2516
2523
2525
2526
2528
2532
2538
2539
2540
2541
2551
2552
2556
2560
2572
2580
2581
2583
2587
2588
2592
2596
2598
2600
2601
2602
2605
2608
2609
2611
2612
2613
2614
2618
2620
2632
2633
2636
2638
2639

2662

2664

2667

2677

2683

2684

2685

2692

2693

2695

2700 2705

2706

2808

2814

2820

2824

2831

2839

2849

2857

2858

2901
Incised copper tablet

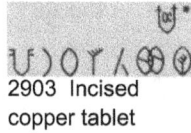

2903 Incised copper tablet

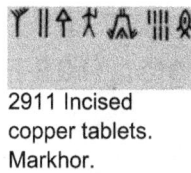

2911 Incised copper tablets. Markhor.

2915

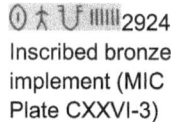

2923
Inscribed bronze implement (MIC Plate CXXVI-2)

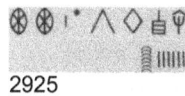

2924
Inscribed bronze implement (MIC Plate CXXVI-3)

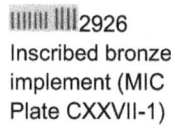

2925
Inscribed bronze implement (MIC Plate CXXVI-5)

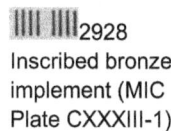

2926
Inscribed bronze implement (MIC Plate CXXVII-1)

2928
Inscribed bronze implement (MIC Plate CXXXIII-1)

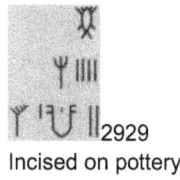

2929
Incised on pottery

2930
Graffiti on pottery

2931 Graffiti on pottery

2934 Graffiti on pottery

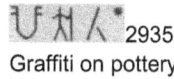

2935
Graffiti on pottery

2936 Graffiti on pottery

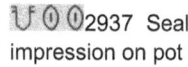

2937 Seal impression on pot

2938Mohenjo-daro, Pottery graffiti. Boat.

2940 Ivory or bone rod

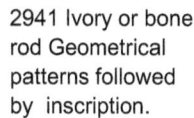

2941 Ivory or bone rod Geometrical patterns followed by inscription.

2944
Ivory or bone rod

2945 Ivory or bone rod

2947

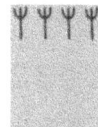

2949 Dotted circles

2950

2951

3001

3002

3010

3016

3019

3021

3023

3024

3035

3038

3042

3044

3051

3052

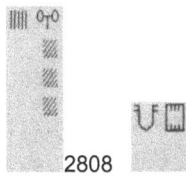

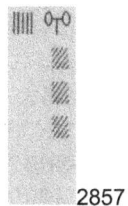

3056
3063
3064
3067
3069
3080
3090
3094
3096
3098 3099
3114
3123
3151
3153
3154
3155
3156
3162
3165
3202
3203
3206
3207
3217
3218
3222

3226
3238
3307
3309
3310
3318
3325
3326
3328
3343
3354
3362
3367
3374
3376
3385
3388
3390
3393
3395
3401
3405
3501

3502
3503
3504
3506
3507 3508
3509
3510
3511
3512 3513

Nindowari-damb01

Squirrel sign

Nindowari-damb02

Nindowari-damb03

Nausharo01

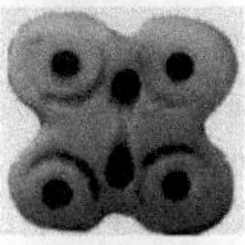

Nausharo02

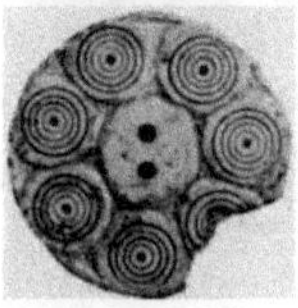

Nausharo03

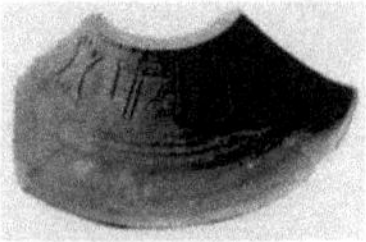

Nausharo04

Nausharo05

Nausharo06

Nausharo07

Nausharo08

Nausharo09

Nausharo10

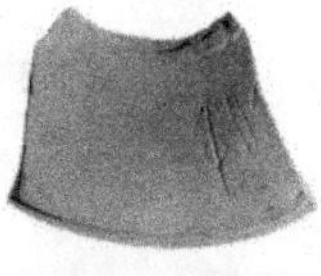

Naro-Waro-dharo01

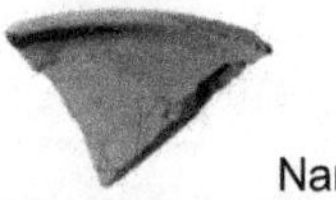

Nar
o-Waro-dharo02

Naro-Waro-dharo03

Pabumath

Prabhas Patan (Somnath) 1A

Prabhas Patan (Somnath)1B

Pirak1

Pirak12

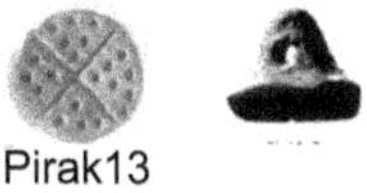
Pirak13

Pirak15

Pirak16

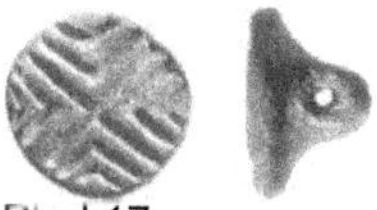
Pirak17

Pirak18

Pirak18A

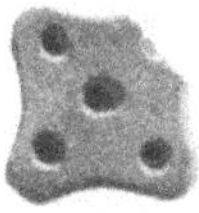
Pirak19

Pirak2

Pirak20

Pirak24

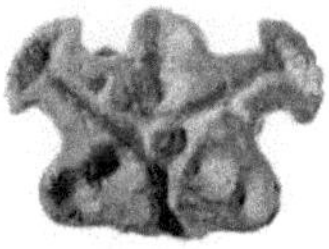
Pirak26Ac

Pirak27

Pirak28

Pirak35

Pirak38

Pirak3 post-harappan

Pirak40

Pirak4

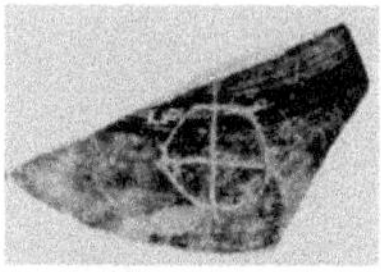
Rangpur

Rakhigarhi1

Rakhigarhi 2

9111

Rakhigarhi 65

Rahman-dheri01A

Rahman-dheri01B

Rahman-dheri120

Rahman-dheri126

Rahman-dheri127

Rahman-dheri150

Rahman-dheri153

Rahman-dheri156

Rahman-dheri158

Rahman-dheri216

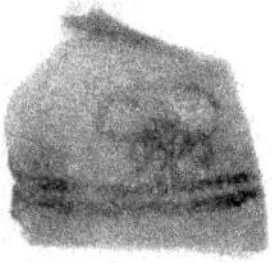

Rahman-dheri241

Rahman-dheri242

Rahman-dheri243

Rahman-dheri254

Rahman-dheri255

Rahman-dheri257

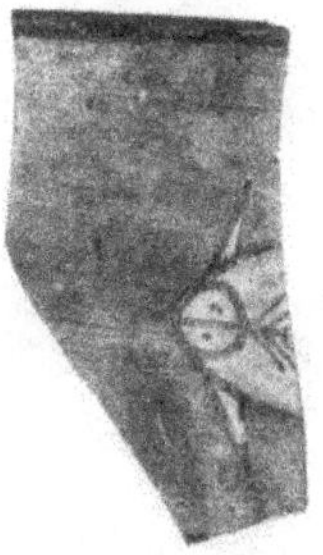

Rahman-dheri258

Rahman-dheri259

Rahman-dheri260

Rahman-dheri90

Rahman-dheri92

Rohira1

Rohira2

Rojdi

9041

9042

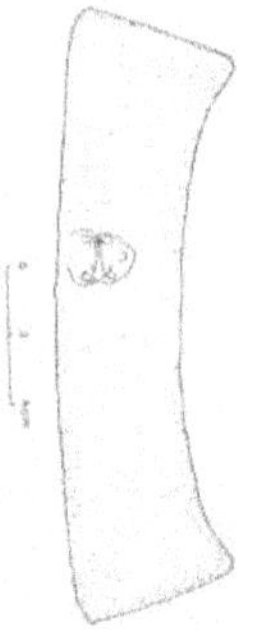

Rojdi. Ax-head or knife of copper, 17.4 cm. long (After Possehl and Raval 1989: 162, fig. 77

Rupar1A

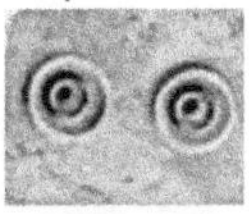

Rupar1B

9021

9022

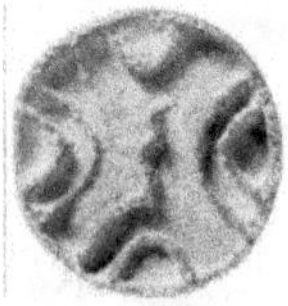

Shahi-tump

Sibri-damb01A

Sibri-damb01B

Sibri-damb02a

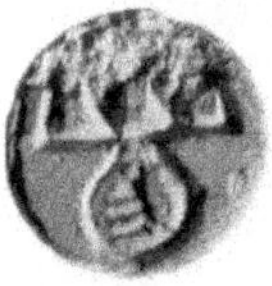

Sibri-damb02E

Sibri-damb03a

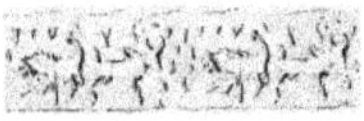

sibri cylinder seal zebu

Surkotada1

9091

Surkotada 2

9092

Surkotada3c

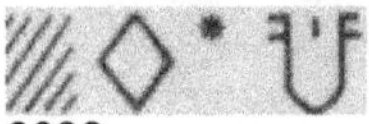

9093

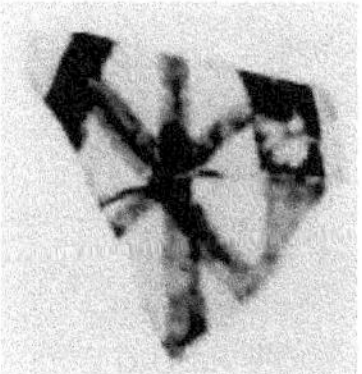

Surkotada 4 
9094

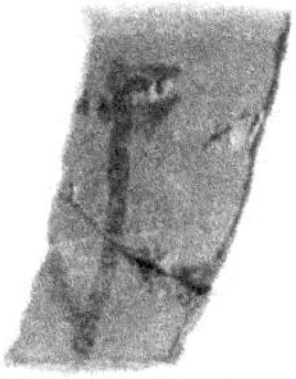

Surkotada 6
9095

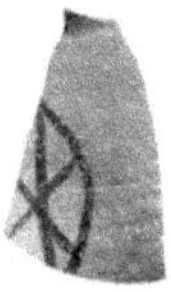

Surkotada 7

Tarakai Qila01A

Tarakai Qila01B

Tarakai Qila02

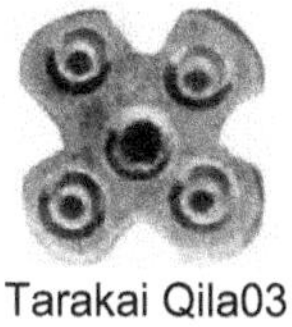

Tarakai Qila03

Tarakai Qila04

Tarakai Qila06

(provenance)
unkn01

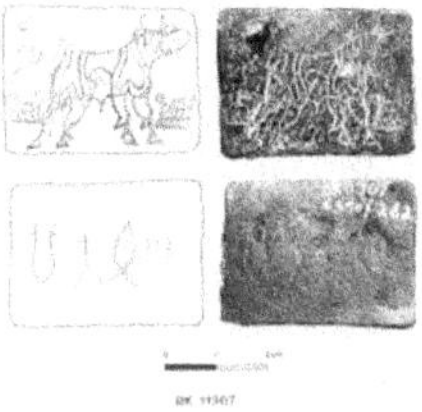

unkn02

unkn03

unkn04

unkn05A

unkn05B

unkn06

Seau l'nde. Musee des Arts Asiatique, Guimet, France

Mohenjo-daro. Copper tablet DK 11307 (SC 63.10/262).

Mohenjo-daro; limestone;

Mackay, 1938, p. 344, Pl. LXXXIX:376.

Mohenjo-daro; Pale yellow enstatite; Mackay 1938, pp. 344-5; Pl. XCVI:488; Collon, 1987, Fig. 607.

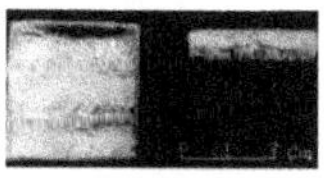

Rakhigarhi: Cylinder Seal (ASI), Lizard or gharial?

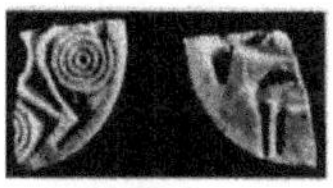

Tarkhanewala-dera1AB

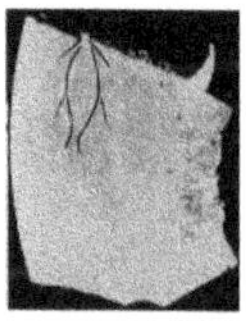

Tarkhanewala-dera 3

9031

Many scholars have noted the contacts between the Mesopotamian and Sarasvati Sindhu (Indus) Civilizations, in terms of cultural history, chronology, artefacts (beads, jewellery), pottery and seals found from archaeological sites in the two areas.

Cylinder seal impression. British Museum (Reg. No. OA 1960.7-18.1). Found in Seistan. Called the

MacMahon cylinder seal. The end of the cylinder shows a combination of triangles (like a range of mountains) reminiscent of a Mohenjo-daro seal (M-443B). The inscription has six signs: a human figures ligatured to three rows of four vertical lines (total count of 12).. Next is a human figure holding in his left hand a rectangular device filled with single hatching (see Marshall 1931, II: 446, no. 196b).

"...the four examples of round seals found in Mohenjo-daro show well-supported sequences, whereas the three from Mesopotamia show sequences of signs not paralleled elsewhere in the Indus Script. But

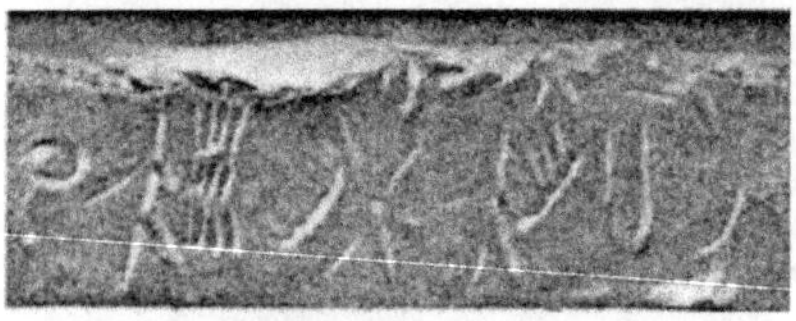

the ordinary square seals found in Mesopotamia show the normal Mohenjo-daro sequences. In other words, the square seals are in the Indian language, and were probably imported in the course of trade; while the circular seals, although in the Indus script, are in a different language, and were probably manufactured in Mesopotamia for a Sumerian- or Semitic-speaking person of Indian descent..." [G.R. Hunter,1932. Mohenjo-daro--Indus Epigraphy, *JRAS*: 466-503]

The acculturation of Meluhhans (probably, Indus people) residing in Mesopotamia in the late third and early second millennium BC, is noted by their adoption of Sumerian names (Parpola, Parpola and Brunswig 1977: 155-159). "The adaptation of Harappan motifs and script to the Dilmun seal form may be a further indication of the acculturative phenomenon, one indicated in Mesopotamia by the adaptation of Harappan traits to the cylinder seal." (Brunswig et al, 1983, p. 110).

[Robert H. Brunswig, Jr. et al, New Indus Type and Related Seals from the Near East, 101-115 in: Daniel T. Potts (ed.), *Dilmun: New Studies in the Archaeology and Early History of Bahrain*, Berlin, Dietrich Reimer Verlag, 1983.]

Mountain topped by a leaf gets stylized as an important motif. Pro-elamite glyptics. Leaf motif. 1-c, After Legrain,L., 1921, Empreintes de cachets elamites, *Mem. Mission Arch. De Perse* 16, Paris: 62-654; d. After Amiet, P., 1961, *La glyptique mesopotamienne archaique*, Paris: 497; Mundigak IV.3; 3. After Casal, J.M., 1961, Fouilles de Mundigak I-II. *Mem. Delegation Arch. Franaise en Afthanistan* 17, Paris: fig. 102: 485; f. Early Harappan. Kalibangan. After Sankalia, 1974: 346, fig. 88d, A. H-L; cf. Fig. 23.45 Asko Parpola, 1996, fig. 23.45. Two goats eating from a tree on a mountain top in proto-Elamite seals from Susa [After Amiet, P., 1972, Glyptique susienne I-II, *Mem. Delegation Arch. En Iran* 43, Paris: 978 and Legrain, L., 1921, Emprientes de cachets elamites, *Mem. Mission Arch. De Perse* 16, Paris: 316].

Nude Bearded Hero Wrestling with Water Buffalo; Bull Man Fighting Lion Cylinder seal and impression Mesopotamia, Akkadian period (ca. 2334–2154 B.C.) Serpentine 36 x 25 mm
Seal no. 159 http://www.themorgan.org/collections/collections.asp?id=193

Texts related to West Asian inscriptions (either not illustrated or not linked):

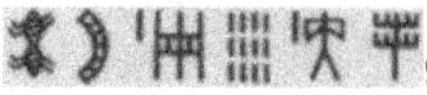9801Susa

9811Djoka (Umma)

9821 Kish

9822 Kish

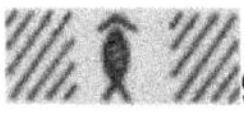9834 Ur

9842 Ur

9852 Telloh

9903 Prob. West Asian find

9904 Prob. West Asian find

A seal made in Meluhha

Susa, Iran; steatite cylinder seal . A bison with head lowered, feeding from a basin. A second bison figure is seen. Inscription on top. Jacques de Morgan Excavatins. Louvre Sb 2425, Delaporte, 1920, s.299 and cf. T.24 from Tello, Iraq; Collon, 1987, Fig. 608.Musee du Louvre and Pierre and Maurice Chuzeville; Legend: Indus script. H.2.3 cm; dia. 1.6 cm. C. 2600 – 1700 BCE. This cylinder seal, carved with a Harappan inscription, originated in the Indus Valley. It is made of fired steatite, a material widely used by craftsmen in Harappa. The animal - a bull with no hump on its shoulders - is also widely attested in the region. The seal was found in Susa, reflecting the extent of commercial links between Mesopotamia, Iran, and the Indus.

[Pierre de talc. Louvre, AO 9036. P. Amiet, Bas-relliefs imaginaries de l'Orient ancien, Paris, 1973, p. 94, no. 274...ils proviendrait de Tello, l'ancienne Girsu, une des cites de l'Etat sumerien de Lagash. Musee National De Arts Asiatiques Guimet, 1988-1989, *Les cites oubliees de l'Indus Archeologie du Pakistan.*] 9851 Telloh

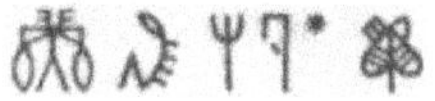

The language of the inscription on this cylinder seal found in Susa (now in the Lourvre museum) reveals

that it wasmade in Harappa in the Indus Valley. In Antiquity, the valley was known as Meluhha.

The seal's chalky white appearance is due to the fired steatite it is made of. Craftsmen in the Indus Valley made most of their seals from this material, although square shapes were usually favored. The animal carving is similar to those found in Harappan works. The animal is a bull with no hump on its shoulders, or possibly a short-horned gaur. Its head is lowered and the body unusually elongated. As was often the case, the animal is depicted eating from a woven wicker manger.

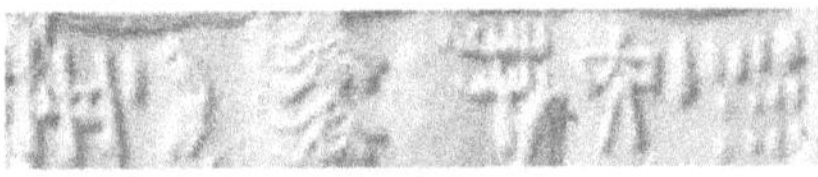
Indus script inscription on Susa cylinder seal

Rebus readings of mleccha (meluhha)

ḍangra 'bull'. Rebus: ḍhangar 'blacksmith'. The text inscription glyphs read rebus: arrowhead, smelter furnace, native metal, black metal.

இறும்பி iṟumpi, *n.* < எறும்பு. [K. *iṟumpu*, M. *iṟumbu.*] Ant; எறும்பு. (யாழ். அக.)

இரும்பு irumpu, *n.* < இரு-மை. cf. செம்பு for செம்மை. [T. *inumu*, M. *irumbu.*] 1. Iron, literally, the black metal; கரும்பொன். (தேவா. 209, 3.) 2. Instrument, weapon: ஆயுதம். இரும்பு மேல் விடாது நிற்பார் (சீவக. 782).

śanku 'twelve-fingers' measure' (Skt.); Rebus: 'arrowhead' (Skt.)

kuṭi 'water carrier' (Te.) Rebus: kuṭhi 'smelter furnace' (Santali) kuṛī f. 'fireplace' (H.); krvṛi f. 'granary (WPah.); kuṛī, kuṛo house, building'(Ku.)(CDIAL 3232)

aḍar 'harrow'; *அடர்¹-. 1. To press down; அமுக்குதல். திருவிரலா லடர்த் தான் வல்லரக்கனையும் (தேவா. 509, 8)*

Rebus: aduru = gan.iyinda tegadu karagade iruva aduru = ore taken from the mine and not subjected to melting in a furnace (Ka.)

dula 'pair' (Kashmiri); rebus: dul 'casting' (Santali).

Trading links between the Indus, Iran, and Mesopotamia

This piece can be compared to another circular seal carved with a Harappan inscription, also found in Susa. The two seals reveal the existence of trading links between this region and the Indus valley. Other Harappan objects have likewise been found in Mesopotamia, whose sphere of influence reached as far as Susa.

The manufacture and use of the seals

Cylinder seals were used mainly to protect sealed vessels and even doors to storage spaces against tampering. The surface of the seal was carved. Because the seals were so small, the artists had to carve tiny scenes on a material that allowed for fine detail. The seal was then rolled over clay to produce a reverse print of the carving. Some cylinder seals also had handles.

Bibliography

Amiet Pierre, L'Âge des échanges inter-iraniens : 3500-1700 av. J.-C., Paris, Éditions de la Réunion des musées nationaux, 1986, coll. "Notes et documents des musées de France", p. 143 et p. 280, fig. 93.
Borne interactive du département des Antiquités orientales.
Les cités oubliées de l'Indus : archéologie du Pakistan, cat. exp. Paris, Musée national des arts asiatiques, Guimet, 16 novembre 1988-30 janvier 1989, sous la dir. de Jean-François Jarrige, Paris, Association française d'action artistique, 1988, pp. 194-195, fig. A5.

http://www.louvre.fr/en/oeuvre-notices/cylinder-seal-carved-elongated-buffalo-and-harappan-inscription

Louvre Museum; Luristan; unglazed, gray steatite; short-honed bull and 4 pictograms

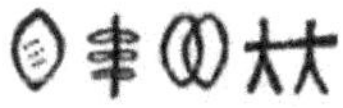

Iraq museum; glazed steatite; perhaps from an Iraqi site; the one-horned bull, the standard are below a six-sign inscription.

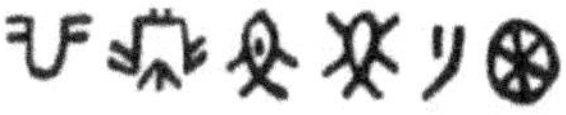

4 Foroughi collection; Luristan; medium gray steatite; bull, crescent, star and net square; of the Dilmun seal type.

TextFailaka; unglazed steatite; an arc of four pictograms above the hindquarter of a bull.

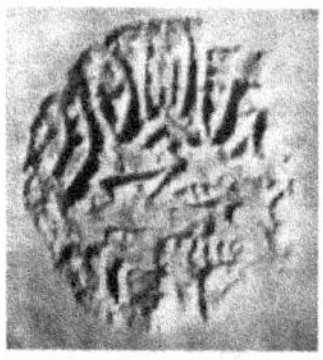

Textseal, impression, Failaka; brownish-grey unglazed steatite; Indus pictograms above a short-horned bull.

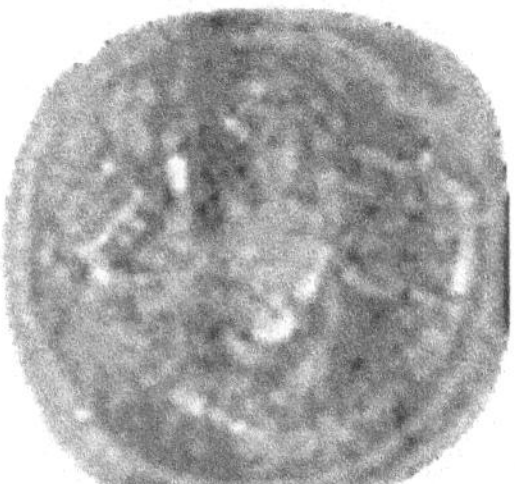

seal, impression; Qala'at al-Bahrain; green steatite; short-horned bull and five pictograms.

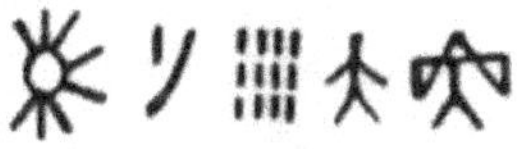

Found in association with an Isin-Larsa type tablet bearing three Amorite names.

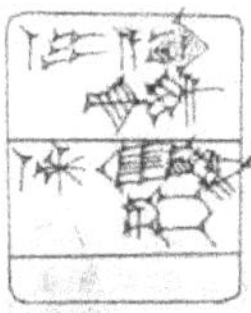

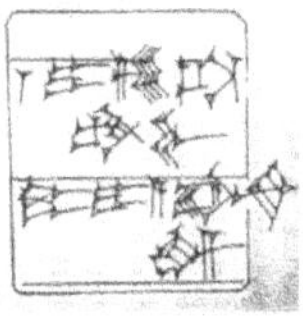

Qala'at al-Bahrain; ca. 2050-1900 BC; tablet, found in the same level where 8 Dilmun seals and six Harappan type weights were found. Three Amorite names are:
Obverse. Janbi-naim; Ila-milkum; Reverse. Jis.i-tambu (son of Janbi-naim). The script is dated to c. 2050-1900 BCE.

Qala'at al-Bahrain; light-grey steatite; hindquarters of a bull and two pictograms.

urseal2 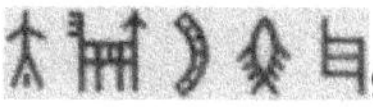 9832 Ur Seal; BM 122187; dia. 2.55; ht. 1.55 cm. Gadd PBA 18 (1932), pp. 6-7, pl. 1, no. 2

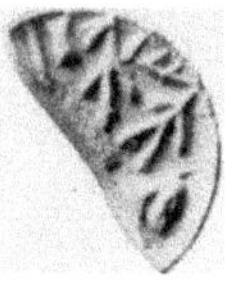

BM 122946; Dia. 2.6; no.3; Legrain, Ur Excavations, X (1951), 629.

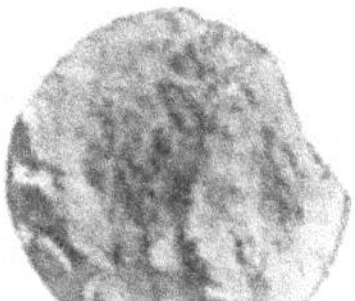

urseal3  9833 Ur Seal; ht. 1.2cm.; Gadd PBA 18 (1932), p. 7, pl. I, no.

urseal8Seal; BM 118704; U. 6020;

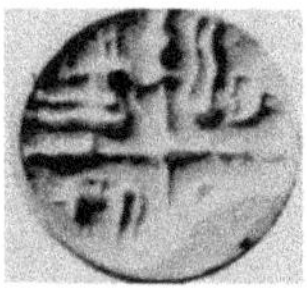

Gadd PBA 18 (1932), pp. 9-10, pl. II, no.8; two figures carry between them a vase, and one presents a goat-like animal (not an antelope) which he holds by the neck.

Human figures wear early Sumerian garments of fleece.

urseal9Seal; BM 122945; U. 16181; dia. 2.25, ht. 1.05 cm; Gadd PBA 18 (1932), p. 10, pl. II, no. o;

each of four quadrants terminates at the edge of the seal in a vase; each quadrant is occupied by a naked figure, sitting so that, following round the circle, the head of one is placed nearest to the feet of the preceding; two figures clasp their hands upon their breasts; the other two spread out the arms, beckoning with one hand.

urseal10 Seal; BM 120576; U. 9265; Gadd, PBA 18 (1932), p. 10, pl. II, no. 10; bull with long horns below an uncertain object, possibly a quadruped and rider, at right angles to the ox (counter clockwise); "...there is, below, a bull with long horns roughly depicted, but above is a rather uncertain addition, which is perhaps an attempt to show one (possibly two) more, in a couching position, as viewed by turning the seal round until the face of the standing bull is downwards. If this is intended, the head of the second bull is turned back, and it is not, perhaps, quite impossible that the remaining part of the design is meant for a bird, such as is fairly often seen perched upon the back of a bull in Sumerian art, a device which has not yet been certainly explained." (C.J. Gadd, Seals of Ancient Indian Style Found at Ur', in: G.L. Possehl, ed., 1979, *Ancient Cities of the Indus*, Delhi, Vikas Publishing House, p. 118).

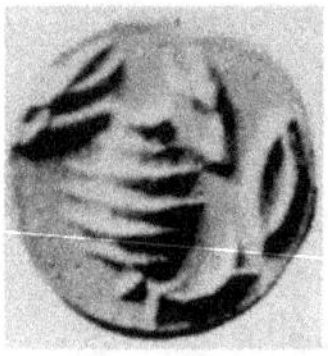

urseal11Seal; UPenn; a scorpion and an elipse [an eye (?)]; U. 16397; Gadd, PBA 18 (1932), pp. 10-11, pl. II, no. 11 [Note: Is the 'eye' an oval representation of a bun ingot made from bica_, sand ore?]

Rectangular stamp seal of dark steatite; U. 11181; B.IM. 7854; ht. 1.4, width 1.1 cm.; Woolley, Ur Excavations, IV (1956), p. 50, n.3. Scorpion.

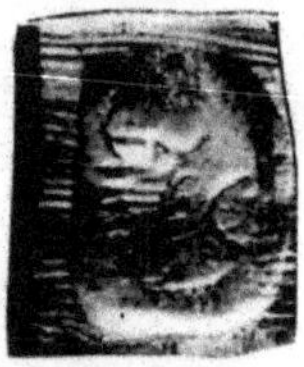

Seal impression, Ur (Upenn; U.16747); dia. 2.6, ht. 0.9 cm.; Gadd, PBA 18 (1932), pp. 11-12, pl. II, no. 12; Porada 1971: pl.9, fig.5; Parpola, 1994, p. 183; water carrier with a skin (or pot?) hung on each end of the yoke across his shoulders and another one below the crook of his left arm; the vessel on the right end of his yoke is over a receptacle for the water; a star on either side of the head (denoting supernatural?). The whole object is enclosed by 'parenthesis' marks. The parenthesis is perhaps a way of splitting of the ellipse (Hunter, G.R., JRAS, 1932, 476). An unmistakable example of an 'hieroglyphic' seal.

urseal13 Seal; BM 122841; dia. 2.35; ht. 1 cm.; Gadd PBA 18 (1932), p. 12, pl. II, no. 13; circle with center-spot in each of four spaces formed by four forked branches springing from the angles of a small square. Alt. four stylised bulls' heads (bucrania) in the quadrants of an elaborate quartering device which has a cross-hatched rectangle in the center.

urseal14Seal; UPenn; cf. Philadelphia Museum Journal, 1929; ithyphallic bull-men; the so-called 'Enkidu' figure common upon Babylonian cylinders of the early period; all have horned head-dresses; moon-symbols upon poles seem to represent the door-posts that the pair of 'twin' genii are commonly seen supporting on either side of a god; material and shape make it the 'Indus' type while the device is Babylonian.

urseal159845 Ur steatite; bull below a PBA 18 (1932), p. 13,

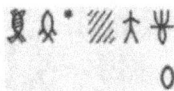

[The first sign looks like an animal with a long tail – as seen from the back and may have been the model for the orthography of Sign 51 as noted in Mahadevan corpus].

Variants of Sign 51.

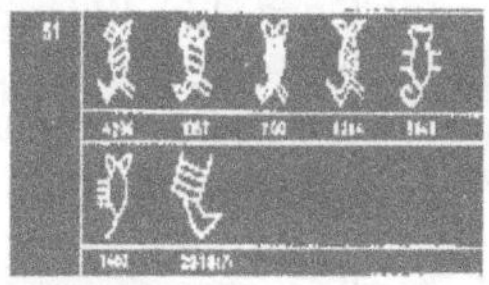

Seal impression; UPenn; scorpion; dia. 2.4cm.; Gadd, Pl. III, no. 15; Legrain, MJ

(1929), p. 306, pl. XLI, no. 119; found at Ur in the cemetery area, in a ruined grave .9 metres from the surface, together with a pair of gold ear-rings of the double-crescent type and long beads of steatite and carnelian, two of gilt copper, and others of lapis-lazuli, carnelian, and banded sard. The first sign to the left has the form of a flower or perhaps an animal's skin with curly tail; there is a round spot upon the bull's back.

9846 UrSeal
123208; found in the filling of a
ond Dynasty of Ur). Dia. 2.3; ht.
1.5 cm.; Gadd, PBA 18 (1932), pp. 13-14, pl. III, no. 16; Buchanan, JAOS 74 (1954), p. 149.

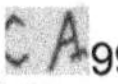
9901 Prob. West Asian find Seal impression, Mesopotamia (?) (BM 120228); cf. cf. Parpola, 1994, p. 132. Note the doubling of the common sign, 'jar'.

an find Pictorial motif: Pict-45 Bull
), from an antique dealer,
cow; the tuft at the end of the tail

of the cow is summarily shaped like an arrow-head; inscription is of five characters, most prominent among them the two 'men' standing side by side. To the right of these is a damaged 'fish' sign.cf. Gadd 1932: no.18; Parpola, 1994, p.219.

urseal6 Cylinder seal; BM 122947; U. 16220 (cut down into Ur III mausolea from Larsa level; U. 16220), enstatite; Legrain, 1951, No. 632; Collon, 1987, Fig. 611.Humped bull stands before a plant, feeding from a round manger or a bundle of fodder (or, probably, a cactus); behind the bull is a scorpion and two snakes; above the whole a human figure, placed horizontally, with fantastically long arms and legs, and rays about his head.

A symbolism of a woman spreading her legs apart, which recurs on an SSVC inscribed object. Cylinder-seal impression from Ur showing a squatting female. L. Legrain, 1936, *Ur excavations, Vol. 3, Archaic*

flanking a similar glyph with legs apart – also

Mohenjo-daro. Sealing. Surrounded by fishes, lizard and snakes, a horned person

of a triangular terracotta amulet (Md 013); surface
shmolean Museum, Oxford.

d storage jar discovered in burn
Kenoyer, 1998, Cat. No. 8.

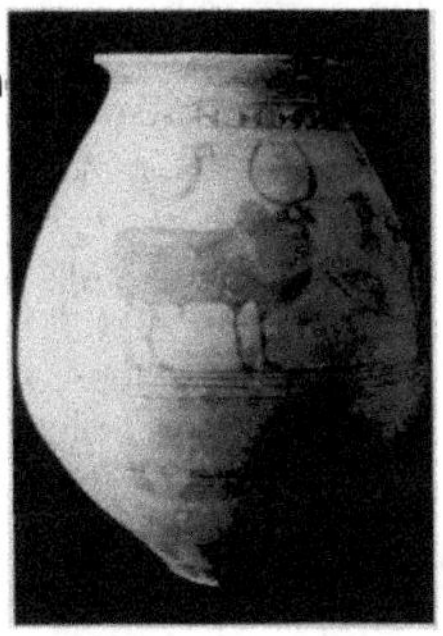

A fish over a short-horned bull and a bird over a one-horned bull; cylinder seal impression, (Akkadian to early Old Babylonian). Gypsum. 2.6 cm. Long 1.6 cm. Dia. [Drawing by Larnia Al-Gailani Werr. Cf. Dominique Collon 1987, *First impressions: cylinder seals in the ancient Near East*, London: 143, no. 609] Tell Suleimeh (level IV), Iraq; IM 87798; (al-Gailani Werr, 1983, p. 49 No. 7).

Cylinder-seal impression; a griffin and a tiger attack an antelope with its head turned back. The upper register shows two scorpions and a frog; the lower register shows a scorpion and two fishes.Syro-Mitannian, fifteenth to fourteenth centuries BCE, Pierpont Morgan Library, New York. [After Fig. 9 in: Jack M. Sasson (ed.), *Civilizations of the Ancient Near East*, p.2705].

Rhinoceros, elephant, lizard.Tell Asmar (Eshnunna), Iraq. IM 14674; glazed steatite; Frankfort, 1955, No. 642; Collon, 1987, Fig. 610.

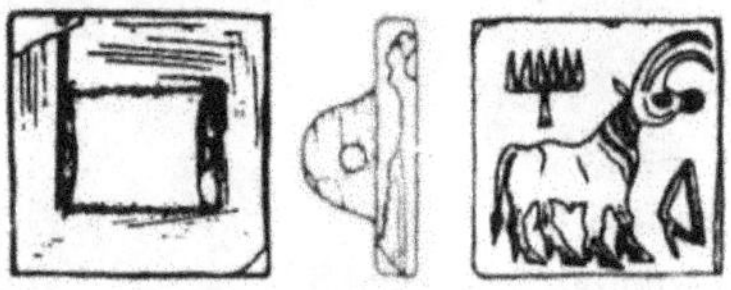

Seal from Shortugai incised with an antelope and two other pictographs. "...Shortugai in Oxus basin, on the Kokcha-Amu Darya doab, has revealed the existence of a Harappan colony for carrying out trade in lapis lazuli. Apart form typical Harappan pottery, a seal bearing the script has also been found to confirm the trading character of the colony." (Six decades of Indus Studies in: BB Lal and SP Gupta, eds., *Frontiers of the Indus Civilization*, Fig. .8, p. 9].

Ur, Iraq; BM 123195; clay, half missing; Collon, 1987, Fig. 613. Probably originated in the east (exact location unknown).

A person with a vase with overflowing water; sun sign. C. 18th cent. BCE. [E. Porada,1971, Remarks on seals found in the Gulf states, *Artibus Asiae*, 33, 31-7].

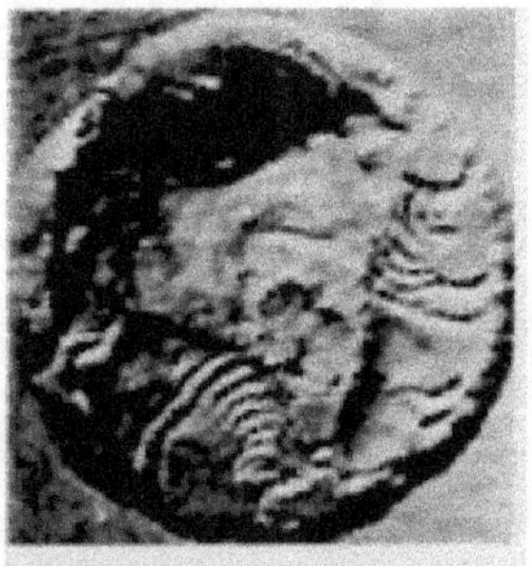

"The main importance of a seal found in 1980 in Maysar-1 (Weisgerber, 1980), is the fact that the Makan/Oman civilisation used seals, as did the great cultures of the Nile, Euphrates/Tigris and Indus. But it is also a convincing proof of contact between Meluhha and Makan. On three sides six animals are engraved: two caprides, an ibex and a wild goat; a zebu cow and a scorpion; a dog and again a wild goat. In our context the zebu cow is the most important. Together with the humped bull painted on a jar from Umm an-Nar (Bibby, 1970: 280) it demonstrates the presence of these animals in the Oman peninsula during the third millennium BCE. This again proves contact with India.

(Not illustrated) "A new seal from Hajjar in Bahrain now gives the same evidence, its shape being nearly identical with the Maysar-1 seal. Among its three engravings are a short-horned bull and an insription in Indus Valley script (Weisgerber, 1981: 218, fig. 54)." (Gerd Weisgerber, Makkan and Meluhha--third millennium BCE copper production in Oman and the evidence of contact with the Indus Valley, in: Parpola, Asko and Petteri Koskikallio (eds.), *South Asian Archaeology 1993,* Helsinki, Suomalainen Tiedeakatemia, 1994).

(Not illustrated) "(At Padri, Gujarat) A of the most significant discoveries is a copper fish-hook, which is 14 cm long and weights 41 gm. A copper fish-hook of such a magnitude has not been reported from any other site so far... The other material equipment include a seal on a stud handle engraved with fish motif, Harappan letters engraved on pot-sherds, cubical chert weights, micro steatite beads, beads of terracotta, carnelian, agate, etc."

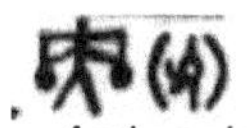

Early Harappan bowl. Fish. [After Fig. 23.35 in, Asko Parpola, New correspondences between Harappan and near Eastern glyptic art, in: in B. Allchin, ed., *South Asian Archaeology*, 1981, Cambridge].

Seal impression; Dept. of Antiquities, Bahrain; three Harapan-style bulls

Nippur; ca. 13th cent. BC; white stone; zebu bull and two pictograms

Tree in front. Fish in front of and above a one-horned bull. Cylinder seal impression (IM 8028), Ur, Mesopotamia. White shell. 1.7 cm. High, dia. 0.9 cm. [Cf. Mitchell 1986 Indus and Gulf type seals from Ur: 280-1, no.8 and fig. 112; Shaikha Haya Ali Al Khalifa and Michael Rice, 1986, *Bahrain through the ages: the archaeology*, London: 280-1, no.8 and fig. 112].

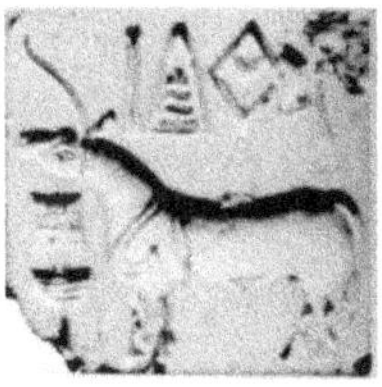

cf. Gadd, PBA 18 (1932), pp. 7-8, pl. I, no.7;; Parpola, 1994, p. 181; fish vertically in front of and horizontally above a unicorn; trefoil design

Terracotta sealing depicting an inscription, 2600 BCE, Western UP, Saharanpur (After Manoj Kumar Sharma). [Source: Page 32 in: Deo Prakash Sharma, 2000, *Harappan seals, sealings and copper tablets*, Delhi, National Museum].

Stamp seals in Metropolitan Museum of Art, New York. 49.40.1 to 3. All three samples show a bull.

"Rendered in strict profile, standing before what might be an altar, the bull is by far the most popular motif in the Indus Valley glyptic art; there is virtually no v ariation in either the style or the iconographic details among the individual examples. The shoulder of the bull is emphasized by an upside-down doubly outlined heart shape that has been interpreted as painted decoration on the body of the bull, but is more likely an artistic convention for representing the muscles of the bull's shoulder."[After Fig. 38 in Holly Pittman, 1984, p. 84].

Mohenjo-daro. Silver seal (After Mackay 1938, vol. 2, Pl. XC,1; XCVI, 520). Two silver seals at Mohenjo-daro, two copper seals at Lothal and at Ras al-Junayz in Oman are rare uses of metal for making seals.

Stamp seal and a modern impression: unicorn or bull and inscription,, Mature Harappan period, ca. 2600–1900 B.C. Indus Valley Burnt steatite; 1 1/2 x 1 1/2 in. (3.8 x 3.8 cm)

http://www.metmuseum.org/toah/ho/02/ssa/ho_49.40.1.htm

Manuscripts in Schoyen Collection

Some manuscripts available in the Schoyen Collection. Located mainly in London and Oslo. URL http://www.nb.no/baser/schoyen/contentnew3.html "The Schøyen Collection comprises most types of manuscripts from the whole world spanning over 5000 years. It is the largest private manuscript collection formed in the 20th century. The whole collection, MSS 1-5245, comprises 13,010 manuscript items, including 2,172 volumes. 6,510 manuscript items are from the ancient period, 3300 BCE – 500 CE. For scholarly research and access the collection is a unique source, uniting materials usually scattered world wide to two locations only. These MSS are the world's heritage, the memory of the world. They are felt not really to belong to The Schøyen Collection and its owner, who only is the privileged, respectful and humble keeper, neither do they belong to a particular nation, people, religion, culture, but to mankind, being the property of the entire world. In the future The Schøyen Collection will have to be placed in a public context that can fulfil these visions...The Schøyen Collection is located mainly in Oslo and London. Scholars are always welcome, and are strongly encouraged to do research and to publish material."

Source:http://www.nb.no/baser/schoyen/intro.html#1.1

Included in the 6,510 manuscripts from the ancient period, 3300 BCE - 500 CE are the following epigraphs which are closely associated with the script of the Sarasvati Civilization.

MS 249 Unidentified Minoan text. Knossos, Crete, 16th cent. BCE, Linear A script?

MS in Minoan on clay, Knossos, Crete, 16th c. BC, 1 black roundel, 3,0x2,7 cm, 4 characters of late Minoan I Linear A script, 2 impressions (1,6x1,0 cm) on opposite edges by an amygdaloid seal with head of papyrus plant.

*Provenance:* 1. Possibly the archive in the West Wing of the Knossos Palace (16th c. BC - ca. 1950); 2. Erlenmeyer Collection, Basel, CMS no. 120 (until 1981); 3. Erlenmeyer Foundation, Basel (1981-1988); 4. Christie's 5.6.1989:99.

*Commentary:* The famous Linear B script of the Mycenean kings, consisting of syllabic signs, ideograms and numerals, resisted decipherment for a generation. When Michael Ventris deciphered it in 1952, the achievement was called the "Everest" in classical archaeology. The language was archaic Greek. Linear A, the earliest script of Europe, has so far resisted all attempts of decipherment, partly because the language is unknown, and the material small, ca. 700 copies only, while Linear B is known in 12,000 - 13,000 examples. This roundel is the only one in private ownership. Outside the Greek museums, they are, in fact, represented in 2 Italian museums only. KN Wc 26 in Erik Hallager: The Knossos roundels, BSA 82(1987).

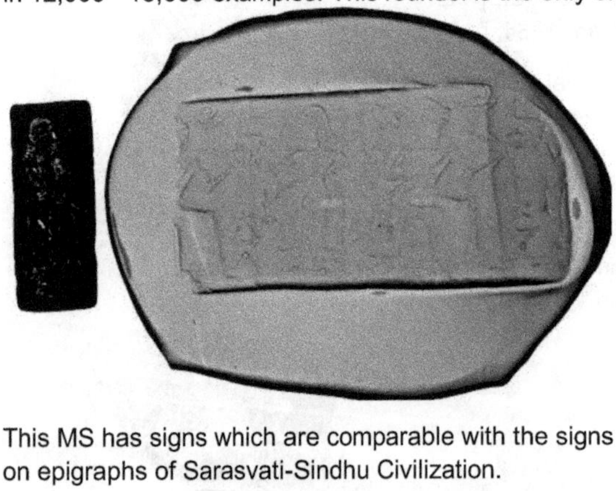

This MS has signs which are comparable with the signs on epigraphs of Sarasvati-Sindhu Civilization.

MS 4625 Cylinder seal with a scene of drinking from a straw, Pakistan ca. 1500-500 BCE

Seal of hard red stone, Coast between Indus and the Persian Gulf, Pakistan, ca. 1500-500 BC, 1 cylinder seal matrix, diam. 1,3x3,2 cm, figure sitting left, holding a long straw from his mouth to a pot with bulbous body and narrow neck, resting on a stand;

behind him a servant holding up a fan; behind the servant another standing person grasping a small quadruped. Above and below him 3 other quadrupeds. Between the 2 main figures a solar disc with rays and a crescent and a full moon combined.

*Provenance:* 1. Found in Baluchistan?, Pakistan (1965); 2. The Waria Collection, Dadu, Pakistan (ca. 1965-2001).

*Commentary:* Drinking beer from a straw is known from Sumer ca. 2700 BC on, but usually a big pot from which a number of persons are all drinking through their own straws. The fan is known in Iranian seals of ca. 1300-1100 BC. While the scene as a whole is Near Eastern, the dress and anklets of the servant is clearly of Indian type. The iconography combined is thus unique.

MS 4602 Indus Valley cylinder seal, ca. 3000 BCE depicting a palm tree and a man between two lions with wings and snakeheads, holding one arm around each, two long fish below, and one fish jumping after one lion's tail or the tail of a sitting monkey above it

Seal matrix on creamy stone or shell, Indus Valley, Pakistan, ca. 3000 BC, 1 cylinder seal, diam. 2,0x3,7 cm, in fine execution influenced by the Jemdet Nasr style of Sumer.

*Provenance:* 1. Found in Mehrgarh, Pakistan; 2. The Waria Collection, Dadu, Pakistan (-2001).

*Commentary:* Similar fish can be found on Indus Valley pottery from the period and later

http://www.nb.no/baser/schoyen/5/5.6/index.html#4602

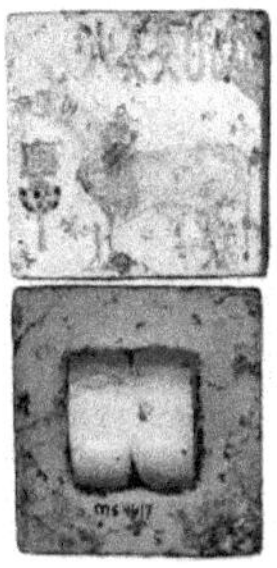

MS 4617 Pakistan, ca. 2200-2000 BCE

White steatite, 1 square seal matrix, 4,3x4,3x1,9 cm, 6 Indus Valley signs in a formal script of high quality, unicorn standing left facing an altar, with loop handle.

*Provenance:* 1. The Waria Collection, Dadu, Pakistan (-2001).

*Commentary:* This seal is among the largest extant. The execution is representing Indus art at its best. The Indus script is still undeciphered, as is the Linear A script from Crete and the Rongo-Rongo script from Easter Island, which has numerous signs in common with the Indus script.

MS 4619, Pakistan, ca. 2200-1800 BCE

White coated grey steatite, Mohenjo-Daro?, Indus Valley, Pakistan, ca. 2200-1800 BC, 1 round seal matrix, diam. 2,3x1,5 cm, 5 Indus Valley signs, bison left eating from a trough, with double loop handle.

*Context:* Only 2 more round seals with inscriptions are known, both with bison and from Mohenjo-Daro (M-415 and M-416).

*Provenance:* 1. The Waria Collection, Dadu, Pakistan (1960'ies-2001).

MS5059 Pakistan, ca. 2200-1800 BCE

White steatite, Mohenjo-Daro, Indus Valley, 2200-1800 BC, 1 square stamp seal matrix, 3,4x3,4x1,7 cm, 9 Indus valley signs

*Provenance:* 1. Found in Mohenjo-Daro (ca. 1950-1970); 2. The Waria Collection, Dadu, Pakistan (-2001).

MS5061 Pakistan, ca. 2200-1800 BCE

White steatite, Mohenjo-Daro, Indus Valley, 2200-1800 BC, 1 square stamp seal matrix, 2,4x2,5x1,2 cm, 3 Indus valley signs

*Provenance:* 1. Found in Mohenjo-Daro (ca. 1950-1970); 2. The Waria Collection, Dadu, Pakistan (-2001).

MS5062 Pakistan, ca. 2200-1800 BCE

White steatite, Mohenjo-Daro, Indus Valley, 2200-1800 BC, 1 square stamp seal matrix, 2,7x2,7x1,6 cm, 4 Indus valley signs

*Provenance:* 1. Found in Mohenjo-Daro (ca. 1950-1970); 2. The Waria Collection, Dadu, Pakistan (-2001).

MS5065 Pakistan, ca. 1800 BCE

MS Indus Valley language on copper, Mohenjo-Daro, Indus Valley, ca. 1800 BC, 1 square stamp seal matrix, 1,3x1,3x0,9 cm, 3 Indus valley signs in script

*Provenance:* 1. Found in Mohenjo-Daro (ca. 1950-1970); 2. The Waria Collection, Dadu, Pakistan (-2001).

*Commentary:* There is only one similar seal known, from Lothal (L-44).

Parallels from Mesopotamia , Anatolia and other contact areas

Administrative tablet with cylinder seal impression of a male figure, hunting dogs, and boars, 3100–2900 B.C.; Jemdet Nasr period (Uruk III script)
Mesopotamia Clay; H. 2 in. (5.3 cm) The seal impression depicts a male figure guiding two dogs on a leash and hunting or herding boars in a marsh environment.

Cylinder seal and modern impression: hunting scene, 2250–2150 B.C.; late Akkadian period Mesopotamia Chert; H. 1 1/16 in. (2.8 cm) This seal, depicting a man hunting an ibex in a mountain forest, is an early attempt to represent a landscape in Mesopotamian art. It was made during the Akkadian period (ca. 2350–2150 B.C.), during which the iconographic repertory of the seal engraver expanded to include a variety of new mythological and narrative subjects. The owner of the seal was Balu-ili, a high court official whose title was Cupbearer.

http://www.metmuseum.org/toah/ho/02/wam/hod_41.160.192.htm

Shaft-hole axhead with a bird-headed demon, boar,and dragon, late 3rd–early 2nd millennium BCE Central Asia (Bactria-Margiana) Silver, gold foil; 5 7/8 in. (15 cm) "Western Central Asia, now known as Turkmenistan, Uzbekistan, and northern Afghanistan, has yielded objects attesting to a highly developed civilization in the late third and early second millennium B.C. Artifacts from the region indicate that there were contacts with Iran to the southwest. Tools and weapons, especially axes, comprise a large portion of the metal objects from this region. This shaft-hole axhead is a masterpiece of three-dimensional and relief sculpture. Expertly cast in silver and gilded with gold foil, it depicts a bird-headed hero grappling with a wild boar and a winged dragon. The idea of the heroic bird-headed creature probably came from western Iran, where it is first documented on a cylinder seal impression. The hero's muscular body is human except for the bird talons that replace the hands and feet. He is represented twice, once on each side of the ax, and consequently appears to have two heads. On one side, he grasps the boar by the belly and on the other, by the tusks. The posture of the boar is contorted so that its bristly back forms the shape of the blade. With his other talon, the bird-headed hero grasps the winged dragon by the neck. The dragon, probably originating in Mesopotamia or Iran, is represented with folded wings, a feline body, and the talons of a bird of prey."

Stamp seal, quatrefoil/maltese cross with infill, whip or snake

MS on grey steatite, North Syria/North Iraq/Iran, 5th millennium BC, 1 square stamp seal, 3,0x3,5x0,6 cm, 1 pictographic sign on reverse, pierced through.

*Provenance:* 1. Erlenmeyer Collection, Basel (before 1958-1981); 2. The Erlenmeyer Foundation, Basel (1981-1997); 3. Sotheby's 12.6.1997:6.

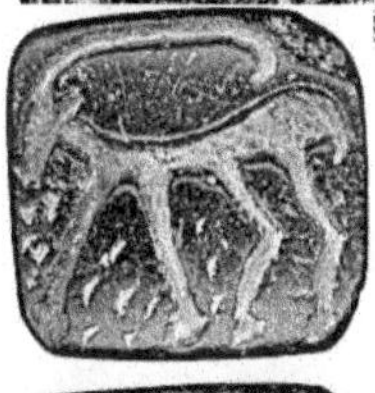

Stamp seal, standing male figure between two horned quadrupeds back to back and head to end

MS on speckled dark-olive steatite or chlorite, North Syria/Iraq/Iran, 5th-4th millennium BC, 1 circular stamp seal, diam. 8,4x1,3 cm, pierced through.

*Provenance:* 1. Erlenmeyer Collection, Basel (before 1958-1981); 2. The Erlenmeyer Foundation, Basel (1981-1997); 3. Sotheby's 12.6.1997:10.

*Commentary:* The earliest stamp seals of Sumer had various geometric patterns, later more elaborate designs and illustrations like the present seal, as a proof of identity and ownership. These can, together with the counting tokens, possibly be considered forerunners to the pictographic script of ca. 3200 BC. http://www.nb.no/baser/schoyen/5/5.6/#2411

Stamp seal, large ibex walking left

MS on black steatite or chlorite, North Syria or Anatolia, 4th millennium BC, 1 rectangular gabled stamp seal, 4,7x5,1x1,3 cm, pierced through.

*Provenance:* 1. Erlenmeyer Collection, Basel (before 1958-1981); 2. The Erlenmeyer Foundation, Basel (1981-1997); 3. Sotheby's 12.6.1997:8.

MS 4631 Bulla-envelope with 11 plain and complex tokens inside, representing an account or agreement, tentatively of wages for 4 days' work, 4 measures of metal, 1 large measure of barley and 2 small measures of some other commodity

Bulla in clay, Adab, Sumer, ca. 3700-3200 BC, 1 spherical bulla-envelope (complete), diam. ca. 6,5 cm, cylinder seal impressions of a row of men walking left; and of a predator attacking a deer, inside a complete set of plain and complex tokens: 4 tetrahedrons 0,9x1,0 cm

(D.S.-B.5:1), 4 triangles with 2 incised lines 2,0x0,9 (D.S.-B.(:14), 1 sphere diam. 1,7 cm (D.S.-B.2:2), 1 cylinder with 1 grove 2,0x0,3 cm (D.S.-B.4:13), 1 bent paraboloid 1,3xdiam. 0,5 cm (D.S.-B.8:14).

*Context:* MSS 4631-4646 and 5114-5127are from the same archive. Only 25 more bulla-envelopes are known from Sumer, all excavated in Uruk. Total number of bulla-envelopes worldwide is ca. 165 intact and 70 fragmentary.

*Commentary:* While counting for stocktaking purposes started ca. 8000 BC using plain tokens of the type also represented here, more complex accounting and recording of agreements started about 3700 BC using 2 systems: a) a string of complex tokens with the ends locked into a massive rollsealed clay bulla (see MS 4523), and b) the present system with the tokens enclosed inside a hollow bulla-shaped rollsealed envelope, sometimes with marks on the outside representing the hidden contents. The bulla-envelope had to be broken to check the contents hence the very few surviving intact bulla- envelopes. This complicated system was superseded around 3500-3200 BCE by counting tablets giving birth to the actual recording in writing, of various number systems (see MSS 3007 and 4647), and around 3300-3200 BC the beginning of pictographic writing. *Exhibited:* The Norwegian Intitute of Palaeography and Historical Philology (PHI), Oslo, 13.10.2003-06.2005.

MS 2963

ACCOUNT OF MALE AND FEMALE SLAVES

MS in Old Sumerian on clay, Sumer, ca. 3300-3200 BC, 1 nearly cubic tablet, 5,2x6,2x4,5 cm, 5 compartments in primitive pictographic script, fine cylinder seal impressions on all sides made prior to writing of 2 men walking left, carrying ostriches, a basket between them and wine amphorae above.

*Context* The tablets MSS 2963, 3149-3151, 4510 and 4511, are all nearly cubic in form, MS 4511 being 4,8x4,8x4,5 cm. There is nothing similar in any public collection apart from 1 in Berlin. They possibly derive from the bulla-envelopes with counting tokens inside (cf. MSS 4631-4632, 4638, ca. 3700-3200 BC). The cubic tablets might represent the next logical step, the adding of pictographs representing the commodities involved, and adapted from the spherical shape of the bullas, to cubic shape, before being reduced to a thinner and more handy tablet. The 2 earliest cubic tablets (MSS 4510 and 3151) are ideonumerographical from Uruk V period, ca. 3400 BC, next to the protopictographical texts Uruk VI, the earliest continous writing know, predating the Tell Brak and Kish tablets (ca. 3200 BC, and the Uruk IV tablets (ca. 3200-3100 BC).

*Commentary:* The present tablet is the earliest written evidence of slavery, see collection 24.13

MS 2645 Indus valley script, and old akkadian illustration. North West Afghanistan, ca. 21$^{st}$ cent.

This seal links Indus Valley and Old Akkadian civilizations. The seal is of blue stone, North West Afghanistan, ca. 23rd-21st c. BC, 1 cylinder seal, 3,9x2,7 cm, 5 Indus valley signs, illustration standing archer aiming his bow at a falling boar, in the style of the best Old Akkadian art in Sumer.

Harappa, potsherd.

Experts believe that this seal may have been used by a merchant from the Indus Valley who was living in Bahrein or Babylon. This seal was found in the

Mesopotamian city of Babylon. The seal shows a bull and has a short inscription in the Indus Valley script. However, it is not square like seals from the Indus Valley. It is round with a knob on the back, which is more like seals from the Gulf island of Bahrein which date from about 2000 B.C. Other seals like this were found in the Sumerian city of Ur. A copy of a square, Indus-type seal with a picture of a bull was also found at Ur. However, this seal had an inscription in cuneiform script rather than in the Indus Valley script.

Harappa, seals, sealings and other miscellaneous objects of faience, stone, etc. selected for the Burdin Fine Arts Exhibition

http://www.photocentralasia.com/specialex/specialexphotos06.html

Seal impression. Royal Ontario Museum, Canada (No ROM number)

Unicorn seal ROM 996.74.5 Royal Ontario Museum, Canada

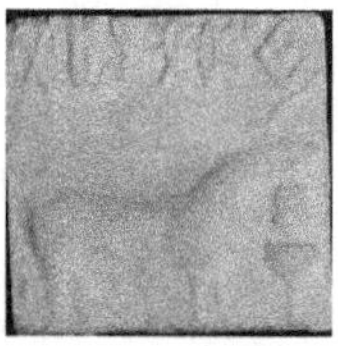

A group of six steatite seals, each with a depiction of an ox before an altar beneath a row of pictographic symbols; the reverse with a pierced boss.
http://www.asianartresource.co.uk/mall/asianartresourcecouk/products/product-823937.stm

(British Museum1892-12-10, 1) Steatite seals in the British Museum

Impression of an Akkadian cylinder seal (ca. 2350-2100 BCE) variously interpreted as potting or cheese-making (after Boehmer 1965: no.693). Another interpretation could be that a man is offering a sword to the eagle-person. The three animals following this man could denote some metallurgical objects. The brazier is inscribing a vessel at the top-left.

Metal artifacts of the Bronze Age from southern Turkmenia. a,c.d Altin-depe; b Anau; e Ashkhabad; f Daina (After fig. 30 in: V.M. Masson and V.I. Sarianidi, 972, *Central Asia: Turkmenia before the*

*Achaemen**ids*, New York, Praeger Publishers) Lead and arsenic was often added to the bronze. Some objects from Namazga-depe contained as much as 8-0 lead and in one case the artifact was even made of brass (an alloy of copper and zinc). Twin moulds were used for casting; precious metals including gold and silver were also used. There are analogies of metal artifacts in the Harappan assemblages; for example, flag daggers without a midrib which were quite atypical for Hissar, were very widespread both in southern Turkmenia and in the Indus Valley.

Artifacts including golden head of bull. Southern Turkmenia, Margiana, Bactria: 4-7 golden head of bull and seals from Altyn depe (Developed Bronze Age); 8-21 seals and amulets of Bactria and Margiana (After Fig.4 in L.P'yankova, Central Asia in the Bronze Age: sedentary and nomadic cultures, in: *Antiquity* 68 (1994): 355-372).4.4 golden head of a bull with a turquoise sickle inlaid in the forehead; 4.5: steatite plate with an image of cross and half-moon.

````

Procession of animals

Bronze dish found by Layard at Nimrud: circular objects are decorated by consecutive chains of animals following each other round in a circle. A similar theme occurs on the famous silver vase of Entemena. In the innermost circle, a troop of gazelles (similar to the ones depicted on cylinder seals) march along in file; the middle register has a variety of animals, all marching in the same direction as the gazelles. A one-horned bull, a winged griffin, an ibex and a gazelle, are followed by two bulls who are being attacked by lions, and a griffin, a one-horned bull, and a gazelle, who are all respectively being attacked by leopards. In the outermost zone there is a stately procession of realistically conceived one-horned bulls marching in the opposite direction to the animals parading in the two inner circles. The dish has a handle. (Percy S.P.Handcock, 1912, *Mesopotamian Archaeology*, London, Macmillan and Co., p. 256). Cf. pasaramu, pasalamu = quadrupeds (Telugu); rebus: pasra = smithy ! (Santali) Smithy for varieties of minerals and metals, indeed.

"Of lasting significance were attempts to lighten the disk wheels, as first seen on a third-millennium seal from Hissar IIIB (fig.2). On it, the central plank, through which the axle passes, is narrowed to a diametral bar; the flanking planks of the Hissar. Depiction of a wheel on a seal from Hissar IIIB. 3rd millennium BCE (After Figure 2, Littauer and Crouwel, 979). tripartite wheel are eliminated, and the former bonding slats are turned into sturdy transverse bars between the diametral bar and the felloe. This crossbar wheel is also clearly illustrated in the second millennium BCE, fixed on a revolving axle; it has remained in use with simple carts in various parts of the world.

Cylinder seal impressions: (a) Nuzi (D. Stein); (b) Ugarit (Schaeffer-Forrer 1983); (c) Alalakh (Collon 1982); (d) Alalakh (Collon 1982); (e) Nuzi (D. Stein); (f) Nuzi (D.Stein); (g) Ugarit (Schaeffer-Forrer
````

1983); (h) Alalakh (Collon 1982).The styles are: juxtaposed antelope, humans and trees framed by geometric patters. The styles have prehistoric roots in Mesopotamia and glyphs such as an antelope with its head turned, jointed animal heads are also seen in Harappan inscription motifs.

ABOUT THE AUTHOR

Dr. S. Kalyanaraman is Director, Sarasvati Research Center, President, Ramasetu Protection Movement in India and BoD member of World Association for Vedic Studies. His research interests relate to rediscovery of Vedic Sarasvati River, roots of Hindu civilization, decoding of Indus Script, National Water Grid and creation of Indian Ocean Community. He has a Ph.D. in Public Administration from the University of the Philippines. He is a multi-lingual scholar versed in Tamil, Telugu, Kannada, Sanskrit, Hindi. He was a senior financial and IT executive in Asian Development Bank, Manila, Philippines and on Indian Railways. His 18 publications include: *Indian Lexicon* - a multilingual dictionary for over 25 Indian languages, *Sarasvati* in 15 volumes, *Indian Alchemy - Soma in the Veda, Indus Script Cipher, Rastram.* He is a recipient of many awards including Vakankar Award (2000), Shivananda Eminent Citizens' Award (2008) and Dr. Hedgewar Prajna Samman (2008).

Website: http://sites.google.com/site/kalyan97

*The book is dedicated to savants who have contributed to an understanding of the roots of written language in the Indian linguistic area – whose contributions are gratefully acknowledged and to children of present and future generations who will continue to cherish the legacy of written language traditions.*

INDEX

## A



## B

C

## I



## J

K



L



M

N



O



P

R



ṛ

R



S

## U



## V

W



Z

www.ingramcontent.com/pod-product-compliance
Lightning Source LLC
Chambersburg PA
CBHW080641270326
41928CB00017B/3155
* 9 7 8 0 9 8 2 8 9 7 1 2 6 *